FAMILY LAW

LONGMAN LAW SERIES

GENERAL EDITORS

PROFESSOR I.H. DENNIS, *University College London*
PROFESSOR J.A. USHER, *University of Edinburgh*

PUBLISHED TITLES

ERIC BARENDT AND LESLEY HITCHENS, *Media Law: Cases and Materials*
ANDREW CHOO, *Evidence: Text and Materials*
R. HALSON, *Contract Law*
JONATHAN HERRING, *Family Law*
NICHOLAS J. MCBRIDE AND RODERICK BAGSHAW, *Tort Law*
BEN PETTET, *Company Law*
ROGER J. SMITH, *Property Law*
ROGER J. SMITH, *Property Law: Cases and Materials*
MAURICE SUNKIN AND ANDREW LE SUEUR, *Public Law*
MARTIN WASIK, THOMAS GIBBONS AND MIKE REDMAYNE, *Criminal Justice: Text and Materials*
WILLIAM WILSON, *Criminal Law: Doctrine and Theory*

FAMILY LAW

SECOND EDITION

—

JONATHAN HERRING

Exeter College
Oxford University

PEARSON

Longman

Harlow, England • London • New York • Boston • San Francisco • Toronto
Sydney • Tokyo • Singapore • Hong Kong • Seoul • Taipei • New Delhi
Cape Town • Madrid • Mexico City • Amsterdam • Munich • Paris • Milan

To Kirsten, Laurel and Joanna

Pearson Education Limited

Edinburgh Gate
Harlow
Essex CM20 2JE
England
and Associated Companies throughout the world

Visit us on the World Wide Web at:
www.pearsoned.co.uk

First published 2001

Second edition published 2004

© Pearson Education Limited 2001, 2004

The right of Jonathan Herring to be identified as author
of this work has been asserted by him in accordance with
the Copyright, Designs and Patents Act 1988.

ISBN-10: 0-582-82280-7
ISBN-13: 978-0-582-82280-1

British Library Cataloguing-in-Publication Data
A catalogue record for this book is available
from the British Library.

Library of Congress Cataloging-in-Publication Data
Herring, Jonathan.
  Family law / Jonathan Herring.—2nd ed.
    p.   cm. — (Longman law series)
  Includes biographical references and index.
  ISBN 0-582-82280-7 (pbk. : alk. paper)
  1. Domestic relations—England.   I. Title. II. Series.

KD750.H47   2004
346.4201'5—dc22   2004044722

10 9 8 7 6 5
09 08 07 06 05

Typeset in 10/12pt Plantin by 3
Printed in Malaysia, PJB

iv

CONTENTS

Preface	xvii
Table of Cases	xix
Table of Statutes	1
Table of Statutory Instruments	lxi
Table of European Legislation	lxii

1 WHAT IS FAMILY LAW?   1
  1. Seeking a definition of the family   1
     A. The person in the street's definition   2
     B. A formalistic definition   2
     C. A function-based definition   3
     D. An idealised definition   3
     E. A self-definition approach   4
     F. Do we give up?   4
     G. Discussion of how the law defines families   5
     H. New families?   6
  2. Should family life be encouraged?   8
     A. Arguments in favour of family life   8
     B. Arguments against families   8
     C. Proposing new visions for families   9
  3. Approaches to family law   10
     A. What is family law?   10
     B. How to examine family law   11
  4. Current issues in family law   18
     A. How the state interacts with families   18
     B. Privatisation of family law   19
     C. The decline in 'moral judgements'   20
     D. Sending messages through the law   22
     E. Legal aid and costs   23
     F. Families in crisis   23
     G. Solicitors and family law   24
     H. Non-legal responses to family law   24
     I. Rights and consequentialism   25
     J. Rules or discretion   25
     K. Partnership   26
     L. Multiculturalism   26
  5. The Human Rights Act 1998 and family law   28
  6. Conclusion   29

2 MARRIAGE AND COHABITATION   30
  1. Introduction   30
  2. Statistics on marriage   31

3. What is marriage? 32
   A. The meaning of marriage 32
   B. The legal definition of marriage 34
   C. Why do people marry? 34
4. Marriage as a status or contract 35
5. The presumption of marriage 36
6. Non-marriages, void marriages and voidable marriages 37
   A. The difference between divorce and nullity 37
   B. The difference between a void marriage and non-marriage 38
   C. The difference between a void and voidable marriage 38
   D. The grounds on which a marriage is void 39
   E. Grounds on which a marriage is voidable 49
   F. Bars to relief in voidable marriages 56
   G. Effects of a decree of nullity 58
   H. Reform of nullity 59
7. Unmarried cohabiting couples 59
8. Comparisons between the legal position of married and unmarried couples 60
   A. Formalities at the beginning and end of a relationship 61
   B. Financial support 61
   C. Children 62
   D. Inheritance and succession 62
   E. Criminal law 63
   F. Contract 64
   G. Tort 64
   H. Evidence 65
   I. Matrimonial property 65
   J. Marital confidences 65
   K. Taxation and benefits 66
   L. Citizenship 66
   M. Statutory succession to tenancies 66
   N. Domestic violence 67
   O. Fatal Accident Act 1976 67
   P. The doctrine of unity 67
   Q. Consortium 67
9. Engagements 68
10. Gay and lesbian relationships 69
11. Should the law treat cohabitation and marriage in the same way? 71
   A. Does the state benefit from cohabitation to the same extent as from marriage? 71
   B. Choice 74
   C. Reflecting current attitudes 75
   D. Should marriage be discouraged? 75
12. What if the state were to abolish legal marriage? 76
13. Conclusion 77

3 DIVORCE AND MEDIATION ... 79

1. Statistics on divorce ... 79
2. Causes of divorce ... 80
3. Social explanations for increasing divorce ... 81
4. What should be the aims of divorce law? ... 82
5. The present law on divorce: Matrimonial Causes Act 1973 ... 85
    A. The background to the Matrimonial Causes Act 1973 ... 85
    B. The current law: The Matrimonial Causes Act 1973 ... 86
6. Problems with the present law ... 93
    A. 'It is confusing and misleading' ... 94
    B. 'It is discriminatory and unjust' ... 94
    C. 'It distorts the parties' bargaining positions' ... 95
    D. 'It provokes unnecessary hostility and bitterness' ... 95
    E. 'It does nothing to save the marriage' ... 95
    F. 'It can make things worse for the children' ... 96
7. Reforming the divorce law: the failure of the Family Law Act 1996 ... 96
    A. General principles of the Family Law Act 1996 ... 96
    B. A timetable for divorce procedures under the Family Law
        Act 1996 ... 97
    C. The information meeting ... 98
    D. Encouragement of reconciliation ... 100
    E. The length of the process ... 101
    F. Counselling and mediation ... 101
    G. Divorce order to be granted only once the financial orders and
        arrangements for children are made ... 102
    H. Protecting children's interests during divorce ... 102
    I. 'Quickie divorce' ... 103
    J. Idealisation of divorce ... 103
8. Some general issues on divorce ... 104
    A. Individualisation of divorce ... 104
    B. No-fault versus fault-based divorce ... 105
    C. Length of time for the divorce process ... 109
    D. Reconciliation and divorce ... 109
    E. The Human Rights Act 1998 and divorce ... 110
    F. Financial arrangements to be made before divorce ... 110
    G. Religion and divorce ... 110
    H. Children and divorce ... 111
9. Pursuing an action for inducing divorce ... 112
10. Separation orders ... 112
11. Death and marriage ... 112
12. Mediation ... 113
    A. Introduction ... 113
    B. What is mediation? ... 114
    C. The role of the mediator ... 115
    D. The benefits of mediation ... 116
    E. The disadvantages of mediation ... 119

F. The false dichotomy of mediation and litigation   122
13. Conclusion   123

4 FAMILY PROPERTY   124
1. The reality of family finances   124
2. The ownership of family property: general theory   126
3. The ownership of personal property   128
   A. Jointly used bank accounts   128
   B. Housekeeping and maintenance allowance   129
   C. Gifts from one partner to the other   129
   D. Gifts to partners from third parties   130
   E. Improvements to personal property   130
   F. Express declarations of trust   130
   G. Criticisms of the present law   130
4. Maintenance during marriage   131
   A. Unmarried cohabitants   131
   B. Married couples   131
5. Ownership of real property: the family home   133
   A. Legal ownership   133
   B. Equitable ownership   134
   C. Improvements to the home   141
   D. Criticism of the present law   142
   E. Reform of the law   144
6. Rights to occupy the home   147
   A. Contractual licences   148
   B. Matrimonial home rights   148
7. The sale of a family home: enforcing trusts   149
8. Protection of beneficial interests against purchasers   150
9. Protection of family property on bankruptcy   151
   A. Protecting creditors from family members   152
   B. Protecting the families from the creditors   154
10. Spouses, partners and mortgages   154
   A. Undue influence: *Barclays Bank* v *O'Brien*   156
11. Conclusion   159

5 PROPERTY ON SEPARATION   160
1. Child support: theoretical issues   160
   A. Does the obligation to support children fall on the state or on the parents?   161
   B. Are the parents' obligations independent or joint?   163
   C. Biological or social parents?   164
   D. What level should the support be?   165
   E. 'The lone parent crisis'   166
   F. Child support and parental support   167
   G. Should child support be a private issue?   168
2. Financial support of children   168
   A. Financial support of children living with both parents   168

	B.	The Child Support Act 1991	169
	C.	The new scheme for child support: Child Support, Pensions and Social Security Act 2000	176
	D.	The Children Act 1989 and child support	180
	E.	The Children Act 1989 and CSA 1991	183
3.	Matrimonial Causes Act 1973 and children		183
	A.	Powers of the court on divorce	183
	B.	'Child of the family'	183
	C.	Applications by children	184
	D.	Factors to be taken into account	184
4.	Financial support for spouses on divorce		184
	A.	The economic realities of divorce	185
	B.	Divorce and redistribution of property	186
	C.	Why should there be any redistribution?	186
	D.	The case for the abolition of maintenance	191
	E.	Certainty or discretion?	192
	F.	Solicitors and negotiations	193
	G.	The Human Rights Act 1998 and maintenance	194
	H.	The importance of discovery	195
	I.	Orders that the court can make	195
	J.	Clean break orders	197
	K.	Interim orders	201
	L.	Factors to be taken into account when making orders	201
	M.	Particular issues relating to redistribution of property on divorce	213
5.	Consent orders		223
	A.	The status of agreement before a court order has been made	224
6.	Enforcement of financial orders		225
	A.	Avoiding enforcement problems	225
	B.	Enforcement of periodical payments	225
	C.	Enforcement of lump sum orders and property adjustment orders	226
7.	Bankruptcy and ancillary relief		226
8.	Variation of, appeals against, and setting aside court orders		227
	A.	Variation	228
	B.	Setting aside a consent order	230
	C.	Appeal	231
9.	Defeating claims: section 37 Matrimonial Causes Act 1973		232
10.	Transfer of tenancies		232
	A.	Who can apply?	232
	B.	Which tenancies can be transferred?	232
	C.	Orders that can be made	233
	D.	Factors to be taken into account	233
11.	Reform of the law on financial support for spouses		234
12.	Conclusion		237

6 DOMESTIC VIOLENCE | | | **238** |
| 1. | Introductory issues | | 238 |

Contents

A. Terminology of topic and definitions 238
B. The incidence of domestic violence 239
C. Causes of domestic violence 241
D. The development of the law on domestic violence 242
2. Injunctions and orders under the Family Law Act 1996 244
A. The non-molestation order 244
B. Occupation orders 250
C. *Ex parte* non-molestation and occupation orders under the
Family Law Act 1996 265
D. Undertakings 266
E. Powers of arrest 266
F. Punishment for breach of an order 267
3. Injunctions under the Protection from Harassment Act 1997 and tort 267
4. The Children Act 1989 and domestic violence 269
5. Domestic violence and housing law 269
A. The definition of 'homeless' 270
B. Priority need 271
C. Unintentionally homeless 272
6. Domestic violence and the criminal law 272
A. The substantive law 272
B. The criminal law in practice 275
C. Reforming the criminal procedure 277
7. State liability 279
8. Why the law finds domestic violence difficult 280
A. The traditional image of the family 280
B. Privacy 280
C. Difficulties of proof 281
D. Occupation or protection 281
E. Victim autonomy 281
F. The law not appropriate 282
G. Solicitors 282
9. Conclusion 282

7 **WHO IS A PARENT?** 284
1. Sociological, psychological and biological notions of parenthood 284
A. Child psychologists 284
B. Sociologists 285
C. Biological perceptions 285
2. The different meanings of being a parent in law 286
3. Who is the child's mother? 287
4. Who is the child's father? 288
A. Legal presumptions of paternity 288
B. Rebutting these presumptions 289
C. Fathers and assisted reproduction 290
D. DIY assisted reproduction 293
E. Fatherless children 294

F.	Parental orders: surrogacy	294
G.	Adoption	296
5.	Losing parenthood	296
6.	Social parents	296
A.	Guardianship	296
B.	Foster parents	300
C.	Special guardians	302
D.	Those who treat a child as a child of the family	302
E.	Step-parents	304
F.	Others caring for the child	305
7.	Relatives	306
8.	The Human Rights Act 1998 and the right to respect for family life	309
A.	What is family life?	309
B.	What is respect?	311
C.	When can infringement be justified?	312
9.	Who has parental responsibility?	312
A.	Outline of the law	313
B.	Consideration of the law in more detail	314
10.	Who should get parental responsibility?	320
A.	Unmarried fathers	320
11.	Losing parental responsibility	325
12.	Wider issues over parenthood	326
A.	What is the basis for granting parenthood?	326
B.	Is there a right to know one's genetic parentage?	330
C.	Is there a right to be a parent?	337
D.	'Illegitimacy'	345
E.	Licensing parenthood	346
13.	Conclusion	346

8 PARENTS' AND CHILDREN'S RIGHTS — 348

1.	When does childhood begin?	348
2.	When does childhood end?	349
3.	The nature of childhood	349
4.	Parents' rights, responsibilities and discretion	350
A.	Parental rights	351
B.	Are parents' rights and responsibilities linked?	352
C.	Why do parents have rights and responsibilities?	353
5.	Parental responsibility	356
A.	What is parental responsibility?	356
B.	Parental responsibility in practice	359
C.	The rights of a parent without responsibility	360
D.	The extent of parental responsibility	361
6.	Sharing parental responsibility	361
A.	Are all parental responsibilities equal?	364
B.	Is the law in a sound state?	364
C.	Co-parenting in practice	366

7.	The welfare principle	366
	A. What does 'welfare' mean?	367
	B. What does 'paramount' mean?	367
	C. When does the welfare principle apply?	368
	D. When does the welfare principle not apply?	368
	E. What if the case involves two children – whose interests are paramount?	370
	F. Conflicts of interests between parents and children	371
8.	The Human Rights Act 1998 and children's welfare and rights	375
	A. Balancing the rights of parents and children under the Convention	376
	B. Is there any practical difference between the approaches of the European Convention and the Children Act 1989?	377
9.	Criticisms of the welfare principle	379
10.	Alternatives to the welfare principle	380
11.	Children's rights	383
	A. Should children have all the rights adults have?	383
	B. The argument against rights for children	387
	C. Extra rights for children	390
	D. Children's rights for adults	391
	E. Children's rights in practice	391
	F. Is there a difference between a welfare-based approach and a rights-based approach?	392
12.	Children and medical law	393
	A. 16- and 17-year-olds	394
	B. Under 16-year-olds	394
	C. Comments on the law	401
13.	Children in court	402
	A. Children bringing proceedings in their own right	403
	B. Representation	406
14.	Children and education	408
15.	Children and criminal law	412
16.	Corporal punishment	414
	A. Reforming the law	415
17.	Children and contract law	417
	A. Parents' liability under children's contracts	418
18.	Children and the law of tort	418
19.	Children's duties	419
20.	Conclusion	420
9	**COURT RESOLUTION OF PRIVATE DISPUTES OVER CHILDREN**	**421**
1.	Introduction	421
2.	Section 8 orders	422
	A. The residence order	422
	B. The contact order	423
	C. Specific issue orders and prohibited steps orders	426

	D.	Restrictions on the use of section 8 orders	426
	E.	Attaching conditions	429
	F.	Variation, discharge and appeals	432
3.		Who can apply for section 8 orders?	432
	A.	Persons who can apply without leave	433
	B.	People who need the leave of the court	433
	C.	How the court decides whether to grant leave	434
	D.	Restricting section 8 applications: section 91(14)	435
4.		Children's welfare on divorce and relationship breakdown	436
5.		How the court decides what is in the child's best interests: the checklist	438
	A.	How the court obtains information on the child's welfare	438
	B.	The statutory checklist	440
6.		Issues of controversy in applying the welfare principle	448
	A.	Is there a presumption in favour of mothers?	448
	B.	The 'natural parent presumption'	449
	C.	Is there a presumption that siblings should reside together?	451
	D.	Racial and cultural background	452
	E.	Religion	452
	F.	Employed parents	454
	G.	Sexual orientation of parents	455
	H.	Disabled parents	456
	I.	Poverty	457
	J.	The 'immoral' conduct of a parent	457
	K.	When is joint residence appropriate?	458
	L.	Publicity	459
	M.	Names	460
	N.	Removal from the UK	466
	O.	When should there be contact between a child and parent?	468
7.		Wardship and the inherent jurisdiction	485
	A.	Wardship	486
	B.	The inherent jurisdiction	488
8.		Child abduction	490
	A.	General	490
	B.	Child Abduction Act 1984	491
	C.	Prevention of abduction and court orders preventing removal	492
	D.	Recovery in the UK	493
	E.	The Hague Convention	494
	F.	The European Convention	502
	G.	Neither convention applies	503
9.		Conclusion	504
10		**CHILD PROTECTION**	506
1.		The Children Act 1989 and child protection	508
2.		The Human Rights Act 1998 and child protection	510
3.		Defining and explaining abuse	512

   A. Explanations for abuse   513
 4. Protection of children by the criminal law   514
 5. Voluntary services provided by local authorities   515
   A. Voluntary accommodation   515
   B. Services for children in need   520
   C. The family assistance order   522
 6. Investigations by local authorities   523
   A. Section 47 investigations   523
   B. Section 37 directions   524
   C. Multi-agency co-operation   525
   D. Child assessment orders   526
 7. Compulsory orders: care orders, supervision orders and emergency
     protection orders   528
   A. Who can apply?   528
   B. Who can be taken into care?   528
   C. The effect of a care order   529
   D. The nature and purpose of the supervision order   530
   E. Care or supervision order?   530
   F. Grounds for supervision and care orders   531
   G. Care plans   544
   H. Interim care orders   545
 8. Emergencies: police protection and emergency protection orders   549
   A. Police protection   549
   B. The emergency protection order   550
 9. Representation of children in child protection proceedings   553
10. Local authorities and section 8 orders   553
11. The problem of ousting the abuser   554
12. Conclusion   556

11 CHILDREN IN CARE   557
 1. Introduction   557
 2. Human Rights Act 1998 and children in care   558
 3. The effect of a supervision order   560
 4. The effects of a care order   561
   A. Distinguishing a child in care and a child voluntarily
       accommodated   561
   B. The legal effects of the care order   561
 5. Questioning local authority decisions   572
   A. Avoiding disputes   572
   B. Procedures to challenge local authority decisions   573
 6. The position of local authority foster carers   578
 7. Duration of care and supervision orders   579
 8. Duties to children leaving care   580
 9. The balance of power between courts and local authorities   581
10. Secure accommodation orders   585
11. Adoption   587

A. The use of adoption today   587
B. Encouraging adoption   591
C. Who can adopt?   592
D. Who can be adopted?   593
E. Selecting adopters and matching adopters and children   593
F. Criminal prohibitions on illegal placements   598
G. The making of an adoption order   598
H. The effect of an adoption order   605
I. Open adoption   606
J. Adoption by a parent   607
K. Adoption by parent and step-parent   608
L. Adoption by relatives   609
M. Post-adoption support   609
N. Revocation of an adoption order   610
O. The breakdown of adoption   611
P. Access to birth and adoption register   611
Q. Intercountry adoption   613
R. Special guardianship   613
12. Conclusion   615

12 FAMILIES AND OLDER PEOPLE   616
1. Introduction   616
2. Statistics on older people   617
    A. Number of older people   617
    B. Older people and their families   617
    C. Income   618
    D. Age discrimination   618
3. Do children have an obligation to support their parents?   619
    A. Moral obligations or legal obligations?   621
    B. What obligations do people actually feel?   621
    C. Integrating family and state care   622
    D. Conclusion   623
4. Financial support for older people and their carers   623
5. Inter-generational justice   625
    A. Health care and older people: health care rationing   626
6. Incapable older people   628
    A. Do older people have rights?   628
    B. When does an older person lose capacity in the eyes of the law?   629
    C. Incapacity and financial matters   629
    D. Reform   632
7. Succession and intestacy   632
    A. Theory   632
    B. The law in cases where there is a will   634
    C. Intestacy   634
    D. The Inheritance (Provision for Family and Dependants) Act 1975   636
8. Elder abuse   642

Contents

A. Defining elder abuse   642
B. The law   643
C. Issues concerning elder abuse   644
9. Conclusion   645

Bibliography and further reading   647
Index   703

PREFACE

This textbook tries to present family law in its context. I hope readers will gain not only an understanding of what the law actually is, but also an awareness of the complex tensions in social, philosophical and political forces which surround 'family life'. This means the book contains much law, but also a little sociology, political theory and philosophy. Of course a little of anything might be said to be a bad thing and the book can only give a flavour of the wide ranging issues surrounding family life and its regulation. Still it is hoped the reader can see that family law is not simply a set of rules cast down from upon high, but rules that have to operate in the messy world of personal relations where many people do not know what the law says, and even if they do, do not care very much about it.

I am extremely grateful for the support of the team at Pearson Education and particularly Michelle Gallagher and Nicola Chilvers. Barbara Massam's editing was outstanding and invaluable. I am also grateful to the support of colleagues and friends and in particular Sandra Fredman, Anne-Marie Forker, and John Eekelaar. Of course my wife, Kirsten, and children, Laurel and Joanna, have given more love and encouragement than words can describe.

The book seeks to present the law as at 1 November 2003, but treats the Adoption and Children Act 2003 as in force.

Jonathan Herring
Exeter College, Oxford University
10 February 2003

TABLE OF CASES

A (A Child) (Change of Name) [2003] 1 FCR 493 CA 464

A (A Child) (Separate Representation in Contact Proceedings),
Re [2001] 2 FCR 55 . . . . 442, 472, 478

A (A Minor) (Care Proceedings), Re [1993] 1 FLR 824 529

A (A Minor) (Cultural Background), Re [1987] 2 FLR 429; (1998) 18
Fam Law 65 452

A (A Minor) (Paternity: Refusal of Blood Tests), Re [1994] 2 FLR 463;
[1994] 2 FCR 908 . . . . 333, 334

A (A Minor) (Residence Order: Leave to Apply), Re [1993] 1 FLR 425;
[1993] 1 FCR 870 . . . . 308, 434

A (A Minor) (Shared Residence Order), Re [1994] 1 FLR 669; [1995] 1 FCR 91 458

A (A Minor) (Supervision Extension), Re [1995] 1 FLR 335; [1995] 2 FCR 114 580

A (Adoption: Agreement: Procedure), Re [2001] 2 FLR 455 602

A (Adoption: Mother's Objections), Re [2000] 1 FLR 665 451

A (Application for Leave), Re [1998] 1 FLR 1; [1999] 1 FCR 127 CA 434, 436

A (Care: Discharge of Application by Child), Re [1995] 1 FLR 599; [1995] 2
FCR 686 580

A (Child of the Family), Re [1998] 1 FLR 347; [1998] 1 FCR 458 303

A (Children) (Shared Residence) [2001] EWCA Civ 1795 [2002] 1 FCR 177 . . 458, 459

A (Children) (Interim Care Order) [2001] 3 FCR 402 539

A (Children) (Specific Issue Order: Parental Dispute), Re [2001] 1 FCR 210;
[2001] 1 FLR 121 452

A (Children: 1959 UN Declaration), Re [1998] 1 FLR 354; [1998] 2 FCR 633
CA 448, 449

A (Conjoined Twins: Medical Treatment), Re [2001] 1 FLR 1; [2000] 3
FCR 577; [2000] 4 All ER 961 CA 352, 371, 398

A (Contact: Separate Representation), Re [2001] FL 540; [2001] 1
FLR 715 . . . . 405, 407

A (Minor) (Wardship: Immigration), Re [1992] 1 FLR 427; [1991] FCR
1013 CA 490

A (Minors) (Abduction: Custody Rights), Re [1992] Fam 106; [1992] 2 FCR 97 498

A (Minors) (Custody), Re [1991] 2 FLR 394; [1991] FCR 569 483

A (Minors) (Residence Orders: Leave to Apply), Re [1992] Fam 182;
[1992] 2 FLR 154; [1992] 2 FCR 174 CA 368, 434, 577

A (Permission to Remove Child from Jurisdiction: Human Rights), Re
[2000] 2 FLR 225; [2001] 1 FCR 210 CA 467

A (Section 8 Order: Grandparent Application), Re [1995] 2 FLR 153; [1996]
1 FCR 467 CA 307, 483

A (Specific Issue Order: Parental Dispute), Re [2001] 1 FLR 121; [2001]
1 FCR 210 441

A v A (A Minor: Financial Provision) [1994] 1 FLR 657; [1995] 1 FCR 309 182

A v A (Family: Unborn Child) [1974] Fam 6; [1974] 2 WLR 106 302

A *v* A (Financial Provision) [1998] 2 FLR 180; [1998] 3 FCR 421 . . . . . . 204, 205, 207

A *v* A (Financial Provision: Conduct) [1995] 1 FLR 345; [1995] 2 FCR 137 208

A *v* B (A Company) [2002] 1 FCR 369 66

A *v* C [1985] FLR 445 343

A *v* J [1989] 1 FLR 110; (1989) Fam Law 63 51

A *v* L (Contact) [1998] 1 FLR 361; [1998] 2 FCR 204 425

A *v* Liverpool CC [1982] AC 363; [1982] 2 FLR 222 HL 487, 490

A *v* M (Family Proceedings: Publicity) [2000] 1 FLR 562; [2000] 1 FCR 1 459

A *v* N (Committal: Refusal of Contact) [1997] 1 FLR 533; [1997] 2 FCR 475
 CA 369, 479

A *v* UK (Human Rights: Punishment of Child) [1998] 2 FLR 959; [1998]
 3 FCR 597, ECtHR 263, 279, 375, 411, 414, 415, 510, 521, 525

A *v* Y (Child's Surname) [1999] 2 FLR 5; [1999] 1 FCR 577 . . . . 463, 465

A and B *v* Essex CC [2002] EWHC 2709 596

A and Byrne and Twenty-Twenty Television *v* UK 25 EHRR 159 CD 460

A NHS Trust *v* D [2000] 2 FCR 577 399

AB (Adoption: Joint Residence), Re [1996] 1 FLR 27; [1996] 1 FCR 633 . . . . . 458, 593

ADT *v* UK [2000] 2 FLR 697 ECtHR 70

A-K (Foreign Passport), Re [1997] 2 FLR 569; [1997] 2 FCR 563 493

A-M *v* A-M (Divorce: Jurisdiction: Validity of Marriage) [2001] 2 FLR 6 . . . . . . 36, 38

AMS *v* Child Support Officer [1998] 1 FLR 955; [1998] 2 FCR 622 CA 175, 196

AZ (A Minor), Re [1997] 1 FLR 682 498

Abbey National Building Society *v* Cann [1991] AC 56; [1990] 2 FLR 112 155

Abbott (A Bankrupt), Re [1983] Ch 45; [1982] 3 WLR 86 226

Abdulaziz et al *v* UK (1985) 7 EHRR 471 310

Adoption Application AA 212/86 (Adoption Payment), Re [1987] 2 FLR 291;
 [1987] 3 WLR 31 . . . . 341, 342

Al Habtoor *v* Fotheringham [2001] FL 352; [2001] 1 FCR 385 . . . . 486, 494

Al Khatib *v* Masry [2002] 2 FCR 539 195

Ampthill Peerage Case, The [1976] 2 WLR 777; [1977] AC 547 HL 35, 287

Archer *v* Archer [1999] 1 FLR 327; [1999] 2 FCR 158 CA 92

Ashburn Anstalt *v* Arnold [1989] Ch 1 CA 250

Ashley *v* Blackman [1988] Fam 85; [1988] FCR 699; [1988] 2 FLR 278 . . . . . . 198, 213

Atkinson *v* Atkinson [1995] 2 FLR 356; [1995] 2 FCR 353 229

Atkinson *v* Atkinson (No. 2) [1996] 1 FLR 51; [1995] 3 FCR 788 CA 203, 229

Attar *v* Attar [1985] FLR 649 206

Attorney General of Hong Kong *v* Humphreys Estate (Queen's Gardens) Ltd
 [1987] AC 114; [1987] 2 WLR 343; [1987] 2 All ER 387 140

Attorney General's Reference (No. 3 of 1994) [1998] AC 245; [1997]
 3 WLR 421 348

Attorney General's Reference (No. 6 of 1980) [1981] QB 715; (1981) 73 CAR 63 . . . 414

Aylesbury FC *v* Watford FC Unreported 12.6.2000 417

B (A Child), Re Unreported 11.11.2003 CA 436

B (A Child) (Adoption Order), Re [2001] EWCA 347; [2001] 2 FCR 89 604

B (A Child) (Immunisation), Re [2003] 3 FCR 156 363

B (A Child: Interim Care Order) [2002] 2 FCR 367; [2002] FL 252 548

B (A Child) (Sole Adoption by Unmarried Father), *Re* [2002] 1 FCR 150 600
B (A Minor) (Abduction), *Re* [1994] 2 FLR 249; [1995] 2 FCR 505 498
B (A Minor) (Care Order: Criteria), *Re* [1993] 1 FCR 565, *Re* [1993] 1 FLR 815 ... 546
B (A Minor) (Disclosure of Evidence), *Re* [1983] 3 FLR 117 399
B (A Minor) (Wardship: Sterilisation), *Re* [1988] AC 199; [1987] FLR 206 338
B (Abduction: Disclosure), *Re* [1995] 1 FLR 774; [1995] 2 FCR 601 493
B (Adoption by One Natural Parent to Exclusion of Other), *Re*
    [2001] 1 FLR 589; [2001] 1 FCR 600; [2002] 1 FLR 196 HL 310, 378, 602, 607
B (Adoption Order: Nationality), *Re* [1999] 1 FLR 907; [1999] 2 FCR 328 HL 593
B (Adoption: Jurisdiction to Set Aside), *Re* [1995] 2 FLR 1; [1994] 2 FLR
    1297; [1995] 3 FCR 671; [1994] 2 FCR 1297 .... 610, 611
B (Adoption: Setting Aside), *Re* [1995] 1 FLR 1; [1995] 3 FCR 671 610
B (Agreed Findings of Fact), *Re* [1998] 2 FLR 968; [1998] Fam Law 583 545
B (Care Order or Supervision Order), *Re* [1996] 2 FLR 693; [1997]
    1 FCR 309 .... 530, 531
B (Care Proceedings: Diplomatic Immunity), *Re* [2003] FL 8 510
B (Change of Surname), *Re* [1996] 1 FLR 791; [1996] 2 FCR 304 CA ... 461, 463, 464
B (Child Immunisation), *Re* [2003] 3 FCR 156 CA 353
B (Children) (Removal from Jurisdiction), *Re* [2001] 1 FCR 108 466
B (Children) (Removal from the Jurisdiction), Re, *Re* S (A Child) (Removal
    from the Jurisdiction) [2003] 3 FCR 637 468
B (Contact: Stepfather's Opposition), *Re* [1997] 2 FLR 579; [1998] 3
    FCR 289 CA 477
B (Disclosure to Other Parties), *Re* [2002] 2 FCR 32 512
B (Minors) (Abduction), *Re* [1993] 1 FLR 988; [1994] 1 FCR 389 .... 495, 497
B (Minors) (Change of Surname), *Re* [1996] 1 FLR 791; [1996] 2
    FCR 304 CA 441
B (Minors) (Removal from the Jurisdiction), *Re* [1994] 2 FLR 309; [1994] Fam
    Law 11 467
B (Minors) (Residence Order), *Re* [1992] 2 FLR 1; [1992] 1 FCR 555 428
B (Minors: Residence: Working Fathers) [1996] CLY 615 455
B (Minors) (Termination of Contact: Paramount Consideration), *Re* [1993]
    Fam 301; [1993] 1 FLR 543; [1993] 1 FCR 363 .... 569, 570
B (Parentage), *Re* [1996] 2 FLR 15; [1996] 3 FCR 697 292
B (Psychiatric Therapy for Parents), *Re* [1999] 1 FLR 701; [1999] 3 FCR 20 CA ... 547
B (Residence Order: Status Quo), *Re* [1998] 1 FLR 368; [1998] 1 FCR 549 CA 443
B *v* B [1954] 2 All ER 598 46
B *v* B [1999] 1 FLR 715; [1999] 2 FCR 251 CA 252–254
B *v* B (A Minor) (Residence Order) [1992] 2 FLR 327; [1993] 1 FCR 211 .... 305, 447
B *v* B (Adult Student: Liability to Support) [1998] 1 FLR 373; [1998] 1 FCR 49 349
B *v* B (Consent Order: Variation) [1995] 1 FLR 9; [1995] 2 FCR 62 230
B *v* B (Custody of Children) [1985] FLR 166 CA 454
B *v* B (Custody of Children) [1985] FLR 462 CA 454
B *v* B (Custody: Conditions) [1979] 1 FLR 385 .... 428, 431
B *v* B (Divorce: Dismissal: Sham Marriages) [2003] FL 372 87
B *v* B (Financial Provision) [1989] 1 FLR 119; [1989] FCR 146 218

B *v* B (Financial Provision: Welfare of Child and Conduct) [2002] 1 FLR
 555; [2002] FL 173 . . . . 202, 210
B *v* B (Grandparent: Residence Order) [1992] 2 FLR 327; [1993] 1 FCR 211 360
B *v* B (M *v* M) (Transfer of Custody: Appeal) [1987] 2 FLR 146 440
B *v* B (Mesher Order) [2003] FL 462 . . . . 199, 212, 221
B *v* B (Minors) (Custody: Care Control) [1991] 1 FLR 402; [1991] FCR 1 . . . . 451, 455
B *v* B (Residence Order: Reasons for Decisions) [1997] 2 FLR 602; [1998] 1
 FCR 409 440
B *v* B (Residence Order: Restricting Applications) [1997] 1 FLR 139; [1997]
 2 FCR 518 CA 435, 451
B *v* El-B [2003] 1 FLR 811 502
B *v* H (Children) (Habitual Residence) [2002] 2 FCR 329 494
B *v* K (Child Abduction) [1993] 1 FCR 382; [1993] Fam Law 17 501
B *v* M [1999] FLP, 16 March 233
B *v* UK [2000] 1 FLR 1; [2000] 1 FCR 289 ECtHR 309, 321, 323, 451, 487
B and G (Minors) (Custody), *Re* [1985] FLR 493; (1985) Fam Law 127 CA 452
B-J (A Child) (Non-Molestation Order: Power of Arrest), *Re* [2000] 2 FLR
 443; [2000] 2 FCR 599 CA 248
B (T) (A Minor) (Residence Order), *Re* [1995] 2 FCR 240 CA 443, 451
Balfour *v* Balfour [1919] 2 KB 571 CA 64, 132, 222
Banbury Peerage Case (1811) 1 Sim & St 153 HL 288
Banik *v* Banik [1973] 3 All ER 45; [1973] 1 WLR 860 92
Bank of Ireland *v* Bell [2001] 3 FCR 134; [2001] 2 FLR 809 153
Banks *v* Banks [1999] 1 FLR 726 249
Barclays Bank *v* O'Brien [1994] 1 AC 180; [1994] 1 FLR 1; [1994]
 1 FCR 357 . . . . 151, 156–158
Barclays Bank *v* Rivett [1999] 1 FLR 730; [1999] 3 FCR 304 157
Barder *v* Barder (Caluori Intervening) [1988] AC 20; [1987] 2 FLR 480 HL . . . 227, 231
Barnes *v* Barnes [1972] 3 All ER 872; [1972] 1 WLR 1381 205
Barrass *v* Harding [2001] 1 FCR 297 640
Barrett *v* Barrett [1988] 2 FLR 516; [1988] FCR 707 204
Barrett *v* Enfield LBC [1999] 3 WLR 79; [1999] 2 FCR 434 577
Basham (decd), *Re* [1987] 1 All ER 405; [1987] 2 FLR 264 139
Baxter *v* Baxter [1948] AC 274; [1948] LJR 479 HL 50
Beaumont, *Re* [1980] Ch 444; [1980] 1 All ER 266 641
Bebee *v* Sales (1916) 32 TLR 413 419
Bedinger *v* Graybill's Trustee (1957) (302) SW (2nd) 594 593
Belcher *v* Belcher [1995] 1 FLR 916; [1994] 2 FCR 143 CA 218
Bellinger *v* Bellinger [2003] UKHL 21; [2003] 2 FCR 1 46
Bennett *v* Bennett [1969] 1 All ER 539; [1969] 1 WLR 430 55
Berkshire CC *v* B [1997] 1 FLR 171; [1997] 3 FCR 88 570
Bernard *v* Joseph [1982] Ch 391; [1982] 2 WLR 1052 150
Bibby *v* Stirling (1998) 76 P&CR 36 139
Billington *v* Billington [1974] Fam 24; [1974] 2 WLR 53 213
Birch *v* Birch [1992] 1 FLR 564; [1992] 2 FCR 564 89
Birmingham CC *v* H [1992] 2 FLR 323; [1993] 1 FCR 247 430

Birmingham City Council *v* H (A Minor) [1994] 2 AC 212; [1994] 1 FLR
224; [1994] 1 FCR 896 370
Bishop, *Re* [1965] Ch 450; [1965] 2 WLR 188 129
Bond *v* Leicester City Council [2002] 1 FCR 566 270
Bouamar *v* Belgium (1987) 11 EHRR 1 586
Bouette *v* Rose [2000] 1 FLR 363; [2000] 1 FCR 385 .... 638, 642
Boyle *v* UK (1994) 19 EHRR 179; [1994] 2 FCR 822 .... 309, 310
Bradford-Smart *v* West Sussex County Council [2002] 1 FCR 425 411
Bradley *v* Bradley [1973] 3 All ER 750; [1973] 1 WLR 1291 90
Bremner (A Bankrupt), *Re* [1999] 1 FLR 912; [1999] Fam Law 293 153
Brett *v* Brett [1969] 1 All ER 1007; [1969] 1 WLR 487 111
Brierley *v* Brierley [1918] P 257 289
Briody *v* St Helens and Knowsley HA [2000] 2 FCR 13 .... 338, 341
Brixley *v* Lynas [1996] 2 FLR 499; [1997] 1 FCR 220 HL 448
Brodie *v* Brodie [1917] P 271 52
Brooks *v* Brooks [1996] AC 375; [1995] 2 FLR 13; [1995] 3 FCR 214 HL 214, 216
Buckingham CC *v* M [1994] 2 FLR 506; [1994] 1 FCR 859 CA 585
Buckland *v* Buckland [1967] 2 WLR 1506; [1968] P 296 .... 53, 54
Buffery *v* Buffery [1988] 2 FLR 365; [1988] FCR 465 CA 88
Bullock *v* Bullock [1960] 2 All ER 307; [1960] 1 WLR 975 58
Burgess *v* Burgess [1996] 2 FLR 34; [1997] 1 FLR 89 199
Burrow *v* Burrow [1999] 1 FLR 508; [1999] 2 FCR 549 215
C (A Baby), *Re* [1996] 2 FLR 43; [1996] 2 FCR 569 488
C (A Child) (HIV Test), *Re* [1999] 2 FLR 1004; [1999] 3 FCR 289 CA .. 353, 426, 431
C (A Minor) (Abduction), *Re* [1989] 1 FLR 403; [1989] FCR 197 CA 495
C (A Minor) (Adoption), *Re* [1994] 2 FLR 513; [1994] 2 FCR 839 CA 579
C (A Minor) (Adoption: Parental Agreement: Contact), *Re* [1993] 2 FLR 260;
[1994] 2 FCR 485 CA 20
C (A Minor) (Care: Children's Wishes) [1993] 1 FLR 832; [1993] 1 FCR 810 442
C (A Minor) (Child Support Agency: Disclosure), *Re* [1995] 1 FLR 201;
[1995] 1 FCR 202 .... 331, 492
C (A Minor) (Interim Residence Order: Residential Assessment), *Re* [1997]
1 FCR 149; [1997] 1 FLR 1 585
C (A Minor) (Leave to Seek Section 8 Order), *Re* [1994] 1 FLR 26;
[1995] 1 FLR 927; [1996] 1 FCR 461 .... 404, 405, 428
C (A Minor) (Wardship: Surrogacy), *Re* [1985] FLR 846 342
C (Abduction: Consent), *Re* [1996] 1 FLR 414; [1996] 3 FCR 222 .... 496, 497
C (Abduction: Grave Risk of Physical or Psychological Harm), *Re* [1999]
2 FLR 478; [1999] 3 FCR 510 499
C (Abduction: Grave Risk of Psychological Harm), *Re* [1999] 1 FLR 1145;
[1999] 2 FCR 507 .... 499, 501
C (Adoption: Religious Observance, *Re* [2002] 1 FLR 1119 596
C (Application by Mr and Mrs X), *Re* [2002] FL 351 .... 295, 341
C (Care Proceedings: Disclosure of Local Authority's Decision-Making Process),
Re [2002] 2 FCR 673 512
C (Change of Surname), *Re* [1998] 2 FLR 656; [1999] 1 FCR 318 CA 463, 464

C (Child Abduction) (Unmarried Father: Rights of Custody), Re [2003] 1 FLR 252 . 496
C (Children) (Residential Assessment) [2001] 3 FCR 164 .... 547, 558
C (Children: Contact) [2002] 3 FCR 183; [2002] 1 FLR 1136 479
C (Contact: No Order for Contact), Re [2000] Fam Law 699;
    [2000] 2 FLR 723 .... 425, 436, 478, 479
C (Contact: Supervision), Re [1996] 2 FLR 314; [1997] 1 FCR 458 474
C (Contempt: Committal), Re [1995] 2 FLR 767 606
C (Detention: Medical Treatment), Re [1997] 2 FLR 180; [1997]
    3 FCR 49 .... 394, 489, 586
C (Family Assistance Order), Re [1996] 1 FLR 424; [1996] 3 FCR 514 522
C (Interim Care Order: Residential Assessment), Re [1997] AC 489; [1997]
    1 FLR 1; [1997] 1 FCR 149 .... 546, 581
C (Leave to Remove from the Jurisdiction), Re [2000] 2 FLR 457; [2000]
    2 FCR 40 CA 467
C (Medical Treatment), Re [1998] 1 FLR 384; [1998] 1 FCR 1 .... 399, 490
C (Minors) (Adoption by Relatives), Re [1989] 1 FLR 222; [1989] FCR 744 298
C (Minors) (Parental Rights), Re [1992] 2 All ER 86; [1992] 1 FLR 1; [1991]
    FCR 865 316
C (Permission to Remove From Jurisdiction), Re [2003] FL 484 468
C (Residence: Child's Application for Leave), Re [1995] 1 FLR 927; [1996] 1
    FCR 461 .... 369, 405
C (Secure Accommodation Order: Representation), Re [1993] 1 FLR 440 407
C v Bury MBC [2002] 3 FCR 608; [2002] 2 FLR 868 .... 512, 574
C v C (A Minor) (Custody: Appeal) [1991] 1 FLR 223; [1991] FCR 254 CA ... 69, 455
C v C (Financial Provision: Personal Damages) [1995] 2 FLR 171; [1996]
    1 FCR 283 .... 203, 207
C v C (Financial Provision: Short Marriage) [1997] 2 FLR 26; [1997] 3
    FCR 360 CA 200, 206
C v C (Minors) (Child Abduction) [1992] 1 FLR 163; [1992] 1 FCR 391 495
C v C (Minors: Custody) [1988] 2 FLR 291; [1988] FCR 411 451
C v C (Non-Molestation Order: Jurisdiction) [1998] Fam 70; [1998] 1 FLR 554;
    [1998] 1 FCR 11 248
C v F (Disabled Child: Maintenance Orders) [1998] 2 FLR 1; [1999] 1
    FCR 39 CA 172, 180, 182
C v K (Inherent Powers: Exclusion Order) [1996] 2 FLR 506; [1996] 3 FCR 488 ... 489
C v S [1987] 2 FLR 505; [1987] 1 All ER 1230 CA 328, 348, 349
C v Solihull MBC [1993] 1 FLR 290; [1992] 2 FCR 341 .... 445, 546
C v W (Contact: Leave to Apply) [1999] 1 FLR 916; [1999] Fam Law 298 435
C and B (Children) (Care Order: Future Harm), Re [2000] 2 FCR 614;
    [2001] 1 FLR 611 CA 511, 559, 604
C and V (Minors) (Parental Responsibility and Contact), Re [1998]
    1 FLR 392; [1998] 1 FCR 57 .... 317, 318, 338, 444
CAFCASS Practice Note (Officers of Legal Services and Special Casework:
    Appointment in Family Proceedings) [2001] 2 FR 151 407
CB (Access: Court Welfare Reports), Re [1995] 1 FLR 622 CA 439
CB (Unmarried Mother) (Blood Test), Re [1994] 2 FLR 762; [1994] 2 FCR 925 ... 333

CH (Care or Interim Care Order), *Re* [1998] 1 FLR 402; [1998] 2 FCR 347 CA 545
CH (Contact Parentage), *Re* [1996] 1 FLR 569; [1996] FCR 768 290
CT (A Minor) (Child: Representation), *Re* [1993] 2 FLR 278; [1993]
    2 FCR 445 .... 403, 408
Cackett *v* Cackett [1950] P 253; [1950] 1 All ER 677 50
Cambridge CC *v* R (An Adult) [1994] 2 FCR 973; [1995] 1 FLR 50 422
Cambridgeshire CC *v* D [1999] 2 FLR 42; [1999] 3 FCR 613 249
Cameron *v* Treasury Solicitor [1996] 2 FLR 716; [1997] 1 FCR 1 CA 197, 640
Camp and Bourimi *v* The Netherlands [2000] 3 FCR 307 ECtHR 346
Campbell and Cosans *v* UK (1982) 4 EHRR 293 ECtHR 376, 415
Campbell *v* Campbell [1977] 1 All ER 1 70
Campbell *v* Campbell [1998] 1 FLR 828; [1998] 3 FCR 63 CA 205
Carmarthenshire CC *v* Lewis [1955] AC 549; [1955] 2 WLR 517 419
Carron *v* Carron [1984] FLR 805 CA 302
Centre for Reproductive Medicine *v* U [2002] FL 267 291
Chalmers *v* Johns [1999] 1 FLR 392; [1999] 2 FCR 110 252–254
Chan Pui Chun *v* Leung Kam Ho [2003] 1 FCR 520, CA 137
Chard *v* Chard [1955] 3 WLR 954; [1956] P 259 113
Chechi *v* Bashier [1999] 2 FLR 489; [1999] 2 FCR 241 CA 246, 247, 266
Chief Adjudication Officer *v* Bath [2000] 1 FLR 8; [2000] 1 FCR 419 .... 37, 42
Citro, *Re* [1991] Ch 142; [1991] FLR 71 151
City of London Building Society *v* Flegg [1988] AC 54; [1988] 1 FLR 98;
    [1987] 3 All ER 435 HL 151
Clark *v* Clark [1999] 2 FLR 498; [1999] 3 FCR 49 CA 208
Clarke *v* Clarke [1943] 2 All ER 540 51
Cleary *v* Cleary [1974] 1 All ER 498; (1974) 117 SJ 834 88
Clibbery *v* Allan [2002] 1 FLR 565; [2002] 1 FCR 385 245
Clutton *v* Clutton [1991] 1 FLR 242; [1991] FCR 265 CA 221
Cole, *Re* [1904] Ch 175 128
Collins, *Re* [1990] Fam 56; [1990] FCR 433 637
Coombes *v* Smith [1986] 1 WLR 808; [1987] 1 FLR 352 140
Cooper *v* Crane [1891] P 369 52
Corbett *v* Corbett (1969) 113 SJ 982; [1971] P 83 .... 44, 45
Cordle *v* Cordle [2002] 1 FCR 97 205
Cornick *v* Cornick (No. 3) [2001] 2 FLR 1240 229
Cossey *v* UK [1991] 2 FLR 492; [1993] 2 FCR 97 ECtHR 45
Costello-Roberts *v* UK (1995) EHRR 112; [1994] 1 FCR 65 ECtHR 415
Council of Civil Service Unions *v* Minister for the Civil Service [1985] AC
    374; [1985] ICR 14 575
Coventry, *Re* [1990] Fam 561 639
Cowan *v* Cowan [2001] 2 FCR 332 210
Crédit Lyonnais Bank *v* Burch [1997] 2 FCR 1; [1997] 1 FLR 11 CA 157
Croydon LB *v* A [1992] Fam 169; [1992] 2 FLR 341; [1992] 1 FCR 522 426
Crozier *v* Crozier [1995] Fam 114; [1994] 1 FLR 26; [1994] 1 FCR 781 175
D (A Child) (IVF Treatment), *Re* [2001] 1 FCR 481 CA 474
D (A Child) (Wardship: Evidence of Abuse) [2001] 1 FCR 707 513

D (A Minor) (Child: Removal From Jurisdiction), *Re* [1992] 1 FLR 637; [1992]
  1 WLR 315 492
D (A Minor) (Contact: Mother's Hostility), *Re* [1993] 2 FLR 1; [1993] 1 FCR 964 .. 473
D (A Minor) (Wardship: Sterilisation), *Re* [1976] Fam 185; [1976] 2
  WLR 279 .... 306, 338, 486
D (A Minor), *Re* [1987] AC 317; [1987] 1 FLR 422 529
D (Abduction: Discretionary Return), *Re* [2000] 1 FLR 24; [2000] 1 FCR 208 498
D (Care or Supervision Order), *Re* [2000] Fam Law 600 530
D (Care: Natural Parent Presumption), *Re* [1999] 1 FLR 134; [1999]
  2 FCR 118 CA 307, 449, 450
D (Care: Threshold Criteria), *Re* [1998] Fam Law 656 CA 533
D (Children) (Shared Residence Orders) [2001] 1 FCR 147 .... 423, 458
D (Contact: Reasons for Refusal), *Re* [1997] 2 FLR 48; [1998] 1 FCR 321 CA 473
D (Jurisdiction: Programme of Assessment or Therapy), *Re* [2000] 1 FCR 436
  CA 547, 548
D (Prohibited Steps Order), *Re* [1996] 2 FLR 273; [1996] 2 FCR 496 CA 427, 430
D (Residence: Imposition of Conditions), *Re* [1996] 2 FLR 281; [1996]
  2 FCR 820 CA 427, 430, 431
D *v* D (Application for Contact) [1994] 1 FCR 694; {1994) 158 JPN 138 ..... 447, 448
D *v* D (Child of the Family) (1981) 2 FLR 93 CA 302
D *v* D (County Court Jurisdiction: Injunctions) [1993] 2 FLR 802;
  [1994] 3 FCR 28 CA 432, 517, 524
D *v* D (Nullity) [1979] Fam 70; [1979] 3 WLR 185 .... 56, 57
D *v* D (Shared Residence Order) [2001] 1 FLR 495; [2001] 1 FCR 147 458
D *v* Hereford and Worcester CC [1991] Fam 14; [1991] 1 FLR 215; [1991]
  FCR 56 316
D *v* N (Contact Order: Conditions) [1997] 2 FLR 797; [1997] 3 FCR
  721 CA 373, 430, 431
D *v* S [1995] 3 FLR 783 319
D and H (Care: Termination of Contact), *Re* [1997] 1 FLR 841; [1997] Fam
  Law 398 CA 570
D, L and LA (Care: Change of Forename), *Re* [2003] 1 FLR 339 465
D-E *v* A-G (1845) 1 Rob Eccl 279 50
DH (A Minor) (Child Abuse), *Re* [1994] 1 FLR 679; [1994] 2 FCR 3 .... 530, 569
DP *v* UK [2002] 3 FCR 385 510
DW (A Minor) (Custody), *Re* [1984] 14 Fam Law 17 445
Da Silva Mouta *v* Portugal [2001] 1 FCR 653 ECtHR 48, 69, 70, 456
Dart *v* Dart [1996] 2 FLR 286; [1997] 1 FCR 21 CA. 205, 214
Dawson *v* Wearmouth [1997] 2 FLR 629 CA; *affirmed*
  [1999] 1 FLR 1167; [1999] 1 FCR 625; [1999]
  2 AC 308, HL 346, 367, 426, 447, 460, 462–465
De Francesco *v* Barnum (1890) 45 Ch D 430 417
Delaney *v* Delaney [1990] 2 FLR 457; [1991] FCR 161 213
Dennis, *Re* (1980) 124 SJ 885; [1981] 2 All ER 140 639
Dennis *v* Dennis [1995] 2 All ER 51 88
Dennis *v* Dennis [2000] 2 FLR 231 110

Devon CC *v* S [1994] Fam 169; [1994] 1 FLR 355; [1994] 2 FCR 409 555
Dharamshi *v* Dharamshi [2001] 1 FCR 492 210
Director of Public Prosecution *v* Tweddell [2002] 1 FCR 348 249
Dodsworth *v* Dodsworth (1973) 228 EG 1115 141
Donaldson *v* McNiven [1952] 2 All ER 691; (1952) 96 SJ 747 419
Dorney-Kingdom *v* Dorney-Kingdom [2000] 3 FCR 20; [2000] 2 FLR 855 172
Douglas *v* Hello! Ltd [2002] 1 FCR 289; [2001] 1 FLR 982 66
Downing *v* Downing [1976] Fam 288; [1976] 3 WLR 335 184
Drake *v* Whipp [1996] 1 FLR 826; [1996] 2 FCR 296 . . . . 139, 144
Dredge *v* Dredge [1947] 1 All ER 29; (1947) 63 TLR 113 . . . . 43, 50
Dudgeon *v* UK (1982) 4 EHRR 149 312
Duxbury *v* Duxbury [1987] 1 FLR 7; (1987) 17 Fam Law 13 . . . . 199, 203, 205
E (A Minor) (Blood Tests: Parental Responsibilities), *Re* [1993] 3 All ER
  596; [1993] 1 FCR 392 332
E (A Minor) (Care Order: Contact), *Re* [1994] 1 FLR 146; [1994] 1 FCR 584
  CA 569, 570
E (A Minor) (Child Support: Blood Test), *Re* [1994] 2 FLR 548; [1995]
  1 FCR 245 170
E (A Minor) (Wardship: Medical Treatment), *Re* [1993] 1 FLR 386;
  [1992] 2 FCR 219 . . . . 395, 397, 397
E (Abduction: Non-Convention Country), *Re* [1999] 2 FLR 642; [1999] 3 FCR 497 . . 504
E (Enduring Power of Attorney), *Re* [2000] 1 FLR 882 632
E (Parental Responsibility: Blood Test), *Re* [1995] 1 FLR 392; [1994] 2 FCR
  709 . . . . 319, 331
E (Residence: Imposition of Conditions), *Re* [1997] 2 FLR 638; [1997]
  3 FCR 245 CA 373, 430
E *v* C (Child Maintenance) [1995] 1 FLR 472; [1996] 1 FCR 612 132
E *v* E (Financial Provision) [1990] 2 FLR 233; [1989] FCR 591 202
E *v* UK [2003] 1 FLR 348; [2002] 3 FCR 700 . . . . 510, 511
Edgar *v* Edgar [1980] 2 FLR 19; [1980] 1 WLR 1410 CA 224
Edwards *v* Edwards [1986] 1 FLR 187 CA 443
Egan *v* Canada [1998] 1 SCR 493 48
Elliott *v* Elliott [2001] 1 FCR 477 . . . . 211, 221
Elsholz *v* Germany [2000] 2 FLR 486; [2000] 3 FCR 385 ECtHR 472
Emmett, *Re* Unreported 15.10.1999 63
Equity and Law Home Loans *v* Prestidge [1992] 1 WLR 137; [1992] 1 FCR 353 . . . 155
Eriksson *v* Sweden (1989) 12 EHRR 183 ECtHR 375, 559
Espinosa *v* Bourke [1999] 1 FLR 747; [1999] 3 FCR 76 641
Essex CC *v* F [1993] 1 FLR 847; [1993] 2 FCR 289 553
Evans *v* Evans [1990] 1 FLR 319; [1990] FCR 498 195
Eves *v* Eves [1975] 3 All ER 768; [1975] 1 WLR 1338 CA 136, 137
Ewing *v* Wheatly (1814) 2 Hagg Cas 175 54
F, *Re* [1990] 2 AC 1; [1989] 2 FLR 376 486
F, *Re* [2002] 1 FLR 217 557
F (A Minor) (Abduction: Custody Rights Abroad), *Re* [1995] Fam 224; [1996]
  1 FCR 379 499

F (A Minor) (Abduction: Jurisdiction), *Re* [1991] Fam 25; [1991] FCR 227 504

F (A Minor) (Adoption: Parental Agreement), *Re* [1982] 3 FLR 101 588

F (A Minor) (Blood Test: Parental Rights), *Re* [1993] Fam 314; [1993] 1 FCR
932; [1993] 1 FLR 598 . . . . 332, 333

F (A Minor) (Child Abduction), *Re* [1992] 1 FLR 548; [1992] 1 FCR 269 CA 495

F (A Minor) (Parental Responsibility Order), *Re* [1994] 1 FLR 504; [1994]
2 FCR 1037 CA 316

F (Abduction: Unmarried Father: Sole Carer), *Re* [2003] FL 222 496

F (Care Proceedings: Contact), *Re* [2000] 2 FCR 481 570

F (Care: Termination of Care), *Re* [2000] FCR 481 . . . . 569, 570

F (Child: Surname), *Re* [1993] 2 FLR 827n; [1994] 1 FCR 110 . . . . 463, 464

F (Children) (Shared Residence Order) [2003] 2 FCR 164 . . . . 423, 459

F (Contact: Child in Care), *Re* [1995] 1 FLR 510; [1994] 2 FCR 1354 . . . . 371, 572

F (Contact: Enforcement: Representation of Child), *Re* [1998] 1 FLR 691;
[1998] 3 FCR 216 . . . . 372, 480

F (Contact: Restraint Order), *Re* [1995] 1 FLR 956; [1996] 1 FCR 81 470

F (In Utero), *Re* [1988] Fam 122; [1988] FCR 529 CA 348, 486, 529

F (Mental Patient: Sterilisation), *Re* [1990] 2 AC 1 . . . . 338, 399

F (Minors) (Denial of Contact), *Re* [1993] 2 FLR 677; [1993] 1 FCR
945 CA 477, 478

F *v* CSA [1999] 2 FLR 244; [1999] 2 FCR 385; [1999] 2 FLR 244 290

F *v* F (Ancillary Relief: Substantial Assets) [1995] 2 FLR 45;
[1996] 2 FCR 397 . . . . 195, 201, 204, 222

F *v* F (Clean Break: Balance of Fairness) [2003] 1 FLR 847 . . . . 198, 199

F *v* F (Contact: Committal) [1998] 2 FLR 237; [1999] 2 FCR 42 CA 480

F *v* F (Divorce: Insolvency: Annulment of Bankruptcy Order) [1994] 1 FLR
359; [1994] 2 FCR 689 226

F *v* Kent CC [1993] 1 FLR 432; [1992] 2 FCR 433 435

F *v* Lambeth LBC [2001] 3 FCR 738 582

F *v* Leeds City Council [1994] 2 FLR 60; [1994] 2 FCR 428 CA 368

F *v* S (Adoption: Ward) [1993] Fam 203 487

F *v* Solfolk [1981] 2 FLR 208 532

F *v* Switzerland (1987) 10 EHRR 411 ECtHR 110

F and R (Section 8 Order: Grandparent's Application), *Re* [1995] 1 FLR 524;
[1995] 1 FCR 563 308

F, F *v* Lambeth LBC, *Re* [2002] FL 8 566

Field *v* Field [2003] 1 FLR 376 216

Fisher *v* Fisher [1989] 1 FLR 423; [1989] FCR 308 CA 198

Fitzpatrick *v* Sterling Housing Association Ltd [2000]
1 FCR 21 HL 3, 5, 6, 29, 48, 66, 69, 637

Flavell *v* Flavell [1997] 1 FLR 353; [1997] 1 FCR 332 CA 200, 229

Flint (A Bankrupt), *Re* [1993] 1 FLR 763; [1993] 1 FCR 518 227

Ford *v* Ford [1987] Fam Law 232 51

Fournier *v* Fournier [1998] 2 FLR 990; [1999] 2 FCR 20 CA 225

Fretté *v* France [2003] 2 FCR 39 EctHR 595

G (A Child) (Contempt: Committal Order) [2003] 2 FCR 231 CA 429, 436

G (A Child) (Domestic Violence: Direct Contact), *Re* [2001] 2 FCR
    134 . . . . 317, 318, 476, 571
G (A Minor) (Care Order: Threshold Conditions), *Re* [1994] 2 FLR 69; [1994]
    2 FCR 216; [1995] Fam 16 545
G (A Minor) (Care Proceedings), *Re* [1994] 2 FLR 69; [1994] 3 WLR 1211 531
G (A Minor) (Parental Responsibility: Education), *Re* [1994] 2 FLR 964; [1995]
    2 FCR 53 CA 363
G (Abduction: Psychological Harm), *Re* [1995] 1 FLR 64; [1995] 2 FCR 22 500
G (Adoption: Contract), *Re* [2003] FL 9 606
G (Care: Challenge to Local Authority's Decision), *Re* [2003] FL 389 559
G (Care Proceedings: Threshold Conditons), *Re* [2001] FL 727 535
G (Child: Contact), *Re* [2002] 3 FCR 377; [2002] EWCA Civ 761 606
G (Decree Absolute: Prejudice), *Re* [2003] 1 FLR 870 92
G (Domestic Violence: Direct Contact), *Re* [2000] Fam Law 789 . . . . 476, 572
G (Minors) (*Ex Parte* Interim Residence Order), *Re* [1993] 1 FLR 910;
    [1992] 2 FCR 720 CA 443
G (Minors) (Interim Care Order), *Re* [1993] 2 FLR 839; [1993]
    2 FCR 557 . . . . 518, 545, 546
G (Parentage: Blood Sample), *Re* [1997] 1 FLR 360; [1997] 2 FCR 325 CA . . . 332–334
G (Secure Accommodation), *Re* [2000] 2 FLR 259; [2000] 2 FCR 385 586
G *v* C (Residence Order: Committal) [1998] 1 FLR 43; [1998] 1 FCR 592 249
G *v* F (Contact and Shared Residence) [1998] 2 FLR 799; [1998] 3 FCR 1 456
G *v* F (Non-Molestation Order: Jurisdiction) [2000] 2 FCR 638 . . . . 244, 245
G *v* G [1924] AC 349 HL 51
G *v* G [1985] FLR 894 HL 432
G *v* G (Maintenance Pending Suit: Costs) [2003] FL 393 132
G *v* G (Occupation Order: Conduct) [2000] 2 FLR 36 . . . . 249, 253, 254
G *v* Kirkless MBC [1993] 1 FLR 805; [1993] 1 FCR 357 308
G *v* The Netherlands [1990] 16 EHRR 38 ECtHR 310
G and M (Child Orders: Restricting Applications), *Re* [1995] 2 FLR 416; [1995]
    3 FCR 514 436
G-A (A Child) (Removal from Jurisdiction: Human Rights), *Re* [2001] 1
    FCR 43 CA 466
GW *v* RW [2003] EWHC 611; [2003] 2 FCR 289; [2003] FL 386 . . . 184, 204, 206, 211
Gammans *v* Ekins [1950] 2 KB 328; [1950] 2 All ER 140 CA 5
Gandhi *v* Patel [2002] 1 FLR 603. 38
Ganesmoorthy *v* Ganesmoorthy [2003] 3 FCR 167 64
Gaskin *v* UK (1989) 12 EHRR 36 579
Gay *v* Sheeran [1999] 2 FLR 519; [1999] 2 FCR 705 232
George *v* George [1986] 2 FLR 347; (1986) 16 Fam Law 294 248
George *v* George [2003] 3 FCR 380 203
Gereis *v* Yagoub [1997] 1 FLR 854; [1997] 3 FCR 755 38
Gillet *v* Holt [2000] 2 FLR 266; [2000] FCR 705 CA 139–141
Gillick *v* W Norfolk and Wisbech AHA [1986] 1 FLR 229; [1986]
    AC 112 HL 349, 352, 358, 394–397, 411, 429, 461, 463, 517, 518
Gissing *v* Gissing [1970] 3 WLR 255; [1971] 1 AC 886 HL 133, 134

Glaser *v* UK [2000] 3 FCR 193; [2000] 1 FCR 153 ECtHR 480
Gloucestershire CC *v* P [1999] 2 FLR 61; [1999] 3 FCR 114 579
Gojkovic *v* Gojkovic [1990] FLR 140; [1990] FCR 119 CA 204
Goldsworthy *v* Brickell [1987] 1 Ch 378; [1987] 2 WLR 133 629
Gollins *v* Gollins [1963] 3 WLR 176; [1964] AC 644 HL 89
Goodchild, *Re* [1996] 1 WLR 694; [1997] 1 FCR 45 641
Goodman *v* Gallant [1986] 1 FLR 513; [1986] Fam 106 134
Goodrich *v* Goodrich [1971] 2 All ER 1340; [1971] 1 WLR 1142 89
Goodwin *v* UK [2002] FCR 577 ECtHR 45, 46
Gorman (A Bankrupt), *Re* [1990] 2 FLR 289; [1990] 1 All ER 717 151
Graham *v* Murphy [1997] 1 FLR 860; [1997] 2 FCR 441 642
Grant *v* Edwards [1986] Ch 638; [1987] 1 FLR 87 CA 136–138, 141
Grant *v* South-West Trains [1998] 1 FLR 839; [1998] 1 FCR 377 ECJ 48
Greasley *v* Cooke [1980] 1 WLR 1306; [1980] 3 All ER 710 CA 140, 141
Griffiths *v* Griffiths [1979] 1 WLR 1350 142
Grimes *v* Grimes [1948] P 323; [1948] 2 All ER 147 50
H (A Child) (Adoption: Disclosure), *Re* ; G (A Child) (Adoption: Disclosure),
   Re [2001] 1 FCR 726 602
H (A Child) (Contact: Mother's Opposition), *Re* [2001] 1 FCR 59 . . . . 473, 481
H (A Child) (Interim Care Order), *Re* [2003] 1 FCR 350 545
H (A Child: Residence), *Re* [2002] 3 FCR 277 CA 451
H (A Minor) (Blood Tests: Parental Rights), *Re* [1997] Fam 89; [1996]
   2 FLR 65; [1996] 3 FCR 201 . . . . 332, 333, 369
H (A Minor) (Care Proceedings: Child's Wishes), *Re* [1993] 1 FLR 440;
   [1993] Fam Law 200 407
H (A Minor) (Contact), *Re* [1994] 2 FLR 776; [1994] FCR 419 CA 305, 483
H (A Minor: Custody), *Re* [1990] 1 FLR 51; [1990] FCR 353 443
H (A Minor) (Custody: Interim Care and Control), *Re* [1991] 2 FLR 109; [1991]
   FCR 985 309
H (A Minor) (Parental Responsibility), *Re* [1993] 1 FLR 484; [1993] 1 FCR 85 319
H (A Minor) (Prohibited Steps Order), *Re* [1995] 1 FLR 638; [1995] 2 FCR 547 . . . 269
H (A Minor) (Role of the Official Solicitor), *Re* [1993] 2 FLR 552; [1993]
   2 FCR 437 . . . . 403, 404
H (A Minor) (S 37 Direction), *Re* [1993] 2 FLR 541; [1993] 2 FCR 277 . . . . . . 342, 343
H (A Minor) (Occupation Order: Power of Arrest), *Re* [2001] 1 FCR 370 267
H (Abduction: Child of 16), *Re* [2000] 2 FLR 51; [2000] 3 FCR 404 . . . . . 494, 497, 498
H (Abduction: Rights of Custody), *Re* [2000] 1 FLR 374; [2000] 1 FCR 225 HL . . . 496
H (Adoption Non-Patrial), *Re* [1996] 1 FLR 717 600
H (Application to Remove from Jurisdiction), *Re* [1998] 1 FLR 848; [1999]
   2 FCR 34 CA 467
H (Child Abduction) (Unmarried Father: Rights of Custody), *Re* [2003] FL 469 496
H (Children. Abduction) [2003] 2 FCR 151 499
H (Children) (Contact Order), *Re* [2001] 1 FCR 49 474
H (Children) (Contact Order) (No 2), *Re* [2001] 3 FCR 385 . . . . 457, 473, 474
H (Children) (Residence Order: Condition), *Re* [2001] 3 FCR 182; [2001]
   2 FLR 1277 . . . . 431, 467

H (Child's Name: First Name), *Re* [2002] 1 FLR 973 465
H (Minors) (Abduction: Acquiescence), *Re* [1998] AC 72; [1997] 2 FCR 257 498
'' (Minors) (Abduction: Custody Rights) [1991] 2 FLR 263; [1992] 1 FCR 45 HL . . 496
      Re [1992] 1 FLR 148; [1992] 1 FCR 70 478
      uthority: Parental Responsibility) (No. 3), *Re* [1991] Fam
      14; [1991] FCR 361 . . . . 316, 318
      :d Steps Order), *Re* [1995] 1 FLR 638; [1995]
      . . . . 424, 427, 428, 555
      buse: Standard of Proof), *Re* [1996] AC 563;
      [1996] 1 FLR 80 HL 536–539, 542, 543
      bility), *Re* [1998] 1 FLR 855; [1998] 2 FCR 89 CA . . 316, 318, 319
      Child's Application for Leave), *Re* [2000]
      . . . . 403–405, 432, 440
      parent), *Re* [2000] Fam Law 715 307
      Parental Responsibility), *Re* [1995] 2 FLR 883; [1996]
      . . . . 320, 458
      849[1954] P 258 . . . . 53, 54
      55 222
H *v* H (Abduction: Acquiescence) [1996] 2 FLR 570; [1996] 3 FCR 425 501
H *v* H (Financial Provision: Special Contribution) [2002] 2 FLR 1021 203
H *v* H (Pension Sharing: Recission of Decree Nisi) [2002] 2 FLR 116 217
H *v* H (Residence Order: Leave to Remove from the Jurisdiction) [1995] 1
    FLR 529; [1995] 2 FCR 469 CA 440
H *v* Norfolk [1997] 1 FLR 384; [1997] 2 FCR 334 CA 576
H *v* P (Illegitimate Child: Capital Provision) [1993] Fam Law 515 182
H *v* West Sussex CC [1998] 1 FLR 862; [1998] 3 FCR 126 570
H and A (Children), *Re* [2002] 2 FCR 469; [2002] 1 FLR 1145 . . . . . 289, 332, 333, 460
HB (Abduction: Children's Objections), *Re* [1998] 1 FLR 422 403
HG (Specific Issue Order: Sterilisation), *Re* [1993] 1 FLR 587; [1993] 1 FCR 553 . . . 435
H-J *v* H-J (Financial Provision: Departing from Equality) [2002] 1 FLR 415 210
HM Customs and Excise and Another *v* A [2002] 3 FCR 481, CA 208
Hadjimilitis (Tsavliris) *v* Tsavliris (Divorce: Irretrievable Breakdown) [2002] FL 883 . . 90
Hale *v* Tanner [2000] 3 FCR 62 249
Hall & Co *v* Simons [1999] 2 FCR 193 CA 224
Hammond *v* Mitchell [1992] 2 All ER 109; [1992] 1 FLR 229; [1991]
    FCR 938 . . . . 136, 137, 251
Hammond *v* Osborn [2002] EWCA Civ 885 629
Hancock (Deceased), *Re* [1998] 2 FLR 346; [1999] 1 FCR 4000 CA 639, 641
Hanlon *v* Hanlon [1978] 2 All ER 889; [1978] 1 WLR 592 219
Hansen *v* Turkey [2003] 3 FCR 97, ECtHR 480
Harnett *v* Harnett [1973] 2 All ER 593; [1973] 3 WLR 1 142
Harper *v* O'Reilly and Harper [1997] 2 FLR 816; [1998] 3 FCR 475 227
Harris *v* Harris [2001] 1 FCR 68 229
Harris *v* Manahan [1997] 1 FLR 205; [1997] 2 FCR 607 CA 223, 230
Harwood *v* Harwood [1991] 2 FLR 274; [1992] 1 FCR 1 218
Haywood *v* Haywood Unreported 13.7.2000 130

Heard v Heard [1995] 1 FLR 970; [1996] 1 FCR 33 CA 231
Hellyer v Hellyer [1996] 2 FLR 579; [1997] 1 FCR 340 227
Hendriks v Netherlands (1982) 5 EHRR 223, 5 D&R 225 ECtHR 377
Heseltine v Heseltine [1971] 1 All ER 952; [1971] 1 WLR 342 128
Hewison v Hewison [1977] Fam Law 207 CA 453
Hewitson v Hewitson [1995] 1 FLR 241; [1995] 2 FCR 588 CA 231
Hill v Hill [1998] 1 FLR 198; [1997] FCR 477 CA 206, 231
Hirani v Hirani (1982) 4 FLR 232 CA 52–54
Hobhouse v Hobhouse [1999] 1 FLR 961 .... 199, 206
Hoffman v Austria [1994] 1 FCR 193; (1993) 17 EHRR 293 ECtHR 453
Hokkanen v Finland [1996] 1 FLR 289; [1995] 2 FCR 320; (1995) 19
    EHRR 139 .... 311, 472, 480
Hollens v Hollens (1971) 115 SJ 327 91
Hoppe v Germany [2003] 1 FCR 176 .... 377, 472
Horrocks v Forray [1976] 1 All ER 737; [1976] 1 WLR 230 CA 148
Horton v Horton [1972] 2 All ER 871 HL 51, 52
Humberside CC v B [1993] 1 FLR 257; [1993] 1 FCR 613 .... 252, 368, 531
Hunter v Canary Wharf Ltd [1997] AC 655; [1997] 2 FLR 342 267
Huntingdon Life Services Ltd v Curtis (1997) *The Times*, 11 December 269
Huntingford v Hobbs [1993] 1 FLR 736; [1993] 1 FCR 45 CA 134
Hyde v Hyde and Woodhouse [1866] LR 1 PD 130 34
Hyett v Stanley [2003] 3 FCR 253 CA 136
I v UK [2002] FCR 613 ECtHR 45
Ignaccolo-Zenide v Romania (2001) 31 EHRR 7 .... 472, 478
Islam v Islam [2003] FL 815 42
Ivin v Blake (1993) 67 P&CR 263; [1993] EGCS 104 137
J (A Minor) (Abduction: Custody Rights), *Re* [1990] 2 AC 562; [1991] FCR 129 ... 495
J (A Minor) (Wardship), *Re* [1988] 1 FLR 65; (1988) 18 Fam Law 91 332
J (A Minor) (Wardship: Medical Treatment), *Re* [1991] Fam 33; [1990] 3 All ER
    930; [1991] 1 FLR 366; [1991] FCR 370 399
J (Abduction: Wrongful Removal), *Re* [2000] 1 FLR 78; [2000] 1 FCR 160 265
J (Adoption: Contacting Father), *Re* [2003] FL 368 602
J (An Infant), *Re* (1913) 108 LT 554 493
J (Children) (Residence: Expert Evidence), *Re* [2001] 2 FCR 44 CA 442
J (Freeing for Adoption), *Re* [2000] 2 FLR 58; [2000] 2 FCR 133 490
J (Income Support Cohabitation), *Re* [1995] 1 FLR 660 59
J (Leave to Issue Application for Residence Order), *Re* [2003] 1 FLR 114 ...... 306, 434
J (Parental Responsibility), *Re* [1999] 1 FLR 784 317
J (Specific Issue Orders), *Re* [2000] 1 FLR 517; [2000]
    1 FCR 307 CA 363, 364, 453, 454
J (Specific Issue Order: Leave to Apply), *Re* [1995] 1 FLR 669; [1995]
    2 FCR 799 .... 519, 520
J (Specific Issue Orders: Muslim Upbringing and Circumcision), *Re* [1999]
    2 FLR 678; [1999] 2 FCR 345 454
J v C [1969] 2 WLR 540; [1970] AC 668 HL 367, 453, 457
J v C [1990] 2 FLR 527; [1990] FCR 716 400

J *v* C (Child: Financial Provision) [1999] 1 FLR 152; [1998] 3 FCR 79 . . . . 165, 182

J *v* J (A Minor: Property Transfer) [1993] 2 FLR 56; [1993] 1 FCR 471 . . . . . . 181, 302

J *v* S-T [1997] 1 FLR 402; [1997] 1 FCR 349 CA 58

JA (Child Abduction: Non-Convention Country), *Re* [1998] 1 FLR 231; [1998]
 2 FCR 159 504

J-PC *v* J-AF [1955] P 215; [1955] 3 WLR 72 CA 204

J-S (A Child) (Contact: Parental Responsibility), *Re* [2002] 3 FCR 433 . . . 319, 471, 477

Jackson *v* Bell [2001] FL 879 153

Jelley *v* Iliffe [1981] Fam 128; [1981] 2 WLR 801 CA 636, 638, 642

Jenkins *v* Howells [1949] 2 KB 218; [1949] 1 All ER 942 409

Jennings (Deceased), *Re* [1994] Ch 256; [1994] 3 All ER 27 639

Jennings *v* Rice [2003] 1 FCR 501 141

Jessell *v* Jessell [1979] 1 WLR 1148; [1979] 3 All ER 645 CA 132

Johansen *v* Norway (1996) 23 EHRR 33 601

Johnson *v* Calvert [1993] 851 P 2d 774 . . . . 287, 329

Johnson *v* Walton [1990] 1 FLR 350; [1990] FCR 568 CA 248, 249

Johnston *v* Ireland (1986) 9 EHRR 203 ECtHR 108, 110, 324

Jones *v* Challenger [1960] 2 WLR 695; [1961] 1 QB 176 CA 150

Jones *v* Jones [1977] 1 WLR 438 141

Jones *v* Jones [2000] 2 FLR 307; [2000] 2 FCR 201 228

Jones *v* Maynard [1951] Ch 572; [1951] 1 All ER 802 128

Judd *v* Brown [1998] 2 FLR 360 153

Julian *v* Julian (1972) 116 SJ 763 92

K, *Re* [1998] Fam Law 567 319

K (A Child) (Secure Accommodation Order: Right to Liberty, *Re* [2001] 1
 FCR 249 CA 586

K (A Minor) (Wardship: Adoption), *Re* [1991] 1 FLR 57; [1991]
 FCR 142 . . . . 301, 346, 449, 450

K (Abduction: Consent), *Re* [1997] 2 FLR 212 498

K (Abduction: Custody), *Re* [1997] 2 FLR 22 497

K (Adoption and Wardship), *Re* [1997] 2 FLR 221; [1997] 2 FLR 230;
 [1997] 2 FCR 389 CA 308, 610

K (Application to Remove from Jurisdiction), *Re* [1988] 2 FLR 1006 466

K (Care Order or Residence Order), *Re* [1995] 1 FLR 675; [1996] 1
 FCR 365 . . . . 422, 541, 542

K (Children: Committal Proceedings), *Re* [2003] 2 FCR 336 480

K (Contact: Mother's Anxiety), *Re* [1999] 2 FLR 703 479

K (Replacement of Guardian ad Litem), *Re* [2001] 1 FLR 663 403

K (Residence Order: Securing Contact), *Re* [1999] 1 FLR 583; [1999] 3
 FCR 365 CA 382, 449

K (Specific Issue Order), *Re* [1999] 2 FLR 280; [1999] 1 FCR 337 333

K (Supervision Orders), *Re* [1999] 2 FLR 303 . . . . 541, 542

K *v* H (Child Maintenance) [1993] 2 FLR 61; [1993] 1 FCR 684 446

K *v* K (Ancillary Relief: Prenuptial Agreement) [2002] FL 877 223

K *v* K (Financial Provision) [1996] 3 FCR 158; [1997] 1 FLR 35 92

K *v* K (Financial Provision: Conduct) [1990] 2 FLR 225; [1990] FCR 372 208

K *v* K (Minors: Property Transfer) [1992] 2 FLR 220; [1992] 2 FCR 253 181

K *v* M (Paternity: Contact) [1996] 1 FLR 312; [1996] 3 FCR 517 . . . . 331, 435

K and T *v* Finland [2000] 2 FLR 79; [2000] 3 FCR 248;
[2001] 2 FCR 673 . . . . 441, 510, 511, 529, 559

K, W, and H (Minors) (Medical Treatment), *Re* [1993] 1 FLR 854; [1993] 1
FCR 240 396

KA *v* Finland [2003] 1 FCR 201; [2003] 1 FLR 696; [2003] 1 FCR 230 . . 550, 551, 559

KD (A Minor) (Ward: Termination of Access), *Re* [1988] AC 806; [1988]
1 All ER 577; [1988] 2 FLR 139; [1988] FCR 657 . . . . 378, 449

KL *v* UK (1999) 26 EHRR CD 113 525

KR (Abduction: Forcible Removal by Parents), *Re* [1999] 2 FLR 542;
[1999] 2 FCR 337 . . . . 53, 488

Katz *v* Katz [1972] 3 All ER 219; [1972] 1 WLR 955 89

Kaur *v* Singh [1972] 1 All ER 292; [1972] 1 WLR 105 51

Kean *v* Kean [2002] 2 FLR 28 231

Keegan *v* Ireland (1994) 18 EHRR 342, ECtHR; [1994] 3 FCR 165 . . . . 309, 310

Kelley *v* Corston [1998] 1 FLR 986; [1998] 1 FCR 554 CA 224

Kelly *v* BBC [2001] 1 FCR 197 . . . . 459, 487

Kemmis *v* Kemmis [1988] 1 WLR 1307; [1988] 2 FLR 223 CA 232

Khan *v* UK (1986) 48 DR 253, ECtHR 43

Khorasandjian *v* Bush [1993] QB 727; [1993] 2 FCR 257; [1993] 2 FLR 66 267

Kilvert *v* Kilvert [1998] 2 FLR 806 154

Kimber *v* Kimber [2000] 1 FLR 232; [2000] 1 FLR 383 . . . . 59, 230

Kingsnorth Trust *v* Tizard [1986] 1 WLR 783 150

Kjeldsen *v* Denmark (1976) EHRR 711 411

Krubert, *Re* [1997] Ch 97 CA 640

Krystman *v* Krystman [1973] 3 All ER 247; [1973] 1 WLR 927 CA 206

Kumar (A Bankrupt), *ex p* Lewis *v* Kumar, *Re* [1993] 2 FLR 382; [1994]
2 FCR 373 226

Kutzner *v* Germany [2003] 1 FCR 249 541

L (A Child) (Contact: Domestic Violence), *Re* [2000] 2 FLR 334; [2000] 2 FCR 404; [2000]
4 All ER 609 CA 24, 25, 377, 382, 383, 425, 450, 469, 471, 475, 476, 480, 483

L (Abduction: Child's Objections to Return), *Re* [2002] 2 FLR 1042;
[1999] 1 FCR 739 . . . . 500, 501

L (Abduction: Pending Criminal Proceedings), *Re* [1999] 1 FLR 433;
[1999] 2 FCR 604 . . . . 491, 497

L (Care: Assessment: Fair Trial), *Re* [2002] 2 FLR 730; [2002] 2 FCR 673 511

L (Contact: Genuine Fear), *Re* [2002] FLR 621 479

L (Contact: Transsexual Applicant), *Re* [1995] 2 FLR 438; [1995] 3 FCR 125 425

L (Medical Treatment: Gillick Competency), *Re* [1998] 2 FLR 810; [1999]
2 FCR 524 . . . . 395, 396

L (Minors) (Financial Provisions), *Re* [1979] 1 FLR 39 203

L (Minors) (Wardship: Jurisdiction), *Re* [1974] 1 All ER 913; [1974] 1 WLR 250 . . . 504

L (Removal from Jurisdiction: Holiday), *Re* [2001] 1 FLR 241 466

L (Residence: Justices' Reasons), *Re* [1995] 2 FLR 445; [1995] 3 FCR 684 443

L (Section 37 Direction), *Re* [1999] 1 FLR 984; [1999] 3 FCR 642 524

L (Sexual Abuse: Standard of Proof), *Re* [1996] 1 FLR 116; [1996]
  2 FCR 352 . . . . 546, 569
L *v* Finland [2000] 2 FLR 118; [2000] 3 FCR 219 . . . 309, 310, 312, 510, 558, 565, 566
L *v* L (Child Abuse: Access) [1989] 2 FLR 16; [1989] FCR 697 571
L *v* L (Leave to Remove Children from Jurisdiction: Effect of Children)
  [2003] 1 FLR 900 467
L *v* Sweden (1982) 40 D&R 140 377
L, V, M, H (Contact: Domestic Violence), *Re* [2000] 2 FLR 334; [2000] 2
  FCR 404 572
LM *v* Essex CC [1999] 1 FLR 988; [1999] 1 FCR 673 586
Laird *v* Laird [1999] 1 FLR 791 150
Lambert *v* Lambert [2002] 3 FCR 673 . . . . 201, 209, 210
Lancashire CC *v* B [2000] 1 FLR 583; [2000] 1 FCR 583; [2000]
  1 All ER 97, HL 306, 506, 539, 540
Lau *v* DPP [2000] 1 FLR 799 268
Le Brocq *v* Le Brocq [1964] 3 All ER 464; [1964] 1 WLR 1085 89
Le Foe *v* Le Foe [2002] 1 FCR 107 137
Leach, *Re [1985] 3 WLR 413;* [1986] Ch 226 CA 637
Leadbeater *v* Leadbeater (1985) 15 Fam Law 280; [1985] 1 FLR 789 . . . . 203, 205
Leeds CC *v* C [1993] 1 FLR 269; [1993] 1 FCR 585 432
Leeds Teaching Hospital NHS Trust *v* A [2003] EWHC 259;
  [2003] 1 FCR 599 . . . . 288, 290–292, 310
Lindsay *v* UK (1986) 49 DR 181 264
Lines *v* Lines (1963) *The Times*, 16 July. 89
Lissimore *v* Downing [2003] 2 FLR 308 . . . . 139, 140
Lister *v* Hesley Hall Ltd [2001] 2 FLR 307; [2001] 2 FCR 97 576
Livesey *v* Jenkins [1985] FLR 813 HL 230
Livingstone-Stallard *v* Livingstone-Stallard [1974] Fam 47; [1974] 2 All ER 766 90
Lloyds Bank *v* Rosset [1991] 1 AC 107; [1990] 2 FLR 155; [1990]
  1 All ER 1111 . . . . 135–138, 143
Lloyds TSB Bank *v* Shoney [2001] EWCA Civ 1161, [2002] 1 FCR 673 155
Logan *v* UK (1994) 22 EHRR 178 174
Lynch *v* DPP [1980] AC 614 53
M, *Re*; R (X and Y) *v* Gloucestershire CC [2003] FL 444 574
M (A Child), *Re* [2002] 1 FCR 88 . . . . 301, 311, 575
M (A Child) (Secure Accommodation), *Re* [2001] EWCA Civ 458; [2001]
  1 FCR 692 587
M (A Minor) (Abduction: Acquiescence), *Re* [1996] 1 FLR 315; [1995] 3 FCR 99 . . 497
M (A Minor) (Adoption), *Re* [1991] 1 FLR 458; [1990] FCR 993 CA 610
M (A Minor) (Care Order: Threshold Conditions), *Re* [1994] Fam 95 CA;
  [1994] 2 AC 424; [1994] 2 FLR 577; [1994] 2 FCR 871, HL 324, 532,
                                                                          534–536, 541, 549
M (A Minor) (Child Abduction), *Re* [1994] 1 FLR 390; [1994] 2 FCR 750 CA 500
M (A Minor) (Custody Application), *Re* [1990] 1 FLR 291; [1990] FCR 424 449
M (A Minor) (Family Proceedings: Affidavits), *Re* [1995] 2 FLR 100;
  [1995] 2 FCR 90 CA 442

M (A Minor) (Immigration: Residence Order), *Re* [1993] 2 FLR 858; [1995]
  2 FCR 793 422
M (A Minor) (Secure Accommodation Order), *Re* [1995] Fam 108; [1995]
  2 FCR 373 369
M (Abduction) (Consent: Acquiescence), *Re* [1999] 1 FLR 171; [1999] 1 FCR 5 . . . 498
M (Abduction: Intolerable Situation), *Re* [2000] 1 FLR 930 499
M (Abduction: Non-Convention Country), *Re* [1995] 1 FLR 89; [1995] 2 FCR 265 . 504
M (Abduction: Undertakings), *Re* [1995] 1 FLR 1021; [1995] 3 FCR 745 499
M (Adoption or Residence Order), *Re* [1998] 1 FLR 570; [1998]
  1 FCR 165 . . . . 422, 600, 614
M (Adoption: Rights of Natural Father), *Re* [2001] 1 FLR 745 602
M (Care: Contact: Grandmother's Application for Leave), *Re* [1995]
  2 FLR 86; [1995] 3 FCR 550 CA 308, 434, 571
M (Care: Leave to Interview Child), *Re* [1995] 1 FLR 825; [1995] 2 FCR 643 578
M (Care Order: Parental Responsibility), *Re* [1996] 2 FLR 84; [1996]
  2 FLR 521 . . . . 533, 535
M (Care Proceedings: Judicial Review) [2003] FL 479 570
M (Challenging Decisions by Local Authority), *Re* [2001] 2 FLR 1300 574
M (Child Support Act: Parentage), *Re* [1997] 2 FLR 90; [1997] 3 FCR 383 287
M (Child's Upbringing), *Re* [1996] 2 FLR 441; [1996] 3 FCR 99 CA 450, 452
M (Contact Order: Committal), *Re* [1999] 1 FLR 810; [1999] 1 FCR 683 480
M (Contact: Welfare Test), *Re* [1995] 1 FLR 274; [1995] 1 FCR 753 . . . . 470, 471
M (Handicapped Child: Parental Responsibility) [2001] 3 FCR 454 . . . . . . 318, 444, 474
M (Intractable Contact Dispute), *Re* [2003] FL 719 479
M (Jurisdiction: Forum Conveniens), *Re* [1995] 2 FLR 224; [1996] 1 FCR 40 CA . . 504
M (Medical Treatment: Consent), *Re* [1999] 2 FLR 1097; [1999] 2 FCR 577 . . 396, 441
M (Minors) (Abduction: Peremptory Return Order), *Re* [1996] 1 FLR 478;
  [1996] 1 FCR 557 504
M (Minors) (Contact: Violent Parent), *Re* [1999] 2 FCR 56 474
M (Minors) (Custody: Jurisdiction), *Re* [1992] 2 FLR 382; [1992] 1 FCR 201 494
M (Minors) (Residence Order: Jurisdiction), *Re* [1993] 1 FLR 495; [1993]
  1 FCR 718 CA 495
M (Official Solicitor's Role), *Re* [1998] 3 FLR 815 525
M (Section 91(14) Order), *Re* [1999] 2 FLR 553 436
M (Section 94 Appeals), *Re* [1995] 1 FLR 546; [1995] 2 FCR 435 452
M (Secure Accommodation Order), *Re* [1995] 1 FLR 418; [1995]
  2 FCR 373 CA 520, 522, 586
M (Sexual Abuse Allegations: Interviewing Techniques), *Re* [1999] 2 FLR 92 425
M (Sperm Donor Father) [2003] FL 94 . . . . 359, 455, 456, 471
M *v* A (Contact: Domestic Violence) [2002] 2 FLR 921 407
M *v* B (Ancillary Proceedings: Lump Sum) [1998] 1 FLR 53;
  [1998] 1 FCR 213 . . . . 184, 202, 218, 219
M *v* Birmingham CC [1994] 2 FLR 141; [1995] 1 FCR 50 445
M *v* C and Calderdale MBC [1993] 1 FLR 505; [1993] 1 FCR 431 CA 433
M *v* H [1996] NZFLR 241 34
M *v* H [1999] 171 DLR (4th) 577 48

M *v* M (Child of the Family) [1984] FLR 796 303

M *v* M (Child: Access) [1973] 2 All ER 81 470

M *v* M (Defined Contact Application) [1998] 2 FLR 244 477

M *v* M (Financial Provision) [1987] 2 FLR 1; (1987) 17 Fam Law 195 200

M *v* M (Minors) (Jurisdiction) [1993] 1 FCR 5 CA 467

M *v* M (Parental Responsibility) [1999] 2 FLR 737 .... 319, 359, 456

M *v* M (Prenuptial Agreement) [2002] FL 177 .... 222, 223

M *v* Newnham [1995] 2 AC 633; [1995] 2 FLR 276; [1995] 3 FCR 337 HL 576

M *v* The Netherlands (1993) 74 D&R 120 310

M *v* Warwickshire [1994] 2 FLR 593; [1994] 2 FCR 121 579

M and B (Children) (Contact: Domestic Violence), *Re* [2001] 1 FCR 116 478

M and N (Minors) (Wardship: Publication of Information), *Re* [1990] Fam
211; [1990] FCR 395; [1990] 1 FLR 149 CA 487

M and R (Child Abuse: Evidence), *Re* [1996] 2 FLR 195; [1996]
2 FCR 617 .... 444, 537, 543

M, T, P, K and B (Care: Change of Name), *Re* [2000] 1 FLR 645 .... 463, 562

MB, *Re* [1997] Med LR 217 396

MB *v* UK (1994) 77 A DR 108 336

MD and TD (Minors) (No. 2), *Re* [1994] Fam Law 489; [1994] 2 FLR 336 579

MG *v* UK [2002] 2 FCR 289 613

MM (Medical Treatment), *Re* [2000] 1 FLR 224 398

MT *v* MT (Financial Provision: Lump Sum) [1992] 1 FLR 362; [1991] FCR 649 ... 204

MW (Adoption Surrogacy), *Re* [1995] 2 FLR 759; [1996] 3 FCR 128 .... 342, 598

McGrath *v* Wallis [1995] 2 FLR 114; [1995] 3 FCR 661 CA 129, 135

McKellar *v* Hounslow LBC Unreported 28.10.2003, QBD 643

McMichael *v* UK [1995] 2 FCR 718; (1995) 20 EHRR 205 ECtHR 323, 512, 559

Manchanda *v* Manchanda [1995] 2 FLR 590; [1996] 1 FCR 733 CA 87

Manchester City Council *v* B [1996] 1 FLR 324; [1996] 3 FCR 118 531

Manchester City Council *v* F [1993] 1 FLR 419; [1993] 1 FCR 1000 544

Martin BH *v* Martin BH [1977] 3 WLR 101; [1978] Fam 12 221

Maskell *v* Maskell [2001] 3 FCR 296 231

Mason *v* Mason (1981) 11 Fam Law 143 90

Mawson *v* Mawson [1994] 2 FLR 985; [1994] 2 FCR 852 175

May *v* May (1985) 16 Fam Law 106; [1986] 1 FLR 325 CA 442

Medway Coucil *v* BBC [2001] FL 883 427

Mendoza *v* Ghaidan [2002] 3 FCR 591 .... 6, 66, 260

Mesher *v* Mesher [1980] 1 All ER 126 CA 220, 221

Messina *v* Smith [1971] P 322; [1971] 3 WLR 118 54

Midland Bank *v* Cooke [1995] 4 All ER 562; [1995] 2 FLR 915;
[1996] 1 FCR 442 CA 130, 138, 139

Mikulic *v* Croatia [2002] 1 FCR 720 .... 310, 332, 336

Miles *v* Chilton (1849) 1 Rob Eccl 684 57

Militante *v* Ogunwomoju [1993] 2 FCR 355; (1994) Fam Law 17 54

Minton *v* Minton [1979] AC 593; [1979] 2 WLR 31 198

Moge *v* Moge (1993) 99 DLR (4th) 456 187

Mordant, *Re* [1996] 1 FLR 334; [1997] 2 FCR 378 .... 226, 227

Morgan v Morgan [1959] P 92; [1959] 2 WLR 487 . . . . 52, 57
Mortgage Corp, The v Shaire [2000] 1 FLR 973; [2000] 2 FCR 222 . . . . 149, 150
Mortimore v Wright [1840] 6 M&W 482 418
Moschetta v Moschetta (1994) 25 Cal App 4th 1218 287
Moss v Moss [1897] P 263 . . . . 54, 55
Mossop v Mossop [1989] Fam 77; [1988] 2 FLR 173 CA 68
Mouncer v Mouncer [1972] 1 All ER 289; [1972] 1 WLR 321 91
Moustaquim v Belgium (1991) 13 EHRR 802 . . . . 309, 451
Moynihan, Re [2000] 1 FLR 113 . . . . 289, 346
Mullin v Richards [1998] 1 All ER 920 419
Murbarak v Murbarak [2001] 1 FCR 193 225
N (Contact: Minor Seeking Leave to Defend and Removal of Guardian),
    Re [2003] FL 154 . . . . 403, 405
N (Leave to Withdraw Care Proceedings), Re [2000] 1 FLR
    134; [2000] 1 FCR 258 . . . . 511, 529, 537, 559, 585
N (Minors) (Abduction), Re [1991] 1 FLR 413; [1991] FCR 765 497
N (Section 91(14) Order), Re [1996] 1 FLR 356; [1996] 2 FCR 377 CA 435
N v N (Abduction: Article 13 Defence) [1995] 1 FLR 107; [1995] 1 FCR 595 499
N v N (Child Abduction: Habitual Residence) [2000] 3 FCR 84 495
N v N (Consent Order: Variation) [1993] 2 FLR 868; [1994] 2 FCR 275 CA 204
N v N (Financial Provision: Sale of Company) [2001] FL 347; [2001] 2 FLR 69 . . 210, 218
N v N (Foreign Divorce: Financial Relief) [1997] 1 FLR 900; [1997] 2 FCR 573 . . . 222
N v N (Jurisdiction: Pre-Nuptial Agreement) [1999] 2 FLR 745;
    [1999] 2 FCR 583 . . . . 223, 426, 430
N-B and Others (Children) (Residence: Expert Evidence), Re [2002] 3 FCR 259 541
Nandu v Nandu Unreported 21.7.2000 231
Nash v Inman [1908] 2 KB 1 417
Newton v Newton [1990] 1 FLR 33; [1989] FCR 521 204
Nicholson (Deceased), Re [1974] 1 WLR 476 142
Nielsen v Denmark (1989) 11 EHRR 175 ECtHR 375, 397
Norris v Norris [2003] 2 FCR 245; [2003] FL 301 . . . . 203, 210, 211
North Yorkshire CC v SA [2003] 3 FCR 118 543
Nottingham CC v October Films Ltd [1999] 2 FLR 347; [1999] 2 FCR 529 490
Nottingham CC v P [1994] Fam 18; [1993] 2
    FLR 134; [1994] 1 FCR 624 CA 424, 428, 524, 525, 554, 555, 581, 584
Nottinghamshire County Council v J, Unreported 26.11.93 518
Nuutinen v Finland (App No 32842/96), Unreported 27.6.2000, ECtHR 480
Nwogbe v Nwogbe [2000] 2 FLR 744; [2000] 3 FCR 345 256
O (A Child) (Supervision Order: Future Harm), Re [2001] 1 FCR 289 541
O (A Minor) (Care Order: Education: Procedure), Re [1992]
    2 FLR 7; [1992] 1 FCR 489 . . . . 409, 410, 532, 534, 541
O (A Minor) (Wardship: Adopted Child), Re [1977] 3 WLR 715; [1978]
    Fam 196 CA 611
O (Abduction: Consent and Acquiescence), Re [1997] 1 FLR 924; [1998] 2 FCR 61 . . 496
O (Abduction: Custody Rights), Re [1997] 2 FLR 702; [1997] 2 FCR 465 495
O (Care or Supervision Order), Re [1996] 2 FLR 755; [1997] 2 FCR 17 530

O (Care: Discharge of Care Order), *Re* [1999] 2 FLR 119 . . . . 580, 582
O (Contact: Imposition of Conditions), *Re* [1995] 2 FLR 124; [1996] 1
    FCR 317 CA 430, 473
O (Family Appeals: Management), *Re* [1998] 1 FLR 431 450
O (Imposition of Conditions), *Re* [2000] Fam Law 631 471
O (Transracial Adoption: Contact), *Re* [1995] 2 FLR 597; [1996] 1 FCR 540 452
O *v* L (Blood Tests) [1995] 2 FLR 930; [1996] 2 FCR 649 331
O *v* O (Jurisdiction: Jewish Divorce) [2000] 2 FLR 147 . . . . 92, 93
O and N (Children) (Non-Accidental Injury) [2003]
    UKHL 18; [2003] 1 FCR 673 . . . . 444, 536, 538, 539, 541–544
Odievre *v* France [2003] 1 FCR 621 336
Olsson *v* Sweden (No. 1) (1988) 11 EHRR 259 ECtHR 311, 559
Omelian *v* Omelian [1996] 2 FLR 306; [1996] 3 FCR 329 CA 229
O'Neill *v* O'Neill [1975] 3 All ER 289; [1975] 1 WLR 1118 89
Oxfordshire CC *v* L (Care or Supervision Order) [1998] 1 FLR 70 . . . . 530, 541
Öztürk *v* Germany (1984) 6 EHRR 409 263
P (A Child) (Expert Evidence), *Re* [2001] 1 FCR 751 478
P (A Child) (Financial Provision) [2003] 2 FCR 481 182
P (A Minor) (Education), *Re* [1992] 1 FLR 316; [1992] FCR 145 CA 410, 441
P (A Minor) (Inadequate Welfare Report), *Re* [1996] 2 FCR 285 439
P (A Minor) (Parental Responsibility Order), *Re* [1994] 1 FLR 578;
    [1994] Fam Law 378 . . . . 318, 319, 364
P (Abduction: Minor's Views), *Re* [1998] 2 FLR 825; [1999] 1 FCR 739 500
P (Adoption: Parental Agreement), *Re* [1985] FLR 635 CA 457
P (Care Orders: Injunctive Relief), *Re* [2000] 3 FCR 426 554
P (Care Proceedings: Father's Application), *Re* [2001] 2 FCR 279 512
P (Children Act 1989, ss 22 and 26: Local Authority Compliance), *Re*
    [2000] 2 FLR 910 . . . . 563, 564
P (Contact Discretion), *Re* [1998] 2 FLR 696; [1999] 1 FCR 566 473
P (Contact: Indirect Contact), *Re* [1999] 2 FLR 893 425
P (Contact: Supervision), *Re* [1996] 2 FLR 314; [1997] 1 FCR 458 CA . . . 372, 457, 471
P (Emergency Protection Order), *Re* [1996] 1 FLR 482; [1996] 1 FCR 637 553
P (Minor) (Wardship: Surrogacy), *Re* [1987] 2 FLR 421; [1988] FCR 140 342
P (Parental Dispute: Judicial Determination), *Re* [2003] 1 FLR 286 447
P (Parental Responsibility), *Re* [1998] 2 FLR 96; [1998] 3 FCR 98 . . . . . . 316, 318, 482
P (Parental Responsibility: Change of Name), *Re* [1997] 2 FLR 722;
    [1997] 3 FCR 739 . . . . 318, 464
P (Section 91(14) Guidelines) (Residence and Religious Heritage),
    Re [1999] 2 FLR 573; [1999] 2 FCR 289 CA 435, 436, 450, 454
P (Terminating Parental Responsibility), *Re* [1995] 1 FLR 1048;
    [1995] 3 FCR 753 326
P *v* B (Paternity; Damages for Deceit) [2001] 1 FLR 1041 . . . . 64, 164
P *v* N (Child: Surname) [1997] 2 FCR 65 461
P *v* P (Contempt of Court: Mental Capacity) [1999] 2 FLR 897 CA 249
P *v* P [1964] 3 All ER 919; (1964) 28 MLR 606 50
P *v* R (Forced Marriage: Annulment: Procedure) [2003] 1 FLR 661 53

P, C, S v UK [2002] 3 FCR 1; [2002] 2 FLR 631 ECtHR 511, 512, 597, 604

PC (Change of Surname), *Re* [1997] 2 FLR 730; [1997]
3 FCR 544 . . . . 362, 363, 365, 461, 462

PJ (Adoption: Practice on Appeal), *Re* [1998] 2 FLR 252 CA 608

Paddington Building Society v Mendelsohn (1985) 50 P&CR 244; (1987)
17 Fam Law 121 155

Park, In the Estate of [1953] 3 WLR 1012; [1954] P 112 55

Parra v Parra [2002] 3 FCR 529; [2002] 3 FCR 513; [2003] 1 FCR 97 . . . 199, 212, 224

Pascoe v Turner [1979] 1 WLR 431; [1979] 2 All ER 945 141

Pasha v Pasha [2001] EWCA Civ 466; [2001] 2 FCR 185 195

Paton v BPAST [1978] 3 WLR 687[1979] QB 276 348

Paton v UK (1981) 3 EHRR 408 ECtHR 337, 348

Payne v Payne [2001] EWCA Civ 166; [2001] 1 FCR 425 . . . . 467, 468

Pazpena de Vire v Pazpena de Vire [2001] 1 FLR 460 37

Pearce (Deceased), *Re* [1998] 2 FLR 705; [1999] 2 FCR 179 641

Penrose v Penrose [1994] 2 FLR 621; [1994] 2 FCR 1167 CA 229

Pereira v Keleman [1995] 1 FLR 428; [1994] 2 FCR 635 418

Pettitt v Pettitt [1969] 2 WLR 966; [1970] AC 777 . . . . 129, 133

Pettkus v Becker (1980) 117 DLR (3d) 257 146

Pheasant v Pheasant [1972] Fam 202; [1972] 1 All ER 587 . . . . 89, 90

Phillips v Pearce [1996] 2 FLR 230; [1996] 2 FCR 237 . . . . 172, 176, 183

Piglowska v Piglowski [1999] 2 FLR 763; [1999]
2 FCR 481 HL 20, 26, 113, 116, 201, 219

Plant v Plant (1982) 12 Fam Law 179; [1983] 4 FLR 305 454

Pounds v Pounds [1994] 1 FLR 775; [1994] 2 FCR 1055 CA 224

Practice Direction [1980] 2 All ER 806 493

Practice Direction [1993] 1 FLR 668 403

Practice Direction [1995] 2 FLR 813 492

Practice Direction (Access: Supervised Access) [1980] 1 WLR 334 425

Practice Direction (Child: Removal from Jurisdiction) [1986] 1 All ER 983 493

Practice Direction (Disclosure of Addresses) [1989] 1 All ER 765 492

Practice Direction (Minor: Change of Surname: Deed Poll) [1995] 1 All ER 832 461

Practice Note (Official Solicitor: Sterilisation) [1993] 2 FLR 222 400

Practice Note (Official Solicitor: Sterilisation) [1996] 2 FLR 111; [1996]
3 FCR 95 400

Practice Note (The Official Solicitor: Application in Family Proceedings)
[1995] 2 FLR 479 408

Preston-Jones v Preston-Jones [1951] AC 391; [1951] 1 All ER 124 HL 288

Price v UK (1988) 55 D&R 1988 . . . . 312, 376

Purba v Purba [2000] 1 FLR 444; [2000] 1 FCR 652 CA 195

Q (Parental Order), *Re* [1996] 1 FLR 369; [1996] 2 FCR 345 . . . . 292, 295, 341

Quoraishi v Quoraishi (1984) 15 Fam Law 308; [1985] FLR 780 90

R (A Child) [2001] EWCA Civ 1344; [2002] 1 FCR 170 . . . . 346, 462, 465, 466

R (A Child) [2003] EWCA 182; [2003] 1 FCR 481, CA 291, 293, 294

R (A Child) (Adoption: Disclosure), *Re* [2001] 1 FCR 238 . . . . 308, 310

R (A Child) (Care Proceedings: Teenage Pregnancy), *Re* [2000] 2 FCR 556 . . . . 529, 590

R (A Minor) (Blood Transfusion), *Re* [1993] 2 FLR 757; [1993] 2 FCR 544 489
R (A Minor) (Contact), *Re* [1993] 2 FLR 762; [1993] 1 FCR 954 CA 471
R (A Minor) (Residence Order: Finance), *Re* [1995] 2 FLR 612; [1995]
   3 FCR 334 CA 455, 458
R (A Minor) (Residence: Religion), *Re* [1993] 2 FLR 163; [1993] 2
   FCR 525 CA 439, 441, 453
R (A Minor) (Wardship: Consent to Medical Treatment),
   Re [1992] 1 FLR 190; [1992] 2 FCR 229; [1992] Fam 11 . . . . 395, 396, 486, 488, 554
R (Abduction: Consent), *Re* [1999] 1 FLR 828 497
R (Adoption: Father's Involvement), *Re* [2001] 1 FLR 302, CA 602
R (Care Proceedings: Adjournment), *Re* [1998] 2 FLR 390; [1998] 3 FCR 654 581
R (Child Abduction: Acquiescence) *Re* [1995] 1 FLR 716; [1995] 2 FCR 609 501
R (Child of Teenage Mother), *Re* [2000] 2 FLR 660 594
R (Enduring Power of Attorney), *Re* [1990] 2 All ER 893; [2000] 1 FLR 882 631
R (Minors) (Custody), *Re* [1986] 1 FLR 6; (1986) Fam Law 15 457
R (On the Application A) *v* Lambeth [2003] 3 FCR 419, HL 610
R (On the Application of AB and SB) *v* Nottingham CC [2001] 3 FCR 350 520
R (On the Application of Assisted Reproduction and Gynaecology Centre
   and H) *v* HFEA [2002] FL 347 . . . . 338, 339
R (On the Application of Denson) *v* CSA [2002] 1 FLR 938; [2002] 1 FCR 460 162
R (On the Application of G) *v* Barnet London Borough Council [2003]
   UKHL 57; [2003] 3 FCR 419 . . . . 521, 522
R (On the Application of L) *v* Manchester CC [2002] FL 13 302
R (On the Application of Montana) *v* Secretary of State for the Home
   Department [2001] 1 FCR 358 346
R (On the Application of National Association of Guardians ad Litem and
   Reporting Officers) *v* CAFCASS [2002] 1 FLR 255 407
R (On the Application of S) *v* Swindon BC [2001] EWHC 334; [2001]
   3 FCR 702 . . . . 523, 524
R (On the Application of the Crown Prosecution Service) *v* Registrar General
   of Births, Deaths and Marriages [2003] 1 FCR 110 . . . . 34, 65
R (On the Application of Williamson) *v* Secretary of State for Education and
   Employment [2003] 1 FCR 1 CA 353, 415
R (Recovery Orders), *Re* [1998] 2 FLR 401; [1998] 3 FCR 321 527
R (Residence: Contact: Restricting Applications), *Re* [1998] 1 FLR 749;
   [1998] 2 FCR 129 436
R (Wardship: Abduction) (No. 2), *Re* [1993] 1 FLR 249; [1993] 1 FCR 710 495
R *v* Avon County Council, *ex p* K [1986] 1 FLR 443 575
R *v* Avon County Council, *ex p* M [1994] 2 FCR 259; [1994] 1 FLR 1006 574
R *v* Bedfordshire CC, *ex p* C [1987] 1 FLR 239; (1987) 17 Fam Law 55 575
R *v* Birmingham City Council, *ex p* A [1997] 2 FLR 841; [1997] 2 FCR 357 520
R *v* Brent LBC, *ex p* Awua [1996] AC 55; [1995] 2 FLR 819; [1995]
   3 FCR 278 HL 270
R *v* Brent LBC, *ex p* S [1994] 1 FLR 203; [1994] 2 FCR 996 CA 573, 576
R *v* Brown [1993] 1 AC 212 63
R *v* C (Kidnapping: Abduction) [1991] 2 FLR 252; [1991] Fam Law 522 492

R v Cambridge District Health Authority, *ex p* B [1995] 1 FLR 1055;
  [1995] 2 FCR 485 399
R v Cardiff Magistrates' Court, *ex p* Czech [1999] 1 FLR 95; [1999] 1 FCR 721 225
R v Central Independent Television plc [1994] Fam 192; [1994]
  2 FLR 151; [1995] 1 FCR 521 . . . . 369, 427, 459, 490
R v Colohan [2001] 3 FCR 409 . . . . 268, 269
R v Cornwall CC, *ex p* LH [2000] FLR 236; [2000] 1 FCR 460 526
R v Court (1912) 7 CAR 127 63
R v Cutts [1987] Fam Law 311 273
R v D [1984] AC 778; [1984] 3 WLR 186 492
R v Derriviere (1969) 53 Cr App R 637 28
R v Devon CC, *ex p* L [1991] 2 FLR 541; [1991] FCR 599 576
R v Ditta, Hussain and Kara [1988] Crim LR 42 64
R v Ealing LBC, *ex p* Sidhu (1982) 3 FLR 438; (1982) 80 LGR 534 271
R v Ethical Committee of St Mary's Hospital (Manchester), *ex p* H [1988]
  1 FLR 512; (1988) 18 Fam Law 165 . . . . 340, 341
R v Griffin [1993] Crim LR 515 493
R v Gwynedd, *ex p* B [1991] 2 FLR 365[1992] 3 All ER 317 326
R v H (Assault of Child: Reasonable Chastisement) [2001] 3 FCR 144 CA 415
R v Hampshire CC, *ex p* H [1999] 2 FLR 359; [1999] 3 FCR 129 576
R v Harrow LBC, *ex p* D [1990] Fam 133 [1990] 1 FLR 79; [1989] FCR 729 CA . . . 526
R v Hereford and Worcester County Council, *ex p* R [1992] 1 FLR 448;
  [1992] FCR 497 575
R v Hills [2001] 1 FCR 569 268
R v Hopely (1860) 2 F&F 202 414
R v Human Fertilisation and Embryology Authority, *ex p* Blood [1999]
  Fam 151; [1997] 2 FCR 501 CA 292, 338
R v Ireland and Burstow [1998] AC 147 . . . . 268, 273
R v Kensington and Chelsea LBC, *ex p* Kihara (1996) 29 HLR 147 CA 271, 520
R v Kent CC, *ex p* S [2000] 1 FLR 155 580
R v Kingston-upon-Thames RB, *ex p* T [1994] 1 FLR 798; [1994]
  1 FCR 232 . . . . 520, 573–575
R v Lambeth LBC, *ex p* Vagiviello (1990) 22 HLR 392; [1990] COD 428 CA 271
R v Lancashire CC, *ex p* M [1992] 1 FLR 109; [1992] FCR 283 CA 574, 575
R v N Yorkshire CC, *ex p* M (No. 3) [1989] 2 FLR 82; [1989] FCR 403 486
R v North West Lancashire HA, *ex p* A [2000] 2 FCR 525 44
R v Northavon DC, *ex p* Smith [1994] AC 402; [1994] 2 FCR 859; [1994]
  2 FLR 671 519
R v Oxfordshire CC (Secure Accommodation Order) [1992] Fam 150; [1992]
  2 FCR 310 440
R v Pearce [2002] 3 FCR 75; [2001] EWCA Crim 2834 65
R v Portsmouth NHS Trust, *ex p* Glass [1999] 2 FLR 905; [1999] 3 FCR 145 398
R v R [1952] 1 All ER 1194; (1952) 96 SJ 362 50
R v R (Private Law Proceedings: Residential Assessment) [2002] 2 FLR 953 . . . 439, 490
R v R (Rape: Marital Exemption) [1991] 4 All ER 481; [1992] 1 AC 599;
  [1992] 1 FLR 217 HL 63, 273

R *v* Rahman (1985) 81 Cr App R 349; [1985] Crim LR 596 492
R *v* Registrar-General, *ex p* Smith [1991] 2 QB 393; [1991] FLR 255;
   [1991] FCR 403 CA 611, 612
R *v* Reid [1972] 3 WLR 395; [1973] QB 299 68
R *v* Renshaw [1989] Crim LR 811 277
R *v* Rossiter (1992) 95 Cr App R 326; [1994] 2 All ER 752 273
R *v* Secretary of State for Defence, *ex p* Perkins [1999] 1 FLR 491 48
R *v* Secretary of State for Social Security, *ex p* Biggin [1995] 1 FLR 851;
   [1995] 2 FCR 595 . . . . 172, 173
R *v* Secretary of State for the Home Office, *ex p* Mellor [2000] 3 FCR 148 . . . . . . 48, 337
R *v* Secretary of State, *ex p* West [1999] 1 FLR 1233; [1999] 3 FCR 574 289
R *v* Senior [1899] 1 QB 283 400
R *v* Sheppard [1980] 3 WLR 960; [1981] AC 394 400
R *v* Surrey Quarter Sessions Appeal Committee, *ex p* Tweedie (1963) 107 SJ
   555; [1963] Crim LR 639 409
R *v* Tameside MBC, *ex p* J [2000] 1 FLR 942; [2000] 1 FCR 173 517
R *v* UK [1988] 2 FLR 445 ECtHR 376, 569
R *v* W [1992] Crim LR 905; (1993) 14 Cr App R (S) 256 273
R *v* Wandsworth LBC, *ex p* P [1989] 1 FLR 387 575
R *v* Westminster CC, *ex p* Bishop [1994] 1 FLR 720; [1994] COD 51 272
R *v* Wilson [1996] 3 WLR 125 63
R *v* Woods (1921) 85 SJ 272 414
R(M) *v* Inner London Crown Court [2003] 1 FLR 994 413
Rampal *v* Rampal (No. 2) [2001] 2 FCR 552 . . . . 26, 58
Raumussen *v* Denmark (1985) 7 EHRR 371 ECtHR 312
Raval, *Re* [1998] 2 FLR 718 153
Ravnsborg *v* Sweden (1994) 18 EHRR 38 , ECtHR 264
Rayatt, *Re* [1998] 2 FLR 264 154
Rees *v* Newbery and the Institute of Cancer Research [1998] 1 FLR 1041 638
Rees *v* UK (1987) 17 Fam Law 157; [1987] 2 FLR 111 ECtHR 45
Richards *v* Richards [1983] 3 WLR 173; [1984] AC 174 . . . . 242, 243, 368
Richardson *v* Richardson [1978] 9 Fam Law 86 215
Richardson *v* Richardson (No. 2) [1997] 2 FLR 617; [1997] 2 FCR 453 . . . . . . 203, 228
Roberts (dec'd), *Re* [1978] 1 WLR 653; [1978] 3 All ER 225 39
Robertson *v* Robertson Unreported 1980 CA 453
Rose *v* Rose [2002] FLR 345 224
Rose *v* Secretary of State for Health [2002] EWHC 1593 (Admin); [2002]
   2 FLR 962; [2002] 3 FCR 731 335
Rowe *v* Prance [1999] 2 FLR 787 130
Royal Bank of Scotland *v* Etridge (No. 2) [2001] 3 FCR 481 . . . . 157, 158
Royal Wolverhampton Hospitals NHS Trust *v* B [2000] 1 FLR 953; [2000]
   2 FCR 76 398
Rukat *v* Rukat [1975] Fam 63; [1975] 2 WLR 201 92
Rye *v* Rye [2002] FL 736 217
S, *Re* W (Children: Care Plan), *Re* [2002] 1 FCR 577, HL 545, 546, 582, 583, 585
S (A Child: Abduction), *Re* [2003] FL 289 493

S (A Child: Abduction: Grave Risk of Harm), *Re* [2002] EWCA Civ
908; [2002] 3 FCR 43 ....499, 500
S (A Child) (Adoption Proceedings: Joinder of Father), *Re* [2001] 1 FCR 158 602
S (A Child) (Identification: Restriction of Publication), *Re* [2003] 2 FCR 577 ...397, 459
S (A Child: Residence Order: Condition) (No 2), *Re* [2003] 1 FCR 713 ....373, 430
S (A Minor) (Abduction), *Re* [1991] 2 FLR 1; [1991] FCR 656 CA 494
S (A Minor) (Abduction: Custody Rights) [1993] Fam 242 501
S (A Minor) (Blood Transfusion: Adoption Order Conditions), *Re* [1994]
2 FLR 416 CA 453, 587
S (A Minor) (Care: Contact Order), *Re* [1994] 2 FLR 222; [1994] 2 FCR 414 570
S (A Minor) (Consent to Medical Treatment), *Re* [1994] 2 FLR 1065; [1994]
1 FCR 604 397
S (A Minor) (Custody), *Re* [1991] 2 FLR 388; [1991] FCR 155 CA 448
S (A Minor) (Custody: Habitual Residence), *Re* [1998] 1 FLR 122; [1997]
3 FCR 293 HL...502
S (A Minor) (Independent Representation), *Re* [1993] Fam 263; [1993]
2 FLR 437; [1993] 2 FCR 1 ....388, 404, 405
S (A Minor) (Medical Treatment), *Re* [1993] 1 FLR 376 396
S (A Minor) (Medical Treatment), *Re* [1994] 2 FLR 1065; [1994] 1 FCR 604 402
S (A Minor) (Parental Responsibility), *Re* [1995] 2 FLR
648; [1995] 3 FCR 225 CA 316–318, 320, 358, 366
S (Abduction) (European Convention), *Re* [1996] 1 FLR 660; [1996] 3 FCR 115 ...502
S (Abduction: Intolerable Situation: Beth Din), *Re* [2000] 1 FLR 454 501
S (Care or Supervision Order), *Re* [1996] 1 FLR 753; [1996] 2 FCR 719 CA 530
S (Care Proceedings: Split Hearing), *Re* [1996] 2 FLR 773; [1996] 3 FCR 578 544
S (Change of Names: Cultural Factors), *Re* [2001] 3 FCR 648 ....454, 464
S (Change of Surname), *Re* [1999] 1 FLR 672; [1999] 1 FCR 304 ....440, 463, 464
S (Contact: Application by Sibling), *Re* [1998] 2 FLR 897;
[1999] Fam 283 ....370, 404, 607
S (Contact: Children's Views), *Re* [2002] 1 FLR 1156 ....441, 478
S (Contact: Grandparents), *Re* [1996] 1 FLR 158; [1996] 3 FCR 30 CA 308, 447
S (Infants), *Re* [1967] 1 All ER 202; [1967] 1 WLR 396 487
S (Minors) (Abduction), *Re* [1994] 1 FLR 297; [1993] 2 FCR 499 504
S (Minors) (Abduction: Acquiescence), *Re* [1994] 1 FLR 819;
[1994] 2 FCR 945 ....498, 500
S (Minors) (Abduction: Custody Rights), *Re* [1991] 2 AC 476; [1992] 1 FCR 45 496
S (Minors) (Abduction: Wrongful Retention), *Re* [1994] Fam 530 495
S (Minors) (Access), *Re* [1990] 2 FLR 166; [1990] 2 FCR 379 ....451, 470
S (Minors) (Access: Religious Upbringing), *Re* [1992] 2 FLR 313; [1993]
1 FCR 283 CA 441, 453
S (Minors) (Inherent Jurisdiction: Ouster), *Re* [1994] 1 FLR 623; [1994]
2 FCR 906 ....489, 555
S v F (Occupation Order) [2000] 1 FLR 255; [2000] 3 FLR 365 ....251, 254
S v P (Contact Application: Family Assistance Order) [1997] 2 FLR 277;
[1997] 2 FCR 185 523
S v S [1955] 2 WLR 246; [1956] P 1 51

S *v* S [1975] 2 WLR 615; [1976] Fam 18n 222
S *v* S [1976] 3 WLR 755; [1977] Fam 127 206
S *v* S [2001] 3 FCR 316 210
S *v* S (Divorce: Staying Proceedings) [1997] 2 FLR 100 222
S *v* S (Recission of Decree Nisi: Pension Sharing Provision) [2002] FL 171 217
S *v* S, W *v* Official Solicitor (or W) [1970] 3 WLR 366; [1972]
    AC 24 HL 289, 331, 368
S and D (Children: Powers of Court), *Re* [1995] 2 FLR 456; [1995] 1
    FCR 26 CA 568
S and G *v* Italy [2000] 2 FLR 771; [2000] 3 FCR 404 ECtHR 569
S(J) (A Minor) (Care or Supervision), *Re* [1993] 2 FLR 919; [1993] 2 FCR 193 530
SC (A Minor) (Leave to Seek Section 8 Orders), *Re* [1994] 1
    FLR 96; [1994] 1 FCR 837 . . . . 369, 405, 422, 518
SH (Care Order: Orphan), *Re* [1995] 1 FLR 746; [1996] 1 FCR 1 . . . . 297, 535
SM (A Minor) (Natural Father: Access), *Re* [1996] 2 FLR 333; [1997] 2 FCR 475 . . 477
SRJ *v* DWJ (Financial Provision) [1999] 2 FLR 176; [1999]
    3 FCR 153 CA 191, 198, 200, 216
SY *v* SY [1962] 3 WLR 526; [1963] P 37 45
Sahin *v* Germany [2003] 2 FCR 619; [2002] 3 FCR
    621 ECtHR 264, 345, 377, 471, 472
Santos *v* Santos [1972] Fam 247; [1972] 2 WLR 889 . . . . 76, 91
Savil *v* Goodall [1993] 1 FLR 755; [1994] 1 FCR 325 CA 136
Schuller *v* Schuller [1990] 2 FLR 193; [1990] FCR 626 203
Scott *v* Selbright (1886) 12 PD 21 53
Scott *v* UK [2000] 1 FLR 958; [2000] 2 FCR 560 . . . . 377, 594
Seaton *v* Seaton [1986] 2 FLR 398; (1986) 16 Fam Law 267 CA 199
Sekhon *v* Alissa [1989] 2 FLR 94; [1989] Fam Law 355 135
Shaw *v* Fitzgerald [1992] 1 FLR 357; [1992] FCR 162 68
Shaw *v* Shaw [2002] 3 FCR 298 232
Sheffield and Horsham *v* UK [1998] 2 FLR 928; [1998] 3 FCR 141 ECtHR 45
Shelley *v* Westbrook (1817) Jac 266n 452
Silver *v* Silver [1955] 1 WLR 728; [1955] 2 All ER 614 56
Simms *v* Simms [2003] 1 FCR 361 399
Simpson *v* Simpson [1989] Fam Law 20; [1992] 1 FLR 601 157
Singh *v* Singh [1971] P 226; [1971] 2 WLR 963 51–53
Slater *v* Slater (1982) 3 FLR 364 CA 205
Smith *v* McInerney [1994] 2 FLR 1077; [1994] 2 FCR 1086 175
Smith *v* Smith [1975] 2 All ER 19n 219
Smith *v* Smith [2000] 3 FCR 374 224
Söderbäck *v* Sweden [1999] 1 FLR 250 . . . . 310, 569, 601
South Glamorgan County Council *v* W and B [1993] 1 FLR 574;
    [1993] 1 FCR 626 . . . . 527, 548, 552
Southwood LBC *v* B [1993] 2 FLR 559; [1993] 2 FCR 607 440
Spence, *Re* [1990] Ch 652; [1990] 2 FLR 278; [1990] FCR 983 58
Spencer *v* Camacho (1983) 127 SJ 155; [1984] 4 FLR 662 248
Sporrong and Lönnroth *v* Sweden (1986) 5 EHRR 35 264

Springette *v* Defoe [1992] 2 FLR 388; [1992] 2 FCR 561 CA 134, 136

St George's Healthcare NHS Trust *v* S [1998] 2 FLR 728; [1998] 2 FCR 685 . . 348, 529

Stephens *v* Avery [1988] 1 Ch 449; [1988] 2 WLR 1280 66

Stephenson *v* Stephenson [1985] FLR 1140 CA 457

Stjerna *v* Finland (1994) 24 EHRR 195 ECtHR 463

Stockport MBC *v* B; Stockport MBC *v* L [1986] 2 FLR 80; (1986) 16 Fam Law 187 445

Stokes *v* Anderson [1991] 1 FLR 391; [1991] FCR 539 141

Stubbings *v* UK (1997) 1 BHRC 316 311

Sullivan *v* Sullivan (1812) 2 Hag Con 238 55

Surtees *v* Kingston-upon-Thames Borough Council [1991] 2 FLR 559;
   [1991] Fam Law 426 418

Suter *v* Suter and Jones [1987] Fam 111; [1987] 2 FLR 232; [1987]
   FCR 52 CA 199, 202

Swift *v* Kelly (1835) 3 Knapp 257 55

Sylvester *v* Austria [2003] 2 FCR 128 501

Szechter *v* Szechter [1971] P 286; [1971] 2 WLR 170 . . . . 52, 53

T (A Child: Contact), *Re* [2003] 1 FCR 303; [2003] 1 FLR 531 478

T (A Child) (DNA Tests: Paternity) [2001] 3 FCR 577; [2001] 2 FLR 1190 . . . 332, 333

T (A Minor) (Care Order: Conditions), *Re* [1994] 2 FLR 423; [1994]
   2 FCR 721 . . . . 528, 568

T (A Minor) (Wardship: Medical Treatment), *Re* [1997] 1 FLR 502;
   [1997] 2 FCR 363 CA 368, 372, 397

T (A Minor) (Wardship: Responsibility), *Re* [1994] Fam 49; [1993] 2
   FCR 445; [1993] 2 FLR 278 . . . . 486, 487

T (Abduction: Child's Objections to Return), *Re* [2000] 2 FLR 193;
   [2000] 2 FCR 159 . . . . 440, 501

T (Accommodation by Local Authority), *Re* [1995] 1 FLR 159; [1995] 1 FCR 517 . . 574

T (Adopted Children: Contact), *Re* [1995] 2 FLR 251; [1995] 2 FCR 537 607

T (Adopted Children: Contact), *Re* [1996] Fam 34; [1995] 2 FLR 792;
   [1996] 2 FCR 118 607

T (Change of Name), *Re* [1998] 2 FLR 620; [1999] 1 FCR 476 463

T (Minor) (Parental Responsibility), *Re* [1993] 2 FLR 450; [1993] 1 FCR 973 318

T (Minors) (Custody: Religious Upbringing), *Re* (1975) 2 FLR 239 CA 452

T (Otherwise H) (An Infant), *Re* [1962] 3 All ER 970; [1962] 3 WLR 1477 461

T (Termination of Contact: Discharge of Order), *Re* [1997] 1 FLR 517 580

T *v* S (Financial Provision for Children) [1994] 2 FLR 883; [1994] 1 FCR 743 . . 143, 182

T *v* T (Financial Relief: Pensions) [1998] 1 FLR 1072; [1998] 2 FCR 364 215

T and E, *Re* [1995] 1 FLR 581; [1995] 3 FCR 260 371

T and M, *Re* [1995] FLR 1 453

TB (Care Proceedings: Criminal Trial), *Re* [1995] 2 FLR 810; [1996] 1 FCR 101 . . . 445

TB *v* JB (Abduction: Grave Risk of Harm) [2001] 2 FCR 497;
   [2001] 2 FLR 515 500

TP and KM *v* UK [2001] 2 FCR 289 . . . . 511, 512, 546

TSB *v* Marshall and Rodgers [1998] 2 FLR 769 149

Tameside MBC *v* M (Injunctive Relief: County Courts: Jurisdiction) [2001] FL 873 . 268

Tanner *v* Tanner [1975] 1 WLR 1346; [1975] 3 All ER 776 CA 148

Tavoulareas *v* Tavoulareas [1998] 2 FLR 418; [1999] 1 FCR 133 CA 208, 222

Taylor *v* Dickens [1998] 1 FLR 806; [1998] 3 FCR 455 140

Tee *v* Tee and Hamilton [1999] 2 FLR 613; [1999] 3 FCR 409 150

Thomas *v* Fuller-Brown [1988] 1 FLR 237; (1988) 18 Fam Law 53 138

Thomas *v* Thomas [1996] 2 FLR 544; [1996] FCR 668 . . . . 195, 203, 218

Thompson and Venables *v* New Group Newspapers Ltd [2001] 1
   FLR 791; [2002] 1 FCR 333 460

Thompson *v* Thompson [1956] P 414; [1956] 2 WLR 814 113

Thurlow *v* Thurlow [1975] 2 All ER 979; [1975] 3 WLR 161 90

Toonen *v* Australia in UN Doc CCPR/C/50/D/488 70

Tuck *v* Robson [1970] 1 All ER 1171; [1970] 1 WLR 741 261

Tyler *v* Tyler [1989] 2 FLR 158; [1990] FCR 22 466

Tyrer *v* UK (1978) 2 EHRR 1 415

U (Application to Free for Adoption), *Re* [1993] 2 FLR 992; [1993] 2 FCR 64 523

U *v* W (Attorney-General Intervening) [1998] Fam 29; [1997] 2 FLR
   282;[1998] 1 FCR 526 . . . . 292, 293

Uddin *v* Ahmed [2001] 3 FCR 300, CA 223

Universal Tankships Inc *v* ITWF [1982] 2 WLR 803; [1983] AC 366 53

V (A Minor) (Wardship), *Re* (1979) 123 SJ 201 489

V (Care or Supervision Order), *Re* [1996] 1 FLR 776; [1996]
   2 FCR 555 CA 531, 532, 560

V (Residence Review), *Re* [1995] 2 FLR 1010; [1999] 2 FCR 371 456

V *v* V (Child Maintenance) [2001] 2 FLR 799 179

V-B (Abduction: Custody Rights), *Re* [1999] 2 FLR 192 495

Valier *v* Valier (1925) 133 LT 830 54

Venema *v* Netherlands [2003] 1 FCR 153; [2003] 1 FLR 551 512

Vervaeke *v* Smith [1982] 2 WLR 855; [1983] 1 AC 145 . . . . 34, 56

W, *Re* A, *Re* B (Change of Name), *Re* [1999] 2 FLR 930; [1999]
   3 FCR 337 CA 462–464

W, *Re* B (Child Abduction: Unmarried Father), *Re* [1998] 2 FLR 146;
   [1998] 2 FCR 549 495

W (A Child) (Contact: Leave to Apply), *Re* [2000] 1 FCR 185 308

W (A Minor) (Contact), *Re* [1994] 2 FLR 441; [1994] 2 FCR 1216 CA 470, 473

W (A Minor) (Medical Treatment: Court's Jurisdiction), *Re*
   [1993] 1 FLR 1; [1992] 2 FCR 785; [1993] Fam 64 CA 394, 396, 397, 488, 518

W (A Minor) (Residence Order), *Re* [1992] 2 FLR 332; [1992] 2 FCR 461 CA . . 362, 448

W (A Minor) (Secure Accommodation Order), *Re* [1993] 1 FLR 692;
   [1993] 1 FCR 693 586

W (Contact Proceedings: Joinder of Child) [2003] 2 FCR 175 393

W (Contact: Application by Grandmother), *Re* [1997] 1 FLR 793; [1997]
   2 FCR 643 434

W (Contact: Application by Grandparent), *Re* [2001] 1 FLR 263 483

W (Minors) (Residence Order), *Re* [1998] 1 FCR 75 532

W (Power of Attorney), *Re* [2001] 1 FLR 832 631

W (Residence), *Re* [1999] 2 FLR 390; [1999] 3 FCR 274 CA 449

W (Residence Order), *Re* [1999] 1 FLR 869; [1998] 1 FCR 75 CA 444, 457

W (Section 34(2) Orders), *Re* [2000] 1 FLR 512; [2000] 1 FCR 752 . . . . 569, 582
W (Wardship: Discharge: Publicity), *Re* [1995] 2 FLR 466;
  [1996] 1 FCR 393 CA 370, 459, 487, 488
W *v* A Local Authority [2000] 2 FCR 662 548
W *v* Essex CC [2000] 1 FCR 568; [2000] 1 FLR 657 HL 577
W *v* Federal Republic of Germany (1985) 50 D&R 219 376
W *v* UK (1988) 10 EHRR 29 ECtHR 376, 511, 558
W *v* W [1984] FLR 796 302
W *v* W [2001] FL 656 210
W *v* W (Child Abduction: Acquiescence) [1993] 2 FLR 211; [1993] 2 FCR 644 498
W *v* W (Decree Absolute) [1998] 2 FCR 304 93
W *v* W (Judicial Separation: Ancillary Relief) [1995] 2 FLR 259; [1996] 3 FCR 641 . . 206
W *v* W (Nullity) [2000] 3 FCR 748 46
W *v* W (Periodical Payments: Pensions) [1996] 2 FLR 480 216
W and B *v* H (Child Abduction: Surrogacy) [2002] FL 345 494
WB (Residence Order), *Re* [1993] Fam Law 395; [1995] 2 FLR 1023 . . . . 320, 459
W(C) *v* C [1987] IR 676 54
Wachtel *v* Wachtel [1973] Fam 72; [1973] 2 WLR 366 CA 207, 235
Wakefield *v* Mackay (1807) 1 Hag Con 394 54
Ward *v* Secretary of State for Social Services [1990] 1 FLR 119; [1990] FCR 361 39
Warwick *v* UK (1986) 60 DR 5 415
Waterman *v* Waterman [1989] 1 FLR 380; [1989] FCR 267 CA 202
Watson, *Re* [1999] 1 FLR 878; [1999] 3 FCR 595 . . . . 637, 638, 642
Wayling *v* Jones [1995] 2 FLR 1029; [1996] 2 FCR 41 140
Wells *v* Wells [1992] 2 FLR 66; [1992] 2 FCR 368 CA 231
Wheatley *v* Wheatley [1999] 2 FLR 205 226
Whiston *v* Whiston [1995] Fam 198; [1995] 2 FLR 268; [1995] 2
  FCR 496 CA 26, 39, 58
White *v* White [1948] P 330 50
White *v* White [2001] AC 596, HL; [2000] 2 FLR 976; [2000] 3 FCR 555 . . . . . 20, 143,
          193, 199, 201, 203, 204, 206, 207, 209–214, 216, 218, 221, 229, 236, 237
Whiting *v* Whiting [1988] 2 FLR 189; [1988] FCR 569 CA 200
Whittaker, *Re* (1882) 21 Ch D 657 128
Wickler *v* Wickler [1998] 2 FLR 326; [1998] 2 FCR 304 92
Wicks *v* Wicks [1998] 1 FLR 470; [1998] 1 FCR 465 CA 201
Wilson *v* Webster [1998] 1 FLR 1097; [1998] 2 FCR 275 267
Windle, *Re* [1975] 3 All ER 987; [1975] 1 WLR 1628 222
Woodley *v* Woodley (No. 2) [1992] 2 FLR 417; [1993] 1 FCR 701 226
Wooton *v* Wooton (1984) FLR 871 CA 249
Worlock *v* Worlock [1994] 2 FLR 689; [1994] 2 FCR 1157 231
Wright *v* Wright [1980] 2 FLR 276 CA 453
X (A Child) (Injunctions Restraining Publication) [2001] 1 FCR 541 . . . . 368, 427
X (Parental Responsibility Agreement), *Re* [2000] 1 FLR 517; [2000]
  1 FCR 379 . . . . 315, 562
X *v* Bedfordshire CC [1995] 2 AC 633; [1995] 2 FLR 276; [1995]
  3 FCR 337 HL 576

X *v* Switzerland (1978) 13 DR 248 310
X *v* X [2002] FL 98 224
X County Council *v* A [1985] 1 All ER 53; (1985) 15 Fam Law 59 490
X, Y, Z *v* UK [1997] 2 FLR 892; [1997] 3 FCR 341 ECtHR 48, 288, 309, 311
Xydhias *v* Xydhias [1999] 1 FLR 683; [1999] 1 FCR 289 CA 224
Y (Children) (Occupation Order), *Re* [2000] 2 FCR 470 .... 252, 254
Y (Mental Incapacity: Bone Marrow Transplant), *Re* [1996] 2 FLR 787; [1997]
    2 FCR 172 400
Y *v* UK (1992) 17 EHRR 238 ECtHR 415
Yackuk *v* Olicer Blais Co Ltd [1949] AC 396; [1949] 2 All ER 150 419
Yaxley *v* Gotts [2000] Ch 162; [1999] 2 FLR 941 141
Yousef *v* The Netherlands [2002] 3 FCR 577; [2000] 2 FLR 118 .... 332, 377
Z (A Minor) (Identity: Restrictions on Publication), *Re* [1996] 1 FLR 191;
    [1996] 2 FCR 164; [1997] Fam 1; [1999] 1 FCR 251 ... 369, 426, 459, 460, 489, 490
Z (Abduction: Non-Convention Country), *Re* [1999] 1 FLR 1270; [1999]
    1 FCR 251 504
Z *v* UK [2001] 2 FCR 246; [2000] 2 FCR 245 EComHR 510, 525

TABLE OF STATUTES

Abortion Act 1967 348
Access to Justice Act 1999 23
Administration of Estates Act 1925—
    s 46 634
    s 55(1)(x) 634
Administration of Justice Act 1970—
    s 36 156
Adoption Act 1976 . . . . 246, 342, 362,
              588, 590, 603, 605, 608
    s 16 362
    s 51 295
    s 72 359
Adoption and Children Act 2002 262,
      302, 304, 312, 314, 588–594, 600,
      601, 605, 607–610, 612, 613, 615
    s 1 . . . . 592, 594, 596, 603
      (4) 599
        (f) 308
      (6) 597, 608
    s 3 591
    s 4 610
      (7) 609
    s 5 . . . . 591, 592
    s 19(1) 596
      (3) 596
    s 20(4) 596
    s 21(3) 596
    s 22 596
    s 24 597
    s 26(1) 597
    s 27 597
      (4) 597
    s 29(1) 598
    s 31 . . . . 596, 604
    s 32 596
    s 34 597
      (1) 597
    s 42 598
      (5) 609
      (6) 609
    s 45 595

s 46(1) 605
    (6) 607
s 47 . . . . 598, 603
    (4) 597
    (9) 593
s 49(2) 593
    (3) 593
    (4) 593
s 50 592
s 51(2) 605
s 52 596
    (1)(a) 603
      (b) 603
    (2) 608
    (5) 602
s 55 610
s 60(3) 612
    (4) 612
s 64(4) 612
s 65(1) 612
s 67 605
    (1)–(3) 605
    (3)(d) 605
s 69 605
s 74(1) 605
s 79 611
s 88(2) 602
s 92 598
s 93 598
s 98(2) 612
    (3) 612
s 144(4) 592
Adoption (Intercountry Aspects)
    Act 1999 613
Adoption of Children Act 1926 587
Attachment of Earnings Act 1971 225
Births and Deaths Registration Act
    1953—
    s 10(1)(a) 289
    s 29 460
    s 34(2) 289

1

British Nationality Act 1981—
  s 1(5) 605
Care Standards Act 2000 . . . . 578, 643
  Pt 2 592
Carers (Recognition and Services)
  Act 1995 624
Child Abduction Act 1984 466,
                        491–493, 503
  s 1(5) 492
  s 2 491
Child Abduction and Custody Act
  1985 491
  s 16(4)(c) 503
Child Support Act 1991 . . . . . . 19, 23, 61,
             131, 160, 162, 164, 165, 167,
          169–176, 178, 179, 182–184, 192,
          193, 197, 198, 214, 237, 290, 299,
             315, 324, 331, 335, 361, 619
  s 1 169
  s 2 173
  s 3 169
    (3) 172
  s 6 . . . . 170, 171
    (2) 171
  s 8(3) 183
    (5) 172
    (6) 172
    (7) 172
    (8) 172, 174
  s 9 170
  s 26 . . . . 170, 288
  s 27 335
  ss 28A–28H 171
  s 46 171
  s 54 169
  s 55 170
  Sch 1 170
  Sch 4B 171
Child Support Act 1995 160,
                        169–171, 192
Child Support, Pensions and Social
  Security Act 2000 . . . . . . 160, 164, 169,
              176, 214, 303, 333, 361
  s 1 177
  Sch 1 177
Children Act 1975 614

Children Act 1989 . . . . 26, 35, 61, 93,
            160, 165, 172, 180–183, 247, 252,
            262, 269, 297, 299–301, 303, 306,
            307, 349, 350, 351, 358, 360–362,
            367, 368, 371, 373, 377, 378, 403,
            407, 421, 422, 435, 441, 444–446,
            448, 472, 487, 489, 490, 508–510,
            515, 518–521, 523, 528, 534, 547,
            549, 553, 556, 557, 561–563, 565,
            572, 581–584, 599, 601, 604, 607
  Pt III 369, 413, 428, 508, 520,
                        521, 573
  Pt IV 391, 555
  Pt X 372
  s 1 . . . . 368, 401, 451, 460, 539,
                        580, 592
    (1) 182, 316, 366, 368, 370,
                  427, 434, 459, 466, 470,
                        527, 531, 545
    (2) 109, 445
    (3) 298, 367, 434, 440, 527,
                        541, 569, 599
      (a) 440, 471
      (b) 442, 471
      (c) 443
      (d) 444, 533
      (e) 444, 471
      (f) 444
      (g) 445, 541
    (4) 440
      (b) 541
    (5) 301, 305, 316, 378,
            446–448, 527, 531, 544, 545
  s 2 312
    (6) 361
    (7) 361, 363, 462, 465
    (8) 358
    (9) 305, 315, 361, 364, 366
    (11) 305
  s 3 . . . . 351, 357
    (5) 519
  s 4 . . . . 312, 314, 316
    (1)(b) 315
    (3) 318, 326
  s 4A 304, 608
  s 5 359

(2) 298	s 13 . . . . 358, 360, 362, 363, 462
(5) 297	(1) 461
(6) 312	(b) 466
(7) 297	(2) 466
(8) 297	s 14A 614
s 6 . . . . 297, 299	(1) 615
(1) 299	(2) 615
(2) 299	(3)(b) 614
(3) 299	(12) 615
(3A) 299	s 14C(3) 613
(4) 299	s 14D 614
(5) 299	(5) 614
(7) 300	s 14F(1) 610
s 7(1) 439	(2) 610
s 8 . . . . 169, 269, 305–307, 360,	s 15 180
362, 368, 403, 406, 410, 422,	s 16 522
426–430, 432–436, 440, 445,	(3) 522
459, 462, 487, 489, 492, 518,	(a) 522
520, 524, 530, 541, 553–555,	(5) 523
567, 571, 577, 579	(7) 522
(1) 422, 424, 426, 429	s 17 . . . . 521, 522
s 9(1) 429	(1) 521
(2) 518	(6) 522
(3) 433, 579	(10) 521, 522
(5) 518	(11) 521
(a) 428	s 18 522
(6) 316, 422, 441	s 20 . . . . 516, 517, 520, 530, 561
(7) 441, 517	(3) 517
s 10 305	(4) 516
(1) 445	(5) 516, 586
(b) 579	(6) 518
(4) 360	(7) 359, 516, 518
(5)(a) 303, 433	(8) 359, 518
(b) 579	s 22 563
(7) 432	(1) 564
(8) 403, 614	(2) 564
(9) 434, 571	(3) 564
(d)(i) 577	(4) 564
s 11 446	(a) 567
(4) 423	(5)(a) 564, 567
(5) 423	(b) 564
(7) 429	(c) 564
s 12 600	s 23(1) 565
(1) 423	(2) 565
(2) 312	(5) 565
(3) 362	(7)(a) 565

(b) 565
s 24(1) 580
(8) 580
(9) 580
s 25(1) 586
s 26(3) 567, 573, 582
(a) 567
s 27 519
s 31 .... 252, 253, 262, 527, 528,
531, 534, 544, 569, 597, 604
(1) 528
(b) 530
(2) 546
(a) 531, 535, 536
(b) 531, 539, 540
(3A) 475, 544, 568
(6) 528
(7) 528
(9) 532, 551
(10) 533
s 32 446
s 33 561
(1) 564
(3) 561, 562
(a) 561
(b) 563
(4) 562
(6) 253, 362
(a) 562
(b)(i) 562
(iii) 562
(7) 462, 562
s 34 ..... 361, 558, 566, 568, 570–572
(1) 570
(2) 567
(3) 569
(b) 571
(4) 567
(6) 568
s 35(1) 560
s 36(4) 410
s 37 .... 343, 479, 523–525
(1) 524
(3) 525
s 38(3) 545
(6) 546–548

s 38A 548, 555
(2) 548
(3) 548
s 39 558
(1) 567, 580
s 43(1) 527
(3) 526
(4) 526
(5) 528
(7) 527
(8) 527
(10) 527
s 44(1)(a)(i) 550
(ii) 550
(b) 551
(4) 551
(c) 314
(5)(b) 552
(6) 552
(b) 552
(7) 527, 552
(8) 552
(10) 552
(13) 361, 552
s 44A 548, 552, 555
s 45(1) 552
(4) 552
(8) 361
(9) 553
(10) 552
s 46 519
(1) 549
(3) 549
(5) 549
(9)(b) 549
(10) 549
s 47 .... 523–526, 644
(1)(b) 524
(6) 524
s 48(3) 551
(4) 551
(9) 551
s 49(1) 572
s 66 300
s 91(1) 580
(7) 326

(8) 326
(14) 318, 434–436, 601
s 100 487
  (2) 489
    (b) 486
    (d) 489
s 105 .... 306, 528
  (1) 182, 302, 349
Sch 1 .... 303, 446
  para 1(2)(d) 257, 258
    (e) 257, 258
  para 4(1) 181
    (2) 181
  para 5(1) 181
Sch 2 522
  Pt II 566
  para 5 554
  para 15 566
    (1)(c) 571
  para 16 566
  para 19(3) 562
  para 21(2) 566
Sch 2A 567
Sch 3 560
  para 3(1) 560
  para 10 580
  para 19 410
Sch 9 372
Sch 13, para 56 294
Children and Young Persons
(Protection from Tobacco) Act
1991 413
Children and Young Persons Act
1933 .... 125, 412, 415
s 1 514
  (1) 399
  (7) 415
s 18 126
Children and Young Persons Act 1969—
  s 12C 410
  s 23 585
Children (Leaving Care) Act 2000 ... 581
Children's Commissioner for Wales
Act 2001 390
Contrast Child (Scotland) Act 1995
  s 1(1) 357

County Courts Act 1984—
  s 38 .... 242, 268
Crime and Disorder Act 1998 413
  Ch 1, Pt 1 523
  ss 8–10 358
  s 8 413
Criminal Injuries Compensation Act
  1995 274
Criminal Justice Act 1925—
  s 47 63
Criminal Justice Act 1988—
  s 23 277
Criminal Justice Act 1991 514
Criminal Justice and Court Service
Act 2000—
  s 11 406
Criminal Justice and Public Order
  Act 1994 63
  s 142 273
Criminal Law Act 1977—
  s 2(2)(a) 64
Crossbows Act 1987 413
Debtors Act 1869 225
Defence of Marriage Act 1996 (US) ... 48
  s 3 48
Divorce Reform Act 1969 .... 84, 86
Divorce (Religious Marriages) Act
  2002 .... 93, 111
Domestic Proceedings and Magistrates'
  Courts Act 1978 242
Domestic Proceedings and Matrimonial
  Causes Act 1978—
  s 1 131
  s 2 131
  s 38 303
Domestic Violence and Matrimonial
  Proceedings Act 1976 .... 242, 267
Education Act 1996 .... 359, 412
  s 7 409
  s 43 413
  s 44 413
  s 241 411
  s 375 412
  s 403 411
  s 443 410
  s 444 410

s 548(1) 415
s 550A 411, 416
Employment Act 1989 412
Employment of Women, Young Persons
  and Children Act 1920 412
Employment of Young People Act 1993—
  s 1(1) 412
Employment Rights Act 1996—
  s 161 125
Enduring Powers of Attorney Act 1985—
  s 6(4) 631
  (5) 631
  s 8(2)(b)(i) 631
     (ii) 631
  (4)(g) 631
Family Law Act 1986 493
  Pt I 493
  s 25 493
  s 33 493
  s 37 493
  s 38 487
  s 55 37
  s 56 335
Family Law Act 1996 . . . . 11, 23, 35,
     65, 82, 83, 86, 96, 97, 99–105,
     109–111, 123, 201, 207, 229, 232,
     244, 246, 249, 251, 252, 254, 258,
     260–262, 264, 265, 267, 269, 281,
     283, 306, 309, 427, 431, 548, 643
  Pt II 96, 101
  Pt III 96
  Pt IV 69, 154, 243, 246, 262,
     427, 554
  s 1 . . . . 11, 82, 96
  (1)(a) 82
  (b) 83
  (c)(i) 83
     (ii) 83
     (iii) 84
  s 5 102
  s 6 97
  (2) 97
  (3) 97
  s 7 97
  (10) 101
  (11) 101

  (13) 101
s 8(2) 100
  (6)(b) 98
  (9) 98
  (b) 102
s 9 . . . . 98, 102
s 10 . . . . 92, 98, 102
s 11 102
s 21 112
s 22A(4) 201
s 23(3) 101
s 27(8) 103
s 29 113
s 30 221
  (1) 148
  (2) 148
  (3) 148
  (8) 148
  (9) 148
s 31(10)(b) 149
s 33 . . . . 148, 153, 250, 256, 257,
     259, 281
  (1)(a)(i) 255
  (3) 251, 255, 256
  (d) 255
  (f) 255
  (g) 248, 255
  (4) 255
  (5) 148, 255
  (6) 256–259
  (7) 251, 259, 260
  (10) 256
s 35 . . . . . 250, 251, 256, 257, 259, 281
  (6) 256
  (e) 257
  (10) 257
s 36 . . . . . 250, 257, 259, 260, 263, 281
  (6) 260
  (7) 260
s 37 . . . . 250, 259
  (3) 259, 260
s 38 . . . . 250, 258, 260
s 40 . . . . 131, 132, 255, 256
  (1)(a)(i) 255
     (ii) 255
  (b) 255

(c) 255
(d) 255
(e) 255
(2) 256
s 41 . . . . 258, 263
s 42 . . . . 244, 282
(2) 247
(b) 247
(5) 247
(6) 248
s 43 . . . . 247, 262
(1) 262
s 44 . . . . 245, 246
(4) 246
s 45 265
(2) 265
(3) 265
s 46(1) 266
(2) 266
(3) 266
(4) 266
s 47(1) 266
(2) 267
(3) 266
(9) 266
s 56 58
s 60 . . . . 247, 282
(1) 247
s 62(1)(a) 245, 257
(2) 252
(3) 244, 245, 257
s 63 . . . . 148, 232, 246
(1) 245, 252
Sch 1 102
Sch 7 . . . . 232, 233
Pt II 233
para 2 232
para 3 232
para 5 233
Family Law Reform Act 1969 . . . 346, 417
s 1 349
s 8(1) 394
s 20 290
s 21 333
(1) 333
(3)(b) 333

s 23(1) 333
s 26 289
Family Law Reform Act 1987 . . . . 62, 346
s 1(1) 34
s 19(14) 346
Family Law (Scotland) Act 1985 127
Fatal Accident Act 1976 67
Female Circumcision Act 1985 363
Firearms Act 1968 413
Firearms Act 1982 413
Fireworks Act 2003 413
Guardianship Act 1973 296
Guardianship of Infants Act 1925 367
Homelessness Act 2002 . . . . 270, 272
Housing Act 1988—
Pt I 232
Housing Act 1996 270
s 175(2)(a) 270
(4) 270
s 177(1) 270
s 189(1) 271
s 190 272
s 191 272
Human Fertilisation and Embryology Act
1990 . . . . . 170, 290, 291, 293, 294, 340
s 2(1) 292
s 13(5) 340
ss 27–29 334
s 27 287
(1) 287
s 28 292
(2) 291, 293, 295, 327
(3) 291, 293, 295, 327
(4) 291
(5) 293
(6) 288, 291, 294
(b) 291
s 29(4) 287
s 30 . . . . 296, 326
(2) 295
(3) 295
(a) 295
(5) 295
(7) 341
(9)(a) 295
s 31(3)(a) 334

(4) 334
   (b) 334
Sch 3 291
  para 5 291
  (3) 292
Human Rights Act 1998 . . 2, 6, 28, 69, 70,
  110, 194, 225, 260, 263, 283, 306,
  309, 323, 332, 336, 344, 345, 373,
  375, 377, 378, 383, 401, 405, 411,
  420, 436, 445, 449, 451, 453, 456,
  459, 472, 480, 501, 510–512, 520,
  521, 525, 556, 558, 563, 565, 566,
  568–570, 574, 576, 577, 583, 601,
        604, 615, 625
s 2 29
s 3 . . . . 29, 46
s 6 28
s 7 . . . . 279, 511, 574, 584
s 8 574
s 12 459
s 22(4) 574
Infant Life (Preservation) Act 1929—
s 1 349
Inheritance (Provision for Family and
Dependants) Act 1975 . . . . 62, 69, 303,
        633–636, 640
s 1(d) 303
s 1(1)(a) 59, 636
  (b) 637, 640
  (c) 637
  (d) 637
  (e) 70, 637
  (2) 639
  (a) 640
  (3) 637
s 1A 637, 642
s 3 639
  (2) 640
  (3) 640
  (4) 641
s 21 639
s 25(4) 59, 636
Insolvency Act 1986 . . . . . . 151, 152, 226
s 282 226
s 283 151
  (2) 154

  (b) 151
s 284 227
s 306 151
s 310(2) 154
s 335A 153
s 336 154
  (1)–(2) 154
s 337 154
s 339 . . . . 153, 226, 226
s 341 153
s 400 226
s 423 . . . . 152, 153
  (3) 153
  (5) 152
s 435 153
s 436 152
Land Registration Act 2002 . . . . . 133, 149
Sch 1 150
Sch 2 150
Sch 3 150
Law of Property Act 1925—
s 27 151
s 52(1) 133
s 53(1) 134
  (b) 134
  (2) 134
Law of Property (Miscellaneous Provisions)
Act 1989—
s 2 133
Law Reform (Husband and Wife) Act
1962 64
Law Reform (Married Women and
Tortfeasors) Act 1935 64
Law Reform (Miscellaneous Provisions)
Act 1970—
s 1 68
s 2(1) 68
s 3(1) 68
  (2) 69
Law Reform (Succession) Act 1995 69
Legal Aid Act 1988—
s 15 123
s 15(F–H) 101
Legitimacy Act 1976 345
s 1 288
  (1) 39, 58

Licensing Act 1964—
  s 169 413
Local Government Act 2003 1
Maintenance Enforcement Act 1991—
  s 1(5) 225
Marriage Act 1949 . . . . 38, 40
  s 1 361
  s 2 41
  s 3 . . . . 41, 360
    (1A) 362
    (6) 487
Marriage Act 1986 39
Marriage Act 1995 42
  s 25 42
  s 49 42
Marriage (Prohibited Degrees of
  Relationship) Act 1986—
  s 6(2) 40
Married Women's Property Act
  1882 . . . . 64, 126
  s 17 126
Married Women's Property Act 1964—
  s 1 129
Matrimonial Causes Act 1857 85
Matrimonial Causes Act 1923 85
Matrimonial Causes Act 1937 85
Matrimonial Causes Act 1973 . 26, 39, 51,
    52, 56, 62, 64, 85, 86, 87, 88, 93,
    101–103, 110, 123, 149, 150, 183,
    184, 201, 216, 221, 222, 226, 237,
           299, 303, 305, 598
  s 1(1) 88
    (2) 88
    (a) 88
    (b) 88, 89
    (c) 90
    (d) 90, 91
    (e) 91, 92
  s 2(1) 88
    (5) 91
    (6) 91
  s 5 92
  s 6 95
    (1) 95
  s 9(2) 87, 92, 93
  s 10(2) 92

    (3) 92
  s 11 39
    (c) 46
  s 12 49
    (e) 50
    (f) 50
  s 13(1) 56
    (2) 57
  s 16 . . . . 39, 58
  s 19 113
  s 21A(1) 217
  s 22 . . . . 132, 201
  s 22A(1) 195
    (4) 132
  s 23 58
  s 23A 197, 257
  s 24 . . . . 58, 226, 257
  s 24A 219, 220
    (6) 197
  s 24B(5) 218
  s 25 . . . . 132, 184, 201, 202, 209,
      212, 213, 218, 219, 223, 224
    (a)(2) 197
    (1) 202, 217, 235, 369
    (2) 217
    (a) 202, 203
    (b) 202, 20
    (c) 202, 205
    (d) 202
    (e) 202, 207
    (f) 207
    (g) 207, 208
    (3) 202
    (4) 184
  s 25A(1) 197, 198
    (2) 197, 198
  s 25B 215
    (1) 215
    (4) 215
    (7) 215
  s 27 132
    (3) 217
  s 28(1)(a) 196
    (b) 196
    (1A) 196, 197, 228
  s 29 184

s 31 227
  (7) 229
    (a) 229
   (7A) 229
s 35(2) 133
s 37 . . . . 226, 232
s 41 . . . . 421, 422
s 52 303
Matrimonial Homes Act 1967 242
Matrimonial Proceedings and Property
  Act 1970 186
  s 37 . . . . 68, 130, 141, 142
Mental Health Act 1983 . . 50, 55, 585, 630
  s 3 629
  s 7 629
Mines and Quarries Act 1954—
  s 124 412
National Assistance Act 1948—
  s 47 643
National Assistance (Amendment) Act
  1951 643
Occupiers Liability Act 1957 418
  s 2(3)(a) 418
Occupiers Liability Act 1984 418
Offences Against the Person Act 1861 . . 514
  s 10 . . . . 273, 414
  s 18 . . . . 268, 273, 414
  s 20 . . . . 268, 273
  s 47 . . . . 268, 273, 358, 414
Pensions Act 1995—
  s 166 215
Police and Criminal Evidence Act
  1984 549
  s 38(6) 585
  s 80 . . . . 65, 277
Prohibition of Female Circumcision Act
  1985 400
Protection from Harassment Act 1997
  . . . . . 243, 244, 246, 267–269, 274, 643
  s 1 . . . . 267, 269, 274
    (1) 268
  s 3 267
    (2) 269
    (3) 269
  s 4 274
    (4) 274

s 5 274
  (3)(b) 274
s 7(2) 268
  (3) 268
Protection of Children (Tobacco) Act
  1986 413
Punishment of Incest Act 1908 514
Registered Homes Act 1984 643
  s 11 643
  s 17 643
Rent (Agriculture) Act 1976 232
Rent Act 1977 . . . . 5, 232, 260
  Sch 1, para 2(2) 6
School Standards and Framework Act
  1998—
  s 70 412
  s 131 415
Sexual Offences (Amendment) Act
  1957 69
Sexual Offences Act 1956 514
  ss 10–11 514
  s 14 514
  s 25 514
  s 28 514
Sexual Offences Act 2003 . . . 69, 412, 514
Social Security Administration Act 1992—
  s 78 299
Supreme Court Act 1981—
  s 37 . . . . 242, 554
  s 41(2) 486
Surrogacy Arrangements Act 1985 . . . 294
  s 1(2) 294
  s 1A 341
  s 2(1) 341
  s 3 341
Theft Act 1968—
  s 30 64
Trusts of Land and Appointment of
  Trustees Act 1996 . . . . 149, 150
  s 13 149
  s 14 . . . . 150, 153, 156
    (1) 149
  s 15 149
    (3) 150
Welfare Reform and Pensions Act
  1999 216

s 29 217
s 85(2)(a) 217
Wills Act 1837 634

Youth Justice and Criminal Evidence Act
1999 514
Pt II 514

TABLE OF STATUTORY INSTRUMENTS

Adoption Support Services (Local
  Authorities) (England) Regulations
  2003, SI 2003/1348 609
Arrangements for Placement of Children
  (General) Regulations 1991, SI
  1991/890—
  reg 4 563
  reg 5(3) 563
  Sch 4 563
Blood Tests (Evidence of Paternity)
  (Amendment) Regulations 2001, SI
  2001/773 333
Child (Secure Accommodation)
  Regulations 1991, SI 1991/1505 . . . 586
Children (Private Arrangements for
  Fostering) Regulations 1991, SI
  1991/2050—
  r 4 301
Children (Protection at Work) Regulations
  1998, SI 1998/276 125
Children's Homes Regulations 1991, SI
  1991/1506—
  reg 11 562
Contact with Children Regulations 1991,
  SI 1991/891 568
Divorce etc. (Pensions) Regulations 2000,
  SI 2000/1123 218
Family Proceedings (Amendment) Rules
  2003, SI 2003/184 225
Family Proceedings Court (Children Act)
  Rules 1991, SI 1991/1395—
  r 4(5) 550
Family Proceedings Rules 1991, SI
  1991/1247—
  r 2 225
  r 4.4(c) 426
  r 4.12 553
  r 4.15(1), Pt IV 446
Family Proceedings Rules 1999, SI
  1999/3491 . . . . 115, 195, 223
  r 2.61 115

r 9.2A 403
Foster Placement (Children) Regulations
  1991, SI 1991/910—
  reg 5(2) 562
Homeless Persons (Priority Need for
  Accommodation) (England) Order
  2002, SI 2002/2051 271
Homeless Persons (Priority Need) (Wales)
  Order 2001, SI 2001/607 271
Insolvency Rules 1986, SI 1986/1925 . . 152
  r 12.3 226
  r 13.3(2)(a) 226
Land Registration (Matrimonial Home
  Rights) Rules 1997, SI 1997/1964 . . 149
Parental Orders (Human Fertilisation and
  Embryology) Regulations 1994, SI
  1994/2767 295
  Sch 1 295
Parental Responsibility Agreement
  Regulations 1994, SI 1994/3157 . . . 315
Pension Sharing (Valuation) Regulations
  2000, SI 2000/1052—
  reg 2 217
Pensions on Divorce etc. (Provision of
  Information) Regulations 2000, SI
  2000/1048 218
Placement with Parents etc. Regulations
  1991, SI 1991/893 565
Registration of Births and Deaths
  Regulations 1987, SI 1987/2088—
  reg 9(3) 460
Representation Procedure (Children)
  Regulations 1991, SI 1991/894 573
Review of Children's Cases Regulations
  1991, SI 1991/895 . . . . 566, 573
Rules of the Supreme Court—
  Ord 53, r 3 574
  Ord 80, r 2 486
Unfair Terms in Consumer Contracts
  Regulations 1999, SI 1999/2083 . . . 155

TABLE OF EUROPEAN LEGISLATION

CONVENTIONS

European Convention of Children's
Rights 1996 439

European Convention on the Legal
Status of Children Born out of
Wedlock 345

European Convention on the Protection
of Human Rights and Fundamental
Freedoms 1950 . . . . 14, 28, 45,
66, 70, 108, 110, 111, 162, 311,
324, 339, 348, 375–378, 397, 401,
408, 411, 414, 415, 436, 453, 467,
472, 511, 529, 539, 545, 558, 595,
604
art 1 375
art 2 399
art 3 . . . . 263, 375, 399, 411,
415, 510, 525, 539, 556
art 5 . . . . 375, 586
(1)(d) 586
art 6 . . . . 173, 174, 225, 263–265,
405–407, 411, 434, 445, 487, 511,
512, 545, 550, 559, 577, 578, 584,
597, 602
art 8 . . . . 4 6, 70, 162, 174, 263,
301, 302, 309, 311, 315, 324, 332,
346, 376, 377, 379, 406, 413, 434,
446, 454, 456, 459, 463, 466, 472,
480, 487, 501, 510, 511, 525, 529,
539, 541, 545, 551, 559, 565, 566,
570, 574, 579, 583, 584, 595, 602,
604, 612
(1) 335
(2) . . . 48, 263, 312, 335, 346, 413,
480, 510, 547, 558, 559, 604
art 9 . . . . 453, 454
art 10 460
art 12 . . . . 43, 45, 46, 48, 76, 337
art 14 . . . . 48, 264, 323, 346, 375,
401, 453, 456, 595
art 35(3) 436

European Convention on the Protection of
Human Rights and Fundamental
Freedoms, Protocol 1—
art 1 . . . . 162, 194, 264, 346
art 2 . . . . 376, 378, 408

European Convention on the Protection of
Human Rights and Fundamental
Freedoms, Protocol 7—
art 5 194

European Convention on Recognition
and Enforcement of Decisions
Concerning Custody of Children and
Restoration of Custody of Children
1980 (Luxembourg Convention) . . . 491,
502, 503
art 1(d) 502
art 8 503
art 9 503
art 10 503
art 12 502
art 15 503
art 23(2) 502

Hague Convention on Civil Aspects of
International Child
Abduction 1980 . . . . 491, 494, 496,
499, 502, 503
art 3 . . . . 495, 496
art 4 494
art 5(a) 495
art 8 494
art 12 497
art 13 497
(a) 496, 497
(b) 498
art 18 497

Hague Private International Law Convention
on Intercountry Adoption 613

United Nations Covenant on Civil and
Political Rights 70

United Nations Convention on the Exercise
of Children's Rights 402

United Nations Convention on the
Rights of the Child 1989 . . . . . 284, 368,
383, 410, 468, 472, 491
art 2(1) 345
art 3 368
art 7 332
art 11 491
art 12 . . . . 402, 439, 440
(1) 439
art 13 491
art 19 415
art 20 557
art 27(3) 516

art 28 411
(1) 408
United Nations Convention on the
Elimination of All Forms of
Discrimination against Women 242
Universal Declaration of Human Rights
1948 8
art 16(2) 52
(3) 8

DIRECTIVES

2000/78/EC (Age Discrimination
Framework Directive) 619

1

WHAT IS FAMILY LAW?

Families can be the scenes of some of the greatest joys, as well as some of the greatest sadnesses, that life can bring. A recent survey found that for a substantial majority of people families are more important to them than jobs or status.[1] The interaction of law and the family therefore gives rise to questions of enormous importance to the individuals who appear before the courts and to society at large.[2] This first chapter will consider some key questions about families: What are families? What is family law? Is family life in crisis? It will also highlight some of the most controversial issues which face family lawyers today and which will appear throughout the book. First, it is necessary to attempt a definition of a family.

1. SEEKING A DEFINITION OF THE FAMILY

The notion of a 'family' is notoriously difficult to define. Many people have a stereotypical image of what the 'ideal family' is like – a mother, a father and two children.[3] Yet this family composition is not the family form that most people will have experienced. So the image of two parents and two children as the ideal family is just that, an ideal; a powerful ideal, but not the most common family form.[4]

The difficulty in defining 'family' is the power of the definition and especially the stigma that follows from denying that a certain grouping of people is a family.[5] In part this explains the objections from within the gay and lesbian community to 'section 28', which refers to gay and lesbian relationships as a 'pretended family relationship'.[6] It is possible to distinguish[7] families (a group of people related by blood, marriage or adoption); a nuclear family (parents and their dependent children); extended families (the nuclear family plus the wider kin, e.g. grandparents); kinships (the larger family groups related by blood or marriage); and households (a group of people sharing accommodation).[8]

'Family' is presently a term that is of limited legal significance. As we shall see, much effort has been made in attempting a legal definition of 'marriage', 'parent' and 'parenthood', but relatively few cases have defined 'a family'. However,

---

[1] Future Foundation (1999).
[2] For a remarkable history of family law during the twentieth century see Cretney (2003a).
[3] Some people insist that a family must involve children: Duckworth (2002b).
[4] Krause and Meyers (2002) provide an excellent discussion.
[5] Douglas (2001: 3).
[6] The section was repealed by the Local Government Act 2003.
[7] See e.g. Day Sclater (2000).
[8] See Archard (2003: ch. 2) for further discussion, although he takes the view that a family must involve children.

following the Human Rights Act 1998 and the importance of the right to respect for family life, the concept of family will grow in legal significance.

How might the law define a family?

A. The person in the street's definition

In an attempt to define a 'family', the law could rely on common usage: how would the person in the street define a family? The difficulty with this is that although there may be some cases where everyone would agree that a particular group of people is a family, there are many other cases where, when asked, people would answer 'I don't know', or there would be conflicting answers, reflecting different values, religious beliefs or cultural perspectives. So asking a person in the street whether a group of people is a family does not help to clarify the definition of family in ambiguous cases. When children have been asked to define families they have revealed a broad understanding of the term and even included pets.[9] Studies of children also suggest that they define families in terms of those people they feel very close to, rather than the standard structure of blood relations.

B. A formalistic definition

The law could rely upon a formalistic approach. Such a definition would focus on whether the group of individuals in question has certain observable traits that can be objectively proved. These definitions often focus on criteria such as marriage or the existence of children. For example, the United Nations Statistical Commission has suggested:

> The family should be defined in the narrow sense of a family nucleus, that is, the persons within a private or institutional household who are related as husband and wife or as parent and never-married children by blood or adoption. Thus a family nucleus comprises a married couple without children or a married couple with one or more never-married children of any age or one parent with one or more never-married children of any age.[10]

The benefit of formalistic definitions is their clarity and ease of proof. The approach therefore has a strong appeal to lawyers. The definitions can be readily proved and would not involve the court in time-consuming or unnecessarily controversial questions.

The main disadvantage is that the approach can be rather technical. If the group of people failed to meet the formal requirements of the definition even though they functioned as a family, should they be denied the status of family? For example, some people argue that it would be bizarre if the law treated an unmarried couple who had lived together for 20 years and raised children together any differently from a married couple who had been married 20 years. Should the fact that the married couple undertook a short ceremony 20 years previously make a difference?

---

[9] Morrow (1998); Smart, Neale and Wade (2001: 52).

[10] Quoted in Hantrais and Letablier (1996: 8). Married couple here includes 'consensual union'.

Those who take such a view may prefer a definition that considers the function the relationship performs, rather than its technical nature.

C. A function-based definition

A function-based definition[11] examines the functions of families in our society.[12] If a group of people perform certain functions then the law can term them a family. The law would be less concerned with the formal nature of relationship between the group of people (e.g. whether they were married or not) and more concerned with their relationship in day-to-day practicalities and their contribution to society. In other words, the approach focuses on what they do, rather than what they are. If such an approach were to be adopted, the law might describe the functions of a family as: providing security and care for its members; producing children; social-ising and raising of children; and providing economically for its members.[13] However, whether a family needs to fulfil all or only some of these functions is con-troversial. Some have argued that a family's existence should be focused around children.[14] Others suggest that a sexual relationship, or a potential sexual relation-ship is essential if families are to be distinguished from friendship.[15]

Opponents of a function-based approach claim that it presupposes that the tra-ditional family is the ideal, and only permits other family forms to be included within the definition if they are sufficiently close to the functions of that ideal.[16] Some such critics suggest that the approach may be too conservative – to be a family you either have to be a married couple with children or equivalent to one, and that makes it difficult for non-traditional family forms (for example, a gay or lesbian couple) to become a family.

D. An idealised definition

Another approach suggests that a workable definition of what a family is does not exist, but that a definition of an idealised family can be provided. In our society many would see this as a married couple with children. The difficulty is that this idealised picture has become tarnished through evidence of domestic violence; abuse of children within the home; and the oppression of women within families. But some still promote a highly traditional family form as the ideal. For example: 'The Conservative Family Campaign aims to put father back at the head of the family table. He should be the breadwinner. He should be responsible for his chil-dren's actions. Those who teach his children should respect him. He should be upheld by social workers, doctors and others who may professionally come into

---

[11] The term 'functionalist definition' would be neater, but within sociological writing the term 'function-alism' has become associated with one particular view of the function of a family: a highly traditional one.

[12] Glennon (2000).

[13] See Veitch (1976); Rusk (1998).

[14] Bainham (1995b).

[15] Diduck and Kaganas (1999: 1) suggest that the law requires the possibility of a heterosexual relation-ship, but see now *Fitzpatrick v Sterling Housing Association Ltd* [2000] 1 FCR 21 HL.

[16] Harvard Law Review (1991).

contact with children.'[17] To others this picture would be far from ideal. We could try to 'update' the traditional image and create an ideal of a mutually supportive family where the children are cared for in a non-patriarchal, caring environment. But such an image of an ideal family is very much a western European one. Where are the grandparents, the uncles and aunts, nephews and nieces? Can a gay or lesbian person not have a family that is 'ideal' for him or her? Some versions of an ideal family involve a large group of people sharing each other's lives. So in a culturally diverse nation such as ours it would be impossible to agree on an idealised family form that would be acceptable to everyone.[18]

E. A self-definition approach

This approach would state 'you are a family if you say you are'. Eekelaar and Nhlapo[19] have suggested that societies are gradually accepting an increasing variety of family forms and are reaching the position that a family is any group of people who regard themselves as a family. The benefit of such an approach is that it does not stigmatise people as 'not family' unless they do not wish to be regarded as a family. Lord Williams of Mostyn, writing as the Attorney-General, has stated: 'We are not in the business of preaching or prescribing. Families in our society vary infinitely. We live in a diverse society ... It is not for me or the Government to define precisely what is a family unit. The mark of a civilised society is to accommodate diversity in others.'[20] The difficulty is that if there is no restriction on who can be a family it is hard for governments to seek to support families or to give family members special rights or responsibilities.

F. Do we give up?

So there are severe difficulties in defining families. There is little agreement within society over exactly what constitutes family or what the purposes of a family are. Does this lead us to throw up our hands and say there is no such thing as a family, as so many sociologists do? The argument for not doing so is that most people regard their family (whatever they mean by that) as of enormous importance, and indeed families are seen as having great social significance. Promoting the family is one of the few political ideals with which most people agree. As Gittens explains: 'The symbolic importance of the family cannot be underestimated, for it goes beyond political allegiances of left or right and has arguably come to be seen as the most important institution of modern industrial society.'[21]

What this demonstrates is that there are dangers in seeking to promote family life or talk about family law unless we are clear what it is we mean by families. We need to be precise about what aspect of the family a law is seeking to promote, or which

[17] G. Webster-Gardiner in a Press Conference quoted in Gittens (1993: 2). Labour politicians too have no embarrassment in referring to families as the building blocks of society: J. Kennedy (2000).
[18] See Bainham (1995b).
[19] Eekelaar and Nhlapo (1998: ix).
[20] Quoted in Bowley (2000).
[21] Gittens (1993: 59).

group of people is intended to be covered by a particular law. Indeed, it may be that some parts of family law will apply to some families and not to others. It is not that some groups are family and some are not, but that some family groups may need the benefits of a particular law and others not.[22] What is clear is that the definition of a family may change over time. Gittens writes: 'Just as it would be ludicrous to argue that a society or an era is characterised by one type of individual, so it is ludicrous to argue that there can only be one type of family. Families are not only complex, but are also infinitely variable and in a constant state of flux as the individuals who compose them age, die, marry, reproduce and move.'[23]

G. Discussion of how the law defines families

The legal definition of families has changed over time. In 1950 in *Gammans* v *Ekins*,[24] talking of an unmarried couple it was stated: 'to say of two people masquerading as these two were as husband and wife, that they were members of the same family, seems to be an abuse of the English Language'. This approach would no longer represent the law.

The leading case on the meaning of family in the law is *Fitzpatrick* v *Sterling Housing Association Ltd*,[25] a decision of the House of Lords. Although their Lordships were careful to explain that they were just considering the meaning of family in the Rent Act 1977, the decision will be highly influential in defining family in other contexts. The case concerned a Mr Thompson and a Mr Fitzpatrick, who had lived together in a flat for 18 years until Mr Thompson died. Under the Rent Act 1977 Mr Fitzpatrick could succeed to the tenancy of the flat, which had been in Mr Thompson's name alone, if he was a member of Mr Thompson's family. So, the core issue was whether a gay or lesbian couple could be a family. By a three to two majority the House of Lords held that Mr Thompson and Mr Fitzpatrick were a family. The majority accepted that the meaning of family is not restricted to people linked by marriage or blood. Lord Slynn suggested that the hallmarks of family life were 'that there should be a degree of mutual inter-dependence, of the sharing of lives, of caring and love, or commitment and support'.[26] He later added that the relationship must not be 'a transient superficial relationship'.[27] Applying these criteria to the couple in question, they were certainly family members. Mr Fitzpatrick had cared for Mr Thompson during the last six years of his illness. Lord Nicholls accepted that the paradigm family unit is a husband and a wife and children.[28] Lord Nicholls stressed that although the meaning of family was wider than blood relationships, the more remote the blood relationship the more evidence will be required to establish that there is a family relationship. However, the same-sex couple in question demonstrated 'the sharing of lives together in a single family unit

---

[22] Ghandhi and MacNamee (1991).
[23] Gittens (1993: 5).
[24] [1950] 2 KB 328 at p. 331, CA.
[25] [2000] 1 FCR 21 HL.
[26] [2000] 1 FCR 21 at p. 32.
[27] [2000] 1 FCR 21 at p. 35.
[28] [2000] 1 FCR 21 at p. 36.

living in one house'[29] that enabled them to be regarded as a family. Lord Clyde, unlike the others in the majority, thought that it would be difficult for a couple to show that they were a family unless there was an active sexual relationship or the potential for one.[30] He felt that the sexual element was important if a distinction was to be drawn between families and acquaintances. The dissenting judges argued that the paradigm of the family was a legal relationship (e.g. marriage or adoption) or by blood (e.g. parent–child). As the couple did not fall into these definitions, nor did they mirror them, they could not be regarded as a family, although the minority added that they believed Parliament should consider reforming the law so that a survivor of a gay or lesbian relationship could take on a tenancy.

In *Mendoza* v *Ghaidan*[31] it was held that a same-sex couple were living 'as [the tenant's] husband or wife' for the purposes of para 2(2) of Sch 1 of the Rent Act 1977 which lists those entitled to succeed to a statutory tenancy. Relying on the Human Rights Act 1998 the Court of Appeal interpreted the paragraph to read 'as if he or she were his wife or husband' and held that this would cover long-term same-sex partners.

So, to summarise the law's approach to defining a family, the law does not restrict the definition of family life to those who are married or those who are related by blood. It is willing to accept that other less formal relations can be family if they can demonstrate a sharing of lives and degree of intimacy and stability. However, it would be wrong to say that the law takes a pure function-based approach because if a couple are married they will be regarded as a family, even though their relationship is not a loving, committed, or stable one. The law therefore, in defining families, uses a combination of a formalist and function-based approach. Despite these developments recognising a variety of family forms Professor Bailey-Harris has argued that there is a hierarchy of families in family law with the top position being taken by married couples, followed by unmarried heterosexual couples, with same-sex couples being at the bottom.[32]

H. New families?

Some commentators believe that at the beginning of the twenty-first century we are witnessing some fundamental changes in the nature of families.[33] Others argue that family life has been in constant flux across the centuries.[34] Certainly some current statistics make dramatic reading. The more detailed figures are given at relevant parts throughout the book, but some of the main changes in family life in recent years include the following:

1. People are now marrying at an older age; the rate of marriage is dropping; and there are projections that fewer and fewer people will marry.[35]

---

[29] [2000] 1 FCR 21 at p. 39.
[30] [2000] 1 FCR 21 at p. 17.
[31] [2002] 3 FCR 591 CA.
[32] Bailey-Harris (2001c).
[33] Silva and Smart (1999). For a discussion of changes in family forms across Europe see Kaufmann; Kuijsten; Schulze and Strohmeier (2002).
[34] Fox Harding (1996).
[35] See Chapter 2.

2. Increasingly people are cohabiting outside of marriage. Whether cohabitation is used as a prelude to marriage, or an alternative to it, is a matter for debate.[36] In 2002 40 per cent of children were born to a mother who was unmarried.[37] In 2000 31 per cent of non-married women aged 18–49 were cohabiting.[38]

3. In the 1970s and 1980s there were sharp increases in the rate of divorce. In recent years the divorce rate appears to have levelled off, and even slightly declined. However, it has been projected that 41 per cent of marriages entered into in the 1990s will end in divorce.[39]

4. An increasing proportion of children lives in lone-parent households. In 2001, 25 per cent of households with dependent children were headed by a single parent.[40]

5. The average size of households is in decline and there is a significant increase in the number of people living alone. In 2001 31 per cent of households contained a single person.[41]

6. The proportion of the population over the age of 65 is ever increasing.[42]

7. There has been a sharp decline in birth rates. It is estimated that 25 per cent of women of child-bearing age will be childless by 2010.[43] A recent survey of women aged 21–23 only 40 per cent said they expected to have a baby in the next five years.[44]

Dench and Ogg have suggested that we are experiencing a dramatic shift from the traditional model of 'mother-father-child' family to one based on 'mother-grand-mother-child', with fathers (and fathers' side of the family) becoming irrelevant for many children. They argue:

> We can see a clear tendency at the moment for matrilineal ties (through the mother) to become the more active, while patrilineal, through the father, may often be very tenuous or even non-existent ... [There is now] a growing frailty in ties between parents ... an increasing marginalisation of men, and of ties traced through men, and a stronger focus-ing of families around women.[45]

However, others have argued the opposite stating that we are witnessing a signifi-cant change in family life because fathers are seeking to play an increasing role in the lives of their children.[46]

---

[36] See Chapter 2.
[37] Office for National Statistics (2003a). See also Eden (2000).
[38] Office for National Statistics (2003a).
[39] Haskey (1996a).
[40] Office for National Statistics (2003a).
[41] Office for National Statistics (2003a).
[42] See Chapter 12.
[43] Office for National Statistics (1996). For a discussion of the extent to which childlessness results from environmental and social factors, rather than a positive choice, see McAllister (2000).
[44] Muir (2003).
[45] Dench and Ogg (2002: x–xiii)
[46] Lewis (2002).

2. SHOULD FAMILY LIFE BE ENCOURAGED?

Most people regard families as beneficial. Indeed the Universal Declaration of Human Rights proclaims that the family is 'the natural and fundamental group unit of society'. However, there are those who oppose families.[47] The benefits and disadvantages of family life will now be briefly summarised.

A. Arguments in favour of family life

1. Emotional security. Family members can provide crucial emotional support and care for each other. Parents can furnish the love and security that children need as they are growing up. As Schaffer has argued:

   > Families are ideally suited for the bringing up of children: they are small, intimate groups, making it easy for children to acquire consistent rules of behaviour; they are linked to various outside settings (other families, work, leisure, and so forth) to which children can gradually be introduced; and they are usually composed of individuals deeply committed to the child whose security and care can therefore be guaranteed. The family is thus the basic unit within which the child is introduced to social living.[48]

2. Families can be regarded as essential to the development of people's identity and to the pursuit of their goals in life. Similarly, families enable children to develop their own characters and personalities.[49]

3. The advantages of family life are not limited to the benefits received by the members themselves. Families benefit the state. Ronald Reagan[50] captured a popular perception that: 'Strong families are the foundation of society. Through them we pass our traditions, rituals and values. From them we receive the love, encouragement and education needed to meet human challenges. Family life provides opportunity and time for the spiritual growth that fosters generosity of spirit and responsible citizenship.' Tony Blair has stated: 'We cannot say we want a strong and secure society when we ignore its very foundation: family life.'[51]

4. The family can also be supported as an institution[52] which protects people from powerful organisations within the state.[53] It is harder for the state to misuse its powers against groups of people living together, than to oppress individuals living alone.

B. Arguments against families

1. A major concern over families is the level of abuse that takes place against the weakest members. It has been claimed that around a quarter of all young

---

[47] Barrett and MacIntosh (1991).
[48] Schaffer (1990: 204).
[49] Parsons and Bales (1955).
[50] Quoted by White House Working Group on the Family (1985).
[51] A. Blair (1997).
[52] Article 16(3) of the Universal Declaration of Human Rights states: 'The family is the natural and fundamental group of society and is entitled to protection by society and the State.'
[53] Mount (1982: 1).

8

females are abused within the home.[54] Levels of domestic violence are strikingly high.[55] Certainly, behind the screen of 'respectable family life' appalling abuse of children and women has occurred. Whether the amount of interpersonal violence would decrease if there were no families may be open to doubt.

2. There is a major concern that families are a means of oppression of women. Delphy and Leonard argue: 'We see men and women as economic classes with one category/class subordinating the other and exploiting its work. Within the family system specifically, we see men exploiting women's practical, emotional, sexual and reproductive labour. For us 'men' and 'women' are not two naturally given groups, which at some point in history fell into a hierarchical relationship. Rather the reason the two groups are distinguished socially is because one dominates the other in order to use its labour.'[56] The argument is not necessarily that every family involves oppression, but that the structure of family life too readily enables oppression to occur.

3. Barrett and MacIntosh[57] argue that families encourage the values of selfishness, exclusiveness and the pursuit of private interest, which undermine those of altruism, community and the pursuit of the public good.[58] They insist: 'The world around the family is not a pre-existing harsh climate against which the family offers protection and warmth. It is as if the family has drawn comfort and security into itself and left the outside world bereft. As a bastion against a bleak society it has made that society bleak.'[59] If, rather than spending time on DIY and gardening, family members spent time on community projects, would society be a better place?

C. Proposing new visions for families

If the law and society were to attempt to promote a radically different form of family life, what might that be?

1. Fineman has suggested that we should view the mother–child relationship as the core element of a family,[60] although she explains that men can carry out the mother role. By using 'mother', she is seeking to promote a relationship of dependency as the foundation of family life. She explains: 'I propose Mother/Child as the substitute core of the basic family paradigm. Our laws and policies would be compelled to focus on the needs of this unit. Mother/Child would provide the structural and ideological basis for the transfer of current societal subsidies (both material and ideological) away from the sexual family to nurturing units.'[61] She is therefore seeking to move away from seeing the sexual

---

[54] Herman (1981) found that 17–28 per cent of women have been abused by men in their homes.
[55] See Chapter 6.
[56] Delphy and Leonard (1992: 258).
[57] Barrett and MacIntosh (1991).
[58] See also Brecher (1994).
[59] Barrett and MacIntosh (1991: 80).
[60] Fineman (1995).
[61] Fineman (1995: 233).

relationship between a man and a woman as the core element of family life and instead focusing on the child–parent relationship.

2. Barret and MacIntosh argue that society should move away from small units towards collectivism. They would like to see a range of favoured patterns of family life, involving larger groups of people living together in a variety of relationship forms.[62]

3. As noted above, increasing numbers of people live alone and this might suggest a model where people throughout their lives engage in a variety of relationships, but without cohabiting with anyone. Sociologists have recognised 'living apart together relationships', where a couple have a monogamous sexual relationship, but live in separate places.[63]

4. Weeks et al. looking at the meaning of 'family' within the gay and lesbian community talk of 'families of choice'. Families were seen as 'an affinity circle which may or may not involve children which has cultural and symbolic meaning for the subjects that participate or feel a sense of belonging in and through it'.[64] Family in this definition are those people to whom a person feels particularly close, rather than those with whom there is a blood tie.

5. Beck-Gernsheim[65] argues that for many people there is a pressure between people pursuing their own goals for their lives and the obligations they feel they owe to their families. She argues this will not lead to the end of the family: 'The answer to the question "What next after the family" is thus quite simple: the family! Only different, more, better: the negotiated family, the alternating family, the multiple family, new arrangements after divorce, remarriage, divorce again, new assortments from your, my, our children, our past and present families.'[66]

3. APPROACHES TO FAMILY LAW

A. What is family law?

There is no accepted definition of family law. Family law is usually seen as the law governing the relationships between children and parents, and between adults in close emotional relationships. Many areas of law can have an impact on family life: from taxation to immigration law; from insurance to social security. Therefore, any book that attempts to state all the laws which might affect family life would be enormous and inevitably textbooks have to be selective in what material is presented. Conventions have built up over the kinds of topics usually covered, but these are in many ways arbitrary decisions. For example, the laws on social security benefits and taxation can have a powerful effect on family life, but they are usually avoided in family law courses.

[62] Barrett and MacIntosh (1991: 134).
[63] Carling (2002).
[64] Weeks, Donovan and Heaphy (2001: 86).
[65] Beck-Gernsheim (2002).
[66] Beck-Gernsheim (2002: 8).

B. How to examine family law

There has been much debate over how to assess family law.[67] What makes good family law? How do we know if the law is working well? This chapter will now consider some of the approaches that are taken to answer these questions, although no one approach is necessarily the correct one and perhaps it is best to be willing to look at the law from a number of these perspectives.

(i) A functionalist approach

This approach regards family law as having a series of goals to be fulfilled. We can then assess family law by judging how well it succeeds in reaching those goals. For example, if we decide that the aim of a particular law has the purpose of increasing the number of couples who marry, then we can look at the rate of marriages to see if the law has succeeded in its aim. So what might be the objectives of family law?

Eekelaar[68] has suggested that, broadly speaking, family law seeks to pursue three goals:

1. Protective – to guard members of a family from physical, emotional or economic harm.
2. Adjustive – to help families which have broken down to adjust to new lives apart.
3. Supportive – to encourage and support family life.

It might be thought that functionalism is such a straightforward approach that it would be uncontroversial. However, there are difficulties with the functionalist approach:

1. One difficulty is that a law rarely has a single clearly identified goal. More often it is attempting a compromise between competing claims. A recent Act on divorce claims that it is seeking both to uphold marriage and to make it possible to divorce with as little bitterness or expense as possible.[69] These are contradictory aims. The Act may or may not strike an appropriate balance between them, but we cannot judge the success of the Act by deciding whether or not it reaches a particular goal, because it has several.
2. Another problem with the functionalist approach is that the law is only one of the influences on the way that people act in their family life. So an Act designed to reduce the divorce rate may have little effect if other social influences cause an increase in the divorce rate. The fact that the divorce rate has not fallen may not be the fault of the Act. The rise might be the result of a complex interaction between the law and all sorts of other influences on family life.[70]
3. With the functionalist approach there is a danger of not questioning whether the aims of the law are the correct ones to pursue. So just asking whether an Act designed to reduce the divorce rate has actually helped reduce divorce sidesteps

---

[67] O'Donnovan (1993).
[68] Eekelaar (1984: 24–6); Eekelaar (1987b).
[69] Family Law Act 1996, s 1.
[70] M. Hill (1995) discusses the wide variety of influences on family life.

asking whether we want to reduce the divorce rate. It is even a little more complex than this because sometimes the law appears to create the very problem it is seeking to fix. For example, it is only because we have legal marriage that we have 'a problem' with divorce.

4. A further difficulty with functionalism is that it overlooks what the law does not try to do. The fact that the law does not regulate a particular area can be as significant as a decision of the law to regulate.

These are powerful criticisms of the functionalist perspective, but do not render it invalid. The approach is so tied to common sense that it cannot be denied as a useful method. However, as the criticisms demonstrate it does have serious limitations.

(ii) Feminist perspectives

Feminist contributions to family law have been invaluable.[71] At the heart of feminist approaches is the consideration of how the law impacts on both men and women; in particular, how the law is and has been used to enable men to exercise power over women. It is important to appreciate the richness of the feminist perspectives:

1. At a basic level, feminist writers point to ways in which the law directly discriminates against women. For example, at one point in history a husband could divorce his wife on the ground of adultery, but a wife could only divorce her husband on the adultery ground if there was also some aggravating feature, for example that the adultery was incestuous. Nowadays there are relatively few provisions that discriminate in such an overt way.

2. Feminist writers also highlight aspects of family law which are indirectly discriminatory: that is laws which on face value do not appear to discriminate against women, but in effect work against women's interests. An example is the rule that financial contributions to a household are far more likely to give rise to a share of ownership in the house than non-financial ones through housework. This indirectly discriminates against women because it is far more likely that women provide only non-financial contributions to a household than men.

3. Feminists have also sought to challenge the norms that form the foundation of the law. Terms which the law might regard as having a given meaning, such as 'family', 'marriage', 'work', and 'mother' have been shown in fact to be 'constructs', images which the law has wished to present as uncontroversial, but which are in fact value-laden. Feminists argue that the law has a construct of what is a 'good mother' and penalises those who are not regarded as 'proper mothers', such as lone parents. Smart[72] suggests that society believes a good mother 'can prevent delinquency by staying at home to look after the children, she can reduce unemployment by staying at home and freeing jobs for men, she can recreate a stable family unit by becoming totally economically dependent on

---

[71] For an excellent recent discussion of family law from feminist perspectives see Diduck (2003).
[72] Smart (1984: 136).

her husband so that she cannot leave him. *She* is the answer.' Mothers who depart from this ideal, for example lone mothers, are penalised by the law and blamed for all kinds of social harms.[73] Rather less work has been done on the way the law constructs men and what makes a good father.[74]

4. Some feminist perspectives have also challenged what are called 'male' forms of reasoning. These feminists have categorised reasoning which focuses on individual rights as 'male' and as undermining the values that women prize, such as relationship and interdependency.[75] Gilligan has written of a distinction between the ethic of care (which rests on responsibilities, relationships and flexible solutions rather than on fixed long-term solutions) and the ethic of justice (which focuses on abstract principles from an impartial stance and stresses the consistency and predictability of results).

5. Feminists have also been concerned with how the law operates in practice and not just with what the law says. For example, although the law might try to pretend that both parents have equal parental rights and responsibilities,[76] in real life it is mothers who carry out the vast majority of the tasks of parenthood. So, it is argued, the legal picture of shared parental roles does not match the reality.[77]

There are, of course, divisions among feminist commentators and there are dangers in referring to 'the feminist response' to a question. Most notably for family law there is a disagreement between those who espouse feminism of difference and those who endorse feminism of equality. Feminism of equality (sometimes called liberal feminism) argues that women and men should be treated identically. Okin,[78] for example, would like to see a world where gender matters as little as eye colour.[79] Feminism of difference argues that the law should accept that men and women are different, but should ensure that no disadvantages follow from the differences. The issue of child-care is revealing. Feminists of equality might argue that we should seek to encourage men and women to have an equal role in child rearing so that they also have an equal role in the workforce. Feminists of difference would contend that we need to ensure that child rearing is valued within society and recompensed financially. Society needs to esteem the nurturing work traditionally carried out by women, rather than forcing women to have to adopt traditionally male roles if they are to receive financial reward. The root problem with these approaches is that they can both work against some women.[80] Feminism of equality might work to the disadvantage of the woman who does not want to enter the world of employment but wants to work at home child caring and home making. Indeed, arguably, middle-class women have only felt able to go out to work because they have been

---

[73] See Moloney (2001) for evidence of this from Australia.
[74] But see Collier (1995; 2000; 2003).
[75] Gilligan (1982).
[76] This is only true if both have parental responsibility. See Chapter 8.
[77] Day Sclater and Yates (1999).
[78] Okin (1992: 171).
[79] For an argument for gender neutrality in family law from a perspective which is not explicitly feminist see Bainham (2000c).
[80] Gregson and Lowe (1994).

able to employ other women to provide housework and child-care services. The difficulty with feminism of difference is that, by stressing differences, it can be seen as exacerbating and reinforcing the traditional roles that men and women play and so can limit the options for women. Much work is therefore being done to produce a third model which values the caring and nurturing work traditionally carried out by women, but at the same time protects the position of women in the workforce.[81] Dunn[82] argues there is a need for:

> recognising and celebrating the value of women's traditional areas of work and influence rather than accepting a masculine and capitalist hierarchy of value which can lead to women passing on their responsibilities to less powerful women. In conjunction with this would be the view that this valuable work is something that male peers can and should do, the aim being to facilitate and insist upon change in men's lives – enabling them to become more like women to the same degree that women have become more like men.

But until men are more willing to undertake this change and value the caring work women do, women are left to carry on their caring work unvalued. As should be clear, the law can only supply part of the impetus for equality for women. Political, cultural and psychological changes are necessary if there is ever to be an end to disadvantages for women.[83]

(iii) The public/private divide

Traditionally it has been thought appropriate to divide life into public and private arenas.[84] Family law has been seen as the protector of private life. Notably, the European Convention on Human Rights upholds 'a right to respect for private and family life'. The significance of this distinction between public and private life is twofold. First, the traditional liberal position is that there are some areas of our lives that are so intimate that it is inappropriate for the state to intervene. It is argued that it is quite proper for the law to regulate aspects of public life, such as contracts, commercial dealings, and governments, but that other areas of life are so private that they are not the state's business. Goldstein et al. argue that protection of family privacy is essential to promote the welfare of the child:

> When family integrity is broken or weakened by state intrusion, her [the child's] needs are thwarted, and her belief that her parents are omniscient and all-powerful is shaken prematurely. The effect on the child's developmental progress is likely to be detrimental. The child's needs for security within the confines of the family must be met by law through its recognition of family privacy as the barrier to state intervention upon parental autonomy.[85]

Not only, it is contended, should the state not intervene in private areas, it cannot. Imagine a law that makes adultery illegal. This might be opposed on the basis that it infringes people's privacy. It might also be argued that it would be unfeasible.

---

[81] For an excellent discussion of equality and discrimination generally see Fredman (2002).
[82] Dunn (1999).
[83] Day Sclater and Yates (1999).
[84] See the discussion in Gavison (1994); Oliver (1999).
[85] Goldstein, Solnit, Goldstein and Freud (1996: 90).

The police cannot keep an eye on the nation's bedrooms and hotels[86] to monitor whether adultery is taking place!

Secondly, it is maintained that where it does intervene in the public arena, the law seeks to promote different kinds of values than it does on the rare occasions when it deals with private law issues. In the public law sector people are presumed to be self-sufficient and able to look after themselves, whereas in the private arena the law stresses mutual co-operation and dependency.[87]

The distinction between private areas of life (into which the law should not intervene) and public areas of life (where the law may intervene) is deeply embedded in many people's thinking and much liberal political philosophy. The differentiation is particularly important in family life, although it is far from straightforward. The following are some of the difficulties with the distinction:

1. Is there really a difference between intervention and non-intervention? Imagine a family where the husband regularly assaults his wife. The law might take the view that this is a private matter and that it should not intervene. But in so doing what is the law doing? It could be argued that by choosing not to intrude, the law has permitted the existing power structure to be reinforced. In other words, the husband's power can be exercised by him only because of the state's decision not to step in. So a decision not to intervene should not be seen in a neutral light, but as a decision to accept the status quo.[88] This makes the distinction between intervention and non-intervention more complex than at first appears.[89]

2. Can we distinguish the public and the private? Take the example of child abuse. Although this takes place within the home, the consequences of it can affect all of society. The state will have the cost of providing alternative care for the child and of dealing with the social harms that flow from child abuse. This indicates that although the conduct takes place in private it has public consequences. Lacey argues that all areas of life – both public and private – involve interlocking arrangements, institutions and relationships between different kinds of people and bodies.[90] To classify a particular area of life as public or private is to oversimplify the complex interplay between governments, corporations and citizens.[91]

3. Why exactly might we want to protect the private? The argument for respecting private life is that it enables people to make decisions about how to live their lives free from state intervention. The traditional liberal approach is that each person should be able to develop his or her own beliefs and personality, free from state intervention unless there is a very good reason for the state to intrude.

---

[86] To make a rather conservative selection of venues.

[87] A distinction is sometimes drawn between *Gemeinshaft*: the values of love, duty, and common purpose (private values) and *Geschellshaft*: the values of individualism, competition and formality (public values).

[88] This may be because the law is happy with the status quo or that the law is concerned that legal intervention would cause even more harm. See further Eekelaar (2000a).

[89] See also Freeman (1985).

[90] N. Lacey (1993).

[91] E. Schneider (2000a: ch. 6).

However, this argument does not necessarily support a neutral stance from the state. Take a wife being regularly assaulted by her husband: it is arguable that to enable her to develop her own beliefs and personality the law must intervene.[92] In other words, the promotion of her autonomy (the freedom to choose how she wishes to live her life) which underpins the notion of privacy doctrine does not necessarily require the law to be non-interventionist. In fact to promote an individual's privacy might require intervention in her private life.

4. Is respecting privacy in fact about promoting societal interests? Eekelaar argues that, rather than dividing the world into public and private, it is more effective to recognise that the state has an interest in all areas of life, and the question is how the state best promotes its interests.[93] In relation to families, non-intervention often best promotes the state's interests. Bainham[94] suggests that: 'Child-rearing may be seen with equal justification as either a private matter, subject to state involvement only when public norms are transgressed, or as a public matter in the sense that the task of giving effect to the community's standards and expectations for child-rearing is delegated to parents.' So this approach would require us to ask whether society's goals are best furthered by intervention or non-intervention in this particular area, rather than asking whether this is a private or public area of life.

5. A further argument is that the image of the home and family as a private place is an ideal that may be true for some middle-class couples, but for those reliant on social housing and benefits the home can be seen as replete with social intrusion. In fact the state may police families in a less obvious way than direct legal intervention: health visitors;[95] teachers; neighbourhood watch schemes; and social workers could all be thought a form of policing of families outside formal legal regulation.[96] The argument here is that to regard legal intervention in family life as the only form of state intervention is unduly narrow.

6. Some commentators challenge not the existence of the public/private distinction, but the way in which it has been used to women's disadvantage. Such people suggest that, for example, the way that the law has classified domestic violence as a private matter, and the 'problem of lone parents' as a public one, works against women's interests. Indeed a critic would argue that those areas of life which are traditionally the preserve of women are labelled as private and so not worthy of legal intervention, whereas the men's world is labelled public and so deserving of regulation.

(iv) Family law and chaos

Any image that family law controls family life in Britain is clearly false. It has been said that 'the law of the family is the law of the absurd'.[97] The point here is that

---

[92] Gavison (1994).
[93] Eekelaar (1989).
[94] Bainham (1990).
[95] Who regularly visit a mother in her house following the birth of a child.
[96] Donzelot (1980); Parton (1991); Rodger (1996).
[97] C. Schneider (1991).

people do not live their family lives only after considering the legal niceties involved. The notion that people treat each other in intimate relationships by following the requirement of the law is clearly unrealistic. The vast majority of people simply do not know what the law relating to families is, and, even if they did, it would be very unlikely that the law would influence the way they would act in their family lives.[98] The government has accepted this: 'The truth is that families are, and always will be, mainly shaped by private choice well beyond the influence of government. That is how it should be. But that is no excuse for government not to do what it can.'[99] This is not to say that family law is utterly powerless. First, in the cases that actually reach the court, a court order usually has a strong influence on the lives of the parties thereafter. Secondly, the law and legal judgments[100] act as one part of the maelstrom of general attitudes within society towards the family, and the general attitudes of society can affect the way people think they ought to behave and hence the way they do behave.

Family law has to deal with people who act in the heat of love, hate, fury or passion, and so it is not surprising that it cannot itself be entirely rational. Like human beings, the law seeks to pursue contradictory objectives with inconsistent means. There is nothing necessarily wrong with this. To seek coherence and consistency in family law may therefore be a false goal. The law is dealing with the chaotic relationships of inconsistent and unreliable people, and so it is not surprising that the law reveals these characteristics too.[101]

(v) Autopoietic theory

Autopoietic theory has been developed from the ideas of Teubner. Its main proponent in the family law arena is Michael King.[102] He argues that society is made up of systems of discourse, and that law is but one system of communication within society.[103] One significance of the theory is that it recognises that there are difficulties in one system of communication working with another. In other words, the law has a certain way of looking at the world and interacting with it. The law classifies people and disputes in particular ways ('a mother'; 'a father'; 'a contact dispute'; 'a child abuse case'), applies the legal rules to it, and produces the appropriate legal response. This process may transform the problem, as the parties understood it, into a quite different form of dispute and then produce an answer inappropriate to the parties' actual needs. Further, when other systems of communication attempt to interact with the legal system, unless they are able to put their arguments into the form of legal communication, the legal system cannot deal with them. For example, when social workers or psychologists are called upon by the courts to advise on what is in the best interests of the child, their evidence will be transformed into a legal communication. This may not be easy for lawyers. The law tends to concentrate on

[98] Rose (1987).
[99] Home Office (1998: para 16), discussed in M. Maclean (2002).
[100] Especially when reported in the media.
[101] Dewar (1998).
[102] M. King (2000); James (1992). For a more critical discussion see Eekelaar (1995).
[103] E.g. M. King (2000).

sharp conclusions: guilty or not guilty; abuse or no abuse. Social workers, by contrast, concentrate on ongoing relationships and working in flexible methods over time, rather than setting down in a written order what should happen to children for the future.

4. CURRENT ISSUES IN FAMILY LAW

Some of the general issues that affect family law will now be considered.

A. How the state interacts with families

Fox Harding has suggested seven ways in which the state could interact with families.[104] Although only sketched here at a superficial level, they demonstrate the variety of attitudes the state could have towards families.

1. *An authoritarian model.* Under this approach the state would set out to enforce preferred family behaviour and prohibit other conduct. The law could rely on both criminal sanctions and informal means of social exclusion and stigmatisation. This approach would severely limit personal freedom.
2. *The enforcement of responsibilities in specific areas.* This model would choose the most important family obligations which the state would then seek to enforce. It is similar to the authoritarian model, but recognises that some family obligations are unenforceable.
3. *The manipulation of incentives.* Here the aim is to encourage certain forms of family behaviour through use of rewards (for example, tax advantages), rather than discourage undesirable behaviour through punishment.[105]
4. *Working within constraining assumptions.* Here the state does not overtly advocate particular family forms, but bases social resources on presumptions of certain styles of family life. For example, especially in the past, benefit and tax laws were based on the presumption that the wife was financially dependent on her husband.
5. *Substituting for and supporting families.* In this model the state's role is limited to supporting or substituting for families if they fail. In other words, the state does not seek to influence the running of the family until the family breaks down, but if it does then the state will intervene.
6. *Responding to needs and demands.* Here the law intervenes only when requested to do so by family members. Apart from responding to such requests, the state does not intrude in family life.
7. *Laissez-faire model.* Under this approach the state would seek to exercise minimal control of family life, which would be regarded as a private matter, unsuitable for legal intervention.

---

[104] Fox Harding (1996).
[105] See further M. Roberts (2001).

B. Privatisation of family law

There is much debate over whether there is a lessening of the legal regulation of family life. Some believe that we are witnessing the privatisation of family life, with the law regulating it less and less. For example, the government has attempted to encourage couples who are divorcing to use mediation to resolve financial disputes and disagreements about what should happen to the children after divorce, rather than using lawyers and court procedures. On the other hand, there are other areas of family law where the law appears more interventionist. For example, the Child Support Act 1991 has created a government agency which enforces support obligations for children – obligations which were often previously left unenforced. So the picture is not a straightforward one of intervention or deregulation. Dewar has argued that, rather than experiencing deregulation, the law is focusing its resources on cases where there is a need for legal intervention.[106] An example to illustrate his argument concerns parental arrangements for children on divorce. Previously, in divorce cases involving children there would be a hearing where a judge would meet the parties and consider the arrangements for the children. However, now there is no such hearing and, unless either party applies for a court order, the judge will not consider the arrangements for the children in depth. This could be seen as privatisation of family law, but it could also be seen as focusing judicial time on those cases which need it – those where the parents cannot agree what should happen to the child.

The law does seem more ready to intervene in family life once the family has broken up. For example, while the family is together there is no direct attempt to ensure that a child is receiving a reasonable level of financial support from his or her parents. However, once the couple separate, the Child Support Act 1991 comes into operation to ensure that a wage-earning parent financially supports the child at a suitable level. The law appears to assume that where a family live together any difficulties can be resolved by the parties themselves within the ongoing relationship; the law is only needed when the parents separate. Eekelaar and Maclean point out that: 'if people live apart, a point of tension or dispute can become the dominant focus of the relationship; there may be a few, if any, compensating benefits which are threatened by legal intervention. It therefore becomes necessary to define more sharply what their legal obligations are and to provide mechanisms for regulating them. Or so one may suppose.'[107]

One error that should not be made is to assume that because most cases are resolved through negotiation rather than actually coming to court, the law is exercising no influence. Eekelaar argues: 'There is . . . a danger that the relative marginalisation of the court in family matters will lead to a belief that *the law itself* has only a marginal role to play. This could be a serious mistake.'[108] It may well be that the matter is not brought before the court because it is obvious what the court would order and therefore the parties' agreement reflects this.

---

[106] Dewar (1992: 6–7).
[107] Eekelaar and Maclean (1997: 2).
[108] Eekelaar (1994c).

Some recent research considered why people seek court orders in relation to children.[109] One might suspect that the reason found was that court orders were sought where the parties were in disagreement. However, the researchers found that this was only one reason why an order might be sought. The other two were:

1. *Authority*. The parents wanted to be able to rely on the authority that a court order gave them, in particular where they felt they lacked control in a specific situation and wanted the confidence that a court order would provide.
2. *Vindication*. Here what was sought was the approval of the court for the parties' agreement and a formal record of it. Also researchers felt that sometimes an application to the court was used to send a message to the child. For example, a father might make an application for a residence order which was doomed to failure so that he could say to the child that it was the court's choice rather than the father's that the child should live with the mother.

Of course, often parties avoid seeking court orders. This may be because of the expense,[110] or the fact that the wrong they wish to be righted is not one recognised by the law. The law cannot usually prevent one spouse spreading gossip about the other, for example.

C. The decline in 'moral judgements'

It is arguable that the law is increasingly reluctant to make what some see as moral judgements.[111] At one time the courts were happy to state what had caused the breakdown of a marriage; who was a good mother or a good father; or what was the best way to raise a child.[112] However, increasingly the courts have been unwilling to do this, and have accepted that there is not necessarily one right answer in difficult cases.[113] In a recent decision of the House of Lords on division of property on divorce, Lord Nicholls stated: 'fairness, like beauty, lies in the eye of the beholder'.[114] In particular, the courts are more and more reluctant to accept that a party's bad conduct should affect the outcome of a case. At one time the question of whether a party had engaged in bad conduct was highly relevant in divorce cases, custody disputes and financial cases. Nowadays behaviour is rarely relevant.

Another notable example of the law's reluctance to impose moral standards is the fact that the House of Lords or Court of Appeal will only overturn a lower court's decision if it is shown that the judgment was clearly outside the range of decisions that the court could reasonably make.[115] The higher courts will not overturn a ruling simply because it is not the decision that they would have made. There is some evidence that judges are becoming increasingly less willing to hear cases and make decisions and rather seek to persuade or encourage the parties to reach their

---

[109] Pearce, Davis and Barron (1999).
[110] And/or being refused legal aid funds to bring the application.
[111] For a discussion of the interaction between legal and social norms see Eekelaar (2000a).
[112] M. King (1999). For a wide-ranging discussion on the role of fault in family law see Bainham (2001a).
[113] *Piglowska* v *Piglowski* [1999] 2 FLR 763 HL.
[114] *White* v *White* [2000] 2 FLR 976, [2000] 3 FCR 555.
[115] *Re C (A Minor) (Adoption: Parental Agreement: Contact)* [1993] 2 FLR 260 at p. 273.

own agreement.[116] Recent research suggests that 'settlement culture' is becoming widespread. This is 'the conviction that if parents can reach agreement, this must necessarily be preferable to any solution that the court can impose'.[117]

This refusal to impose moral standards has been supported by Finch, who argues:

> The aim of policies should be to facilitate flexibility in family life, rather than to shape it into a particular form. It is a proper role for the state to ensure that people have maximum opportunity to work out their own relationships as they wish, to suit the circumstances of their own lives. It is not the proper role of governments to presume that certain outcomes would be more desirable than others.[118]

It may be that the law's increasing reluctance to make moral judgements represents increasing uncertainty over moral absolutes in society at large.[119] Bainham[120] questions the assumption that there is a shared body of common values about family life and the role of family in society. He even questions whether it can be said that society accepts that adultery is morally wrong. He argues: 'It seems likely that if we were to concentrate on the practice rather than the theory of matrimonial obligations, at least as strong a case could be made for identifying a community norm of marital infidelity.' If we cannot even agree that adultery is wrong, there are few areas indeed where the law could set down moral judgements. However, Regan has argued that the law cannot avoid making moral judgements.[121] Even declining to express a moral judgement is in a way expressing a moral view. Also, as Bainham argues, the courts are willing to use bad behaviour as evidence of how an individual may behave in the future. So, although a father who has been violent may not be denied contact with his child on the basis that he has behaved immorally, he might be denied contact on the basis that his past bad conduct indicates that he might pose a risk to the child in the future.[122]

Criticism of the law's reluctance to uphold moral principles has come from a leading feminist writer, Carol Smart.[123] She argues that there is an overemphasis on 'psy professions' who focus on children's welfare and fathers' rights, while a mother's interests are lost. She is not, of course, calling for the courts to uphold 'traditional morality', but rather wishes to emphasise 'the morality of caring'. This is tied in with an argument that the law should focus on what family members 'do' rather than what their rights are. She argues that the 'doing' of parenthood – providing the day-to-day care of the child – should be given far more weight than in the present law, which instead emphasises rights, such as 'the father's right to contact the child'.

---

[116] E.g. Bailey-Harris, Barron and Pearce (1999).
[117] Bailey-Harris, Barron and Pearce (1999: 54).
[118] Quoted in Neale and Smart (1999: 24).
[119] Bainham (2000c).
[120] Bainham (1995b: 239).
[121] Regan (2000).
[122] Bainham (2001a). See Chapter 9 for a discussion of the law on contact.
[123] Smart (1991).

D. Sending messages through the law

The number of cases where the courts actually decide what happens to a family is small. Of far more importance is the general message that the law sends to individuals and to the solicitors who advise them. The ability of the law to send messages has been recognised by the Law Commission, which concluded, in a discussion on the law of divorce, that: 'for some of our respondents, as for our predecessors, it was important that divorce law should send the right messages, to the married and the marrying, about the seriousness and the permanence of the commitment involved. We agree.'[124] The law can also send messages through the language it uses.[125] For example, judges have said that is no longer appropriate in legal terms to speak of illegitimacy, because whether a child's parents are married or not does not affect the child's status.[126]

The problem with using the law as a means of sending messages is that, as regards the general public, the message that the law wishes to send is transmitted by the news media. The reliability of the media as conveyors of legal messages is certainly open to doubt. The government can, of course, send messages of its own about family life outside the context of the law. For example, the government recently created the National Family and Parenting Institute to advise people on parenting and family matters.[127] However, Eekelaar has expressed some concern that using the law to send 'messages' concerning how individuals live their intimate lives may infringe the principle that 'aspects of an individual's life are matters for determination by that individual alone'.[128] The tension between encouraging behaviour while not 'preaching' is seen in the following quotation from the government paper, *Supporting Families*:[129]

> Families do not want to be lectured about their behaviour or what kind of relationship they are in. They do not want to be nannied themselves or to be nagged about how they raise their children. But they do want support: advice on relationships; help with overcoming difficulties; support with parenting; and, should the couple's relationship break down irretrievably, a system of divorce which avoids aggravating conflict within the family.

Michael King has suggested that the law in this area is better understood as 'stabilising normative expectations' rather than resolving disputes.[130] He argues that the law cannot predict the future. It cannot at one hearing properly decide what is in the welfare of a child, for example. What it can do is set out the expectations generally of the law for particular kinds of cases.

---

[124] Law Commission Report 192 (1990: para 3.4).
[125] Bainham (1998b). This question becomes particularly important in discussing the enforcement of court orders: see Bainham (2003).
[126] Though it is not as straightforward as this; see Chapter 7.
[127] Home Office (1998).
[128] Eekelaar (2001c: 190).
[129] Home Office (1998: 30).
[130] M. King (2000).

E. Legal aid and costs

The role that costs and legal aid plays in family law is crucial.[131] The aim of legal aid, as defined by the Lord Chancellor at the time, 'is to provide a reasonable level of help in legal matters to people in genuine need, who could not afford that help without some subsidy or guarantee from the public'.[132] If legal aid is not available for certain kinds of proceedings then access to that part of the law is effectively denied to a section of the population. One notable example is the right to defend a divorce petition. Although this right exists in theory, it would be very unlikely that someone would be granted legal aid to defend a divorce petition. So the right to defend a divorce petition in effect is a right only for the wealthy. Further there is some evidence that at least in some parts of the country it has become difficult to find a solicitor or barrister to deal with legal aid work.[133] Therefore in some places the only sources of advice are through volunteers who are not legally qualified (e.g. at a Citizens' Advice Bureau).

A further significant effect of the costs issue is that now all questions of reform of family law must consider the potential impact on the legal aid bill and the general cost to government. Arguably, the Child Support Act 1991 and the divorce reform in the Family Law Act 1996 were both driven at least in part by a desire to cut the cost to the government of legal aid.

F. Families in crisis

There are some who believe that families are in crisis. For example, Lord Ashbourne in a House of Lords debate over the Family Law Bill stated:[134]

> If the Government are really concerned about the problems of law and order and child abuse they must end the policies that encourage the one-parent family and introduce measures that build up and support the traditional nuclear family ... Unless the Government are prepared to confront the threat which the collapse of the traditional family presents to the nation the problems will continue to escalate.[135]

There is also political talk of promoting family values,[136] by which is usually meant: stable marriages; gendered division of roles; the confinement of sexuality to the married heterosexual unit; and the support of these patterns through government policy.[137] These have been championed in particular by some on the 'new right'. Diduck has suggested that when people mourn the loss of the traditional family they are in fact grieving for the loss of the values of loyalty, stability, co-operation, love and respect, rather than the traditional image of the married couple with children.[138] Others speak of the 'new family', where the traditional notions of family

---

[131] Glancy (1997). The detailed law on legal aid is now found in the Access to Justice Act 1999.
[132] Lord Chancellor's Department (1996).
[133] Davis, Finch and Barnham (2003).
[134] HL col 170, 20 November 1996.
[135] P. Morgan (1999b).
[136] For a discussion of the difficulty in finding agreed 'family values' in today's society see Carbone (2000).
[137] Jagger and Wright (1999: 1–2).
[138] Diduck (2003: 23).

have been cast aside to make room for multifarious forms of family life. So whether family life is in crisis or simply undergoing change is a matter for debate.[139]

Giddens[140] suggests that there has been a fundamental shift in the nature of intimate relationships. He suggests that today the typical relationship is one

> entered into for its own sake, for what can be derived by each person from a sustained association with another; and which is continued only in so far as it is thought by both parties to deliver enough satisfaction for each individual to stay within it . . .

This is a highly individualised concept of relationships. It has been criticised by some feminist commentators for failing to recognise the role that dependency and caring plays in the lives of women particularly.

G. Solicitors and family law

As we have already noted, the vast majority of disputes between family members do not reach the courts. Many are resolved by negotiation using solicitors. Hence the position of the family law solicitor is a crucial one in the working out of family law in everyday life. Ingleby has suggested the term 'litigotiation'[141] as appropriate to explain what many family lawyers do. The word suggests a combination of litigation and negotiation, meaning that the parties negotiate through the mechanisms put in place to prepare for litigation. The 'guess' or prediction of what a court will order shapes the bargaining of the solicitors. If, for example, the solicitors are negotiating a financial settlement after divorce, they will normally be able to estimate the range within which a court is likely to make an order. The negotiations will then concern where in that range the parties can reach agreement. Further, there is increasing interest in the attitudes and practices of family lawyers.[142] Piper has suggested that 'solicitors appear to have internalised an agreed set of "rules" which must be followed by those aspiring to be good family lawyers'.[143]

H. Non-legal responses to family law

No family lawyer would claim that the law provides the solutions to all problems that families might face. The importance of the role played by social workers, psychiatrists, psychologists and mediators in resolving difficulties families face should not be underestimated. In an important decision heard recently in the Court of Appeal, *Re L (A Child) (Contact: Domestic Violence)*,[144] Thorpe LJ stressed that sometimes lawyers had to accept that counselling and social work may be far more effective than lengthy and costly legal proceedings. Talking of disputes over contact, he suggested:

> The disputes are often driven by personality disorders, unresolved adult conflicts or egocentricity. These originating or contributing factors would generally be better treated

---

[139] Howard and Wilmot (2000).
[140] Giddens (1992: 58).
[141] Ingleby (1992).
[142] Eekelaar, Maclean and Beinart (2000).
[143] Piper (1999: 101). See also Diduck (2000).
[144] [2000] 2 FCR 404 CA.

therapeutically, where at least there would be some prospect of beneficial change, rather than given vent in the family justice system.[145]

In Chapter 3 the benefits and disadvantages of using mediation rather than lawyers will be discussed and it will be noted that recent suggestions of reform of the divorce law have been dominated by attempts to encourage parties to rely on mediation, rather than using lawyers.

I. Rights and consequentialism

This tension in family law between the wish to promote the welfare of the child and the concern to protect the rights of family members has been emphasised by many writers and it gives rise to some fascinating theoretical issues. In an insightful article[146] Stephen Parker has analysed how the approach of family law has swung between 'utility' and 'rights'. A utilitarian approach, he argues, 'evaluates acts and institutions in terms of their consequences for reaching' a goal; in this context the goal is the promotion of the welfare of the child, whereas a rights-based approach seeks 'not to evaluate an act or institution solely in terms of its consequences' (for example, promoting the welfare of the child) but in terms of 'the right of an actor to do it'. Parker suggests that in Anglo-Australian law there had been a gradual shift from rights to utility, but there is now gradual reversion to rights. In fact the picture is confused, as Parker acknowledges, because there is not a clear attachment to either rights or utility across family law at present. He suggests that this represents 'normative anarchy'[147] and Dewar has stated that this is part of the 'normal chaos of family law'.[148] Dewar argues that rights and utility are 'simply different and incompatible ways of approaching the tasks of conceptualising children and their needs and of decision making in such cases'.[149]

J. Rules or discretion

There is a debate over the extent to which family law cases should be resolved by relying on rules and the extent to which they should be decided on a discretionary basis.[150] Put simply, should a judge decide each case on its merits and be given a wide discretion in reaching a solution appropriate to a particular case or should we have rules to ensure consistency,[151] save costs, and protect the rights of individual family members?[152] In fact the distinction is not that sharp because there is a continuum between wide discretion and inflexible rules.[153] The more family law is seen

---

[145] [2000] 2 FCR 404 at p. 439.
[146] S. Parker (1992). See also Eekelaar (1994d); S. Parker (1998).
[147] S. Parker (1992: 312).
[148] Dewar (1998).
[149] Dewar (1998: 472).
[150] C. Schneider (1991).
[151] As Dewar (2000b) points out, clear rules would ensure that there is consistency between decisions reached not only in the courtroom but also between settlements negotiated by the parties and their lawyers.
[152] Dewar (1997).
[153] C. Schneider (1991).

as a set of fixed rights and responsibilities, the more likely it is for a rule-based system to be used; but if family law is seen as about achieving justice for the particular individuals involved, the more likely a discretionary-based system will be employed. With a discretionary-based system, if the case is going to be decided on its own special facts then the court will require all the relevant evidence to be heard, and this creates more costs in both the preparation of and hearing of a case. So the expense involved is another important factor in deciding the balance between the two regimes.[154]

Family law in England and Wales has examples of both inflexible rules and wide discretion.[155] The Child Support Acts are based on rigidly applied formulae with only limited scope for departure, while the standard of the best interests of the child which is at the heart of the Children Act 1989 is notoriously vague and in effect gives a wide discretion to a judge. Lord Hoffmann in the House of Lords in *Piglowska v Piglowski*,[156] considering the issue of judicial discretion in redistributing property on divorce, stated: 'These are value judgements on which reasonable people may differ. Since judges are also people, this means that some degree of diversity in their application of values is inevitable and, within limits, an acceptable price to pay for the flexibility of the discretion conferred by the [Matrimonial Causes Act 1973].'

K. Partnership

One theme that runs through the Children Act 1989 – the leading piece of legislation on the law relating to children – is 'partnership'. The public law in particular places much stress on the concept of a voluntary partnership between local authorities and parents. There is support for parents carrying out their roles as parents; there is emphasis on the partnership between the parents if both have parental responsibility together; there is also much stress on the need for co-operation between the different agencies which are involved with children. So local education, housing and health authorities are under a statutory duty to assist the social services departments. The aim is to achieve a more co-ordinated approach to families, rather than different agencies working in opposition to one other.

L. Multiculturalism

To what extent should family law take into account the variety of cultural practices in British society?[157] The question can be framed as how to balance the desire to protect the values of the dominant culture with a need to recognise and respect the values of minority cultures. For example, in relation to marriage, should the law permit polygamous marriages out of respect for minority cultures which may

---

[154] For further discussion see Dewar and Parker (2000).
[155] An interesting recent example is *Rampal v Rampal (No. 2)* [2001] 2 FCR 552 which preferred to retain discretion on whether a court can award ancilliary relief to a bigamist, rather than the strict bar which the Court of Appeal in *Whiston v Whiston* [1995] 2 FLR 268 had appeared to suggest.
[156] [1999] 2 FLR 763 at p. 785.
[157] For some useful discussions see Brophy (2000); Khaliq and Young (2001); Banda (2003).

encourage polygamy, or should it rather reflect the disapproval of the majority culture towards polygamy? Corporal punishment of children is another issue over which different cultures may have different practices. Alternatively, the issue can be seen as this: does the law believe that people have rights which should be protected, regardless of their cultural background, or does the law encourage cultural groups to adopt different practices, regardless of whether the majority approves of them?[158]

There are various strategies that could be adopted including the following:[159]

1. *Absolutism.* This view is that the values of the majority are the only correct values. Absolutism would lead to a strategy of complete non-recognition of the values of minority cultures. Minority cultures would have to adopt the values of the majority. This is not an approach that would be acceptable to most western democracies.

2. *Pluralism.* This approach recognises that there are some issues where minority values should be protected, but others where the majority's values must be preserved.[160] Poulter argues that minority cultural values should be restricted in instances where human rights as set out in international agreements must be protected.[161] For example, if the practices of a minority culture infringe children's rights, the law is permitted to outlaw those practices. Parkinson suggests that 'the importance of preserving the inherited cultural values of the majority must be balanced against the effects of such laws on the minority's capacity for cultural expression'. Parkinson insists, in reference to Australia, that there are some aspects of the majority's culture which are fundamental and should be fixed.[162] He refers to the minimum age of marriage, to laws prohibiting incest, and to the need for consent for marriage as being some of the fundamental values. On these issues, minority family practices which contravened these principles could be outlawed. However, on less fundamental values, the minority practices should be respected, even if the majority found them distasteful.

3. *Relativism.* This view states that there are no moral absolutes; that different values may be acceptable for particular cultures at particular times.[163] Therefore, if a form of conduct is accepted in a minority culture the majority has no ground upon which to forbid it. If this approach were adopted there might be difficulties over issues where the minority practice is based on a mistaken factual premise. For example, if female circumcision was acceptable in a minority culture because it was thought to provide medical benefits, would the majority be entitled to forbid it because they 'know' that it has no medical benefits? In a more positive light, relativism claims that society benefits from there being a wide variety of different cultural practices and beliefs – it creates a richer and more diverse society.[164] However, most relativists accept that there might be some forms of cultural practice that so infringe the rights of others to live their

---

[158] Mouffe (1995).
[159] For a thorough discussion see Freeman (1997a; 2002b).
[160] For further discussion see Raz (1994).
[161] Poulter (1987).
[162] Parkinson (1996).
[163] See the discussion in Tilley (2000).
[164] Raz (1994).

lives as they wish that they should be prohibited.[165] Opponents of relativism argue that once society accepts that people have certain rights, these rights should not be lost simply because a citizen is from a minority culture. If, for example, children's rights require that the law forbids corporal punishment, children should not lose those rights because they belong to a culture which accepts corporal punishment.

Freeman has argued that a degree of scepticism is justifiable when considering cultural practices:

> Many cultural practices when critically examined turn upon the interpretation of a male elite (an oligarchy, clergy or judiciary): if there is now consensus, this was engineered, an ideology construction to cloak the interests of only one section of society.[166]

He stated that the way ahead is to develop through dialogues across communities versions of 'common sense' values.[167]

One of the few occasions on which the English courts[168] have addressed these issues was *R v Derriviere*,[169] where a father gave his son, aged under 13, heavy corporal punishment because he had stayed out late at night. The father argued that the level of punishment was normal by the standards of his culture. However, the Court of Appeal held: 'Once in this country, this country's laws must apply; and there can be no doubt that, according to the law of this country, the chastisement given to this boy was excessive and the assault complained of was proved.' However, in sentencing the father, the fact that he was unaware of the acceptable standards of corporal punishment was taken into account.[170]

5. THE HUMAN RIGHTS ACT 1998 AND FAMILY LAW

The Human Rights Act 1998 protects individuals' rights under the European Convention on Human Rights. That convention sets out the minimum standards of treatment under the law that people are entitled to expect.[171] The Human Rights Act 1998 has had a significant impact on the way that family cases will be argued. Parents, children and families now regularly bring cases referring to their rights under the Act. There are two important aspects of the Human Rights Act. First, the rights in the Act (which are essentially the rights protected in the European Convention on Human Rights) are directly enforceable against public authorities (e.g. local authorities) and all public authorities must act in a way that is compatible with these rights unless required to do so by other legislation.[172] The court is a public authority and hence it is generally thought that no court order should infringe an individual's rights as defined in the Human Rights Act, unless com-

---

[165] Raz (1994).
[166] Freeman (2000d: 13).
[167] Freeman (2002b).
[168] Poulter (1998) provides a thorough discussion of the response of English law to cultural diversity.
[169] (1969) 53 CAR 637.
[170] For a useful discussion of how cultural values and human rights interrelate see Freeman (2002a: ch. 6).
[171] This point is emphasised in Bainham (2000c).
[172] Human Rights Act 1998, s 6.

pelled to do so by other legislation. Secondly, under s 3 of the Human Rights Act all legislation is to be interpreted, if at all possible, in line with the Convention rights. If it is not possible to interpret the legislation in accordance with these rights, then the legislation should be enforced as it stands and a declaration of incompatibility issued: this requires Parliament to confirm or amend the offending legislation. In interpreting the extent of the rights protected in the Human Rights Act, the decisions of the European Court of Human Rights and European Commission will be taken into account by the courts.[173] The possible relevance of rights under the Act will be considered at the relevant points throughout this book.

6. CONCLUSION

This chapter has considered the nature of families and family law. One point that has emerged is that the terms 'family' and 'law' do not have a fixed meaning. The understanding of a family has changed over time. For example, although at one point a family would have been defined as a married couple with children, recently the House of Lords has accepted that a gay couple can be a family.[174] Despite the lack of clarity over what a family is, it is clear that it is a powerful ideal: no major political party would openly advocate 'family unfriendly policies'. The chapter has also noted the diversity of ways that family law can be approached. There is no one correct way of viewing the law and each approach has its benefits and limitations. What, however, the discussion demonstrates is that the interaction between families, law and socio-political forces is complex. The tensions between the traditional ideal of what a family should be like and the realities of family life today are revealed in the topical issues discussed at the end of the chapter. As these controversies indicate, family law today is quite different from family law 30 years ago; and where family law will be in 30 years' time is a question requiring guesswork.

---

[173] Human Rights Act 1998, s 2.
[174] *Fitzpatrick v Sterling Housing Association Ltd* [2000] 1 FCR 21 HL.

2

MARRIAGE AND COHABITATION

1. INTRODUCTION

In most societies around the world it is widely accepted that it is best for children to be brought up in 'stable intimate partnerships' and that such partnerships can provide adults with much personal fulfilment. The regularisation of these stable relationships has in England and Wales been channelled through marriage, but marriage worldwide is a hugely varied phenomenon. For example, there is no agreement over whether marriage is polygamous or monogamous (i.e. how many parties there should be to a marriage); whether or not the upbringing and/or nurturing of children is central to the concept of marriage; whether marriage partners should be chosen by the parties themselves or by their wider family; or at what age marriage is appropriate. In Britain, in our culturally diverse society, it would be difficult to say anything about the nature of marriage that would be true for all married couples. Traditionally, it has been the Christian conception of marriage which has been dominant, although it is far from clear exactly what that conception is.[1] Increasingly, there is a divide between the church's and the law's understanding of marriage. Legal marriages can take place in circumstances which would not be approved by many churches. It is interesting that some religious groups have seen the need for legal marriages to be bolstered by special religious pledges, involving commitments beyond the legal obligations of marriage.[2]

Marriage used to be the main focus of family law. Textbooks would concentrate on discussion of the formalities of marriage, the consequences of marriage, and its dissolution. However, today, many commentators on family law feel that parenthood is the core concept in family law and that marriage is of limited legal significance. That said, marriage still creates some important legal consequences – it would not be possible for a lawyer to advise a client over a family matter unless the lawyer knew whether the couple were married. There are two particular challenges that threaten to limit the legal significance of marriage even further. First, there are calls for the traditional definition of marriage to be widened, for example that two people of the same sex be permitted to marry and that divorce should be more readily available. As marriage has become easier to enter and to exit, any claim that it is a special relationship deserving of particular respect becomes harder to maintain. Secondly, there are arguments that those who are unmarried but live together in many ways like a traditionally married couple should be treated in the same way as

---

[1] Thatcher (1999).
[2] E.g. the Promise Keepers movement in the United States.

a married couple. These pressures make it harder to claim a unique status for marriage.

2. STATISTICS ON MARRIAGE

There is much debate over whether marriage is in decline. Some statistics certainly suggest that it is. There has been a 40 per cent drop in the number of marriages between 1972 and 1998.[3] In 2001 there were 249,227 marriages in England and Wales, the lowest figure since 1897.[4] Although there has been a gradual decline in the number of marriages over the past few decades, there was a 1.7 per cent increase in the number of marriages between 1999 to 2000.[5] However, for 2001 the number of marriages again declined, so any hope that the figures for the year 2000 indicated a resurgence in the popularity of marriage appear misplaced.[6] The number of men marrying per 1,000 unmarried men aged 16 or over was 27.8 in 2001; for women the rate was 23.8. These rates were a drop from the rates in the year 2000 which were 29.5 and 25.7. Significantly in 2001, 40 per cent of marriages were second or further marriages.[7] This suggests that there are numbers of people marrying, divorcing and remarrying who are keeping the numbers of marriages at their present rate. In 1961 about 330,000 first-time marriages and 50,000 remarriages took place but by 2001 these figures had dropped to fewer than 148,642 first-time marriages, with 100,585 remarriages.[8] The number of people who choose not to marry at all has greatly increased. It has been estimated that by 2005 less than half of the adult population will be married.[9] Some would say England and Wales are moving closer to the position in Sweden, for example, where marriage is the exception and unmarried cohabitation the norm.

It is, however, possible to point to statistics which indicate that marriage is in a healthy state. As Bernardes argues '. . . around 90% of all women marry in the UK today, compared to 70% in the Victorian era. Britain has one of the highest rates of marriage in the European Union. By the age of 40 years 95% of women and 91% of men have married.'[10] Whether marriage is in terminal decline or not remains to be seen. What is clear is that the nature of marriage is changing. Three points in particular are worth noting. First, the average age of first marriage in England and Wales has changed – for women the average age of marriage has risen from 21.4 in 1975 to 32.2 in 2001.[11] Secondly, it is now commonplace for a couple to cohabit

---

[3] Barton (2002b: 437).
[4] Office for National Statistics (2003a).
[5] Office for National Statistics (2003a).
[6] It is possible that the popularity of marriage overseas may impact on the apparent rate of marriage. Carter (2003) quotes a figure of 60,000 people going abroad to marry.
[7] Office for National Statistics (1999).
[8] Eden (2000).
[9] Thorpe (2002: 891).
[10] Bernardes (1997: 137). According to National Family and Parenting Institute (2001a); 95 per cent of British women will have been married by the time they are 49.
[11] Murphy and Wang (1999).

before marriage.[12] Thirdly, the likelihood that marriage will end in divorce has greatly increased.[13]

3. WHAT IS MARRIAGE?

A. The meaning of marriage

It is impossible to provide a single definition of marriage. Indeed, one approach is to say that one cannot define marriage because marriage is whatever the parties to a marriage take it to mean. Thus a Christian couple seeking to base their marriage on biblical principles may well see their marriage in very different terms from a couple who understand their marriage to be open and short-term, entered into for tax purposes. Further, the wife's experience and understanding of marriage may be very different from the husband's. The lack of a clear definition of marriage may be a sign of the times. As Glendon writes:

> the lack of firm and fixed ideas about what marriage is and should be is but an aspect of the alienation of modern man. And in this respect the law seems truly to reflect the fact that in modern society more and more is expected of human relationships while at the same time social changes have rendered those relationships increasingly fragile.[14]

But it would be too easy to see marriage as simply being whatever the parties want it to be because this denies a wider understanding of marriage within society. The concept of marriage is an important symbol within our society – marriage is not just a personal matter between the parties.

Marriage can be examined from a number of perspectives:

(i) Functional

From a functionalist approach it would be necessary to decide what the purpose of marriage is. Some insist that children are at the heart of marriage. Hoggett et al. suggest: 'If nothing else, then, marriage is about the licence to beget children.'[15] Engels, on the other hand, saw the role of marriage and family as an integral part of the regulation of private property and the creation of legitimate heirs. Others would emphasise the role of creating an environment of love and comfort for the husband, wife and any children.

(ii) Psychological

Others analyse marriage by considering the psychological need to marry and the psychological interactions between the two marriage partners. For example, one perspective is to see marriage as a conversation between the spouses, formulating

---

[12] Kiernan and Mueller (1999). In 2001, of 249,227 marriages 189,711 couples gave the same address as their place of residence.
[13] See Chapter 3.
[14] Glendon (1989).
[15] Hoggett, Pearl, Cooke and Bates (2003).

their own relationship and their common view of the world.[16] Giddens has argued that modern intimate relations are entered into 'for what can be derived by each person from a sustained association with another; and . . . is continued only in so far as it is thought by both parties to deliver enough satisfaction for each individual to stay within it'.[17] In other words, people are now more individualistic and are only willing to stay in relationships so long as they feel they personally are benefiting from them.[18] Regan,[19] taking a different approach, has written of the need to appreciate both the external and internal elements of marriage. Couples constantly seek to balance the interests of each individual spouse and the interests they have as a couple together. He sees both the legal and social difficulties in marriage as involving a resolution of the tension between these elements.[20]

(iii) Political

It is also possible to consider the role marriage plays in wider society. Some see the subjugation of women as the essence of marriage. Marriage has been described as 'a public form of labour of relationship between men and women, whereby a women pledges for life (with limited rights to quit) her labour, sexuality and reproductive capacity, and receives protection, upkeep and certain rights to children'.[21] Others reject the idea that marriage is a conservative institution. Mount has suggested that marriage can be regarded as subversive, protecting individuals from the power of the state and the church.[22] The government has announced that it would like to strengthen marriage, but it does not want to pressure people into marry or penalise those who do not.[23] The difficulty is that any 'rewards' given to those who marry can be seen as penalising those who choose not to.

(iv) Religious

There is a wide variety of religious understandings of marriage.[24] Some religions teach of a spiritual union between spouses on marriage, with the spouses' love reflecting God's love.[25] Some religions regard marriage as indissoluble, although others do not take a hard line on divorce. In England and Wales the law's understanding of marriage has historically been strongly influenced by Christian theology.[26]

---

[16] Berger and Kellner (1980).
[17] Giddens (1992: 58).
[18] Beck and Beck-Gernsheim (1995); Lewis (2001a; 2001b).
[19] Regan (1999).
[20] For a discussion on the link between marriage and commitment, see Lewis (1999).
[21] Lenard (1980).
[22] Mount (1982).
[23] Home Office (1998).
[24] Thatcher (1999).
[25] Pontifical Council for the Family (2000).
[26] For a collection of writing on modern theological understandings of marriage see Scott and Warren (2001).

B. The legal definition of marriage

The most widely accepted definition of marriage in the law is that in *Hyde* v *Hyde and Woodhouse*:[27] 'the voluntary union for life of one man and one woman to the exclusion of all others'. This is perhaps better understood as an ideal promoted by the law rather than a definition as such. As we shall see, it is quite possible to have a legally valid marriage which is entered into involuntarily,[28] is characterised by sexual unfaithfulness, and is ended by divorce. In truth, it is probably not possible to provide a purely legal definition of marriage. The law has had much to say about who can marry whom and how the relationship can be ended, but says very little explicitly about the content of the relationship itself. In fact, it would be possible for a couple to be legally married but never to have lived together or had any kind of relationship.[29] In *R (on the Application of the Crown Prosecution Service)* v *Registrar General of Births, Deaths and Marriages*[30] the Crown Prosecution Service sought an order preventing a marriage between a man charged with murder and the woman intended to be the main prosecution witness at his trial. It was argued that the marriage was being entered into so that she would not be a compellable witness against him. However, the Court of Appeal refused to grant the order. It would not examine the reason why the couple wanted to marry and consider if it was a valid one. [31] This is not surprising because the law cannot force a married couple to live in any particular relationship. The law on marriage merely provides parameters within which the couple are free to develop the content of their marriage as they wish.

C. Why do people marry?

Several recent studies have sought to discover why people marry.[32] Hibbs et al.[33] carried out an interesting study into why people married. Forty-two per cent of those engaged people questioned gave 'love' or 'love and . . .' as the reason for marriage. A further 13 per cent stated the reason for marriage being a sign of commitment and 9 per cent as marriage being a sign of progression of their relationship. Three per cent said they did not know why they were getting married! Three factors which might have been expected to appear were rarely mentioned: only 4 per cent mentioned children being a reason to marry, and less than 1 per cent mentioned religion;[34] and none gave legal reasons for getting married.[35] In fact 41 per cent of those questioned thought (quite incorrectly) that marriage would not

---

[27] (1866) LR 1 PD 130 at p. 133, per Lord Penzance. This definition is discussed in Poulter (1979).
[28] If a marriage is not entered into voluntarily then the marriage will be voidable, which will mean it is a legally valid marriage, but can still be set aside if the pressurised party wishes to have the marriage annulled.
[29] *Vervaeke* v *Smith* [1983] 1 AC 145.
[30] [2003] 1 FCR 110.
[31] See also *M* v *H* [1996] NZFLR 241 where the New Zealand court upheld the marriage of two students entered into solely so that their parents' wealth would not be taken into account in calculating the level of their grant.
[32] Much less research has been carried out on why people cohabit, but see Smart (2000a).
[33] Hibbs, Barton and Beswick (2001). See also Barlow, Duncan, James and Park (2003).
[34] Kiernan (2001) found a strong link between marriage rates and religious belief.
[35] Although 3 per cent stated that legal considerations had influenced their decision to get married.

change their legal rights and responsibilities towards each other. A different study found that the attraction of marriage was to demonstrate commitment.[36] Notably the commitment was not only a commitment to the partner the person was marrying, but also to a particular lifestyle: settling down and entering a stable family life.[37]

Another study, looking at why people did *not* marry found that the most common reason given was that people could not afford it (21.8 per cent of those questioned).[38] The cost of marriage is also sometimes given as a reason for delaying marriage. One report[39] suggested that the average cost of marriage was between £15,000 and £17,000. This will represent many years' savings for most couples.[40]

4. MARRIAGE AS A STATUS OR CONTRACT

Marriage could be regarded as either a status or a contract. In law, a status is regarded as a relationship which has a set of legal consequences which flow automatically from that relationship, regardless of the intentions of the parties. A status has been defined as 'the condition of belonging to a class in society to which the law ascribes peculiar rights and duties, capacities and incapacities'.[41] So the status view of marriage would suggest that, if a couple marry, then they are subject to the laws governing marriage, regardless of their intentions or choices.[42] The alternative approach would be to regard contract as governing marriage. The legal consequences of marriage would then flow from the intentions of the parties as set out in an agreement rather than any given rules set down by the law.

Marriage is perhaps best regarded as a mixture of the two.[43] Dewar and Parker have suggested marriage should be regarded as 'a contractually acquired status'.[44] There are some legal consequences which flow automatically from marriage and other consequences which depend on the agreement of the parities. The law sets out: who can marry; when the relationship can be ended; and what are the consequences for the parties of being married. However, following the Children Act 1989 and Family Law Act 1996, increasing emphasis is placed on encouraging the parties to resolve their disputes at the end of their relationship themselves without referring them to court.

Some have argued that it would be preferable to move towards a more contractarian view of marriage.[45] The law could require each couple wishing to marry to decide for themselves exactly what the legal consequences of their marriage would be in a pre-marriage contract. If necessary, the law could produce some sample contracts that people might choose to use.[46] The supporters of such a proposal tend

---

[36] Reynolds and Mansfield (1999).
[37] Kiernan (2001) found a link between marriage rates and whether an individual had experienced his or her parents' divorce.
[38] Lewis (2001b: 135).
[39] Carter (2003).
[40] According to Lewis (2001b) the average spent on weddings in 2000 was £10,500.
[41] *The Ampthill Peerage Case* [1977] AC 547 HL.
[42] For support for marriage as a status see Regan (1993a).
[43] Weyrauch (1980).
[44] Dewar and Parker (2000: 125).
[45] Rasmusen and Evans State (1998).
[46] Pre-marriage forms are available on the Internet according to Kavanagh (2000).

to fall within three camps. First, some feminists argue that a contractarian view of marriage would enable women to avoid the traditional marital roles that are disadvantageous to them. Secondly, from a libertarian perspective some argue that the law should not impose upon people any regulation of their intimate lives. Spouses should choose their own form of regulation[47] rather than there being one kind of marriage sanctioned by the state.[48] After all, there are many different kinds and understandings of marriages and a contractual-based approach can recognise those differences.[49] Thirdly, there are traditionalists who believe that the present law on marriage is too liberal and that a couple should be allowed to contract to enter a 'traditional' marriage, for example severely restricting access to divorce.[50]

Opponents of contractual marriage argue that pre-marriage contracts are unpopular among the general public because they are 'not very romantic'.[51] They implicitly accept that marriage may not be for life. Perhaps more significantly, it is argued that entering a fair contract is only possible if the parties are fully aware of each other's financial position, are independently advised and have equality of bargaining power.[52] In only a few cases will this be so. Even if the parties do have full information and equality of bargaining power, the parties cannot foresee the future, and so the contract may rapidly become outdated and need to be continually renegotiated.[53] Other opponents argue that the contract approach overlooks the interests the state might have in the marriage: the state might wish to support marriage because it has benefits for society as a whole. If this is so, the state will not want to leave the law of marriage entirely up to the parties themselves. A compromise solution would be for the state to offer people who wish to marry a range of alternative forms of marriage from which they can choose. For example, some states in the United States offer as an alternative to the standard marriage, 'covenant' marriage, which only permits divorce in limited circumstances.[54]

5. THE PRESUMPTION OF MARRIAGE

If a man and a woman live together, believe themselves to be married, and present themselves as married, the law presumes that they are legally married.[55] So anyone who seeks to claim that the couple are not married must introduce evidence to rebut this presumption. The policy behind this is that a couple who believe themselves to be married should not suffer the disadvantages that would follow from being found not to be married without there being clear evidence.[56]

The presumption is most often used where the marriage took place a long time ago or abroad[57] and so official records are not be available. The presumption can

---

[47] McLellan (1996).
[48] Evans State (1992).
[49] Shultz (1982).
[50] See Chapter 3 for a discussion of these arguments.
[51] S. Bridge (2001: 27).
[52] McLellan (1996).
[53] Alexander (1998).
[54] Waddington (2000: 251–2).
[55] A detailed discussion of the presumption is found in Borkowski (2002).
[56] Borkowski (2002).
[57] *A-M v A-M (Divorce: Jurisdiction: Validity of Marriage)* [2001] 2 FLR 6.

be rebutted if it can be shown that the parties did not undergo a legal marriage. However, the longer the parties have cohabited, the stronger the presumption is that they are legally married.[58] In order to rebut the presumption of marriage, clear and positive evidence must be introduced.[59] In *Pazpena de Vire* v *Pazpena de Vire*[60] a distinction was drawn between cases where there the couple have cohabited following a ceremony, but there are doubts whether the ceremony is valid, and cases where there is no evidence of a ceremony, but there has been a lengthy cohabitation, with the couple believing themselves to be, and being regarded as being, married. Where there has been some kind of ceremony then it must be shown beyond reasonable doubt that the ceremony was an invalid marriage, otherwise the presumption will apply. Where there is no evidence of a ceremony there must be firm evidence that there was no marriage. It is important to appreciate that the law is not saying that couples who live together are married because they cohabit, but that there is a presumption that they have undergone a ceremony of marriage unless proved otherwise. If the validity of a marriage is ambiguous, there is power under s 55 of the Family Law Act 1986 for a court to make a declaration clarifying the status of the marriage.

6. NON-MARRIAGES, VOID MARRIAGES AND VOIDABLE MARRIAGES

Although it is relatively rare for a party to seek to have a marriage annulled in law, nullity is particularly important because, in effect, it defines who may or may not marry and reveals what the law sees as the essential ingredients of marriage. What might appear to be a ceremony of marriage can either be:

1. a valid marriage;
2. a voidable marriage;
3. a void marriage; or
4. a non-marriage; a ceremony of no legal significance.[61]

It is necessary to draw some important distinctions at this point:

A. The difference between divorce and nullity

The law relating to marriage draws an important distinction between those marriages which are annulled and those which are ended by divorce.[62] Where the marriage is annulled the law recognises that there has been some flaw in the establishment of the marriage, rendering the marriage ineffective. Where there is a divorce the creation of the marriage is considered proper but subsequent events demonstrate that the marriage should be brought to an end.

---

[58] *Chief Adjudication Officer* v *Bath* [2000] 1 FLR 8.
[59] *Chief Adjudication Officer* v *Bath* [2000] 1 FLR 8.
[60] [2001] 1 FLR 460.
[61] See the useful discussion on the distinction between these in Probert (2002b).
[62] Prior to the Reformation in the sixteenth century there was no divorce, but Canon Law recognised the possibility that a marriage could be annulled.

B. The difference between a void marriage and non-marriage

A void marriage is one where, although there may have been some semblance of a marriage, there is in fact a fundamental flaw in the marriage which means that it is not recognised in the law as valid. This needs to be distinguished from a non-marriage, where the ceremony that the parties undertook was nothing like a marriage and so is of no legal consequence. It is a nothing in the eyes of the law. The distinction is of great practical significance because if it is a void marriage then the court has the power to make financial orders, redistributing property between the couple. If the ceremony is a non-marriage the court has no power to redistribute property and the couple will be treated as an unmarried couple. The distinction is clarified by *Gereis* v *Yagoub*,[63] where the couple went through a purported marriage at a Coptic Orthodox Church without going through the legal formalities. The priest had encouraged the parties to have a civil ceremony of marriage, but they had not done so. After the church service the couple cohabited together, but the relationship later broke down. When the case came to court, the question was whether the service was a void marriage, thereby allowing some financial orders to be made, or whether the marriage was simply a nothing and so no orders could be made. Judge Aglionby stressed the following facts in deciding this was a void marriage: the ceremony had the 'hallmarks of an ordinary Christian marriage'; the parties regarded themselves as married (they had sexual intercourse only after the service); the couple held themselves out as a married couple by, for example, claiming married couples' tax allowance. He therefore decided that the marriage was void in that the parties had knowingly and wilfully intermarried in disregard of the formalities under the Marriage Act 1949. He contrasted the position with that of one where a couple have pretended to marry as part of a play or a charade, a scenario in which there would be a non-marriage. It may be that the test developed by Aglionby J may discriminate against ethnic minorities because their ceremonies do not 'bear the hallmarks of a Christian marriage'.[64] Perhaps a better test would be whether a reasonable observer would believe they were witnessing an effective marriage. Indeed an Islamic ceremony in a private flat[65] and a Hindu ceremony in a restaurant[66] have been held to be non-marriages, being too far distant from what one would expect from a marriage ceremony.

C. The difference between a void and voidable marriage

A void marriage is one that in the eyes of the law has never existed. A voidable marriage exists until it has been annulled by the courts and, if it is never annulled by a court order, it will be treated as valid. This distinction has a number of significant consequences:

1. The first is that technically a void marriage is void even if it has never been declared to be so by a court, although a voidable marriage is valid from the date

---

[63] [1997] 1 FLR 854, [1997] 3 FCR 755.
[64] See the discussion in Probert (2002b).
[65] *A-M* v *A-M (Divorce: Jurisdiction: Validity of Marriage)* [2001] 2 FLR 6.
[66] *Gandhi* v *Patel* [2002] 1 FLR 603.

of the marriage until the court makes an order. That said, a party who believes his or her marriage to be void would normally seek a court order to confirm this to be so. This avoids any doubts over the validity of the marriage and also permits the parties to apply for court orders relating to their financial affairs.[67]

2. A child born to parties of a void marriage would be technically 'illegitimate', unless at the time of the conception either parent reasonably believed that they were validly married to the other parent.[68] The concept of illegitimacy is now not part of the law, but still there are a few consequences that depend on whether a child's parents are married or unmarried.[69]

3. The distinction between a void and a voidable marriage may also be important in determining one person's rights to the other's pension.[70]

4. Any person may seek a declaration that the marriage is void,[71] but only the parties to the marriage can apply to annul a voidable marriage. This reflects a fundamental distinction in the grounds on which marriage can be declared void or voidable. The grounds on which a marriage may be declared void are those circumstances in which there is an element of public policy against the marriage – hence any interested person can seek a declaration of nullity. The grounds on which a marriage may be voidable do not indicate that there is a public policy objection to the marriage, but rather that there is a problem in the marriage which is so significant that, if one of the parties wish, the marriage can be annulled.[72]

Having discussed these distinctions it is now necessary to consider the grounds on which a marriage may be void or voidable.

D. The grounds on which a marriage is void

As already noted, the grounds on which a marriage is void are those which reflect a public policy objection to the marriage. The grounds[73] are set out in the Matrimonial Causes Act 1973, s 11:

(a) that it is not a valid marriage under the provisions of the Marriages Acts 1949 to 1986 (that is to say where—
   (i) the parties are within the prohibited degrees of relationship;
   (ii) either party is under the age of sixteen; or
   (iii) the parties have intermarried in disregard of certain requirements as to the formation of marriage);
(b) that at the time of the marriage either party was already lawfully married;
(c) that the parties are not respectively male and female;

---

[67] *Whiston v Whiston* [1995] 2 FLR 268, [1995] 2 FCR 496 CA; discussed Cretney (1996a).
[68] Legitimacy Act 1976, s 1(1).
[69] See Chapter 7.
[70] See *Ward v Secretary of State for Social Services* [1990] 1 FLR 119, [1990] FCR 361.
[71] Matrimonial Causes Act 1973 (hereafter MCA 1973), s 16. This section applies to decrees after 31 July 1971.
[72] *Re Roberts (dec'd)* [1978] 1 WLR 653 at p. 656, per Walton J.
[73] Walton J suggested that the set of grounds set out in MCA 1973 is exhaustive and so there is no jurisdiction for the courts to create new grounds: *Re Roberts (dec'd)* [1978] 1 WLR 653 at p. 658.

(d) in the case of a polygamous marriage entered into outside England and Wales, that either party was at the time of the marriage domiciled in England and Wales.

These grounds will now be considered separately.

(i) Prohibited degrees

The marriage between two people who are related to each other in certain ways is prohibited. It is interesting that nearly all societies across the world have bars on marriages between people who are related. In Britain the restrictions are based on two groups of relations: those based on blood relationships (consanguinity) and those based on marriage (affinity). The details of the law are set out in the Marriage (Prohibited Degrees of Relationship) Act 1986, s 6(2).

1. The prohibited consanguinity restrictions mean that marriage between the following is not permitted: parent–child; grandparent–grandchild; brother–sister; uncle–niece; aunt–nephew. These include relations of the half-blood as well as those relationships based on the whole blood. It will be noted that cousins may marry under English law.
2. The affinity restrictions are traditionally based on the 'unity of husband and wife'. This is the notion that, on marriage, a husband and wife become one. These prohibited degrees based on marriage are controversial because some believe the doctrine of unity upon which they are based is outdated. There are only two that remain, following the Marriage Act 1949:
   (a) *Marrying a stepchild.* A step-parent can marry the child of a former spouse if:
      (i) both parties are aged 21 or over; and
      (ii) the younger party has not been a child of the family in relation to the other while under the age of 18.
      The effect of the law is that if a step-parent acts in a parental role towards a stepchild, the two can never marry.
   (b) *Marrying a parent-in-law.* A person (X) can only marry his former spouse's parent (Y) if:
      (i) X and Y are over the age of 21; and
      (ii) the marriage is solemnised after both X and Y's spouses have died.
      The aim of the law here is to ensure that a parent-in-law cannot marry a child-in-law if the potential marriage could be regarded as a cause of the divorce of either party.
3. Even though adoption normally ends the relationship between the adopted child and his or her birth family, the restrictions on marriage between an adopted child and members of his or her birth family apply as above. An adoptive child and adoptive parent are also within the prohibited degrees of relationship.[74] However, an adopted child can marry other relations that arise from the adoption. So a man could marry the daughter of his adopted parents.[75]

---

[74] This is a permanent bar and even applies if the child is adopted for a second time.
[75] Assuming the daughter is not his half-sister.

The restrictions based on these relationships are justified by three arguments.[76] The first is the fear of genetic dangers involved in permitting procreation between close blood relations. This would not justify bars based on affinity[77] and with the availability of genetic screening may be harder to support. A second argument in favour of these bars is that permitting marriage between close relations may undermine the security of the family. The argument is that children should be brought up without the possibility of approved sexual relations later in life with members of their family. A third argument can be based on the widespread instinctive moral reaction against such relationships.

It should be recalled that although these restrictions prevent, say, a father marrying his daughter, there would be nothing to prevent them cohabiting, although any sexual relations would constitute the crime of incest.

(ii) Age

There are two requirements that relate to the age of the parties:

1. A marriage will be void if either party to the marriage is under 16.[78] All western societies have some kind of age restrictions on who may marry and a minimum age for legal sexual relations, although exactly what that age is varies from state to state[79] and generation to generation.[80] The choice of the age 16 in England and Wales reflects the policy of the criminal law that it is unlawful for a man to have sexual intercourse with a girl under 16. It also reflects the concern of society about any children that may be born of such a union: the parents may be too young to care for the children and the burden could then fall on the state. There is also the argument that, below that age, the parties may not fully understand the consequences of marriage.[81]
2. The second requirement is that if either party is between the age of 16 and 18 then it is necessary to have the written consent of each parent with parental responsibility.[82] It is possible for the teenager to apply to the court to have the parental consent requirement revoked. However, if the marriage goes ahead without that consent (or on the basis of a forged consent), it would still be valid. The significance of this requirement, then, is that it permits a registrar to refuse to carry out a wedding without this consent.

---

[76] For an argument that the list of prohibited relationships should be added to, see Cretney, Masson and Bailey Harris (2002: 42).
[77] Interestingly, Australia has removed all restrictions on marriage based on affinity: see Finlay (1976).
[78] Marriage Act 1949, s 2.
[79] Douglas (2001: 27) records that in Europe the minimum age of marriage varies from 15 (Belgium) to 20 (Switzerland).
[80] Indeed, until 1929 in England a girl could marry from the age of 12.
[81] There can be problems where a marriage takes place abroad involving a child under 16, which is valid in that country: see Lowe and Douglas (1998: 47–52).
[82] Unless there is a residence order, in which case only the parents with parental responsibility and residence order need consent: Marriage Act 1949, s 3, as amended. A guardian or local authority can also provide consent in certain circumstances.

(iii) Formalities

There are complex rules governing the legal formalities required for a marriage. The exact requirements depend on whether the marriage was performed within the rites of the Church of England or outside. The detailed provisions will not be discussed here.[83]

The purposes of having formalities can be said to be as follows:

1. The formality requirements help draw a clear line between a marriage, an engagement, and an agreement to cohabit.
2. The formality requirements ensure that the parties do not enter into marriage in an ill-considered or frivolous way. To fulfil the requirements takes some time and effort. Further, they ensure that the moment of marriage is a solemn event. This reinforces the seriousness of marriage to the parties and those present.
3. The existence of the formalities helps ensure that there is a formal record of marriages.[84]
4. The formalities also ensure that anyone who wishes to object to the marriage can do so.

There are, however, dangers that formalities can be too strict. There are two particular concerns. The first is that couples may be discouraged from marrying if the formalities are too onerous. This concern led to the passing of the Marriage Act 1995, which has greatly increased the number of places where a marriage can take place.[85] Secondly, if the law were interpreted too strictly, a minor breach of the rules could invalidate what might appear to be a valid marriage. The law has dealt with this concern under ss 25 and 49 of the Marriage Act 1995, which state that a marriage is only void for breaching the formalities if the parties marry knowingly and wilfully in breach of the requirement.[86]

One further issue is whether the parties should be required to undergo biological tests, in order to see if either party is suffering from an infectious illness. There have been calls for genetic testing to be carried out on the parties before marriage.[87] At present no biological tests are required in England and Wales. The reason may be that a requirement of tests would discourage marriage.

There have also been some calls that couples be required to attend marriage counselling sessions before marriage. The closest the government has come is the proposal that a 'clear and simple guide' detailing the rights and responsibilities of marriage should be made available to all couples planning to marry.[88] This seems very sensible given the lack of understanding over the legal consequences of mar-

---

[83] See Cretney, Masson and Bailey-Harris (2002: ch. 2).
[84] Although see the remarkable case of *Islam* v *Islam* [2003] FL 815 where although the evidence showed that the woman had been married she was not able to show she had married the man she claimed to be her husband. The judge asked the papers to be sent to the Crown Prosecution Service so that it could consider possible criminal proceedings against the wife.
[85] See Home Office (2002) for further proposals to liberalise the law.
[86] See *Chief Adjudication Officer* v *Bath* [2000] 1 FCR 419, [2000] 1 FLR 8 for an example of a case where the parties were unaware of the non-compliance with the formalities.
[87] Discussed in Deech (1998).
[88] Home Office (1998: 4.15).

riage.[89] In the USA a computer questionnaire has become a popular way for a couple to check compatibility before marriage. Apparently, having taken the test and considered the results 10 per cent of couples decided not to marry.[90]

(iv) Bigamy

If at the time of the ceremony either party is already married to someone else, the 'marriage' will be void. The marriage will remain void even if the first spouse dies during the second 'marriage'.[91] So if a person is married and wishes to marry some-one else, he or she must obtain a decree of divorce or wait until the death of his or her spouse. If the first marriage is void it is technically not necessary to obtain a court order to that effect before marrying again, but that is normally sought to avoid any uncertainty. In cases of bigamy, as well as the purported marriage being void, the parties may have committed the crime of bigamy.[92]

Many cultures do permit polygamous marriages, although in British society monogamous marriages are the accepted norm, which is rarely challenged.[93] There are concrete objections to polygamous marriages. Some argue that polygamy may create divisions within the family, with one husband or wife vying for dominance over the others, and particularly that divisions may arise between the children of different parents.[94] Supporters of polygamous marriage argue that polygamy leads to less divorce and provides a wider family support network in which to raise children. Polygamy could also be regarded as a form of sex discrimination unless both men and women were permitted to take more than one spouse. There have also been suggestions that permitting polygamous marriages involves an insult to the religious sensitivities of the majority.[95]

(v) The parties must be respectively male and female

A marriage is void if the parties are not respectively male and female in a biological sense. This gives rise to two separate issues. The first is deciding what is a man and what is a woman: in particular, how the law should deal with transsexual and inter-sex people. The second is whether the law should permit two people of the same sex to marry if they wish. As these situations raise different problems they will be considered separately.

---

[89] Hibbs, Barton and Beswick (2001).
[90] Hibbs, Barton and Beswick (2001). See Simons (1999) for a detailed discussion of marriage preparation.
[91] *Dredge* v *Dredge* [1947] 1 All ER 29.
[92] In *Khan* v *UK* (1986) 48 DR 253 the European Court of Human Rights rejected an argument that the bar of polygamous marriage infringed the parties' rights under article 12 of the European Convention.
[93] For a detailed discussion see Bradney (1993); Parkinson (1996).
[94] See Bala and Jaremko Bromwich (2002: 166–9) for a discussion of the arguments against polygamy.
[95] Devlin (1965).

(a) Transsexual people[96]

The question of deciding how to define sex has arisen in particular because of the law's treatment of transsexual people. These are people who are born with some or all of the biological characteristics of one sex, but psychologically feel they belong to the other sex.[97] There is a treatment available on the National Health Service[98] and in private hospitals, known as 'gender realignment surgery' (popularly known as a 'sex change operation'[99]). This, combined with hormonal drug treatment, has the effect that the outward appearance of the patient matches their 'psychological sex'. Such a person can then operate in society to a large extent as the sex they feel they ought to be. It should be stressed that this complaint is well recognised medically and some clinicians believe that the condition may have a physical, rather than a psychological, cause.

The issue for the law is how the sex of such people should be treated. At present a transsexual person can apply to amend their passport, national insurance number and other official documents to reflect their declared sex. However, the one document a transsexual person cannot change is their birth certificate, which remains as a record of the 'sex with which they were born'. This is crucial because this is the document used to determine sex for the purpose of marriage.

The leading case on transsexual people and marriage is *Corbett v Corbett*,[100] a decision of Ormrod J. He argued that for the purpose of the law an individual's sex is fixed at birth: 'The law should adopt in the first place the first three of the doctor's criteria, i.e., the chromosomal, gonadal and genital tests, and if all three are congruent, determine the sex for the purpose of marriage accordingly, and ignore any operative intervention.'[101] So, in the case before him, April Ashley, born as a man but having undergone a 'sex change operation' and living as a woman, was a man and could not enter into a marriage with a man. For the purposes of marriage he retained the sex with which he was born, the sex determined by chromosomal, gonadal and genital factors. Ormrod J left open the question of what should happen if these factors produce conflicting results, but he suggested that in such a case the original appearance of genital organs was to be the overriding factor. Ormrod J justified his approach by arguing that people who had undergone a sex change operation were not able to engage in 'full natural sexual intercourse'.

This decision still represents the law although it has been strongly criticised by many commentators. Before considering the criticisms it is useful to consider the possible benefits of Ormrod J's approach. The main benefit is certainty. If it is important for the law to distinguish male and female then stating that it is determined and fixed at birth promotes certainty. The alternative is that people might fluctuate between maleness and femaleness throughout their lives. This argument

---

[96] Taitz (1988); Khaliq (1996); Sharpe (2002); Whittle (2002).

[97] There is no definitive data on the number of transsexual people, but estimates vary between 2,000 and 5,000: Home Office (2000a).

[98] Although there is no right to such treatment: *R v North West Lancashire HA, ex p A* [2000] 2 FCR 525.

[99] This term is disliked by many transsexual people who argue that the operation is not changing their sex, but rather is bringing their body in line with their true sex.

[100] [1971] P 83.

[101] At p. 106.

is not convincing because it would not be difficult to enable transsexuals to change their birth certificate while retaining a high degree of certainty. One could have a system where sex is fixed by the birth certificate but then the certificate could be modified if appropriate medical evidence is produced.[102]

The objections to the *Corbett* decision are many.[103] First, there is Ormrod J's argument that full natural sexual intercourse is impossible in a marriage involving a transsexual person. It is unclear why 'full natural sexual intercourse' is not possible. The decision appears inconsistent with *SY* v *SY*,[104] where a woman was born without an effective vagina, but the court decided that even though what she now had was an artificial vagina, she could still engage in 'full natural intercourse' and consummate a marriage.

Secondly, the inability to engage in intercourse is a ground for a marriage being voidable, but not void, as was the result in *Corbett*. Further, many question whether heterosexual intercourse is essential for marriage. Do not tenderness, mutual respect and love play at least as important a role in marriage as sexual intercourse?[105] However, the criticism of *Corbett* is not limited to the reasoning used. The decision has been said to reflect the law's obsession with categorising people into being either male or female. Some commentators have argued that far from there being two boxes for male and female, there is rather a scale of maleness and femaleness.[106]

As a result of these and other objections, *Corbett* has come under attack in subsequent cases. In particular the decision has been challenged by reference to the European Convention on Human Rights and Fundamental Freedoms, relying on two main provisions. The first is the right to marry. Article 12 states: 'Men and women of marriageable age have the right to marry and to found a family, according to the national laws governing the existence of this right.' The British law was unsuccessfully challenged in the European Court of Human Rights in *Rees* v *UK*;[107] *Cossey* v *UK*;[108] and *Sheffield and Horsham* v *UK*.[109] But recently the European Court of Human Rights in *Goodwin* v *UK*[110] and *I* v *UK*[111] have accepted that the refusal of the UK to permit a post-operative male to female transsexual to marry interfered with her rights under article 12. Looking in detail at the medical evidence the Court held that the *Corbett* criteria could no longer be regarded as decisive in determining someone's sex. However, significantly the European Court restricted their ruling to transsexual people who have undergone gender realignment surgery. Transsexual people who live in one sex but decide not to undergo surgery (for example, because of the medical risks associated with it) cannot rely on *Goodwin* to claim a right to marry in their declared sex.

---

[102] As imagined in the Gender Identity Bill.
[103] Whittle (2002: ch. 7) provides a detailed analysis.
[104] [1963] P 37.
[105] See, e.g., Chau and Herring (2002: 347–51).
[106] O'Donnovan (1993).
[107] [1987] 2 FLR 111 ECtHR.
[108] [1991] 2 FLR 492 ECtHR.
[109] [1998] 2 FLR 928 ECtHR.
[110] [2002] 2 FCR 577 ECtHR.
[111] [2002] 2 FCR 613 ECtHR.

Following *Goodwin*, the case of, *Bellinger* v *Bellinger*[112] was brought to the House of Lords in which it was argued that under s 3 of the Human Rights Act 1998 the words male and female in s 11(c) of the Matrimonial Causes Act 1973 had to be interpreted to include post-operative transsexual people. The House of Lords felt unable to agree with the argument. It would be stretching the words male and female too much to include within their definition transsexual people in their declared sex. Further, had the application succeeded it would have required the House of Lords to define precisely what forms of surgery (if any) a person would have to undergo before being recognised in their sex. The issue involved a 'major change in the law' calling for 'extensive enquiry and the widest public consultation and discussion'.[113] It was better, their Lordships felt, for Parliament, rather than the courts, to make this change in the law. Their Lordships therefore issued a declaration that s 11(c) of the Matrimonial Causes Act 1973 was incompatible with the articles 8 and 12 of the European Convention on Human Rights. The government has responded by producing a consultation paper[114] and a Gender Identity Bill.[115] Under the proposals an individual can apply for a gender recognition certificate, which can be issued by a Gender Recognition Panel. The certificate will be available only to a person who has 'gender dysphoria' and has lived in their 'acquired gender' for two years before the certificate has been issued. Notably it is not required that an individual undergo any form of surgery, unless the panel requires such surgery before issuing a certificate,[116] and the legislation is expressed in terms of recognising a change in gender, rather than sex. However, once the certificate is granted the individual can marry in accordance with their declared sex.

(b) Intersexual people

Transsexual people must be clearly differentiated from intersex people who are born with sexual or reproductive organs of both sexes. As the biological sex of an intersex person is ambiguous at birth, the doctors, in consultation with the family, will select a sex for the child.[117] Tragically it can later become clear that the doctors made the wrong choice and the child's body develops in a way clearly in line with the opposite sex. In such cases it is possible to amend the birth certificate to reflect the fact that an error was made in determining the sex at birth and the child will be regarded as having the sex they have come to have.

The leading case in this area is now *W* v *W* *(Nullity)*,[118] where Charles J held that if a person was born with ambiguous genitalia the individual's sex was to be determined by considering: (i) chromosomal factors; (ii) gonadal factors; (iii) genital factors; (iv) psychological factors; (v) hormonal factors; and (vi) secondary sexual characteristics (such as distribution of hair, breast development, etc.). Notably

---

[112] [2003] UKHL 21, [2003] 2 FCR 1.
[113] Lord Nicholls, para 73.
[114] There was an attempt in 1995 to introduce a Gender Identity (Registration and Civil Status) Bill but it did not receive government support and failed. See now the Gender Identity Bill 2003.
[115] Home Office (2000a).
[116] See Sharpe (2002); Whittle (2002) for possible legislation in this area.
[117] For a detailed discussion of the medical and legal issues surrounding intersexual people see Chau and Herring (2002).
[118] [2000] 3 FCR 748; discussed in Herring and Chau (2001). See also *B* v *B* [1954] 2 All ER 598.

Charles J accepted that a decision as to someone's sex could be made at the time of the marriage, taking these factors into account. Some commentators take the view that the position of intersexual people reveals that there is no hard and fast division between male and female, and rather there is a scale between maleness and femaleness and people are placed at various points on that scale.[119] To them we should simply treat everyone as a person and not classify people as male or female. That would mean in this context that any two people should be allowed to marry. Objectors to this view might reply that it overlooks the reality that the vast majority of people clearly do strongly regard themselves as either male or female. For the law to ignore this would be highly artificial.

(c) Same-sex marriage

The law on same-sex relationships is clear: two men or two women may live together and, if both over 16, engage in sexual relations, but they cannot marry. Is the law acceptable?

One way of approaching the question would be to consider whether gay and lesbian relationships provide the same advantages to the state as married heterosexual couples.[120] If they do it would be hard to justify denying them the privileges of marriage. Some of the possible advantages marriage might provide the state are discussed later in this chapter. Clearly a homosexual married couple would contribute some of the benefits that a heterosexual married couple would. They would provide the state with the benefits of economic mutual support and concern for the wider community and environment.[121] Many see the crucial issue as the ability to have children. The immediate response is that a homosexual couple cannot bear children, but then many married heterosexual couples may not produce children, through infertility, old age, or choice. However, one could reply that the law has to be practical: the state could not realistically test or question every heterosexual couple coming forward to marry as to their ability to have children. So the law may be entitled to assume that heterosexual couples have the potential to produce children, while we can be sure that a gay couple will not be able to have children of their own accord. In reply it could be pointed out that changes in artificial reproduction which make it easier for gay couples to produce children may make this argument harder to sustain, particularly in relation to lesbian couples.[122]

One approach in favour of gay marriage is to argue that to deny the benefits of marriage to homosexuals is a form of sexual discrimination: 'If I were a woman I would be able to marry this man but because I am a man I cannot. Therefore I am discriminated against because of my sex.' The argument is not, however, conclusive because in reply it could be said that 'whether I am a man or a woman the position is the same: I cannot marry someone of the same sex and so the law is not

---

[119] The argument is developed in Chau and Herring (2002). See also the interesting discussion of the meaning of sex in Grenfell (2003).

[120] For an argument against gay marriage, see Wardell (1998).

[121] Although Duckworth (2002a: 91) claims that same-sex marriages are less consistent or dependable than opposite-sex couples. It is hard to see how such a claim could be proved (or disproved).

[122] Bamforth (2001) argues for same-sex marriage as a matter of justice.

discriminatory'.[123] Thus it has been accepted by the European Court of Justice in *Grant* v *South-West Trains*[124] and the European Court of Human Rights in *X, Y, Z* v *UK*[125] that the bar on gay marriage does not amount to sex discrimination.[126]

Rather than relying on sex discrimination, it might be more productive to face the issue head on and claim that the law is discriminatory on the grounds of sexual orientation.[127] The key question is whether sexual orientation should be added to the traditionally accepted grounds of unlawful discrimination, such as sex and race.[128] However, in *Da Silva Mouta* v *Portugal*[129] the European Court of Human Rights has held that discrimination on the grounds of sexual orientation could amount to discrimination in breach of article 14 of the European Convention on Human Rights.[130] A powerful argument can therefore be mounted that a bar on same-sex marriage interferes with a gay or lesbian's right to marry under article 12 in a way which is discriminatory under article 14. This could only be justified if there were reasonable and objective justification for the state's approach.

If the UK government were faced with such an action it might seek to raise two defences. One would be that article 12 only permits opposite-sex couples to marry and so the bar on same-sex couples does not infringe article 12.[131] The other would be to seek to raise an objective and reasonable justification for the discrimination. This would be difficult. The argument the Court might be most likely to accept is that to permit a same-sex couple to marry would be to cause grave offence to those who hold a traditional religious view of marriage.[132] In a recent survey it was found that 50 per cent of British people questioned expressed the view that sex between two men is always or mostly wrong,[133] although it should be pointed out that the level of opposition to same-sex relationships appears to drop dramatically every time such surveys are performed as same-sex relationships gain social acceptability. Even if the argument about the traditional understanding of marriage was accepted the argument would not provide an explanation for why a same-sex couple should

---

[123] This was the approach taken by the European Court of Justice in *Grant* v *South-West Trains* [1998] 1 FLR 839 ECJ.

[124] [1998] 1 FLR 839 ECJ.

[125] [1997] 2 FLR 892, [1997] 3 FCR 341 ECtHR.

[126] Lord Slynn in *Fitzpatrick* v *Sterling Housing Association Ltd* [2000] 1 FCR 21 at p. 27 seemed to think it was open to debate whether the Human Rights Act would permit discrimination between homosexual and heterosexual couples.

[127] An excellent discussion is J. Gardner (1998).

[128] In the United States the legislature has passed the Defence of Marriage Act 1996 specifically to protect the traditional understanding of marriage. Section 3 states: 'A legal union between one man and one woman as husband and wife, and the word "spouse" refers only to a person of the opposite sex who is a husband or a wife.'

[129] [2001] 1 FCR 653, discussed in Herring (2002a). See also *Grant* v *South-West Trains* [1998] 1 FLR 839; *R* v *Secretary of State for Defence, ex p Perkins* [1999] 1 FLR 491.

[130] See *Egan* v *Canada* [1998] 1 SCR 493 and *M* v *H* [1999] 171 DLR (4th) 577 for the approach in the Canadian courts.

[131] In *R* v *Secretary of State for the Home Office, ex p Mellor* [2000] 3 FCR 148 the Court of Appeal held that the state was entitled to prohibit the right to marry in article 12 if circumstances analogous to those in article 8(2) were found. This requires a significant amount of reading into the convention, where article 12 is presented as an absolute right.

[132] Regan (1993a); Finnis (1994); Jones-Purdy (1998); George (1999: ch. 8); Pontifical Council for the Family (2000); Duckworth (2002b) outline some of the non-religious arguments against permitting same-sex marriage. Bamforth (2001) and Woelke (2002) respond to some of these arguments.

[133] Johnson, Mercer, Evans et al. (2000).

not be permitted to enter an alternative to marriage (e.g. a registered partnership) giving them the same rights as a married couple.[134]

Those countries that have been willing to recognise same-sex partnerships have not extended the meaning of marriage but have created an alternative status which imparts similar legal rights to those of a married couple. In Denmark, Sweden, Belgium, Iceland, Finland and Norway, for example, same-sex couples can apply to register their partnership and thereby acquire many of the rights of marriage.[135] It is noteworthy that even in such liberal states there has not been a willingness to extend marriage to include gay couples.[136] This indicates the strength of the traditional image of marriage.[137] It has led one advocate of gay rights to state that gay marriage is not politically achievable.[138]

Some gay and lesbian commentators have argued that same-sex couples should not seek to take up a heterosexual institution (i.e. marriage).[139] They argue that rather than same-sex couples trying to conform to the standards of heterosexual relationships, heterosexuals should learn much from gay relationships.[140] Other gay and lesbian commentators feel that marriage should be available to same-sex couples and that setting up any alternative system specifically for same-sex couples will send the message that such relationships are 'second best'.

(vi) Marriages entered into abroad

Complex issues of private international law arise over the recognition of marriages conducted abroad and these are not discussed here.[141]

E. Grounds on which a marriage is voidable

The grounds on which a marriage is voidable are set out in the Matrimonial Causes Act 1973, s 12:

(a) that the marriage has not been consummated owing to the incapacity of either party to consummate it;

(b) that the marriage has not been consummated owing to the wilful refusal of the respondent to consummate it;

(c) that either party to the marriage did not validly consent to it, whether in consequence of duress, mistake, unsoundness of mind or otherwise;

(d) that at the time of the marriage either party, though capable of giving a valid consent, was suffering (whether continuously or intermittently) from mental disorder within

---

[134] The Mayor of London has set up a London Partnerships Register which permits same-sex couples and heterosexual couples to register their partnership. It does not automatically confer any rights.

[135] See Nielsen (1990); Dupuis (1995); Broberg (1996); Inglis (2001a); Rowthorn (2002).

[136] The one exception is the Netherlands which now permits same-sex marriage.

[137] Lind (1995).

[138] Inglis (2001a: 897).

[139] A government study found that 86 per cent of members of the lesbian, gay and bisexual community said they would be interested in having their relationship recognised formally: Women & Equality Unit (2003: 17).

[140] Homer (1994), and see Cooper (2001).

[141] See e.g. Lowe and Douglas (1998: 48–52).

the meaning of the Mental Health Act 1983 of such a kind or to such an extent as to be unfitted for marriage;

(e) that at the time of the marriage the respondent was suffering from venereal disease in a communicable form;

(f) that at the time of the marriage the respondent was pregnant by some person other than the petitioner.

These grounds will now be considered separately.

(i) Inability or wilful refusal to consummate

The importance of consummation was originally based on the theological ground that the act of sexual intercourse united the two spouses in a spiritual union and was therefore necessary to complete the sacrament of marriage. The requirement of consummation can also be explained in non-religious terms in that it is the act of sexual intercourse that most clearly distinguishes marriage from a close relationship between two platonic friends. However, given the increase in sexual relations outside of marriage it is harder to argue that sexual intercourse has a unique place in marriage. The importance of consummation could also be said to amount to an encouragement for married couples to produce children.[142]

In order for a marriage to be consummated there need only be one act of consummation; but the act must take place after the solemnisation of the marriage.[143] So in *P* v *P*,[144] where a husband only had sexual relations eight times in 18 years, the marriage was not voidable and divorce was the only way to end the marriage. There are two grounds of voidability connected to consummation. The first ground is a wilful refusal by a spouse to consummate the marriage, and the second is the incapacity of either party to consummate the marriage. The applicant for the nullity application can rely on his or her own inability to consummate but not on his or her own wilful refusal. This is because a party should not be able to rely on his or her own decision not to consummate in order to annul a marriage. It is useful to have the two alternative grounds as it may be difficult in a particular case to discover whether the non-consummation was due to inability or wilful refusal.

What is meant by consummation? 'Consummation' is defined as an act of sexual intercourse. Consummation can only be carried out by the penetration of the vagina by the penis. No other form of sexual activity will amount to consummation. Intercourse needs to be 'ordinary and complete, and not partial and imperfect'.[145] There needs to be full penetration, but there is no need for an ejaculation or orgasm.[146] In *Baxter* v *Baxter*[147] the House of Lords held that consummation took place even though the man was wearing a condom.[148] There have even been cases

---

[142] *Baxter* v *Baxter* [1948] AC 274.
[143] *Dredge* v *Dredge* [1947] 1 All ER 29.
[144] [1964] 3 All ER 919.
[145] *D-E* v *A-G* (1845) 1 Rob Eccl 279 at p. 298.
[146] *R* v *R* [1952] 1 All ER 1194.
[147] [1948] AC 274. Discussed in Gower (1948).
[148] There is some doubt about *coitus interruptus* (where the man withdraws before ejaculation): *Cackett* v *Cackett* [1950] P 253; *White* v *White* [1948] P 330; *Grimes* v *Grimes* [1948] 2 All ER 147. The issue was left open in *Baxter* v *Baxter* [1948] AC 274.

where a pregnancy resulted from a sexual act but the court decided there was no consummation because there was no penetration.[149] This reveals that the consummation requirement is not explained by the state's interest in the potential production of children.

'Inability to consummate' means that the inability cannot be cured by surgery[150] and is permanent. Inability can either be physiological or psychological. Inability also includes 'invincible repugnance', where one party is unable to have sexual intercourse due to 'paralysis of the will',[151] but this must be more than lack of attraction or a dislike of the other partner.[152]

There has been much debate over whether the incapacity to consummate marriage has to exist at the time of the marriage. In other words, what would happen if the husband was rendered impotent as a result of a fight he had with the bride's father during the reception? Under Canon Law impotence could only be relied upon if the impotence existed at the time of marriage. This reflected the crucial distinction between nullity and marriage: nullity applies when defects exist at the time of marriage, while divorce is used when defects occur after the time of the marriage itself. However, the Matrimonial Causes Act makes no reference to the inability existing 'at the time of the marriage', whereas it makes explicit reference to 'at the time of the marriage' in relation to other grounds of voidability. It is therefore submitted that there is a strong case that the inability can occur at any time before or during the marriage as long as the union has not yet been consummated.

'Wilful refusal to consummate' requires a 'settled and definite decision not to consummate without wilful excuse'.[153] If there has been no opportunity to consummate the marriage[154] then it will be hard to show that there has been a wilful refusal unless one party has shown 'unswerving determination' not to consummate the marriage.[155] 'Wilful refusal' may also occur where the parties have agreed only to have intercourse under certain circumstances (e.g. after a religious ceremony). In such a case then a refusal by one party to abide by the condition may constitute 'wilful refusal'.[156] For example, in *Kaur v Singh*[157] a couple agreed they would be legally married and then undergo a religious ceremony, and only after that would the marriage be consummated. The couple were legally married but the man then refused to undergo the religious ceremony, although he was willing to consummate the marriage. The wife was unwilling to consummate the marriage until the religious ceremony was performed. She applied for and was granted a nullity decree on the basis of wilful refusal to consummate.[158] There is some doubt over the position of the law where the parties agree before the marriage that they would not consummate

---

[149] *Clarke* v *Clarke* [1943] 2 All ER 540. The marriage here had lasted 15 years.
[150] If the inability to consummate can only be cured by potentially dangerous surgery then the inability will be permanent: *S* v *S* [1956] P 1.
[151] *G* v *G* [1924] AC 349 HL.
[152] *Singh* v *Singh* [1971] P 226.
[153] *Horton* v *Horton* [1972] 2 All ER 871 HL.
[154] Perhaps because the parties are living in different places (e.g. the husband is in prison).
[155] *Ford* v *Ford* [1987] Fam Law 232.
[156] *A* v *J* [1989] 1 FLR 110.
[157] [1972] 1 All ER 292.
[158] See also *A* v *J* [1989] 1 FLR 110.

the marriage at all. It seems to be that such an agreement would be regarded as contrary to public policy[159] unless the parties have a good reason for the agreement.[160] The marriage will not be annulled on the ground of wilful refusal if the lack of consummation is due to a just excuse,[161] although the case law reveals very little on the exact meaning of this.[162]

(ii) Lack of consent

The Matrimonial Causes Act recognises four circumstances which may cause a person to be unable to give consent so as to render a marriage voidable. These are 'duress, mistake, unsoundness of mind or otherwise'.[163] The law seeks to resolve a tension here. On the one hand there is the view that it should not be too easy to have a marriage annulled. On the other hand, at least in the West, consent is regarded as a highly important factor in marriage. At one time the law required that the lack of consent was apparent at the time of the ceremony.[164] Although the appearance of consent may be important as a matter of evidence, it is now clear that it is not a formal requirement.

It should be noted that lack of consent renders a marriage voidable rather than void. This means that if a party does not consent to the marriage but later changes his or her mind and is happy with the marriage, the marriage will be valid and there is no need to remarry. The separate ways in which a lack of consent may be demonstrated will now be discussed.

(a) Duress

If it could be shown that someone was compelled to enter a marriage as a result of fear or threats, the marriage may be voidable due to duress. The following issues have been discussed in the case law:

1. *What must the threat or fear be of?* At one time it was thought that it was only possible for duress to render a marriage voidable if there was a threat to 'life, limb or liberty'.[165] The Court of Appeal in *Hirani* v *Hirani*[166] suggested that the test for duress should focus on the effect of the threat rather than the nature of the threat. In other words, the threats can be of any kind, but it must be shown that 'the threats, pressure or whatever it is, is such as to destroy the reality of the consent and overbear the will of the individual'.[167] In the case of *Hirani* v *Hirani*[168] the court accepted that social pressure could overbear the consent. The woman was threatened with ostracism by her community and her family if she did not

---

[159] *Brodie* v *Brodie* [1917] P 271.
[160] *Morgan* v *Morgan* [1959] P 92.
[161] Borkowski (1994).
[162] *Horton* v *Horton* [1972] 2 All ER 871 HL.
[163] Article 16(2) of Universal Declaration of Human Rights 1948 states that: 'Marriage shall be entered into only with the free and full consent of the intending spouses.'
[164] *Cooper* v *Crane* [1891] P 369.
[165] *Szechter* v *Szechter* [1971] P 286; *Singh* v *Singh* [1971] P 226.
[166] (1982) 4 FLR 232 CA; noted Bradney (1983).
[167] *Hirani* v *Hirani* (1982) 4 FLR 232 at p. 234 CA.
[168] (1982) 4 FLR 232.

go through with the marriage and the fear of complete social isolation was such that there was no true consent. In *P v R (Forced Marriage: Annulment: Procedure)*[169] Colderidge J followed *Hirani* and held that severe emotional pressure could be such as to mean that there was no genuine consent to marry. *Hirani* should be contrasted with *Singh v Singh*,[170] where the couple had not met before the marriage and the wife agreed to marry only out of respect for her parents. As the wife entered the marriage, not out of fear, but out of a sense of duty, it could not be said that she did not consent to the marriage. The effect of the *Hirani* decision is that those who have undergone an arranged marriage in the face of a serious threat have the choice of either accepting their culture and the validity of the marriage or accepting the dominant culture's view that marriage should be made voidable.[171] This could be regarded as an appropriate compromise between respecting the cultural practice of arranged marriages and respecting people's right to choose whom to marry.[172] The government has recently published a report which seeks to tackle the problem of forced marriages.[173]

The Law Commission has suggested that really what is at issue is the legitimacy of the threat rather than the lack of consent. This approach is reflected in other areas of law where duress is an issue, for example contract law, where reference to the 'overborne will' has largely been abandoned.[174] When someone is acting under duress it is not that they do not make a choice but rather that the choice is made in circumstances in which it should not lead to legal effect. This then requires the court to make a judgment on whether the horrors of the alternative meant that the choice should not be given effect, rather than considering whether there was true consent.[175] It may be that when the issue next comes before the Court of Appeal it will focus on the legitimacy of the threat as well as the impact of the threat on the victim.

2. *Must the fear be reasonably held?* What if a threat was made, but a reasonable person would not have taken it seriously? In *Szechter* it was suggested that duress could not be relied upon unless the fear was reasonably held.[176] Against this is *Scott v Selbright*,[177] in which it was suggested that as long as the beliefs of threats were honestly held, duress could be relied upon. The *Scott v Selbright* view seems preferable because it would be undesirable to punish a person for their careless mistake by denying them an annulment.

3. *Was the threat reasonably made?* In *Buckland v Buckland*[178] a man was alleged to have made a young woman pregnant while he was in Cyprus. The police

---

[169] [2003] 1 FLR 661.
[170] [1971] P 226.
[171] See also *Re KR (Abduction: Forcible Removal by Parents)* [1999] 2 FLR 542, where the court were willing to use wardship to protect a 17-year-old from being taken abroad for an arranged marriage. Home Office (2000c) sets out the proposals to deal with enforced marriages.
[172] Parkinson (1996).
[173] Home Office (2000c).
[174] *Lynch v DPP* [1980] AC 614; *Universal Tankships Inc v I.T.W.F.* [1983] AC 366. See Atiyah (1982).
[175] Bradney (1994).
[176] *Buckland v Buckland* [1968] P 296 at p. 301 (per Scarman J); *H v H* [1954] P 258 at p. 269 (per Karminski J).
[177] (1886) 12 PD 21 at p. 24.
[178] [1968] P 296.

threatened him with arrest and prosecution unless he married the woman. He denied the allegation but, fearing the police's threats, agreed to marry the woman. Simon J agreed that the marriage was voidable due to lack of consent on the grounds of duress. However, he stressed that this was because he believed the young man's version of events, namely that he had barely met the woman and was not responsible for the pregnancy. The threat was therefore 'unjust'. However, had he been responsible for the pregnancy Simon J's judgment seems to imply that the marriage would not have been annulled. Some commentators have argued that this is a wrong approach and that if there is a genuine lack of consent the marriage should be voidable regardless of whether the party was at fault in causing the duress. Even if *Buckland* is followed in future cases, surely it can never be reasonable to impose a threat requiring someone to enter into a marriage?[179]

4. *By whom must the threat be made?* The threat can emanate from a third party; it need not emanate from the spouse.[180]

(b) Mistake

A mistake can also negate consent. So far the law has only allowed two kinds of mistake to negate consent. The first is a mistake as to the other party's identity. It must be a mistake as to identity rather than a mistake as to attribute.[181] So, for example, a marriage would not be voidable if one party wrongly thought the other was rich,[182] or a marvellous cook. But a marriage would be voidable if a party to the marriage thought the person they were marrying was someone else (e.g. if there was a case of impersonation).[183] The second kind of mistake that will make a marriage voidable is when there is a mistake as to the nature of the ceremony. So if one party believes the ceremony is one of engagement, say, then this can invalidate the marriage.[184] However, a mistake as to the legal effects of marriage is insufficient.[185]

It is arguable that in the light of *Hirani* this area of the law is open to reconsideration; that the law should focus not on the kind of mistake, but the effect of the mistake on a person's consent. So, for example, if it was crucial to a wife that her husband belonged to a particular religion then a mistake as to his religion could invalidate her consent. Only future cases will tell whether such a liberal approach can be taken, or whether the traditional approach of only accepting mistakes as to the person or the nature of the ceremony will negate consent.

(c) Unsoundness of mind

Unsoundness will only lead to a marriage being voidable if it exists at the time of the marriage. So a marriage will not be void if someone becomes mentally ill after

---

[179] In Ireland a teacher who was threatened with dismissal from her job unless she married the father of the child she was carrying was able to have the marriage annulled on the grounds of lack of consent: *W(C)* v *C* [1987] IR 676.
[180] *H* v *H* [1954] P 258.
[181] *Moss* v *Moss* [1897] P 263.
[182] *Wakefield* v *Mackay* (1807) 1 Hag Con 394 at p. 398; *Ewing* v *Wheatly* (1814) 2 Hagg Cas 175.
[183] E.g. *Militante* v *Ogunwomoju* [1993] 2 FCR 355.
[184] An example of this can be found in *Valier* v *Valier* (1925) 133 LT 830.
[185] *Messina* v *Smith* [1971] P 322.

the marriage. There is a presumption that people are of sound mind, and so the burden of proof lies on the person seeking to have the marriage annulled. To determine whether there is sufficient unsoundness of mind to render the marriage voidable Singleton LJ in *In the Estate of Park*[186] stated it is necessary to ask whether the person was:

> capable of understanding the nature of the contract into which he was entering, or was his mental condition such that he was incapable of understanding it? To ascertain the nature of the contract of marriage a man must be mentally capable of appreciating that it involves the responsibilities normally attaching to marriage. Without that degree of mentality, it cannot be said that he understands the nature of the contract.

(d) Otherwise

The statute refers to a lack of consent through factors other than duress or mistake. These include the following:

1. *Drunkenness.* There is no clear authority on whether the marriage is voidable where one party was drunk and so did not consent to the marriage. There are two views here. One is that drunkenness should be seen as analogous to being of unsound mind and so would make a marriage voidable. Another view is that a party should not be able to rely on a lack of consent that arises due to their own fault and so voluntary intoxication should not render a marriage voidable. In *Sullivan* v *Sullivan*[187] it was suggested that the groom was so drunk that he was unable to understand the nature of the ceremony and so the marriage was voidable.
2. *Fraud and misrepresentation.* Neither fraud nor innocent misrepresentation will on its own affect the validity of the marriage.[188] However, if the fraud or misrepresentation leads to a mistake as to the identity of the other party or the nature of the ceremony then, as discussed above, the marriage will be voidable.

(iii) Mental disorder

A marriage is also voidable if either party is suffering a mental disorder[189] at the time of the marriage to such an extent that they are unfit for marriage: that is, 'incapable of carrying out the ordinary duties and obligations of marriage'.[190] It is necessary to distinguish this from the lack of consent through unsoundness of mind. The mental disorder ground covers those who are able to understand the nature of a marriage but are unable to perform the duties of marriage due to a mental illness.

It should be stressed that both the grounds relating to mental illness only make the marriage voidable and not void, so there is nothing to stop those with mental illnesses, even extreme ones, from marrying.[191]

---

[186] [1954] P 112.
[187] (1812) 2 Hag Con 238 at p. 246.
[188] *Swift* v *Kelly* (1835) 3 Knapp 257 at p. 293; *Moss* v *Moss* [1897] P 263.
[189] As defined by the Mental Health Act 1983.
[190] *Bennett* v *Bennett* [1969] 1 All ER 539.
[191] In Ireland this ground has been interpreted extensively so that people who have married people with 'personality disorders' which mean they are not suited to marriage have been able to obtain nullity decrees: O'Connor (1993).

(iv) Venereal disease and pregnancy

A marriage is voidable if the respondent is suffering from venereal disease[192] at the time of the ceremony or if the respondent was pregnant by someone other than the petitioner. It should be noted that a wife cannot seek nullity on the ground that the husband has fathered a child through another woman prior to the marriage. It may be thought that venereal disease and pregnancy should no longer be regarded as sufficient grounds to annul a marriage, although, as we shall see, a petitioner will not be able to use these grounds if they were aware of the disease or the pregnancy at the time of the marriage. The continued use of the term 'venereal disease' is a little unfortunate because it is not one that is now used in medical circles. 'Sexually transmitted disease' is the preferred phrase.[193]

(v) Sham marriages

What is the position of a couple who go through a marriage purely for the purpose of pretending to be married, even though they never intend to live together as husband or wife? This is most likely to arise in a case involving immigration. The House of Lords in *Vervaeke* v *Smith*[194] suggested that such marriages are valid, even though in that case the parties only saw each other on a few occasions after the marriage and that the aim of the marriage was to enable the wife to obtain British citizenship and so avoid deportation.[195]

F. Bars to relief in voidable marriages

There are no bars to a marriage being void, although there are some circumstances which prevent the petitioner from seeking to annul a voidable marriage. These bars are found in s 13(1) of the Matrimonial Causes Act 1973. If the bar is established the court may not annul the marriage. The burden is on the respondent to raise the bar as a defence. If the respondent does not mention the bar, the court cannot raise it on his or her behalf. If no statutory bar is established the court cannot bar the annulment on the basis of public policy.[196] This indicates that the bars exist not for public policy reasons but for the protection of the petitioner. We will now consider the different bars.

(i) Approbation

Section 13(1) of the Matrimonial Causes Act 1973 states:

> The court shall not ... grant a decree of nullity on the ground that a marriage is voidable if the respondent satisfies the court—

---

[192] The term is not defined in the Act.
[193] It is not clear whether the courts would be willing to stretch the meaning of venereal disease to include HIV.
[194] [1983] 1 AC 145.
[195] Divorce may well be possible, of course: e.g. *Silver* v *Silver* [1955] 1 WLR 728.
[196] *D* v *D (Nullity)* [1979] Fam 70.

(a) that the petitioner, with knowledge that it was open to him to have the marriage avoided, so conducted himself in relation to the respondent as to lead the respondent reasonably to believe that he would not seek to do so; and

(b) that it would be unjust to the respondent to grant the decree.

It is essential that both paragraphs (a) and (b) be proved to the court's satisfaction.[197] The basis of this bar is that it is seen as contrary to public policy and unjust to allow a person to seek to annul the marriage after leading the other party to believe he or she would not challenge the marriage. For example, in *D v D (Nullity)*[198] the husband relied on his wife's refusal to consummate the marriage in a nullity petition. However, he had previously agreed to the adoption of a child. It was held that his action indicated to the wife that he intended to treat the marriage as valid. Similarly, a man marrying a woman who he knows suffers from a mental disorder or is pregnant would be barred from seeking to annul the marriage on these grounds.[199] It may be that if the marriage has lasted some time the court might imply from the delay in bringing the petition that the petitioner had consented to the marriage.

In order to establish the bar it must be shown that to annul the marriage would be unjust. For example, in *D v D* it might have been unjust to leave the wife caring for the children on her own. However, in that case the wife consented to the nullity decree and so it was thought not to be unjust to her to grant the decree. In considering justice under (b) the court is likely to consider factors such as the length of the marriage, financial implications of the nullity, and social implications of granting a decree.

(ii) Time

A decree of nullity will normally not succeed unless brought within three years of the date of the marriage,[200] the exception being a petition based on impotence. The policy behind this is clear: parties need a degree of security in their marriage – if three years have passed, then to claim that the marriage is fundamentally flawed seems unrealistic.

(iii) Estoppel

Can a party ever be prevented from obtaining a nullity decree on the basis of estoppel? There are two kinds of estoppel that might be relevant. The first is estoppel by conduct where one party so conducts himself or herself that it would be unjust for him or her to deny the facts that he or she has led the other to believe are true. *Miles v Chilton*[201] provides an example of the kind of situation under discussion. A husband sought annulment on the ground that his wife was already married at the time

---

[197] *D v D (Nullity)* [1979] Fam 70.
[198] [1979] Fam 70.
[199] See e.g. *Morgan v Morgan* [1959] P 92.
[200] MCA 1973, s 13(2). There is an exception if the petitioner suffered from some kind of mental disorder.
[201] (1849) 1 Rob Eccl 684.

of the marriage. The wife argued that the husband had deceived her into believing that her 'first' husband had divorced her. The court held that this was no answer to the husband's petition, because otherwise the court would be prevented from discovering the true state of affairs.[202] So estoppel by conduct was not found relevant in this case.

The other kind of estoppel is *estoppel per rem judicatam*, meaning that a party cannot seek to overturn a court's decision. A decree of nullity is what is known as a judgment *in rem*: proceedings cannot be started which seek to undermine such a judgment. However, if the nullity petition is dismissed this only affects the parties themselves. So, if a man is granted a nullity petition on the ground that the wife is married to another man, no one can seek to undermine the basis of the annulment by suggesting in a court that the first marriage was invalid. However, if the petition had been dismissed on the ground that the first marriage was invalid this does not bar anyone except the parties themselves from seeking to show that the first marriage was in fact valid.

G. Effects of a decree of nullity

Section 16 of the Matrimonial Causes Act 1973 states:

> A decree of nullity granted after 31st July 1971 in respect of a voidable marriage shall operate to annul the marriage only as respects any time after the decree has been made absolute, and the marriage shall, notwithstanding the decree, be treated as if it had existed up to that time.

A child of a void marriage is treated as legitimate due to s 1(1) of the Legitimacy Act 1976, as long as at the time of the marriage either (or both) parties reasonably believed that the marriage was valid.[203] *Re Spence*[204] has clarified the law and said that if the marriage was annulled after the birth then the child was legitimate.

Due to ss 23 and 24 of the Matrimonial Causes Act 1973 on granting a decree of nullity, the court has the power to make ancillary relief orders to the same extent as if a divorce order was being made. However, following *Whiston* v *Whiston*,[205] as interpreted in *Rampal* v *Rampal (No. 2)*,[206] if the marriage is void on the ground of bigamy then the court might decide that the applicant's conduct was such that the court should not award her any ancillary relief.[207] In *J* v *S-T*[208] the applicant was born a woman, underwent a partial sex-change operation, lived as a man, and then married a woman. After 17 years of marriage the wife[209] petitioned for a declaration that the marriage was void on the ground that the parties were not respectively male and female. The husband applied for ancillary relief. The court held that there was

---

[202] There are contrary *dicta* in *Bullock* v *Bullock* [1960] 2 All ER 307 at p. 309.
[203] Under the Family Law Act 1986, s 56 a declaration of legitimacy can be made if there is any doubt.
[204] [1990] 2 FLR 278, [1990] FCR 983.
[205] [1995] 2 FLR 268, [1995] 2 FCR 496 CA; discussed Cretney (1996a).
[206] [2001] 2 FCR 552.
[207] Although for an argument that *Rampal* misinterpreted *Whiston* see Sharp (2003).
[208] [1997] 1 FLR 402, [1997] 1 FCR 349 CA.
[209] It took the wife 17 years to find out her husband had not been born a man. The facts of the case reveal the dangers of looking in a man's sock drawer.

a discretion in the court to award ancillary relief. However, in exercising their discretion the court decided not to make any award bearing in mind his deception as to his sex.[210]

H. Reform of nullity

There were 657 petitions for annulments in 2001.[211] Interestingly there appears, in the last few years, to have been an increase in the number of nullity petitions (an 8 per cent increase between 1999 and 2000).[212] It is notable that in those countries where divorce is forbidden or heavily restricted the law on nullity tends to be more liberal.[213]

The concept of a void marriage is necessary if there are to be limits on who may marry and whom. However, there has been some debate over whether the concept of voidable marriage should be abolished. The Law Commission[214] supported the retention of voidable marriage by arguing that to some couples it is particularly important that annulment rather than divorce ends their marriage. This tends to be for religious reasons. Cretney has argued that the law on voidable marriage could be abolished, leaving questions of annulment to the church or other religious bodies.[215] There is much to be said for this approach, given that the vast majority of annulment petitions are brought for religious reasons.

7. UNMARRIED COHABITING COUPLES

There is enormous difficulty in discussing unmarried couples because there are so many forms of cohabitation. The term 'cohabiting couple' can range from a group of students living together in a flat-share, to a boyfriend and girlfriend living together while contemplating marriage, to a couple who have deliberately decided to avoid marriage but wish to live together in a permanent stable relationship. The law has not yet provided a coherent approach to cohabitation, but in several statutes married and unmarried couples have been treated in the same way. Apart from these special provisions, the law treats unmarried couples as two separate individuals, without regard to their relationship. If there is no specific statutory provision then the law treats an unmarried couple in the same way as it would two strangers.[216]

Some indication of the law's definition of cohabitation can be given by those social security cases which have considered when a couple can be regarded as living together as if they were husband and wife.[217] Tyrer J in *Kimber v Kimber*[218]

---

[210] As a result of ss 1(1)(a) and 25(4) of the Inheritance (Provision for Family and Dependants) Act 1975 a person who in good faith has entered into a void marriage may apply to the court for reasonable provision out of the estate.

[211] Office for National Statistics (2001).

[212] Brunner (2001).

[213] See O'Connor (1993).

[214] Law Commission Report 33 (1970).

[215] Cretney (1972).

[216] See Smart and Stevens (2000) for a discussion of the wide range of cohabiting relationships.

[217] N. Harris (1996).

[218] [2000] 1 FLR 232. See also *Re J (Income Support Cohabitation)* [1995] 1 FLR 660.

suggested the following factors be considered in deciding whether there is cohabitation:

1. whether the parties were living together under the same roof;
2. whether they shared in the tasks and duties of daily life (e.g. cooking, cleaning);
3. whether the relationship had stability and permanence;
4. how the parties arranged their finances;
5. whether the parties had an ongoing sexual relationship;
6. whether the parties had any children and how the parties acted towards each other's children; and
7. the opinion of the reasonable person with normal perceptions looking at the couple's life together.

What is clear is that more and more couples are choosing to cohabit.[219] One in eight couples is unmarried.[220] Of women in the age group 18 to 49, 23 per cent were cohabiting outside marriage. In 2002, 40 per cent of children were born to couples who were unmarried.[221] Eighty per cent of births to unmarried couples are registered by both parents.[222] One in sixteen of all dependent children are now being raised by couples living together in stable relationships outside marriage.[223]

What is not clear is whether those who are cohabiting are doing so prior to marriage or in place of marriage. In one study only 9.7 per cent of cohabiting couples said that they were not considering getting married,[224] although 22.7 per cent stated that they did not regard marriage as important. Certainly cohabitation before marriage has become the norm: 80 per cent of couples now cohabit before marriage.[225] Where cohabitation does not end in marriage it tends to break up. The average length of cohabitation is about two years, after which the couple tend either to marry or split up.[226] But, as already emphasised, we must be careful not to make generalisations: some long-term cohabiting relationships do exist.

8. COMPARISONS BETWEEN THE LEGAL POSITION OF MARRIED AND UNMARRIED COUPLES

It is surprisingly difficult to compile a complete list of the differences between the legal positions of married and unmarried couples, primarily because the law does not provide a clear statement of the rights and responsibilities of marriage. Some of the main differences in the legal treatment of married and unmarried couples will now be discussed.

---

[219] This is a Europe-wide phenomenon, see Kiernan (2001). For a thorough discussion of the statistics on cohabitation see Kiernan and Estaugh (1993); Haskey (2001).
[220] Haskey (2001: 66).
[221] Eden (2000); Matheson and Babb (2003).
[222] Matheson and Babb (2003).
[223] C. Gibson (2000: 34).
[224] Lewis (2001b: 135).
[225] Haskey (2001: 57).
[226] Ermisch and Francesconi (1998).

A. Formalities at the beginning and end of a relationship

The law closely regulates the beginning and end of a marriage. It sets out certain formalities that must be complied with in order for a legal marriage to start, and marriage only ends when the court grants a decree absolute of divorce. An unmarried cohabiting relationship can, by contrast, begin or end without any notification to any public body. While every marriage is centrally registered, there is no such record of cohabitation. One consequence of these formalities is that although the law can restrict who can or cannot marry and whom they can marry, there is obviously no restriction as to who may cohabit – there is nothing to stop any number of men or women, unmarried or married, from cohabiting.

It is easy to overestimate the practical importance to the parties of the legal formalities at the beginning and end of a relationship. The legal requirements of marriage are not particularly difficult for a heterosexual couple, and the legal formalities take up little time when compared with the non-legal trappings that often accompany marriage which take up much more of the money and attention of the parties. Similarly, in relation to separation, although divorce does include legal formalities, when compared with the paperwork and practical arrangements of the ending of a long-term relationship the legal formalities of divorce can be of minor importance. The paperwork concerned over, for example, separating joint bank accounts, resolving the occupation of the home, dealing with the mortgage or tenancy, changing arrangements over electricity, gas bills etc. can make the formalities connected to the divorce itself seem small.

B. Financial support

During the marriage itself each party can seek a court order requiring one spouse to pay maintenance to the other,[227] but one unmarried cohabitant cannot seek maintenance from another. In fact, it is very rare for one spouse to seek maintenance from the other except in the context of divorce. Where it is sought, the amounts awarded tend to be low and difficult to collect.[228]

Of far more significance is the fact that on divorce the court has the power to redistribute property owned by either party. However, on the ending of an unmarried relationship the court only has the power to declare who owns what and has no power to require one party to transfer property to the other or to pay maintenance. Although this is a crucial distinction between married and unmarried couples, three important factors need to be stressed. The first is that for many couples the Child Support Act 1991 and Children Act 1989 cover the maintenance for children. These Acts apply equally to married and unmarried couples. Secondly, once the child support has been resolved there is often not enough spare money to consider spousal support. In fact, in fewer than half of all divorces do the courts make any order dealing with the parties' financial resources.[229] The third distinction is that,

---

[227] See Chapter 5.
[228] It seems there is a common law duty to maintain a spouse, although there is no method to enforce this obligation: Cretney, Masson and Bailey-Harris (2002: 73–5).
[229] Barton and Bissett-Johnson (2000).

as we shall see later, in resolving disputes between unmarried cohabitants over property the courts have utilised various equitable doctrines (for example, constructive trusts) which have in effect given the courts wide discretion in deciding the appropriate share of the equitable interest. Indeed in some cases involving unmarried couples the results using the equitable doctrines are those which would be expected if the couple were married and the court were hearing the case under the Matrimonial Causes Act 1973.

C. Children

There used to be a crucial distinction drawn between 'legitimate' and 'illegitimate' children. This affected the status of children and the nature of parental rights over children. The label of illegitimacy has now been abolished by the Family Law Reform Act 1987 and only minor differences exist in the legal position of 'legitimate' and 'illegitimate' children.[230] However, there are still important differences between the legal position of married and unmarried fathers. As we shall see, one of the key concepts of the law relating to parenthood is parental responsibility. Every mother of a child automatically acquires parental responsibility for her child, but the father of the child will only automatically acquire parental responsibility if he is married to the mother. An unmarried father may acquire parental responsibility by being registered as the father on the child's birth certificate, lodging at the court a parental responsibility agreement, or the father may apply to the court for a parental responsibility order. This is a significant difference between married and unmarried fathers, but it is of less importance than it might at first appear, for two reasons. First, the courts have been very willing to award parental responsibility to a father who applies for it. The second is that in day-to-day issues parental responsibility is of limited importance. Many unmarried fathers carry out their parental role unaware that they do not have parental responsibility. Whether or not a father has parental responsibility is only really of significance when major decisions have to be made in respect of the child, such as whether a child should have a medical operation.

D. Inheritance and succession

Where a person dies without having made a will, the person is intestate. In such a case the deceased's spouse will be entitled to some or all of the estate, depending on the application of various rules which will be discussed in Chapter 12. However, an unmarried partner of the deceased is not automatically entitled to an intestate estate. All an unmarried partner can do is to apply under the Inheritance (Provision for Family and Dependants) Act 1975 for an order that in effect alters the intestacy rules and awards them a portion of the estate. So a bereaved unmarried partner must apply to the court in order to be put in the same position as the bereaved spouse if his or her partner is intestate.

---

[230] See Chapter 7.

E. Criminal law

There used to be important distinctions between married and unmarried couples in criminal law, but many of these have been removed.

1. *Rape*. It used to be a common law rule that a husband could not be guilty of raping his wife.[231] This was justified in two ways. First, there was an emphasis on the concept of the unity of husbands and wives – as a husband and wife are one in the eyes of the law, sexual intercourse between them could be no crime.[232] Secondly, it was argued that on marriage the wife impliedly consents to intercourse at any time during that marriage and that such consent was irrevocable. Eventually the House of Lords in *R v R (Rape: Marital Exemption)*[233] abolished the marital exception for rape and this was confirmed by Parliament in the Criminal Justice and Public Order Act 1994. Lord Keith explained that marriage 'is in modern times regarded as a partnership of equals and no longer one in which the wife must be the subservient chattel of the husband'.[234] So now the substantive law on rape is the same whether the defendant be the victim's husband or not.[235]

2. *Actual bodily harm and grievous bodily harm*. There is some confusion in the criminal law over the circumstances in which one person may injure another with their consent. In *R v Brown*[236] the House of Lords confirmed the conviction of some sado-masochists who were convicted of assaulting each other even though their 'victims' had consented to the infliction of the pain. In *R v Wilson*[237] a husband was convicted of assault occasioning actual bodily harm for branding his initials on his wife's buttocks in spite of her consent. The Court of Appeal overturned the conviction. There is some dispute over how to reconcile these two cases. One argument is that the courts distinguished between injuries caused within marriage and injuries caused by gay couples.[238]

3. *Coercion*. The defence of coercion[239] is available to a wife who has committed a crime (apart from murder or treason) as a result of threats from her husband. If a wife commits an offence in the presence of her husband there is a rebuttable presumption that she should not be convicted because she was acting as a result of her husband's coercion. The defence is very similar to duress, the main difference being that coercion does not require a threat of death or serious injuries. The defence is not available to an unmarried couple[240] or even to those with void

---

[231] Although he could be guilty of other criminal offences against his wife.
[232] This was never a very convincing explanation, because a husband could be convicted of assaulting his wife.
[233] [1991] 4 All ER 481, [1992] 1 FLR 217 HL. See now Sexual Offences Act 2003, s 1.
[234] [1991] 4 All ER 481 at p. 484.
[235] Although it appears that marital rapists still receive lower sentences than non-marital rapists (Warner (2000)).
[236] [1993] 1 AC 212.
[237] [1996] 3 WLR 125.
[238] Although in *Emmett* 15.10.99 (unreported) a man's conviction following injuries caused to his partner during an (alleged) sado-masochistic incident with his fiancée was upheld. For an alternative explanation and discussion see Herring (2002c: 144).
[239] Criminal Justice Act 1925, s 47.
[240] *R v Court* (1912) 7 CAR 127.

marriages.[241] It has been widely criticised as based on an outdated presumption that wives are under the thumb of their husbands.

4. *Theft.* Under s 30 of the Theft Act 1968 a person can only be prosecuted for theft against his or her spouse if the Director of Public Prosecutions has given consent.

5. *Conspiracy.* A person cannot be guilty of conspiring with his or her spouse, unless it is alleged that they conspired with other people.[242]

F. Contract

It was only after the Law Reform (Married Women and Tortfeasors) Act 1935 that wives were able themselves to enter contracts that were legally effective. Husbands and wives can enter into contracts with each other, but will have to show that there is intent to create legal relations. For example in *Balfour* v *Balfour*[243] the Court of Appeal held that a promise by a husband to pay his wife £30 per week while he was abroad was found to be unenforceable. This was because there is a presumption that spouses do not intend to be legally bound by such agreements. The rule does not apply to spouses who have separated. A married couple cannot enter into an enforceable contract which excludes the jurisdiction of the divorce court. So a court can make orders in relation to children or financial matters regardless of any contracts the spouses have signed. The position for unmarried couples is similar. Although they may enter a contract they must persuade a court that their agreement was intended to be legally binding. A crucial difference is that a married couple cannot enter into a contract which governs what would happen to their property in the event of their divorce because that would be to interfere with the court's jurisdiction under the Matrimonial Causes Act 1973. An unmarried couple can sign a contract which will determine what happens to their property when the relationship ends.

G. Tort

The rule that a spouse could not sue his or her spouse in tort was revoked by the Law Reform (Husband and Wife) Act 1962 and the rule that a husband had to be joined in any tortious action brought by or against a wife was abolished by statute in 1935.[244] In relation to tort, married and unmarried couples are therefore now treated in the same way. The most remarkable case of partners suing in tort is *P* v *B (Paternity; Damages for Deceit)*[245] where a man sued in deceit after his partner had falsely told him he was the father of her child as a result of which he claimed he paid her £90,000 to support the child. His action was held not to be barred on the grounds of public policy.[246]

---

[241] *R* v *Ditta, Hussain and Kara* [1988] Crim LR 42.

[242] Criminal Law Act 1977, s 2(2)(a).

[243] [1919] 2 KB 571 CA.

[244] Married Women's Property Act 1882 and Law Reform (Married Women and Tortfeasors) Act 1935.

[245] [2001] 1 FLR 1041.

[246] A spouse will not be permitted to sue a former spouse in tort if this is regarded as an attempt to unsettle the financial orders reached on divorce: *Ganesmoorthy* v *Ganesmoorthy* [2003] 3 FCR 167 CA.

H. Evidence[247]

There are two issues here: can a spouse give evidence against the other spouse (is he or she competent), and can a spouse be forced to give evidence against the other spouse (is he or she compellable)? At one time spouses were not compellable[248] witnesses in civil or criminal proceedings against their spouses, the idea being that a spouse should not be forced into the appalling dilemma of either committing perjury or giving evidence which would harm his or her spouse in the proceedings. The spouse was considered an incompetent witness in criminal proceedings because the evidence would be so tainted that a jury would not be able to treat it fairly. These positions have been changed by statute.

The present law is now that in civil proceedings a spouse is both a compellable and a competent witness. In criminal proceedings generally the spouse is competent, but not compellable.[249] In other words, if a spouse is willing to give evidence against his or her spouse he may do so, but will not be forced to. The exceptions are that if the husband and wife are jointly charged for an offence, then neither is competent to give evidence for the prosecution (unless the charges against them are dropped or they plead guilty). Under s 80 of the Police and Criminal Evidence Act 1984 there is a shortlist of offences for which the spouse is compellable. These are offences which involve an assault or injury or threat of injury to the spouse or any person under 16 or a sexual offence against a person under 16.[250] There are no special rules relating to the evidence of cohabitants.[251]

I. Matrimonial property

The Family Law Act 1996 provides married couples with matrimonial home rights which provide a right to occupy the matrimonial home.[252] There are also special provisions relating to matrimonial property during bankruptcy and also pension rights, which we will discuss later.[253] These provisions do not apply to cohabitants, who are given no particular protection on bankruptcy.

J. Marital confidences

The law on protection of confidence applies to confidential communications between spouses. The information must be given in confidence, there must be an

---

[247] Creighton (1990).
[248] By saying a witness is compellable it is meant that a witness can be forced to give evidence.
[249] In *R (on the application of the Crown Prosecution Service)* v *Registrar General of Births, Deaths and Marriages* [2003] 1 FCR 100 a defendant to a charge of murder married the chief prosecution witness to take advantage of this rule. The Crown Prosecution Service in that case unsuccessfully applied to prevent that marriage.
[250] This includes attempting, conspiring, aiding, abetting, counselling, procuring or inciting their commission.
[251] This was confirmed by the Court of Appeal in *R* v *Pearce* [2001] EWCA Crim 2834, [2002] 3 FCR 75. It rejected an argument that following the Human Rights Act 1998 cohabitants should not be compellable witnesses.
[252] See Chapter 4.
[253] See Chapter 4.

unauthorised use of that information, which harms the confiding party, and the information must 'have the necessary quality of confidence about it'. The law may then prevent the disclosure of confidential information. Information passed from one spouse to another spouse will be presumed to be confidential. However, the court may well also find that information passed between unmarried partners was confidential.[254] Now when considering such cases the courts must balance the need to protect privacy with the freedom of expression protected under the European Convention on Human Rights.[255]

K. Taxation and benefits

There are special exemptions from tax that apply to married couples but not unmarried couples. The most important are in respect of inheritance tax and capital gains tax allowance.[256] The Labour government removed the married couple's tax allowance, which was an allowance against income tax available to married couples, but not unmarried couples. The removal of this tax advantage has been strongly criticised. For example, Mary Corbett of the Catholic Family Group wrote: 'Only naive people would think that the marriage allowance would have kept anyone together, but the allowance was a symbol worth keeping because it pointed to marriage as a worthwhile commitment.'[257] It is significant that the government has replaced the married couple's tax allowance with a tax credit for those who care for children. In relation to state benefits, unmarried couples and married couples are generally treated in the same way.

L. Citizenship

Anyone who is not a citizen of the UK and colonies does not become a citizen by marrying someone who is. She or he may obtain nationality by naturalisation or by one of the other methods. The spouse's requirements for naturalisation are less strict than for others. If a person is settled in the UK then the spouse will be given entry clearance as long as he or she can show the marriage is not a sham and that the couple are able to accommodate and maintain themselves. There is a similar power for engaged couples, but not unmarried cohabitants.[258]

M. Statutory succession to tenancies

Statute has provided rights to a tenant's family to succeed to the tenancy on the death of a tenant. The phrase 'family' has been interpreted to include heterosexual or homosexual cohabitants.[259] The phrase 'as husband and wife' includes heterosexual or same-sex couples.[260]

---

[254] *Stephens v Avery* [1988] 1 Ch 449; *A v B (a company)* [2002] 1 FCR 369.
[255] *Douglas v Hello! Ltd* [2002] 1 FCR 289, [2001] 1 FLR 982.
[256] Tax Law Review Committee (2003) provides a useful summary of the differences between married and unmarried couples' taxation.
[257] Corbett (1999).
[258] Cretney, Masson and Bailey-Harris (2002: 92–3) for the detail of the law.
[259] *Fitzpatrick v Sterling Housing Association Ltd* [2000] 1 FCR 21.
[260] *Mendoza v Ghaidan* [2002] 3 FCR 591 CA.

N. Domestic violence

Married couples and cohabitants are associated persons and so can apply for non-molestation injunctions. Cohabitants can also apply for occupation orders, although if the female applicant does not have property rights in the property she will be treated less favourably than she would have been had she been married.[261]

O. Fatal Accident Act 1976

The Fatal Accident Act 1976 permits a spouse of a deceased killed in an accident to claim damages under certain circumstances. Under this Act a cohabitant is able to have a claim in the same way as a married person if he or she had been living with the deceased in the same household as husband or wife for at least two years immediately before the date of death. It is generally thought that the requirement that the couple were living together as 'husband and wife' limits this availability to men and women living together as couples and excludes a homosexual couple or a group of people.

The next two issues are differences of a theoretical rather than practical nature.

P. The doctrine of unity

The principal effect of marriage at common law is that the husband and wife become one. The doctrine of unity finds its basis in Christian theology.[262] Blackstone[263] wrote:

> By marriage, the husband and wife are one person in law; that is, the very being or legal existence of the woman is suspended during the marriage, or at least is incorporated and consolidated into that of the husband; ... Upon this principle of a union of person in husband and wife, depend almost all the legal rights, duties, and disabilities, that either of them acquire by the marriage.

The effects of this doctrine were never fully explained in the law and today the doctrine is regarded with cynicism. Lord Denning MR in *Midland Bank Trust Co Ltd v Green (No. 3)*[264] explained that the position used to be that '... the law regarded the husband and wife as one and the husband as that one'. However, he made it clear that the doctrine of unity is now of very limited application.

Q. Consortium

The concept of consortium is not clear but has been defined in *Bromley's Family Law*[265] as 'an abstract notion which appears to mean living together as husband and wife with all the incidents (insofar as these can be defined) that flow from that

---

[261] See Chapter 6.
[262] The Bible, Genesis 2: 24; Genesis 3: 16.
[263] Blackstone (1770: 442).
[264] [1982] Ch 529 at p. 538.
[265] Lowe and Douglas (1998: 55).

relationship'. At one time there was an obligation on the wife to provide her husband with 'society and services', although a husband did not owe the wife a corresponding duty. This is clearly obsolete and today the concept of consortium is rarely relied upon. For example, in *R v Reid*[266] it was confirmed that a husband could be guilty of kidnapping his wife and that the right of consortium did not provide a defence to such a charge.

9. ENGAGEMENTS

Before marriage it is common for couples to enter into an engagement, when the parties agree to marry one another.[267] In the past, under common law, such agreements were seen as enforceable contracts, and so if either party, without lawful justification, broke the engagement then it would be open for the other to sue for breach of promise and to obtain damages. Such an action was abolished by the Law Reform (Miscellaneous Provisions) Act 1970, s 1,[268] which stated that no agreement to marry is enforceable as a contract. The abolition was justified on the basis that it was contrary to public policy for people to feel forced into marriages through fear of being sued.

In general, engaged couples are treated in the same way as unmarried couples, though engagement still has legal significance in a number of ways:

1. *Property of engaged couples.* When resolving property disputes between an engaged couple s 37 of the Matrimonial Proceedings and Property Act 1970 applies.[269] The effect of this provision is described in detail in Chapter 4, but, in brief, it states that if someone improves a house he or she thereby acquires an interest in it. Apart from this provision, the property of an engaged couple is treated in the same way as that of an unmarried couple.[270]

2. *Gifts between engaged couples.* The Law Reform (Miscellaneous Provisions) Act 1970, s 3(1) states that: 'A party to an agreement to marry who makes a gift of property to the other party to the agreement on the condition (express or implied) that it shall be returned if the agreement is terminated shall not be prevented from recovering the property by reason only of his having terminated the agreement.' So each case will turn on its own facts and depend on whether the gift was subject to an implied condition that the gift should be returned if the marriage did not take place. For example, furniture bought for the intended matrimonial home may be thought to be conditional upon marriage and therefore should be returned if the engagement is broken. A Christmas gift would probably be regarded as unconditional.

---

[266] [1973] QB 299.
[267] It is possible for a party to be engaged even though he or she is married to someone else: *Shaw v Fitzgerald* [1992] 1 FLR 357, [1992] FCR 162.
[268] Law Commission Report 26 (1969), although Bagshaw (2001) discusses the possibility of an action being brought in the tort of deceit if a person promised to marry another, without ever intending to do so.
[269] *Mossop v Mossop* [1988] 2 FLR 173 CA, because of s 2(1) of the Law Reform (Miscellaneous Provisions) Act 1970.
[270] See Chapter 5.

The gift of an engagement ring is presumed to be an absolute gift and there-fore can be kept by the recipient, but this presumption can be rebutted if it can be shown there was a condition that the ring be returned in the event of the mar-riage not taking place.[271] For example, if the ring had belonged to the man's grandmother and was intended to be passed down within her family, it may be presumed that the ring should be returned if the engagement is broken.

3. *Domestic violence.* Engaged couples are 'associated' people for the provisions of Part IV of the Family Law Act 1996 and so can automatically apply for a non-molestation order against one another. However, the Act requires the engage-ment be proved in one of a number of distinct ways (see Chapter 6).

10. GAY AND LESBIAN RELATIONSHIPS[272]

In recent years gay and lesbian relationships have become more widely accepted. No longer is it an offence for two adult males to engage in sexual relationships.[273] As discussed above, in 1999 the House of Lords in *Fitzpatrick* v *Sterling Housing Association Ltd*[274] accepted that a gay person was a member of his partner's family. However, the law has not gone so far as to give gay and lesbian couples the same rights as heterosexual couples. The following are some of the differences in the treatment between homosexual and heterosexual relationships in the family law context:

1. If a couple with children separate and one of the parents forms a gay or lesbian relationship this is a relevant factor to be taken into account if there is a dispute over where the child should live.[275] The court will be willing to award residence to the gay or lesbian parent, but will require persuasion that this is in the best interests of the child.[276] The courts may be required to reconsider this response in the light of the Human Rights Act 1998 which prohibits discrimination on the grounds of sexual orientation. If a gay parent can show he or she was treated dif-ferently from a heterosexual parent then this must be justified with objective and reasonable grounds which justify the discrimination.[277]
2. It will be easier for a heterosexual couple than a gay or lesbian couple to obtain an occupation order in the domestic violence context under the Family Law Act 1996, Part IV.[278]
3. Under the Inheritance (Provision for Family and Dependants) Act 1975 (which enables one party to seek a court order granting him or her a share in the estate of a deceased person) there is a newly created category of claimants[279] who have

---

[271] Law Reform (Miscellaneous Provisions) Act 1970, s 3(2).
[272] Wintemute and Andenaes (2001) provides a very useful collection of essays.
[273] Sexual Offences (Amendment) Act 1957. See also the Sexual Offences Act 2003 which seeks to draw distinction between same-sex and opposite-sex sexual activity.
[274] [2000] 1 FCR 21.The case is discussed in Glennon (2000) and Diduck (2001).
[275] See Chapter 9. For a general discussion see Bradley (1987).
[276] *C* v *C (A Minor) (Custody: Appeal)* [1991] 1 FLR 223, [1991] FCR 254; see generally Golombok (1999); Barton (1996b).
[277] *Da Silva Mouta* v *Portugal* [2001] 1 FCR 653 ECtHR.
[278] See Chapter 6.
[279] Created in the Law Reform (Succession) Act 1995.

cohabited for two years but which applies only to heterosexual couples and not to gay and lesbian couples.[280]

4. A gay or lesbian couple cannot marry.[281]

5. At present a same-sex relationship does not fall within the scope of respect for family life under article 8 of the European Convention on Human Rights, although it would fall within the definition of private life.[282] However it is unlawful under the European Convention to discriminate upon the grounds of sexual orientation.[283]

These distinctions between same-sex and opposite-sex couples are unjustifiable. At the very least there should be a means whereby a same-sex couple can acquire official recognition of their relationship. Bailey-Harris[284] asserts that the arguments for the recognition of same-sex relationships can be made on the basis of equality and self-determination and in addition she has produced a list of some interests that the state has in providing some formal recognition of same-sex relationships:

- The promotion of pluralism and party autonomy.
- The promotion of equality and equal access to legal rights.
- The encouragement of stability in family life.
- The safeguarding and promotion of the welfare of any children involved.
- The achievement of economic justice between parties on the breakdown of a relationship.
- The protection of the public purse through the effective enforcement of individual obligation.

The government has responded to arguments such as these by producing a paper proposing a civil registration of relationships which would be open to same-sex couples.[285] The proposal is that same-sex couples (and only same-sex couples) will be able to register their partnerships. A registered partnership will acquire many of the same rights and responsibilities of marriage.[286] Registered partnerships would only be available to adult couples who are not presently in a registered partnership or married.[287] The partnership could be dissolved if it was shown that the relationship had broken down irretrievably. On dissolution the court would have the power

---

[280] Although in the light of the Human Rights Act 1998 a court may be willing to interpret the provision to include a same-sex couple. They may also be able to apply under the category of being maintained by the deceased: Inheritance (Provision for Family and Dependants) Act 1975, s 1(1)(e).

[281] Although see Bowley (1995); Lind (1995); S. Katz (1999). Several European countries have taken the route of allowing same-sex couples to register their relationships. For a discussion of the French forms of registered relationships see Martin and Thery (2001). See Murphy (2002) and Tan (2002) for a discussion of the difficulties English and Welsh law may face when dealing with a same-sex couple who have married or entered a registered partnership overseas.

[282] *ADT v UK* [2000] 2 FLR 697.

[283] *Da Silva Mouta v Portugal* [2001] 1 FCR 653 ECtHR. Lady Turner's Sexual Orientation Discrimination Bill 1998 was not passed. See *Toonen v Australia* in UN Doc CCPR/C/50/D/488 for arguments that the UN Covenant on Civil and Political Rights prohibits discrimination on the ground of sexual orientation.

[284] Bailey-Harris (2001c: 605; 2000).

[285] Women & Equality Unit (2003).

[286] If one has a child a registered partner can acquire parental responsibility in the same way a step-parent can.

[287] There will also be restrictions on the basis of blood relationships.

to make orders enabling a fair distribution of property and making arrangements for children. Registered partners would also acquire many of the rights that a spouse has at the death of a partner. Although a registered partnership will resemble marriage, it is not identical and the government has made it clear that it has no plans to permit same-sex marriage.[288] The government hopes that not only will registered partnerships improve the legal position of same-sex partners, but they will also increase the social acceptability of same-sex relationships.

11. SHOULD THE LAW TREAT COHABITATION AND MARRIAGE IN THE SAME WAY?

It should be noted that many European countries have legislated to treat married and unmarried couples in the same way.[289] There are various ways of considering this question.

A. Does the state benefit from cohabitation to the same extent as from marriage?

The state has traditionally favoured marriage and sought to encourage people to marry, most explicitly by providing tax advantages to married couples which are not available to unmarried people. However, marriage is not encouraged only through such explicit means. As O'Donnovan explains: 'Marriage endures as symbol ... it may be presented as private but it is reinforced everywhere in public and in political discourse.'[290] An example of her argument is that the government has proposed that teachers in schools sing the praises of marriage.[291] A study of attitudes among the general public towards marriage revealed that two-thirds of those interviewed saw marriage as an ideal family form, although notably only 28 per cent of respondents thought marriage made couples better parents.[292] But why is it that the government, through public statements and policies, seeks to encourage marriage? There are five particular advantages to the state which are often cited:

1. Sir George Baker, a former President of the Family Division, has argued that marriage provides the 'building blocks' of society and is 'essential to the well-being of our society, as we understand it'.[293] Lady Thatcher argued that marriage is 'the basic unit of our society'.[294] The Home Office paper, *Supporting Families*,[295] states: 'Marriage does provide a strong foundation for stability for the care of children. It also sets out rights and responsibilities for all concerned. It remains the choice of the majority of people in Britain. For all these reasons, it makes sense for the Government to do what it can to strengthen marriage.'

---

[288] Women & Equality Unit (2003: 13).
[289] Thorpe (2002: 893).
[290] O'Donnovan (1993: 57).
[291] This is discussed in Eekelaar (2000c: 649).
[292] Barlow, Duncan, James and Park (2001).
[293] *Campbell* v *Campbell* [1977] 1 All ER 1 at p. 6.
[294] Thatcher (1981).
[295] Home Office (1998: 4.12).

This view, although a popular notion amongst politicians, lacks precision. What does it mean that marriage is a building block or the foundation of society? It could be argued that a married couple may feel they have a greater stake in society than two single people, and so may be more willing to contribute to it.[296] This is certainly open to debate as, for example, single people may well be more likely to use public transport and perhaps even be more vulnerable to crime. It could be suggested that marriage provides psychological benefit to the couple themselves, which might in turn make them better citizens.[297] These arguments are all hard to prove either way. We have not tried a society without marriage, and so do not know whether society would be different without marriage.

2. It may be that the state wishes to support marriage in order to promote the production of and caring for children. The government's view is that: 'many lone parents and unmarried couples raise their children every bit as successfully as married parents. But marriage is still the surest foundation for raising children and remains the choice of the majority of people in Britain. We want to strengthen the institution of marriage to help more marriages to succeed.'[298] Some statistical support might be found for this in that in considering whether a mother was still living with the father five years after the birth of a child it was found that she was in 92 per cent of cases where the couple were married; but it was 48 per cent where the couple were unmarried, and 75 per cent where the couple were unmarried at the time of the birth but then married.

3. A third alleged benefit to the state is that by managing the start of a relationship the state is able to regulate the relationship if it breaks down. The state may wish to ensure that at the end of a relationship the arrangements for children will promote the child's welfare, and that the spouses' property is divided between them in a way that is just. If a marriage breaks down the couple must turn to the courts for a divorce so that the marriage can be officially terminated; however, if an unmarried couple separate the court may well not be involved at the end of the relationship. The strength of this view is weakened in the light of the present law. First, the law, in both financial and child-related matters, essentially allows the parties themselves to resolve these matters and intervenes only if there is a dispute. Secondly, this view does not explain why the law does not try to provide the same intervention for unmarried couples.[299]

4. A fourth benefit is economic. If a person falls ill, or becomes unemployed, and so no longer has an income, then the financial responsibility is likely to fall on the state if that person is single, whereas a married couple would depend on each other. A further economic benefit is the straightforward fact that a couple sharing accommodation require less housing than two single people.

5. Marriage can be used as an effective evidential tool. If the law were to abolish the legal significance of marriage then it would be necessary to create some kind of alternative in order legally to regulate family life. Perhaps cohabitation would

---

[296] Berger and Kellner (1980).
[297] There is some evidence of a higher incidence of premature death among unmarried rather than married men: McAllister (1995).
[298] Home Office (1998).
[299] Horowitz and Harper (1995).

provide that alternative. The difficulty is that a couple might be sharing a house, but not necessarily sharing their lives. The definition of cohabitation and the investigation that would be necessary to decide whether or not a couple were sharing their lives would be far more complex and expensive than deciding whether a person is married. The couples who marry therefore save the state and courts' time and effort in formally establishing the nature of their relationship.

Many of these benefits of marriage to the state are also provided by cohabiting relationships. However, the core question is whether unmarried cohabiting couples are as stable as married ones.[300] This is especially important when considering their role in raising children. It is very difficult to obtain statistics on cohabiting relationships because there are no formalities marking their beginning and end. The evidence available suggests that unmarried cohabiting relationships are shorter lived.[301] One study found that cohabiting couples are three to four times more likely to separate than married couples.[302] Half of first-time cohabiting partnerships dissolve their relationship before their child is five.[303] However, it is also clear that unmarried cohabitants tend to be economically less well off, and it may be their economic position rather than their marital status that truly affects the stability of their relationship. In other words, even if the cohabiting couple had married, their relationship would not have lasted any longer. Eekelaar and Maclean draw these conclusions after conducting research in Britain:

> ... we should identify the socio-economic status of the parents rather than their formal relationship as having the most significant effect on the social capital which they provide for their children. However, marriage may play an important role in symbolising and confirming an achieved degree of economic security, and therefore be a desirable context in which parenthood is to be exercised. We cannot determine from this study how much *being married* might *in itself* add to the security created by socio-economic circumstances, or whether other types of institutional arrangements (for example, making parental responsibility agreements) might have similar effects. We can see value in institutionalising the expectations inherent in the joint exercise of parenthood and note that, insofar as this is done through marriage, most people make the public commitment which marriage symbolises when their socio-economic circumstances are such that their chances of providing the most favourable social capital for their children are at their highest. For this reason, whatever might be the position regarding childless marriages, our evidence reveals marriage in a positive light as an institution which supports parenthood.[304]

We might ask if there are any rational reasons why married relationships are stronger than unmarried ones. Four reasons will be suggested. The first is that marriage may indicate a deeper commitment to the relationship.[305] This may be true

---

[300] For the case that cohabitation does not benefit the state to the same extent as marriage, see P. Morgan (2000). She argues that there are higher rates of domestic violence, child abuse and alcohol abuse. For a study arguing for similar findings in the United States (including an argument that married couples record higher levels of sexual satisfaction than unmarried ones) see Waite (2000).

[301] McRae (1997); Haskey (2001); Kiernan (2001).

[302] Buck and Ermisch (1995). For a survey of the material, see P. Morgan (2000); Lewis (2001b). C. Gibson (2000: 35) suggests that the breakdown rate for unmarried cohabitants is twice that of married couples.

[303] Lewis (2001b: 39).

[304] Eekelaar and Maclean (1997: 143).

[305] P. Morgan (2000).

for many couples but is clearly not true for all. The current divorce rate demonstrates that marriage is not a guarantee of lifelong commitment. The second is that the social pressure against ending a marriage may be greater than the pressure against ending an unmarried relationship. Again this may be true, depending on the attitude and culture of the parties, their families and communities. Thirdly, the legal barriers to divorce may slow down the marital breakdown process, which might increase the chance of reconciliation. The strength of these arguments is very much open to debate. Even if it could be shown that marriage itself makes couples more stable, it could still be argued that the state should do more to encourage and support unmarried relationships rather than privileging married relationships. Fourthly, it can be suggested that the characteristics or values of cohabiting couples differ from married ones and these make them more likely to separate.[306]

An argument that is sometimes made in this debate is that treating unmarried couples in the same way as married couples will discourage marriage, thereby harming society.[307] This argument is weak. As has already been mentioned, it is very unlikely that people decide not to marry because of the legal consequences. Simply put, few people know the law in this area.[308] Even those who do are more likely to base their decision to marry on religious and social views, or to be influenced by their families, friends and culture.

B. Choice

An alternative approach is to focus on 'choice'.[309] Deech[310] has argued that if a couple choose not to marry it is wrong for the law to treat them as if they were married as this would negate their choice and show a lack of respect for their decision. There are perhaps three difficulties with this view, despite its persuasive power. The first is that it is doubtful to what extent many couples *choose* not to marry, at least to what extent they choose not to take on the legal consequences of marriage.[311] In reality few couples decide positively not to get married because of the legal differences in treatment and, indeed, few marry because of the legal benefits.[312] Indeed in one survey 69 per cent of those questioned thought living together outside marriage created legal rights.[313] A second problem is that some couples disagree over whether or not to marry. It may be, for example, that the woman wants to get married but the man does not. It seems a little harsh to say she has chosen not to marry. Deech, rather bluntly, replies that such a person should either leave her partner or accept the unmarried status. A third argument is that some of the legal consequences of marriage do not reflect the couple's decision but rather the justice of the situation or the protection of a state interest (for example, protecting the interests of children). One might take the view that it should not be possible to choose not

---

[306] See e.g. Axin and Thornton (1992); Lye and Waldron (1997).
[307] P. Morgan (2000).
[308] Smart and Stevens (2000).
[309] Deech (1980); Dnes (2002).
[310] Deech (1980).
[311] Oliver (1982).
[312] Hibbs, Barton and Beswick (2001).
[313] Hibbs, Barton and Beswick (2001: 202).

to have justice or not to protect a state interest. Alternatively it could be said that although cohabiting couples might not want all of the consequences of marriage, this does not mean they do not want the law to intervene at all at the end of their relationship.[314] In spite of these responses, where both members of a couple have decided firmly to reject the legal consequences of marriage, to deny respect to that choice seems unduly interventionist.

It may be that Deech's argument is more persuasive when seen as a call for marriage to be treated in the same way as cohabitation. In other words, regardless of whether the couple are married or not, the law's response should focus on their commitment to each other, rather than having the consequences of the status of marriage 'imposed upon them'.

C. Reflecting current attitudes

Another approach is to argue that the law should reflect current attitudes. Studies suggest that many people do not regard cohabitation outside marriage as immoral and indeed there is often talk in the media of 'a common law wife', suggesting that if a couple have lived together for a certain time they are treated as married. This meaning of 'common law marriage' is not legally recognised. Unmarried couples are often under the misapprehension that once they have cohabited for a while they will be treated as if they are married.[315] It may be argued that the law should reflect this popular (mis)understanding. Of those interviewed in a recent survey, 61.4 per cent suggested that cohabitants who had lived together for ten years should have the same maintenance rights as married couples, and 92.1 per cent thought they should have the same inheritance rights.[316] However, another study[317] found a significant difference in the attitudes towards financial matters of those married couples divorcing and cohabiting couples who were separating. Divorcing couples talked about ensuring there were fair financial arrangements for the children and then dividing what was left, while separating cohabitants talked about each partner taking back what they had brought into the relationship. Interestingly the role of children appeared to play a much smaller part in the discussions of cohabitants.

D. Should marriage be discouraged?

There are, of course, arguments that the state should not encourage marriage.[318] Some feel that marriage is an institution which has helped perpetuate disadvantage against women.[319] O'Donnovan has sought 'to break free from marriage as a timeless unwritten institution whose terms are unequal and unjust '.[320] The argument is that marriage ensures the maintenance of patriarchal power, through the power

---

[314] Haskey (2001: 53).
[315] Pickford (1999).
[316] Barlow, Duncan, James and Park (2001; 2003).
[317] Maclean, Eekelaar, Lewis et al. (2002).
[318] See Chapter 1.
[319] For an economic analysis supporting this conclusion see Slaughter (2002).
[320] O'Donnovan (1993).

given to husbands as 'head of the household'.[321] Other criticisms have been similar to those launched against the family, namely that marriage can be self-centred, with the couple focusing on preparing their home rather than working in the community around them. From an opposite perspective, marriage can be seen as anti-individualist. O'Donnovan summarises Weitzman's view of marriage: 'this unwritten contract, to be found in legislation and case-law, is tyrannical. It is an unconstitutional invasion of marital privacy, it is sexist in that it imposes different rights and obligations on the husband and wife, and it flies in the face of pluralism by denying heterogeneity and diversity and imposing a single model of marriage on everyone.'[322] Other commentators detect a modern understanding of marriage among younger people which is based on a partnership of equals, sharing the burdens of homemaking, child-caring and wealth creation,[323] although the extent to which such marriages occur in reality, rather than as an aspiration, is a matter of debate.

12. WHAT IF THE STATE WERE TO ABOLISH LEGAL MARRIAGE?

One point of view is that marriage should cease to have any legal significance, although holders of this view would be happy for marriage to continue to have religious and social significance. This would mean that any legal regulation of relationships would not depend on whether couples are married or not, but rather on different criteria, for example, on whether a couple have children, or on the length of time a cohabitation has existed.[324] So, for example, if the government wishes to give benefits to stable couples who care for children, these could be directed towards couples with children who have stayed together for five years, rather than giving the benefit to all married couples, which would be over-inclusive. Glendon foresaw the withering away of marriage. She argued that the law was moving to 'break the family down into its component parts and treat family members as separate and independent'.[325]

If the law does not rely on marriage, how might the law distinguish two strangers from two people in a close relationship, assuming it wishes to?[326] The following are some possibilities:

1. The law could rely on cohabitation. The difficulty is in defining cohabitation. Does it require staying overnight: how many nights a week are necessary?[327] Proof of cohabitation (or non-cohabitation) may also prove difficult.
2. An alternative approach is to focus on the kind of relationship. Has the relationship reached a depth where it deserves a particular benefit? Simon Gardner, in

---

[321] Smart (1984).

[322] O'Donnovan (1984: 114).

[323] Schwartz (2000) describes such marriages as 'peer' marriages.

[324] Clive (1994). But see S. Bridge (2001: 9) who questions whether such an approach is compatible with article 12 of the European Convention on Human Rights.

[325] Glendon (1989: 296).

[326] For a discussion of whether family law could be reduced to a network of personal rights and obligations, without obligations emanating from 'the family', see Eekelaar (2000a).

[327] Cf. *Santos v Santos* [1972] Fam 247.

the context of property rights, has suggested considering whether the relationship displays 'communality'. The difficulty with this approach is that it is very
difficult for a third party (e.g. a judge) to understand the nature of a particular
relationship. Some people, for example, would attach great significance to a
sexual relationship; others would pay little attention to this.

3. Another approach is to focus on the agreement between the parties.[328] This
could require or encourage the parties to prepare and sign a legal agreement.
This is only satisfactory where the parties are aware of the benefits of doing so.
It is notoriously difficult to persuade people to make wills. It is doubtful we will
be more successful in persuading people to make cohabitation contracts. In any
event, even if such contracts were drafted there is a fear that they would too
quickly become out of date. For example, a contract could be entered into on
the assumption that the man will be the main breadwinner; but if he becomes
unemployed and the woman takes over being the main earner, the contract
would need to be updated. In any event, even if the contract was kept up to date
there would be difficulties in the contract being liable to challenge on the
grounds of misrepresentation or undue influence. Further, it is unlikely that we
would want such contracts to cover all areas. Either the court would feel that
they should override the contract or inventively construe it. For example, we
may not want such contracts to be upheld in relation to children if the terms
would be contrary to the interests of the children. It would also be necessary to
persuade couples to enter these contracts. At present the evidence shows that
the idea of entering a contract at the start of the relationship is strongly
opposed.[329]

4. It would be possible for the state to create an alternative to marriage, for
example registered partnerships.[330] However, it is unlikely that people who do
not wish to marry would choose to register their partnerships. Partnerships
would, however, be useful for those who are legally barred from marriage.

5. To some commentators the significance attached to parenthood reflects the
decreasing importance of marriage. Dewar[331] suggests 'that family law is increasingly emphasising the maintenance of economic and legal ties between parents
and children after separation, as if to create the illusion of permanence in the
face of instability. Since, by definition, neither marriage nor cohabitation are
available for the purpose, these continuing links are founded on parenthood.'

13. CONCLUSION

This chapter has considered the nature of marriage and cohabitation. Increasing
numbers of people are deciding to live together outside marriage and, in response,
the legal distinctions between married and unmarried couples are lessening. Most
significantly, the tax advantages awarded to married couples have been replaced by
a tax credit to those caring for children (whether married or not). This reflects a

[328] For a useful discussion see Lewis (2001b).
[329] Lewis (1999: 184).
[330] Anderson (1997); Bradley (2001).
[331] Dewar (2000a: 63).

suggestion that it is parenthood rather than marriage which is at the heart of family law. This is not to say there are no legal differences between married and unmarried couples, but those differences that remain are controversial and many argue that the distinctions should be removed. As the legal consequences of marriage lessen, it is harder to justify the restrictions on who can marry whom. Further, if marriage is not to be the touchstone for deciding who are a legally recognised couple, what should replace it? There are great difficulties in finding an alternative: cohabitation or the intentions of the parties, for example, are not susceptible to ready proof, particularly when compared to examining the marriage register to see if a couple are married. The bureaucratic difficulties caused by defining cohabitation might ultimately lead to the law deciding that intimate relationships between adults give rise to no legal obligations whatsoever and that obligations should flow instead from parenthood.

3

DIVORCE AND MEDIATION

1. STATISTICS ON DIVORCE

It is easy to paint a gloomy picture of the number of divorces in England and Wales. Between 1961 and 1991 there was a fivefold rise in the divorce rate. By 2002 there were 147,735 divorces and 249,227 marriages in England and Wales.[1] The divorce rate (the number of divorces per 1,000 marriages per year) had risen from 4.7 in 1970 to 13.7 in 1999, but dropped to 13.0 in 2001.[2] In 1971, 82,000 children were involved in divorce; by 2002 there were over 149,335 children involved in divorce.[3] Now, one in four children will be affected by divorce by the time they are 16.[4] All of these figures are particularly surprising given the low rate of marriage.[5]

That said, the picture of gloom painted by these figures could give a misleading picture. Between 1978 and 1988 the total number of divorces rose by 6 per cent but the number of *first* marriages ending in divorce fell by 6 per cent.[6] Indeed 30 per cent of those divorcing in 2001 had been divorced previously.[7] What this reveals is that the divorce rate figures are somewhat skewed by the number of people marrying, divorcing, remarrying and divorcing again. Further, it is clear that the divorce rate for marriages which have lasted at least eight years is the same today as it was in 1970. In other words, well-established marriages are as stable now as they were 30 years ago. As Eekelaar and Maclean explain, 'the increase in the divorce rate for people marrying in the 1970s is almost entirely an increase during the first four to eight years of marriage'.[8] Further, since 1993 there has been a decline in the divorce rate. In 1998, 12.9 per 1,000 marriages ended in divorce, which was the lowest rate since 1990.[9]

The projected rate of divorce now stands at about 37 per cent.[10] This means that for every 100 couples marrying now, 37 of those marriages will probably end in divorce. However, it is crucial to appreciate that this is the rate for the average marriage. A couple both marrying for the first time in their mid-twenties, who have not cohabited before marriage, will have a much lower projected rate of divorce.

---

[1] National Statistics (2003b).
[2] Office for National Statistics (2003b).
[3] Office for National Statistics (2003b)
[4] Office for National Statistics (2002).
[5] As fewer people marry and more cohabit prior to marriage, it might be thought that only the stronger relationships result in marriage.
[6] Eekelaar (1991a: 55).
[7] Office for National Statistics (2000); The Stationery Office (2000c).
[8] Eekelaar and Maclean (1997: 22).
[9] Office for National Statistics (1999).
[10] C. Gibson (1994).

79

2. CAUSES OF DIVORCE

Here we will consider the factors that are statistically linked to divorce. It must be stressed that these are only statistical links, so it does not mean that because one of these factors is present the couple will divorce; it is simply more likely that they might.

1. *Age.* There is a close link between divorce and being married at a young age. An 18-year-old bride has twice the risk of marital breakdown as that of a 21-year-old. This is particularly so where the marriage follows a pregnancy.[11]

2. *Previously married.*[12] A second marriage is much more prone to divorce than a first marriage.[13] However, this does depend on the cause of the end of the first marriage. A woman who remarries after divorcing her first husband is six times more likely to be divorced a second time than a woman who remarries after the death of her first husband. Some argue that the existence of stepchildren puts particular strains on second marriages.[14]

3. *Education.* There is a link between low-level educational achievement and the divorce rate, although most of the evidence to support this is based on studies in the USA. It may be that poor education is reflected in poor communication skills, which could be directly linked to divorce.

4. *Poverty.* There is a strong link between divorce and poverty, unemployment and receipt of benefits.[15] A man who becomes unemployed is nearly two and a half times more likely to separate within the year following the loss of the job than an employed man.[16] There is also some evidence that where the husband earns less than the wife this can increase the likelihood of divorce significantly.[17]

5. *Cohabitation prior to marriage.* If a couple cohabit prior to marriage there is clear evidence that they are more likely to divorce than a couple who do not cohabit prior to marriage.[18] For example, between 1980 and 1984 a couple who cohabited prior to marriage were 50 per cent more likely to divorce within the first five years than a couple who had not cohabited.[19] Even 15 years from the start of the relationship the fact that a couple cohabited before marriage affects the likelihood of their divorce by a 20 per cent increase.[20] To many these are surprising statistics. Two explanations are offered. First, if a couple cohabit and then choose to marry, it must be asked why they have decided to marry. It may be that the cohabiting couple decide to marry in order to feel more secure within their relationship, whereas the feeling of a lack of security may, in fact, indicate a weakness in the relationship. This explanation could be supported by reference

---

[11] E.g. Bracher, Morgan and Trussell (1993).
[12] E.g. Haskey (1983).
[13] C. Gibson (1994: 163).
[14] Kiernan and Wicks (1990).
[15] Kiernan and Mueller (1999).
[16] Haskey (1984).
[17] Cronin and Curry (2000).
[18] E.g. M. Murphy (1985); Haskey (1992); A. Booth (1999). Although see Kiernan (1999) for a contrary finding looking at statistics across Europe.
[19] Kiernan and Mueller (1999).
[20] Kiernan and Mueller (1999).

to the fact that the longer the cohabitation before marriage the greater the risk of divorce. The second explanation of why cohabitation affects the divorce rate is that those who choose not to cohabit prior to marriage may do so because of religious beliefs and those same religious beliefs may disincline a couple to divorce.[21]

6. *Experiencing divorce in childhood.* Those whose parents divorce during their childhood are more likely to experience divorce in their own marriages.[22]

3. SOCIAL EXPLANATIONS FOR INCREASING DIVORCE

Although the factors above are statistically linked to divorce, they do not necessarily provide an explanation for why the divorce rate has risen. The following have been proposed as some of the reasons why the divorce rate has increased:

1. One explanation for the increased divorce rate is that society's attitude towards marriage has changed. Some have argued that a higher degree of satisfaction is now expected from marriage.[23] Giddens has maintained that in modern times people stay in intimate relationships only for as long as the relationships meet their own goals of personal autonomy and fulfilment.[24] Day Sclater summarises his view: 'we no longer look for Mr or Mrs Right, but rather we search for the perfect relationship; when one fails to satisfy, the individual in late modernity increasingly feels free to move on to try another'.[25] This increased individualism and the increased expectations of marriage may therefore help explain the increase in divorce rates. Notably, the majority of divorce petitions are presented by women. It may be that women are increasingly less willing to accept a traditional subservient role in marriage.

2. Another explanation is that increased life expectancy affects the divorce rate.[26] The potential length of marriages has increased by 15 years during the course of the twentieth century.[27] In other words, the average length of a marriage is now similar to that in the Victorian era; marriages now end in divorce at a time when they used to be ended by death.

3. Hochschild[28] has suggested that increased work pressures mean that there is less time to spend on family activities and this causes marital breakdown. Further, combining the career aspirations of both the husband and the wife with childcare can cause great tensions within a marriage.

4. One factor that affects the divorce rate is that now divorce is economically a possibility for women. Improvements in benefits for lone parents and increased employment opportunities for women mean that a wife can leave her husband without falling into utter poverty. In the first half of the twentieth century the

---

[21] Kiernan and Wicks (1990) suggest that seven out of ten couples cohabit prior to marriage.
[22] E.g. McLanahan and Bumpass (1988).
[23] C. Gibson (1994: 214).
[24] Giddens (1992).
[25] Day Sclater (2000: 68).
[26] C. Gibson (1994: 127).
[27] Eekelaar and Maclean (1997: 17).
[28] Hochschild (1996).

wife was dependent on her husband to support her; few women would have been economically able to leave their husbands.

4. WHAT SHOULD BE THE AIMS OF DIVORCE LAW?

There has been much debate over what the role of the law is on divorce: what is the purpose of divorce law? Some of the possible answers to this question will now be considered. The first six are set out as the guiding principles for the divorce law in s 1 of the Family Law Act 1996. Notably, when the Lord Chancellor announced that the proposals in the Act would not be implemented, he confirmed the government's support for the principles declared in s 1.[29]

1. Divorce law should seek to support the institution of marriage.[30] Divorce is not only a tragedy for the couple; it also involves expense to the state. It has been suggested that the cost of supporting on benefits families who have separated is 5p in the pound of income tax.[31] Divorce may also be said to shake social stability by challenging the image of the family as comforting, secure and enduring.[32] However, these arguments assume that there is a link between divorce law and the rate of divorce. Deech argues:

    > every successive attempt during this century to bring statute law into line with 'reality' has resulted in an increase in the divorce rate. The increased divorce rate results in greater familiarity with divorce as a solution to marital problems, more willingness to use it and to make legislative provision for its aftermath. The resultant pressure on the divorce system leads to a relaxation of practice and procedure ..., then to a call for a change in the law in order to bring it into line with 'reality', and then to yet another increase in divorce.[33]

    In this way, she argues, the changes in divorce law have led to an increase in the divorce rate. Indeed the statistics appear to support Deech's argument, although some commentators see the legislation as a response to the divorce statistics, rather than a cause of them.[34] What is far from clear is *how* changes in the divorce law could cause marital breakdown.[35] Clearly the rate of divorce and law on divorce are linked. We could have no legal divorce at all, and so a divorce rate of nil. That would not mean, of course, that all the couples who would have divorced would still be living together. No doubt, they would simply separate. We would therefore have a large number of 'empty shell' marriages. So, the real question is whether the divorce law affects the marital *breakdown* rate. If the divorce procedure is perceived to be difficult, spouses may be reluctant to seek the advice of a solicitor until they think that they would be entitled to a divorce.

---

[29] Lord Chancellor's Department (2001).
[30] Family Law Act 1996 (hereafter FLA 1996), s 1(1)(a).
[31] Quoted in Mostyn (1999: 97).
[32] Day Sclater (1999: 4).
[33] Deech (1994: 121). Deech (1990); Eekelaar and Maclean (1990); Brinig (2000) and Ellman (2000a) discuss whether the law on divorce can affect the rates of breakdown.
[34] Davis and Murch (1988: 22–3). Mansfield, Reynolds and Arai (1999) claim that changes in the law have only a slight impact on divorce rates.
[35] M. Richards (1996b).

Delaying the visit to the solicitor and the institution of legal proceedings may possibly help reduce breakdown rates. So it is possible that the *perception* of the divorce law might affect the breakdown rate. However, it should be stressed that there is a whole range of factors that might affect marital breakdown.

If the law did wish to discourage divorce, it might do so more effectively by making marriage – rather than divorce – harder.[36] Increasing the age at which one could marry might well reduce the divorce rate, as might requiring the parties to have a year of reflection and consideration before being permitted to marry. However, both of these proposals might lead to a reduction of the marriage rate,[37] as well as the divorce rate. Certainly the government has accepted that much more than manipulation of the divorce law is required if marriages are to be supported by the state.[38]

2. Divorce law should seek to save marriages if possible.[39] The argument here is that if a couple seeks a divorce the legal procedure should do all it can to persuade them to be reconciled and to turn back from divorce.[40] However, opponents of this aim argue that people do not normally turn to lawyers when their marriage first hits the rocks, but only when it is irreparable,[41] and often at the time when one or both of the parties wishes to remarry. It is also argued that some marriages should not be saved: for example, where there has been serious domestic violence or the unhappy marriage is harming the children.[42]

3. If there is to be a divorce, the law should not exacerbate the bitterness between the parties.[43] This aim, one might think, is uncontroversial; however, opponents point out that increased bitterness is an inevitable aspect of divorce. To expect a legal system to enable the parties to separate happily and then have a good post-divorce relationship is pure idealism. This is why the stated purpose is that the law should not *exacerbate* the bitterness, rather than *remove* it. The difficulty is that the parties often come to divorce with expectations of the law that are unrealistic. The parties might expect the judge to make a clear statement as to who is to blame for the breakdown of the marriage. However, nowadays the law refuses to do this. Whether this increases or decreases the bitterness of the parties is open to debate.

4. The divorce law should seek to promote a continuing relationship between the spouses as far as possible, particularly where there are children.[44] This is clearly desirable. As Beck and Beck-Gernsheim explain: 'Only someone equating marriage with sex, loving and living together can make the mistake that divorce means the end of marriage. If one concentrates on problems of material support, on the children and on a long common biography, divorce is quite obviously not

---

[36] Scott (1990).
[37] Which may or may not be objectionable.
[38] Home Office (1998).
[39] FLA 1996, s 1(1)(b).
[40] For a discussion of how the FLA 1996 sought to encourage reconciliation, see McCarthy, Walker and Hooper (2000).
[41] Walker (2000a).
[42] Richards and Dyson (1982).
[43] FLA 1996, s 1(1)(c)(i).
[44] FLA 1996, s 1(1)(c)(ii).

even the legal end of marriage but transforms itself into a new phase of post-marital "separation marriage" '.[45] Whether the divorce process is the correct mechanism for helping the parties to communicate after divorce, or is used at the best time, may be open to debate, but if the law can do anything to improve the parties' relationship after divorce, clearly it should.

5. The divorce process should not involve unnecessary expenditure for the state or the parties.[46] This is relatively uncontroversial. The difficulty is over the meaning of the word 'unnecessary'. In the bitterness of the moment, the parties might wish their lawyers to dispute every fact claimed by the other party or to hide as many assets as possible from the other party. Lawyers are certainly expensive, but that is in part, and only in part, because the parties misuse their lawyers' time to negotiate about matters which are, from one perspective, not worth the money involved. That said, it is much easier for an outsider to state what is and is not worth litigating, than it is for the divorcing couples themselves.

6. The divorce law should ensure that any risk to one of the parties, and to any children, of violence from the other party during the breakdown of the relationship, so far as is reasonably practicable, be removed or diminished. This is certainly a laudable aim of the divorce law. It may, however, conflict with the above aims. For example, the 'harder' divorce is, in the name of reinforcing the institution of marriage, the more likely it is that the abused party may have to put up with higher levels of abuse.

7. Some argue that the law should permit divorce in order to enable remarriage because otherwise there will be increased unmarried cohabitation after the breakdown of the spouses' relationship. One of the major aims of the Divorce Reform Act 1969 was to reduce the number of children born to unmarried parents by enabling people to remarry after divorce. In fact the number of such children increased.

8. The law should seek to deal with the emotional turmoil of the parties.[47] As Richards[48] points out:

> Any family lawyer can provide numerous examples of what has to be regarded as typical behaviour: he broke into her house and tipped the contents of the dustbin into the double bed where she and her new partner sleep; she went through the family photograph album cutting him out of each photo; he slashed the tyres of her, once their, car; she burnt the postcard he sent to the children while he was away on a business trip. We expect them both to be calm and rational, yet we present them with a system that allows them to take their irrational behaviour into the public arena of the court where it may be validated by the professionals who have become drawn into their warring world. Court contests seem to be designed to allow the trivia of everyday life to become elevated to a point where it becomes the basis of long-term decision-making ... I suggest that until we begin to address the feelings of the participants at divorce we cannot expect people to make sensible decisions about the long-term interests of their children.

---

[45] Beck and Beck-Gernsheim (1995: 147).
[46] FLA 1996, s 1(1)(c)(iii).
[47] Brown and Day Sclater (1999).
[48] M. Richards (1994: 312).

Whether the emotional side of divorce should be dealt with through the legal process itself or by co-ordinating counselling and legal services is open to debate. There is particular concern with the lack of support children receive when their parents separate. One recent study found that one-quarter of children said that no one had talked to them about their parents' separation. Only 5 per cent felt they had been given a full explanation and the opportunity to ask questions.[49]

5. THE PRESENT LAW ON DIVORCE: MATRIMONIAL CAUSES ACT 1973

A. The background to the Matrimonial Causes Act 1973

Prior to 1857 the ecclesiastical (church) courts determined the law on divorce.[50] This meant that although nullity decrees could be made, divorce was not available through the courts. The only form of divorce was by an Act of Parliament. This was a hugely expensive procedure that was open only to a few people. The Matrimonial Causes Act 1857 was the first Act to create an alternative to divorce by Act of Parliament. The Act created a divorce procedure through the courts. However, there was a difference between the grounds available to a husband and to a wife. For example, a husband could rely on his wife's adultery, but a wife could rely on a husband's adultery only if there were aggravating circumstances (e.g. the adultery was incestuous or there was some 'unnatural offence'). The Matrimonial Causes Act 1923 put the husband and wife in the same position – simple adultery was a ground of divorce for both. The grounds were extended further in the Matrimonial Causes Act 1937 to include cruelty, desertion or incurable insanity. The last ground was of particular significance because for the first time it recognised that a party could be divorced even though they had not behaved in a blameworthy way.

The Second World War led to an increase in the number of divorces. During the 1960s there was an increasing acceptance of divorce, even by religious bodies. There were growing calls for divorce to be available simply on the ground that the marriage had irretrievably broken down. The arguments in favour of making divorce easier particularly focused on couples whose marriages had failed and who were forced to form relationships out of marriage with new partners because they were unable to prove the grounds of divorce. There were particular concerns over the number of children being born to unmarried parents. It was argued that liberalising the divorce law would lead to a reduction in the number of children born outside marriage.[51] Rather surprisingly, in 1966 a group created by the Archbishop of Canterbury produced one of the leading documents (*Putting Asunder*) in favour of liberalising the law. The fact that the Church of England had come to accept the need for a liberalisation of the divorce law indicated that society's attitude towards divorce had truly changed. The report was referred to the Law Commission, who

---

[49] Dunn, J. and Deater-Deckard, K. (2001).
[50] For a discussion of the history of divorce law see Smart (2000a); Cretney (2003a).
[51] In fact the number of children born to unmarried parents did not fall following the relaxing of the divorce laws.

produced their own report: *Reform of the Grounds of Divorce: The Field of Choice.*[52] The Archbishop's group had suggested that the judge should consider each and every case to decide whether the marriage had irretrievably broken down. But the Law Commission thought the ideal was not practical, and instead proposed creating a new ground of divorce based on a period of separation.

The government decided not to adopt all of the Law Commission's proposals and the Divorce Reform Act 1969 sought to create a compromise between the different views. The decision was to abolish the old grounds for divorce and replace them with a single ground for divorce – that the marriage had irretrievably broken down. However, the only way of proving irretrievable breakdown was by establishing one of five facts. The divorce law was consolidated in the Matrimonial Causes Act 1973. Before turning to the present law, it is important to appreciate that the Family Law Act 1996 has since been passed, which sets out a complete reform of the law. However, the Lord Chancellor has announced that the Act will not be implemented.[53] This means that the present law is in a strange hiatus: the Matrimonial Causes Act 1973 is the present law but Parliament has indicated that it believes the Act needs to be reformed.[54] This chapter will therefore consider the current law in the Matrimonial Causes Act 1973; the rejected proposals of the Family Law Act 1996; and how the law might be reformed in the future.[55]

B. The current law: The Matrimonial Causes Act 1973

To understand how the Matrimonial Causes Act 1973 works in practice it is crucial to appreciate the court procedures that are in place to deal with petitions for divorce.

(i) The special procedure

Prior to 1973 each divorce required a hearing where the petitioner in open court would have to present evidence to support the grounds set out in the petition, by introducing witnesses if necessary. This was expensive, embarrassing and stressful for the parties and it involved the judiciary in lengthy hearings. This led to a special procedure that, by 1977, covered all grounds for divorce where the petition was undefended.[56] Under the special procedure the petitioner simply needs to lodge at the court the petition outlining the grounds for the divorce; a statement concerning the arrangements for the children; and an affidavit confirming the truth of these documents.[57] If the petition is undefended the case is entered onto the special procedure list and the district judge just has to read through the documents and, if satisfied that the petitioner has proved his or her case, pronounces a decree nisi. This

[52] Law Commission Report 6 (1966).
[53] Dyer (2000).
[54] Lord Chancellor's Department (2001).
[55] According to Thorpe LJ (2000), there is a widespread feeling amongst family lawyers that there is a need for some reform.
[56] The procedural change was reinforced by the withdrawal of legal aid for divorce.
[57] It is also necessary to provide other documents in some cases.

86

is done in an open court, although usually the parties are not present and the judge simply announces that a decree nisi is granted in cases numbered one to twenty (for example). So although there is some scrutiny to ensure that the formal paperwork is present, there is no attempt to ensure that what is stated on the petition is true. Indeed the petition may be entirely false; there is no need to prove the veracity of what is stated, unless the respondent defends the divorce. The law works on the assumption that if the respondent does not attempt to defend the petition then it can be assumed to be true. This assumption is in fact unreliable. If a respondent receives a petition based on falsehoods, he or she must decide whether or not to defend the petition. The expense involved in defending the petition (there is no legal aid available) and the reluctance of lawyers to become involved in defended divorces[58] means that very few petitions are defended. Even where divorces are defended, the vast majority of defences are unsuccessful.[59] The procedure can be said to increase bitterness between the parties, by denying the respondents opportunity to defend themselves from the allegations in the petition.[60] There would therefore be more than an element of truth in saying that the present law of divorce in England and Wales is *in effect* divorce on demand.

In *B v B (Divorce: Dismissal: Sham Marriages)*[61] a judge refused to grant five undefended petitions of divorce, having received evidence from the Queen's Proctor that the marriages had been entered into purely for immigration purposes and that the divorces were being sought shortly after indefinite leave to remain in the country had been granted. To grant the divorces in such a case, it was held, would be an abuse of the divorce system, although it must be said that there is something a little strange in punishing such abusers of the system by requiring them to remain married.

The divorce decree is completed in two stages. First the decree nisi is pronounced and later the decree absolute is declared. The divorce does not take effect until the decree absolute. Any time after six weeks from the decree nisi the petitioner can apply for a decree absolute; if the petitioner fails to apply then the respondent can apply for the decree to be made absolute any time after three months from the decree nisi.[62] The purpose of the gap in time between the decree nisi and decree absolute is to give time for any appeal against the decree nisi to be lodged.

About three-quarters of petitions are based on either adultery or unreasonable behaviour as these grounds do not involve delay. In 1994 the median length of time the divorce procedure took when the petition was based on one of the fault facts was 6.8 months for petitioning wives and 6.3 months for petitioning husbands.[63]

---

[58] They are widely regarded by lawyers as a waste of time. If one party is determined to obtain a divorce, is there any practical benefit in preventing them?

[59] In only four in 1,000 divorces did the judge reject the petition in 1988: Law Commission Report 170 (1988).

[60] Cretney (2003a: 383).

[61] [2003] FL 372.

[62] Although if the respondent applies the court has a discretion to refuse to make the decree absolute if there are financial matters unresolved (Matrimonial Causes Act 1973 (hereafter MCA 1973), s 9(2)). See e.g. *Manchanda v Manchanda* [1995] 2 FLR 590 CA.

[63] Haskey (1996a).

(ii) The ground for divorce

Divorce under the Matrimonial Causes Act 1973 is granted on the basis of a petition where one party (the petitioner) presents an application for divorce which the other party (the respondent) may choose either to defend or not. It is not possible to petition for divorce until the couple have been married for one year. The sole ground for divorce is set out in s 1(1) of the Matrimonial Causes Act 1973: that the marriage has irretrievably broken down. But the only way of proving irretrievable breakdown is by proving one of the five facts in s 1(2). If none of the five facts is proved then a divorce cannot be granted, even if the court is convinced that the marriage has irretrievably broken down.[64] Even if one of the facts is made out, if the court is convinced that the marriage has not irretrievably broken down, a divorce should not be granted. The five facts are as follows.

(a) The respondent's adultery

Section 1(2)(a) of the Matrimonial Causes Act 1973: 'that the respondent has committed adultery and the petitioner finds it intolerable to live with the respondent'.

The petitioner can rely on the fact that the respondent has committed adultery and that the petitioner finds it intolerable to live with the respondent. Three points should be stressed. First, a petitioner cannot rely on his or her own adultery. Secondly, it is not enough just to show that the respondent had committed adultery – it is also necessary to demonstrate that the petitioner finds it intolerable to live with the respondent. Thirdly, in *Cleary* v *Cleary*[65] it was established that it is not necessary to show that the reason why the petitioner cannot live with the respondent is due to the adultery. So if the husband commits adultery which the wife forgives, but then later the relationship breaks down for some other reason, the adultery fact can be made out. This suggests that the law believes that adultery is a symptom of a broken marriage, but does not of itself indicate that a marriage has broken down. However, s 2(1) of the Matrimonial Causes Act 1973 states that if the parties live together for more than six months after an act of adultery then the petition cannot be based on that act of adultery.

Adultery is defined as involving a voluntary act of sexual intercourse between the husband or wife and a third party of the opposite sex.[66] Homosexual intercourse or other forms of sexual activity not involving sexual intercourse will not constitute adultery, but may well constitute unreasonable behaviour under s 1(2)(b). If the respondent defends the petition and denies the adultery then the petitioner must prove it. The court will be willing to find that adultery took place if it could be demonstrated that the parties had the inclination and opportunity to commit adultery. For example, if the husband was seen dining with a woman and then retiring to a room to spend the night with her the court may be willing to assume that adultery took place.

---

[64] *Buffery* v *Buffery* [1988] 2 FLR 365, [1988] FCR 465 CA.
[65] [1974] 1 All ER 498.
[66] *Dennis* v *Dennis* [1995] 2 All ER 51.

In relation to the intolerability, the question is whether *this* petitioner finds it intolerable to live with this respondent. It does not matter whether most people would or would not find it intolerable with the respondent; it is only the reaction of the petitioner which is relevant.[67]

(b) The respondent's behaviour

Section 1(2)(b) of the Matrimonial Causes Act 1973: 'that the respondent has behaved in such a way that the petitioner cannot reasonably be expected to live with the respondent'.

The petitioner can rely on the ground that the respondent has behaved in such a way that the petitioner cannot reasonably be expected to live with him or her. A crucial point is that it is not enough just to prove that the respondent has engaged in unreasonable behaviour. It must be behaviour that a right-thinking person would think was such that this petitioner cannot reasonably be expected to live with the respondent.[68] So the court should take into account the personality of the parties in deciding whether the conduct was sufficient to prove the ground.[69] However, if the petitioner is reacting unreasonably to the respondent's behaviour the petitioner may fail.

Domestic violence would obviously fall within the definition of unreasonable behaviour, but a wide range of conduct can be included under this heading. It is also possible to rely on a series of incidents which, although minor in themselves, cumulatively establish that the petitioner cannot live with the respondent. There are probably few marriages where a party would not be able to recall a few incidents of unreasonable behaviour by his or her spouse. The Law Commission has acknowledged that 'virtually any spouse can assemble a list of events which, taken out of context, can be presented as unreasonable behaviour sufficient to found a divorce petition'.[70] The cases reveal a wide range of conduct constituting unreasonable behaviour, ranging from a DIY enthusiast husband who removed the door of the toilet and took eight months to replace it,[71] to a husband who required his wife to tickle his feet for hours every evening leaving his wife with uncontrollable movements in her hands.[72]

It should be stressed that although the behaviour must be unreasonable, there is no need for the respondent to be blameworthy.[73] For example, if a spouse suffers from an illness which causes him or her to behave in an unreasonable way, the fact that the behaviour was 'not their fault' would be irrelevant.[74] However, this rule causes difficulties. In *Pheasant* v *Pheasant*[75] the husband presented a petition on the behaviour factor, based on a claim that the wife did not provide spontaneous displays

---

[67] *Goodrich* v *Goodrich* [1971] 2 All ER 1340.
[68] *Birch* v *Birch* [1992] 1 FLR 564, [1992] 2 FCR 564.
[69] *Birch* v *Birch* [1992] 1 FLR 564, [1992] 2 FCR 564.
[70] Law Commission Report 170 (1988: 3.8).
[71] *O'Neill* v *O'Neill* [1975] 3 All ER 289.
[72] *Lines* v *Lines* (1963) The Times, 16 July. See also *Le Brocq* v *Le Brocq* [1964] 3 All ER 464 where the wife claimed that her husband's submissive character and refusal to argue infuriated her.
[73] *Gollins* v *Gollins* [1964] AC 644 HL.
[74] *Katz* v *Katz* [1972] 3 All ER 219.
[75] [1972] 1 All ER 587.

of emotion. It was held that this could not constitute unreasonable behaviour, as the wife had not breached any marital obligation. The case is perhaps better understood as revealing a reluctance of the courts to accept that omissions by a spouse can constitute unreasonable behaviour,[76] rather setting up a requirement that behaviour has to constitute a breach of an obligation in order to constitute unreasonable behaviour. However, it would be wrong to suggest that a decree cannot be based on the omissions of a spouse; it is just that the court will require more convincing that omissions can constitute unreasonable behaviour.[77] *Pheasant* v *Pheasant* can be contrasted with *Livingstone-Stallard* v *Livingstone-Stallard*,[78] where the divorce was granted on the basis of the constant criticisms and rudeness of the husband. In *Hadjimilitis (Tsavliris)* v *Tsavliris (Divorce: Irretrievable Breakdown)*[79] the unreasonable behaviour was claimed to be the husband's constant criticism; lack of warmth; controlling and demanding behaviour; public humiliation; lack of respect, insight, sensitivity and understanding, causing the wife depression and nervous strain.

If the spouses live together for six months after the last incident of unreasonable behaviour referred to in the petition then the court must take this into account when considering whether it was reasonable to expect the petitioner to live with the respondent.[80] However, if the period is less than six months the fact the parties lived together after the incident cannot be taken into account. The reason for this is that parties should not be deterred from attempting reconciliation for fear that it would make it harder to establish a fact.

(c) The respondent's desertion

Section 1(2)(c) of the Matrimonial Causes Act 1973: 'that the respondent has deserted the petitioner for a continuous period of at least two years immediately preceding the presentation of the petition'.

If the petitioner can show that the respondent has deserted the petitioner for a continuous period of two years preceding the petition, this could form the basis of the divorce application. Desertion has been defined as an unjustifiable withdrawal from cohabitation, without the consent of the remaining spouse and with the intent of being separated permanently. If the desertion is justifiable then it cannot be relied upon. It was justifiable for a wife to leave when the husband took in a 'second wife'.[81] Because it is also possible to rely on two years' separation with consent to the divorce,[82] desertion is rarely used.[83]

---

[76] The courts have been reluctant to accept that refusal to engage in sexual relations was necessarily unreasonable behaviour: *Mason* v *Mason* (1981) 11 Fam Law 143.

[77] *Thurlow* v *Thurlow* [1975] 2 All ER 979.

[78] [1974] 2 All ER 766.

[79] [2002] FL 883.

[80] It is still quite possible for a petition to be granted, despite the period of living together, where for example there was no alternative accommodation available for the petitioner: *Bradley* v *Bradley* [1973] 3 All ER 750.

[81] *Quoraishi* v *Quoraishi* [1985] FLR 780.

[82] MCA 1973, s 1(2)(d).

[83] Less than 1 per cent in 1994, according to Haskey (1996a).

(d) Two years' separation with the respondent's consent to the divorce
Section 1(2)(d) of the Matrimonial Causes Act 1973: 'that the parties to the marriage have lived apart for a continuous period of at least two years immediately preceding the presentation of the petition . . . and the respondent consents to a decree being granted'.

If the petitioner can establish that there has been two years' separation immediately before the presentation of the petition and that the respondent consents to the petition a divorce can be granted. This ground is significant because the law has accepted that divorce can be obtained by consent without proof of wrongdoing. The intention was that this would be the most commonly used ground, but in fact it has never exceeded 26.7 per cent of all divorces.[84]

A couple are living apart unless they are living with each other in the same household.[85] It is possible for them to be living apart in the same accommodation, if they are living separate lives. For example, in *Hollens v Hollens*[86] the husband and wife both lived in a house but did not speak, eat or sleep together. They were held to be living apart. However, in *Mouncer v Mouncer*,[87] where the spouses ate together and spoke to each other, it was decided that they were not living apart. The strict interpretation has been criticised on the basis that the more civilised the parties are towards each other during the 'separation', the more likely it is that the courts will find the fact not made out.[88] The situation can be particularly harsh on a couple who cannot afford alternative accommodation and where one of the first three grounds cannot be made out. The courts' approach can be explained on the basis that the more liberal the interpretation given to living apart, the closer the law is to accepting divorce on demand.

Not only must the parties be physically apart, there must also be a wish by one spouse to live apart, explained the Court of Appeal in *Santos v Santos*.[89] This need not be a mutual wish, nor need it be communicated. So if the husband is imprisoned and the spouses live separately for over two years this ground can be made out if one of the parties formed the intention to live separately. The requirement in *Santos v Santos*[90] of a mental element is controversial because there is no reference to it in the statute.

Section 2(5) permits the spouses to resume living together for one or more periods totalling six months. Such a period will not count towards the two years' living apart, but it will not stop the period running.

(e) Five years' separation
Section 1(2)(e) of the Matrimonial Causes Act 1973: 'that the parties to the marriage have lived apart for a continuous period of at least five years immediately preceding the presentation of the petition . . .'

---

[84] In 1979: Law Commission Report 170 (1988: Appendix B).
[85] MCA 1973, s 2(6).
[86] (1971) 115 SJ 327.
[87] [1972] 1 All ER 289.
[88] Hayes and Williams (1999: 529).
[89] [1972] Fam 247.
[90] [1972] Fam 247.

The petitioner can rely on the fact that the parties have been separated for five years prior to the date of the petition. This was the most controversial ground because it permitted divorce to be ordered against a spouse without his or her consent and without any proof of wrongdoing. Opponents called the section a 'Casanova's charter', although with a five-year wait between marriages, a Casanova would require patience!

(iii) Defences to petitions

1. If the petitioner relies on the ground of five years' separation[91] s 5 of the Matrimonial Causes Act 1973 provides a defence to a respondent who does not wish the divorce to go through.[92] The defence is available if the divorce would result in grave financial or other hardship to the respondent and that it would be wrong in all the circumstances to dissolve the marriage. A good example of how s 5 could be used is *K v K (Financial Provision)*,[93] where the court lacked the power to require the husband to make certain orders to equalise the position of the parties in respect of pension provision. The court felt that in the absence of such provision the wife would suffer grave financial hardship. The court adjourned the husband's petition for divorce until the husband voluntarily made the necessary financial arrangements. In *Archer v Archer*,[94] where the wife had considerable assets, the court refused to find that she would suffer grave financial hardship if the divorce were granted. In general the courts have been very reluctant to use s 5 even if divorce causes financial losses[95] or social ostracism.[96] It should be stressed that it is not enough just to show the hardship; it is also necessary to show that it would be wrong in all the circumstances to grant the decree.
2. If the petition is based on the two or five years' separation grounds then decree absolute should not be made unless the court is satisfied that the petitioner should not be required to make financial provision for the respondent, or that the financial provision made by the petitioner for the respondent is reasonable and fair, or the best that can be made in the circumstances.[97]
3. Under s 9(2) if three months have passed from the making of the decree nisi and the petitioner has not applied to have it made absolute then the respondent can apply to have the decree nisi made absolute. However, the court has the power to refuse to make the decree absolute on the respondent's application if that is appropriate in all the circumstances. In *O v O (Jurisdiction: Jewish Divorce)*[98] the

---

[91] MCA 1973, s 1(2)(e).
[92] FLA 1996, s 10 proposed a similar provision to the divorce procedure under MCA, s 5. Notably, s 10 would have also permitted a court to make an order preventing divorce if there was evidence that the children involved would suffer substantial harm.
[93] [1996] 3 FCR 158, [1997] 1 FLR 35.
[94] [1999] 1 FLR 327.
[95] *Julian v Julian* (1972) 116 SJ 763.
[96] *Banik v Banik* [1973] 3 All ER 45; *Rukat v Rukat* [1975] Fam 63.
[97] MCA 1973, s 10(2), (3). *Wickler v Wickler* [1998] 2 FLR 326 for an example of when the section was used and *Re G (Decree Absolute: Prejudice)* [2003] 1 FLR 870 where it was not.
[98] [2000] 2 FLR 147.

respondent husband refused to supply his wife with a *get*, which she required if her divorce was to be recognised within the Jewish religion. The wife petitioner therefore refused to apply to have the decree made absolute. The respondent husband applied under s 9(2) but the court refused to make the decree absolute until he supplied the *get*.[99]

4. Viljeon J in *O v O (Jurisdiction: Jewish Divorce)*[100] also suggested a court had the power to delay making absolute a decree nisi under the inherent jurisdiction if there were special reasons for doing so. The failure of the husband in that case to supply the *get* was a sufficiently special circumstance.

5. Under the Divorce (Religious Marriages) Act 2002 the court can refuse to make a decree absolute until the arrangements for a religious divorce have been made. The Act will be discussed further, below.

6. Where the couple have children of the family under the age of 16, the court when considering whether to make a decree nisi must consider the parties' proposals concerning the future of the child. On divorce the court must decide whether it should make any orders under the Children Act 1989. The same is true if the court directs that it should consider the arrangements for a child over 16. The court rarely so directs, but may do so if there are special circumstances, for example if the child is disabled. The court may ask for further evidence and even delay the making of the decree absolute in exceptional cases until it is in a position to make any appropriate orders in respect of the children. In practice, whatever the age of the child, unless either spouse has applied for an order, the court is unlikely to make one of its own volition. As Douglas et al. explain: 'The assumption which lies behind this approach is that parents may be trusted in most cases, to plan what is best for their children's futures, and that, where they are in agreement on this, it is unnecessary and potentially damaging for the state, in the guise of the court, to intervene.'[101]

6. PROBLEMS WITH THE PRESENT LAW

Moves to reform the Matrimonial Causes Act 1973 started with the Booth Committee Report in 1985. The report argued that defended divorces led to increased bitterness and disappointment. Parties, it was argued, should resolve issues themselves and disputes taken to court should be kept to a minimum. Subsequently, Law Commission Report 192[102] suggested significant reforms of the law. The report began by criticising the present law. These criticisms will now be considered.

---

[99] For another example, where there was a fear that the respondent would leave the jurisdiction without enabling the court to make effective ancillary relief orders, see *W v W (Decree Absolute)* [1998] 2 FCR 304.

[100] [2000] 2 FLR 147.

[101] Douglas, Murch, Scanlan and Perry (2000).

[102] Law Commission Report 192 (1990).

A. 'It is confusing and misleading'

The confusion is said to flow from the fact that although irretrievable breakdown is stated to be the ground for all divorces, it is in fact insufficient simply to show that the marriage is irretrievably broken down: one of the five facts must also be proved. A linked complaint is that the law requires the parties to cite a fact as the cause of the marital breakdown, a fact that might not actually be the real cause of the marital breakdown. Mears,[103] however, claims that the law is not misleading because lawyers can always explain the true position of the law to their clients. This is not, it must be said, a very satisfactory excuse for having a confusing law. That said, as Mears points out, this is not an area of the law which the public complains about on the grounds of it being impenetrable.

The law can also be criticised on the basis that its practice differs so much from the law as it appears in the statute books. Cretney puts it this way:

> English divorce law is in a state of confusion. The theory of the law remains that divorce is a matter in which the State has a vital interest, and that it is only to be allowed if the marriage can be demonstrated to have irretrievably broken down. But the practical reality is very different: divorce is readily and quickly available if both parties agree, and even if one of them is reluctant he or she will, faced with a divorce petition, almost always accept the inevitable: there is no point in denying that the marriage has broken down if one party firmly asserts that it has.[104]

B. 'It is discriminatory and unjust'

The Law Commission suggests that the ground of two years' separation is not readily available to those who are unable to afford alternative accommodation for those two years.[105] Those who cannot afford to live separately must use one of the fault-based grounds or wait for five years.[106] Mears[107] argues that this is also an unfair criticism because the only discrimination is against those who are unable to prove the ground of divorce. The validity of his objection depends on whether there is a good reason for requiring separation. If there is not the Law Commission's argument is valid.

It is also said by some to be unjust that the fault-based grounds do not reflect necessarily who is really responsible for the marital breakdown. For example, the fact that one party has committed adultery might imply that he or she is solely responsible for the breakdown of the relationship – while in fact the other party's bad behaviour may be said to have caused the adultery.

---

[103] Mears (1991).
[104] Cretney (2003a: 391).
[105] If the couple are in local authority housing they may not be entitled to separate housing until they have officially divorced.
[106] It is possible for two parties to live separately under one roof.
[107] Mears (1991).

C. 'It distorts the parties' bargaining positions'

The argument here concerns the situation where one spouse is desperate for the divorce to go through as quickly as possible but the other spouse is happy for there to be a delay in the divorce. As the party who is desperate for a divorce is dependent on the other party's consent (if it is a two-year petition) or willingness not to defend the petition, either way, this gives the non-consenting spouse a weapon that they can use to their advantage in the bargaining process. For example, if the spouses had separated and found new partners, and the husband for religious reasons wished to marry his new partner, but the wife was happy to cohabit with hers, then the wife could use the husband's desire for a divorce as soon as possible to extract a more generous settlement from him, by threatening not to consent to the divorce and thereby requiring him to wait until five years after their separation. Those who would seek to counter this argument would reply that the non-consenting spouse only has a tool if the consenting spouse cannot prove one of the grounds that Parliament has set down and, if so, the non-consenting spouse is within his or her rights to withhold consent.

D. 'It provokes unnecessary hostility and bitterness'

The system encourages the parties to use the fault-based grounds because they are so much quicker to use.[108] This can produce distress, bitterness and embarrassment in the making of that allegation, particularly because such allegations are made in public documents. The legal process, it is said, requires the parties to look to the past and at the bad aspects of their marriage. This might destroy any last hope of reconciliation. If a wife visits her solicitor and informs him or her that she wants to divorce her husband then the first thing the solicitor will do[109] will be to ask the wife to recount all the very worst things that her husband has done during the marriage. These will be typed up into a draft petition and sent to the husband. It would be hard to imagine a procedure better designed to increase the parties' ill feelings towards each other. Supporters of the present law would argue that ill feeling and bitterness are an inevitable part of divorce. This will be discussed further below.

E. 'It does nothing to save the marriage'

The parties are required to concentrate on making allegations rather than saving the marriage. The only provision specifically designed to assist reconciliation in the Matrimonial Causes Act 1973 is s 6. This states that if a petitioner consults a solicitor in connection with a divorce, the solicitor is required to certify whether or not the possibility of a reconciliation has been discussed and, if appropriate, whether the names and addresses of organisations or people that can help have been provided.[110] The aim is to ensure that a solicitor reflects carefully on whether the

---

[108] A divorce based on the fault-based grounds can often take between four and six months to complete.
[109] After discussing fees.
[110] MCA 1973, s 6(1).

parties ought to consider reconciliation. The provisions are, of course, of little use to those who do not instruct a solicitor.[111]

F. 'It can make things worse for the children'

Children whose parents divorce may suffer more if the parents are in conflict. The law does not attempt to reduce conflict; indeed, it may exacerbate conflict by focusing on one party's blameworthy conduct.

7. REFORMING THE DIVORCE LAW: THE FAILURE OF THE FAMILY LAW ACT 1996

Although the criticisms have persuaded many commentators and practitioners that the divorce law is in urgent need of reform, it must be pointed out that (unlike many other areas of family law) members of the public do not appear to get particularly agitated about it. There have not been demonstrations in the streets calling for reform of divorce law, even though there have in several other areas of the law. Nevertheless the criticism contained in the Law Commission report persuaded the government and Parliament decided to reform the law through the Family Law Act 1996. However, before putting the Act into effect, it was decided to try out the proposals in various pilot studies around the country. The results of the pilot studies were regarded by the government as very disappointing. It therefore decided not to implement the Family Law Act 1996 and Part II of the Act (which deals with the divorce procedure) will be repealed.[112] This chapter will still discuss the Act in outline because there is a widespread acceptance that the divorce law should be reformed in some way.[113] The reasons for the rejection of the law as set out in the Family Law Act 1996 will play a key role in discussions over how the divorce law should be reformed in the future.

A. General principles of the Family Law Act 1996

Section 1 of the Family Law Act, which sets out the general principles which would govern the law under the divorce part of the Act, provides:

> The court and any person, in exercising functions under or in consequence of Parts II and III, shall have regard to the following general principles—
>
> (a) that the institution of marriage is to be supported;
>
> (b) that the parties to a marriage which may have broken down are to be encouraged to take all practicable steps, whether by marriage counselling or otherwise, to save the marriage;
>
> (c) that a marriage which has irretrievably broken down and is being brought to an end should be brought to an end—
>
> (i) with minimum distress to the parties and to the children affected;

---

[111] Booth J (1985: paras 4.42–4.23).

[112] Lord Chancellor's Department (2001).

[113] The Lord Chancellor indicated he would continue to consider ways of reforming the divorce procedure despite the failure of the Family Law Act 1996 (Lord Chancellor's Department 2001).

(ii) with questions dealt with in a manner designed to promote as good a continuing relationship between the parties and any children affected as is possible in the circumstances; and

(iii) without costs being unreasonably incurred in connection with the procedures to be followed in bringing the marriage to an end; and

(d) that any risk to one of the parties to a marriage, and to any children, of violence from the other party should, so far as reasonably practicable, be removed or diminished.

These general principles were to guide not only judges but others carrying out activities relating to the divorce, including lawyers acting for clients, mediators, and Legal Aid Board officers.

B. A timetable for divorce procedures under the Family Law Act 1996

At the heart of the thinking behind the Act is that divorce should be a process over time rather than a one-off event. Before looking at some of the detailed provisions of the Act, a general outline of the proposed procedures will be provided by means of a timetable.[114] The procedures set out in the Act were in fact complicated, and this timetable is a simplification. It is based on the parties moving through the procedure as quickly as possible.

0 months	The spouse wishing to initiate the procedure must attend an 'information meeting'. The other spouse, if he or she wishes, can also attend the meeting. Following the information meeting the parties should spend the next three months considering whether they really want to get divorced.
3 months	One or both parties may file a statement of marital breakdown.[115] The statement of marital breakdown cannot be made until the parties have been married at least one year.[116]
3 months, 14 days	The period of reflection and consideration starts.[117] During this time the parties should continue to consider whether they want to get divorced. Marriage counselling facilities will be available. The parties should also look to the future and consider their relationship after divorce. In particular, arrangements should be made for residence and contact relating to any children, and any financial arrangements should be considered. The parties may consult a lawyer or mediator, if they have not done so already.
12 months, 14 days	If there are no children and neither party has applied for an extension of time, the parties can apply for the divorce order.[118]

---

[114] Bird and Cretney (1996) provide a useful analysis of the Act.

[115] FLA 1996, s 6.

[116] FLA 1996, s 6(2), (3).

[117] The 14 days are the period allowed for service of the statement of marriage breakdown on the other party.

[118] In cases where there are children of the parties or one spouse has applied for an extension of time, the period of reflection and consideration will be extended by a further six months. This extension will not apply if an occupation order or non-molestation order is in force, or if the court is satisfied that delaying the making of the divorce order would be significantly detrimental to the welfare of any child: FLA 1996, s 7.

The court will grant the divorce order if applied for providing the parties have been able to satisfy s 9 (requiring in essence that the arrangements over the parties' finances and children have been resolved). A party can apply for an order under s 10 to prevent the granting of the divorce order if there would be substantial financial or other hardship to the applicant spouse or the child if the divorce order were granted.

18 months, 14 days Those unable to apply at the 12-month stage (e.g. those with children or where a party has applied for an extension) may apply for a divorce order. The court will grant a divorce order subject to ss 9 and 10.

Some of the more controversial aspects of the proposals and the difficulties with them revealed by the pilot studies will now be considered in further detail.

C. The information meeting

The information meeting was to start the whole divorce procedure. Apart from a few exceptions,[119] anyone intending to initiate divorce proceedings was to attend an information meeting. It was not necessary for both spouses to attend a meeting but they could. The aims of the information meeting were as follows:[120]

1. To communicate a range of information on the divorce process and its consequences. This would cover information about the procedure of the divorce; the availability of mediation; the existence of free marriage guidance facilities and other counselling facilities; the possibility of seeking legal advice; and advice on matters associated with marriage breakdown such as housing and domestic violence.
2. To 'mark the seriousness of the step taken'. The parties were to be informed of the possible consequences of divorce and in particular the ways in which a child may suffer during a divorce. They were to be encouraged to think again about whether they really wished to obtain a divorce. The parties at the meeting were to be offered marriage guidance counselling and were to be encouraged to take it.[121]
3. To encourage the parties to use mediation, rather than relying on lawyers.

The pilot studies used a range of styles of information meetings including one-to-one meetings; group sessions; using CD-ROMs and computer technology; or a mixture of the three. The meetings were conducted by 'information providers', who were not necessarily lawyers, and who were employed on the basis of their communication skills.[122] The highest levels of satisfaction in the pilot studies were found with individual meetings; next came the group sessions and the least popular were the CD-ROMs.[123]

---

[119] Famous and disabled people were to be exempt from attending the meetings.
[120] FLA 1996, s 8(9) provides a complete list.
[121] FLA 1996, s 8(6)(b).
[122] Out-of-work actors were a popular category.
[123] Walker (2001a), although in part the lack of satisfaction with the CD-ROMs may result from lack of familiarity with computers.

The government's decision to abandon the implementation of the 1996 Act was largely caused by the lack of satisfaction with the information meetings.[124] The major concern was that the meetings did not succeed in encouraging the parties to attend mediation. Other statistics reveal successes: 90 per cent of attendees found the meetings useful and 13 per cent of those attending went to see a marriage counsellor, half of those with their spouse.[125] Most people found the meetings positive.[126] These have led at least one leading researcher to suggest the government should not have regarded the meetings as a failure, but rather that it had unrealistic expectations about what they could achieve.[127]

The key complaint made about the information meetings was that they were too 'structured, impersonal and routine'.[128] Many participants felt that they were being subjected to a prepared package, rather than being treated as individuals. In particular there were complaints that:

1. The 'information providers' were able only to provide information and were not able to give individual advice. This meant that although the parties were given general principles, they could not be given advice on how these principles applied to their particular case. This was particularly frustrating for some participants.
2. Some of the information given at the meeting was not relevant. For example, some participants found it irritating to listen to information about domestic violence injunctions when such information was not useful for them. Those who did not have children found the information relating to children unnecessary.
3. Part of this dissatisfaction was caused by the fact that those attending the information meeting had different purposes in mind. Some were attending the meeting in order to gain advice on a particular question; some simply had problems with their marriage and were not sure how to proceed; and some wished to pursue divorce proceedings.[129] It is not surprising that the same information was not appropriate for all these groups.
4. There were concerns that members of religious or ethnic minorities would be deterred from attending information meetings because the meetings were public and alien to their culture.[130]

What lessons for future law reform are to be learned from the failure of the information meetings in the pilot studies? First, no two divorces are the same. The information that one couple may require to guide them through their divorce may be quite irrelevant for another divorcing couple.[131] As Professor Walker, in her in-depth of study of the pilot information meetings, explains:

---

[124] Walker (1998; 1999; 2001a).
[125] Walker (2001a).
[126] Walker (2001b).
[127] Walker (2001b). See also Hale LJ (2000) who suggests that there were unrealistic expectations for the information meetings.
[128] Walker (2000b: 6).
[129] Walker (2000b).
[130] C. Bridge (2000).
[131] Arnold (2000). Interestingly, only 66 per cent of women who said that in theory information about violence was relevant to them found the information provided useful: C. Bridge (2000: 546), although it should be noted that there are concerns that victims of domestic violence may be reluctant to describe themselves as such: Richards and Stark (2000).

People want an individual meeting to be sensitive to their personal situation and the stage they have reached in the process of marriage breakdown, and flexible enough to focus on providing information which is relevant to their needs at that time. Relevance and timing are key factors in the provision of information.[132]

Secondly, those involved in the divorcing process strongly dislike being 'lectured to' and prefer discussions with information providers to being passive recipients of information. Indeed, attempts by the state to force divorcing couples to 'behave well' during divorce are likely to be of very limited effect. However, research in Scotland reported very positive outcomes to programmes aimed to assist separating parents understand and support their children.[133]

One aspect of the information meeting that proved useful is that they enabled participants to have access to a wide range of information and services. The government has now encouraged solicitors to take up the role of providers of information about services that may be useful to divorcing couples. Solicitors are to be encouraged to be part of Family Advice and Information Networks which will provide information and resources to those considering divorce.[134]

D. Encouragement of reconciliation

One of the main aims of the Family Law Act 1996 was to persuade couples to become reconciled.[135] At the information meeting couples were to be encouraged to consider saving their marriage and counsellors were available to assist those who wished to pursue this option. Further, the Act required a three-month gap between the information meeting and the making of the statement of marital breakdown.[136] The aim of this gap was to provide a 'cooling off' period, a time for the parties to consider reconciliation and the offer of marriage guidance facilities. These facilities were to be available free of charge throughout the period of 'reflection and consideration'. Indeed it was hoped that through the process of mediation the couple might decide to seek reconciliation. Mediators, it was thought, might be more willing than lawyers to encourage parties to consider reconciliation.[137]

The research from the pilot studies indicated that this aim was not being achieved. In fact, there was some evidence that the information meetings inclined those who were uncertain about their marriage towards divorce. Further, the information meetings were usually attended by only one of the parties (the one seeking the divorce), in which case talking about reconciliation was of little effect.[138] Interestingly, just under a half of respondents at the pilot studies attended a meeting with a marriage counsellor. However, many of those did not want to save their marriages, but wanted emotional support.[139] As the Lord Chancellor has indi-

---

[132] Walker (2001a).
[133] Mayes, Gillies, MacDonald and Wilson (2000).
[134] R. Carter (2001); Douglas and Murch (2002b); James (2003: 141).
[135] Mackay (2000).
[136] FLA 1996, s 8(2). There were exceptional circumstances where this requirement could be waived.
[137] This appears to be an unfounded hope: Dingwall and Greatbatch (2001).
[138] Walker (2001a).
[139] McCarthy (2001).

cated,[140] the story of the Family Law Act's attempts to save marriages is that efforts to rescue marriages need to focus on the period of time *before* the parties reach the stage of considering divorce. Indeed the government has recently announced that £5 million was to be given to Marriage and Relationship Support, a body which offers marriage guidance for couples whose relationship is going through a difficult time before they reach the stage of divorce.[141]

E. The length of the process

As noted earlier, under the present law (under the Matrimonial Causes Act 1973) a divorce could take four months where reliance is placed on a fault-based ground. Under the Family Law Act' 1996 the length of the proposed divorce procedure was a minimum of 12 months and 14 days. Where the divorcing spouses have children under 16[142] or one of the parties requests extra time for consideration,[143] the minimum could[144] increase to 18 months and 14 days. Cretney had doubts about whether people will spend the period of reflection and consideration reflecting and considering: 'May not some of those concerned prefer to spend their time in the far more pleasurable activity of conceiving – necessarily illegitimate – babies?'[145] It was comments like these that led the Lord Chancellor to mention the length of time for the divorce procedures in the Family Law Act 1996 as one of the reasons for proposing the repeal of Part II of the Act.

F. Counselling and mediation

When the Family Law Act 1996 was passed, the government intended mediation to be at the heart of the new divorce law.[146] For example, at the information meeting the parties were to be informed of the availability of mediation and they were to be encouraged to use it during the period of reflection and consideration.[147] There were to be special provisions to encourage those on legal aid to use mediation.[148] The pilot studies found that mediation was not popular. Only 7 per cent of those attending the information meetings wanted to use mediation and 39 per cent said that they were *more* likely to see a solicitor than they had been before the meeting. This was said by the Lord Chancellor to be a disappointment.[149] It may be that in

---

[140] Lord Chancellor's Department (2001).
[141] Lord Chancellor's Department (2003c). Such money has been used to support, for example, the 'Keep Love Alive' campaign.
[142] FLA 1996, s 7(11).
[143] FLA 1996, s 7(10), (13).
[144] The extensions to the period of reflection would not have applied automatically, for example, if the delay in making the divorce order would be significantly detrimental to the welfare of any child.
[145] Cretney (1996b).
[146] In Home Office (1998) mediation is presented as being generally preferable to litigation for disputes between family members.
[147] Although this is only open to those eligible for free legal aid and mediation (FLA 1996, s 23(3)). Others must fund mediation themselves.
[148] Legal Aid Act 1988, ss 15F–15H. Discussed in A. King (1988).
[149] Whether these findings should be regarded as a failure is discussed in Collier (1999) and Walker (2000b).

the light of the experience of the Family Law Act the government will be less keen to promote mediation than it was. As Wilson J (writing extra-judicially) put it:

> Mediation is a seductive figure whom government has been quick to embrace. But, like a mistress whose lover expected not to have properly to support her, she currently senses that her affair with government has cooled and is left worried about its long-term intentions.[150]

G. Divorce order to be granted only once the financial orders and arrangements for children are made

Under the procedure as set out in the Family Law Act 1996[151] the divorce order could normally only be granted when parties had made arrangements for the future.[152] This included arrangements concerning financial matters and their children. This marks a crucial difference between the law under the Family Law Act 1996 and that under the Matrimonial Causes Act 1973. Under the Family Law Act, in most cases, the divorce would only be granted if the parties had reached an agreement over the financial matters. However, under the Matrimonial Causes Act it is perfectly possible (and quite common) to obtain a divorce and only then turn to consider the financial orders that should be made. It is likely that in this regard, in any future reform, the Family Law Act's proposals will be adopted.

H. Protecting children's interests during divorce

The Family Law Act 1996 had a number of other special provisions seeking to promote the interests of children:

1. There was no general duty on the courts to consider the interests of the children during the divorce procedure. Under s 11 the court had a duty to pay particular regard to the wishes and feelings of children. However, it seems the section only operated where the court was considering whether or not to permit a divorce if the arrangements concerning the children were not yet resolved, and was not of wider application.
2. Under s 10 an order preventing divorce could be made if a divorce would cause a child substantial financial or other hardship and it would thus be wrong to dissolve the marriage. However, there was no wider power to prevent divorce in order to promote the interests of any child.
3. The information meetings were to stress to the attendees the importance of promoting any child's welfare and might offer advice on how to help children through the divorce. Information about counsellors trained to work with children was to be offered (s 8(9)(b)). There is much evidence that during a divorce children can feel helpless and do not understand what is happening.[153] The

---

[150] Wilson J (2003: 35).
[151] FLA 1996, s 5.
[152] FLA 1996, s 9. There were various exceptional circumstances in which this requirement need not be complied with, which are set out in FLA 1996, Sch 1.
[153] Lyon (1997b: 70).

research on pilot study information meetings indicated that the information on children was useful, although parents 'found it difficult to bridge the gap between knowing what to do to help their children and actually doing it'.[154]

4. The Lord Chancellor was empowered to make rules requiring lawyers to inform their clients that children's wishes, feelings and welfare should be considered.

5. There were duties on state-funded mediators: they were required 'to have arrangements designed to ensure that the parties are encouraged to consider the wishes and feelings of each child'; and to consider whether the children should attend the mediation sessions (s 27(8)).[155]

I. 'Quickie divorce'

There was concern that some of the media, having picked up on the fact that under the proposals proof of fault would no longer be required, had presented the proposed law as a 'quick and easy' divorce. In fact, as noted above, the procedure under the 1996 Act was to take much longer in most cases than the present law under the Matrimonial Causes Act 1973. The worry was that such misinformed perceptions might undermine marriage. Further, those who seek a divorce might be disappointed to find that a divorce could actually take over one and a half years. Supporters of the present law argue that the Matrimonial Causes Act 1973 presents a clever fiction: it appears very difficult to divorce, but in fact it can be quick and easy to do so.[156] Indeed, Cretney has argued that the government should have been more open about this effect of its proposals: 'It is concealing the reality – that divorce is to be available at the unilateral wish of either party, behind a comforting façade of consideration, reflect, reconciliation and counselling – that the government's proposals are most vulnerable to the charge of perpetuating the tradition of hypocrisy and humbug.'[157]

J. Idealisation of divorce

The Family Law Act 1996 can be criticised for presenting an idealised vision of divorce. It assumes that a fair number of couples will be reconciled; that people will wish to sit in a room together and mediate their dispute; and that time will be spent reflecting on and considering their relationship and the future. The pilot studies show that such aspirations for divorcing couples may be unrealistic. The law may hope that divorcing couples will behave in a 'sensible' way, but such wishes may ignore the psychological effects of divorce.[158] The law has only limited ability to influence social behaviour.[159] As Hasson puts it 'marital breakdown is a fact of life to be dealt with, rather than something to be corrected or discouraged.'[160]

---

[154] Walker (2001b: 4).
[155] There are codes of practice for mediators which cover when children should be involved: UK College of Mediators (1998).
[156] Deech (1990).
[157] Cretney (1996b: 52).
[158] Brown and Day Sclater (1999).
[159] James (2002).
[160] Hasson (2003: 362).

Reece has interpreted the Family Law Act as an attempt to encourage people to divorce responsibly.[161] It was recognising that people's relationships are based on choice; you cannot force someone to be happily married. However, when people make the momentous choice of divorce the law should ensure that that decision is taken with proper care and due consideration of the consequences. The information meetings and times for reflection and consideration were an attempt to do this. Other commentators have interpreted these periods of reflection as a punishment (a 'time out') imposed by the state on divorcing couples.[162]

Cynically, perhaps, Davis has suggested that giving the couple time for reflection was more about assuaging society's anxieties about divorce, than being for the benefit of the couple.[163] He argues that we must never forget that there is little the law can offer to heal the pain of divorce and there is much the law can do to make it worse.[164]

8. SOME GENERAL ISSUES ON DIVORCE

Following the failure of the Family Law Act 1996 it is 'back to the drawing board' so far as reform of the divorce law is concerned. This section will now consider some key issues which will need to be taken into account when deciding how the law should be reformed.

A. Individualisation of divorce

In the United States in particular there have been moves towards offering people a range of marriages from which they can choose the model which suits them best.[165] For example, a couple could choose a marriage that could end in divorce whenever either party chooses, in other words divorce on demand. However, if they wished, the parties could select a divorce clause stating that the marriage could only come to an end if adultery was proved, or maybe even that the marriage could never be ended.[166] These are sometimes known as 'covenant marriages'. The main argument in favour of this approach is that it provides freedom of choice, that parties should be able to choose to limit their freedom to divorce in order to give deeper commitment to the marriage. The argument can be made that in some marriages sacrifices need to be made early on in the marriage, for the long-term benefits of a committed relationship. For a party to leave after the other party has made sacrifices and before the benefits arrive is unjust. For example, a wife may decide to give up work, and concentrate on caring for the children and making the home. From her perspective, entering into a marriage where her husband is bound to stay with her for at least ten years may in fact be a more attractive option than a marriage where he

---

[161] Dewar (1998); Eekelaar (1999); Reece (2003).
[162] Reece (2000).
[163] Davis (2001).
[164] See the discussion in Douglas, Murch, Scanlan and Perry (2000); Davis (2001).
[165] Scott (1990); Lacey (1992); Rasmusen and Evans State (1998); Shaw Spaht (2002). The take-up rate for the 'covenant marriage' (with fault-based divorce) has been low (Ellman (2000b)).
[166] See discussion in Brinig (2000).

could leave at any time. Opponents of this approach argue that it would be very difficult to enforce. In the above example, preventing the husband from divorcing for ten years will not keep him from simply leaving his wife. Alternatively, the proposed clause could be redefined so that if either party ceases to cohabit with the other there would be a financial penalty. This could create particular problems of its own; in particular, there are concerns that it could lead to domestic violence. Further, the financial penalty might work against the interests of a poorer spouse who would be unable to make the payments necessary if she or he wished to separate.

Reece[167] sees a post-liberal approach to divorce in the Family Law Act 1996: that divorce should be an exercise of choice, but that this choice should be a carefully thought out and considered one. She explains: 'For the post-liberal, it is no longer sufficient to establish whether the subject wants to divorce: instead, we need to discover whether divorce would help him or her to realise himself or herself, or whether remaining married would more authentically reflect him or her.'[168]

B. No-fault versus fault-based divorce

There has been much debate over whether there should be a fault- or no-fault-based divorce system. In fact this rather simplifies the options available to the law. The forms of divorce law most discussed have been the following:

1. *A pure fault-based system.* This system allows divorce only if one party proves that the other party has wronged them in a particular way. The most common faults cited are that one party has committed adultery, or otherwise behaved in an unacceptable way.
2. *Requiring proof of irretrievable breakdown.* Here divorce would be granted if there is proof that the marriage has broken down and cannot be saved.
3. *Divorce over a period of time.* Divorce would be available after the spouses had waited a period of time following an indication that they wished to separate.
4. *Divorce by agreement.* If both parties agreed to a divorce, that would be available without proof of any fault on either side.
5. *Divorce on demand.* In this form divorce is granted at the request of one of the parties. There is no need to prove fault or irretrievable breakdown.

In modern times models 1 and 2 have few supporters, mostly on the basis that it is impossible for a court to ascertain whether there is irretrievable breakdown or who was at fault in causing the end of the marriage.[169] Around the world, legal systems have been moving towards a no-fault divorce procedure. Thorpe LJ[170] argues that no-fault divorce is 'the highest legislative priority for the family justice system'. Despite the wide support in academic circles for no-fault divorce, the arguments are not all one way and it is useful to consider the advantages and disadvantages of both fault and no-fault systems.

---

[167] Reece (2003).
[168] Reece (2003: 18).
[169] Bainham (2001a) discusses the role fault plays in family law generally.
[170] Thorpe LJ (2000).

(i) Arguments in favour of fault-based divorce

(a) Psychology

Richards argues that although the law may seek to discourage parties from asking who is to blame for the ending of the marriage, this is unrealistic:

> The coming of legal 'no fault' divorce has perhaps allowed us to believe that couples separate with a similar detached view of divorce. They don't. Blame, accusation, and strong feelings of injustice are the norm at divorce and they get in the way of couples making reasonable arrangements about children and money. Neither legal fiction of the lack of fault or imposed orders do anything to relieve the situation, rather the reverse.[171]

A no-fault system can therefore be criticised on the basis that it does not deal with the issues which really concern the parties.[172] Indeed, in one study of divorcing couples' attitudes to divorce the law's failure to address who was at fault in causing the breakdown of the marriage was cited as a major flaw.[173] To some divorcing spouses justice is only served if the court declares that the other party was the cause of the marriage breakdown.[174] Psychologists argue that blame is a psychologically crucial part of the divorce process,[175] and that making allegations of fault can even be cathartic. As one experienced mediator put it, for most of his clients: 'their marriage has not died, it has been killed'.[176]

While these arguments reveal the importance to divorcing parties of finding fault, some argue that it is not the place of the courtroom to explore these issues, especially at the taxpayer's expense.[177] Perhaps one benefit of mediation is that it can do something to deal with the parties' allegations of fault in a private setting, although most mediators try to persuade clients to focus on the future rather than the past.

(b) Justice

Linked to the argument above is a further point that it is not only the parties' psychological needs that are relevant here, but that it is the law's responsibility to uphold society's values and to discourage conduct which damages society.[178] Where one spouse is to blame for ending the marriage and thereby harming the children, the law should declare the wrongdoing and, if appropriate, punish it.[179] However, others reply that the law cannot prevent marital misconduct or even be responsible for deciding who has caused the end of a relationship.[180] For example,

---

[171] M. Richards (1994).
[172] Davis and Murch (1988); Day Sclater (1999). See also the discussion in Smart and Neale (1999: 138) suggesting the law fails to appreciate the different kinds of power exercisable on divorce.
[173] Davis and Murch (1988); Deech (1990).
[174] Davis, Cretney and Collins (1994).
[175] Day Sclater and Piper (1999).
[176] C. Richards (2001).
[177] Rasmusen (2002) surveys the range of legal remedies there may be to penalise adultery, apart from denying divorce.
[178] Law Commission Report 192 (1990: 181) found that 84 per cent of people in a survey agreed with the present law that adultery should be a ground for divorce (suggesting that the general public favours fault-based grounds).
[179] Swisher (1997).
[180] O'Donnovan (1993).

Bainham[181] has argued that the party who commits adultery may not be the one who is at fault, because they may have been driven to do so as a result of the coldness of their spouse. This is controversial but demonstrates that it is far from easy to determine who is at fault.

(c) Marriage

It can be argued that having no-fault divorce undermines marriage: no-fault divorce permits a spouse to end a marriage whenever she or he wishes and this undermines the ideal of marriage being a life-long obligation. As Baroness Young has argued:

> The message of no fault is clear. It is that breaking marriage vows, breaking a civil contract, does not matter. It undermines individual responsibility. It is an attack upon decent behaviour and fidelity. It violates common sense and creates injustice for anyone who believes in guilt and innocence.[182]

Others reply that if a couple are only staying together because of what the law says, their marriage is worth little; what makes marriages strong or weak is the love and commitment of the spouses and not the legal regulation. As already noted, there is much debate over whether the law on divorce can in fact affect the rate of marital breakdown.[183]

Some economists have entered the debate to argue in favour of using divorce to maintain the stability of marriage. Rowthorn[184] argues that a no-fault divorce system undermines the notion of commitment that is key to the nature of marriage.[185] It provides men, in particular, the opportunity to leave the marriage when it is opportune for them, leaving women severely disadvantaged. Cohen puts the argument this way:

> At the time of formation, the marriage contract promises gains to both parties. Yet the period of time over which these gains are realized is not symmetrical. As a rule, men obtaining early in the relationship, and women late. This follows from women's relative loss in value. Young women are valued as mates by both old and young men. When they choose to marry a particular man they give up all their other alternatives. . . . The creation of this long-term imbalance provides the opportunity for strategic behaviour whereby one of the parties, generally the man, will perform his obligations under the marriage contract only so long as he is receiving a net positive marginal benefit and will breach the contract unless otherwise constrained once the marginal benefit falls below his opportunity cost.[186]

Scott is sympathetic to the aims of those who seek a fault-based system of divorce. She argues that the law should impose restrictions on exiting marriage as these will 'discourage each spouse from pursing transitory preferences that are inconsistent with the couple's self-defined long-term interest' and therefore 'each spouse, knowing the other's commitment is enforceable, receives assurance that his or her investment in the relationship will be protected'.[187] However Scott argues

---

[181] Bainham (1995b).
[182] Baroness Young, Hansard (HL) Vol. 569, col. 1638.
[183] Ellman (2000b).
[184] Rowthorn (1999).
[185] Lewis (1999: 125).
[186] Cohen (2002: 25).
[187] Scott (2003: 162).

that fault is not the most effective way of doing this and instead suggests three other ways of providing a disincentive to divorce: mandatory waiting periods before divorce;[188] mandatory marital counselling before a divorce petition can be presented; and that on divorce most marital property be held on trust to provide for the children. Reece considers a similar argument from a different perspective. She suggests that it could be argued that no-fault divorce denies the parties the opportunity of engaging in a long-term committed project, fully immersing themselves in the marriage, confident that the other party cannot (without good reason) withdraw from the marriage.[189]

(ii) Arguments in favour of no-fault systems

(a) 'Empty shell'
It has been maintained that if one spouse wishes to divorce there is little value in forcing the couple to stay married. There is no point in keeping 'empty shell' marriages alive. Making divorce available only on proof of fault does not lead to happier marriages, but to parties separating, although legally married, or to cantankerous divorce. After all 'no statute, no matter how carefully and cleverly drafted can make two people love each other'.[190]

(b) The 'right to divorce'
Some argue that it is now a human right to divorce.[191] Forcing someone to remain married against their wishes is an infringement of their right to marry or right to family life. However, the European Court of Human Rights has made it clear that the European Convention does not include a right to divorce.[192]

(c) Bitterness
A common complaint is that a fault-based system promotes bitterness. By focusing the spouses' minds on the past and the unhappiness of the marriage and making these public, it is argued that fault-based systems exacerbate the anger and frustration they feel towards each other.

(d) The impossibility of allocating blame
We have already referred to this argument – that the law cannot really determine who was truly to blame for the break-up. There are practical difficulties in discovering the facts of the case, particularly as the husband and wife are often the only two witnesses. But even if all the facts were known, the court may still not be in a position to allocate blame. Bainham suggests that many people would take the view that for 'a very large number of people, the obligation of *lifelong* fidelity to one partner was at best an impossible dream'.[193]

---

[188] Ellman (2000b) argues that such waiting periods do more harm than good.
[189] Reece (2003: 121).
[190] Lord Chancellor's Department (1995: para 3).
[191] Bradley (1998).
[192] *Johnston v Ireland* (1986) 9 EHRR 203.
[193] Bainham (2002c: 177).

Although this chapter has summarised the arguments for and against fault-based divorce, it should be noted that the weight of opinion among practising and academic family lawyers is in favour of a no-fault-based system. Future reforms of the divorce law in England and Wales are very likely to abandon fault-based grounds of divorce. Indeed Cretney has argued that the courts on divorce should seek to do little more than they do on marriage, namely record-keeping. The court cannot even properly decide whether or not a marriage has irretrievably broken down.[194]

C. Length of time for the divorce process

The length of time a divorce should take is inherently problematic. On the one hand, there is concern that if the process moves too quickly then people who are having difficulties with their marriage and consult a solicitor for advice might find themselves divorced before they have had time to think about whether divorce is appropriate. Indeed, under the present law some people have complained that once they consulted a solicitor the matter was taken out of their hands and they lost control of what was happening. On the other hand, the longer the divorce takes, the greater the risk of increased domestic violence and bitterness, especially if the couple are not able to fund two homes until the financial settlement is made. Others suggest that the increased length of the divorce process will discourage people from marrying in the first place.[195] Certainly the length of a divorce under the proposals in the Family Law Act do not sit easily with the 'no delay' principle in s 1(2) of the Children Act 1989.[196] The most obvious effect of the length of time that the divorce procedure takes is that it delays remarriage. It might be argued that, given the vulnerability of second marriages to divorce, this might be seen as sensible.[197]

D. Reconciliation and divorce

We have already discussed the difficulties of using the law on divorce to encourage reconciliation. Attempting to save a marriage once one of the parties has taken the drastic step appears to be far too late. As indicated by the Lord Chancellor, in future, attempts to save marriages in trouble will primarily focus on the period of time before the parties seek to divorce.[198] Indeed, perhaps the possibility of requiring couples who are planning to marry to receive advice and counselling may be investigated.[199]

---

[194] Cretney (2002).
[195] Bainham (1998b).
[196] See Chapter 9.
[197] Eekelaar and Maclean (1997: 145) are concerned that the length of the period of reflection might increase cohabitation.
[198] Lord Chancellor's Department (2001). Concrete proposals are found in Lord Chancellor's Department (2002b).
[199] Barton (2003).

E. The Human Rights Act 1998 and divorce

According to *Johnston* v *Ireland*,[200] although the European Convention recognises a right to marry, this does not necessarily include a right to divorce. In *F* v *Switzerland*[201] it was confirmed that it was contrary to the Convention to forbid a man who had divorced three times from marrying for a fourth time until three years had elapsed. It was held that although stability of marriage was a legitimate aim, the length of the time restriction was unreasonable and disproportionate. These cases suggest that the Convention will allow the state to restrict access to divorce, but not unduly restrict access to marriage or remarriage.[202] These cases suggest that neither the law of divorce as set out in the Matrimonial Causes Act 1973 nor the rejected proposals under the Family Law Act 1996 could be challenged under the Human Rights Act 1998.

F. Financial arrangements to be made before divorce

As noted above, one of the significant effects of the Family Law Act 1996 was to be that a divorce order could not be granted until the arrangements for the future were resolved. By contrast, the present law under the Matrimonial Act 1973 allows divorce to be granted without the arrangements concerning financial matters and children being completely resolved. In fact, it might be years after the divorce when the financial orders are finally made. The government justified the Family Law Act approach by arguing that 'people who marry should discharge their obligations under-taken when they contracted their earlier marriage and also their responsibilities which they undertook when they became parents, before they become free to remarry'.[203] But there was more to it than that, because it was hoped that, as the parties made their arrangement for the future, they might in fact decide to abandon their divorce plans. For example, the hope was that a father, upon realising he would see his children only once a fortnight after the divorce, might decide to be reconciled with his wife.

Another argument in favour of the Family Law Act approach is that it ensures that the negotiations over the financial matters do not go on indefinitely. In contrast, the argument in favour of the Matrimonial Causes Act's approach is that a spouse may not be able emotionally to face deciding what should happen after the divorce until the divorce order is actually made, particularly if that spouse is opposed to the making of the decree.

G. Religion and divorce

Problems arise when the requirements for divorce in a religion do not match the legal requirements. For example, under Jewish religious law unless the former hus-band provides what is known as a *get*, the wife is not permitted to remarry.[204] She

---

[200] (1986) 9 EHRR 203 ECtHR.
[201] (1987) 10 EHRR 411 ECtHR.
[202] *Dennis* v *Dennis* [2000] 2 FLR 231.
[203] Lord Chancellor's Department (1995 para 4.26).
[204] She will then be an *agunah* (a 'chained wife').

can remarry under secular law, but not under religious law.[205] At first sight this appears to be solely a religious matter and it would be inappropriate for the law to intervene. But Hamilton has suggested four reasons why the state might want to intervene in these types of situations:[206]

1. To promote remarriage. Marriage and family are seen as the framework of society and the state should have the power to intervene to permit remarriage and to require a religion to recognise the marriage.
2. The right to marry under the European Convention[207] could be said to justify intervention by the law to recognise remarriage.
3. General perceptions of fairness and equality require that the courts and legislature intervene where a religious divorce is unjustly withheld.
4. An unscrupulous husband may use his control of the religious divorce to get a more favourable settlement.

However, there are serious problems for legal intervention in this area. The main one is that under Jewish law the *get* must be provided voluntarily, and so a court order to provide a *get* might be counter-productive.[208] So far the courts have been very unwilling to intervene where a *get* has not been provided.[209]

The Divorce (Religious Marriages) Act 2002 enables the courts to refuse to make a decree of divorce absolute unless a declaration has been made by both parties that they have taken such steps as are required to dissolve the marriage in religious terms. This does not resolve all the problems because it does not help in situations where the wife seeks a divorce but the husband refuses to grant it or in cases where the couple have already divorced.

H. Children and divorce

There has been much concern expressed that discussion of reform of divorce does not take sufficient account of the feelings and wishes of children. Day Sclater has summarised the research on children and divorce in this way: 'they want their views to be taken account of; they do not want to choose between parents, neither do they want to feel responsible for post-divorce arrangements for their care, but they do want to be involved in the changes that affect their lives, and to have a chance to contribute to the decision-making process'.[210] As we have seen, in relation to the present system and the Family Law Act 1996 proposals there are only limited procedures that permit children's voices to be heard. A recent survey found that only 34 per cent of parents in the sample had discussed the arrangements concerning children after divorce with their children.[211] This alone lends weight to a requirement that the court should consider the interests of children.[212] To what extent the

---

[205] There can be similar problems under Islamic law.
[206] Hamilton (1995: ch. 3).
[207] Article 12.
[208] Schuz (1996).
[209] *Brett v Brett* [1969] 1 All ER 1007.
[210] Day Sclater (2000: 80).
[211] Murch, Douglas, Scanlan et al. (1999).
[212] Lowe and Murch (2003).

law can or should seek to involve children in the divorce and court proceedings will be discussed further in Chapter 9.

9. PURSUING AN ACTION FOR INDUCING DIVORCE

There has been some debate over whether a spouse can sue a person who has broken up the marriage. For example, could a wife sue the woman who committed adultery with her husband if the adultery was the cause of the marital breakdown? This has been done in the United States, but it is very unlikely that such an action would be recognised in the UK. The action would have to be based in tort and probably on inducing a breach of contract. However, it is very likely that the court would see such an action as contrary to public policy.[213]

10. SEPARATION ORDERS

The effect of a separation order is that although the parties remain married, there is no legal obligation to cohabit. The significance of the order lies in the fact that it enables the court to make orders relating to financial provision for spouses.[214] A separation order is likely to be made where the parties have religious objections to divorce but have decided to live separately, or where there are financial benefits to the parties if they remain married (e.g. a widow's pension that will only be payable to a woman who has remained married to her husband). Few judicial separation orders are made: only 925 were made in 2001.[215]

11. DEATH AND MARRIAGE

A marriage comes to an end on the death of one of the parties. Usually there will be no doubt that a person has died.[216] However, there can be situations where, although it is suspected that someone has died, it cannot be proved. For example, if a husband fails to return home from work and his car is found abandoned near a cliff but his body is never found. This kind of situation puts the wife in a difficult position. Is she free to remarry or is she prevented from remarrying until she can prove that her husband has died?

There are two circumstances in which a person is entitled to assume that his or her spouse has died. The first is based on the seven-year ground. To rely on the seven-year ground it is necessary to show that there is no affirmative evidence that the person was alive for the seven years or more since their disappearance, and:

1. that there are persons who would be likely to have heard from the spouse during that period;

---

[213] See Pascoe (1998). See also Bagshaw (2001) and the possible use of the tort of deceit in family cases.
[214] Under FLA 1996, s 21, if one spouse dies intestate then the property shall devolve as if the other spouse had died prior to the intestacy.
[215] National Statistics (2001).
[216] Normally death and marriage are clearly evidenced by the registers of death and marriage.

2. that those persons have not heard from him or her; and
3. all appropriate enquiries have been made.[217]

This will give rise to a presumption of death, which could be rebutted if other evidence arises that shows that the spouse might still be alive. In *Thompson* v *Thompson*[218] it was stressed that 'pure speculation' that the spouse may be alive is insufficient to defeat the presumption of death.

The second ground for presuming death under s 19 of the Matrimonial Causes Act 1973 is:

> Any married person who alleges that reasonable grounds exist for supposing that the other party to the marriage is dead may present a petition to the court to have it presumed that the other party is dead and to have the marriage dissolved, and the court may, if satisfied that such reasonable grounds exist, grant a decree of presumption of death and dissolution of marriage.[219]

There is no need to show that seven years have passed since the spouse was last seen, but there must be convincing circumstantial evidence of death. It may be that the discovery of the car by the cliff in the example mentioned above would be insufficient on its own. In *Chard* v *Chard*,[220] where there was no reason why anyone would have heard from the missing wife, the court refused to presume her death even some 16 years after the wife was last seen. She had broken contact with her family and her husband, but it could not be presumed from the fact that she had not contacted anyone that she was dead.

12. MEDIATION

A. Introduction

In recent years there have been attempts to persuade divorcing couples[221] to make greater use of mediation rather than resorting to lawyers.[222] Indeed before their solicitors can be granted legal aid all legal aid clients must meet with a mediator and their case be assessed to see if it is suitable for mediation.[223] Three particular motivations are behind this change in emphasis. The first is a concern over the expense of lawyers. Lawyers' fees can be so high that they take up a large percentage of a divorcing family's assets.[224] Mediation is thought usually to be a cheaper option. Secondly, there is an ideological belief that better results for the parties will be obtained if they reach decisions for themselves rather than have the result imposed upon them by a judge. Thirdly, there is a perception that the legal system does not

---

[217] MCA 1973, s 19.
[218] [1956] P 414.
[219] MCA 1973, s 19.
[220] [1956] P 259.
[221] Indeed, in many areas of the law there have been moves to encourage the use of alternative dispute resolution techniques.
[222] Davis (1988); Walker, McCarthy and Timms (1994).
[223] FLA 1996, s 29. See the discussion and criticism of this provision in Davis, Bevan and Pearce (2001).
[224] In *Piglowska* v *Piglowski* [1999] 2 FLR 763 HL the total legal costs exceeded the total family assets.

deal with the psychological and emotional problems that parties face on divorce and that mediation offers the parties an opportunity to address these. Each of these alleged benefits is controversial, as we shall see. However, first, mediation must be defined.

B. What is mediation?

It is important to distinguish between reconciliation and mediation. The aim of reconciliation is to encourage the parties to abandon the divorce petition and to rescue their marriage. Mediation, however, accepts the fact of breakdown and attempts to assist the parties in deciding what should happen in the future. It may happen that in the course of working together to arrange their life post-divorce, the parties become reconciled, but that is not the purpose of mediation. The government White Paper on divorce reform defines mediation as 'a process in which an impartial third person, the mediator, assists couples considering separation or divorce to meet together to deal with the arrangements which need to be made for the future'.[225] The core goal in mediation is 'to help separating and divorcing couples to reach their own agreed joint decisions about future arrangements; to improve communications between them; and to help couples work together on the practical consequences of divorce with particular emphasis on their joint responsibilities to co-operate as parents in bringing up their children'.[226] A variety of different styles of mediation have been developed.[227] There are two main points of distinction. The first lies in how closely the mediation process is tied in with the court. The second involves the role played by the mediator. Regarding the first point of distinction, there are two basic forms of mediation in use: out-of-court mediation and in-court mediation.

(i) Out-of-court mediation

Out-of-court mediation is mediation that takes place outside of the court system. The benefit of this scheme is that it can be used before the legal process has begun: the parties have not yet met lawyers and do not yet have entrenched positions. Indeed, there is no need for the court to be notified that the mediation is taking place. At the end of the mediation it is common for the court to be presented with the agreement and be asked to formalise it by means of a consent order.[228]

(ii) In-court mediation

The aim of in-court mediation is to incorporate mediation within a court-based process. A typical system might be as follows: the district judge would meet the solicitors and the parties. If it is an appropriate case the district judge may direct

---

[225] Lord Chancellor's Department (1995: para 5.4).
[226] Lord Chancellor's Department (1995: para 6.17). See also S. Roberts (1995).
[227] Lord Chancellor's Advisory Committee on Legal Education and Conduct (1999) for recommendations to improve the training and accreditation of mediators.
[228] See Chapter 11.

the parties to attend a mediation meeting with a court welfare officer who will help the parties reach an agreement. A mediation meeting may involve any children over the age of nine, and the parties' solicitors may attend as well. The district judge will be available to make consent orders. If the parties cannot reach an agreement, a different court welfare officer may be required to produce a report. So although the mediation itself does not involve the judge, the mediation procedure is in a sense supervised by the judge and can be taken into account if the judge has to resolve the dispute.

The main disadvantage of the in-court mediation scheme is the fact that the parties may feel under pressure from the district judge to reach an agreement. Some have felt that in-court mediation blurs the distinction between adjudication and mediation.[229] In other words, although the mediated agreement is meant to be determined by the parties, in reality the judge or welfare officer makes the final decision and they persuade the parties to agree to it. Therefore, to talk of the decision as the parties' agreement is something of a fiction. Certainly with in-court mediation, the exact line between mediation and a court-imposed solution becomes ambiguous.

Under the Family Proceedings Rules 1999 a couple using court procedures to resolve financial issues between them must attend a Financial Dispute Resolution appointment,[230] where the judge will encourage the parties and the lawyers to reach a settlement. The parties and their lawyers will be expected to attend and make offers to settle. The Rules are designed to encourage lawyers to negotiate a settlement in as many cases as possible.

C. The role of the mediator

The other variable in forms of mediation is the function that the mediator plays. Roberts has suggested three roles a mediator could adopt:[231]

1. *Minimal intervention.* This model requires the mediator to ensure there is effective communication between the parties, but it is not the job of the mediator to influence the content of the agreement. So even if the mediator believes that the parties are reaching an agreement that is wholly unfair to one side, the mediator should not try to correct the balance. At the heart of this model is the notion that the agreement should be the parties' own decision. If the agreement seems fair to them then it is not for anyone else to declare it unfair.
2. *Directive intervention.* Under this model the mediator might provide additional information and seek to influence the content of the agreement if the proposed agreement is clearly unfair to one side or the other. He or she may try to persuade one or both parties to change their views, and may attempt to persuade the parties to agree to the arrangements the mediator believes are most suitable. However, ultimately the decision is for the parties to reach themselves.

---

[229] Davis, Cretney and Collins (1994: ch. 8).
[230] Family Proceedings Rules 1999, r. 2.61 SI 1999/3491.
[231] S. Roberts (1988).

3. *Therapeutic intervention.* Here the mediator focuses on the relationship between the parties. This model promotes the belief that the dispute is merely a symptom of a broken relationship. The time spent in mediation may not therefore focus on the actual issues in dispute, but on trying to improve the parties' relationship generally.

In the English and Welsh family law context the model of minimalist intervention is often used.[232] But this model does not render the mediator powerless. Most mediators hold a screening meeting before starting mediation and if, for example, it becomes clear that there has been serious violence in the past, they will refuse to go ahead with the mediation. Further, if during the course of the mediation the mediator is concerned that one party is being taken advantage of, it is always open to the mediator to stop the mediation and suggest that the parties seek legal advice.

Now the arguments over the benefits and disadvantages of mediation must be considered.[233]

D. The benefits of mediation

The following are some of the possible benefits of mediation:

1. Central to the arguments in favour of mediation is the idea that there is no 'right answer' to a particular dispute. If the parties reach a solution which is right for them, no one else should be able to regard their agreement as the wrong one. It could be said to be none of the state's business to seek to interfere in the arrangement the parties have reached. In part, mediation is fuelled by a belief that the court cannot claim that there is a particular solution that is 'just' or 'in the best interests of the child' because there are no agreed community values the law could use as a basis for such a solution. Indeed the House of Lords itself has accepted that in many cases a variety of solutions could be appropriate and there is not necessarily a right or wrong one.[234]

   There are three key issues here. The first is whether it is correct that there is no right answer for a court to declare. If there is not, then the solution reached by the parties is likely to be as good as the solution reached by anyone else. If, however, you do not accept this and believe that it is possible to state that some solutions are better than others, then the second key issue is whether there is a good reason to believe that the court is more likely to find a better solution than the parties in mediation. Thirdly, even if you accept that some solutions are better than others and that the court is more likely than the parties to find a better solution, there is still the issue of whether the state, through the courts, should be able to impose the right answer (or *a* right answer) on the parties. The law might want to set down a right answer on the divorcing couple because there are interests of either third parties or of the state which justify forcing a solution

---

[232] But see S. Roberts (2000) who suggests there is variation in practice over the style of mediation used.
[233] As Mantle (2001: 151) argues, much more research is required before it is possible properly to assess the advantages of mediation.
[234] *Piglowska* v *Piglowski* [1999] 2 FLR 763 HL.

on the parties.[235] So, for example, many argue that mediation is not acceptable because it does not adequately protect the interests of the child. There is nothing to prevent the parents reaching an agreement in mediation which does not promote the interests of the child. However, such an argument would need to demonstrate that allowing judges to resolve disputes over children has a better chance of promoting children's interests than letting parents reach the decision.

2. Supporters of mediation claim that the solutions agreed by the parties are more effective than court orders in the long term,[236] although one study found that only half of all mediated agreements were intact six months after they were reached.[237] There are three aspects to the argument that mediation produces more effective results. The first is that because the parties have reached the agreement themselves they will more easily be able to renegotiate it together if difficulties with the agreement subsequently arise. Secondly, the solution reached through mediation will be one which the parties can tailor to their particular lifestyles rather than being a formula applied by lawyers or judges to deal with 'these kinds of cases'. Thirdly, it is argued that as mediation can be hard work and emotionally exhausting, the parties will therefore feel more committed to the agreement than if it had been given to them by a judge.

3. Mediation enables the parties to communicate more effectively. The White Paper on mediation criticises the use of lawyers as detrimental to communication:

> Marriage breakdown and divorce are ... intimate processes, and negotiating at arm's length through lawyers can result in misunderstandings and reduction in communication between spouses. Lawyers have to translate what their clients say and pass it on to the other side. The other party's lawyers then translate again and pass this on to his or her client. There can thus be a good deal of misunderstanding and a good deal of anger about what is said and how it is said.[238]

Opponents of mediation argue that lawyers can filter out particularly offensive communications and so in fact reduce bitterness, while mediation, by contrast, can increase bitterness. It is said that placing people whose relationship is breaking down in a room together is bound to generate animosity and discord. Despite these arguments, it must be agreed that if mediation enables the parties to talk to each other effectively it has given them an invaluable gift. The question is: how many couples are helped and how many might find the process of mediation exacerbates bitterness? To this we have no clear answer.

Another aspect of this argument is that supporters of mediation claim that family disputes are unsuitable for court hearings. It is argued that court hearings work reasonably well in finding out past facts: 'who did what to whom and when'; but are less effective in building up ongoing relationships. In other

---

[235] Or even that there are rights that the divorcing couple have themselves which they should not be permitted to negotiate away in the process of mediation.
[236] For a discussion of the evidence against this proposition see Eekelaar, Maclean and Beinart (2000: 16).
[237] Mantle (2001: 141). He regards this rate as impressive, given the level of conflict between many parties in court cases.
[238] Lord Chancellor's Department (1995: para 5.19).

words, the court procedure works best if the parties are never going to have to see one another again. Mediation, it is claimed, is a more suitable basis for a long-term relationship.

4. A linked argument to the one made above is that mediation is a better forum for resolving the emotional issues involved in divorce. The mediation process can not only help resolve the dispute but perhaps also help the parties come to terms with their feelings about the other person and begin the post-breakdown healing process. One mediator claims that mediation enables parties to express their anger and expressions of blame more effectively than the legal process.[239] This might be why, on successful mediation, parties report high levels of satisfaction with the result.[240] While this is true where the procedure is successful, where it is unsuccessful the failure might simply increase the emotional anguish.

5. Mediation gives time for all issues which are important to the parties to be discussed. It has been a complaint of the legal process that it 'transforms' the parties' disputes. Their arguments are put into legal terminology and some issues that might be of concern to them are ignored.[241] For example, if a husband and wife were using lawyers and wanted help in resolving a dispute over who should keep their goldfish, lawyers would refuse to spend much time on this, regarding it as a trivial issue. Certainly a judge would not be impressed if asked to rule on who should keep the goldfish. By contrast, in mediation any matter which is important to the parties can be discussed and they can put their arguments in the language they wish to use rather than transforming the issue through legal terminology. Perhaps the real issue here is legal aid. Should public funds be used to resolve what appear to be trivial issues, whether in mediation or the courts? It could also be argued that the use of formal lawyer's language helps avoid antagonism between the parties, which might occur if more open language was used.

6. Mediation saves costs, or at least the government certainly hoped that mediation would save costs. By using just one mediator rather than two lawyers, and with the hourly rate for mediators being generally less than lawyers', savings could be made. The Law Commission suggested that the average mediation was £550 per case, while £1,565 was the average legal aid bill per case using lawyers.[242] In fact, whether or not mediation saves money depends on the success rate of mediation. The present research indicates that if all couples were required to attend state-subsidised mediation it would be likely to lead to increased, not reduced, costs. This is because of the extra costs involved where mediation fails. The Newcastle study (based on people volunteering for mediation) suggested that only about 39 per cent of mediations were wholly successful, 41 per cent were partially successful and 20 per cent failed.[243] For the 20 per cent of totally failed mediations[244] there are inevitably greater costs than if the parties had gone

[239] C. Richards (2001).
[240] Teitelbaum and Dupaix (1994).
[241] Sarat and Felstiner (1995).
[242] Law Commission Report 192 (1990).
[243] Newcastle Conciliation Project (1989). In Davis's (2000) research there was 45 per cent agreement on all issues and 24 per cent on some.
[244] The success rate would be likely to be significantly lower if mediation were forced on all divorcing couples, as the survey covered those who had volunteered to participate in mediation.

to lawyers to begin with, without using mediation.[245] If mediation is partly successful the parties still need to consult lawyers to resolve the remaining issues. But asking a lawyer to resolve 50 per cent of a dispute does not mean incurring only 50 per cent of what the cost would have been had he or she been asked to resolve the whole of the dispute. This is because it is the gathering together of all the facts and information that takes up most of a lawyer's time and this will need to be done whether the lawyer is resolving all or only a part of a dispute. So resolving 50 per cent of a dispute may cost 75 per cent of what the fee would have been for resolving all of a dispute, in which case it is not clear that mediation actually saves costs.[246] Even if the mediation is completely successful, there are some who believe the costs will be greater.[247]

An important study looking at the comparative costs of mediation and solicitor-based negotiation found that mediation could cost between 65 per cent and 115 per cent of the solicitor-based negotiation.[248] The study suggested that if the success rate for mediation fell below 60 per cent (which the evidence suggests it would be very likely to do), there would be no savings. The success rate of mediation for couples who sought mediation after attending an information meeting under the study for the Legal Services Commission was only 34 per cent for financial cases and 45 per cent for children cases.[249] A recent study found that the modal costs for non-for-profit mediators was £700; and £1,200 for solicitor-mediators. However, it is impossible to know how much these would have cost had lawyers dealt with these cases. More importantly it should not just be a question of whether mediation is cheaper, but whether its benefits (or disadvantages) are worth the expenditure (or savings).

E. The disadvantages of mediation

1. Some opponents of mediation argue that it is in fact impossible for a mediator to be purely impartial.[250] A mediator can influence the content of the agreement, through explicit as well as indirect means, such as body language or the way a mediator responds to one party's proposal.[251] For example, a husband might make a proposal and whether the mediator immediately asks the wife what she thinks about the proposal or asks the husband to expand on the proposal might have a profound effect on the course of the negotiation. Piper,[252] in her study of mediation, notes that a mediator's summaries of what has been said to date plays a crucial role in the mediation and yet often excludes what the mediator believes to be 'non-relevant matters'.[253]

---

[245] Ogus, Jones-Lee, Cloes and McCarthy (1990).
[246] Davis, Clisby, Cumming et al. (2003: 5) found that 57 per cent of their sample stated that their partner was not keen to resolve the legal disputes and compromise.
[247] Burrows (2000).
[248] Bevan and Davis (1999).
[249] Davis, Finch and Barnham (2003: 9). See similar figures for the success rate for mediation in the pilot studies:Walker (2001b: 3).
[250] Piper (1993); Dingwall and Greatbatch (1994).
[251] Dingwall (1988).
[252] Piper (1996).
[253] See also Kruk (1998).

Dingwall and Greatbatch found that mediators had 'the parameters of the permissible',[254] in other words a band of orders they thought acceptable. There would be no intervention as long as the negotiations were within that band, but if the mediation appeared to be going beyond that band the mediator would seek to influence the discussion.[255]

If the mediator does directly or indirectly affect the content of the agreement then there are concerns that mediation will become, in effect, adjudication in secret. The mediator will act like a judge but without having to give any reasons or be publicly accountable for the outcome. For example, one recent study suggested that mediators often spoke of a father's right of contact with his children, even though the courts have expressly denied such a right.[256]

2. One powerful criticism of mediation is that mediation can work against the interests of the weaker party.[257] Weakness in the bargaining position may stem from three sources. First, a lack of information, coupled with the inability to verify presented information. Every family lawyer would say that it is common for rich spouses to portray themselves as impoverished. As mediation has a less effective method of checking levels of wealth compared with disclosure mechanisms used by lawyers, it is likely to work against the interests of the less well-off spouse.[258] A party's lack of personal expert knowledge may also impede their bargaining position. For example, if one party is a trained accountant and the other has an aversion to figures then when the parties discuss what should happen to the pension or the endowment mortgage there might be an inequality of power. The second weakness in the bargaining process may result from a lack of negotiation skills. One party may regularly take part in negotiations in the course of his or her work and may be trained to push for an agreement, while the other may not. The third weakness can be psychological. Women,[259] it is argued by some, are, in general, by nature conflict-adverse.[260] They may more readily agree rather than argue, partly as a result of being socially conditioned to avoid conflict.[261] There is also an argument that women generally may put greater value on things that are not material in value and/or they may have lower self-esteem.[262] It may well be that the wife's primary concern is that she keeps the children and is willing to agree to anything in order to achieve that goal.[263]

[254] Dingwall and Greatbatch (2001).
[255] One example given was that the mediator did not mind whether the father saw the children one weekend in three or four, but would not be happy if the father was to have no contact.
[256] Davis, Pearce, Bird et al. (2000). See further the discussion on contact in Chapter 9.
[257] One study of mediation at a county court found that a quarter mediated without being legally represented.
[258] In their sample Davis, Clisby, Cumming et al. (2003: 5) found high levels of mistrust among those who were mediating.
[259] One does not have to accept the gendered way the argument is presented in order to appreciate its weight. For example, if one party is conflict-adverse, regardless of whether they are a man or a woman, they may be at a disadvantage.
[260] Dingwall and Greatbatch (1994) express concerns that mediation may work against people from certain cultural and ethnic backgrounds.
[261] Grillo (1991) argues that women are more concerned than men with keeping the relationship amicable.
[262] P. Bryan (1992).
[263] Davis and Roberts (1989) argued that there was no evidence that women did worse in mediation but P. Bryan (1992), for example, strongly disagrees.

There is some evidence that women are more likely to suffer depression than men at the end of a relationship, and this may affect their bargaining ability.[264] However, these points are controversial and there is in fact much debate over whether women do better or worse using mediation.

There are particular concerns about using mediation where the relationship has been characterised by violence.[265] In such cases mediators themselves accept that mediation is unsuitable because co-operation and proper negotiations can only take place where there is no abuse or fear. The concern is whether the mediators can always ascertain those cases where there has been domestic violence.[266] Particularly difficult are cases where the parties do not regard themselves as victims of domestic violence.[267]

3. Mediation can be skewed by the norms of society. Neale and Smart have argued that even if one accepts that the mediators and the law are not influencing the agreement, it is wrong to believe that the values of the parties are the only ones that shape the agreement. The norms of society (which may not be legal norms) will predominate.[268] Researchers have found that 'folk myths' concerning what should happen on divorce can play an important part in the mediation.[269] Specifically, Neale and Smart are concerned that if the parties focus on protecting the children's welfare then the burden of caring for the children will fall mostly on mothers, based on the common assumption that the woman should look after the children.[270] Further, Neale and Smart are concerned that the money and property will be seen as belonging to the wage earner, most often the husband. So the wife will be in the weaker position of arguing for some of 'his' money, rather than discussing how to distribute 'their' money.[271] This may be partly circumvented by allowing the parties to receive legal advice before or during mediation, although the more legal advice is used the greater the costs.

4. There is concern that if mediation becomes widely used, the quality of the court-based procedure and the law itself will suffer, because it will be less often used.[272]

5. As already mentioned, there are concerns over whether mediation affects children's interests. As Richards explains:

> while mediation may do much to help parents reach agreements and set up workable arrangements for children, it cannot protect children's interests. It must rely on the information about children that the parties bring to the sessions. Necessarily this information will be presented in the light of parental perceptions, hopes, fears, anxieties, and guilt. In

---

[264] P. Bryan (1992).
[265] Kaganas and Piper (1994). Contrast S. Roberts (1996).
[266] Diduck and Kaganas (1999: 360–1).
[267] Davis, Clisby, Cumming et al. (2003: 5) found that 41 per cent of women and 21 per cent of men in their sample stated that fear of violence made it difficult to resolve issues in their case.
[268] Neale and Smart (1997).
[269] Piper (1996).
[270] Walker, McCarthy and Timms (1994) found that women felt greater guilt at the occurrence of the divorce and might therefore be in a weaker bargaining position.
[271] The difficulty in distinguishing offers from threats is discussed in Altman (1996).
[272] Ingleby (1997: 400).

most cases this will serve children's interests well enough, but it cannot be termed protection as it is not based on an independent view.[273]

As well as the question of whether mediation will protect the interests of children, there is another question of whether children should be involved in the proceedings. Many think that children should not be involved in mediation, especially given the tension that is often felt early on in a mediation. There may be a case for having a session with the children once the parties have reached a basic agreement.

6. There are doubts whether mediators have the expertise to consider the complex tax and financial issues which may have to be dealt with on divorce.[274] For example, even experienced solicitors struggle with the valuation and sharing of pensions on divorce and most seek expert advice. To expect mediators and the couple to deal with such issues is to expect too much.

7. An argument can be made that mediation does not acknowledge the psychological realities of many divorces.[275] Although it would be nice if every divorcing couple amicably reached an agreement over their children and finances, and that would reassure us that all was well with 'the family', the anger, fear and bitterness means such a pleasant picture is for the few. It is anger, bitterness and fear that dominates, rather than a desire to sit down and talk the matter out.

F. The false dichotomy of mediation and litigation

In considering the benefits and disadvantages of mediation it is important to stress that the choice is not between mediation and litigation in the courtroom, but rather between mediation and negotiation between lawyers.[276] Images of lawyers aggressively fighting cases out in the court room is exceptional.[277] In fact, few cases actually reach the courts for settlement. In a major study by Ingleby not one case in his sample resulted in a contested final hearing.[278] Davis et al. noted:

> ... some solicitors gave us the impression that they regarded trials of the ancillary relief issue in much the same light as they viewed the white rhino – a possibly mythical creature which was outside their immediate experience.[279]

A recent study of clients' experiences of solicitors and mediators found no evidence of lawyers as 'aggressive troublemakers'.[280]

Supporters of a lawyer-based approach argue that negotiations between lawyers ensure that the bargaining process is on an equal footing and that values which the law wishes to promote can infiltrate the negotiations. The lawyer also plays an important role in being partisan: being on the side of the client.[281] It is, of course,

---

[273] M. Richards (1995b: 225).
[274] Dingwall and Greatbatch (2001).
[275] Day Sclater (1999).
[276] Eekelaar, Maclean and Beinart (2000).
[277] Davis (2000).
[278] Ingleby (1992).
[279] Davis, Cretney and Collins (1994: 40).
[280] Davis, Finch and Fitzgerald (2001).
[281] Davis, Finch and Fitzgerald (2001).

possible to go through the divorce procedure without using lawyers and mediators. To many clients having someone to take their side and fight their corner is of great psychological benefit during the trauma of divorce. Interestingly of clients who had used both lawyers and mediators in one study, 60 per cent stated their lawyers had been helpful, but only 35 per cent their mediators.[282]

Section 15 of the Legal Aid Act 1988 requires all people seeking legal aid for a family dispute to attend a meeting with a mediator, who will assess their suitability for mediation.[283] They are only entitled to legal aid if their case is unsuitable for mediation. Research suggests that few of those attending such meetings are enthusiastic or interested in mediation and that in the majority of cases the mediator assesses the case unsuitable for mediation.[284] However, worryingly, a recent study found that 57 per cent of parents who indicated a fear of violence were still deemed suitable for mediation by mediators at the initial meeting.[285] This scheme can be regarded as putting pressure on legal aid clients to use mediation rather than lawyers (a pressure that privately funded clients do not have).

13. CONCLUSION

The present law on divorce is in a strange state. Although the Matrimonial Causes Act 1973 represents the present law, Parliament had indicated that it regards it as unsatisfactory and proposed reforms through the Family Law Act 1996. However, because of the difficulties revealed in the pilot studies, the Act's divorce reforms have been abandoned. The chapter has focused on the complexity of the role of the state during divorce. On the one hand, there are concerns that if divorce is 'too easy' this may be thought to destabilise marriage. On the other hand, any attempt to make divorce available only to those who can prove that their marriage has broken down may involve the parties in costly and bitter disputes over whether the marriage can be saved. The Family Law Act 1996 can be seen as an attempt by the law to persuade the parties to behave in particular ways on divorce: namely to act without anger or bitterness and to reach amicable settlements. The pilot studies reveal that human nature is not so readily manipulated. The difficulty for the law here is how to channel the strong feelings often produced during divorce through a legal system traditionally designed to be governed by rational thought rather than wild emotion. As Eekelaar suggests:

> We may, however, become uncomfortable when the government intervenes at these points in the institutional processes of marriage and divorce and attempts to impose its own vision of how people should be behaving at these times. At best it risks being made to appear foolish and ineffectual. Worse it can appear heavy-handed, domineering and insensitive . . .[286]

---

[282] Davis, Clisby, Cumming et al. (2003: 11).
[283] Davis, Clisby, Cumming et al. (2003) discuss the operation of this provision in practice.
[284] Davis, Pearce, Bird et al. (2000); Davis, Clisby, Cumming et al. (2003).
[285] Davis, Pearce, Bird et al. (2000: 58).
[286] Eekelaar (1999: 387).

4

FAMILY PROPERTY

The courts' power to redistribute the property of spouses on divorce and make orders for maintenance will be discussed in Chapter 5. In this chapter the parties' financial position during their relationship, whether they are married or unmarried, will be considered. There are two themes which run through the chapter. The first is to what extent the family should be regarded as individuals each with their own property interests, and to what extent the law should recognise that property is owned by the family as a group of people. The second is how to deal with disputes between family members and third parties. The difficulty is this: in cases involving disputes between family members the law may want to protect the interests of each member by giving them each an interest in the property, even if the property is formally in the name of only one person. However, so doing causes difficulties when a third party is involved because property which might appear to belong to one person may be subject to the rights of other family members.

1. THE REALITY OF FAMILY FINANCES

As shall be seen, the law does not normally intervene in the way in which the family distributes its money among its members. It is therefore important to understand how families deal with their money and property in the absence of formal legal regulation.

One notable feature of the latter half of the twentieth century was the increasing number of women in paid employment. Now three-quarters of all women aged 35–45 are employed.[1] Indeed it has been argued that the lifestyle of many families can only be maintained by having two wage earners.[2] This has led Morgan to maintain that some men cannot afford a 'traditional marriage' (i.e. where the husband is employed, but the wife does not seek paid employment) and married couples relying on one income cannot afford to have children.[3]

Although at one time stigma attached to a mother who was in employment while raising children, a survey into women's attitudes to combining paid work and raising children suggested that the stigma is now less.[4] Eight out of ten women accepted that most mothers have to do paid work to support their families these days. However, more than eight out of ten women said that they thought mothers felt guilty about 'leaving' their children, especially if below school age. Notably, the

[1] Office For National Statistics (1994: 57).
[2] Irvine (1999).
[3] P. Morgan (1999b: 82).
[4] Bryson, Budd, Lewis and Elam (2000).

government has launched a scheme known as the 'New Deal',[5] specifically designed to encourage lone parents (the large majority of whom are women) to seek employment.

Despite the widespread existence of families with dual earners, there is still a common presumption that men are the main breadwinners and this presumption has a powerful effect. Pahl argues that:

> inequality in the wider society meshes with inequality within the household. A woman may contribute a higher proportion of her earnings to housekeeping than her husband, but her income is still likely to be regarded as marginal; a man may contribute a lower proportion of his earnings, but he still feels justified in spending more than his wife on leisure because both define him as the breadwinner.[6]

Many more women than men fall into the category of homemakers. Homemakers are largely unpaid and have no access to unemployment or sickness benefits.[7] Further, in social terms the work is undervalued and lacks prestige.

Pahl has identified four systems of money management adopted in families:

1. *Wife management or the whole wage system.* The wife is responsible for managing the finances of the household and is responsible for all expenditure, except for the personal spending of the husband.
2. *Allowance system.* Typically this involves the husband giving the wife a set amount every week or month. She is responsible for paying for specific items of household expenditure and the rest of the money remains under the control of the husband.
3. *Pooling system or shared management.* Here the couple have a joint account or common kitty into which both pay in and from which both draw out.
4. *Independent management system.* Here each spouse has his or her own separate fund and there is no mixing of funds. They reach an agreement over who pays which bills.

Pahl argues that the system adopted can have important consequences on the way money is spent. She explains:

> Where wives control finances a higher proportion of household income is likely to be spent on food and day-to-day living expenses than is the case where husbands control finances; additional income brought into the household by the wife is more likely to be spent on the food than additional money earned by the husband ... husbands are more likely to spend more on leisure than wives.[8]

Children are also engaged in unpaid work, particularly in babysitting or working in the family business.[9] Children are protected by the Children and Young Persons Act 1933 and the Children (Protection at Work) Regulations 1998, which provide that no child under 14 can be employed in any work other than on an occasional basis or as an employee of the parents in light agricultural or horticultural work.

---

[5] Outlined in Douglas (2000a).
[6] Pahl (1989: 170).
[7] Employment Rights Act 1996, s 161.
[8] Pahl (1989: 151–2).
[9] Discussed in Diduck and Kaganas (1999: 174).

The light work must not jeopardise the child's safety, health, development, attendance at school, or participation in work experience.[10]

2. THE OWNERSHIP OF FAMILY PROPERTY: GENERAL THEORY

Who owns the family's property?[11] Of course, most of the time there is no need for members of a family to know who in law owns a particular piece of family property. In most families 'who owns the television?' is not a question that is usually asked. (Ownership of the remote control unit is, of course, another question!) There are, however, a number of reasons why it can be important to know who owns a certain piece of property:

1. If the couple are unmarried then it is crucial to know who owns what because there is no power in the court to redistribute property if the relationship breaks down. Therefore when the couple separate each person is entitled to take whatever property is theirs.
2. If someone becomes bankrupt then all of their property falls into the hands of the trustee in bankruptcy. The property of the bankrupt's spouse or partner does not. It is therefore necessary to know whether certain property belongs to the bankrupt person or their partner.
3. If a third party wishes to purchase property it may be important to know who is the owner. Particularly when a house is to be sold, it is necessary to know who the owner of the house is so that he or she can sign the appropriate paperwork. There have been cases where husbands have sold the family home behind their wives' backs. In such cases it is important to know whether the wife had an interest in the property and, if so, whether the purchaser is bound by her interest.
4. On the death of a family member it is important to know who owns what. So, if a wife left all her books to her brother in her will, it would be important to know which books were hers and which books belonged to her husband.
5. Ownership of family property has important symbolic power. At one time the husband owned all of his wife's property. This reflected the fact that he was regarded as in control of all of the family's affairs. It is arguable that if the law were to state that family property is jointly owned, this would reflect a principle of equality between spouses in marriage.

Law in this area should seek to pursue three particular aims. First, the law should produce as high a degree of certainty as possible. Secondly, the law should reflect the wishes and expectations of most couples. Thirdly, the law should be practical and easy to apply. Some of the approaches the law could take are as follows:

1. *Sole ownership.* The law could decide that one spouse owns all the family's property. Historically, a woman could not own property in her own right[12] and so the

---

[10] Children and Young Persons Act 1933, s 18.
[11] Under s 17 of the Married Women's Property Act 1882 an application can be made to a court for a declaration of ownership if the couple are married.
[12] The Married Women's Property Act 1882 has removed the incapacity of the wife to own property.

husband owned all the family's property. This approach might have the benefit of certainty, but it would not reflect the expectations of many couples nowadays and would be unacceptable in a society committed to equality between men and women.

2. *Community of property.*[13] The law could state that on marriage (or cohabitation) all property becomes jointly owned.[14] This may be thought to reflect the expectations of most couples, but does it? On marriage would the husband expect a half interest in his wife's collection of shoes? The law could deal with such concerns by producing exceptions to the rule, but these might create uncertainty.[15]

3. *Community of gains.* The law could be that each party owns the property he or she owned before the marriage (or cohabitation), but all property acquired during the relationship will be jointly owned. Many countries that have adopted this approach have created exceptions for special gifts or inheritance received during the relationship.

4. *Community of common property.* The law could take the approach that all items intended for joint use would be jointly owned.[16] So the car, television, cooker etc. would be jointly owned but the wife's golf clubs would not. This approach could be criticised on the basis that in some cases there might be doubt whether a particular item was for common use and this could cause uncertainty over ownership.

5. *Purchaser-based ownership.* Another option is simply to use the normal rules of property and not create any particular regime for couples. In effect this would mean that the person who buys a piece of property owns it. The objection to this is that it may be a matter of chance whose money happened to be used to buy a piece of property.

6. *Intention-based ownership.* The law could decide that ownership would be determined by the intentions of the parties. There would have to be rules that would apply if it were not possible to discover the parties' intentions. This approach would have the disadvantage of making it particularly difficult for third parties to ascertain the ownership of a piece of property.

As we shall see, the law of England and Wales does not plump for one or other of these approaches but instead is based on a rather arbitrary set of rules, which have developed over the years. The Law Commission did produce a report in an attempt to formulate a more coherent approach, although it found it difficult to find a single principle that could apply across the board and its proposals were not implemented by Parliament.[17]

Before setting out the law it is necessary to distinguish between real property and personal property. Basically, real property is land and buildings, personal property is all other kinds of property (e.g. books, cars, CDs).

---

[13] Some countries have 'deferred community of property', which only comes into play on separation.
[14] See e.g. Family Law (Scotland) Act 1985.
[15] Law Commission Report 175 (1988: para 3.2).
[16] Basically the approach proposed by Law Commission Report 175 (1988).
[17] Law Commission Report 175 (1988).

3. THE OWNERSHIP OF PERSONAL PROPERTY

So how do the courts decide who owns what? The law can be summarised with the following statements:

1. Income belongs to the person who earns it.[18] So if a wife is employed, her salary belongs to her.
2. Personal property prima facie belongs to the person whose money was used to buy the property. This is a presumption which can be rebutted.[19] For example, if a husband bought his wife a pair of socks it may well be that the court would find the presumption rebutted and that the socks belong to the wife, not the husband.
3. Ownership of property can be transferred from one person to another if there is effective delivery of the property[20] with evidence that it is intended as a gift. So if a wife hands a piece of property to her husband saying that it is a present for him, this would be an effective transfer of ownership from her to him.
4. The act of marriage, engagement or cohabitation itself does not change ownership of property.

There are a number of scenarios where the law is a little more complicated, and these will now be discussed in detail.

A. Jointly used bank accounts

Where the parties pool their incomes into a common account, it seems that normally they both have a joint interest in the whole fund.[21] The crucial question is: what is the purpose for which the fund is held? The leading case is *Jones* v *Maynard*.[22] The husband authorised his wife to draw from his bank account. Although the husband's contribution to the account was greater than the wife's, they treated the account as a joint account. When the marriage was dissolved the ownership of the account became an issue. Vaisey J argued:

> In my view a husband's earnings or salary, when the spouses have a common purse and pool their resources, are earnings made on behalf of both; and the idea that years afterwards the contents of the pool can be dissected by taking an elaborate account as to how much was paid in by the husband or the wife is quite inconsistent with the original fundamental idea of a joint purpose or common pool. In my view the money which goes into the pool becomes joint property.

So the court should focus on the intentions of the parties. Was the account intended to be a 'common purse'? If the account was in both names then it is very likely it will be regarded as joint. Even if it was only in one spouse's name the court will examine whether in fact the fund was used jointly.

---

[18] *Heseltine* v *Heseltine* [1971] 1 All ER 952.
[19] *Re Whittaker* (1882) 21 Ch D 657.
[20] *Re Cole* [1904] Ch 175.
[21] This is so regardless of in whose name the account stands.
[22] [1951] Ch 572.

Property bought using money from the common fund is jointly owned if the property was purchased for the parties' joint use. However, if the property was bought for the use of one of the parties then it seems likely that it will be regarded as belonging to that party. So if the wife bought a rare stamp for her stamp collection using money from a joint bank account then the stamp is likely to be seen as hers, but if she bought a sofa it will probably be seen as for joint use and therefore jointly owned.[23] In *Re Bishop*[24] investments were purchased from the common fund. Some were purchased in joint names, others in the name of the husband and one in the wife's name. It was held that the fact that the investments were put in specified names indicated they were owned by the named parties.

B. Housekeeping and maintenance allowance

According to s 1 of the Married Women's Property Act 1964:

> If any question arises as to the right of a husband or wife to money derived from any allowance made by the husband for the expenses of the matrimonial home or for similar purposes, or to any property acquired out of such money, the money or property shall, in the absence of any agreement between them to the contrary, be treated as belonging to the husband and wife in equal shares.

The Act only applies if the allowance is paid by the husband. It does not apply to payments made by a wife to her husband nor between cohabitants, nor engaged couples. However, for engaged couples and cohabitees the courts may still decide that the parties intended to share such property. Little use seems to be made of the Act, perhaps because it is based on a rather outdated scenario of family finances.

C. Gifts from one partner to the other

Where it is clear that one party intended to make a gift and transferred possession of the property to the other party, then ownership passed from one to the other. So if a wife purchased a book using money from her own bank account the law will presume it belongs to her. However, if she wrapped it up and presented it to her husband on his birthday ownership passed to him. If, however, it is unclear whether the transfer of possession was intended to be a gift, the law is rather odd. In the absence of any evidence to the contrary, a transfer from a husband to a wife is a gift[25] but a transfer from a wife to a husband will result in the husband holding the property on trust for the wife, so effectively she will still be the owner. If the couple are unmarried and there is no evidence as to the nature of the transfer then it will be presumed that the recipient is to hold the property on trust for the 'donor', whether the donor was a man or a woman.

---

[23] A specific agreement could rebut these presumptions.

[24] [1965] Ch 450.

[25] This is as a result of the presumption of advancement. However, it is clear that even the smallest amount of evidence can rebut this: *Pettitt* v *Pettitt* [1970] AC 777. In *McGrath* v *Wallis* [1995] 2 FLR 114 (at p. 122) it was even suggested that the lack of a reason for making the gift could rebut the presumption, which means one questions whether the presumption exists at all.

D. Gifts to partners from third parties

Where a third party makes a gift to a couple, ownership of the gift depends on the donor's intention. This intention can be inferred from the surrounding circumstances. For example, it is reasonable to assume that a wedding gift was intended for joint ownership unless there is evidence to the contrary.[26] By contrast, a birthday present given to the husband will be presumed to belong to him alone.

E. Improvements to personal property

If a spouse or fiancé(e) (but not a cohabitant) does work that improves a piece of property (for example, if a wife fixes up an antique car and so makes it a valuable commodity), then he or she can rely on s 37 of the Matrimonial Proceedings and Property Act 1970 to establish an interest in the property. We will discuss this provision later when real property is considered.

F. Express declarations of trust

An owner of a piece of personal property can declare him- or herself trustee of it. The declaration can be oral and does not require the use of formal language. For example, in *Rowe* v *Prance*[27] a man bought a boat and wrote to his lover referring to what he would like to do with her on 'our boat'. This was held by the court to be sufficient evidence of an express declaration of trust and he therefore shared equitable ownership with his lover.[28]

G. Criticisms of the present law

The present law has been widely criticised.[29] The Law Commission has characterised the existing rules as arbitrary, uncertain and unfair.[30] There is too much emphasis placed on who purchased a piece of property, while this is often a matter of chance. Some of the presumptions seem out of date and based on sexist presumptions no longer appropriate for our law. Further, there is also much uncertainty over when an express trust can be found. The case of *Rowe* v *Prance*, which we have just discussed, demonstrates that even casual comments can have legal significance attached to them, perhaps out of all proportion to their intended effect. By contrast, there may be couples whose general lifestyle demonstrates that they wish to share everything, but if there are no statements which reflect this, they may have difficulty in proving co-ownership.[31] An unmarried couple who go to court for an order deciding who owns their collection of CDs could find themselves in for a protracted court case.

[26] *Midland Bank* v *Cooke* [1995] 4 All ER 562, [1995] 2 FLR 915 CA.
[27] [1999] 2 FLR 787.
[28] See also *Haywood* v *Haywood* Unreported 13.7.2000.
[29] See, e.g, Tee (2001).
[30] Law Commission Report 175 (1988: para 1.4).
[31] Although the court have shown a willingness to find a common intention in *Haywood* v *Haywood* Unreported 13.7.2000.

4. MAINTENANCE DURING MARRIAGE

The law on the payment of maintenance on divorce will be discussed in Chapter 5. This section will consider maintenance payments during marriage and cohabitation.

A. Unmarried cohabitants

There is no obligation on one unmarried partner to support the other. However, there is an obligation on a parent to provide for children whether the parents are married or not. This will be discussed in Chapter 5. Income could result, however, from an order under s 40 of the Family Law Act 1996, requiring a party to make payments of maintenance for the dwelling house, or rent or mortgage, in connection with an occupation order.[32]

B. Married couples

There are two potential sources of maintenance liability for spouses while the couple are married: from statutes and from separation agreements reached between themselves.[33] We will discuss the liability to maintain spouses on divorce in Chapter 5.

(i) Statutory obligations to maintain

Research suggests that although there are statutory means of enforcing an obligation to pay maintenance during the marriage, in practice very small sums are involved and they are rarely collected.[34] No doubt many spouses who have separated rely on benefits or earnings while pursuing divorce proceedings. The liability to support a child under the Child Support Act 1991 dominates the financial relationship between parties prior to divorce.

There are four statutory provisions that are relevant for spousal maintenance during marriage:

1. Under s 2 of the Domestic Proceedings and Matrimonial Causes Act 1978, periodical payments orders and lump sum orders for less than £1,000[35] can be made. Section 1 sets out the criteria:

   Either party to a marriage may apply to a magistrates' court for an order under section 2 of this Act on the ground that the other party to the marriage—
   (a) has failed to provide reasonable maintenance for the applicant; or
   (b) has failed to provide, or to make a proper contribution towards, reasonable maintenance for any child of the family; or
   (c) has behaved in such a way that the applicant cannot reasonably be expected to live with the respondent; or
   (d) has deserted the applicant.

---

[32] Discussed in Chapter 6.
[33] At common law the husband is under a duty to provide his wife with the necessities of life.
[34] Lowe and Douglas (1998: 755–6).
[35] There is no such limitation if there is a consent order.

In calculating the level of spousal maintenance, the first consideration is the welfare of any minors and there is a list of factors to consider, virtually identical to those in s 25 of the Matrimonial Causes Act 1973.[36] Sums that are awarded are usually small. In *E v C (Child Maintenance)*[37] it was held to be inappropriate to order a man on income support to pay £5 per week. In fact if someone is on income support it would only be appropriate to order a nominal sum. Applications under this statute are made to the magistrates' court. This is a cheaper procedure than the other three provisions and is therefore the most popular.

2. Under s 27 of the Matrimonial Causes Act 1973 periodic payment and lump sum orders can be made without limit. It is necessary to show that the respondent has failed to provide reasonably for the spouse or for a child of the family. The provision is only available for married couples.
3. Prior to divorce and nullity or judicial separation it is possible to apply for maintenance pending suit.[38] Interim lump sum orders can now be made.[39]
4. Section 40 of the Family Law Act 1996 can require the payment of rent, mortgage, and outgoings in respect of a property when an occupation order is made.[40]

(ii) Separation agreements

Especially before divorce became more readily available, private agreements were a popular option for couples who could not divorce (or did not want to divorce) but intended to separate. Nowadays separation agreements are often used by couples to deal with the parties' financial affairs while waiting for the final financial orders to be made. The law's approach to such agreements is that they can be legally enforced, but are open to alteration by the courts. In other words, the court's jurisdiction cannot be ousted by private agreements.[41]

An agreement is only binding if the normal requirements of contract law are in place. In particular, there must be an intention to create legal relations. There is a presumption that agreements between married couples are not intended to be legally binding.[42] The question is whether the parties intended their agreement to be enforceable by the courts or whether it was merely made as a record of their informal understanding. The court will readily find an intention to create legal relations where the parties have separated and the circumstances in which the agreement was reached had the kind of solemnity associated with binding contracts. The contract may not be binding where there is fraud, misrepresentation or undue influence.[43] If the agreement constitutes a legally binding agreement it can be enforced like any other contract.

---

[36] Discussed in Chapter 5.
[37] [1995] 1 FLR 472, [1996] 1 FCR 612.
[38] Matrimonial Causes Act 1973 s 22; see *G v G (Maintenance Pending Suit: Costs)* [2003] FL 393.
[39] Matrimonial Causes Act 1973, s 22A(4).
[40] See Chapter 6.
[41] *Jessell v Jessell* [1979] 1 WLR 1148 at p. 1152 CA.
[42] *Balfour v Balfour* [1919] 2 KB 571 CA.
[43] See Beatson (2002).

Where there is a binding contract the court can revise the agreement on the basis:

(a) that by reason of a change in the circumstances in the light of which any financial arrangements contained in the agreement were made or, as the case may be, financial arrangements were omitted from it (including a change foreseen by the parties when making the agreement), the agreement should be altered so as to make different, or, as the case may be, so as to contain financial arrangements, or

(b) that the agreement does not contain proper financial arrangements with respect of any child of the family . . .[44]

This then would enable the courts to increase or decrease the amounts payable under the agreement.

5. OWNERSHIP OF REAL PROPERTY: THE FAMILY HOME

The home is the most valuable asset that many people own. This is true not just in monetary terms but in emotional terms: to many people the home is of great psychological importance. A dispute over ownership of the home can therefore be particularly heated. We will first consider how the law determines who owns a house.[45] This is particularly important for unmarried couples because at the end of their relationship the court has no jurisdiction to require one party to transfer their share of the home to the other and can only declare who at the moment owns the house.

English and Welsh law has not developed a special regime for dealing with family homes.[46] So the law governing the family home is the same as that concerning any two people who happen to share a house, whether they be business partners or lovers.[47] Because of the way that the law has evolved, it is necessary to distinguish ownership of property at law and at equity.

A. Legal ownership

Determining ownership of land[48] is not difficult. If the land is registered,[49] the legal owner can be determined by discovering who is registered as the owner of the land. If the land is not registered, it is necessary to discover into whose name the lease or property was conveyed. Section 52(1) of the Law of Property Act 1925 makes clear that legal title can only be conveyed by deed.[50] So words alone cannot transfer legal ownership.

Just because someone owns the property at common law, it does not mean they are the absolute owner, because the legal owner may hold the property on trust for someone else. It is therefore necessary to consider who owns the property in equity.

---

[44] Matrimonial Causes Act 1973, s 35(2).
[45] Although references will be made to a house, the law is essentially the same over flats.
[46] For an excellent discussion see Mee (1999).
[47] *Pettitt* v *Pettitt* [1970] AC 777 HL; *Gissing* v *Gissing* [1971] 1 AC 886 HL.
[48] Land here includes ownership of the house on the land.
[49] Eventually the Land Registration Act 2002 will end unregistered title.
[50] Law of Property (Miscellaneous Provisions) Act 1989, s 2.

B. Equitable ownership

In the eyes of equity it matters not in whose name the property is registered, nor into whose name the property was conveyed. In equity the legal owner of the property may be found to hold the property on trust for someone else who will then have an equitable interest in the property. A trust may be express or implied.

(i) Express trusts

The leading statutory provision is s 53(1)(b) of the Law of Property Act 1925, which states that a declaration of trust in respect of land must be manifested and proved in writing. So an oral statement from the owner that they wish to hold the land on trust for someone else would not be sufficient for an express trust.[51] It may be that there is a trust deed that sets out the shares of the parties in equity. The deed may be part of the conveyance (for example, the conveyance may specifically state that the property is transferred 'to A to hold on trust for A and B in shares of 60 per cent and 40 per cent respectively') or there may be a separate document signed by the owner setting out the terms of the trust. In these cases, unless there is any fraud or mistake, this document will identify the shares and there will be no need for the court to consider the ownership question further. This was made clear in *Goodman* v *Gallant*.[52] It is therefore highly advisable for a couple purchasing a house to make it quite clear the shares they are to own in equity.[53]

However, all too often there is no written declaration of interests. Typically this arises where one person buys a house and later on his or her partner moves in. The parties do not think about seeing a lawyer to produce a written document. In such cases s 53(2) of the Law of Property Act 1925 is crucial, because it states that s 53(1) does not affect the creation of implied, resulting and constructive trusts. So in the absence of a formal document it is necessary to turn to the law of implied trusts.[54]

(ii) Implied trusts

There are three areas that need to be considered: resulting trusts, constructive trusts and proprietary estoppel. As we shall see, the role now played by resulting trusts in relation to the family home is small.

(a) Resulting trusts

The presumption of a resulting trust is that if A and B both contribute to the purchase price[55] of a house and the property is put into B's name, then although B will be owner at common law she will hold it on trust (a resulting trust) for herself and A and B. Similarly, if A transfers property into B's name, without B providing any

---

[51] Although such a statement may well form the basis of an implied trust.
[52] [1986] 1 FLR 513.
[53] *Springette* v *Defoe* [1992] 2 FLR 388 at p. 390 per Dillon LJ.
[54] *Gissing* v *Gissing* [1971] AC 886 HL.
[55] See *Huntingford* v *Hobbs* [1993] 1 FLR 736 CA for a discussion of the position where a mortgage is used.

consideration,[56] then B will hold the property on trust solely for A. Both of these resulting trusts are presumptions, based on the belief that people do not give money or property expecting nothing in return. The presumption can be rebutted if it can be shown that the contribution to the purchase price was given as a gift or a loan.[57] For example, if an aunt helps provide the purchase price for her nephew's first house it may readily be shown that she intended this money to be a gift and did not intend him to hold it on trust for her.

The presumption of the resulting trust does not apply if A is B's husband or father. In such a case the presumption is that A intended to make a gift to B. This is known as the presumption of advancement. So if a father helps a child buy a house and the house is put in the child's name, the presumption would be that the child owns the house absolutely.[58] However, this presumption is a rebuttable one. The Court of Appeal has suggested that the presumption of advancement should only be relied upon as a 'last resort', if there is no evidence of the parties' intentions.[59] Given the archaic and gendered nature of the presumption, there is much to be said for this approach.[60]

(b) Constructive trusts

The law on constructive trusts is now governed by the decision of the House of Lords in *Lloyds Bank* v *Rosset*.[61] To appreciate the decision it is important to consider some of the earlier case law. Some of the cases prior to *Rosset* had suggested that the court could find a constructive trust if it thought that the fairness of the case demanded it; other cases had suggested that a constructive trust could be found if this accorded with the parties' intentions, but that these intentions could be inferred (invented, critics would say) by the courts. Lord Bridge feared that such approaches led to too much uncertainty and so he sought to tighten up the circumstances in which the courts could find a constructive trust. Lord Bridge stated that a constructive trust could only be found if: (1) there is a common intention to share ownership; and (2) the party seeking to establish the constructive trust has relied on the common intention to his or her detriment. These two requirements need to be considered in further detail.

1. Common intent

There are only two ways of establishing common intent:

1. If there is 'any agreement, arrangement or understanding reached between them that the property is to be shared beneficially'.[62]
2. A common intent can be inferred from a direct contribution to the purchase price or mortgage instalment.

[56] See Beatson (2002) for explanation of this term.
[57] *Sekhon* v *Alissa* [1989] 2 FLR 94.
[58] Although if a mother or wife gave property to her child or husband then the presumption of resulting trust would apply.
[59] *McGrath* v *Wallis* [1995] 2 FLR 114, [1995] 3 FCR 661 CA.
[60] For a discussion of resulting trust in cases of fraud, see R. Smith (2000: 117–19).
[61] [1991] 1 AC 107.
[62] *Lloyds Bank* v *Rosset* [1991] 1 AC 107.

In the absence of these, a common intention cannot be found in any other way.[63] These two means of establishing a common intention will now be considered separately.

The agreement. This requires evidence of an actual conversation between the parties in which it was agreed that the parties would share ownership. It is not enough that there is a mutual, but uncommunicated, belief. There must be proof that a conversation took place.[64] It should be stressed that the agreement must be to share ownership, not just to share occupation.[65]

Lord Bridge accepted that it is not easy to prove an oral agreement, but that evidence of agreements can be introduced 'however imperfectly remembered and however imprecise their terms must have been'. The difficulties with this have been recognised in *Hammond* v *Mitchell* by Waite J who noted that:

> the tenderest exchanges of a common law courtship may assume an unforeseen significance many years later when they are brought under equity's microscope and subjected to an analysis under which many thousands of pounds of value may be liable to turn on this fine question as to whether the relevant words were spoken in earnest or in dalliance and with or without representational intent.[66]

Cases following *Rosset* have been very willing to find evidence of common intention. The following comments have been evidence of an agreement: 'Don't worry about the future because when we are married [the house] will be half yours anyway and I'll always look after you and [our child]';[67] and 'You need a secure home'.[68] These examples are controversial because the promises appear to relate to rights in the future, rather than being agreements to share in the present, which is what Lord Bridge required. It may be that the judgments after *Rosset* are trying to loosen the strictness of the approach taken by Lord Bridge.

Lord Bridge stated there were two 'outstanding examples' of the kind of agreements revealing common intention that he had in mind. Both cases involved property which was in the man's name and he gave an excuse to his partner for not putting the property into their joint names. In *Eves* v *Eves*[69] the man (untruthfully) stated that his partner was too young to be put on the title deed. In *Grant* v *Edwards*[70] the man involved (again untruthfully) said he would not put the property into their joint names because it would prejudice a dispute between her and her husband (whom she was divorcing). Some commentators have pointed out that these cases, far from showing a common intention that the property was to be

---

[63] Lord Bridge stated that it was 'extremely doubtful' there would be any other way of establishing the interest.

[64] Although the Court of Appeal has suggested it might be willing to infer from the surrounding circumstances that there was a conversation agreeing to share the property: *Springette* v *Defoe* [1992] 2 FLR 388 at p. 395. In *Hyett* v *Stanley* [2003] 3 FCR 253 the fact that the parties had executed a charge over the house for which they were jointly responsible was evidence that they must have agreed to share the property.

[65] *Lloyds Bank* v *Rosset* [1990] 1 All ER 1111 at p. 1115.

[66] *Hammond* v *Mitchell* [1992] 2 All ER 109 at p. 121.

[67] *Hammond* v *Mitchell* [1992] 2 All ER 109, [1992] 1 FLR 229.

[68] *Savil* v *Goodall* [1993] 1 FLR 755, [1994] 1 FCR 325 CA.

[69] [1975] 3 All ER 768.

[70] [1987] 1 FLR 87 CA.

shared, in fact indicate that the men did not intend that their partners should have a share. Others have supported these cases on the basis that in each instance the men, having led the women to believe it was their intent that the property should be in their joint names, cannot deny there was a common intention to share ownership.

One question which is not clearly answered in the case law is at what time the agreement to share must take place. In *Rosset* Lord Bridge suggested that the agreement should be at the point of purchase, 'or exceptionally' at a later date. Subsequent cases have been ready to rely on agreements made many years after the purchase.[71] This is an important issue because, as explained earlier, most of the cases concerning constructive trusts have arisen where one party moved in with the owner of the house.

Inferring common intent from payments. The only circumstance in which Lord Bridge was willing to accept that a common intention to share could be found in the absence of an oral agreement was where there was a direct contribution to the purchase price or at least one of the mortgage instalments. It should be stressed that Lord Bridge required a *direct* contribution. This appears to mean that if the woman paid all of the household expenses while the man paid the mortgage instalments then she would not be able to rely on an implied common intention, even if it was only because she had paid the household bills that the man could meet the mortgage instalments.[72] However in *Le Foe* v *Le Foe*[73] Mostyn QC suggested that indirect contribution to the mortgage could be evidence to infer a common intention. He picked up on Lord Bridge's statement that it was 'at least extremely doubtful whether' anything less than a direct contribution would do; and argued this indicates he accepted that there may be cases when indirect contributions would suffice.[74]

2. Detrimental reliance

A common intent to share is not in and of itself sufficient for a constructive trust. There must also be acts that show a party has relied on that common intention to his or her detriment, as was recently emphasised by the Court of Appeal in *Chan Pui Chun* v *Leung Kam Ho*.[75] The problem is that it is far from clear what constitutes detrimental reliance.

The approach with the most authority is that detrimental reliance requires conduct upon which the claimant 'could not reasonably have been expected to embark unless she was to have an interest in the house'.[76] In *Eves* v *Eves*[77] the act of reliance was the woman's manual work on the property, including breaking up concrete, demolishing and rebuilding a shed, and renovating the house. This conduct was

---

[71] *Hammond* v *Mitchell* [1992] 2 All ER 109, [1992] 1 FLR 229.
[72] *Ivin* v *Blake* (1993) 67 P&CR 263.
[73] [2002] 1 FCR 107.
[74] For an article supporting this approach see Pawlowski (2002).
[75] [2003] 1 FCR 520 CA.
[76] Nourse LJ in *Grant* v *Edwards* [1986] Ch 638, [1987] 1 FLR 87 CA. See also *Chan Pui Chun* v *Peung Kam Ho* [2003] 1 FCR 520 CA.
[77] [1975] 3 All ER 768 CA.

held to be detrimental reliance because it was not the kind of conduct one would expect from a 'normal' female cohabitee. It could therefore be inferred that she must have acted in this way because she believed she had an interest in the property. By contrast, in *Thomas v Fuller-Brown*[78] a man who moved in with a woman and carried out various pieces of DIY around the house did not thereby acquire an interest in it. This was partly because the acts of DIY were the kind of things a man living in the house could be expected to have done, and so was not the type of conduct he would only have performed had he believed he had an interest in the property. In *Rosset* the wife's conduct in supervising the builders because her husband was abroad was insufficient to amount to detrimental reliance as 'it would seem the most natural thing in the world for any wife, in the absence of her husband abroad, to spend all the time she could'[79] working on the house, and therefore did not reveal she believed that she had an interest in the house. These examples demonstrate the danger that gender stereotyping can determine whether a party is able to establish detrimental reliance or not.

There is some authority for alternative approaches. Sir Nicholas Browne-Wilkinson V-C (as he then was) suggested that detrimental reliance requires any conduct of the kind that relates to a couple's 'joint lives' together.[80] This is a very liberal interpretation of the requirement. It simply stipulates that there were detrimental acts that related to the couple's joint lives. This might include caring for the couple's children or a substantial amount of housework. If a couple were living together it would almost be inevitable that there would be acts that were referable to their joint lives together. Whichever approach is taken a direct contribution to the purchase price or mortgage instalments can constitute detrimental reliance. This means that such payments will be evidence from which both a common intention can be inferred and detrimental reliance shown and therefore in and of them establish a constructive trust.

3. Calculating what share a party is entitled to under a constructive trust
The shares the parties are entitled to under a constructive trust are determined by the parties' intentions. In *Midland Bank v Cooke*[81] a wedding present of £1,000 given by Mr Cooke's parents was used to place a deposit on a house. The cash was seen as given to the couple jointly, and so £500 of the purchase price came from Mrs Cooke. This was a direct contribution to the purchase price and so, under *Rosset*, the court could find a common intention to share ownership and detrimental reliance upon that common intention. However, in deciding what share Mrs Cooke was entitled to, the court were not restricted to the percentage share she had contributed, but rather her share was calculated by reference to the share she was intended to have. Waite LJ explained:

> to determine (in the absence of express evidence of intention) what proportions the parties must be assumed to have intended for their beneficial ownership, the duty of the judge

[78] [1988] 1 FLR 237.
[79] [1990] 1 All ER 1111 at p. 1117.
[80] *Grant v Edwards* [1986] Ch 638 at p. 657.
[81] [1995] 2 FLR 915 CA.

is to undertake a survey of the whole course of dealing between the parties relevant to their ownership and occupation of the property and their sharing of its burdens and advantages. That scrutiny will not confine itself to the limited range of acts of direct contribution of the sort that are needed to found a beneficial interest in the first place. It will take into consideration all conduct, which throws light on the question what shares were intended. Only if that search proves inconclusive does the court fall back on the maxim that 'equality is equity'.

So when considering what proportion of shares the parties intended in the property, the court is not restricted to taking into account actual conversations or direct contributions to the purchase or mortgage. The court can consider all the circumstances of the parties' relationship.

The Court of Appeal in *Midland Bank* v *Cooke*[82] found an 'inescapable' inference that the parties were to share the property equally. They were a couple who had 'agreed to share everything'.[83] They shared child-care, business endeavours, and marriage. It could therefore be presumed that they intended to share ownership of the house. By contrast, in *Drake* v *Whipp*[84] the woman provided 19.4 per cent of the purchase price but was entitled to one-third of the house's value. The contrast between the awards to Mrs Cooke and Ms Drake shows how hard it can be to predict the court's response, and that perhaps this is very much an issue for the judge's individual discretion.[85] It may be that the difference between the two was that Mrs Cooke was married while Ms Drake was an unmarried cohabitant. Alternatively, it may be that in *Drake* a significant factor was that the man had spent a large amount of time and effort in improving the property, thereby greatly increasing its value.

(c) Proprietary estoppel

For A to establish a proprietary estoppel claim over B's property it is necessary to show:[86]

1. A believes she has or is going to be given an interest over B's property;
2. A must act to her detriment in reliance on this belief;
3. B must be aware of his own interests in the property; and
4. B must have known of and encouraged A's belief.

However, having said this, the Court of Appeal in *Gillet* v *Holt* has recently stressed that the crucial principle underlying proprietary estoppel is conscionability.[87] Conscionability in essence means fairness. So proprietary estoppel cannot be tied down to a firm set of rules: each case turns on what is conscionable in all the circumstances. Indeed it may be that if A acted greatly to her detriment the court will be less strict about proof of B having encouraged the belief, and a vague statement will be sufficient.[88] Similarly, if B makes a very clear statement that A is to have an

---

[82] [1995] 2 FLR 915 CA.
[83] At p. 928.
[84] [1996] 1 FLR 826.
[85] For criticism on this basis see Battersby (1996).
[86] *Re Basham (Deceased)* [1987] 1 All ER 405; *Gillet* v *Holt* [2000] FCR 705 CA.
[87] *Gillet* v *Holt* [2000] FCR 705 CA.
[88] *Bibby* v *Stirling* (1998) 76 P&CR 36. But see *Lissimore* v *Downing* [2003] 2 FLR 308 where the promise was found to be too vague to found the basis of an estoppel claim.

interest in the property, the court may be willing to accept acts that are only detrimental to a small extent. The representation must relate to a specific piece of property. So a representation that a person would not want for anything could not form the basis of an estoppel claim.[89] A good example of a successful proprietary estoppel claim is *Greasley* v *Cooke*,[90] where Doris Cooke moved in with a family. She formed a relationship with one son and nursed and cared for other members of the family. She had been led to believe that she would be able to live in the house for the rest of her life. This led to a successful proprietary estoppel claim.

A number of elements of proprietary estoppel have given rise to difficulties.

1. *Must the promise or assurance be irrevocable?* The difficulty here is demonstrated by *Taylor* v *Dickens*,[91] where an older woman who owned her house promised to make a will leaving her gardener her house if he performed extra work for her. It transpired that she did make the will but later changed it. The gardener did the extra work and claimed an interest in the house against the estate under a proprietary estoppel. He failed because it was said that the woman had not made an irrevocable promise: she promised to make a will and leave him the property, but she did not promise never to change the will. This decision has been doubted by *Gillet* v *Holt*.[92] The Court of Appeal said that the question to be asked is whether in the light of the detrimental reliance it is conscionable for the maker of the promise to go back on his or her word. However, if a party makes it clear the promise is not intended to be binding, it is extremely unlikely that it could form the basis of a proprietary estoppel.[93]

2. *What does reliance mean?* One element that gives rise to particular difficulties for those seeking to establish a proprietary estoppel is that it is necessary to show that the claimant has acted to his or her detriment in reliance on a promise or mistaken belief of an interest in the property. In *Coombes* v *Smith*[94] Parker QC took the view that the plaintiff who had left her husband to move in with her lover had done so out of love, rather than in reliance on a promise by her lover that he would provide for her. She therefore was unable to establish a proprietary estoppel. However, in *Wayling* v *Jones*[95] the Court of Appeal took the view that once it was established that the promise had been made then the burden of proof was on the defendant to establish that the plaintiff had not relied on the promise. It is clear there must be a sufficient link between the promise and the conduct, although it was enough if the promise was *an* inducement, even if not *the sole* inducement, for the reliance. In *Wayling* v *Jones* there was deemed sufficient reliance because, even if Wayling had acted to his detriment partly out of love, had he known that Jones's promise to leave him the property on his death was a lie he would not have acted in the way he had.

---

[89] *Lissimore* v *Downing* [2003] 2 FLR 308.
[90] *Greasley* v *Cooke* [1980] 3 All ER 710 CA.
[91] [1998] 1 FLR 806.
[92] [2000] 2 FLR 266 CA.
[93] *A-G of Hong Kong* v *Humphreys Estate (Queen's Gardens) Ltd* [1987] AC 114.
[94] [1986] 1 WLR 808.
[95] [1995] 2 FLR 1029.

3. *What acts can constitute detriment?* The courts have not set down strict criteria for what constitutes detriment. There is no need for detrimental conduct to be in monetary terms, although it must involve substantial disadvantage.[96] The following are examples of conduct which constitutes detriment: leaving a job;[97] looking after the family of the owner;[98] and 'setting up house together, having a baby, making payments to general housekeeping expenses ...'.[99] As mentioned earlier, the amount of detriment will be one factor in considering whether it is conscionable to award a proprietary estoppel.

4. *What remedy is granted?* Having established a proprietary estoppel claim, the next question is what interest in the property should thereby be acquired by the plaintiff? The simple answer is that the remedy given is that which would 'satisfy the equity'. In other words, that remedy which would be just. The courts have been willing to grant a wide range of remedies including a fee simple[100] or a sum of money.[101] In particular the courts will consider the nature of the interest that was promised or assured by the owner and the amount of detriment suffered by the claimant.[102] Although ultimately the question is a matter for the court's discretion, any remedy should be proportionate to the financial value of the detriment.[103]

(d) The interrelation of constructive trusts and proprietary estoppel

It will have been noticed that the requirements of a constructive trust and proprietary estoppel are very similar. Indeed some commentators take the view that proprietary estoppel and constructive trusts should be amalgamated.[104] Certainly the courts have not taken great efforts to distinguish the two. Lord Bridge, for example, said that where a person has acted to his or her detriment on reliance of an agreement to share property, this will 'give rise to a constructive trust or proprietary estoppel'. The Court of Appeal has accepted that the requirements for the two are very similar.[105] However, the current view of the courts is that although at some point the doctrines might be merged, they are not yet assimilated.[106]

C. Improvements to the home

Section 37 of the Matrimonial Proceedings and Property Act 1970 states that if a spouse or fiancé(e) (but not an unmarried cohabitant) makes a substantial contribution to the improvement of property[107] in which the other spouse or fiancé(e) has

---

[96] *Gillet v Holt* [2000] FCR 705 CA.
[97] *Jones v Jones* [1977] 1 WLR 438.
[98] *Greasley v Cooke* [1980] 1 WLR 1306.
[99] *Grant v Edwards* [1986] Ch 638 at p. 657.
[100] *Pascoe v Turner* [1979] 1 WLR 431. A fee simple is absolute ownership.
[101] *Dodsworth v Dodsworth* (1973) 228 EG 1115.
[102] *Jennings v Rice* [2003] 1 FCR 501.
[103] *Jennings v Rice* [2003] 1 FCR 501.
[104] See the debate between Hayton (1993) and Ferguson (1993). See also the discussion in Nield (2003).
[105] *Yaxley v Gotts* [2000] Ch 162, [1999] 2 FLR 941.
[106] *Stokes v Anderson* [1991] 1 FLR 391.
[107] The section applies to real and personal property.

an interest, the improvement will create an interest in the property. However, the section states that this rule is subject to any agreement that the parties reach. A number of requirements need to be satisfied if the section is to apply:

1. The improvement must be of monetary value. Section 37 applies whether the contribution is in real money or money's worth. The improvement may be made by the claimant him- or herself or by someone employed by the claimant.[108] So if an incompetent husband carries out DIY work on the house, which in fact decreases the value of the house, he will be unable to invoke this section, as no improvement of monetary value has been made.
2. The contribution must be identifiable with the improvement in question. So if it could be shown that a wife pays the household expenses thereby enabling the husband to pay for the improvements to a piece of property, s 37 could be relied upon by the wife.[109]
3. The contribution must be of a substantial nature. *Re Nicholson (Deceased)*[110] provides a good example of this. Installing central heating worth £189 in a house worth £6,000 was substantial, but spending £23 on a gas fire was not.
4. The contribution must constitute an improvement to the property and not merely maintenance of it.[111]

The share acquired will be that which reflects any agreement of the parties, and if there is not one, then what the court regards as just. Normally the party will receive a share in the property reflecting the increase in the value of the property that the improvements caused.

There is some debate over the policy behind this section. It could be regarded as putting into legal effect the presumed intentions of the parties: that is, what the parties themselves would have expected to happen as a result of their actions to improve the property had they thought about it. Alternatively, s 37 could be seen as a way of achieving a just result in recognition of a party's contribution to improving the house, regardless of the parties' intentions. The fact that the parties can reach an agreement which negates the effect of the section would suggest that the statute is primarily seeking to reflect the parties' intentions.[112] The section is rarely relied upon because works carried out on the house will often form the basis of a proprietary estoppel or constructive trust claim.

D. Criticism of the present law

The law on ownership of the family home has been heavily criticised. The Law Commission has stated that: 'The present rules are uncertain and difficult to apply and can lead to serious injustice.'[113] The law can especially lead to great injustice

---

[108] *Griffiths v Griffiths* [1979] 1 WLR 1350.
[109] *Harnett v Harnett* [1973] 2 All ER 593 at p. 603.
[110] [1974] 1 WLR 476.
[111] *Re Nicholson (Deceased)* [1974] 1 WLR 476.
[112] It is therefore analogous to the working of resulting trusts.
[113] Law Commission Report 234 (1995: 34).

for unmarried cohabitants. Injustice was revealed in the following *dicta* of Johnson J in *T* v *S (Financial Provision for Children)*:[114]

> the sadness here is that, after a long and seemingly happy relationship, this mother of five children, never having been married to their father, has no rights against him of her own. She has no right to be supported by him in the short, still less in the long term; no right in herself to even have a roof over her head.

There is much academic support for the need to change the law.[115] The following are some of the main criticisms:

1. The requirement in *Rosset* for an oral agreement between the parties or a direct financial contribution has been heavily criticised. It is unrealistic to expect all couples to discuss the legal ownership of their property.[116] The cases demonstrate that the courts have had to pick up on casual comments made during the relationship.[117] A further difficulty with the approach in *Rosset* is that the parties' recollections of their 'tenderest exchanges' may well be contradictory and the only way to decide which of the two is telling the truth would be to look at the nature of their relationship (which was the kind of approach Lord Bridge was trying to move away from).

2. The emphasis on requiring a spoken promise in both constructive trusts and proprietary estoppel works against the less articulate or assertive partner, who may not seek an unequivocal promise from the owner.[118]

3. It has been argued that the law reveals gender bias. In the absence of a conversation, common intention can only be established through a direct contribution to the purchase price or mortgage instalments. It is far more likely that men will be able to contribute in these ways than women, given the greater rates of employment among men. Further, the law devalues non-financial contributions to the household by treating them as insufficient to establish a constructive trust. Olsen suggests that the law reveals an underlying distrust of unmarried women. She argues: 'Unmarried women involved in sexual relations are either good women who should be married or bad women who should not be able to make demands upon a man beyond whatever he chooses to give her.'[119] Notably in relation to the redistribution of property of married couples on divorce the House of Lords has recently held that there should be no discrimination between the money-earner and the homemaker or child-carer.[120]

4. We have already noted that the results of these cases can be particularly unpredictable. This produces uncertainty and causes particular difficulties for negotiations between the parties before the case reaches the court.

---

[114] [1994] 2 FLR 883.
[115] See S. Gardner (1993); Bailey-Harris (1995; 1996); Law Commission Report 278 (2002).
[116] Hayes and Williams (1999: 688).
[117] Rippon (1998).
[118] S. Gardner (1993); Mee (1999).
[119] Olsen (1998).
[120] *White* v *White* [2001] AC 596 HL; see Chapter 5.

5. The overlap between resulting trusts, constructive trusts and proprietary estoppel has been said to be a cause of unnecessary confusion.[121]

E. Reform of the law

The Law Commission for many years has been considering the law relating to the ownership of property of unmarried couples and in 2002 it produced its report on the question, *Sharing Homes*.[122] The Commissioners accepted that the issue raised profound legal and social questions to which there is no ready answer. It is important to appreciate the task the Law Commission set itself: how to ascertain the ownership of property shared by two or more people. So the Law Commission was starting with the approach of the present law towards cohabiting couples: that the law can only seek to declare ownership of property. The Commission was not therefore considering the option of setting up a scheme by which the court could redistribute property of both married and unmarried couples at the end of their relationships. The Law Commission also did not restrict its discussion to cohabitants, but considered the position of any two or more people sharing a home.

The paper does not produce a set of definitive proposals as such, but rather it seeks to promote and focus discussion. One proposal which the Commissioners found attractive was the following:

> We considered that the basis of the law should continue to derive from the circumstances immediately prior to the determination of ownership of the shared home, rather than, for instance, to require the court to address the future needs and resources of the parties. This approach reflected the nature of the project and its focus on how the ownership of the shared home should be determined as a matter of property law. We therefore considered that:
> (1) the ascertainment of property rights should be based on the contributions made by the parties;
> (2) the contributions relevant to this assessment should not be exclusively confined to those that are referable to the acquisition of the property.[123]

However, ultimately they rejected it, deciding that 'the infinitely variable circumstances affecting those who share homes have rendered it impossible to propose the scheme as a viable and practicable reform of the law'.[124]

Also rejected was a scheme whereby the court would be given a discretion looking at a range of factors in deciding what property interests a party held. It was thought such a scheme would be too uncertain.[125] On the other hand the Law Commission also rejected schemes which it considered would be rigid and unbending.[126] The Law Commission discussed the option of giving the courts the power to redistribute the property of unmarried couples who had lived together for a period of time, as is

---

[121] Acknowledged in *Drake* v *Whipp* [1996] 1 FLR 826, [1996] 2 FCR 296.
[122] Law Commission Report 278 (2002), discussed in Probert (2002a). See Fox (2003) for a discussion of how other jurisdictions have dealt with this issue.
[123] Para 3.21.
[124] Para 1.27.
[125] Paras 3.47–3.48.
[126] S. Bridge (2002).

done with married couples. However, the Law Commission, as already mentioned, regarded such a scheme as outside its remit. In any event it thought that such a change in the law involved consideration of political and social issues, which meant that it was better considered by the government rather than the Law Commission.[127]

Here is a summary of some of the alternative ways which could be used to reform the law in this area:

1. The law could give the courts the power to redistribute the property of cohabitants in the same way as they can redistribute the property of married couples.[128] The Law Society has suggested that once couples[129] have cohabited for two years or have a child, a court could redistribute their property taking into account a list of factors, including whether there were any children and whether there was a sexual relationship.[130] However, the power to redistribute would only arise where the parties had not entered a cohabitation contract which dealt with the financial issues in the event of a breakdown of relationship.

   In many ways this would be the easiest solution. Bailey-Harris argues that in this area the law should not distinguish between married and unmarried couples, saying:

   > The content of a legal rule should be determined by its functional context; the function of the law of financial provision is identical for all couples whatever the status of their relationship: to redress the economic inequalities between the parties which have arisen from the relationship. Furthermore, to deny unmarried couples of whatever sexuality the protection of an adjustive financial regime afforded to their married counterparts is discriminatory and runs counter to the support of a variety of different family forms required in a pluralist society. The same model of maintenance and property division regime should apply to all cohabitation relationships (subject to a minimum duration), whether formalised by marriage or not.[131]

   The objections to such a proposal were discussed in Chapter 2. However, to recap some of the objections:

   (a) To treat unmarried and married couples alike would devalue the status of marriage.
   (b) To treat unmarried couples as if they were married would be contrary to the wishes of the couple who have deliberately chosen not to marry for the purpose of avoiding court intervention in their property affairs on the breakdown of their relationship. Therefore to treat them as married would undermine their autonomy.
   (c) There are great difficulties in defining cohabitation.

---

[127] The Law Commission noted that it would be possible for the government to give a court some, but not all, of the powers available to a court on divorce; e.g., to give the court power to distribute assets, but not require maintenance payments.

[128] Discussed in Bailey-Harris (1996).

[129] Law Society (2002). Their proposal would include same-sex and opposite-sex couples. See also S. Bridge (2002).

[130] S. Bridge (2002) argues that such a scheme could only be introduced after a public education campaign to inform people of the law. See also Atkin's discussion (2003) of the approach to this issue in New Zealand.

[131] Bailey-Harris (1998a).

2. The law could focus on the intentions of the parties. This approach might encourage unmarried cohabitants to draw up cohabitation contracts, but, if they did not, the courts would seek to ascertain the parties' intentions from what was said and done during the relationship. The benefit of this approach is that it would promote the parties' autonomy – the law would be seeking to enforce their intentions, rather than telling them what to do. The disadvantages are shown by the law on constructive trusts. Snippets of vaguely recalled conversations may have far more emphasis placed upon them than was intended. Further, in many of these cases the intention of the owner of the property may be quite different from the intention of the cohabitee, and so seeking any kind of *common* intention could be a futile task.

3. The law could focus on the reasonable expectations of the party who is seeking an interest in the property. The difficulty with this approach is revealed by the following scenario. An owner tells the claimant that she can live with him but she will never acquire an interest in his house. If the claimant were then to move in and spend an enormous amount of effort in maintaining and improving the property, she could not reasonably expect the owner to intend that she thereby acquires an interest in the house, even though justice may call out for her to be awarded an interest. The approach also suffers from the difficulty that establishing that the claimant's belief that she had an interest in the property was reasonable is likely to require proof of conversations of the kind which bedevil the present law.

   These concerns have produced an interesting variant of the reasonable expectation approach and this is to focus on what share the claimant might reasonably believe he or she *ought* to have.[132] In the scenario discussed in the previous paragraph, although the owner made it clear that the claimant was not to acquire an interest in the property and so she cannot reasonably believe that she was to acquire an interest, she might nevertheless reasonably expect that she ought to. The problem of this variant centres on the concept of reasonableness. Our society does not have a fixed set of views on when people should be entitled to a share in houses, so it is hard to say what is reasonable or not. In effect this model is similar to option 1 above – it is simply a question of judicial discretion. So it may be more desirable to give the judiciary such discretion explicitly.

4. The courts could focus on the actions performed on the property by the party who has no legal interest in the property. The law should then seek to value the work they have performed. This approach could be based on a form of unjust enrichment. This means that if the owner has received a benefit of the other party's work, the owner would be unjustly enriched by retaining the benefits for the work unless the other party acquires an interest in the property.[133] The benefit of this approach is that by focusing on what was done (rather than said, foreseen or intended), a more concrete concept is used. It is certainly easier to prove. The difficulty with this approach is twofold. The first is valuation of the benefit. This is a particular problem where the benefit is in the form of work which is not

---

[132] Eekelaar (1994b).
[133] See e.g. Dickson J in *Pettkus v Becker* (1980) 117 DLR (3d) 257 at p. 274.

usually valued in economic terms, such as housework, and which at the time the parties themselves may not have regarded as of economic value. Secondly, there is difficulty with the unjustness element. Could the owner argue that in return for housework he permitted the claimant to stay in the house, or provided for her financially in other ways and it is therefore not unjust to deny her an interest in the property?

5. The court could focus on the nature of the parties' relationship. Gardner[134] has argued that the court should consider whether the relationship of the parties has reached the stage of 'communality'. He criticises the present approach for being individualistic: dealing with disputes using the values of commercial law. It would be better to use values which governed the parties' relationship to resolve their dispute. Gardner suggests that the values promoted by a loving relationship are sharing and communality: 'that the parties have committed themselves to sharing the incidents of the relationship between them – good and bad; wealth and costs; work and enjoyment'.[135] The example he gives, however, demonstrates the great difficulties with his approach. He considers a situation where one person invites another to a meal, but the other is unable at the last minute to turn up. He suggests that if they were not yet a couple there would be no expectation to pay for their share of the food, but if they had reached communality, the one unable to attend would expect to pay for his or her share of the meal. Whether most couples would regard there to be an obligation to pay in such cases is very much open to question. Therein lies the problem: it is extremely difficult for someone from the outside to judge the nature of a relationship. Take sexual relations. For some couples the onset of sexual relations may indicate that the relationship has become a deeply committed one; for other couples sexual relations may not indicate this at all. These concerns are greater if one considers that judges may not be best placed to assess the nature of younger people's relationships. The communality approach might also require deeply personal details of a relationship to be aired before the court. A further difficulty is that one party may regard the relationship to have reached communality and the other party not. These arguments suggest that although this approach might be the most attractive in theory, there are grave practical problems with it.

6. RIGHTS TO OCCUPY THE HOME

A person has the right to occupy the house if they have an interest in the property under an express trust, resulting trust, constructive trust or a proprietary estoppel. Even if the claimant is unable to establish such an interest, he or she may be able to establish a constructive trust, or a spouse may have a right to occupy the property under a contractual licence or a matrimonial home right.

[134] S. Gardner (1993).
[135] S. Gardner (1993).

A. Contractual licences

A contractual licence is a contract under which the owner permits the licensee to occupy the property.[136] The claimant needs to show all the requirements of an ordinary contract. There can be particular difficulties for family members in demonstrating that the owner intended to create legal relations.[137] The holder of the contractual licence might be able to obtain damages if the owner excludes him or her but the contractual licence will not bind third parties.[138]

B. Matrimonial home rights

(i) When are matrimonial home rights conferred?

Section 30(1) of the Family Law Act 1996 explains when a matrimonial home right is bestowed. Matrimonial home rights are conferred in respect of a dwelling-house,[139] which has been or was intended to be the home of the spouses where:

    (a) one spouse is entitled to occupy a dwelling-house by virtue of—
        (i) a beneficial estate or interest or contract; or
        (ii) any enactment giving that spouse the right to remain in occupation; and
    (b) the other spouse is not so entitled.

The right is also awarded to spouses who have an equitable interest in the home.[140] The matrimonial home right ceases on divorce or death of either spouse,[141] unless a court orders otherwise.[142]

(ii) What do matrimonial home rights consist of?

A matrimonial home right consists of:

    (a) if in occupation, a right not to be evicted or excluded from the dwelling-house or any part of it by the other spouse except with the leave of the court given by an order under section 33;
    (b) if not in occupation, a right with leave of the court so given to enter into and occupy the dwelling-house.[143]

The real significance of the right is that, otherwise, the spouse without it could be evicted by the other.

Section 30(3) of the 1996 Act states that payments made by the person with the matrimonial home right in respect of rent or mortgage should be treated by the recipient as if made by the owner or tenant of the property. So if a husband stops

---

[136] *Tanner* v *Tanner* [1975] 3 All ER 17 CA.
[137] *Horrocks* v *Forray* [1976] 1 All ER 737 CA.
[138] *Tanner* v *Tanner* [1975] 3 All ER 17 CA.
[139] Defined widely in Family Law Act 1996 (hereafter FLA 1996), s 63 to include, e.g., a caravan.
[140] FLA 1996, s 30(9).
[141] FLA 1996, s 30(8).
[142] FLA 1996, s 33(5).
[143] FLA 1996, s 30(2).

paying rent on a house taken in his name, the wife can pay the rent and the land-lord would have to accept the payment as if made by the husband, and so cannot evict her for non-payment of rent.

(iii) Protection of matrimonial home rights against third parties

The matrimonial home rights should be protected by a notice on the land register if the land is registered under the Land Registration Act 2002,[144] or as a class F Land Charge if the land is unregistered.[145] The significance of this is that if the owner sells the house to a third party and the matrimonial home right is registered then the third party must permit the matrimonial home rights holder to occupy the property.

7. THE SALE OF A FAMILY HOME: ENFORCING TRUSTS

If a cohabiting couple split up there are two questions for the court. The first is: who owns or has the right to occupy the property? That is the question we have just discussed. The second is whether the property should or may be sold. This is the question which will now be addressed.

If two unmarried cohabitants[146] co-own a property (for example, under a constructive trust), there may then be a dispute over whether or not the property should be sold. The Trusts of Land and Appointment of Trustees Act 1996 governs the present law. Land that is co-owned is now held under a trust of land. The trustees have a power to sell and also a power to postpone sale. Section 14(1) permits any trustee or beneficiary under a trust to apply to the court for an order. The court then has the power to make any order relating to the exercise of the trustees' functions as they see fit. Most significantly, the court can order the trustees to sell the property and pay the beneficiaries their cash share of the property.[147] The court could also refuse to order sale but require the party remaining in occupation of the home to pay the other 'rent'.[148]

There is a set of guidelines to be considered by the court when deciding whether to exercise their powers.[149] These do not rob the courts of a wide discretion, but rather give them some factors to take into account.[150] The guidelines are set out in s 15 of the Trusts of Land and Appointment of Trustees Act 1996:

(a) the intentions of the person or persons (if any) who created the trust,
(b) the purpose for which the property subject to the trust is held,

---

[144] Land Registration (Matrimonial Home Rights) Rules 1997, SI 1997/1964.
[145] The matrimonial home right is not an overriding interest, even if the holder is in occupation: FLA 1996, s 31(10)(b).
[146] Disputes between married couples over whether a house should be sold should be resolved under the Matrimonial Causes Act 1973.
[147] Trusts of Land and Appointment of Trustees Act 1996, s 15.
[148] Trusts of Land and Appointment of Trustees Act 1996, s 13.
[149] These were intended to consolidate the previous case law.
[150] *TSB v Marshall and Rodgers* [1998] 2 FLR 769; *The Mortgage Corp v Shaire* [2000] 1 FLR 973.

(c) the welfare of any minor who occupies or might reasonably be expected to occupy any land subject to the trust as his home, and

(d) the interests of any secured creditor of any beneficiary.[151]

There are different guidelines which apply to a trustee in bankruptcy, which will be discussed shortly.

The general attitude of the courts has been that a house is bought by the couple as a home, but if they split up then the purpose of the trust has failed (factor (b) above) and a sale can be ordered.[152] If there are children living in the house, the interests of the children will often be an important consideration, particularly if ordering the sale of the property will disrupt their education.[153] The aim of the Act is to give the courts wide discretion and so each case will be decided on its own special facts.[154] Notably this is one of those areas of the law where the interests of children are not made paramount.[155]

There have been some attempts to use s 14 where the parties are divorcing or have divorced. The courts have adopted a strict approach. Couples who are divorcing or have divorced must apply for orders under the Matrimonial Causes Act 1973 and may not use the Trusts of Land and Appointment of Trustees Act 1996.[156]

8. PROTECTION OF BENEFICIAL INTERESTS AGAINST PURCHASERS

We have seen how a cohabitant or spouse who is not a legal owner can establish an interest in a property via a constructive trust or a proprietary estoppel. However, this interest would be of limited value if the owner could sell the property and thereby extinguish the other party's interest. Imagine this situation: A owns a house in law; his girlfriend, B, moves in and in due course acquires an interest in the house under a constructive trust; A then sells the house to C: what is B's position?

The answer depends on whether the land is registered or not. If the land is registered then B's interest can be protected if her interest is registered on the land register with a caution, or if she can claim to have an overriding interest under Schedules 1, 2 and 3 to the Land Registration Act 2002. If the land is not registered then the question is whether the purchaser had notice of the interest, that is whether the purchaser was aware or ought to have been aware of B's interest.[157] Both of these provisions have the same basis: C ought to have been able to discover the interests of B by following ordinary conveyancing practice, and by failing to do so deserves to be bound by B's interests.

The position would be slightly different if there are two legal owners (for instance, in our example if A owned the house with D). In such a case the interests of the beneficiaries are 'overreached' and so will not bind the purchaser. The

---

[151] Under s 15(3) the wishes of the majority of the beneficiaries should be taken into account.
[152] *Jones* v *Challenger* [1961] 1 QB 176 CA.
[153] *Bernard* v *Joseph* [1982] Ch 391.
[154] *The Mortgage Corp* v *Shaire* [2000] 1 FLR 973.
[155] Warren (2002) discusses the impact of bankruptcy on children.
[156] *Laird* v *Laird* [1999] 1 FLR 791; *Tee* v *Tee and Hamilton* [1999] 2 FLR 613.
[157] *Kingsnorth Trust* v *Tizard* [1986] 1 WLR 783.

beneficiaries will be able to claim their proportion of the purchase price from the trustees.[158]

9. PROTECTION OF FAMILY PROPERTY ON BANKRUPTCY

The law in relation to bankruptcy and the family requires a delicate balance between the rights of the creditors and the rights of the bankrupt's family. There are strong economic arguments in favour of encouraging people to embark on entrepreneurial activities, even if there is a risk of failure. Part of this incentive is to ensure that it is not too difficult for business people to acquire capital for the start-up and support of their businesses. In practice, banks and other lending institutions are only willing to provide credit where there is a degree of security and this involves enabling business people to use their family home as collateral or security for loans. Few people have any other assets which would provide adequate security. The effect of using a family home as collateral or security for a loan is that if the debtor fails to make the required payments the bank can then seize the house, sell it and pay off the loan with the proceeds. However, the consequences of this on bankrupts and their families are severe. The Court of Appeal has referred to the 'melancholy consequences of debt and improvidence with which every civilised society has been familiar'.[159] The problem for the law is that if it protects the interests of the bankrupt's family members too strongly, then the family home will cease to be regarded as valuable security and this will discourage loans to entrepreneurs, which will have undesirable economic consequences. The difficulty was neatly summarised by Lord Browne-Wilkinson in *Barclays Bank* v *O'Brien*: 'It is essential that a law designed to protect the vulnerable does not render the matrimonial home unacceptable as security to financial institutions.'[160] Creditors may have no way of knowing whether the debtor has (or will have) a family, and any protection for family members would create greater uncertainty in the loan market. On the other hand, is it fair that a person should lose his or her home due to the business failure of someone else? This is connected to the questions of to what extent the law should regard family members as each having their own property and to what extent the law should recognise a kind of community property. It has been pointed out that if a wife can gain from the family business when it does well, she should suffer if it does not.

The law on bankruptcy as it affects family members will now be briefly discussed. On bankruptcy all of the bankrupt's property[161] is vested in the trustee in bankruptcy.[162] The trustee in bankruptcy is appointed by the court to act on behalf of the creditors and is 'in charge' of the bankrupt's assets, with the power to sell or transfer them.[163] The trustee in bankruptcy is under a duty to sell the assets and to

---

[158] Law of Property Act 1925, s 27. *City of London Building Society* v *Flegg* [1988] 1 FLR 98 HL.
[159] *Re Citro* [1991] Ch 142 at p. 157.
[160] [1994] 1 AC 180 at p. 188.
[161] Defined in the Insolvency Act 1986 (hereafter IA 1986), s 283, notably excluding clothes, bedroom furniture, and provisions for satisfying the basic domestic needs of the bankrupt and his family (s 283(2)(b)).
[162] IA 1986, s 306.
[163] The bankruptcy will sever a joint tenancy: *Re Gorman (A Bankrupt)* [1990] 2 FLR 289.

distribute the proceeds among the creditors.[164] It is a fundamental principle of the law of bankruptcy that the trustee steps into the shoes of the bankrupt and so cannot assume rights that a bankrupt does not have. There are two main issues. The first is how the law protects creditors from family members. It would be all too easy for bankrupts to transfer their assets to their family members in an effort to put the assets out of the reach of the creditors, and the law shields creditors from such attempts. The second issue is how the law guards family members from creditors.

A. Protecting creditors from family members

(i) Setting aside transactions

There is the danger that if one spouse is engaged in a business which is in severe financial difficulties he or she will attempt to avoid the unpleasant consequences of bankruptcy by transferring assets to his or her spouse in an attempt to keep them out of the hands of creditors. This danger has been addressed by two provisions in particular:

1. Section 423 of the Insolvency Act 1986 deals with transactions which defraud creditors. If a person enters into a transaction at an undervalue in order to defeat the claims of his or her creditors, the transaction can be set aside. So, for example, if a wife whose business is failing transfers some shares into her husband's name without receiving sufficient payment from him, this transaction can be set aside and the shares returned to the wife (in effect therefore to her trustee in bankruptcy). For the provision to operate it is necessary to show:

    (i)   There was a transaction. A transaction includes any kind of transfer, gift or arrangement.[165]
    (ii) That the transaction was at an undervalue. It will be regarded as at an undervalue if there was no consideration,[166] or the consideration given was significantly less than the value of the asset.
    (iii) The purpose of the transaction must be to place the asset outside the reach of the creditors or any person who might at some point in time become a creditor. This can be inferred from the circumstances if necessary.
    (iv) The transaction cannot be set aside if the property was acquired in good faith for value[167] and without awareness of the facts on which an order under s 423 could be made.

    Proceedings to set aside the transaction can be brought by anyone prejudiced by the transaction; by a party to the transaction; or by the trustee in bankruptcy.[168]

---

[164] Insolvency Rules 1986, SI 1986/1925, and IA 1986 set out the law in detail.
[165] IA 1986, s 436.
[166] That is, nothing of value in the eyes of the law was given in return for the transfer.
[167] In other words, that a reasonable price was paid.
[168] IA 1986, s 423(5).

Courts will order that assets are returned so that the parties are in the position they would have been in had the transaction not been made.[169]

2. Section 339 deals with transactions at an undervalue entered into by a bankrupt. It is therefore different from s 423, which addresses situations where a debtor is seeking to avoid the consequences of bankruptcy, but need not actually be bankrupt. Under s 339 the trustee of the bankrupt's estate may apply to the court for an order if the bankrupt entered into a transaction at an undervalue. The application can be made in respect of any transaction entered into up to five years prior to the bankruptcy. But if the transaction was more than two years prior to the bankruptcy then it is necessary to show that the bankrupt was insolvent at the time of the transaction. The insolvency will be presumed if the transaction was entered into with 'an associate' (which includes a spouse, former spouse, reputed spouse[170] or relative).[171] There is no need to prove an intent to defraud, and so the section is simpler to prove than s 423.

These provisions sit a little uneasily with the general law on personal property of family members which regards cohabitants or spouses as two separate individuals. In this context, the law in effect treats the property of the family as a single unit and not owned as individuals.

(ii) Bankruptcy and the family home

The trustee in bankruptcy, acting on behalf of the creditors, can seek an order for sale of the family home under s 14 of the Trusts of Land and Appointment of Trustees Act 1996.[172] The court may make such order as is just and reasonable: having regard to the interests of the creditors, to the conduct of the spouse or former spouse so far as contributing to the bankruptcy, to the needs and resources of that person, to the needs of any children and to all the circumstances of the case other than the needs of the bankrupt.[173] If the application is lodged more than one year after the making of the bankruptcy order, the interests of the creditors should outweigh any other consideration unless the facts of the case are exceptional. The court has accepted that a case may be exceptional where the bankrupt's spouse is seriously ill.[174] But if there are not extreme circumstances of this kind, the law explicitly prefers the interests of the creditors. However, the Court of Appeal has suggested that although the courts have greater flexibility they should not forget that it is always a 'powerful consideration' whether the creditor is receiving proper recompense for not receiving their money.[175] It is arguable that the present law does not pay adequate regard to article 8 rights of the family members.[176]

---

[169] IA 1986, s 423(3).

[170] The meaning of the phrase is unclear, but presumably it is intended to include a stable cohabiting relationship.

[171] IA 1986, ss 339, 341, 435.

[172] An occupation order under FLA 1996, s 33 may be available, but s 14 seems more appropriate.

[173] IA 1986, s 335A.

[174] *Re Raval* [1998] 2 FLR 718; *Judd v Brown* [1998] 2 FLR 360. In another case, *Re Bremner (A Bankrupt)* [1999] 1 FLR 912, the spouse's needs in looking after the seriously ill bankrupt were regarded as exceptional.

[175] *Bank of Ireland v Bell* [2001] 3 FCR 134, [2001] 2 FLR 809.

[176] See the discussion in *Jackson v Bell* [2001] FL 879.

B. Protecting the families from the creditors

Clarke[177] argues that there is certainly a public interest in discouraging bankruptcy, but on the other hand it would not be in the public interest if the bankrupt's family could be left with literally nothing. Section 283(2) of the Insolvency Act 1986 states that 'such clothing, bedding, furniture, household equipment and provisions as are necessary for meeting the basic domestic needs of the bankrupt and his family' are excluded from the bankrupt's estate. Section 310(2) states that the income of the bankrupt should not fall 'below what appears to the court to be necessary for meeting the reasonable needs of the bankrupt and his family'. In deciding the appropriate sum it is important to achieve 'proportionality' between the creditors and the bankrupt;[178] this does not necessarily mean that the bankrupt and his or her family are limited to the minimum sum requisite for the family to survive and so could even include private school fees.[179] This provision should ensure that the bankrupt and his or her family do not become dependent on benefits, and shows that society's interest of saving public costs is even more important than the interests of any creditors.

Section 336 of the Insolvency Act 1986 offers some protection to the occupation rights of the bankrupt's spouse. Once the bankrupt's property is placed in the hands of the trustee, no matrimonial homes rights[180] can be acquired. However, existing rights will bind a trustee, even if they are unregistered.[181] This is because the trustee steps into the shoes of the bankrupt and takes the property with the same limitations that bound the bankrupt. Children are offered some protection under s 337. If the bankrupt was entitled to occupy a dwelling-house by virtue of any estate or interest, and any person under 18 was living with the bankrupt when the petition was presented, the trustee cannot evict the child. The protection is in addition to any protection available under s 336.

10. SPOUSES, PARTNERS AND MORTGAGES

There are particular problems where one spouse or cohabitant signs a mortgage, with the family home as security, and then defaults on the mortgage. Imagine a husband who takes out a loan or mortgage, using the family home as collateral, and fails to make the necessary payments.[182] The bank will then try to enforce the security by seeking an order for sale of the property. If the wife is seeking to prevent the sale, she will have an uphill task.[183] The following stages indicate the approach the law would take.

1. The first question is whether the wife has an interest in the property. She might seek to demonstrate that she has an interest under an express or implied trust,

---

[177] Clarke (1993).
[178] *Kilvert* v *Kilvert* [1998] 2 FLR 806.
[179] *Re Rayatt* [1998] 2 FLR 264.
[180] Under FLA 1996, Part IV.
[181] The trustee can apply to have the rights terminated under IA 1986, s 336 (1)–(2).
[182] The law will be the same if it is the wife who takes out the loan and substantially the same if the couple are unmarried, but in the section that follows it will be assumed that the husband takes out the loan.
[183] Davey (1997).

or has rights of occupation under a matrimonial home right. If she has no interest[184] then she will not be in a position to halt the order for sale.

2. The next question is whether the mortgage covers the wife's share of the property or whether it only covers the husband's share. Clearly if the wife was a party to the mortgage (i.e. if she signed the mortgage) and the mortgage states that it covers the wife's share, it would.[185] However, even if she did not sign the mortgage she may have ceded priority of her interest over to the bank. This means that her share in the property would only be paid over to her after the bank was paid the sum owed to it. So if the house is worth £100,000 and there is a mortgage of £70,000 and the wife's share in the house is 50 per cent (i.e. £50,000), then when the house is sold the bank's mortgage would be paid first and the wife could claim her share from what was left (i.e. about £30,000 in this example). In fact this scenario is not realistic, as attempts to enforce an order for sale by the bank are likely to be preceded by a period of non-payment of mortgage instalments and second mortgages. Usually, therefore, the mortgage would take up the total value of the house, leaving nothing for the wife.

The wife would be deemed to have ceded priority of her interest to the bank in the following cases:

(i) She signed a document ceding priority.

(ii) She knew that her husband had taken out the mortgage and had voiced no objection.[186]

(iii) The mortgage was essential to the purchase of the property.[187]

(iv) The mortgage was a second mortgage, replacing a mortgage to which the wife had ceded priority.[188]

The case law developments in (ii), (iii) and (iv) are controversial. In effect they make it very unlikely that a wife or cohabitant would be able to claim priority of a mortgage in respect of a mortgage on the family home.

3. There are three ways in which a wife may attempt to prevent the mortgagee from enforcing a sale:

(i) The wife could argue that the mortgage was void or voidable. She could show that she and/or her husband had signed the mortgage as a result of misrepresentation or undue influence, or that the mortgage was unconscionable. Alternatively, she could rely on the Unfair Terms in Consumer Contracts Regulations 1999.[189] The normal rules of contract law would apply. A special set of rules has been developed in this area in relation to undue influence and we will discuss these in detail shortly.

---

[184] A wife will inevitably have a matrimonial home right if the home was intended to be both spouses' home together.

[185] Unless the contract specifically states otherwise, the creditor cannot increase the liability of a guarantor in a way which prejudices the position of the guarantor without the consent of the guarantor (*Lloyds TSB Bank* v *Shoney* [2001] EWCA Civ 1161, [2002] 1 FCR 673).

[186] *Paddington Building Society* v *Mendelsohn* (1985) 50 P&CR 244.

[187] *Abbey National Building Society* v *Cann* [1990] 2 FLR 112.

[188] *Equity and Law Home Loans* v *Prestidge* [1992] 1 WLR 137.

[189] SI 1999/2083.

(ii) If the wife's share in the home is independent of the mortgage she and the trustee in bankruptcy will be co-owners. The trustee can make an application under s 14 of the Trusts of Land and Appointment of Trustees Act 1996. This has already been discussed.

(iii) The wife could seek an order suspending enforcement of the mortgage under s 36 of the Administration of Justice Act 1970.[190]

Dewar has pointed out that this area of the law involves give and take. On the one hand, the law has been making it increasingly easy for the spouse or cohabitant to establish an interest in the family home. However, this interest is almost inevitably worthless if the bank or building society seeks to enforce a mortgage on the home. The law here is seeking to protect the cohabitant or spouse as against his or her partner, but not so as to prejudice the rights of the lending institutions.

A. Undue influence: Barclays Bank v O'Brien

There have been a large number of recent cases resulting from the decision of the House of Lords in *Barclays Bank* v *O'Brien*.[191] The kind of situation under discussion has arisen where one spouse or cohabitee (it has most often been the wife or female cohabitant) agreed to act as a surety or guarantee for her spouse's or cohabitant's loan. When the bank came to enforce the surety or guarantee, the wife or cohabitant sought to escape liability from acting as surety because of her husband's undue influence. At first sight such a claim seems unlikely to succeed. Normally, a contract between two parties (here the bank and the wife) will not be set aside on account of the wrongdoing of a third party (the husband). However, in *Barclays Bank* v *O'Brien*[192] the House of Lords found a novel way around this difficulty by arguing that the bank could be bound by the misrepresentation or undue influence of the husband if it had notice of it. So if the spouse or partner could show: (1) there was undue influence or a misrepresentation made by her husband or cohabitant; and (2) the bank had notice of the undue influence or misrepresentation, then the contract of surety or guarantee signed by the wife or cohabitant would be unenforceable.

The requirements will be considered separately.

(i) Proof of undue influence or misrepresentation

The concept of misrepresentation is clearly governed by contract law and does not really occasion particular difficulties in this area.[193] The doctrine of undue influence, however, needs some explanation. Undue influence arises in cases where there is a relationship where one party has a measure of influence over another and takes unfair advantage of the relationship. Unfair advantage may be taken by

---

[190] For a discussion of the recent case law, see Dixon (1998); Thomson (1998); Pawlowski and Brown (2002).
[191] [1994] 1 FLR 1, [1994] 1 FCR 357.
[192] [1994] 1 FLR 1, [1994] 1 FCR 357.
[193] See Beatson (2002).

blatant acts of persuasion or by less overt acts of relationship.[194] The burden of proving the undue influence is on the wronged person. The kind of evidence which will establish undue influence was explained by Lord Nicholls in *Royal Bank of Scotland* v *Etridge (No. 2)*:[195]

> Proof that the complainant placed trust and confidence in the other party in relation to the management of the complainant's financial affairs, coupled with a transaction which calls for explanation, will normally be sufficient, failing satisfactory evidence to the contrary, to discharge the burden of proof.[196]

This can be broken down into the following elements:

1. that the relationship between the parties was of a kind in which undue influence could be exercised; and
2. the transaction calls for an explanation; and
3. there is no evidence to rebut the presumption that there was undue influence.

Regarding element 1, there are some relationships which automatically give rise to a presumption that undue influence could be exercised. An example would be a doctor and patient relationship.[197] Others depend on the facts of the particular circumstances. So in one case, involving a man and his gardener, it was held that the presumption of undue influence could apply because the gardener had come to dominate the man. In later cases the courts have also been very willing to find that a variety of relationships have been of the kind that undue influence could be exercised.[198] But what about husbands and wives? Lord Browne-Wilkinson in *Barclays Bank* v *O'Brien* held that there is no automatic presumption that the relationship between a husband and wife is one where undue influence could be exercised. However, on the facts of a particular case a claimant may be able to persuade a court that he or she relied on his or her spouse in all financial matters, therefore was open to having his or her trust abused. [199]

In relation to element 2 it used to be the law that it was necessary to show that the claimant suffered manifest disadvantage as a result of the transaction. However, in *Royal Bank of Scotland* v *Etridge (No. 2)*[200] Lord Nicholls took the view that the correct test is to ask whether the transaction was readily explicable by the relationship of the parties. The significance of this is twofold. First, there may be a transaction which is to the disadvantage of the weaker party, but which is readily explicable by the relationship between the parties and so does not give rise to a presumption of undue influence (for example, where a child gives her father a Christmas present). Secondly, there may be a transaction which does call for

---

[194] *Royal Bank of Scotland* v *Etridge (No. 2)* [2001] 3 FCR 481, para 11.

[195] [2001] 3 FCR 481.

[196] Para 14.

[197] Others include guardian and ward, trustee and beneficiary, solicitor and client (*Royal Bank of Scotland* v *Etridge (No. 2)* [2001] 3 FCR 481, para 18).

[198] E.g. *Crédit Lyonnais Bank* v *Burch* [1997] 2 FCR 1 CA.

[199] Most cases have involved husbands taking advantage of their wives, but *Simpson* v *Simpson* [1992] 1 FLR 601 and *Barclays Bank* v *Rivett* [1999] 1 FLR 730 are examples of cases where a wife was found to have exercised undue influence over her husband.

[200] [2001] 3 FCR 481, paras 21–31.

explanation, even if not to the manifest disadvantage of the parties (for example, where a client sells his solicitor his house for the market value). Applying that to the kind of cases under discussion, is a transaction where a wife guarantees payment of her husband's business debts one which calls for explanation? Lord Nicholls in *Royal Bank of Scotland* thought not, 'in the ordinary case'.[201] He explained that 'the fortunes of husband and wife are bound up together. If the husband's business is the source of the family income, the wife has a lively interest in doing what she can to support the business'.[202]

In relation to the third element the most common way of rebutting a presumption of undue influence is by showing that the claimant received independent financial advice. However, even though a claimant received independent financial advice it may still be found that the transaction was the result of undue influence. Further, there may be other ways, apart from independent advice, which would rebut the presumption of undue influence.

(ii) Notice to the bank of undue influence or misrepresentation

The bank will be put on inquiry where a wife offers to stand surety for her husband's debts. Similarly in relation to unmarried couples where the bank is aware of the relationship. This can be where the couple are heterosexual or homosexual, or may or may not be cohabiting.[203] A joint advance to a couple will not put the bank on inquiry. Once the bank is on inquiry it is under an obligation to take reasonable steps to satisfy itself that the wife understood the practical implications of the transaction. In *Etridge* Lord Nicholls accepted that this would not mean that the wife was not suffering from undue influence, but it would mean that the wife was aware of the basic elements of the transaction. The most common way for a bank to carry out its obligation would be to ensure that the wife receives independent legal advice.

(iii) Discussion of the O'Brien/Etridge case law

Lord Bingham has described transactions whereby a partner guarantees a loan as being of 'great social and economic importance'.[204] The law is seeking to protect the position of a spouse (or partner) who is offering their interest in a matrimonial home to secure the borrowing of a spouse. It is necessary to ensure that that he or she fully understands the transaction into which the party entered. On the other hand it is necessary also to protect the position of lenders, so that they can advance money confident that the transaction will not be undone if appropriate procedures are undertaken.[205]

The ultimate effect of *O'Brien* cases is that banks now ensure that any spouse or partner guaranteeing a loan will be required by the bank to see a solicitor first.[206]

[201] Para 30.
[202] Para 28.
[203] *Royal Bank of Scotland* v *Etridge (No. 2)* [2001] 3 FCR 481, para 47.
[204] *Royal Bank of Scotland* v *Etridge (No. 2)* [2001] 3 FCR 481, para 21.
[205] *Royal Bank of Scotland* v *Etridge (No. 2)* [2001] 3 FCR 481 HL, para 2.
[206] Oldham (1995).

Arguably, all this does is lead to increased expenses for the spouse, with little practical benefit to him or her. However, others see it as an attempt by the law to do the best it can to protect the independent financial interests of wives, without unduly prejudicing the interests of banks and other lending institutions. The law recognises that the financial interests of husbands and wives may not be identical. The normal privacy that surrounds marital finances does not apply here. Under *O'Brien* the courts will be willing to look at the way in which money matters were dealt with within the marriage.

Some complain that the law 'depicts wives as passive, ill-informed and obedient to the will of their partners'.[207] Then again, there is evidence that the majority of wives do defer to their husbands over important financial decisions and so the law is perhaps simply being realistic.[208] Gardner neatly sums up the alternative approaches here:

> Some may see [the law] as appropriately standing for the recognition and correction of what they see as the disadvantaged position of wives and other emotional dependants in the kind of matter under discussion. Others, however, whilst agreeing that wives and other emotional dependants occupy a disadvantaged position, may believe that the appropriate answer is to encourage such people to take better care of themselves, and/or to alter social structures in such a way that the disadvantage is less likely to arise; and that the law should remain neutral as between classes of citizens, seeing this as important either as the correct position for the law in principle, or as marking the equal status which it is hoped wives and other emotional dependants will attain. Others still may find the very idea that specially generous treatment is merited an insulting one.[209]

11. CONCLUSION

This chapter has revealed that the law has failed to find a consistent approach to family property. On the one hand, generally the law treats spouses or cohabitants as two individuals and the normal property rules apply. On the other hand, some of the rules on bankruptcy or mortgages accept that even if property may be technically owned by one family member, in practice it is enjoyed by them all and so there are special rules designed to ensure that one family member does not avoid the consequences of insolvency by claiming that his or her property is actually owned by other family members. This law in this area is interesting in its treatment of the ownership of the family home. Because there is no discretion in the court to redistribute the property of unmarried couples on the breakdown of their relationship, the law on who owns the family home is particularly important for them. This has led the court to develop (manipulate, some would say) land law to enable a cohabitant to establish an interest in a home even if the normal formality requirements that attach to the transfer of interests in land have not been complied with.

---

[207] M. Thornton (1997: 491).
[208] Fehlberg (1997).
[209] S. Gardner (1999: 6).

5

PROPERTY ON SEPARATION

While a couple are married the law does little to interfere in the property interests of the parties. By contrast, on separation the law is willing to intervene to ensure that the spouses' financial interests are adequately protected. The law distinguishes financial support for children from financial support for partners. In relation to child support, the law is largely governed by the Child Support Act 1991, Child Support Act 1995, Child Support, Pensions and Social Security Act 2000 and to a lesser extent the Children Act 1989. These pieces of legislation apply equally to parents who are married and those who are unmarried. However, in relation to financial support for partners an important distinction is drawn between married and unmarried couples. For married couples the courts have the power to redistribute the family's property between the spouses as they consider just, taking into account all the circumstances of the case. For unmarried couples the courts can simply declare who owns what, and have no power to require one party to transfer property to another, except as a means of providing child support.

1. CHILD SUPPORT: THEORETICAL ISSUES

There is grave concern over the economic circumstances in which many children are brought up in the UK. More than one in three children live in poverty.[1] There are particular concerns about children of lone parents. One study found that in 1999 62 per cent of children with lone parents were living in poverty.[2]

Poverty for children is not restricted to children of lone parents. Seven per cent of children do not have properly fitting shoes; 3 per cent go without three meals a day; 10 per cent go without celebration on special occasions; 6 per cent without a waterproof coat.[3] Eighteen per cent of children suffer from poverty, defined as lacking two or more necessities in a list widely agreed by parents.[4] Such statistics are particularly concerning because poverty is linked with low birth weight,[5] poor levels of psychological health,[6] higher levels of exclusions from schools and teenage pregnancies,[7] drug misuse and high unemployment.[8] Poverty in childhood even leads to

---

[1] Douglas (2000a: 132).
[2] National Family and Parenting Institute (2001c). See also Family Policy Studies Centre (1997).
[3] Gordon, Adelman, Ashworth et al. (2000: 34).
[4] Middleton and Adelman (2003).
[5] Palmer, Rahman and Kenway (2002: 32 and 38).
[6] Meltzer and Gatward (2000).
[7] Palmer, Rahman and Kenway (2002: 31–2).
[8] Child Poverty Action Group (2001: 136–140).

subsequent generations of children suffering.[9] The government has pledged to end child poverty within 20 years. But the policies are directed towards encouraging parents to work (e.g. by increasing the provision of child-care), not by giving increased benefits to non-working parents. This is explained in this way: 'Having a parent in work provides children with an active, valuable role model. It helps provide the parent with self-respect and a social network. And most important of all, a waged family is less likely to be poor and benefit-dependent than an unwaged one'.[10] Fortin is critical of such an approach. She claims that 'motivated by concerns about the public purse and by policies over encouraging parents to seek employment, the state maintains a safety-net approach to family support. Such short-term policies ignore the long-term impact on society of large numbers of children being brought up in severely impoverished conditions.'[11]

As this discussion demonstrates, the question of financial support is crucial if children's interests are to be adequately protected. The issue raises some important questions of theory, which will now be discussed.

A. Does the obligation to support children fall on the state or on the parents?

A key issue concerning child support is: on whom does the burden of support for children primarily fall? Ultimately, is the state responsible for the financial support of children (although the state can recoup the money from parents) or are the parents responsible (although the state can step in to support children if the parents fail)?[12] In other words, is it the state's primary role to enforce parental responsibility to pay child support, or to provide guaranteed support itself for the child? Krause suggests that the obligation is shared between society and the parents: 'children have a right to a decent start in life. This right is the obligation of the father and equally of the mother, and in recognition of a primary and direct responsibility, equally the obligation of society.'[13]

Looking at this question from another angle, it is possible to regard the question as one of children's rights. If it is accepted that children should have rights then it seems inevitable that children have a right to the financial support necessary so that they can, at least, be fed and clothed.[14] Given that the state is a more reliable supporter than the parent, it is in the child's interests that the state should have the primary obligation to ensure children receive sufficient support, but how the state's obligation is performed may vary from family to family. The government's White Paper, *Children's Rights and Parents' Responsibilities*,[15] regards the burden of child support as clearly on the parents, and sees the government's role as 'helping' parents

---

[9] Department of Work and Pensions (2002: 10–11). Ghate and Hazel (2002) report the real difficulties of parenting while in poverty.
[10] Department of Social Security (1998: ch. 7, para 5).
[11] Fortin (2003b: 303).
[12] Garrison (1998).
[13] Krause (1994: 232).
[14] See Chapter 8.
[15] Department of Social Security (2000).

to meet their responsibility.[16] The question is made even more complex in that the state's approach to child support may seek to pursue a variety of aims. As well as ensuring that the child is adequately provided for, a scheme may also endeavour to discourage births out of marriage; to punish unmarried fathers; or to decrease the legal aid costs associated with relationship breakdown.[17]

The position in practice in England and Wales is that the financial support for children is supplied by the state for low-income and unemployed parents, and by parents for better-off households. However, the state does recognise some obligation to *all* children by providing child benefit payments to all parents regardless of wealth.[18] There are two main aspects of the government's response to poverty among children. On the one hand, there is the 'New Deal' for lone parents,[19] which is aimed at encouraging lone parents to seek employment. On the other hand, there is the Child Support Agency, which seeks to collect money from non-residential parents (those parents who no longer live with the child). The most recent government White Paper sets out the government's approach:

> Every child has the right to the best possible start in life. And parents have a clear responsibility to protect and provide for their children so that the children can make the most of their lives. This is a responsibility that endures regardless of family separation. The Government helps parents fulfil their responsibility in a number of ways. It does so directly – for example through payment of Child Benefit – and indirectly by ensuring that parents discharge their responsibilities especially where they live apart from their children. We are determined to put in place a new system to ensure that the children of parents who live apart get the care and support they need and to which they are entitled.[20]

In *R (On the application of Denson) v Child Support Agency*[21] Mumby J rejected an argument that the Child Support Act 1991 was incompatible with the non-resident parent's rights under the European Convention of Human Rights. Mumby J held that the Act achieved a proportionate response between the non-resident parent's rights under articles 8 and 1 of the first protocol; the non-resident parent's responsibilities towards his or her children; the need for a system that produced fair and consistent results; and the interests of taxpayers in being relieved of the support of parents with care of the children.

Sheldon, by contrast is not convinced that the present law adequately protects the interests of children. She argues: 'Leaving children dependent on the economic means of their parents has contributed significantly to the widespread poverty of women and children and, in countries where the wealth to rectify this situation exists, this should be cause for national shame.'[22] She therefore argues that the state should be regarded as primarily responsible for the financial support of children. This view has also received support from Bainham[23] who rejects an argument that

[16] Department of Social Security (2000: 1).
[17] Krause (1994).
[18] Millar (1996).
[19] A useful summary in Douglas (2000a).
[20] Department of Social Security (2000: 1).
[21] [2002] 1 FCR 460.
[22] Sheldon (2003: 193).
[23] Bainham (2001a).

men who have a 'one night stand' should be taken to accept responsibility for the resulting child.[24] As Kapp has argued:

> To saddle a man with at least eighteen years of expensive, exhausting child support liability on the basis of a haphazard vicissitude of life seems to shock the conscience and be arbitrary, capricious, and unreasonable, where childbirth results from the mother's free choice . . . a man no longer has any control over the course of a pregnancy he has biologically brought about [and] it is unjust to impose responsibility where there is no ability to exercise control.[25]

On the other hand the burden of raising children in lone-parent households most commonly falls on women. To deny that fathers are financially responsible and render lone mothers dependent on the state for financial support is likely to increase poverty among women, and lone mothers particularly, unless there is a sea of change in political attitudes towards lone parents.[26] Others argue that child support can be justified on the basis that it is pre-payment of the support the parent will receive in old age from the child.[27] This argument will be discussed further in Chapter 12, but the fact that children are not legally obliged to support their aged parents somewhat weakens it.

Scott has argued that parents can be said to be liable to pay child support because they have wronged the child by allowing their relationship to become unhappy.[28] The enforcement of child support punishes this wrong and deters such behaviour. It also requires people to consider carefully about having children if they are unsure that their relationship is going to last. To some this argument will appear to be an expression of moral disapproval for sexual behaviour outside committed relationships, which is inappropriate in a pluralistic society.[29]

B. Are the parents' obligations independent or joint?

Accepting that parents are obliged to support their children, the question is then whether parents are separately responsible for the support of the child or whether they share this burden, in that each parent should only be expected to pay their own half of the child support. If, for example, a mother who is receiving income support is raising the child, should a non-residential employed father be required to pay all the expenses of the child or only 'his half' of them? The father may try to argue that he was only 'half responsible for the birth' and so should pay no more than half of the costs of the child. On the other hand, it is arguable that the residential parent provides her 'share' of the child support through the time and effort she puts in day to day for the child, and that therefore the full financial burden should fall on the non-residential parent.[30]

---

[24] O'Neil and Ruddick (1979); Nelson and Nelson (1989).
[25] Kapp (1982: 376–7).
[26] Blustein (1982) justifies child support on the basis that parents are best placed to meet the needs of vulnerable children.
[27] For an interesting theory based on gratitude see Loken (1999).
[28] Altman (2003).
[29] Bainham (2001a).
[30] Eekelaar (1991a: 111).

As we shall see, the approach taken in England and Wales is that each parent can be liable to pay the full costs of the support of the child, but if both are able to pay then the burden may be shared.

C. Biological or social parents?

If children should be supported jointly by their parents, the next question is: what is meant by parents in this context? Specifically, where a parent has both stepchildren and biological children, how should his or her resources be shared between them?[31] Imagine A and B have a child, Y. A moves out and later lives with C, who has a child, X, by a previous relationship. Should A support Y or X? Or should he try to support both? Prior to the Child Support Act 1991, the practice in many cases was that if a man left his first family and later moved in with a second family, he would provide for the second family and the state would support the first family through benefits. The Child Support Act 1991 and Child Support, Pensions and Social Security 2000 have changed this fundamentally and now liability is attached to biological parenthood. So, in our example, A is liable in law to support Y and not X.[32] Interestingly, a recent study suggests that this is in line with the views of children whose parents have separated.[33]

There are a number of issues here:

1. *Should financial responsibility be linked with parental responsibility?* Is it fair that under English and Welsh law an unmarried father is automatically required to support the child financially, but is not automatically granted parental responsibility? It can be argued that as it is inevitably in the child's interests to receive financial support from his or her father, but not inevitably in the child's interest for his or her father to have parental responsibility, the position can be justified. For example, if the father does not know the child at all, it may be in the child's interests to require him to pay but not to permit him to make decisions on the child's behalf. However, from a father's perspective the position appears most unjust.[34] Indeed there is some evidence that both mothers and fathers in their minds link the payment of child support and contact.[35]

2. *Should financial responsibility be coupled with social parenting?* It could be argued that the law should match fiscal legal liability with the feelings of social or moral obligation that parents have. This, it has been maintained, would make the law more effective and acceptable. Eekelaar and Maclean found in their survey that fathers thought financial obligations should be tied to the social role played by fathers, but mothers thought the obligations should follow the blood tie.[36] The study demonstrated that there was a strong link between payment of financial

---

[31] Bennett (1997).

[32] See Chapter 7 for a general discussion on the differences between biological and social parenthood.

[33] Clarke, Craig and Glendinning (1996a).

[34] By contrast, in *P v B (Paternity; Damages for Deceit)* [2001] 1 FLR 1041 a father sued in deceit his cohabitant whom he claimed had falsely told him her child was his, leading to him paying £90,000 by way of child support.

[35] Clarke, Craig and Glendinning (1996b).

[36] But these might not reflect the views of the public at large: see Herring (1998b: 214).

support and contact with the child. Where the father had contact with the child he was more likely to support the child than where he did not. Eekelaar and Maclean argued:

> A support obligation which accompanies or arises from social parenthood is embedded in that social parenthood; thus the payment of support can be seen as part of the relationship maintained by continued contact. But an obligation based on natural parenthood rests on the policy of instilling a sense of responsibility for individual action and equity between fathers who do and fathers who do not exercise social parenthood.[37]

The workings of the Child Support Act 1991 in practice have revealed that where there is an ongoing level of contact between the non-resident parent and the child there is more likely to be payment of child support and that such payments are perceived to be fair.[38] Indeed, interviews with non-resident fathers have shown that fathers regard their payments of child support of symbolic importance in that they maintain the father's position as the 'breadwinner' in the family. Some fathers indicate that payments of support can make up for feelings of guilt about not being with their children.[39]

3. *Should it matter whether the pregnancy was planned or not?* Hale J in *J* v *C (Child: Financial Provision)*[40] confirmed that liability under the Children Act 1989 and the Child Support Act 1991 did not depend on whether the pregnancy was planned or not. Although it may be understandable that, from a parent's perspective, whether the pregnancy was planned or not should be relevant in determining liability, from the child's viewpoint he or she should not be prejudiced because of his or her parents' attitudes at the time of the conception.[41]

D. What level should the support be?

There are many options for setting the correct level of child support. Some of the options are:

1. *Subsistence costs.* This would be the amount of money that would be necessary to support the child at a minimally decent level. This sum could be assumed to be the amount of the welfare payment from the state that would be paid in respect of the child.
2. *Acceptable costs.* This would be the estimated level of support required to keep a child at a reasonably acceptable standard of living. It might be appropriate to look at the level of payments made by local authorities to foster parents as a guide for the appropriate figure.
3. *Expected lifestyle costs.* This would be the amount needed to keep the child at the lifestyle level the child would have expected to enjoy had the parents not separated.

---

[37] Eekelaar and Maclean (1997: 150).
[38] Davis and Wikeley (2002).
[39] Bradshaw, Stimson, Skinner and Williams (1999). See also Brasse (2002).
[40] [1999] 1 FLR 152, [1998] 3 FCR 79.
[41] Spon-Smith (2002: 29) notes a case in which a man who was deceived into thinking that he was the father of a child was refunded by the CSA £30,000 that he had paid by way of child support when it turned out he was not the father.

Another way of putting this test is that the child should be kept at the lifestyle standard enjoyed by children in two-parent households of the separating parents' income level.[42]

4. *Actual expenditure.* The law could focus on the amount actually spent by the residential parent, in so far as it was reasonable, and require the non-residential parent to share these costs. The difficulty with this approach would be the ambiguity which surrounds the term 'reasonableness'. The average cost of raising a child until the age of 21 has recently been calculated at £140,398.[43]

5. *Income percentage.* The level of child support could be a fixed percentage of the non-residential parent's income.

6. *Cost-effective level.* The amount of support should be fixed at a level which can be regularly paid. This approach is highly pragmatic. It focuses not on the child but on the expense to the state of enforcing and collecting the payments. It argues that, whatever the ideal, if the level is fixed at too high a rate and seen as unfair, then the money will not be paid. It is therefore better to set a lower rate which is more likely to be paid and thereby avoid the costs of enforcement.

7. *Equality of households.* This approach would seek to achieve an equal standard of living between the father's and mother's household.[44] This would not necessarily mean fixing equal income, because the cost of caring for the child would involve the residential parent in greater expense. This method requires integration of the maintenance of the parent with support for the child.

8. *Utilitarian.* This approach would fix child support at a level at which the removal of any asset from the non-residential parent's house would lead to a greater reduction in that household's welfare than the gain which would be received by the residential parent's household. The approach focuses not on sums of money, but on the welfare and happiness of the parties. It would, however, be extremely difficult to measure these.

E. 'The lone-parent crisis'

In the present political climate it is difficult to separate the question of child support from the concerns over the 'crisis of lone parents'.[45] There has been a substantial increase in the number of lone-parent households. In 2001 in England and Wales a lone parent headed 25 per cent of households;[46] in 1972 the figure was 7 per cent.[47] The reaction to the increase in lone parenthood has been varied.[48] Some see lone parents as an alarming sign of social disintegration, while others view lone parenthood as a crucial aspect of the liberation of women from the traditional family. Those who see lone parents as a major problem in our society quote statistics that show the percentage of lone parents in receipt of benefits rose from 37 per

---

[42] S. Parker (1991).
[43] BBC (2003).
[44] S. Parker (1991).
[45] For criticism of lone parents families see e.g. Galston (1991); for a more positive response see Young (1999).
[46] Office for National Statistics (2001).
[47] Office for National Statistics (1996).
[48] Fox Harding (1996).

cent in 1971 to 66 per cent 1989;[49] that 85–92 per cent of lone parents receive benefits at some stage;[50] and that benefits for lone parents cost £10 billion in 1997/98.[51] Further, there is evidence that children of lone parents (or at least some categories of lone parents) suffer in various kinds of ways (e.g. they are more likely to commit crime).[52] However, there is much debate as to why this is so. Some argue that the root cause of the disadvantage faced by children of lone parents is the poverty associated with lone parenthood, while others cite the lack of a father figure or stable family background as the primary cause.[53] In political terms, these arguments lead to debates over whether state benefits to lone parents encourage lone parenthood and so should be restricted or whether such benefits help alleviate the disadvantages attached to lone parenthood and should be increased.

It is important to realise that the average time spent as a child of a lone parent is just under four years.[54] This indicates that although children may spend some of their childhood with lone parents, the likelihood is that the lone parent will repartner. It should also be noted that lone parenthood is not a novel phenomenon; in previous centuries even higher percentages of children lived with lone parents than today, with death being the main cause of lone parenthood.[55]

Although it is common to refer to 'the problem of lone mothers', it might be more appropriate to refer to 'the problem of non-residential fathers'. One survey found that only 77 per cent of non-residential fathers had paid maintenance at least once and 57 per cent were doing so currently. Twenty-one per cent had not seen their children in the last year, although 47 per cent saw their children at least every week.[56] Lady Thatcher, who as Prime Minister had steered the Child Support Act 1991 through Parliament, notably recalled in her memoirs that she was 'appalled by the way in which men fathered a child and then absconded, leaving the single mother – and the tax payer – to foot the bill for their irresponsibility and condemning the child to a lower standard of living'.[57]

F. Child support and parental support

If a parent is obliged to support a child, should he or she necessarily be required to provide for the residential parent? There is no point in supplying a child with food and clothing if there is no one to feed or clothe the child. So a strong case can be made that if a child is to be cared for by a residential parent, then the non-residential parent should be liable to support the residential parent at some level. Another key question is how to balance the claims of children and spouses on divorce. A straightforward approach could be that first the courts should resolve the issues related to the child's support, and then turn to spousal support. Deech suggests

[49] P. Morgan (1999b).
[50] Noble, Smith and Chong (1998).
[51] P. Morgan (2000: 9).
[52] P. Morgan (2000). See Gingerbread (2002) for the harsh realities of life for many lone parents.
[53] Edwards and Halpern (1992).
[54] Bradshaw and Millar (1991).
[55] Laslett (1979).
[56] Bradshaw, Stimson, Skinner and Williams (1999).
[57] Thatcher (1995: 630).

that, for most couples nowadays, child support takes up such a large part of income that very limited resources are available for spousal support. She predicts that:

> A survey of property and maintenance on divorce in ten years' time is likely to find that spousal maintenance has been abolished; that non-residential fathers are paying child maintenance collected through income tax or in some other relatively painless form; and that private agreements are being reached over matrimonial homes. Yet such a report is unlikely to find reduced rates of unhappiness, divorce and legal expense.[58]

G. Should child support be a private issue?

Should the level of child support be fixed by the government or is it a private matter to be left to negotiation between the parties? In considering this issue it is useful to distinguish cases where the child and resident parent are receiving state benefits and cases where they are not. For such cases where they are the state has a clear interest in ensuring that the non-resident parent recompenses the state for the amount paid out in benefits, if he or she can afford to do so. But if neither party is in receipt of benefits does the state have an interest, justifying intervention in how the parties decide to receive child support? For example, if a couple decide that the best way to arrange their post-separation finances is that the wife and children will receive the former matrimonial home, but to compensate the husband for his loss in the share of the house he will have to pay less by way of financial support than he would have done, is it proper for the state to intervene to require the husband to pay a certain minimum amount? Or should this be regarded as a private matter which should be left to the decision of the couple themselves? It could be argued that the issue of child poverty is an important one for the state and parents should not be permitted to enter an agreement which leaves the child only barely provided for.[59]

2. FINANCIAL SUPPORT OF CHILDREN

A. Financial support of children living with both parents

A crucial point about the present law is that generally it does not intervene in the financial affairs of a family who are living together. As long as the child is provided for at a basic level and the child is not suffering significant harm, the state will not interfere. Indeed many fathers have complained that they are required to pay more for their child after the separation than they did when living with the child. It is on parental separation that the law intervenes and can require a parent not just to provide for the basic needs of the child, but also to apply a fair level of support. This non-intervention in family life except upon the separation of parents is one aspect of the weight the law places on the protection of the private life of the family.[60] In fact, a child who wishes to complain that he or she is not being given enough pocket

---

[58] Deech (1996: 104).
[59] Wikeley (2001).
[60] See Chapter 1.

money could seek an order under s 8 of the Children Act 1989, but it is hard to imagine a court being willing to hear such a case.

B. The Child Support Act 1991

The original child support scheme is found in the Child Support Act 1991. However, the scheme is being replaced by that found in the Child Support, Pensions and Social Security Act 2000. All new claimants since 3 March 2003 have fallen under the 2000 Act. Existing clients are being gradually transferred from the Child Support Act 1991 (hereafter CSA 1991) to the 2000 Act. This chapter will therefore discuss both Acts.

The CSA 1991 was born out of a deep dissatisfaction with the system of child support that existed at the time. The White Paper, *Children Come First*, described the problems:

> The present system of maintenance is unnecessarily fragmented, uncertain in its results, slow and ineffective. It is based largely on discretion. The system is operated through the High and County Courts, the Magistrates' Courts ... and the offices of the Department of Social Security. The cumulative effect is uncertainty and inconsistent decisions about how much maintenance should be paid. In a great many instances, the maintenance award is not paid or the payments fall into arrears and then take weeks to re-establish. Only 30% of lone mothers and 3% of lone fathers receive regular maintenance for their children. More than 750,000 lone parents depend on income support. Many lone mothers want to go to work, but do not feel able to do so.[61]

The previous system was administered by the courts. The burden lay on the residential parent to apply to the court for an order against the other parent. Many parents did not think it was worth applying or found the system too difficult to use. Given the strain of bringing up a child alone, it is not surprising that few lone parents successfully pursued their applications. When the cases came to court there was great inconsistency over the levels of support ordered. Even once made, there were enormous difficulties in enforcing the court orders. In effect, then, maintenance was rarely paid and lone parents were dependent on benefits for financial support.

The Child Support Act 1991 attempted to bring in an entirely new procedure. As the 1991 Act is being phased out, it will not be discussed in detail, but we will only consider in outline the 1991 Act, as amended by the Child Support Act 1995 (hereafter CSA 1995). The key features of the Acts are as follows:

1. The Acts are only concerned with 'absent' (non-residential) parents. They do nothing to ensure financial support for a child whose parents are still living together.[62] It should be noted that the CSA 1991 also operates if both parents are 'absent' (e.g. if the child was being cared for by a relative).
2. The CSA 1991 imposes liability on 'parents'.[63] This only covers those who are in law the mother or father of the child.[64] A person who has treated the child as

---

[61] Department of Social Security (1990).

[62] The Acts only apply to 'qualified parents', that is to parents who are sharing a household with the child (Child Support Act 1991, hereafter CSA 1991, s 3).

[63] CSA 1991, s 1.

[64] CSA 1991, s 54.

a child of the family, but is not the child's parent is not liable under the Acts. The term 'parent' includes natural parents, adoptive parents and people treated as parents under the Human Fertilisation and Embryology Act 1990. If a person denies parentage, then, unless a finding of parentage has been made in a previous court hearing,[65] biological tests must be carried out.[66] The nature of the parents' relationship (whether they are married or not) does not affect the parents' liability under the CSA 1991.

3. Under the Child Support Acts parents have a duty to maintain their children until the child is 16, or until their 19th birthday if they are receiving full-time education.[67]

4. The CSA 1991 is concerned with periodical payments. Capital payments or transfers of property cannot be ordered under the CSA 1991.

5. The Child Support Agency has responsibility for administering the Acts.[68] This means that the duty for assessing and enforcing the payments lies with the Agency and not with the residential parent or the courts. Indeed if the residential parent is receiving benefits, he or she must notify the Agency of the identity of the other parent.[69] The Agency will then enforce the orders for payments made against the non-residential parent, whether the residential parent wishes the Agency to become involved or not.[70]

6. The Acts provide a formula which determines the liability of parents. The formula results in a target figure which it is hoped the non-residential parent will be able to pay. This target is called 'the maintenance requirement'. The maintenance requirement is basically set at the amount that would be paid by the state in respect of income support benefit for the child and their carer.[71] The non-residential parent is required to pay 50 per cent of his or her 'assessable income' to the Agency, that is the income he or she has after deduction of tax, less a sum representing his or her very basic needs (the 'exempt income').[72]

The formula is designed to ensure that the non-residential parent is not reduced to a level of income close to that which he or she would have if on benefits, because then he or she would have no incentive to work. So the formula must not operate to reduce his or her income below a level known as the 'protected income'. If paying 50 per cent of his or her income would exceed the maintenance payment then the calculation is different. The non-residential parent pays 50 per cent of his or her income up to the point that the maintenance requirement is met and then he or she pays between 15 per cent and 25 per

[65] In certain specified hearings, as set out in CSA 1991, s 26.
[66] CSA 1991, s 26. The blood tests should be carried out unless to do so would be contrary to the child's interests (*Re E (A Minor) (Child Support: Blood Test)* [1994] 2 FLR 548).
[67] CSA 1991, s 55.
[68] CSA 1991, Sch 1.
[69] CSA 1991, s 6.
[70] CSA 1991, s 9.
[71] This would include 'personal allowances', which the parent who has care would receive, and the 'family premium'. From this total is deducted the amount of child benefit payable in respect of the family. Essentially, the maintenance requirement is the amount a lone parent with a child would receive from the state, excluding child benefit.
[72] Rent or mortgage payments are included and, after the Child Support Act 1995 (hereafter CSA 1995), there is now an allowance for children living with him or her.

cent (depending on the number of relevant children) on the remaining part of his or her assessable income,[73] although there is a maximum figure, which no award can exceed. If the residential parent has an income then the maintenance obligation is divided between the parents, roughly in proportion to their incomes.

After complaints that the formula was too rigid, the CSA 1995 amended the law so that the Secretary of State was permitted to operate various 'departure directions'.[74] Either parent can seek a direction that the formula be departed from under certain circumstances. The circumstances which might permit a departure include:[75] where there are special expenses;[76] where under a court order or agreement entered into before 5 April 1993 a lump sum or capital payment was made in lieu of child support; when a person's lifestyle is inconsistent with their level of income; or where a person's housing costs are unreasonably high. There is then discretion to decide whether or not there will be a departure from the formula.

7. There is no general obligation on the residential parent to apply for an assessment of the liability of the non-residential parent under the Child Support Acts. If neither parent is in receipt of benefits it is open to them to reach their own maintenance agreement in connection with child support and they do not need to involve the Agency. However, where the female parent with care of the child is in receipt of income support or family credit, she must authorise steps to recover payment and provide information about the identity of the father.[77] Failure to do so leads to a reduction in benefit (by a reduced benefit direction).[78] There is an exception where:

> there are reasonable grounds for believing that—
>> (a) if the parent were to be required to give that authorisation; or
>> (b) if she were to give it,
> there would be a risk of her, or any child living with her, suffering harm or undue distress as a result.'[79]

It is not clear what constitutes 'harm or undue distress' in this context, but presumably it covers serious cases of domestic violence.[80]

8. There are broad powers of collection and enforcement in the Child Support Acts. If there has been wilful and culpable neglect, the non-payer can be sent to prison. There are also powers to ascertain information from the employers of those involved. Inspectors have power to enter premises used for carrying out a trade, profession, vocation or business, unless it is the individual's dwelling-house.

---

[73] In other words, he or she pays the maintenance requirement and 25 per cent of the amount his or her available income exceeds twice the maintenance requirement.

[74] CSA 1991, ss 28A–28H.

[75] CSA 1991, Sch 4B.

[76] E.g. costs in travelling to work; costs in maintaining contact with a child for whom he or she is liable to pay child support.

[77] CSA 1991, s 6.

[78] CSA 1991, s 46. From 1996 the deduction was increased to 40 per cent.

[79] CSA 1991, s 6(2).

[80] Hayes and Williams (1999: 722) discuss this issue in some detail.

(i) Child Support Acts and court orders

Where the CSA 1991 applies and a child support officer has the power to make a maintenance order, then the courts are normally prohibited from making periodical payment orders in respect of those children and parents.[81] A court still has jurisdiction to make financial orders in respect of children who are under the Agency's jurisdiction in the following circumstances:

1. The court has a power to make a periodical payments order if the maximum child maintenance assessment is in force.[82] The court would need to be satisfied that the maintenance as it stands is inadequate. This is only likely to occur where the non-residential parent is exceptionally rich or the child has particular needs.[83]
2. If the child is receiving education, instruction or training for a trade, profession or vocation, the court can make an order for the purpose of meeting the costs of the education or training.[84]
3. Where the child is disabled the court can require the non-residential parent to meet some of the expense in connection with the disability.[85] A good example of this is *C v F (Disabled Child: Maintenance Orders)*,[86] where an application was made under the Children Act 1989. It was held that the order could be made under the Children Act 1989 beyond the child's 19th birthday, even though a person is never liable to support a child over 18 under the CSA 1991.
4. The court may exercise its power where 17- and 18-year-old dependants are not in full-time education because such children do not fall within the ambit of the CSA 1991.
5. Where there is a maintenance agreement in writing, it can be enforced, but not so as to exclude the operation of the CSA 1991.[87] In other words, it would be possible to increase the liability of a non-residential parent through the enforcement of a maintenance agreement, but not to decrease it.[88]
6. There is nothing in the CSA 1991 that prevents a court from making a lump sum order or property adjustment order under other legislation, although the courts will not be willing to make lump sum orders that are in effect capitalised maintenance orders.[89]

(ii) Using the courts to challenge the Child Support Acts

Various attempts have been made to seek a judicial review of an assessment made under the CSA 1991. These have been largely ineffective. Most notably in *R v*

---

[81] CSA 1991, s 3(3). The bar does not apply if the child support officer has no jurisdiction to make a maintenance order – for example, if the non-residential parent is not habitually resident in the UK.
[82] CSA 1991, s 8(6).
[83] CSA 1991, s 8(6).
[84] CSA 1991, s 8(7).
[85] CSA 1991, s 8(8).
[86] [1998] 2 FLR 1, [1999] 1 FCR 39 CA.
[87] CSA 1991, s 8(5).
[88] See for futher discussion *Dorney-Kingdom* v *Dorney-Kingdom* [2000] 3 FCR 20, [2000] 2 FLR 855.
[89] *Phillips* v *Pearce* [1996] 2 FLR 230, [1996] 2 FCR 237.

Secretary of State for Social Security, ex p Biggin[90] one father sought to challenge the Agency by relying on s 2 of the CSA 1991, which states:

> Where, in any case which falls to be dealt with under this Act, the Secretary of State is considering the exercise of any discretionary power conferred by this Act, he shall have regard to the welfare of any child likely to be affected by his decision.

The father sought to argue that in his case it would not promote the child's interests for the amount assessed under the formula to be enforced against him, in particular because it would mean that he would not be able to afford to have contact with his son. He failed in his attempt, with Thorpe J arguing that the section did not affect the application and enforcement of the formula. It was accepted that this left s 2 with little or no role to play in the 1991 Act.[91]

(iii) Criticisms of the 1991 Act

The Child Support Act has been strongly criticised. In fact, the ferocity of the opposition has been startling. The main criticisms are as follows:

1. *Miscalculations.* In 1994 the National Audit Office, in examining the work of the Agency, found that half of all assessments made under the 1991 Act were wrong. This was not due to maliciousness, but to the complexity of the formula.[92] The Child Support Agency Annual Report[93] stated that by 2002 at least 82 per cent of cases were correct. However, the Agency was still being criticised for its high level of errors by the National Audit Office.[94] Also there are concerns that in over 28 per cent of cases the Agency was working on false information provided by clients.[95]

   There are particular difficulties in calculating correctly the appropriate payments for those whose income is constantly changing; for example those who are self-employed.[96] This may involve the Agency in constantly recalculating the appropriate level of payment.

2. *The state is favoured over children.* It has been argued that the CSA 1991 put the Treasury, rather than the child, first.[97] There is much to support such an allegation. If payments are made to the Agency they will not actually benefit the residential parent and the child because any payment received will lead to a 'pound for pound' reduction in the benefits they receive. It is therefore only if the non-residential parent pays more than the total the residential parent receives in benefits that the residential parent will actually be better off because of the CSA. Notably between 50 and 70 per cent of spending on children came

---

[90] [1995] 1 FLR 851.

[91] See *Logan* v *UK* (1994) 22 EHRR 178 CD for a failed attempt to argue that the Child Support Act breached article 6 of the European Convention on Human Rights.

[92] Deas (1998). For claims that the CSA has greatly improved its accuracy rates see Ten Downing Street (2003).

[93] Child Support Agency (2000).

[94] National Audit Office (2000).

[95] Pirrie (2003).

[96] Department of Social Security (2000: 1.4).

[97] Child Poverty Action Group (1994).

from income support. This is important because income support is a benefit that is paid to parents with care for themselves.[98] Clearly parents with care were spending less on themselves, in order to provide for their children.

The scheme was designed to maximise the chance of the state recouping the amount being paid out in benefits to lone parents. Notably, once the state, in a particular case, has achieved its objective of recouping the expense it has incurred (the maintenance requirement), a lower percentage is required for additional income from the non-residential parent.[99] It is not surprising that there have been strong objections from men who have had to contribute half of their available income to the Agency. It is also striking that the targets set by the government for the Agency were in terms of the amount of money that the Treasury would save, rather than the amount of money that lone parents and their children received.[100] Some 1.5 million children are under the Agency's umbrella, but only 250,000 children receive more money than they would without the existence of the Act.[101] It is clear that the scheme is far more effective at saving the government money than it is in alleviating poverty among lone-parent households, but saving taxpayers' money is no bad thing.

In *Logan* v *UK*[102] a father claimed that he was required to pay so much under the CSA 1991 that he was unable to finance contact with his children and that this constituted an infringement of his right to respect for family life under article 8 of the European Convention. The European Commission held that there was no infringement of article 8 because it had not been shown that the operation of the Act was such as to render him unable to retain contact. The Commission seemed to leave open the possibility that the Act could infringe article 8 if it could be shown that the Act rendered it impossible for a father to see his children.[103]

3. *The high proportion of payers on low income.* Nearly equal numbers of those non-residential parents assessed by the Agency are on benefits, as are in employment.[104] Even if a non-residential parent is in receipt of income support, he or she may be liable to pay a small sum. In cases where the payer is on benefits then money is in effect moved from one section of the social security department to another.

4. *Lack of collection.* In 1997 only 31 per cent of those assessed were paying the full amount due; 36 per cent part of what was due and 33 per cent nothing.[105] For the year prior to March 1997 non-residential parents had failed to pay £513 million (about half of the total collectable amount).[106] The Child Support Agency spends 90 per cent of its time assessing maintenance and only 10 per cent collecting it.[107] However, things had improved by 2002 when by

---

[98] Fortin (2003b: 294).
[99] CSA 1991, s 8(8).
[100] Gillespie (1996); Glendinning, Clarke and Craig (1996).
[101] Department of Social Security (2000: 1.3). See also Marsh, Ford and Finlayson (1997).
[102] (1994) 22 EHRR 178.
[103] The Commission also rejected an argument based on article 6.
[104] Davis, Wikeley and Young (1998).
[105] Davis, Wikeley and Young (1998).
[106] Department of Social Security (1997).
[107] Department of Social Security (2000: 1.8).

then in 73 per cent of cases money was being collected.[108] However, by February 2002 only 49 per cent of non-residential parents were fully compliant with their maintenance obligations.[109] In 2002 the Child Support Agency wrote off £2 billion in unpaid child support.[110] These figures indicate both the complexities of the formula and significant flaws in the way the agency operates in practice. There is widespread evidence of non-residential parents seeking to avoid payments. It may be that in part this is because the payer is aware that payments made will not actually benefit the child.[111]

5. *Unfairness*. One of the most common complaints is that the scheme is unfair. There has been particular opposition from fathers who feel that it was not their fault that the relationship broke up, but that they have been required to suffer financially as a consequence. There have also been complaints from fathers who feel they are being denied contact by mothers, and yet are still expected to pay child support.[112] Both of these criticisms are valid from the point of view of the father, but from the child's perspective financial support is required whoever ended the relationship. Bradshaw et al.[113] found that 57 per cent of non-residential fathers were paying child support. The main reasons given by the fathers who were not paying child support was that the father was unemployed or could not afford the payments. Mothers also complained that the formula's use of the child's age was unfair. The formula is based on the unrealistic assumption of that 11-year-olds cost only 61 per cent of the cost of a 16-year-old.[114]

6. *Inflexible system*. There are strong claims that the formula is inflexible and does not take into account particular circumstances of the parties.[115] For example, in *Crozier v Crozier*,[116] on a divorce (which was granted before the CSA 1991 was in operation) the husband transferred his interest in the former home to his wife on the understanding that this would constitute payment of his child support in the future. The wife received income support. The husband subsequently received an assessment under the Child Support Act for £29 per week. By the time the assessment was made, the parties had formed new relationships. Booth J refused leave to appeal out of time against the original order. It was held that the public liability to maintain children remained on both parents, whatever the agreement between the parties. The state was not bound by any agreement between the husband and wife. One can understand why the father felt that he was being required to pay twice for child support and

---

[108] Pirrie (2003).
[109] Davis and Wikeley (2002: 525).
[110] Hencke (2002).
[111] Department of Social Security (2000: 1.15).
[112] Davis, Wikeley and Young (1998).
[113] Bradshaw, Stimson, Skinner and Williams (1999).
[114] Middleton, Ashworth, and Braithwaite (1997).
[115] Pirrie (2002).
[116] [1994] 1 FLR 26, [1994] 1 FCR 781. See also *Mawson v Mawson* [1994] 2 FLR 985, [1994] 2 FCR 852; *Smith v McInerney* [1994] 2 FLR 1077, [1994] 2 FCR 1086; *AMS v Child Support Officer* [1998] 1 FLR 955, [1998] 2 FCR 622 CA.

that the formula was being applied in an inflexible way in not taking account of his earlier transfer.[117]

   To some extent the criticism that the Act is inflexible has been met by the creation of the departure directions that can be sought, although these can involve time-consuming and complex applications to the Secretary of State.

7. *Insufficient regard for new children.* Some claim that the formula takes insufficient account of the costs of children who are now living with the father and his new partner. It is possible to apply for a departure direction in respect of costs of supporting a child living with the 'absent parent' who is not his own. However, the liability of the parents of that child will be taken into account.

8. *Infringing privacy.* One effect of the 1991 Act is that virtually all mothers on benefits must inform the state of the identity of the father of the child, whereas there is no such obligation on non-benefit-dependent spouses. This can be regarded as a significant infringement of privacy for lone parents. In fact there is evidence that over 70 per cent of mothers on income support try to avoid making a child support application.[118]

9. *Residential parent's new partner.* The income of a residential parent's partner is not taken into account in the formula. The mother could be living with a millionaire, but the non-residential father would still be expected to contribute to the child's maintenance.

10. *Creation of tension between the parents.* There have been claims[119] that the formula has created tension between the parents. In particular, the non-residential parent may see it as the residential parent's fault that the Agency has become involved. Indeed one way of understanding the Act is as an attempt to retain the ideal of a two-parent family, but maintaining the link between a lone parent and his or her spouse.[120] The operation of the CSA means that the father is not seen as the provider of the child. That the money for the child comes from the Agency, not the father, undermines that role.[121] The inability of fathers to provide gifts to their children as a demonstration of their love greatly distressed fathers.

11. *Link with contact.* Complaints by fathers that they were required to pay too much has been found by researchers to be particularly strong where the father had problems with contact.[122]

C. The new scheme for child support: Child Support, Pensions and Social Security Act 2000

At its core the new scheme will be refreshingly simple. Indeed one of its key aims is to be easy to use. Only four pieces of information will be required for assessment: the non-residential parent's income; the number of children they have; the number

---

[117] Now a departure direction could be sought. See as *Phillips* v *Pearce* [1996] 2 FCR 237.
[118] Department of Social Security (1998).
[119] Department of Social Security (2000: 1.4).
[120] Diduck (1995).
[121] Lewis (2002).
[122] Davis and Wikeley (2002).

of nights the children stay overnight with the non-resident parent; and whether they live in a household with other children. This should be contrasted with the present formula which requires over a hundred items of information.[123] If the non-residential parent earns over £200 per week net and has one qualifying child, he or she must pay 15 per cent of his income;[124] if he or she has two qualifying children he or she must pay 20 per cent; if he or she has three or more he or she must pay 25 per cent.[125] The maximum assessable weekly income is £2,000 per week. So the most a non-resident parent would have to pay under the new scheme is £26,000 per year for three or more children. There is a slight variation for lower-income parents.[126] If the non-residential parent earns under £100 per week net then a fixed sum will be paid, and if between £100 and £200 a lesser percentage. The minimum sum payable for most people will be £5 per week.[127]

There is some account taken of any other children living with the non-residential parent. So, if a father (F) leaves his partner (M) and their child (A) and moves in with another woman (W) who has a child (B) by another man, the existence of B will affect the amount payable by F for A.[128] His notional income is reduced in relation to the number of children living with him by 15 per cent, 20 per cent or 25 per cent, as above. So if F earned £1,000 per week, because of B his notional income would be reduced by 15 per cent, making it £850. He would then have to pay 15 per cent of that for A (i.e. £127.50).

There will be a special tribunal of the Child Support Agency to deal with exceptional cases where the payment would be unreasonable, either because of special expenses or because other forms of support are or have been provided. Expenses would include those relating to contact; long-term care of an ill or disabled child; the payment of debts incurred for the child's benefit when the parents were living together; and boarding school fees.[129] There will also be circumstances set out concerning when residential parents can apply to increase the amount payable. Examples include where the non-residential parent has diverted income in order to reduce the child support liability or enjoys a lifestyle which is inconsistent with his or her alleged income.[130]

One important rule is that if the non-residential parent has his or her child to stay with him or her for more than 52 nights per year there will be a reduction in the levels paid. If the child stays with the payer 52 to 103 nights per year[131] the level payable will be reduced by one-seventh; 104 to 155 nights by two-sevenths; 156 to

---

[123] Department of Social Security (2000: 1.7).
[124] This is income after tax, national insurance and pension contributions.
[125] Child Support, Pensions and Social Security Act 2000 (hereafter CSPASSA 2000), s 1, Sch 1.
[126] Foley (1996) even suggests that unemployed fathers should be sent to work camps to enable them to pay child support!
[127] Although a nil rate band is available in very limited circumstances (e.g. if the non-resident parent is a student or a person whose income is below £5 per week).
[128] CSPASSA 2000, s 1, Sch 1.
[129] CSPASSA 2000, Sch 1.
[130] Department of Social Security (2000: 6.11).
[131] That is one or two nights a week.

174 by three-sevenths;[132] and 175 or more by a half. Payers whose income is less than £100 per week need make no payment at all if there is staying contact for one or more nights per week. This policy may well lead to an increase in the level of overnight contact.[133] Whether this will always be in the interests of the child is open to debate.[134]

The residential parent and child will receive a child maintenance payment from the state worth up to £10 per week, if the non-resident parent is paying child support.[135] This will mean that all children will see an immediate financial benefit from the fact that their non-residential parents are paying towards their care. In addition, a new working families' tax credit will provide assistance for those residential parents in low-paid jobs.

The position where neither parent is on benefit will continue: they will not be required to apply to the Agency. They will be allowed to reach an agreement between themselves and register the agreement, and the court can collect the maintenance due to them when necessary. However, unlike the present scheme, the parent who has a court order agreement will be able to apply for an assessment by the Agency from 12 months after the agreement has been registered. So a residential parent should receive at least the amount they would under the CSA 1991 and if the amount required to be paid under the agreement is less than the CSA 1991 would order, the parent should apply to the Agency, who will make the calculation and enforce payment.

The government accepts that the new percentages are likely to lead to lower levels of payment (except perhaps for the wealthy), but justify the scheme for three reasons. The first is that the scheme can be educative. These financial figures can be widely publicised and can, in effect, then be a deterrent against fathering children, as the consequences of fatherhood would be made obvious. Secondly, the figures will be easy to understand and so there should be less of a sense of grievance about the sum claimed as it will be transparent as to how it has been calculated. It is hoped that a lesser sense of grievance will mean that non-residential parents will be more willing to pay, and so there should be fewer difficulties in enforcement. Thirdly, the Child Support Agency will have to spend less time calculating how much is payable and therefore will have more time to enforce the sums.

(i) Criticisms of the new scheme

1. The formula is a little rough and ready, even more so than the present scheme as it takes fewer factors into account. No account is taken for exceptional costs, except under an application to the tribunal.[136] The government hopes that, although the formula is a little crude, the percentages are low enough that only

---

[132] At first sight, reduction by three-sevenths seems appropriate but, according to the pressure group Families Need Fathers, a six-sevenths reduction is appropriate, as the non-residential parent has one day a week less care than the residential parent, although this overlooks the fact that the non-residential parent has to provide support for the primary carer.

[133] A one-seventh reduction in child support for the cost of a burger and video is a bargain.

[134] See Chapter 9 for a discussion about the benefits of contact.

[135] Department of Social Security (2000: 1.14).

[136] Gillespie (2002) regards the ability to apply to the tribunal as a significant improvement.

rarely will the tribunal have to depart from the calculation.[137] The figure of 15 per cent was justified on the basis that an unseparated two-parent family spent 30 per cent of their income on their children and so the non-resident parent should pay his or her half on separation.[138] The flaw in this explanation (as the White Paper admitted) is that normally the father contributes far more than half of the costs of the child's upbringing and so he will be paying far less under the new Act than he would have done when the couple were together.

2. There is some dispute over whether the new formula will result in lower or higher payments.[139] This could well mean that the burden on the taxpayer will be greater. It depends on whether because of the lower and simpler calculation there will be a higher rate of payment among those who at present do not pay. It appears that where a non-resident parent has children with several different women there will be a notable reduction in the amount each child receives.[140]

3. The new scheme fails to take into account the income of the parent with care of the child. This is quite deliberate, as the Green Paper explains: 'the new scheme will not take account of the parent with care's income. Every child who lives with a parent shares automatically in her living standards and income. And non-residential parents still have a responsibility to their children, however much support and financial provision the residential parent provides.'[141] Mostyn responds: 'Each child needs a finite amount of support. That obligation should be shared rateably between the parents in the ratios of their respective incomes.'[142]

4. The court's powers to deal with issues of child support will be severely restricted. For new cases after the Act comes into force the only power the court will have is to make 'top-up' orders, increasing the amount payable for wealthy couples. Under the old law if the couple could agree on the appropriate level of child support then the court could make a consent order in those terms.[143] Under the new law a couple cannot agree to 'contract out' of the Child Support Act, except for the first 12 months of the making of the order. Once the 12 months have passed, either parent on two months' notice can apply to the Child Support Agency to carry out a calculation.

The proposal has been criticised for enabling parties to enter agreements, but then allowing them to turn to the Agency for payment obligations one year after the initial agreement. This could be said to undermine the certainty that such agreements are designed to create. It certainly limits the freedom of the parties to reach such agreement over child support as they think fit, at least to the extent that if the agreement is that the non-residential parent pays less than the Agency would order, it is liable to be upset if the residential parent decides to apply to the Agency.

---

[137] Department of Social Security (2000: 1.12).

[138] Department of Social Security (2000: 9).

[139] Mostyn (1999) claims that the payments will be lower.

[140] Gillespie (2002: 530).

[141] Department of Social Security (1998: ch. 6).

[142] Mostyn (1999).

[143] But there were problems if the parents could not agree: *V v V (Child Maintenance)* [2001] 2 FLR 799.

5. Gillespie, interviewing people involved with the Child Support Agency, found that the most common concerns about the new scheme were about the impact it might have on their relationship. There were concerns that if the new scheme required non-resident parents to pay more or led to pressure to increase overnight contact this might cause further tensions between separated families.
6. It may be argued that it is unfair that a father can claim a deduction for children with whom he is living even if those children's father is paying support for them. To some this will appear unfair.[144] If those children are being financially supported by another man, why are they a financial burden on him? This provision could be explained on the basis that it ensures a man paying child support is not deterred from moving in with a woman with children.

D. The Children Act 1989 and child support

The Children Act 1989 can require parents to support children, regardless of whether the parents are married or unmarried. This is an important part of ensuring that the law governing the financial support of children does not depend on whether the parents were married or not. However, in practice the Children Act 1989 has been very little used, in part because so few separating cohabitants seek advice from solicitors.[145]

(i) Who can apply under the Children Act 1989?

The following people can apply for a financial order under s 15 of the Children Act 1989 in respect of a child:

1. A parent. This includes adoptive parents as well as natural parents. It also includes 'any party to a marriage (whether or not subsisting) in relation to whom the child . . . is a child of the family'.[146] A step-parent would be covered by the definition.
2. A guardian.
3. Any person who has a residence order in force in respect of a child.
4. An adult student, or trainee, or other person who can show special circumstances can apply for an order against his or her parents.[147] This order cannot be made if both parents are living together in the same household. So, for example, if the child's parents are still happily married or cohabiting the law will not intervene to force them to provide for the student's upkeep.[148]

The court in its own discretion can make an order under the section, even if there has been no application. For example, if the child has been made a ward of court, the court might make an award under the Act.

---

[144] Barton and Hibbs (2002: 85).
[145] Maclean, Eekelaar, Lewis et al. (2002).
[146] See Chapter 7 for further discussion of this term.
[147] E.g. *C v F (Disabled Child: Maintenance Orders)* [1999] 1 FCR 39, [1998] 2 FLR 1.
[148] The only orders these applicants can claim are periodical payments or lumps sum orders.

(ii) Who is liable to pay?

1. *Parents.* This includes biological parents and adoptive parents. A parent is liable to pay even if he or she does not have parental responsibility or never sees the child.
2. *Those who have treated the child as a child of the family.* An unmarried cohabitant of the mother, who is not the father of the child, will not be liable.[149]

(iii) Orders which can be made

Under the Children Act 1989 periodical payments and lump sum orders can be made.[150] A party can also be required to make a transfer of property. This is most likely to be used in relation to the family home and may, for example, direct that a child and the residential parent stay in a property until the child ceases education. There is also the power to transfer a secure tenancy to the other parent for the child's benefit.[151]

(iv) Factors that the court will consider

The courts will take into account the following factors in deciding whether to make an order:

  (a) the income, earning capacity, property and other financial resources which [the applicant, parents and the person in whose favour the order would be made] has or is likely to have in the foreseeable future;
  (b) the financial needs, obligations and responsibilities which [each of those persons] has or is likely to have in the foreseeable future;
  (c) the financial needs of the child;
  (d) the income, earning capacity (if any), property and other financial resources of the child;
  (e) any physical or mental disability of the child;
  (f) the manner in which the child was being, or was expected to be, educated or trained.[152]

Where the liability of a person who is not the child's legal parent is taken into account the court should also consider:

  (a) whether that person had assumed responsibility for the maintenance of the child and, if so, the extent to which and basis on which he assumed that responsibility and the length of the period during which he met that responsibility;
  (b) whether he did so knowing that the child was not his child;
  (c) the liability of any other person to maintain the child.[153]

---

[149] *J v J (A Minor: Property Transfer)* [1993] 1 FCR 471, [1993] 2 FLR 56.
[150] This can include a lump sum to meet expenses incurred before the court hearing, including expenses connected to the birth of a child (Children Act 1989, Sch 1, para 5(1)).
[151] *K v K (Minors: Property Transfer)* [1992] 2 FCR 253, [1992] 2 FLR 220; although the courts have indicated they will be cautious in exercising this power: *J v J (A Minor: Property Transfer)* [1993] 1 FCR 471, [1993] 2 FLR 56.
[152] Children Act 1989, Sch 1, para 4(1).
[153] Children Act 1989, Sch 1, para 4(2).

The welfare of the child is not the paramount consideration because, as is made clear by s 105(1), property orders are not deemed concerned with the upbringing of the child and so fall outside the scope of s 1(1) of the Children Act 1989.[154] The following points will influence the court in deciding the appropriate level of the award:

1. The level of the award should not depend on whether the child's parents were married or not.[155]
2. The child should be brought up in a way which is in some way commensurate with the non-residential parent's lifestyle.[156] In *J v C (Child: Financial Provision)*[157] the child's non-residential father became a millionaire and it was held that the child should be brought up in a way appropriate for a millionaire's daughter, including living in a four-bedroomed house and being driven around in a Ford Mondeo. In *Re P (A Child)(Financial Provision)*[158] the mother's claim for a top-of-the-range Range Rover from the very wealthy father was found to be excessive. However, she could expect a £20,000 car and £450,000 for a house in a 'suitable' part of London.
3. The court should be wary of making an award which will benefit the resident parent but not the child.[159] Of course some provision for the child will inevitably also benefit the resident parent (e.g. a house) and there can be no objection to this. Payment for nanny care could be expected, even if the mother was not working.[160] In *Re P (Child: Financial Provision)*[161] it was held that mother was entitled to an allowance in her capacity as the child's carer, even though she could not make any claim in her own right.
4. A parent is only liable to support a child during the child's minority. So if a large sum is provided for accommodation for the child, the sum will normally be held on trust to revert to the paying parent on the child reaching the age of 18 or finishing his or her education.[162] This means that when the child reaches 18, if a house was provided it may be sold and the sum returned to the paying parent.[163]
5. If the court is considering the liability of a step-parent, the court will take into account their liability to support any biological child of theirs.
6. Where the applicant is a disabled adult, they can claim against their parents. Although the expenses are restricted to expenses that directly relate to the disability while under the jurisdiction of the Child Support Act, under the Children Act other expenses can be considered.[164]

---

[154] *J v C (Child: Financial Provision)* [1999] 1 FLR 152; *Re P (A Child) (Financial Provision)* [2003] 2 FCR 481.

[155] In *A v A (A Minor: Financial Provision)* [1994] 1 FLR 657 at p. 659.

[156] *H v P (Illegitimate Child: Capital Provision)* [1993] Fam Law 515.

[157] [1999] 1 FLR 152.

[158] [2003] 2 FCR 481.

[159] *Re P (A Child)(Financial Provision)* [2003] 2 FCR 481.

[160] *Re P (A Child)(Financial Provision)* [2003] 2 FCR 481.

[161] [2003] 2 FCR 481.

[162] *H v P (Illegitimate Child: Capital Provision)* [1993] Fam Law 515; *T v S (Financial Provision for Children)* [1994] 1 FCR 743, [1994] 2 FLR 883.

[163] Although the order may provide for the residential parent to have an option to purchase the house.

[164] *C v F (Disabled Child: Maintenance Orders)* [1999] 1 FCR 39, [1998] 2 FLR 1 CA.

E. The Children Act 1989 and CSA 1991

The CSA 1991 has greatly lessened the significance of the powers under the Children Act 1989. Where a CSA assessment has been made, the court cannot make a periodical payment order under the Children Act, unless the maximum award under the CSA has been made.[165] The following are examples of the kind of case where financial orders under the Children Act may be made:

1. Where the award under the CSA 1991 is inadequate, it may be appropriate to use the Children Act for an additional lump sum. Under *Phillips* v *Pearce*[166] the father was assessed by the Child Support Agency as liable to pay nothing, even though he lived in a house worth £2.6 million. This was because the father's wealth was hidden in various companies. The mother applied under the Children Act. Because of the nil assessment, a periodical payments order could not be made under the Children Act.[167] However, the Children Act could still be used to grant lump sum orders. So in this case the Children Act was relied upon to order lump sums to purchase a house and provide furniture.
2. Children who fall outside the operation of the Child Support Acts (e.g. children over the age of 18 who are disabled or in full-time education) can be provided for under the Children Act 1989.
3. An award against a step-parent can only be made under the Children Act 1989. So if the child's birth father had disappeared or was unable to provide for the child, an application could be made under the Children Act to seek financial support against a step-parent.

3. MATRIMONIAL CAUSES ACT 1973 AND CHILDREN

A. Powers of the court on divorce

On divorce the court has wide powers to redistribute the parties' property. This includes the power to make orders especially designed to benefit children. For example, an order could demand regular payment of money to the child or, more commonly, a payment to the resident parent for the benefit of the child. However, as with the Children Act 1989, an order under the Matrimonial Causes Act 1973 cannot be made if the Child Support Agency has jurisdiction to make an assessment.

B. 'Child of the family'

Many of the court's powers to redistribute in divorce proceedings apply in respect of 'a child of the family'. The meaning of this phrase will be discussed in Chapter 7. The definition most notably includes a stepchild. Such a child can be treated under the CSA 1991 as the biological parents' responsibility, but under the

---

[165] CSA 1991, s 8(3).
[166] [1996] 2 FCR 237, [1996] 2 FLR 230.
[167] CSA 1991, s 8(3).

Matrimonial Causes Act 1973 (hereafter MCA 1973) as the step-parents' responsibility.

The MCA 1973 does list special considerations that apply where a step-parent is being asked to pay. The following factors must be taken into account:

    (a) to whether that party assumed any responsibility for the child's maintenance, and, if so, the extent to which, and the basis upon which, that party assumed such responsibility and the length of time for which that party discharged such responsibility;

    (b) to whether in assuming and discharging such responsibility that party did so knowing that the child was not his or her own;

    (c) to the liability of any other person to maintain the child.[168]

C. Applications by children

A child who is over 18 can apply for a financial or property order if his or her parents are divorcing, or apply for a variation of an order made earlier.[169] Although normally orders will cease once the child attains 18, the court can order that periodical payments extend beyond the 18th birthday if the child is or will be receiving instruction at an educational establishment or undergoing training and there are special circumstances which justify the order.[170]

D. Factors to be taken into account

The factors to be considered in deciding the appropriate level of an award under the MCA 1973 will be discussed in detail shortly. It should be noted that the welfare of any child is to be regarded as the first consideration[171] and the courts regard ensuring the children are adequately housed as especially important.[172] The courts have indicated that the amount that would be awarded under the CSA will be a starting point.[173]

4. FINANCIAL SUPPORT FOR SPOUSES ON DIVORCE

The redistribution of property on divorce is a controversial issue. There is a wide range of competing policies that the law seeks to hold together. There is a desire, on the one hand, to ensure that on divorce a fair redistribution of the property takes place so that one party is not unduly disadvantaged by the divorce; but, on the other hand, to do so in a way that enables the parties to achieve truly independent lives after the divorce is often impossible. The truth is that for many couples suitable financial orders cannot be made. Neither party will be able to live at a standard of living they regard as acceptable. As Symes explains:

---

[168] Matrimonial Causes Act 1973 (hereafter MCA 1973), s 25(4).
[169] See *Downing* v *Downing* [1976] Fam 288.
[170] MCA 1973, s 29.
[171] MCA 1973, s 25.
[172] *M* v *B (Ancillary Proceedings: Lump Sum)* [1998] 1 FLR 53, [1998] 1 FCR 213.
[173] *GW* v *RW* [2003] FL 386.

Quite clearly, marriage as it has traditionally been practised, is not intended to be ended by divorce. Indeed, traditional housewife marriage has a most potent feature of indissolubility built right into it – dependency ... The accumulation of responsibilities and obligations, the consequences of an unequal partnership based on dependency – all mean that an absolute severance of the bond without massive adjustment would be manifestly unjust, more likely impossible.[174]

There is simply not enough money for most married couples to support two individuals in separate households after divorce, certainly not at the level to which they had become accustomed.[175]

A. The economic realities of divorce

There is convincing evidence that following divorce women who are caring for children suffer a detrimental downturn in their finances, while their ex-husbands do not.[176] Weitzman, in an American study, found that men gain a 42 per cent improvement in their post-divorce standard of living, while women suffer a 73 per cent decline.[177] The extent of disadvantage for women on divorce is closely related to their work history during marriage.[178] However, it is still more common for husbands than wives to be in employment. Gregory and Foster found that at the time of separation 98 per cent of husbands and 62 per cent of wives were in employment.[179] Seventy per cent of husbands, but only 21 per cent of wives, had worked continually throughout their marriage. Twenty-five per cent of wives had not worked at all during the marriage.[180] Even when women do work during marriage, the employment tends to be part-time,[181] lower paid, and provide fewer benefits.[182] In part, ex-wives' financial hardships also reflect the wage differences which exist generally between men and women: average full-time earnings of women are 40 per cent lower than men.[183] Women face discrimination in finding employment, both on the basis of their sex and on the basis that they are caring for children and therefore in a weaker position to advance their careers.[184] It is not just child-care than can restrict a woman's ability to advance her career. Women still carry the primary duty of housework.[185] Bergman has found that women do on average 28.1 hours' unpaid work per week in the home and men 9.2 hours per week.[186]

---

[174] Symes (1985: 57).
[175] Barton and Bissett-Johnson (2000) noted that in the majority of cases no financial orders are made by the court. In some cases this will reflect the fact that there are simply no assets to redistribute.
[176] Davis, Cretney, Barder and Collins (1991); Perry, Douglas, Murch et al. (2000).
[177] Weitzman (1985).
[178] Funder (1988).
[179] Gregory and Foster (1990: 38).
[180] Gregory and Foster (1990: 38).
[181] Family Policy Studies Centre (1995).
[182] Morris and Nott (1995).
[183] Stationery Office (2000a).
[184] M. Maclean (1991).
[185] Brannen, Meszaros, Moss and Poland (1994).
[186] Bergman (1986: 263).

B. Divorce and redistribution of property

The core question in this area is: why should one spouse be required to transfer property to another? Before looking at this issue, it is necessary to draw two distinctions which affect how a divorcing couple's finances are dealt with:

1. It is possible to distinguish the question who owns what[187] and the question of whether one spouse be required to transfer property or money to the other.
2. It is possible to distinguish cases where the couple have one or more children and where they have none.[188] Some take the view that if the couple have no children to take care of, it is harder to claim that the marriage has caused financial disadvantage to either party.

C. Why should there be any redistribution?

To assist in the discussion of this question, it will be assumed that the husband is in the stronger position economically, and that the wife is seeking a court order. Similar arguments can, of course, be made if it is the wife who is the higher earner.

1. *Spousal support and the care of children.* It must be noted that supporting the child will inevitably involve providing benefits to the residential parent. So if it is decided that the child should live in a luxury-level house, this will benefit both the child and the parent with whom they are living. Further, included in the support required for the child must be an element to provide personal care for the child. So one ground for spousal support is that the spouse be maintained at the level required to ensure adequate care of the child. Eekelaar and Maclean have supported the 'equalisation of the standard of living of the two households, and thus of the children within them'.[189] They argue that this equalisation is not due to any kind of implied undertaking between the parents (as some of the models below emphasise), but due to the moral claim of the child. That is, the child's household should not be disadvantaged to the benefit of the non-residential parent's household.
2. *Contract.* It could be argued that it is a part of the marriage contract that, on breach of the contract, one party will pay the other 'damages'; that on marriage the spouses promise to support each other for the rest of their lives. If a husband decides to divorce his wife he must pay her damages so that she is in the economic position she would have been had he not broken the contract. This would mean that the husband would have to pay the wife financial support so that she could enjoy the level of wealth she experienced during the marriage.[190] Nowadays this theory does not really explain the English law: first, because it might be questioned whether marriage does include a promise to remain with the other spouse forever, given the ready availability of divorce; secondly,

---

[187] Discussed in Chapter 4.
[188] Eekelaar and Maclean (1997: 30–1).
[189] Eekelaar and Maclean (1997: 197).
[190] This would justify the minimal loss theory behind the Matrimonial Proceedings and Property Act 1970.

because the law has abandoned trying to work out which party breached the contract, that is, who it is that has caused the marriage breakdown. However, as will be seen, in cases involving very rich couples, aspects of this approach are still used in the reasoning of the courts.

3. *Partnership.* The view here is that marriage should be regarded as analogous to a partnership.[191] The husband and wife co-operate together as a couple as part of a joint economic enterprise.[192] It may be that one spouse is employed and the other works at home, but they work together for common benefits. Therefore, on divorce each spouse should be entitled to their share, normally argued to be half each.[193] It could also be argued that on marriage the parties will bring to the relationship a variety of different assets, skills, personalities, interests etc. Throughout the marriage each party will enjoy and share their personalities, interests and skills. If the relationship involves the mutual sharing of all aspects of their lives, this should include their material assets.

At first consideration this argument might justify redistributing assets that have accumulated during the marriage, but would not apply to assets owned by the parties before entering the marriage or assets acquired after the marriage breakdown. However, the approach can be developed to extend to future assets. It is possible to argue that the partnership assets are not limited to tangible assets, but extend to the earning capacity of the parties.[194] So if the wife had supported the husband at home while he developed his career, she could argue that he has only been able to reach the position where he is able to earn as much money as he does because of the help she provided. This argument would entitle the wife to a share in his future earnings, reflecting the increase in his earning potential acquired during the marriage. The approach could also be said to justify a sharing of assets acquired before the marriage.

But there are difficulties with the partnership approach:

(i) Some argue that the partnership approach is inappropriate in the absence of an express agreement to share the family assets. It could be replied that the partnership concept is part of the marriage package, and is an obligation which the parties accept by marrying. Another response is that the partnership approach is not necessarily designed to reflect the intentions of the parties, but rather what is conscionable or fair; that, as the spouses worked together on a common enterprise, they should share the fruits, even if they had not explicitly agreed to do so. Regan has argued that marriage is a distinctive relationship based on mutuality, interdependence and care. Therefore responsibilities can arise from it even though there has not been an express agreement to undertake them.[195]

(ii) Where the argument extends to future earnings, the partnership approach requires the court to calculate what share of the husband's earning

---

[191] See the approach of the Canadian Supreme Court in *Moge* v *Moge* (1993) 99 DLR (4th) 456, discussed in Diduck and Orton (1994). See also Bailey-Harris (2001b).
[192] Gray (1977: 24).
[193] See Burch (1983).
[194] This argument is developed in Frantz and Dagan (2002).
[195] Regan (1999: 188).

capacity is a result of the marriage. This is difficult to ascertain. Also, if the husband could show that, had he not married, he would have done just as well in his career, he could argue that no proportion of his earning capacity could be said to result from the partnership.[196]

(iii) It can be argued that the approach takes insufficient account of the needs of the parties. Particularly where one spouse is raising the child, a half:half share may not adequately meet his or her needs.[197] In other words, dividing the assets equally might leave the spouse with the child in effectively a worse-off financial position (because of the extra expenses of child-care) and not receiving a 'fair' share of the economic benefits of the joint enterprise.

Despite these objections, the partnership approach certainly provides a sound basis for financial support. It is important to appreciate that the approach is not arguing that one spouse should transfer money to the other, but rather that the family assets are jointly owned. So a home-working mother is not asking for some of her husband's money on divorce; she is seeking her share of their assets.[198]

4. *Equality.* Some argue that on the breakdown of the marriage the parties should be treated equally. As Eekelaar has pointed out, this could mean two things: first, equality of outcome; and secondly, equality of opportunity.[199] Equality of outcome requires that at the point of divorce each spouse has the same total value of assets. Equality of opportunity is that 'each former spouse should be in an equal position to take advantage of the opportunities to enhance her or his economic position in the labour market'.[200] Neither in its most simple form is satisfactory. The difficulty with equality of outcome is that as the needs of the parties (particularly in relation to children) are different, giving the parties equal assets will not truly produce an equal standard of living. The problem with the equality of opportunity approach is that the prevailing social structures (such as discrimination against women in the employment market) are such that perfect equality of economic opportunity would be impossible to achieve.

A more sophisticated version of equality of income for both households post-divorce would have to take carefully into account the costs of raising children. As Weitzman argues:

As long as women are more likely than men to subordinate their careers in marriage, and as long as the structure of economic opportunity favours men, and as long as women contribute to their husband's earning capacities, and as long as women are likely to assume the major responsibilities of child rearing, and as long as we want to encourage the care and rearing of children, we cannot treat men and women as equals in the divorce settlement. We must find ways to safeguard and protect women, not only to achieve fairness and equality, but also to encourage and reward those who invest in and care for our children and, ultimately, to foster true equality for succeeding generations.[201]

[196] Singer (1997).
[197] Forder (1987).
[198] Weitzman (1985: 360).
[199] Eekelaar (1988).
[200] Eekelaar (1988: 192).
[201] Weitzman (1985).

Parker[202] suggests that the law should start with the assumption that spouses will equally share the tasks of parenting, homemaking and earning. Where each contributes equally in each of these three areas then a 50:50 split should be ordered of the parties' assets. However, where the spouses have departed from the equal sharing (e.g. where one spouse has undertaken an unequal share of the parenting or homemaking tasks) then the court can redress any imbalance by reason of lost opportunity.

5. *Compensation.* Here the argument is that on divorce the non-earning spouse should be compensated for all the unpaid work that she put into the relationship from which the earning spouse benefited. The compensation argument can take two forms (assuming the wife to be the non-earning spouse):

   (i) The non-earning spouse should be compensated for loss of the earnings which she would have gained had she not been at home caring for the children or the home.

   (ii) The non-earning spouse should in retrospect be paid an appropriate wage for her work by the husband. A court could assess how much the house-cleaning and child-caring would have cost the husband had he employed people to do it. Some who adopt this approach accept that, as the non-earning spouse herself benefits from the housework, the cost should be shared and so the husband should only pay for half of this work.

There are difficulties with the compensation approach. Those criticising the first option argue that the non-earning spouse chose to bear and raise children, maybe for personal motives. She may have chosen the joys of child-raising over the world of work, just as some people take a lower-paid job due to the pleasure it provides. Therefore, any loss is as a result of her choice and is not a ground for compensation. This argument, however, overlooks the fact that the choice of bearing and raising children is one that is essential to society's well-being. It is therefore a choice which society must seek to encourage and support. Others argue that the costs that women who care for children suffer are due to the inequalities of society, rather than being married. It is the state's failure to provide adequate child-care facilities and employment protection for mothers that is the root cause of the disadvantages suffered. The losses women suffer should be compensated for by the state rather than by husbands. However, in the absence of state support, surely it is unfair for mothers alone to have to carry the burden of financial sacrifice for the raising of children.

Eekelaar sees a different objection to the compensation approach, arguing that even if the wife had not married her husband she would have married someone else, and so it is not realistic to claim that the lack of development in her career is *this* man's fault.[203] Funder has argued that if, say, the wife gives up her career to care for the children then the resulting loss of income is a loss for both parties because they would have shared her income. The wife cannot therefore claim compensation for it, because the couple would have already equally shared

---

[202] S. Parker (1998).
[203] Eekelaar (1988).

the loss of the income.[204] Carbone and Brinig[205] refute these kinds of arguments by suggesting that, as the husband himself has benefited from his wife's sacrifices (by having the pleasure of fatherhood and a pleasant home life), it can be seen as reasonable to require him to compensate the wife for her loss of earnings.

6. *The state's interests.* The arguments so far have assumed that the issue is about achieving fairness between the parties themselves.[206] It is arguable that financial orders on divorce can be justified by interests of the state, regardless of what would be fair or just between the parties. So what state interests are there here? Bailey-Harris identifies the following interests of the state in family breakdown:

    (i)   the equalisation of the effects of the relationship on the parties' economic positions;

    (ii)   the prevention of exploitation where there is or was a power imbalance;

    (iii) the recognition of pluralism in contemporary society;

    (iv) the removal of discrimination on the basis of marital status, gender or sexuality;

    (v)   the promotion of party autonomy;

    (vi) the clear definition of legal rights;

    (vii) the promotion of methods of dispute resolution which minimise conflicts and costs;

    (viii) the avoidance of an unjustified burden on the public purse.[207]

This is, of course, a controversial list, with which not everyone would agree, and there are also conflicts between these objectives, especially (i) and (v). The key question is to what extent the state is entitled to force these objectives upon the spouses. In other words, if the spouses are happy to separate with unequal economic consequences, should the state force them to adopt an equal distribution? Clearly the state has an economic interest in avoiding either spouse claiming benefits, but, beyond that, are these other reasons strong enough to justify intervention here when the same reasons are not taken seriously in other areas of the law (for example, in ensuring there is equality between employers and employees)?

One issue not addressed by Bailey-Harris's list is whether the state wants to encourage a spouse to give up earning in order to take up the care of the child. The state might take the view that each member of society should be as economically productive as possible, and so it would want to discourage a spouse giving up employment to take up child-care, in which case the state might want to limit financial awards on divorce. If there were no financial orders on divorce then this would discourage a spouse thinking of giving up employment to care for children, instead they would be likely to rely on day care. However, the state might believe that children's interests are promoted if one spouse gives up work to care for the children, in which case some form of protection from financial disadvantage would

---

[204] Funder (1994).

[205] Carbone and Brinig (1991).

[206] Many commentators make the assumption that redistribution of property on divorce is a private matter: see e.g. Cretney (2003b).

[207] Bailey-Harris (1998b).

be necessary. Hale J in the Court of Appeal in *SRJ* v *DWJ (Financial Provision)*[208] has stated:

> It is not only in [the child's] interests but in the community's interests that parents, whether mothers or fathers, and spouses, whether husbands or wives, should have a real choice between concentrating on breadwinning and concentrating on home-making and child-rearing, and do not feel forced, for fear of what might happen should their marriage break down much later in life, to abandon looking after the home and the family to other people for the sake of maintaining a career.

Such arguments can lead to calls for the state to place a far higher value on the unpaid work of raising children than is done at present.[209] Through property orders on divorce the state is able to demonstrate that it values child-care as an important social activity. Property orders on divorce are necessary if the taking up of child-care is not to be regarded as a financially dangerous choice for spouses.

Many of the difficulties that this chapter deals with are caused by the unequal sharing of child-care. Although there is evidence of fathers seeking to play an increased role in child-care[210] the vast majority is still undertaken by women.[211] Some commentators take the view that the government should attempt to encourage a more equal division of child-caring roles. However, the trend is for those working to be working for longer and longer hours, making it harder for couples to share child-care and work.[212] The alternative is to encourage both parties to work and for ever greater use to be made of day care. However, this raises the debate over whether day care or care at home is preferable for children. This is a heated debate. Although the evidence suggests that there some advantages and disadvantages to both, whether overall one is preferable is controversial.[213]

Another possible societal interest is that imposing maintenance obligations and redistributing property may discourage divorce. Dnes[214] fears that more high-earning spouses would leave low-earning spouses if the law did not require them to compensate the poorer spouse for their losses. Whether the level of maintenance does affect the level of divorce is a matter of debate.

D. The case for the abolition of maintenance

There is a case for the abolition of maintenance. The argument is that the existence of maintenance perpetuates the fact that women are dependent upon men.[215] A vicious circle exists in that because wives are and feel themselves to be dependent upon husbands, they are willing to take lower-paid jobs. If maintenance were

---

[208] [1999] 2 FLR 176 at p. 182.
[209] Burggraf (1997). See the National Family and Parenting Institute (2001b) for the data on work and family life.
[210] Maushart (2001: 129–134).
[211] E.g. Eekelaar and Maclean (1997: 137).
[212] Moen (2003). Hakim (2003) argues that although most couples want a better home life/work balance most believe that one spouse should be primarily responsible for raising the children.
[213] Ermisch and Francesconi (2001; 2003) argue that children whose parents both work suffer in a variety of ways. The Daycare Trust (2003) paints a much more positive view of day care.
[214] Dnes (1998).
[215] In practice it is far more common for a wife to be awarded maintenance than a husband.

abolished and financial independence encouraged, women would have to find jobs that paid adequately.[216] Although there may be a short period during which women would suffer from the lack of maintenance, over time the market would have to provide adequately paid jobs for women, or provide economic rewards for homemaking and child-rearing activities. O'Donnovan,[217] although sympathetic to this argument, has suggested that the abolition of maintenance can only fairly be accomplished when there:

1. is equality of division of labour during marriage, including financial equality;
2. is equal participation in wage-earning;
3. are wages geared to people as individuals and not as heads of families;
4. is treatment of people as individuals (rather than family units) by the state in taxation and benefit provision.

A second objection to maintenance has already been mentioned: that the economic disadvantages that women suffer are due to inequalities within society, such as the lack of provision of child-care services and family-friendly working practices etc. Therefore, the state, and not husbands, should recompense wives on the breakdown of their marriage for the losses that society has caused.

E. Certainty or discretion?

Another major issue in the area of spousal financial support is whether the financial support for spouses should be based on some formula to ensure certainty of result and consistency or whether the case should be resolved in reliance upon discretion. As we shall see, spousal financial support is at present based on a very broad discretion, considering a list of factors. This can be contrasted with the Child Support Acts, where the level of the award is based upon a mathematical calculation, with only a limited discretion to depart from the calculation. Some of the arguments for and against discretion will now be considered:

1. *Enforcement*. One of the arguments against discretion is that enforcement is easier if the system is seen to be fair and consistent. One common reason for non-payment of maintenance is that the amount payable is seen to be unfair. Having a clearly applied formula, which the parties could be made aware of before marriage, might improve enforcement levels.[218]
2. *Certainty*. Another argument against discretion is that the parties in negotiations are assisted by having clear guidance on what amount the law regards as fair in a particular case.[219] The problem with the present law is that it can be very difficult for solicitors to predict how much a court will award a client.[220] Not only

---

[216] Although the levels of maintenance are low and it is unlikely that women would choose not to work in the hope of getting maintenance should they divorce. Perhaps more convincing is the argument that maintenance is symbolic of the culture of dependency.
[217] O'Donnovan (1982).
[218] Jackson, Wasoff, Maclean and Dobash (1993).
[219] Jackson, Wasoff, Maclean and Dobash (1993).
[220] Davis, Cretney and Collins (1994).

does a discretion-based system make negotiations harder, it also increases the powers of solicitors.[221] As Jackson et al. argue:

> along with discretion goes uncertainty; the elevation of professional judgement (because only lawyers, who deal with these matters all the time, have the necessary knowledge and skill to weigh up the competing factors); an almost limitless need for information about family finances (because discretion, if it is to [be] justified at all, has to be based on a minute examination of differing circumstances) and the demand for large amounts of professional time (because discretion, if it is not to be exercised arbitrarily, takes time).[222]

Dewar, however, argues that there is no evidence that less discretion means it will be easier for the parties to reach an agreement, because the parties can disagree how even a rigid formula should apply.[223]

3. *Flexibility*. A benefit of the discretion-based system is that it can apply unique solutions that may better fit the circumstances of individual parties. As discussed when considering the CSA1991, one of the most common complaints about the formula around which the Act is based is that it is too rigid and creates injustices in many cases.

The benefits or disadvantages of discretion change from case to case.[224] Davis et al. suggest that:

> One possible conclusion to draw from our research is that a discretionary system is not geared to mass proceedings such as we have in divorce these days. The proposal that outcomes may be determined by the application of a formula, and usually by an administrative authority can certainly be supported in relation to the relatively straightforward cases which comprised the bulk of our sample.[225]

Perhaps the core question is: to what extent are we willing to put up with injustices in a few cases to enable speedy and efficient responses for the majority?

Lord Nicholls in *White* v *White*[226] accepted that there were both advantages and disadvantages to a discretion-based system. He argued that even though English and Welsh law had a discretionary system, there still should be principles which guide the discretion:

> It goes without saying that these principles should be identified and spelled out as clearly as possible. This is important, so as to promote consistency in court decisions and in order to assist parties and their advisers and mediators in resolving disputes by agreement as quickly and inexpensively as possible.

F. Solicitors and negotiations

Financial disputes on divorce are one of the areas where negotiations between solicitors play an important role. Very few financial disputes reach the courts for a

---

[221] Davis, Cretney and Collins (1994).
[222] Jackson, Wasoff, Maclean and Dobash (1993: 256).
[223] Dewar (1997).
[224] Acknowledged by Lord Nicholls in *White* v *White* [2000] 3 FCR 555, [2000] 2 FLR 976.
[225] Davis, Cretney and Collins (1994: 270).
[226] [2000] 2 FLR 976, [2000] 3 FCR 555.

contested hearing.[227] The vast majority of cases are resolved by negotiations between the parties' solicitors. Research on their performance is mixed. Davis et al. found that negotiations between solicitors were often characterised by delay, and in some cases the solicitors did virtually nothing.[228] The significance of this is that delay benefits the party who is better off. Typically this will be the husband. As he is earning he will have no difficulty in coping financially. If his wife is raising young children and seeking financial support from him, she will grow increasingly desperate for a resolution of the financial issues, and will therefore be in a weaker bargaining position.

G. The Human Rights Act 1998 and maintenance

Article 1 of the first Protocol of the European Convention on Human Rights protects the right to peaceful enjoyment of property:

> Every natural or legal person is entitled to the peaceful enjoyment of his possessions. No one shall be deprived of his possessions except in the public interest and subject to the conditions provided for by the law and by the general principles of international law. The preceding provisions shall not, however, in any way impair the right of a State to enforce such laws as it deems necessary to control the use of property in accordance with the general interest or to secure the payment of taxes or other contributions or penalties.

At first sight, a person ordered to make any payment on divorce could invoke this article. No case has yet been brought on this basis in relation to ancillary relief, so it is unclear how it would be interpreted. As was noted earlier, some theories justifying redistribution of property on divorce involved a wife seeking 'her share' in the property, rather than a transfer to her of the husband's property, and if such an approach is taken the article loses its bite.

Article 5 of the seventh Protocol on the equality between spouses states:

> Spouses shall enjoy equality of rights and responsibilities of a private law character between them, and in their relations with their children, as to marriage, during marriage and in the event of its dissolution. This article shall not prevent States from taking such measures as are necessary in the interests of the children.

There is an explanatory memorandum which states that article 5 'should not be understood as preventing the national authorities from taking due account of all relevant factors when reaching decisions with regard to the divisions of property in the event of the dissolution of marriage'. This article was not included within the Human Rights Act due to potential conflict with English and Welsh law,[229] although the government has promised to implement the Protocol in due course. Even if it does, these provisions are unlikely greatly to affect English and Welsh law, given the uncertainty over the term equality, discussed above.

---

[227] Barton and Bissett-Johnson (2000).
[228] Davis, Cretney and Collins (1994).
[229] Home Office (1997: 4.15, 4.16).

H. The importance of discovery

Crucial to the success of the parties' negotiations and any court hearing is having full disclosure of each party's assets, income and liabilities. There is a duty on both clients and lawyers to make a full and frank disclosure of the parties' present assets. An affidavit must be filed with the court, which sets out their income and assets. However, it is 'all too common'[230] for people to try to hide their assets. This can be by simple failure to disclose, but in more sophisticated forms can involve hiding income and property behind companies or trusts controlled by the parties. Although there are powers that the courts have for ordering discovery of relevant documents, too often it is never possible to know for sure that all the relevant material has been provided. The court has two further tools at its disposal if it cannot ascertain a party's true financial position. First, the court can order that the non-disclosing party be punished by being ordered to pay all or some of the legal costs incurred in the attempt to ascertain his or her wealth. Further, the court can, if it is convinced that it does not have the full picture, presume that a party has a certain level of wealth.[231] This will certainly be done where the court decides that a person's lifestyle is not commensurate with their claimed income.[232]

The difficulty in ascertaining the wealth of the parties is likely to work in favour of the richer party. It is far harder to hide the income of a part-time worker than to hide the true income of a managing director of a company whose salary may be but a small portion of his or her true income.

At the other end of the spectrum, the courts have complained of solicitors seeking too much information from the other side in the hope of uncovering assets which may be available to their clients. Intensive financial questioning[233] can lead to enormous solicitors' costs; £1.5 million in one notorious case.[234] The Family Proceedings Rules 1999[235] are designed to prevent unnecessary investigation, but the practitioner is in a difficult position. There is a danger that if he or she does not follow up a lead in disclosure, they may be sued in negligence, but if the practitioner does they may be penalised in costs for unnecessary work.

I. Orders that the court can make

The court has a range of orders that it can make. It is useful to divide these up into those orders that relate to income, and those that relate to capital and property.

(i) Income orders

The main income order is the periodical payments order (PPO) under s 22A(1) of the MCA 1973. These payments can be weekly, monthly or annual. For example,

---

[230] Thorpe LJ in *Purba v Purba* [2000] 1 FLR 444 CA.
[231] *Pasha v Pasha* [2001] EWCA Civ 466, [2001] 2 FCR 185 CA.
[232] *Thomas v Thomas* [1996] 2 FLR 544, [1996] FCR 668; *Al Khatib v Masry* [2002] 2 FCR 539.
[233] *Evans v Evans* [1990] 1 FLR 319, [1990] FCR 498; see also Booth J (1992).
[234] *F v F (Ancillary Relief: Substantial Assets)* [1995] 2 FLR 45.
[235] SI 1999/3491.

a husband could be ordered to pay his ex-wife £400 per month. The order can be secured or unsecured. If it is a secured PPO and the payments are not made, then the property providing the security can be sold to enable payment. The security could be, for example, shares or the matrimonial home. This is an attractive option for the recipient, as she will not have to worry about non-payment, and also secured periodical payments can continue after the death of the payer. However, if there are sufficient assets to provide security for periodical payments, then it might be better simply to transfer those assets over to the wife as a lump sum instead of requiring regular payments. It is therefore not surprising that Thorpe LJ has suggested that secured PPOs 'have [been] virtually relegated to the legal history books'.[236]

A payments order will cease on any of the following events:

1. The death of either party.[237] However, if the order is a secured periodical order, the order need not cease on the death of the payer.[238]
2. The remarriage of the recipient.[239] The explanation is that on remarriage the new spouse would be financially responsible for the recipient.
3. The court order may specify a date on which the payments will end. For example, the order may state that there are to be periodical payments for the next three years only.[240]

Maintenance orders can be made against either parent for the benefit of a child. If the child is over 18 then PPOs can be made only if the child is in full-time education or under specific circumstances, such as disability.

(ii) Property orders

There are three main types of property orders:

1. *Lump sum orders.* A lump sum order (LSO) requires a lump sum of money to be handed over by one spouse to the other. The LSO may be made to a parent for the benefit of a child. It is possible to order the LSO be paid in instalments. The LSO is often used when considering housing issues: assuming one party is to stay in the matrimonial home, the other will need some money to use as a deposit to rent or buy a home.
2. *Transfer of property orders.* The most common transfer of property order is an order that one party transfers a share in the matrimonial home to the other. A transfer of property order could also be used to transfer ownership of other property, such as a car or piece of furniture. The court can make an order to transfer property to the other spouse or to an adult for the benefit of a child under a trust.

---

[236] *AMS* v *Child Support Officer* [1998] 1 FLR 955 at p. 964.
[237] MCA 1973, s 28(1)(a).
[238] MCA 1973, s 28(1)(b).
[239] MCA 1973, s 28(1)(a).
[240] The recipient could apply to vary the order so as to extend that period unless the order contains a direction under s 28(1A) or the date on which the payments are due to cease has passed, in which case it is not possible to apply for variation.

3. *Power to order sale.* Under s 24A of the MCA 1973 the court can order the sale of property which either spouse owns outright or which the spouses own jointly. The order is effectively ancillary to a LSO. The owner is normally required to sell the item and then the proceeds are divided between the spouses by means of a LSO.[241]

J. Clean break orders

(i) What is a clean break order?

When considering what financial order to make, the court must consider whether to make a clean break order. If a clean break order is not made then the parties can potentially have further financial obligations placed upon them after divorce for the rest of their lives. For example, if on divorce the husband is required to pay the wife £100 per month, and two years after the divorce the husband wins the national lottery, the wife could apply to the court for a significant increase in the amount she should receive. Similarly, if she won the national lottery, the husband could apply to have the payments ended. By contrast, if a clean break order is made, it ends any continuing obligation between the spouses. So the court may make a lump sum or property adjustment order, and neither party would be able to make any further applications to the court.[242] The financial responsibilities to each other in relation to the divorce are at an end.[243] However, it should be stressed that the clean break cannot end the possibility that a spouse may be liable under the CSA 1991. It is only spousal support that can be cleanly broken; child support cannot.

A delayed clean break order is also possible.[244] This is where the periodical payments order is set for a certain period, say two years, and after that period the payments will end, with no option for the spouse receiving the payments to apply to extend that period.

(ii) The statutory provisions

In every divorce case there is an obligation on the court to consider whether to make a clean break order. Under section 25A(1) of the MCA 1973 there is a duty on the court in all cases to consider 'whether it would be appropriate so to exercise [its] powers that the financial obligations of each party towards the other will be terminated as soon after the grant of the decree as the court considers just and reasonable'.[245]

If the court is making a periodic payments order, it should consider whether to limit the length of time over which payments will be made, and whether a delayed

---

[241] MCA 1973, s 24A(6): if a third party has an interest in the property this does not mean that there cannot be an order for sale, but that third party's interests must be taken into account.

[242] Although it would be possible to appeal against the making of the order, discussed below.

[243] A clean break order should also contain a term making it impossible to apply under the Inheritance (Provision for Family and Dependants) Act 1975 should the paying spouse die: *Cameron v Treasury Solicitor* [1996] 2 FLR 716 CA.

[244] MCA 1973, s 28(1A).

[245] MCA 1973, s 25(1)(a)(2).

clean break order would be appropriate.[246] A clean break should not be regarded as something to be achieved at all costs. Certainly it would be wrong to make an order which produced an unfair or unjust division in the name of achieving a clean break order.[247]

(iii) The benefits and disadvantages of a clean break order

The benefits of a clean break order include:

1. The parties are each free to pursue their own careers or start new careers without fear that their actions will lead to applications to vary maintenance payments. If the husband is paying maintenance, he may be reluctant to increase his income for fear that such an increase would simply result in his ex-wife seeking a larger maintenance payment. The wife might be deterred from seeking a new job for fear that if she had more income her husband would seek to have the maintenance payments reduced.
2. There may be emotional reasons for having a clean break: the parties may not feel that they are completely released from the marriage until all financial issues are resolved;[248] although if there are children the parties will be encouraged to keep in contact,[249] and so the strength of this benefit may be questioned.[250]
3. If the recipient intends to remarry, she may prefer a lump sum clean break arrangement as this will free her to remarry without the risk of losing her maintenance.

The main disadvantage of the clean break is that the court ties its hands and, whatever tragedy befalls the parties, the courts cannot reopen the court order. For example, if the court assumes that the wife will be able to support herself with the income from a new job and therefore makes a clean break order, nothing can be done if, a few months later, she is made redundant.

(iv) When a clean break order is appropriate

Although the court must consider in each case whether or not to make a clean break order,[251] there is no presumption in favour of making the order.[252] Clean break orders have been considered appropriate in the following circumstances:

1. *When continuing support offers no benefit to the wife.* In *Ashley* v *Blackman*[253] the wife was unemployed. The husband was of limited means. The court accepted that the wife would see a very limited benefit if the husband were ordered to pay maintenance because any small amounts of money transferred to her would lead

---

[246] MCA 1973, s 25A(2).
[247] *F* v *F (Clean Break: Balance of Fairness)* [2003] 1 FLR 847,
[248] Lord Scarman in *Minton* v *Minton* [1979] AC 593 at p. 608 HL.
[249] And financial liability may continue under the CSA 1991.
[250] See Hale J in *SRJ* v *DWJ (Financial Provision)* [1999] 2 FLR 176 CA.
[251] MCA 1973, s 25A(1).
[252] *Fisher* v *Fisher* [1989] 1 FLR 423, [1989] FCR 308 CA.
[253] [1988] FCR 699, [1988] 2 FLR 278.

to a corresponding reduction in her state benefits.[254] The court therefore made a clean break order.

2. *Short, childless marriages.* If the marriage was short and childless, and the parties are easily able to return to the position they were in before they married, a clean break order may be appropriate.[255] Even if the marriage is short, if there is a child the court may well decide that the future for mother and child is too uncertain to make a clean break order.[256]

3. *The very wealthy.* With wealthy people it is often particularly appropriate to require one spouse to pay the other a substantial lump sum as part of a clean break order.[257] A '*Duxbury*' calculation is widely used, which involves calculating a lump sum which, if suitably invested, will produce enough income to meet the reasonable requirements of the recipient spouse for the rest of their life.[258] The House of Lords in *White* v *White*[259] have, however, referred to the *Duxbury* paradox, which is that the longer the marriage, the older the claimant will be, and so the shorter the life expectancy, and so the lower the award.

4. *Both spouses have well-established careers.* In *Burgess* v *Burgess*[260] the wife was a doctor in general practice and the husband was a partner in a firm of solicitors. Both were well established in their careers and their children were students at university. It was held that dividing all the family assets equally and making a clean break order was the most appropriate course, given that they were both clearly able to support themselves from their careers.

5. *Where there is antagonism between the spouses.* A clean break between spouses is appropriate where the relationship has broken down. In such a case continuing financial responsibility may only increase the bitterness affecting the relationship. However, even if the relationship is an unhappy one it might still be impossible to make a clean break order which achieves fairness.[261]

(v) When a clean break order is inappropriate

1. *Where there are still young children.* In *Suter* v *Suter and Jones*[262] there were children, but very limited capital assets. It was held that it was not appropriate to make a clean break order and that the husband should be required to pay a nominal sum of £1 a year. The court stressed that simply because there were dependent children did not mean that there was no possibility of making a clean break order. However, in this case it was necessary to provide a 'backstop' in

---

[254] *Seaton* v *Seaton* [1986] 2 FLR 398 CA.

[255] E.g. *Hobhouse* v *Hobhouse* [1999] 1 FLR 961.

[256] *B* v *B (Mesher Order)* [2003] FL 462.

[257] For a rare case where despite the parties' wealth clean break was not appropriate see *F* v *F (Clean Break: Balance of Fairness)* [2003] 1 FLR 847.

[258] Actuarial calculations are made, estimating the life expectancy of the recipient spouse, the rate of inflation, etc. For a criticism of *Duxbury* calculations see Merron, Baxter and Bates (2001).

[259] [2000] 2 FLR 976, [2000] 3 FCR 555 HL.

[260] [1996] 2 FLR 34, [1997] 1 FLR 89.

[261] *Parra* v *Parra* [2002] 3 FCR 513, although the judgment was overturned on the facts by the Court of Appeal ([2003] 1 FCR 97).

[262] [1987] 2 FLR 232, [1987] FCR 52 CA.

case there were future unforeseen events which might lead the court to want to make ancillary relief orders.

2. *Where there is too much uncertainty over the recipient's financial future.* In *Whiting* v *Whiting*[263] the wife had, at the time of the divorce, started a job. The husband, who had been well paid, had recently been made redundant, but had become self-employed earning at that time £4,500. The trial judge decided that the husband should be ordered to pay a nominal sum and declined to make a clean break order. This was because although it appeared that the wife was in a position where she would be able to become financially independent, it was not possible to predict her future. The majority of the Court of Appeal decided that the judge's decision could not be said to be entirely wrong, even though they would have made a clean break order. Balcombe LJ, in the minority, thought the trial judge's ruling was fundamentally wrong and should be overturned. Less controversial was *M* v *M* *(Financial Provision)*,[264] where a woman, aged 47, had a limited earning capacity. Here the court declined to make a clean break order as she had not worked for the last 20 years and there was no certainty that she would be able to become self-sufficient in the future.

3. *Where there is a lengthy marriage.* In *SRJ* v *DWJ* *(Financial Provision)*[265] the couple had been married for 27 years, during which the wife had spent most of her time caring for the children and the house. The Court of Appeal felt that this strongly militated against a clean break order.

(vi) Deferred clean break orders

If the court decides that a clean break order is not appropriate, then the next question is whether a delayed clean break order can be made. A delayed clean break order is useful where a party could adjust, without undue hardship, to the termination of financial provision orders in the foreseeable future.

In *Flavell* v *Flavell*[266] Ward LJ was concerned that the lower courts were too ready to make these delayed clean break orders. He stated:

> There is in my judgment, often a tendency for these orders to be made more in hope than in serious expectation. Especially in judging in the case of ladies in their middle years, the judicial looking into a crystal ball very rarely finds enough of substance to justify a finding that adjustment can be made without undue hardship. All too often these orders are made without evidence to support them.

As Ward LJ put it in *C* v *C* *(Financial Provision: Short Marriage)*,[267] 'Hope, without pious exhortations to end dependency, is not enough.' The court therefore must have clear evidence that the recipient will certainly be financially independent come the end of the period of maintenance payments if a delayed clean break order is to be appropriate.

---

[263] [1988] 2 FLR 189, [1988] FCR 569 CA.
[264] [1987] 2 FLR 1.
[265] [1999] 2 FLR 176 CA.
[266] [1997] 1 FLR 353, [1997] 1 FCR 332 CA.
[267] [1997] 2 FLR 26, [1997] 3 FCR 360 CA.

K. Interim orders

Given the length of time that litigation and negotiations can take, it is understandable that a divorcing spouse might need financial support before the making of a final court order. Hence the MCA 1973 permits the court to order interim support under s 22. There are no formal guidelines, but the courts will take into account all the circumstances of the case. In fact, it seems that interim awards are 'almost unknown', according to Thorpe J in *F v F (Ancillary Relief: Substantial Assets)*.[268] This is because the courts do not want to tie their hands before they have heard all the facts in a full hearing.

In *Wicks* v *Wicks*[269] the court held that there is no power to grant interim lump sum orders. Since the Family Law Act 1996 there is the power to make interim lump sum orders under s 22A(4). It has been suggested that such orders may be useful to enable a party to pay their lawyers' fees![270] More particularly, interim lump sum orders will be helpful in paying for alternative accommodation. There is, however, no power in the Family Law Act 1996 to make an interim property adjustment order.

L. Factors to be taken into account when making orders

(i) Discretion not formula

The key to understanding the way judges decide what financial orders to make under the MCA 1973 is to appreciate that they are given wide discretion. The House of Lords have accepted that different judges may quite properly reach different conclusions as to what the most appropriate order is in a particular case.[271] The factors to be taken into account by a court in deciding which orders to make are listed in s 25 of the MCA 1973. The Act deliberately has no one overall objective[272] and it is permissible for the court to take into account factors not listed in s 25, if they believe them to be relevant.[273] However, Lord Nicholls in the House of Lords in *White* v *White*[274] has suggested that fairness is the overriding purpose of the Act. Fairness here means the judge's objective assessment of fairness, not the parties' subjective assessment of what they think might be fair.[275] That said, the concept of fairness is not particularly useful. Lord Nicholls accepted this guidance was not of enormous assistance, as he put it 'fairness, like beauty, lies in the eye of the beholder'.[276]

We shall now consider the various factors which s 25 of the MCA 1973 requires the court to take into account.[277]

---

[268] [1995] 2 FLR 45.
[269] [1998] 1 FLR 470.
[270] *F v F (Ancillary Relief: Substantial Assets)* [1995] 2 FLR 45.
[271] *Piglowska* v *Piglowski* [1999] 2 FLR 763 HL.
[272] *White* v *White* [2001] AC 596 HL at pp. 316–17.
[273] See e.g. the discussion in *Thomas* v *Thomas* [1996] 2 FLR 544, [1996] FCR 668.
[274] [2000] 2 FLR 976, [2000] 3 FCR 555 HL.
[275] *Lambert* v *Lambert* [2002] 3 FCR 673, para 39.
[276] *White* v *White* [2000] 3 FCR 555, para 1.
[277] It is important to note that less than half of cases lead to ancillary relief orders (Barton and Bisset-Johnson (2000)). Many couples have so few assets that a court order is unnecessary.

(ii) The welfare of children[278]

The court must take into account all the factors listed in s 25. However, it is required 'to have regard to all the circumstances of the case, first consideration being given to the welfare while a minor of any child of the family who has not attained the age of eighteen'.[279] It was made clear in *Suter v Suter and Jones*[280] that although the child's welfare is the first consideration, that does not mean that it is the overriding consideration. That is to say, it is the most important factor, but not the only factor. The Court of Appeal explained that, as well as protecting the child's interests, it is necessary to reach 'a financial result, which is just as between husband and wife'.

The criteria to be taken into account when considering awards to spouses with children are set out in s 25(3):

(a) the financial needs of the child;
(b) the income, earning capacity (if any), property and other financial resources of the child;
(c) any physical or mental disability of the child;
(d) the manner in which he was being and in which the parties to the marriage expected him to be educated or trained;
(e) the considerations mentioned in relation to the parties to the marriage in paragraphs (a), (b), (c) and (e) of [s 25(2) of the MCA 1973].

The child's interests are obviously significant when considering the appropriate level of child support but are also very relevant when deciding the financial support for spouses. The child's interests can be pertinent in a number of ways:

1. It has been held that it would be contrary to the child's interests if either of his or her parents had to live in straightened circumstances, as this would cause the child distress[281] and affect the parents' ability to care for him or her.
2. The child's interests can also be important in deciding what should happen to the matrimonial home. It may well be thought that it is in the child's best interests if he or she and the parent who is caring for him or her remain in the matrimonial home. In *B v B (Financial Provision: Welfare of Child and Conduct)*[282] the need to ensure that the child (who had had a disturbed background) had a secure and satisfactory home meant that there was no money to enable the husband to purchase a house.[283] This was justified by Connell J on the basis that the child's welfare was to be the first consideration.
3. The child's interests are also relevant in deciding whether or not the court should expect the residential parent to go out to work to support him- or herself, or order the other spouse to pay maintenance support.[284] The courts gen-

---

[278] The court will consider the award for child support as part of the overall package which we will consider shortly.
[279] MCA 1973, s 25(1). 'Child' here includes any child of the family of the couple (see Chapter 7 for further discussion of this term).
[280] [1987] 2 FLR 232, [1987] FCR 52 CA.
[281] *E v E (Financial Provision)* [1990] 2 FLR 233 at p. 249.
[282] [2002] 1 FLR 555.
[283] Contrast *M v B (Ancillary Proceedings: Lump Sum)* [1998] 1 FLR 53.
[284] *Waterman v Waterman* [1989] 1 FLR 380, [1989] FCR 267 CA.

erally accept that a parent caring for young children should not be expected to seek employment.[285]

The court will take into account the future interests of children, even beyond their minority, as well as the interests of children already over the age of minority, even though the interests of such children are not the first consideration.[286]

(iii) Financial resources

The income, earning capacity, property and other financial resources which each of the parties to the marriage has or is likely to have in the foreseeable future, including in the case of earning capacity any increase in that capacity which it would in the opinion of the court be reasonable to expect a party to the marriage to take steps to acquire.[287]

Clearly, the financial resources of the parties are a key element, although the truth is that in most cases the courts are dealing with the debts, rather than the assets, of the parties.[288] A number of controversial issues have been discussed by the courts in regard to financial resources:

1. The court cannot take into account the resources of a third party.[289] So if the wife now has a rich boyfriend, his income cannot be taken into account. However, the court may assume that a spouse's new partner might be in a position to contribute to her household expenses thereby reducing her needs.[290] Another circumstance in which this issue is relevant is if a spouse's wealth is hidden within a company that he or she controls. The court may assume that the company could make payments to the spouse to meet any order that the court may impose,[291] as long as there are no third party's interests which may be endangered.[292]

2. 'Other resources' includes income from discretionary trusts; personal injury damages;[293] and even inheritance received after the divorce.[294] Property inherited during the marriage can be divided on divorce, although the fact that it was inherited by one spouse should be taken into account in determining whether it would be fair to distribute it.[295] Only very rarely will the court assume

---

[285] *Leadbeater* v *Leadbeater* [1985] 1 FLR 789.
[286] *Richardson* v *Richardson (No. 2)* [1997] 2 FLR 617.
[287] MCA 1973, s 25(2)(a).
[288] Eekelaar and Maclean (1986); Fisher (2002).
[289] *Re L (Minors) (Financial Provisions)* [1979] 1 FLR 39; *Duxbury* v *Duxbury* [1987] 1 FLR 7.
[290] *Atkinson* v *Atkinson (No. 2)* [1996] 1 FLR 51, [1995] 3 FCR 788 CA.
[291] Especially where the company has provided the paying spouse with money when needed in the past.
[292] *Thomas* v *Thomas* [1996] 2 FLR 544, [1996] FCR 688. A similar point was made in this case about a discretionary trust.
[293] *C* v *C (Financial Provision: Personal Damages)* [1995] 2 FLR 171, [1996] 1 FCR 283. But the court will not assume an outcome in proceedings which are yet to be concluded: *George* v *George* [2003] 3 FCR 380.
[294] *Schuller* v *Schuller* [1990] 2 FLR 193, [1990] FCR 626.
[295] *White* v *White* [2000] 2 FLR 976, [2000] 3 FCR 555 HL, applied in *Norris* v *Norris* [2003] 2 FCR 245, [2003] FL 301, although in *H* v *H (Financial Provision: Special Contribution)* [2002] 2 FLR 1021 Peter Hughes QC said the husband's inheritance was not available for division because he had kept it entirely separate from the family finances. This decision does not sit comfortably with the other cases.

that one spouse will receive money under someone's will at some point in the future.[296]

3. The court will consider not only the spouse's present income, but also the extra earnings that could be gained by working overtime[297] or taking out loans.[298] If a person is unemployed then he or she may be expected to find work. One difficult issue involves the earning capacity of spouses, normally wives, who have dedicated their lives to child-care. The courts will not generally expect a middle-aged spouse who has been out of the job market to find employment.[299] Hence in *A v A (Financial Provision)*[300] it was held not to be reasonable to expect a woman of 45 to seek full-time employment or set up her own business, even though she had an engineering degree. Had she been much younger, or had there been no children, the court might have reacted differently.[301]

4. The courts are not limited to considering those assets which a party has acquired during the marriage.[302] So if one party has substantial wealth which he or she inherited before the marriage, this wealth can still be redistributed, even though it was not gained in the course of the marriage. However, the fact that one party brought wealth to the marriage could be regarded as a contribution to the marriage which the court should take into account when deciding what would be a fair distribution of property.[303]

(iv) The needs, obligations and responsibilities of the parties

The financial needs, obligations and responsibilities which each of the parties to the marriage has or is likely to have in the foreseeable future.[304]

Having looked at the plus side (the resources of the parties), the court will then turn to the minus side (the needs, obligations and responsibilities of the parties). The concept of 'needs' is inevitably subjective. Do you *need* a sofa? If so, should it be from Argos, Habitat, or Harrods? The courts have interpreted 'needs' loosely. The needs of a rich couple are not the same as the needs of a poor couple. This has, in fact, caused the courts some embarrassment, in that saying a spouse *needs* three houses[305] sounds peculiar, and so the courts have suggested that, at least in the context of the rich, 'reasonable requirements' of the spouses should be referred to, rather than their 'needs'. Reasonable requirements are not limited to essentials, and so, for example, in *Gojkovic v Gojkovic*[306] £1.3 million was given to enable a wife to start up her own business.

---

[296] Although in rare cases it might even be appropriate to adjourn the court until a relative's death has occurred: *MT v MT (Financial Provision: Lump Sum)* [1992] 1 FLR 362, [1991] FCR 649.
[297] *J-PC v J-AF* [1955] P 215 CA.
[298] *Newton v Newton* [1990] 1 FLR 33, [1989] FCR 521.
[299] *Barrett v Barrett* [1988] 2 FLR 516, [1988] FCR 707.
[300] [1998] 2 FLR 180, [1998] 3 FCR 421.
[301] See *N v N (Consent Order: Variation)* [1993] 2 FLR 868, [1994] 2 FCR 275 CA.
[302] *GW v RW* [2003] EWHC 611, [2003] 2 FCR 289.
[303] *White v White* [2001] AC 596, at p. 610.
[304] MCA 1973, s 25(2)(b).
[305] *F v F (Ancillary Relief: Substantial Assets)* [1995] 2 FLR 45.
[306] [1990] FLR 140, [1990] FCR 119 CA.

In many cases the first need the court will consider is housing. As Thorpe LJ put it in *Cordell* v *Cordell*: 'nothing is more awful than homelessness'.[307] The court will therefore always seek to ensure that the children and their carer are housed. Where possible the next concern will be to provide money for the non-resident parent to be rehoused.

The court will not normally take into account obligations which are voluntarily assumed. If a spouse has increased expenditure because he or she insists on living in an unduly large house,[308] or lives a long way from work and so has high travel expenses[309] then the court may regard these as voluntarily assumed obligations and therefore will not include them when considering the appropriate award. But the court may be willing to take into account the costs of a new family and the needs of a new spouse.[310]

It should be stressed that the courts are concerned with what a spouse needs, not with what he or she might actually spend the money on. The court's responsibility is to ensure that there is enough money, as far as possible, to meet the spouse's needs, and it is the spouse's responsibility to spend it appropriately.[311] A spouse cannot refuse to pay maintenance on the basis that the recipient would spend it in an inappropriate manner.[312]

(v) 'The standard of living enjoyed by the family before the breakdown of the marriage'[313]

This factor tends to be relevant to rich couples in particular.[314] For wealthy couples a spouse's reasonable requirements are calculated by considering the expenditure during the marriage.[315] So if the wife during the marriage normally spent £50,000 per annum on clothes then, when calculating her reasonable requirements, it will be assumed that that figure represents her reasonable requirements for clothing. An exception to this approach was highlighted in *A* v *A (Financial Provision)*,[316] where the spouses lived a frugal life despite being extremely wealthy.[317] In such a case the court suggested that the wife's reasonable requirements could be calculated by asking what standard of life she might have expected to enjoy being married to a man of that wealth.

---

[307] [2002] 1 FCR 97 at para 33.
[308] *Slater* v *Slater* (1982) 3 FLR 364 CA.
[309] *Campbell* v *Campbell* [1998] 1 FLR 828, [1998] 3 FCR 63 CA.
[310] *Barnes* v *Barnes* [1972] 3 All ER 872.
[311] *Duxbury* v *Duxbury* [1987] 1 FLR 7.
[312] *Duxbury* v *Duxbury* [1987] 1 FLR 7.
[313] MCA 1973, s 25(2)(c).
[314] *Leadbeater* v *Leadbeater* [1985] 1 FLR 789.
[315] *Dart* v *Dart* [1996] 2 FLR 286, [1997] 1 FCR 21 CA.
[316] [1998] 2 FLR 180, [1998] 3 FCR 421.
[317] Singer J suggested that their frugality was revealed by the fact their sofa was purchased at Ikea rather than Harrods.

(vi) 'The age of each party to the marriage and the duration of the marriage'[318]

The shorter the marriage, the less likely the court will make a substantial award.[319] In *Attar* v *Attar*,[320] where the couple had lived together as a married couple only for six months, it was suggested that the sum awarded should reflect the amount necessary to return the parties to the position they were in before they were married.[321] However, just because a marriage is short does not mean that an order will not be made. This was clearly revealed in *C* v *C* *(Financial Provision: Short Marriage)*,[322] where the marriage had lasted only nine months. However, a child had been born during the marriage. As the wife could not be expected to enter employment[323] and the child's health was uncertain, there was no likelihood that the wife would be able to become independent. Therefore, a substantial lump sum order and periodical payments order were made.

In considering the length of the marriage the court will also take into account the total length of the relationship. In *Krystman* v *Krystman*[324] a couple were married for 26 years but they had actually lived together for only two weeks and so no order was made. Where the couple have cohabited before the marriage the court will take into account the total length of the relationship. Ewbank J in *W* v *W* *(Judicial Separation: Ancillary Relief)*[325] and Mostyn QC in *GW* v *RW*[326] drew no distinction between the period of cohabitation and the period of marriage. Courts have also had to consider cases where the same couple have divorced, later cohabited and then broken up again. The cohabitation can be taken into account in reopening the original divorce.[327]

Sometimes in cases involving elderly divorcing couples the real issue is who will have the family assets on the couple's death, because each spouse wants to be the one who decides who will have those assets after their death. In *S* v *S*[328] an elderly couple divorced after a short marriage. The court ordered the husband to transfer money to the wife which was to be held on trust, reverting to the husband or his estate on the wife's death, therefore ensuring that, ultimately, the husband would keep control of the property. Lord Nicholls in *White* v *White*[329] has accepted that it is permissible for a judge to take into account the wish of a spouse to leave money to her relatives in her will and this could constitute a 'need'.

---

[318] MCA 1973, s 25(2)(d).
[319] See the discussion in Eekelaar (2003c).
[320] [1985] FLR 649.
[321] See also *Hobhouse* v *Hobhouse* [1999] 1 FLR 961.
[322] [1997] 2 FLR 26, [1997] 3 FCR 360 CA.
[323] The wife had worked as a prostitute (her husband had met her in her 'professional capacity') but the husband could not expect her to return to her former 'occupation'.
[324] [1973] 3 All ER 247 CA.
[325] [1995] 2 FLR 259.
[326] [2003] EWHC 611, [2003] 2 FCR 289.
[327] *Hill* v *Hill* [1998] 1 FLR 198, [1997] FCR 477 CA.
[328] [1977] Fam 127.
[329] [2000] 2 FLR 976, [2000] 3 FCR 555 HL.

(vii) 'Any physical or mental disability of either of the parties to the marriage'[330]

In reality this factor is subsumed under the needs heading. The most notable case is *C* v *C* *(Financial Provision: Personal Damages)*[331] where a husband who was badly disabled was held entitled to £5 million, even though the wife was to be left on social security benefits. The husband's disabilities meant he required constant care and complex equipment, and this meant that he had to have all the assets.

(viii) Contributions to the welfare of the family

The contributions which each of the parties has made or is likely in the foreseeable future to make to the welfare of the family, including any contribution by looking after the home or caring for the family.[332]

Under this heading the courts have discussed two issues. The first is the position of the spouse (normally wife) who has not been earning, but who has worked as a homemaker and child-carer. The courts have recognised this to be an important contribution to the welfare of the family. Certainly the courts will not accept the argument that a wife should receive less maintenance because she has not brought any financial income into the marriage. In *A* v *A* *(Financial Provision)*[333] the court stated that the wife's adultery did not diminish the fact that she had undertaken the day-to-day care of the children in her traditional role as homemaker and companion. In *White* v *White*[334] Lord Nicholls explained:

whatever the division of labour chosen by the husband and wife, or forced upon them by circumstances, fairness requires that this should not prejudice or advantage either party when considering [MCA 1973, s 25(2)(f)] ... If in their different spheres, each contributed equally to the family, then in principle it matters not which of them earned the money and built up the assets. There should be no bias in favour of the money earner and against the home-maker and the child-carer.

(ix) Conduct

The conduct of each of the parties if that conduct is such that it would in the opinion of the court be inequitable to disregard it.[335]

At one time conduct was considered very important. A wife who was regarded as guilty of marital misconduct could expect a low award.[336] However, in line with the trend generally in family law, it is now rare for conduct to be taken into account.[337] As the statute states, the conduct must be 'such that it would ... be inequitable to

---

[330] MCA 1973, s 25(2)(e).
[331] [1995] 2 FLR 171, [1996] 1 FCR 283.
[332] MCA 1973, s 25(2)(f).
[333] [1998] 2 FLR 180, [1998] 3 FCR 421.
[334] [2000] 2 FLR 976, [2000] 3 FCR 555 HL.
[335] MCA 1973, s 25(2)(g), as amended by the Family Law Act 1996.
[336] *Wachtel* v *Wachtel* [1973] Fam 72 CA marked the change in the courts' attitude.
[337] Eekelaar (1991a), although Inglis (2003) argues that judges should be far more willing to allow domestic violence to affect the level of the award.

disregard'. The cases suggest that the conduct must be of an extreme kind in order to be relevant. Sir George Baker P suggested that conduct should be 'of the kind that would cause the ordinary mortal to throw up his hands and say, "surely that woman is not going to be given any money" or "is not going to get a full award" '. For example, in *K v K (Financial Provision: Conduct)*[338] the wife helped her depressed husband's suicide attempt as she wished to acquire his estate and to set up a new life with her lover. Her conduct was such that it should be taken into account and her award was reduced from the £14,000 she would have received but for her misconduct to £5,000.[339] Notably conduct, even in these extreme cases, does not lead to the award being reduced to nil.

Where a court decides that conduct is sufficiently serious to be taken into account, the judge must explain how it affects the level of the award. In *Clark v Clark*[340] the Court of Appeal held that the wife's misconduct was so bad 'it would be hard to conceive graver misconduct'.[341] The Court of Appeal criticised the lower court judge, who accepted that the conduct was bad but had decided that it should not affect the level of the award. The Court of Appeal felt that serious misconduct should be taken into account in deciding the appropriate order, although it was open to a court to decide that no deduction would be made.

The court will consider not only the bad conduct, but also the good conduct of the spouses. In *A v A (Financial Provision: Conduct)*[342] the husband gave up his job and made no effort to work, while the wife undertook a degree course and started a new career. The court thought that the contrast between what they regarded as the good conduct of the wife and the bad conduct of the husband should be taken into account in calculating the correct award.

In *Tavoulareas v Tavoulareas*[343] Thorpe LJ suggested that it is necessary to distinguish conduct which affects the level of the award and conduct which leads to being penalised in costs. He stated:

> it does seem to me that a clear distinction must be drawn in all these cases between what might loosely be described as marital conduct and what might conventionally be described as litigation conduct … It seems to me as a matter of construction that s 25(2)(g) is plainly aimed at marital misconduct.

Whether conduct should or should not be relevant has given rise to some debate.[344] There are some who argue that if the court is to achieve justice, it must ensure that grossly wrong conduct is taken into account. Others argue that, with the increasing acceptance of no fault divorce, it is harder to justify the relevance of fault here, except in the most extreme cases.

---

[338] [1990] 2 FLR 225, [1990] FCR 372.
[339] *HM Customs and Excise and another v A* [2002] 3 FCR 481 CA held that the fact that the husband was a convicted drug dealer was conduct which it was inequitable to ignore.
[340] [1999] 2 FLR 498 CA.
[341] [1999] 2 FLR 498 at p. 509. The wife (described by the judge as a woman of considerable charm and physical attraction) was in her early 40s and the husband nearly 80. She oppressed the husband, refused to consummate the marriage and virtually imprisoned the husband in a caravan in the garden of his house.
[342] [1995] 1 FLR 345.
[343] [1998] 2 FLR 418, [1999] 1 FCR 133 CA.
[344] Carbone and Brinig (1991). See also Carbone and Brinig (1988).

(x) Loss of benefits

> The value to each of the parties to the marriage of any benefit (for example, a pension) which by reason of the dissolution or annulment of the marriage, that party will lose the chance of acquiring.[345]

The most obvious issue here is the pension rights that a spouse may lose the right of acquiring, although rights under an inheritance might be relevant. The law on pensions will be discussed shortly.

(xi) The 'yardstick of equality'

In a major reconsideration of the exercise of discretion, the House of Lords in *White v White* has suggested that equality of division of the family assets should be seen as a 'yardstick'. Lord Nicholls explains:

> As a general guide equality should only be departed from if, and to the extent that, there is good reason for doing so. The need to consider and articulate reasons for departing from equality would help the parties and the court to focus on the need to ensure the absence of discrimination. This is not to introduce a presumption of equal division under another guise.[346]

Equal division is an appropriate starting point because each party has contributed to the marriage, be it financially or through child-care or housework. Lord Nicholls, however, makes it clear then that the equality principle is not to be regarded as a presumption, but rather a yardstick. In *Lambert* Thorpe LJ described the yardstick of equality as a 'cross check'.[347] In other words the judge should consider all the factors in s 25 to decide on the appropriate division of assets. The judge should then consider whether he or she has departed from equality and if so whether there was a good reason for doing so. Lord Nicholls made it clear that very often there will be a reason for departing from equality. The decision in *White* has left many questions unanswered:

(a) When should the principle of equality be departed from?
The following are some of the circumstances in which it may be appropriate to depart from the equality:

- *The needs of the parties*. In many cases the needs of the children and resident parent will require a departure from equality. Couples may lack sufficient assets to meet the most basic needs of the children and primary carer. In such a case an equal distribution will be unacceptable; indeed the children and carer may well need all of the assets and in addition ongoing maintenance payments. Only where the couple are very rich will there be sufficient assets to meet the basic needs of the parties and equal division can be considered as a possibility. In *Lambert* Lord Justice Thorpe suggested that in many cases the courts should seek to divide

---

[345] MCA 1973, s 25(2)(h).
[346] *White v White* [2000] 3 FCR 555, para 24. Singer HHJ (2001) provides a useful discussion of discrimination in this context.
[347] [2002] 3 FCR 673, para 38.

equally those assets which were surplus once the needs of the parties had been met.[348] In *S* v *S*[349] the husband was living with a woman and her children. It was held he therefore had greater needs than the wife who was living alone. This justified giving him slightly more than half the assets. However, subsequently *H-J* v *H-J (Financial Provision: Departing from Equality)*[350] and *Norris* v *Norris*[351] have suggested that it is wrong in principle for a wife to get less than she would otherwise because her husband had left her for another woman and had children with her.

- *Extraordinary contribution.* In *Cowan* v *Cowan*[352] the husband was an extremely successful business person. The Court of Appeal suggested that his contribution was 'stellar' or 'really special'. After that case there was much discussion over what sort of contributions could be regarded as 'really special'.[353] Subsequently in *Lambert* v *Lambert*[354] Thorpe LJ made it clear that only in exceptional cases will the contribution of one of the parties be regarded as a good reason for departing from equality.[355] He made the point that if the money-earner's contribution can be assessed to ascertain whether it was outstanding, then in fairness the child-carer's or homemaker's contribution should be assessed to see if it was outstanding.[356] The obstacle is, of course, that it is extremely difficult to calculate how good someone is at being a mother.[357] As Thorpe LJ put it in *Lambert*: 'I do not accept that the duty requires a detailed critical appraisal of the performance of each of the parties during the marriage. Couples who cannot agree division are entitled to seek a judicial decision without exposing themselves to the intrusion, indignity and possible embarrassment of such an appraisal.'[358]
- *Parental contribution.* In *White* itself and *Dharamshi* v *Dharamshi*[359] the fact that the family business had been started by money from the father's parents was a reason for giving him slightly more than half the family assets.
- *Obvious and gross misconduct.* In *B* v *B (Financial Provision: Welfare of Child and Conduct)*[360] the husband's non-disclosure, removal of the assets and failure to support the children justified a departure from equality.
- *Difficulties in liquidation.* If it is not possible to liquidate assets (e.g. they are tied up in a business in a way which makes their extraction impossible) this will be a reason to depart from equality.[361]

---

[348] *Lambert* v *Lambert* [2002] 3 FCR 673, para 39. This proposal was supported in *Supporting Families* para 4.49.

[349] [2001] 3 FCR 316.

[350] [2002] 1 FLR 415.

[351] [2003] 2 FCR 245, [2003] FL 301.

[352] [2001] 2 FCR 332.

[353] Claims were unsucessfully made that a reason for departing from equality was that the wife had made a particularly negative contribution to the marriage: *W* v *W* [2001] FL 656.

[354] [2002] 3 FCR 673, discussed in Brasse (2003).

[355] See *Norris* v *Norris* [2003] 2 FCR 245 where the wife's contribution to the marriage was 'as full as it could have been', but not exceptional.

[356] Hodson, Green and De Souza (2003). It will be no easier if it is the wife who is claiming to be exceptional: *Norris* v *Norris* [2003] 2 FCR 245, [2003] FL 301.

[357] At para 27.

[358] Para 38.

[359] [2001] 1 FCR 492.

[360] [2002] FL 173.

[361] *N* v *N (Financial Provision: Sale of Company)* [2001] FL 347.

(b) What property is to be divided equally?

Is the property to be divided equally under the *White* yardstick only the property which was acquired by the couple during the marriage, or is it all of the property that the couple possess available for redistribution? The position the courts appear to have reached at present is that all of a couple's property is available for redistribution, but the fact that one of the parties brought it into the marriage (or acquired it through inheritance) may be good reason to depart from equality and permit that party to retain it.[362]

(c) Does White only apply to lengthy marriages?

Most of the cases where the *White* v *White* principle of equality has applied have been lengthy marriages of over 20 years. In *GW* v *RW*[363] Mostyn QC suggests that although an equal division is obvious where the marriage is over 20 years, it is 'more problematic' where the marriage is less than 20 years, although he does not explain precisely what he means by this.[364] He stated: 'I find it to be fundamentally unfair to be required to find that a party who has made domestic contributions during a marriage of 12 years should be awarded the same proportion of the assets as a party who has made the domestic contributions for a period in excess of 20 years.'[365] However, until we receive approval of the Court of Appeal of this approach it would be dangerous to assume it represents the law.[366]

(d) Does White only apply to rich couples?

Lord Nicholls's judgment is unclear on this question. At one point he describes the principle of non-discrimination between the money-earner and child-carer as one of 'universal application'. However, earlier in his judgment he described his approach as one which is appropriate in cases where the assets exceed the parties' financial needs for housing and basic living expenses. It appears that the yardstick of equality does apply to all marriage, regardless of wealth, but that in less well-off cases the needs of the parties are likely to be the dominant consideration and always provide a reason for departing cases.[367] It should be added that there has been concern that if *White* v *White* is misinterpreted by solicitors to imply an equal division of assets in middle- and low-income families wives and children will be far less well off as a result of *White*.[368]

(e) Equality when?

Lord Nicholls did not make it clear whether what he was proposing as a yardstick was that at the day of divorce the couple's assets be added up and divided between them equally, or whether the court should seek to ensure some kind of financial

---

[362] *Norris* v *Norris* [2003] 2 FCR 245.
[363] [2003] EWHC 611, [2003] 2 FCR 289. Barton and Hibbs (2002) suggest *White* should be used only where the total assets exceed the needs of the parties.
[364] See Eekelaar (2003c) for a useful discussion.
[365] [2003] EWHC 611, [2003] 2 FCR 289, para 43.
[366] Bailey-Harris (2003).
[367] *White* was relied upon in *Elliott* v *Elliott* [2001] 1 FCR 477, a case in which the couple were not particularly well off.
[368] Fisher (2002).

equality into the foreseeable future. If one spouse is a wage earner and the other is not, then equal division of assets on divorce will mean equality at that point in time, but a few years down the line there is likely to be a sharp inequality.[369] At present the courts are yet to address which of these versions of equality are to be relied upon by the law.

In an interesting judgment, *B* v *B (Mesher Order)*,[370] Munby J refused to make an order that the wife sell the former matrimonial home in which she and the child were to live when the child reached the age of 18 or she remarried. This was because, although to give the husband a half share would be to promote equality on the day of divorce, by the time the house had to be sold it was likely that the husband (who was able to earn significantly more than the wife) would be far richer than her and so to give him half the house would produce inequality. This indicates a willingness to attempt to achieve some kind of equality and fairness not only at the date of divorce, but also off into the future.

(f) A discussion of White

There has been much debate over the ruling in *White* v *White*.[371] Perhaps it is still too early to assess properly the impact of the decision because its ramifications are still being worked out by the Court of Appeal. But the essential argument that in all but exceptional cases the contributions of the money-earner and the child-carer/homemaker should be regarded as equal is controversial. Stephen Cretney asks

> is it far-fetched to suggest that there is something rather simplistic about the notion that home-making contributions are to be equated in terms of economic value with commercially motivated money-making activity? And even if right-thinking people now want to make such an equation, is this not essentially a matter of social judgment for decision by Parliament rather than the courts?[372]

Cretney's point about whether the approach in *White* was a matter for Parliament rather than the courts is a matter for debate. If the House of Lords felt that the lower courts' interpretation of the word 'contribution' in s 25 was effecting gender discrimination and was misconceived were they not right to set out what the word should mean? That is a normal aspect of the House of Lords' role in statutory interpretation. Interestingly the yardstick of equality appears to accord with the general public's views on what is appropriate on the breakdown of a relationship. One study found that equal division was felt by many people to be a fair way of dividing matrimonial assets on divorce, although (*inter alia*) where one party had given up earning prospects to look after a child or there was fault in the ending of relationships many felt there should be a departure from equality.[373]

Another criticism of *White* v *White* is that although at the heart of Lord Nicholls's judgment is a rejection of the earlier law which he suggested focused too much on

---

[369] But see the warning of Thorpe LJ in *Parra* [2003] 1 FCR 97, at para 27 of relying on speculation as to what the parties' financial position might be in the future.
[370] [2003] FL 462.
[371] See Duckworth and Hodson (2001); Eekelaar (2001a).
[372] Cretney (2001: 3).
[373] Lewis, Arthur, Fitzgerald and Maclean (2000).

one aspect of the s 25 criteria – the parties needs – arguably his yardstick of equality is based on only one criterion – the parties' contributions.[374]

An aspect of *White* which has been less discussed by the courts and commentators is Lord Nicholls's argument that focusing on the needs of the party would mean that an older wife after a long marriage would receive less than a younger wife with a shorter marriage. Focusing on contributions rather than needs avoided this. Eekelaar has suggested that this indicated a shift from a welfare-based approach (meets the needs of the parties) to an entitlement-based approach (what the spouse has 'earned' through the marriage).[375] In other words, it is no longer a case of the money-earner having to give the child-carer/homemaker some of 'his' money, rather it is the court dividing the couple's joint assets. Opponents of this suggestion might argue that English and Welsh law clearly does not recognise community of property (i.e. that on marriage the couple's property becomes jointly owned).[376]

M. Particular issues relating to redistribution of property on divorce

(i) The poor

The case law has established that a spouse cannot expect the state to meet his or her liability towards the other spouse. The problem is that if a spouse is on benefits and receives maintenance this can lead to a reduction in the level of benefits and hence there will be little practical gain in receiving the maintenance. If the wife is on benefits and the husband is on low pay, there is a danger that any maintenance order will mean that the husband will see no benefit in working and the wife will not gain financially from the order.

It is very unusual for a party on benefits to be ordered to make payments.[377] More common is a nominal order that is made but could be varied if the person ever got a job. The courts have also made it clear that a payer in employment should not be made to pay so much that he or she has left only the same income he or she would have if receiving benefits, because that would rob him or her of the incentive to be employed. In *Ashley* v *Blackman*[378] the wife was a 48-year-old schizophrenic on state benefits and the husband was a 55-year-old on an income of £7,000 per annum. The judge thought it important to allow the husband to see the 'light at the end of the tunnel' and be spared paying the few pounds that separated him from penury as there was no corresponding benefit to the wife. In *Delaney* v *Delaney*[379] the husband was left with insufficient income to pay his mortgage and support his new cohabitant. The Court of Appeal balanced the availability of state benefits and the husband's need to support his new cohabitant. A nominal payments order in favour of the children was all the court was willing to make. The court thought it important to be aware that there was 'life after divorce'. However, it must be

---

[374] Bailey-Harris (2001a).
[375] Eekelaar (2001a).
[376] Eekelaar (2003c).
[377] *Billington* v *Billington* [1974] Fam 24 at p. 29.
[378] [1988] FCR 699, [1988] 2 FLR 278.
[379] [1990] 2 FLR 457, [1991] FCR 161.

appreciated that, after the Child Support Act 1991 and Child Support, Pensions and Social Security Act 2000, any attempt by the courts to make a clean break order is impossible in regard to children.

(ii) The rich

The leading case in this area is *White* v *White*.[380] Their Lordships criticised the approach of the Court of Appeal in the case of *Dart* v *Dart*.[381] Mr Dart was worth hundreds of millions of pounds. Before the Court of Appeal the wife argued that she should be awarded a percentage of his wealth, perhaps one-third. However, the husband argued that the court should focus on the reasonable requirements of the wife. The Court of Appeal followed the husband's approach. Having calculated her reasonable requirements, by considering her annual expenditure on herself during the marriage, the court awarded her some £9 million, which it was calculated, if appropriately invested, could provide her with income which would meet those requirements.

In *White* v *White* the House of Lords took the view that *Dart* v *Dart* had placed too much emphasis on the wife's reasonable requirements. Lord Nicholls asked: 'where the assets exceed the financial needs of both parties, why should the surplus belong solely to the husband?' The court should, instead of focusing on the needs of the spouse, look at what would be a fair division of the family's assets, bearing in mind the yardstick of equality.

(iii) Pensions[382]

For most couples the home and pension are the two most valuable family assets. The difficulty arises where one spouse, normally the husband, has substantial pension provision, but the other, normally the wife, has wholly inadequate provision. As Lord Nicholls in *Brooks* v *Brooks*[383] explained, the 'major responsibility for family care and home-making still remains with women' and 'the consequent limitations on their earning power prevents them from building up pension entitlements comparable with those of men'. Only 37 per cent of women workers are occupation scheme members, although overall 48 per cent of workers are. Only 16 per cent of part-time workers (the majority of whom are women) belong to pension schemes.[384] Twice as many women as men (two-thirds of the female population) have an income below poverty level on their retirement.[385] If the couple remain married then the wife will be able to share in her husband's pension and if her husband dies while he is receiving a pension, his widow will be entitled to payments. However, if they divorce the wife's financial position will be much weaker than had she remained married. Joshi and Davis state:

[380] [2000] 2 FLR 976, [2000] 3 FCR 555 HL.
[381] [1996] 2 FLR 286, [1997] 1 FCR 21 CA.
[382] R. Ellison (1998); Salter (2000); Hanlon (2001).
[383] [1995] 2 FLR 13 at p. 15.
[384] Government Actuary's Department (1994: table 2.3).
[385] Masson (1996: 109).

where domestic responsibilities have not been divided it is not equal treatment to expect women to carry the double burden of society's unpaid work and earn themselves as individuals the pension rights that their husbands and ex-husbands managed to earn freed from the need to run the unpaid side of life.[386]

A different view is expressed by Deech, who suggests that it is arguable that wives who do not ensure that they have adequate pension provision in their own name are negligent.[387]

There is now a duty on the court to consider the pension position of the parties on divorce under the MCA 1973, s 25B.[388] Under s 25B(1) of the Act the courts are under a duty to consider the parties' pension entitlements:

(a) ... any benefits under a pension scheme which a party to the marriage has or is likely to have, and

(b) ... any benefits under a pension scheme which, by reason of the dissolution or annulment of the marriage, a party will lose the chance of acquiring.

Singer J in *T v T (Financial Relief: Pensions)*[389] has made it clear that this provision does not require the courts to compensate a party for loss of a share in pension, but it does mean the courts have to consider any loss of pension rights. The court in deciding what (if any) order to make have the following options. In explaining these options it will be assumed that it is the husband who has substantial pension provision and the wife whose pension position is inadequate.

1. *'Set off'*. The husband could be ordered to pay the wife money in order to ensure she has adequate provision.[390] So a husband might be ordered to pay his wife a lump sum which the wife should invest so that it will provide for her retirement. The difficulty is that there are few couples who have sufficient funds to provide an adequate sum for a pension.

2. *'Earmarking' part of pension*. This is a delayed LSO or PPO. The court has power to order the trustees or managers to make payments (including lump sums) for the benefit of a pensioner's spouse when sums become payable to the pensioner under the terms of the pension.[391] From 1 December 2000 earmarking orders must be expressed in percentage terms.

3. *Delay*. The court may prefer to delay deciding what should happen to the pension until the husband retires.[392] On divorce the court will therefore make a PPO and not dismiss the application for a LSO. The issue will therefore be delayed until the husband retires and at that point the wife should apply for a LSO and/or a variation of the PPO.

4. *Commutation of pension*.[393] The court can order the pension to be commuted.[394] That is, that the pension fund be turned into a lump sum, which can then be

---

[386] Joshi and Davies (1992).
[387] Deech (1996).
[388] Pensions Act 1995, s 166.
[389] [1998] 1 FLR 1072, [1998] 2 FCR 364.
[390] *Richardson v Richardson* [1978] 9 Fam Law 86.
[391] MCA 1973, s 25B(4).
[392] *Burrow v Burrow* [1999] 1 FLR 508.
[393] MCA 1973, s 25B(7).
[394] From 1 December 2000 the court can require a portion of the pension to be commuted (MCA 1973, s 25B(7)).

divided by means of a LSO. Normally, to commute a pension is financially disadvantageous and is therefore rarely ordered.[395]

5. *Undertakings.* If the court lacks the jurisdiction to order a particular kind of provision, it may still be able to accept an undertaking. For example, a court cannot order a husband to take out a policy of insurance on his own life for his wife's benefit, but the court may be willing to accept an undertaking from a husband that he will do so.[396]

6. *Pension sharing.* From November 2000 the court is able to split the husband's pension into two portions on the spouses' divorce. The husband will thus have his share and the wife will have her share and each will be responsible for paying into their pensions as appropriate. This order is only available as a result of the Welfare Reform and Pensions Act 1999.[397] The wife will be entitled to keep her share of the pension with the provider of her husband's pension scheme or transfer her share to a different company. The government has stressed that there is no presumption that there should be a 50:50 split or indeed any form of order at all.[398] It may be that *White* v *White* implies that an equal split of the pension should be ordered unless there is a good reason not to.[399] However, it is arguable that account should be taken of what proportion of the pension was referable to the marriage and what proportion relates to payments made before the marriage.[400]

The pension sharing option is certainly the most desirable option for many wives.[401] As mentioned already, a set-off is only available for the richest of couples. The difficulty with earmarking and delay (options 2 and 3 above) is that if the wife remarries this will end her PPO. A further difficulty with earmarking is that the husband may be deterred from paying into the pension scheme after the order is made and may prefer to set up a separate pension scheme.[402] There is also a concern that the parties may not want to have their relationship reawakened maybe 20 years after the divorce when the husband retires. It is not surprising to learn that the number of earmarking orders has been small.[403] With option 3 there is the difficulty that, by the time the husband retires, he may have several ex-wives who seek to claim a portion of the pension. We will now look in further detail at pension sharing which will be the most appropriate option for most couples with a substantial pension.

---

[395] *Field* v *Field* [2003] 1 FLR 376.
[396] *W* v *W (Periodical Payments: Pensions)* [1996] 2 FLR 480.
[397] In the unusual facts of *Brooks* v *Brooks* [1995] 2 FLR 13, [1995] 3 FCR 214 the House of Lords were willing to split a one-person pension scheme under the MCA 1973, treating it as prenuptial contract.
[398] Baroness Hollis, Official Report (HL) 6 July 1999, col. 776.
[399] *SRJ* v *DWJ (Financial Provision)* [1999] 2 FLR 176.
[400] Da Costa (2002); Salter (2003).
[401] Ginn and Price (2002).
[402] There are also difficulties where the husband dies before the pension is payable.
[403] Bird (2000).

(a) What pensions can be split?

Pension sharing is available 'in relation to a person's shareable rights under any pension arrangement other than an excepted public service pension scheme'.[404] The basic state pension cannot be split, although the State Earnings Related Pension Scheme (SERPS) can be.

(b) What is a pension sharing order?

A pension sharing order is defined in s 21A(1) of the MCA 1973 as:

'... an order which—
(a) provides that one party's—
  (i) shareable rights under a specified pension arrangement, or
  (ii) shareable state scheme rights,
  be subject to pension sharing for the benefit of the other party, and
(b) specifies the percentage value to be transferred.[405]

The essence of the order is therefore that a portion of one party's shareable rights are transferred to the other party. The order transfers rights to the other party and it must specify the percentage value to be transferred.[406]

(c) The effects of pension sharing

The effects of pension sharing are defined in s 29 of the Welfare Reform and Pensions Act 1999:

(a) the transferor's shareable rights under the relevant arrangement become subject to a debit of the appropriate amount, and
(b) the transferee becomes entitled to a credit of that amount as against the person responsible for that arrangement.

The transferor therefore loses the percentage required to be transferred, so that his pension fund is reduced in value, and the transferee acquires the right to require the pension scheme trustee or manager to credit her with that amount so that she gains a pension fund of that value. The transferee in effect has a pension of her own.

(d) Factors to be taken into account

Under s 25(2) of the MCA 1973 the court is to have regard to all the circumstances of the case and include 'any benefits under a pension arrangement which a party to the marriage has or is likely to have' and 'any benefits under a pension arrangement which ... a party to the marriage will lose the chance of acquiring'.

---

[404] MCA 1973, s 27(1) explains that a person's shareable rights under a pension arrangement are 'any rights of his under the arrangement' other than rights of a description specified by regulations made by the Secretary of State for Social Security (MCA 1973, s 27(3)). See also Pension Sharing (Valuation) Regulations 2000, SI 2000/1052, reg 2.

[405] A pension sharing order can only be made in respect of petitions filed after 1 December 2000 (Welfare Reform and Pensions Act 1999, s 85(2)(a)). If the petition is filed before that date there is conflicting case law on whether a decree nisi can be rescinded in order to permit the petitioner to re-petition and be able to take advantage of the new provisions (*S v S (Rescission of Decree Nisi: Pension Sharing Provision)* [2002] FL 171; *H v H (Pension Sharing: Rescission of Decree Nisi)* [2002] 2 FLR 116; but see *Rye v Rye* [2002] FL 736).

[406] The order must rely on percentages rather than a cash sum.

The court cannot make a pension sharing order if there is in force an earmarking order in respect of that pension.[407] Similarly, an earmarking order cannot be made if a pension sharing order is in force.

(e) Valuation

One problem with the law in this area is that valuing a pension is extremely expensive.[408] Masson[409] highlights the difficulty in valuing the pension. As it is impossible to know for certain how much will be paid on retirement, the transfer value is used (that is, the value of the fund which could be used if a person wished to transfer a fund from one pension fund to another).

(iv) Family businesses

If a husband and wife co-own a business, effectively as business partners, the law treats financial settlements differently from other divorce cases.[410] The court starts by deciding what share in the business each spouse has. In many cases this will be 50:50, but the proportion is determined by commercial law principles. The court must then decide who should continue running the business (assuming that the couple cannot continue running the business together after the divorce). If the business is profitable then only as a last resort should the court stop the business operating.[411] However, following *White v White*, the need in some cases to achieve equality may require the sale of businesses more often than before.[412] The court begins with a presumption that the spouse leaving the business should receive compensation for their share. Only if the factors in s 25 of the MCA 1973 compel it, will this be departed from. The other spouse can be required to transfer their shares and assets of a co-owned partnership or company as payment of an order.[413] The most difficult problem is to find a way for one spouse to buy the other spouse's share of the business.[414] One option is to give the spouse who lost his or her share in the business a charge[415] over the business property and over the profits made by the business.[416]

(v) Housing

In many cases the matrimonial home is the most valuable asset that the parties have. There is real difficulty in balancing the interests of the husband, the wife and the children in deciding who should occupy the family home. *M v B (Ancillary*

---

[407] MCA 1973, s 24B(5).
[408] See e.g. Divorce etc. (Pensions) Regulations 2000, SI 2000/1123; Pensions on Divorce etc. (Provision of Information) Regulations 2000, SI 2000/1048 for detailed regulations.
[409] Masson (1996).
[410] For a useful discussion of such cases see Marshall (2003).
[411] *B v B (Financial Provision)* [1989] 1 FLR 119, [1989] FCR 146.
[412] Although see *N v N (Financial Provision: Sale of Company)* [2001] 2 FLR 69 where the difficulty in liquidating assets provided a reason for departing from equality.
[413] *Harwood v Harwood* [1991] 2 FLR 274, [1992] 1 FCR 1.
[414] See e.g. *Thomas v Thomas* [1996] 2 FLR 544, [1996] FCR 668.
[415] A little like a mortgage.
[416] *Belcher v Belcher* [1995] 1 FLR 916 CA.

Proceedings: Lump Sum)[417] provides some indication of how these interests are to be ranked:

> In all these cases it is one of the paramount considerations, in applying the s 25 criteria, to endeavour to stretch what is available to cover the need of each for a home, particularly where there are young children involved. Obviously the primary carer needs whatever is available to make the main home for the children, but it is of importance, albeit it is of lesser importance, that the other parent should have a home of his own where the children can enjoy their contact time with him. Of course there are cases where there is not enough to provide a home for either. Of course there are cases where there is only enough to provide for one. But in any case where there is, by stretch and a degree of risk-taking, the possibility of a division to enable both to rehouse themselves, that is an exceptionally important consideration and one which will inevitably have a decisive impact on the outcome.[418]

These *dicta* were approved by the House of Lords in *Piglowska v Piglowski*.[419] So the first aim is to house the children and then, if possible, to enable both spouses to be housed. There are three good reasons for permitting the children to remain in the matrimonial home if at all possible. First, the children will benefit from the security of staying in the house they have been brought up in, given the other huge changes that are going on around them. Secondly, there are educational reasons for keeping the children in their present home, as they can continue to attend their present school. Thirdly, it may be important for the children's psychological welfare that they keep up their friendships with other children who live nearby.

As well as housing the children, if at all possible both spouses should be housed. However, there is no rigid rule that both spouses have a right to be housed.[420] The housing of the spouses can be justified in the name of the children's interests. If fathers are to have contact with their children then normally they will need a home where the children can visit them. It is concerning to discover that 22 per cent of all homeless families (22,880 of them) were homeless as a result of relationship breakdown.[421]

Clearly, whether the parties have alternative accommodation is an important consideration. So in *Hanlon v Hanlon*,[422] where the husband had a flat that came with his job, the court readily required him to transfer to his wife his interest in the matrimonial home. By contrast, if a spouse has special needs then this is an important factor. In *Smith v Smith*[423] the wife was awarded the house as she suffered from a kidney complaint. Despite these observations, the House of Lords has stressed that the court in each case has a discretion and that it would be wrong to see these cases as setting down any rigid rule.[424]

The harsh truth is that if the house were to be sold and the equity divided[425] then it may be that neither spouse would have sufficient cash to purchase another house

[417] [1998] 1 FLR 53 at p. 60.
[418] Approved in *Piglowska v Piglowski* [1999] 2 FLR 763 HL.
[419] [1999] 2 FLR 763 HL.
[420] *Piglowska v Piglowski* [1999] 2 FLR 763 HL.
[421] Office of the Deputy Prime Minister (2003).
[422] [1978] 2 All ER 889.
[423] [1975] 2 All ER 19n.
[424] *Piglowska v Piglowski* [1999] 2 FLR 763.
[425] Under MCA 1973, s 24A.

of the same size. On the other hand, not selling the house and permitting the children and the residential parent to remain in the house may seem harsh on the non-residential spouse. So the courts have sought ways of enabling one spouse to stay in the house with the children while seeking to protect the other spouse's financial interest in the property. If the couple own a house then on divorce the court can consider the following options:

1. The court might order one spouse to pay money in exchange for the other's share in the property. So if the husband is ordered to give up his share in the matrimonial home so that the wife and children can stay there, the wife may be required to pay money to the husband by way of compensation. This is likely to be an option only for reasonably well-off couples. The money given in exchange for the share in the property should be sufficient as to enable the husband to purchase his own property, with the aid of a mortgage if necessary.
2. The court could order that the house be sold under s 24A of the MCA 1973 and the proceeds be divided between the parties in such proportion as the court orders. This might be particularly appropriate if there are no children and the sale would provide enough money to enable both parties to buy their own homes. Such orders require careful wording over payment of mortgage until sale, occupation with the sale, and control of the sale. There is obviously a fear that the party who is allowed to occupy the house until the sale might try to delay the sale.
3. The court can postpone the sale of the property until a specified event has occurred. There are two main kinds of orders that can been used:

   (i) A *Mesher* order.[426] The parties will hold the property as equitable tenants in common and the sale will be deferred until the children reach the age of 17; or complete their full-time education; or the wife dies or remarries; or until further order. If one of these events occurs, the house will be sold and the equity divided as decided by the court. The option 'or until further order' enables the court to preserve a discretion in cases where an unforeseen event occurs. Until the sale the wife (or residential parent) will be permitted to occupy the property with the children.

   Until recently it had been thought that the *Mesher* had fallen out of favour.[427] There are a number of disadvantages with it:

   (a) The wife and husband will have to communicate and discuss the sale many years after the divorce. It thereby keeps a certain tie between the couple years after the marriage has formally ended.
   (b) When the children have finished their education they may still be reliant on the mother for accommodation, and the sale of the house could cause them harm.
   (c) The time when the mother is forced to leave her home is at a time in her life when she is most vulnerable. She may be middle-aged, with

---

[426] *Mesher* v *Mesher* [1980] 1 All ER 126 CA.
[427] Eekelaar (1991a) found that only 18 per cent of registrars regarded *Mesher* orders in a favourable light.

limited earning capacity and in no position to find appropriate alternative housing.

However, in *Elliott* v *Elliott*[428] the Court of Appeal supported the making of a *Mesher* order on the basis of *White* v *White*. It was held that to avoid gender discrimination and to promote equality the husband was prima facie entitled to half the value of the family home. Although the needs of the children justified delaying the husband's access to his share, once the children no longer needed the home the husband should be entitled to his share. A *Mesher* order enabled that to occur. *White* might therefore lead to an increase in the number of *Mesher* orders.[429] However, against this trend is *B* v *B (Mesher Order)*,[430] where Munby J took the view that to order sale and divide the proceeds when the child reached 18 or the mother remarried would result in inequality and so be against the spirit of anti-discrimination in *White* v *White*. He pointed out that by the time the triggering events occurred the husband, with his successful career, would have been able to earn substantial sums, while the wife, whom it was predicted would spend much of her time in child-care, would have been able to earn relatively little. Such a result would not, therefore, promote equality.

(ii) A *Martin* order.[431] The *Martin* order is similar to a *Mesher* order in that the property is jointly owned, but the wife (or residential parent) can stay in the home for as long as she wishes. A common form of the order is that she can stay in the house until she dies or remarries. In *Clutton* v *Clutton*[432] the Court of Appeal approved a *Martin* order where the sale was to take place on the death, remarriage or cohabitation of the wife. There is concern over this kind of 'cohabitation clause', as it might lead to spying by the husband and involve an invasion of the wife's privacy.[433] The Court of Appeal in *Clutton* suggested that this concern was outweighed by the bitterness the husband would otherwise feel if the wife were to cohabit in 'his' house with another man.[434]

4. The court can give a spouse occupation rights. If, say, a husband was the beneficial owner of the property, it would be possible to give the wife a right to occupy without giving her ownership of the property. There is no provision for such an order under the MCA 1973, but it can be achieved through an order under s 30 of the Family Law Act 1996 that a wife's matrimonial home rights continue after divorce.

5. The court could order a transfer of the house from one spouse to the other, subject to a charge in the transferor's favour. For example, a husband could be

---

[428] [2001] 1 FCR 477.
[429] Fisher (2002: 111).
[430] [2003] FL 462.
[431] *Martin BH* v *Martin BH* [1978] Fam 12.
[432] [1991] 1 FLR 242, [1991] FCR 265 CA.
[433] For an example of such spying see *B* v *B (Mesher Order)* [2003] FL 462.
[434] M. Hayes (1994).

ordered to transfer to his wife his share in the house, subject to a charge in his favour. So he would not own the house, but when the house is sold he would be entitled to a share in the proceeds.[435] The benefit of this order is that, as the wife would be the owner, she would decide when the house should be sold, but the husband does not completely lose his financial interest in the property.

6. The court could order that the house be held on trust for the child. In *Tavoulareas* v *Tavoulareas*[436] the husband was ordered to purchase a house to provide accommodation for his wife and child during the child's dependency. The house was to be held on trust for the husband with the fund reverting to the child rather than to the husband. Once the child reached majority he could, in theory, remove his mother from the home.

(vi) Pre-marriage or prenuptial contracts

The basic position in English and Welsh law is that pre-marriage contracts carry little weight in a court's consideration of an application under the MCA 1973. There are two particular reasons for this. First, it is presumed that an agreement between a couple before they marry is ineffective on the basis that they do not intend to create legal relations.[437] This is not to say that a couple cannot intend to create legal relations, it is simply that the parties will need to demonstrate that they did so intend. Secondly, contracts between couples concerning the settlement of their divorce or what should happen in the event of the marriage breaking down are not enforceable. It is the court which determines how property should be distributed on divorce, and the parties cannot rob the court of its jurisdiction. So pre-marriage or prenuptial contracts are not binding on the courts. It used to be said that pre-marriage contracts were contrary to public policy in that they require people to enter marriage while contemplating its breakdown. However, the courts do not seem to find this a convincing argument given the high rates of divorce.[438]

They can be read by the court and be taken into account, but the weight given to them depends on the particular case. In *F* v *F (Ancillary Relief: Substantial Assets)*[439] the pre-marriage contract was 'of very limited significance'.[440] However, other cases have placed much more weight on the pre-marriage contract.[441] In *N* v *N (Foreign Divorce: Financial Relief)*[442] it was reaffirmed that the contract could be a factor to be taken into account, and in *S* v *S (Divorce: Staying Proceedings)*[443] Thorpe J stated:

> There will come a case ... where the circumstances surrounding the prenuptial agreement and the provision therein contained might, when viewed in the context of other circum-

---

[435] It is not normally appropriate to phrase the order in terms of a sum of money but rather a percentage, as a specific sum would be ravaged by inflation: *S* v *S* [1976] Fam 18n at p. 21.

[436] [1998] 2 FLR 418, [1999] 1 FCR 133 CA.

[437] *Balfour* v *Balfour* [1919] 2 KB 571; *Re Windle* [1975] 3 All ER 987.

[438] Connell J in *M* v *M (Prenuptial Agreement)* [2002] FL 177.

[439] [1995] 2 FLR 45.

[440] See also *H* v *H* [2002] 1 FCR 55.

[441] For an argument that the law may gradually be changing see Francis and Phillips (2003).

[442] [1997] 1 FLR 900.

[443] [1997] 2 FLR 100 at p. 102.

stances of the case, prove influential or even crucial ... I can find nothing in s 25 to compel a conclusion ... at odds with personal freedoms to make agreements for ourselves ... carefully struck by informed adults. It all depends.[444]

It should be stressed that in both of these cases the couple were married in countries where the contract was enforceable and in both cases the parties were independently advised.[445] In *K v K (Ancillary Relief: Prenuptial Agreement)*[446] Smith QC decided to implement the aspects of the pre-marriage contact relating to the capital aspects of the financial dispute, but not the maintenance aspects of it. In *M v M (Prenuptial Agreement)*[447] Connell J, taking the pre-marriage contract into account, given the circumstances of the case, stated that it guided him towards a more modest award to the wife than he might otherwise have been minded to make. In *N v N (Jurisdiction: Pre-Nuptial Agreement)*[448] Wall J refused to enforce a prenuptial agreement governing the religious aspects of the couple's divorce.[449]

In *Uddin v Ahmed*[450] the Court of Appeal refused to enforce an agreement signed by the couple and their fathers which set out financial arrangements in the event of the parties separating. To enable the parents of the spouses to enforce such an agreement would be to undermine the rule governing the non-enforceability of a pre-marriage contract.

5. CONSENT ORDERS

Increasingly, parties are being encouraged to resolve their financial disputes on divorce without going to court, either through negotiation between their lawyers, or more rarely through mediation. Further impetus is given by the Family Proceedings Rules 1999, which have as their aim the enabling of parties to reach agreement. If the parties do reach an agreement then it is normally incorporated into the form of a draft court order which is presented to court for formal approval. The court retains the power to examine the contents of the agreement and consider the factors in s 25 of the MCA 1973. Ward LJ in *Harris v Manahan*[451] described the role of the court in these cases: 'the court is no rubber stamp nor is it some kind of forensic ferret'. In other words, the court will not blindly accept the parties' proposed orders, nor will it spend enormous effort considering the proposal with a high level of scrutiny.[452] The court will assume that if the parties were advised independently then the terms are reasonable and will make an order on the terms agreed by

---

[444] In *K v K (Ancillary Relief: Prenuptial Agreement)* [2002] FL 877 Smith QC held that the capital aspects, but not the maintenance aspects of the agreement, should be followed in a court order.
[445] There is an odd contrast here between separation agreements and pre-marriage contracts. Separation agreements are prima facie enforceable, but pre-marriage contracts are not.
[446] [2002] FL 877.
[447] [2002] FL 177.
[448] [1999] 2 FLR 745.
[449] In Home Office (1998) the government encouraged married couples to draw up pre-marriage contracts.
[450] [2001] 3 FCR 300 CA.
[451] [1997] 1 FLR 205, [1997] 2 FCR 607 CA.
[452] Davis, Pearce, Bird et al. (2000) in empirical research found that there was rarely sufficient information before a judge properly to evaluate the proposed order.

the parties.[453] Once the consent order has been made, it has the same legal effect as if it had been made by the court after a contested hearing.

A. The status of agreement before a court order has been made

What if the parties have reached an agreement, but before the agreement is turned into a consent order by the court one of the parties seeks to resile from it? The position is that the court must then hold a contested hearing, but, as was made clear in *Edgar* v *Edgar*,[454] it will take the agreement into account. In *Edgar* a very rich man and his wife signed a separation deed. Before the agreement was made into a court order the wife tried to withdraw from the agreement. The court decided to follow the agreement they had reached. This was correct, the Court of Appeal thought, although it pointed out there could be some circumstances when a party should not be bound by their agreement: namely where there was duress, undue influence, unforeseen circumstances, or injustice. Although *Edgar* has represented the law for some time, the Court of Appeal in *Pounds* v *Pounds*[455] suggested that the law was not satisfactory. It thought that the law as set out in *Edgar* was 'the worst of both worlds' since 'the agreement may be held to be binding, but whether it will be can be determined only after litigation'. The law was recently reconsidered in *Xydhias* v *Xydhias*.[456] The Court of Appeal confirmed that there was a strong presumption that if the parties had reached an agreement the court would implement that agreement.[457] But the court has an overriding duty to ensure the overall fairness of the proposed settlement.[458] The Court of Appeal held that deciding whether the parties' agreement should be implemented was a question for discretion.[459] Subsequently in *Parra* v *Parra*[460] it was suggested that where a couple had throughout their marriage ordered their affairs to achieve equality (e.g. by ensuring they each had equal shares in the business they ran) 'considerable weight' should be attached to those arrangements. In *X* v *X*[461] Munby J held that where the parties had reached their own agreement, having been independently advised, that was a 'very important' factor in deciding what would be a just and fair order under s 25. These cases reflect the tension the courts feel between on the one hand ensuring that parties are not bound by grossly unfair agreements, while on the other hand not undermining the ability of the parties to resolve their dispute themselves free from court interference.

---

[453] *Xydhias* v *Xydhias* [1999] 1 FLR 683, [1999] 1 FCR 289 CA.
[454] [1980] 2 FLR 19 CA.
[455] [1994] 1 FLR 775, [1994] 2 FCR 1055 CA.
[456] [1999] 1 FLR 683, [1999] 1 FCR 289 CA, noted in Cretney (1999).
[457] Although the court should still consider all the circumstances of the case: *Smith* v *Smith* [2000] 3 FCR 374.
[458] *Kelley* v *Corston* [1998] 1 FLR 986, [1998] 1 FCR 554 CA; *Hall & Co* v *Simons* [1999] 2 FCR 193 CA.
[459] See also *Rose* v *Rose* [2002] FLR 345. The court emphasised the importance between a consent order made by a court which cannot be resiled from and an agreement by the parties which can be.
[460] See also *Parra* v *Parra* [2003] 1 FCR 97, para 27, discussed by Scully (2003).
[461] [2002] FL 98.

6. ENFORCEMENT OF FINANCIAL ORDERS

A. Avoiding enforcement problems

At least half of the financial orders made are not paid without the use of enforcement.[462] Problems over enforcement are so common that it is better to find a way of avoiding having to use enforcement in the first place. For example, obtaining a lump sum order instead of a periodical payments order can help, as it would only need to be enforced once. Indeed, if there are difficulties in enforcing a periodical payments order, the court may order a lump sum order in its place.[463] The problem is that few couples have sufficient spare capital to enable such a lump sum to be ordered. For some couples a more realistic option is for the court to make a secured periodical payments order. Such an order means that an asset (such as a house) is used as collateral so that if the periodical payments are not made the asset can be sold to supply the necessary money to meet the order.

B. Enforcement of periodical payments

Bankruptcy cannot be used as a means of enforcing periodical payments orders, but if the orders are not secured then the following forms of enforcement may be used:

1. A judgment summons under the Debtors Act 1869. This means that if a payment is not made then the debtor can be liable to imprisonment.[464]
2. An attachment of earnings order.[465] This requires payment to be made by the employer directly out of the earnings of the payer.
3. An order can be made requiring the payer to set up a standing order from a bank account to the recipient.[466]

The debtor who is in arrears may apply to have a periodical payments order varied, or even to have the arrears remitted. There is a general rule that arrears should not be allowed to build up for over 12 months and leave is required before arrears of more than 12 months.[467] This approach can be justified on the basis that, if no attempt is made to enforce the arrears, the recipient can be deemed to have acquiesced in the non-payment. In practice this means that arrears need to be enforced reasonably swiftly.

---

[462] Edwards, Gould and Halpern (1990). See also Eekelaar and Maclean (1986).
[463] *Fournier* v *Fournier* [1998] 2 FLR 990, [1999] 2 FCR 20 CA.
[464] Family Proceedings Rules 1991, SI 1991/1247, r 2. The Court of Appeal in *Murbarak* v *Murbarak* [2001] 1 FCR 193 warned that great care had to be taken to ensure that the requirements of article 6 of the European Convention were complied with when relying on a judgment summons. See now Family Proceedings (Amendment) Rules 2003 (SI 2003/184), which should ensure the procedures are Human Rights Act compliant.
[465] Attachment of Earnings Act 1971; Maintenance Enforcement Act 1991, s 1(5).
[466] Maintenance Enforcement Act 1991, s 1(5).
[467] *R* v *Cardiff Magistrates' Court, ex p Czech* [1999] 1 FLR 95.

C. Enforcement of lump sum orders and property adjustment orders

Lump sums are not payable on the bankruptcy of the payer spouse,[468] although in exceptional circumstances a bankruptcy order could be made to enable payment of a lump sum.[469] They can be enforced in the same way as any other debt. The most common means will be through the attachment of an earnings order, or by a judgment summons.

7. BANKRUPTCY AND ANCILLARY RELIEF[470]

There are some complex provisions dealing with the interaction of bankruptcy and ancillary relief orders. Here the bankrupt's estate is subject to competing claims: from the bankrupt's creditors and from the bankrupt's spouse. How should the law reconcile these? The key elements of the law are as follows:

1. *Using bankruptcy to avoid financial orders on divorce.* If a spouse has petitioned for bankruptcy merely as a device to avoid ancillary relief orders then the bankruptcy order can be set aside.[471]
2. *Financial relief orders on bankruptcy.* A financial obligation arising from a divorce order is not provable in bankruptcy.[472] This means that if a husband is ordered to pay his wife a lump sum on divorce under the MCA 1973 and before he pays it he becomes bankrupt, his wife will not be able to claim against the trustee in bankruptcy along with other creditors.[473] However, in the unlikely event that all the creditors are paid off and there are still funds available, she may be able to enforce the order.

    Normally, the fact that a person goes bankrupt will not upset any earlier transfers of property to the former spouse. However, this rule is subject to provisions of the Insolvency Act 1986 designed to secure for the benefit of creditors certain property transferred by the bankrupt within a specified period before the bankruptcy, which were discussed in Chapter 4.[474] In *Re Abbott (A Bankrupt)*[475] it was held that where a consent order provided for sale of the matrimonial home and the proceeds to go to the wife in return for which the wife had given up her right to pursue a claim for a property transfer under s 24 of the MCA 1973, then the wife had given up valuable consideration, and so the transaction should not be set aside under s 339 of the Insolvency Act 1986. However, if she has not provided what could be regarded as consideration, the transfer is vulnerable to attack.[476] In *Re Kumar (A Bankrupt), ex p Lewis v Kumar*[477] it was decided that

---

[468] Insolvency Rules 1986, SI 1986/1925, r 13.3(2)(a).
[469] *Wheatley* v *Wheatley* [1999] 2 FLR 205. For a thorough discussion see Miller (2002).
[470] Mendoza (1995).
[471] Insolvency Act 1986, s 282. *F* v *F (Divorce: Insolvency: Annulment of Bankruptcy Order)* [1994] 1 FLR 359. Ewbank J in *Woodley* v *Woodley (No. 2)* [1992] 2 FLR 417, [1993] 1 FCR 701 suggested that bankruptcy itself can be a reviewable disposition under s 37 of the MCA 1973.
[472] Insolvency Rules 1986, r 12(3). *Woodley* v *Woodley (No. 2)* [1992] 2 FLR 417, [1993] 1 FCR 701.
[473] Although if the lump sum order referred to money in a specific account, the order may have had the effect of transferring the equitable interest in it: *Re Mordant* [1996] 1 FLR 334.
[474] See Insolvency Act 1986 (hereafter IA 1986), ss 339, 400.
[475] [1983] Ch 45.
[476] *Re Kumar (A Bankrupt), ex p Lewis v Kumar* [1993] 2 FLR 382.
[477] [1993] 2 FLR 382.

the transfer of a house to the wife was at an undervalue, even though she undertook to be responsible for the mortgage payments.

3. *Transfers after the bankruptcy.* Once a spouse has become bankrupt then any
   transfers of his or her property will be void,[478] unless leave of the court is
   given.[479] *Re Flint (A Bankrupt)*[480] stated that where a husband transferred the
   house to his wife after he was bankrupt, but under the terms of a consent order
   made before the bankruptcy, the transfer was void. The same will be true if the
   order had been one made by a court following a contested hearing. This does
   not mean that the court cannot make an order against a bankrupt, although it
   would usually only be appropriate to do so if there is likely to be a surplus at the
   end of the bankruptcy (*Hellyer* v *Hellyer*).[481]

These cases demonstrate a clear preference for the bankrupt's creditors above the
interests of the bankrupt's divorcing wife. As was noted earlier in this chapter, there
is much debate over whether the financial orders on divorce are providing the wife
(or whoever is the less well-off spouse) with *her* share of the assets or whether the
husband (or better-off spouse) is required to pay her some of *his* assets. The law in
bankruptcy seems based on the latter view.

8. VARIATION OF, APPEALS AGAINST, AND SETTING ASIDE COURT ORDERS

It may be that some time after the order has been made, one of the parties believes
that the order is no longer appropriate. It may be that since the making of the order,
the needs of one of the parties has increased (for example, he or she suffers a serious
injury following a car crash) or that one of the parties has greater resources (for
example, he or she has won the national lottery). One of the most dramatic
examples of events after the making of an order which justified amending the order
is *Barder v Barder (Caluori Intervening)*,[482] where following a divorce the wife killed
the family's two children and committed suicide. In her will left she left the property to her mother.

It is important to distinguish three ways of challenging an order.

1. The applicant could apply to vary or discharge orders. The amount payable
   under a periodical payments order may be increased or decreased, or the order
   discharged and brought to an end.[483] An application to vary an order is based
   on an argument that although the order was correct at the time when it was
   made, subsequent events mean that the order should be varied to reflect the new
   positions of the parties.

---

[478] Though if a bankrupt has been ordered to transfer property to a spouse it is possible that the effect
of the order is that the beneficial interest ceases to belong to the bankrupt: *Harper v O'Reilly and
Harper* [1997] 2 FLR 816; *Re Mordant* [1996] 1 FLR 334.
[479] IA 1986, s 284.
[480] [1993] 1 FLR 763.
[481] [1996] 2 FLR 579.
[482] [1987] 2 FLR 480 HL.
[483] MCA 1973, s 31.

2. The applicant could appeal against an order. Here the claim is that there was a fundamental flaw in the judge's reasoning, and the order should not have been made.
3. The applicant could apply to have the order set aside. This is normally done on the grounds of fraud or non-disclosure of property. The approach is similar to an appeal but the crucial difference is that the application to set aside accepts that the correct decision was made by the judge on the facts as presented, but that the other party misled the court into making the wrong order.

A. Variation

The power of the courts to vary the order is highly controversial (unlike the power to vary or set aside the order which exists for all court orders). If the couple have divorced and an appropriate order made by the court, why should the fact that, say, the husband wins the national lottery justify the wife in being entitled to more money? Looking back at the justifications discussed earlier in this chapter, apart from the contract approach the others would not seem to justify a claim to the lottery winnings. However, a case can be made to justify variation. This is that on divorce all too often there are not sufficient assets to make the order that the court may believe just, bearing in mind all the circumstances. For example, even though the marriage may be a long one and the wife may have contributed significantly to it through care of the children and the home, the husband may have disposed of his assets and so there are not enough to give her the level of income she deserves. In such a case, if the husband subsequently does receive a lottery winning and the court can now make the order which would be just and appropriate, should it not do so? Against this is the argument that court orders should represent finality, so that the parties can plan for the future. Further, there is a fear that the power to vary court orders may discourage the parties from seeking to improve their financial position. Payers may fear that if they increase their income the payee will apply to increase the level of payments; similarly, payees may be concerned that any improvement in their standard of living will lead to an application to reduce the level of payments.

(i) Which orders can be varied?

An application can be made to vary a periodical payments order. The court could increase, decrease or terminate the payments, or could vary for how long the payments are to be made. Any application for variation must be made before the order expires.[484] In other words, if the order states that periodical payments are to be made to the wife until 1 January 2005, the wife can only apply to extend the period of payments if she applies to do so before 1 January 2005. If a court wants to make an order for periodical payments which cannot be extended then an order under s 28(1A) of the MCA 1973 must be made.[485] On hearing an application for variation

---

[484] *Jones* v *Jones* [2000] 2 FCR 201 CA.
[485] *Richardson* v *Richardson (No.2)* [1997] 2 FLR 617, [1997] 2 FCR 453; discussed in Cooke (1994).

the court could decide to terminate payments altogether.[486] The court can also vary a PPO by making a LSO in its place.[487] So if a husband had been paying a wife £1,000 per year maintenance and he acquired some capital, the court might decide to order him to make a lump sum payment of, say, £25,000 and then end his PPO.

As property adjustment orders (PAOs) and lump sum orders are designed to produce finality the general principle is that they cannot usually be varied.[488]

(ii) Factors to be taken into account

In considering variation of a PPO the court will have regard to all the circumstances of the case and first consideration being the welfare of the child. This includes any change in matters to which the court had regard when first making the order. Under s 31(7) of the MCA 1973, in considering variation the court is also to consider:

    (a) ... whether in all the circumstances and after having regard to any such change it would be appropriate to vary the order so that payments under the order are required to be made or secured only for such further period as will in the opinion of the court be sufficient to enable the party in whose favour the order was made to adjust without undue hardship to the termination of those payments;

    (b) in a case where the party against whom the order was made has died, the circumstances of the case shall also include the changed circumstances resulting from his or her death.

Section 31(7)(a) therefore specifically requires the court to consider the possibility of ending the payments altogether to enable the parties to become financially independent. Most cases for variation will involve a fundamental change in circumstances since the order was made,[489] although this is not essential according to the Court of Appeal in *Flavell* v *Flavell*.[490]

There is a strict rule that if the spouse who is in receipt of periodical payments remarries then the payments will automatically come to an end. But what if she or he cohabits rather than remarries? In *Atkinson* v *Atkinson (No. 2)*[491] the Court of Appeal rejected an argument that as the wife was now cohabiting the periodical payments should come to an end. However, the Court of Appeal accepted that the ex-wife's needs were less on the basis that her cohabitant could be expected to contribute to her household expenses and so the level of maintenance should be reduced. On the husband's behalf it was argued that an ex-wife who remarries should not be disadvantaged compared to an ex-wife who cohabits and that

---

[486] *Penrose* v *Penrose* [1994] 2 FLR 621 CA.

[487] MCA 1973, s 31(7A), as inserted by the Family Law Act 1996 (hereafter FLA 1996). See *Harris* v *Harris* [2001] 1 FCR 68 where the Court of Appeal refused to set down guidelines on how the power under this section should be used, although in *Cornick* v *Cornick (No. 3)* [2001] 2 FLR 1240 it was suggested that the principles in *White* v *White* could be applied.

[488] Although the time of payment can sometimes be changed: *Omelian* v *Omelian* [1996] 2 FLR 306, [1996] 3 FCR 329 CA.

[489] A party will be prevented from seeking to vary an order if they have led the other party to act to his or her detriment on an assumption that they will not apply for variation.

[490] [1997] 1 FLR 353, [1997] 1 FCR 332 CA.

[491] *Atkinson* v *Atkinson* [1995] 2 FLR 356, [1995] 2 FCR 353; *Atkinson* v *Atkinson (No. 2)* [1996] 1 FLR 51, [1995] 3 FCR 788 CA.

therefore cohabitation and marriage should automatically end the payments. The court rejected this argument, stating that if the court did end the wife's payments on cohabitation this would pressurise her into marrying her new cohabitant to ensure she had financial security. The court stated that it would be wrong for the law to place such pressure on her.

It is possible to draft the PPO or PAO to cease if there is cohabitation. For example, a typical order relating to the home is 'the wife to have occupation of the former matrimonial home, sale of the property to be postponed until such time as she remarry or cohabit with another man'; a typical PPO is that 'the order for periodical payments shall terminate in the event of the wife's cohabitation with another man'.[492] There are difficulties with such orders. The first is the complexity of cohabitation. If the wife has a partner who visits her regularly, when does this amount to cohabitation?[493] Further, such clause can even lead to spying by the paying spouse to try to discover whether there is cohabitation.

B. Setting aside a consent order

Once a consent order has been made by the court, the court will be very reluctant to permit any challenges to the order. The following are examples of the circumstances upon which an application can be made to set aside a consent order:

1. *Non-disclosure.* The court, in deciding whether to set aside a consent order on the basis of non-disclosure, will consider whether the non-disclosure was fundamental enough to merit setting the order aside. In *Livesey* v *Jenkins*[494] the House of Lords thought the failure by the wife to reveal that she was engaged to remarry was of sufficient importance that the order should be set aside. The test, their Lordships suggested, was that had the court been aware of the information that had not been disclosed it would have made a substantially different order. This test strikes the balance between on the one hand ensuring fairness between the parties and discouraging non-disclosure, and on the other hand preventing a large number of appeals on the basis of the tiniest non-disclosures.

2. *Bad legal advice.* In *B* v *B (Consent Order: Variation)*[495] it was accepted that 'manifestly bad advice' could be a ground for setting aside a consent order. In *Harris* v *Manahan*[496] the Court of Appeal seemed to restrict this to cases where there was an exceptional case of the 'cruellest injustice'. It might be more profitable in such cases for a person to bring negligence proceedings against his or her solicitors.

---

[492] Hayes (1994).
[493] See *Kimber* v *Kimber* [2000] 1 FLR 383.
[494] [1985] FLR 813 HL.
[495] [1995] 1 FLR 9, [1995] 2 FCR 62.
[496] [1997] 1 FLR 205, [1997] 2 FCR 607 CA.

C. Appeal

It is possible to appeal against a court order. However, there are time restrictions on when an application can be made. A crucial issue is when it is possible to appeal against an order out of time. This is particularly relevant in relation to clean break orders when variation cannot be relied upon. There is a balance to be drawn between on the one hand ensuring there is finality of litigation, so that the parties are not constantly challenging the orders made in the court, while, on the other hand, it could be seen to be contrary to justice to uphold a judgment known to be based on a falsehood. The leading case is *Barder v Barder (Caluori Intervening)*,[497] which suggested that an application to appeal out of time will only occur if the following conditions are shown:

1. The basis of the order, or a fundamental assumption underlining the order, has been falsified by a change of circumstances since the making of an order. Perhaps the most common example of this is where a valuation relied upon by the court of, for example, a business or a house has proved inaccurate,[498] although it should be stressed that an applicant for leave can only rely on an unsound valuation as the basis of appeal if they have sought leave as quickly as possible and are not at fault for the misvaluation.[499] Another example may be where one spouse dies shortly after an order has been made.[500] In *Wells v Wells*[501] the wife had remarried just six months after the husband had been ordered to provide a home for the wife. It was held that the remarriage so shortly after the order had been made justified giving leave out of time. Also where the couple reconcile and cohabit after the divorce only to separate many years later it is open to appeal out of time against the original order; the reconciliation and cohabitation is an event of sufficient importance to justify giving leave out of time.[502] In *Maskell v Maskell*[503] it was held that the husband's redundancy could not be regarded as a supervening event.
2. Such change is within a relatively short time of the order, usually two years at most.[504] However, the court may be sympathetic if the applicant has applied as quickly as could reasonably be expected once he or she knew of the change of circumstances.
3. The application for leave must have been made reasonably promptly once the change of circumstances were known about.
4. The granting of leave should not prejudice unfairly third parties who had acquired interests for value in the property affected.

---

[497] [1988] AC 20 HL.
[498] E.g. *Heard v Heard* [1995] 1 FLR 970 CA; *Kean v Kean* [2002] 2 FLR 28.
[499] *Kean v Kean* [2002] 2 FLR 28.
[500] *Barder v Barder (Caluori Intervening)* [1988] AC 20; *Nandu v Nandu* Unreported 21.7.2000.
[501] [1992] 2 FLR 66 CA.
[502] *Hewitson v Hewitson* [1995] 1 FLR 241; see *Hill v Hill* [1998] 1 FLR 198 CA for an alternative way of dealing with these cases.
[503] [2001] 3 FCR 296 CA.
[504] *Worlock v Worlock* [1994] 2 FLR 689 (four years after application and two years after change then 'far too late').

Only in an 'exceptionally small number of cases' will these factors justify the over-ruling of a decision in a family law case.[505]

9. DEFEATING CLAIMS: SECTION 37 MATRIMONIAL CAUSES ACT 1973

The MCA 1973, s 37 seeks to prevent people disposing of assets in an attempt to minimise the award that can be made to their husbands or wives. The court has wide powers to prevent or set aside dispositions of property which have been made for the purpose of defeating a financial relief claim. The difficulty is often in proving that the intent of the person was to defeat a spouse's claim, although there is no need to show it was his or her sole – or even dominant – intention.[506]

10. TRANSFER OF TENANCIES

Under Sch 7 to the Family Law Act 1996[507] the court has the power to transfer certain tenancies from one spouse or cohabitant to another.

A. Who can apply?

Spouses can apply where 'one spouse is entitled, either in his own right or jointly with the other spouse, to occupy a dwelling-house by virtue of a relevant tenancy'.[508] Cohabitants or former cohabitants can apply where 'one cohabitant is entitled, either in his own right or jointly with the other cohabitant, to occupy a dwelling-house by virtue of a relevant tenancy'.[509] Cohabitants are defined in the Family Law Act 1996 as 'a man and a woman who, although not married to each other, are living together as husband and wife'.[510] So a gay couple, or two siblings renting together, cannot apply for a transfer of a tenancy.

B. Which tenancies can be transferred?

The statute applies only to certain kinds of tenancy[511] and the tenancy must be of a dwelling-house which was the home of the spouses or cohabitants. A tenancy must still be in existence when the application for a transfer is made. An important restriction on the availability of the schedule was revealed in *Gay* v *Sheeran*,[512] where Mr Sheeran was a joint tenant with Ms Gunn of a property. Ms Gunn moved

---

[505] *Shaw* v *Shaw* [2002] 3 FCR 298 at para 44.
[506] *Kemmis* v *Kemmis* [1988] 1 WLR 1307 CA.
[507] Which has been implemented.
[508] FLA 1996, Sch 7, para 2.
[509] FLA 1996, Sch 7, para 3.
[510] FLA 1996, s 63.
[511] A protected tenancy or statutory tenancy within the meaning of the Rent Act 1977; a statutory tenancy within the meaning of the Rent (Agriculture) Act 1976; a secure tenancy within the meaning of s 79 of the Housing Act 1985; and an assured or assured agricultural occupancy within the meaning of Part I of the Housing Act 1988.
[512] [1999] 2 FLR 519.

out; Ms Gay subsequently moved in; and finally Mr Sheeran moved out. Ms Gay sought an order transferring the tenancy to her. However, she failed because neither she nor Mr Sheeran were 'entitled in [their] own right or jointly with the other cohabitant' to occupy the property. So a cohabitant cannot seek a transfer of a tenancy which is jointly held by his or her partner and a third party.

C. Orders that can be made

In essence the tenancy can be transferred from one spouse or cohabitant to the other; or be transferred from the joint names of both cohabitants or spouses into the name of one of them.[513] If the tenancy is transferred then the new tenant takes on the tenancy subject to all the burdens as well as the benefits of the tenancy. There is no power to alter the terms of the agreement. But there is the power to require the transferee to pay compensation to the transferor for the loss of any interest in the tenancy.[514]

D. Factors to be taken into account

The court must consider:

1. the circumstances in which the tenancy was granted;
2. the housing needs and resources of the parties and any relevant child;
3. the financial resources and obligations of the parties and any child;
4. the likely effect of transferring or not transferring the tenancy on the health, safety or well-being of the parties and any relevant child; and
5. the suitability of the parties as tenants.[515]

In a case involving cohabitants the courts should also consider:

1. the nature of the parties' relationship, including the fact that they have not given each other the commitment involved in marriage;
2. the length of time the parties have cohabited;
3. the length of time since they ceased to cohabit;
4. whether they have any children together or whether they had parental responsibility for any children.[516]

B v M[517] gives a good example of where an order to transfer a tenancy may be appropriate. A woman moved in to her partner's rented property. She started up a successful florist business in the property. On the breakdown of the relationship she successfully applied for a transfer of the tenancy. The court focused on the fact that her business was flourishing and that the man could find alternative accommodation, as he was in receipt of housing benefit.

---

[513] The detailed terms are set out in FLA 1996, Sch 7, Part II.
[514] A list of the effects to be taken into account is found in Sch 7 to the FLA 1996.
[515] FLA 1996, Sch 7, para 5.
[516] FLA 1996, Sch 7, para 5.
[517] [1999] FLP, 16 March.

11. REFORM OF THE LAW ON FINANCIAL SUPPORT FOR SPOUSES

The Report to the Lord Chancellor of the Ancillary Relief Advisory Group indicated that solicitors, barristers and judges involved in this area of the law are broadly satisfied with the present law. Nevertheless, there has been some discussion about whether the law needs to be reformed to give it a clearer structure.[518] There are a number of options that have been mooted including the following:

1. In the government paper, *Supporting Families*, some overarching criteria were proposed as giving the courts clearer guidance:

   > First, to promote the welfare of any child of the family under the age of eighteen, by meeting housing needs of any children and the primary carer, and of the secondary carer; both to facilitate contact and to recognise the continuing importance of the secondary carer's role. Second, the court would take into account the existence and content of any written agreement about financial arrangements ... third, ... the court would then divide any surplus so as to achieve a fair result, recognising that fairness will generally require the value of the assets to be divided equally between the spouses. Fourth, the court would try to terminate financial relationships between the parties at the earliest date practicable.[519]

2. *Pre-marriage contracts*. Mr Hoon, a Home Office minister, has argued in favour of prenuptial contracts:

   > anything that can be done to increase the certainty of the process, and hopefully, therefore, to reduce the conflict involved, must, in my view, be worth pursuing. Clearly, however, if we were to go down this route, much work would need to be done to ensure such agreements were workable – we would need to consider mechanisms for registration, and for ensuring that such agreements were fair and workable – not just for each spouse, but also for any third party, such as a pension provider.[520]

   The evidence from the United States is that pre-marriage contracts can give rise to just as much litigation as the present law. This results from spouses claiming that pre-marriage contracts should be set aside on the basis of misrepresentations, non-disclosure, or undue influence. So it is unlikely that pre-marriage contracts could, on their own, provide solutions to all difficulties. There are also concerns that enforcement of pre-marriage contracts would lead to results that work against the interests of women who on average have less bargaining power than a man might have.[521] It is unlikely that many couples in preparing for marriage will want to discuss what should happen when they divorce.[522] Studies of the attitudes of the general public to pre-marriage contracts suggests that they are regarded as unromantic and pessimistic.[523]

---

[518] Thorpe LJ (1998a); Bird (2002).
[519] Home Office (1998: para 4.49).
[520] Thorpe LJ (1998b).
[521] Slaughter (2002).
[522] Lewis (2001a).
[523] Hibbs, Barton and Beswick (2001); Lewis (2001a).

Eekelaar predicts that the basis of the law in the future will take into account the agreements of the parties. He suggests that the law is moving towards the following position:

> the law should first look to securing the circumstances of children when any relationship breaks down, then to making sure (if possible) that the role of the children's carer is properly recognized, and that includes characterizing that role as one which generates entitlements to capital or, in some cases, to ongoing support. Beyond that, parties will be given wide freedom to determine their own interests.[524]

3. *Equal distribution.* Some have proposed that there should be a presumption of equality in distribution of assets.[525] A modified version of this approach appears in *Supporting Families*,[526] where it was suggested that the court should 'exercise its powers so as to endeavour to do that which is fair and reasonable between the parties and any child of the family'. It was suggested that the court first ensure that the housing needs of the child and any primary carer be met; then that the non-residential parent be given a sufficient award to enable him or her to continue in a parenting role. The court would also take into account any written agreement the parties had reached. The government suggested that, so far as could be achieved consistently with these aims, the law should seek to ensure the parties would be treated fairly, which would normally involve dividing the assets equally. This proposal has been rejected by a report of the 17 judges of the Family Division:[527]

> Our view is that the principle of primacy for the children [in s 25(1)] is valuable and we question how any principle of equal asset division can be reconciled with [the principle of equal division]. Either the principle of equal division would be subordinate, in which case its effect would be severely emasculated; or the two principles would stand together, in which case their frequent clashes might not easily be resolved; or the children principle would become subordinate which, we sense, would be as unacceptable to the public as ourselves.[528]

The opposition is partly due to a desire to keep the discretion of the judiciary to tailor the solution to the particular case. In particular, as mentioned above, a straightforward division of the assets will work against the interests of the spouse who will be caring for the children.

4. In *Wachtel v Wachtel*[529] Denning LJ suggested that the wife should be entitled to one-third of the family's assets. He explained that the husband would have to find 'some woman to look after his house', while it would be unlikely a woman would need to. This view has few supporters nowadays. It is clearly based on traditional gender roles and, even from its own sexist perspectives, overlooks the need of the wife to employ a handyman to help with house repairs!

---

[524] Eekelaar (2000b: 421).
[525] Thorpe LJ (1998c).
[526] Home Office (1998), discussed in Cretney (2000).
[527] Wilson J (1999).
[528] Wilson J (1999: 161).
[529] [1973] Fam 72 CA.

5. Eekelaar[530] has suggest oed an approach which attaches greater significance to the length of time the parties have lived together. He accepts that in a lengthy marriage equality is appropriate, but where one party brings to the marriage substantial assets the poorer party should be regarded as gradually earning an increasing share in the other's assets. He suggests 2.5 per cent per annum, leading to an equal share after 20 years. His argument is strongest when considering an extreme case: if, for example, a woman marries a multi-millionaire but the marriage lasts only a few weeks she should not be entitled to half the fortune. But if the marriage has lasted 30 years she has a strong claim for an equal share of the fortune. Against his argument is the view that it does not accord with how most couples understand their marriage and finances. The notion of the child-carer/homemaker day by day earning a little more in his or her spouse's assets is not one many couples would feel an affinity with. Bailey-Harris[531] also argues that it is discriminatory that domestic contributions earn equal value only over time, whereas financial ones do not. Eekelaar responds to this comment by suggesting that unlike financial contributions homemaking is linked to duration. His point is that one day's housework cannot be worth more or less than one day's housework; however, the money-earner's value depends on the amount brought home. So homemaking can be valued only by time, but money-earning need not be.[532] Housework may be of equal value to money-earning, but that does not mean it is of equal worth, he argues. Further he asserts that the *White* equality is best understood on the basis that over time the couple's interests merge. His argument, if accepted, does not necessarily mean that contributions must be rejected as a basis for redistributing property on divorce, but means that contributions cannot (in relation to shorter marriages) be used for doing so. Critics of Eekelaar's argument may suggest that the claim that money-earning contributions and financial contributions are equal is a social or political statement, rather than a point of logic or economics.

6. Others argue that if there is to be financial fairness between spouses on divorce, some fundamental change in society is required. Diduck and Orton look forward to a better future:

> Along with true equality in employment and pay and affordable good quality child care, an adequate valuation of domestic work would mean it would not be necessary that each partner play exactly the same role in wage earning ... Roles in marriage could be adopted based on the partners' actual interests and skills. Maintenance on divorce would still sometimes be necessary, then, but it would no longer overwhelmingly be women who require it and it would no longer result in economic disadvantage for the recipient. Maintenance would be seen as a right, expected and earned, rather than as a gift, act of benevolence or based on a notion of women's dependency on men.[533]

---

[530] Eekelaar (2001a; 2003c).
[531] Bailey-Harris (2003).
[532] The argument is less convincing if one includes as a contribution to the marriage not only money-earning, child-care and household tasks, but also emotional support, love etc.
[533] Diduck and Orton (1994: 686–7).

12. CONCLUSION

This chapter has focused on the financial position of partners on the breakdown of their relationship. For many couples it is the financial support for children which is the key issue, with limited resources available for spousal support. For both married and unmarried couples, child support is calculated by means of a rigid formula, set out in the Child Support Act 1991. This is by contrast with the wide discretion the courts have to determine spousal support under the Matrimonial Causes Act 1973. The two systems reveal the contrasting benefits and disadvantages of rule-based and discretion-based systems. The chapter also reveals the different bases upon which financial support obligations are based. In *White* v *White* the House of Lords has stressed the importance of fairness between spouses, which will often require an equal division of assets between a husband and wife. However, the issue is not one which just involves the interests of the couple themselves. The Child Support Act 1991, despite its focus on the parental obligation to support children, primarily seeks to reduce government expenditure on welfare payments. Running through this chapter is the requirement for the law to be realistic. Imposing obligation which cannot be enforced, or requiring people to support those to whom they feel no particular moral obligation, is unlikely to result in an effective law. That said, finding a law on financial support for family members which is regarded as fair, reflects the social obligations which people feel, and is practicably enforceable, might be an impossible task.

6

DOMESTIC VIOLENCE

1. INTRODUCTORY ISSUES

A. Terminology of topic and definitions

There is no agreement over the correct terminology to be used to describe violence that takes place between adults in a close relationship. At one time it was common to talk about domestic violence or 'battered wives', but now the violence between those in close emotional relationships is seen as a wider problem, being restricted not just to wives nor even to domestic situations. Despite its drawbacks, the term 'domestic violence' will be employed here because it has become so widely accepted.[1]

The definition of domestic violence used by the police for statistical purposes is 'any violence between current or former partners in an intimate relationship, wherever and whenever the violence occurs. The violence may include physical, sexual, emotional or financial abuse.'[2] The forms of abuse are distressingly varied.[3] The abuse is not limited to physical abuse, but includes emotional abuse and intimidation.[4] Of course, physical abuse can also in turn lead to depression and other mental disorders.[5]

The government's interdepartmental initiative, *Raising the Standards*, used the following explanation:

> Domestic Violence and Abuse is best described as the use of physical and/or emotional abuse or violence, including undermining of self-confidence, sexual violence or the threat of violence, by a person who is or has been in a close relationship. Domestic violence can go beyond physical violence. It can also involve emotional abuse, the destruction of a spouse's or partner's property, their isolation from friends, family or other potential sources of support, threats to others including children, control over access to money, personal items, food, transportation and the telephone, and stalking.[6]

To some extent the phrase 'domestic violence' is a 'culturally specific term'. What this means is that the understanding of domestic violence is determined by the norms of a particular culture. So, in some cultures, if a husband refused to permit his wife to leave the home unaccompanied, this would not be regarded as

---

[1] E.g. Home Office (2000d)
[2] Home Office (2000d: 1.10).
[3] Home Office (2000d: 1.15). The variety of forms of abuse is revealed in Jones, Lockton, Wood and Kashef (1995).
[4] A powerful and perceptive discussion can be found in Edwards (1996: ch. 5) and L. Smith (1989).
[5] Golding (1999).
[6] Quoted in Lord Chancellor's Department (2003b: 3).

abuse, whereas in other cultures it would. There are real difficulties here. Should the definition of abuse be determined by the victim or by society? Are there rights that should not be infringed even if it is acceptable to do so in a particular culture? This refers back to the discussion of cultural pluralism that was undertaken in Chapter 1. One difficulty is that victims do not necessarily regard themselves as victims of domestic violence.[7] A woman might think that she deserved to be hit, for example, or that pushing and punching is normal in intimate relationships. Smart and Neale have found that the versions of events given by men and women of an incident of domestic violence are often quite different.[8] This means that even if a woman believes an incident constitutes domestic violence, her partner may not see it in that way.

The vast majority of domestic violence takes place against women,[9] although many men are subject to violence from their partners.[10] It has been argued that most violence by women against men is quite different from violence by men against women because women's violence is often in self-defence rather than being an aspect of an ongoing oppressive relationship.[11] Also where men are the victims the injuries involved tend to be less serious.

Domestic violence can also include abuse against elderly people. This raises particular issues and will be considered separately in Chapter 12.

B. The incidence of domestic violence

The occurrence of domestic violence is often underestimated in the public consciousness. Giddens has written: 'The home is, in fact, the most dangerous place in modern society. In statistical terms, a person of any age or of either sex is far more likely to be subject to physical attack in the home than on the street at night.'[12] It is not easy to gather comprehensive statistical information on domestic violence, given that so little of it is reported. However, the following shocking array of statistics demonstrates the prevalence of domestic violence:

- The British Crime Survey found that one in four women and one in six men had been physically assaulted by a current or former partner at some point in their lives.[13]
- An incident of killing, stabbing or beating takes place on average every six minutes in a home in Britain.[14]
- An incident of domestic violence is reported to the police every minute on average.[15]

---

[7] Mahoney (1991); Smart and Neale (1999).
[8] Smart and Neale (1999); Mahoney (1991).
[9] For a discussion of the ethnic issues in domestic violence see Mama (2000). For a discussion of violence in lesbian relations see Eaton (1994).
[10] Mirless-Black (1999). Where men are abused the degree of violence tends to be less: Buzawa and Buzawa (2003: 13). See Families Need Fathers (2003) for an argument that it is too often assumed that domestic violence is only perpetrated by men against women.
[11] Day Sclater (2000: 105–6).
[12] Giddens (1989).
[13] Mirless-Black and Bayron (2000).
[14] Stanko (2000).
[15] Home Office (2003b: 3).

- On average 46 per cent of assault cases referred to the Crown Prosecution Service were of domestic violence.[16]
- 150 people per year are killed by a current or former partner.[17]
- Domestic violence is the single largest category of violent crime, representing 25 per cent of all assaults.[18]
- Mooney found that 61 per cent of women questioned said that they could imagine their male partners using violence against them in a hypothetical scenario.[19]
- It has been estimated that there were 6.6 million incidents of domestic violence in 1995.[20]
- The Law Commission Report in 1992 estimated that 22 per cent of divorce petitions refer to domestic violence.[21]
- Eekelaar and Maclean found that 22 per cent of their sample of married mothers discussed personal protection with lawyers.[22]

This litany of statistics clearly demonstrates that the problem of domestic violence is widespread.

Domestic violence is far more likely to occur at the end of a relationship. Only 2 per cent of married women reported being assaulted in the previous year in the British Crime Survey; while the figure was 22 per cent for those who had separated from a cohabiting partner that year.[23] It also appears that those under 25 are most at risk of being assaulted, as are those who are in low-income households.[24] There is also disturbingly a link between pregnancy and domestic violence with 30 per cent of cases of domestic violence starting during the victim's pregnancy.[25]

It should not be thought that domestic violence only impacts adults. According to Women's Aid of 54,000 people who sought refuge in a shelter in 1997 32,017 were children and 22,492 were women.[26] There is widespread acceptance that children raised in a household where there is domestic violence suffer in many ways, as compared to households where there is not.[27] Indeed one study of children who had suffered abuse showed that 39 per cent of them had come from families in which there was domestic violence.[28]

In the light of these statistics the government has produced an important consultation paper, *Protection and Justice*,[29] which outlines the government's commitment

---

[16] Cretney and Davis (1996).
[17] Home Office (2003a: 8).
[18] Mirless-Black (1999).
[19] Mooney (2000).
[20] Home Office (2000b: 3.7).
[21] Law Commission Report 207 (1992: Appendix C).
[22] Eekelaar and Maclean (1997).
[23] Mirless-Black and Bayron (2000).
[24] Mirless Black and Bayron (2000).
[25] Home Office (2003a: 20).
[26] Women's Aid (1998).
[27] Humphreys (2001). Children are aware of the domestic violence in half of all reported cases (Home Office (2003a).
[28] Farmer and Pollock (1998).
[29] Home Office (2003a; 2003b).

to tackle domestic violence by a variety of means and seeks consultation on changes to the law.

C. Causes of domestic violence

The explanations of the causes of domestic violence fall into three categories:[30]

1. *Psychopathological explanations.* These tend to see the problem of domestic violence as flowing from the psychological make-up of the abuser. It is said that domestic violence is caused by the abuser having an underdeveloped personality, including an inability to control his anger or deal with conflict. There is also a strong link between alcohol and abuse, although the alcohol may just exacerbate other factors.[31] Some even argue that male violence is natural, pointing to the fact that male animals are more violent than female animals. The psychopathological approach is criticised by others on the ground that pathology cannot be the only explanation for domestic violence, as abusers are able to control their tempers outside the home, when dealing with people at work, for example. The government has sought opinions on whether there should be a register of domestic violence abusers.[32]

2. *Theories about the position of women in society.* These theories focus on patriarchy and the domination of women by men, throughout society.[33] One argument is that the attitude of the law and state authorities perpetuates abuse. Society, through the multifarious ways that men are permitted to exercise power over women, makes domestic abuse appear acceptable to the abuser. This can be supported by evidence which shows that violence often occurs when women do not fulfil their traditional roles and men use violent means to reassert their authority.[34] Further, the lack of an effective response by the law means that women are unable to find suitable ways to escape from abuse. Although this is a convincing explanation of domestic violence, there is a danger that it can lessen the responsibility of the individual abuser for his actions. One disturbing recent survey found that one in five young men and one in ten young women think that violence against a partner is acceptable in some situations such as where it is found that a partner has been unfaithful.[35]

3. *The family relationship.* Some argue that the failure of family relationships leads to domestic violence. Poor communication skills or volatile partnerships are to blame as the causes of violence.[36] This is a controversial approach, because it suggests that it is the fault of both the abuser and the victim that the violence

---

[30] A useful discussion on the causes of domestic violence is found in Miles (2001: 80–7).

[31] Home Office (2003a: 18) reports that 32 per cent of victims of domestic violence reported that their abusers were drunk at the time.

[32] Home Office (2003a: 36).

[33] See, for example, Freeman (1984); Hanmer (2000).

[34] Yllo and Bograd (1988).

[35] Home Office (2003a: 17). Home Office (2003a: Part II) describes how the government will attempt to challenge public attitudes towards domestic violence. See also Home Office (2003b)

[36] Borkowski, Murch and Walker (1983).

has occurred. Dobash and Dobash point out that this fails to explain why it is the man rather than the woman who is usually violent.[37]

The truth, no doubt, is that domestic violence occurs as a result of the complex interaction between these and many other factors.

D. The development of the law on domestic violence

A famous statement of the lawyer Hale describes the attitude of the law to domestic violence in the past: he suggested that a husband could beat his wife with a stick no wider than his finger.[38] This was seen as an aspect of the husband's right to control his household. The law did not really recognise domestic violence until the feminist movement brought it to the attention of a male-dominated media and legislature in the 1970s. It was either regarded as so rare as not appropriate for legal intervention, or as simply part of the 'rough and tumble of marital life'. It was the refuge/shelter movement and the growth of feminist writings, in particular *Scream Quietly or the Neighbours will Hear* by Pizzey, which made domestic violence a public issue.[39] There was subsequently a report of a Select Committee of the House of Commons which found there was a strong case for improving the assistance available to women who were the victims of domestic violence.[40] At that time legal remedies were limited to the general criminal law and tort law. The increased interest in protecting human rights led to arguments that safeguarding victims of domestic violence was an aspect of protecting their human rights. Indeed, domestic violence was the subject of an optional protocol attached to the United Nations Convention on the Elimination of All Forms of Discrimination against Women.

In the UK a series of statutes was passed by Parliament, presenting a rather haphazard scheme of protection: Matrimonial Homes Act 1967; Domestic Violence and Matrimonial Proceedings Act 1976; and Domestic Proceedings and Magistrates' Courts Act 1978. We will not go into the details of these pieces of legislation, but they displayed a confusing array of law. The three Acts used different criteria; were available to different kinds of relationships; used different courts; and provided different kinds of remedies. In addition to the statutes, the courts sometimes relied upon their power to make orders under tort and the courts' inherent jurisdiction.[41] When the Law Commission came to consider domestic violence[42] it felt that there was a strong case for changing the law. There were three particular concerns. First, orders were too difficult to obtain. The House of Lords in *Richards* described an order removing someone from their home as a 'draconian order'. It was therefore necessary to show serious misconduct before such an order could be justified. The Law Commission recommended that the focus of the court should shift away from considering the conduct of the parties and more towards their needs and resources. Secondly, there was no protection to former cohabitants

---

[37] Dobash and Dobash (1992).
[38] Doggett (1992).
[39] Pizzey (1978).
[40] Select Committee (1975; 1977).
[41] Reserved by s 37 of the Supreme Court Act 1981 and s 38 of the County Courts Act 1984.
[42] Law Commission Report 207 (1992).

at all (apart from tortious remedies) and this was seen as unjustifiable. Thirdly, as Lord Scarman pointed out when discussing the law at the time:

> The statutory provision is a hotchpotch of enactments of limited scope passed into law to meet specific situations or to strengthen the powers of specified courts. The sooner the range, scope and effect of these powers are rationalised into a coherent and comprehensive body of statute law, the better.[43]

The Law Commission believed that the law should be reformed to remove the anomalies and gaps that existed in the present law; to provide at least as much protection as presently afforded; and to enable the law to minimise hostilities.[44] The Law Commission Report was implemented by the government and the Family Homes and Domestic Violence Bill was presented to Parliament. It was widely thought that the rationalisation of the laws would be seen as uncontroversial. However, late in the legislative process there was a campaign against the Bill by part of the tabloid press, most notably the *Daily Mail*. The campaign was particularly concerned that by providing unmarried couples with similar remedies to domestic violence as married couples, marriage would be undermined. How it was thought that denying protection to unmarried victims of domestic violence would bolster marriage is a mystery. The proposed changes were more by way of clarification and reorganisation than effecting a substantial change in the protection of the law. A number of MPs were persuaded by this campaign and the Bill was withdrawn in its second reading. The Bill was reintroduced as Part IV of the Family Law Act 1996. However, a number of changes were made and these were reflected in the eventual form of the Act.

To understand the law on domestic violence fully it is necessary to appreciate aspects of criminal law, tort law and housing law, as well as legislation specifically designed to deal with domestic violence.[45] Traditionally, a distinction has been drawn between civil proceedings and criminal proceedings. In civil proceedings it is the victim herself who is bringing the proceedings to pursue applications against the abuser, as compared with the criminal law, where the proceedings are brought on behalf of the state. The rest of the chapter will proceed as follows. First, it will consider the injunctions and orders that can be obtained to protect a victim of domestic violence from abuse under the Family Law Act 1996. Secondly, the remedies available under the Protection from Harassment Act 1997 will be examined. Thirdly, the chapter will outline the provision of alternative accommodation by local authorities to victims of domestic violence. Fourthly, it will consider the criminal law's response to this problem. The chapter will end with a consideration of why the law finds domestic violence such an intractable problem.

---

[43] *Richards v Richards* [1984] AC 174 at pp. 206–7.
[44] Law Commission Report 207 (1992: 1.2).
[45] Humphreys, Hester, Hague et al. (2002) discuss the importance of a multifaceted response to domestic violence.

2. INJUNCTIONS AND ORDERS UNDER THE FAMILY LAW ACT 1996

This section will discuss orders available under the Family Law Act 1996. There are essentially two kinds of order available. First, the victim of domestic violence (the applicant) can seek a court order that the abuser (the respondent) does not molest her and, secondly, that he leave and stay away from the family home. These are known as non-molestation orders and occupation orders respectively. Both are primarily designed to deter the respondent from abusing the applicant in the future. If he does so in breach of a non-molestation or occupation order, he could face imprisonment.

A. The non-molestation order

The non-molestation order is an order that one party does not molest the other.[46] Molestation here is not defined in the Act but includes conduct that harasses or threatens the applicant. Such an order is less intrusive than an order forcing someone to leave his or her home and so is more readily and widely available. Indeed, many acts that would constitute molestation are crimes (especially after the Protection from Harassment Act 1997). So viewed, the non-molestation order can be regarded as odd – an order that someone not commit a crime against another. Cynics argue that the use of molestation orders is merely a means of delaying treating an act as a crime. It is common for police to suggest that a victim seek non-molestation injunctions, rather than themselves having to institute criminal proceedings.

(i) Who can apply for a non-molestation order?

There was much debate over who should be able to apply for non-molestation injunctions under the Act. On the one hand, there was a desire that people who needed protection receive it; on the other hand, if too many people could seek non-molestation injunctions this could lead to excessive litigation. For example, it was thought inappropriate that disputes between neighbours and employees should be resolved by using non-molestation injunctions. Hence the Law Commission Report preceding the Family Law Act 1996 suggested that remedies should be limited to those who have an especial emotional tie.[47] The Law Commission had suggested that people who had had a 'sexual relationship with each other (whether or not including sexual intercourse)' should be included in the definition of those who could apply for an injunction. However, practical problems of proof and difficulties in defining a 'sexual relationship'[48] led to that category being abandoned. So it was decided that only those who were 'associated persons' could apply for a non-molestation order. 'Associated persons' are defined in s 62(3). Before listing those who come under this heading, it is important to note that Wall J in *G v F (Non-*

---

[46] Family Law Act 1996 (hereafter FLA 1996), s 42.
[47] Law Commission Report 207 (1992), paras 3.17 and 3.19.
[48] No one thought to consult President Clinton on this issue.

244

Molestation Order: Jurisdiction)[49] suggested that if it is unclear whether the relation-ship between two people falls within one of these definitions, it should be treated as if it does. Indeed, he thought that unless it was clear that the couple were not associated, it should be presumed that they were. A person is associated with another person if:

1. *They are or have been married to each other.*
2. *They are cohabitants or former cohabitants.* Under s 62(1)(a) 'cohabitants' are defined as 'a man and a woman who, although not married to each other, are living together as husband and wife'. A gay couple, then, would not fall within the definition of cohabitants, although they will fall into the next category (3).[50] In *G v F (Non-Molestation Order: Jurisdiction)*[51] the respondent stayed with the applicant a few nights a week in her home and she visited him for two nights a week at his home. Wall J held that this should be regarded as cohabitation. Particular weight was placed on the fact that they had had a sexual relationship, had lived in the same household, and had had a joint account.[52]
3. *They live or have lived in the same household, otherwise than merely by reason of one of them being the other's employee, tenant, lodger or boarder.* This category includes many people living together and would cover, for example: a gay couple; stu-dents living together in a student house; or two elderly people sharing accom-modation companionably. A sexual relationship is not required. It should be noted that just because a couple are each other's employee, tenant, lodger or boarder does not mean the couple are necessarily excluded: the question is whether they live together *merely* because of that relationship. So if a landlord and tenant are lovers they may be associated.
4. *They are relatives.* This is given a very wide definition in s 63(1):

   (a) the father, mother, stepfather, stepmother, son, daughter, stepson, stepdaughter, grandmother, grandfather, grandson, or granddaughter of that person or of that person's spouse or former spouse, or
   (b) the brother, sister, uncle, aunt, niece or nephew (whether of the full blood or of the half blood or by affinity) of that person or of that person's spouse or former spouse; and includes, in relation to a person who is living or has lived with another person as husband and wife, any person who would fall within paragraph (a) or (b) if the parties were married to each other.

   This is a wide definition and is rather arbitrary. It includes, for example, a former cohabitant's half-niece, although it does not include cousins.
5. *They have agreed to marry one another (whether or not that agreement has been termi-nated).* It should be stressed that this is not as broad a category as it may at first appear. This is because there are only three ways one can prove that there is an agreement to marry.[53] First, that there is evidence in writing of the agreement to

---

[49] [2000] 2 FCR 638.
[50] Home Office (2003a: 33) states the government's intention to amend the definition of 'cohabitants' to include a same-sex relationship.
[51] [2000] 2 FCR 638.
[52] See *Clibbery v Allan* [2002] 1 FLR 565 CA where the couple were not found to be cohabiting.
[53] FLA 1996, s 44.

marry. Secondly, that there was the gift of an engagement ring by one party to the agreement to the other in contemplation of the marriage. Thirdly, that there was a 'ceremony entered into by the parties in the presence of one or more other persons assembled for the purpose of witnessing the ceremony'.[54] There has been some debate over whether an engagement party would be sufficient for the third method of proof. It seems unlikely that a court would accept a party as 'a ceremony', although a religious service on engagement would certainly be sufficient. It is rather odd that if a couple can prove that they are engaged, but not in one of the ways above, they would not necessarily be associated. It should be noted that a formerly engaged couple can only apply for a non-molestation order if the agreement to marry was terminated less than three years previously.[55] There are no restrictions in the statute on the means of proving the termination of the agreement.

6. *In relation to any child (a parent of a child or someone who has parental responsibility for the child).*

7. *They are parties to the same family proceedings (other than proceedings under Part IV of the 1996 Act).* Family proceedings are defined in s 63. The list includes, for example, parties to a contact application. The list also includes the Adoption Act 1976 and so if there was tension between the potential adopters and the genetic parents an application for a non-molestation injunction can be made.

The most notable omission from this list of associated persons are those couples who have 'dated' each other, but have not actually cohabited.[56] This is controversial. Lowe and Douglas ask 'why it is felt appropriate to permit an applicant to obtain an order against a former cohabitant's stepmother . . . but not against the "boyfriend" from whom they have split up after a lengthy period of non-cohabitational courtship'.[57] After the Family Law Act 1996 was passed there was increasing concern in the media about stalking and this led to the passing of the Protection from Harassment Act 1997, under which injunctions are available, even if there is no kind of relationship between the victim and the harasser. The fact that anyone can use the 1997 Act means that the argument that access to the 1996 Act should be limited for fear of creating a flood of litigation has been greatly weakened.

If the applicant is associated with the respondent she can apply for a non-molestation injunction against him, even if the dispute between them is not a family dispute. In *Chechi* v *Bashier*[58] the Court of Appeal rejected the argument that the Family Law Act 1996 could not apply to two brothers who had a business dispute. Although their dispute was not a family one, they were associated by virtue of being brothers and so the court had jurisdiction to make a non-molestation order.[59]

---

[54] FLA 1996, s 44.
[55] FLA 1996, s 44(4).
[56] The government are considering whether or not to reform the law to include such couples: Home Office (2003a: 33).
[57] Lowe and Douglas (1998: 198).
[58] [1999] 2 FLR 489.
[59] But declined to do so.

The court can make a non-molestation order on its own motion.[60] This might be appropriate where the court decides that a party or a child needs the protection of the order but is for some reason (maybe fear) unwilling to apply for the order.[61] Similar concerns have led to s 60 being inserted into the 1996 Act, which permits approved third parties to bring proceedings on behalf of victims of domestic violence. Nobody has yet been approved, although it is suspected that in due course the police and perhaps organisations working on behalf of victims of domestic violence will be named.

A child can apply for an order with the leave of the court if he or she is under 16 but the 'court may grant leave for the purposes of subsection (1) only if it is satisfied that the child has sufficient understanding to make the proposed application for the occupation order or non-molestation order'.[62] In making its decision the court is likely to consider the kinds of factors that are relevant when a child applies for an order under the Children Act 1989.[63]

(ii) On what grounds can the order be granted?

Under s 42(5) of the Family Law Act 1996:

> In deciding whether to exercise its powers under this section and, if so, in what manner, the court shall have regard to all the circumstances including the need to secure the health, safety and well-being—
> (a) of the applicant or, in a case falling within subsection (2)(b), the person for whose benefit the order would be made; and
> (b) of any relevant child.

This is clearly a very widely drawn test, permitting the court to take into account any circumstances it believes relevant. The aim of the test is to focus on the need for protection in the future rather than requiring proof of the fact or threat of violence in the past.[64] 'Health' is defined to include 'physical or mental health' and so it is not necessary to show that there is even a threat of physical violence. One factor the court will consider is whether the order may be misused. If the court fears that the order will simply be used as a weapon in the party's disagreements, rather than to provide protection, the court may decline to make the order.[65]

The court should not be unduly reluctant to make a non-molestation injunction, as the making of a non-molestation injunction is hardly a serious infringement of the liberty of the respondent (the person against whom the order is made). By contrast, an occupation order removing someone from his or her home is a grave infringement of his or her rights and so is much harder to obtain than a non-molestation injunction.

---

[60] But only to protect parties to the proceedings before it.
[61] FLA 1996, s 42(2).
[62] FLA 1996, s 43.
[63] See Chapter 8.
[64] Law Commission Report 192 (1990: 3.6).
[65] *Chechi v Bashier* [1999] 2 FLR 489.

(iii) What can the order contain?

A non-molestation order will prohibit one person from molesting another. Molestation is not defined in the statute. That is a deliberate omission and was recommended by the Law Commission, which argued that there should not be a definition for fear that it might provide loopholes that a respondent could exploit.[66] It was noted that the lack of a definition had not led to grave difficulties with the law to date. The Law Commission stated that molestation could encompass 'any form of serious pestering or harassment and applies to any conduct which could properly be regarded as such a degree of harassment as to call for the intervention of the court'.[67] It could range from rifling through a handbag[68] to shouting obscenities.[69] In *C* v *C (Non-Molestation Order: Jurisdiction)*[70] the Court of Appeal stated that a husband could not obtain a non-molestation order to prevent his former wife making revelations in newspapers about their relationship. It was explained that molestation does not involve simply a breach of privacy but 'some quite deliberate conduct which is aimed at a high degree of harassment of the other party'. Here it was felt that the husband was seeking protection of his reputation rather than protection from molestation. This case might be contrasted with *Johnson* v *Walton*,[71] where a man sent semi-naked photographs of his former girlfriend to the press. It was held that this could constitute molestation. A distinction between these cases may be made on the basis that the press involvement was directly aimed at humiliating the woman in *Johnson* v *Walton*, whereas in *C* v *C (Non-Molestation Order: Jurisdiction)*[72] the wife's conduct was intended to explain her version of events rather than disgracing her husband.[73]

Under s 42(6) the order can refer to specific acts of molestation. This might be appropriate where the applicant wishes to prevent a particular kind of conduct which the respondent (or the police) might not appreciate would constitute molestation. Persistent telephone calls might be an example. There are some lower court unreported decisions which indicate that s 42(6) can include prohibiting a person from entering a specified area around a person's house.[74] This may well be open to challenge before the Court of Appeal, as it could be seen as obtaining an occupation order through the back door.[75] It seems certain that a non-molestation order could not be used to remove someone from a house.

There is no limit to the duration of a non-molestation order. It can be stated to last until a further order is made.[76]

---

[66] Law Commission Report 207 (1992: 3.1).
[67] Law Commission Report 207 (1992: 3.1).
[68] *Spencer* v *Camacho* [1984] 4 FLR 662.
[69] *George* v *George* [1986] 2 FLR 347.
[70] [1998] 1 FLR 554, [1998] 1 FCR 11.
[71] [1990] 1 FLR 350, [1990] FCR 568 CA.
[72] [1998] 1 FLR 554, [1998] 1 FCR 11.
[73] The court in *C* v *C (Non-Molestation Order: Jurisdiction)* [1998] 1 FLR 554, [1998] 1 FCR 11 also took into account the importance of freedom of the press.
[74] These unreported decisions are discussed in Da Costa (1998).
[75] See FLA 1996, s 33(3)(g).
[76] *Re B-J (A Child) (Non-Molestation Order: Power of Arrest)* [2000] 2 FCR 599 CA.

(iv) Can the order be made against someone who is unable to control his or her actions?

Prior to the Family Law Act 1996, case law suggested that only deliberate acts could constitute molestation.[77] This is probably no longer correct. In *Banks v Banks*[78] it was seen as inappropriate to make a non-molestation injunction against a woman who was suffering from a manic depressive disorder and therefore unable to control her behaviour. The reasoning was that it would be wrong if she were to be guilty of contempt of court through conduct that was beyond her control.[79] This was only a decision of a county court and so is not a strong precedent. The concern is that a similar argument could be used to prevent an injunction being made against an alcoholic abuser. It is arguable that in this area the law should focus on protection of the victim rather than fairness to the perpetrator of the violence. In the light of these arguments and the decision of the Court of Appeal in *G v G (Occupation Order: Conduct)*[80] that an occupation order could be made after unintentional conduct,[81] it is submitted that a non-molestation injunction should be able to be made even following unintentional conduct. However, it should be borne in mind that a person can only be guilty of contempt if he or she has sufficient mental capacity to understand that a court order has been made forbidding certain conduct, under threat of punishment.[82]

(v) Enforcement of the orders

If the order is breached by acts of violence then the respondent is likely to be brought before the court and imprisoned for contempt of court.[83] In deciding what sentence is appropriate, the court should focus on the act that constitutes the breach, rather than the facts that led to the making of the injunction in the first place. In *Cambridgeshire CC v D*[84] a non-molestation injunction was obtained after serious violence. In breach of the injunction D wrote love letters. The Court of Appeal overturned a sentence of 12 months for contempt, saying that that was an excessive punishment for writing love letters, despite the serious violence in the past.[85]

---

[77] *Johnson* v *Walton* [1990] 1 FLR 350, [1990] FCR 568 CA, but contrast *Wooton* v *Wooton* (1984) FLR 871 CA.
[78] [1999] 1 FLR 726.
[79] A useful discussion is found in Ashton DJ (2000).
[80] [2000] 2 FLR 36.
[81] *G v G (Occupation Order: Conduct)* [2000] 2 FLR 36.
[82] *P v P (Contempt of Court: Mental Capacity)* [1999] 2 FLR 897 CA.
[83] *G v C (Residence Order: Committal)* [1998] 1 FLR 43. It is perfectly proper to imprison a person for contempt who is also due to face criminal proceedings for the same incident (*DPP* v *Tweddell* [2002] 1 FCR 348).
[84] [1999] 2 FLR 42.
[85] For a general discussion on sentencing in these cases, see *Hale* v *Tanner* [2000] 3 FCR 62.

B. Occupation orders

An occupation order can remove an abuser from the home and can give a right to the victim to enter or remain in the home. Although the occupation order is most commonly used in cases of domestic violence it can be applied for if there is no violence, but simply a dispute over who should occupy the property. Where the order is that someone be removed from their home, this is a severe infringement of the rights of the person who is removed from their home. However, the order may be the only way that it is possible to provide effective protection for the victim(s). In the very worst cases it might be crucial that the abuser does not know where the victim is, in which case alternative accommodation will be essential. Because of the greater infringement of the rights of the respondent, access to occupation orders is far more restricted than to molestation orders. There are five different sections, which apply to different groups of applicants, and each section has slightly different requirements, some being harder to satisfy than others.

It is only possible for an applicant to obtain an occupation order against a respondent to whom she is associated. If the applicant is married to the respondent or is entitled to occupy the property, she should use s 33.[86] However, if the applicant is not entitled to occupy the property, the key question is whether the applicant is the ex-spouse of the respondent or is the cohabitant or former cohabitant of the respondent. If she is the ex-spouse, s 35 is appropriate; if she is the cohabitant or ex-cohabitant then an application should be made under s 36. In the very unlikely event that neither the applicant nor the respondent are entitled to occupy the dwelling-house then s 37 or s 38 should be used. This chapter will now consider these different sections in further detail.

(i) Section 33: married and entitled applicants

(a) Who can apply?
'Entitled' applicants can use s 33. An entitled person is a person who:

(i) is entitled to occupy a dwelling-house by virtue of a beneficial estate or interest or contract or by virtue of any enactment giving him the right to remain in occupation, or

(ii) has matrimonial home rights in relation to a dwelling-house.

Nearly all spouses are therefore 'entitled' because they will have matrimonial home rights.[87] Also, anyone who has a right to occupy a dwelling-house is entitled. This includes those who own the house (for example, those who are registered owners) and those who, although not registered owners, have a beneficial interest in the property by virtue of a resulting trust, a constructive trust, a proprietary estoppel or an interest under a trust for land.[88] The question of whether a person has a right to reside in the property under a proprietary estoppel or trust can be highly complex.

---

[86] Except in the very unusual situation where neither spouse is entitled to occupy their home (e.g. if they are squatters).

[87] The exception being where neither is entitled to occupy the house, in which case either s 37 or s 38 applies.

[88] But not a contractual licence: *Ashburn Anstalt* v *Arnold* [1989] Ch 1 CA.

Cases deciding such issues have been known to go on for weeks.[89] It might seem odd that an applicant seeking urgent protection from violence could need to introduce evidence of promises made often years earlier in order to determine which section of the Act should be used.[90]

(b) In respect of what property can the order be sought?
There are two requirements here. The first is that the property is a dwelling-house. So if a couple ran a business together it would not be possible to get an order in respect of the business premises. The second is that the home must be or was intended to be the home of the applicant and a person to whom she is associated. So if a flat was bought with the sole intention of it being the wife's pied-à-terre while she worked in London, an occupation order could not be obtained concerning the flat as it was never meant to be the home of the couple together. Similarly, if the applicant left the marital home and moved in with her mother she could not get an occupation order requiring the respondent to stay away from her mother's home.[91] Whether a holiday cottage would be defined as a home is open for debate.

(c) Against whom can the order be made?
The order can be sought by the applicant against any person with whom she is associated and with whom she shared or intended to share a home.

(d) What factors will the court take into account?

The 'significant harm test'
The starting point for the court's deliberations is the significant harm test set out in s 33(7):

> If it appears to the court that the applicant or any relevant child is likely to suffer significant harm attributable to conduct of the respondent if an order under this section containing one or more of the provisions mentioned in subsection (3) is not made, the court shall make the order unless it appears to it that—
> (a) the respondent or any relevant child is likely to suffer significant harm if the order is made; and
> (b) the harm likely to be suffered by the respondent or child in that event is as great as, or greater than, the harm attributable to conduct of the respondent which is likely to be suffered by the applicant or child if the order is not made.

The court must first ask itself what will happen if the court makes no order: is it likely that the applicant or relevant child will suffer significant harm attributable to the conduct of the respondent? If the answer is 'no' then the significant harm test is not satisfied. If the answer is 'yes' then the court must consider what will happen if the court does *not* make an order: will the respondent or any relevant child suffer significant harm? If the answer to that question is 'no' then the court *must* make an

---

[89] *Hammond* v *Mitchell* [1992] 1 FLR 229, [1991] FCR 938.
[90] In *S* v *F (Occupation Order)* [2000] 1 FLR 255 Judge Cryan found there was not enough time at the hearing to hear all the evidence necessary to decide whether the applicant had an interest and so treated the application as if made under s 35.
[91] Although a non-molestation order may offer some protection here.

occupation order. If the answer is 'yes', then the question is whose risk of harm is greater. If the harm the applicant or child will suffer is greater than that which the respondent will suffer then an order *must* be made. Otherwise the significant harm test is not satisfied.

B v *B*[92] shows how the subsection operates. The case concerned a married couple who had two children living with them: the husband's son from his previous relationship and a baby of their own. The husband was extremely violent and so the wife and baby moved out to temporary accommodation, leaving the husband and his son in the flat. The court considered the significant harm test. They were satisfied that if they made no order the mother and baby who were living in unsatisfactory temporary accommodation would continue to suffer significant harm and that this was attributable to the husband's violence. However, the court also accepted that if the husband and his son were ordered from the flat they would suffer significant harm too. In particular, the local authority would not be under any obligation to house them and so the son's education and general welfare would suffer.[93] The court decided that the harm, especially to the son, if the order was made would be greater than the harm that the mother and baby would suffer if the order was not made, and so the significant harm test was not satisfied.

A few points on the wording of the test will now be considered:

1. *Who is a 'relevant child'?* A relevant child here is broadly defined to include 'any child whose interests the court considers relevant'.[94] The child does not need to be the biological child of either the applicant or the respondent. In most cases the child will be living with the applicant and respondent, but conceivably the interests of a child not living with them will also be relevant, for example if the making or not making of an occupation order prevents the child having contact with the parties.

2. *What is harm?* Harm is defined as including 'ill-treatment and the impairment of health' (which includes emotional health).[95] For a child, harm also involves impairment of development. Ill-treatment 'includes forms of ill-treatment which are not physical and, in relation to a child, includes sexual abuse'.[96] It is rather surprising that the statute makes it clear that sexual abuse is harm to a child but does not state this in respect to an adult. There is probably no significance in this because sexual abuse of an adult would inevitably constitute ill-treatment or impairment of health. Also, although the definition of harm in the Children Act 1989[97] does not specifically apply to the Family Law Act 1996, presumably the court would willingly accept that a child who witnessed domestic violence was being harmed.

3. *What is significant harm?* There is no definition of significant harm in the Family Law Act 1996, although in a similar context Booth J suggested it was harm that was 'considerable, noteworthy or important'.[98] In *Chalmers* v *Johns*[99] the Court

---

[92] [1999] 1 FLR 715, [1999] 2 FCR 251 CA.
[93] A similar fear was expressed in *Re Y (Children) (Occupation Order)* [2000] 2 FCR 470.
[94] FLA 1996, s 62(2).
[95] FLA 1996, s 63(1).
[96] FLA 1996, s 63(1).
[97] Section 31.
[98] *Humberside CC* v *B* [1993] 1 FLR 257 at p. 263.
[99] [1999] 1 FLR 392.

of Appeal rejected an argument that a one-and-a-half mile walk to school for the mother and child was 'significant harm'. The court stressed that in order to be 'significant harm' some kind of exceptional harm needed to be shown.

4. *What does 'attributable' mean?* One point of particular importance on the wording of the test is that when considering whether the applicant or relevant child will suffer significant harm it must be shown that the significant harm will be attributable to the conduct of the respondent. In *B v B*, the facts of which are explained above, the mother was able to show that it was her husband's extreme violence which had forced her from the house and so the significant harm was attributable to her husband's conduct. If there had been no violence and she had moved out simply because she did not like her husband any more, she would have had grave difficulty in showing that the significant harm was attributable to the husband's conduct. However, notably, when considering the risk of significant harm to the respondent there is no need to show that it is attributable to the conduct of the applicant. So in *B v B* it was irrelevant that the significant harm that the son and husband would suffer if the order was made would not be due to the wife's conduct. *G v G (Occupation Order: Conduct)*[100] makes it clear that conduct is attributable to the respondent even if it is unintentional conduct: the court's focus is on the effect of the respondent's conduct, not his or her intention.

5. *What does 'likely' mean?* It is not clear what 'likely' means here. The word 'likely' in s 31 of the Children Act 1989 has been defined by the House of Lords to signify 'a real possibility'. It is suggested that a similar interpretation is given to the term here. It seems that the degree of likelihood of significant harm is not relevant in the significant harm test. In other words, if it is almost certain that the applicant will suffer significant harm, but there is a real possibility that the respondent will suffer a higher level of harm, the significant harm test will not be satisfied.

6. *What if the risks of significant harm are equal?* It should be noted that if the harm likely to be suffered by the applicant is equal to the harm that may be suffered by the respondent then an order does not have to be made.

The significant harm test sets out the circumstances in which the court *must* make an order. It is important to appreciate that simply because the significant harm test is not satisfied does not mean that an order cannot be made.[101]

General factors

If the significant harm test is satisfied then the court must make an order. If, however, it is not, the court must then consider the general factors. These are set out in s 33(6):

(a) the housing needs and housing resources of each of the parties and of any relevant child;

(b) the financial resources of each of the parties;

---

[100] [2000] 2 FLR 36.
[101] *Chalmers v Johns* [1999] 1 FLR 392 CA.

(c) the likely effect of any order, or of any decision by the court not to exercise its powers
     ..., on the health, safety or well-being of the parties and of any relevant child; and
(d) the conduct of the parties in relation to each other and otherwise.

The courts have in fact been reluctant to grant occupation orders.[102] Thorpe LJ in
Chalmers v Johns[103] held that when considering the general factors a judge should
bear in mind that an occupation order 'overrides proprietary rights and . . . is only
justified in exceptional circumstances'.[104] Occupation orders should be seen as
'draconian'.[105] In *G v G (Occupation Order: Conduct)* it was stressed that to succeed
an applicant must show that more tensions exist than normally surround a family
during a divorce.[106] In *Re Y (Children) (Occupation Order)*[107] Sedley LJ suggested
occupation orders should be seen 'as a last resort in an intolerable situation'.[108]
These decisions of the Court of Appeal emphasise that occupation orders should be
made only in exceptional cases. Critics would argue that these statements are
excessively restrictive. Had Parliament intended that occupation orders should only
be available in exceptional cases, it would have said so.

The Court of Appeal in *B v B*[109] considered the position had the father not had
the son with him. The court suggested that in that case, even if the significant harm
test might not have been satisfied,[110] the court would still be minded to make an
order, when looking at the general factors and in particular bearing in mind his violence towards the wife. This suggests that where the court is dealing with a violent
spouse the conduct factor ((d)) may become very important.

However, it would be wrong to state that an occupation order is only available
when there is serious violence. In *S v F (Occupation Order)*[111] the children were
residing with the mother, who had decided to leave London to live in the country.
One son wished to remain in London, especially because he was soon going to be
taking examinations at school. The court was willing to make an occupation order
granting the father the right to live in the matrimonial home in London so that he
could provide a house for his son for the completion of the schooling, while the
mother moved to the country.

---

[102] Although evidence looking at cases shortly after the Act was implemented suggests that more occupation orders are being granted than were under the previous legislation (Edwards (2000)).
[103] [1999] 1 FLR 392 CA.
[104] [1999] 1 FLR 392 at p. 397; see also *Re Y (Children) (Occupation Order)* [2000] 2 FCR 470 at
p. 477.
[105] See also *G v G (Occupation Order: Conduct)* [2000] 2 FLR 36.
[106] [2000] 2 FLR 36.
[107] [2000] 2 FCR 470.
[108] [2000] 2 FCR 470 at p. 480.
[109] [1999] 1 FLR 715, [1999] 2 FCR 251 CA.
[110] Because the husband being rendered homeless would be a greater harm than the mother and baby
living in poor accommodation.
[111] [2000] 1 FLR 255.

(e) What orders can be made?

These will be divided in three categories:

1. *Declaratory orders under s 33(4) and (5)*. These orders simply enable the court to declare that a party has a right to remain in the property. This may forestall any attempt by the respondent to bring court proceedings to evict the applicant.
2. *Orders under s 33(3)*:

   An order under this section may—
   (a) enforce the applicant's entitlement to remain in occupation as against the other person ('the respondent');
   (b) require the respondent to permit the applicant to enter and remain in the dwelling-house or part of the dwelling-house;
   (c) regulate the occupation of the dwelling-house by either or both parties;
   (d) if the respondent is entitled as mentioned in subsection (1)(a)(i), prohibit, suspend or restrict the exercise by him of his right to occupy the dwelling-house;
   (e) if the respondent has matrimonial home rights in relation to the dwelling-house and the applicant is the other spouse, restrict or terminate those rights;
   (f) require the respondent to leave the dwelling-house or part of the dwelling-house; or
   (g) exclude the respondent from a defined area in which the dwelling-house is included.

   These orders can be divided into three categories; first, there are those which enforce the applicant's existing rights ((a), (b)); secondly, orders used to regulate the rights of both parties ((c)); thirdly, those that prevent the respondent from enforcing his rights ((d), (e), (f), (g)). The strongest order that the court could make would require the respondent to leave the dwelling-house;[112] remove his rights to re-enter;[113] and exclude him from the area surrounding the house.[114] Subsection (c) gives the court great flexibility and permits the court to make all kinds of arrangements for the occupation of the home. It might decide that the applicant can live there during the weekdays and the respondent at the weekends, or that the respondent live on the top floor and the applicant on the ground floor.
3. *Section 40 orders*. There would be little point in removing the respondent from the house if the applicant was unable to pay for the rent for the house or meet the mortgage payments and so could be removed by the landlord or mortgagee. Therefore, under s 40 four kinds of supplemental orders can be made. First, either party can be ordered to pay the rent, mortgage payments, or general household expenses;[115] secondly, either party can be ordered to maintain or repair the house;[116] thirdly, the party who is to remain in the property can be required to make payments to the party who is to be removed (in effect this will be equivalent to a payment of rent);[117] and, fourthly, orders can be made to deal with disputes over use and care of furniture.[118] When considering an application

---

[112] FLA 1996, s 33(3)(f).
[113] FLA 1996, s 33(3)(d).
[114] FLA 1996, s 33(3)(g). There is some debate over what exactly an 'area' is in this context. Would it be possible to exclude someone from the village in which the home is situated?
[115] FLA 1996, s 40(1)(a)(ii).
[116] FLA 1996, s 40(1)(a)(i).
[117] FLA 1996, s 40(1)(b).
[118] FLA 1996, s 40(1)(c), (d), (e).

under s 40 the court should only consider the parties' financial needs, obligations and resources.[119] Unfortunately, because statute does not provide for any method of enforcing orders requiring payment under s 40, the Court of Appeal in *Nwogbe v Nwogbe*[120] has recommended that financial orders are not made under s 40 until Parliament has rectified this error.[121]

(f) Duration

An order under s 33 can be of fixed or unlimited length, until the court next hears the matter.[122] The length of the order does not seem to be limited by the extent of the property right or the duration of the marriage.

(ii) Section 35: one ex-spouse with no existing right to occupy

(a) Who can apply?

This section applies only to situations where the applicant has no right to occupy the property but the respondent (the applicant's ex-spouse) does. If the couple are still married or the applicant is entitled to occupy the property then s 33 should be used.

(b) In respect of what property?

An order under s 35 is only available in respect of a dwelling-house which was the actual or intended matrimonial home of the applicant and the respondent.

(c) What orders are available?

The list of orders is similar to those in s 33(3). However, there is an important difference in that if the court is going to make any order under s 35 then the applicant must be given the right to enter or remain in the property, and the respondent must be prohibited from evicting the applicant. These orders are known as the mandatory orders. The thinking behind these provisions is that it would be quite wrong to evict the respondent but not give the applicant the right to enter or remain in the property. Otherwise, it would be possible to end up with a situation where neither party would have the right to live in the property. In addition to the mandatory orders, the court can make a discretionary order. Those are any of the other orders available under s 33(3), for example an order excluding the respondent from a defined area around the dwelling-house.

(d) What factors are to be taken into account?

When considering a mandatory order the general factors as listed in s 33(6)[123] apply, although there are some extra factors which are to be taken into account for the ex-spouse, and these are (s 35(6)):

---

[119] FLA 1996, s 40(2).
[120] [2000] 2 FLR 744, [2000] 3 FCR 345.
[121] Parliament's response is still awaited.
[122] FLA 1996, s 33(10).
[123] See pages 253, 254.

   (e) the length of time that has elapsed since the parties ceased to live together;

   (f) the length of time that has elapsed since the marriage was dissolved or annulled; and

   (g) the existence of any pending proceedings between the parties—

       (i)   for an order under section 23A or 24 of the Matrimonial Causes Act 1973 (property adjustment orders in connection with divorce proceedings, etc.);

      (ii)   for an order under paragraph 1(2)(d) or (e) of Schedule 1 to the Children Act 1989 (orders for financial relief against parents); or

     (iii) relating to the legal or beneficial ownership of the dwelling-house.

These three factors are to turn the court's mind to the nature of the parties' marriage. The shorter the marriage and the longer the time since the divorce, the harder it will be for the applicant to succeed.

If the court decides to make a mandatory order the court should then consider making a discretionary order. When considering whether to make a discretionary order the court must first consider the significant harm test which operates in exactly the same way as described above in relation to s 33. If the test does not require the court to make an order, the court will then consider the general factors listed in ss 33(6) and 35(6)(e). This is rather odd because it means that a more wide-ranging investigation is made when the court considers making the discretionary order than when it makes a mandatory order, even though the mandatory orders involve a greater invasion of the respondent's property rights. The explanation may be that having found that the applicant deserves to have a right to occupy the property (in deciding whether to make a mandatory order) the case then involves two people who both should be entitled to occupy the dwelling-house and so the case is similar to a case involving an entitled applicant under s 33 and the criteria for further orders should then be the same.[124]

(e) Duration

The duration of an order under s 35 is more limited than a s 33 order. The order cannot exceed six months, although at the end of the six months the applicant can reapply for further extensions not exceeding six months each.[125]

(iii) Section 36: one cohabitant or former cohabitant with no existing right to occupy

(a) Who can apply?

This section applies to an applicant who is not entitled to occupy the property and who is the cohabitant[126] or former cohabitant of the respondent. Cohabitants are defined as 'a man and a woman who, although not married to each other, are living together as husband and wife'.[127]

---

[124] Although that would not explain why (e) is taken into account when considering the discretionary stage.

[125] FLA 1996, s 35(10).

[126] As defined in FLA 1996, s 62(3).

[127] FLA 1996, s 62(1)(a).

(b) In respect of what property?
The orders are available only in respect of a property that was or was intended to be the home of the applicant and the respondent.

(c) What orders can be made?
The orders available are exactly the same as under s 35.

(d) What factors are to be taken into account?
When considering whether to make a mandatory order the court must consider the general factors listed in s 33(6) and in addition the following extra criteria:

  (e) the nature of the parties' relationship;
  (f) the length of time during which they have lived together as husband and wife;
  (g) whether there are or have been any children who are children of both parties or for whom both parties have or have had parental responsibility;
  (h) the length of time that has elapsed since the parties ceased to live together; and
  (i) the existence of any pending proceedings between the parties
      (i) for an order under paragraph 1(2)(d) or (e) of Schedule 1 to the Children Act 1989 (orders for financial relief against parents); or
      (ii) relating to the legal or beneficial ownership of the dwelling-house.

Under s 41: 'When the court is required to consider the nature of the parties' relationship, it is to have regard to the fact that they have not given each other the commitment involved in marriage.' This was one of the provisions added to appease those who feared the Act was undermining marriage. Whether the provision will ever have an effect on the outcome of a case is doubtful.

When considering whether to make a discretionary order the court begins by asking the 'significant harm' questions. These are:

  (a) whether the applicant or any relevant child is likely to suffer significant harm attributable to conduct of the respondent if [a discretionary order is not made]; and
  (b) whether the harm likely to be suffered by the respondent or child if [the discretionary order is made] is as great as or greater than the harm attributable to conduct of the respondent which is likely to be suffered by the applicant or child if the provision is not included.

This is very similar to the significant harm test, but it does not compel the court to make an order if the applicant's significant harm is greater than the respondent's harm would be. The significant harm that the parties are at risk of suffering are simply factors to be considered, along with the general factors in s 33(6). Given the argument earlier that once a mandatory order is made an applicant should be viewed in the same light as an entitled applicant under s 33(6), it is hard to justify using the significant harm questions rather than the significant harm test.[128]

---

[128] The significant harm questions are one of the provisions inserted late in the legislative process to distinguish the treatment of married and unmarried couples.

(e) Duration

An order under s 36 cannot exceed six months in duration and can be extended on one occasion for a period of six months. This is similar to s 35, with the important limitation that under s 36 only one extension can be applied for, but there is no limit on the number of extensions under s 35.

(iv) Section 37: neither spouse nor former spouse entitled to occupy

(a) Who can apply?

This section applies to spouses or former spouses where neither spouse is entitled to occupy the property. It would, in fact, be very unusual for neither spouse to be entitled to occupy the matrimonial home. If the spouses were squatters then this may be so.[129] There will be very few applications under this section.

(b) In respect of what property?

The orders are available only in respect of a property that was or was intended to be the home of the applicant and the respondent.

(c) What can the order contain?

Under s 37(3):

> An order under this section may—
> (a) require the respondent to permit the applicant to enter and remain in the dwelling-house or part of the dwelling-house;
> (b) regulate the occupation of the dwelling-house by either or both of the spouses;
> (c) require the respondent to leave the dwelling-house or part of the dwelling-house; or
> (d) exclude the respondent from a defined area in which the dwelling-house is included.

These orders are much more limited than those under ss 33, 35 and 36 because neither party is entitled to occupy the home and so they have no rights that can be restricted or removed.

(d) What factors are to be taken into account?

Section 33(6) (the general factors) and (7) (the significant harm test) apply.

(e) Duration

An order under s 37 can be made for a period not exceeding six months, but may be extended on any number of occasions for a further period not exceeding a total of six months.

---

[129] Or if they were bare licensees (e.g. if a friend had invited the couple to stay).

(v) Section 38: neither cohabitant nor former cohabitant entitled to occupy

(a) Who may apply?
This section applies to a cohabitant or former cohabitant where neither the applicant nor the respondent are entitled to occupy the property. Again it will be very rare for applications to fall within this section.

(b) In respect of what property?
The orders are available only in respect of a property that was or was intended to be the home of the applicant and the respondent.

(c) What orders can be made?
The same orders that were listed as available under s 37(3) (quoted above) are available under s 38.

(d) What factors are to be taken into account?
Section 36(6) (the general factors) and (7) (the significant harm questions) apply.

(e) Duration
As under s 36, the order can be for a maximum of six months, and be extended on one occasion for a maximum period of six months.

(vi) Those who cannot apply for an occupation order

As should be clear from the above, a person who is not entitled to occupy the property and is not the spouse, former spouse, cohabitant or former cohabitant of the respondent cannot apply for an occupation order. In particular, gay partners, relatives and non-cohabiting engaged couples cannot apply for an occupation order in respect of a dwelling-house unless they are entitled to occupy it.[130] However, in *Mendoza v Ghaidan*[131] the phrase in Rent Act 1977 'living with the original tenant as his or her wife or husband' was interpreted to include a same-sex couple after the Human Rights Act 1998. It might be that a similar line of reasoning would be used to mean that a same-sex couple fell within the definition of a cohabiting couple for the purposes of the Family Law Act.

(vii) Some core issues in occupation orders

(a) Conduct
The original Law Commission proposals did not refer to the conduct of the parties.[132] Orders, it was suggested, should be granted solely by considering the parties'

---

[130] The government has confirmed its intention to amend the definition of 'cohabitant' to include a same-sex couple: Home Office (2003a: 33).
[131] [2002] 3 FCR 591.
[132] Nor in the significant harm test (s 33(7)) did the applicant's significant harm have to be attributable to the respondent's conduct.

needs, resources, and obligations – in effect a 'no fault' scheme to resolve disputes over the occupation of the home. It is understandable that Parliament was reluctant to follow these proposals. It would have meant that if there was a case where the violent party was less well off and not in a position to find alternative accommodation then the victim of domestic violence could be the one ordered out of the house for her own protection. This would be unacceptable to the majority of people. That said, the parts of the Family Law Act 1996 relating to domestic violence do not sit easily with the parts intended to deal with divorce, which stress the importance of 'no fault' divorce and discourage the parties from making allegations of misconduct against one another.

(b) Property interests

When considering occupation orders, property rights are of significant importance. Cohabitants and former spouses with property interests are treated differently from those without property interests. The importance of property interests is also revealed by the fact that cohabitants with property interests are treated in the same way as married couples with property interests. A critic would argue that considering the property interests of the parties is inappropriate when deciding how to protect an applicant from violence: are not people more important than property rights?[133] Can it be justifiable that if two victims of domestic violence in similar circumstances need the protection of an occupation order, one may be granted the order and one not because of their property entitlement under the rules of land law? Those who seek to justify the relevance of property interests do so on two bases. First, it has been argued that an order removing a party's property rights is a greater infringement of a party's rights than removing a party from a house in which they have no property interest, and therefore requires stronger justification. Secondly, it has been maintained that entitled and non-entitled applicants should be treated differently because they involve different kinds of issues. The Law Commission suggested that cases involving non-entitled applicants are 'essentially a short-term measure of protection intended to give them time to find alternative accommodation or, at most, to await the outcome of an application for a property law remedy'.[134] By contrast, cases of entitled applicants may involve imposing long-term solutions. These arguments, although powerful in theory, lose some of their force when it is recalled that the law on whether or not a person has an interest in property under a constructive trust or proprietary estoppel is so controversial and appears to draw arbitrary distinctions.[135] Another argument is that a property right carries with it obligations, including the obligation not to enable the property to be used for criminal purposes.[136] Could it be said that a person who commits violence in his or her home thereby forfeits his or her property right?

[133] Law Commission Report 207 (1992).
[134] Law Commission Report 207 (1992: para 4.7).
[135] See Chapter 4.
[136] *Tuck* v *Robson* [1970] 1 All ER 1171.

(c) Children's interests
It is notable that the interests of children are not paramount, as they are in other issues involving children. The Law Commission were concerned that placing children's interests paramount 'might lead to more specious applications by fathers for custody, and encourage more mothers to use "I've got the kids so kick him out" arguments'.[137] The concern is understandable, but a similar argument could be used in many circumstances where the welfare test applies. Although the child's welfare is not paramount under the Family Law Act 1996, the Act does have provisions which protect children.[138] There are three in particular:

1. Children can now under s 43 apply for an occupation or non-molestation order. If under 16, the child needs the leave of the court and can apply only if 'the child has sufficient understanding to make the proposed application'.[139] If a child has applied to the court for a non-molestation order, the court is likely to make one if possible.[140]
2. When considering the significant harm test it is important to note that if there is a relevant child who is likely to suffer significant harm attributable to the conduct of the respondent, the court must make an order unless greater or equal harm will be caused to the respondent if the order is made. However, it is notable that there is no attempt to attach greater importance to the harm suffered by the child than the harm suffered by the respondent or applicant.
3. The needs of the child are factors that should be taken into account when considering the general factors.

The failure to prioritise the needs of the child in the Family Law Act 1996, Part IV does not fit comfortably with the weight placed on children's interests under the Children Act 1989 and Adoption and Children Act 2002. Notably, children who are suffering significant harm can be removed from their parents and taken into care under s 31 of the Children Act 1989. However, the fact that the child is suffering significant harm does not necessarily require the making of an occupation order under the significant harm test, if it can be shown that the respondent will suffer a greater level of harm.[141] This may be a particular concern because there is increasing evidence that children who witness domestic violence suffer in a variety of ways.[142]

(d) The distinction between married and unmarried couples
The Family Law Act 1996 does distinguish between unmarried and married couples, but only where the applicant has no interest in the property. If the applicant does have an interest in the property there is no difference in the law that applies. Where the applicant does not have interest in the home the law draws three distinctions:

[137] Law Commission Report 207 (1992).
[138] For a discussion of the impact of domestic violence on children see McGee (2000).
[139] FLA 1996, s 43(1).
[140] Bainham (1998a: 428).
[141] Although the court may still make an occupation order when considering the general factors.
[142] Parkinson and Humphreys (1998).

1. The significant harm test is not used for non-entitled applicants, the significant harm questions are used and only once using the general factors it has been decided that a mandatory order must be made.[143]
2. There is a difference in the general factors that are taken into account. In particular, under s 41 the court is required to consider the fact that the parties have not given each other the commitment involved in marriage.
3. The maximum duration of orders for non-entitled cohabitants is shorter than for non-entitled spouses or ex-spouses.

As suggested earlier, it is hard to see how any of these differences could be thought to uphold marriage, and some commentators have suggested that in this context no distinction should be drawn between married and unmarried couples.

(e) Human Rights Act 1998
The Human Rights Act 1998 may be relevant to domestic violence in the following ways:

1. Article 3 requires the state to protect citizens from torture or inhuman or degrading treatment.[144] If the police or a court fails to take positive steps to provide an effective remedy for someone suffering torture or inhuman or degrading treatment, they will be in breach of article 3. The court must ensure, in considering an application for an occupation order, that an applicant who is suffering torture or inhuman or degrading treatment is provided protection.
2. An occupation order requiring someone to leave their home would appear clearly to breach the right under article 8 of the Convention to respect for private and family life. However, the making of orders could readily be justifiable under para 2 of article 8 on the grounds of public safety; prevention of disorder or crime; protection of health or morals; or protection of rights and freedoms of others. In particular, an occupation order could be justified in order to protect the rights of the applicant or the child. A more interesting question is whether the high hurdles placed in the way of obtaining occupation orders adequately protect the right to respect for the private and family life of the applicant and child.
3. Article 6 is relevant in requiring a public hearing. As will be discussed later, it is arguable that an *ex parte* occupation order infringes a party's rights under article 6. Of potentially more significance is a suggestion that an occupation order could be regarded as punishment following a criminal charge and so the requirements of article 6 must be complied with,[145] the argument being that being removed from one's home is equivalent to a criminal punishment.[146] In deciding whether a law involves punishment, the European Court of Human Rights has suggested that there are three factors to be taken into account: the legal classification of the provision; the nature of the offence; and the nature and

---

[143] FLA 1996, s 36.
[144] *A v UK (Human Rights: Punishment of Child)* [1998] 2 FCR 959, [1998] 3 FCR 597.
[145] See Swindells, Neaves, Kushner and Skilbeck (1999: ch. 13).
[146] *Öztürk v Germany* (1984) 6 EHRR 409.

degree of severity of the penalty.[147] If article 6 does apply, then all the paragraphs of article 6 apply:

    (a) a presumption of innocence;
    (b) a right to be informed of the accusation;
    (c) a right to have adequate time and facilities for the defence;
    (d) the right to defend oneself, to have representation and legal aid;
    (e) the right to call and cross-examine witnesses.

It is not clear that (a) would be protected in law on occupation orders. The other requirements may be infringed in relation to *ex parte* applications (which will be discussed later). However, there are good reasons for arguing that occupation orders do not constitute criminal proceedings and punishment. First, the application is not brought by the state but by an individual. Secondly, the purpose of the remedy is not to punish the respondent, but to protect the applicant.

4. Article 1 of the first Protocol of the European Convention states that: 'Every person shall be entitled to the peaceful enjoyment of his possessions. No one shall be deprived of his possessions except in the public interest and subject to the conditions provided for by the law and by the general principles of international law.' Although an occupation order might deprive a person of his or her right to enjoyment of his or her possession, in most cases where such an order will be made it could be justified as being in the public interest.[148]

5. It might also be argued that the law on occupation orders discriminates against unmarried and same-sex couples. If an applicant is able to show that because she was in a same-sex or unmarried relationship she was not able to get an order under the Family Law Act she could argue that this amounts to discrimination contrary to article 14.[149] The Home Office has announced that it intends to consider amending the Family Law Act so that same-sex couples without property interests will be able to apply for an occupation order.[150]

(f) Wider consequences of domestic violence orders

As well as resolving a dispute between two parties as to who can live in a property, the occupation order can in fact have far wider impact. For example, there can be consequences in relation to the children. If, say, the husband is removed from the house and the wife and children remain there, it may well be that the father will lose contact with the children. Certainly by the time the court comes to consider the residence of the children, the children will have settled with the mother and the 'status quo principle' (see Chapter 9) will mean that the father will be very unlikely to obtain a residence order. Further, in ancillary relief applications, if the husband has found alternative accommodation and the children and wife are living in the house, the court may well make an order transferring the house into the wife's name.[151]

---

[147] *Ravnsborg* v *Sweden* (1994) 18 EHRR 38.
[148] *Sporrong and Lönnroth* v *Sweden* (1986) 5 EHRR 35.
[149] Contrast *Lindsay* v *UK* (1986) 49 DR 181 and *Sahin* v *Germany* [2003] 2 FCR 619.
[150] Home Office (2003a).
[151] See Chapter 5.

Indeed studies have suggested that in a significant number of cases domestic violence is connected in complex ways with a whole range of family disputes.[152]

C. Ex parte non-molestation and occupation orders under the Family Law Act 1996

An *ex parte* application is an application made by one party without the other party being present or being given notice of the proceedings. Such an application will most often be used when there is a need for the immediate protection of the victim and any delay in serving papers on the respondent and giving him time to reply may endanger the applicant. In offering the applicant some immediate protection, the statute makes it clear that an *ex parte* hearing should be followed by an *inter partes* hearing, at which both parties will be able to put their arguments forward.[153] It should be stressed that the *ex parte* court order is only effective once it has been served on the respondent. So there is no danger that a respondent will breach an order of which he or she is unaware. There is a careful balancing exercise required here. On the one hand, there is the difficulty of ensuring that the evidence is sufficient to make an order, particularly an order removing someone from his or her home, when only one side of the case is heard. On the other hand, it is necessary to make available fast and effective remedies to those in dire need of them. Section 45 of the Family Law Act 1996 states that a court can make an *ex parte* occupation or non-molestation order 'in any case where it considers that it is just and convenient to do so'. In deciding whether this is so the court shall have regard to all the circumstances, including:

(a) any risk of significant harm to the applicant or a relevant child, attributable to conduct of the respondent, if the order is not made immediately;
(b) whether it is likely that the applicant will be deterred or prevented from pursuing the application if an order is not made immediately; and
(c) whether there is reason to believe that the respondent is aware of the proceedings but is deliberately evading service and that the applicant or a relevant child will be seriously prejudiced by the delay involved [in effecting service or substituted service].[154]

It is arguable that making an *ex parte* order could deny people the right to a fair and public hearing under article 6 of the European Convention of Human Rights. However, in a different context, the Court of Appeal in *Re J (Abduction: Wrongful Removal)*[155] rejected such an argument on the basis that the right to the full *inter partes* hearing and the right to apply to have an *ex parte* order set aside protects the right to a fair hearing.

---

[152] Pleasence, Balmer, Buck et al. (2003).
[153] FLA 1996, s 45(3).
[154] FLA 1996, s 45(2).
[155] [2000] 1 FLR 78.

D. Undertakings

An undertaking is a promise by the respondent in clear terms which is made formally in court. The court can accept an undertaking in any case where it has the power to make a non-molestation or occupation order. Where the court accepts the undertaking, an order is normally not made.[156] Section 46(4) states that an undertaking can be enforced as if it were an order of the court.[157] However, some have claimed that the police are far less willing to intervene if a victim claims that an undertaking has been breached than where she claims that a court order has been breached.[158]

The one restriction on the power of the court to accept an undertaking is s 46(3), which provides that 'the court shall not accept an undertaking . . . in any case where apart from this section a power of arrest would be attached to the order'.[159] The significance of this is that, under s 47(1), if the respondent has used or threatened violence against the applicant or a relevant child, a power of arrest *must* be attached to an occupation order or a non-molestation order unless the court is satisfied that the applicant or relevant child will be adequately protected without such a power of arrest.[160] It is therefore arguable that where the court is required to attach a power of arrest under s 47(1) it cannot accept an undertaking. However, it may be that the court will readily hold that if an undertaking is offered the applicant and child will be adequately protected without the power of arrest and so the undertaking can be accepted. Certainly research suggests that it has become the norm to accept undertakings in non-molestation cases when offered.[161]

E. Powers of arrest

Section 47(1) (referred to above) creates a strong presumption in favour of attaching a power of arrest in nearly all cases of non-molestation or occupation injunctions because it is rare for one of those injunctions to be applied for unless there is at least a threat of violence.[162] The significance of having a power of arrest attached to an order is that if a person breaches the order, the police automatically have the power to arrest him or her. If a power of arrest is not attached, then the victim will have to apply to the court for a warrant for arrest,[163] unless the actions constitute a criminal offence. The Law Commission regarded the previous law on powers of arrest as unsatisfactory because the courts seemed very reluctant to grant them.[164]

---

[156] FLA 1996, s 46(1).

[157] FLA 1996, s 46(4), although a power of arrest cannot be attached to an undertaking (s 46(2)).

[158] Baron (1990).

[159] It is unclear whether the court can issue a warrant for arrest on the basis of a breach of an undertaking: Gerlis (1996).

[160] A more restrictive test applies where the application is *ex parte* (FLA 1996, s 47(3)).

[161] Bird (1996: 4.12). The government has proposed that breach of a non-molestation or occupation order should become a criminal offence: Home Office (2003a: 34).

[162] In *Chechi* v *Bashier* [1999] 2 FLR 489 CA the requirement to attach a power of arrest led the Court of Appeal to decide that it was better not to make a non-molestation injunction at all.

[163] The application needs to be supported by a statement on oath and there must be reasonable grounds to believe that a respondent has failed to comply with the order (s 47(9)).

[164] Law Commission Report 192 (1990: 5.15).

In 1996 there were 22,652 injunctions made under the Domestic Violence and Matrimonial Proceedings Act 1976, of which only 10,099 had powers of arrest attached. One of the aims of the Family Law Act 1996 is to encourage the use of powers of arrest. In 2002, 22,053 non-molestation injunctions were made, of which 19,198 had a power of arrest attached, suggesting that there has been an increase in the use of powers of arrest.[165]

In *Re H (A minor)(Occupation Order: Power of Arrest)*[166] a father obtained an occupation order against his 17-year-old son, following his violent and abusive behaviour towards his parents. Under section 47(2) the judge attached a power of arrest. The appeal to the Court of Appeal centred on the argument that a power of arrest could not be attached where the respondent is a minor because there is effectively no sanction for contempt of court that can be imposed on a minor. Although the Court of Appeal felt that the lack of effective sanction required reform, it did not prevent the court attaching the power of arrest because that would enable the police to arrest the son and remove him from the home.

F. Punishment for breach of an order

If a person has breached a non-molestation or occupation order then he or she is liable to be punished for contempt of court. This may involve imprisonment or a fine. Where the act breaching an occupation or non-molestation order is a violent one then there should be an immediate custodial sentence.[167]

3. INJUNCTIONS UNDER THE PROTECTION FROM HARASSMENT ACT 1997 AND TORT

Prior to the Protection from Harassment Act 1997, the law of tort had been strained in the attempt to find a tort of harassment. For example, one case found that persistent telephone calls constituted the tort of nuisance.[168] Stretching the traditional categories of the law of tort is no longer necessary, as the 1997 Act in effect creates a new tort of harassment. It is possible to obtain an injunction if there is an actual or anticipated breach of s 1.[169] Under s 1:

(1) A person must not pursue a course of conduct—
    (a) which amounts to harassment of another, and
    (b) which he knows or ought to know amounts to harassment of the other.
(2) For the purposes of this section, the person whose course of conduct is in question ought to know that it amounts to harassment of another if a reasonable person in possession of the same information would think the course of conduct amounted to harassment of the other.

---

[165] Lord Chancellor's Department (2003). Home Office (2003a) proposes making the breach of a domestic violence injunction a criminal offence.
[166] [2001] 1 FCR 370.
[167] *Wilson v Webster* [1998] 1 FLR 1097, [1998] 2 FCR 275.
[168] *Khorasandjian v Bush* [1993] 2 FCR 257, [1993] 2 FLR 66; overruled in *Hunter v Canary Wharf Ltd* [1997] 2 FLR 342.
[169] Protection from Harassment Act 1997, s 3.

(3) Subsection (1) does not apply to a course of conduct if the person who pursued it shows—

    (a) that it was pursued for the purpose of preventing or detecting crime,

    (b) that it was pursued under any enactment or rule of law or to comply with any condition or requirement imposed by any person under any enactment, or

    (c) that in the particular circumstances the pursuit of the course of conduct was reasonable.

This section requires proof of three elements:

1. First, it must be proved that the defendant harassed the victim. The Act does not define harassment and so the word is to be given its normal meaning. However, the Act makes it clear that 'references to harassing a person include alarming the person or causing the person distress'.[170] This reveals that there is no need to demonstrate that physical harm is caused, nor that the victim suffers a psychological injury.[171] Only a person can be harassed for the purposes of the Act, a local authority cannot.[172]

2. The offence can only be committed where there is a course of conduct, which must involve conduct on at least two occasions.[173] So a single incident, however terrifying, cannot amount to an offence under the Act. Two incidents separated by four months were found not to be a 'course' of conduct in *Lau v DPP*.[174] However, it all depends on the nature of the conduct. If there was a threat to do an act and a year later the threat was carried out, this linked form of conduct could constitute a course of conduct.[175] In *R v Hills*[176] there were two incidents of violence separated by six months. However, between the two incidents the couple had cohabited and had sexual relations. This, the Court of Appeal felt, meant that there could not be a course of conduct. Indeed they doubted that the Protection from Harassment Act 1997 was suitable in cases where the defendant and victim were living together, as such cases were a long way from the stalking cases at which the Act was primarily aimed. That said, the 1997 Act has been used for a wide variety of cases beyond the traditional stalking cases, ranging from animal rights protesters, to neighbours falling out with each other, and it is hard to see why cohabitants should be seen as outside the Act's scope.

3. It is enough if it is shown that the defendant *ought* to have been aware that his or her conduct was harassing. It is therefore no defence for defendants to claim that they were unaware that their behaviour was harassing. In *R v Colohan*[177] the schizophrenic defendant argued that the jury should consider whether a reasonable

---

[170] Section 7(2). There is no need for the prosecution to prove that the victim suffered a psychologically recognised illness, as is required under the Offences Against the Person Act 1861, ss 47, 20 and 18.

[171] Although Lord Steyn in *R v Ireland and Burstow* [1998] AC 147 thought that most cases under the Act would involve violence.

[172] *Tameside MBC v M (Injunctive Relief: County Courts: Jurisdiction)* [2001] FL 873, although in that case the judge in the county court was willing to use the court's statutory jurisdiction under s 38 of the County Courts Act 1984 to protect the council and its staff.

[173] Protection from Harassment Act 1997, s 7(3). Conduct includes speech.

[174] [2000] 1 FLR 799.

[175] *Lau v DPP* [2000] 1 FLR 799.

[176] [2001] 1 FCR 569.

[177] [2001] 3 FCR 409.

schizophrenic person would be aware that his or her conduct was harassing. The argument was rejected: the jury or magistrates should simply consider what an ordinary reasonable person would have known.

There are various defences available listed in s 3(3). The one most likely to be relied upon is the defence that the course of conduct was reasonable. A defendant's mental illness will not render his or her conduct reasonable.[178] Once s 1 is established then an injunction can be made. In addition, s 3(2) states that damages can be awarded for anxiety and any financial loss.

It should be stressed that this Act does not require there to be any kind of relationship between the parties. It is therefore potentially very wide. Interestingly, the first reported case under the section involved animal rights protesters picketing an animal laboratory.[179] This was not the kind of case the government had in mind in passing the legislation, but demonstrates the potential width of the statute.

4. THE CHILDREN ACT 1989 AND DOMESTIC VIOLENCE

It is not possible to obtain a prohibited steps order or specific issue order under s 8 of the Children Act 1989, which has the same effect as an occupation or non-molestation order.[180] There are two reasons for this. The first is that the basis of making an order under the Children Act 1989 is the welfare principle, whereas Parliament has set out different criteria in the Family Law Act 1996 for occupation and non-molestation orders. To allow someone to be able to get an occupation order under the Children Act 1989 would be to by-pass the criteria in the Family Law Act 1996. The second is that an order under s 8 of the Children Act 1989 can only be made in respect of an issue which relates to an exercise of parental responsibility. An order that one partner does not molest the other would not relate to an exercise of parental responsibility and so could not be made under s 8 of the Children Act 1989.

5. DOMESTIC VIOLENCE AND HOUSING LAW

A crucial part of legal protection for abused adults is the provision of alternative affordable accommodation by the state.[181] One scandalous aspect of the law's present approach is the lack of support for battered women's refuges to which women can turn in emergencies.[182] These are largely run by voluntary agencies on very tight budgets.[183] However, shelters are only intended as a short-term solution. For long-term solutions the local authorities need to provide housing. The abused spouse, who is not able to afford rented accommodation and is seeking alternative

---

[178] *R v Colohan* [2001] 3 FCR 409.

[179] *Huntingdon Life Services Ltd v Curtis* (1997) The Times, 11 December.

[180] *Re H (A Minor) (Prohibited Steps Order)* [1995] 1 FLR 638, [1995] 2 FCR 547.

[181] Recognised by the government in Home Office (2000b: 12.1). See also Conway (2002)

[182] The government has accepted the shortcomings in provision of emergency accommodation of this kind and promised increased funding and resources to improve the position: Home Office (2003a: 42).

[183] Humphreys, Hester, Hague et al. (2002).

accommodation, must rely on the legislation relating to homelessness. Indeed it has been suggested that 15 per cent of those who are homeless have been victims of domestic violence.[184] For the year 2002/3 22 per cent of homeless families had become homeless following relationship breakdown. In 70 per cent of these cases violence had caused the breakdown.[185]

Under the Housing Act 1996 there is a duty on all local authorities:

1. To ensure that any person who requires support in their area has access to advice and information about homelessness.
2. To enquire whether a person is eligible for assistance if the local authority have reason to believe that a person is threatened with homelessness.
3. To house a person who is in priority need, and not intentionally homeless.[186]

It is this third duty which is of the most practical significance and so we will consider it in more detail.

A. The definition of 'homeless'

A person is homeless if they have no accommodation available for their use in the UK or elsewhere. The accommodation must be available[187] for the person together with any other person who lives with them as a member of their family, or any other person who might reasonably be expected to live with them. However, to be available it must be reasonable to expect the person to occupy the property. It would not be reasonable for the person to occupy a property they have had to leave due to domestic violence.[188] The relevant section of the Housing Act 1996 (s 177(1)) states:

> It is not reasonable for a person to continue to occupy accommodation if it is probable that this will lead to domestic violence against him, or against—
> (a) a person who normally resides with him as a member of his family; or
> (b) any other person who might reasonably be expected to reside with him.

Hence once it is shown that the person is likely to be the victim of domestic violence from a person with whom they live they will automatically be found to be homeless.[189] 'Domestic violence' here means 'violence from a person with whom he is associated, or threats of violence from such a person which are likely to be carried out'.[190] The Homelessness Act 2002 provides that violence from a non-associated person may also be included if it is racially motivated, for example. Accommodation need not be settled or permanent.[191] Thus it can include temporarily staying with

---

[184] Morley and Pascall (1996: 328).
[185] Shelter (2003).
[186] Housing Act 1996, s 175(4).
[187] This includes property which the person has an interest in or a licence to occupy or a right not to be evicted from.
[188] Or if the property is, for example, occupied by a squatter who could only be removed by legal action or force (s 175(2)(a)).
[189] *Bond* v *Leicester City Council* [2002] 1 FCR 566.
[190] Housing Act 1996, s 177(1).
[191] *R* v *Brent LBC, ex p Awua* [1995] 2 FLR 819, [1995] 3 FCR 278 HL.

friends or relatives. This is problematic because it is common for victims of domestic violence to seek refuge with friends or relatives.[192] More importantly, the question has been raised whether a shelter may be regarded as accommodation. In *R v Ealing LBC, ex p Sidhu*[193] it was held that a shelter should not be regarded as accommodation.[194]

B. Priority need

Those who are in priority need include, *inter alia*:

(a) a pregnant woman or a person with whom she resides or might reasonably be expected to reside;

(b) a person with whom dependent children reside or might reasonably be expected to reside;

(c) a person who is vulnerable as a result of old age, mental illness, or handicap, or physical disability or other special reason,[195] or with whom such a person resides or might reasonably be expected to reside.[196]

Category (b) includes those with whom a child stays only several days a week.[197] To fall within category (b) the courts[198] have held that it is not necessary for a parent to have a residence order in respect of a child, although some local authorities might still require this.[199] Under category (c) a victim of domestic violence will be regarded as a vulnerable person.[200] In 2002 statutory instruments[201] added to the categories of those in priority need, including (in England[202]) those who are vulnerable as a result of ceasing to occupy accommodation by reasons of violence or realistic threats of violence from another person. The requirement of vulnerability is meant to distinguish between cases where a person flees domestic violence but is surrounded by a network of friends and family and cases where the person in flight is left desperate and destitute.[203]

---

[192] Department of Health (2002a: para 6.37) accepts that overcrowding may mean that staying with a relative or friend is no longer feasible.

[193] (1982) 3 FLR 438.

[194] This view was accepted in the Department of Health (2002a: para 6.26).

[195] This has been said to include a young person escaping a violent home life: *R v Kensington and Chelsea LBC, ex p Kihara* (1996) 29 HLR 147 CA.

[196] Housing Act 1996, s 189(1). See also Homeless Persons (Priority Need for Accommodation) (England) Order 2002 (SI 2002/2051) and Homeless Persons (Priority Need) (Wales) Order 2001 (SI 2001/607) which add to this list for England and Wales respectively.

[197] *R v Lambeth LBC, ex p Vagiviello* (1990) 22 HLR 392 CA.

[198] *R v Ealing LBC, ex p Sidhu* (1982) 3 FLR 438.

[199] Yell (1992: 20).

[200] *R v Kensington and Chelsea LBC, ex p Kihara* (1996) 29 HLR 147 CA.

[201] Homeless Persons (Priority Need for Accommodation) (England) Order 2002 (SI 2002/2051) and Homeless Persons (Priority Need) (Wales) Order 2001 (SI 2001/607).

[202] The provisions for Wales are slightly wider, most notably not requiring proof of vulnerability.

[203] Conway (2002: 914); Department of Health (2002a: para 8.26).

C. Unintentionally homeless[204]

A person is intentionally homeless if they do or fail to do something that leads to them not occupying property that it would have been reasonable for them to carry on occupying.[205] A person is unintentionally homeless unless it is shown that they caused their own homelessness.

The difficulty is that local authorities have found the burden of caring for homeless people a heavy one, so it is not surprising that they have attempted to treat their obligations as strictly as possible. But this has worked to the disadvantage of many victims of domestic violence, so some authorities have taken the view that a woman who is the victim of violence should seek an occupation order (or ouster order as it was), and a failure to do this and simply to leave her home may make her intentionally homeless.[206] Such an attitude was strongly criticised by the Court of Appeal in *R v Westminster CC, ex p Bishop*.[207] However, the approach reveals the reluctance of local authorities to house victims of domestic violence unless they feel compelled to do so by the state. The Home Office has recently stressed to local authorities the importance of ensuring that victims of domestic violence are provided with accommodation.[208]

6. DOMESTIC VIOLENCE AND THE CRIMINAL LAW[209]

The fact that a violent incident occurred in a home does not affect its position in the criminal law. An assault in a home is as much an assault as if it took place in a pub. At least that is the theory. However, the history of the criminal law in this area shows that the police and courts have often regarded domestic violence as a less serious offence than other crimes. In recent years Parliament, the courts and police have shown an increasing awareness of the problems of molestation, domestic violence and stalking, but there is still much dissatisfaction with the operation of the criminal law.

A. The substantive law

As already stated, the fact that an offence takes place in a home makes no difference to the substantive law. This section will concentrate on how the criminal law has responded to the increasing awareness of domestic violence problems.

---

[204] If the person is intentionally homeless then the duty is only to give accommodation for such period as is reasonable for him or her to find alternative accommodation and provide advice and assistance to help find accommodation.
[205] Housing Act 1996, s 191 (as amended by Homelessness Act 2002). If a person is intentionally homeless then only temporary accommodation and advice and assistance need be offered (s 190).
[206] R. Thornton (1989).
[207] [1994] 1 FLR 720.
[208] Home Office (2000c: 2c.iii.1). See also Department of Health (2002a: ch. 7).
[209] S. Edwards (1996: ch. 5).

(i) Rape

There used to be a common law rule that a husband could not be guilty of raping his wife. The reasoning behind this rule was that, on marriage, a wife gave her irrevocable consent to sexual relations throughout marriage. In *R v R (Rape: Marital Exemption)*[210] the House of Lords stated that the traditional view that a husband could not be guilty of raping his wife was now unacceptable and the common law rule was abolished. Now a husband can be guilty of raping his wife. The fact that the law did not change until 1992 reveals the reluctance of Parliament and the courts to deal with domestic violence.

(ii) Assaults

Concerning the law on assaults, there have been difficulties with the areas of stalking and harassment. The House of Lords has been willing to extend the understanding of assault occasioning actual bodily harm[211] and causing grievous bodily harm[212] to cover harassing conduct. In *R v Ireland and Burstow*[213] the House of Lords accepted that the phrase 'bodily harm' included psychological injuries as well as physical injuries. This enabled the House of Lords to uphold the conviction of a man who had been persistently telephoning women with silent phone calls, for an offence contrary to s 47 of the Offences Against the Person Act 1861. Their Lordships also confirmed the conviction of a man for causing grievous bodily harm contrary to s 18 of the Offences Against the Person Act 1861 after he fought a campaign of harassment against a woman and caused her a severe psychological illness.

(iii) Sentencing of domestic crimes

The Court of Appeal has recently made it clear that marital disharmony will never in itself constitute a justification for violence.[214] Also, the fact that the parties are married is not a reason for giving a lower sentence.[215] However, a survey of cases by Edwards has suggested that some judges regard domestic violence as less serious than other assaults.[216] Another survey has found widespread use of binding over to keep the peace in these cases.[217]

---

[210] [1992] 1 AC 599 HL. The decision was put into statutory form in Criminal Justice and Public Order Act 1994, s 142 and see now Sexual Offences Act 2003.

[211] Offences Against the Person Act 1861, s 47.

[212] Offences Against the Person Act 1861, ss 18 and 20.

[213] [1998] AC 147. Discussed by S. Gardner (1998); Herring (1998c).

[214] *R v Rossiter* [1994] 2 All ER 752 at p. 753.

[215] *R v W* (1993) 14 CAR (S) 256; *R v Cutts* [1987] Fam Law 311.

[216] Edwards (1996).

[217] Cretney and Davis (1996) found that domestic violence resulted in a bind-over in 16 per cent of cases, whereas for assaults in non-domestic assaults only 4 per cent of cases resulted in a bind over.

(iv) Protection from Harassment Act 1997

The Protection from Harassment Act 1997 was produced after a number of high profile cases involving stalking were thought to reveal inadequacies in the law.[218] Stalkers may be complete strangers to the victim or be former partners. In fact this statute covers a far wider range of behaviour than stalking. It is an offence to breach s 1 of the Protection from Harassment Act 1997, which was quoted above. The maximum sentence for the offence under s 1 is six months[219] and it is possible for the court to make a restraining order.[220] A more serious offence is set out in s 4 of the Act:

(1) A person whose course of conduct causes another to fear, on at least two occasions, that violence will be used against him is guilty of an offence if he knows or ought to know that his course of conduct will cause the other so to fear on each of those occasions.

(2) For the purposes of this section, the person whose course of conduct is in question ought to know that it will cause another to fear that violence will be used against him on any occasion if a reasonable person in possession of the same information would think the course of conduct would cause the other so to fear on that occasion.

(3) It is a defence for a person charged with an offence under this section to show that—

    (a) his course of conduct was pursued for the purpose of preventing or detecting crime,

    (b) his course of conduct was pursued under any enactment or rule of law or to comply with any condition or requirement imposed by any person under any enactment, or

    (c) the pursuit of his course of conduct was reasonable for the protection of himself or another or for the protection of his or another's property.

The requirements for this offence are similar to s 1, with two main differences: the focus is on causing fear of violence rather than on harassment; and the reasonableness defence is only available if the conduct is deemed reasonable for the protection of the defendant or the defendant's or another's property. The maximum sentence is five years.[221]

(v) Compensation

Financial compensation is probably very low down the list of priorities for a victim of domestic violence but payment can have practical importance as well as being a public recognition of the wrong done to the victim.[222] It is unrealistic that a victim will sue a perpetrator in tort, and so any compensation is likely to come from the Criminal Injuries Compensation Scheme.[223] An award under the scheme is available where there is a conviction and domestic violence is covered by the scheme, although awards are not high.[224]

---

[218] C. Wells (1997).

[219] Or a level 5 fine (s 5)

[220] This order prohibits the defendant from conduct which would constitute harassment or cause a fear of violence. The order can be of fixed or indefinite duration (s 5(3)(b)).

[221] Section 4(4).

[222] Cobley (1998).

[223] Now set out in the Criminal Injuries Compensation Act 1995.

[224] CICB (1990: Appendix C).

(vi) Crimes committed by victims of domestic violence

There have been several cases where a victim of domestic violence has killed her abuser and been charged with murder. The courts have been willing to develop the law on the defence of provocation and diminished responsibility to deal with such cases.[225] The Court of Appeal has acknowledged that on a charge of murder the existence of battered women's syndrome is relevant as evidence that the woman killed while suffering from diminished responsibility or that she killed while acting under provocation.[226]

B. The criminal law in practice

There has been a history of the criminal law not, in practice, taking domestic violence seriously. There are basically three stages at which an incident of domestic violence may fail to lead to a successful prosecution: the arrest; the decision to prosecute; and the trial.[227]

(i) Arrest policies

Criminologists have written much on the importance of police culture[228] and have argued that in police culture domestic violence is often not taken seriously enough. Using the database of one domestic violence unit, Stanko[229] found that only 12 per cent of recorded cases of domestic violence resulted in arrest. There are three main problems which limit the likelihood of arrest. First, for various reasons, the victim may fail to contact the police after an assault. For example, the victim may feel that what happened was not a crime, or she may feel that she would not be taken seriously. Secondly, the police may not make an arrest because they themselves do not regard domestic violence as a 'proper crime', or because they find it impossible to discover what actually happened. The police arrive at scenes which are often emotionally charged and not easy to deal with.[230] Certainly a domestic violence incident is not as clear-cut an issue as dealing with a fight outside a pub. Thirdly, the victim, even though she may have contacted the police, may not actually want an arrest, but just want the man to be removed.[231] This decision might be encouraged explicitly or implicitly by the police's reaction to the situation.[232]

Some of these concerns have led to a reconsideration of the police's attitude towards domestic violence. A Home Officer Circular[233] sent to all police authorities recommended that:

---

[225] McColgan (1993) and Kaganas (2002) for a critical discussion of the law.
[226] McColgan (1993). Law Commission Consultation Paper 173 (2003) proposes reform of the law.
[227] Hoyle (1998).
[228] Edwards (1996: 196–8).
[229] Stanko, Crisp, Hale and Lucraft (1998).
[230] Edwards and Halpern (1991).
[231] Hoyle (1998: 214) found that only a third of the women in her study wanted the police officers to arrest the suspect and many of those did not want the matter taken further.
[232] Akerstrom (1998).
[233] Home Office Circular 60/1990.

1. police take a more interventionist approach in domestic violence, with a presumption in favour of arrest;
2. domestic violence be recorded and investigated just in the same way as other
   crimes; and
3. police be more sympathetic and understanding towards victims and inform
   them of the range of organisations which could be of assistance.

A Home Office Research Study[234] considered the effects of this circular. The study
noted that many police stations have a domestic violence unit, although the emphasis given to the units varied. Victims spoke well of most units, but one-third of oper-
ational officers had not heard of the Home Office Circular and half had not received
any new guidelines on handling domestic violence. The Home Office has recently
issued new guidance[235] on arrest and domestic violence, suggesting that there
should be an arrest in all cases of domestic violence unless there are exceptional circumstances.[236]

(ii) 'Down-criming' and decisions not to prosecute

Some people have alleged that although there has been an increase in the number
of arrests for domestic violence following changes made in police practice, the
number of convictions has not changed, because of the attitude of the Crown
Prosecution Service (CPS).[237] It is the job of the CPS to decide either to prosecute
the offence; to 'down-crime' (that is, to charge a lesser offence than the one the
victim alleges); or not to pursue the case to a court hearing.[238] Following arrest, 30
per cent of cases are withdrawn; 7 per cent are not charged; and 52 per cent are dis-
continued. Only 11 per cent of cases are brought to trial.[239] The decision not to
prosecute or to 'down-crime' may be caused by difficulties of proof, especially as
often the only witnesses to the incident are the victim and the defendant. It may be
that the victim is unwilling to pursue the prosecution because of her fear of reprisals
or because she believes there will not be any tangible benefit to her from the prosecution. Indeed the imprisonment of the abuser might cause the victim financial
and emotional harm. One study found that in 46 per cent of cases victims withdrew
their support for a prosecution, having initially reported the incident to the
police.[240] In cases where a victim withdraws her testimony, the CPS have been
instructed to investigate to ensure her decision truly reflects her wishes.[241] The
Home Office has suggested that it may be appropriate to bring proceedings even if
the victim does not wish to give evidence, and that the CPS should consider adopting such a policy.[242] However, in practice it is rare for there to be a prosecution if

[234] Grace (1995).
[235] Home Office (2000c: ch. 2).
[236] Home Office Circular 19/2000.
[237] National Inter-Agency Working Party (1992).
[238] 'Down-criming' occurs in all offences but it appears particularly common in offences of domestic
violence: Cretney and Davis (1996).
[239] Cretney and Davis (1996).
[240] Crown Prosecution Service Inspectorate (1998).
[241] Home Office (2000c: 2b:ii.4).
[242] Home Office (2000c: 2b.ii.6).

the victim is unwilling to co-operate. The Home Office has indicated that it will implement measures to encourage the CPS to prosecute domestic violence wherever appropriate.[243]

(iii) The trial

Even if the case reaches trial, a conviction is, of course, not guaranteed. There are particular problems if the victim does not want to give evidence.[244] Under s 23 of the Criminal Justice Act 1988 a written statement of the victim of an assault may[245] be admissible as evidence.[246] So in suitable cases there may be no need for the victim to give evidence in court. That said, live evidence is likely to be more persuasive to a jury. It would be possible to compel the victim to give oral evidence, by threatening them with contempt of court if they fail to testify in person.[247] In one case a victim refused to give evidence and this led to the case being dropped against her attacker, but as a result the judge decided to sentence the victim to prison for contempt of court.[248]

So the low rate of successful prosecutions results from victims not wishing to pursue criminal prosecutions, and the state agencies being reluctant to press for such prosecutions.[249]

C. Reforming the criminal procedure

A more radical approach could be taken by the criminal law in dealing with domestic violence. Some of the options are as follows.

(i) Pro-arrest guidelines or pro-prosecution

Some jurisdictions have adopted 'pro-arrest' policies or even 'mandatory arrest' policies. With these the police are required or strongly encouraged to arrest an abuser if the victim of domestic violence makes a complaint.[250] Even if the victim subsequently withdraws her consent the prosecution should still continue. In the UK the closest statement we have got to a mandatory arrest policy is the most recent guidance of the Home Office, suggesting that, unless there are good reasons not to, an arrest should be carried out in cases of domestic violence.[251]

One argument in favour of a mandatory arrest and prosecution policy is that a potential abuser, aware of the high likelihood of being arrested, may be deterred

---

[243] Home Office (2003a: 27).
[244] Home Office (2000b: ch. 2) sets out guidance for courts in order to make the experience of giving evidence as untraumatic as possible.
[245] The court has a discretion to decide whether to admit the statement, and in particular to rule whether the evidence can be subject to the scrutiny of cross-examination.
[246] Although only if the witness was able to give that evidence 'live'.
[247] Police and Criminal Evidence Act 1984, s 80.
[248] *R v Renshaw* [1989] Crim LR 811.
[249] Cretney and Davis (1996).
[250] L. Ellison (2002).
[251] Home Office (2000c: ch. 2).

from violence. Others suggest that it is unlikely that batterers would be aware of the policy, and, even if they were, it would not operate as a deterrent in the 'heat of the moment'. A further justification of a pro-arrest or mandatory arrest policy is that the batterer will automatically be publicly labelled as an abuser. The publicity that would surround such a policy might make a powerful statement to society in general that domestic violence is unacceptable. The policy would also lead to less pressure being put on victims, who would not have to decide whether or not to seek arrest or prosecution, and because of this might also be more willing to assist police officers.[252] This, supporters claim, will disempower batterers, by removing their ability to thwart criminal procedures by terrifying the victim into withdrawing her complaint.[253] Critics could reply that such policies in fact disempower the victim by assuming that society knows what is best for her, rather than letting her decide whether to pursue her complaint.

One well-known example of a mandatory arrest policy in practice was the Minneapolis Experiment in the United States. Although this policy led to a reduction in the rate of reported domestic violence, it was unclear whether this was because victims were not reporting violence because of the policy or whether the policy did indeed reduce the level of violence.[254] Further replica studies in Omaha, Nebraska and Charlotte, North Carolina failed to replicate the Minneapolis results.[255] There is therefore no conclusive evidence that such a policy would lead to a reduction in the level of violence. The argument that such a policy would send out a clear message of society's disapproval of domestic violence still stands.

(ii) 'Rehabilitative psychological sentences'

An alternative approach would be for the criminal law to focus on the rehabilitation of domestic violence offenders rather than on punishment. In other jurisdictions those arrested for domestic violence offences can be sent on 'batterers' programmes'. These focus on the apparent psychological inadequacies of the aggressor: they can teach the aggressor acceptable ways of expressing anger; challenge the abuser's general attitude towards women; or treat both the abuser and the victim together by finding ways to improve their communication.[256] Supporters of such programmes suggest that in this way the law can actually prevent future violence, but opponents argue that the method fails to take violence seriously enough and treats it as an illness rather than as criminal behaviour. Hoyle's study[257] found that a large majority of victims did not want prosecutions of the alleged abuser, some

[252] L. Ellison (2002).
[253] Hanna (1996); E. Schneider (2000b: 488).
[254] Buzawa and Buzawa (2003).
[255] A further difficulty with the approach is that it might lead to both parties being arrested, if both have been violent. It might be possible to require arrest of the primary aggressor, but this would not be an easy policy to implement on the ground.
[256] Adams (2000), Dobash and Dobash (2000) and Bowen, Brown and Gilchrist (2002) describe such programmes.
[257] Hoyle (1998: 214).

because they did not want to break up their relationships.[258] For such cases the psychological course may find favour with victims. The Home Office has recognised the benefits of some programmes of this kind, but has not suggested that they should replace the sanctions of the criminal law.[259] There is, however, much debate over the effectiveness of such programmes.[260]

(iii) Not using the criminal law at all

It could be argued that the criminal law is inappropriate in cases of domestic violence. Because there are such difficulties in proof and in finding punishments that meet the victims' needs, rather than developing criminal law and policing the law should focus on attempting to find alternative housing for abused women. Some say that imprisoning the abuser can only worsen the position of the victim.[261] However, this approach fails to recognise the interest that society has in preventing domestic violence and in expressing its condemnation of such acts through the criminal law. Offering alternative accommodation can be used in conjunction with the criminal law, but should not be a replacement for it.

7. STATE LIABILITY

One issue which has not been discussed in much detail in English and Welsh courts is whether the state can be liable in tort for failing to protect a victim of domestic violence. This claim would be likely to be one based on the tort of negligence or an action under s 7 of the Human Rights Act 1998. Arguably, if the police are aware that a person has been the victim of domestic violence in the past and such a person contacts the police seeking urgent protection then there may be a duty on the police to ensure that such protection is offered. Further, in the light of *A v UK (Human Rights: Punishment of Child)*,[262] there is a duty on the state to ensure that citizens do not suffer torture or inhuman or degrading treatment and to provide remedies to prevent that occurring. A person suffering serious violence who is not protected by the police may have this right infringed. The Home Office have recently proposed creating a register of domestic violence offenders,[263] similar to the one that presently exists for sex offenders.[264] The aim is that the register could be consulted by police or the CPS deciding whether to arrest or prosecute, rather than being available to members of public wanting to know if a person they fancy is a known abuser.

---

[258] Some victims are concerned that informing public authorities about violence will lead to investigation by social workers into their children: McGee (2000).

[259] Home Office (1999).

[260] Morley and Mullender (1992: 284–5).

[261] Hoyle (1998).

[262] [1998] 2 FLR 959, [1998] 3 FCR 597.

[263] This includes both those who have committed criminal offences and those against whom civil orders have been taken out.

[264] Home Office (2003a).

8. WHY THE LAW FINDS DOMESTIC VIOLENCE DIFFICULT

Around the world, legal systems struggle to find the correct response to domestic violence. There are a number of reasons for the difficulties.

A. The traditional image of the family

Domestic violence challenges the traditional images within family law of the family as a place of safety, a haven in a harsh world.[265] The presumption of non-intervention in family life is based on this peaceful view of families, although, as we saw when considering the statistical information on domestic violence, abuse is common in the home. The strength of the image of the family may explain why some victims refuse to regard themselves as the victims of crime, even regarding violence as an aspect of 'normal life'.[266]

B. Privacy

In Chapter 1 the importance of the concept of privacy in family law was stressed.[267] O'Donnovan[268] suggests: 'Home is thought to be a private place, a refuge from society, where relationships can flourish uninterrupted by public interference.' So not only is the home regarded as a refuge, it is seen by some as essential that the law should 'stay out of the home'. However, despite the strength that has traditionally been attached to the privacy argument, there are good reasons in favour of state intervention in cases of domestic violence.

1. Battering can be seen as causing public harm: it can cause increased costs to the NHS; extensive loss to the economy of police time, victims having to take time off work; etc. It has been estimated that domestic violence alone costs Greater London £278 million per year.[269] Half of women seeking help for mental health problems had been the victim of domestic violence.[270]
2. It could be said that domestic violence is caused by and reinforced by patriarchy. As the state upholds and maintains patriarchy, it has responsibility for it and so is under a duty to mitigate its effects.
3. Intervention in domestic violence could be required in order to uphold the equal rights of men and women. If there is to be equality between the sexes in the home, there must be effective remedies for domestic violence.
4. It has been argued that if society focuses on the victim's privacy rather than the privacy of the 'home', intervention is justified. Schneider[271] maintains that the state needs to promote 'a more affirmative concept of privacy, one that encom-

---

[265] Lasch (1977).
[266] Kaganas and Piper (1994).
[267] E. Schneider (1994).
[268] O'Donnovan (1993: 107).
[269] Home Office (2000b).
[270] Home Office (2003a: 10).
[271] E. Schneider (1994: 37).

passes liberty, equality, freedom of bodily integrity, autonomy and self-determination, which is important to women who have been battered'. Intervention in domestic violence can therefore be justified in order to promote the privacy of the victim.

C. Difficulties of proof

One of the difficulties of domestic violence is that often the only witnesses to the violence are the two parties themselves. In many cases it is one person's word against another's. This requires the courts to make orders that may infringe important rights of either party on the basis of meagre evidence. If the court makes the wrong decision, an innocent person may be removed from his or her home or a victim may be denied protection from further violence.

D. Occupation or protection

There are two kinds of cases in which someone may apply for an order relating to the occupation of a home. The first is those which involve domestic violence, where the applicant is seeking protection. The second kind of case is where there is no violence and the dispute is one of who should occupy the home until a final resolution of the financial affairs of the couple is reached. This is more in the nature of a property dispute. Although these are quite different kinds of cases, the Family Law Act 1996 deals with them both under ss 33, 35 and 36.

E. Victim autonomy

There can be real difficulties in finding a correct solution to a situation once domestic violence is proved. In some cases the ideal solution from the victim's point of view is that her partner returns to the home but ceases to be violent.[272] The victim may be emotionally and financially dependent on the abuser and to imprison him might cause her further harm.[273] It can be argued that a victim who wishes to remain in a violent relationship is not expressing her genuine wishes, and that, rather than respect what the victim says she wants, we should seek to put the victim where the victim, free from violence, can make genuine choices.[274] Another argument is that the common attitudes of victims to domestic violence – 'I want the relationship to continue, but the violence to stop' – represent incompatible wishes. The law is not able to respect both of these desires of the victim. The law could take the view that the desire for the violence to stop is the more important aspect of the wishes of the victim.

There may also be a conflict here between the interests of the state and the victim. The state may wish to express its abhorrence of domestic violence by a severe punishment, whereas the victim may not seek such stern treatment. This tension is

---

[272] Hoyle (1998).
[273] In certain cultures there may be severe social disadvantages following public intervention in domestic violence.
[274] The argument is discussed in Miles (2001: 101).

revealed in civil law in that s 60 of the Family Law Act 1996 permits third parties to bring proceedings on a victim's behalf, but the courts may make orders on their own motion under s 42 of the Family Law Act 1996. Both sections suggest that it may be proper to provide a victim with protection which she does not want. In criminal law, encouraging arrest and pressurising a victim into providing evidence demonstrates the tension between protecting the victim's right to choose what should happen and voicing society's opposition to domestic violence. At the extreme it might even be alleged that a victim's autonomy is threatened, on the one hand, by her abusive partner and, on the other, by state agencies acting to 'protect her' contrary to her wishes. However, whether an abused woman is in a position to exercise autonomy following what might be years of abuse is also open to question.[275] Further it could be argued that the interests of potential future victims of domestic violence justify a tough approach against current incidents of violence.[276]

F. The law not appropriate

Some feminists argue that the law's treatment of domestic violence is doomed to fail, given the patriarchal domination of the language, procedures and personnel of the legal process.[277] They maintain that domestic violence can only be combated if the domination of women by men throughout society is brought to an end. Until then the law can only tinker at the edges of the problem.

G. Solicitors

The professionals involved can create problems in the law's response to domestic violence. We have already discussed the attitudes of the police, but there may be problems with the mindset of those whose role is to assist the victim. Lawyers are traditionally seen as slow acting and the hectic life of many practising solicitors makes problematic the rapid applications that are necessary in domestic violence cases. Ingleby, in his work on family solicitors, argues: 'The solicitor's role in these violent situations might be seen in terms of preserving non-violent arm's-length lines of communication within which to negotiate the other aspects of the dispute in the hope that the passage of time will defuse the situation.'[278] It may also be that some solicitors lack awareness of the problems surrounding domestic violence. One study suggested that solicitors do not, as a matter of routine, ask family clients about domestic violence.[279]

9. CONCLUSION

This chapter has considered the law on domestic violence. This is an area where the notion of privacy has been particularly influential: that behaviour between partners

---

[275] Hoyle and Sanders (2000).
[276] L. Ellison (2002).
[277] Smart (1984).
[278] Hester, Pearson and Radford (1997).
[279] Kaganas and Piper (1999: 194).

in their home is their own business and the state should not interfere. In recent years the extent of domestic violence has become more widely acknowledged, both in terms of the severity of the violence and the number of people involved. However, acknowledgement of the problem is but a small step to providing a solution. The Family Law Act 1996 and the judicial interpretation of that statute reveal that ousting abusive partners runs counter to the protection of property rights and (now) the right to respect for family and private life under the Human Rights Act 1998. So even if ousting will provide the most effective protection to a victim of domestic violence, the courts will require convincing evidence before being willing to do so. A further difficult issue is to what extent the law should respect the right of autonomy of the victim of domestic violence and therefore rely on her to pursue the remedy she wishes; and to what extent the state should seek to protect the victim (regardless of whether she wants the intervention). This is an area where, perhaps, the solution lies not so much in the hands of the law, but in a wholesale change in attitudes towards violence in the home.[280]

---

[280] Home Office (2000d and 2000e) discuss how the government intends to change attitudes towards domestic violence.

7

WHO IS A PARENT?

It may seem rather odd to ask, 'who is a parent?'[1] But the concept of parenthood is far from straightforward. In the vast majority of cases the parents of a child are those who genetically produce the child. The woman whose egg and the man whose sperm together ultimately produce the child are its parents. In the past, although there may have been practical problems in proving who was the biological father, that definition of parenthood was generally agreed. In recent times this definition has become problematic. Three developments in particular have caused a re-examination of the concept of parenthood. The first is the advent of new reproductive technologies. Now the woman who carries the child need not be genetically related to the child and a man may donate sperm to a hospital without ever intending to play a parental role. Secondly, with increased rates of divorce and breakdown of relationships it is now common for a child to be cared for by someone who is not necessarily a genetic parent but, for example, a step-parent. Indeed a child may have a series of adults who carry out the social role of being a parent.[2] For such children there has been a separation between who is the person caring for them day to day and who is their genetic parent. Thirdly, there has been an increased interest in child psychology among lawyers, and an acceptance that children may have a 'psychological parent' who is not genetically the parent.

Shortly, the law on parenthood will be considered, but it will be useful to consider briefly the understanding of parenthood from three other disciplines.

1. SOCIOLOGICAL, PSYCHOLOGICAL AND BIOLOGICAL NOTIONS OF PARENTHOOD

A. Child psychologists

One influential group of child psychologists has argued that, from a child's perspective, 'psychological parenthood' is of greater significance than biological parenthood.[3] Goldstein et al. write:

> Whether any adult becomes the psychological parent of a child is based on day-to-day interaction, companionship and shared experiences. The role can be fulfilled either by a biological parent or by an adoptive parent or by any other caring adult – but never by an absent, inactive adult, whatever his biological or legal relationship to the child may be.[4]

---

[1] The United Nations Convention on the Rights of the Child does not include a definition of a parent.

[2] Haskey (1997) states that only three-quarters of children in their mid-teens live with both their biological parents.

[3] For discussion of the psychological importance to a child of 'attaching' to a parent-figure see Bowlby (1973); Howe, Brandon, Hinings and Schofield (1999).

[4] Goldstein, Solnit, Goldstein and Freud (1996: 19).

They explain that children's and adults' perceptions of parenthood may differ:

> Unlike adults, children have no psychological conception of blood tie relationship until quite late in their development. For the biological parents, the experience of conceiving, carrying and giving birth prepares them to feel close to and responsible for their child. These considerations carry no weight with children who are emotionally unaware of the events leading to their existence. What matters to them is the pattern of day-to-day interchanges with adults who take care of them and who on the strength of such interactions, become the parent figures to whom they are attached.[5]

Although this notion of a psychological parent is important, research on adopted children suggests that children may also regard genetic parentage of great importance,[6] as it provides an important part of the child's sense of identity.

B. Sociologists

Some sociologists have argued that parenthood is a socially constructed term, meaning that the rules on who is a parent reflect common norms within society, rather than reflecting an inevitable truth. Indeed anthropologists looking at different societies in different parts of the world and at different times have found a wide variety of understandings of parenthood. For example, Goody has noted the following different aspects of parenthood: bearing and begetting children; endowment with civil and kinship status; nurturance; and training and sponsorship into adulthood.[7] Different people in different cultures may carry out these roles.

C. Biological perceptions

Johnson has usefully distinguished four kinds of parenthood in a biological sense.[8] First, there is genetic parentage. At present, there is a need for sperm from the man and an egg from the woman to produce a conceptus which will ultimately develop into a person.[9] Secondly, coital parentage, which involves the meeting or joining of the sperm and egg.[10] Thirdly, there is the gestational or uterine component of parentage, involving the rearing and support of the foetus, which in humans is undertaken by the mother in pregnancy. Finally, there is the post-natal component: the raising of the child after birth.

It is clear from this very brief outline that the definition of a parent is unclear and the term 'parent' can cover a wide range of ideas. Eekelaar[11] has looked at different aspects of parenthood and has usefully suggested that it is necessary to distinguish three key elements: legal, social and biological parenthood. Legal parenthood is who is deemed in the eyes of the law to be the parent. Biological parenthood would

---

[5] Goldstein, Solnit, Goldstein and Freud (1996: 9).
[6] Thoburn (1988).
[7] E. Goody (1982).
[8] Johnson (1999).
[9] It may be that technology will develop so that in the future more than two people could be genetically related to a child.
[10] For the majority of human parents this will be through sexual intercourse.
[11] Eekelaar (1991c)

be who is biologically (by which he means genetically) the parent. Thirdly, the social parent is the person who carries out the day-to-day nurturing role of a parent. These roles are often acted out by the same person, but can be carried out by different people. For example, a step-parent may be the social parent of a child without being the biological or legal parent.

2. THE DIFFERENT MEANINGS OF BEING A PARENT IN LAW

It is not surprising that the law has a variety of understandings on being a parent. Bainham has usefully explained that the law distinguishes between parentage, parenthood and parental responsibility:[12]

1. *Parentage*: those who are genetically related to the child. In other words, the man who provided the sperm and the woman who provided the egg, which were combined to produce the foetus which became the child.[13]
2. *Parenthood*: those who are regarded in the law as parents. In many cases they will be those who have parentage, but it need not be so. For example, the law may decide that a man who donates sperm to a clinic will not be legally regarded as the father of the child.
3. *Parental responsibility*: those who are to have the legal responsibilities and rights that are attached to being a parent.

The benefit to the law in having these different understandings of 'parent' is that it increases flexibility. The law can decide that some people will have parenthood but not parental responsibility, or indeed that some people will be regarded as having parental responsibility but not parenthood. For some children it is possible that different people will have parentage, parenthood and parental responsibility under the present law. For example, imagine a woman who gives birth following assisted reproductive services provided to her and her unmarried partner but using the sperm of a sperm donor. After the birth she leaves her partner and marries another man, who is awarded a residence order in respect of the child. In such a case the sperm donor would have parentage; the partner parenthood; and the husband parental responsibility.

The law could be much simpler. We could have just two categories for adults: they either are or are not parents of a child. But having only two categories would lead to a less subtle law. By accepting different forms of parents the law is able to capture the variety of ways in which an adult can act in a parental role. Bainham argues that having different ways of being a parent assists in the debate over whether social or biological parenthood should be regarded by the law as the crucial element of parenthood: 'Increasingly the question will not be whether to prefer the genetic or social parent but how to accommodate both on the assumption that they both have distinctive contributions to make to the life of the child.'[14]

[12] Bainham (1999).
[13] See Archard (1995) for a discussion of the significance that should attach to a genetic link between an adult and a child.
[14] Bainham (1999: 27).

However, Bainham's enthusiasm for accepting a wide range of different kinds of parent is controversial. It is important to note that the 'problem' in defining parenthood is largely one of defining fathers. There is relatively little difficulty in defining motherhood. In the vast majority of cases there is no separation between parentage, parenthood and parental responsibility for mothers, as they relate to the same person. Increasing the number of people who can be regarded as parents is in reality increasing the number of people who can be regarded as fathers. From the mother's viewpoint, the greater the recognition given to different kinds of fathers, the weaker the mother's position may become.[15] For example, a requirement that mothers should consult with a child's father(s) over important issues is a more onerous requirement if several men are regarded as father, rather than just one.

This chapter will now consider the legal definitions of who is the mother and who is the father of a child.

3. WHO IS THE CHILD'S MOTHER?

The mother of a child is the woman who gives birth to the child.[16] This is so even where there is assisted reproduction and the woman who carries and gives birth to the child is not genetically related to the child. Section 27(1) of the Human Fertilisation and Embryology Act 1990[17] states:

> The woman who is carrying or has carried a child as a result of the placing in her of an embryo or of sperm and eggs, and no other woman, is to be treated as the mother of the child.[18]

This indicates that, in relation to motherhood, it is the gestational rather than the genetic link which is crucial. In fact the genetic link is irrelevant in establishing legal motherhood.[19] This could be explained in any one of three ways. The most convincing argument is that the pain and effort of childbirth and the closeness of the bond which develops through pregnancy[20] and birth justifies the status of motherhood.[21] The gestational mother has given more of herself to the child than the genetic mother. Secondly, the law could be justified on the basis of certainty. It is far easier to discover who gave birth to the child than to ascertain who (if anyone) donated the egg.[22] Thirdly, the law might be seen as a way of encouraging egg donation.[23] Egg donors may be deterred from donating if they were to be regarded as the parents of the child.

---

[15] See further Herring (2001: 137).

[16] *Ampthill Peerage Case* [1977] AC 547 at p. 577.

[17] Human Fertilisation and Embryology Act 1990 (hereafter HFEA 1990), s 27 applies only from 1 August 1991 and the legislation is not retrospective: *Re M (Child Support Act: Parentage)* [1997] 2 FLR 90.

[18] There is one exception involving matters relating to succession of any dignity or title of honours (HFEA 1990, s 29(4)).

[19] Contrast *Johnson v Calvert* [1993] 851 P 2d 774. Discussed in Douglas (1994b). See also *Moschetta v Moschetta* (1994) 25 Cal App 4th 1218.

[20] There is some psychological evidence for such a bond which is discussed in J. Hill (1991).

[21] Douglas (1991).

[22] This argument was stressed by the Warnock Report (1984: 6.6–6.8).

[23] Kandel (1994).

A woman can also become a child's mother through the making of an adoption order or a parental order.[24]

4. WHO IS THE CHILD'S FATHER?

A man[25] who wishes to prove that he is the father of a child must show:

1. that he is genetically the father of the child;[26] or
2. that one of the legal presumptions of paternity applies and has not been rebutted; or
3. that he is a father by virtue of one of the statutory provisions governing assisted reproduction; or
4. that an adoption order or parental order has been made in his favour.

The core notion of paternity has traditionally been seen as a biological or genetic concept. A man is the father of a child genetically related to him.[27] Until recently it was difficult to prove whether a father was genetically related to a child and so the law had to rely on certain presumptions. Although DNA testing can now prove conclusively whether a man is the father of a child, the legal presumptions are still of importance because they explain who the father of a child is if no tests have been carried out.

A. Legal presumptions of paternity

These are the circumstances in which fatherhood is presumed:

1. If a married woman gives birth it is presumed that her husband is the father of the child.[28] This presumption is sometimes known as *pater est quem nuptiae demonstrant* (or *pater est* for short). It does not apply to unmarried cohabitants.[29] If the birth takes place during the marriage but conception took place before the marriage the *pater est* presumption still applies. The presumption also applies if it is clear[30] that the conception took place during a marriage, even if death or divorce has ended that marriage by the time the birth occurs.[31] There will therefore be conflicting presumptions if the child could have been conceived during a first marriage but is born during the course of the wife's second marriage. It is not clear who the law would regard as the father in such a situation. It is suggested that the second husband should be regarded as the father, it being

---

[24] These will be discussed shortly.
[25] Only a man can be a father: *X, Y, Z v UK* [1997] 2 FLR 892, [1997] 3 FCR 341 ECtHR, discussed in Lind (1997).
[26] A sperm donor to a licensed clinic cannot rely on this ground (HFEA 1990, s 28(6)).
[27] This was recently confirmed in *Leeds Teaching Hospital NHS Trust v A* [2003] EWHC 259, [2003] 1 FCR 599.
[28] *Banbury Peerage Case* (1811) 1 Sim & St 153 HL. The Lord Chancellor's Department (1999) suggested that the *pater est* presumption should be put on a statutory footing. The presumption does not apply in cases of disputed fatherhood under the Child Support Act 1991 (s 26).
[29] Although it does to parties in a void marriage: Legitimacy Act 1976, s 1.
[30] The court will refer to the normal gestation period, although the House of Lords in *Preston-Jones* v *Preston-Jones* [1951] AC 391 HL could not agree on the definition of a gestational period.
[31] A cynic might regard this presumption as unrealistic in some cases. If a child is conceived and shortly afterwards there is a divorce, that may well suggest a third party is the father.

more likely that he is the genetic father. He is also the man who would act in the parental role during the child's upbringing. Against this view is the argument that it would be wrong to presume that the wife committed adultery.

The *pater est* presumption is controversial, although no doubt statistically it is more likely than not that a husband is the father of his wife's child. It is also possible to see the presumption as being based on the policy of seeking to avoid a child not having a father. Thorpe LJ in *Re H and A (Children)*[32] has doubted the relevance of the presumption. He explained 'as science has hastened on and as more and more children are born out of marriage it seems to me that the paternity of any child is to be established by science and not by legal presumption of inference'.[33] Without the presumption, however, children will have no legal father until tests are carried out.

2. The law presumes that if a man's name appears on the birth certificate of a child, he is the child's father.[34] If the couple are married then there is a statutory obligation on both parties to register the birth within 42 days. If the mother is unmarried the obligation rests on the mother alone. The unmarried father does not have a right to have his name registered and a blank can be left in that space if the mother wishes. If the unmarried father wishes to be registered as the father then it is necessary for either the mother to consent or for the father to prove his genetic fatherhood through a court order.[35]

3. It is not clear whether the making of a parental responsibility agreement will be regarded as prima facie evidence of paternity, although the Lord Chancellor's Consultation Paper[36] believes it does. *R v Secretary of State, ex p West*[37] suggests that a parental responsibility order by consent can be regarded as evidence of paternity by the Child Support Agency.

4. The court may also infer paternity simply from the facts of the case. For example, if it were shown that the mother and the man spent the night together at the time the conception is said to have taken place, this would be evidence of the man's paternity.

B. Rebutting these presumptions

Section 26 of the Family Law Reform Act 1969 states that the legal presumptions can be rebutted on the balance of probabilities. In *S v S, W v Official Solicitor (or W)*[38] Lord Reid thought that the presumptions should be regarded as weak, and could be rebutted with only a little evidence.[39] There are two main ways that a man presumed to be the father could rebut the presumption. The first and most reliable is to seek a court order for genetic tests (normally through comparing DNA

---

[32] [2002] 2 FCR 469.
[33] At p. 479.
[34] Births and Deaths Registration Act 1953, s 34(2); *Brierley v Brierley* [1918] P 257.
[35] Births and Deaths Registration Act 1953, s 10(1)(a).
[36] Lord Chancellor's Department (1998).
[37] [1999] 1 FLR 1233.
[38] [1972] AC 24 HL.
[39] In *Re Moynihan* [2000] 1 FLR 113 a higher standard of proof was suggested, but the Court of Appeal in *Re H and A (Children)* [2002] 2 FCR 469 preferred *S v S*.

samples). There is power to order such tests under s 20 of the Family Law Reform Act 1969, although, as will be noted later, the court in some cases will refuse to order tests to be performed. If a man is shown to be the father of the child through genetic tests then he is legally the father of the child, and if another man was presumed to be the father he is no longer regarded as the father. In *F v CSA*[40] it was unclear whether the father of the child was the mother's husband or her lover. The lover was assessed by the Child Support Agency. He refused to undergo blood tests. His refusal to undergo the blood test led to a presumption that he was the father. This presumption was held to be stronger than the presumption of legitimacy. The second way that a man could seek to rebut a presumption that he was the father would be to introduce evidence to undermine the logical basis of the presumption. So a husband could rebut the presumption that he was the father of his wife's child by introducing evidence that he was abroad at the time of the alleged conception, or that he was impotent.

C. Fathers and assisted reproduction[41]

There are various forms of assisted reproduction:[42]

1. *Assisted insemination.* This refers to the placing of sperm into the mother (other than by sexual intercourse) leading to fertilisation. It is common to distinguish insemination using the husband's sperm (AIH) and insemination using a donor's sperm (AID).[43]
2. *In vitro fertilisation (IVF).* This technique involves mixing in a dish an egg and sperm. The fertilised egg is then placed in the woman's uterus. The sperm and/or egg may come from the couple themselves or donors.
3. *Gamete intrafallopian transfers (GIFT).* Here a donated egg is placed with the sperm (either of the husband or a sperm donor) in the womb.

The law governing assisted reproduction is found in the Human Fertilisation and Embryology Act 1990. The starting point in ascertaining parenthood in cases of assisted reproduction is that the same rules that govern fatherhood in other cases apply. The genetic father, or a man presumed to be the father by virtue of one of the presumptions above, will be the father in a case of assisted reproduction unless he can find a statutory provision that states otherwise. In other words, the 'default' position, in the absence of any provision to the contrary, is that the genetic father is the legal father. Any man who is a father as a result of provisions in the Act is a father in the full sense of the law and cannot, for example, seek to escape liability under the Child Support Act 1991 on the basis that he is not the biological father.[44]

The Human Fertilisation and Embryology Act 1990 provides for the following exceptions to the basic rule that the genetic father is the child's father:

[40] [1999] 2 FLR 244.
[41] For a useful discussion see S. Bridge (1999).
[42] A thorough analysis can be found in Douglas (1991: ch. 6).
[43] Less than 10 per cent of cases involving assisted reproduction use donated sperm or eggs (see HFEA 1990).
[44] *Re CH (Contact Parentage)* [1996] 1 FLR 569, [1996] FCR 768, *Leeds Teaching Hospital NHS Trust v A* [2003] EWHC 259, [2003] 1 FCR 599.

1. Section 28(6) makes clear that a man who donates sperm to a licensed clinic is not the father of any child born using that sperm as long as his sperm is used in accordance with his consent under Sch 3.[45] The protection does not cover the donor who consents to sperm for use with his wife, but it is used for another woman.[46] He will be regarded as the father of any child born. The donor must trust the clinic not to use his sperm outside the terms of his consent.

2. A man who has died before his sperm is used in procedures leading to pregnancy is not the father of any child born using that sperm.[47] A dead man's sperm can only be used where he has consented to its use.[48] The Human Fertilisation and Embryology (Deceased Fathers) Act 2003 will, when it comes into force, enable a deceased provider of sperm to be a father.

The Act also provides that a man not genetically related to a child is the legal father in the following circumstances:

1. Under s 28(2) the husband of a woman who gives birth as a result of a licensed clinic's assisted reproductive treatment is presumed to be the child's father unless he shows that he did not consent *and* that he is not the child's genetic father.[49] It should be noted that a clinic is very unlikely to provide services to a married woman without her husband's consent[50] and so it should be rare that the question of consent will be raised. In *Leeds Teaching Hospital NHS Trust v A*[51] a wife's egg was mixed by mistake with the sperm of Mr B, rather than that of her husband (Mr A). It was held that Mr A had not consented to the treatment of his wife *with that sperm* and therefore he was not the father under s 28. Because Mr B's sperm had been used without his consent s 28(6) (discussed below) did not apply and so he was the father.

2. Under s 28(3) a man will be treated as the father of a child born to a woman[52] 'in the course of treatment services provided for her and a man together by a person to whom a licence applies'. If the man is the father as a result of this section then 'no other person is to be treated as the father of the child'.[53] The section is remarkable[54] in that a man becomes a father without a genetic link to the child and without being married to the mother.[55] This is unique in English law. The section requires some explanation:

---

[45] HFEA 1990, Sch 3, para 5.
[46] *Leeds Teaching Hospital NHS Trust v A* [2003] EWHC 259, [2003] 1 FCR 599.
[47] HFEA 1990, s 28(6)(b).
[48] In *Centre for Reproductive Medicine v U* [2002] FL 267 Butler-Sloss P rejected an argument that the husband's withdrawal of his consent before his death was the result of undue influence.
[49] HFEA 1990, s 28(2).
[50] The Human Fertilisation and Embryology Authority Code of Practice, para 5.7 makes this clear.
[51] [2003] 1 FCR 599, discussed Ford and Morgan (2003).
[52] The provision does not apply to married women receiving treatment with their husbands (s 28(2) is the relevant provision for them): *Leeds Teaching Hosptal NHS Trust v A* [2003] EWHC 259, [2003] 1 FCR 599.
[53] HFEA 1990, s 28(4).
[54] Hale LJ has called it 'unusual' (*Re R (A Child)* [2003] 1 FCR 481, para 20).
[55] The section does not apply if the woman is married. If she is married the situation is governed by HFEA 1990, s 28(2).

(a) *'Services'*. Section 2(1) defines services as 'medical, surgical or obstetric services provided to the public or a section of the public for the purpose of assisting women to carry children'.

(b) *'Services together'*. It should be stressed that it is not enough just to show that the mother's partner consented to the treatment; it is necessary to show that the mother and the partner received the treatment services together. In *Re Q (Parental Order)*[56] Johnson J suggested that it was necessary to show that the man himself received medical, surgical or obstetric treatment. This was a highly restrictive interpretation because it would be very unlikely the man himself would be receiving treatment unless he was donating sperm for the procedure, in which case he would not need to rely on s 28.[57] However, this approach has not been adopted by more recent cases. In *Re B (Parentage)*[58] Bracewell J decided that the couple were receiving treatment services together because the partner had donated sperm and attended the clinic with the mother.[59] Bracewell J *obiter* suggested that the question was whether the parties had embarked on a joint enterprise to produce a child and give birth. In other words, the phrase 'services together' could include cases where the woman received the medical treatment, but the man supported her emotionally and attended the treatment services with her, even if he did not himself receive services. Bracewell J's approach was approved by Lord Woolf MR in *R v Human Fertilisation and Embryology Authority, ex p Blood*[60] and in *U v W (Attorney-General Intervening)*.[61] In *U v W* it was held that the couple were receiving treatment together as they had 'jointly attended' the fertility clinic. *Obiter* Wilson J held that they had been receiving treatment together as the doctor had been 'responding to a request for that form of treatment by the woman and the man as a couple, notwithstanding the absence in the man of any physical role in such treatment'. In *Leeds Teaching Hospital NHS Trust v A*[62] Butler-Sloss P suggested (*obiter*) that a fundamental mistake concerning the treatment provided (e.g. the sperm of another man, rather than the woman's partner was used) would mean that the treatment would not be regarded as being received 'together'.[63]

So the law now interprets receiving treatment together as requiring the couple to attend together and to seek treatment as a couple as part of a joint enterprise. Although this more recent approach is a rather stretched interpretation of the words 'receiving services together' it is a pragmatic and sensible interpretation of the provision.[64]

---

[56] [1996] 1 FLR 369, [1996] 2 FCR 345.
[57] A point which Johnson J himself acknowledged.
[58] [1996] 2 FLR 15, [1996] 3 FCR 697.
[59] The case in fact concerned the use of the phrase 'treatment services together' in para 5(3) of Sch 3 to the HFEA 1990.
[60] [1997] 2 FCR 501 CA.
[61] [1997] 2 FLR 282, [1998] 1 FCR 526.
[62] [2003] EWHC 259, [2003] 1 FCR 599.
[63] Para 37.
[64] See S. Bridge (1999).

The Human Fertilisation and Embryology Authority Code of Practice correctly recommends that the partner of any woman receiving treatment signs a form acknowledging that he is receiving treatment together with the woman, and this should mean that there will be few disputes over the meaning of this section.

In *Re R (A Child)*[65] the Court of Appeal held that it was necessary to show that the couple were receiving treatment services together at the time when the embryo was placed inside the woman. In that case a woman and her partner approached a clinic for assisted reproductive services. They signed paperwork stating that they would be receiving treatment services together. Some time later the couple separated, but they did not inform the clinic. Later an embryo was placed into the mother and in due course she gave birth. It was held that her ex-partner was not the father, because at the time of the placing of the embryo he and the mother were not receiving services together.

(c) '*Licensed clinic*'. In order for a partner to be able to rely on s 28(3) the clinic must be registered by the British Human Fertilisation and Embryology Authority. In *U v W (Attorney-General Intervening)*[66] a man could not rely on the subsection, as the couple had received treatment in Rome, Italy, at a clinic which was not licensed by the British authority. He was not married to the woman and had no genetic tie to the child, and so he could not be a father in the eyes of the law.

(d) '*Child born in the course ...*' This phrase suggests that if the child is born in the course of the treatment this is sufficient for s 28(3) to operate. There is no need to prove that the child was born as a result of the procedure.

D. DIY assisted reproduction

In a case of do-it-yourself insemination, where, for example, a woman obtains sperm via the Internet[67] or from a friend and uses a syringe to impregnate herself, the normal rules apply. The donor of the sperm will be treated as the father and the woman who gives birth as the mother. The Human Fertilisation and Embryology Act 1990 does not alter these basic rules as the procedures do not take place within a licensed clinic. There is one exception to this and this is that s 28(2) and (5) of the Human Fertilisation and Embryology Act 1990 suggest that if the mother is married then her husband (and not the sperm donor) is the father, unless it can be shown that the husband did not consent to the use of the sperm.[68]

---

[65] [2003] EWCA Civ 182, [2003] 1 FCR 481 CA.

[66] [1997] 2 FLR 282, [1998] 1 FCR 526.

[67] Try http://www.mannotincluded.com if you are interested! There have been reports of the first child born in the UK as a result of Internet sperm (BBC (2003).

[68] An unmarried couple cannot rely on s 28(3) because that only applies where the couple receive treatment in a licensed clinic.

E. Fatherless children

As a result of the provisions in the Human Fertilisation and Embryology Act 1990, some children can be deemed fatherless. This might arise where a single woman (or a married woman acting without her husband's consent) becomes pregnant as a result of AID provided by a licensed clinic. The donor could not be the father due to s 28(6), and the Act does not provide for anyone else to be the father. A similar situation arises if a man's sperm is used after his death. Some have criticised the fact that the law allows a child to be fatherless. But without breaching the principle of anonymity of sperm donors it is hard to see how the law can avoid this.

One interesting observation on these legally fatherless children is that the law here, for the first time, is moving away from the view that a child must have one father and one mother. Hale LJ has stated that it is clearly in the child's interests to have a father, if possible.[69] However she went on to accept that that was not always possible. One prominent theme within the present law is that a child, as far as possible, should have one father and one mother, and can never have more than one mother or one father. Richards has complained of the 'very persistent prejudice that children should never have more than two parents and when a new one arrives, an old one has to go'.[70]

F. Parental orders: surrogacy[71]

A married couple can become parents through a parental order. This is designed for use following a surrogacy arrangement. Surrogacy involves an agreement whereby the 'gestational mother'[72] agrees to bear a child for someone else ('the commissioning parent or parents'). The Surrogacy Arrangements Act 1985 defines a surrogacy arrangement as one made before the woman began to carry the child 'with a view to any child carried in pursuance of it being handed over to, and parental responsibility being met (so far as practicable) by another person or persons'.[73] The aim is that the gestational mother will hand over the baby after birth to the commissioning parent and that the gestational mother will not exercise parental responsibility. Surrogacy can cover a wide range of different forms. The genetic link between the commissioning parents can vary: the gestational mother could be impregnated with both the sperm and the egg of donors; or the child could be born through the gestational mother being artificially inseminated with either the father's or a sperm donor's sperm.[74]

Whatever the form of the surrogacy, the legal attribution of parenthood is straightforward. It is clear that the gestational mother is the mother and the genetic father is the legal father unless he is a sperm donor providing sperm to a licensed

---

[69] *Re R (A Child)* [2003] 1 FCR 481 CA, para 27.

[70] M. Richards (1995a: 21). See also Kandel (1994).

[71] Harding (1987); Douglas (1991: ch. 7); Hibbs (1997); and Cook, Day Sclater and Kaganas (2003) provide useful discussions of surrogacy.

[72] Often known as the surrogate mother, although there has been some debate over whether it is the commissioning mother or the gestational mother who is the surrogate: see D. Morgan (1994).

[73] Section 1(2) (as amended by Children Act 1989, Sch 13, para 56).

[74] Many clinics will refuse to aid a surrogacy arrangement: Douglas (1993: 63).

clinic. However, it is possible for the commissioning couple to apply to a court for a parenting order, the effect of which is that they will be treated as the parents of the child. On the making of the order the child will be treated as the child of the applicants.[75] The order will vest parental responsibility exclusively in the applicants and the parental status and parental responsibility of anyone else (and specifically the gestational mother) will be thereby extinguished.[76] The order will be registered in the Parental Order Register.[77] To obtain an order it is necessary to show:

1. Either the sperm, or eggs, or both, came from the commissioning husband or wife.
2. The treatment that resulted in the pregnancy was provided by a licensed clinic.
3. The applicants must be married.
4. The applicants must both be over 18.
5. At least one of the applicants must be domiciled in UK.[78]
6. The child must, at the time of the order, live with the applicants.[79]
7. The order must be made within six months of the child's birth.[80]
8. The genetic father[81] must give full and unconditional consent[82] to the making of the order.[83]
9. The gestational mother must give her full and unconditional consent to the making of the order, at least six weeks after the birth.
10. The husband of the woman who gave birth to the child must give his full and unconditional consent.
11. Money or other benefits have not been given to the surrogate mother, unless they are reasonable expenses[84] or the court has retrospectively authorised the payments.[85]
12. The pregnancy was not the result of sexual intercourse between the surrogate mother and male applicant.
13. The court must decide to make the order with the child's welfare being the first (but not paramount) consideration.[86]

---

[75] Although the child will still be within the prohibited degrees of the birth family for marriage purposes and the law of incest.
[76] HFEA 1990, s 30(9)(a) and Parental Orders (Human Fertilisation and Embryology) Regulations 1994, SI 1994/2767.
[77] When someone is 18 he or she can be supplied with a copy of his or her birth certificate (which will reveal the identity of the birth family) and counselling facilities will be available: Adoption Act 1976, s 51, applied by Parental Orders (Human Fertilisation and Embryology) Regulations 1994.
[78] This includes the Channel Islands or Isle of Man.
[79] HFEA 1990, s 30(3)(a).
[80] HFEA 1990, s 30(3)(a).
[81] This includes someone who is a father by virtue of s 28(2) or s 28(3) of the HFEA 1990.
[82] The consents mentioned are unnecessary if the person cannot be found or is incapable of giving agreement.
[83] This requirement is of consent to the order, not just consent to the application: HFEA 1990, s 30(2), (3), (5).
[84] E.g. maternity clothes, loss of earnings.
[85] *Re Q (Parental Order)* [1996] 1 FLR 369 at p. 373, where expenses of £8,280 were authorised. £12,000 was authorised in *Re C (Application by Mr and Mrs X)* [2002] FL 351.
[86] Parental Orders (Human Fertilisation and Embryology) Regulations 1994, Sch 1.

It should be stressed that this is a highly restrictive list of requirements. Most notably, the applicants must be married and at least one of them have a genetic link to the child. However, there is no requirement that the couple be approved by the local authority as suitable parents, as would be the case if they wished to adopt the child. If the commissioning couple are unable to apply for a parenting order, or if the application fails, then it is still open to ask for a residence order authorising that the child live with the commissioning couple.

G. Adoption

Adoption will be discussed in detail in Chapter 11. There are two points to be stressed here. The first is that before adoption takes place, prospective adoptive parents must undergo close scrutiny through the adoption panel of the local authority. The court will further consider whether the adoption is in the child's best interests. The court can make the order only if the parents consent or, *inter alia*, the court decides that it would be in the child's welfare for the parents' consent to be dispensed with. Secondly, once the adoption order is made, the adoptive couple acquire the full status of parenthood. They do not merely obtain parental responsibility but are considered by the law to be the child's parents.

5. LOSING PARENTHOOD

Legal parenthood will only come to an end if an adoption order is made or a parental order under s 30 of the Human Fertilisation and Embryology Act 1990 is awarded.[87] In either of these cases the original parents (the parents at birth) cease to be the legal parents and the applicants take over as parents.

6. SOCIAL PARENTS

Under this heading we will discuss the various ways the law treats those who are caring for the child in a parental way, even though they may not actually be the parents. There are several categories: guardianship; foster parents; special guardians; treating a child as a child of the family; step-parents; and others caring for children.

A. Guardianship

The law is naturally concerned about children whose parents die. In part this is dealt with by enabling parents with parental responsibility to appoint someone to be a guardian of their children in the event of their death.[88] The courts can also appoint a guardian. There is no restriction over who can be appointed as a

---

[87] See page 294.

[88] At one time the law stated that the father was the 'guardian' of his children and therefore had a higher status than the mother, but this notion of a parent being a guardian was abolished by the Guardianship Act 1973.

guardian[89] and more than one guardian can be appointed.[90] The parents may appoint anyone they choose, although step-parents are common choices. A local authority cannot be appointed as a guardian.[91]

(i) The appointment of guardians by parents

Parents with parental responsibility can appoint guardians,[92] as can people who are guardians themselves. But a father without parental responsibility cannot appoint a guardian; nor can a non-parent with parental responsibility. The appointment of a guardian must be written, dated, and signed.[93] Usually the appointment is made as a term in a will, although this is not necessary.

At what point does the guardianship come into effect? This depends upon whether or not one of the parents has a residence order at the time when a parent dies:

1. Where a residence order has been made in favour of one of the parents the guardianship will take effect on the death of the parent with the residence order, even if the other parent is still alive and has parental responsibility. In such a case the child will have both a parent and a guardian.
2. Where there is no residence order in place, the guardianship only comes into effect once the last remaining parent with parental responsibility dies.[94] So if a couple are married and the mother appoints a guardian and then dies, the appointed guardian will not actually become a guardian until the father also dies. By contrast, if a father is unmarried and without parental responsibility then the mother can appoint a guardian who will take office immediately on her death.

The explanation for the distinction between cases where there are or are not residence orders seems to lie in the fact that if there has been a residence order the court may have decided not to give residence to the other parent because they were unsuitable. In such a case enabling the parent with the residence order to appoint a guardian may in effect protect the child. However, the law has been criticised. There are two particular concerns. The first is that the law produces uncertainty. Both the parent and the guardian may have parental responsibility,[95] but the law does not say with whom the child should live. This need not cause us too much concern because the parties could resolve any dispute by applying to the court for a residence order if they are not able to reach agreement between themselves. The second concern is one of principle. Bainham argues that the position is contrary to the principle of continuing parental responsibility.[96] In theory, both parents with

---

[89] It seems even a child can be a guardian of a child, but this would be highly unusual.
[90] Children Act 1989 (hereafter CA 1989), s 6.
[91] Nor can the director of social services be appointed in order to circumvent this restriction (*Re SH (Care Order: Orphan)* [1995] 1 FLR 746 at p. 749).
[92] Although a guardian can only be appointed by a person over the age of 18.
[93] CA 1989, s 5(5).
[94] CA 1989, s 5(7), (8). The surviving parent can apply for the appointment to be ended if he or she wishes.
[95] If the parent was an unmarried father he may not have parental responsibility.
[96] Bainham (1998a: 181–5).

parental responsibility are on an equal footing and if one dies the other should take over. Certainly the law does not sit easily with the 'natural parent presumption' (that the child is better off with the natural parent unless the natural parent is manifestly unsuitable).[97] The law could be supported on the basis that the parent with the residence order has been given the right to decide with whom the child will live and that this power should continue after death. More convincing is the argument that, by giving both the guardian and the parent the authority to care for the child, the law maximises the chances that someone will be able to take over care of the child on the death of the parent with the residence order.

The person appointed to be guardian does not need to have been approved by the court or the local authority. It is notable that there is a very limited control on the making of an appointment. The absence of control over such appointments is in marked contrast to adoption or fostering.[98] However, there is power in the court to revoke a guardianship and this power could be used if the guardian was unsuitable. It is still arguable that a power to revoke guardianship once it has become apparent the guardian is unsuitable is not as effective protection for a child as requiring a would-be guardian to undergo some kind of vetting process.

(ii) The appointment of guardians by courts

The court may consider appointing a guardian where the parents have both died without either of them appointing anyone as guardian of their children.[99] The court can also appoint a guardian even though the parents have appointed other guardians. This might occur if the person appointed by the parents as guardian is unable or unwilling to carry out the role. The court only has the power to appoint a guardian if there is no parent with parental responsibility who is alive, or if the parent with the residence order has died.[100] Usually this will follow an application to the court by the proposed guardian, although the court can act on its own motion. In deciding who to appoint, the child's welfare is to be the paramount consideration.[101] Clearly the court is likely to want to appoint someone who knows the child well.[102]

(iii) The legal effects of guardianship

The effects of guardianship are as follows:

1. The guardian acquires parental responsibility.
2. The guardian can object to adoption.
3. The guardian can appoint a guardian to replace them on their death.

---

[97] Discussed further in Chapter 9.
[98] Douglas and Lowe (1992).
[99] Or appointing an unsuitable or unwilling guardian.
[100] CA 1989, s 5(2).
[101] Though there is no requirement to consult the checklist in s 1(3) of CA 1989.
[102] *Re C (Minors) (Adoption by Relatives)* [1989] 1 FLR 222, [1989] FCR 744.

4. A guardian is not liable to provide financially for a child under the Children Act 1989 or child support legislation, nor under social security legislation.[103]
5. There are no succession rights on the intestate death of the guardian.[104]
6. No citizenship rights pass through a guardian.

It should be noted that guardians are given more 'rights' than a non-parent with parental responsibility (e.g. the rights on adoption), although they are not given all of the rights and responsibilities of a parent with parental responsibility. Although guardians are not liable for assessment under the child support legislation, guardians are under a legal duty to maintain the children and provide education, adequate food, clothing, medical aid and lodging. The explanation is that there was a fear that guardians would be deterred from accepting guardianship if they could become financially responsible for the child under the child support legislation.

(iv) Revoking an appointment

Section 6 of the Children Act 1989 deals with revocation of a guardianship appointment. The guardianship can be revoked in the following ways:

1. The parent who made the appointment makes a subsequent appointment. This will revoke the first appointment unless it is clear the parent was seeking to appoint a second guardian.[105]
2. The parent who made the appointment can revoke it by a signed and dated document.[106]
3. If the appointment is made in a will it is revoked if the will or codicil is revoked.[107]
4. If the appointment is made by a document, the destruction of the document will end the appointment.[108]
5. If a spouse is appointed as guardian[109] this will be revoked by a subsequent divorce.[110]

(v) Disclaimer

A guardian can disclaim the appointment within a reasonable length of time.[111] The disclaimer must be in writing. Once someone disclaims guardianship he or she ceases to have the rights and responsibilities of guardianship. There is no need for

---

[103] Social Security Administration Act 1992, s 78. It should be noted that guardians might be liable to support the child on their divorce under the Matrimonial Causes Act 1973 if the child were regarded as a 'child of the family'.
[104] Nor can the guardian claim in the event of the child's death.
[105] CA 1989, s 6(1).
[106] CA 1989, s 6(2).
[107] CA 1989, s 6(4).
[108] CA 1989, s 6(3).
[109] For example, if a step-parent is appointed as guardian.
[110] CA 1989, s 6(3A).
[111] CA 1989, s 6(5).

a person to consent to becoming a guardian, so the burden rests on the guardian to make the non-acceptance of the appointment clear as soon as possible.

(vi) Termination

A court order can terminate guardianship. Anyone with parental responsibility, or the child him- or herself, can apply for a revocation, as can the court on its own motion.[112] The welfare principle governs the issue. The court may also decide to appoint a replacement guardian. The kind of circumstances in which the court may terminate a guardianship are where the guardian is failing properly to care for the child or where there is a dispute between, say, an unmarried father and the guardian which cannot be resolved, and the court decides the child's long-term future is with the father.

Termination of guardianship will occur on the death of the child; the death of the guardian; or on the child reaching majority. It may well be that the guardian's powers will terminate on the minor's marriage, but there is no clear provision to this effect.

B. Foster parents

(i) The nature of foster parenthood

Foster parents[113] are people who look after children on a long-term basis, but are not related to them. The term therefore covers a wide variety of arrangements: from a friend asked by a mother to care for her child while the mother has a lengthy time in hospital; to a family approved by a local authority to look after children who have been taken into local authority care. The law draws an important distinction between those placements which are private (arranged by parents) and those which are public (arranged by the local authority).

(ii) Private foster parents

The Children Act 1989 defines a 'privately fostered child'[114] as a child under 16 years of age cared for by someone who:

1. is not a parent;
2. does not have parental responsibility for the child;
3. is not a relative; and
4. has accommodated the child for at least 28 days.

The requirement that a foster parent must accommodate a child for at least 28 days means that babysitters, day-care centres, playgroups and nurseries are not classified as foster parents.

---

[112] CA 1989, s 6(7).

[113] Although the statute refers to 'foster parents', local authorities prefer to refer to 'foster carers'.

[114] CA 1989, s 66. See Laming (2003) for a call that the government reconsider the law on private foster arrangements.

There is, in practice, limited regulation of private foster parents.[115] There is no need for a court or local authority to approve a private fostering arrangement, although the local authority should be notified by the foster parents of the fact they are fostering or intend to foster.[116] The local authority, in theory, can inspect the house where the child is living to check that it is suitable for fostering and may even supervise the fostering. In practice, many private fostering arrangements go unreported to any organ of the state.[117] Even where the local authority is notified of the arrangement, it is unlikely to intervene unless there is evidence that the child is being harmed.

Foster parents do not automatically acquire parental responsibility.[118] They are normally in the same position as anyone else who happens to be caring for a child at a particular time. They can rely on s 3(5) of the Children Act 1989:

A person who—
(a) does not have parental responsibility for a particular child; but
(b) has care of the child
may (subject to the provisions of this Act) do what is reasonable in all the circumstances of the case for the purpose of safe-guarding or promoting the child's welfare.

The courts are most likely to become involved in private fostering arrangements when the parent asks the private foster parent to return the child and the carer refuses. A notable case of this kind was *Re K (A Minor) (Wardship: Adoption)*,[119] where the biological parents handed over a child to an older childless couple when their child was only six weeks old. The biological parents later sought the return of the child. The older couple were well educated, wealthy, and close to the child. By contrast, the biological parents were poor, had a criminal record and a history of drug abuse. Nevertheless, the court preferred the natural parents. The Court of Appeal said that it could not be permitted for a court to order that children be removed from their parents simply because the children would be better off with foster carers. This case demonstrates that if the matter comes to court the position of the foster carers is weak. Unless the parents are utterly unsuitable, the child will be returned to them. However, if the genetic parents are happy with the fostering arrangement then the foster carers are in a reasonably secure position, unless a local authority could establish that the grounds for a care order could be established.

(iii) Local authority foster parents

Local authority foster parents have a very special position in the Children Act 1989. The details of their position will be discussed in Chapter 11, but the law seeks to hold together two policies. On the one hand, there is the realisation that foster parents and

---

[115] It is now possible for a person who is thought by a local authority to be unsuitable to be a foster parent to be disqualified.

[116] Children (Private Arrangements for Fostering) Regulations 1991, SI 1991/2050, r 4.

[117] Barton and Douglas (1995: 107) suggest that compiling the register is not high on the list of priorities of a local authority and that the power of inspection is rarely used; see Laming (2003).

[118] In *Re M (a child)* [2002] 1 FCR 88 the child was found to have family life with the foster carers for the purposes of article 8 of the European Convention on Human Rights.

[119] [1991] 1 FLR 57, [1991] FCR 142.

children can form a close relationship which should be recognised and protected.[120]
On the other hand, local authority foster parents are not normally intended to be permanent carers and it is necessary to ensure that local authorities can remove the child
(perhaps with a view to placing the child with prospective adopters) when necessary.
The balance is struck by restricting the foster parent's ability to apply for a residence
order until the foster parents have cared for the child for three years.

C. Special guardians

The Adoption and Children Act 2002 created the status of special guardianship.
This is intended to cover those who are full-time carers of children but are not
going to take on the full status of parenthood. This is discussed further in Chapter
11.

D. Those who treat a child as a child of the family

Even if an adult is not a child's genetic parent, legal consequences will follow if he
or she treats a child as 'a child of the family'.

(i) What does 'a child of the family' mean?

The phrase 'child of the family' means any child of a married couple and any child
treated by a married couple as a child of their family.[121] The definition therefore
covers both genetic children of the marriage and a child to whom the spouses are
not genetically related, but whom they have brought up as their child.[122] It covers
stepchildren who are treated by step-parents as their own child. The phrase does
not cover children brought up by unmarried couples.[123] To decide whether a child
is a child of the family the Court of Appeal has proposed the test: 'the independent
outside observer has to look at the situation and say: "does the evidence show that
the child was treated as a member of the family?" '.[124] Therefore, the test focuses
on the conduct of the adult rather than their beliefs.[125] The child must be treated
as a child of *a family*. There must be a family – a husband and wife living
together.[126] The child cannot be treated as a child of a family due to actions before
he or she was born.[127] In *A v A (Family: Unborn Child)*[128] the man married a pregnant woman, believing the child to be his, but after the marriage, yet before the
birth, the wife left the man. It was decided that he had not treated the child as a

---

[120] Foster carers and their children can have family life together for the purposes of article 8: *R (on the application of L) v Manchester CC* [2002] FL 13.
[121] CA 1989, s 105(1).
[122] Foster children placed by a local authority or voluntary agency are excluded from the definition.
[123] *J v J (A Minor: Property Transfer)* [1993] 2 FLR 56, [1993] 1 FCR 471.
[124] *D v D (Child of the Family)* (1981) 2 FLR 93 at p. 97 CA, per Ormrod LJ.
[125] *Carron v Carron* [1984] FLR 805 CA.
[126] Cohabiting for a fortnight was sufficient in *W v W* [1984] FLR 796.
[127] *A v A (Family: Unborn Child)* [1974] Fam 6.
[128] [1974] Fam 6.

child of the family because the only way in which the husband had treated the child as if it were his own was before the birth. The decision has been criticised by some as being unduly narrow. It certainly could be that a wife could decide to go ahead with a pregnancy because of her husband's support. If he leaves her just before the birth there is an argument that he should be responsible for financial support.

One case which indicates how difficult the definition can be to apply is *Re A (Child of the Family)*.[129] Here two grandparents were looking after their grandchild after the mother fell ill. The grandparents in due course divorced and the issue arose whether the child was treated as a child of their family. The grandfather argued that he had treated the child as a grandchild and not as a child of his marriage. The court disagreed, relying on the following facts: the child called him 'dad'; the grandparents made important decisions relating to the child without referring to the mother; and the grandparents paid for the child's food and expenses without seeking recompense from the mother.[130]

(ii) The consequences of treating a child as a child of the family

1. On divorce a spouse is liable to provide financial support for any child he or she treated as a child of the family under s 52 of the Matrimonial Causes Act 1973.[131]
2. A person who has treated a child as a child of the family may be liable to provide financial support under Sch 1 to the Children Act 1989.[132]
3. A person who has treated a child as a child of the family may be liable to provide financial support under the Domestic Proceedings and Matrimonial Causes Act 1978, s 38.
4. A person who has treated a child as a child of the family can apply as of right for a residence or contact order without needing to apply to the court for leave.[133]
5. A child may be able to claim against the estate of a deceased adult who has treated them as a child of the family under the Inheritance (Provision for Family and Dependants) Act 1975.[134]

By using the concept of a child of the family the law gives some recognition to social parenthood, although it is restricted to those who are married. The emphasis is on the imposition of responsibilities rather than granting rights. The person treating the child as if the child is his or hers acquires responsibilities towards the child as listed above, although he or she does not thereby acquire parental responsibility. The biological parents will still be liable to support the child under the Child Support, Pensions and Social Security Act 2000, the Children Act 1989 or the Matrimonial Causes Act 1973; and the social parent may also be liable to support

---

[129] [1998] 1 FLR 347.
[130] Financial support on its own is not sufficient to establish that a man is treating the child as a child of the family: *M v M (Child of the Family)* [1984] FLR 796.
[131] See Chapter 5.
[132] See Chapter 5.
[133] CA 1989, s 10(5)(a).
[134] Inheritance (Provision for Family and Dependants) Act 1975, s 1(d). See Chapter 12.

the child under the concept of a child of the family. From the child's viewpoint this greatly increases the chances that someone will support them financially.

E. Step-parents

(i) The legal position of step-parents

A step-parent is a person who marries the mother or father of a child.[135] Inaccurately, but commonly, the term is also used for an unmarried cohabitant who moves in with a child's parent. It has been estimated that one in eight children will at some point in their childhood live in a household with a step-parent.[136] Step-parents, and particularly stepmothers, have often been stigmatised in fairy tales as terrifying figures for children. Research backs up the common perception that relationships between children and step-parents can be difficult, particularly where there are stepbrothers and stepsisters.[137] Of course, the quality of relationship between stepchildren and step-parents varies enormously, as indeed does the relationship between genetic parents and their children.[138] A recent study by Marjorie Smith found that many step-families did not describe themselves using the label 'step-' but simply as families.[139] Another recent study on step-parenthood found that most children felt a continuing commitment to blood ties *and* a commitment to their stepfamilies.[140] In other words, the child felt able to accept the new step-parent but also wished to retain the relationship with the genetic parent. The researchers found 'commitment to the idea of family as a set of flexible interconnecting and supportive relationships'.[141] However, the research suggested that, in times of family stress, the stepfamily emphasised the genetic relationships, rather than the step-relationships.[142] However, another study suggests that socio-economic class plays an important role in whether the child's ties to the biological family or the stepfamily are emphasised.[143]

The law's treatment of step-parents is ambiguous. Even though step-parents in practice often act towards the child as parents and indeed may be treated by a child as if they were their biological parents, step-parents do not automatically acquire parental responsibility on marrying the parent.[144] However, if the step-parent reaches an agreement with the child's parents with parental responsibility he or she can thereby gain parental responsibility.[145] It should be noted that a step-parent will

---

[135] The social and legal position of step-parents is discussed in M. Smith (2003). Ribbens McCarthy, Edwards and Gillies (2003) found that many stepfamilies reject the 'step-' terminology and regarded themselves simply as families.

[136] Haskey (1994).

[137] Bar-Hava and Pryor (1998).

[138] Ferri and Smith (1998); Ribbens McCarthy, Edwards and Gillies (2003).

[139] M. Smith (2003).

[140] Bornat, Dimmock, Jones and Peace (1999).

[141] Bornat, Dimmock, Jones and Peace (1999).

[142] See also Edwards, Gillies and McCarthy (1999).

[143] Ribbens McCarthy, Edwards and Gillies (2003).

[144] Bartlett (1984: 914) argues that the step-parent should gain parental rights on marriage to the parent, but lose them on divorce.

[145] CA 1989, s 4A. This section was added by the Adoption and Children Act 2002. For a discussion of the vulnerable position of the step-parent before these reforms see Masson (1984: ch. 14); Lowe (1997c).

need the consent of the non-resident parent (if he or she has parental responsibility) for this to happen. The alternative for a step-parent is to apply to the court for a parental responsibility order. This will be used, no doubt, mainly where the non-resident parent is refusing to consent to the sharing of the parental responsibility. The step-parent who acquires parental responsibility in either of these two ways will not lose it if their marriage to the parent comes to an end. However, they can have that parental responsibility brought to an end by a court order.[146] These provisions apply only to a person who marries a parent; they do not apply to a cohabitant of a parent. Another option for a step-parent is to adopt the child.[147] The step-parent is not under a legal obligation to support stepchildren, although if he or she treats a child as a child of the family he or she may be liable on divorce or separation to support the child, under the Matrimonial Causes Act 1973. On divorce a court may award a step-parent a contact order, but there is no presumption in favour of such an order.[148]

F. Others caring for the child

A family friend or relative may care for a child on a day-to-day basis without having an official role. Such a person does not acquire parental responsibility simply because he or she is caring for a child. However, the law does provide some ways in which day-to-day carers are regulated by the law:

1. It is possible to delegate parental responsibility. Under s 2(9) of the Children Act 1989 a person with parental responsibility may 'arrange for some or all of it to be met by one or more persons acting on his behalf'.[149] There is no need to obtain court approval of the delegation. However, delegation does not absolve someone with parental responsibility from any legal liability. For example, a parent may be guilty of a criminal offence involving neglect of children, even though they have delegated parental responsibility to someone else, as s 2(11) makes clear.
2. Under s 3(5) of the Children Act 1989 if an adult is caring for a child he or she 'may ... do what is reasonable in all the circumstances of the case for the purpose of safeguarding or promoting the child's welfare'. The exact scope of this power and to what extent such a carer must consult with the parent is unclear.[150] It is generally accepted that a person relying on s 3(5) cannot overrule a decision of a person with parental responsibility, but there is no provision explicitly to this effect.
3. A social parent with leave could apply to the court for a s 8 order.[151] If the child is living with that adult then he or she could acquire parental responsibility by virtue of a residence order.

---

[146] The application to do so can be brought by a person with parental responsibility or the child.
[147] See further, Chapter 11.
[148] A contact order is available but there is no presumption of contact between a child and a step-parent, as was made clear in *Re H (A Minor) (Contact)* [1994] 2 FLR 776, [1994] FCR 419.
[149] CA 1989, s 2(9).
[150] In *B v B (A Minor) (Residence Order)* [1992] 2 FLR 327, [1993] 1 FCR 211 a grandmother caring for a child without parental responsibility had difficulty in dealing with doctors and the educational authority in cases relating to children.
[151] CA 1989, s 10.

4. A carer could seek to use wardship. The best-known circumstances are *Re D (A Minor)*,[152] in which there were plans to sterilise an 11-year-old girl. Her parents did not object, but an educational psychologist who had been seeing the girl was concerned and used wardship to bring the issue to the court. However, wardship is only available in extreme cases. Following the Children Act 1989, in most cases an application for such a s 8 order will be most appropriate.
5. People caring for children have responsibilities. They commit criminal offences if they assault, ill-treat, neglect, abandon or expose a child in a way likely to cause unnecessary suffering or injury. Also a child can be taken into care on the basis of the lack of care provided by a carer.[153]

7. RELATIVES

Here we will consider the position of those who are a child's relatives.[154] First, we will look at the rights of family members under the Children Act 1989. It will also be necessary to examine the right to respect for family life protected under the Human Rights Act 1998. The Children Act defines relatives as including 'a grandparent, brother, sister, uncle, or aunt (whether of the full blood or half blood or by affinity) or step-parent'.[155] In the Children Act there is no clear legal status which flows from being a relation. There are some who argue for a more formalised position for relatives, giving them a clear set of rights. The arguments are made especially in respect of grandparents.[156] Sociological studies demonstrate that most children hold their grandparents in special affection[157] and indeed grandparents often play a major role in child-care arrangements.[158] Over half of women in paid work with a child under five left the child with the child's grandparents.[159] Where a child is disabled, the role played by grandparents can be particularly significant.[160] There are dangers in talking about grandparents as a general group. One study suggested that grandmothers tended to play a more significant role in children's lives than grandfathers, and maternal grandparents than paternal grandparents.[161] In a recent study it was found that, on parental divorce, paternal grandparents often lost contact with their grandchildren and that grandparents suffered depression as a result.[162] This has led some to call for the law to grant grandparents a special legal status with attendant rights.

---

[152] [1976] Fam 185.
[153] *Lancashire CC* v *B* [2000] 1 FLR 583 HL.
[154] For a useful discussion of the psychological role that relatives can play, see Pryor (2003).
[155] CA 1989, s 105. The Family Law Act 1996 gives a much longer list of relatives, which is discussed in Chapter 6.
[156] *Re J (Leave to Issue Application for Residence Order)* [2003] 1 FLR 114. Home Office (1998) expresses the government's views that grandparents play an important role in many children's lives and should be encouraged to do so.
[157] Step-grandparents can play a significant role too.
[158] Hill and Tisdall (1997: 89–90); Douglas and Murch (2002a). For a discussion of the support siblings can offer each other see Beckett and Hershman (2001).
[159] Social and Community Planning Research (2000).
[160] *Re J (Leave to Issue Application for Residence Order)* [2003] 1 FLR 114.
[161] Douglas and Ferguson (2003).
[162] Merrick (2000).

Opponents of such suggestions reply that giving wider family members rights will impinge on the rights of parents to raise their children as they think fit.[163] Further, that to give grandparents and others rights would be to give them rights without having responsibilities for the child.[164] Douglas and Ferguson,[165] arguing against giving grandparents special legal rights, argue that this would work against the norms that generally govern relations between grandparents, their children and grandchildren. They argue that these relationships are governed by 'the norm of non-interference': that is, that grandparents seek to support but not interfere in the role carried out by parents. Further, that the sacrifices that grandparents make for their grandchildren are not seen as part of a reciprocal relationship (i.e. grandparents do not expect anything back from their labours of love for their grandchildren).

This is a complex issue, partly because the nature of the relationships varies so much. For example, some children never see their aunts and to others an aunt may be a 'second mother'. It is therefore perhaps not surprising that the law is reluctant to set out specified rights and obligations flowing from a particular blood relationship. One danger in this area is that, by giving relatives parental responsibility, the child might become confused. An aunt is an aunt, not a parent. That said, parental responsibility is a legal term of art and a phrase unlikely to be used in everyday family life.

Under the Children Act 1989 there are various consequences of being a relative:

1. A relative can apply for a residence order or contact order without leave of the court where the child has lived with the relation for three years (or with the consent of the parents). Even if the child has lived with the relatives less than three years, the relative can still apply for a s 8 order, but leave of the court will be required.[166] A relative is unlikely to be successful in applying for a residence order against the wishes of the parents unless it is shown that the parents are clearly unsuitable.[167] In *Re D (Care: Natural Parent Presumption)*,[168] for example, the court had to decide whether a child should live with his father or grandmother. The Court of Appeal preferred the father, even though he had a history of drug abuse and had a number of children with different women, with some of whom he had no links. However, in *Re H (Residence: Grandparent)*[169] grandparents who had cared for a child for six years were granted a residence order, which was confirmed, despite the mother's objection. This was because there was such a strong relationship between the child and the grandparents. More commonly, a relative may apply for a contact order. In *Re A (Section 8 Order: Grandparent Application)*[170] the grandmother wanted contact with her young grandchildren after a bitter divorce. The Court of Appeal stated that although

---

[163] See Crook (2001).
[164] Kaganas and Piper (2001: 268).
[165] Douglas and Ferguson (2003).
[166] For an argument that in relation to grandparents leave should not be required see Drew and Smith (1999).
[167] *Re D (Care: Natural Parent Presumption)* [1999] 1 FLR 134 CA.
[168] [1999] 1 FLR 134.
[169] [2000] Fam Law 715.
[170] [1995] 2 FLR 153, [1996] 1 FCR 467.

there was a presumption in favour of contact between a parent and a child there was no such presumption of contact between a grandparent and a child, nor between any other relative and a child. It is clear that in each case the court will need to be persuaded that the relationship between the grandparent and the child is a close one and that contact will benefit the child. In many cases the court will be readily persuaded that the relationship is close.[171] The courts have acknowledged that to force a parent to permit contact between a child and a grandparent may be counter-productive if, for example, the parents regard the grandmother as interfering.[172] Siblings, of course, have a strong right to contact, but more distant relatives have been less successful than grandparents in contact cases.[173]

2. A grandparent and other relatives will have a strong case for contact with a child who is in care. If a local authority is 'looking after a child' then it is under a duty to promote contact between the child and the wider family.[174] The cases certainly suggest that contact between a grandparent and a child in care will normally be granted. So in *Re M (Care: Contact: Grandmother's Application for Leave)*[175] the Court of Appeal granted an order in favour of reasonable contact between a child and the grandparent. The court noted that grandparents have a special place in any child's affections. The court felt that when a child was in care a local authority had the burden of proof in proving why contact should not go ahead. In *Re W (A Child) (Contact: Leave to Apply)*[176] Wilson J accepted that the question of whether there was a presumption of contact between grandparents and children would need to be reconsidered.

3. Where the parents of a child have died without appointing a guardian, the courts are likely to consider appointing a relative as guardian.

4. The local authority is under an obligation to consider placing a child with relatives before taking a child into care.[177] Further, a local authority which is considering putting a child up for adoption should consider the possibility of placing a child with a relative before considering adoption by a stranger.[178] In *Re K (Adoption and Wardship)*,[179] where a Bosnian child was adopted in the UK, the fact that the grandfather and extended family were not consulted was seen as a serious flaw in the procedure, although in *Re R (A Child) (Adoption: Disclosure)*[180] Holman J held that the relatives should not be informed of the proposed adoption of a new-born baby, after the mother asked that the birth be kept confidential.

---

[171] *Re M (Care: Contact: Grandmother's Application for Leave)* [1995] 2 FLR 86, [1995] 3 FCR 550.

[172] *Re F and R (Section 8 Order: Grandparent's Application)* [1995] 1 FLR 524. See also *Re S (Contact: Grandparents)* [1996] 1 FLR 158, [1996] 3 FCR 30 CA.

[173] *G v Kirkless MBC* [1993] 1 FLR 805, [1993] 1 FCR 357 and *Re A (A Minor) (Residence Order: Leave to Apply)* [1993] 1 FLR 425, [1993] 1 FCR 870.

[174] See Chapter 11.

[175] [1995] 2 FLR 86, [1995] 3 FCR 550 CA.

[176] [2000] 1 FCR 185.

[177] Adoption and Children Act 2002, s 1(4)(f) requires the court to consider the child's relationship with her relatives before making an adoption order.

[178] *Re R (A Child) (Adoption: Disclosure)* [2001] 1 FCR 238.

[179] [1997] 2 FLR 221; [1997] 2 FLR 230 CA.

[180] [2001] 1 FCR 238.

5. Domestic violence injunctions. Under the Family Law Act 1996 non-molestation injunctions are available between 'associated persons', which includes relatives.[181]
6. Relatives may treat a child as a child of their family and this will trigger a series of rights and responsibilities.[182]
7. In certain circumstances a relative may be in a position to invoke wardship.[183]

8. THE HUMAN RIGHTS ACT 1998 AND THE RIGHT TO RESPECT FOR FAMILY LIFE

Under the Human Rights Act 1998:

1. Everyone has the right to respect for his private and family life, his home and his correspondence.
2. There shall be no interference by a public authority with the exercise of this right except such as is in accordance with the law and is necessary in a democratic society in the interests of national security, public safety or the economic well-being of the country, for the prevention of disorder or crime, for the protection of health or morals, or for the protection of the rights and freedoms of others.[184]

This is a clear recognition that family members other than parents can be protected through the law. The relevance of this article will be discussed throughout the book, but here a few general points will be made.

A. What is family life?

In defining family life it is clear that the paradigm of family life for the European Court of Human Rights has been a husband and wife and children.[185] In *B v UK*[186] the European Court expressed this when explaining that there could be a variety of kinds of unmarried father, ranging from an ignorant or indifferent father to the relationship with the child being 'indistinguishable from the conventional family based unit'. Clearly, here the court regarded the 'conventional family-based unit' as a married couple with children. However, the European Court has not restricted family life to married couples and relationships through blood.[187] Article 8 has been found to cover unmarried couples;[188] siblings;[189] uncle/nephew;[190]

---

[181] See Chapter 6.
[182] See page 302.
[183] See *Re H (A Minor) (Custody: Interim Care and Control)* [1991] 2 FLR 109, [1991] FCR 985.
[184] Article 8 of the European Convention.
[185] Liddy (1998). For a discussion of the understanding of family life under the European Court of Justice see Stalford (2002).
[186] [2000] 1 FLR 1, [2000] 1 FCR 289.
[187] *X, Y, Z v UK* [1997] 2 FLR 892, [1997] 3 FCR 341 ECtHR.
[188] *X, Y, Z v UK* [1997] 2 FLR 892, [1997] 3 FCR 341 ECtHR. A suggestion that, on divorce, a couple ceases to have family life was made by the court in *L v Finland* [2000] 2 FLR 118 at p. 148; but this seems inconsistent with the general approach in the previous cases: e.g. *Keegan v Ireland* (1994) 18 EHRR 342 ECtHR.
[189] *Moustaquim v Belgium* (1991) 13 EHRR 802. See also the discussion in Beckett and Hershman (2001).
[190] *Boyle v UK* (1994) 19 EHRR 179.

grandparents/grandchild;[191] and foster parents/foster-child.[192] However, it appears that the further the relationship departs from the paradigm (i.e. the more remote the blood relationship), the more evidence is needed to show that there was a close social relationship between the parties. For example, in *Boyle v UK*[193] it was accepted that the uncle and nephew had 'family life' because the uncle proved he was a father figure to the boy. Had he actually been the boy's father, the court would readily have accepted that their relationship constituted family life and there would have been no need to show that their relationship was especially close. The English courts have been more willing to assume family life exists with wider relatives. In *Re R (A Child) (Adoption: Disclosure)*[194] Holman J was willing to accept to hold that a new-born baby had family life with her wider family, including uncles and aunts.

If the case involves a married couple the court will willingly find family life even if the spouses are not living together.[195] An unmarried couple can demonstrate family life, but it depends on the nature of the relationship: the court will consider whether the parties live together; the length of the relationship; and whether they have demonstrated commitment to each other, for example by having children.

Perhaps the most controversy surrounds fathers and children. Although mothers inevitably have family life with their children,[196] this is not true of fathers. It appears that fathers can acquire family life with their children in two ways:

1. By actually caring for the child in a practical way.[197] This does not require the father to live with the child, but must involve some kind of contact.[198]
2. If the conception of the child takes place in the context of a committed relationship. Therefore if the father was married, engaged or in a permanent cohabiting relationship at the time of the conception he will have family life with the resulting child.[199]

This means that if the conception is part of a casual relationship and the man does not undertake a significant role in the care of a child, he will not be regarded as having family life with a child. In *G v The Netherlands*[200] a man donated sperm to a lesbian couple. After the child's birth he sought to have regular contact with the child. The European Court held that he did not have family life with the child.[201] Similarly in *Leeds Teaching Hospital NHS Trust v A*[202] it was held that a man who

---

[191] *L v Finland* [2000] 2 FLR 118.
[192] *X v Switzerland* (1978) 13 DR 248.
[193] (1994) 19 EHRR 179.
[194] [2001] 1 FCR 238.
[195] *Abdulaziz et al. v UK* (1985) 7 EHRR 471.
[196] *Re B (Adoption by One Natural Parent to Exclusion of Other)* [2001] 1 FLR 589, per Hale LJ.
[197] This does not seem to require that the father live with the child: *Söderbäck v Sweden* [1999] 1 FLR 250.
[198] *Söderbäck v Sweden* [1999] 1 FLR 250.
[199] *Keegan v Ireland* [1994] 3 FCR 165 ECtHR although subsequently the European Commission on Human Rights in *M v The Netherlands* (1993) 74 D&R 120 stated that there had to be some close personal ties to establish family life.
[200] [1990] 16 EHRR 38.
[201] See also *Mikulic v Croatia* [2002] 1 FCR 720 ECtHR where a father who had only ever had a casual relationship with the mother and had played no significant role in the care of the child was held not to have family life.
[202] [2003] 1 FCR 599.

provided sperm to enable a woman to become pregnant through assisted reproduction could not thereby claim to have family life with the child. To some these cases constitute gender discrimination and there is no justification for assuming that a mother, but not a father, deserves family life with the child. To others the courts are recognising that through pregnancy and birth all mothers have demonstrated a relationship which deserves protection under the European Convention on Human Rights, while fathers' relationships with their children can be so minimal that they do not automatically justify protection.

The European Court has not yet faced the difficulty that deciding who is a family can depend upon from whose perspective one views the case. For example, in *X, Y, Z v UK*[203] Bainham argues it was understandable that from the point of view of the adults concerned the family consisted of the transsexual, his partner and their child. However, Bainham suggests that from the child's perspective the sperm donor may be regarded as part of the child's family. Indeed by focusing on what the father has 'done' in deciding whether or not he has family life, might be said to be an adult way of considering the issue.[204] Should a child lose his or her right to family life with his or her father because of the father's lack of concern over the child? A similar point can be made about *Olsson v Sweden (No. 1)*[205] where a child was removed from her parents and placed with foster parents. The court regarded that the placement infringed the parents' right to respect for family life. However, it was arguable that from the child's point of view the foster parents were now as much part of her family as her parents, and returning her to her parents would infringe part of her right to respect for family life with the foster parents.[206] Even more could be made of this point. At least one study suggests that during divorce children are more likely to seek and find support and comfort from friends than their relatives.[207] Does this suggest that from the perspective of children the significance the law attaches to family and the irrelevance of friendship is misplaced?

B. What is respect?

The European Court has made it clear that the requirement of respect for family life places both positive and negative obligations on the state. Article 8 may not only require the state not to interfere in family life but it may on occasions require the state to act positively to promote family life. For example, in *Hokkanen v Finland* the European Court held that the failure of the state to provide an effective mechanism for enforcing a contact order between a father and his child was an infringement of the right to respect for family life.[208] In *Stubbings v UK*[209] it was explained:

> although the object of article 8 is essentially that of protecting the individual against arbitrary interference by the public authorities, it does not merely compel the state to abstain

---

[203] [1997] 2 FLR 892, [1997] 3 FCR 341 ECtHR; Bainham (1998a).
[204] Bainham (2002a).
[205] (1988) 11 EHRR 259 ECtHR.
[206] Such an argument was accepted in *Re M (a child)* [2002] 1 FCR 88.
[207] Butler, Scanlan, Robinson et al. (2002).
[208] [1996] 1 FLR 289, [1995] 2 FCR 320 ECtHR; Feldman (1997).
[209] (1997) 1 BHRC 316.

from such interference: there may, in addition to this primary negative undertaking, be positive obligations inherent in an effective respect for private or family life. These obligations may involve the adoption of measures designed to secure respect for private life even in the sphere of the relations of individuals between themselves.

Thus the Court has reasoned that some positive acts may be a necessary part of respect for family or private life and so a failure to provide these can be an interference with respect for family life. For example, *Raumussen v Denmark*[210] suggests that respect for family life may involve providing an effective and accessible remedy so that a man can establish that he is the father of a child. Another important example will be discussed in Chapter 11 and that is that if the state takes a child into care then the state is under an obligation to enable contact between the child and his or her family to take place, unless to do so would harm the child.

C. When can infringement be justified?

Paragraph 2 of article 8 sets out the circumstances in which an infringement of the right to respect for family life is justified. To justify the interference in the right it must be shown that:

1. The interference was in accordance with the law.
2. The interference was in pursuance of one of the listed aims (e.g. national security).
3. The interference must be necessary. It is not enough to show that the interference was reasonable or desirable. It must be shown that there was a pressing need for the interference.[211] Further it must be shown that the extent of the intervention was proportionate. In other words there was not a less interventionist measure which would have adequately protected national security (or whichever of the listed aims was being pursued).

It is submitted that the nature of the quality of relationship between the parties is relevant, not only in deciding whether there is family life, but also in deciding whether the interference is justified under para 2. The further the applicant is from the paradigm of a married parent/child relationship, the more likely it is that state action will not be regarded as interference in the relationship; or if it is interference that it will be seen as justifiable. Thus to prevent a grandparent from visiting a child in care requires less justification than preventing a parent from having contact.[212]

9. WHO HAS PARENTAL RESPONSIBILITY?

In many ways this is a more important question than 'who is a parent?', but, as we shall see, 'who is a parent?' and 'who has parental responsibility?' are actually linked questions. It is necessary to distinguish the way mothers, fathers, non-parents and

---

[210] (1985) 7 EHRR 371 ECtHR.
[211] *Dudgeon v UK* (1982) 4 EHRR 149.
[212] *Price v UK* (1988) 55 D&R 1988, *L v Finland* [2000] 2 FLR 118.

local authorities may obtain parental responsibility. First, the law will be set out in broad outline and then more detailed points will be discussed.

A. Outline of the law

(i) Mothers

All mothers[213] automatically have parental responsibility.

(ii) Fathers

A father[214] will have parental responsibility in any of the following circumstances:

1. he is married to the mother;[215] or
2. he is registered as the father of the child on the birth certificate;[216] or
3. he enters into a parental responsibility agreement with the mother; or
4. he obtains a parental responsibility order from the court;[217] or
5. he has been granted a residence order;[218] or
6. he has been appointed to be a guardian;[219] or
7. he has adopted the child.

(iii) Non-parents

Someone who is not a parent can obtain parental responsibility in the following ways:

1. He or she will acquire parental responsibility if appointed as a guardian.[220]
2. A person who is not a parent or a guardian will acquire parental responsibility when he or she obtains a residence order.
3. A person who is granted an emergency protection order thereby acquires parental responsibility.

It should be noted that, in these circumstances, although the non-parent will have parental responsibility, he or she will not obtain the rights that flow from being a parent.

(iv) Local authorities

Local authorities can acquire parental responsibility as follows:

---

[213] That is, the woman regarded as the mother in the eyes of the law.
[214] That is, a man who is regarded as a father under the legal definition.
[215] The phrase 'married to the mother' has a wide definition. This includes a child born as a result of assisted reproduction (CA 1989, s 2).
[216] CA 1989, s 4, as amended by the Adoption and Children Act 2002.
[217] CA 1989, s 4.
[218] CA 1989, s 12(2).
[219] CA 1989, s 5(6).
[220] CA 1989, s 5(6).

1. When a local authority obtains a care order it acquires parental responsibility.[221]
2. When a local authority obtains an emergency protection order it acquires parental responsibility.

B. Consideration of the law in more detail

It is necessary to discuss some specific aspects of some of the points above.

(i) Mothers

The rule that all mothers automatically have parental responsibility for their children can be explained on the basis that the mother throughout the pregnancy has sustained the child and has undergone great sacrifices for her child. Because she has demonstrated her commitment to the child through pregnancy and has accepted that she will be involved in the care for the child after the birth, it is in the child's interests that she obtains parental responsibility.

(ii) Fathers

There is much debate over whether all fathers should automatically obtain parental responsibility. The present law restricts which fathers might obtain parental responsibility. For a father there are two sources of parental responsibility: first, the mother (if she has married him or has permitted him to be registered as the father on the birth certificate or has entered a parental responsibility agreement with him); secondly, the court (if the unmarried father is granted one of the orders mentioned above). The law appears to take the view that a father needs to be vetted and approved before he can acquire parental responsibility. But it should also be noted that a father (unlike the mother) has a choice: if a man wishes to father a child without having parental responsibility he may do so. There is no way that a mother can force the unmarried father of her child to have parental responsibility against his wishes.[222] The mother does not have the option of giving birth to a child but not taking parental responsibility. This may well indicate cultural assumptions that it is 'natural' for mothers to care for children, but this is not necessarily expected of fathers.

We shall consider in further detail the different ways in which an unmarried father can acquire parental responsibility.

(a) The registered father

The Adoption and Children Act 2002 amends s 4 of the Children Act 1989 to provide that fathers who are registered as the father of the child on the birth certificate will automatically acquire parental responsibility. This significant change in the law will greatly increase the number of unmarried fathers who have parental responsibility. Eighty per cent of births to unmarried couples are registered by both mother

---

[221] CA 1989, s 44(4)(c).
[222] She cannot register him on the birth certificate without his consent.

and father. However, it is important to appreciate that a father can only appear on the birth certificate if the mother agrees to this. So in a way this is simply a particular kind of parental responsibility agreement.[223] On the birth of the child the mother is specifically given the chance to share responsibility with the father. There have been concerns that this change in the law will in fact deter fathers from being registered because they falsely believe that if they are given parental responsibility they will become financially liable for the child.[224] Eekelaar voices a different concern, that mother's may be deterred[225] from registering the father's name for fear that doing so would give him rights he could use to interfere with her upbringing of the child.[226] If either of these concerns materialised this would work against the policy of enabling children readily to discover the identity of their birth parents, discussed later in this chapter.

(b) Parental responsibility agreements

A father and a mother can enter a parental responsibility agreement under s 4(1)(b) of the Children Act 1989. The agreement must be in the prescribed form and recorded.[227] It must be signed by both parties and taken to a court where the certificate will be witnessed and signed. Critics of the procedure argue that the technicalities that surround it deters fathers from using it. Indeed, the number of parental responsibility agreements has not been high.[228] The reason, no doubt, is that if the parents are happy together they do not see the need for a formal agreement, but if they are in dispute then there will be no agreement. On the other hand, there are those who suggest that the procedure is too easy. There is no effective check to ensure that the applicant is the father of the child; that the mother's consent is freely given;[229] or that the man is suitable to have parental responsibility.

In *Re X (Parental Responsibility Agreement)*[230] the Court of Appeal regarded the right of a mother and father to enter into a parental responsibility agreement 'free from state intervention'[231] as an important aspect of the right of respect for family life under article 8. The right to enter into the parental responsibility agreement exists even though the child has been taken into care.[232]

---

[223] For an argument that the new provision robs mothers of their powers to control a father's access to parental responsibility see Wallbank (2002a). However, it should be noted that an unmarried father does not have an automatic right to place his name on the birth certificate, without the mother's consent.

[224] In fact fathers are liable under the Child Support Act 1991 whether or not they have parental responsibility.

[225] In fact he suggests they would be 'well advised' not to (Eekelaar (2001d: 430)).

[226] Although he points out having the father registered may make it easier to claim child support against him.

[227] An oral agreement could amount to a delegation of parental responsibility under CA 1989, s 2(9).

[228] About 3,000 parental responsibility agreements are registered each year. This is, of course, a tiny percentage of the children born to unmarried parents.

[229] There was some evidence that the mother's signature could be forged (CAAC (1993: 13)), although since the Parental Responsibility Agreement Regulations 1994, SI 1994/3157 the agreement must now be signed in the local court and witnessed by a court official before being lodged at the court. A copy is then sent to the mother and father.

[230] [2000] 1 FLR 517.

[231] This is perhaps a little misleading, as the agreement does have to be lodged at the court and so the state is involved.

[232] In *Re X (Parental Responsibility Agreement)* [2000] 1 FLR 517.

(c) Section 4 applications

If the father is not registered on the birth certificate and is unable to obtain the mother's consent, he can apply under s 4 of the Children Act 1989 for a parental responsibility order. Only genetic fathers can apply under s 4, and if there is any doubt whether the applicant is the father, DNA evidence will be required. Orders are only available in respect of a child under 18.[233]

In deciding whether to grant parental responsibility, s 1(1) of the Children Act 1989 applies,[234] and therefore the welfare of the child is to be the paramount consideration.[235] Although the Court of Appeal in *Re H (Parental Responsibility)*[236] have stated that it is wrong to suggest that there is a presumption in favour of awarding parental responsibility, we shall see that the cases demonstrate that only in unusual circumstances will parental responsibility not be granted. The statistics show that in 90 per cent of cases the application succeeds.[237]

Most of the cases considering applications under s 4 use as a starting point *Re H (Minors) (Local Authority: Parental Responsibility) (No. 3)*,[238] where it was stated that these factors should be taken into account:

(1) the degree of commitment which the father has shown towards the child;
(2) the degree of attachment which exists between the father and the child; and
(3) the reasons of the father applying for the order.

A little more focus to the test was set out by Mustill LJ in *Re C (Minors)*:

> ... was the association between the parties sufficiently enduring; and has the father by his conduct during and since the application shown sufficient commitment to the child to justify giving the father a legal status equivalent to that which he would have enjoyed if the parties had married?[239]

The fact that the applicant has applied for an order shows commitment in itself,[240] but the Court of Appeal has stressed that even if there is attachment and commitment the court still might not award parental responsibility if other factors indicate that it would be contrary to the child's interests.[241] Each case depends very much on its own facts, but the following points have arisen in previous cases and will be considered:[242]

1. *Contact with the child.* Where there is regular contact and financial support the court will readily find there is sufficient commitment between the father and

---

[233] Even if the child is under 16. There is no need to demonstrate that the circumstances are exceptional: cf. CA 1989, s 9(6).
[234] As does CA 1989, s 1(5): *Re P (Parental Responsibility)* [1998] 2 FLR 96, [1998] 3 FCR 98, although Gilmore (2003) suggests that whether the welfare principle applies to applications for a parental responsibility order is yet to be definitively decided.
[235] Ward J in *D v Hereford and Worcester CC* [1991] 1 FLR 215, [1991] FCR 56; *Re F (A Minor) (Parental Responsibility Order)* [1994] 1 FLR 504 CA; *Re H (Parental Responsibility)* [1998] 1 FLR 855 CA.
[236] [1990] 1 FLR 855 CA.
[237] Six per cent of the applications are refused and in 4 per cent of cases no order is made.
[238] [1991] FLR 214, [1991] FCR 361.
[239] *Re C (Minors) (Parental Rights)* [1992] 2 All ER 86 at p. 93.
[240] *Re S (A Minor) (Parental Responsibility)* [1995] 2 FLR 648 at p. 659.
[241] *Re P (Parental Responsibility)* [1998] 2 FLR 96, [1998] 3 FCR 98.
[242] Gilmore (2003) provides a very useful discussion of the case law.

the child for a parental responsibility order to be appropriate.[243] However, just because there has never been contact between the father and the child, it does not necessarily mean that parental responsibility will not be granted, especially if the father can demonstrate that the lack of contact was due to the mother's actions. That said, as yet there is no case where a father has never seen the child but was awarded parental responsibility. Indeed in *Re J (Parental Responsibility)*[244] parental responsibility was refused on the basis that the child never knew her father, he was 'almost a stranger'.

2. *Status.* In *Re S (A Minor) (Parental Responsibility)*[245] the Court of Appeal emphasised that parental responsibility gave an unmarried father the status 'for which nature had already ordained that he must bear responsibility'. This judgment suggests that the parental responsibility order merely confirms what the father's status is according 'to nature'. The parental responsibility order was referred to as a 'stamp of approval'. In this case, even though the father had been convicted of possessing paedophilic literature, he was still awarded parental responsibility. It is not clear what to make of these statements of the Court of Appeal. They certainly suggest that there need to be good reasons if an unmarried father is not to be granted parental responsibility.

3. *Child's reaction to failed application.* In *C and V (Minors) (Parental Responsibility and Contact)*[246] Ward LJ stated that it was good for a child's sense of self-esteem that the child thought positively about an absent parent and so 'wherever possible the law should confer on a concerned father that stamp of approval because he has shown himself willing and anxious to pick up the responsibility of fatherhood and not to deny or avoid it'. Similarly, in *Re S (A Minor) (Parental Responsibility)*[247] it was stated that:

> ... the law confers upon a committed father that stamp of approval, lest the child grow up with some belief that he is in some way disqualified from fulfilling his role and that the reason for the disqualification is something inherent which will be inherited by the child, making her struggle to find her own identity all the more fraught.[248]

4. *The child's view.* If the child is sufficiently mature, the child's views on whether the application should succeed can be taken into account.[249] In *Re G (A Child) (Domestic Violence: Direct Contact)*[250] the fact that a child (aged nearly 4) did not want to have any contact with the father and was fearful when he was mentioned led Butler-Sloss P to hold that it was inappropriate to grant him parental responsibility.

---

[243] *Re S (A Minor) (Parental Responsibility)* [1995] 2 FLR 648.
[244] [1999] 1 FLR 784.
[245] [1995] 2 FLR 648.
[246] [1998] 1 FLR 392, [1998] 1 FCR 57; see Eekelaar (1996).
[247] [1995] 2 FLR 648.
[248] At p. 657. A cynic might doubt whether the child will appreciate the significance of parental responsibility if he or she does not see his or her father. The order is more likely to affect the father's image of himself than his child's.
[249] *Re J (Parental Responsibility)* [1999] 1 FLR 784.
[250] [2001] 2 FCR 134.

5. *Misuse.* A father should not be denied a parental responsibility order simply because there are fears that the father may misuse the order.[251] If necessary, the court can make orders restricting the father's use of parental responsibility[252] or requiring him to obtain the leave of the court before bringing any proceedings.[253] It is even possible to remove parental responsibility from a father.[254] In *Re S (A Minor) (Parental Responsibility)*[255] the mother's argument that the father might misuse the order on the basis that he had been unreliable about providing financial support for the child and had been convicted of possessing paedophilic literature failed. It was stated that it was wrong to focus on the potential misuse of the order and, instead, a father wishing to undertake the responsibilities associated with parenthood should be entitled to do so. That said, if there is very clear evidence that the father is determined to disrupt the mother's care of the child and is applying for parental responsibility to enable him to do so then the court will decline to grant the order.[256]

6. *Parental responsibility and other orders.* A parental responsibility order can be made even though a contact or residence order is inappropriate.[257] In other words, it is not necessary to show that the father will ever practically be able to exercise parental responsibility in order for him to be awarded it. So, parental responsibility can be ordered even though the child is about to be adopted.[258] A good example of this point is *Re C and V (Minors) (Parental Responsibility and Contact)*,[259] where a father had a close relationship with a child. Unfortunately, the child had severe medical problems and needed constant medical attention. The mother had learned the skills necessary to care for the child, but the father had not. It was therefore felt inappropriate to grant contact to the father, but still he was granted parental responsibility as a mark of his commitment to the child.

7. *Reprehensible conduct of the father.* Simply because the father has harmed the child in the past does not necessarily mean that a father will be denied parental responsibility. However, in *Re T (Minor) (Parental Responsibility)*[260] the application was denied because the father had shown no understanding of the child's welfare and had treated the mother with violence and hatred.[261] In *Re P (Parental Responsibility: Change of Name)*[262] the Court of Appeal refused to interfere with a refusal to grant parental responsibility on the basis that the father's repeated criminal offences and resulting imprisonment demonstrated (the court felt) his lack of commitment to the child. In *Re H (Parental*

---

[251] *Re S (A Minor) (Parental Responsibility)* [1995] 2 FLR 648 at p. 657.
[252] For example, through a prohibited steps order or a specific issue order.
[253] CA 1989, s 91(14).
[254] CA 1989, s 4(3).
[255] [1995] 2 FLR 648.
[256] *Re P (Parental Responsibility)* [1998] 2 FLR 96, [1998] 3 FCR 98; *Re M (Handicapped Child: Parental Responsibility)* [2001] 3 FCR 454.
[257] *Re P (A Minor) (Parental Responsibility Order)* [1994] 1 FLR 578.
[258] *Re H (Minors) (Local Authority: Parental Responsibility) (No. 3)* [1991] FLR 214, [1991] FCR 361.
[259] [1998] 1 FLR 392, [1998] 1 FCR 57.
[260] [1993] 2 FLR 450, [1993] 1 FCR 973.
[261] See also *Re G (A Child) (Domestic Violence: Direct Contact)* [2001] 2 FCR 134.
[262] [1997] 2 FLR 722, [1997] 3 FCR 739.

Responsibility)[263] the father had injured the son deliberately and there was even some suggestion that sadism was involved, and therefore the court did not grant parental responsibility as there was a future risk. So it appears that if the misconduct reveals a lack of commitment to the child or that the man is a danger to the child then the misconduct may be a strong reason to deny parental responsibility.

8. *Mother's possible reaction to the granting of the order.* The fact that the mother might bitterly oppose the order and there is hostility is not a reason for refusing the order,[264] although if the child's mother will be so upset that this may affect her parenting ability and causes the child to suffer, then parental responsibility may be denied.[265]

9. *Mother's death.* In some cases the argument had been accepted that parental responsibility should be granted to a father so that he can take over care of the child if anything happens that might prevent the mother from caring for the child, for example if she dies.[266]

10. *The father's ability to exercise parental responsibility.* In *M v M (Parental Responsibility)*[267] the father suffered from learning disability and head injuries and Wilson J argued that therefore he was incapable of exercising the rights and responsibilities of parental responsibility.

11. *The father's standing under the Hague convention.* If there are concerns that the child may be abducted and the father needs to use the Hague convention, the father needs parental responsibility to do so. In *Re J-S (A Child) (Contact: Parental Responsibility)*[268] the mother was Australian and the father English, and this was, the Court of Appeal held, an argument in favour of granting the father parental responsibility.

As the above discussion demonstrates, the cases do not always reveal a consistent approach, but it appears that if a father has shown sufficient commitment to the child then a parental responsibility order will be made unless there are serious concerns that he may harm the child. Indeed it is striking that we needed a decision of the Court of Appeal (in *Re H (Parental Responsibility)*[269]) to tell us that a father who had sadistically injured his child should not have parental responsibility.

The readiness of the courts to award parental responsibility is controversial. In discussing these cases it is crucial to remember that they all involve families where the mother is opposing the grant of parental responsibility. If she was in accord, the couple would lodge a parental responsibility agreement. What from one perspective appears to be the court encouraging the father to play his role in the child's life might appear to the mother to be a licence to the man who may have abused her child to interfere in every aspect of the child's life. The real difficulty here is that

---

[263] [1998] 1 FLR 855 CA.
[264] *D v S* [1995] 3 FLR 783; *Re P (A Minor) (Parental Responsibility Order)* [1994] 1 FLR 578.
[265] *Re K* [1998] Fam Law 567.
[266] *Re E (Parental Responsibility: Blood Test)* [1995] 1 FLR 392, [1994] 2 FCR 709; *Re H (A Minor) (Parental Responsibility)* [1993] 1 FLR 484, [1993] 1 FCR 85.
[267] [1999] 2 FLR 737.
[268] [2002] 3 FCR 433.
[269] [1998] 1 FLR 855 CA.

perhaps the notion of parental responsibility is not sufficiently fine-tuned. There is a strong argument for perhaps creating two levels of parental responsibility: one giving all the rights of parenthood and the other giving a lesser level of rights (for example, the right to be consulted on a list of crucial decisions). Returning to *Re S (A Minor) (Parental Responsibility)*, discussed above, to give a father who had a conviction for possession of paedophilic literature the right to clothe, feed, and bathe a child might seem inappropriate, even if there is an argument that he can have a say in fundamental issues, such as where the child should be educated. The difficulty is that the present law on parental rights requires us to give him all or none of the legal rights of a parent.

(iii) Non-parents

It is sensible that if a non-parent is given a residence order, parental responsibility will also be granted because this will reflect the fact that he or she will be carrying out the parental roles. At present only parents or those with residence orders can be granted parental responsibility. There is an argument that the court should have a wider power to make parental responsibility orders. The court has certainly called for this. A good example of the problems of the present law is *Re WB (Residence Order)*,[270] where a man had brought up and cared for a child with the mother. He separated from the mother but it was found (to his surprise) that he was not a father. The court could only grant him parental responsibility by giving him a residence order, but the court felt unable to do so as it was in the child's welfare to stay with her mother. However, the courts have shown greater willingness to make a shared residence order in order to grant parental responsibility if to do so would not be completely artificial.[271]

(iv) Local authorities

This will be discussed in Chapter 10.

10. WHO SHOULD GET PARENTAL RESPONSIBILITY?

A. Unmarried fathers[272]

As we have explained, unmarried fathers in English law do not obtain parental responsibility automatically. An unmarried father may acquire parental responsibility in three ways. The first is by agreement with the mother and being registered as the father on the birth certificate or registering a parental responsibility agreement with the court. The second is by marrying the child's mother.[273] The third is

---

[270] [1995] 2 FLR 1023.

[271] *Re H (Shared Residence: Parental Responsibility)* [1995] 2 FLR 883, [1996] 3 FCR 321 CA.

[272] There has been a real problem in finding a term to describe the father of a child who is not married to the mother. The phrase unmarried father has become widely accepted, although he may well be married – to someone other than the mother.

[273] Only the father of a child obtains parental responsibility of the child by marrying the mother. A stepparent does not thereby acquire parental responsibility.

by persuading the court to make a parental responsibility order. Whether this law is satisfactory is hotly disputed and there is much debate over whether unmarried fathers should get parental responsibility automatically.[274]

The difficulty is that the term 'unmarried father' covers a wide range of relationships. The European Court of Human Rights in *B v UK*[275] has explained the dilemma: 'The relationship between unmarried fathers and their children varies from ignorance and indifference to a close stable relationship indistinguishable from the conventional family-based unit.' In 2002, 40 per cent of births in England and Wales were outside marriage, but in the same year only 8,240 parental responsibility orders were made.[276] About 3,000 parental responsibility agreements are registered each year.[277] This indicates that only a tiny proportion of unmarried fathers have parental responsibility, even though 80 per cent of births to unmarried parents were joint registrations, suggesting that at least that percentage of fathers intended to play an important role in the child's life. Research by Pickford[278] found that although four-fifths of fathers were aware that they were financially liable to support their children, only a quarter of all fathers were aware that there was a difference in the legal rights of married and unmarried fathers.

Very broadly, five approaches could be taken to unmarried fathers and parental responsibility:

1. All unmarried fathers could be given unmarried parental responsibility automatically.
2. All unmarried fathers could be given parental responsibility, but this could be removed on application to the court.[279]
3. A group of unmarried fathers could be given parental responsibility. There could be removal or addition to this group on application to the court.
4. No unmarried fathers could be automatically given parental responsibility, but a procedure could exist whereby they could acquire parental responsibility (or to remove parental responsibility). This is the position in England and Wales at present.
5. No unmarried father is given parental responsibility.

The essential question is where should the burden lie? Should it be on the mother or the state to establish that the father is unsuitable, or on the father to show that he is suitable? At the heart of this issue is what parental responsibility means. The stronger the 'rights' that parental responsibility provides, the more reluctant the law will be in granting it to a wide group of people. However, the more limited the rights the more willing a legal system may be to grant all fathers parental responsibility. The meaning of parental responsibility is discussed in Chapter 8. There is also a dispute over the role of the law here. On the one hand, there are those who

---

[274] Bainham (1989); Lowe (1997c); Lord Chancellor's Department (1998).
[275] [2000] 1 FLR 1 at p. 5.
[276] Lord Chancellor's Department (2003d).
[277] Lord Chancellor's Department (1998).
[278] Pickford (1999).
[279] Parental responsibility for mothers cannot be revoked, except when following the making of an adoption order or a parental order.

emphasise the 'message' that the law gives. They often argue that fathers should be encouraged and expected to fulfil their role as parents and this should be emphasised by giving as many unmarried fathers as possible parental responsibility. Others emphasise the practical effect of giving unmarried fathers parental responsibility and are concerned by the fact that parental responsibility could be misused.

Some of the key issues that have been raised in the debate are as follows:

1. *The balance of power between mothers and fathers.* The case for awarding parental responsibility to only a selection of unmarried fathers runs as follows. Why does the father need parental responsibility? He can carry out all the duties and joys of parenthood (feeding, clothing, playing with the child) without parental responsibility. He only needs parental responsibility when he is dealing with third parties such as doctors and schools. At such times the mother can provide the necessary consent. He would only need parental responsibility if he were wishing to exercise parental responsibility in a way contrary to the mother's wishes.[280] An unmarried father who has been fully involved in the raising of the child might be thought validly to have an important say in the raising of children. But an unmarried father who had limited or no contact with the child should surely not be able to override the mother's wishes. Deech has argued that parental responsibilities:

   > include feeding, washing and clothing the child, putting her to bed, housing her, educating and stimulating her, taking responsibility for arranging babysitting and day-care, keeping the child in touch with the wider family circle, checking her medical condition, arranging schooling and transport to school, holidays and recreation, encouraging social and possibly religious or moral development. Fatherhood that does not encompass a fair share of these tasks is an empty and egotistical concept and has the consequence that the man does not know the child sufficiently well to be able sensibly to take decisions about education, religion, discipline, medical treatment, change of abode, adoption, marriage and property.[281]

   More recently Wallbank[282] has argued that because women assume the primary responsibility for the child their views should be given priority in decisions about whether the father should acquire parental responsibility. She suggests that those who support giving all fathers parental responsibility rely on the 'ethic of justice' (which emphasises the importance of formal equality and general rules), rather than 'the ethic of care' (which emphasises the importance of responsibilities and relationships).[283] She supports privileging the position of mothers who undertake the bulk of the day-to-day work with the child. Opponents of such views will claim that it is wrong to presume that unmarried fathers do not take part in the 'work' of parenting or do not have relationships with their children that are of equal worth to those mothers have.

2. *Fears of misuse.* There is a concern that the non-residential father may misuse parental responsibility. He may see it as a justification for 'snooping' on the

---

[280] Eekelaar (1996); Kaganas (1996).
[281] Deech (1993: 30).
[282] Wallbank (2002a).
[283] See further Sevenhuijsen (1997); Smart and Neale (1999).

mother and continuing to exercise power over her, although it may be said that if a man is of the kind who will pester the mother with legal actions and 'snooping' to check she is being a good mother, he will do so whether or not he has parental responsibility.

3. *Parental responsibility should reflect the social reality.* The argument here is that if a father is carrying out a parental role he should receive parental responsibility. This would mean that the legal position of the father and his social position would match. The parental responsibility could then be seen as the law's stamp of approval for the task he is carrying out.[284]

4. *Rights of the child.*[285] The issue could be examined from the perspective of the rights of the child. It could be argued that a child has a right to have the responsibilities of parenthood imposed on both his or her mother and father. Deech strongly opposes such an argument: 'The basic rights of the child are not furthered by delivering more choice to the unmarried father. Legal rights which he may acquire are choices for him; that is, he may or may not choose to exercise them. Such choice is a limitation on the rights of the child.'[286]

5. *The rights of the father.* Some claim that the English law, in failing to provide an unmarried father with parental responsibility, breaches the Human Rights Act 1998. There are ways that such a claim may be made:

   (a) *Discrimination on the grounds of sex.* Article 14 states: 'The enjoyment of the rights and freedoms set forth in this convention shall be decreed without discrimination on any ground such as sex, race, colour, language, religion, political or other opinion, natural or social origin in association with a natural minority, property, birth or other status.' It might be argued that, by giving mothers but not fathers automatic parental responsibility, this is discrimination on the ground of sex. However, this was rejected in *McMichael* v *UK*[287] and *B* v *UK.*[288] This, it is argued, is correct because of the greatly differing roles that men and women play during pregnancy.

   (b) *Discrimination on the grounds of marital status.* Again, referring to article 14, it could be said that the list of prohibited grounds of discrimination is not closed (the article says 'such as', indicating there could be other grounds apart from the ones mentioned in the article). It could therefore be argued that marital status could be added as another prohibited ground and that denying automatic parental responsibility to unmarried fathers is therefore prohibited. *B* v *UK*[289] accepted that it is permissible under the European Convention on Human Rights for a state to treat married and unmarried couples in different ways, if a sound reason for doing so existed. They suggested that, given the wide varieties of unmarried

---

[284] Eekelaar (1996).
[285] See also Fortin (1998a: 323).
[286] Deech (1993: 30).
[287] [1995] 20 EHRR 205 ECtHR.
[288] [2000] 1 FLR 1, [2000] 1 FCR 289 ECtHR.
[289] [2000] 1 FLR 1, [2000] 1 FCR 289 ECtHR.

fathers, it was legitimate for the state to restrict which could receive parental responsibility.

(c) *Breach of right to respect for family life.* Article 8 of the European Convention on Human Rights states that: 'Everyone has the right to respect for his private and family life, his home and his correspondence.' This article certainly protects unmarried fathers[290] but this does not require automatic legal status. The approach taken by the European Court seems to be that, as long as there is a route available by which a father can establish that he should be given parental responsibility, there is no breach of the Convention.

6. *Wrong to impose responsibilities but no rights.* An unmarried father is liable to pay child support under the Child Support Act 1991 but is not automatically awarded parental responsibility. Is it fair that he should suffer the burdens but not gain the benefits that flow from parental responsibility? Deech has argued the opposite. If the father is not willing to show the commitment to the mother and the child by marriage, he should not receive parental responsibility, but should bear financial responsibility.[291] Indeed it could be argued that although it always promotes a child's welfare to have both parents under a duty to support him or her financially, it is not true that it is necessarily in a child's interests to have both parents having the power to make decisions over his or her upbringing. This is true especially if a parent with that power does not know the child.

7. *The rapist father.* The argument that carried much weight in the parliamentary discussion of the issue was that a man who fathered a child through rape should not obtain parental responsibility. To require a victim of rape to persuade a court that the rapist father should have his parental responsibility removed was clearly inappropriate and it was therefore better not to give the unmarried father automatic parental responsibility.[292] This argument is perhaps not as strong as might at first sight appear. It would be possible to have a specific statutory provision preventing convicted rapists[293] (although this would deal only with those rapists who were convicted). In any event there is a danger in relying on a rare situation to establish a general rule.

8. *Uncertainty.* This is one of the strongest arguments in favour of the present law. One benefit of the present law is that it is relatively easy to know whether a man has parental responsibility for a child. He will need to produce his certificate of marriage with the mother, the child's birth certificate, a parental responsibility order or copy of a parental responsibility agreement. If the law were to state that all unmarried fathers automatically obtained parental responsibility then, unless biological tests were done, it would be impossible to know whether a man claiming to have parental responsibility was or was not the father of the

[290] E.g. *Johnston v Ireland* (1986) 9 EHRR 203 ECtHR.
[291] Deech (1993).
[292] The argument overlooks the fact that a husband who rapes his wife gets parental responsibility under the law.
[293] Bainham (1989: 231).

child. As the most common situation where it really matters whether a man has parental responsibility or not is when a child needs medical treatment, it is important that doctors can readily discover whether a father has parental responsibility.

9. *Efficiency and public resources.* The present law seems to suggest that it is not at all difficult for an unmarried father to obtain parental responsibility (although it does involve expense and time) and, if so, it may be asked whether there is any point in having these administrative hoops, with the public costs they involve.[294] On the other hand, it may be that increasing the number of people with parental responsibility will merely increase the scope for bringing disputes to court.

10. *Marriage promotion.* It might be argued that the distinction between married and unmarried fathers is important as part of the promotion of marriage. The belief of the majority of people that marriage does not affect parental rights undermines this argument to a large extent.[295]

The arguments are well balanced.[296] The difficulty is that the cases where parental responsibility matters the least (where the mother and father are jointly raising the child together) are the cases where there are strongest arguments for awarding both parents parental responsibility and the cases where parental responsibility matters the most (the parents have separated and are in dispute over the raising of the child) are the cases where there is the strongest case for putting special weight on the wishes of the parent who carries out the bulk of the day-to-day caring for the child. The truth is that the law is requiring too much of responsibility. A single concept cannot do the job of an acknowledgement of a parent's commitment; be a stamp of approval for their parenting role; provide a parent with all the rights and responsibilities of parenthood; and decide who can make important decisions in relation to children. At risk of further complicating the law, it is suggested the law develops two categories of parental responsibility: those which acknowledge that the father has shown commitment to the child and those which reflect the reality that he is sharing in the day-to-day upbringing of the child.

11. LOSING PARENTAL RESPONSIBILITY

A person with parental responsibility cannot give up parental responsibility just because he or she does not want it any more. Even if the child has to be taken into care because of the parent's abuse, parental responsibility does not come to an end.[297] In *Re M (A Minor) (Care Order: Threshold Conditions)*[298] the father had killed the mother in front of the children and was sentenced to a lengthy term of imprisonment. He still retained parental responsibility. However, parental responsibility can be extinguished in a few ways:

---

[294] In terms of judicial resources and legal aid.
[295] Pickford (1999).
[296] Although most of the academic writing supports a change in the law to permit all fathers to acquire parental responsibility automatically (see Gilmore (2003)).
[297] See Chapter 11.
[298] [1994] 2 FLR 577, [1994] 2 FCR 871 HL.

1. Anyone with parental responsibility will lose it when an adoption order is made. Once an adoption order is made, only the adoptive parents will have parental responsibility.
2. A child's birth mother and her husband will lose parental responsibility when a parental order under s 30 of the Human Fertilisation and Embryology Act 1990 is made.[299]
3. Once a child reaches 18, all parental responsibility for the child comes to an end.[300]
4. If a father has parental responsibility through a parental responsibility order, this can be brought to an end if the court so orders under s 4(3) of the Children Act 1989. An application to do so can be brought by someone with parental responsibility (including the father applying himself) or the child.[301] The welfare principle governs the issue. However, the court may not end a parental responsibility order if there is a residence order still in force in favour of the father. In *Re P (Terminating Parental Responsibility)*,[302] although the parents had made a s 4 agreement, it became clear that the father had caused the baby severe injuries, causing permanent disability. It was held that by his conduct he had forfeited his entitlement to parental responsibility and it was removed. It will require extreme conduct of this kind if the court is to remove parental responsibility under s 4(3).
5. If a person has parental responsibility by virtue of being granted a residence order then when the residence order comes to an end so does the connected parental responsibility. However, a father who has been awarded a residence order (and therefore parental responsibility) will retain parental responsibility even if the residence order is ended.
6. Parental responsibility will, of course, end on the death of the child, although there may be separate rights in respect of burial of the child's body.[303]

12. WIDER ISSUES OVER PARENTHOOD

Having looked through the law regulating parents, we can now look at some of the key issues of debate in this area.

A. What is the basis for granting parenthood?

There has been much discussion on what is at the heart of the concept of parenthood. Four main views will be considered: first, that genetic parenthood is the core idea in the law; secondly, that the law focuses on intent to be a parent; thirdly, that parenthood is earned by commitment to and care of the child. Fourthly, that social parenthood (the day-to-day caring of the child) is the most important part of parenthood. Before considering the arguments in favour of these approaches, it should

[299] See page 294.
[300] CA 1989, s 91(7), (8).
[301] With leave of the court: see Chapter 9.
[302] [1995] 1 FLR 1048, [1995] 3 FCR 753.
[303] *R v Gwynedd, ex p B* [1992] 3 All ER 317.

be noted that they are not necessarily incompatible. All four could be persuasive. As Bainham has argued, by using a variety of understandings of 'parent' the law can recognise different aspects of parenthood. For example, it is then possible for the law to acknowledge that both genetic parent *and* social parent have a role to play in a child's life.

(i) Genetic parentage

It could be claimed that the core notion of parenthood is genetic parenthood. It is clear that there is not an exact correlation between genetic parentage and legal parenthood. The circumstances where a man who is not biologically the father of the child can still be recognised as the father were discussed above. The circumstances where the legal father will not be the genetic father are as follows:

1. A husband may be presumed to be the father of his wife's child, but in fact not be the genetic father. If the genetic father does not seek to challenge the presumption, the husband will be treated as the father.
2. In cases of AID treatment where either the husband is the father under s 28(2) or the partner is the father under s 28(3) of the Human Fertilisation and Embryology Act 1990, the child's father will not be the genetic father.
3. An adopted father will be a father in the eyes of the law, even if he is not the genetic father.
4. Where a father has the benefit of a parental order, he will be the legal father but may not be the genetic father.

However, these circumstances are all rare. The vast majority of genetic parents are parents in law, although not all genetic fathers are awarded parental responsibility, as we have seen. That said, if genetic parentage is at the heart of legal parenthood, it is surprising that the law does not take stronger steps to determine genetic parenthood. It would be possible for our legal system to require genetic testing of every child born to ensure that paternity is known, but it does not. Instead, we are happy to rely on the presumptions of law. One journalist[304] has suggested that 30 per cent of husbands are unaware that they are not the father of their wife's children. If this figure is anything like accurate, then it must bring into question whether genetic parentage is in reality of significance for parenthood, because these husbands will be presumed to be the father in the law's eyes without being genetically the father. Further, there are claims that emphasise that genetic parentage can be unfair in cases of 'sperm bandits' (where men claimed that women obtained their sperm either by lying about whether they were using contraception or when the men were asleep or unconscious).[305]

But why should genetic links be regarded as important at all? There are two main arguments that have been relied upon in favour of biology:[306]

---

[304] Illman (1996).
[305] Sheldon (2001).
[306] J. Hill (1991).

1. *Genetic identity.* It is argued that our genetic parents play a crucial role in our self-identity. The strongest evidence for this is in relation to adopted children, who often seek to find information about their genetic parents. To recognise genetic parenthood acknowledges the importance to the child of the genetic link. It also recognises the importance many parents place on the genetic link to their children.
2. *Genetic contribution.* Some argue that the genetic link is important because the child has been born out of the genetic contribution of the parents. As the child's being results from the contribution of the two genetic parents that contribution must be recognised.

Even if there is not a logical principle to justify the emphasis on genetic parentage, amongst most people in our society the genetic link is regarded as important.

(ii) Intent

Some have argued that the law should now place less emphasis on genetic parentage and that, instead, intent to be a parent is of far more importance. A parent is a parent only if he or she intends to be a parent. There is no doubt that there are some situations where intent to be a parent can be seen as crucial:

1. In assisted reproduction a man jointly receiving treatment with a woman can be treated as the father, even though he has no genetic link. Here his intention to be a parent is respected.
2. A sperm donor can waive his parental status. Here the law respects an intention not to be a parent.
3. Guardianship seems based on intention, but in a negative way in that, unless the guardian expressly disclaims the guardianship, they will be a guardian.[307]
4. Adoption is intent based. An adoption order is made only after a person volunteers to be an adoptive parent.

However, there are problems in emphasising intent when considering the most common origin of parenthood, where normal sexual intercourse is involved. It could be argued that to have sexual intercourse reveals an intent to be a parent. At first this seems an implausible argument, given the rate of unintended pregnancies. However, it is possible to argue that, given the availability of contraception and abortion, where the couple decide to go ahead with a pregnancy they manifest their intent to be parents. But there are difficulties with this. First, a father will have a limited role in law in the decision whether or not the mother has an abortion.[308] Secondly, the decision not to abort may be due to religious or moral beliefs and not necessarily indicate an intention to become a parent. It could be argued that each time a couple engage in sexual intercourse they willingly accept the risk of becoming parents, and this is sufficient intent to be a parent. However, where contraception is used but fails such a presumption would appear to fly in the face of the

---

[307] It does reflect the intention of the parent of who should carry on the parenting role.
[308] A father cannot stop a mother having an abortion: *C v S* [1987] 2 FLR 505 CA. For a critique of such arguments see Sheldon (2003).

facts.[309] Further, it seems a very odd test for parenthood. If I notice that a neighbour is pregnant and would like to act as a father of the child, I cannot claim I have an intent to be the child's parent, which should be recognised in the law. There is also a concern that such an approach would lead to uncertainty. For example, how does one prove one's intent? What exactly is an intent to be a parent? There are also fears that, under the guise of using intent to be a parent, different policies could be used.[310] Could it be said, for example, that a drug addict could have no intent to be a parent because he or she would not be capable of being an effective parent?[311] There are also concerns that focusing on intent might lead to the burdens of parenthood falling on more women than men because it is more likely that a man than a woman will successfully be able to argue that he did not intend to be a parent.[312]

There might, however, be an argument that the intent to be a parent is useful where there are competing claims based on biology. For example, in *Johnson* v *Calvert*,[313] a Californian case, the mother gave birth following a surrogacy arrangement, the commissioning mother having provided the egg. Here both could be said to be the biological parent (the commissioning mother by providing the egg, the gestational mother through the care provided during the pregnancy). The court said that intent could be used to resolve the dispute. The court argued that 'but for' the intent of the commissioning parents, the child would not have been born and so they should therefore be regarded as the parents. It was held by Panelli J that it was the commissioning mother 'who intended to procreate the child – that is, she who intended to bring about the birth of a child that she intended to raise as her own – is the natural mother under Californian law'. The argument is not straightforward, as it could equally be suggested that if the gestational mother had not been involved, the child would not have been born. A similar claim could be made for the medical team involved in the assisted reproduction.

It is certainly true that intent-based parenthood would help avoid gender stereotypes or overemphasis of traditional family structures.[314] Recognising intent rather than the stereotypical male and female roles would acknowledge a variety of parenting forms. It would permit more than two people to be parents of a child, and parents would not need to be of the opposite sex. This could be seen as a great benefit of the approach or a great disadvantage, depending on one's view on the traditional family form.[315]

(iii) Earned parenthood

It can be argued that parenthood must be earned. That is that the mother, through pregnancy, has demonstrated her commitment to the child and has formed a bond with the child. If the father has married the mother and can therefore be presumed

[309] Stumpf (1986: 187).
[310] Dolgin (1998).
[311] Douglas (1991: ch. 9).
[312] See the interesting discussion in Sheldon (2001).
[313] [1993] 851 P 2d 774.
[314] Shultz (1990), discussed in Douglas (1994b).
[315] See Chapter 1.

to have offered the mother support through the pregnancy, this also indicates a commitment to the child. But the unmarried father has not earned the parenthood, as he has not shown the commitment to the mother and child by marrying the mother. Although this could be a test for parental responsibility, it is not an explanation of who is a parent. A genetic father can be regarded as a father even though he has done nothing to 'earn the parentage'.

(iv) Social parenthood

At the start of this chapter it was noted that psychologists have stressed the importance of psychological parents. This has led some to argue that the law should recognise the day-to-day work of parenting, rather than the more abstract notions of intended parenthood or genetic parenthood.[316] As noted earlier, psychological evidence suggests that, for children, it is the person who provides their constant care and with whom they have an emotional relationship who is most important. The emphasis on social parenthood would also appeal to those who would argue that the law should emphasise and value caring interdependent relationships between parties.

B. Is there a right to know one's genetic parentage?

(i) What could such a right entail?

The question: 'Does a child have a right to know genetic parentage?' is often asked, but is ambiguous. It is necessary to be quite clear about what such a right would entail. The following could be included:

1. A right to know some non-identifying information about genetic parents.
2. A right to be told the names of genetic parents.
3. A right to meet one's genetic parents.

These rights might arise from as early an age as possible, or only once the child has reached the age of majority. It should be borne in mind that it is arguable that a child has a right *not* to know his or her genetic parentage. Even if we recognise the child's rights, it is necessary to appreciate that as well as these rights there are rights of parents that might also be relevant. There may be a right for a genetic parent to be acknowledged as the parent of a child. There may also be said to be a right of privacy: the right *not* to be acknowledged as the parent. There may also be rights of the social parent – that unwanted revelation of genetic parentage may amount to interference with their family life. Some countries in Europe offer mothers the opportunity to denounce her status of motherhood, the state will arrange alternative carers for the child and there will be no link between the mother and child.[317] Such laws are said to encourage women not to abandon their babies or to abort unwanted children. There are no equivalent laws in England and Wales.[318] There

---

[316] Schaffer (1990).
[317] See the discussion in O'Donnovan (2000).
[318] Although a mother can shortly after birth place her child with the local authority and ask for an adoption to be arranged.

may also be rights of the social parent – that unwanted revelation of genetic parentage may amount to interference with their family life.

(ii) Does the law recognise the right to know one's genetic parentage?

It is clear that the law does not recognise this right as a general one. We do not test every child at birth to determine genetic parentage. That said, with the Child Support Act 1991 and the expense that can fall on a non-residential father, it is likely that more fathers will seek to deny parentage and require tests which will establish the genetic truth. There are certain specific circumstances where the right to know one's genetic parentage arises.

(a) Children born as a result of sexual intercourse

A child can discover from his or her birth certificate who is registered as his or her parents. Once a child is 18 he or she can obtain a copy of the birth certificate, although the name of the father might have been left blank on the certificate. Even if it was filled in, there is no guarantee that the named man is the true father. A child might also discover his or her genetic parenthood if his or her mother is assessed by the Child Support Agency. However, the child has no right to be told who his or her father is by the Child Support Agency.[319]

An adult may seek to rebut one of the presumptions of parentage. However, it is not possible to make a free-standing application for a declaration of parenthood.[320] In other words, a man cannot seek a declaration that he is or is not the father simply out of curiosity. Instead, there must be some other application to which parenthood is relevant; for example, if a man is seeking to have contact with the child or if there is a dispute over whether a man should be financially responsible for a child. Even then the court may decide that the application can be decided without recourse to tests. For example, in *O v L (Blood Tests)*[321] the mother argued that her husband was not the father of the child three years after their separation when the husband sought contact. During the marriage the husband had assumed that he was the father of the child and the court held that, given the close relationship between the husband and the child, contact would be ordered regardless of what the blood tests showed. There was therefore no need to pursue the tests.[322]

When should tests be ordered?

In deciding whether to order tests, the child's welfare is not the paramount consideration. This is because the child's upbringing is not in question and so s 1 of the Children Act 1989 does not apply. Instead, the test is as set out in *S v S, W v Official Solicitor (or W)*,[323] a decision of the House of Lords: 'the court ought to permit a blood test of a young child to be taken unless satisfied that that would be

---

[319] *Re C (A Minor) (Child Support Agency: Disclosure)* [1995] 1 FLR 201.
[320] *Re E (Parental Responsibility: Blood Test)* [1995] 1 FLR 392.
[321] [1995] 2 FLR 930, [1996] 2 FCR 649.
[322] See also *K v M (Paternity: Contact)* [1996] 1 FLR 312, [1996] 3 FCR 517.
[323] [1972] AC 24 HL.

against the child's interests'.[324] The case law on whether tests should be ordered reveals that the courts are pulled by two countervailing arguments. On the one hand, the courts have placed importance on the child's right to know their genetic origins; on the other hand, the courts have placed weight on the concern that if it is found that the child's father is not the mother's husband or present partner, the child's family unit will be disrupted and this will harm the child. The cases show that it can be hard to predict which argument will carry the day.

The leading case emphasising the importance of the child knowing the truth is the Court of Appeal decision in *Re H (A Minor) (Blood Tests: Parental Rights)*.[325] The mother and her husband cared for three children. It was alleged that the youngest of the children was the result of an affair the mother had had. All three children and the husband had a good relationship. Ward LJ argued that 'every child has a right to know the truth unless his welfare clearly justifies the cover-up'.[326] He claimed that such a right was apparent in article 7 of the UN Convention on the Rights of the Child: 'The child should be registered immediately after birth and shall have the right from birth to a name, the right to acquire a nationality and, as far as possible, the right to know and to be cared for by his or her parents.'[327] Ward LJ did add that it was important here that the child's relationship with the husband was not likely to be harmed by finding out the truth about his biological paternity and that the child was likely to find out in any event, as the older brothers were aware of the doubt over the child's paternity. It was better to have the issue resolved now than for the child to find out later.[328]

The arguments in favour of ordering tests have been strengthened after the Human Rights Act 1998. In *Mikulic v Croatia*[329] the European Court of Human Rights held that a child had a right to know her biological parenthood as part of her right to respect for private life under article 8. The state was required to put in place procedures which would protect that right. Notably the court did not claim that a father has the right to establish his paternity under article 8.[330] Indeed in *Yousef v The Netherlands*[331] the European Court held that even though a father had family life with his child it was not in the child's interests to declare formally that he was the father. However, *Yousef* could be criticised on the basis that it failed to consider the child's rights to have his paternity declared. The strength the court might put on the right to know one's genetic background was revealed in *Re J (A Minor) (Wardship)*,[332] where the court accepted that an injunction could be granted to prevent a mother (who was seeking to avoid the carrying out of tests) leaving the country.[333]

---

[324] As summarised in *Re F (A Minor) (Blood Test: Parental Rights)* [1993] Fam 314 at p. 318; see also Fortin (1996).

[325] [1996] 2 FLR 65, [1996] 3 FCR 201.

[326] *Re H (A Minor) (Blood Tests: Parental Rights)* [1996] 2 FLR 65 at p. 80.

[327] The importance of ascertaining the truth was emphasised by the Court of Appeal in *Re H and A (Children)* [2002] 2 FCR 469, [2002] 1 FLR 1145.

[328] This case has been followed in several other cases, e.g. *Re G (Parentage: Blood Sample)* [1997] 1 FLR 360, [1997] 2 FCR 325.

[329] [2002] 1 FCR 720 ECtHR.

[330] *Re T (A Child) (DNA Tests: Paternity)* [2001] 3 FCR 577.

[331] [2002] 3 FCR 577.

[332] [1988] 1 FLR 65.

[333] *Re E (A Minor) (Blood Tests: Parental Responsibilities)* [1993] 3 All ER 596.

The leading case in favour of not ordering tests is *Re F (A Minor) (Blood Test: Parental Rights)*.[334] A wife became pregnant at a time when she was having sexual relations with both her husband and another man. After the affair she was reconciled with her husband and they raised the child together. There had been no contact between the alleged father and the child. The lover applied for parental responsibility. It was claimed that the blood tests would not benefit the child. Indeed there was evidence that the mother's marriage would be harmed and the security of the child's upbringing would be diminished if the blood tests showed the lover to be the father. The Court of Appeal stressed that the welfare of the child depended upon the stability of the family unit, which included the mother's husband. The advantages to the child of the blood tests were, the court thought, minimal, when compared with the benefits of a secure family upbringing.[335] In *Re K (Specific Issue Order)*[336] Hyam J stated that the child's right to know the identity of his father could be outweighed by the child's welfare. There the mother had an obsessive hatred of the biological father, and if the child was told about the father's identity the child would suffer due to the mother's emotional turmoil. He therefore refused to require the mother to inform the child who her father was.

The most recent cases have favoured ordering tests: *Re H (A Minor) (Blood Tests: Parental Rights)*;[337] *Re T (A Child) (DNA Tests: Paternity)*[338] and *Re H and A (Children)*.[339] This suggests that only in cases where there is overwhelming evidence that children will suffer grave harm if tests are ordered are the courts likely to decline to order tests.

Tests and consent

Section 21 of the Family Law Reform Act 1969 states that the court can direct biological tests but not force adults to take blood tests.[340] A child can be tested if the person with 'care and control' of the child consents, or if they do not then the court can order that the tests be carried out if that would be in the best interests of the child.[341]

Adverse inferences and refusals to be tested

Section 23(1) of the Family Law Reform Act 1969 states that if a person fails to take a biological test then the court will draw inferences.[342] If a man is seeking to show that he is the father of a child but refuses to undergo blood tests it will be presumed that he is not the father.[343] Similarly, if a man is seeking to show he is not the father but refuses to undergo blood tests, it will be presumed that he is the

---

[334] [1993] Fam 314, discussed in Fortin (1996).
[335] A similar attitude was taken in *Re CB (Unmarried Mother) (Blood Test)* [1994] 2 FLR 762, [1994] 2 FCR 925.
[336] [1999] 2 FLR 280.
[337] [1996] 3 FCR 201.
[338] [2001] 3 FCR 577, [2001] 2 FLR 1190.
[339] [2002] 2 FCR 469, [2002] 1 FLR 1145.
[340] Section 21(1).
[341] Section 21(3)(b), inserted by Child Support, Pensions and Social Security Act 2000. Blood Tests (Evidence of Paternity) (Amendment) Regulations 2001, SI 2001/773.
[342] *Re A (A Minor) (Paternity: Refusal of Blood Tests)* [1994] 2 FLR 463 CA.
[343] *Re G (Parentage: Blood Sample)* [1997] 1 FLR 360, [1997] 2 FCR 325 CA.

father.[344] If a mother refuses to allow a child to be tested when a man claims he is the father it will be presumed that the man is the father. If a mother refuses to consent to the child being tested when her husband claims he is not the father then it will be presumed that the husband is not the father. In effect, the law is saying that if a person refuses to undergo blood tests, which will establish the truth, then it must be that he or she knows the test will show his or her claim to be false. The position is summarised by Ward LJ in *Re G (Parentage: Blood Sample)*:[345] 'the forensic process is advanced by presenting the truth to the court. He who obstructs the truth will have the inference drawn against him.' The inferences are also a way of encouraging the parties to undergo tests.

An adverse inference will not be drawn if there is a reason for refusing a biological test which is fair, just and reasonable,[346] rational, logical and consistent.[347] For example, if it was contrary to someone's religious beliefs to give a sample for testing then this might be accepted as a valid reason.

(b) Children born as a result of assisted reproduction

As set out in s 31(4) of the Human Fertilisation and Embryology Act 1990, a person can apply to find out whether there is someone who would be their parent but for ss 27–29 of that Act.[348] That is information about the sperm donor whose sperm led to the creation of the child. The information available will, however, be limited and, in particular, the donor's identity must not be revealed for fear that this might deter people from donating.[349] Once the child is over 16 he or she can be told whether they are related to a person they wish to marry.[350]

However, all those sources of information presume that a child knows that he or she has been born as the result of assisted reproductive technology. There is no requirement that a child's birth certificate indicate that a child was born as a result of donated sperm or eggs and there is no legal obligation on parents to tell their children of the circumstances of their conception.[351] There is evidence that over 70 per cent of parents who use reproductive techniques do not tell children of their genetic origins,[352] although the Human Fertilisation and Embryology Authority encourages parents to tell their children. Freeman cites evidence that 60–70 per cent of donors do not object to information being revealed, even if it is identifying information. Indeed, Sweden does not respect the secrecy of genetic parentage,

---

[344] *Re A (A Minor) (Paternity: Refusal of Blood Tests)* [1994] 2 FLR 463 CA.

[345] [1997] 1 FLR 360, [1997] 2 FCR 325 CA.

[346] *Re A (A Minor) (Paternity: Refusal of Blood Tests)* [1994] 2 FLR 463 CA.

[347] *Re G (Parentage: Blood Sample)* [1997] 1 FLR 360, [1997] 2 FCR 325 CA.

[348] The sperm donor's identity could be revealed under this provision. An egg donor would not be considered a mother apart from under HFEA 1990, ss 27–29 and, technically, information concerning an egg donor would not be available under s 31(4).

[349] HFEA 1990, s 31(3)(a). Counselling is available but superficial: Blyth (1995). The government is considering allowing more information to be available to those born following assisted reproduction: Woolf (2000).

[350] HFEA 1990, s 31(4)(b). Marrying your half-sibling may seem fanciful, but in cities where there is a severe shortage of sperm donors (such as Glasgow apparently) this is not so far-fetched.

[351] See M. Roberts (2000) for further discussion.

[352] Maclean and Maclean (1996). See also the studies by Cook (2002) and Golombok, MacCallum, Goodman and Rutter (2002) also finding widespread secrecy surrounding assisted reproduction.

although Deech has argued that this has led some couples seeking assisted reproductive help to go abroad.[353] It is notable that in the UK children born as a result
of assisted reproduction are in a less advantageous position than adopted children,
who can discover the names of their genetic parents.[354]

In *Rose v Secretary of State for Health*[355] two children born as a result of assisted
reproduction using donated sperm sought to find out information about their
sperm donor fathers. The litigation is ongoing, but Scott Baker J has ruled that the
claimants did have a right under article 8(1) of the European Convention to find
out information about their genetic parentage. However, he left open the question
of whether denying them the information could be justified under article 8(2).[356]

(c) Adopted children

This is discussed in Chapter 11.

(d) Establishing parentage

The court has two jurisdictions under which it may seek to determine or declare
parenthood. Under s 56 of the Family Law Act 1986 a child can seek a declaration
that a named person is his or her parent.[357] Section 27 of the Child Support Act
1991 also allows the Secretary of State or person with care to apply for a declaration
of parentage in connection with the operation of the Child Support Act.

The Lord Chancellor's Department[358] suggested that the law should have a unified
procedure so that:

> In any civil proceedings in which the parentage of any person falls to be determined, the
> court may, either on its own motion or an application by any party to the proceedings, give
> a direction—
> (a) for the use of scientific tests to ascertain whether such tests show that a person is or
>   is not the father or mother of that person . . .

This proposal is not yet law.

If the law took seriously a child's right to know his or her genetic origins the legal
position would be quite different. At present the birth register is not an accurate
source of genetic information.[359] The state could require tests to be carried out at
birth to ensure there was an accurate statement of a child's genetic background. At
the very least there could be a requirement for children born using donated gametes
to have that registered as such.[360] The effect of the present law is that the child's
right to know who his or her father was is only given effect when the father seeks to
establish his paternity. It would be more accurate to say that the present law
protects a father's rights to establish his paternity than that a child has a right to
know his or her genetic parents. Notably children whose mothers are in receipt of

---

[353] Deech (1998) see also Gottlieb, Lalos and Lindblod (2000).
[354] Maclean and Maclean (1996).
[355] [2002] 2 FLR 962.
[356] For further discussion of the issues see Sutherland (2001).
[357] Lord Chancellor's Department (1998).
[358] Lord Chancellor's Department (1998).
[359] Freeman (1992b).
[360] Glazebrook (1984: 209).

benefits have the right protected, because their mother will be required to declare who their father is by the Child Support Agency.[361] Any father receiving an assessment from the agency who has any doubts over whether or not he is the father of the child is likely to insist that tests are carried out.

(e) The Human Rights Act 1998 and the right to know one's parentage

As already indicated, the Human Rights Act can be relied upon to support a claim that a child has a right to know his or her genetic origins. Although the European Courts have not been sympathetic to a claim that a father has a right to establish his paternity if he is unable to establish that he has family life with the child,[362] they have been more accepting of the argument that a child has a right to know who his or her parents are. In *Mikulic v Croatia*[363] the European Court of Human Rights found that a child's right to respect for private life included the right to establish who is his or her father. However, this right is not an absolute right. In *Odievre v France*[364] it was held to be permissible for France not to inform adopted children of their biological origins in the name of protecting the privacy of mothers who had given up their children for adoption.[365]

(iii) Should there be a right to know one's parentage?

The main arguments in favour of recognising a right to know one's parentage include the following:[366]

1. Eekelaar argues that there is a right to be informed of one's parentage. He asks whether anyone would choose to live their life on the basis that they had been deliberately deceived about their genetic origin.[367] On that basis he suggests we should recognise the right to know one's parentage.
2. There are claims that knowing parentage produces psychological benefits.[368] There is evidence that some adopted children feel that unless they find out about their genetic origins they suffer psychologically.
3. There is no evidence that children of assisted reproduction are harmed on discovering their origins.[369] Freeman notes that Sweden, Germany, Austria and Switzerland do permit disclosure, without there being disadvantageous consequences.[370]
4. O'Donnovan[371] notes that there are medical reasons why one needs to know one's parentage. For example, if a child is aware that they are genetically predis-

---

[361] See further Chapter 5.
[362] *MB v UK* [1994] 77 A DR 108.
[363] [2002] 1 FCR 720.
[364] [2003] 1 FCR 621.
[365] The argument was that if confidentiality was not respected women who did not want to care for the children they were carrying would be more likely to abort or abandon them.
[366] M. Richards (2003) provides a useful summary of the arguments in favour of the right to know in the context of children born as a result of assisted reproduction.
[367] Eekelaar (1994a).
[368] S. Wilson (1997).
[369] Golombok, Cook, Bish and Murray (1995).
[370] Freeman (1996).
[371] O'Donnovan (1988).

posed to a particular illness, it might be possible to receive preventative treatment.

The main arguments against the right to know one's parentage are:

1. Some argue that social parents have an interest in not having their family life disrupted by information being given to the child they are caring for about his or her genetic origins.[372]
2. The genetic parents may have a right to privacy, which would be infringed by informing the child of their existence.
3. The child may have the right not to know his or her genetic parentage. This argument would be that the law should wait until the child is old enough to be able to decide for him- or herself. The fact that some adopted children choose not to discover their genetic parentage suggests that they would rather not know the information.
4. In the context of assisted reproduction there are concerns that giving children the right to discover their parentage may discourage donation.[373] Many donors are not particularly interested in contact.[374] This will depend on the motivation behind the donation of the sperm or egg. Empirical evidence suggests that the typical sperm donor is a student donating for beer money.[375] Egg donors seem to be motivated more strongly by altruism; indeed egg donation (unlike sperm donation) is not paid.[376] This is partly because egg donation involves a higher degree of risk and injury[377] than sperm donation. More controversially, the technology exists to extract eggs from foetuses. The benefit of this might be thought to be that there would be no possible genetic mother who could seek to play a role in the resulting child's life.

C. Is there a right to be a parent?

(i) What might the 'right to procreate' mean?

It is hard to claim a positive right to procreate, not least because natural procreation requires two people. Few people would seriously suggest that the state should be obliged to provide partners for anyone who wishes to produce a child! Article 12 of the European Convention states that 'men and women of marriageable age have the right to marry and according to national laws governing the exercise of this right found a family'. Although this might suggest a positive right to procreate on a literal reading, this notion has been rejected in *Paton v UK*.[378] In *R v Secretary of State for the Home Office, ex p Mellor*[379] the Court of Appeal held that a married prisoner had no right under article 12 to have access to artificial insemination services to

---

[372] Discussed in Maclean and Maclean (1996).
[373] Price and Cook (1995).
[374] Lui and Weaver (1994).
[375] Golombok and Cook (1993).
[376] Plomer and Martin-Clement (1996).
[377] Smith and Cook (1991).
[378] (1981) 3 EHRR 408 ECtHR.
[379] [2000] 3 FCR 148.

enable his wife to have a child. Such services were a privilege or benefit and no one could claim them as of right.[380] However, the Court of Appeal went on to suggest that there might be exceptional circumstances in which it would be a disproportionate interference in a prisoner's article 8 rights to deny access to assisted reproduction.[381]

First, it can be said there is a right not to have one's natural ability to procreate removed by the state.[382] The notion of compulsory sterilisation, or having to be approved as a suitable parent before engaging in sexual intercourse, would not be acceptable in most democracies.[383] Further, in some of the cases involving sterilisation of mentally handicapped adults, references have been made to the 'right of a woman to reproduce'.[384] The issue was considered by the courts in *Briody v St Helens and Knowsley HA*,[385] where, due to the alleged negligence of a health authority, the claimant was unable to bear children. She sought damages to enable her to enter a surrogacy contract in California, so that a surrogate could be impregnated with the claimant's egg, fertilised with her partner's sperm. She failed but, interestingly, Ebsworth J did not reject the claim on the basis that she had no right to a child but on the basis that she was seeking money to acquire a child by means of a commercial contract that would not comply with UK law. He foresaw that there may be cases where an award could be made to enable a woman rendered infertile to acquire a child.[386]

The second sense in which one might claim a right to procreate is to argue that one should not be denied fertility treatment without good reason.[387] For example, lesbian women, gay men or single people should not be prevented from using such techniques, without good reason.[388] It can be claimed that infertility should be treated as an illness and a would-be parent should be entitled to treatment for this as with any other medical condition. The law governing the provision of treatment by fertility clinics will be discussed shortly, but it should be noted that if there is such a right, it is limited. Under the NHS any right to claim treatment must be regarded in the context of the whole NHS system and there may be monetary or medical reasons why a particular form of treatment is not available.[389] It should be noted that those who are able to afford it may well be able to obtain infertility treatment that is not available on the NHS. This means that maybe the question 'can you buy a baby in the UK?' cannot be answered with a definite 'no'.[390] In *R (On*

---

[380] For an interesting discussion of this case see C. Williams (2002).

[381] Para 45.

[382] Although not expressed in such terms, *R v Human Fertilisation and Embryology Authority, ex p Blood* [1999] Fam 151, [1997] 2 FCR 501 CA could be regarded as accepting a right to procreate.

[383] Archard stresses that a right to bear children must be conditional on the ability to provide for one's offspring: Archard (1993a).

[384] *Re B (A Minor) (Wardship: Sterilisation)* [1988] AC 199; *Re F (Mental Patient: Sterilisation)* [1990] 2 AC 1; *Re D (A Minor) (Wardship: Sterilisation)* [1976] Fam 185.

[385] [2000] 2 FCR 13. The Court of Appeal upheld the judgement in [2002] QB 856.

[386] [2000] 2 FCR 13 at p. 37.

[387] For further discussion see Robertson (1994); J. Harris (1999); Sutherland (2003).

[388] Douglas (1991: 21). Deech (2000: 172) states that the Human Fertilisation and Embryology Authority has taken the line that there is no 'right to a baby'.

[389] *R (On the Application of Assisted Reproduction and Gynaecology Centre and H) v HFEA* [2002] FL 347.

[390] Brazier (1999).

the Application of Assisted Reproduction and Gynaecology Centre and H) v HFEA[391]
Sedley LJ took the view that neither articles 8 nor 12 gave a woman a right to a particular type of assisted reproductive treatment. However, if they did the HFEA
might well be able to show reasons justifying why it should not be provided. That
said if a clinic refused to provide treatment on the grounds of race or sex (or perhaps sexual orientation) it is arguable that the rights under the European
Convention would be engaged.

Some writers have claimed there is a right to reproductive autonomy – the right
to choose whether or not to reproduce. It is argued that the choice to have a child
is intimately bound up with our sense of identity and can therefore be analogous to
other rights that are protected such as the right to religion. The argument most
often made to support such a claim is that as there are no tests or restrictions on
fertile couples who wish to produce a child there should be no restrictions on those
who need the assistance of fertility treatment.[392] Indeed to impose such restriction
could amount to discrimination on the grounds of disability. Opponents of such a
right reject these arguments. O'Neill points out that the right to reproduce involves
the creation of a third party, and this distinguishes it from other rights, such as to
religion or free speech.[393] She argues that reproduction 'can never be justified
simply by the fact that it expresses the individual autonomy of one or two (or more)
would-be reproducers'.[394]

(ii) Should assisted reproduction be permitted?

Although assisted reproduction is now commonly available, whether it should be
permitted is a topic which still engenders debate. Giesen[395] argues:

> Assisted reproduction with both gametes donated must be prohibited as departing too far
> from the traditional setting; donation of female gametes as well disturbs the natural unity
> of bearing and genetic motherhood. We feel that a separation of biological and social
> fatherhood should be avoided as well. Still, we must answer to reality: prohibiting AID
> would turn out to be unenforceable, since AID does not require medical assistance.

So wherever possible reproductive techniques should use gametes from the couple
concerned. The validity of this argument partly turns on the idea of the 'natural'.
Some would say that allowing a couple medical assistance to have a child is allowing them to have what nature intended (a child); others might argue that AID is
equivalent to adultery. Whatever the views of individuals, it appears that Giesen's
approach is in a minority.

Another argument against assisted reproductive techniques is that the world is
already overpopulated and there is no need to create more people. However, the
number of children born through reproductive techniques is too small for this argument to carry much weight. Others argue that assisted reproduction overlooks the

---

[391] [2002] FL 347.
[392] Robertson (1994); J. Harris (1998).
[393] O'Neill (2002: 61).
[394] O'Neill (2002: 62).
[395] Giesen (1997: 260).

real problems connected with the issue: society's expectations which create the sadness often associated with infertility, and emphasises treating the symptoms of infertility, rather than considering its causes.[396]

(iii) Restricting access to assisted reproductive techniques

(a) The legal restrictions

Although the Human Fertilisation and Embryology Act 1990 provides regulations requiring the licensing of clinics it does not restrict who is permitted to have access to the treatment. The crucial provision is s 13(5), which requires clinics, in deciding whether to provide treatment to a particular patient, to take account of 'the welfare of any child who may be born as a result of the treatment (including the need of the child for a father), and of any other child who may be affected by the birth'.[397] This requirement was added after pressure from Conservative MPs and reveals a desire that the traditional concept of the two-parent family be adhered to. There is also a non-binding code of practice. This code of practice encourages clinics to consider, among other things, the capacity of an applicant to parent and the ability to provide otherwise for the child's needs. In law, then, the clinics have a wide discretion in deciding whether to provide treatment in individual cases. Jackson[398] has argued that the section should be deleted, stating that it is not possible to assess the potential welfare of a child born as a result of assisted reproduction. Further, we do not use this criterion to assess whether fertile people can become parents

(b) Restrictions in practice[399]

There is much evidence that clinics, in effect, ration access to reproductive treatments. Studies show that age, sexual orientation, and marital status are taken into account.[400] There have been complaints that clinics follow their own internal guidelines rather than considering each case on its own merits. Certainly there is a lack of consistency in approach, no doubt because the notion of the child's welfare is such an ambiguous concept.[401] Jackson has challenged the restrictions on access to assisted reproduction. She argues that doctors, legislators and regulators are ill-equipped to make the decision about whether an individual deserves to be able to procreate.[402]

(iv) Challenging a refusal to treat

If a parent wishes to challenge the decision of a health authority, the starting place is with the authority's own internal complaints procedure. The only legal remedy for an individual patient is to seek a judicial review.[403] But in *R v Ethical Committee*

---

[396] D. Morgan (1995).

[397] Discussed in Douglas (1993); Jackson (2002).

[398] Jackson (2002),

[399] Douglas (1993).

[400] Six out of 66 clinics did not exclude for treatment anyone on principle. Three of 65 clinics did not treat unmarried couples; 30 of 64 had a maximum age: Douglas (1993); Blyth (1995).

[401] Blyth (1995).

[402] Jackson (2002: 259).

[403] *R v Ethical Committee of St Mary's Hospital (Manchester), ex p H* [1988] 1 FLR 512.

of St Mary's Hospital (Manchester), ex p H[404] it was indicated that it is very unlikely that the court will look into the merits of the decision made by a clinic. However, the court accepted that in extreme cases judicial review could succeed if, for example, the clinic denied treatment on grounds of race.

(v) Should surrogacy be permitted?

(a) Criminal offences

One writer has claimed that there are one hundred surrogate births per year.[405] Section 2(1) of the Surrogacy Arrangements Act 1985 states:

> No person shall on a commercial basis do any of the following acts in the United Kingdom, that is—
> (a) initiate or take part in any negotiations with a view to the making of a surrogacy arrangement,
> (b) offer or agree to negotiate the making of a surrogacy arrangement, or
> (c) compile any information with a view to its use in making, or negotiating the making of surrogacy arrangements;
> and no person shall in the United Kingdom knowingly cause another to do any of those acts on a commercial basis.[406]

To constitute an offence the arrangement needs to be made before the gestational mother becomes pregnant. It should be stressed that the gestational mother and the commissioning mother are not liable for the offence; only third parties who make the arrangements can be guilty of the offence. The UK will therefore never allow the situation which arises in the United States, where companies will advertise mothers at varying rates depending on their age, intelligence and health.[407]

It is also an offence to pay money that constitutes a reward or profit to the gestational mother under a surrogacy arrangement, but payment can cover expenses.[408] Any payments can be authorised under s 30(7) of the Human Fertilisation and Embryology Act 1990: *Re Q (Parental Order)*.[409] Some regard this as effectively permitting commercial surrogacy.[410]

Section 1A of the Surrogacy Arrangements Act 1985 states: 'No surrogacy arrangement is enforceable by or against any of the persons making it.' Without this provision a surrogacy contract might be thought to be enforced in the same way as any other contract. In *Briody v St Helens and Knowsley HA*,[411] the case mentioned earlier where a woman sought damages from a health authority which she claimed had rendered her infertile through negligence to enable her to enter a surrogacy contract, Ebsworth J stated: 'It is one thing for a court retrospectively to sanction breaches of statute in the paramount interests of an existing child, it is quite another

---

[404] [1988] 1 FLR 512.
[405] Laurance (2000).
[406] Section 3 outlaws advertising in relation to surrogacy.
[407] Ince (1993).
[408] *Re Adoption Application AA 212/86 (Adoption Payment)* [1987] 2 FLR 291. In *Re C (Application by Mr and Mrs X)* [2002] FL 351 £12,000 has been accepted as a payment covering expenses.
[409] [1996] 1 FLR 369, [1996] 2 FCR 345.
[410] Jackson (2002: 265).
[411] [2000] 2 FCR 13.

to award damages to enable such an unenforceable and unlawful contract to be entered into.'[412] However, it was left open whether in the future such damages may be available.

(b) What happens when the baby is born?

If the arrangement goes to plan and the baby is handed over to the commissioning parents the following legal options are available:

1. The commissioning parents could take no legal steps. The gestational mother would be the mother and the genetic father the father. The commissioning parents (without a court order) would not have parental responsibility and so would be bringing up the child without formal legal authority. If the child's status ever did come to court, the judge may have little choice but to affirm the status quo and grant a residence order to the commissioning parents. This is demonstrated by *Re H (A Minor) (S.37 Direction)*,[413] where a mother gave birth, but did not want to care for the child. She handed the baby over to two friends, a lesbian couple. One had a history of mental illness and the other had a criminal conviction. Nine months after the birth the matter was brought to the court's attention. By now the child had bonded with the couple and the court accepted that unless there was danger of significant harm to the child it would have to affirm the present arrangements. Had the matter come to court shortly after the birth, with the couple applying for a residence order, it would have been highly unlikely that the court would have made the order. This case demonstrates the difficulties of legal intervention in this area. A surrogacy arrangement may not come to the court's attention until so much time has passed that the court has little option other than to affirm the transaction.
2. The commissioning parents could apply for a parental order. This has been discussed above.
3. The commissioning couple could apply for a residence order.[414] Leave to make the application will be required unless the commissioning husband is the genetic father of the child. In considering the application the court's paramount consideration will be the welfare of the child and the court will not in any sense feel bound by the terms of the surrogacy agreement. However, if the gestational mother does not oppose the application it is likely to be granted.[415]
4. The commissioning parents may also apply for an adoption order if a parental order is not available.[416] One problem that may arise is that the Adoption Act 1976 clearly forbids any 'payment or reward' in private adoption placements. However, the courts have in practice been willing to overlook any payments made under the surrogacy arrangement and have authorised the adoption.[417]

---

[412] At p. 36.
[413] [1993] 2 FLR 541, [1993] 2 FCR 277.
[414] *Re C (A Minor) (Wardship: Surrogacy)* [1985] FLR 846; *Re P (Minor) (Wardship: Surrogacy)* [1987] 2 FLR 421, [1988] FCR 140.
[415] E.g. *Re C (A Minor) (Wardship: Surrogacy)* [1985] FLR 846.
[416] *Re MW (Adoption Surrogacy)* [1995] 2 FLR 759, [1996] 3 FCR 128.
[417] *Re Adoption Application AA 212/86 (Adoption: Payment)* [1987] 2 FLR 291; *Re MW (Adoption: Surrogacy)* [1995] 2 FLR 759.

5. The local authority may wish to investigate in order to decide whether to use any of its powers: for example, to apply for a care order. It may be that the court will make a direction under s 37 of the Children Act 1989,[418] asking the local authority to investigate the child's situation.

If there is a dispute between the commissioning parents and the gestational mother who refuses to hand over the child then the commissioning parents could apply for a residence order. However, by the time the matter reaches the court it may well be that the child will have bonded with the gestational mother. This, in conjunction with the 'natural parent' presumption,[419] is likely to mean that the court will not grant the order and the child will stay with the gestational mother unless she is for some reason clearly unsuitable.[420]

The law's response to surrogacy is in a sense ambiguous. Surrogacy itself is not illegal, but on the other hand surrogacy contracts are not enforceable. Notably two leading government reports on the subject found surrogacy widely 'accepted', but there were grave concerns that it was unethical.[421] The British Medical Association has described surrogacy as acceptable, 'as a last resort'.[422] Yet, as Deech has pointed out, where surrogacy runs smoothly there are no objections to surrogacy; it is when it does not that the media and general public become concerned.[423] The arguments for and against encouraging surrogacy arrangements will now be summarised.

(c) Arguments against surrogacy

1. It has been argued that surrogacy arrangements are contrary to the best interests of children. Bainham has suggested that: 'It is difficult to see how it could be argued that surrogacy is designed *primarily* for the benefit of the child.'[424] However, he adds that talking of the benefits for the child is a little odd in this context. Would it be in a child's interests not to be born? Perhaps the strongest way the argument can be put is that it is not desirable for a child to be born in circumstances that are so likely to result in a dispute between adults, which may well harm the child. Some argue that children born as a result of surrogacy will be confused as to their identity.[425]

2. Surrogacy can be seen as demeaning to women – they are being used as little more than 'walking incubators'. There are some areas of life, it is argued, that are too intimate to be the subject of a contract.[426] Alternatively, it may be argued that the decision to give up a child is such a complex one that it cannot validly be made until after the birth.[427] There are particular concerns where women are forced through poverty to offer themselves as surrogate mothers.[428]

---

[418] *Re H (A Minor) (S.37 Direction)* [1993] 2 FLR 541, [1993] 2 FCR 277.
[419] See Chapter 9.
[420] *A v C* [1985] FLR 445.
[421] Warnock Report (1984: para 8.17); Brazier, Campbell and Golombok (1998: para 2.23).
[422] British Medical Association (1996).
[423] Deech (1998).
[424] Bainham (1998a: 209).
[425] British Medical Association (1996).
[426] Field (1989), although S. Maclean (1990) provides arguments to the contrary.
[427] See the discussion in Lane (2003).
[428] Rao (2003).

3. Surrogacy does not challenge the attitude of society towards infertility and means resources are not directed towards discovering the causes of infertility.

4. The Roman Catholic Church has argued that surrogacy is analogous to adultery, in that it brings a third party into the marriage.[429]

5. There are concerns expressed by some that the child after birth might be rejected by both the gestational mother and the commissioning parents, particularly if the child is born disabled.[430] Even if this does not happen, there are concerns that children will be confused over their biological origins[431] or that the child will be harmed by being denied contact with his or her birth mother.[432] Whether these concerns are such that it would be better for the child not to be born is hotly debated.

6. Commercial surrogacy arrangements commodify children and treat them as chattels to be bought and sold. Of course this argument is only really of weight when considering commercial surrogacy.

(d) Arguments in favour of surrogacy

1. A woman should be allowed to do with her body as she wishes. If she wishes to enter into a surrogacy arrangement and use her body in that way, she should be allowed to. Surrogacy can also be argued as an aspect of procreative freedom. Indeed it is possible to regard surrogacy as a 'gift' to be encouraged.[433]

2. Some people believe that surrogacy is a more appropriate solution for infertile couples than AID or other forms of treatment.[434] However, as Bainham notes, 'surrogacy will be triggered by a man's desire to have his own *genetic* child where his wife or partner is unable to conceive or bear a child'.[435]

3. Surrogacy is inevitable, and therefore best regulated by the law. Its history goes back to biblical times, and even were it to be outlawed, this would simply lead to a black market in surrogacy.

4. It has been argued that surrogacy encourages and enables a variety of family forms. For example, a gay couple would be able to have a child through a surrogate. In early 2000 the media paid much attention to a gay couple who travelled over to the United States and produced a child, using a surrogacy arrangement, and then returned to Britain with the child.[436] In a different case a couple sought unsuccessfully to use a surrogate mother and the sperm of their dead son so that they could have a grandchild.[437] Some will see these examples as a welcome break from the traditional nuclear family form, but others as a misuse of technology.

---

[429] See also the opposition of the Roman Catholic Church (1987).

[430] For a disturbing example of where this occurred see Tong (1985: 56).

[431] See D. Morgan (2003) for argument that could be made in this regard under the Human Rights Act 1998.

[432] Lane (2003: 131).

[433] See the discussion of the use of gift in this context: Ragoné (2003).

[434] Even the BMA states that surrogacy is an acceptable option of last resort: British Medical Association (1996).

[435] Bainham (1998b: 202) (italics changed from the original).

[436] Independent on Sunday (2000).

[437] Laurance (2000).

The government has reviewed the law on surrogacy following the disquiet concerning publicity surrounding Karen Roche.[438] The media claimed that she entered into a surrogacy arrangement with a Dutch couple but ended the arrangement, claiming (untruthfully) that she had terminated the pregnancy. It was alleged that she then entered into a second arrangement with a different couple. In 1998 there was review of surrogacy[439] which led to proposals for a new Code of Practice aimed at controlling the payments to surrogate mothers and the regulation of surrogacy by the UK.[440]

(vi) The right not to procreate

The law, to a limited extent, recognises a right not to procreate. We will not consider the law relating to contraception and abortion in any detail here, only recognising that there is no legal impediment to access to contraception (at least for those over 16), while access to abortion is restricted. Douglas summarises the law's attitude to pregnancy:[441]

> The law therefore gives the woman the right to control her capacity to reproduce through contraception, through its recognition of a right to bodily autonomy in the sense of non-interference. But once the child has been conceived, her freedom to have an abortion depends on a balance which gradually shifts in the foetus's favour though never so far as to favour the life of the foetus over that of the woman.

D. 'Illegitimacy'

Historically, in England and Wales a lesser status has been accorded to children whose parents are not married. At common law an illegitimate child was referred to as a *filius nullius* and had no legal relationship with his or her father, nor even, at one time, with his or her mother. There has been a gradual shifting of the position by permitting a child to be legitimated by the parents' subsequent marriage,[442] and there has been a gradual removal of the legal disadvantages of children born outside of marriage. Now, as we shall see, very few consequences flow from illegitimacy. The key argument behind the reforms is that a child's legal position should not be affected by the parents' decision whether or not to marry. This is reflected in article 2(1) of the UN Convention on the Rights of the Child and in the European Convention on the Legal Status of Children Born out of Wedlock, which both state that a child's status should not depend on whether his or her parents were married. Some jurisdictions have removed the status of the illegitimate child altogether.[443] As confirmed by the European Court of Human Rights in *Sahin* v *Germany*[444] the Human Rights Act 1998 means that any distinction between legitimate and illegitimate children

---

[438] See Hibbs (1997).
[439] Department of Health (1998a).
[440] As D. Morgan (2003) emphasises the use of the Internet for 'procreative tourism' means that if surrogacy were banned in the UK it would be easy for someone to access surrogacy overseas.
[441] Douglas (1991: 18).
[442] Legitimacy Act 1976.
[443] E.g. New Zealand.
[444] [2003] 2 FCR 619.

may infringe article 8 in conjunction with article 14, unless that distinction can be justified as necessary under paragraph 2 of article 8.[445]

The Family Law Reform Acts of 1969 and 1987 have done much to limit the distinction made between legitimate and illegitimate children. Now children whose parents are not married have nearly the same rights as children whose parents are married. Section 1(1) of the Family Law Reform Act 1987 states that for all future legislation any reference to a parent would (unless there was contrary indication) cover both married and unmarried parents. However, there are a few distinctions between children whose parents were married and those whose parents were unmarried, in the areas of citizenship,[446] titles of honour[447] and maintenance.[448] There is also a distinction drawn in the father's legal position because an unmarried father, unlike a married father, does not acquire parental responsibility. In *R (On the Application of Montana) v Secretary of State for the Home Department*[449] it was held that the denial of citizenship to the child of an unmarried father was not an infringement of the right to respect for family life, and therefore article 14 could not be invoked. It could be argued that the fact that children of unmarried parents do not benefit from their fathers having parental responsibility for them is discrimination on the grounds of their illegitimacy. It is also notable that the judiciary still in judgments refer to 'illegitimate' children, even in the House of Lords.[450]

E. Licensing parenthood

As mentioned earlier, it would be possible to have a legal system where parents would only be able to keep children if they were approved by the state as suitable. This is sometimes known as licensing parenthood.[451] Few would support licensing; in fact there is a positive fear of 'social engineering'. In one case Butler-Sloss LJ stated: 'The mother must be shown to be entirely unsuitable before another family can be considered, otherwise we are in grave danger of slipping into social engineering.'[452] Despite this, there are some forms of parenting which are in effect licensed. Most obviously, adoption and parenting orders are made after the court is convinced that the parents are suitable.

13. CONCLUSION

It was not long ago when to ask 'what is a parent?' would have appeared to ask the obvious; but now the question is the subject of lengthy books. The complex sets of

---

[445] *Camp and Bourimi v The Netherlands* [2000] 3 FCR 307 ECtHR.
[446] Discussed in detail in Cretney (1997: 606). In *Re Moynihan* [2000] 1 FLR 113 the House of Lords took the view that this was not in breach of article 8 of the European Convention, nor article 1 of the first Protocol.
[447] Family Law Reform Act 1987, s 19(14).
[448] See Chapter 5.
[449] [2001] 1 FCR 358.
[450] *Dawson v Wearmouth* [1999] 1 FLR 1167; for criticism of them doing so see Bainham (2000b: 482). Hale LJ in *Re R (A Child)* [2001] EWCA Civ 1344 was critical of case reporters who had used the word 'illegitimate' in the title of a case.
[451] Lafollete (1980).
[452] *Re K (A Minor) (Wardship: Adoption)* [1991] 1 FLR 57, [1991] FCR 142.

relationships within which children are raised requires the law to recognise that a variety of people may act towards the child in a parental or quasi-parental way and those who are the child's genetic parents may play little part in the child's life. One major debate in this area is over whether the greater legal recognition should be given to those who are the genetic parents of the child or to those who act socially as the parents of the child. The law is developing ways of recognising both these understandings of parenthood, but the 'balance of power' between the adults involved is controversial. This chapter has also considered other complex issues which have been created by the advent of assisted reproduction: is there a right to be a parent? Does a child have a right to know his or her genetic origins? The future development of reproductive technologies will, no doubt, create many more legal problems.

8

PARENTS' AND CHILDREN'S RIGHTS

This chapter will consider the legal position of parents and children. What rights do parents and children have? How can the law balance the interests of parents and children? Chapter 9 will look at how the courts resolve disputes between children and parents. This chapter is concerned with the legal position if no court order has been made. The chapter will start by considering when childhood begins or ends. It will then examine the position of parents: what obligations and rights does the law impose upon parents? The chapter will then turn to the legal position of children: how does the law protect the interests of children? Do children have any rights? The complex questions of how to deal with clashes between the interests of children and parents and also between different children will be examined. The chapter will conclude by looking at particular issues to see how, in practice, the interests of children and parents are balanced.

1. WHEN DOES CHILDHOOD BEGIN?

English law takes the position that a person's life begins at birth. Before birth the foetus is not a person. But this does not mean that the unborn child is a 'nothing'. In the eyes of the law the foetus is a 'unique organism'[1] which is protected by the law in a variety of ways.[2] For example, it is an offence to procure a miscarriage unless the procedure is permitted under the Abortion Act 1967. However, the law is unwilling to protect the foetus at the expense of the rights of the mother to bodily integrity and self-determination. For example, in *Re F (In Utero)*[3] the social services were concerned about the well-being of the unborn child and wanted to make it a ward of court. The court stated that the unborn child could not be made a ward of court, as it was not a child; although once the child was born there was nothing to stop the court warding him or her.[4] It was held that to enable an unborn child to be warded would give the court inappropriate control over the mother's life. An even more dramatic example is the acceptance by the Court of Appeal that if a mother is competent and refuses to consent to a Caesarean section it is unlawful to carry out the operation on the mother, even if without it the unborn child and the mother would die.[5]

Fathers have no rights in relation to foetuses and are therefore not able to prevent an abortion.[6] The only possible route for a father seeking to prevent an abor-

---

[1] *Attorney-General's Reference (No. 3 of 1994)* [1998] AC 245 at p. 256.
[2] *St George's Healthcare NHS Trust* v *S* [1998] 2 FLR 728.
[3] [1988] Fam 122 CA; Fortin (1988).
[4] See Chapter 11 for further discussion of when a care order can be obtained in such cases.
[5] For a general discussion of the law, see Herring (2000a); Seymour (2000).
[6] *C* v *S* [1987] 2 FLR 505 CA; *Paton* v *BPAST* [1979] QB 276. Approved by the European Convention on Human Rights: *Paton* v *UK* (1981) 3 EHRR 408 ECtHR.

tion is to argue that the proposed abortion is illegal. However, in *C* v *S*[7] it was suggested that the Director of Public Prosecutions is the person who should be bringing any such proceedings, rather than the father.[8]

2. WHEN DOES CHILDHOOD END?

Childhood is a concept in flux. Societies at different times and in different places have had a variety of ideas about when childhood ends.[9] In 1969 the legal age at which a child ceased to be a minor in England and Wales was reduced from 21 to 18.[10] The Children Act 1989 confirms this by defining a child as 'a person under the age of eighteen'.[11] However, there is not a straightforward transformation in the status of the child at age 18. For example, 16 is the age at which a child is entitled to perform some activities[12] and there are still some legal limitations that apply until the person is 21.[13] Further, in *Gillick* v *W Norfolk and Wisbech AHA*[14] the House of Lords accepted that the law must recognise that children develop and mature at different rates and a child under 16 should be recognised as competent to make some decisions for himself or herself. We shall discuss the notion of '*Gillick* competence' and when under 16-year-olds can make decisions for themselves in further detail shortly.

Although childhood legally ends at age 18, the parental role does not necessarily end then. Many over 18-year-olds continue to live with parents, who will continue to provide them with practical, financial and emotional support. Indeed, under certain circumstances parents can be legally obliged to support children financially beyond the age of 18.[15]

3. THE NATURE OF CHILDHOOD

As we have seen already there is no hard and fast line between childhood and adulthood. This has led some to claim that childhood is a social construction.[16] Certainly the notion of childhood is a powerful one in our society and the media are constantly concerned by the position of children. To some we are living in times when childhood is disappearing, with children becoming exposed to adult life at an earlier and earlier stage. In particular there are concerns about the sexualisation and commercialisation of children.[17] These are, it is said, rushing children through what should be an innocent and stress-free time of life.[18] However, others claim that the

---

[7] [1987] 2 FLR 505 CA.
[8] Infant Life (Preservation) Act 1929, s 1.
[9] Ariès (1986); Freeman (1997a).
[10] Family Law Reform Act 1969, s 1.
[11] Children Act 1989, s 105(1); subject to exemptions relating to financial support.
[12] A child can marry at age 16.
[13] For example, applicants for adoption need to have reached the age of 21.
[14] [1986] 1 FLR 229, [1986] AC 112 HL.
[15] E.g. *B* v *B (Adult Student: Liability to Support)* [1998] 1 FLR 373 and see Chapter 5.
[16] In other words, that there is not an objectively true definition of childhood, rather the concept is created by society. See further Fionda (2001); Stainton Rogers (2001); Smart, Neale and Wade (2001: 11).
[17] Although children's materialism may simply reflect society's: Ashworth and Walker (1994).
[18] Stainton Rogers (2001); Mayall (2002: 3).

lines between childhood and adulthood are being reinforced more than ever. Children are being excluded from public places either because their parents fear for their safety or because of concerns about their behaviour. Much government legislation has been directed towards tackling truants and children with anti-social behaviour. It may, in fact, be that both these perspectives have an element of truth:[19] that children are simultaneously being treated as dangerous young people in need of control in some areas of life, but also as vulnerable minors needing protection and/or restraint.[20]

A similar division of opinion can be found in assessment of the position of children in society. Much has been written of the innocence of children and the need to protect them from the vast array of dangers the modern world poses to them, the latest being Internet chatrooms. However, others challenge this view. Jenks argues that children now have taken a central place in meeting the needs of adults. He argues:

> As we need children we watch them and we develop institutions and programmes to watch them and oversee the maintenance of that which they, and they only, now protect. We have always watched children, once as guardians of their own future and now because they have become the guardians.[21]

Jenks then suggests that adults' concern over the vulnerability of children says far more about the insecurity of adults than it does about the reality for children. He also challenges the orthodox view that children are nowadays economically unproductive and are (until they are older) a drain on the economy. James, Jenks and Prout suggest that such a view overlooks the way children contribute to the economy by the time they spend caring for themselves rather than relying on an adult to look after them; by caring for sick or disabled adults and working for their parents in unpaid work.[22]

The last couple of decades have seen increasing interest in childhood from psychologists[23] and sociologists. The common perception that children are passive in family life, the victims of the decisions of the adults around them, has been challenged. Increasingly children are recognised as active participants in family life, sometimes offering as much support and help as they receive from their parents.[24]

4. PARENTS' RIGHTS, RESPONSIBILITIES AND DISCRETION

Parental responsibility is the key legal concept which describes the legal duties and rights that can flow from being a child's parent. It is significant that the Children Act 1989 talks of 'parental responsibility' rather than 'parental rights', because this

---

[19] Smart Neale and Wade (2001) suggest that in the media children are often represented as either little angels or little devils.

[20] Robb (2001) argues that there is no straightforward answer to the question whether children are better off now than they were in the past.

[21] Jenks (1996: 69).

[22] Solberg (1997); James, Jenks, Prout (1998).

[23] E.g. Graham, Turk and Verhulst (1999).

[24] Smart Neale and Wade (2001: 12).

stresses that children are not possessions to be controlled by parents, but instead children are persons to be cared for.[25] However, when the Children Act comes to define parental responsibility in s 3, it states:

> In this Act 'parental responsibility' means all the rights, duties, powers, responsibilities and authority which by law a parent of a child has in relation to the child and his property.

It will be noted that the first word used to describe parental responsibility is 'rights'. This demonstrates that it would be quite wrong to say that parents do not have rights.

A. Parental rights

Two important distinctions need to be made when we consider parental rights. The first is that when talking about parents' rights it is important to distinguish:

1. The rights a parent may have as a human being. These will be called a parent's human rights. These would include, for example, the right to life, free speech etc.
2. The rights that a parent may have because he or she is a parent. These will be called a parent's parental rights. These would include the right to decide where the child will live.

Secondly, when talking about a parent's parental rights it is important to be clear what might be meant by such a phrase. Take, for example, the parent's right to feed the child. By this could be meant one (or more) of three things:

1. Third parties or the state cannot prevent the parent carrying out this particular activity. So, no one is entitled to prevent a parent feeding the child what food the parent believes appropriate.
2. The state must enable the parent to perform this activity. For example, in relation to the right to feed, the state is obliged to ensure that parents have sufficient money so that they can supply the food the child needs.
3. The acts of the parents are lawful. This means that although it may be unlawful for a stranger to feed a child,[26] the parental right means it is not unlawful for a parent to feed a child.

Having made these distinctions there are some difficult questions concerning parental rights that must be faced.[27]

---

[25] See Hendricson (2003) for a discussion of a government code setting out the rights and responsibilities of parents.

[26] It is far from clear whether this would be a criminal offence (assuming the substance is not harmful), although it could be a battery.

[27] See Archard (2003; ch. 2) for a useful discussion of parents' rights.

B. Are parents' rights and responsibilities linked?

Lord Scarman in the House of Lords decision in *Gillick* argued that parents' rights exist only for the purpose of discharging their duties to children. He argued that: 'Parental rights are derived from parental duty and exist only so long as they are needed for the protection of the person and property of the child.'[28] Lord Scarman is talking here about a parent's parental rights and is making the important point that any parental rights a parent has exist for the purpose of promoting children's interests. Bainham, however, suggests that the position is not that straightforward. He has suggested that parents have rights *because* they have responsibilities and they have responsibilities *because* they have rights.[29]

McCall Smith[30] has argued that not all parental rights exist for the benefit of children. He suggests that parents have two kinds of parental rights: parent-centred and child-centred rights. Child-centred rights are rights given to parents to enable them to carry out their duties. So, the parent has the right to clothe the child as an essential part of enabling the parent to fulfil his or her duty of ensuring the health of the child. By contrast, parent-centred rights exist for the benefit of the parent. One example McCall Smith gives is that of the parental right to determine the religious upbringing of children. He argues that this right is given to enable parents to bring up children as they think is most appropriate. Parent-centred rights, he explains, are justified not because they positively promote the welfare of the child, but because they cannot be shown to harm the child, but can benefit the parent.

The distinction between child-centred and parent-centred rights is an important one, but there are difficulties with McCall Smith's approach. It can be difficult to decide whether a right is a parent-centred or child-centred right. Is the right to feed the child parent- or child-centred? Such a right is essential for the health of the child and so appears to be child-centred. But what kind of food is provided (for example, whether the parents choose to feed their children only vegetarian food) appears to be a parent-centred right. Further, it could be argued that parental rights do promote a child's welfare and do not exist solely for the benefit of parents. This is because many believe that living in a society where people like different kinds of food, have different religious beliefs, and different senses of humour is part of what makes life enjoyable. If so, it could be said to be in a child's interests to be brought up in a diverse society.

What is most useful about McCall Smith's distinction is that it stresses that there are certain areas of parenting over which parents do not have a discretion: they may not starve their child, the child must be adequately fed. There are, however, other areas of parenting where there is no state-approved standard of parenting (e.g. what kind of clothes the child should wear) and so the issue is left to the discretion of each individual parent. So while it is clear that if an issue relating to a child's upbringing comes before the court it will give 'respect' to the wishes of a responsible parent, at the end of the day it is for the court to decide what is in the best interests of the child,[31] However, if the court finds that it is unclear what is in the

---

[28] Lord Scarman *Gillick v W Norfolk and Wisbech AHA* [1986] AC 112 at p. 184.
[29] Bainham (1998a).
[30] McCall Smith (1990), discussed in Bainham (1994b).
[31] *Re A (Conjoined Twins: Medical Treatment)* [2000] 3 FCR 577.

best interests of the child, the court will permit the parent to make the decision. The court may take the view that the court cannot in practical terms force a parent to treat a child in a particular way and so to make an order would be meaningless.[32] This can mean that it is difficult for a non-resident parent to obtain a court order seeking to change the behaviour of the resident parent. Nonetheless the Court of Appeal in *Re B (Child Immunisation)*[33] was willing to permit the vaccination of a child with the MMR vaccine, against the wishes of the resident parent, following an application for such an order by the non-resident parent. This may be explained on the basis that the order did not involve an invasion of the resident parent's rights on how to live her day-to-day life. It would, no doubt, have been quite different if the non-resident parent had sought an order that the resident parent feed the child at least five portions of fresh fruit or vegetables a day. It is unlikely that a court would make such a court order, despite the clear scientific evidence of the benefits of such a diet.

C. Why do parents have rights and responsibilities?

It may seem self-evident that on the birth of a child the mother and father are under legal and moral obligations concerning the child and have the right to care for the child. But this need not be so. We could have a society where the state takes care of every child at birth in giant children's homes and the parents have no legal standing in relation to the child; or where on birth the child is handed over to the person who has scored highest in a parenting examination organised by the state. Most people would regard these alternatives with horror, but why is it that it seems so 'natural' that parents should be responsible for and should have rights over 'their' children? Philosophers and lawyers have struggled with this question and in truth there is no entirely satisfactory answer, but some of the suggestions are as follows:

(i) Children as property

Children can be seen as the fruit of the parent's labour through procreation and therefore as the property of the parent.[34] This could be seen as the basis of parental rights. At first sight, this is a rather unpleasant way of seeing children and such a theory has great difficulties.[35] We do not normally regard people as pieces of property which can be owned, and to describe parents' legal relationship with their children in the same terms used to describe their relationship with their cars seems clearly inappropriate.[36]

---

[32] *Re C (A Child)(HIV Test)* [1999] 2 FLR 1004, although see Strong (2000) for criticism of the argument on the facts of that case.
[33] [2003] 3 FCR 156 CA.
[34] Montgomery (1988). Rix LJ in R *(On the Application of Williamson v Secretary of State for Education and Employment)* [2003] 1 FCR 1 CA suggested that the view that children are the property of their parents explained why historically parents could use corporal punishment against them (para 241), although he added that such a view might need to be reconsidered.
[35] Archard (1993b).
[36] Not least because once a child reaches majority parental rights cease.

Despite these objections, Barton and Douglas[37] argue that the property notion has something to be said for it. If a child is removed from a hospital by a stranger shortly after birth, parents might naturally say 'their' baby had been stolen. Our society is based on a strong belief that parents should normally be allowed to bring up 'their' children, and children can only be removed from parents if there is sufficient justification. Such claims are similar to those made in respect of items of property. However, despite some similarities there are many other ways in which children are treated quite differently from property. One can legally destroy one's computer but not one's child, for example.

(ii) Children on trust

This theory is that children have rights as people. As the child is unable to exercise these rights, the parents exercise these rights on the child's behalf. This version of explaining parents' rights is more popular than the property formulation.[38] It can take three forms:

1. The parents hold the rights of the child on trust for the child until he or she is old enough to claim these rights for him- or herself.
2. The parents hold the rights of the child on trust for the state. The parents care for the child until the child is able to become a citizen and a member of the state him- or herself.
3. The parents hold the rights of the child on a purpose trust – the purpose being the promotion of the welfare of the child.

The exact formulation matters little in practice, but the alternative approaches indicate important theoretical differences. The crucial difference is to whom the parent is responsible for the exercise of their rights: under 1 the parent is responsible to the child, whereas under 2 the parent is responsible to the state, while 3 leaves it unclear who has responsibility for enforcing the trust. The point to stress in all of these formulations is that the rights that parents exercise are not theirs, but those of the child and so should not be exercised for the benefit of the parent, but of the child.

There are three particular benefits of the trust analysis.[39] First, the law on trustees (fiduciaries) has been specifically developed to deal with fears that the trustee will misuse his or her powers as a trustee for his or her own benefit, rather than for the benefit of the subject of the trust. Such rules may be used for the law in ensuring that parents do not misuse their parental rights. Secondly, the law on trusts has developed realistic standards in policing the fiduciary's behaviour. The trustee cannot be expected always to make perfect choices, and is allowed a degree of discretion, but this does not permit the trustee to make manifestly bad decisions. These rules may also be useful in the parenting context. Thirdly, the trust approach

[37] Barton and Douglas (1995).
[38] See Beck, Clavis, Barnes Jenkins and Nadi (1978); Scott and Scott (1995).
[39] O'Donnovan (1993).

means that the law would not need to see parents' interests and children's interests as in conflict.

There are, however, difficulties with the trusts approach. There are some uncertainties of a technical nature:[40] precisely what is the subject of the trust? (the rights of the child is the most common answer); who created the trust? Other problems are more practical. It may be justifiable to place on fiduciaries heavy obligations never to consider their own interests when dealing with the trust property, but for parents the obligation to care for children is a 24-hour-a-day obligation, involving decisions which profoundly affect their own private lives. To require the same standards as trustee (and never to consider their own interests) may seem therefore overly onerous.[41] Further, although the law can readily establish a widely accepted standard on, for example, the duty of investment upon a trustee, finding community standards as to what is reasonable parenting would be well-nigh impossible on many issues.[42] Also the trust model does not readily capture the notion that children may have the right to make decisions for themselves. This could be dealt with by stating that the number of rights which are the subject of the trust lessen as the child becomes older and the child is able to exercise these for him- or herself.

(iii) Imposition by society

The flip side of the question why should parents have rights is to ask: why should parents be under a duty to care for children? Eekelaar argues that there are two aspects of a parent's obligations to care for a child.[43] First, he suggests that every person owes a basic duty to other people to promote human flourishing. Secondly, on top of that basic duty there are special duties that society chooses to impose on particular people in particular circumstances. Our society chooses to impose special duties on parents to care for children. This is because children are vulnerable and need to be cared for by someone if society is to grow. Parents are best placed to provide the required care and that is widely accepted within our society. In other words, parents are only obliged especially to care for children because that is the choice of our society, not because of some underlying moral principle. Barton and Douglas are unhappy with this approach because it suggests that there would be nothing morally objectionable for a state to require all children at birth to be removed from their parents and raised by state approved agencies. They argue that most people would find such a system objectionable, even if it could be shown not to be particularly harmful to children, which is why they think that parents have something akin to an ownership right in respect of the child.

(iv) Voluntary assumption by parents

Barton and Douglas argue that the key element behind imposing the responsibilities of parenthood is that parents have voluntarily accepted the obligation. A parent

---

[40] See e.g. M. Bryan (1995).
[41] C. Schneider (1995).
[42] C. Schneider (1995).
[43] Eekelaar (1991b).

who does not want to care for the child is not necessarily obliged to. For example, they argue that if a mother gives birth to a child following a rape she is not obliged to raise the child, although she is under a duty to ensure the child receives some care, as would someone who came across an abandoned baby. However, any parent who chooses to undertake the parental role is under a duty to carry out the role reasonably well. There is much to be said for this theory, but it cannot completely explain why parents are under parental obligations.[44] If I notice my neighbour has just had a baby and I steal it and undertake to care for it, this does not give me the rights and duties of parenthood, despite my intent to be a parent. So, as Barton and Douglas[45] suggest, an element of the property argument or Eekelaar's argument needs to be relied upon in addition to the argument based on voluntary assumption of obligation if this theory is to explain the law's attitude towards parents.

(v) The 'extensions claim'

It can be said that the rights of parents to raise their children as they think fit is connected with the right that the state should not interfere with parents' private lives. As Fried has put it 'the right to form one's child's values, one's child's life plan and the right to lavish attention on the child are extensions of the right not to be interfered with in doing those things for one's self'.[46] The difficulty with such a claim is that it could be made in respect of close friends or fellow employees.[47]

So far we have been looking at parents' rights and responsibility from a theoretical perspective. What is the law itself?

5. PARENTAL RESPONSIBILITY

The law on the duties and rights of parenthood is covered by the notion of parental responsibility.

A. What is parental responsibility?

Given that parental responsibility is one of the key concepts in family law you might have thought it would be easy to define it, but it is not. The root cause of the uncertainty is that the notion of parental responsibility is required to fulfil a wide variety of functions.[48] Eekelaar has suggested that there are two aspects of parental responsibility:[49]

---

[44] See Chapter 5 for further discussion of such arguments in the context of child support.
[45] Barton and Douglas (1995).
[46] Fried (1978: 152).
[47] Archard (2003: 92).
[48] Piper (1999) discusses the difficulties solicitors face in practice when trying to explain what parental responsibility means.
[49] See Eekelaar (1991c).

1. *What that responsibility means.* It encapsulates the legal duties and powers that enable a parent to care for a child or act on the child's behalf. Parents must exercise their rights 'dutifully'[50] towards their children.
2. *Who has the responsibility?* It explains that the law permits the person with parental responsibility rather than anyone else[51] to have parental responsibility. It determines who has the authority to make a decision relating to a child.

In an attempt to explain further what parental responsibility means we need to look at the legislative and judicial understanding of parental responsibility:

(i) The Children Act

The starting point is section 3 of the Children Act 1989:

> In this Act 'parental responsibility' means all the rights, duties, powers, responsibilities and authority which by law a parent of a child has in relation to the child and his property.

This leaves unanswered as many questions as it answers, because it fails to explain what those rights etc. are. The Law Commission decided against a statutory definition of the responsibilities of parents because they change from case to case and depend on the age and maturity of the child.[52] For example, parental responsibility in relation to a disabled child might be thought to impose different obligations on a parent than if the child were not disabled.[53] In any event, it would not be possible to list all the responsibilities that attend parental responsibility. Douglas and Lowe have attempted a list and have suggested the following:

1. providing a home for the child;
2. having contact with the child;
3. determining and providing for the child's education;
4. determining the child's religion;
5. disciplining the child;
6. consenting to the child's medical treatment;
7. consenting to the child's marriage;
8. agreeing to the child's adoption;
9. vetoing the issue of a child's passport;
10. taking the child outside the UK and consenting to the child's emigration;
11. administering the child's property;
12. protecting and maintaining the child;
13. naming the child;
14. representing the child in legal proceedings;
15. disposing of the child's corpse;
16. appointing a guardian for the child.[54]

---

[50] Lowe and Douglas (1998: 31–3).
[51] A point stressed in Lowe (1997b).
[52] Contrast Children (Scotland) Act 1995, s 1(1).
[53] See Corker and Davis (2000) for a discussion of the legal treatment of disabled children.
[54] Lowe and Douglas (1998: 350). See also Hendricson's proposals (2003) for a parenting code, setting out clearly the rights and responsibilities of parents.

No doubt this is not a complete list, but it gives an indication of the range of issues for which parents may be responsible. Occasionally Parliament adds to the responsibilities of parents. For example, under ss 8–10 of the Crime and Disorder Act 1998 the court may make a parenting order if a child has committed certain offences. This may require parents to control their child and require parents to attend guidance sessions. This in effect imposes on parents a duty to ensure their children do not commit crimes.

Rather than trying to list the issues over which parents can make decisions about a child, it may be more profitable to consider what limitations there are on the parental power to decide how to raise a child. The parent can make decisions about all areas of the child's life, subject to the following:

1. *The criminal law.* For example, it is a criminal offence to assault a child,[55] which restricts the power of parents to administer corporal punishment.
2. *Any requirement to consult or obtain the consent of anyone else with parental responsibility.* For example, s 13 of the Children Act 1989 requires a parent wishing to change a child's surname to obtain the consent of anyone else with parental responsibility, before doing so.
3. *The power of the local authority to take a child into care.* If a child is taken into care by a local authority then this effectively restricts the powers of parents to make decisions about their child's upbringing.[56]
4. *Any orders of the court.* There may be a court order in force which deals with a specific aspect of a child's upbringing, in which case a parent may not act in a way contrary to the court order.[57]
5. *The ability of a child who is sufficiently mature* (Gillick *competent*) *to make decisions for him- or herself.* This will be discussed shortly.

The Children Act 1989 appears then to see parental responsibility in terms of being able to make decisions about a child's upbringing, even if it is not quite clear what those rights are.

(ii) Judicial understanding of parental responsibility

Unfortunately the courts have not been consistent in their understanding of parental responsibility. Some cases have described parental responsibility as a 'stamp of approval' to mark the 'status' which nature has bestowed on the father.[58] The Court of Appeal has spoken of the way in which parental responsibility may create a positive image of the father in the child's eyes.[59] So understood, parental responsibility appears to be little more than a pat on the back, official confirmation that the father is a committed father. This is especially so in cases where the father is given parental responsibility, but then denied contact with the child.

---

[55] Offences Against the Person Act 1861, s 47.
[56] See Chapter 11.
[57] Children Act 1989, s 2(8).
[58] E.g. *Re S (A Minor) (Parental Responsibility)* [1995] 2 FLR 648, [1995] 3 FCR 225 CA; *Re C and V (Minors) (Parental Responsibility and Contact)* [1998] 1 FLR 392, [1998] 1 FCR 57.
[59] *Re S (A Minor) (Parental Responsibility)* [1995] 2 FLR 648, [1995] 3 FCR 225 CA.

Other cases have, however, seen parental responsibility about real rights and about the exercise of parental responsibility. For example in *M v M (Parental Responsibility)*[60] despite his obvious love and commitment to his child the father was denied parental responsibility because he lacked the mental capacities to make decisions on behalf of the child. In *Re M (Sperm Donor Father)*[61] the court ordered contact to a father who did not know the child, and suggested that after a while the court might award him parental responsibility once he had got to know the child. The view that parental responsibility is about the making of decisions over children is further supported by those cases (which will be discussed shortly) which indicate that over important issues the resident parent must consult with all parents with parental responsibility. As this discussion shows, there is a real tension in the case law over whether parental responsibility is about real decision-making power, or whether it is of more symbolic value, recognising the father's commitment to the child.

B. Parental responsibility in practice

A person who does not have parental responsibility can, of course, act as a parent towards a child in a variety of ways. He or she can feed, clothe, educate, and play with the child. Indeed, no doubt, some people without parental responsibility act more like a parent towards a child than other people with parental responsibility. Eekelaar suggests that over a million fathers carry out a parental role without having parental responsibility.[62] So when does it actually matter whether a person has parental responsibility? The following are rights and responsibilities that a father with parental responsibility has, which a father without parental responsibility does not have.[63]

1. He can withhold consent to adoption and freeing for adoption.[64]
2. He can object to the child being accommodated in local authority accommodation[65] and remove the child from local authority accommodation.[66]
3. He can appoint a guardian.[67]
4. He can give legal authorisation for medical treatment.[68]
5. He has a right of access to his child's health records.
6. He can withdraw a child from sex education and religious education classes and make representations to schools concerning the child's education.[69]

---

[60] [1999] 2 FLR 737.
[61] [2003] FL 94.
[62] Eekelaar (2001d: 426).
[63] The issue only relates to fathers because all mothers have parental responsibility.
[64] Adoption Act 1976, s 72.
[65] Children Act 1989, s 20(7).
[66] Children Act 1989, s 20(8).
[67] Children Act 1989, s 5.
[68] See p. 393 for a discussion on children and medical law. Eekelaar (2001d: 429) argues that a father without parental responsibility can give effective consent to medical treatment because he has a duty to promote the health of his children and that duty can only realistically be imposed if he has the right to provide the consent necessary for that treatment.
[69] Education Act 1996. Eekelaar (2001d) argues that a father without parental responsibility can make decisions in relation to the child's education.

7. His consent is required if the child's mother seeks to remove the child from the jurisdiction.[70]
8. He can sign a child's passport application and object to the granting of a passport.[71]
9. He has sufficient rights in relation to a child to invoke the international child abduction rules.[72]
10. He can consent to the marriage of a child aged 16 or 17.[73]
11. He will automatically be a party to care proceedings.[74]

Although this is a lengthy list, in fact these rights do not arise very often in practice. The most common situations are where a third party wishes to treat a child in a particular way which would be a crime or tort without the consent of someone who has parental responsibility;[75] for example, a doctor wishes to provide medical treatment for a child.[76] Ros Pickford found that over 75 per cent of fathers were unaware that they lacked parental responsibility. Many of these fathers were fathers of teenagers. This indicates that it is quite possible to carry out a full parental role without having to rely on parental responsibility. Notably, even those fathers who were aware they lacked parental responsibility rarely went on to seek it.

If parental responsibility is of limited practical significance then why is it so important? Eekelaar sums up the position well: 'parental responsibility can best be understood as legal recognition of the exercise of social parenthood. It thus comprises a factual (recognition of a state of affairs) and a normative (giving the state of affairs the "stamp of approval") element.'[77]

As this implies, parental responsibility is more about confirming an existing situation or sending a message of approval to the parent, rather than actually creating rights. However, as most unmarried fathers are unaware of whether they have parental responsibility or not,[78] the effectiveness of such a stamp of approval may be questioned.

C. The rights of a parent without responsibility

Although parental responsibility is the primary source of parental rights, there are rights and responsibilities that flow simply from being a parent. These are the benefits and responsibilities that follow from parenthood in and of itself, whether or not a parent has parental responsibility.

1. A parent has a right to apply without leave for a s 8 order.[79]
2. A parent has rights of succession to the estate of the child.[80]

---

[70] Children Act 1989, s 13.
[71] See Passport Agency (1994).
[72] See Chapter 9.
[73] Marriage Act 1949, s 3.
[74] A father without parental responsibility can also be a party in certain limited circumstances: Children Act 1989, Appendix 3.
[75] Or the consent of the court.
[76] *B v B (Grandparent: Residence Order)* [1992] 2 FLR 327, [1993] 1 FCR 211.
[77] Eekelaar (2001d: 428).
[78] Pickford (1999).
[79] Children Act 1989, s 10(4).
[80] See Chapter 12.

3. There is a presumption that a child in local authority care should have reasonable contact with each parent.[81]
4. On application for an emergency protection order there is a duty to inform the child's parents.[82]
5. A parent can apply to discharge an emergency protection order.[83]
6. Rights of citizenship pass primarily through parentage.[84]
7. Parents are liable persons under social security legislation.[85]
8. A parent cannot marry his or her child.[86]
9. The criminal law on incest forbids sexual relations between parents and children.
10. A parent who is not living with his or her child will be liable to make payments under the Child Support Act 1991 and Child Support, Pensions and Social Security Act 2000.

D. The extent of parental responsibility

Parental responsibility is for life. Once a parent has parental responsibility, this cannot be removed, except in a few special cases.[87] Even if the parent has behaved in such a way that the child has to be taken into care, he or she will not lose parental responsibility.[88] Although a parent cannot surrender parental responsibility, it is possible to delegate it.[89] The fact that a new person acquires parental responsibility does not mean that anyone else loses it.[90] As shall be seen later, the nature of parental responsibility may change with the age and development of the child.

6. SHARING PARENTAL RESPONSIBILITY

It is clear from the scheme of the Children Act 1989 that there will be many situations where several people have parental responsibility. Although a child can have only two parents, any number of people can have parental responsibility. The question therefore arises whether each person with parental responsibility can exercise his or her parental responsibility alone or whether it is necessary to have the agreement of all those with parental responsibility in respect of each decision concerning the upbringing of the child.[91]

Although there are a few exceptions, s 2(7) appears to give a clear answer:

---

[81] Children Act 1989, s 34.
[82] Children Act 1989, s 44(13).
[83] Children Act 1989, s 45(8).
[84] Cretney, Masson and Bailey-Harris (2002: 105–6).
[85] Cretney, Masson and Bailey-Harris (2002: ch. 11).
[86] Marriage Act 1949, s 1.
[87] If a non-parent has parental responsibility through a residence order then when the order comes to an end the parental responsibility ceases.
[88] See Chapter 10.
[89] Children Act 1989, s 2(9).
[90] Children Act 1989, s 2(6), although an adoption order will end any existing parental responsibility.
[91] See the discussion in Maidment (2001b).

Where more than one person has parental responsibility for a child, each of them may act alone and without the other (or others) in meeting that responsibility; but nothing in this Part shall be taken to affect the operation of any enactment which requires the consent of more than one person in a matter affecting the child.

There are two crucial points that appear clear from this subsection. The first is that, except where the statute provides otherwise, each person with parental responsibility can exercise parental responsibility alone without obtaining the consent of the others with parental responsibility or even consulting them. It has been suggested that in this way the Act promotes 'independent' rather than 'co-operative' parenting.[92]

The second is that there is no hierarchy among those with parental responsibility. So, in the Children Act 1989 there is no preference given to mothers over fathers, or between those with whom the child lives and those with whom the child does not live. If a child who normally lives with her mother is visiting her father (with parental responsibility), he can take her to a church service; arrange for her to have an unusual haircut; or feed her meat, even if the mother strongly opposes these activities. The mother could apply for a prohibited steps order[93] to prevent the father doing this, but in the absence of such an order he is free to do this.[94] Similarly, when the child lives with the mother, she can bring up the child as she believes best. The purpose of shared parental responsibility is to enable each parent to feel responsible for the welfare of the child and act as a parent in as full a way as possible.[95]

There are a number of exceptions to the rule that there is no need to consult, although in all of these situations if the consent is not provided then the court may be able to dispense with the consent and authorise the act:

1. Adoption and freeing for adoption can only take place if *all* parents[96] with parental responsibility consent.[97]
2. If the child aged 16 or 17 wishes to marry then *all* parents with parental responsibility and any guardians must consent.[98]
3. If the child is to be accommodated by the local authority then *none* of those with parental responsibility must have objected.[99]
4. Section 13 of the Children Act 1989 states that if a residence order has been made and one party wishes to change the surname of the child then the consent of all those with parental responsibility is required.[100] In *Re PC (Change of Surname)*[101] it was suggested that even if there was not a residence order in force

---

[92] Bainham (1990).
[93] Under Children Act 1989, s 8.
[94] A local authority has a duty to consult parents and people with parental responsibility about all decisions unless this is not reasonably practicable.
[95] There is no question of the parties being bound by pre-birth agreements: *Re W (A Minor) (Residence Order)* [1992] 2 FLR 332.
[96] And guardians.
[97] But not others with parental responsibility: Adoption Act 1976, s 16; Children Act 1989, ss 12(3), 33(6).
[98] Marriage Act 1949, s 3(1A).
[99] See Chapter 10.
[100] Children Act 1989, s 13.
[101] [1997] 2 FLR 730.

then it was necessary to have the consent of all those with parental responsibility.[102]

5. Section 13 of the Children Act 1989 states that if there is a residence order it is not possible to remove a child from the UK without the consent of all those with parental responsibility.[103] It is arguable, by analogy with the decisions relating to surnames, that in order to remove a child from the UK the consent of all those with parental responsibility is required.

6. There are cases which suggest that the consent of all those with parental responsibility is required for any decision which is of fundamental importance to the child and is irreversible.[104] Which decisions are of fundamental importance? This will, it seems, be decided on a case-by-case basis. We know the following are issues of fundamental importance:

- Education. In *Re G (A Minor) (Parental Responsibility: Education)*[105] it was suggested that there is a duty to consult over long-term decisions relating to education. Here the question was whether the child should be moved from one school to another.
- Circumcision. In *Re J (Specific Issue Orders)*[106] the Court of Appeal held that if a male child[107] is to undergo a circumcision all of those with parental responsibility should be consulted.
- The changing of a child's surname. Before the change in a child's name all those with parental responsibility should be consulted.[108]
- The MMR vaccine. If the resident parent decides not to give her child the MMR vaccine she should consult with the non-resident parent if he has parental responsibility.[109]

It is arguable that these decisions fly in the face of s 2(7) of the Children Act 1989,[110] which makes it clear that, in the absence of statutory provisions to the contrary, a parent can exercise parental responsibility without consultation.

It appears from the case law that the duty on the resident parent is to consult, rather than obtain the non-resident parent's consent. The significance of this consultation requirement is therefore that it gives the non-resident parent the opportunity to bring legal proceedings to prevent the resident parent from acting in the proposed way. However, it is far from clear what the court will do if the resident parent fails to consult. For example, if the mother arranges for the circumcision without consultation with the father, there is not much the law can do. The requirement to consult appears unenforceable in many cases.

---

[102] Indeed, as we shall see in Chapter 9, it may be necessary to obtain the consent of every parent.
[103] Children Act 1989, s 13.
[104] Eekelaar (1998).
[105] [1994] 2 FLR 964, [1995] 2 FCR 53 CA.
[106] [2000] 1 FLR 517, [2000] 1 FCR 307 CA.
[107] Female circumcision is forbidden under the Female Circumcision Act 1985.
[108] *Re PC (Change of Surname)* [1997] 2 FLR 730.
[109] *Re B (A Child) (Immunisation)* [2003] 3 FCR 156.
[110] Eekelaar (2001d).

A. Are all parental responsibilities equal?

It seems clear from s 2(9) of the Children Act 1989 that each parent with parental responsibility is equal. However, in *Re P (A Minor) (Parental Responsibility Order)*[111] the courts have suggested that the parent with whom the child lives is to have the power to decide 'day-to-day' issues relating to the child. So the non-residential parent cannot use his or her parental responsibility to upset the day-to-day parenting of the residential parent.[112]

B. Is the law in a sound state?

If a residential parent (the parent with whom the child lives) exercises parental responsibility in a way objected to by the non-residential parent, the latter could bring the matter before the court by way of a specific issue order or prohibited steps order. There is therefore a sense that it matters little whether there is a formal duty to consult because, whether or not there is a requirement to consult, if those with parental responsibility disagree, the matter will be brought before a court. There are, however, three points of practical significance in whether or not there is a duty to consult. The first is that it determines whose responsibility it is to bring the matter before the court. For example, if the law is that one parent cannot change the name of the child without the other's consent then the parent seeking to change the name will have the burden of bringing the matter before the court. However, if the law was that a parent could independently change a name, then it would be the responsibility of the person objecting to the change to bring the matter before the court. Secondly, the issue of who should be liable to pay the legal costs of both parties if the matter is brought before the court may depend on whether there was a duty to consult, with which a parent did not comply. Thirdly, there is the 'message' that the law wishes to send out. Does the law wish to encourage co-operative or independent parenting?

The following are some of the approaches that the law could take regarding those who share parental responsibility:

1. All those with parental responsibility must agree on every issue relating to the child.
2. The residential parent can make all decisions relating to the child and the non-residential parent has rights only to bring a matter to court.
3. The residential parent should make all important decisions, although the non-residential parent can make day-to-day decisions when the child is spending time with him or her.
4. The parents must consult on all important issues, otherwise each parent can take day-to-day decisions when the child is spending time with him or her.
5. Each parent with parental responsibility can exercise parental responsibility independently and does not need to consult with the other over any issue.

It should be clear that approach 1 is impractical. It would not be realistic to expect

---

[111] [1994] 1 FLR 578.
[112] E.g. *Re J (Specific Issue Orders)* [2000] 1 FLR 517, [2000] 1 FCR 307 CA.

a parent to contact and discuss with the other parent the contents of every meal, for example. Approach 2 is likewise impractical, at least if the non-residential parent is to have contact with the child. The choice is therefore between the last three options. The issues seem to be as follows:

1. *Fears of misuse.* There are fears that giving the non-residential parent a say in how the child is brought up by the residential parent could constitute a major infringement of the rights of private life of the residential parent. For example, if the non-residential parent could compel the vegetarian parent to prepare meat for the child to eat, this may be seen as an infringement of the residential parent's rights. There are particular concerns in cases where there has been domestic violence, where there is evidence that abusers continue to exercise control over their victims through whatever route is available.[113] Giving powers to the non-residential parent to direct how the residential parent brings up the child is therefore open to abuse.

2. *Involvement of the non-residential parent.* There are concerns that the non-residential parent will be excluded from the child's life. If there is no duty to consult, the non-residential parent may not even be aware that there is a crucial issue to be decided in respect of the child and will not be able to carry out an effective parenting role.

3. *Lack of knowledge of non-residential parent.* Some claim that non-residential parents do not know the child well enough to make important decisions in relation to the child. Of course, this is a generalisation, but the law in this area must rest on generalisations and it may well be argued that, as a general rule, the residential parent will be better poised to make a decision in respect of a child than a non-residential parent.

4. *Onerous obligation on residential parent.* Some are concerned that an obligation to obtain consent could be unduly time-consuming, stressful and burdensome for the residential parent, especially where the other parent may be difficult to contact.[114]

5. *Disruption for child.* There is a concern that permitting each parent to exercise parental responsibility will lead to disruption for the child by constantly changing lifestyles. For example, in *Re PC (Change of Surname)*[115] it was argued that if each parent with parental responsibility could change the child's surname, this would lead to the child's name constantly being changed, first by one parent and then by the other. Similarly, a child receiving religious instruction from one parent and conflicting religious instruction from another could feel confused and pressurised.

6. *Law should stress 'doing'.* Smart and Neale[116] criticise the law for failing to place sufficient emphasis on the 'doing' aspects of caring. They argue it is wrong to stress 'caring about' children above 'caring for' children. They see a danger in

---

[113] Hester and Radford (1996).
[114] Law Commission Report 172 (1988: para 2.10).
[115] [1997] 2 FLR 730, [1997] 3 FCR 544.
[116] Smart and Neale (1999).

giving non-residential parents rights, without having to perform the day-to-day care for children.

7. *Ignorance of the law.* Given the ignorance of the requirements of family law, it seems wrong to impose an obligation to consult, as it is likely to be unknown by most people. It would therefore be honoured more in the breach than the observance and would, as suggested above, effectively be unenforceable.

8. *Reality.* It could be argued that there is little the law can do here. Whether there will be co-operative or independent parenting will depend on the relationship and personality of the parties, rather than the requirements of the law. Compelling consultation or co-operation is unlikely to be productive.

As can be seen from the above, there are strong arguments on both sides. Whatever the law is, there will some cases where a consultation requirement will be beneficial and others where it is open to abuse. This key issue is whether it is worth running the risks of misuse in the name of sending a message encouraging co-operation. Further, although we may generally want parents to consult over important issues over their children's upbringing, that does not meant that we should turn that into a legal obligation.[117] Also, it is arguable that if there is to be a duty to consult we need to be a little more careful in deciding who should have parental responsibility. Should the father in *Re S (A Minor) (Parental Responsibility)*,[118] who was known to be a possessor of paedophilic literature, be consulted about his daughter's medical treatment? Even if he has not seen her for years? Should a mother be required to consult a father if he has been violent towards her in the past?

C. Co-parenting in practice

It seems that in practice there is only a limited degree of co-parenting after separation. This is particularly so where one of the parents remarries or starts cohabiting with a new partner. Maclean and Eekelaar write: 'Joint decision-making of any serious nature probably occurs in about one in ten cases where contact is regularly exercised, and then usually only on a limited number of issues.'[119] Indeed, the Law Commission accepted that, in reality, parental responsibility 'ran with child'. This might suggest that the independent parenting envisaged in s 2(9) of the Children Act 1989 is realistic, whatever the ideal may be.[120]

7. THE WELFARE PRINCIPLE

At the heart of the law relating to children is the principle that whenever the court considers a question relating to the upbringing of children the paramount consideration should be the welfare of the children. Section 1(1) of the Children Act 1989 clearly states the central principle of children law:

---

[117] Eekelaar (2001d).

[118] [1995] 2 FLR 648, [1995] 3 FCR 225 CA.

[119] Eekelaar and Maclean (1997: 137). For an interesting American study of joint custody, see Macooby and Mnookin (1992).

[120] See Backett (1982) and Smart and Neale (2000) for explanations for the lack of consultation.

When a court determines any question with respect to—

(a) the upbringing of a child; or

(b) the administration of a child's property or the application of any income arising from it

the child's welfare shall be the court's paramount consideration.

This apparently simple principle is in fact complex. Several issues require explanation.

A. What does 'welfare' mean?

The Children Act has attempted to add some flesh to the concept of a child's welfare.[121] There is no definition of 'welfare' in the Children Act 1989, although there is a list of factors which a judge should consider when deciding what is in the child's welfare. These are listed in s 1(3):

(a) the ascertainable wishes and feelings of the child concerned (considered in the light of his age and understanding);

(b) his physical, emotional and educational needs;

(c) the likely effect on him of any change in his circumstances;

(d) his age, sex, background and any characteristics of his which the court considers relevant;

(e) any harm which he has suffered or is at risk of suffering;

(f) how capable each of his parents, and any other person in relation to whom the court considers the question to be relevant, is of meeting his needs;

(g) the range of powers available to the court under this Act in the proceedings in question.

The interpretation of these factors is discussed in detail in Chapter 9.

B. What does 'paramount' mean?

The courts' interpretation of the word 'paramount' is based on the decision of the House of Lords in *J* v *C*,[122] which considered the meaning of the words 'first and paramount' in the Guardianship of Infants Act 1925. Lord McDermott explained that the phrase means:

> more than the child's welfare is to be treated as the top item in a list of items relevant to the matter in question. [The words] connote a process whereby, when all the relevant facts, relationships, claims and wishes of parents, risks, choices and other circumstances are taken into account and weighed, the course to be followed will be that which is most in the interests of the child.[123]

This clearly expresses the view that the welfare of the child is the sole consideration. The interests of adults and other children are only relevant in so far as they might affect the welfare of the child in question.[124] *J* v *C*[125] itself was especially significant

---

[121] For an interesting discussion that it would be preferable to talk in terms of well-being rather than welfare see Eekelaar (2002a: 243).

[122] [1970] AC 668.

[123] At pp. 710–11.

[124] See e.g. Lord Hobhouse in *Dawson* v *Wearmouth* [1999] 1 FLR 1167 HL.

[125] [1970] AC 668.

because the House of Lords made it quite clear that the interests of the children outweigh the interests of even 'unimpeachable' (perfect) parents.[126] So whether an order is 'fair' or infringes the rights of parents is not relevant; all that matters is whether the order promotes the interests of children. This is a surprising interpretation because, had Parliament intended welfare to be the only consideration, it could have said so. There was no need to interpret the word 'paramount' to mean sole. It is interesting to note that the UN Convention on the Rights of Children, in article 3, states that the child's welfare should be the primary consideration. This appears to place slightly less weight on children's interests than s 1 of the Children Act 1989.

C. When does the welfare principle apply?

The welfare principle applies when the court is asked to determine any question that concerns a child's upbringing or the administration of their property. Bracewell J in *Re X (A Child) (Injunctions Restraining Publication)*[127] stated that upbringing means 'the bringing up, care for, treatment, education, and instruction of the child by its parents or by those who are substitute parents'. It is of wide application and not restricted to the Children Act 1989. For example, s 1(1) applies where the court considers making an order under s 8 of the Children Act 1989; where the High Court is exercising the inherent jurisdiction;[128] and when the court considers public law orders such as care orders.[129] Rather than listing all the orders when the welfare principle applies, it is in fact easier to consider the issue from the opposite perspective and ask when the welfare principle does not apply.

D. When does the welfare principle not apply?[130]

The welfare principle does not apply in the following cases:

1. *If the issue does not relate to the child's upbringing.* It is clear from the wording of s 1 of the Children Act 1989 that the welfare principle applies only if the issues involve the upbringing of the child. Even if the issue does not involve the upbringing of the child, the court may still pay special attention to the welfare of the child, although the welfare of the child will not be paramount.[131] It is not always easy, however, to know whether an issue relates to the upbringing of the child, as is clear from some of the following examples:

   (a) In *Re A (Minors) (Residence Orders: Leave to Apply)*[132] the Court of Appeal held that deciding whether or not to grant leave to an adult to apply for an order under s 8 of the Children Act 1989 was not an issue that

---

[126] Freeman (2000a) states that unimpeachable parents were always fathers.
[127] [2001] 1 FCR 541 at 546f.
[128] *Re T (A Minor) (Wardship: Medical Treatment)* [1997] 1 FLR 502, [1997] 2 FCR 363 CA.
[129] *Humberside CC v B* [1993] 1 FLR 257, [1993] 1 FCR 613, per Booth J; applied in *F v Leeds City Council* [1994] 2 FLR 60, [1994] 2 FCR 428 CA.
[130] Lowe (1997b).
[131] *S v S, W v Official Solicitor (or W)* [1972] AC 24; *Richards v Richards* [1984] AC 174.
[132] [1992] 2 FCR 174, [1992] 2 FLR 154 CA.

involved the upbringing of a child and so the child's welfare was not paramount. However, the welfare principle does apply where a child is seeking leave to bring a s 8 application.[133]

(b) In considering whether to order blood tests to determine who is the father of a child, the welfare principle does not apply, as the taking of blood does not relate to the child's upbringing.[134]

(c) It is held that the welfare principle does not apply when a court is deciding whether a parent should be committed to prison for breach of a court order concerning a child.[135]

(d) In *Re Z (A Minor) (Identity: Restrictions on Publication)*[136] the Court of Appeal held that the decision whether a television company be allowed to film a programme about a child's education related to her upbringing and so the welfare principle applied. However, if the television programme relates not to the child's upbringing, but rather to publicity about the child's parent, then the child's welfare is not paramount, although it may be a factor to be taken into account.[137]

2. *Part III of the Children Act.* The welfare principle does not apply to Part III of the Children Act 1989, which sets out the various duties that a local authority owes to children in its area. This was made clear in *Re M (A Minor) (Secure Accommodation Order)*.[138] The explanation is that, in considering what services to provide to children in its area and how to exercise its powers, the local authority must consider the needs of all children in its area and the financial limitations it faces. The welfare of a particular child cannot, therefore, be paramount.

3. *Express statutory provision.* The welfare principle does not apply if a statute expressly states it should not. A notable example is in relation to redistribution of property and financial issues on divorce: the child's interests are said to be 'first',[139] but not paramount. Perhaps most significantly, in deciding whether or not to grant a divorce to a child's parents, the child's welfare is not paramount; indeed, the courts are not even required to consider the child's welfare.

4. *Outside the context of litigation.* It is arguable that the welfare principle does not apply to parents with respect to their day-to-day decisions relating to the child. As Lowe and Douglas explain: 'parents are not bound to consider their children's welfare in deciding whether to make a career move, to move house or whether to separate or divorce'.[140] However, there are some *dicta* which have suggested that the welfare principle does affect a parent's day-to-day life. Ward LJ suggested:

---

[133] *Re SC (A Minor) (Leave to Seek Section 8 Orders)* [1994] 1 FCR 837, [1994] 1 FLR 96; *Re C (Residence: Child's Application for Leave)* [1995] 1 FLR 927, [1996] 1 FCR 461.
[134] *Re H (A Minor) (Blood Tests: Parental Rights)* [1996] 2 FLR 65, [1996] 3 FCR 201.
[135] *A v N (Committal: Refusal of Contact)* [1997] 2 FCR 475, [1997] 1 FLR 533 CA.
[136] [1997] Fam 1.
[137] *R v Central Independent Television plc* [1994] Fam 192.
[138] [1995] Fam 108.
[139] Matrimonial Causes Act 1973, s 25(1).
[140] Lowe and Douglas (1998: 326).

a parent may choose to conduct himself in a way which has insufficient regard to his responsibilities to his children. If a person has no parental responsibilities, he is at liberty to conduct himself as he chooses ... if he has parental responsibilities, those responsibilities may restrict his freedom of action. He is required, where his children's upbringing is involved, to have regard also to the welfare of his children.[141]

It is far from clear how to interpret these *dicta*. Perhaps the best way to understand the law is that there is a duty on parents to avoid causing the child harm, but not a duty positively to promote the child's welfare.[142]

E. What if the case involves two children – whose interests are paramount?

There is a real difficulty in using the welfare principle in cases where two or more children are concerned and their interests are in conflict.

(i) The basic rule: 'who is the subject of the application?'

Birmingham City Council v H (A Minor)[143] involved a mother who was herself a minor, being under 16, and her baby. The mother and baby had been taken into care, but had been separated. The mother applied for contact with the baby. It was felt that it was in the minor mother's interest that contact take place but that contact was not necessarily in the baby's interests. It was therefore crucial for the court to determine whose interest was paramount: the mother's or the baby's. The House of Lords took the view, relying on the wording of s 1(1) of the Children Act 1989, that it was the child who was the subject of the proceedings whose welfare was paramount. It was held that because the mother was applying for contact with the baby, the baby was the 'subject of the proceedings' and so it was the baby's interests which were paramount and therefore contact was not ordered.

This is not a very satisfactory approach because it may be a matter of chance what form the application takes and which child happens to be the subject of the application.[144] Although the approach of the House of Lords was correct as a matter of statutory interpretation, the House of Lords could have approached the issues on a more theoretical level: either by saying that in such cases the interests of the two children had to be balanced with each other; or that a minor mother's interests were always lower than her baby's. However, the House of Lords rejected these alternatives.

Birmingham City Council v H (A Minor)[145] has been applied in later cases. For example, in *Re S (Contact: Application by Sibling)*[146] Y (an adopted child) sought leave to bring an application for contact with her birth sister, S (also adopted, but by other parents). In such a case it was S's and not Y's welfare which was para-

---

[141] *Re W (Wardship: Discharge: Publicity)* [1995] 2 FLR 466 at p. 477 CA.
[142] B. Dickens (1981: 471).
[143] [1994] 2 AC 212.
[144] See Douglas (1994a).
[145] [1994] 2 AC 212; see Douglas (1994a).
[146] [1998] 2 FLR 897.

mount, because S was the 'subject' of the application.[147] In this case it was not in S's welfare to make a contact order, and so, however much contact may benefit Y, contact could not be ordered.

(ii) Where there are two or more children who are the subject of an application under the Children Act 1989

What if an application[148] were made in respect of two children and it was in the interests of one child that the order be made, but not in the interests of the other? Wilson J in *Re T and E*[149] explained that in such a case both children's welfare had to be taken into account and balanced against each other. So if the order would greatly benefit one child and slightly disadvantage the other, the order should be made. This approach was applied in *Re A (Conjoined Twins: Medical Treatment)*,[150] where there were two conjoined twins, J and M. If no medical treatment was provided then both would die. It was, however, possible to separate the twins with the result that J would live, but M would die. The operation would therefore be in J's interests, but not in M's (she would die sooner if the operation were performed than if it were not). The Court of Appeal was willing to balance the interests of the children. The interests of J were held to be more weighty than the interest of M and so the operation was authorised.

(iii) Where there are two or more children who are the subject of applications under different pieces of legislation

What if two children are the subject of connected applications under different pieces of legislation with different versions of the welfare principle? In *Re T and E*[151] T and E were half sisters. Both were in care. T's father wanted to revoke T's care order and sought a residence order under the Children Act 1989. The local authority sought an adoption order, hoping that T and E would be adopted together with the same family. The court decided that it was in T's interests for her to live with her father, but in E's interests for T and E to be adopted together. Wall J decided that under the adoption application the interests of both children were the 'first' consideration, but under the application for the revocation of the care order, T's welfare was paramount. The care order therefore had to be revoked, because it was in T's welfare to live with her father (even if that was contrary to E's interests).

F. Conflicts of interests between parents and children

One might expect that, given the welfare principle, if there is a clash between the interests of the children and parents, the interests of the child would be preferred.

---

[147] See also *Re F (Contact: Child in Care)* [1995] 1 FLR 510, [1994] 2 FCR 1354.
[148] Or two applications are heard together.
[149] [1995] 1 FLR 581, [1995] 3 FCR 260. Noted in Cromack and Parry (1996).
[150] [2001] 1 FLR 1, [2000] 3 FCR 577 CA.
[151] [1995] 1 FLR 581, [1995] 3 FCR 260.

As was stated by the Court of Appeal in *Re P (Contact: Supervision)*,[152] 'the court is concerned with the interests of the mother and the father only in so far as they bear on the welfare of the child'. So, however great the sacrifice demanded of parents, if there is overall a marginal increase in the child's welfare, the order should be made. In fact, despite the existence of the welfare principle, the English courts have been able to protect the interests of parents.[153] Four of the ways that have been used to do this will now be briefly examined, although there are more:

1. The law makes no attempt to ensure that everything that adults do in relation to children day to day promotes their welfare. There is no direct supervision of the way parents treat their children, unlike the close direct regulation of day-care centres or childminders.[154] Although there are regular inspections and assessments of day-care centres, there are no equivalent investigations into the way parents raise children. If the parents bring up the child in a way that harms the child then unless one of the parents or the local authority or the child brings the matter before a court, there is unlikely to be any formal legal intervention.[155]

2. As already noted, there are various issues to which the welfare principle does not apply, even though the interests of the child may still be an important consideration. Such circumstances include the granting of a divorce; domestic violence; financial redistribution of property on divorce; and enforcement of court orders.[156] It may be noted that these are hardly topics where children's interests are insignificant, but rather cases where parents' interests are particularly weighty. A cynic may suggest that the law is only willing to promote a child's welfare where that does not greatly inconvenience adults.

3. A third way that the courts have protected the rights of parents is through closely identifying the interests of children and parents. Perhaps the best recent example to illustrate this is *Re T (A Minor) (Wardship: Medical Treatment)*.[157] This case concerned a dispute over whether life-saving medical treatment should be given to a child. The unanimous medical opinion was in favour, but the parents opposed it. The court decided that it would not be in the child's best interests for the treatment to go ahead, bearing in mind the pressure that this would put on the parents. Butler-Sloss LJ reasoned: 'the mother and this child are one for the purpose of this unusual case and the decision of the court to consent to the operation jointly affects the mother and son and so also affects the father. The welfare of the child depends upon his mother.'[158]

   By suggesting that the interests of the parent and the child were 'one', the Court of Appeal was able to take account of the parents' interests under the umbrella of the child's welfare. It can be argued that this case failed to consider fully the possibility of the child being cared for by alternative carers if the parents felt unable to cope, and, further, that the court placed excessive weight on

---

[152] [1996] 2 FLR 314 at p. 328.
[153] Herring (1999a).
[154] Children Act 1989, Part X, Sch 9; Department of Health (1991d).
[155] Though see Donzelot (1980) for discussion of indirect policing of families.
[156] *Re F (Contact: Enforcement: Representation of Child)* [1998] 1 FLR 691, [1998] 3 FCR 216.
[157] [1997] 1 FLR 502.
[158] [1997] 1 FLR 502 at p. 510.

the parents' views and insufficient weight on the child's right to life. By seeing the mother and child as one, the child's independent interests were hidden.

4. The courts have sometimes protected parents' interests by explicitly limiting their jurisdiction. So, for example, in *Re E (Residence: Imposition of Conditions)*[159] the court refused to make it a condition of a mother's residence order that she remain in London because that would be to intervene in the mother's right to choose where to live.[160] There is nothing in the Children Act 1989 that limits the courts' jurisdiction in such a way, but decisions of this kind enable the court to protect the interests of parents.[161]

These indicate that, in fact, the courts are able to give effect to the interests of the parents despite purporting to uphold the welfare principle as a principle requiring the interests of parents to be subservient to the interests of children. In the light of the Human Rights Act 1998 the court will have to acknowledge explicitly that parents have human rights which cannot be automatically overridden simply by reference to the welfare principle. So how should the law deal with clashes between the rights and interests of parents and children? Here are some of the possibilities that could be adopted:[162]

1. *The welfare principle.* It could be argued that despite the acknowledgment of parents' rights in the Human Rights Act the court should continue to assert that the interests of children are the sole consideration.

2. *Primary and secondary interests (Bainham).* One of the most developed considerations of how to balance the conflicting rights and interests of family members is the analysis made by Bainham. He suggests that the answer is to categorise parents' and children's interests as either primary or secondary interests.[163] A child's secondary interests would have to give way to a parent's primary interests and similarly a parent's secondary interests must give way to a child's primary interests. In addition, the court should consider the 'collective family interest'.[164] This, he argues, should also be taken into account in the balancing exercise, so that the interests of one family member may have to be weighed against the good of the family as a unit.

3. *Relationship-based welfare (Herring).* This theory[165] argues that children should be brought up in relationships which overall promote their welfare. It argues that families, and society in general, are based on mutual co-operation and support. So it is important to encourage a child to adopt, to a limited extent, the virtue of altruism and an awareness of social obligation. Children should only be expected to be altruistic to the extent of not demanding from parents excessive sacrifices in return for minor benefits. It is beneficial for a child to be brought up in a family that is based on relationships which are fair and just. A relationship based on

[159] [1997] 2 FLR 638. Constrast *Re S (A Child: Residence Order: Condition) (No. 2)* [2003] 1 FCR 138.
[160] See Chapter 9 for further discussion.
[161] See also *D v N (Contact Order: Conditions)* [1997] 2 FLR 797, [1997] 3 FCR 721 CA.
[162] When considering these theories it may be useful to look at the facts of an actual case. Consider, for example, *Re S (A Child: Residence Order: Condition) (No. 2)* [2003] 1 FCR 138.
[163] Bainham (1998c).
[164] Bainham (1998c).
[165] Herring (1999b).

unacceptable demands on a parent is not furthering a child's welfare. So a court can legitimately make an order which benefits a parent, but not a child, if that can be regarded as appropriate in the context of their ongoing relationship.

4. *Modified least detrimental alternative (Eekelaar)*. Eekelaar summarises his theory in this way:

> The best solution is surely to adopt the course that avoids inflicting the most damage on the well-being of any interested individual ... [I]f the choice was between a solution that advanced a child's well-being a great deal, but also damaged the interests of one parent a great deal, and a different solution under which the child's well-being was diminished, but damaged the parent to a far lesser degree, one should choose the second option, even though it was not the least detrimental alternative for the child.'[166]

However, he adds an important qualification to this test and that is that 'no solution should be adopted where the detriments outweigh the benefits for the child, unless that would be the result of *any* available solution, so that is unavoidable.'[167] He also adds that there may be a degree of detriment to which a child should never be subjected, if that is avoidable.[168] He is concerned about cases where, for example, a disabled spouse would greatly suffer if on divorce the child were to live with the other parent.

5. *Balancing all interests*. This perspective[169] simply requires the courts to weigh up the interests of each party. There would be no particular preference for the interests of each of the parties. This approach would suggest that the court should make the order which would produce the most benefit and least detriment for the parties.

The difference between these approaches can be clarified by looking at the benefit or disadvantage of the proposed orders on a scale of +50 (the most beneficial) to −50 (the least beneficial). Consider these four possible orders (F being the father, M the mother and C the child):

> Solution 1: C (−30); F (+30); M (+30)
> Solution 2: C (−5); F (−5); M (+35)
> Solution 3: C (+10); F (−30); M (−40)
> Solution 4: C(+5); F (−5); M (−5)

The approach of balancing all the interests would support solution 1 because this is the one that produces the greatest total benefit adding together all the disadvantages and benefits for each party and treating them equally. Solution 1 would be unacceptable to the welfare principle because it harms the child. It would be unacceptable to Bainham because it involves the infringement of a primary interest of the child. It would also be unacceptable to Eekelaar because he refuses to accept making an order which causes a detriment to a child unless any order the court would make would cause a detriment to a child.

---

[166] Eekelaar (2002a: 243–4).
[167] Eekelaar (2002a: 243).
[168] Eekelaar (2002a: 245).
[169] This appears to be supported by Reece (1996).

The welfare principle approach would promote solution 3. Despite the fact this may harm (quite seriously) the father and mother, under the welfare principle the harms caused to the parents are irrelevant and this is the solution that would best promote the child's welfare. Eekelaar would prefer solution 4. Although solution 3 promotes the child's welfare to the greatest extent, it does so by causing the parents significant harm. Solution 4 manages still to promote the child's welfare (albeit to a lesser extent than solution 3) and it does so causing less harm to the parents. Bainham might also approve of solutions 2 or 4 because they do not involve the infringement of anyone's primary or secondary interests.

Herring's approach is less straightforward because it requires an understanding of the nature of the relationship in the past, and the foreseeable future. If, for example, in the past the mother and father have had to make unusual and extreme sacrifices for the benefit of the child solution 2 or even 1 may be acceptable.

8. THE HUMAN RIGHTS ACT 1998 AND CHILDREN'S WELFARE AND RIGHTS[170]

It is generally accepted that the European Convention on Human Rights does not provide adequately for the rights of children.[171] The Convention was clearly drawn up with adults (rather than children) as the focus of attention.[172] Indeed, there are no articles in the Convention explicitly dealing with children. However, that is not to say that children receive no protection under the Convention.[173] Children are entitled to the same rights under the Convention as adults.[174] Article 1 states: 'The High Contracting Parties shall secure to everyone within their jurisdiction the rights and freedoms in this Convention.'[175] The European Court has accepted that 'everyone' in article 1 includes children.[176] To give two examples: children have been able to bring applications before the European Court of Human Rights claiming that they are entitled to state protection under article 3 (to protect them from corporal punishment which constitutes torture or inhuman or degrading treatment)[177] and article 5 (to complain of being wrongfully detained in a hospital).[178] Children's interests can also sometimes be protected when an adult enforces his or her own rights. So the enforcement of a parent's rights of contact with his or her child inevitably leads to an enforcement of the right of the child to contact with his or her parent.[179]

---

[170] Fortin (1999a); Herring (1999b).
[171] Fortin (2002).
[172] Douglas (1988).
[173] For a thorough discussion of the rights of children under the European Convention see Kilkelly (2000).
[174] L. Smith (1993).
[175] Article 14 states that the rights must be granted without discrimination 'on any ground such as sex, race, colour ...' Although age is not specifically mentioned, the use of the words 'such as' indicates that the list is not intended to be exhaustive and so it could be argued that age should be included as a prohibited ground of discrimination.
[176] *Nielsen v Denmark* (1989) 11 EHRR 175 ECtHR.
[177] *A v UK (Human Rights: Punishment of Child)* [1998] 2 FLR 959.
[178] *Nielsen v Denmark* (1989) 11 EHRR 175 ECtHR.
[179] E.g. *Eriksson v Sweden* (1989) 12 EHRR 183 ECtHR.

Although children are in theory entitled to claim these rights, one leading commentator on child law has complained of the 'pitifully inadequate response thus far by the European Institutions to the equally independent rights of children under the Convention'.[180] This complaint is made because often the rights of the children concerned are not explicitly mentioned by the courts when cases are brought by adults even though the case concerns children. It is notable that many of the cases which have concerned children have involved parents bringing proceedings in respect of a breach of a parent's rights. For example, some of the leading cases on the corporal punishment of children in schools concern claims by parents that hitting children infringes the rights of parents.[181]

The relevance of particular rights of children under the Convention will be discussed where appropriate throughout the book; but now the way the Convention deals with clashes between the interests of adults and children will be considered.

A. Balancing the rights of parents and children under the Convention

The Convention, rather surprisingly, includes no explicit reference to ensure that the enforcement of adult rights does not harm a child's welfare. However, the European Court has been able to give weight to the interest of the child by considering the wording in the articles which restrict rights. For example, the most quoted article in cases concerning children is article 8:

1. Everyone has the right to respect for his private and family life, his home and his correspondence.
2. There shall be no interference by a public authority with the exercise of this right except such as is in accordance with the law and is necessary in a democratic society in the interests of national security, public safety or the economic well-being of the country, for the prevention of disorder or crime, for the protection of health or morals, or for the protection of the rights and freedoms of others.

So a permitted interference of a right must be in accordance with the law;[182] it must pursue a legitimate aim; it must be proportionate[183] and necessary.[184] It is clearly established that a 'legitimate aim' includes preserving the rights and welfare of children.[185] In other words, an infringement of an adult's right to respect for private and family life can be justified if necessary to protect the children's interests. However, as yet, the European Court of Human Rights has not developed a clear approach as to how to balance the rights and interests of parents and children. It is clear that in cases involving families, the interests of children must be considered. In *W v Federal Republic of Germany*[186] the Commission held that a national court

---

[180] Bainham (1995a: 258).
[181] Under article 2 of Protocol 1; *Campbell and Cosans v UK* (1982) 4 EHRR 293 ECtHR
[182] The procedure must be accessible, foreseeable and reasonably quick: *W v UK* (1988) 10 EHRR 29 ECtHR.
[183] *Price v UK* (1988) 55 D&R 1988.
[184] States have a margin of appreciation in deciding whether the intrusion is necessary.
[185] E.g. *R v UK* [1988] 2 FLR 445 ECtHR.
[186] (1985) 50 D&R 219.

should take into consideration the interests of children.[187] In *Hendriks* v *Netherlands*[188] it was stated: 'the Commission has consistently held that, in assessing the question of whether or not the refusal of the right of access to the non-custodial parent was in conformity with article 8 of the Convention, the interests of the child would predominate'. This was accepted as an accurate statement of the approach of the Convention by the Court of Appeal in *Re L (A Child) (Contact: Domestic Violence)*.[189] Most recently, the European Court of Human Rights in *Scott* v *UK*[190] has stated that the interests of the child are 'of crucial importance' in cases involving the interests of parents and child. In *Hoppe* v *Germany*[191] it was said the interests of children were of 'particular importance'.[192] In *Yousef* v *The Netherlands*[193] it was held that under the European Convention where the rights of children and parents conflict the rights of children will be the 'paramount consideration'. This is very close to the interpretation by the English and Welsh courts of the welfare principle, but falls short of holding that the welfare of the child is the sole consideration.

Despite these findings there are concerns that the Human Rights Act 1998, by explicitly giving parents rights, will weaken the interests of children. As Fortin[194] argues:

> It is of fundamental importance that the judiciary shows a willingness to interpret the European Convention in a child-centred way, as far as its narrow scope allows. It would be unfortunate in the extreme, if such a change heralded in an increased willingness to allow parents to pursue their own rights under the Convention at the expense of those of their children.

Kaganas and Piper[195] predict that the rights of adults under the Human Rights Act will only be upheld where these correspond to the current understanding of the welfare of the child. This will mean that there will be no conflict between the Human Rights Act and the welfare principle.

B. Is there any practical difference between the approaches of the European Convention and the Children Act 1989?

It has been seen that the European Convention, based upon rights, can take into account the welfare of children and that the Children Act 1989, based upon the welfare principle, has taken into account the rights of parents. It is therefore inevitable that the question be asked: is there any practical difference between the two approaches?[196]

---

[187] *L* v *Sweden* (1982) 40 D&R 140.
[188] (1982) 5 D&R 225.
[189] [2000] 2 FCR 404 CA.
[190] [2000] 2 FCR 560 at p. 572.
[191] [2003] 1 FCR 176, at para 49.
[192] See also *Sahin* v *Germany* [2003] 2 FCR 619.
[193] [2000] 2 FLR 118 at para 118.
[194] Fortin (1998a: 56).
[195] Kaganas and Piper (2001).
[196] See Herring (1999b); Choudhry (2003).

It may certainly be argued that the difference between the approach in the Human Rights Act 1998 and that in the Children Act 1989 is semantic only. Indeed, when the House of Lords directly faced the question whether the welfare principle and the rights protected in the Convention were consistent, it suggested that the difference was negligible. Bainham has argued that the courts see it 'as business as usual' in applying the welfare principle after the Human Rights Act.[197] In *Re KD (A Minor) (Ward: Termination of Access)*[198] Lord Templeman specifically compared the welfare principle and the Convention: 'In my opinion there is no inconsistency of principle or application between the English rule and the Convention rule.' Lord Oliver suggested that:

> Such conflict as exists is, I think, semantic only and lies only in differing ways of giving expression to the single common concept that the natural bond and relationship between parent and child gives rise to universally recognised norms which ought not to be gratuitously interfered with and which, if interfered with at all, ought to be so only if the welfare of the child dictates it.[199]

Such an approach has been confirmed by the House of Lords in *Re B (Adoption by One Natural Parent to Exclusion of Other)*.[200] It is respectfully suggested that this statement is not entirely accurate and that there are important differences between the approach of the Children Act 1989 and the European Convention on Human Rights. Imagine a case concerning contact between a child and a non-residential parent. Under the European Convention, the starting point is the parent's right to respect for family life which will be infringed if contact is denied. In order to justify the breach there must be clear and convincing evidence that the contact would infringe the rights and interests of the child to such an extent that the infringement was necessary and proportionate. However, under the Children Act there is a factual assumption that contact will promote the child's welfare, although this could be rebutted by evidence that contact would not promote the child's welfare in this particular case.

The difference between the two approaches is twofold. First, less evidence would be required under the Children Act to show the assumption that contact promotes a child's welfare than would be required under the Convention to show that infringement of the parent's rights is necessary and proportionate. Secondly, the nature of the question is different. Under the Children Act the question is a factual one (will contact promote the child's welfare?), whereas under the European Convention approach it is a question of legal judgment – whether the harm to the child is sufficient to make the breach 'necessary' as understood by the law.

A further difference between the approach of the welfare principle and the Convention is that the Convention is in this area essentially restrictive – it tells governments and courts what they may not do; while the welfare principle requires the court to act positively to promote the child's welfare.[201] A good example is article 2

---

[197] Bainham (2002b: 290). See also Harris-Short (2002: 338) for concerns that the courts have not taken the impact of the Human Rights Act seriously enough.
[198] [1988] 2 FLR 139, [1988] FCR 657.
[199] [1988] 1 All ER 577 at p. 588.
[200] [2002] 1 FLR 196.
[201] Although note s 1(5) of the Children Act 1989.

of the first Protocol: 'no person shall be denied the right to education'. It should be noted that this does not give a positive right to education, just a right not to be denied any education offered by the state. Similarly, article 8 requires that the state should not interfere with respect for family life, but the wording does not appear to require the state to promote family life. That said, as seen in Chapter 7, article 8 has been interpreted to require the state in some circumstances to act positively to promote the child's welfare.

9. CRITICISMS OF THE WELFARE PRINCIPLE

The welfare principle seeks to ensure that children are not exploited for the interests of adults.[202] At least, judicial decisions concerning children's upbringing must be phrased in terms of benefit for children. This can be justified on the basis that children are likely to be the least responsible for the difficulties that have led to the court case. They are also the least likely to be able to escape from the family difficulties and be least equipped to respond positively to the effect of any order which is against their interests.

Despite its predominance in the law relating to children, the welfare principle has been criticised.[203] Some of the main objections will be now be outlined.

1. *The law has a narrow perception of welfare.* King and Piper have argued that 'the broad range of factors – genetic, financial, educational, environmental and relational – which science would recognise as capable of affecting the welfare of a child are narrowed by law to a small range of issues which fall directly under the influence of the judge, the social workers or the adult parties to the litigation process'.[204] The court does not consider issues such as pollution, the quality of public housing and wider political questions which can have a powerful effect on the interests of children.

2. *Uncertainty.* Mnookin[205] argues that the welfare principle gives rise to uncertainty and unpredictability. The uncertainty arises from the great many unknowns concerning welfare. The facts are not known because often there is only the conflicting evidence of the father and mother as to the history of the parents' relationship. Even if the facts are established, it is impossible to predict how well the parties will be able to care for children. Even if the court could predict how the parents will act, it may be hard to choose who is the better parent, given the lack of agreed values over what makes an ideal parent. These uncertainties in effect give a judge a wide discretion in deciding what is in a child's welfare. This creates problems for parents in negotiating. As it is hard to anticipate how a judge might decide a case, the parties may well prefer chancing a judicial hearing, rather than reaching a negotiated settlement. By contrast, if it was predictable how a judge would resolve a dispute between the parties then

---

[202] Eekelaar (2002a).
[203] See e.g., Reece (1996).
[204] King and Piper (1995: 50). This is based on autopoietic theory: see Chapter 1.
[205] Mnookin (1975).

there would be little point in incurring the expenses involved in taking the matter to court.

3. *Smokescreen.* There is a concern that, given the uncertainty surrounding the welfare principle, the real basis for the decision will be hidden.[206] In particular, the prejudices of the professionals involved (the judiciary, the expert witnesses and the lawyers) provide the true reason behind the decision. For example, an individual's ideology of what makes a good mother or father can be extremely significant.[207] This then can lead to the welfare presumption being used in a way which works against the interests of women.[208]

4. *Increased costs.* It can be argued that the welfare principle simply increases the costs for the parties. Its unpredictability means that it is harder to negotiate a settlement and the complexity of the test means that court hearings take longer and require more substantial preparation.

5. *Unfairness.* The welfare principle can be attacked for failing to give adequate (or indeed any) weight to the interests of adults.[209] Eekelaar explains: 'the very ease of the welfare test encourages a laziness and unwillingness to pay proper attention to all the interests that are at stake in these decisions and, possibly, also a tendency to abdicate responsibility for decision making to welfare professionals'.[210]

6. *Unrealistic.* If there is a dispute over the medical treatment for a child and the matter is brought before the court a judge deciding what is the best for the child may decide that the child should be flown to the top medical hospital in America to be treated by the world's leading expert in the field, with no expense spared.[211] Of course a court could not make such an order. As this indicates, it is often for practical reasons impossible to make the order that would best promote the child's welfare.

10. ALTERNATIVES TO THE WELFARE PRINCIPLE

If the law were to abandon the welfare principle, what alternatives could be used?[212]

1. *Maternal presumption.* There could be a strong presumption that children should live with their mothers and the views of the mother should be preferred over the view of the father in any issue of dispute. In fact, few would support such an overtly gender-based standard.[213] Indeed, such a presumption would be opposed by many feminists on the ground that it would reinforce and perpetuate the view that child-care is 'women's work'.[214]

---

[206] Reece (1996: 296–7).
[207] Boyd (1996).
[208] Fineman (1988).
[209] Reece (1996: 303), although Ribbens McCarthy, Edwards and Gillies (2003: 140) argue that the position that the interests of children should be first is one of the few 'unquestionable moral assertions'.
[210] Eekelaar (2002a: 248).
[211] Archard (2003: 41).
[212] Meli (1993).
[213] Although, as we shall see in Chapter 9, the courts have been willing to assume that babies' interests are normally best pursued by living with their mothers.
[214] Carbone (1996).

2. *Primary carer principle.*[215] This approach suggests that the child should reside with the parent who was the primary carer of the child before the breakdown and that the law should uphold the views of the primary care-taker in respect of any dispute concerning the upbringing of the child, unless it would demonstrably harm the child.[216] The primary care-taker principle could be justified on three grounds. First, the parent who was primarily responsible for the care of the child is the person who is most likely to know the child the best and have the strongest relationship with the child. This has led Minow to suggest that the primary carer principle is strongest when the child is younger, and weakens when he or she is older.[217] Secondly, it can be argued that it has benefits over the welfare approach because it is fact-based (who undertook the majority of the care for the child before the separation?) rather than judgement-orientated (who is the best parent?). Those who fear that the welfare principle is too vague or open to misuse by the judge's prejudices may therefore prefer this test. Thirdly, the primary carer principle rewards the parent who has sacrificed the most during the relationship in caring for the child. The principle might even be thought to compensate for the lack of recognition that society otherwise accords to those who care for children. It might even encourage both parents to be involved as much as possible with the child's care, during the relationship.[218]

Those who oppose the primary carer principle fall into three main camps. Some claim that it is in effect a thinly disguised maternal presumption: women are nearly always the primary carers. The principle is therefore anti-fathers.[219] This is a little unfair, as it is only anti-fathers to the extent that fathers choose not to perform at least half of the child-care. That said, it is certainly true that society in some ways makes it easier for women rather than men to care primarily for the child. In fact evidence from West Virginia, USA, which for a time experimented with using the primary carer presumption, suggests that it worked against mothers, at least those mothers who did not fall into the traditional mould.[220] There is a second objection and that is that the approach does not place sufficient emphasis on the welfare of the child. The primary carer during the relationship may not be the best person to care for the child after the relationship. If there is strong evidence that the child's welfare would be promoted by the non-primary carer, should not the primary carer principle be overridden? Supporters of the principle would argue that such a prediction would be no more than guesswork. Thirdly, opponents of the primary carer principle suggest that the claimed benefit of certainty may be exaggerated; it may in fact be far from clear who was the primary carer.[221]

3. *Presumption of joint residence and parenting.* It would be possible to create a presumption that, after separation, the child should split his or her time between

---

[215] Boyd (1996).
[216] Chambers (1984).
[217] Minow (1986).
[218] Brophy (1985).
[219] Bainham (1990).
[220] Bartlett (1999).
[221] Elster (1987).

each parent and that all important issues should be resolved by joint agreement. Although at one time popular in the United States, it has never been a common solution in England and Wales. Unless the parents have a good relationship, joint residence is not likely to work effectively. Further, there are fears that children will feel unsettled and insecure if they are in constantly changing environments.

4. *Promoting co-operative parenting.*[222] It has been suggested that even if joint residence is not to be presumed, residence should be granted to the parent who will best promote contact with the other parent.[223] The hope is that the law will thereby encourage both parents to play as full a role in the life of the child as possible. Such an approach could be supported by evidence that children benefit from contact with the non-residential parent,[224] but it would be very difficult to predict which parent would truly encourage contact, as inevitably, if this approach were adopted, both parents would promise to permit contact.

5. *Letting the child decide.* There is much evidence that although children wish to be listened to when their parents separate, most do not want to be forced to decide between their parents.[225] It is therefore unlikely that this would be appropriate except for mature teenagers who have strong views. There are further dangers that the approach might encourage parents to manipulate the child's views.

6. *Tossing a coin.* Elster suggests that resolving disputes over children could be resolved by tossing a coin.[226] In part this approach is a counsel of despair: the courts are not able to predict what will promote the welfare of the child and so they may as well toss a coin. The approach is cheap and treats each side equally. However, the approach cannot really be acceptable, because it abdicates responsibility for children. It is true there are some cases where it is impossible to know what is in a child's interest, but there are many others where the court can ascertain what is in a child's interests or at least what is not in a child's interests. Not to protect the child in such a case would appear irresponsible.[227]

7. *Non-legal solutions.* It is perhaps too readily assumed that disputes between family members should be resolved by a court hearing.[228] It is certainly arguable that social work to assist the family may be more effective than legal intervention. Masson,[229] considering disputes over contact, suggests that rather than spending resources on lengthy bitter disputes in deciding whether or not there should be contact, resources may be better spent encouraging the parties to reach their own decision and facilitating contact. Thorpe LJ in *Re L (A Child) (Contact: Domestic Violence)*,[230] also talking about disputes over contact, has suggested:

---

[222] Bainham (1990) see also Kaganas and Piper (2002).
[223] *Re K (Residence Order: Securing Contact)* [1999] 1 FLR 583 CA.
[224] See Chapter 9.
[225] Cantwell and Scott (1995).
[226] Elster (1987).
[227] C. Schneider (1991).
[228] M. King (2000).
[229] Masson (2000b).
[230] [2000] 2 FCR 404 at p. 437.

The disputes are particularly prevalent and intractable. They consume a disproportionate quantity of private law judicial time. The disputes are often driven by personality disorders, unresolved adult conflicts or egocentricity. These originating or contributing factors would generally be better treated therapeutically, where at least there would be some prospect of beneficial change, rather than given vent in the family justice system.[231]

Whether such an approach could be justified in the light of the Human Rights Act 1998, and the requirement that the state protects the rights of parents and children, is open to debate. This gives rise to some of the debates over mediation which were considered in Chapter 3.

11. CHILDREN'S RIGHTS

So far we have looked at the law's attempts to promote the welfare of the child. However, in the last few decades there have been calls that, rather than adults attempting to promote the child's welfare, the law should recognise that children have rights of their own.[232] After all it is hard to resist the argument 'children have human rights, because children are human'.[233] Indeed children's rights are protected by a variety of international instruments, including most notably the United Nations Convention on the Rights of the Child.[234]

There are those who argue that it is not helpful (or not possible) to talk about humans having rights. They are in a minority and so here it will be assumed that people should have (or do have) some rights and we will focus on the questions of whether children have rights. There are two key questions:

1. Should children have all the rights that adults have or should we limit the rights available to children?
2. Should children be given extra rights over and above those given to adults?[235]

A. Should children have all the rights adults have?

A simple approach is that children are people and so should have all the rights that adults have.[236] These will include the right to vote, work, travel, use drugs and to engage in sexual relations.[237] Such an approach is taken by a group of thinkers known as child liberationists[238] or colloquially as 'kiddy libbers'.[239] For example,

---

[231] *Re L (A Child) (Contact: Domestic Violence)* [2000] 2 FCR 404 at p. 439.
[232] For a consideration of children's rights from a global perspective see John (2003). Woodhouse (2000) provides a useful discussion of children's rights.
[233] Herring (2003b: 146).
[234] Fortin (2003b: ch. 2) provides an invaluable discussion on the rights of children in international law. The government has been criticised for failing to implement the Convention by the United Nations Committee on the Rights of the Child (2002).
[235] See Herring (2003b) for more detailed discussion.
[236] Although still today some academic commentators take the view that it is appropriate to call a child 'it'. I'll refrain from naming and shaming!
[237] Holt (1975: 18).
[238] Children's liberationists include Foster and Freund (1972) and Holt (1975). For criticism see Archard (1993a); Fox Harding (1996).
[239] Mnookin (1981).

Holt[240] has written that the law supports the view of a child 'being wholly sub-servient and dependent ... being seen by older people as a mixture of expensive nuisance, slave and super-pet'. Initially, the approach seems unacceptable: surely we cannot accept a society where children have the same rights to sexual freedom, to marry, or to drive cars as adults?[241] The child liberationist position is often crit-icised for failing to appreciate the physical and mental differences between children and adults.[242] But this is not quite what most child liberationists nowadays claim. They argue that the same laws should apply to adults and children. It is quite per-missible to ban from driving those incapable of driving competently, but the state should not ban people from driving on the grounds of age. So children should not be barred from driving simply on the basis of their age, but can be on the basis of their inability at driving. Similarly, in sexual matters, if the child is not competent to consent then it would be unlawful for someone to have sexual relations with him or her. But that would be true for all who have sexual relations with those who do not consent. Another way of putting this argument is that children should not be discriminated against on the grounds of their age.[243] It must be admitted that the present law on at what age young people are able to do something is illogical. To give one example: a 16-year-old is deemed old enough to consent to sexual relations with her or his MP, but not to vote for her or him![244]

This more moderate liberationist approach is harder to rebut. It is necessary to show some morally relevant distinction between children and adults in order to jus-tify rejection of the liberationist position.[245] One argument may be based on bureaucratic difficulties in assessing competence. To expect a bar-tender to inter-view every person who orders a drink to ascertain whether they have sufficient understanding of the potential harms of alcohol to make a reasoned decision to pur-chase it would be unworkable.[246] A slightly different point is that using age provides a clear impersonal requirement, because the assessment of each individual's capacity can involve 'contested norms'.[247] Age also provides a predictable criterion which enables people to plan their lives, without fearing that they will be found incompetent.[248]

As can be seen already, much of the discussion about children's rights centres on the right to autonomy. The right to autonomy is essentially the right to decide how you wish to live your life. Eekelaar has called autonomy 'the most dangerous but precious of rights: the right to make their own mistakes'.[249] Most people accept that if an adult wishes to spend all his or her free time playing computer games or watch-ing television or writing a law textbook he or she can, providing these activities do

---

[240] Holt (1975).
[241] Archard (2003: 9) suggests that some writers are 'rhetorical child liberationists' in that they do not really mean that children should have all the rights of adults, but that to make such a claim is eye-catching and therefore politically a useful way of increasing the number of rights children have.
[242] Fortin (2003b: 5).
[243] Herring (2003b).
[244] Children's Law Centre (1999) provides a useful guide as to what a young person can do at what age.
[245] Roche (1999).
[246] How many adults would pass the test?
[247] Haldane (1994).
[248] Teitelbaum (1999).
[249] Eekelaar (1986: 161).

not harm anyone else. Sometimes writers talk about each person being permitted to pursue their own vision of the 'good life'. This is generally regarded as not only good for each individual but also good for society. Our society would be a less culturally rich society if everyone were to spend all their free time jogging, for example. It is good for society that there is diversity in the kinds of hobbies people enjoy. The difficulty is in applying this approach to children. Specifically, children do not have the capacity to develop their own version of their 'good life', at least in the sense of defining long-term goals. The essential problem is this: the way a child lives his or her childhood affects the range of choices and options available later on in life.[250] A simple example is that allowing a child to pursue their vision of a good life and allowing them not to go to school may mean that they will be prevented from pursuing what they regard as the good life once they reach majority because they will not have the education needed to pursue their goals. It may therefore be justifiable to infringe a child's autonomy during minority in order to maximise their autonomy later on in life. This, then, could explain why children cannot be treated as adults and why the state may be entitled to restrict autonomy rights in the name of promoting the child's welfare and ultimately their autonomy. Eekelaar has developed a well-respected version of children's rights.[251] He started with Raz's definition of a right that: 'a law creates a right if it is based on and expresses the view that someone has an interest which is sufficient ground for holding another to be subject to a duty'.[252] Eekelaar suggests that three kinds of interest are relevant for children:

1. *Basic interests.* These are the essential requirements of living – physical, emotional and intellectual interests. They would include the interest in being provided with food and clothing and in developing emotionally and intellectually. Eekelaar argues that the duty to promote these basic needs lies on parents, but there is also a duty on the state to provide these where parents fail to do so.
2. *Developmental interests.* Eekelaar describes these as 'all children should have an equal opportunity to maximise the resources available to them during their childhood (including their own inherent abilities) so as to minimise the degree to which they enter adult life affected by avoidable prejudices incurred during childhood'.[253] Eekelaar accepts that, apart from education, these would be hard to enforce as legal rights.
3. *Autonomy interest.* This is the freedom for the child to make his or her own decisions about their life.

Of these three interests, Eekelaar would rank the autonomy interest as subordinate to the developmental and basic interests.[254] So children would not be able to claim autonomy interests in a way that would prejudice their basic or developmental interests. He would therefore allow children to make decisions for themselves, even

---

[250] Eekelaar (1994b).
[251] Eekelaar (1994b). Bevan (1989: 11) proposes a simple division of children's rights which are protective and those which are self-assertive. This has received the support of Fortin (2003b: 17).
[252] Raz (1994).
[253] Eekelaar (1994b).
[254] Eekelaar (1994b). Freeman (1997a) proposes a similar theory and agrees with the subordination of autonomy to other basic needs of the child.

if those were bad mistakes, unless the decision involved infringing one of the basic or developmental interests. This would mean that a child's decision not to go to school would be overridden, because this would be infringing their developmental interests. But their decision to wear jeans should not be overridden as it would not infringe their interests.[255] Of course, there may be borderline cases (would nose piercing be permitted?) but such borderline cases are present in every theory. Eekelaar's approach has the benefit of providing an explanation of why children do not have all the rights of adults – so that they can have greater autonomy as adults – and provides a sensible practical model enabling children to make some decisions for themselves, but not so as to cause themselves serious harm.[256]

Eekelaar has developed his thinking by suggesting that the law should promote a child's welfare by encouraging dynamic self-determinism.[257] He explains that:

> The process is dynamic because it appreciates that the optimal course for a child cannot always be mapped out at the time of decision, and may need to be revised as the child grows up. It involves self-determinism because the child itself is given scope to influence the outcome.'[258]

The aim of this approach is:

> To bring a child to the threshold of adulthood with the maximum opportunities to form and pursue life-goals which reflect as closely as possible an autonomous choice.[259]

This approach would therefore give children an increasing role in making decisions for themselves as they grow up.

One way to test Eekelaar's theory would be to ask (as Eekelaar has) how as adults looking back on our childhood we would have wished to have been raised. The answer is probably that we would not have wanted every desire we had as children to be granted. It may well be that we would come up with a set of guidelines similar to Eekelaar's. However, this approach is problematic. Archard [260] considers parents who face a choice of encouraging a child to play sport or music. If we ask what as an adult the child would want, this is problematic because what the child when he or she grows up would think will depend on the choice. If the parents choose music and the child grows up a talented musician he or she will approve of his or her parents' decisions. However, if the parents choose sport and the child becomes a successful sportsperson then the child will approve of that decision. There are also problems because the hypothetical adult will decide using adult eyes. Would the adult let the child go to an expensive Santa's grotto at Christmas, or would the hypothetical adult regard that as a waste of money?

There are also difficulties with applying Eekelaar's theory practically in modern society. Imagine a child who is a highly gifted musician. What are the parents to do? Should the parents permit or encourage the child to devote most of her life to devel-

---

[255] Unless he or she were not allowed to attend school while wearing jeans.

[256] Giddens (1998: 191–2) argues for the democratisation of family life, with children being treated as equal citizens in the family.

[257] Eekelaar (1994a).

[258] Eekelaar (1994a: 48).

[259] Eekelaar (1994a: 156).

[260] Archard (2003: 51).

oping this talent? If the parents do, is it not arguable that that will limit the child's range of lifestyles in adulthood: she will be aged 18, a gifted musician, but with a limited range of alternatives in life. If, however, the parent seeks to encourage her to develop a wide range of interests and hobbies and not dedicate a large portion of her life to music, it is unlikely that she will be sufficiently skilled to become a professional musician. With increased specialisation (especially in artistic, academic and sporting activities), dedication in childhood is essential in order to live out some life goals. A more common example is of children whose parents have undergone a bitter divorce. The court may have to decide whether the child will live with the mother or the father, knowing that contact with the other parent is unlikely to be effective. In such a case the court cannot keep the options open for the child to decide when they are an adult; the court must decide on some basis which is best for the child.[261]

A second problem with Eekelaar's approach is that it is not clear why it is restricted to childhood. The university student who fails to work towards their degree and ends up failing their examinations could be said to have lessened their ability to choose their life choices. Is there a good reason for not permitting a child to limit their life choices but allowing young adults to do so?

A third objection is that Eekelaar's approach may lead to an open-ended solution. Leaving the question so that the child can make decisions when they are old enough may leave issues connected with the child's upbringing unresolved and open-ended.[262] For example, in relation to a dispute over religious upbringing, Eekelaar's approach may suggest that a child be brought up within both religions so that they can decide their religion for themselves later on in life. However, this may leave the child confused and unsettled. Despite these difficulties it is submitted that Eekelaar's approach provides the best approach to examining children's rights.

B. The argument against rights for children

1. There are two main theories of rights: the will theory and the interest theory.[263] The will theory argues that rights can only exist where the right-holder can have choice in deciding whether or not to enforce the rights. This would mean that children (especially if very young) could not have rights.[264] MacCormick and other supporters of children's rights argue that this would be unacceptable and hence he rejects the will theory of rights in favour of the interest theory, which protects the interests of the right-holder and is not dependent on the ability to make a choice.[265] The arguments for and against these theories are discussed in detail in books on jurisprudence.[266]

---

[261] C. Smith (1997b).

[262] C. Smith (1997b).

[263] MacCormick (1976).

[264] It could be argued by supporters of the will theory who wish to support children's rights that if children are not competent to choose whether or not to enforce their rights, parents are entitled to enforce those rights on children's behalf. See the discussion in Archard (2003: 7).

[265] The benefits and disadvantages of these approaches are beyond the scope of this book.

[266] See e.g. MacCormick (1976); Archard (2003: ch. 1).

2. A second objection would be that focusing on rights does not provide adequate protection for children.[267] Children are vulnerable and need protection from adults who can seek to take advantage of them and from children's own foolish decisions. As Archard puts it:

> [Children] need to be nurtured, supported and, more particularly, subjected to control and discipline. Without that context, giving children the rights that adults have is not only bad for the children but is also bad for the adults they will turn into, and for the society we share as adults and children.[268]

A moderate version of children's rights, such as Eekelaar's, would seem to diffuse such fears. However, there are still concerns that too much weight may be placed on children's wishes. Sir Thomas Bingham MR in *Re S (A Minor) (Independent Representation)*[269] has explained:

> First is the principle, to be honoured and respected, that children are human beings in their own right with individual minds and wills, views and emotions, which should command serious attention. A child's wishes are not to be discounted or dismissed simply because he is a child. He should be free to express them and decision-makers should listen. Second is the fact that a child is after all a child. The reason why the law is particularly solicitous in protecting the interests of children is that they are liable to be vulnerable and impressionable, lacking the maturity to weigh the longer term against the shorter, lacking the insight to know how they will react and the imagination to know how others will react in certain situations, lacking the experience to match the probable against the possible . . .

3. A further difficulty with rights for children is that an enforcement of a right of autonomy for a child will mean in many cases an infringement of a parent's or other carer's rights. Children live much of their childhood dependent on adults and their relationship with adults is crucial. It is arguable that the language of rights is quite inappropriate in intimate family relationships, where sacrifice and mutual support are the overriding values of the family unit, rather than the individual market-place philosophy where rights might make more sense.[270] It may be possible to produce a vision of rights that promotes individual autonomy *and* interpersonal connection, but these would not be identical to rights as they are commonly understood.[271]

Much work among feminist writers has been in developing an 'ethic of care'.[272] Sevenhuijsen explains that the ethic of care: 'is encapsulated in the idea that individuals can exist only because they are members of various networks of care and responsibility, for good or bad. The self can exist only through and with others and vice versa . . .'[273]

---

[267] Purdy (1994).
[268] Archard (2003: 16).
[269] [1993] 2 FLR 437, [1993] 2 FCR 1.
[270] Regan (1993a); Diamantides (1999).
[271] Minow (1986); Herring (1999a).
[272] See e.g. Sevenhuijsen (2000); Noddings (2003).
[273] Sevenhuijsen (2002: 131).

Such a model would seem to emphasise the values of interdependence and relationships, rather than individualistic versions of rights. Smart has explained that the ethic of care:

> need not be carried forward on the basis of individual rights in which the child is construed as an autonomous individual consumer of oppositional rule-based entitlements, but more where the child is construed as part of a web of relationships in which outcomes need to be negotiated (not demanded) and where responsibilities are seen to be reciprocal.[274]

4. O'Neill[275] has suggested that it would be more profitable to focus on the notion of duties that adults owe towards children, than to stress the rights of children.[276] She is particularly concerned with impressive-sounding rights when it is unclear who has the duty to provide the child with the benefit. She warns:

> many of the rights promulgated in international documents are not perhaps spurious, but they are patently no more than 'manifesto' rights ... that cannot be claimed unless or until practices and institutions are established that determine against whom claims on behalf of a particular child may be lodged. Mere insistence that certain ideals or goals are rights cannot make them into rights ...[277]

She therefore argues that there are obligations owed to children, which cannot be recognised as rights, but that should still be recognised as obligations. The main remedy she suggests to deal with children's powerlessness is to grow up.

5. A further argument is that even if in theory children's rights are beneficial, in practice children's rights can be used to the disadvantage of women and children.[278] The fear is that rights are of use to those who have strength within society and, in particular, rights are of use to men to be used as tools of oppression. For example, children's rights could be used to investigate and control the intimate lives of women.

There are also concerns that children's rights reflect the norms within society, which may be discriminatory. Olsen asks why getting children to help mother bake cookies at home is not a form of child labour.[279] This question, although a little tongue in cheek, does lead us to enquire how many of what we regard as human rights are in fact just a reflection of the cultural values of our society.

6. There is a concern over the enforcement of children's rights. If children's rights can only realistically be enforced by adults, it may be that such rights will be used only for the benefit of adults. For example, the courts have held that a child has a right to know his or her genetic origins, but in practice this only occurs when a father seeks to have biological tests carried out to determine whether or not he is the father. This example may lead one to conclude that in reality this is a right for fathers to establish paternity, rather than for children to know their genetic identity.

---

[274] Smart (2003: 239).
[275] O'Neill (1992). For a response, see Coady (1992).
[276] For a discussion over whether too much is expected of children's rights see Wardle (1996); M. King (1997); Freeman (2000c).
[277] Discussed further in Freeman (1997a).
[278] Olsen (1992).
[279] Olsen (1992).

This has led some to call for a children's rights commissioner who can enforce rights on behalf of children who are unable to enforce such rights themselves.[280] The House of Commons Joint Committee on Human Rights has said that a children's commissioner should be appointed for England.[281] Wales already has one.[282] The government Green Paper, *Every Child Matters*,[283] suggests that England should have one too.

A slightly different point is that children in our society are not used to being listened to. In schools and homes children become accustomed to not being expected to make decisions for themselves.[284] Lowe and Murch also raise difficulties over communication between children and adults:

> children, in certain respects, inhabit different cultural worlds from adults. Moreover, they can be baffled by the language of adults, especially by professional jargon. Equally, adults are often unfamiliar with children's language codes which, in any event, can differ from age group to age group.[285]

The ease of misconception is demonstrated by the finding of one study which suggested that children associated courts with criminal wrongdoing, even if in fact the court is a family one.[286]

7. Some commentators have argued that the most important right children have is 'the right to be a child'.[287] This argument emphasises that children should not be expected to bear the responsibilities of adulthood. There is, for example, evidence from psychologists interviewing children whose parents are divorcing which suggests that although children do wish to be listened to by their parents and the courts, they do not wish to be required to choose between their parents.[288] Critics suggest that such arguments are based on an idealised childhood – a time of innocence, free from the concerns and responsibility of the adult world – that is a far cry from the poverty, bullying and abuse which is the lot of all too many children.[289]

C. Extra rights for children

So far the chapter has focused on whether children are entitled to all the rights that adults have. But can children claim rights which adults do not have? It certainly seems so. Children may be thought to have rights to education, protection from

---

[280] United Nations Committee on the Rights of the Child (2002).
[281] House of Commons Joint Committee on Human Rights (2003).
[282] Children's Commissioner for Wales Act 2001, discussed Hollingsworth and Douglas (2002). The Commissioner discusses his work in Rees (2002). A survey carried out by UNICEF of children in the UK found that more than 90 per cent wanted a children's rights commissioner (BBC (2002a)). Recently the government appointed a Minister for Children.
[283] Department for Education and Skills (2003).
[284] Schofield and Thoburn (1996: 62).
[285] Lowe and Murch (2001: 145).
[286] Lowe and Murch (2001: 152).
[287] Campbell (1992).
[288] Cantwell and Scott (1995).
[289] See Phillips (2003) who discusses the pervasive violence faced by many children in their everyday lives.

abuse[290] and financial support to a greater extent than might be claimed by adults. These would reflect the developmental interests expounded in Eekelaar's approach. A clear example is that a parent is liable to support a child financially until (normally) the child reaches the age of 18.[291] These rights, then, are the rights of the child to enable him or her to become an adult and take on the full mantle of rights an adult has.

D. Children's rights for adults

Most of the discussion on children's rights has centred on the debate whether children are as competent as adults. Although difficult to gauge, probably most commentators appear to accept that the vulnerability of children and their dependency on their parents means that children cannot be granted the same rights as adults. However, it is interesting to ask the question the other way around: are adults as vulnerable and dependent as children? Although the law tends to assume that adults are self-sufficient, fully competent adults, this is an ideal which is unrealistic for many adults.[292] It can be argued that 'once co-operative, care-giving relationships among vulnerable people (rather than autonomous individuals) are seen as the basis around which rights work, the difficulties with children having the same rights to a large extent fall away'.[293]

E. Children's rights in practice

As we have seen, most of the academic discussion on children's rights has centred on children's rights of autonomy. However, this discussion of children's rights is skewed from a western perspective. Notably, looking at the main English and Welsh textbooks on family law it is easier to find a discussion on whether children should be allowed to pierce their noses than on children's right to clean water. We tend to take for granted that the basic needs of children are met.[294] However, Britain need not be complacent:

- The number of children recorded as living in poverty in 2000/01 was 3.9 million.[295]
- Seven per cent of children suffer serious physical abuse at the hands of their parents. [296]
- One-quarter of 16-year-olds failed to achieve any GCSEs above a grade D in 2001.[297]
- One-third of British teenagers are overweight.[298]

---

[290] E.g. Children Act 1989, Part IV.
[291] See Chapter 5.
[292] Minow (1986); Lim and Roche (2000).
[293] Herring (2003b: 172).
[294] See UNICEF (2000) for an outline of the agonies facing the world's children.
[295] Child Poverty Action Group (2002). There are clear links between race and child poverty: Oppenhein and Lister (1996). The government has said it is determined to eradicate child poverty, see the discussion in M. Roberts (2001).
[296] NSPCC (2000).
[297] New Policy Institute (2002).
[298] BBC News Online, 17 September 2002.

- The president of the Family Division pointed out that Britons give far more money by way of charitable giving to donkey sanctuaries than to children in need.[299]

Indeed the United Nations Committee on the Rights of the Child had no difficulty in providing extensive criticism of the position of children within the UK.[300]

F. Is there a difference between a welfare-based approach and a rights-based approach?

Does it really make any difference whether the law talks in terms of children's rights or their welfare?[301] Traditionally there has been seen to be a clash between those who are paternalists and those who are supporters of children rights.[302] Paternalism takes as its starting point that children are vulnerable and in need of protection from the dangers posed by adults, other children and themselves. Children lack the knowledge, experience or strength to care for themselves, and therefore society must do all it can to promote the child's welfare.[303] Within paternalism there is some dispute over who should decide what is in the child's best interests: the child's parents or the state, taking the advice of expert psychologists.

After all, the rights of children to clothing, food, education etc. could all equally be supported in terms of a child's right to their basic needs and as necessary in order to promote a child's welfare. Indeed, as Eekelaar has pointed out, 'if people have rights to anything, it must include the right that their well-being be respected'.[304] In fact, in the vast majority of situations there would be no difference in result whether a rights-based approach or a welfare-based approach was taken. But, in practical terms, when would it matter which approach is taken? Looking at Eekelaar's approach, the welfare approach would justify promoting a child's basic or developmental interests. The difference between the approaches is revealed when considering the autonomy approach. The rights-based approach would permit children to make decisions for themselves as long as there is no infringement of the developmental or basic interests. A welfare approach would also permit children to make some decisions for themselves. This is because it could be said to be in a child's interests to learn from their own mistakes. Alternatively, it could be argued that refusing to follow the child's wishes would cause the child emotional distress. The difference between a welfare approach and Eekelaar's rights-based approach would be over a small band of cases where allowing a child to decide for him- or herself would not infringe their basic or developmental interests, but would cause enough harm for a welfare approach to decide that more harm would be caused by allowing them to make the decision than not. Consider also this state-

---

[299] Butler-Sloss (2003).
[300] United Nations Committee on the Rights of the Child (2002).
[301] See the very useful discussion in Bainham (2002).
[302] Although interestingly the United Nations Committee on the Rights of the Child (2002) called for the UK to use the welfare principle in all areas which affect children.
[303] Fox Harding (1996).
[304] Eekelaar (2002a: 243).

ment of Dame Butler-Sloss: 'The child has a right to a relationship with his father even if he [the child] does not want it.'[305] Indeed, it could be said that children have a right to have their welfare promoted. However, Eekelaar[306] has rejected any suggestion of such a right:

> A claim simply that some should act to further my welfare as they define it is in reality to make no claim at all. Running behind these explicit propositions lies the suggestion that to treat someone fully as an individual of moral worth implies recognizing that that person makes claims and exercises choices: that is, is a potential right-holder.

Even if in practical terms there are few cases when the approaches would produce different results, there are important conceptual differences between the two approaches. The first is that although both rights and welfare models can be explained on the basis that they protect the child's interest, in the welfare model the courts or parents determine what children's interests are, whereas the rights-based model seeks to promote the interests as the child sees them to be, or would see them were they capable. A second important difference is that the existence of rights implies that there are duties. That is that the child (or those acting on behalf of the child) can make claims against the court or parents. However, a welfare approach imposes no obligation on the parents or courts, unless we merge the two approaches and give the children a right to have their welfare promoted by the courts and their parents.[307] A third is that there may be rights which a child has, which cannot necessarily be demonstrated to promote his or her welfare. For example, it is increasingly recognised that a child has a right to know his or her genetic origins, even though it might not be possible to demonstrate that this knowledge promotes a child's welfare.

To see how the theoretical discussion operates in practice, this chapter will now briefly discuss cases where the interests of children, parents and the state have had to be balanced. The area that reveals the issues better than any other is medical law.

12. CHILDREN AND MEDICAL LAW

Many of the cases involving disputes between children and adults have concerned medical treatment. The cases are useful beyond the medical arena because they give some general guidance on how disputes between children and adults should generally be resolved.

The law on when a doctor can treat a child can now be summarised with the following propositions:

1. Unless there has been a court order forbidding the carrying out of the treatment, a doctor can provide treatment to a child which he or she believes to be in the child's best interests if, and only if:

   (a) the child is competent and consents to the treatment; or

---

[305] *Re W (Contact Proceedings: Joinder of Child)* [2003] 2 FCR 175.
[306] Eekelaar (1992: 221).
[307] Eekelaar (1994d).

    (b) those with parental responsibility consent; or

    (c) the court declares the treatment lawful; or

    (d) the defence of necessity applies.

2. The court cannot force a doctor to provide treatment which the doctor does not wish to provide.

An understanding of the law must start with the fact that a doctor who touches a patient commits a battery, which is a criminal offence, unless he or she has a defence. A defence is provided in any one of the four circumstances listed above. These will now be considered in further detail.

A. 16- and 17-year-olds

Section 8(1) of the Family Law Reform Act 1969 states:

> The consent of a minor who has attained the age of sixteen years to any surgical, medical or dental treatment ... shall be as effective as it would be if he were of full age; and where a minor has by virtue of this section given an effective consent to any treatment it shall not be necessary to obtain any consent for it from his parent or guardian.

This indicates clearly that a child aged 16 or 17 can give legal effect to treatment, unless they are shown to be incompetent, using the same rules as for an adult. This might arise if they suffered from a mental disability.

What if a child aged 16 or 17 refused to consent but their parents did consent to the treatment? Following *Re W (A Minor) (Medical Treatment: Court's Jurisdiction)*,[308] a doctor can rely on the consent of the parents of a 16- or 17-year-old, despite the opposition of the child. However, this decision is subject to an important caveat. The doctor can only treat a patient if he or she believes the treatment is in the best interests of the patient. It would be most unusual for a doctor to decide that it would be in the interests of a 16- or 17-year-old to receive medical treatment against their wishes. Even if a doctor did wish to treat such a patient, relying on the consent of the parents, he or she may well prefer to obtain the authorisation of the court before so doing.[309] In *Re C (Detention: Medical Treatment)*[310] C, aged 16, suffered from anorexia nervosa. The court under the inherent jurisdiction directed that C should remain as a patient at a clinic until discharged by her consultant or further order of the court. This power included the use of reasonable force to detain her for the purposes of treatment.[311] This is a highly controversial decision because it is unlikely that, had C been over 18, it would have been lawful to detain her.

B. Under 16-year-olds

The leading case here is *Gillick*.[312] In 1980 the Department of Health and Social Security provided a notice that in 'exceptional circumstances' a doctor could give

---

[308] [1993] 1 FLR 1, [1992] 2 FCR 785 CA.
[309] *Re W (A Minor) (Medical Treatment: Court's Jurisdiction)* [1993] 1 FLR 1, [1992] 2 FCR 785 CA.
[310] [1997] 2 FLR 180, [1997] 3 FCR 49.
[311] De Cruz (1999).

contraceptive advice to a girl under 16 without parental consent or consultation. Victoria Gillick, a committed Roman Catholic, sought to challenge the legality of the notice after she unsuccessfully requested assurances that none of her five daughters under 16 would receive advice without her permission. She lost at first instance, but won unanimously at the Court of Appeal, but lost 3–2 in the House of Lords.[313] The fact that the majority of judges who heard the case decided in her favour, even though she lost at the end of the day, reveals the difficulty of the issues involved.

The majority of the House of Lords accepted that if a doctor decided that it was in the best interests of an under 16-year-old that she be given the contraceptive advice she sought and that she was competent to understand the issues involved, then the doctor was permitted to provide the treatment without obtaining the consent of the parents first. This was a hugely important decision because it recognised that under 16-year-olds had the right to give effective legal consent to medical treatment.

The decision left a number of issues unanswered:

(i) When is a child competent to give consent?[314]

The term '*Gillick* competent' has been widely used to describe children who are sufficiently competent to give consent to treatment. In considering whether a child is *Gillick* competent or not, the court will consider a number of issues:

1. *Does the child understand the nature of their medical condition and the proposed treatment?* Relevant here is not just the fact that the child understands what it is that is proposed to be done, but the possible side-effects of any treatment.[315] The child must also understand what will happen if the treatment is not performed. Rather controversially, in *Re L (Medical Treatment: Gillick Competency)*[316] L was found not to be competent because she did not appreciate the manner of her death if the treatment was not performed. The reason why she did not was because the doctors thought it would cause her undue distress if they were to tell her. It seems highly unsatisfactory that a child can be found not competent because the doctors have failed to give her the relevant information that she needs to be competent.[317]

2. *Does the child understand the moral and family issues involved?* This was stressed by Lord Scarman in *Gillick*. It was also thought relevant in *Re E (A Minor) (Wardship: Medical Treatment)*,[318] where the court was concerned that the child did not appreciate how much grief his parents would suffer if he were to die.

---

[312] Noted in Bainham (1986); Eekelaar (1986).

[313] The case also gave rise to some interesting issues of criminal law, which will not be discussed here.

[314] Alderson (1993). The British Medical Association has produced guidelines to assist doctors in determining a child's competence: British Medical Association (2001).

[315] *Re R (A Minor) (Wardship: Consent to Medical Treatment)* [1992] 1 FLR 190, [1992] 2 FCR 229 CA.

[316] [1998] 2 FLR 810.

[317] Indeed since this decision the British Medical Association has suggested that doctors should not fail to give minor patients information on the basis that to do so would cause them distress.

[318] [1993] 1 FLR 386.

3. *How much experience of life does the child have?* The courts have relied on this ground in particular when considering children brought up by parents of strong religious views. In *Re L (Medical Treatment: Gillick Competency)*[319] a 14-year-old had been brought up by Jehovah's Witness parents. The court felt that she had lived a sheltered life and had not been exposed to a variety of different religious views. This pointed to the fact she was not competent.[320]

4. *Is the child in a fluctuating mental state?* If the child is fluctuating between competence and incompetence then the court will treat the child as not competent. This was the approach taken in *Re R (A Minor) (Wardship: Consent to Medical Treatment)*.[321] The decision could be justified on the basis that, otherwise, the hospital would be in a very difficult position in having to decide each time the child was touched whether she was competent or not. Opponents of the decision would argue that inconvenience for medical professionals should not justify not taking the rights of children seriously.

5. *Is the child capable of weighing the information appropriately to be able to reach a decision?*[322] Here the court will consider not only the child's ability to understand facts, but also the ability to weigh the facts in reaching a decision.

(ii) When the doctor can rely on the parent's consent

Lord Scarman had suggested in *Gillick* that 'the parental right yields to the child's right to make his own decisions when he reaches a sufficient understanding and intelligence to be capable of making up his own mind on the matter requiring decision'. This seemed to suggest that if the child was competent and refused to give consent then this refusal could not be overridden by someone with parental responsibility. However, the Court of Appeal has made it clear in cases following *Gillick* that, even if a competent child does not consent, the doctor can still treat a child if he or she believes that to do so would promote the welfare of the child and someone with parental responsibility for the child gives consent. In *Re W (A Minor) (Medical Treatment: Court's Jurisdiction)*[323] it was explained that a doctor who wishes to treat a patient needs a 'flak jacket' of consent that would provide protection from liability in criminal or tort law. It was stated that this flak jacket could be provided by either the competent child *or* a person with parental responsibility. So the fact that the child had refused to provide the flak jacket did not prevent someone with parental responsibility providing one. Indeed, in *Re K, W, and H (Minors) (Medical Treatment)*[324] it was held that where someone with parental responsibility gives consent, it was unnecessary and inappropriate to bring the matter before the court; the doctors should simply provide the treatment. In *Re M (Medical Treatment: Consent)*[325] a 15-year-old girl refused a heart transplant, stating that she

---

[319] [1998] 2 FLR 810.
[320] See also *Re S (A Minor) (Medical Treatment)* [1993] 1 FLR 376. For criticism of such cases see Eekelaar (1994a: 57).
[321] [1992] 1 FLR 190, [1992] 2 FCR 229 CA.
[322] *Re MB* [1997] Med LR 217.
[323] [1993] 1 FLR 1, [1992] 2 FCR 785.
[324] [1993] 1 FLR 854, [1993] 1 FCR 240.
[325] [1999] 2 FLR 1097.

did not want to have someone else's heart. Her mother consented to the treatment. The Court of Appeal authorised the operation, stating that the preserving of the girl's life justified overriding her views. Notably here the Court of Appeal did not state whether she was or was not *Gillick* competent. This was because it did not matter. Someone with parental responsibility had provided the flak jacket and the operation was in the best interests of the girl so her views were irrelevant. In *Nielsen v Denmark*[326] the European Court of Human Rights appeared to accept that the European Convention would permit treatment to be carried out on children against their wishes, relying on the consent of the parent.[327]

(iii) If the matter is brought before the court, how should the court resolve the issue?

Where cases involving disputes over the medical treatment of children have been brought before them, the courts have been very willing to approve the treatment proposed by the doctors, even if the treatment is opposed by the parents and the children.[328] The cases that have come before either court have tended to be extreme: the children of Jehovah's Witnesses refusing to consent to a blood transfusion necessary to save their lives;[329] an anorexic girl refusing treatment necessary to treat her illness.[330] It would be quite wrong, however, to conclude that parents' wishes are largely ignored. The fact that only these rather extreme cases come before the court indicates that, normally, doctors abide by the parent's wishes and, if not, try very hard to persuade the child or parent to consent to the treatment.[331]

There is one notable case where the court sided with the parents, rather than the medical establishment: *Re T (A Minor) (Wardship: Medical Treatment)*.[332] Here a baby, C, had a life-threatening liver complaint. There was a unanimous prognosis from the medical experts that, without a liver transplant, C would not live beyond two-and-a-half years of age. However, if a transplant could be found the prognosis was very good. The parents refused to consent to the transplant. This time the courts sided with the parents and refused to authorise the transplant without the consent of the parents. Before examining the court's reasoning, it should be stressed that there were several facts that made the case rather unusual. First, both parents were health care professionals who had experience of caring for sick children. Secondly, C had undergone earlier unsuccessful surgery and this had caused C much pain and distress. Thirdly, the parents at the time of the case had moved

---

[326] (1989) 11 EHRR 179.

[327] In an obiter comment in *Re S (A Child) (Identification: Restriction on Publication)* [2003] 2 FCR 577 Hale LJ suggested that a child might be competent enough to consent to an interview with a newspaper and her parents not have any power to stop her.

[328] *Re E (A Minor) (Wardship: Medical Treatment)* [1993] 1 FLR 386, [1992] 2 FCR 219; *Re S (A Minor) (Consent to Medical Treatment)* [1994] 2 FLR 1065, [1994] 1 FCR 604.

[329] E.g. *Re E (A Minor) (Wardship: Medical Treatment)* [1993] 1 FLR 386, [1992] 2 FCR 219; *Re S (A Minor) (Consent to Medical Treatment)* [1994] 2 FLR 1065, [1994] 1 FCR 604.

[330] E.g. *Re W (A Minor) (Medical Treatment: Court's Jurisdiction)* [1993] 1 FLR 1, [1992] 2 FCR 785.

[331] C. Bridge (1999).

[332] [1997] 1 FLR 502, [1997] 2 FCR 363; discussed Bainham (1997); Fox and McHale (1997); Michalowski (1997).

(for job reasons) to a distant Commonwealth country. The Court of Appeal, in deciding not to authorise the treatment, relied upon the welfare principle. It was stated that although there was a presumption in favour of prolonging a child's life, this was not the court's sole objective. Ward LJ stated: 'in the last analysis the best interest of every child includes an expectation that difficult decisions affecting the length and quality of its life will be taken for it by the parent to whom its care had been entrusted by nature'.[333] The decision seemed to place much weight on the intrusion that ordering the treatment would make in the lives of the parents: they would need to return from their new country and would be required to provide extensive care for the child. Arguably, these concerns were misplaced, because even if the parents were unwilling to make these sacrifices, they could hand the child over to be cared for by a local authority. In fact, despite the Court of Appeal's ruling, the parents did return to the UK and the child received treatment.[334] The decision may be contrasted with *Re MM (Medical Treatment)*,[335] where the Russian parents opposed the treatment proposed by the doctors for what the court described as 'rational reasons' (they were not sure the treatment could be provided on their return to Russia; and did not want to depart from a treatment which had worked in the past). However, Black J authorised the proposed treatment, confirming the approach of most cases of this kind which have stressed that parents are not to be permitted to make martyrs of their children. A similar approach was taken in *Re A (Conjoined Twins: Medical Treatment)*[336] where the Court of Appeal authorised the separation of the conjoined twins despite the objections of the parents. Ward LJ, added, however, that had the hospital decided to abide by the wishes of the parents and not operate this would have been a 'perfectly acceptable response'. However, that suggestion appears to overlook the rights of J (the stronger of the twins) to the life-saving treatment which the Court decided she should receive.[337]

There have been tragically difficult cases involving children who have been born severely disabled and there is dispute over the appropriate medical treatment for the child.[338] The criminal law prohibits any acts of doctors designed to end the child's life,[339] or acts aimed at shortening the child's life (as opposed to aimed at relieving pain).[340] What is strictly forbidden is the performing of any act designed to end the life of the child: that would be murder. However, the courts may authorise the doctors to refrain from offering treatment. The general approach has been that, if there is medical evidence that the child's life will be intolerable if the child lives, the court will approve the non-treatment, even if the parents are in favour of providing treatment.[341] If the child's life will not be intolerable, the doctors should provide the

---

[333] The use of the term 'it' in reference to the child is revealing.
[334] C. Bridge (1999: 11).
[335] [2000] 1 FLR 224.
[336] [2000] 4 All ER 961.
[337] See further the discussion in Bainham (2001b).
[338] If there is a dispute between the parents and doctors, such cases should be brought before the court: *R v Portsmouth NHS Trust, ex p Glass* [1999] 2 FLR 905.
[339] Not reported but discussed in Gunn and Smith (1985).
[340] *Royal Wolverhampton Hospitals NHS Trust v B* [2000] 1 FLR 953 at p. 956, per Bodey J.
[341] *Re C (Medical Treatment)* [1998] 1 FLR 384; Fortin (1998b).

treatment, even if the parents object to it (*Re B (A Minor) (Disclosure of Evidence)*)[342]. In *Re J (A Minor) (Wardship: Medical Treatment)*[343] it was explained:

> I consider that the correct approach is for the court to judge the quality of the life the child would have to endure if given the treatment and decide whether in all the circumstances such a life would be so afflicted as to be intolerable to that child. I say 'to that child' because the test should not be whether the life would be intolerable to the decider. The test must be whether the child in question, if capable of exercising sound judgement, would consider life intolerable ... it takes account of the strong instinct to preserve one's life even in circumstances, which an outsider, not himself at risk of death, might consider unacceptable.[344]

This approach has been held by Cazalet J in *A NHS Trust v D*[345] not to be in breach of a child's right to life under article 2 of the European Convention on Human Rights. Indeed, not providing treatment which would extend an intolerable life was necessary under article 3, which required the state to ensure that the child was not subjected to inhuman or degrading treatment.

(iv) Can a doctor be forced to treat a child?

The issue here relates to the situation where the doctor refuses to treat a child. This may be because the doctor believes that the treatment is not appropriate, or may be because of health care rationing (e.g. that the treatment is too expensive). It is clear that if a doctor declines to offer treatment then the court cannot force him or her to perform the operation.[346] One option in such a case is for a patient to apply for judicial review, although such an option is unlikely to succeed unless there is strong evidence that the decision is unreasonable.[347] In any event, even if judicial review is successful the NHS trust would only be required to reconsider the decision and would not necessarily be required to perform the operation. If a doctor is unsure about the propriety of treatment (e.g. because it is a risky, untried, procedure) the matter could be brought before a court for guidance.[348]

(v) Can the parents be criminally liable for failing to arrange suitable medical care for a child?

It is an offence when anyone over 16 with responsibility for a child 'wilfully assaults, ill-treats, neglects, abandons, or exposes him ... in a manner likely to cause him unnecessary suffering or injury to health'.[349] This means that a parent who wilfully fails to ensure that the child receives adequate medical treatment commits an

---

[342] [1983] 3 FLR 117.
[343] [1990] 3 All ER 930, [1991] 1 FLR 366, [1991] FCR 370.
[344] [1990] 3 All ER 930 at p. 945.
[345] [2000] 2 FCR 577.
[346] Although *dicta* in *Re F (Mental Patient: Sterilisation)* [1990] 2 AC 1 that there is a duty on doctors to perform a sterilisation raises doubts about this.
[347] *R v Cambridge District Health Authority, ex p B* [1995] 1 FLR 1055.
[348] E.g. *Simms v Simms* [2003] 1 FCR 361.
[349] Children and Young Persons Act 1933, s 1(1).

offence. It should be stressed that it must be shown that the failure to arrange treatment is wilful. Therefore, as *R* v *Sheppard*[350] suggests, if parents do not provide treatment due to their low intelligence they will not be punished.[351] If the child dies after his or her parents fail to organise suitable medical treatment there is even the possibility of a manslaughter or murder conviction.[352]

(vi) Are there some kinds of treatment which cannot be carried out on children?

Is there a limit to what the doctors, with the parents' consent, can do to a child? The dispute here surrounds non-therapeutic treatment, that is, treatment which has no direct medical benefit to the child. It seems that some non-therapeutic treatment can be carried out, but only if it can be shown that the treatment benefits the child in the wider sense. So, for example, the parent can consent to a blood test to determine a child's paternity. Although such a blood test does not provide medical benefits, it is thought to be in a child's interests as it enables his or her paternity to be ascertained. However, problems may arise where the child is asked to donate bone marrow or organs for the treatment of someone else. If the bone marrow or organ is to a close relative it may be possible to find a benefit to the child. For example, if a child is donating an organ to their sister and without the treatment the sister will die, the benefit to the child of maintaining the relationship with the sister may be sufficient to make the donation in the child's benefit.[353]

A procedure that is clearly to the detriment of a child may not be lawful. For example, it may be that a parent could not effectively consent to multiple body piercing of a child.[354] One particularly controversial issue is circumcision.[355] Female circumcision is unlawful, unless necessary for medical reasons.[356] But the position of male circumcision seems to be that it is lawful. There are those who claim that this is an irreversible operation, which is an attack on the child's physical integrity, and unless there are medical benefits to the child it should be unlawful. There are others who argue that a child has a right to a religious or cultural heritage and, at least where circumcision is an aspect of religious background, it should be permissible.[357]

---

[350] [1981] AC 394.

[351] It is no defence to show that even had one attempted to obtain medical assistance there would have been none available.

[352] *R* v *Senior* [1899] 1 QB 283, where for religious reasons a parent refused to obtain medical treatment.

[353] By analogy with the reasoning in *Re Y (Mental Incapacity: Bone Marrow Transplant)* [1996] 2 FLR 787.

[354] Similarly, sterilisation may be permitted if the child suffers from mental handicap, if that sterilisation can be said to be in the best interests of the child and the court has given its approval: *J* v *C* [1990] 2 FLR 527, [1990] FCR 716; *Practice Note (Official Solicitor: Sterilisation)* [1993] 2 FLR 222 and *Practice Note (Official Solicitor: Sterilisation)* [1996] 2 FLR 111.

[355] I. Katz (1999).

[356] Prohibition of Female Circumcision Act 1985.

[357] Circumcision of boys is regarded by many Jews and Muslims as an important aspect of their religious practice.

C. Comments on the law

(i) The case law and children's rights

Some have argued that the present law is illogical, by arguing as follows: the law permits a competent minor to consent to treatment, but not to refuse it. If the child is competent to decide the question, it seems a bit odd to say to him or her: 'You can decide this issue but only if you decide to answer "yes". If you decide "no" we may override your wishes.' It is especially odd because it is a far greater infringement of a child's rights to operate on him or her without their consent than to deny them treatment that they would like to have. If anything, the law would be more logical if it said that the doctor cannot operate on the child if he or she refuses but has a discretion if he or she consents. Such arguments have led Fortin to suggest that the present law may be open to challenge under the Human Rights Act in that forcing treatment on young people breaches their rights to protection from inhuman and degrading treatment and right to liberty and security of the person.[358]

However, the law is perfectly logical once it is recalled that the basis of the law relating to children is set out in s 1 of the Children Act 1989 – the welfare principle. The law is based on the view that, if the doctor wants to perform treatment, this is in the best interests of the child because it is the view of the medical expert. The law is then engineered to make it as easy as possible to enable the doctor to go ahead. The doctor can operate if either the mature minor consents, or the parents consent, or the courts give approval. The law could hardly do more to enable the doctor to treat, once he or she has decided that the treatment is in the best interests of child. Put this way, the law is a clear example of ensuring that the child's best interests are promoted. However, as the previous paragraph makes clear, the law is not logical if one looks at the question as one of children's autonomy rights.

(ii) The importance of doctors

There is some concern that the law places too much weight on the opinions of doctors. It has just been argued that the law relating to children is best understood on the basis that the doctor is presumed to make decisions that are in the child's interests. In effect, if the parent consents and the child does not, it is the doctor who has the final say unless the child decides to bring the matter before the court. Of course, generally, doctors will be best placed to decide whether a medical treatment is in a patient's best interests. However, where the issue involves moral as well as medical issues (abortion for example), giving so much power to doctors may be controversial.[359] Also, in many areas of medicine there is more than one point of view as to the best kind of medical treatment. The present law favours the views of

---

[358] Fortin (2003b: 129). She also suggests that the law could be challenged using article 14 of the European Convention on Human Rights, arguing that the present law amounts to discrimination on the grounds of age. Although age is not included in article 14 as a prohibited ground of discrimination, the list of grounds under article 14 is not closed and a strong case can be made for adding age.

[359] Herring (1997).

the particular doctor dealing with the patient, over what might be the reasonable objections of the patient.[360]

(iii) Misuses of competence

It has been argued that the test for competence for children is too strict. Certainly the test of competence for children is stiffer than that for adults.[361] Further, there is a danger that the child will be found incompetent if the doctor or court believes the child's decision to be wrong, but the child will be found competent if the decision is one which is thought to promote his or her best interests.[362] However, arguments over the appropriate test for competence are complex. If the law was that a competent child's decision could not be vetoed by the courts or the parents, the law would wish to have a very strict test of competence. A further complaint about the law on competence for children is that it is wrong for the law to categorise children as either competent or not and, instead, decisions should be made with children, enabling them to participate in the decision-making process to as great an extent as possible.[363]

(iv) Is the law not adequately protecting children?

As mentioned above, if the parents oppose a form of treatment, the doctors will seek to find alternative forms of treatment or persuade the parents to change their minds. It is only where this fails that the doctors are likely to turn to the courts for authorisation to treat the child contrary to the parents' wishes. For example, where a child's parents are Jehovah's Witnesses, who oppose blood transfusions, doctors may try to use non-blood substitutes before eventually seeking court intervention.[364] Bridge[365] has argued that this delay in providing the ideal treatment could be seen as protecting the parents' rather than the child's interests.

13. CHILDREN IN COURT

Children's rights would mean little without an effective mode of enforcement. It is therefore crucial that children have access to courts.[366] The fact that children should be heard in proceedings does not require that their views will necessarily determine the question. The right of a child to be heard is therefore less contentious than a right to autonomy. However, there is a delicate balance to be drawn between listening to children and not placing them in the position where they have to decide

---

[360] Douglas (1992).
[361] See Dickenson and Jones (1995) for a general discussion of children's competence.
[362] Shaw (2002).
[363] Herring (1997).
[364] *Re S (A Minor) (Medical Treatment)* [1994] 2 FLR 1065, [1994] 1 FCR 604.
[365] C. Bridge (1999).
[366] UN Convention on the Rights of the Child, article 12. See also the European Convention on the Exercise of Children's Rights, not yet signed by the UK. See Lowe and Murch (2001) for an excellent discussion.

between their parents.[367] Many commentators have been persuaded by the view that if children have autonomy rights then they must have a means to bring applications to enforce those rights. However, there are also serious concerns about involving children in litigation.[368] There is much evidence that requiring a child to choose whether they live with their father or mother causes the child much harm. There is also a concern that children's rights to bring matters before a court are open to misuse, either from parents seeking to manipulate the children[369] or even from solicitors keen to promote their professional standing.[370]

There are three ways in which a child may be directly involved in family proceedings:

1. The child may bring proceedings through a solicitor in their own right.
2. The child's 'next friend' (normally one of their parents) can bring proceedings on the child's behalf.
3. The child's interests can be represented in the case between adults by a Guardian ad Litem.

A. Children bringing proceedings in their own right

Under rule 9.2A of the Family Proceedings Rules 1999, SI 1999/3491, a minor can bring (or defend) proceedings under the Children Act 1989 or involving the inherent jurisdiction either:

1. if the court gives leave; or
2. where a solicitor, acting for the child, considers[371] that the child is able to give instructions in relation to the proceedings.[372] However, the most likely proceedings that a child will want to bring is for an order under s 8 of the Children Act 1989 and, for such an application, the court must give leave, even if the child's solicitor is satisfied that the child is competent.[373]

There was a fear when the Children Act 1989 was first introduced that the courts would be swamped with applications from children seeking to 'divorce' their parents (although this has proved to be unfounded). Before granting leave, the court must be satisfied 'that [the child] has sufficient understanding to make the proposed application'.[374] There has been some dispute over whether the welfare of the child is relevant when considering whether or not to grant leave. Following *Re H*

---

[367] M. King (1987: 190).
[368] This was recognised by Thorpe LJ in *Re HB (Abduction: Children's Objections)* [1998] 1 FLR 422.
[369] In *Re K (Replacement of Guardian ad Litem)* [2001] 1 FLR 663 the court decided that the child had been pressurised by his father into applying to dispense with the services of his guardian.
[370] Thorpe LJ (1994).
[371] Sawyer (1995).
[372] *Re H (A Minor) (Role of the Official Solicitor)* [1993] 2 FLR 552. Even if the solicitor decides that the child is competent, it is open to the court to stop the proceedings if the court is not satisfied that the child is competent: *Re CT (A Minor) (Child Representation)* [1993] 2 FLR 278, [1993] 2 FCR 445.
[373] *Practice Direction* [1993] 1 FLR 668; *Re N (Contact: Minor Seeking Leave to Defend and Removal of Guardian)* [2003] FL 154.
[374] Section 10(8).

(*Residence Order: Child's Application for Leave*),[375] it now seems to be accepted that the welfare of the child is not the paramount consideration. This was significant in that case because H was 15, and since the age of 6 he had come under the influence of a Mr R, who had been arrested for committing offences against children. As H was a mature and intelligent young man, it was held that he should have separate representation, even though there were grave concerns surrounding his desire to have unrestricted contact with Mr R. In considering whether to grant leave, the court will consider the following factors:

1. *Is the matter serious enough to justify a court hearing?* In *Re C (A Minor) (Leave to Seek Section 8 Order)*[376] a 14-year-old wanted to go on holiday with her friend's family to Bulgaria. Her parents opposed this and she applied for a specific issue order that she be permitted to go on the holiday. Johnson J refused to grant leave, claiming that the issue was too trivial an issue to be suitable for resolution by the courts. If this issue is too trivial, it is likely that many other issues which children may want to raise before a court (e.g. what time they go to bed) will also be too trivial. Freeman has forcefully argued that, where the child has instituted proceedings, this is an indication that, to the child, this is an important issue and that there is therefore a need for some kind of intervention for the child's benefit.[377] This is correct, but whether the intervention need be in the form of a court hearing or some kind of informal social work is a matter for debate. It should be recalled that issues that may appear trivial to adult, may appear hugely important from a child's perspective.

2. *Should the family resolve the issue themselves?* Johnson J in *Re C (A Minor) (Leave to Seek Section 8 Order)*[378] also considered the girl's application that she be allowed to move in with her friend's family. He also refused to grant leave for that application on the basis that he thought the issue should be left to the family to sort out between themselves, rather than involving the courts. The court feared that giving the child leave might give her an advantage in her dispute with her parents, although it might be thought that denying her leave gave her parents an advantage point.

3. *How mature is the child?* In *Re S (A Minor) (Independent Representation)*[379] it was stressed that the real issue is not the child's age but her understanding.[380] The very fact that the child had applied to the court would indicate maturity.[381] In *Re H (A Minor) (Role of the Official Solicitor)*[382] it was stressed that what had to be considered was whether the child would be able to give instructions in the light of the evidence that would be produced to the court. Where the evidence might be complex there may be difficulty in demonstrating this. The court may

---

[375] [2000] 1 FLR 780.
[376] [1994] 1 FLR 26.
[377] Freeman (1997a: 168; 2000c).
[378] [1994] 1 FLR 26.
[379] [1993] 2 FLR 437, [1993] 2 FCR 1.
[380] In *Re S (Contact: Application by Sibling)* [1999] Fam 283 a 9-year-old was found to have sufficient understanding to apply for leave for a contact order with her half-brother.
[381] *Re C (A Minor) (Leave to Seek Section 8 Order)* [1995] 1 FLR 927, [1996] 1 FCR 461.
[382] [1993] 2 FLR 552.

also take the view that the emotional turmoil that would be caused to the child by becoming involved in the litigation would be contrary to his or her welfare.[383]

4. *What is the likelihood of the success of the application?*[384] In *SC (A Minor) (Leave to Seek Section 8 Orders)*[385] it was confirmed that the fact that the application was not a hopeless application would be a factor in favour of granting leave.

5. *Would the child suffer from being involved in a protracted dispute between their parents?* In *Re S (A Minor) (Independent Representation)*[386] an 11-year-old boy wanted to replace his Guardian ad Litem. In the Court of Appeal, Bingham MR said that it was necessary to respect the child's wishes but at the same time protect the child from danger. It was held here that the effect of being closely involved with a bitter dispute between parents could harm a child and it was better for the boy to have the 'buffer' of a Guardian ad Litem. In *Re C (Residence: Child's Application for Leave)*[387] it was thought not to be to the child's benefit to hear the evidence of his warring parents. Fortin has argued that, rather than using this as a reason for denying access to the courts, consideration should be given as to how court procedures can be altered to protect child litigants' psychological welfare.[388]

6. *Will all the arguments that a child wishes to raise be presented to the court?* In *Re H (Residence Order: Child's Application for Leave)*[389] a 12-year-old boy sought to apply to the court for a residence order in his father's favour on his parents' divorce. Although he was mature enough to make the application, Johnson J held that the child would not bring before the court any argument that the father would not be making in his application for a residence order. There was therefore nothing to gain from granting leave. This argument fails to appreciate the importance to the child of feeling that he or she is being listened to.

7. *The impact of the Human Rights Act.* A child may have a right to be represented and heard in proceedings with which they are involved.[390] *Re A (Contact: Separate Representation)*[391] accepted that a boy who wished to alert the judge to the dangers he believed his father posed to his young half-sister should have leave to do so.

In the light of this list of reasons for not permitting access, it is not surprising that it is rare for children successfully to bring applications before the court, or to find that research suggests that, generally, judges are opposed to children even attending court hearings.[392] It has been argued that the leave requirement improperly infringes a child's right to a fair hearing under article 6 of the European Convention, in a way which improperly discriminates on the basis of age, contrary

---

[383] *Re N (Contact: Minor Seeking Leave to Defend and Removal of Guardian)* [2003] FL 154.
[384] *Re C (A Minor) (Leave to Seek Section 8 Order)* [1995] 1 FLR 927, [1996] 1 FCR 461.
[385] [1994] 1 FLR 96, [1994] 1 FCR 837.
[386] [1993] 2 FLR 437, [1993] 2 FCR 1.
[387] [1995] 1 FLR 927, [1996] 1 FCR 461.
[388] Fortin (1998a: 202–3).
[389] [2000] 1 FLR 780, discussed in Sawyer (2001).
[390] Henley and Hershman (2003).
[391] [2001] 1 FLR 715.
[392] Masson and Winn Oakley (1999).

to article 14.[393] In reply it could be said that children may need protection from the rigours of the court procedures such as cross-examination and this justifies the imposition of the leave requirement.[394] The ability of children to represent themselves would mean that the court could hear the child's views in his or her own words, rather than mediated through the reports of welfare officers.[395] Notably, Dame Margaret Booth has argued that children should not be required to seek leave from the high court before applying for a section 8 order.[396]

If leave is granted, the full application will be heard. The welfare principle will govern the issue. The law governing the case is as discussed in Chapter 9.

B. Representation

In 2001 the government created the Children and Family Court Advisory Support Service (CAFCASS).[397] This agency was created to provide courts with services in cases involving children.[398] It is in charge of ensuring that children's interests are properly represented in court cases. It is necessary to distinguish public and private law cases.

(i) Public law cases

In public law cases (e.g. where a child is being taken into care) the child's interests will be protected by a guardian. The guardian will appoint a solicitor whose job it will be to represent the child's interests in any court hearing. The guardian and solicitor will work together to ascertain the wishes of the child and present these to the court. Courts can allow children who are the subject of public law proceedings to attend their hearing, although research indicates that at present many children who wish to attend the court are not allowed to do so.[399] Fortin[400] suggests that the awareness of children's rights under articles 6 and 8 might lead to a change in practice.

(ii) Private law cases

The representation of children's interests in private law cases is less effective. In a private case any of the following could occur:

1. The case proceeds without the court ever hearing of the child's views.
2. The court requests a child and family reporter[401] to prepare a report on the child, which will include a summary of the child's views.

---

[393] Lyon (2000).
[394] Lowe and Murch (2001).
[395] Butler and Williamson (1994).
[396] Her views are noted and discussed in Children Act Sub-Committee (2002a: para 12.6).
[397] Criminal Justice and Court Service Act 2000, s 11.
[398] Murch (2003) provides an excellent discussion of the issues.
[399] Ruegger (2001).
[400] Fortin (2003b: 236).
[401] A specialist social worker attached to CAFCASS.

3. The child could have party status (i.e. be treated as a party to the proceedings) and his or her interests be represented by his or her own lawyer.[402]
4. The child may be able to litigate and bring applications on his or her own behalf with the leave of the court.[403]

Many commentators have expressed concern that all too often 1 is what happens and that children's wishes and interests are not specifically addressed in a court proceeding. The United Nations Committee on the Rights of Children has expressed concern about the lack of representation of children's wishes in private cases.[404] Fortin has gone so far as to complain that 'The most serious procedural weakness undermining the Children Act's direction to the courts to consider the child's wishes and feelings is that there is no guarantee that the court will receive any evidence indicating what those wishes are.'[405] In part the reluctance to call for reports can be explained by the delays that can result while a report is being prepared.[406]

As this last point suggests, serious difficulties have beset CAFCASS.[407] This has led to divisions within the organisation,[408] the resignation of its chief executive, and long delays in the preparation of reports. Many of these problems can be explained by inadequate funding of the service by government.

In the last few years there has been an increasing acknowledgment of the need to ensure that children are heard in disputes over their upbringing. [409] Even if children's wishes are not to determine the case they should at least be heard and have their views taken seriously.[410] The judiciary itself now recognises the importance of listening to the views of children.[411] This is even true (perhaps particularly true) where the parents appear to agree over what is best for the child. Indeed arguably a child has a right under article 6 of the European Convention on Human Rights to have her or his views given due consideration.[412] This may require, as well as a report, separate representation of the child's interests.[413]

Despite the acknowledgment that listening to and appreciating children's wishes is important there are still grave concerns over the way in which reports concerning

---

[402] Although see Masson and Winn Oakley (1999) for an argument that even though children's interests may be separately represented the child may have only limited communication with their lawyer.

[403] It is very difficult for children to get leave in such cases: see *Re H (A Minor) (Care Proceedings; Child's Wishes)* [1993] 1 FLR 440 and *Re C (Secure Accommodation Order: Representation)* [1993] 1 FLR 440.

[404] Fortin (2003b: 213).

[405] Fortin (2003b: 215).

[406] In *M v A (Contact: Domestic Violence)* [2002] 2 FLR 921 there was a seven-month delay in the preparation of a report.

[407] Hunt and Lawson (1999).

[408] *R (on the Application of National Association of Guardians ad Litem and Reporting Officers) v CAFCASS* [2002] 1 FLR 255.

[409] Ruegger (2001); Murch (2003). Thomas (2001) emphasises that listening to children is also more likely to produce good decisions.

[410] Archard (2003: 54) emphasises that children have a right not just to be listened to, but also to be heard.

[411] *Re A (Contact: Separate Representation)* [2001] 1 FLR 715.

[412] Fortin (2003b: 223).

[413] *Re A (Contact: Separate Representation)* [2001] 1 FLR 715 CA. But *CAFCASS Practice Note (Officers of Legal Services and Special Casework: Appointment in Family Proceedings)* [2001] 2 FR 151 suggests that separate representation is only appropriate in special cases.

children are prepared and the length of time taken to prepare them.[414] The difficulty that many commentators report is that it is difficult for social workers to ascertain and report the wishes of children accurately. Children may feel intimidated and unable to say what they wish. Further, the questions asked of them by the reporter may not reflect the way the problem is perceived by the child.[415] The reporter therefore (unintentionally) deprives children of the ability to express their views in their own terms.[416]

As well as preparing the reports the child and family reporter can be responsible for communicating with the child after the order has been made. This is also important because part of taking a child's views seriously is reporting back to the child the court's decision and discussing it with him or her.[417]

There has been much dispute over whether or not the law should go further and encourage the active participation of children in court cases involving them. It could be said that simply having a report of the child's views is inadequate and that the court should see the child her- or himself. However, most commentators reject this as a general presumption. There is evidence that many children find appearing in court traumatic, particularly if it is felt they are being made to make a choice between their parents.[418]

(iii) Appointment of Official Solicitor

The Official Solicitor has traditionally represented children in wardship. It is in the discretion of the Lord Chancellor whether the Official Solicitor should intervene. If the child is not represented by a Guardian ad Litem, then a judge may decide, in exceptional cases, to ask the Official Solicitor to become involved.[419] This will occur only in cases in the High Court and the office of the Official Solicitor should be used sparingly.[420]

14. CHILDREN AND EDUCATION[421]

Article 2 of the first Protocol to the European Convention on Human Rights states:

> No person shall be denied the right to education. In the exercise of the functions which it assumes in relation to education, and to teaching, the state shall respect the right of parents to ensure such education and teaching is in conformity with their own religious and philosophical convictions.[422]

There are two notable points about this article of the Convention. First, rather than granting a positive right to education, the article says that children should not be

---

[414] Hunt and Lawson (1999); Lyon, Surrey and Timms (1999).
[415] Mayall (2002: 166).
[416] Buchanan, Hunt, Bretherton and Bream (2001); Murch (2003).
[417] Buchanan, Hunt, Bretherton and Bream (2001: 93).
[418] Piper (1999: 396); Smart, Neale and Wade (2001: 166).
[419] *Practice Note (The Official Solicitor: Application in Family Proceedings)* [1995] 2 FLR 479.
[420] *Re CT (A Minor) (Child: Representation)* [1993] 2 FLR 278, [1993] 2 FCR 445.
[421] For a discussion of the law on education, see Bainham (1998a); Fortin (2003b: ch. 6).
[422] Contrast the UN Convention on the Rights of the Child in article 28(1).

denied education. This seems to imply that if the state decides to provide education, it must not prevent a child using the education, rather than requiring the state positively to provide education. Secondly, the article protects the religious and philosophical beliefs of the parents, but not of the child.

Children spend a large portion of their childhood in schools. Generally, our society believes that education is a crucial part of enabling a child to develop his or her own personality and become a productive member of society. Education gives rise to some interesting clashes between the rights of parents, children and the state over who should decide the form of education. This area is one where, surprisingly, the notion of children's rights has little sway and some children complain that being at school is like living under a dictatorship.[423] Monk has argued that it is meaningful to talk of children having rights in education: rights to be treated as subjects, not objects, and a recognition that children are social agents and active participants within the education system.[424] Others complain of suffering racial disadvantage within the education system and hope that recognising rights in education will combat that.[425]

There is no legal duty on a child to attend school. The legal obligation is placed on the parents. Under s 7 of the Education Act 1996:

> The parents of every child of compulsory school age shall cause him to receive efficient full-time education suitable—
> (a) to his age, ability and aptitude, and
> (b) to any special educational needs he may have,
> either by regular attendance at school or otherwise.

The compulsory school age is from 5 to 16.[426]

This, then, is one of the few areas where there is a statutory limitation on parents' freedom to bring up children in whatever way they like. Parents have some choice, however, over the form of education. Most parents send children to school but they can choose to home school their child,[427] although this is increasingly difficult in the light of the requirements of the national curriculum. If parents are using the education system, the parents' duty is to register the child at a school and to secure attendance at school. A child may only fail to attend school if one of the statutory excuses apply: for example, that the child is sick.[428]

The local authority is in charge of ensuring that parents provide their children with adequate education.[429] The local education authorities can enforce the parents' duty in the following ways:

1. *Care order or emergency protection order.* The local authority could enforce the duty by applying for a care order or an emergency protection order in respect of the child.[430]

---

[423] See also Hill and Tisdall (1997: ch. 7). For a useful collection of writings on children's rights in the education context see Hart, Cohen, Erickson and Flekkoy (2001).
[424] Monk (2002: 45).
[425] Owusu-Bempah (2001).
[426] Jeffs and Smith (1996) argues against the compulsory nature of education.
[427] *R v Surrey Quarter Sessions Appeal Committee, ex p Tweedie* (1963) 107 SJ 555.
[428] This must be the child not the parents: *Jenkins v Howells* [1949] 2 KB 218.
[429] For the government's response to the problems of truancy, see Social Exclusion Unit (1998).
[430] *Re O (A Minor) (Care Order: Education: Procedure)* [1992] 2 FLR 7.

2. *School attendance order.* The education authority can serve on the parents a notice requiring them to satisfy the authority that their children are receiving suitable education. If the parents do not, then the education authority must serve a school attendance order. Failure by the parent to comply with such an order can lead to a fine or imprisonment.[431]

3. *Education supervision order.* Where a child is not attending school regularly the local education authority could prosecute the parents under s 444 of the Education Act 1996. This is available if it can be proved that the child is of compulsory school age and 'is not being properly educated'. Being 'properly educated' means that the child is 'receiving efficient full-time education suitable to his age, ability and aptitude and any special educational needs he may have'.[432] The effect of the order is to place the child under the supervision of a 'designated authority'. The education supervision order will last one year. The parents are under a duty to comply with any direction given under the education supervision order. A social worker will be appointed whose duty it is to 'advise, assist and befriend the parents and the child'. It is an offence for a parent persistently to fail to comply with the supervisor's advice.[433] If the child is failing to comply then the social services will be informed and they may consider whether to exercise any of their powers, the most extreme being to place the child in care.

4. *Section 8 order.* It may be that a specific issue order would be appropriate where a child's parents are in disagreement over how the child should be educated.[434] The court would then decide which parent's wishes were to be followed.

5. *Truancy.* Under the Children and Young Persons Act 1969, s 12C, a school attendance requirement can be made in response to truancy.[435]

Thus, the way that children's rights to education are enforced is by requiring local authorities to supply education and demanding that parents ensure that their children are educated. Children have no say over which school they attend, although they could apply for a s 8 order if they disagreed with their parents' choice of school.[436] Some argue that competent children should be given the choice of attending school or seeking employment.[437]

This legal structure appears an inadequate solution to the problem of truancy in schools.[438] There are two difficulties here. First, there is the issue of whether children should be required to attend schools. As we have already seen child liberationists would argue that children have the right to decide not to attend school. Others argue that compulsory attendance at schools brings teaching into disrepute and is counter-productive.[439] However, the majority of commentators take the view that children should be required to attend school. Indeed the UN Convention on

[431] Education Act 1996, s 443.
[432] Children Act 1989, s 36(4).
[433] Children Act 1989, Sch 3, para 19.
[434] A care order was made on the basis of truancy in *Re O (A Minor) (Care Order: Education: Procedure)* [1992] 2 FLR 7.
[435] Ball and Connolly (1999).
[436] *Re P (A Minor) (Education)* [1992] 1 FLR 316, [1992] FCR 145 CA.
[437] R. Lindley (1989).
[438] Department for Education and Employment (2002).
[439] Jenks (2002).

the Rights of the Child requires states to 'take measures to encourage regular attendance at schools'.[440] Secondly, assuming that children should be required to attend
schools, how is this to be achieved? Should the state use the deterrence of criminal
punishment to threaten parents who do not ensure their children attend schools?
Or should it be the children who are threatened with punishment for failing to
attend? Or is the problem with schools failing to stimulate children sufficiently? The
problem of truancy is a serious one because not only does it lead to a lack of education but it is also linked to a range of antisocial behaviour and subsequent social
exclusion.[441]

In the educational setting there are grave concerns that, all too often, the rights
of children are not adequately protected. There are serious concerns at the level of
bullying at schools.[442] Although this is an intractable problem, after the implementation of the Human Rights Act 1998 article 3 of the European Convention will
require the state to ensure that children are protected from bullying that reaches the
level of being torture or inhuman or degrading treatment.[443] There are also concerns that the disciplining of children in schools, including exclusion[444] and detention,[445] are being unfairly used. Arguably, article 6 of the Convention may in some
cases require a fair and public hearing before a punishment can be imposed.[446]

Another controversial aspect of children's rights in schools is sex education. The
basic position is that parents have a right to remove children from sex education
classes, unless they form part of the national curriculum.[447] The national curriculum covers the key biological elements of sexual reproduction and human
biology.[448] There is, beyond this, no right of a child to sex education, although it is
arguable that a *Gillick* competent child can decide for him- or herself whether to
attend sex education classes.[449] Alternatively, a child could apply to the court for a
specific issue order that he or she be permitted to attend the classes. Controversially,
classes on sex education should emphasise the nature of marriage and its importance in bringing up children.[450] There is ample evidence of the benefits of good sex
education[451] and that sex education far from encouraging early sexual activity actually delays the beginning of sexual relationships.[452] Some commentators argue that

[440] Article 28.
[441] Social Exclusion Unit (1998). Flood-Page, Campbell, Harrington and Miller (2000) indicate that
half of 12–16-year-old boys who were persistently truant were offenders.
[442] E.g. Commission on Children and Violence (1995); Department for Education and Employment
(2000b). For a discussion of the tortious liability for schools when a child is bullied see *Bradford-
Smart* v *West Sussex County Council* [2002] 1 FCR 425.
[443] *A* v *UK (Human Rights: Punishment of Child)* [1998] 2 FLR 959, [1998] 3 FCR 597.
[444] Social Exclusion Unit (1999b). For a very useful discussion of exclusions from schools see Fortin
(2003b: ch. 6).
[445] The use of force in schools by teachers is now severely limited: see Education Act 1996, s 550A.
[446] Fortin (1999a).
[447] Education Act 1996, s 241. Parents do not automatically have a right to remove their children from
sex education classes under the European Convention on Human Rights, providing the classes are
balanced and objective: *Kjeldsen* v *Denmark* (1976) EHRR 711.
[448] Primary schools are required to have a policy on sex education, but not to provide sex education
classes. This is criticised in Fortin (2003b: 189).
[449] See Bainham (1996).
[450] Department of Education and Employment (2000a: 1.21) and Education Act 1996, s 403.
[451] Wellings (1995).
[452] Jepson (2000).

children have a right to sex education,[453] especially given the alarming rate of teenage pregnancy.[454] Notably, research indicates that the major source of information about sexual issues for most children is not parents or friends, but schools.[455]

A further controversy is over religious education. Here the law recognises that children have the right to be informed about religious matters.[456] The Education Act 1996 requires all agreed syllabuses for religious education to 'reflect the fact that the religious traditions in Great Britain are in the main Christian whilst taking account of the teaching and practices of the other principal religions represented in Great Britain'.[457] Further, the Education Act 1996 now requires all pupils to 'take part in an act of collective worship on each school day'.[458] There is an interesting contrast with the approach in the United States, where the view is taken that the state should not be seen to promote any one religion and so religious education within state schools is prohibited. In England and Wales, by contrast, it is required.[459]

15. CHILDREN AND CRIMINAL LAW

Children are protected under the general criminal law.[460] There are also special offences that are designed to protect children from particular forms of abuse. The extreme child liberationists would be opposed to these laws on the ground that children should be treated in exactly the same way as adults and any special protection under the criminal law denies a child the autonomy that an adult has. It is important in considering the protection offered to children by the criminal law to note that a high proportion of crimes against children are committed by members of the child's family or household.

The offences involving children can be divided into three main groups. First, there are those which are designed to protect children from abuse by adults. For example, there are special sexual offences against children[461] and the offence of neglecting children.[462] Secondly, there are offences designed to protect children's basic interests. For example, there are a host of protections for children from being employed in dangerous activities or for long periods.[463] Thirdly, there are offences which may be seen as protecting the general public from children. For example, there are a huge number

---

[453] Fortin (1998a: 152).
[454] Social Exclusion Unit (1999a), noting that the United Kingdom has the second highest level of teenage births in the world.
[455] Ofsted (2002: para 77).
[456] For criticism, see Hamilton (1995); Hamilton and Watt (1996).
[457] Education Act 1996, s 375.
[458] School Standards and Framework Act 1998, s 70.
[459] Hamilton (1995).
[460] See e.g. W. Wilson (1998).
[461] E.g. Sexual Offences Act 2003.
[462] E.g. Children and Young Persons Act 1933.
[463] E.g. Employment of Young People Act 1993, s 1(1); Employment of Women, Young Persons and Children Act 1920; Mines and Quarries Act 1954, s 124; Employment Act 1989.

of offences restricting what might be sold to a child under 16. These include alcohol,[464] tobacco,[465] firearms,[466] crossbows and fireworks.[467]

A different issue is how the law deals with children who have committed crimes. Here the state needs to balance the protection of the public from criminal youngsters with the desire to help children who have committed crime. On the one hand, there are those who believe criminal activity in those under 18 reveals that the child is in need of social work assistance and support. On the other, criminal activity among the under 18s constitutes a large percentage of criminal acts and protection of the public might call for harsh treatment of young criminals. The Crime and Disorder Act 1998 now governs this area of the law. Children under 10 cannot be convicted of a criminal offence, however heinous their crime. Such a child may, of course, be subject to protective measures under Part III of the Children Act 1989.

In recent years Parliament[468] has accepted that, in some cases, parents have parental responsibility for the criminal acts of their children.[469] There are two main arguments against the proposals. The first was that those families whose children are committing crimes are often the most deprived and it would be better for resources to be channelled into providing support for such families. The second was that it might encourage a greater use of corporal punishment which could become child abuse. Under s 8 of the Crime and Disorder Act 1998 a court may make a parenting order where a child safety order is made;[470] or where an antisocial behaviour order or a sex offender order is made in respect of a child or young person;[471] or if the child or young person is convicted of an offence (in which case the court shall make a parenting order unless it decides that to do so would be not desirable, in which case it must explain why in open court); or a person is convicted of an offence under s 43 or s 44 of the Education Act 1996.[472] The order requires a parent to attend counselling or guidance sessions. These last no more than 12 weeks and occur no more than once a week. There may be additional requirements. The most likely would be that a parent must ensure that a child attends school or that a child be home by a particular time. These requirements can last 12 months. The new order is controversial, as Bainham suggests:

> The new order might be viewed by some as an attempt to provide support and encouragement to the parents of young offenders, while others will see it as fundamentally authoritarian, an

---

[464] Licensing Act 1964, s 169.
[465] Protection of Children (Tobacco) Act 1986; Children and Young Persons (Protection from Tobacco) Act 1991.
[466] Firearms Acts 1968 and 1982.
[467] Crossbows Act 1987 and Fireworks Act 2003, respectively.
[468] Home Office (1990a: paras 8.1 and 8.2).
[469] Gelsthorpe (1999).
[470] This order is available where a child under 10 commits an act that would be a crime if the child were over 10, or where such an order is considered necessary to prevent the child committing such acts.
[471] Very basically, these orders are available where a person has caused distress, alarm or harassment to one or more people not in the person's own household and so their behaviour is deemed antisocial.
[472] *In R (M) v Inner London Crown Court* [2003] 1 FLR 994 it was accepted that a parenting order did infringe a parent's rights under article 8 of the European Convention to a right to respect for family life, but that such an intervention was justifiable under para 2.

attack on civil liberties and an extraordinary invasion by the State into family autonomy – so richly prized elsewhere in the law.[473]

16. CORPORAL PUNISHMENT

Corporal punishment has been defined as 'the use of physical force with the intention of causing a child to experience pain but not injury for the purposes of correction or control of the child's behaviour'.[474] Corporal punishment is one of the most controversial topics surrounding parenting.[475] Although nearly everyone agrees that children require some form of discipline, there is much dispute about what form that discipline should take. For some, the issue is straightforward: 'Hitting people is wrong – and children are people too.'[476] Indeed, it can be regarded as a basic human right not to be hit.[477] Others argue that corporal punishment is an important part of bringing children up well and even cite some biblical support.[478] A third group (perhaps the majority of parents) do not think that corporal punishment is necessarily a positive good but admit that when at the end of their tether they use corporal punishment. A survey revealed that corporal punishment is widespread: 81 per cent of interviewees supported corporal punishment by parents of own children; 45 per cent by carer or nannies; 67 per cent by teachers; 71 per cent by head teachers; and (remarkably) 70 per cent by courts.[479] A survey in 1985 suggested that two-thirds of children were smacked during their first year.[480] More recently, 88 per cent of parents stated that they found it sometimes necessary to hit their children.[481]

The present criminal law is under review, after the European Court of Human Rights in *A v UK (Human Rights: Punishment of Child)*[482] has declared English and Welsh law in breach of the Convention. The present law is that corporal punishment is prima facie an assault. It could be a battery, an assault occasioning actual bodily harm,[483] or wounding or inflicting or causing grievous bodily harm,[484] depending on the severity of the punishment. However, under common law there is a defence to these offences if the conduct constitutes 'lawful chastisement'. Precisely what 'lawful chastisement' is, is not clear. The nearest that the case law has come to providing a definition is a statement that the punishment must be 'moderate and reasonable'.[485] There is also a specific offence of ill-treatment or

---

[473] Bainham (1998a: 491).
[474] Strauss and Donnolly (1993: 420).
[475] For a useful discussion of the use of force against children in a variety of contexts see Fortin (2003a).
[476] Newell (1989).
[477] United Nations Committee on the Rights of the Child (2002) called on the UK to remove the defence of 'reasonable chastisement'.
[478] Proverbs 13: 24.
[479] ICM poll (*The Guardian*, 7 November 1996).
[480] Newell (1995).
[481] Sawyer (2000).
[482] [1998] 2 FLR 959, [1998] 3 FCR 597.
[483] Contrary to Offences Against the Person Act 1861, s 47.
[484] Contrary to Offences Against the Person Act 1861, s 18 or s 10.
[485] *R v Hopely* (1860) 2 F&F 202; *Attorney General Reference (No. 6 of 1980)* (1981) 73 CAR 63. The defence applies only to a person *in loco parentis*. So a brother cannot administer corporal punishment to a sister: *R v Woods* (1921) 85 SJ 272.

wilful neglect 'in such a way as to cause a child unnecessary suffering or injury to health'.[486] In respect of this offence there is a particular defence in s 1(7) of the Children and Young Persons Act 1933: 'Nothing in this section shall be construed as affecting the right of any parent, teacher or other person having the lawful control or charge of a young person to administer punishment to him.' In deciding whether or not the punishment was reasonable and moderate the jury should consider the nature and context of the defendant's behaviour; its duration; its physical and mental consequences for the child; the child's age, sex and characteristics; and the reasons given by the defendant for the punishment.[487]

As well as involving potential criminal charges, corporal punishment might also lead to investigation by a local authority. Corporal punishment is now forbidden in state and independent schools[488] and in residential care homes.[489] The European Court and Commission have had to address the issue of corporal punishment on a number of occasions.[490] The most recent case, *A v UK (Human Rights: Punishment of Child)*,[491] has had the biggest impact. A cane was used on more than one occasion by a mother's partner on her child. The European Court of Human Rights did not make a general statement on chastisement but did state that article 3 was breached. The defence of 'reasonable chastisement' was too vague and inadequately protected the child from inhuman and degrading treatment.[492] The European Court of Human Rights took the view that corporal punishment breached article 19 of the UN Convention, which requires the state to protect children from all forms of violence.[493]

A. Reforming the law

The government is at present considering the reform of the law on corporal punishment.[494] The following issues appear of particular significance:

1. The psychological evidence seems to suggest that corporal punishment harms children.[495] Opponents of corporal punishment argue that it teaches children that violence is an appropriate way to deal with situations of conflict and that it

---

[486] Children and Young Persons Act 1933.
[487] *R v H (Assault of Child: Reasonable Chastisement)* [2001] 3 FCR 144 CA. Note the criticisms of that decision in the Northern Ireland Consultation Paper (Northern Ireland Office of Law Reform (2001: 40–1)).
[488] Education Act 1996, s 548(1) as amended by the Schools Standards and Framework Act 1998, s. 131 abolished corporal punishment in independent schools. A challenge that this provision infringed parents' rights under the European Convention on Human Rights failed in *R (On the Application of Williamson) v Secretary of State for Education and Employment* [2003] 1 FCR 1 CA; discussed Eekelaar (2003b).
[489] Home Office (1993: para 5).
[490] Including *Tyrer v UK* (1978) 2 EHRR 1; *Campbell and Cosans v UK* (1982) 4 EHRR 293; *Warwick v UK* (1986) 60 DR 5; *Y v UK* (1992) 17 EHRR 238; *Costello-Roberts v UK* (1995) EHRR 112; *A v UK (Human Rights: Punishment of Child)* [1998] 2 FLR 959, [1998] 3 FCR 597; discussed Barton (1999).
[491] [1998] 2 FLR 959, [1998] 3 FCR 597.
[492] The court left open a possible claim under article 8.
[493] United Nations Human Rights Committee (1995: paras 16 and 31).
[494] Department of Health (2000a; 2001a).
[495] Orentlicher (1998); Gershoff (2002); Newell (2002).

is appropriate for larger people to injure smaller people.[496] Further, it is argued that corporal punishment cultivates a culture within society which accepts violence towards children. Some fear that where there is regular corporal punishment this can too easily escalate to more serious abuse and violence for the child.[497] That said there are many children who have been corporally punished, whom it cannot be shown have suffered particular harm as a result.

2. The most straightforward approach is that hitting children is an infringement of their rights. Freeman has stated that 'nothing is a clearer statement of the position that children occupy in society, a clearer badge of childhood, than the fact that children alone of all people in society can be hit with impunity'.[498]

3. It would be possible to reform the law so as to forbid the hitting of the child with certain kinds of implements or hitting children on certain parts of the body. However, any such list would draw arbitrary lines and would be unlikely to be effective.

4. It is difficult to distinguish physical restraint and corporal punishment. It is generally accepted that on occasion it is necessary to use force to restrain a child. Some believe there is a very fine dividing line between restraining children who are about to harm themselves or another and punishment.[499] The same act (e.g. pushing a child) could be restraining a child who was about to harm him- or herself or a punishment, depending on the intention of the parent. This demonstrates that there is some difficulty in saying that the issue is simply that a child should not be hit.

5. Some fear that if corporal punishment is outlawed then trivial assaults (e.g. a light smack) might be seen as corporal punishment. However, in Sweden, in the 14 years since corporal punishment was made illegal[500] there has been only one punishment of a parent after a complaint by a child.[501] This suggests that fears that any prohibition would lead to a major intrusion into family life are exaggerated.

6. In a survey 88 per cent of those questioned thought it sometimes necessary to smack naughty children.[502] It must be questioned whether a prohibition against all corporal punishment which would go against the views and practice of the vast majority of parents would be justifiable. Perhaps, however, a useful analogy could be made with speeding whilst driving. Clearly not all speeding is punished, and most people do break the speeding laws, yet the laws are still generally accepted.

The Department of Health has published a consultation paper on the issue, *Protecting Children, Supporting Parents*.[503] This proposes that it will be an offence to

---

[496] Commission on Children and Violence (1995).
[497] Scottish Law Commission Report 135 (1992).
[498] Freeman (1997a).
[499] See e.g. Education Act 1996, s 550A, which sets out when teachers can use force.
[500] Sweden, Finland, Denmark, Norway, Austria, Latvia, Croatia and Cyprus have all prohibited corporal punishment.
[501] Sawyer (2000).
[502] Department of Health (2000a: Annex A).
[503] Department of Health (2000a).

smack children with a cane, slipper or belt or any implement likely to injure the head, eyes or ears. Whether restricting where a child may be hit and with what will provide workable and effective guidance to parents and protection for children will be much debated during the consultation. The document starts with the premise that it would not be appropriate to render unlawful all smacking or physical rebuke of children.[504] It is perhaps surprising in a document that wishes to review the law that this supposition is not challenged or at least carefully justified.[505] The justification appears to be that an outright ban on corporal punishment would not command public acceptance.[506] At present the government appears minded to leave the law as it is.[507]

17. CHILDREN AND CONTRACT LAW

Children do, of course, enter into contracts.[508] The purchase of clothes, music or food play a central part in the life of many a teenager. If the teenager is a prestigious film star or musician, the contracts may involve substantial amounts of money. The law is concerned to protect minors who enter into contracts that they do not fully understand, and also to protect those who, in good faith, enter into contracts with minors. Of course, a child may seek to rely on the ordinary rules of contract law and claim that, for example, he or she entered the contract as a result of a misrepresentation. We will consider here only cases where minority in and of itself is a ground for making the contract unenforceable. The basic rule is that contracts entered into by minors are unenforceable, although there are exceptions to this.[509] The main exceptions are

1. A child is bound by contracts for necessities[510] if the contract is for the benefit of the minor and does not contain onerous terms. In *Aylesbury FC* v *Watford FC*[511] a contract with an under 18-year-old footballer, which tied him to one club, was held not to be for his benefit because it curtailed his ability to pursue his footballing career.
2. A minor is bound by contracts of employment.[512]
3. There are four categories of contracts which are voidable. These are binding on minors, unless they repudiate them during minority, or shortly after attaining majority. The four are:

---

[504] Department of Health (2000a: para 1.5).
[505] Barton (2002a).
[506] Department of Health (2001a: para 5–6).
[507] Department of Health (2001a).
[508] See Cooke (1998) for a discussion of the ownership of property by children.
[509] A minor is someone who is under 18. However, many of the leading cases deal with individuals who were over 18 and under 21 and were decided prior to the Family Law Reform Act 1969.
[510] So in *Nash* v *Inman* [1908] 2 KB 1 a Savile Row tailor failed in an action against a Cambridge undergraduate for failure to pay for 11 fancy waistcoats. It had not been shown that the waistcoats were necessities. Indeed, the court specifically noted there was no evidence that the undergraduate was not in full supply of waistcoats.
[511] Unreported 12.6.2000.
[512] *De Francesco* v *Barnum* (1890) 45 Ch D 430.

(i) contracts concerning land;
(ii) the acquisition of shares in companies;
(iii) partnership agreements; and
(iv) marriage settlements.

There is no accepted explanation as to why these particular kinds of contracts have been set aside for special treatment. One view is that these four categories of contracts involve a degree of permanence. They involve the minor acquiring an interest in property and to which there are continuing obligations. Where the minor repudiates the contract he or she will be freed from any future liabilities but, unless there has been a complete failure of consideration, he or she will be required to retain his or her interests in the subject matter. Treitel has suggested that the special social and economic factors that explained the special treatment for these kinds of contracts have passed away and they should be treated like other contracts.[513]

A. Parents' liability under children's contracts

Parents are not liable for contracts entered into by their children[514] unless they have appointed the child to act as their agent or ratified the contract.[515]

18. CHILDREN AND THE LAW OF TORT

The way the law of tort deals with children is a huge topic and so only a few of the issues can be highlighted here.[516] First, the law has been willing to expect people (and landowners in particular)[517] to take special steps to ensure that they (or their property) do not cause injury to children. For example, in s 2(3)(a) of the Occupier's Liability Act 1957 'an occupier must be prepared for children to be less careful than adults'.[518]

Secondly, in theory, children would be able to sue their parents for negligent parenting.[519] Normally there will be little point in a child suing parents because any damages would be taken from the parents and, in effect, returned to them. However, there is one situation where it may well make sense for a child to sue a parent and this is where the child is injured as a result of the parent's negligent driving. Here the insurance company would cover the parent's award of damages to the child.[520] The leading case on injuries caused by carers of children is *Surtees v Kingston-upon-Thames Borough Council*.[521] Here a foster child suffered severe foot injuries after the child put her foot into a bath and turned on the hot water tap. The

---

[513] Treitel (2003).
[514] *Mortimore v Wright* [1840] 6 M&W 482.
[515] The parents may also be liable under the doctrine of estoppel.
[516] Bagshaw (2001) provides a very useful discussion.
[517] Occupier's Liability Act 1957 and Occupier's Liability Act 1984; discussed in Kidner (1988).
[518] Occupier's Liability Act 1957, s 2(3)(a).
[519] For a useful discussion see Maidment (2001a).
[520] See *Pereira v Keleman* [1995] 1 FLR 428 for an example of a child suing her abusive father.
[521] [1991] 2 FLR 559.

crucial point was that the child was unaccompanied at the time. The Court of Appeal decided that the foster mother was not liable in tort. The court made the point that it did not wish to impose too high a standard of care on parents and that inevitably children will be unsupervised for short periods of time and that this injury was unforeseeable: 'We should be slow to characterise as negligent the care which ordinary loving and careful mothers are able to give individual children, given the rough-and-tumble of home life.' In the light of this case accidental injuries caused by parents are unlikely to lead to successful action against a parent unless there is clearly blameworthy neglect.

Thirdly, children are liable for torts and there is no defence of minority. In fact it is rare for the child to have sufficient money to be worth suing and so most of the actions have concerned contributory negligence. That is where the child has been harmed by the defendant's act but the defendant claims that the injuries were also partly caused by the child's acts. The test seems to be whether the child exercises the degree of care one could expect of a child of his or her age.[522]

Fourthly, normally parents are not liable for the torts of their children except in two particular situations: first, where the parents have authorised the child's actions;[523] secondly, where the parents are themselves negligent in failing to prevent the act which injured the third party. So in *Bebee* v *Sales*[524] a father was liable after he gave his son an air gun, which the boy used to damage a neighbour's property and injure another child. This case can be contrasted with *Donaldson* v *McNiven*,[525] where the father did make attempts to supervise his son and his son promised not to use the gun outside. In a different kind of case, *Carmarthenshire CC* v *Lewis*,[526] a local authority-run nursery had inadequate supervision and a 4-year-old child ran out into a street, causing a crash. This led to the local authority being liable for the death of the lorry driver involved in the crash.

19. CHILDREN'S DUTIES

Although much has been written on children's rights, there is very little said about children's duties.[527] Indeed, children appear to be under few duties under the law. By far the most significant is the duty to obey the criminal law, at least once they have reached the age of 10.[528] However, there is not even an obligation upon children to attend school.[529]

At a theoretical level, as children's rights are increasingly recognised, it is arguable that greater emphasis should be placed on children's responsibilities. If children are thought to have sufficient capacity to be able to make decisions for themselves, then

---

[522] *Yackuk* v *Olicer Blais Co Ltd* [1949] AC 396; *Mullin* v *Richards* [1998] 1 All ER 920.
[523] Or where the child is employed by the parents.
[524] (1916) 32 TLR 413.
[525] [1952] 2 All ER 691.
[526] [1955] AC 549.
[527] Bainham (1998c).
[528] Notably a young offender can be subject to a curfew order. Such orders cannot be made against adults.
[529] The obligation to ensure attendance at school is placed upon the parents, rather than the child.

it is arguable that they have sufficient capacity to have responsibilities. As Sir John Laws has written:

> A society whose values are defined by reference to individual rights is by that very fact already impoverished. Its existence says nothing about individual duty, nothing about virtue, self-discipline, self-restraint, to say nothing of self-sacrifice.[530]

However, the difficulty arises in enforcing any duties imposed upon children. Even though children are subject to the criminal law, the punishments imposed on children are not the same as those placed on adults.

20. CONCLUSION

This chapter has considered the ways in which the law looks at children. Two particular approaches have been contrasted: those in which the law seeks to promote the child's welfare and those in which the law protects the rights of the child. In respect of many issues, despite their important theoretical differences, these approaches would adopt the same solution. The issue of most disagreement is over whether a child should be able to make decisions for him- or herself. The leading cases in this area have in fact focused on the medical arena. In the rather extreme circumstances of those cases, the courts have not been willing to permit children to make decisions which have the effect of ending their lives. These cases might give the impression that children's wishes will be readily overridden by the courts, whereas in fact forcing any form of action on an unwilling teenager is rare, although this may be as much because of the practical problems in compelling a person to do something against their will as any theoretical principle. The chapter has also considered the ways that the law must balance the interests of parents and children. The issue is often not made explicit in the case law. The simple approach that the interests of children are paramount and always trump those of the parent has been shown not to represent the law and not to be appropriate in theory. The Human Rights Act 1998 will no doubt lead to many more cases where the court will be required to balance the interests of parents, children and the state and, hopefully, more well-thought-out principles will be developed.

---

[530] Laws (1998: 255).

9

COURT RESOLUTION OF PRIVATE DISPUTES OVER CHILDREN

1. INTRODUCTION

This chapter will consider the law in situations when the court is required to resolve a private dispute concerning children. Chapter 10 will examine public law cases, that is, where the local authority is seeking to protect a child who they fear is in danger of being abused. Here we will concentrate largely on the cases which involved disputes between parents over the upbringing of children, although, as will become apparent, adults other than parents, and indeed children themselves, may seek court orders over children.

The law is based on the assumption that parents promote the welfare of their children, and so there is no need normally for the intervention of the court. The courts only become involved if there is a dispute between the parents over the upbringing of their child or, rarely, if the child him- or herself applies to the court. One exception is on divorce. Under s 41 of the Matrimonial Causes Act 1973:

> In any proceedings for a decree of divorce or nullity of marriage, or a decree of judicial separation, the court shall consider—
> (a) whether there are any children of the family to whom this section applies; and
> (b) where there are any such children, whether (in the light of the arrangements which have been, or are proposed to be, made for their upbringing and welfare) it should exercise any of its powers under the Children Act 1989 with respect to any of them.

So on the making of each divorce decree the court must consider the statement of arrangements concerning the children produced by the parents and decide whether it should exercise any of its powers in relation to the children of the divorcing couple. In practice, if neither party applies for an order, the court will normally assume that there is no need to make an order.[1] The thinking behind this approach has been explained by Douglas et al. in this way: 'parents may be trusted, in most cases, to plan what is best for their children's futures, and that, where they are in agreement on this, it is unnecessary and potentially damaging for the state, in the guise of the court, to intervene'.[2]

Research into the operation of s 41 has indicated that the procedure is flawed.[3] There are no means of checking whether the proposals in the statement are accurate. More significantly, researchers found that the parents' proposals were rarely

---

[1] Douglas, Murch, Scanlan and Perry (2000).
[2] Douglas, Murch, Scanlan and Perry (2000: 183–4).
[3] Murch, Douglas, Scanlan et al. (2000).

discussed with the children.[4] The government has indicated that it is willing to consider reform of s 41. The proposal is to improve the information available to courts and to encourage the use of Parenting Plans, which will set out clearly the intentions of the parents regarding the children.[5] It is hoped that these will focus the minds of parents on the key questions to be addressed and provide the courts with the information they need to make a proper assessment of the situation.

The Children Act 1989 brought together the orders appropriate for most private disputes involving children, but sometimes the courts must use their inherent jurisdiction if it is not possible to make the order needed to protect a child under the Children Act 1989. This chapter will begin by setting out the orders available under the Children Act, then consider how the courts decide what order to make, followed by a discussion of the inherent jurisdiction, and concluding with the rules relating to child abduction.

2. SECTION 8 ORDERS

In private cases involving children the courts may make one of the orders mentioned in s 8 of the Children Act 1989. A s 8 order cannot be made in respect of a person over the age of 18.[6] If the child is 16 or 17 then a s 8 order should not be made unless the 'circumstances of the case are exceptional'.[7] There are a few cases where the court has thought it appropriate to make an order in respect of a 16- or 17-year-old. In *Re M (A Minor) (Immigration: Residence Order)*[8] the fact that the child did not have any relatives living in the UK was sufficiently exceptional to justify the making of an order that would last until the 18th birthday of the child.

The different orders that can be made under s 8 will now be considered.

A. The residence order

(i) The effect of a residence order

A residence order is 'an order settling the arrangements to be made as to the person with whom a child is to live'.[9] It will normally be made in favour of one of the child's parents, but can be made in favour of a grandparent, an aunt, or, in fact, anyone.[10] It is even possible to impose a residence order on people against their wishes,[11] although it is very rare.

---

[4] Douglas, Murch, Scanlan and Perry (2000).
[5] Lord Chancellor's Department (2002d:8).
[6] For a discussion of how contact with adults may be restricted see *Cambridge CC v R (An Adult)* [1994] 2 FCR 973.
[7] Children Act 1989 (hereafter CA 1989), s 9(6).
[8] [1993] 2 FLR 858.
[9] CA 1989, s 8(1).
[10] Booth J in *Re SC (A Minor) (Leave to Seek Section 8 Orders)* [1994] 1 FLR 96 at p. 100, suggested that a residence order could not be made in favour of a child. However, there is no statutory provision to this effect. It would not be impossible to imagine circumstances when it might be appropriate: for example, where a mature 15-year-old sister is to care for her younger sibling.
[11] *Re M (Adoption or Residence Order)* [1998] 1 FLR 570, [1998] 1 FCR 165; *Re K (Care Order or Residence Order)* [1995] 1 FLR 675, [1996] 1 FCR 365.

The residence order confers upon those to whom it is granted parental responsibility, if they do not have it already. It is therefore impossible to have a residence order without having parental responsibility. The reason for this is that if the child is to live with an adult then that adult will be exercising all the duties and responsibilities of parenthood on a day-to-day basis, and so giving him or her parental responsibility will make the legal position reflect the factual position. However, if the court is granting a residence order in favour of an unmarried father, then s 12(1) of the Children Act 1989 obliges the court to make a separate parental responsibility order. The significance of this is that, if the residence order is subsequently revoked, the unmarried father will retain parental responsibility, whereas a non-parent with a residence order would cease to have parental responsibility if the residence order was revoked.

(ii) Joint residence orders

A residence order can be made in favour of two people under s 11(4), even if they do not live together.[12] The subsection explains that an order can require a child to spend a certain amount of time with one person and a certain amount of time with the other. For example, the order may state that the child should spend alternate weeks with the mother and father. The precise dividing line between a joint residence order and liberal contact order is blurred. It has been suggested that a joint residence order is one which involves each parent seeing the child a substantial amount of time.[13] Some commentators suggest a joint residence order occurs when each parent sees the child between 30 per cent and 70 per cent of the time.[14] If the percentages are more or less than these, then a residence and contact order may be more appropriate than a joint residence order. If there is a residence order requiring a child to live with one of two parents, the order will cease if the parents live together for longer than six months.[15]

B. The contact order

(i) The effect of a contact order

As well as deciding with whom the child should live, the court must also consider whether the child should have regular meetings with their other parent (the contact parent), or indeed with other relatives or family friends. The hope is that regular meetings will enable the child to continue his or her relationship with both parents and both sides of the family. As is often (rather glibly) stated, the fact that the parents have separated should not affect their relationship with the child: parenthood

---

[12] Hoggett (1994); Baker and Townsend (1996); C. Bridge (1996).

[13] *Re D (Children) (Shared Residence Orders)* [2001] 1 FCR 147, at para 32.

[14] Macooby and Mnookin (1992). In *Re F (Children) (Shared Residence Order)* [2003] 2 FCR 164 a shared residence order where the father saw the children 38 per cent of the time was approved, although Wilson J suggested that the court could just as well have made a residence order in favour of the mother and a generous contact order in favour of the father (para 32).

[15] CA 1989, s 11(5).

is for life. Following a bitter separation, the residential parent[16] may be deeply opposed to the child seeing the other parent. This is particularly so if the residential parent remarries and tries to form a 'new family' with his or her new spouse. On the other hand, the contact parent will seek to do all he or she can to retain contact with the child and make the most of the contact permitted. This means that contact applications are often very bitterly disputed.

The contact order is defined as 'an order requiring the person with whom a child lives, or is to live, to allow the child to visit or stay with the person named in the order, or for that person and the child otherwise to have contact with each other'.[17] This wording gives rise to some interesting questions about the effect of the order.

(ii) Who has the obligation of enabling contact?

The definition of a contact order is interesting. It seems to suggest that there are two kinds of contact order available. First, and normally, the order can be directed at the residential parent requiring her or him to permit the child to have contact with the person named in the order. So if the residential parent prevents contact then she or he will be in breach of the order and could ultimately be imprisoned for contempt. Secondly, the order can simply state that the child and another person are to have contact. This seems to impose no obligation on the residential parent, and the residential parent would not be in breach of the order if the contact did not take place. In fact, no one would be in breach of the order if contact did not take place. However, the distinction between these different wordings of the orders has not been made explicit by the courts, and *Re H (Minors) (Prohibited Steps Order)*[18] appeared to assume that only the first kind of order could be made.

(iii) Is a 'no contact' order a contact order?

The courts have interpreted the definition of a contact order to include an order that there is to be *no* contact between the child and a named person.[19] It is not clear whether such an order binds both the named party and the residential parent. *Re H (Minors) (Prohibited Steps Order)*[20] seemed to suggest that if a court wishes to bind the residential parent then a no contact order should be made, but if the aim is to bind a person who is not to have contact then a prohibited steps order should be made.[21] A no contact order may be appropriate where the residential parent has a friend who is a known paedophile and the courts wish to prevent the residential parent from introducing the friend to the child. A prohibited steps order may be appropriate where a stepfather has abused his stepchildren and has then separated from the mother, but has been seeking to contact the children.[22] In such a case a

---

[16] A 'residential parent' is the parent with whom the child is to live.
[17] CA 1989, s 8(1).
[18] [1995] 1 FLR 638, [1995] 2 FCR 547.
[19] *Nottingham CC v P* [1994] 2 FLR 134, [1994] 1 FCR 624 CA.
[20] [1995] 1 FLR 638, [1995] 2 FCR 547.
[21] *Re H (Minors) (Prohibited Steps Order)* [1995] 1 FLR 638, [1995] 2 FCR 547.
[22] *Re H (Minors) (Prohibited Steps Order)* [1995] 1 FLR 638, [1995] 2 FCR 547.

no contact order may be inappropriate because there is little the mother could do to stop the step-parent seeing the children, if he was persistent enough.[23] It would therefore be more appropriate to make a prohibited steps order, directed against the step-parent. In some cases it might be best to make both a no contact and a prohibited steps order.

(iv) Can the parent be forced to have contact with the child?

The law has not yet directly addressed the question of whether the non-residential parent can be *required* to have contact with the child. If the evidence is clear that the child would benefit from regular contact with the non-resident father, but the father does not wish to have contact, can he be compelled to see the child?[24] The definition of a contact order would not seem to include an order that binds the person named to have contact.[25] Indeed, Thorpe LJ in *Re L (A Child) (Contact: Domestic Violence)*[26] explicitly denied that a parent could be ordered to spend time with a child against the parent's wishes. In any event, it would probably be counter-productive to compel a reluctant parent to see a child.[27]

(v) What can 'contact' involve?

A contact order will normally involve face-to-face meetings, but contact orders can also involve indirect contact, for example in the form of letters, e-mails or telephone calls. An indirect contact order may be appropriate if the contact parent cannot see the child, for example if he or she is in prison.[28] An indirect contact order may also be appropriate if the child and the contact parent do not have a relationship at present, and they need to establish or re-establish links before direct contact would be appropriate. In *Re L (Contact: Transsexual Applicant)*[29] two teenage boys found it very uncomfortable visiting a father who had had a 'sex change'. Indirect contact was ordered with the hope that direct contact would be possible in the future once the boys had come to terms with their father's new sex. It would be most unusual for a court to decide that even indirect contact would be inappropriate.[30]

If contact is to be face to face, it can be supervised by the social services.[31] This may be particularly appropriate where there is a fear that the contact parent may endanger the child.[32] If contact is to be supervised then it will often take place at a contact centre, a place set up by the local authority to assist in meetings between

---

[23] *Re C (Contact: No Order for Contact)* [2000] Fam Law 699, [2000] 2 FLR 723.
[24] Of course, he could not physically be forced to do so, but he could be ordered to do so under threat of punishment.
[25] Although a specific issue order may have this effect.
[26] [2000] 2 FCR 404, at para. 43.
[27] But see the discussions on the duties of contact later in this chapter.
[28] *A v L (Contact)* [1998] 1 FLR 361, [1998] 2 FCR 204.
[29] [1995] 2 FLR 438, [1995] 3 FCR 125.
[30] *Re P (Contact: Indirect Contact)* [1999] 2 FLR 893.
[31] *Practice Direction (Access: Supervised Access)* [1980] 1 WLR 334.
[32] Although where there has been sexual abuse indirect contact is normally ordered: *Re M (Sexual Abuse Allegations: Interviewing Techniques)* [1999] 2 FLR 92.

contact parents and children.[33] The effectiveness of these centres will be considered later in this chapter.

C. Specific issue orders and prohibited steps orders

A specific issue order (SIO) is 'an order giving directions for the purpose of determining a specific question which has arisen, or which may arise, in connection with any aspect of parental responsibility for a child'.[34] A prohibited steps order (PSO) is 'an order that no step which could be taken by a parent in meeting his parental responsibility for a child, and which is of a kind specified in the order, shall be taken by any person without the consent of the court'.[35]

The SIO may require someone to act positively in some way or may require someone to refrain from a particular activity. It is designed to deal with a particular one-off issue relating to the child's upbringing; for example, in *Re C (A Child) (HIV Test)*[36] a SIO was made that a baby be tested for HIV. It is not designed to deal with ongoing disputes – for example, what kind of clothes the child may wear. The PSO is entirely negative – it tells a parent what he or she may not do in respect of their child. The order can be used, for example, to prevent a child being known by a different name,[37] or to prevent a child being removed from the United Kingdom.[38]

D. Restrictions on the use of section 8 orders

The s 8 orders are loosely defined and so could be open to abuse were they not restricted in their scope in the following ways.

(i) The order must relate to an aspect of parental responsibility

This means that the order must relate to an issue concerning the upbringing of the child and not just concerning the relationship between the parents. So, for example, s 8 orders cannot prevent contact between adults,[39] nor require a husband to provide the wife with a *get* so that their divorce can be recognised within Jewish law.[40] However, it is not always easy to tell whether a particular question does relate to an aspect of parental responsibility. For example, there has been some dispute over whether restricting publicity about children is an aspect of parental responsibility. In *Re Z (A Minor) (Identity: Restrictions on Publication)*[41] the issue was whether a

---

[33] The government has announced that it will spend £2.5 million on improving contact centres: Home Office (2003a: 39).

[34] CA 1989, s 8(1). It is possible to apply for an *ex parte* specific issue order: Family Proceedings Rules 1991, SI 1991/1247, r 4(4)(c).

[35] CA 1989, s 8(1). In 1995, 8,730 applications were made and 5,780 orders granted.

[36] [1999] 2 FLR 1004 CA.

[37] *Dawson* v *Wearmouth* [1999] 1 FLR 1167, [1999] 1 FCR 625 HL.

[38] Law Commission Report 172 (1988: 4.20).

[39] *Croydon LB* v *A* [1992] 2 FLR 341, [1992] 1 FCR 522.

[40] *N* v *N (Jurisdiction: Pre-Nuptial Agreement)* [1999] 2 FLR 745.

[41] [1996] 1 FLR 191, [1996] 2 FCR 164 CA.

television company could film a child who was attending a specialist medical unit. It was decided that the question was whether the child's right of confidentiality should be waived. The Court of Appeal held that waiving confidentiality was an aspect of parental responsibility and so a PSO could be made. However, in *R v Central Independent Television plc*[42] it was held that broadcasting a television film about the arrest of the father did not involve an aspect of parental responsibility, even though the showing of the film might cause distress to the child. This was because the making of the film did not require the child's involvement and so did not involve an aspect of the child's upbringing. The distinction is not always easy to draw. In *Re X (A Child) (Injunction Restraining Publication)*[43] a local authority sought to prohibit the publication of details of a case where white foster parents had been prevented from adopting a black child, allegedly on the basis of their race. It was held that because the key issue was the policy of the local authority, rather than the raising of this child as such, a PSO could not be made. In *Medway Council v BBC*[44] because the film had already been made and its broadcast did not involve an aspect of the boy's upbringing a PSO preventing the broadcast could not be ordered.

Although the order can only concern an exercise of parental responsibility, the person at whom the order is directed need not actually have parental responsibility. It is sufficient if the order is stopping someone from doing something that would be an exercise of parental responsibility if he or she had parental responsibility.[45] So it would be possible for a neighbour to be ordered not to speak to a child, even though the neighbour has no parental responsibility, because if the neighbour had parental responsibility speaking to the child would be an exercise of it.

(ii) There is no power to make an occupation or non-molestation order through a s 8 order

A specific issue or prohibited steps order cannot be made if the effect is the same as an occupation or non-molestation order.[46] Any such order must be sought under the Family Law Act 1996, Part IV.[47] However, if it can be shown that the order sought is not identical to an order available under the Family Law Act 1996 then the order can be made. In *Re H (Minors) (Prohibited Steps Order)*[48] a PSO preventing a step-father visiting a child could be made because a non-molestation order would only prevent molestation and not prohibit all contact with the child. The PSO was therefore not identical to a non-molestation order.

---

[42] [1994] Fam 192.
[43] [2001] 1 FCR 541.
[44] [2001] FL 883.
[45] *Re H (Minors) (Prohibited Steps Order)* [1995] 1 FLR 638, [1995] 2 FCR 547.
[46] *Re D (Prohibited Steps Order)* [1996] 2 FLR 273, [1996] 2 FCR 496 CA; *Re D (Residence: Imposition of Conditions)* [1996] 2 FLR 281, [1996] 2 FCR 820 CA.
[47] See Chapter 6.
[48] [1995] 1 FLR 638, [1995] 2 FCR 547.

(iii) There is no power to make a disguised residence or contact order using a PSO or SIO

Section 9(5)(a) of the Children Act 1989 states that neither a PSO nor a SIO can be made 'with a view to achieving a result which could be achieved by making a residence or contact order'.[49] The real significance of this restriction relates to local authorities: they can apply for specific issue orders or prohibited steps orders, but cannot apply for contact or residence orders. In *Nottingham CC v P*[50] the Court of Appeal held that a local authority could not apply for a s 8 order that a father vacate a matrimonial home. Such an order was essentially a residence order and local authorities were prohibited from applying for that. In *Re H (Minors) (Prohibited Steps Order)*[51] an order was made preventing a stepfather from contacting a child. This was not a no contact order in disguise because a contact order compels the residential parent to permit or forbid contact, but here the order was directed to be effective against the stepfather and so could not have been made as a contact order.

(iv) A s 8 order cannot be made if the High Court would not be able to make the order acting under the inherent jurisdiction

The practical effect of this restriction is that a local authority is prevented from accommodating the child or obtaining the care or supervision of a child through a specific issue order. If the local authority wishes to accommodate, care for, or supervise a child, they must use their powers under the Children Act 1989, Part III, rather than use s 8 orders.

(v) The courts will not normally make a PSO or SIO in relation to trivial matters

In *Re C (A Minor) (Leave to Seek Section 8 Order)*[52] Johnson J refused to give leave to apply for a SIO permitting a child to go on holiday to Bulgaria with her friend's family against her parents' wishes. This was held to be too trivial an issue to be suitable for a s 8 order. If going on holiday is too trivial an issue for a SIO, many other questions that may concern a child or non-residential parent (such as whether the child has to eat green vegetables) can also be seen as too trivial.[53] Section 8 orders should deal with issues of great significance in the child's life, such as where the child is to go to school or whether he or she should have a medical operation. However, there is nothing in the wording of the statute to suggest that s 8 orders should not deal with what might appear to be trivial matters. A court might feel it is appropriate to deal with a 'trivial issue' (for example, what hairstyle the child should have)[54] if the issue has come to dominate the parents' and child's relationship to such an extent that it is harming the child. So the better view is that SIOs

---

[49] *Re B (Minors) (Residence Order)* [1992] 2 FLR 1, [1992] 1 FCR 555.
[50] [1993] 2 FLR 134, [1994] 1 FCR 624 CA.
[51] [1995] 1 FLR 638, [1995] 2 FCR 547, discussed in M. Roberts (1995).
[52] [1994] 1 FLR 26.
[53] *Re C (A Minor) (Leave to Seek Section 8 Orders)* [1994] 1 FLR 26.
[54] E.g. what time the child should go to bed: *B v B (Custody: Conditions)* [1979] 1 FLR 385.

or PSOs can be made in relation to trivial issues, but only rarely will it be appropriate to do so.

(vi) The orders must be in precise terms

A prohibited steps or specific issue order must be in clear terms. An order prohibiting the publishing of 'any information' about two children was found to be in too general terms and restricted by the Court of Appeal to information that identified the children.[55]

(vii) Only residence orders are available if the child is in care

Under s 9(1) of the Children Act 1989 the only s 8 order that can be applied for if a child is in care is a residence order. The reasoning is that the local authority, rather than the court, should make decisions relating to the upbringing of a child in care.[56]

(viii) There may be restrictions on s 8 orders where the child is competent

There is some dispute over whether a PSO can overrule the decision of a competent child. For example, if a competent child and doctor agree on a form of contraception, could a court make a PSO to prevent the doctor providing the contraception? One view is that the PSO can only prevent an exercise of parental responsibility. As a parent cannot overrule the consent of a competent child to such treatment, neither can a PSO.[57] The opposite view is that the PSO can overrule the wishes of a competent minor because the definition of a PSO in s 8(1) refers to the decision that 'a' parent, rather than 'the' parent, could make. The best view of the present law is that the court is unlikely to make a s 8 order against the wishes of a competent child, but it is open to the court to do so if necessary for the child's welfare. Even if this view were not taken, it would still be open to the court to overrule the child's wishes through the use of the inherent jurisdiction.

E. Attaching conditions

When making any order under s 8, the court can attach conditions to the order. This power enables the court to 'fine-tune' the order. The conditions can give detailed arrangements as to how the order should be carried out. For example, there may be conditions stating where the contact is to take place. There is a fine balance here between encouraging the parties to be flexible and resolve minor issues between themselves, and making the order sufficiently detailed that it is clear what is required. Section 11(7) provides that an order under s 8 can:

---

[55] *Re G (A Child) (Contempt: Committal Order)* [2003] 2 FCR 231 CA.
[56] See Chapter 11 for further discussion.
[57] *Gillick v W Norfolk and Wisbech AHA* [1986] 1 FLR 229, [1986] AC 112 HL.

(a) contain directions about how it is to be carried into effect;
(b) impose conditions which must be complied with by any person—
    (i) in whose favour the order is made;
    (ii) who is a parent of the child concerned;
    (iii) who is not a parent of his but who has parental responsibility for him; or
    (iv) with whom the child is living,
    and to whom the conditions are expressed to apply;
(c) be made to have effect for a specified period, or contain provisions which are to have effect for a specified period;
(d) make such incidental, supplemental or consequential provision as the court thinks fit.

It will be noted that the conditions do not necessarily apply to the person who has the benefit of the s 8 order. They might bind the partner of the person who has the benefit of a contact order, for example. However, the power to attach conditions is not as wide as it might at first appear, and the courts have developed a number of restrictions on the use of the power:

1. Conditions are intended to be supplemental to the s 8 order and should not be used as the primary purpose of the order.[58] Hence a Jewish wife failed in an application for a condition to be attached to a contact order that a husband provided her with a *get* so that she could obtain a religious divorce. It was held that this condition would not be appropriate as it was not supplemental to a contact order and was raising a completely new issue.[59] What is 'supplemental' may be open to debate. For a while there was some doubt over whether a residential parent could be ordered to read correspondence from the contact parent to the child. It is now clear that this can be ordered, as it is supplemental to an indirect contact order.[60]

2. The condition must not be incompatible with the main order. In *Birmingham CC v H*[61] Ward J said that a residence order could not contain a condition that the mother had to live at a specialised unit for mothers and children and comply with reasonable instructions from the staff at the unit. The court explained that the basis of a residence order is that the person with the benefit of the order can choose where the child should live and how to raise the child; the condition was inconsistent with both of these.

3. The condition cannot affect the fundamental rights of a parent. In *Re E (Residence: Imposition of Conditions)*[62] the judge sought to impose a condition on a residence order that the mother remain at a particular address. This was held by the Court of Appeal to be an inappropriate use of a condition, as it limited the mother's right to choose where to live. However, in *Re S (A Child) (Residence Order: Condition) (No.2)*[63] the Court of Appeal took the view that in the truly

---

[58] *Re D (Prohibited Steps Order)* [1996] 2 FLR 273, [1996] 2 FCR 496 CA.
[59] *N v N (Jurisdiction: Pre-Nuptial Agreement)* [1999] 2 FLR 745.
[60] *Re O (Contact: Imposition of Conditions)* [1995] 2 FLR 124, [1996] 1 FCR 317 CA.
[61] [1992] 2 FLR 323.
[62] [1997] 2 FLR 638, [1997] 3 FCR 245 CA. Two other examples are *Re D (Residence: Imposition of Conditions)* [1996] 2 FLR 281, [1996] 2 FCR 820 CA; and *D v N (Contact Order: Conditions)* [1997] 2 FLR 797, [1997] 3 FCR 721 CA.
[63] [2003] 1 FCR 138 CA.

exceptional circumstances of the case before it was permissible for the judge to make a residence order prohibiting the mother from moving to Cornwall to be with her new partner.[64] The exceptional circumstances were that the child in question suffered from Down's Syndrome and other complications. She had a very good relationship with the mother and father. The judge was concerned that if the mother moved to Cornwall this would have the effect of dramatically reducing the contact between the father and child. The daughter would lack the capacity to understand why this had happened and would therefore suffer great distress. The condition was therefore necessary in the interests of the child, even though the condition would cause a significant infringement into the rights of the mother.

By contrast in *Re D (Residence: Imposition of Conditions)*[65] children were returned to the mother under a residence order with a condition that the children should not be brought into contact with her partner and that her partner should not reside with her and the children. The Court of Appeal allowed an appeal against the imposition of the condition. Ward LJ explained that:

> the case concerned a mother seeking, as she was entitled to, to allow this man back into her life because that is the way she wished to live it. The court was not in a position so to override her right to live her life as she chose. What was before the court was whether, if she chose to have him back, the proper person with whom the children should reside was herself or whether it would be better for the children that they lived with their father or with the grandmother.

In other words, the court should not use conditions attached to residence orders to 'perfect' a parent. Instead, in deciding who should have a residence order, the court should choose between the parents as they are.

4. The condition cannot be used as a back-door route to obtaining an order that is available under other pieces of legislation. So in *D v N (Contact Order: Conditions)*[66] the Court of Appeal stated that it was inappropriate to use conditions to prevent the father molesting the mother, as such an order was available under the Family Law Act 1996.

5. The condition must be enforceable. In *B v B (Custody: Conditions)*[67] a condition that the child be in bed before 6.30 pm was struck out. There was no way that the court could realistically enforce such an order. Similarly, in *Re C (A Child) (HIV Test)*[68] the Court of Appeal agreed that it would be inappropriate to order a mother not to breastfeed her child, as this would be unenforceable.[69]

6. There is no power to use conditions to interfere with the local authority's exercise of its statutory or common law powers. So a condition cannot be used to

---

[64] See also *Re H (Children) (Residence Order: Condition)* [2001] 3 FCR 182 where a father with a residence order was prevented from taking the children to live with him in Northern Ireland.

[65] [1996] 2 FCR 820, at p. 825.

[66] [1997] 2 FLR 797, [1997] 3 FCR 721.

[67] [1979] 1 FLR 385.

[68] [1999] 2 FLR 1004 CA.

[69] For criticism of this see Strong (2000).

require a local authority to supervise contact[70] or to exercise its powers in a particular way.[71]

F. Variation, discharge and appeals

It is possible to appeal against the granting of a s 8 order. However, it is clear from *G v G*[72] that there is no power in an appeal court to overturn a decision simply because it disagrees with the lower court's decision. It has to be shown that the lower court's decision was flawed in one of the following ways:

1. the lower court made an error of law;
2. the lower court relied upon evidence which should not have been taken into account;
3. the lower court failed to consider evidence that should have been taken into account; or
4. the decision of the lower court was 'plainly wrong'.

The aim is to provide a degree of certainty and to discourage appeals.

Section 8 orders can be discharged or varied. People who can apply as of right for a s 8 order can also apply for a variation or discharge of the order. In addition, a person can apply for variation of an order if the order was made on his or her application. A person who is named in a contact order can also apply for a variation or discharge of the order,[73] but that does not include the child who is the subject of the order.[74]

3. WHO CAN APPLY FOR SECTION 8 ORDERS?

When considering who can apply for s 8 orders it is necessary to distinguish two separate groups of applicants: those who have the automatic right to apply for a s 8 order, and those who have the right to apply only if the court grants leave. The detailed law will be discussed shortly but, generally, those who have a very close link with the child can automatically apply for a s 8 order. Anyone else must first seek the leave of the court to bring the application. Only if the court thinks there is an issue which requires a full hearing will it give leave for the application to be heard. If it thinks the application is frivolous or mischievous, the court will refuse to grant leave. The law in this area is seeking to strike a balance between making the court accessible to all those who have legitimate concerns about the upbringing of children, and protecting those who care for children from the stress of facing challenges to their parenting in the courts. The requirement for leave enables the court to filter out applications that the court thinks are inappropriate, without causing the resi-

---

[70] *Leeds CC v C* [1993] 1 FLR 269, [1993] 1 FCR 585.
[71] *D v D (County Court Jurisdiction: Injunctions)* [1993] 2 FLR 802, [1994] 3 FCR 28 CA.
[72] [1985] FLR 894 HL.
[73] CA 1989, s 10(7) states that additional categories can be added, although these powers have not been used.
[74] *Re H (Residence Order: Child's Application for Leave)* [2000] 1 FLR 780.

dential parent the expense and stress of preparing a defence and attending the hearing.

A. Persons who can apply without leave

Those who can apply for any s 8 order without leave of the court are:

1. Parents. This includes an unmarried father without parental responsibility. It does not include former parents, for example those whose children have been freed for adoption.[75]
2. Guardians.
3. Those with the benefit of a residence order.

There is a special category of people who can apply without leave only for residence or contact orders. The explanation seems to be that the listed people have a sufficiently close relationship with the child to have a say in where the child should live (particularly where the parents have become incapable of caring for the child), but they do not have a right to have a say in the details of how the parent should bring up the child.[76] Those who can apply for residence or contact orders (but not other orders) without leave are:

1. Any party to a marriage[77] if the child has been treated by the applicant as a 'child of the family'.[78] This includes stepparents.
2. Any person with whom the child has lived for at least three years.[79]
3. Any person who has the consent of:

    (a) each of the persons in whose favour any residence order is in force; or
    (b) the local authority, if the child is subject to a care order; or
    (c) in any other case, each of the people who have parental responsibility for the child.

B. People who need the leave of the court

Anyone else can apply for a s 8 order once they have obtained the leave of the court. This includes the child him- or herself. The one exception to this is local authority foster carers, who must have the consent of the local authority to apply for a s 8 order unless they are related to the child or the child has been living with them for at least three years preceding the application.[80]

---

[75] *M v C and Calderdale MBC* [1993] 1 FLR 505, [1993] 1 FCR 431 CA.
[76] Bainham (1998a: 173).
[77] Even if the marriage has been dissolved.
[78] CA 1989, s 10(5)(a).
[79] The period need not be continuous but needs to have started more than five years before the application and be subsisting three months before the making of the application.
[80] CA 1989, s 9(3).

C. How the court decides whether to grant leave

If it is necessary to obtain the leave of the court, the factors that the court will take into account in deciding whether to give leave depend on whether the applicant is an adult or a child.

(i) Adults seeking leave

The factors to be considered are listed in s 10(9) of the Children Act 1989:[81]

    (a) the nature of the proposed application for the section 8 order;
    (b) the applicant's connection with the child;
    (c) any risk there might be of that proposed application disrupting the child's life to such an extent that he would be harmed by it; and
    (d) where the child is being looked after by a local authority—
        (i) the authority's plans for the child's future; and
        (ii) the wishes and feelings of the child's parents.

In *Re A (Minors) (Residence Orders: Leave to Apply)*[82] the Court of Appeal held that the paramountcy principle under s 1(1) of the Children Act 1989 does not apply when considering whether to grant leave. This is because the question of leave does not itself involve an issue relating to the child's upbringing.[83] The court can consider factors that are not listed in s 10(9), most notably the child's wishes.[84] In deciding whether or not to grant leave the courts must now take account of the applicant's rights under articles 6 and 8 of the European Convention.[85] This suggests that only where the application is thought frivolous, vexatious or otherwise harmful to the child will leave not be granted.[86] There is no need to show that the applicant has 'a good arguable case' before being granted leave.[87] Special considerations apply if the application concerns a child in care, and these will be discussed in Chapter 11.

It is clear that if leave is granted there is no presumption that the application will succeed at the full hearing.[88]

(ii) Children seeking leave

This was discussed in Chapter 8.

---

[81] These do not apply to an application for leave following a s 91(14) application: *Re A (Application for Leave)* [1998] 1 FLR 1, [1999] 1 FCR 127 CA.
[82] [1992] 2 FLR 154, [1992] 2 FCR 174 CA.
[83] The Court of Appeal also argued that the criteria in s 10(9) would be otiose if s 1(3) applied.
[84] *Re A (A Minor) (Residence Order: Leave To Apply)* [1993] 1 FLR 425, [1993] 1 FCR 870.
[85] *Re J (Leave to Issue Application for Residence Order)* [2003] 1 FLR 114 CA.
[86] *Re M (Care: Contact: Grandmother's Application for Leave)* [1995] 2 FLR 86, [1995] 3 FCR 550 CA.
[87] *Re J (Leave to Issue Application for Residence Order)* [2003] 1 FLR 114 CA.
[88] *Re W (Contact: Application by Grandmother)* [1997] 1 FLR 793, [1997] 2 FCR 643.

(iii) Applying for s 8 orders in favour of someone else

It is not clear whether it is possible to apply for a s 8 order on behalf of someone else, although, as there is no statutory bar, it is presumably possible. Certainly an adult can apply for leave on behalf of a child.[89] It also seems that a child can apply for leave for a residence order in favour of someone else.[90] There is some debate over whether a local authority can apply for a residence order in favour of a third party. Such an application would fail if it were thought that a local authority was seeking to circumvent the prohibition on a local authority to apply for a residence or contact order themselves.

D. Restricting section 8 applications: section 91(14)

One parent may be intent on pursuing applications against the other out of bitterness or desperation. For example, a non-residential parent may constantly apply to the court for SIOs relating to tiny aspects of the child's upbringing.[91] Repeated fruitless applications to the court could cause severe distress to the child and their carer, not least because each application must be defended in court.[92] In order to restrict such applications, the court under s 91(14) can require a party to obtain the leave of the court before applying for any further orders. This way the child and their carer will not be bothered by having to defend an application unless the court has considered it worthy of a full hearing and granted leave. A court can make a s 91(14) order whenever it disposes of an application for any order under the Children Act 1989. It is possible under the subsection to restrict only a certain kind of application; for example, applications for a residence order. One interesting example of the use of the order was *K* v *M (Paternity: Contact)*,[93] where a lover was prevented from bringing further applications to establish that he was the father of a woman's child, after the woman had decided to remain with her husband and to raise the child with him. The court thought the use of the order necessary to prevent the spreading of rumours over the child's paternity.

A s 91(14) order is only appropriate where there is evidence that future applications are likely to be unreasonable, vexatious, or frivolous.[94] In deciding whether or not to make an order under s 91(14) the court should keep in mind, *inter alia*, the following factors:[95]

---

[89] There may be financial reasons for doing this, as the child may then be able to obtain legal aid: *Re HG (Specific Issue Order: Sterilisation)* [1993] 1 FLR 587, [1993] 1 FCR 553.

[90] So a child cannot apply for a residence order that he or she live by him- or herself.

[91] *Re N (Section 91(14) Order)* [1996] 1 FLR 356 CA.

[92] *C* v *W (Contact: Leave to Apply)* [1999] 1 FLR 916.

[93] [1996] 1 FLR 312, [1996] 3 FCR 517.

[94] *F* v *Kent CC* [1993] 1 FLR 432, [1992] 2 FCR 433. So if there is no history of making inappropriate applications a s 91(14) order should not be made: *B* v *B (Residence Order: Restricting Applications)* [1997] 1 FLR 139, [1997] 2 FCR 518 CA.

[95] A complete list of relevant factors is listed in *Re P (Section 91(14) Guidelines) (Residence and Religious Heritage)* [1999] 2 FLR 573 CA.

1. The welfare of the child is the paramount consideration.[96]
2. It is a draconian order[97] which should be used sparingly and only as a last resort.[98]
3. The court should weigh up the child's interests in being protected from inappropriate applications with the fundamental right of access to the courts: *Re R (Residence: Contact: Restricting Applications)*.[99]
4. The order is appropriate if there have been repeated and unreasonable applications.[100] Where, however, the party has not been making inappropriate applications and there is no evidence that he or she will do so, the order will be inappropriate.[101]

If a s 91(14) order is made against a party, he or she can still apply for leave to make an application.[102] The important point is that the hearing for leave will not require the attendance of the residential parent; indeed, they need not even know of the application.[103] This protects the residential parent from the worry that such applications may cause. If an application for leave is made then the test in deciding whether to grant leave is whether the application for leave demonstrates a need for renewed investigation by the court.[104]

It might be argued that s 91(14) is inconsistent with the Human Rights Act 1998. However, the Court of Appeal explained in *Re P (Section 91(14) Guidelines) (Residence and Religious Heritage)*[105] that, as s 91(14) does not constitute a complete bar of access to the court but simply requires leave, it is probably consistent with the Act. Indeed, the European Convention itself includes similar provisions to prevent inappropriate applications to the European Court of Human Rights,[106] so it is unlikely that s 91(14) would infringe the Human Rights Act. However, in *Re B (A Child)*[107] the Court of Appeal suggested that to make a s 91(14) order that would last for the whole of the child's minority was a disproportionate infringement of the father's rights, given that the father had never sought to misuse court proceedings. It was held that the order should last only two years.

4. CHILDREN'S WELFARE ON DIVORCE AND RELATIONSHIP BREAKDOWN

The most common circumstance in which an application for a s 8 order is made is when the relationship of the parents breaks down. We will now consider the evi-

---

[96] *Re M (Section 91(14) Order)* [1999] 2 FLR 553.
[97] Butler-Sloss P in *Re G (A Child) (Contempt: Committal Order)* [2003] 2 FCR 231.
[98] *Re R (Residence: Contact: Restricting Applications)* [1998] 1 FLR 749.
[99] [1998] 1 FLR 749 CA.
[100] *Re R (Residence: Contact: Restricting Applications)* [1998] 1 FLR 749.
[101] *Re C (Contact: No Order for Contact)* [2000] Fam Law 699, [2000] 2 FLR 723.
[102] It may be appropriate to limit the duration of the order: *Re M (Section 91(14) Order)* [1999] 2 FLR 553.
[103] In *Re G and M (Child Orders: Restricting Applications)* [1995] 2 FLR 416 it was expressly ordered that the mother should not be informed of applications for leave.
[104] *Re A (Application for Leave)* [1998] 1 FLR 1, [1999] 1 FCR 127 CA.
[105] [1999] 2 FLR 573.
[106] Article 35, para 3.
[107] Unreported 11.ll.2003 (CA).

dence of child psychologists that children suffer on the breakdown of their parents' relationship and how the law responds to this.

It is widely accepted that, statistically, children whose parents separate are more likely to suffer in various ways than those whose parents stay together.[108] Divorce is regarded by children as a crisis.[109] As one of the leading experts in the field, Martin Richards, has stated:

> Compared with those of similar social backgrounds whose parents remain married, children whose parents divorce show consistent, but small differences in their behaviour throughout childhood and adolescence and a somewhat different life course as they move into adulthood. More specifically, the research indicates on average lower levels of academic achievement and self-esteem and a higher incidence of bad conduct and other problems of psychological adjustment during childhood. Also during childhood a somewhat earlier social maturity has been recorded. A number of transitions to adulthood are typically reached at earlier ages; these include leaving home, beginning heterosexual relationships and entering cohabitation, marriage and child bearing. In young adulthood there is a tendency toward more changes of job, lower socio-economic status, a greater propensity to divorce and there are some indications of a higher frequency of depression and lower measures of psychological well-being. The relationship (in adulthood) with parents and other kin relationships may be more distant.[110]

It is important to appreciate what is *not* being claimed here. Clearly not all children whose parents separate suffer in these ways and some children whose parents do not separate do suffer in these ways. The point is merely that, on average, children whose parents separate are more likely to suffer these harms than those whose parents have not separated. In fact, only a minority of children whose parents separate suffer in these ways,[111] although they appear to be twice as likely to do so as children whose parents stay together.[112] It should also be stressed that although children whose parents have separated can suffer in these various ways, it does not necessarily follow that this is because their parents have separated. It may not be the separation that causes these problems, but the earlier tensions in the marital relationship;[113] or poverty connected to relationship breakdown; or society's reaction to separated families, although there is some evidence that the quality of parenting declines immediately following a divorce as the parents come to terms with lone parenthood.[114] Further, the research does not support the view that parents should 'stay together for the sake of the children'. Indeed, evidence suggests that children brought up in continually warring families do even less well than children whose parents separate.[115] Despite all these caveats, the fact that 28 per cent of children will experience divorce by the age of 16[116] must give cause for grave concern.

---

[108] Poussin and Martin-LeBrun (2002), although for a discussion on the limitations of such research, see Pryor and Seymour (1996).

[109] Butler, Scanlan, Robinson et al. (2003).

[110] M. Richards (1997: 543); Pryor and Seymour (1996).

[111] Although nearly every child reports feelings of pain or distress at the time of divorce (Emery (1999)).

[112] Rogers and Pryor (1998).

[113] Kelly (2003). Notably, children who experience the death of a parent do not suffer in these ways to the same extent as children whose parents have divorced.

[114] Emery (1998).

[115] M. Richards (1994); Eekelaar and Maclean (1997: 53–7).

[116] Rogers and Pryor (1998).

There do seem to be some factors that are particularly linked to the problems children suffer on their parents' divorce, namely: poverty before or after the separation; conflict before, during or after the separation;[117] a parent's psychological distress; multiple changes in family structures;[118] and a lack of high quality contact with the non-residential parent.[119] Richards[120] suggests that there are steps that can be taken to lessen the harm caused to children on divorce. He argues that society should seek to encourage the maintenance of ties with both parents and kin; ensure adequacy of income for the child; reduce conflict over children involved; provide emotional support for parents; and limit the need for the child to move house or school.[121] As will be seen, these aims are pursued by the law only to a limited extent. There is also ample evidence that listening to children and keeping them informed during the separation process is important to their welfare.[122] Particularly significant is the way children are first told about the breakdown.[123] Research suggests that both children and parents avoid talking about the separation and this may exacerbate the harm suffered by children.[124] In a recent important study[125] children expressed the range of fears they felt when hearing of the parental separation. They were concerned at not only losing contact with the non-resident parent, but of losing friends or changing schools. Although children reported receiving support from their resident parents, best friends were found to be extremely important.[126]

5. HOW THE COURT DECIDES WHAT IS IN THE CHILD'S BEST INTERESTS: THE CHECKLIST

In resolving any dispute relating to the upbringing of the child, the court must decide what is in the child's best interests. Before looking at the kinds of issues that the courts have considered in deciding what will promote a child's welfare, the ways in which the court receives information about a child's well-being will be examined.

A. How the court obtains information on the child's welfare

Obviously not all children are alike and the arrangements which might promote one child's welfare will not benefit another.[127] Therefore the court needs to consider the position of each child before it as an individual. In deciding what is in the interests of the child's welfare the judge does not rely on his or her own instincts, but seeks

---

[117] As Wild and Richards (2003) emphasise, the child may experience conflict even though the parents attempt to keep the conflict under wraps in the presence of the child.
[118] E.g. living with a parent who has a number of partners during the child's minority.
[119] Rogers and Pryor (1998); Hawthorne, Jessop, Pryor and Richards (2003).
[120] M. Richards (1994).
[121] See also Richards and Connell (2000).
[122] Rogers and Pryor (1998).
[123] Douglas, Murch, Robinson et al. (2001).
[124] Douglas, Murch, Robinson et al. (2001).
[125] Butler et al (2003).
[126] Butler, Scanlan, Robinson et al. (2003: 188).
[127] Smart, Neale and Wade (2001: 166).

expert advice.[128] Although the parties themselves are free to call witnesses to support their case, the court often needs independent evidence about a child and may seek a report, known as a welfare report.[129] The report is not requested in every case, but only when there is no realistic possibility that the parties can be persuaded to mediate the dispute.

These reports are normally provided by the child and family reporter.[130] The report considers issues over which there is dispute; the options that are available to the court; and, if appropriate, recommends a course of action. In preparing the report the child and family reporter should interview each party as well as the child. Normally quite a number of visits will be needed. The importance placed on the report means that great care should be taken in its preparation.[131] Often the report will be highly influential on the eventual outcome of the case, although it would be wrong to think that the court must follow the welfare report.[132] If the judge is minded to depart from the report, he or she should obtain oral evidence from the reporter.[133] The welfare report often records the child's wishes. However, there is increasing recognition of the desirability to the court of hearing the child's voice directly.[134] If necessary the judge can interview the child in private to protect them from the ordeal of appearing in court.[135]

There has been a growing interest in the right of children to express their views in any court case concerning their upbringing. [136] Indeed such a right is protected under article 12 of the United Nations Convention on the Rights of the Child 1989 and the European Convention of Children's Rights 1996.[137] There are, however, concerns that in difficult cases there may be difficulties in listening to children. Children may not be used to being listened to by adults and find it disturbing talking to professionals.[138] One report on children's experiences of professionals depressingly concluded: 'Professionals may be perceived as inflexible, intrusive, condescending, deceitful and reinforcing in a myriad of ways their superiority to the child.'[139] Another research team found that children wanted a conversation with their parents about the separation, rather than being asked for a formal expression of their views.[140]

---

[128] In a private law case it is not possible to order a residential assessment of one parent and child against the wishes of the other parent (*R v R (Private Law Proceedings: Residential Assessment)* [2002] 2 FLR 953). This is possible in a public law case.

[129] CA 1989, s 7(1).

[130] Who is normally a social worker.

[131] *Re P (A Minor) (Inadequate Welfare Report)* [1996] 2 FCR 285.

[132] *Re P (A Minor) (Inadequate Welfare Report)* [1996] 2 FCR 285.

[133] *Re CB (Access: Court Welfare Reports)* [1995] 1 FLR 622 CA.

[134] Indeed this is required under article 12(1) of the UN Convention on the Rights of the Child. See further e.g. in Smart and Neale (2000).

[135] *Re R (A Minor) (Residence: Religion)* [1993] 2 FLR 163, [1993] 2 FCR 525 CA.

[136] Lowe and Murch (2003); Murch (2003).

[137] To which the UK is not a signatory.

[138] Lowe and Murch (2003: 18–19).

[139] Neale and Smart (1999: 33).

[140] Smart, Neale and Wade (2001: 169).

B. The statutory checklist

When considering applications under s 8, the court must take into account the checklist of factors in s 1(3), in deciding what is in the welfare of the child.[141] The court is required to consider all the different factors and weigh them in the balance, although the court can also take into account other factors not mentioned in the list.

There are contrasting attitudes towards the checklist among the judiciary. Waite LJ in *Southwood LBC v B*[142] referred to the checklist as an aide-mémoire.[143] To Staughton LJ in *H v H (Residence Order: Leave to Remove from the Jurisdiction)*[144] the checklist was not 'like the list of checks which an airline pilot has to make with his co-pilot, aloud one to the other before he takes off'. By contrast, *B v B (Residence Order: Reasons for Decisions)*[145] described going through the individual items on the checklist as a good discipline. This suggests that the exact use of the checklist differs from judge to judge. What is clear is that if it can be shown that a judge failed to take into account one of the factors on the checklist which was relevant to the case in hand, then the decision would be liable to be overturned on appeal.

The various factors listed in s 1(3) will now be considered.

(i) The ascertainable wishes and feelings of the child concerned (considered in the light of his age and understanding)[146]

The child's wishes are only one of the factors to be taken into account, but where the child is mature it is likely to be the most important factor.[147] Sturge and Glaser, two leading psychologists, suggest that the wishes of children under 6 should be regarded as indistinguishable from the wishes of the main carer, and the wishes of children over 10 should carry considerable weight, while those between 6 and 10 are at an intermediate state.[148] In deciding whether a child's views should be taken into account the court will consider whether the child is competent.[149] 'Full and generous' weight should be given to a mature child's wishes.[150]

Even if a judge believes the child to be mistaken, it may still be appropriate to follow the child's views. There are two reasons why a judge may do this. First, there are practical considerations. If a teenager insists on not living with a particular parent then the child may simply ignore any court order awarding residence to that parent. There will be little point in making an order that the child will simply dis-

---

[141] CA 1989, s 1(4).

[142] [1993] 2 FLR 559 at p. 573.

[143] Magistrates use a pro forma listing the factors to guide their reasoning: *R v Oxfordshire CC (Secure Accommodation Order)* [1992] Fam 150 at p. 160.

[144] [1995] 1 FLR 529 at p. 532 CA.

[145] [1997] 2 FLR 602.

[146] CA 1989, s 1(3)(a).

[147] *B v B (M v M (Transfer of Custody: Appeal)* [1987] 2 FLR 146; *Re T (Abduction: Child's Objections to Return)* [2000] 2 FLR 193. UN Convention on the Rights of the Child, article 12, requires the court to give due weight to children's views in accordance with their age and maturity.

[148] Sturge and Glaser (2000: 624).

[149] *Re S (Change of Surname)* [1999] 1 FLR 672.

[150] *Re H (Residence Order: Child's Application for Leave)* [2000] 1 FLR 780.

obey. Secondly, the judge may also believe that it is beneficial for the child to learn from his or her mistakes. Indeed, it may damage a child psychologically to ignore his or her wishes. As Butler-Sloss LJ has argued:[151] 'nobody should dictate to children of this age, because one is dealing with their emotions, their lives, and they are not packages to be moved around. They are people entitled to be treated with respect.' That is not to say that the wishes of a mature minor can never be overridden, because the welfare principle is the paramount criterion.[152] There have, for example, been several cases where the court has approved the provision of life-saving medical treatment, despite the opposition of the teenager who needed it.[153]

When the court considers the views of the child it will have regard to the following factors:

1. The weight to be attached to the child's views will depend on the maturity of the child.[154] In *Re B (Minors) (Change of Surname)*[155] it was held that it would be exceptional for a court to make orders contrary to the wishes of a teenager. The Children Act states that the facts of the case must be exceptional before an order can be made in respect of children over 16.[156] In *Re S (Contact: Children's Views)*[157] Tyrer J followed the views of a 16- and a 14-year-old stating that their views were carefully thought out. He stated that if the law required young people to respect the law then the law must respect them. This might even mean permitting them to make mistakes.
2. The importance of the issue is clearly relevant. The more important the issue, the more willing the court may be to overrule the wishes of a child. For example, if the child refuses to consent to medical treatment which would save his or her life, the court will readily override the child's decision.[158]
3. The courts are also concerned with the possibility that an adult may heavily influence the views of the child. So before attaching weight to the child's views, the court will try to ensure that they truly are the views of the child and he or she is not simply repeating what they have been told by one of their parents.[159]
4. There is some psychological evidence that requiring children to choose between parents is very harmful.[160] The court will readily be prepared to accept that the child has no wishes in such cases.[161] Interestingly, in one study only 55 per cent of children interviewed said they would like to have been asked whether they

---

[151] *Re S (Minors) (Access: Religious Upbringing)* [1992] 2 FLR 313 at p. 321 CA.
[152] *Re P (A Minor) (Education)* [1992] 1 FLR 316, [1992] FCR 145 CA. Contrast the position in Finland where children over the age of 12 can veto court decisions concerning residence and access (the Finnish law is conveniently summarised in *K and T v Finland* [2000] 2 FLR 79).
[153] *Re M (Medical Treatment: Consent)* [1999] 2 FLR 1097.
[154] A 9-year-old's wishes were overridden in *Re R (A Minor) (Residence: Religion)* [1993] 2 FLR 163, [1993] 2 FCR 525 CA.
[155] [1996] 1 FLR 791, [1996] 2 FCR 304 CA.
[156] CA 1989, s 9(6), (7).
[157] [2002] 1 FLR 1156.
[158] *Re M (Medical Treatment: Consent)* [1999] 2 FLR 1097.
[159] There are particular concerns where the child has been the victim of sexual abuse: see Jones and Parkinson (1995).
[160] M. King (1987: 190). Such an argument was influential in *Re A (Specific Issue Order: Parental Dispute)* [2001] 1 FLR 121.
[161] Schofield (1998).

would prefer to live with their mother or father after the separation of their parents.[162] Another study reported that many children wanted to talk to the family court welfare officer, but did not want them to tell their parents or the court what they had said, largely for fear that to do so would hurt a parent they loved.[163]

5. The court will wish to examine the basis of the child's views. In *Re M (A Minor) (Family Proceedings: Affidavits)*[164] the wishes of a 12-year-old girl to live with her father were overridden because her decision was based on occasional visits to her father while she lived with her grandparents. It was felt that her occasional visits did not give her a clear view of what life with her father would be like.[165] The case indicates that where a child has a strong view based on factual error, the court will readily override that view. The courts have also expressed a concern that children may put undue weight on short-term gains and not take a long-term view of their welfare.[166]

The court may be able to find the child's views by means of a welfare report. However, in difficult cases it may be appropriate for the child to be separately represented by their own counsel.[167] The National Youth Advocacy Service and other organisations can assist with the legal representation of children in court cases. This might remedy the widespread perception elicited by one study of children involved in private law cases concerning them, that although they were listened to they were not involved in the decision-making process.[168] Other studies have found that practitioners lack the skills necessary to listen effectively to children.[169]

Of course, what has been said so far deals with cases which reach the courts. Where the dispute is resolved without recourse to the court process children may have little voice in what happens to them. Remarkably 45 per cent of children in one study said that on the breakdown of their parent's relationship they were not asked whether they preferred to live with their mother or father.[170]

(ii) The child's physical, emotional and educational needs[171]

In many cases the child's needs, together with the parents' capacity for meeting those needs, are the crucial issue. The emotional welfare of the child is particularly important.[172] The welfare report will consider the closeness of the relationship between the child and each of the parents. This might require the court to compare different styles of parenting. In *May v May*[173] the court preferred the father's par-

---

[162] Douglas, Murch, Robinson et al. (2001).
[163] Bretherton (2002).
[164] [1995] 2 FLR 100, [1995] 2 FCR 90 CA.
[165] In particular, she did not appreciate that she might have to do a lot of housework!
[166] *Re C (A Minor) (Care: Children's Wishes)* [1993] 1 FLR 832, [1993] 1 FCR 810.
[167] *Re A (A Child) (Separate Representation in Contact Proceedings)* [2001] 2 FCR 55.
[168] Bretherton (2002).
[169] Sawyer (1995); O'Quigley (1999).
[170] Douglas, Murch, Robinson et al. (2001).
[171] CA 1989, s 1(3)(b).
[172] *Re J (Children) (Residence: Expert Evidence)* [2001] 2 FCR 44 CA.
[173] [1986] 1 FLR 325 CA.

enting, partly because he stressed the importance of academic achievement, to the mother's more relaxed attitude towards school. As will be noted shortly, the courts have accepted that it is normally in the emotional interests of children to retain contact with both parents.

(iii) The likely effect on the child of any change in his circumstances[174]

The courts have stressed the importance of maintaining the status quo for children if possible. Changing children's schools and housing can cause even further disturbance for children at a time when their lives are already under stress. In practice, as empirical evidence shows, the court will normally confirm the presently existing arrangements for the child.[175] In effect, then, if a child has a settled life with one parent, good reasons will be needed to justify a move to the other parent.[176] This was stressed by the Court of Appeal in *Re B (Residence Order: Status Quo)*,[177] where the trial judge was criticised for being willing to move the child from the mother to the father in the speculative hope that he would be more willing to let the child have contact with the mother than she would with him. It was held that maintaining the status quo was too important to be challenged on the basis of a speculative hope. Indeed, in some cases the importance of maintaining the status quo has even been sufficient to prefer a third party over a natural parent[178] and to separate two siblings.[179] Of course, there are also cases where the status quo is disrupted, but they tend to involve fairly extreme factors, such as the drug-taking of parents.[180]

There are three particular concerns about placing much weight upon the status quo. The first is that it might encourage a parent to snatch their child from the other parent and then go into hiding, and later seek to rely on this principle. However, the courts have accepted that the status quo is not relevant if it is achieved by abduction.[181] The second concern is that there is a danger the principle will encourage the party with whom the child is living to delay the proceedings. There are now, however, various procedures that can be used by a court to speed up litigation if necessary. A third concern is that the status quo principle means that the parties in reality resolve the dispute between themselves when deciding where the child is to live while awaiting the court's decision, while often not appreciating the significance of their decision.

---

[174] CA 1989, s 1(3)(c).
[175] Eekelaar and Clive (1977: 13–14).
[176] *Re L (Residence: Justices' Reasons)* [1995] 2 FLR 445.
[177] [1998] 1 FLR 368, [1998] 1 FCR 549 CA.
[178] *Re H (A Minor: Custody)* [1990] 1 FLR 51.
[179] *Re B (T) (A Minor) (Residence Order)* [1995] 2 FCR 240 CA.
[180] *Re G (Minors) (Ex Parte Interim Residence Order)* [1993] 1 FLR 910 CA.
[181] *Edwards v Edwards* [1986] 1 FLR 187 CA.

(iv) The child's age, sex, background and any characteristics of his which the court considers relevant[182]

These factors are likely to be of special relevance in choosing foster parents and potential adopters for children. The Children Act 1989 requires a local authority to take account of the child's 'religious persuasion, racial origin and cultural and linguistic background' in deciding what care arrangements are appropriate for the child. As we shall discuss shortly, there has been some debate in the case law over whether girls are better looked after by their mothers and boys by their fathers.

(v) Any harm which the child has suffered or is at risk of suffering[183]

The court, of course, would never make an order which it thought might place a child in a situation where there was a risk that the child would suffer harm. It has been made clear by the Court of Appeal in *Re M and R (Child Abuse: Evidence)*[184] that, before taking a risk into account, the court must find proved facts on the balance of probabilities which reveal that risk.[185] So the court must first consider what facts are proved. Once facts are proved, the next issue is whether those proven facts indicate a risk of harm.[186]

It is not always easy to tell whether an arrangement will cause harm to a child. In *Re W (Residence Order)*[187] the mother and her new partner had an uninhibited attitude towards nudity and were often nude in front of the children. The Court of Appeal thought the trial judge had been misled in assuming that this would harm the children. There was no clear evidence that the nudity would harm the children and so it should not have been taken into account.

(vi) How capable each of the child's parents (and any other person in relation to whom the court considers the question to be relevant) is in meeting his needs[188]

This factor must be read in conjunction with the needs of the child. If, for example, the child has a medical condition requiring careful management which only one parent is capable of providing, this would be a crucial consideration.[189] In *Re M (Handicapped Child: Parental Responsibility)*[190] the father's inability to care effectively for his disabled daughter was fatal to his application for a residence order. The phrase 'other person' could include the new partner of the parent. The court

---

[182] CA 1989, s 1(3)(d).
[183] CA 1989, s 1(3)(e).
[184] [1996] 2 FLR 195, [1996] 2 FCR 617.
[185] This is explained and discussed further in Chapter 10.
[186] This was approved *obiter* and without full argument by Lord Nicholls in *Re O and N (Children) (Non-Accidental Injury)* [2003] 1 FCR 673 at para 45.
[187] [1999] 1 FLR 869 CA.
[188] CA 1989, s 1(3)(f).
[189] *Re C and V (Minors) (Parental Responsibility and Contact)* [1998] 1 FLR 392, [1998] 1 FCR 57.
[190] [2001] 3 FCR 454.

may regard it as an advantage to the child to live in a two-adult household rather than a single-person one.[191]

(vii) The range of powers available to the court under the Children Act 1989 in the proceedings in question[192]

The court has the power to make orders other than those sought by the parties.[193] The court, in considering an application for a particular order, must therefore decide whether the order sought would be better than any other order available under the Children Act 1989.

As well as the checklist of factors, the court must also take into account two further provisions of the Act which are relevant in deciding whether to make a s 8 order.

(viii) The principle of no delay

Section 1(2) states:

> In any proceedings in which any question with respect to the upbringing of a child arises, the court shall have regard to the general principle that any delay in determining the question is likely to prejudice the welfare of the child.

The legal process is notoriously slow, but the longer the court takes in cases involving children, the greater the uncertainty for the children and the higher the levels of stress felt by the parents.[194] It is therefore not surprising that the judiciary have been particularly critical of delay in family cases.[195] Indeed, article 6 of the European Convention on Human Rights may require a public hearing within a reasonable timescale, and so avoiding unnecessary delay is now required by the Human Rights Act 1998.[196]

The no delay principle in s 1(2) applies to all proceedings concerning a child's upbringing, except financial orders.[197] It should, however, be stressed that while delay is not necessarily detrimental to a child, unnecessary delay is.[198] There are occasions when delay may be beneficial. It might be important for there to be a delay in order that further crucial information can be obtained or for the parties' circumstances to settle so that the best long-term decision can be reached. But any delay should be planned and purposeful.[199]

This subsection on its own would probably do little to prevent delay. The Children Act 1989 gave more powers to the judges to speed up cases. In both

---

[191] *Re DW (A Minor) (Custody)* [1984] 14 Fam Law 17; *M v Birmingham CC* [1994] 2 FLR 141.
[192] CA 1989, s 1(3)(g).
[193] CA 1989, s 10(1).
[194] Lord Chancellor's Department (2002c) .
[195] Ewbank J in *Stockport MBC v B; Stockport MBC v L* [1986] 2 FLR 80.
[196] Finlay (2002).
[197] See *Re TB (Care Proceedings: Criminal Trial)* [1995] 2 FLR 810, [1996] 1 FCR 101 for a discussion of how criminal and care proceedings should be co-ordinated.
[198] *C v Solihull MBC* [1993] 1 FLR 290, [1992] 2 FCR 341.
[199] *C v Solihull MBC* [1993] 1 FLR 290, [1992] 2 FCR 341.

private[200] and public[201] cases the court must draw up a timetable for the case and ensure that the timetable is followed. The timetable cannot be departed from unless the court grants leave.[202] The Law Commission set the goal for resolving cases within 12 weeks,[203] but this has not been met.[204] In fact the average length of public law cases is ten months[205] and private cases 74 days.[206] In 2002 Booth J published a study of why cases under the Children Act were still suffering from delay.[207] As a result the Lord Chancellor's Department has produced a variety of procedural measures, designed to speed up children's cases.[208] There is a tension here between the desire to encourage speedy litigation and the desire to persuade the parties to settle without a court hearing. The faster the parties are propelled towards a court hearing, the less time there is for negotiation.[209]

(ix) The no order principle

This fundamental principle is set out in s 1(5) of the Children Act 1989:

> Where a court is considering whether or not to make one or more orders under this Act with respect to a child, it shall not make the order or any of the orders unless it considers that doing so would be better for the child than making no order at all.

This provision emphasises that before making an order under the Children Act concerning the upbringing of children,[210] there should be a demonstrable benefit to the child by making the order. If no positive benefit can be obtained by making the order then no order should be made. The Law Commission was particularly concerned that orders should not be made where parents were in complete agreement, and there was therefore no specific need for an order. This is sometimes referred to as the 'no order' principle. It can be argued that this principle is really just an aspect of the welfare principle: if an order does not promote a child's welfare, it should not be made. However, it was clearly thought necessary to stress this particular application of the welfare principle.

Some commentators have read more into s 1(5) and have suggested that it represents the principle of deregulation or non-intervention.[211] That is, that the subsection reflects the presumption that the parents are the best people to care for the child and they should decide what should happen to the child. Only if there are strong reasons should the law intervene. It can be said that this is in line with article 8 of the European Convention on Human Rights, which protects family

---

[200] CA 1989, s 11.
[201] CA 1989, s 32.
[202] Family Proceedings Rules 1991, SI 1991/1247, r 4.15(1), Part IV.
[203] Law Commission Report 172 (1988: para 4.54).
[204] Children Act Advisory Committee (1993: ch. 2).
[205] Children Act Advisory Committee (1993: 81).
[206] Butler, Noaks, Douglas et al. (1993).
[207] Booth, J (2002).
[208] Lord Chancellor's Department (2002c; 2003a).
[209] Bailey-Harris, Davis, Barron and Pearce (1998: 26).
[210] *K v H (Child Maintenance)* [1993] 2 FLR 61, [1993] 1 FCR 684 states that s 1(5) does not apply to applications under Sch 1 to CA 1989 for financial provision for children.
[211] See e.g. Cretney and Masson (1997: 658).

privacy. However, other commentators stress that the statute itself does not suggest that there is a presumption that no order is best. Rather, it is neutral on the question of whether intervention is desirable.[212] All the subsection is saying is that it is necessary to show there is a positive benefit to be gained from making an order.[213] The disagreement over the meaning of the subsection is reflected in a study which found that practitioners and district judges took a variety of approaches to the subsection.[214] In *Dawson* v *Wearmouth*[215] Lord Mackay interpreted s 1(5) to mean that a court should only make an order if there was some evidence that to do so would improve the child's welfare. In *Re P (Parental Dispute: Judicial Determination)*[216] the Court of Appeal stressed that if a dispute is brought before a court it must be adjudicated on and s 1(5) should not be used to abdicate responsibility.

An example of the subsection in operation is *B* v *B (A Minor) (Residence Order)*,[217] where a child had been living with her grandmother for ten years. The grandmother applied for a residence order because she had encountered difficulties in providing consent to various school activities because she lacked parental responsibility. The court held that there were good reasons for making the order, even though there were only a few occasions when it would provide practical benefit. It was wrong to think that s 1(5) meant it was necessary to show that the making of the order would significantly benefit the child; it was enough if it was seen, on balance, as better to make the order than not to. The Court of Appeal have also warned of the dangers which might result from deciding to make no order simply because the parties appear to be in agreement. In *Re S (Contact: Grandparents)*[218] a grandparent sought a contact order. By the time the matter came to court, the judge was persuaded that the mother would permit contact, and therefore did not make a contact order, relying on s 1(5). The Court of Appeal felt that, having decided that it was in the child's welfare to have contact with the grandparent, the contact order should be made, even if the parties were in agreement at the time of the court hearing. The making of the order would ensure that contact did take place and avoid the need to return to court in the event of a disagreement. It should be stressed that this was a case where there was a history of antagonism between the parties and therefore there was a risk that the arrangement would break down. If the parties have consistently been in agreement, s 1(5) may operate to make no order appropriate. This reflects the practical reality that the role played by grandparents after divorce depends greatly on the relationship between the grandparents and children and parents before the divorce.[219]

If the court does not grant an order, it must be made clear whether the court is dismissing the application or is deciding to make 'no order'. This was stressed in *D*

---

[212] Bainham (1990: 221).
[213] As argued in Bainham (1998b: 2–4).
[214] Bailey-Harris, Barron and Pearce (1999).
[215] [1999] 2 AC 308.
[216] [2003] 1 FLR 286.
[217] [1992] 2 FLR 327, [1993] 1 FCR 211.
[218] [1996] 1 FLR 158, [1996] 3 FCR 30 CA.
[219] Douglas and Ferguson (2003).

v *D (Application for Contact)*.[220] The actual number of 'no orders' has not been great. For example, in 2002, in relation to contact applications, 945 were disposed of by no order, while 61,356 orders were made.[221] That said, the number of applications for residence orders has fallen, especially when compared with the equivalent number before the Children Act 1989.[222] So it may be that s 1(5) has the effect of discouraging applications.[223]

Now some of the issues which have caused the courts particular difficulty in applying the welfare principle will be considered.

6. ISSUES OF CONTROVERSY IN APPLYING THE WELFARE PRINCIPLE

A. Is there a presumption in favour of mothers?

One hotly disputed issue is whether there is or should be a presumption that children are better brought up by mothers rather than by fathers.[224] At one time it was thought that there was a presumption that babies and girls should be brought up by mothers, and boys by fathers.[225] It was made clear by the Court of Appeal in *Re A (Children: 1959 UN Declaration)*[226] that although there is still a presumption that babies are better off with mothers,[227] with regard to other children there is no principle or presumption in favour of mothers or fathers.[228] The rule in relation to babies is partly based on the benefits of breastfeeding. The psychological evidence seems to support the view that there is no convincing evidence that girls are better off with mothers, or boys with fathers.[229] That said, there is some research that children prefer to be brought up by the parent of the same sex after divorce.[230]

Even though there is no presumption in favour of mothers, the sex of the parent can still be important in issues relating to children.[231] Lord Jauncey in the House of Lords in a Scottish case (*Brixley* v *Lynas*[232]) explained:[233]

> the advantage to a very young child of being with its mother is a consideration which must be taken into account when deciding where lie its best interests in custody proceedings in which the mother is involved. It is neither a presumption nor a principle but rather recognition of a widely held belief based on practical experience and the workings of nature. Its

---

[220] [1994] 1 FCR 694.
[221] Lord Chancellor's Department (2003b).
[222] Lord Chancellor's Department (2000).
[223] Bailey-Harris, Barron and Pearce (1999).
[224] There is in fact little psychological evidence for this: see M. King (1974); Chambers (1984: 515–24).
[225] See *Re W (A Minor) (Residence Order)* [1992] 2 FLR 332, [1992] 2 FCR 461 CA.
[226] [1998] 1 FLR 354, [1998] 2 FCR 633 CA.
[227] *Re W (A Minor) (Residence Order)* [1992] 2 FLR 332, [1992] 2 FCR 461 CA.
[228] See also *Re S (A Minor) (Custody)* [1991] 2 FLR 388 CA.
[229] Downey and Powell (1993).
[230] Kaltenborn and Lemrap (1998).
[231] Much media attention was paid to a judgment of Lord Justice Thorpe which was reported as denying a residence order to a 'house husband' on the basis of the different roles that women and men played (Rabinovitch (2002)). The case was never fully reported.
[232] [1996] 2 FLR 499, [1997] 1 FCR 220 HL, discussed in Sutherland (1997).
[233] [1996] 2 FLR 499 at p. 505.

importance will vary according to the age of the child and to the other circumstances of each individual case such as whether the child has been living with or apart from the mother and whether she is or is not capable of providing proper care. Circumstances may be such that it has no importance at all. Furthermore it will always yield to other competing advantages which more effectively promote the welfare of the child. However, where a very young child has been with its mother since birth and there is no criticism of her ability to care for the child only the strongest competing arguments are likely to prevail.

So the position seems to be that although there is no legal presumption in favour of the mother,[234] the court will more easily be persuaded that the child is better cared for by the mother than by the father.[235] This is especially so in the case of younger children. The Court of Appeal in *Re K (Residence Order: Securing Contact)*[236] in awarding residence of a 2-year-old to a father admitted that this was 'somewhat unusual'. Indeed, the research indicates that, on separation, it is far more common for children to live with mothers than with fathers.[237] The courts are wary of explicitly creating a presumption in favour of mothers, as this might constitute discrimination on the grounds of sex and so be in breach of the Human Rights Act 1998.[238] However, there is evidence that girls are particularly vulnerable to sexual abuse following divorce. Fretwell Wilson[239] points to a study which found that 50 per cent of girls living solely with their father reported sexual abuse by someone (not necessarily their father) and argues that these concerns must be addressed when the court is making decisions over residence.

B. The 'natural parent presumption'

Where there is a dispute between a parent and a third party there is a strong presumption that: '[t]he best person to bring up a child is the natural parent. It matters not whether the parent is wise or foolish, rich or poor, educated or illiterate, provided the child's moral and physical health are not endangered.'[240] As the Court of Appeal in *Re D (Care: Natural Parent Presumption)*[241] has suggested, there need to be compelling factors if the right of a child to be brought up by their 'natural parent' is to be overridden. The psychological evidence to support the presumption is ambiguous.[242] Although there is clear evidence that once a child has established a strong relationship with his or her parents it would harm them to remove them to other carers, there is no strong evidence from psychologists that if from birth a baby is brought up by someone who is not his or her parent, the baby suffers.[243] The presumption can be

---

[234] Stressed in *Re A (Children: 1959 UN Declaration)* [1998] 1 FLR 354, [1998] 2 FCR 633 CA.
[235] *Re W (Residence)* [1999] 2 FLR 390 CA.
[236] [1999] 1 FLR 583 CA.
[237] Priest and Whybrow (1986). Moloney's (2001) study of Australian decisions found that fathers tended to succeed in residence disputes only where mothers were found to be inadequate.
[238] Sutherland (1997).
[239] Fretwell Wilson (2002).
[240] *Re KD (A Minor) (Ward: Termination of Access)* [1988] 1 All ER 577 at p. 578.
[241] [1999] 1 FLR 134 CA. For another leading example of the principle in practice, see *Re K (A Minor) (Wardship: Adoption)* [1991] 1 FLR 57, [1991] FCR 142 CA. For a rare case where the presumption was not applied, see *Re M (A Minor: Custody Application)* [1990] 1 FLR 291, [1990] FCR 424.
[242] For an examination of the presumption from a philosophical perspective see Archard (1995).
[243] Schaffer (1990); Weyland (1997).

regarded as being as much about a protection of the rights of natural parents as a promotion of the child's welfare.[244] In part, the presumption is prompted by aversion to social engineering. Ours is a society so horrified by the possibility that the state could decree who is and who is not suitable to raise children that the law is only willing to remove the child from the natural parents if they are clearly unsuitable.[245]

Where there is a dispute over where the child should live, the court should first consider whether the 'natural parents' are suitable. Only if they are unsuitable should the court consider other people as carers. It would be wrong to balance the benefits of living with the natural parent with the benefits of living with someone else, because that would not place sufficient weight on the presumption.[246]

The potential strength of the 'natural parent' presumption is revealed in the controversial case of *Re M (Child's Upbringing)*.[247] The Court of Appeal had to consider what should happen to a 10-year-old Zulu boy who had been handed over by his parents to a white couple and raised in England for four years. The child had settled into life in England and expressed a strong wish to stay with the white couple. There was expert evidence that his immediate return to South Africa would cause psychological harm. However, his parents successfully applied for his return and Neill LJ in the Court of Appeal stated:

> Of course there will be cases where the welfare of the child requires that the child's right to be with his natural parents has to give way in his own interest to other considerations. But I am satisfied that in this case, as in other cases, one starts with the strong supposition that it is in the [child's] best interests . . . that he should be brought up with his natural parents.

The Court of Appeal therefore ordered his immediate return to the natural parents. The story did not end there because, following the court hearing and some unsuccessful attempts to force him onto the aeroplane, the boy was returned to South Africa. However, he failed to settle there and his family later consented to his being returned to the couple in England.[248]

However, in recent years there has been a move against the natural parent presumption. Thorpe LJ in *Re O (Family Appeals: Management)*[249] suggested that the Court of Appeal in *Re M (Child's Upbringing)*[250] had fallen into error.[251] His view, expressed in *Re L (A Child) (Contact: Domestic Violence)*,[252] is that the strength of the presumption depends on the nature of the relationship between the child and the natural parent. The presumption is a strong one where the child knows the parent well. However, where the child does not know the parent at all, or the parent

---

[244] Eekelaar (1991d).
[245] *Re K (A Minor) (Wardship: Adoption)* [1991] 1 FLR 57, [1991] FCR 142 CA.
[246] *Re D (Care: Natural Parent Presumption)* [1999] 1 FLR 134 CA, discussed Fortin (1999b).
[247] [1996] 2 FLR 441, [1996] 3 FCR 99 CA.
[248] Freeman (1997b).
[249] [1998] 1 FLR 431.
[250] [1996] 2 FLR 441 CA.
[251] See also *Re P (Section 91(14) Guidelines) (Residence and Religious Heritage)* [1999] 2 FLR 573 for a case where the natural parents failed in their attempt to have the children returned to them because the children were well settled with foster parents.
[252] [2000] 2 FLR 334, [2000] 2 FCR 404 CA.

has harmed the child, the presumption is weaker. In *Re H (A Child: Residence)*[253] Thorpe LJ suggested that 'the biological parent may not always be the natural parent in the eyes of the child'.[254] In that case a grandmother had undertaken sole care of the child and Thorpe LJ suggested that she had become the psychological parent of the child. He added 'presumptions in favour of a natural parent are nowhere to be found within' s 1 of the Children Act 1989.[255] It is submitted that his approach is in tune with that of the European Court of Human Rights in, for example, *B v UK*,[256] and has much to commend it.[257] Certainly research among children suggests that children regard the psychological bond to be more important than the blood tie.[258]

C. Is there a presumption that siblings should reside together?

The evidence of psychologists stresses the importance of the sibling relationship, especially on the breakdown of the parental relationship.[259] It is therefore not surprising that the courts have suggested that siblings should be kept in the same household unless there are strong reasons against this.[260] However, the further the siblings are apart in age, the weaker the presumption that they should stay together.[261] Of course, there still will be cases where the separation of the siblings is necessary. For example, in *B v B (Residence Order: Restricting Applications)*[262] the court decided that the mother should bring up two brothers, but the older brother simply refused to stay with the mother and lived with the father. The court felt that, as the older brother was intent on staying with the father and the younger brother had a close attachment to the mother, it was necessary for the brothers to live apart.[263] If the siblings are to live in different places, there is a strong presumption that there should be contact between them.[264] It is clear that the relationship between two siblings will be regarded as family life and so protected under the Human Rights Act 1998.[265] This supports the presumption that there must be good reasons for separating siblings.

---

[253] [2002] 3 FCR 277 CA. See also *Re A (Adoption: Mother's Objection)* [2001] 1 FLR 665.
[254] [2002] 3 FCR 277 CA, para 41.
[255] Para 285.
[256] [2000] 1 FLR 1, [2000] 1 FCR 289 ECtHR.
[257] See further Weyland (1997).
[258] Smart, Neale and Wade (2001: 58).
[259] Hill and Tisdall (1997: 85–9), although in the study by Douglas, Murch, Robinson et al. (2001: 376) siblings were not found to be a significant source of emotional support on family breakdown and friends were far more important.
[260] E.g. *C v C (Minors: Custody)* [1988] 2 FLR 291.
[261] *B v B (Minors) (Custody: Care Control)* [1991] 1 FLR 402, [1991] FCR 1.
[262] [1997] 1 FLR 139, [1997] 2 FCR 518 CA.
[263] See also *Re B (T) (A Minor) (Residence Order)* [1995] 2 FCR 240 CA.
[264] *Re S (Minors: Access)* [1990] 2 FLR 166, [1990] 2 FCR 379.
[265] *Moustaquim v Belgium* (1991) 13 EHRR 802 at para 36.

D. Racial and cultural background

Racial and cultural backgrounds are important issues which the court should not ignore.[266] Normally, a child should be brought up by carers who share his or her racial and cultural background. In *Re M (Section 94 Appeals)*[267] the Court of Appeal reversed the first instance judgment which did not consider the racial issues involved when denying a mixed-race girl contact with her father.[268] Although there may be concern that children who are raised by people of a different racial background to their own will suffer confusion,[269] these concerns can be lessened by arranging contact with relatives of the same background.[270] In *Re A (Children) (Specific Issue Order: Parental Dispute)*[271] the Court of Appeal approved of a judge's decision that children of a French father and an English mother should live with the mother, but attend a French school in London. This would enable the children to have close links with both aspects of their background. Despite these points, as was stressed in *Re A (A Minor) (Cultural Background)*,[272] racial and cultural issues are but one factor to be taken into account when considering a child's welfare. A child's racial or cultural interests will not be promoted at the cost of the child's overall welfare.

E. Religion

Although at one time issues concerning a child's religious upbringing may have been a very important factor, they rarely arise now in reported cases.[273] In one well-known eighteenth-century case, the poet Shelley was denied custody of his child on the basis that he was an atheist.[274] Nowadays the court would not deny a parent a residence order on the basis of their religious beliefs. Generally, if the child has no religious views, the present law is summed up in the *dicta* of Scarman LJ in *Re T (Minors) (Custody: Religious Upbringing)*[275] that the court should not 'pass any judgement on the beliefs of parents where they are socially acceptable and consistent with a decent and respectable life'. However, it may be that the court can be persuaded that a parent's religion is 'immoral and obnoxious'. In *Re B and G (Minors) (Custody)*[276] the court felt that this was true of Scientology, and ordered custody to the non-Scientologist parent. The court should consider whether the religion involves practices that directly harm the child. So, for example, if the religion requires lengthy periods of fasting, causing medical harm to the child, then the court would be willing to take the parent's religious practices into account. The

---

[266] *Re M (Section 94 Appeals)* [1995] 1 FLR 546 at p. 550.
[267] [1995] 1 FLR 546.
[268] *Re M (Child's Upbringing)* [1996] 2 FLR 441, [1996] 3 FCR 99 CA (discussed above) can be explained on these grounds.
[269] Gill and Jackson (1983).
[270] *Re O (Transracial Adoption: Contact)* [1995] 2 FLR 597, [1996] 1 FCR 540.
[271] [2001] 1 FCR 210.
[272] [1987] 2 FLR 429.
[273] For a discussion of the issues, see Hamilton (1995); Mumford (1998); M. Freeman (2003).
[274] *Shelley v Westbrook* (1817) Jac 266n.
[275] (1975) 2 FLR 239 CA.
[276] [1985] FLR 493 CA.

court might be willing to consider an argument that a religion caused the child to suffer social isolation[277] or indoctrination.[278] The court should always bear in mind that particular issues can be dealt with by means of a specific issue order. For example, the court should not be deterred from awarding a residence order to a Jehovah's Witness parent for fear that the parent might refuse to consent to a blood transfusion should the child require it, because if that issue arose the court could overrule the parents' decision by means of a specific issue order.[279]

Simply to deny residence to a parent on the basis of religious beliefs would be contrary to the Human Rights Act 1998 because the European Convention on Human Rights protects freedom of religion and outlaws discrimination on the grounds of religion.[280] In *Hoffman* v *Austria*[281] it was held that it would be contrary to the Convention for a state to deny custody to a parent simply because of her religion, although it would be permissible for courts to take into account the effect of any religious practices on a child. This approach seems in line with that of the English and Welsh courts,[282] although it is often impossible to distinguish a religion and its practices. To say: 'the law does not discriminate against you on the grounds of your religion but on the grounds that you attend religious services' is to disguise the truth.[283] It may be more honest to accept that there are limits to religious freedom, and that discrimination against a religion that demonstrably harms children is permitted.[284]

If a child has religious beliefs[285] of his or her own the court is likely to make an order which enables the child to continue their religious practices.[286] Indeed, if the child has strong religious views shared by one parent but not the other, this might be a factor in that parent's favour.[287] If the child has religious views of his or her own, the residential parent could be required to permit the child to exercise their religious beliefs. For example, there could be a specific issue order requiring the residential parent to permit the child to attend religious services[288] or indeed preventing the parent from involving a child in his or her religion.[289] For example, in *Re T and M*[290] two boys were baptised as Roman Catholics and the mother converted to Islam. The mother wished to move the children from a Church of England school

---

[277] *Hewison* v *Hewison* [1977] Fam Law 207 CA.

[278] *Wright* v *Wright* [1980] 2 FLR 276 CA.

[279] *Re S (A Minor) (Blood Transfusion: Adoption Order Conditions)* [1994] 2 FLR 416 CA.

[280] Article 9 and article 14 respectively.

[281] (1993) 17 EHRR 293 ECtHR.

[282] Adhar (1996).

[283] Bainham (1994c).

[284] See the general discussion in Mumford (1998).

[285] The court will focus on the religious practices of the child and will *not* automatically assume that a child acquires a religion simply through being born to parents of a particular religion: *Re J (Specific Issue Orders)* [2000] 1 FLR 517 CA.

[286] *Re R (A Minor) (Residence: Religion)* [1993] 2 FLR 163, [1993] 2 FCR 525 CA.

[287] E.g. *Robertson* v *Robertson* Unreported 1980 CA, although that would be only one factor: *Re R (A Minor) (Residence: Religion)* [1993] 2 FLR 163, [1993] 2 FCR 525 CA.

[288] *J* v *C* [1970] AC 668 HL (Protestants gave an undertaking to bring up the child as a Roman Catholic); *Re R (A Minor) (Residence: Religion)* [1993] 2 FLR 163 (where the Exclusive Brethren aunt was permitted contact on condition that she did not discuss religion).

[289] *Re S (Minors) (Access: Religious Upbringing)* [1992] 2 FLR 313 CA.

[290] [1995] FLR 1.

to an Islamic school. A prohibited steps order was made to stop the change of schools, although the mother was permitted to talk to the children about Islam. Such cases would now involve careful consideration of both the parents' and children's rights to freedom of religion in article 9 and private life in article 8 of the European Convention.[291] Even if the child does not have beliefs of his or her own as they are too young the court may still take into account the religious heritage into which they were born. So when a child who was born to an Orthodox Jewish couple was taken into care then the court confirmed that the local authority should try to find Jewish foster parents and adopters if possible.[292]

Where the parents of a child have different religions there might be disputes over the religious upbringing of a child. If the child is not old enough to form his or her own religious beliefs the courts are likely to allow the resident parent to determine the religious upbringing of the child. In *Re S (Change of Names: Cultural Factors)*[293] Wilson J rejected the father's argument that the child should be raised as both a Muslim and a Sikh. Instead he should be raised in the religion of the mother (Islam), although he should be made aware of his Sikh identity and encouraged to respect Sikhism. Wilson J was persuaded that having decided that the mother should have the residence order the child would inevitably become integrated into the Mulsim community of which she was part.

In *Re J (Specific Issue Orders: Muslim Upbringing and Circumcision)*[294] Wall J suggested that although the father might be able to claim to have his child circumcised in accordance with his freedom of thought, conscience and religion under article 9 of the European Convention, so too did the mother have the right not to have her son circumcised under the same article. In such a case, where two parents disagree, the Convention permits the courts to choose the approach which best furthers the welfare of the child. The Court of Appeal confirmed his approach and did not require the circumcision to be performed. In particular they rejected the argument that the child was a Muslim boy, arguing that the child was not yet old enough to belong to any faith.[295]

F. Employed parents

It used to be thought that a parent who stayed at home to spend as much time as possible with a child would be favoured regarding residency over a parent who spent substantial time in employed work. Such an approach tends to favour mothers over fathers; indeed a father who gave up work to look after a child was at one time criticised by a court for 'deliberately giv[ing] up work in order to go on social security'.[296] However, it seems now that a working parent will not necessarily be

---

[291] Barnett (2000).
[292] *Re P (Section 91(14) Guidelines) (Residence and Religious Heritage)* [1999] 2 FLR 573.
[293] [2001] 3 FCR 648.
[294] [1999] 2 FLR 678; approved in *Re J (Specific Issue Orders)* [2000] 1 FLR 517. Contrast in *Re S (Change of Names: Cultural Factors)* [2001] 3 FCR 648.
[295] For further discussion of how the religion of a child is ascertained see Van Praagh (1997).
[296] *Plant v Plant* [1983] 4 FLR 305 at p. 310. See also *B v B (Custody of Children)* [1985] FLR 166 CA; contrast *B v B (Custody of Children)* [1985] FLR 462 CA.

disadvantaged over a non-working parent.[297] In *Re R (A Minor) (Residence Order: Finance)*[298] the court preferred to make a joint residence order so that both parents were able to continue in employment, rather than giving sole residence to the mother, because that would mean she would have to give up her job which would cause financial disadvantage to the children and involve the Child Support Agency in the family's finances.

G. Sexual orientation of parents

There have been a few cases where the court has had to consider whether the fact that one of the parents is in a gay or lesbian relationship should have any bearing on a dispute over the residence of the child. The cases to date suggest that this is a relevant factor: 'It is still the norm that children are brought up in a home with a father, mother and siblings (if any) and, other things being equal, such an upbringing is most likely to be conducive to their welfare.'[299] This was the approach taken in the case of *C v C (A Minor) (Custody: Appeal)*,[300] where the Court of Appeal had to decide between a mother who was in a lesbian relationship and a father who had remarried. It was noted: 'If [the child's] house was to be with the father that would be a normal home by the standards of our society; that would not be the case if the home were with the mother.'[301] Balcombe LJ was critical of the original hearing, where the judge had placed no weight on the fact that the mother was now in a lesbian relationship and ordered a rehearing. Notably at the rehearing the mother was granted custody.[302] In *B v B (Minors) (Custody: Care and Control)*[303] two particular factors were thought to be relevant in cases involving gay parents. The first was that a child brought up by a gay or lesbian parent might suffer from teasing at school and, secondly, the child may suffer confusion over his or her sexual identity. As to the latter, it is not clear whether the reference is to confusion over sexual orientation or gender identity.[304] In this case both these fears were set aside. It was noted by Callman J that the mother was not a 'militant lesbian' trying to convert people to lesbianism, and so there would be less chance of the child suffering stigmatisation. Secondly, the judge found that the mother had several male friends who, along with the father, could provide male role models for the child. The court also noted that the boy in question was very boyish in appearance and so it thought he was less likely to suffer confusion over his identity. In future cases the courts are likely to consider these two concerns, but, as shown, these fears may be abated on the facts of the case. Recently Black J in *Re M (Sperm Donor Father)*[305] has confirmed that a

---

[297] Although see *Re B (Minors: Residence: Working Fathers)* [1996] CLY 615. Moloney (2001) provides evidence that Australian judges are sceptical about fathers who offer to reduce their work commitments to raise a child.
[298] [1995] 2 FLR 612, [1995] 3 FCR 334 CA.
[299] Balcombe LJ in *C v C (A Minor) (Custody: Appeal)* [1991] 1 FLR 223 at p. 231.
[300] [1991] 1 FLR 223, [1991] FCR 254 CA.
[301] [1991] 1 FLR 223 at p. 232.
[302] Tasker and Golombok (1991).
[303] [1991] 1 FLR 402, [1991] FCR 1 CA.
[304] Although the court presumed both to be harmful for the child.
[305] [2003] FL 94.

court could not ignore that there were special concerns where a child was being raised in a lesbian household, in particular about teasing at school and confusions a child may have about his or her background.

These cases will have to be reconsidered in the light of the Human Rights Act 1998. The European Court of Human Rights decision in *Da Silva Mouta* v *Portugal*[306] found that it was unlawful discrimination contrary to articles 14 and 8 to deny residence or contact to a parent on the ground of sexual orientation. The fact that a gay family was 'abnormal' did not constitute an objective or reasonable justification.[307] Whether concerns over possible teasing of a child will amount to a justification for discrimination remains to be seen; certainly convincing evidence of it would be required before the court could take it into account.[308]

The court should hear expert views on this issue. It is difficult to conduct research on how being raised by a gay parent affects a child, due to the relatively small number of children involved. However, the research to date does suggest that the courts are wrong to foresee any adverse side-effects. After a thorough review of the research, Golombok concludes: 'What the findings appear to suggest is that whether their mother is lesbian or heterosexual may matter less for children's psychological adjustment than a warm and supportive relationship with their parents and a harmonious family environment.'[309]

H. Disabled parents

The courts will take into account the abilities of parents to meet the needs of a child and any disability of a parent will therefore be relevant. In *M* v *M* *(Parental Responsibility)*[310] Wilson J decided that it would be inappropriate to give a father parental responsibility because he suffered from learning disabilities, aggravated by an accident, which meant that he would not be capable of exercising the rights and responsibilities of parenthood. Cases involving disabled parents must now be reconsidered in the light of the Human Rights Act 1998. Although the Human Rights Act does not explicitly prohibit discrimination on the basis of disability, it is arguable that it should be added to the list of prohibited grounds in article 14.[311] The English and Welsh courts' approach is demonstrated in *Re V* *(Residence Review)*,[312] where a father suffered a collapse after witnessing the drowning of one

---

[306] [2001] 1 FCR 653 ECtHR, discussed in Herring (2002a).

[307] See *G* v *F* *(Contact and Shared Residence)* [1998] 2 FLR 799 where it was held that there should be no discrimination against a lesbian applicant and that a mother and her lesbian partner should be given the benefit of a joint residence order.

[308] Concerns over teasing were seen as legitimate in *Re M* *(Sperm Donor Father)* [2003] FL 94.

[309] Golombok (1999: 175). See also Patterson, Fulcher and Wainright (2002) who likewise conclude that children do not suffer by being raised by a same-sex couple. But P. Morgan (2002) argues that such studies fail to establish a convincing case and that it is wrong to carry out social experiments on children.

[310] [1999] 2 FLR 737.

[311] Article 14 of the European Convention states: 'The enjoyment of the rights and freedoms set forth in this Convention shall be secured without discrimination on any ground such as sex, race, colour, language, religion ... or other status.' The use of the phrase 'such as' suggests that the list is not necessarily a complete one.

[312] [1995] 2 FLR 1010.

of his children. He suffered post-traumatic stress syndrome and lost his job. The court decided it would be better for the child to live with the mother, although this was against the boy's wishes and the recommendation of the welfare report. The father had received severe head injuries which the court felt deprived him of the ability to react appropriately to the child. Direct contact would be dangerously destabilising to the child and therefore only indirect conduct was deemed suitable.[313] It is suggested that, before taking such an approach, the court should ensure that a disabled parent cannot be enabled by the provision of suitable equipment or assistance to meet the child's needs.

I. Poverty

The court should not place much weight on the fact that one parent can offer a higher standard of living than another.[314] This is explained on the basis that 'anyone with experience of life knows that affluence and happiness are not necessarily synonymous'.[315] Although this is true, if given a choice most children would rather their parents be rich than poor, all other factors being equal. In reality it is easier to explain the irrelevance of wealth on the basis that it would be unjust to distinguish rich and poor parents. The significance of this factor is lessened in relation to married couples because the court has the power to redistribute the couple's property.

J. The 'immoral' conduct of a parent

In general, the conduct of a parent will only be relevant if it affects his or her ability to be a parent. So, for example, the fact a parent has committed adultery will nowadays, in and of itself, not be relevant to a dispute over residence or contact.[316] In *Re R (Minors) (Custody)*[317] the father had a drink problem and a criminal record and it was held that this affected his ability to be a parent. By contrast, in *Re P (Contact: Supervision)*[318] the fact that the father wore Nazi uniforms and had extreme political views did not mean that a contact order in his favour should not be made, as the court felt that this did not relate directly to his child-raising abilities.

It should be stressed that the court will not seek to achieve justice between the parents. So the fact that one party to the marriage may have behaved in a deeply reprehensible way and the other in an exemplary way will not necessarily affect how the court decides who is the best person to care for the child.[319] That said, the court will consider which parent is best able to bring up the child in the whole sense and this may include instilling moral values. It might therefore, for this reason, be open to a judge to consider a parent's lifestyle. However, as *Re W (Residence Order)*[320]

---

[313] See also *Re H (Children) (Contact Order) (No. 2)* [2001] 3 FCR 385.
[314] *Stephenson v Stephenson* [1985] FLR 1140 CA at p. 1148.
[315] *Re P (Adoption: Parental Agreement)* [1985] FLR 635 CA at p. 637.
[316] Although see Wardell (2002) for an argument that adultery should be a relevant factor.
[317] [1986] 1 FLR 6.
[318] [1996] 2 FLR 314, [1997] 1 FCR 458 CA.
[319] *J v C* [1970] AC 668.
[320] [1999] 1 FLR 869 CA.

(the case involving the nudist parent of a child) reveals, unless a particular way of life can be shown positively to harm a child, the court is unlikely to criticise it.

K. When is joint residence appropriate?

There are two situations where a court might consider a shared residence order. The first is where it is intended that the child split his or her time between the two parents. For example, the child may spend alternate weeks with their mother and father. The second situation is where the primary purpose of the joint residence order is to grant parental responsibility to both parents.

A joint residence order where the child is genuinely sharing his or her time between the two parents is not common, although it should not be regarded as appropriate only in exceptional circumstances.[321] In most cases the court will decide that it is better for a child to have the security of being based at one home. Only where the joint residence order is in the interests of the child should it be made.[322] Where the child has a good relationship with each parent and the child can move from one parent to the other without undue inconvenience (for example, if they live close to each other) the order may be suitable.[323] One interesting possibility is that the child stays in one house and the parents move in and out.[324] A joint residence order is usually only suitable where there is a good relationship between the parents.[325] This is because, if a shared residence order is to work, it is essential that the parties can talk effectively to each other. One benefit of a shared residence order is that it may minimise the conflict between parents and rebut the all too common perception that disputes over custody involve a winner and a loser.[326] On the other hand, some express concern that a joint residence order is an ideal compromise for the two parents but not for the child, who can find it artificial and alienating.[327]

An alternative reason for making a joint residence order is to confer parental responsibility upon one party. In *Re H (Shared Residence: Parental Responsibility)*[328] it was accepted that the child should live with the mother. However, it was felt that there was a strong case for the stepfather, who had brought up the child as his own and whom the child regarded as a father figure, to have parental responsibility. The court was willing to grant a joint residence order to the mother and stepfather pri-

---

[321] *Re A (A Minor) (Shared Residence Order)* [1994] 1 FLR 669; *Re A (Children) (Shared Residence)* [2002] 1 FCR 177.
[322] *D v D (Shared Residence Order)* [2001] 1 FLR 495 CA. See Weyland (1995), arguing that in practice the courts are reluctant to make the orders.
[323] Dunn, J. and Deater-Deckard, K. (2001) found that children in such arrangements were very positive about them.
[324] C. Bridge (1996).
[325] *Re R (A Minor) (Residence Order: Finance)* [1995] 2 FLR 612, [1995] 3 FCR 334 CA, though see *Re D (Children) (Shared Residence Orders)* [2001] 1 FCR 147 for a case where the Court of Appeal held that there should be a shared residence order even though there was much animosity between the parents.
[326] C. Bridge (1996).
[327] Macooby and Mnookin (1992); Baker and Townsend (1996).
[328] [1995] 2 FLR 883, [1996] 3 FCR 321 CA. See also *Re AB (Adoption: Joint Residence)* [1996] 1 FLR 27, [1996] 1 FCR 633.

marily in order to give the stepfather parental responsibility, even though the child would spend most of her time with the mother. However, where the making of a joint residence order would be wholly artificial, it should not be granted solely for the purpose of awarding parental responsibility, as was made clear in *Re WB (Residence Order)*,[329] where there was to be virtually no contact between the step-father and the child. In *Re F (Children) (Shared Residence Order)*[330] the Court of Appeal held that a shared residence order must reflect the reality of the case.[331]

L. Publicity

There have been a series of cases concerning publicity over children. The position seems to be as follows:

1. Where the child is not the subject of the publicity, the court has jurisdiction to prevent the publicity, but will rarely do so. So in *R v Central Independent Television plc*[332] a mother sought to prevent the broadcast of a television pro-gramme concerning the facts around the arrest of the child's father over charges of indecency. As the child was not the subject of the programme, the child's wel-fare was not paramount. In fact the child's welfare was not relevant at all, and the Court of Appeal stated that in such cases the freedom of the press pre-vailed.[333] Subsequently in *Re S (A Child) (Identification: Restriction on Publication)*[334] the Court of Appeal said that in such cases the Human Rights Act 1998 had an important impact. The child's rights under article 8 had to be taken into account. In this case a child's parents were facing criminal proceedings and an injunction was sought to prevent revelation of their names. The court must weigh up, on the one hand, the effect the publicity will have on the child and the effect of the order on the ability of the court to carry out any subsequent care proceedings in relation to the child and, on the other hand, the effect of the order on the ability of the press to provide the public with a full and fair report of the proceedings, thereby providing the public with an accurate record of the public trial.

2. Where the child is the subject of the publicity, a parent can apply to the court for a s 8 order and in such circumstances the welfare of the child will be the paramount consideration.[335] Similarly, if a parent permits publicity about the child, the other parent could seek a s 8 order to prohibit the publicity, or the court could prohibit it under the inherent jurisdiction.[336] If the court is very con-cerned about a parent seeking to use a child for publicity purposes, the court may even make the child a ward of court.[337] Section 12 of the Human Rights

---

[329] [1995] 2 FLR 1023.
[330] [2003] 2 FCR 164.
[331] See also *Re A (Children) (Shared Residence)* [2002] 1 FCR 177.
[332] [1994] 2 FLR 151.
[333] Although the right to respect for private life is now relevant because of the Human Rights Act 1998: *A v M (Family Proceedings: Publicity)* [2000] 1 FLR 562; *Kelly v BBC* [2001] 1 FCR 197.
[334] [2003] 2 FCR 577.
[335] CA 1989, s 1(1).
[336] *Re Z (A Minor) (Identity: Restrictions on Publication)* [1996] 1 FLR 191, [1996] 2 FCR 164.
[337] *Re W (Wardship: Discharge: Publicity)* [1995] 2 FLR 466, [1996] 1 FCR 393 CA.

Act 1998 requires the courts to pay particular regard to the importance of the right to freedom of expression under article 10 of the European Convention. This means that, in future, the court will not be able to state that the sole consideration is the child's welfare.[338] This led Butler-Sloss P in *Thompson and Venables* v *News Group Newspapers Ltd*[339] to make an injunction preventing the publication of information about the two boys who had killed Jamie Bulger. She relied on the law on protection of confidential information to do so, in this exceptional case.

It should be noted that the distinction between cases where the subject of the publicity is the child and those where it is someone else is artificial. Its basis is the wording of s 1 of the Children Act 1989, which states that the welfare of the child is paramount in cases involving the upbringing of the child. However, the child can be as harmed by publicity which indirectly relates to the child as by publicity which directly relates to the child. The issues of balancing the welfare of the child and the freedom of the press should be the same in both.

M. Names

(i) Registration of birth

A child must be registered within 42 days of the birth and the person registering the birth can declare 'the surname by which at the date of the registration of the birth it is intended that the child shall be known'.[340] The birth can be registered by the mother or the father, if he is married to the mother. An unmarried father has no right to register the birth. The father has no ground to insist that the child be given his surname. This position has been criticised.[341] It gives the unmarried father no say in the name of his child. It also enables the married father who has separated from the mother to register the child without consulting the mother.[342]

If a father (or mother) objects to the initial registration he (or she) can apply for a specific issue order that the child have his (or her) surname. The Court of Appeal decision in *Dawson* v *Wearmouth*[343] suggests that as long as the mother's decision was not 'a maliciously or manifestly absurd choice', the courts will uphold her choice. So, presumably, if a mother chooses her own or the child's father's surname it could not successfully be challenged in court. If, however, she chooses the surname of a popular television personality, the father would be more likely to succeed in his appeal. Once the name is registered it cannot be changed unless there has been a clerical error.[344]

---

[338] *Re Z (A Minor) (Identity: Restrictions on Publication)* [1996] 1 FLR 191, [1996] 2 FCR 164 was approved by the European Commission in *A and Byrne and Twenty-Twenty Television* v *UK* 25 EHRR 159 CD,

[339] [2001] 1 FLR 791.

[340] Registration of Births and Deaths Regulations 1987, SI 1987/2088, reg. 9(3).

[341] Gosden (2003).

[342] This appeared to happen in *Re H and A (Children)* [2002] 2 FCR 469.

[343] [1997] 2 FLR 629 CA at p. 635.

[344] Births and Deaths Registration Act 1953, s 29.

(ii) What is a child's name?

In law a child's name is not necessarily the name which appears on the birth register. *Re T (Otherwise H) (An Infant)*[345] makes it clear that the child's surname in law
is simply that by which he or she is customarily known, which does not, of course,
have to be the registered name. It is possible through a deed poll to provide formal
evidence of a change from the registered surname, although it is not essential.[346] If
a deed poll is used to recognise the new surname of a child, it must be signed by all
those with parental responsibility.[347]

(iii) Can a parent allow a child to be known by a name with which he or she was not registered?

It is clear that only a person with parental responsibility can change the name of a
child. What is not clear is whether a person with parental responsibility must consult with anyone else with parental responsibility before doing so. The following
situations need to be distinguished.

(a) Where a residence order is in force

Where a residence order is in force the position is governed by s 13(1) of the
Children Act 1989:

> Where a residence order is in force with respect to a child, no person may—
> (a) cause the child to be known by a new surname; or
> (b) remove him from the United Kingdom
> without either the written consent of every person who has parental responsibility for the
> child or leave of the court.

So where a residence order is in force, the name of the child cannot be changed
without the consent of all those with parental responsibility or the leave of the court.
P v N (Child: Surname)[348] suggested that the section does not apply where the name
is to be changed to a hyphenated name, including the existing name. However, this
is a county court decision and is therefore of very limited weight as a precedent. It
seems a little surprising that this would not be regarded as a 'change' in the name
of the child on a literal reading of the statute.

The section does not state that the consent of the child is needed. It was left open
in *Re PC (Change of Surname)*[349] whether the consent of a *Gillick*-competent child
was necessary or sufficient to change the name. Given that the mature child can in
effect ensure that he or she is known by friends and others by a particular name,
there may be little point in ordering an older child to be known by a particular
name.[350]

---

[345] [1962] 3 All ER 970.
[346] The procedure for this is set out in *Practice Direction (Minor: Change of Surname: Deed Poll)* [1995] 1
All ER 832.
[347] *Practice Direction (Minor: Change of Surname: Deed Poll)* [1995] 1 All ER 832.
[348] [1997] 2 FCR 65.
[349] [1997] 2 FLR 730, [1997] 3 FCR 544.
[350] *Re B (Change of Surname)* [1996] 1 FLR 791, [1996] 2 FCR 304 CA.

(b) Where there is no residence order in force and both parents have parental responsibility

It had been thought that the implication of s 8 was that if there was no residence order then s 13 did not apply, and so relying on s 2(7) of the Children Act 1989 one person with parental responsibility could change the name of a child without having the consent of the other parent with parental responsibility or the leave of the court. This was rejected by the Court of Appeal in *Dawson v Wearmouth*.[351] The explanation was that if s 2(7) applied then each person with parental responsibility could independently change the child's name and this could lead to a chaotic situation with the name being constantly changed and re-changed by each parent. *Dawson v Wearmouth* argued that s 13 was simply making it clear that a residence order did not extend to the power of unilaterally changing a name. So, after *Dawson v Wearmouth*, it seems that if two people have parental responsibility, the child's name cannot be changed without the agreement of both, or, if that is not possible, the court's approval.

(c) Where one person has parental responsibility

Holman J in *Re PC (Change of Surname)*[352] suggested that if only one parent has parental responsibility then he or she could unilaterally change a child's name. An unmarried father without parental responsibility could object to this by applying for a prohibited steps order, but the mother is entitled to change the name and the burden is on the father to bring the matter to the court if he wishes to object. However, the law is unclear. Lord Mackay in *Dawson v Wearmouth*[353] in the House of Lords stated: 'Any dispute [over the registration of a child's name] should be referred to the court for determination whether or not there is a residence order in force and whoever has or has not parental responsibility. No disputed registration or change should be made unilaterally.'[354] This implies that even if only the mother has parental responsibility she will need to apply to the court for permission to change a child's name. In *Re W, Re A, Re B (Change of Name)*[355] it was suggested that if only one person has parental responsibility, they ought to obtain the consent of the other parent or the leave of the court, although it is unclear where this requirement comes from and what the penalty is for breaching it. However, in *Re R (A Child)* Hale LJ appeared to suggest that a parent without parental responsibility did not have a right to be consulted over the surname of a child, but did have the right to challenge the choice in court.[356]

(iv) Child in local authority care

Under s 33(7), if a child is in care then a child's name can only be changed in writing, if all those with parental responsibility consent or the court gives leave. It

---

[351] [1997] 2 FLR 629 CA; affirmed [1999] 1 FLR 1167, [1999] 1 FCR 625 HL.
[352] [1997] 2 FLR 730, [1997] 3 FCR 544.
[353] [1999] 1 FLR 1167, [1999] 1 FCR 625 HL.
[354] [1999] 1 FLR 1167 at p. 1173.
[355] [1999] 2 FLR 930 CA.
[356] [2002] 1 FCR 170, para 9.

would be open for a child in care, if sufficiently competent, to apply him- or herself to have their name changed.[357] In *Re M, T, P, K and B (Care: Change of Name)*[358] a local authority was given leave to change the surname of children in care because they lived in fear that their parents would discover their whereabouts. This was seen as a valid reason for giving leave to change the surname.

(v) How will the court resolve a disputed case?

If a dispute over a child's name is brought before the court then the child's welfare will be the paramount consideration.[359] The cases indicate that a court seeking to resolve a dispute over the surname of a child will consider the following issues:[360]

1. *The registered name.* The person seeking to change the name from the registered name has the burden of persuading the court that the change of name is in the child's welfare. Ward LJ in *Re C (Change of Surname)*[361] stated that the person seeking to change the name must provide 'good and cogent reasons' to support the change. On the other hand, it would be wrong to suggest that registration should be regarded as decisive;[362] rather that if the arguments for or against changing the name are equally balanced the registered name should prevail.[363]

2. *The child's views.* The child's views will be important, but not the sole consideration. Wilson J in *Re B (Change of Surname)*[364] ordered that three children (two teenagers) keep their father's surname, despite their opposition, in order to maintain the link with their father. However, it might be thought that little more could be done to damage the relationship between a father and teenagers than forcing them to keep his name. Despite this decision, it was made clear in *Re S (Change of Surname)*[365] that the views of a *Gillick*-competent child over a surname should be given careful consideration.

3. *Embarrassment.* It seems that simply arguing that the child is going to be embarrassed by having a different name from their residential parent is not a strong enough argument to justify changing the name.[366] In fact 'there [is] no opprobrium nowadays for a child to have a different surname from that of adults in the household'.[367] So if the child has his or her father's name and the parents separate and the mother remarries, taking her new husband's surname, the court

---

[357] *Re S (Change of Surname)* [1999] 1 FLR 672.
[358] [2000] 1 FLR 645.
[359] *Dawson v Wearmouth* [1999] 1 FLR 1167, [1999] 1 FCR 625 HL.
[360] *Stjerna v Finland* (1994) 24 EHRR 195 ECtHR. A man wanted to change his surname about which he was regularly taunted. The European Court accepted that article 8 included the right to change one's name, although the public interest in that case justified infringing his right.
[361] [1998] 2 FLR 656, [1999] 1 FCR 318 CA.
[362] *Re W, Re A, Re B (Change of Name)* [1999] 2 FLR 930 CA.
[363] *A v Y (Child's Surname)* [1999] 2 FLR 5.
[364] *Re B (Change of Surname)* [1996] 1 FLR 791, [1996] 2 FCR 304 CA.
[365] [1999] 1 FLR 672.
[366] *Re F (Child: Surname)* [1993] 2 FLR 827n, [1994] 1 FCR 110; *Re T (Change of Name)* [1998] 2 FLR 620, [1999] 1 FCR 476.
[367] *Re B (Change of Surname)* [1996] 1 FLR 791, [1996] 2 FCR 304 CA; *Re T (Change of Name)* [1998] 2 FLR 620, [1999] 1 FCR 476.

will not place much weight on the argument that the child should have the same surname as the mother to avoid embarrassment.

4. *Informal use of names.* There is a difficulty where the child's surname has informally been changed and the child has used the new name for some time before the matter is brought before the court. In such circumstances the court may easily be persuaded that it would be harmful for the child to have the name changed back to the original name. For example, in *Re C (Change of Surname)*[368] the Court of Appeal felt that although the mother's initial decision to change the surname had been undesirable, given the length of time the children had been known by the new surname it would be inappropriate to revert to the original name. It may be that a court will accept that the formal name will be different from the informal name. However, Lord Hobhouse in *Dawson v Wearmouth*[369] confirmed that the formal name and the name in everyday use should be the same, but there was no need to regard this as 'all important'. Wilson J in *Re B (Change of Surname)* accepted that, in practice, there is little the law can do to control the name by which a child is to be known on a day-to-day basis. The court can only control the name by which the child will be known in formal documents.[370]

5. *Strength of the child's relationship with their parents.* Where the residential parent is seeking to change the child's surname from the surname of the non-residential parent then the strength of the relationship between the child and non-residential parent will be taken into account.[371] However, it is not easy to tell how this relationship will be taken into account. If the child sees the non-residential parent only rarely then that is an argument *in favour* of retaining the non-residential parent's name, because the name may be the strongest link between the child and the non-residential parent. However, in the *B* case in *Re W, Re A, Re B (Change of Name)*[372] approval was given to a change of name from the father's after the father had been imprisoned, because there was not likely to be a meaningful relationship between the child and her father in the future. In *Re S (Change of Surname)*[373] the fact that the children alleged the father had abused them was recognised as a strong reason for justifying a change from the father's name.

6. *Cultural factors.* A court might place weight on normal rules governing surnames from the parent's cultural background.[374] In *Re S (Change of Names: Cultural Factors)*[375] Wilson J held that the child's name should be changed for day-to-day purposes from a Sikh name to a Muslim name. This was because he had ordered residence to the Muslim mother and therefore the child would inevitably become part of the Muslim community and the child should be helped to

---

[368] [1998] 2 FLR 656 CA.
[369] [1999] 1 FCR 625.
[370] [1996] 2 FCR 304. Accepted also in *Re F (Child: Surname)* [1993] 2 FLR 837n, [1994] 1 FCR 110.
[371] *Re P (Parental Responsibility: Change of Name)* [1997] 2 FLR 722, [1997] 3 FCR 739.
[372] [1999] 2 FLR 930.
[373] [1999] 1 FLR 672.
[374] *Re A (A Child) (Change of Name)* [2003] 1 FCR 493 CA.
[375] [2001] 3 FCR 648.

become accepted within that community. However, for formal purposes he held that the name should remain the Sikh name to remind him of his Sikh origins.

7. *Double-barrelled names.* It might be thought that suggesting the child have a double-barrelled name, linking the child to both the mother and father, would be a suitable compromise in many cases. In *Re R (A Child)*[376] it was suggested that using a combination of both surnames was to be encouraged because it would recognise the importance of both parents to the child.

(vi) First names

In *Re H (Child's Name: First Name)*[377] it was held that the rules in relation to surnames do not apply to forenames. A court will not stop the resident parent from using whatever forename she wishes. The father had registered the child with one first name and that would remain the registered name, but for all practical purposes the mother could choose the name she wished. Foster carers and adoptive parents should not change their children's first names (even by using a shortened form of the name) without the local authority's approval. If there is no agreement the matter should be taken to the High Court.[378] To some this might sound bizarre, but the President of the Family Division so held, explaining that changes of forenames raised important issues. Notably however, she held that the foster carers, who were 'marvellous people' in caring for a severely disabled child should not be caused unhappiness or difficulty by requiring them not to use the name they wished.

(vii) What should the law be?

There are two main issues here.[379] The first is whether the question of the surname is an important one. The House of Lords has accepted that changing the surname of the child is a 'profound issue',[380] so much so that the normal rule of independent parenting does not apply. Lord Jauncey in *Dawson v Wearmouth*[381] suggested that 'the surname is ... a biological label which tells the world at large that the blood of the name flows in its veins'. But is it really a 'profound issue'?[382] More so than dispute over religious upbringing or medical issues to which s 2(7) does apply? It is arguable that although the surname may be important to the parents, it is rarely a profound issue for children, for whom first names are usually far more important.[383] The fact that the House of Lords felt it necessary to hear a case over surnames, when there are so many other issues of greater significance to children's

---

[376] [2002] 1 FCR 170. The option did not appeal to Tyrer J in *A v Y (Child's Surname)* [1999] 2 FLR 5 who thought that only the mother's half (the latter half) of the name would be used.
[377] [2002] 1 FLR 973.
[378] *Re D, L and LA (Care: Change of Forename)* [2003] 1 FLR 339.
[379] Bond (1998); Eekelaar (1998); Herring (1998a).
[380] *Dawson v Wearmouth* [1999] 1 FLR 1167 HL at p. 1173 (Lord Mackay).
[381] [1999] 1 FLR 1167 HL at p. 1175.
[382] Thorpe LJ in *Re R (A Child)* [2002] 1 FCR 170 called the surname issue a 'small issue' (para 1).
[383] Lord Hobhouse in *Dawson v Wearmouth* [1999] 1 FLR 1167 at p. 1178 was insistent the issue was one of the welfare of the child rather than the rights of parents.

welfare, may be thought to reveal how the court's involvement in the lives of children is driven by the concerns of adults, rather than the needs of children.

The second issue is how the law should treat stepfamilies. Many of these cases involve the mother remarrying or repartnering and wanting to take on her new partner's name. The issue then arises whether the child's name should be changed to reflect the mother's new name and so tie in the child to the new family, or whether the child should keep his or her biological father's name to retain the link with him. Hale LJ in *Re R (A Child)*[384] expressed her view forcefully:

> It is also a matter of great sadness to me that it is so often assumed, and even sometimes argued, that fathers need that outward and visible link in order to retain their relationship with, and commitment to, their child. That should not be the case. It is a poor sort of parent whose interest in and commitment to his child depends upon that child bearing his name. After all, that is a privilege which is not enjoyed by many mothers, even if they are not living with the child. They have to depend upon other more substantial things.

N. Removal from the UK

It is clear from s 13(1)(b) of the Children Act 1989[385] that if there is a residence order in force then a child cannot be removed from the UK unless there is the written consent of every person with parental responsibility, or the leave of the court. Section 13(2) permits a child to be removed for less than one month by the person with the residence order without the consent of others with parental responsibility.[386] If there is a dispute between the parents over removal of the child from the UK an application for a specific issue order could be made.[387]

If leave to remove the child from the jurisdiction[388] is sought, the child's welfare is the paramount consideration.[389] The court must take a long-term view in deciding whether leave to remove will promote the child's welfare.[390] The most difficult cases involve the residential parent seeking to emigrate with a child. Refusing leave may be regarded as an infringement of the parent's right to respect for private and family life, which includes being able to choose where to live.[391] The non-residential parent may well object on the ground that permitting emigration will severely restrict the practicability of any contact with the child and infringe that parent's rights under article 8. The approach that the courts have taken is that leave will be granted if the request to emigrate is reasonable and bona fide,[392] unless it is shown

---

[384] [2002] 1 FCR 170, para 13.

[385] See page 461.

[386] See also Child Abduction Act 1984.

[387] See *Re L (Removal from Jurisdiction: Holiday)* [2001] 1 FLR 241 where permission was given on condition (*inter alia*) that the mother and her family made solemn declarations on the Koran that they would return the child to the UK.

[388] That is to remove the child from the country.

[389] CA 1989, s 1(1).

[390] *Re B (Children) (Removal from Jurisdiction)* [2001] 1 FCR 108.

[391] European Convention on Human Rights, article 8; *Re G-A (A Child) (Removal from Jurisdiction: Human Rights)* [2001] 1 FCR 43 CA.

[392] That is, it is not being made solely for the purpose of bringing the contact arrangement to an end. See e.g. *Tyler v Tyler* [1989] 2 FLR 158, [1990] FCR 22; *Re K (Application to Remove from Jurisdiction)* [1988] 2 FLR 1006.

that emigration would be contrary to the welfare of the child.[393] Where the children are older their views will be given weight.[394] Where leave is granted this may well be on the basis that the children will return to the UK for lengthy holidays.[395]

The leading case[396] on this issue is now *Payne v Payne*[397] where Thorpe LJ explained 'refusing the primary carer's reasonable proposals for the relocation of her family life is likely to impact detrimentally on the welfare of her dependant children. Therefore her application to relocate will be granted unless the court concludes that it is incompatible with the welfare of the children.'[398] He went on to confirm that such an approach was consistent with the European Convention.[399] Thorpe LJ went on to warn of the dangers of stating that there was a legal presumption that if the primary carer's plans were reasonable she would be given leave. In each case the judge must assess what would be in the welfare of the child, using the following approach:

(a) Pose the question: is the mother's application genuine in the sense that it is not motivated by some selfish desire to exclude the father from the child's life? Then ask is the mother's application realistic, by which I mean founded on practical proposals both well researched and investigated? If the application fails either of these tests refusal will inevitably follow.

(b) If, however, the application passes these tests then there must be a careful appraisal of the father's opposition: is it motivated by genuine concern for the future of the child's welfare or is it driven by some ulterior motive? What would be the extent of the detriment to him and his future relationship with the child were the application granted? To what extent would that be offset by extension of the child's relationships with the maternal family and homeland?

(c) What would be the impact on the mother, either as the single parent or as a new wife, of a refusal of her realistic proposal?

(d) The outcome of the second and third appraisals must then be brought into an overriding review of the child's welfare as the paramount consideration, directed by the statutory checklist in so far as appropriate.'[400]

Subsequent decisions show that normally leave will be granted.[401] In *L v L (Leave to Remove Children from Jurisdiction: Effect on Children)*[402] leave was granted to the mother to remove the children to the USA after her new husband had been offered a major job advancement and there was evidence that the medical care for one of the children was better in the USA than in the UK. Interestingly Johnson J also placed weight on the fact that the father had left the mother and children and could be said to have been to blame for the ending of the parents' relationship. In

---

[393] *Re H (Application to Remove from Jurisdiction)* [1998] 1 FLR 848, [1999] 2 FCR 34 CA.
[394] *M v M (Minors) (Jurisdiction)* [1993] 1 FCR 5 CA.
[395] *Re B (Minors) (Removal from the Jurisdiction)* [1994] 2 FLR 309; *Re H (Application to Remove from Jurisdiction)* [1998] 1 FLR 848, [1999] 2 FCR 34 CA.
[396] As confirmed in *Re H (Children) (Residence Order: Condition)* [2001] 2 FLR 1277.
[397] [2001] 1 FCR 425.
[398] [2001] 1 FCR 425, para 26.
[399] *Re A (Permission to Remove Child from Jurisdiction: Human Rights)* [2000] 2 FLR 225 CA.
[400] *Payne v Payne* [2001] 1 FCR 425, para 40.
[401] See *Re C (Leave to Remove from the Jurisdiction)* [2000] 2 FCR 40 CA for a controversial decision denying leave to remove the children.
[402] [2003] 1 FLR 900.

Re C (Permission to Remove from Jurisdiction)[403] the court held that the ideal solution would be for the mother to decide to stay in the UK rather than return to the country of birth. However, to order her to do so would in the long term harm the children because of its potential impact on the mother. The court asked the mother to reconsider her decision to leave, but refused to prevent her doing so.[404]

While holding that the decision in *Payne* was justifiable, Bainham is concerned that the reasoning used 'apparently attached more significance to the security and stability of the child with her mother, than it did to the preservation of the child's relationship with the father, as secondary carer, and the father's family. This, again, might be criticized as an inadequate response to the child's identity rights under the UN Convention.'[405] Hayes and Williams[406] argue that: 'The courts have been too ready to indulge the selfish feelings of mothers and second husbands ... Restrictions on mobility should simply be regarded as one of the burdens of bringing up children.'

O. When should there be contact between a child and parent?

Cases concerning whether there should be contact between the non-resident parent and the child are some of the most controversial issues that courts hear.[407] Before considering the approach the courts have taken, the findings of psychologists on the benefits of contact will be considered.

(i) Psychological evidence of the benefits of contact

There is much support among child psychologists for 'attachment theory': that at an early age a child forms a psychological attachment with a parent or parent figure. This normally takes place within the first three months of the child's life, but may occur even up to age 7.[408] Removing that child from the adult to whom they have become attached can cause the child serious harm. Of course, the quality of the attachment is of great significance, but the breaking of any attachment can cause harm.[409] The dominant view in England and Wales is that contact between a child and both parents is in general beneficial.[410] It has been argued that contact with the non-resident parent provides a number of benefits:

1. It avoids the child feeling rejected by the non-residential parent.
2. It enables the parent and child to maintain a beneficial relationship.

---

[403] [2003] FL 484.
[404] See also *Re B (Children) (Removal from the Jurisdiction)*, *Re S (A Child) (Removal from the Jurisdiction)* [2003] 3 FCR 637 where the Court of Appeal gave leave to take children out of the jurisdiction so that the resident parents could marry men living abroad.
[405] Bainham (2002a: 285). See also Barton (1997).
[406] Hayes and Williams (1999: 316–17).
[407] Geldof (2003) is a vivid expression of the emotions that arise in disputed contact cases. See generally Bainham, Lindley, Richards and Trinder (2003) for a useful discussion of the issues.
[408] Schaffer (1990).
[409] See e.g. Schofield (1998).
[410] Willbourne and Stanley (2002).

3. Contact may dispel erroneous fantasies that the child could have about the non-residential parent.
4. Contact helps the child develop or retain a sense of identity. In particular, it may help in maintaining a sense of cultural identity.
5. Contact can help the child understand the parental separation.
6. It can ensure the child retains contact with the wider family of the non-residential parent.
7. It can help the child feel free to develop relationships with a step-parent without a sense of betrayal to his or her birth parent.[411]

However, proof of these benefits is not established beyond doubt.[412] As Eekelaar and Maclean explain:

> What has not been established is whether a child whose separated parents behave gently and reasonably to her and to one another, but who sees the outside parents rarely or never, somehow does 'less well' than a child of similar parents who sees the outside parent often.[413]

Others argue that benefits do not flow from the mere existence of the contact; what matters is the frequency and quality of the contact.[414] As Pryor and Daly Peoples put it:

> Fathers who are able to have a nurturing and monitoring role have a positive impact on their children in a variety of ways . . . Those fathers whose participation is confined to outings and having fun will, then, have little influence on their children's adjustment.[415]

After a major investigation of the research to date by Rogers and Pryor,[416] they concluded:

> the relationship between the amount of access to the non-residential parent and child adjustment is not straightforward. Some studies find that frequent contact is associated with better adjustment for children; however, others find no relationship. A few find a negative relationship between frequent levels of contact and child well-being. These diverse findings suggest that the relationship between contact and well-being is moderated by other factors.[417]

Even if there are benefits of contact, it must be recognised that there are also potential disadvantages:[418]

1. Contact often leads to bitter disputes between the resident and non-resident parent and this atmosphere of conflict may harm the child.

---

[411] Hill and Tisdall (1997: 227).
[412] As Eekelaar (2002b) points out, a number of studies cast doubt on the assumption that contact is beneficial: e.g. Emery (1994); Poussin and Martin-LeBrun (2002).
[413] Eekelaar and Maclean (1997: 55).
[414] Rogers and Pryor (1998: 40); Hetherington and Kelly (2002: 133).
[415] Pryor and Daly Peoples (2001: 199).
[416] Rogers and Pryor (1998).
[417] Rogers and Pryor (1998: 42).
[418] Discussed in *Re L (A Child) (Contact: Domestic Violence)* [2000] 2 FCR 404 CA.

2. The child may feel torn between the residential and non-residential parent, which may be exacerbated by emotionally intense contact sessions. This may cause psychological disturbance.[419]

3. The relationship between the child and the non-residential parent may be an abusive or bullying one whose continuance will harm the child.[420]

A recent study on children in stepfamilies[421] found that contact with the non-resident parent had no discernable impact on children's welfare. What was crucial to a child's welfare were the relationships in the home where the child was living. This suggests that the law should not seek to promote contact where this will cause severe disturbance in the child's home.[422]

To conclude on the current state of the evidence on the benefits of contact between a child and non-resident parent: What the evidence certainly does show is that it should not be assumed that contact is always beneficial.[423] On the other hand, there are many benefits that *can* flow from contact in many cases where the contact is part of a constructive relationship.[424] Certainly there is evidence that children value the contact they have with their non-resident parent and would like to have more.[425] It should not be forgotten in all the debate over whether children benefit or not from contact that contact arrangements can have significant impact on the welfare of fathers[426] and mothers.[427] Despite the ambiguity of the research, the law has been willing to accept that contact promotes the welfare of the child.

(ii) The courts' approach to contact: is there a right to contact?

Some cases have talked of children having a right to contact.[428] Sir Stephen Brown suggested in *Re W (A Minor) (Contact)*:[429] 'It is quite clear that contact with a parent is a fundamental right of a child, save in wholly exceptional circumstances.' Those cases which have referred to a right to contact have stressed that contact is the right of the child and not the parent.[430] However, to talk of a right to contact is a misnomer because s 1(1) of the Children Act 1989 applies to contact applications and so the key question is whether or not the contact will promote the child's welfare.[431] In *Re M (Contact: Welfare Test)* it was held that contact was not a fundamental right of the child. Instead, the Court of Appeal accepted that there was a strong presumption in favour of contact and the test was:

---

[419] Wallerstein and Kelly (1980: 311).
[420] Jones and Parkinson (1995).
[421] Smith, Robertson, Dixon and Quigley (2001).
[422] Maclean and Mueller-Johnson (2003).
[423] Rogers and Pryor (1998); Kaganas and Piper (1999).
[424] Hetherington and Kelly (2002); Poussin and Martin-LeBrun (2002); Trinder (2003).
[425] Dunn (2003).
[426] Simpson, Jessop and McCarthy (2003).
[427] Day Sclater and Kaganas (2003).
[428] E.g. *Re S (Minors) (Access)* [1990] 2 FLR 166 at p. 170, Balcombe LJ; *Re F (Contact: Restraint Order)* [1995] 1 FLR 956 at p. 963.
[429] [1994] 2 FLR 441 CA at p. 447.
[430] *M v M (Child: Access)* [1973] 2 All ER 81. See further the discussion in Wallbank (1998).
[431] See the discussion in Bailey-Harris (2001d).

whether the fundamental emotional need of every child to have an enduring relationship with both his parents [s 1(3)(b)] is outweighed by the depth of harm which in the light, inter alia, of his wishes and feelings [s 1(3)(a)] this child would be at risk of suffering [s 1(3)(e)] by virtue of a contact order.[432]

This quotation has been approved in the Court of Appeal in *Re L (A Child) (Contact: Domestic Violence)*,[433] where Thorpe LJ and Butler-Sloss P explained that it was not appropriate to talk of a right to contact. Thorpe LJ was not keen even on referring to a presumption in favour of contact and preferred to talk of an assumption of the benefit of contact which was 'the base of knowledge and experience from which the court embarks upon its application of the welfare principle'.[434] He suggested that the strength of the case in favour of contact depended on the quality of the relationship between the non-resident parent and the child. Where there is a high-quality existing relationship, the case for contact is at its strongest, but if the child does not know the parent, or the relationship is an abusive one, the argument for contact is much weaker.[435] Whether the father is married or not to the mother should not be a relevant characteristic.[436] However, Kaganas and Day Sclater[437] suggested that Butler-Sloss P, who gave the other main judgment in *Re L*, was more willing than Thorpe LJ to assume that contact was to the benefit of the child. She agreed with statements in *Re O (Imposition of Conditions)*[438] that contact was 'almost always' in the child's interests. However, it is submitted that, rather than suggesting a different approach, Butler-Sloss P was agreeing with Thorpe LJ that each case should be considered on its own merits, and only pointed out that in most cases contact will be found beneficial.[439]

It seems that in future the courts will consider more carefully what benefits and disadvantages contact would provide, both in the short and long term.[440] In *Re M (Sperm Donor Father)*[441] a lesbian couple used a sperm donor to father a child. He applied for a contact order. It was held that on balance it would be beneficial for occasional contact to take place, so that the child could, at an early stage, be comfortable about his origins.

Bainham is adamant that there is a right to contact. He explains that by a right he is talking about 'fundamental presumptions' which may be rebutted – but only for good reasons.[442] He claims that 'those who assert that there is no right or presumption of contact are not merely misguided, but are plainly wrong'.[443] He argues that children have a right of contact with mothers and fathers and mothers and

---

[432] [1995] 1 FLR 274, at p. 275. A useful summary of the law is set out in *Re P (Contact: Supervision)* [1996] 2 FLR 314 at p. 318.
[433] [2000] 2 FLR 334, [2000] 2 FCR 404 CA.
[434] *Re L (A Child) (Contact: Domestic Violence)* [2000] 2 FCR 404 at p. 437. See by contrast *Re R (A Minor) (Contact)* [1993] 2 FLR 762 CA.
[435] *Re L (A Child) (Contact: Domestic Violence)* [2000] 2 FCR 404 at p. 437.
[436] *Sahin* v *Germany* [2003] 2 FCR 619 ECtHR.
[437] Kaganas and Day Sclater (2000).
[438] [2000] Fam Law 631.
[439] This appears to be her view in an extra-judicial article: Butler-Sloss (2001).
[440] *Re J-S (A Child) (Contact: Parental Responsibility)* [2002] 3 FCR 433.
[441] [2003] FL 94.
[442] Bainham (2003: 75).
[443] Bainham (2003: 74).

fathers have rights of contact with their children.[444] This is a bold statement in the light of the clear statement of Lord Justice Thorpe that there is no right or presumption in favour of contact in English and Welsh law. Bainham's argument is focused on the right to contact which parents and children have under the European Convention on Human Rights.[445] The European Court of Human Rights has made it quite clear that the right to respect for family and private life under article 8 of the European Convention on Human Rights includes the right of contact between parents and children.[446] In *Elsholz* v *Germany*[447] it was confirmed that to deny contact between a father and a child where they had an established relationship infringed article 8, although denial of contact could be justified under paragraph 2 if necessary in the interests of the child.[448] When weighing up the interests of parents and child in relation to contact, the welfare of the child will be of 'crucial importance'.[449] However, it must be shown that the concerns over the welfare of the child render the infringement of the father's right necessary.[450] In other words, contact should not be denied simply because it will very slightly harm the child; a significant harm to the child is required to justify denying contact. However, Bainham also accepts that violence of the father against the mother or child may lead to a forfeiture of his right to contact.[451]

It is perhaps possible to reconcile the approach of Thorpe LJ with the approach of the European Convention. Thorpe LJ appeared to take the view that the human rights to contact were protected by the application of the welfare principle used by the English courts. So Thorpe LJ was not denying that the rights existed, but believed that their existence did not require the court to depart from the statutory formulation under the Children Act, based on the welfare principle. Thorpe LJ's argument could be that given the court's willingness to assume that contact was beneficial, the English court, just like the European Court, will order contact unless there is clear evidence that the child will be harmed by it.

The Court of Appeal has accepted that the Human Rights Act 1998 has had an impact on contact cases. In *Elsholz* v *Germany*[452] the failure of the state to obtain a psychological report meant that it could not be demonstrated that termination of the contact was necessary.[453] Similarly in *Sahin* v *Germany*[454] the German courts in failing to hear the child directly or receive an expert report recording her view on contact infringed the human rights of the father who was seeking contact. Not surprising you might think, except that the child was aged 4. In the light of these cases in *Re A (A Child) (Separate Representation in Contact Proceedings)*[455] the Court of Appeal suggested that following the Human Rights Act it may be necessary for a

---

[444] Bainham (2003: 74).
[445] He also relies on the United Nations Convention on the Rights of the Child.
[446] *Hokkanen* v *Finland* (1995) 19 EHRR 139 and *Ignaccolo-Zenide* v *Romania* (2001) 31 EHRR 7.
[447] [2000] 2 FLR 486 ECtHR.
[448] *Sahin* v *Germany* [2003] 2 FCR 619 ECtHR.
[449] *Sahin* v *Germany* [2002] 3 FCR 321 ECtHR at para 40.
[450] *Elsholz* v *Germany* [2000] 2 FLR 486 ECtHR.
[451] Bainham (2003: 72).
[452] [2000] 2 FLR 486 ECtHR.
[453] *Hoppe* v *Germany* [2003] 1 FCR 176 is an example of where the procedural requirements were met.
[454] [2002] 3 FCR 321 ECtHR.
[455] [2001] 2 FCR 55.

child to be separately represented to ensure that their views are heard by the court. Further, if a parent is to be denied contact expert reports may be required before contact is denied to ensure that the infringement of rights is justified.

In summary, the present law on contact is that the courts will consider the benefits and disadvantages of contact in each particular case. There is no presumption in favour of contact, although its benefits will readily be found in an appropriate case. In each case the courts will weigh up the benefits and disadvantages of contact. The courts have therefore not accepted the arguments of some commentators that there should be a presumption in favour of equal parenting after divorce.[456] We will now consider certain types of contact cases which have raised particular difficulties.

(iii) The opposition of the residential parent

There has in recent years been a change in approach in cases where the resident parent is strongly opposed to contact.[457] At one time opposition was thoroughly castigated. In *Re O (Contact: Imposition of Conditions)*[458] it was stated:

> The courts should not at all readily accept that the child's welfare will be injured by direct contact ... Neither parent should be encouraged or permitted to think that the more intransigent, the more unreasonable, the more obdurate and the more uncooperative they are, the more likely they are to get their own way.

As explained in *Re W (A Minor) (Contact)*,[459] the mother has no right to deny the child the benefit of contact. More recently in *Re P (Contact Discretion)*,[460] the courts have accepted that there may be very good reasons for the residential parent to oppose contact and it is now necessary to distinguish two types of cases.[461] First, where the opposition of the parent is justified: in such a case if the residential parent's fears are 'genuine and rationally held'[462] then the court may refuse contact.[463] Where the resident parent claims that there is a risk of violence to the children that would be a reasonable ground to oppose contact, unless that risk can be eliminated.[464] The resident parent may also reasonably fear that the non-resident parent will during a contact session seek to abduct the child and take him or her out of the jurisdiction.[465] Secondly, those cases where the opposition is 'emotional' and there is no rational basis for it: in such a case contact will be ordered unless it can be shown that the residential parent will suffer such distress if forced to permit contact

---

[456] Bartlett (1999).
[457] Wallbank (1998) discusses these cases.
[458] [1995] 2 FLR 124 at pp. 129–30.
[459] [1994] 2 FLR 441, [1994] 2 FCR 1216 CA.
[460] [1998] 2 FLR 696, [1999] 1 FCR 566.
[461] See also *Re D (Contact: Reasons for Refusal)* [1997] 2 FLR 48, [1998] 1 FCR 321 CA.
[462] *Re D (Contact: Reasons for Refusal)* [1997] 2 FLR 48 at p. 53.
[463] For a thorough discussion see Children Act Sub-Committee (2002) and *Re H (A Child) (Contact: Mother's Opposition)* [2001] 1 FCR 59.
[464] *Re H (Children) (Contact Order) (No. 2)* [2001] 3 FCR 385. The court may leave open the possibility of contact in the future: *Re D (A Minor) (Contact: Mother's Hostility)* [1993] 2 FLR 1, [1993] 1 FCR 964.
[465] D. Smith (2003).

that the child will be harmed.[466] In *Re H (Children) (Contact Order) (No. 2)*[467] Wall J held that the child's need to have a competent and confident primary carer outweighed their need to have direct contact with their father in a case where there was evidence that the mother might have a nervous breakdown if contact was ordered. In *Re M (Handicapped Child: Parental Responsibility)*[468] a father's contact with his severely disabled daughter was reduced on the basis that there had been ferocious arguments between the mother and father over her upbringing and it was in her welfare that she and her carers be freed from the stresses and strains of these arguments. In *Re H (Children) (Contact Order)* Hale LJ supported such an approach, explaining that research showed that having a competent and confident primary carer was a better predictor of a child's success following separation than contact.[469]

A few recent cases have focused on the father's conduct and have accepted the argument that the father, if he wishes to have contact, must behave in a more suitable way.[470] This is important because the earlier case law had concentrated on the mother and regarded her opposition as the problem, rather than considering whether it was the father's behaviour which created the difficulties.[471] Some commentators have suggested that the law is predicated on an image of a 'good' or 'bad' mother or father. A mother is automatically 'bad' if she denies contact to a father, even when she fears that the father may harm the child; whereas a father is 'good' if he seeks contact with the child, even though he may have shown disregard of the child's welfare during the parents' relationship.[472] There are concerns that the increased emphasis on encouraging contact will reinforce this message.[473]

There are also practical issues here. In *Re D (A Child) (IVF Treatment)*[474] Butler-Sloss P held that in relation to a young baby who did not know the father it would be impossible to remove the child from the mother to enable contact to take place, at least until she was aged 3. In other words the co-operation of the resident parent may be essential to the working of the contact order. This may mean that if the resident parent strongly opposes contact, then to order it may be ineffective. Some commentators take the wider point that for contact to be productive there must be trust and co-operation between the parents.[475] Contact where the parents still fear and distrust each other (whether justifiably or not) is likely to lead to the child being used as a pawn in their dispute. Research suggests that the most common reason for resident mothers refusing contact is fear that violence or sexual abuse will be carried out against them or the child.[476] Where these fears are justified, of course, contact will not be ordered. But even if they are unjustified fears some commenta-

---

[466] *Re C (Contact: Supervision)* [1996] 2 FLR 314 suggested that it may be difficult to persuade a court of this.
[467] [2001] 3 FCR 385.
[468] [2001] 3 FCR 454.
[469] [2001] 1 FCR 49, para 58.
[470] *Re M (Minors) (Contact: Violent Parent)* [1999] 2 FCR 56.
[471] Smart and Neale (1999).
[472] Boyd (1996).
[473] Rhoades (2002).
[474] [2001] 1 FCR 481 CA.
[475] Herring (2003a).
[476] Rhoades (2002); Day Sclater and Kaganas (2003).

tors argue that contact in the context of such fear is likely to be traumatic for the child, rather than beneficial.[477]

(iv) Domestic violence and contact

In recent years there has been much debate in the courts and among commentators concerning cases in which there is a dispute over contact where the parental relationship had been marked by domestic violence.[478] One study of separated parents found 56 per cent of parents interviewed reported domestic violence and 78 per cent feared it.[479] Some commentators have argued in favour of a legal presumption against contact where there has been domestic violence.[480] Those who take such an approach point to the following:

1. Children who live in an atmosphere of domestic violence suffer psychological harm,[481] even if they do not actually witness the abuse.[482]
2. There is evidence that there are statistical links between child abuse and spousal abuse.[483] Judge Wall[484] quoted research that if a man is abusing his wife there is a 40–60 per cent chance he is also abusing his child.[485]
3. There is also a fear that a father may be able to continue to dominate and exercise power over the mother through the arrangements over contact. For example, contact arrangements can be used to discover the mother's address, or to threaten or abuse her.[486] Hale LJ has expressed her concern 'that some women are being pursued and oppressed by controlling or vengeful men with the full support of the system'.[487]
4. One survey which looked at cases where contact had been ordered even though there had been domestic violence, suggested that 25 per cent of children were abused[488] as a result of the contact.[489]

The leading case on the law is *Re L (A Child) (Contact: Domestic Violence)*.[490] The Court of Appeal decided to hear four cases together so as to analyse the law in this

---

[477] Imagine what a mother with such fears will say to her child as she sends him or her off for the contact session.
[478] For the government view see Lord Chancellor's Department (2001). See also Harrison (2002) on the Australian position. She suggests that the Australian law's emphasis on encouraging contact has caused the judiciary to order contact even where there are serious concerns about the safety of children.
[479] Buchanan, Hunt, Bretherton and Bream (2001: 15).
[480] Kaye (1996); Hester and Pearson (1997); Fineman (2002). See Wallerstein and Lewis (1998: 375–7) for a general discussion of these cases.
[481] Kaye (1996); Barnett (2000); Hester, Pearson and Harwin (2000).
[482] *Re L (A Child) (Contact: Domestic Violence)* [2000] 2 FCR 404 CA. Note also the definition of harm in CA 1989, s 31(3A) including the witnessing of ill-treatment of another.
[483] Bowker, Arbitell and McFerron (1989).
[484] Wall HHJ (1997).
[485] See also Bowker, Arbitell and McFerron (1989).
[486] Hester and Radford (1996); Wall HHJ (1997: 817); Women's Aid (2003).
[487] Hale LJ (1999).
[488] A term the researchers used to include emotional harm. Ten per cent were sexually abused and 15 per cent physically abused.
[489] Radford (1999); Hester (2002) .
[490] [2000] 2 FCR 404 CA.

area.[491] It was emphasised that the fact that there had been domestic violence is not a bar to contact. However, it is one important factor in the balancing exercise. The Court of Appeal stressed that a judge should approach such cases in two stages:

1. If domestic violence is alleged, the court has to decide whether the allegations are made out or not.[492]
2. The court should weigh up the risks involved, and the impact of contact on the child, against the positive benefits (if any) of contact. Any risk of harm to the residential parent should also be considered.

Butler-Sloss P explained:

> a court hearing a contact application in which allegations of domestic violence are raised, should consider the conduct of both parties towards each other and towards the children, the effect on the children and on the residential parent and the motivation of the parent seeking contact. Is it a desire to promote the best interests of the child or a means to continue violence and/or intimidation or harassment of the other parent? In cases of serious domestic violence, the ability of the offending parent to recognise his or her past conduct, to be aware of the need for change and to make genuine efforts to do so, will be likely to be an important consideration.[493]

In particular, the court should consider the following factors when considering contact where there has been domestic violence:

1. The child might be abused during contact.
2. Contact might exacerbate the bitterness between the parents, and this would be detrimental to the child.
3. A bullying or dominating relationship between the child and contact parent might be perpetuated.
4. If the child had witnessed domestic violence between their parents then contact might reawaken old fears.[494]
5. If the child opposes contact, weight should be placed on their views.

When considering the benefits the court should recall in particular:

1. That seeing a father may be beneficial to the child's identity.
2. The 'male contribution to parenting'[495] that a father can offer.
3. The loss of opportunity to know the paternal grandparents if contact does not take place with the father.
4. The opportunity 'to mend the harm done' may be lost if contact is not ordered.

---

[491] The Court of Appeal paid particular attention to Children Act Sub-Committee (2002). See further Sturge and Glaser (2000).
[492] In cases of interim contact when it is not possible to assess the facts, special care should be taken to protect the child.
[493] *Re L (A Child) (Contact: Domestic Violence)* [2000] 2 FCR 404 CA, at p. 416. In *G (A Child) (Domestic Violence: Direct Contact)* [2001] 2 FCR 134 the father's failure to recognise the distress caused by the past violence was a powerful consideration in denying contact.
[494] This factor was relied upon when denying contact in *Re G (Domestic Violence: Direct Contact)* [2000] Fam Law 789.
[495] It is not clear exactly what this means.

However, overriding all such factors it is the welfare of the child which is the para-mount consideration and domestic violence is but one factor to be taken into account. Hence in *Re J-S (A Child) (Contact: Parental Responsibility)*[496] despite the fact that the father had thrown a shoe at the mother, forced his way into her home, had pushed a hot tea bag in her face, and hit her across the face chipping her tooth, he was permitted contact. It was explained that the child had established a strong attachment with the father and that to end contact with the father would therefore harm the child. Such cases will be opposed by those commentators who are con-cerned that too great a willingness to permit contact following serious domestic violence may endanger mothers and children.[497]

(v) Step-parents and hostility

Sometimes the courts are willing to accept the opposition of a step-parent to the contact order as reason enough for denying contact. In *Re SM (A Minor) (Natural Father: Access)*[498] the fear that contact with the natural father would destabilise the relationship between the mother and the stepfather was seen as a reason for deny-ing contact. A similar finding was made in *Re B (Contact: Stepfather's Opposition)*,[499] where the stepfather gave evidence that he would leave the mother if the father were allowed contact with the child. The Court of Appeal accepted that the stepfather was sincere[500] and noted that, had contact with the father been ordered, the con-tact would have been very limited. These cases are very controversial with some arguing that a step-parent's views should not be taken into account.

(vi) The relevance of the child's opposition

As has already been discussed, in deciding what is in the welfare of a child the court will place much weight on the child's views,[501] taking into account the age of the child, the reasons behind the child's views and the seriousness of the issues.[502] In *M v M (Defined Contact Application)*[503] a father was granted residence of his chil-dren. The eldest daughter insisted on regularly visiting her mother. Her father sought a defined contact order to limit the contact between the mother and the daughter. The court made 'no order'; the argument being that if a defined order was made, the child would be in a position deliberately to flout it. In effect, the court accepted that in relation to mature children the law can do little to encourage or discourage contact with parents and so there is usually little benefit in making

---

[496] [2002] 3 FCR 433.
[497] Hester (2002).
[498] [1996] 2 FLR 333, [1997] 2 FCR 475.
[499] [1997] 2 FLR 579, [1998] 3 FCR 289 CA.
[500] Evidence was given that his attitude was common among the Asian community.
[501] Buchanan, Hunt, Bretherton and Bream (2001: 18) suggest that children often feel that their views are not properly taken into account in contact cases.
[502] In *Re F (Minors) (Denial of Contact)* [1993] 2 FLR 677, [1993] 1 FCR 945 CA contact was not ordered because the children (aged 12 and 9) strongly opposed contact following the father's 'sex change' operation.
[503] [1998] 2 FLR 244.

contact orders.[504] For younger children courts may not be unduly perturbed by the apparent distress of children,[505] believing that the long-term benefits of contact normally outweigh short-term distress.[506] However, in *Re C (Contact: No Order for Contact)*[507] the child (aged nearly 4) was terrified of the father and this justified an order that even indirect contact be prohibited. In *Re M and B (Children) (Contact: Domestic Violence)*[508] Thorpe LJ held that it was a misdirection for the trial judge to hold that an 8-year-old was too immature to express a view on contact. Less controversially in *Re S (Contact: Children's Views)*[509] the strong views of 16-, 14- and 12-year-olds that they did not want to have contact with their father were followed by the court. The Court of Appeal wisely stated:

> They [the children] might obey, perhaps they will obey an order of the court, but with what result? What would be the quality of what is being asked of them by me to do if I order them to do it? . . . If young people are to be brought up to respect the law, then it seems to me that the law must respect them and their wishes, even to the extent of allowing them, as occasionally they do, to make mistakes.[510]

In recent years some commentators have sought to attach significance to what has been called 'parental alienation syndrome'.[511] This controversial 'syndrome' is said to lead to the resident parent turning the child against the non-resident parent. Supporters claim that appreciation of this syndrome means that if the child opposes contact the court should readily ignore his or her view and order contact. Indeed, the opposition of the child may indicate that the residential parent suffers from this syndrome and that residence should be changed. In fact most commentators argue such a syndrome does not exist.[512] Indeed evidence from Australia suggests that it is far more common for non-resident parents to seek to turn children against resident parents than vice versa. The courts, to date, have not found evidence to support the existence of the syndrome,[513] although they do recognise the importance of ensuring that the expressed views of the children are genuinely their own views.[514] Indeed the UK courts have accepted that in complex cases the child should be separately represented to ensure their views are clearly heard by the court.[515] This is in line with the approach taken by the European Court of Human Rights.[516]

---

[504] See Smart and Neale (1999: 189) for an argument that children could be said to have a right not to have contact with parents against their wishes.

[505] *Re H (Minors) (Access)* [1992] 1 FLR 148, [1992] 1 FCR 70.

[506] *Re F (Minors) (Denial of Contact)* [1993] 2 FLR 677, [1993] 1 FCR 945, where the boys did not want contact to see their transsexual father.

[507] [2000] Fam Law 699.

[508] [2001] 1 FCR 116, para 19.

[509] [2002] 1 FLR 1156.

[510] At p. 1169.

[511] Hobbs (2002a) provides a basic introduction to this alleged syndrome.

[512] Sturge and Glaser (2000); Burch (2002).

[513] *Re P (A Child) (Expert Evidence)* [2001] 1 FCR 751; *Re S (Contact: Children's Views)* [2002] 1 FLR 1156.

[514] *Re T (A Child: Contact)* [2003] 1 FCR 303, [2003] 1 FLR 531.

[515] *Re A (A Child) (Separate Representation in Contact Proceedings)* [2001] 2 FCR 55 CA.

[516] *Ignaccolo-Zenide* v *Romania* (2001) 31 EHRR 7.

In *Re C (Children: Contact)*[517] Butler-Sloss P thought that the more likely explanation for the children's objection to seeing their father was that he had left his wife and children for another woman, rather than parental alienation syndrome. Indeed, she suggested the father's obsession with his view that the mother suffered from the syndrome was blocking his appreciation of the reality. However, in *Re M (Intractable Contact Dispute)*[518] Wall J found that the mother had falsely persuaded the boys aged 14 and 10 that their father had sexually and physically abused them. Wall J made a direction under s 37 of the Children Act 1989 that the local authority investigate the children's welfare and consider whether or not to apply for a care order. This resulted in care proceedings being brought and the children being taken into care.[519]

(vii) Indirect contact

Even if direct contact is not appropriate, the court will make an order for indirect contact in all but exceptional cases.[520] In *Re L (Contact: Genuine Fear)*,[521] indirect contact was ordered even though the mother suffered a 'phobia' of the father (he had been a Hell's Angel who had stabbed his ex-wife, and her solicitor and boyfriend). Although it was felt the 'phobia'[522] meant that direct contact could not take place, this was no reason for denying indirect contact. The judge asked for professional help in ensuring the indirect contact took place because it was feared that the mother might destroy any correspondence. Only very rarely will the court not even order in direct contact. In *Re C (Contact: No Order for Contact)*[523] the child was terrified of his father and destroyed all letters sent by the father. This persuaded Connell J to make an order which prohibited indirect contact between the father and the child.

(viii) Enforcement of contact orders

There is much debate over how the court should enforce contact.[524] For example, if a mother refused to permit a father to have contact with a child, despite the existence of a contact order, should she be sent to prison? In such a case, *A v N (Committal: Refusal of Contact)*,[525] it was confirmed that, when considering imprisonment, the welfare of the child was a material consideration but was not the paramount consideration. Holman J accepted that the daughter would suffer if the mother were imprisoned but held that this was not due to the law's approach but

---

[517] [2002] 3 FCR 183, [2002] 1 FLR 1136. Hobbs (2002b) claims that the decision supports the existence of the syndrome, but this appears to be a misinterpretation (Masson (2002b)).
[518] [2003] FL 719.
[519] Although the children escaped from care and returned to the mother. Later they changed their allegiances and expressed their wish to live with their father.
[520] *Re K (Contact: Mother's Anxiety)* [1999] 2 FLR 703.
[521] [2002] 1 FLR 621.
[522] Bruce Blair QC described her fears as 'irrational', perhaps surprisingly.
[523] [2000] Fam Law 699.
[524] Smart and Neale (1997).
[525] [1997] 1 FLR 533, [1997] 2 FCR 475 CA.

that 'this little child suffers because the mother chooses to make her suffer'.[526] However, in more recent cases the courts have sought to avoid such a drastic conclusion. In *Re F (Contact: Enforcement: Representation of Child)*,[527] where the baby suffered cerebral palsy, it was held that the harm to the child if the mother was imprisoned was such that it would be inappropriate to attach a penal notice to a contact order. In *Re K (Children: Committal Proceedings)*[528] the Court of Appeal emphasised that imprisonment of the resident parent would infringe the article 8 rights of both the mother and child and therefore before committal the court should ensure that the committal is justifiable under article 8(2).[529] The Court of Appeal in *Re M (Contact Order: Committal)*[530] stated that, before committal to prison, other remedies such as further contact orders, family therapy and even changing residence should be explored. Thorpe LJ[531] has suggested that treatment rather than imprisonment is more likely to succeed in cases where contact orders are flouted.[532]

The European Court of Human Rights in *Hokkanen v Finland*[533] interpreted article 8 to mean that not only may the state prevent contact between a parent and child only where permitted to do so under paragraph 2 of article 8, but, further, that there is a positive obligation on the state to ensure that other people do not prevent contact.[534] In that case a father had been granted rights of contact, but the grandparents, who were caring for the child, refused to permit him to have access to the child. The state was found to be in breach of article 8 because it failed to provide an effective means by which the father could enforce his right of contact. However, the state is only required to take reasonable steps to enforce contact. The European Court in *Glaser v UK*[535] accepted that, at the end of the day, if the only means of enforcement were imprisonment of the residential parent or changing residence, the state may justifiably decide not to take these steps. In *Nuutinen v Finland*[536] the European Court recognised that the obligation on a state to use coercion to enable contact to take place was limited.

Commentators are divided on the issue. Here are some of the views that have been expressed on how (if at all) contact should be enforced:

1. Smart and Neale[537] have suggested: 'Questions must be asked about where family law is going, because in its current form the law is beginning to look like a lever for the powerful to use against the vulnerable, rather than a measure to safeguard the welfare of children.' They see these cases as too often involving strong fathers using the law on contact as a tool against mothers they have

---

[526] See also *F v F (Contact: Committal)* [1998] 2 FLR 237, [1999] 2 FCR 42 CA.
[527] [1998] 1 FLR 691, [1998] 3 FCR 216.
[528] [2003] 2 FCR 336.
[529] The non-resident parent's and child's rights under article 8 must also be considered.
[530] [1999] 1 FLR 810.
[531] *Re L (A Child) (Contact: Domestic Violence)* [2000] 2 FCR 404 at p. 439.
[532] The approach may be consistent with the Human Rights Act 1998: *Glaser v UK* [2000] 3 FCR 193.
[533] [1996] 1 FLR 289, [1995] 2 FCR 320.
[534] See also *Hansen v Turkey* [2003] 3 FCR 97 ECtHR.
[535] [2000] 3 FCR 193 ECtHR.
[536] App no. 32842/96, unreported 27.6.2000 ECtHR.
[537] Smart and Neale (1997: 336).

abused or terrified. Bainham has maintained that such an argument is in danger of equating the interests of children with those of their mothers.[538]

2. Some groups promoting the interests of fathers have claimed that the non-enforcement of contact orders means that they are not worth the paper they are written on. If court orders are not enforced the law is seen as powerless and unwilling to enforce people's rights.[539] Opponents of this view may argue that if contact has taken place only following threats of imprisonment or pressure from judges or professionals there will not be effective contact.[540]

3. Bainham suggests that there must be an attempt to enforce contact in order to send the message that contact is an important right of the child which the law will protect.[541] He emphasises the importance of the court order in acknowledging that there is a right of contact. Even if the court is ultimately unable to enforce the right the order should be made, and some steps taken to enforce it, so that it officially acknowledges that there should be contact in this case.

4. Eekelaar has warned: 'it is important not to jump from the fact that an outcome is optimally desirable to the conclusion that it should, therefore, be legally enforceable'.[542] It certainly seems odd to enforce an order designed to further a child's welfare in a way that harms a child. However, the law might be justified by the argument that the imprisonment of the mother in the case harms the child, but this promotes the welfare of children generally by encouraging parents to obey court orders.

5. Some commentators[543] have argued that where contact orders are ignored the solution lies not in imprisonment but the use of extra-legal facilities. In *Re H (A Child) (Contact: Mother's Opposition)*[544] the mother opposed contact. The Court of Appeal took the view that the mother's opposition was without foundation and amounted to an attempt to blackmail the court. The Court of Appeal sought the assistance of a psychiatrist who was to assist the family and advise on how contact could be progressed. This indicates a recognition that some cases of this kind involve emotional and psychological difficulties more suitable for the help of a counsellor or psychiatrist than a judge or a lawyer.

6. Many commentators take the view that there is little the law can do in these cases.[545] We have to acknowledge that family law cannot always provide an answer. A recent study[546] found that couples who rely on the law to resolve their contact disputes risk making matters worse for everyone concerned. By contrast those parents who resolve matters without recourse to the law avoid stress and distress. The researchers argued that in dealing with contentious contact cases it would be more profitable to spend time and money on services to improve the

---

[538] Bainham (1998b: 7).
[539] Jolly (1995: 234).
[540] Herring (2003a).
[541] Bainham (2003). See also Jolly (1995); Willbourne and Stanley (2002: 688).
[542] Eekelaar (2002b: 272).
[543] E.g. Masson (2000b); Buchanan and Hunt (2003).
[544] [2001] 1 FCR 59.
[545] Trinder, Beek and Connolly (2002) emphasise the harm children can suffer due to stress and dispute over contact.
[546] Trinder, Beek and Connolly (2002).

relations between the parents and children, rather than on lawyers and the legal process.

7. Several commentators[547] have noted the contrast in treatment of resident and non-resident parents. If the resident parent deprives the child of the benefit of contact he or she risks imprisonment. However, if the non-resident parent does not want contact with the child (equally depriving the child of the benefit of contact) he or she will not face any legal sanction.

The government has considered the enforcement of contact orders. *Making Contact Work*[548] emphasises the government's keenness to increase the level of contact between children and non-resident parents after family breakdown, but that at the same time contact must be positive and safe for all involved. *Making Contact Work* does not propose one solution to the problem. However, it advocates the use of non-legal methods of encouraging contact, including the use of counselling services, mediation,[549] parenting programmes[550] and contact centres.

(ix) Contact centres

There has been increased interest in and use of contact centres.[551] These provide a neutral venue in which contact can take place. Although not designed to deal with potentially violent cases, they are often used by courts and solicitors in cases where the resident parent has concerns over his or her own or his or her child's safety.[552] The contact can be supervised by a social worker or untrained volunteer, who can make sure that there is no abuse of the child. Also it would be possible for the arrangements to be such that the resident parent and contact parent do not meet.

Not everyone is convinced that the use of contact centres is the solution to the intractable problem of contact. Key to the success of such studies is that they create a safe and pleasant atmosphere for contact. One study suggested that (predictably) resident parents feel that the supervision at such centres is inadequate, while non-resident parents feel that the supervision is unnecessarily invasive and humiliating.[553] The study went on to note that in a significant minority of centres the well-being of women and children was being compromised due to a lack of staff and expertise, leading to inadequate supervision.[554] Indeed, it should be appreciated that in the UK many contact centres are run in community buildings such as church halls.[555] It should also be recalled that very young children might require the resident parent to remain in sight during the contact session.[556]

---

[547] E.g. Smart and Neale (1997).
[548] Lord Chancellor's Department (2002d), a response to Children Act Sub-Committee (2002a).
[549] Kaganas and Piper (1994) take the view that mediation is not appropriate where there has been domestic violence. This view is taken by many mediators too.
[550] See Rhoades (2003) for the negative Australian experience of these.
[551] Lord Chancellor's Department (2002); Humphreys and Harrison (2003).
[552] Humphreys and Harrison (2003).
[553] Aris, Harrison and Humphreys (2002).
[554] There is grave concern over decisions like *Re P (Parental Responsibility)* [1998] 2 FLR 96 where a paedophilic father who had been 'grooming a child' was allowed contact at a contact centre.
[555] Maclean and Mueller-Johnson (2003).
[556] Aris, Harrison and Humphreys (2002) found this to be so in a significant minority of cases.

(x) Linking contact and residence

The court might take the parents' attitudes to contact into account when deciding to whom to grant a residence order, and this can be an important consideration.[557] If, for example, the mother is bitterly opposed to contact and the father is happy to allow contact, that will be a factor in favour of awarding residence to the father. Richards has even suggested it should be the most important factor.[558] Some supporters of 'parental alienation syndrome'[559] have argued that if a child is manipulated in this way by the residential parent, the residence should be changed.

(xi) Other relatives

Step-parents[560] and grandparents[561] can apply for contact, but there is not the same assumption of the benefits of contact that exists in relation to parents.[562] Step-parents and grandparents must persuade the court that they have a close relationship with the child and that the child will benefit from continued contact. In *Re W (Contact: Application by Grandparent)*[563] Hollis J accepted that it can be extremely beneficial for a child to have contact with her grandparents, even if that contact is opposed by the parents. However, some campaigners claim that other judges too readily deny contact to grandparents, especially if that is opposed by the child's parents.[564]

(xii) Duties of contact

Although there has been much discussion of the rights of contact, there has been less about the duties of contact. Yet as Bainham has pointed out: 'to talk of contact as a *right* of anyone is devoid of meaning unless considered alongside the *obligations* which go with that right'.[565]

Bainham argues that if we acknowledge that children have a right of contact then parents have a duty to exercise it. This is controversial because it suggests that a parent who does not want to have contact with his or her child could be required by a court order (on pain of imprisonment) to have contact. Bainham accepts that such a duty may be unenforceable, but this does not mean that the duty should not be recognised as a way of underlining the fact that society values relationships between parents and children. Thorpe LJ in *Re L (A Child) (Contact: Domestic Violence)* suggested that such an order cannot be made: 'The errant or selfish parent cannot be ordered to spend time with his child against his will however much the child may yearn for his company and the mother desire respite.'[566]

---

[557] *Re A (Minors) (Custody)* [1991] 2 FLR 394 at p. 400.
[558] M. Richards (1989).
[559] Maidment (1998).
[560] *Re H (A Minor) (Contact)* [1994] 2 FLR 776, [1994] FCR 419 CA.
[561] *Re A (Section 8 Order: Grandparent Application)* [1995] 2 FLR 153, [1996] 1 FCR 467 CA.
[562] For a useful discussion of grandparents and contact see Kaganas and Piper (2001).
[563] [2001] 1 FLR 263.
[564] Drew and Smith (1999).
[565] Bainham (2003: 61).
[566] [2000] 4 All ER 609 at p. 637e–f.

Bainham[567] also controversially suggests that if a parent has a right of contact with a child then the child can be said to be under a duty to permit that contact. Without such a duty the parent's right is not meaningful. Again he accepts there may be difficulties in enforcing children to see parents they do not want to see, but he suggests attempts should be made to do so.

(xiii) Encouraging contact

The problem of the lack of contact between children and non-resident parents is only partly due to non-resident parents wanting, but not being able to have, contact. A far more common cause of the lack of contact is that non-resident parents do not seek contact with children. It is notable that those who seek to emphasise the right of the child to contact use this right as a means of forcing resident parents (normally mothers) to have contact with the non-resident parents (normally fathers) but arguably more could be done by those wishing to promote the child's rights to contact if those fathers who do not have contact with their children were encouraged to do so.[568] The reality is that after separation many non-resident fathers find their relationship with their children strained.[569] Further, it is often difficult to fit in contact sessions with the work life of the non-resident parent and the social life of the child.[570]

(xiv) The role of solicitors in contact disputes

There is evidence that family law solicitors,[571] mediators[572] and district judges[573] are keen to promote contact and will strongly discourage opposition to contact. This creates a culture where contact is seen as the norm. It may be that the attitudes of these professionals is in practical terms more important than the views of the Court of Appeal.[574]

(xv) Contact in practice

The statistics suggest that contact arrangements often break down. Eekelaar and Clive[575] found that although two-thirds of non-residential parents had contact in the first six months, by five years after the divorce only one-third did. However, other studies have shown higher rates of contact. Eekelaar and Maclean in their study found contact rates of 69 per cent where the parents had been married, but 45 per cent where unmarried.[576] In the survey by Bradshaw et al.[577] only 21 per cent

---

[567] Bainham (2003).
[568] See Herring (2003a) for a discussion of how the law might do this.
[569] Bradshaw, Stimson, Skinner and Williams (1999).
[570] Buchanan, Hunt, Bretheron and Bream (2001: 18); Buchanan and Hunt (2003).
[571] Neale and Smart (1997).
[572] Piper (1993: 118).
[573] Bailey-Harris, Davis, Barron and Pearce (1998).
[574] Eekelaar, Maclean and Beinart (2000).
[575] Eekelaar and Clive (1977).
[576] Eekelaar and Maclean (1997).
[577] Bradshaw, Stimson, Skinner and Williams (1999).

of the sample had not seen their children in the last year. In their survey, Trinder et al.[578] found that for only 27 of the 61 families were contact arrangements 'working'. However, all the studies show a decline in the rate of contact as the years since parental separation pass. This drop-off has been explained on three grounds. The first is that some fathers may (falsely) believe they do not have to pay (or can escape payment) of child support if they do not see the child; secondly, some find occasional contact painful;[579] thirdly, some fathers believe that the child will settle down better if contact is stopped. Another important factor is that the father may remarry or repartner[580] and his new partner may discourage contact, especially once the new couple have children of their own. Long-term contact works best where both the resident and non-resident parent are committed to making contact succeed and are willing to work through the practical difficulties.[581]

As already mentioned contact disputes are often the most bitter cases. Many believe that too often fathers are denied contact: the courts refuse to order contact and where they do the orders are not enforced. Others claim that the courts too readily order contact, placing mothers and children in danger. In fact the evidence is that where contact is applied for it is nearly always granted. In only 1.3 per cent of cases in 2001 was contact refused.[582] Indeed most contact disputes are resolved through negotiations.[583]

7. WARDSHIP AND THE INHERENT JURISDICTION

The inherent jurisdiction provides the court with powers which do not originate from statute but from the common law. The jurisdiction flows from the ancient *parens patriae* jurisdiction which the Crown owes to those subjects who are unable to protect themselves. The classic example of such subjects are children. The basis of the jurisdiction is that if a child needs protection the courts should not be inhibited from acting merely because of 'technical' difficulties. It is readily understandable that children should not be left without the protection of the law. However, there is concern that use of the inherent jurisdiction bypasses the protection of the rights of children and adults in statutes. It is notable that, following the Children Act 1989, there is a limited role for the inherent jurisdiction.

There are two main aspects of the *parens patriae* jurisdiction that are relevant today: wardship and the inherent jurisdiction.[584] In the case of wardship the child is placed under the care of the court. This means that any important decision in respect of a child must be made by the court. The inherent jurisdiction does not have that effect. The inherent jurisdiction is used to resolve one-off decisions concerning children.

---

[578] Trinder, Beek and Connolly (2002).
[579] Trinder, Beek and Connolly (2002) found that children experienced difficulty in establishing a meaningful relationship with the non-resident parent.
[580] Eekelaar and Maclean (1997) found that sometimes repartnering encouraged contact and sometimes discouraged it.
[581] Trinder, Beek and Connolly (2002).
[582] Humphreys and Harrison (2003).
[583] Humphreys and Harrison (2003).
[584] Bainham (1998a: 405).

For example, if a child needs an urgent operation and the approval of the court is sought, the inherent jurisdiction may be relied upon.

A. Wardship

The effect of wardship is that the legal control of a child's person and property is vested in the court. The court not only takes on the parents' powers, but also further powers. Lord Donaldson MR explained:

> the practical jurisdiction of the court is wider than that of parents. The court can, for example, forbid the publication of information about the ward or the ward's family circumstances. It is also clear that this jurisdiction is not derivative from the parents' rights and responsibilities, but derives from, or is, the delegated performance of the duties of the Crown to protect its subjects.[585]

(i) Who can be warded?[586]

Only minors, that is children under the age of 18, can be warded.[587] A foetus cannot be warded,[588] nor can a child in care.[589] The child must be habitually resident in the UK.[590]

(ii) Initiating wardship

Under s 41(2) of the Supreme Court Act 1981 the moment an application for wardship is made the child becomes a ward of court.[591] This means that wardship offers immediate and effective protection of children. On the other hand, it is also open to potential misuse. Simply by means of lodging an application, the primary responsibility for a child can be taken away from parents. A parent intending to take a child on holiday may be stopped at the airport simply because someone has applied for wardship. Any person who has a proper interest may apply to make a child a ward.[592] In one case a child's psychologist applied to have a child made a ward of court because she opposed the proposals of the parents and doctors to sterilise the child.[593] A child can even ward him- or herself by making a wardship application through a next friend.[594] If necessary, the High Court can make a child a ward on its own motion, without anyone applying for wardship.[595]

---

[585] *Re R (A Minor) (Wardship: Consent to Medical Treatment)* [1992] Fam 11 at p. 24.
[586] For a fuller discussion of who can be warded, see Lowe (1988).
[587] *Re F* [1990] 2 AC 1, [1989] 2 FLR 376 made it clear that a mentally incompetent adult cannot be warded.
[588] *Re F (In Utero)* [1988] Fam 122, [1988] FCR 529 CA.
[589] CA 1989, s 100(2)(b).
[590] *Al Habtoor v Fotheringham* [2001] FL 352.
[591] I.e. as soon as an originating summons is lodged.
[592] *Re T (A Minor) (Wardship: Responsibility)* [1994] Fam 49, [1993] 2 FCR 445, [1993] 2 FLR 278.
[593] *Re D (A Minor) (Wardship: Sterilisation)* [1976] Fam 185.
[594] Rules of Supreme Court, Order 80, r 2.
[595] *R v N Yorkshire CC, ex p M (No. 3)* [1989] 2 FLR 82, [1989] FCR 403.

As a result of s 100 of the Children Act 1989, local authorities can no longer apply for wardship. Prior to the Children Act 1989, wardship was often relied upon by local authorities, but that is no longer an option. The local authority must now use the protective powers under the Children Act 1989 to care for the child.

A child does not cease to be a ward of court until there is an order specifically ending the wardship or when the child reaches his or her majority. The European Court of Human Rights has suggested that it may be 'inappropriate' for a child to become a ward without a contested hearing.[596] It did not state which article would be breached, but presumably articles 6 and 8.

(iii) The effect of wardship

Once the child is a ward of court, 'no important step in the child's life can be taken without the court's consent'.[597] If the court's consent is not obtained, imprisonment or a fine may be imposed.[598] The difficulty is that it is unclear what would be regarded as an 'important step'. It seems that marriage;[599] removing a child from the jurisdiction;[600] or consenting to adoption of a child[601] would require the court's permission, although other situations will depend on the facts of the case.

(iv) When is wardship appropriate?

In deciding whether a child should be made a ward of court, the child's welfare will be the paramount consideration.[602] There are two particular situations in which wardship is *not* appropriate:

1. The Court of Appeal decisions in *Re T (A Minor) (Wardship: Responsibility)*[603] and *Re W (Wardship: Discharge: Publicity)*[604] make it clear that wardship should not be used unless it has advantages that cannot be obtained by making an order under s 8 of the Children Act 1989. If there is a single issue that concerns someone – for example that the parent is refusing to consent to a medical procedure recommended by the doctors, or if the child is being taken abroad – then a prohibited steps order or an order under the inherent jurisdiction would be appropriate. It is only where there is a fear about the child's general welfare that wardship may be appropriate. It is likely that in many cases a care order would be the most suitable route.
2. Wardship cannot be used to overrule the exercise of a discretion by a local authority: *A v Liverpool CC*.[605] This case has given rise to the '*Liverpool* principle',

---

[596] *B v UK* [2000] 1 FLR 1.
[597] Cross J in *Re S (Infants)* [1967] 1 All ER 202 at p. 209.
[598] *F v S (Adoption: Ward)* [1993] Fam 203.
[599] Marriage Act 1949, s 3(6).
[600] Family Law Act 1986, s 38.
[601] *F v S (Adoption: Ward)* [1973] Fam 203. An interview with the BBC is not an important step: *Kelly v BBC* [2001] 1 FCR 197.
[602] *Re M and N (Minors) (Wardship: Publication of Information)* [1990] Fam 211, [1990] FCR 395, [1990] 1 FLR 149 CA.
[603] [1994] Fam 49, [1993] 2 FCR 445, [1993] 2 FLR 278 CA.
[604] [1995] 2 FLR 466, [1996] 1 FCR 393 CA.
[605] [1982] AC 363, [1982] 2 FLR 222 HL.

namely that the courts should generally not intervene via wardship in matters where statute has given the local authority the discretion to decide what should happen to a child.

The following are examples of cases where wardship has proved useful:

1. Wardship might be appropriate where the parents refuse to consent to medical treatment and it is necessary to take long-term decisions about the child.[606] In *Re C (A Baby)*[607] a child was abandoned and there was no one with parental responsibility for the child who could be found. Sir Stephen Brown suggested that wardship was useful, especially as the child was severely ill, having developed brain damage after meningitis.
2. Wardship might also be useful if third parties such as the press are intruding on the child's life. A prohibited steps order or specific issue order cannot be obtained against someone who is not exercising an aspect of parental responsibility. Wardship would be able to protect the child as the court has the power under wardship to prevent publicity relating to children.
3. In *Re W (Wardship: Discharge: Publicity)*[608] a father had care and control of four sons. He permitted the children to talk to the press, which led to the publication of various articles. The father also changed the children's schooling without consulting the mother. The Court of Appeal saw the need for wardship because a specific issue order could not be made which was wide enough – it was not possible to predict how the father might act in the future. It was also thought beneficial that the Official Solicitor could remain involved in the case and act as a buffer between the parents.
4. In *Re KR (Abduction: Forcible Removal by Parents)*[609] wardship was used to protect a child whom, it was feared, was about to be removed from the jurisdiction to be forced to enter an arranged marriage.

B. The inherent jurisdiction

(i) The effect of the inherent jurisdiction

The exercise of the inherent jurisdiction is quite different from wardship. The order will simply resolve a single issue relating to the child and have no wider effect. It does not provide ongoing supervision by the court of the child's welfare. The Court of Appeal has stated that its powers under the inherent jurisdiction are unlimited.[610] Specifically, it is accepted that the court, acting under the inherent jurisdiction, has wider powers than a parent.[611]

---

[606] Eekelaar and Dingwall (1990).
[607] [1996] 2 FLR 43, [1996] 2 FCR 569.
[608] [1995] 2 FLR 466, [1996] 1 FCR 393 CA.
[609] [1999] 2 FLR 542.
[610] *Re W (A Minor) (Medical Treatment: Court's Jurisdiction)* [1993] Fam 64, [1992] 2 FCR 785, [1993] 1 FLR 1.
[611] *Re R (A Minor) (Wardship: Consent to Medical Treatment)* [1992] Fam 11 at p. 25.

(ii) The court's powers

The court can use the inherent jurisdiction on its own motion, even if no one else has applied for an order. The court will prefer to use the s 8 orders but these may not be available (either because what is sought is outside the scope of s 8 orders or because the child is already in care), in which case the inherent jurisdiction may be used. If necessary, under the inherent jurisdiction, the court has the power to authorise the use of force to restrain a young person.[612]

(iii) Restrictions on the use of the inherent jurisdiction

Although in theory the powers of the court are unlimited,[613] there are in practice a number of situations where the court will not utilise the inherent jurisdiction:

1. Under s 100(2) of the Children Act 1989 the inherent jurisdiction may not be used:

    (i) to place a child in care; or
    (ii) to place a child under the supervision of a local authority; or
    (iii) to place or accommodate the child by a local authority.

   Section 100(2)(d) also prevents the inherent jurisdiction being used: 'for the purpose of conferring on any local authority power to determine any question which has a risen, or which may arise, in connection with any aspect of parental responsibility for the child'.
      The thinking behind these provisions is that the powers and responsibilities of the local authority are set out in the Children Act 1989 and should not be added to by using the inherent jurisdiction. These provisions do not prevent a local authority asking a court to exercise the inherent jurisdiction, as long as it is not seeking to gain any extra powers.[614]

2. The inherent jurisdiction can be used only to protect the child and not to protect the parent.[615]

3. The inherent jurisdiction should be used only if there is no statutory power available which can protect the children. In *Re R (A Minor) (Blood Transfusion)*,[616] which involved a child who needed a blood transfusion, the court suggested that the inherent jurisdiction was not appropriate because a suitable order under s 8 of the Children Act 1989 could be made. Similarly, the inherent jurisdiction cannot be used to make what is in effect an occupation or non-molestation order.[617]

4. The inherent jurisdiction cannot be used in contravention of a statute. That said, the court may interpret any potential infringement of a statute in any way

---

[612] *Re C (Detention: Medical Treatment)* [1997] 2 FLR 180, [1997] 3 FCR 49.
[613] *Re Z (A Minor) (Identity: Restrictions on Publication)* [1997] Fam 1 at p. 23.
[614] The local authority must first obtain the leave of the court.
[615] *Re V (A Minor) (Wardship)* (1979) 123 SJ 201.
[616] [1993] 2 FLR 757, [1993] 2 FCR 544.
[617] But see *Re S (Minors) (Inherent Jurisdiction: Ouster)* [1994] 1 FLR 623 and *C v K (Inherent Powers: Exclusion Order)* [1996] 2 FLR 506, [1996] 3 FCR 488, which could be seen as cases where this principle was not followed.

that does not limit the court's powers.[618] In *R* v *R (Private Law Proceedings: Residential Assessment)*[619] Holman J held that the fact that the Children Act 1989 did not provide for a judge to order a residential assessment in a private law case was a deliberate omission and that it would be improper to use the inherent jurisdiction to enable him to do so.

5. It will be rare for the court to use the inherent jurisdiction to restrict the actions of non-parents. In *X County Council* v *A*[620] the press were restrained from revealing the identity or whereabouts of the daughter of Mary Bell (a notorious woman who had been convicted of manslaughter).[621] In *Nottingham CC* v *October Films Ltd*[622] the local authority asked the court to make an order under the inherent jurisdiction to prevent a 'fly on the wall documentary' on children in care and at risk. But these were exceptional cases and generally a court cannot compel a local authority to treat the child in a particular way,[623] nor the immigration service,[624] nor a doctor.[625]

8. CHILD ABDUCTION

There is a special set of rules that deals with child abduction: that is, where a child is removed from the care of the residential parent, often to another jurisdiction. This area of law is complex, and what follows is an outline of the legal position.

A. General

The popular image of child abduction is the harrowing one of a father, having lost his battles in the court, who steals his child from their school and removes the child to another country: the distraught mother despairs of seeing her child again. While there are cases such as this, in fact the majority of child abductions are carried out by women. It has been suggested that many women are removing themselves and their children to other countries to escape from their partner's abuse and violence.[626]

As one would expect, there is clear evidence that abducted children suffer distress. However, this is one of those areas of the law where there is a difference between the interests of the child in the case and the interests of children generally. If a child is abducted and lives with his or her abducting parent for several years before they are finally traced, it may be in the child's interests to stay with the abducting parent with whom they may have settled into a new way of life. On the

---

[618] The inherent jurisdiction could be used to fill in the gaps within legislation: *Re J (Freeing for Adoption)* [2000] 2 FLR 58.
[619] [2002] 2 FLR 953.
[620] [1985] 1 All ER 53.
[621] See also *R* v *Central Independent Television plc* [1994] Fam 192 CA; *Re Z (A Minor) (Identity: Restrictions on Publication)* [1997] Fam 1, [1996] 2 FCR 164, [1996] 1 FLR 191.
[622] [1999] 2 FLR 347.
[623] *A* v *Liverpool CC* [1982] AC 363, [1982] 2 FLR 222 HL.
[624] *Re A (Minor) (Wardship: Immigration)* [1992] 1 FLR 427 CA.
[625] *Re C (Medical Treatment)* [1998] 1 FLR 384, [1998] 1 FCR 1.
[626] Lowe and Perry (1998) show that 70 per cent of abductions are by mothers and a high proportion of those may be mothers escaping violence.

other hand, to make such an order may send the wrong message, suggesting that parents who abduct children and keep them hidden for long enough will be permitted to keep the children.[627] Such a message may harm the interests of children generally.

It is partly a sign of the growth of international travel and cross-national relationships that international child abduction has become a growing problem. In 1986 there were 16 reported abductions under the Hague Convention in the UK; by 1997 the figure had grown to 200.[628] No doubt the number of actual abductions is much higher than this. It must not, of course, be assumed that once the child is returned the difficulties for the resident parent are over. Fear of repeat abduction and harassment of the family may continue for some time.[629]

In a united effort to combat the problem of child abduction two international conventions have been produced which aim to facilitate the location and return of abducted children.[630] The UK has signed both the Hague Convention[631] and the European Convention[632] which are effected by the Child Abduction and Custody Act 1985.[633] There seems widespread agreement that the Hague Convention works well. This is not to say that there are not enormous problems in recovering abducted children, but the Hague Convention provides as effective a legal response as might reasonably be expected. In England and Wales the returns are completed within six and a half weeks on average (in outgoing cases the average is eleven and a half weeks).

Before considering the Conventions, this section will look at attempts to prevent children being taken from the country. First, there are the criminal offences created by the Child Abduction Act 1984.

B. Child Abduction Act 1984

The Child Abduction Act 1984 states that it is an offence for a person unconnected with a child to remove or keep a child under 16 from a person who has lawful control of the child.[634] Of perhaps greater significance for the purposes of this topic is that it is an offence for a person connected with a child to remove a child under 16 from the UK,[635] without the consent[636] of everyone with parental responsibility,

---

[627] For explicit recognition of this argument see Wilson J in *Re L (Abduction: Pending Criminal Proceedings)* [1999] 1 FLR 433 at p. 442.

[628] Lowe and Douglas (1998: 479).

[629] Marilyn Freeman (2003).

[630] Required by the United Nations Convention on the Rights of the Child 1989, articles 11, 13.

[631] The full title is the Hague Convention on Civil Aspects of International Child Abduction 1980 (1981 Cmnd 8281).

[632] The European Convention on the Recognition and Enforcement of Decisions Concerning Custody of Children and Restoration of Custody of Children 1980 (Luxembourg Convention) (1981 Cmnd 8155).

[633] Although see Armstrong (2002) for an argument that the 1985 Act has failed to implement effectively the 1980 Hague Convention.

[634] Child Abduction Act 1984, s 2.

[635] England, Wales, Scotland and Northern Ireland. The Channel Islands and Isle of Man are not included.

[636] Written or oral.

unless the leave of the court has been granted.[637] So, even if the parents are happily married, it could be an offence for a husband to take the children out of the country without the consent of the mother.[638] However, it is not an offence for a mother of a child to take the child out of the UK without the consent of a father without parental responsibility. There is one exception and that is where a parent has a residence order, in which case he or she can remove the child for a period of up to one month without the consent of others with parental responsibility, unless there is a prohibited steps order in effect to prevent it.

There is no offence if one of the defences under s 1(5) is proved. These are that the removal was done:

(a) ... in the belief that the other person—
    (i) has consented; or
    (ii) would consent if he was aware of all the relevant circumstances; or
(b) he has taken all reasonable steps to communicate with the other person but has been unable to communicate with him; or
(c) the other person has unreasonably refused to consent.

There are other offences which could be relied upon in a child abduction case, most notably kidnapping and false imprisonment.[639]

C. Prevention of abduction and court orders preventing removal

Once a child has been removed to a foreign country, locating the child and obtaining effective court orders for the return of the child is extremely difficult. It is therefore far better, if possible, to prevent removal from the UK. Although the Child Abduction Act makes it clear that removal of a child can be a criminal offence, there is much to be said for applying for a court order specifically prohibiting the removal if there is a fear that the child is about to be removed. Having the court order will help in obtaining the assistance of the police and public authorities in preventing a removal.[640] For example, it will assist in utilising the 'port alert' facility, which will be discussed shortly. There are two main kinds of order that may be appropriate:

1. *Prohibited steps orders.* A prohibited steps order under s 8 of the Children Act 1989 can prohibit a parent from removing a child from the jurisdiction.[641] If there is any doubt in the mind of the would-be abductor that he or she might be permitted to take the child abroad, a court order will make it clear that they are not.

---

[637] There are a number of limited defences in s 1(5).
[638] Although there is a defence if the father believes that the mother consents even though she does not in fact (Child Abduction Act 1984, s 1(5)).
[639] E.g. *R v D* [1984] AC 778; *R v Rahman* (1985) 81 CAR 349; *R v C (Kidnapping: Abduction)* [1991] 2 FLR 252.
[640] The obtaining of the court order can assist in acquiring the help of government agencies (such as the Office for National Statistics or National Health Service) to locate the child or the abductor: *Practice Direction (Disclosure of Addresses)* [1989] 1 All ER 765 and *Practice Direction* [1995] 2 FLR 813. The court can order the Child Support Agency to disclose information: *Re C (A Minor) (Child Support Agency: Disclosure)* [1995] 1 FLR 201.
[641] *Re D (A Minor) (Child: Removal From Jurisdiction)* [1992] 1 FLR 637.

2. *Wardship*. If the child is made a ward of court then there is an automatic ban on taking the child out of the country. The bar operates as soon as the application for wardship is received by the court, and so is the swiftest way of obtaining the desired protection. To remove a warded child would be a contempt of court, even if the abductor were unaware of the wardship.[642]

If there are concerns that a child may be abducted, a court may be persuaded to make additional orders that can assist in preventing the child's removal. For example, the High Court can require a person who has information concerning an abducted child to reveal it to the court.[643] The court can also order the return of a child's passport[644] or that a passport not be issued for a child.[645]

(i) All ports warning system[646]

The police national computer can warn all airports and ports throughout the country of a suspected abduction. The warning includes descriptions of the individuals concerned; how it is feared they may try to leave the country; and a statement of the likely ports of exit. The police organise this facility[647] and must be persuaded that the complaint is bona fide and that the danger of removal is real and imminent (i.e. within the next 24 to 48 hours). The existence of a court order is clear evidence to the police of the gravity of the issue. Of course, although the system is effective, it is by no means foolproof. The police will have the right to arrest anyone they believe to be taking a child out of the country contrary to the Child Abduction Act 1984.[648]

D. Recovery in the UK

If the child is removed from one part of the UK to another then the situation is dealt with by the Family Law Act 1986.[649] Under Part 1 of the Family Law Act 1986 an order made by a court in one part of the UK is recognised and enforceable in any other part of the UK.[650] For example, if a father was granted the benefit of a contact order by a Scottish court and the child was removed to England, the father could register the Scottish court order in the local English court and then apply to have the order enforced. Once the order is registered it can be enforced as if the order had been made in that court. The only objection to registration that can be raised is that the court which made the original order had no jurisdiction to do so,

---

[642] *Re J (An Infant)* (1913) 108 LT 554.

[643] Family Law Act 1986, s 33. This includes a solicitor: *Re B (Abduction: Disclosure)* [1995] 1 FLR 774. See also *Practice Direction* [1980] 2 All ER 806.

[644] Family Law Act 1986, s 37. This can include surrender of a foreign national's passport: *Re A-K (Foreign Passport)* [1997] 2 FLR 569.

[645] Passport Agency (1994).

[646] Home Office Circular No. 21/1986.

[647] *Practice Direction (Child: Removal from Jurisdiction)* [1986] 1 All ER 983.

[648] *R v Griffin* [1993] Crim LR 515.

[649] The Act is not to be used where the dispute is between England and another country which is not part of the UK (*Re S (A Child: Abduction)* [2003] FL 298).

[650] Section 25. For an excellent critique of the Act see Lowe (2002).

or that in the light of subsequent events the local court is persuaded that it should reconsider the original order.[651]

E. The Hague Convention

The Hague Convention on the Civil Aspects of International Child Abduction is a remarkably successful example of international legal co-operation. The concern over the harm that child abduction can cause has led to over 50 countries signing the Convention. The principle at the heart of the Hague Convention is that disputes over children should be resolved in the child's country of habitual residence. For example, if a child is removed from Australia and brought to Britain, there is a presumption that the dispute should be resolved in Australia. The Hague Convention is also useful in non-abduction cases, where for example a parent living in Britain has a right of contact with a child living abroad but is being prevented from seeing that child.[652]

(i) Who can invoke the Convention?

Article 8 of the Hague Convention provides that 'any person, institution or other body claiming that a child has been removed or retained in breach of custody rights' can invoke the Convention. So anyone can claim that the child has been wrongfully removed or retained, even the child him- or herself. However, the applicant must have some interest in the matter.

(ii) To whom does the Convention apply?

Article 4 explains that the Convention applies to any child under the age of 16[653] who is habitually resident in one contracting state but has been wrongfully removed to or retained in another contracting state.[654] These terms need some clarification.

(a) Habitual residence[655]
The key question is where the habitual residence of the child is immediately before the wrongful removal.[656] Normally children will take on the residence of their parents,[657] but if the parents agree that a child should live elsewhere, this may change a child's residence. If parents separate then the child's residence normally follows

---

[651] *Re M (Minors) (Custody: Jurisdiction)* [1992] 2 FLR 382 at pp. 386–7.

[652] Lowe (1994).

[653] The Convention does not apply to over 16-year-olds: *Re H (Abduction: Child of 16)* [2000] 2 FLR 51, although the inherent jurisdiction could be invoked for over 16-year-olds who have been abducted.

[654] See *Al Habtoor v Fotheringham* [2001] FL 352 for an unsuccessful attempt to use wardship in relation to a child who was no longer habitually resident in the UK.

[655] For a fuller discussion of habitual residence, see Stone (1992).

[656] *Re S (A Minor) (Abduction)* [1991] 2 FLR 1 CA. For a case where a new-born child was found to have no country of habitual residence see *W and B v H (Child Abduction: Surrogacy)* [2002] FL 345.

[657] It seems that older children may be able to form the necessary intention to establish a residence apart from their parents. This was suggested obiter in *B v H (Children) (Habitual Residence)* [2002] 2 FCR 329.

that of the primary carer.[658] A wrongful removal cannot change a child's habitual residence.[659] To change habitual residence it is necessary to show a settled purpose to stay in the new country.[660]

These tests can be difficult to apply where a family is in the course of moving from one country to another. Balcombe LJ in *Re M (Minors) (Residence Order: Jurisdiction)*[661] usefully explained:

> There is a significant difference between a person ceasing to be habitually resident in country A, and his subsequently becoming habitually resident in country B. A person may cease to be habitually resident in country A in a single day if he or she leaves it with a settled intention not to return to it but to take up long-term residence in country B instead. Such a person cannot, however, become habitually resident in country B in a single day. An appreciable period of time and a settled intention will be necessary to enable him or her to become so. During the appreciable period of time the person will have ceased to be habitually resident in country A but not yet have become habitually resident in country B.[662]

(b) 'Wrongful' removal or retention

In order to use the Convention it is necessary to find the taking or retention to be wrongful, within the meaning of article 3. The removal or retention is wrongful if the act is contrary to the rights of custody under the law of the contracting state in which the child is habitually resident.[663] Article 5(a) explains that: ' "rights of custody" includes rights relating to the care of the person of the child, and, in particular, the right to determine the child's place of residence'. Clearly the removal will be wrongful if it is contrary to an express court order[664] or contrary to the general law of the relevant state,[665] although the Court of Appeal in *Re V-B (Abduction: Custody Rights)*[666] stated that a right to be consulted before removing a child, but not to veto the removal, did not amount to custody rights. The removal is wrongful even if the taker was ignorant of the wrongfulness.[667]

The majority of the Court of Appeal in *Re B (Minors) (Abduction)*[668] and Cazalet J in *Re O (Abduction: Custody Rights)*[669] gave a wider meaning to rights of custody and accepted that rights of custody could include factual day-to-day care of the

---

[658] But not always. See e.g. *Re M (Minors) (Residence Order: Jurisdiction)* [1993] 1 FLR 495, [1993] 1 FCR 718.

[659] *Re R (Wardship: Abduction) (No. 2)* [1993] 1 FLR 249. See also *N v N (Child Abduction: Habitual Residence)* [2000] 3 FCR 84.

[660] *Re B (Minors) (Abduction) (No. 2)* [1993] 1 FLR 993 at p. 995.

[661] [1993] 1 FLR 495, [1993] 1 FCR 718 CA.

[662] See also *Re F (A Minor) (Child Abduction)* [1992] 1 FLR 548 CA, which accepted that a family had acquired a new habitual residence within a month of arriving in a new country.

[663] It is necessary to show that the rights of custody were actually exercised or would have been exercised but for the removal or retention.

[664] *Re C (A Minor) (Abduction)* [1989] 1 FLR 403 CA.

[665] *C v C (Minors) (Child Abduction)* [1992] 1 FLR 163.

[666] [1999] 2 FLR 192. See also the discussion in *Re S (Minors) (Abduction: Wrongful Retention)* [1994] Fam 530.

[667] *C v C (Minors) (Child Abduction)* [1992] 1 FLR 163.

[668] [1993] 1 FLR 988. Stressed in *Re W, Re B (Child Abduction: Unmarried Father)* [1998] 2 FLR 146, per Hale J, although the *dicta* are hard to reconcile with the House of Lords' decision in *Re J (A Minor) (Abduction: Custody Rights)* [1990] 2 AC 562.

[669] [1997] 2 FLR 702.

child, even though this is not technically supported by a legal right. So if a relative had for some time been caring for a child without the formal legal right to do so and the father of the child suddenly removed the child, that could still be regarded as a wrongful taking.[670] However, if the unmarried father did not have parental responsibility and was not the primary carer of the child then he will not have custody rights.[671] These are controversial decisions, not readily justified by the meaning of the Convention, but they do recognise that often children are cared for by those who do not formalise their position as carers in the eyes of the law.

If an application is made to a court to decide the child's future, the court thereby acquires rights of custody over the child. This was confirmed by the House of Lords in *Re H (Abduction: Rights of Custody)*.[672] This means that if a father or relative who does not have legal rights of custody applies to have rights over the child, then any removal of the child will be wrongful as in breach of the *court's* rights of custody. Although this may appear a rather strained interpretation of the phrase 'rights of custody', it overcomes the problem of a parent removing a child when an application for custody rights has been lodged but the court has not yet heard the case. Rather controversially in *Re H (Child Abduction) (Unmarried Father: Rights of Custody)*[673] it was held that a letter written by the mother's solicitor confirming that the mother was happy to leave the children with the father, granted the father an 'inchoate right' to determine the child's place of residence.

There has been some doubt over whether a removal or retention is wrongful if it has been done with the consent of the parent with custody rights. In *Re C (Abduction: Consent)*[674] it was suggested that consent could not render a wrongful removal justifiable, because consent is specifically mentioned as a defence under article 13(a) and the issue should be relevant under article 13(a), rather than as negating the wrongfulness of the custody. However, Bennett J in *Re O (Abduction: Consent and Acquiescence)*[675] disagreed and said that consent is relevant for both article 3 and article 13(a).[676]

(c) Removal or retention

The Convention refers to both removal and retention. In *Re H, Re S*[677] the House of Lords stressed that removal and retention were different concepts. Removal was defined as:

> when a child, which has previously been in the state of its habitual residence, is taken away across the frontier of that state, whereas retention occurs where a child, which has pre-

---

[670] See *Re F (Abduction: Unmarried Father: Sole Carer)* [2003] FL 222; *Re G (Abduction: Rights of Custody)* [2002] FL 732.
[671] *Re C (Child Abduction) (Unmarried Father: Rights of Custody)* [2003] 1 FLR 252.
[672] [2000] 1 FLR 374 HL.
[673] [2003] FL 469.
[674] [1996] 1 FLR 414.
[675] [1997] 1 FLR 924.
[676] The agreement may be vitiated by deceit.
[677] *Re H (Minors) (Abduction: Custody Rights)* [1991] 2 FLR 263, [1992] 1 FCR 45 HL; *Re S (Minors) (Abduction: Custody Rights)* [1991] 2 AC 476.

viously been for a limited period of time outside the state of its habitual residence, is not returned on the expiry of such limited period.[678]

(iii) The presumption in favour of returning the child

Under article 12 of the Convention, if an application is brought within 12 months of the removal, the court must order the return of child unless one of the defences in article 13 applies. If more than a year has passed then the child should be returned 'unless it is demonstrated that the child is now settled in its new environment'. The courts have clarified some of the terminology. 'Now' refers to the date of the commencement of the proceedings and not the date of the hearing, explained Bracewell J in *Re N (Minors) (Abduction)*.[679] As to 'settled', Bracewell J stated that this involves both a physical element of being established in a community and an emotional one, indicating security.[680] Wilson J in *Re L (Abduction: Pending Criminal Proceedings)*[681] suggested that a year living in hiding could not lead to 'a settled life'.[682]

There are, however, exceptions to the general principle that the child should be returned and these are set out in article 13.[683] The burden of proving the existence of the exception lies on the party seeking to establish it. Even if the exception is established, the court still has discretion to order a return of the child under article 18.[684] It has been suggested that in the most exceptional of cases the court might be willing to refuse to return the child on grounds other than those set out in articles 12 and 13,[685] but that would be most unusual. It should be emphasised that the child's welfare is not the paramount consideration when deciding child abduction cases.[686]

(iv) The exceptions in article 13

(a) Article 13(a): consent or acquiescence

Under article 13(a) of the Hague Convention, the child might not be returned if 'the person, institution or other body having care of the child was not actually exercising the custody rights at the time of the removal or retention, or has consented to or acquiesced in the removal or retention'.

The evidence of consent needs to be clear and unequivocal, although it need not be in writing, as was made clear in *Re K (Abduction: Custody)*.[687] Holman J in *Re C (Abduction: Consent)*[688] suggested that consent could even be inferred from

---

[678] [1991] 2 AC 476 at p. 500, per Lord Brandon.
[679] [1991] 1 FLR 413.
[680] See also *Re M (A Minor) (Abduction: Acquiescence)* [1996] 1 FLR 315, where Thorpe LJ stressed the psychological and emotional needs.
[681] [1999] 1 FLR 433.
[682] See also *Re H (Abduction: Child of 16)* [2000] 2 FLR 51.
[683] Caldwell (2001) provides a useful discussion of these defences.
[684] *Re L (Abduction: Pending Criminal Proceedings)* [1999] 1 FLR 433.
[685] *Re B (Minors) (Abduction)* [1993] 1 FLR 988.
[686] *Re R (Abduction: Consent)* [1999] 1 FLR 828.
[687] [1997] 2 FLR 22.
[688] [1996] 1 FLR 414.

conduct.[689] The fact that the consent is reluctant does not negate the fact that it is consent,[690] although the fact that it was obtained as a result of a fraud would.[691] Once acted upon, consent cannot be withdrawn.[692]

What is acquiescence? *Re H (Minors) (Abduction: Acquiescence)*[693] is the leading case on the topic. It involved an Orthodox Jewish couple. The mother and children moved to the UK without the father's consent. The father pursued the matter in the religious rabbinical courts in Israel. Only later did he turn to the secular court. The House of Lords rejected the distinction which had been drawn in some earlier cases[694] between active and passive acquiescence. The new approach was set out by Lord Browne-Wilkinson, who stated that the question of whether or not there is acquiescence is a subjective question. It depends on the actual state of mind of the person said to have acquiesced and not whether the other parent believed them to have acquiesced. However, he qualified this by adding:

> Where the words or actions of the wronged parent clearly and unequivocally show and have led the other parent to believe that the wronged parent is not asserting or going to assert his right to the summary return of the child and are inconsistent with such return, justice requires that the wronged parent be held to have acquiesced.[695]

Delay can be evidence of acquiescence,[696] but there may be an explanation for the delay that negates any suggestion that the delay implies acquiescence.[697] For example, if the applicant failed to make any attempt to have the child returned as a result of wrong legal advice then the delay would not necessarily indicate acquiescence.[698] The fact that a parent has not applied for custody does not, in and of itself, indicate that there is acquiescence. An abductor who hides the children and takes steps to prevent the other parent discovering their whereabouts will find it difficult to show that the other acquiesced in the removal.[699]

In *Re D (Abduction: Discretionary Return)*[700] Wilson J stressed that even where there is consent to the removal, the court still has a discretion to decide whether to order the return of the child. He suggested that on the facts of that case the benefit of the case being decided in a court of the country from which the child originated justified ordering their return, despite there being acquiescence.

(b) Article 13(b): grave risk

Under article 13(b) of the Convention the court may refuse to return the child if 'there is a grave risk that his or her return would expose the child to physical or psychological harm or otherwise place the child in an intolerable situation'. In what

---

[689] Approved in *Re M (Abduction) (Consent: Acquiescence)* [1999] 1 FLR 171.
[690] *Re M (Abduction) (Consent: Acquiescence)* [1999] 1 FLR 171.
[691] *Re B (A Minor) (Abduction)* [1994] 2 FLR 249.
[692] *Re K (Abduction: Consent)* [1997] 2 FLR 212.
[693] [1998] AC 72; noted McClean (1997).
[694] E.g. *Re A (Minors) (Abduction: Custody Rights)* [1992] Fam 106.
[695] *Re H (Minors) (Abduction: Acquiescence)*, at p. 90.
[696] *W v W (Child Abduction: Acquiescence)* [1993] 2 FLR 211.
[697] *Re S (Minors) (Abduction: Acquiescence)* [1994] 1 FLR 819; *Re AZ (A Minor)* [1997] 1 FLR 682.
[698] *Re S (Minors) (Abduction: Acquiescence)* [1994] 1 FLR 819.
[699] *Re H (Abduction: Child of 16)* [2000] 2 FLR 51.
[700] [2000] 1 FLR 24, [2000] 1 FCR 208.

might be regarded as a rather strained piece of statutory interpretation Ward LJ in *Re S (A Child) (Abduction: Grave Risk of Harm)*[701] suggested that it is necessary to show both that there was a risk of physical or psychological harm, *and* that that risk of harm put the child in an intolerable situation.

It should be noted that if the child returned this does not mean that the other parent will automatically take over care of the child. So in *Re H (Children: Abduction)*[702] although there were grave concerns about the father's past violence and threats the Court of Appeal ordered the return of the child to Belgium. It was held that there was no evidence that the father was such an uncontrollable risk that the Belgian authorities were not able to control him.

The courts have been reluctant to find that a case falls into these categories and the evidential burden is high.[703] A mere allegation, even of serious abuse, will not necessarily be sufficient.[704] There must be clear and compelling evidence[705] of a grave and serious harm.[706] Ward LJ justified setting the hurdle high in order that it not prevent the dominant purpose of the Convention, namely to return the child to the country of habitual residence. In *Re M (Abduction: Intolerable Situation)*[707] the mother argued that if she were forced to return to Norway with the child, she would be at risk of physical harm from her husband, who had been imprisoned for murdering a man whom he thought was having an affair with the mother. He was soon to be released, but Charles J was willing to assume that the Norwegian authorities would be able to protect the mother and would keep her address secret. This suggests that the courts will rarely find the defence proved. In *Re S (A Child) (Abduction: Grave Risk of Harm)*[708] concerns of returning the child to Israel, given the security situation in the Middle East, were insufficient to justify not returning the child.[709] The Court of Appeal in *Re C (Abduction: Grave Risk of Physical or Psychological Harm)*[710] indicated that it was necessary to distinguish cases where the intolerable situation existed before the abduction itself (e.g. where the abductor removed the child from an abusive situation), and where the risk of harm arose from the abduction (e.g. where the child has become attached to the abductor and it would harm the child to be returned). In the latter kind of case it would be very rare for the defence to succeed, although in the former kind of case there was a higher chance of success.

Despite the courts' reluctance to find this defence made out, there have been cases where it has succeeded. For example, in *Re F (A Minor) (Abduction: Custody Rights Abroad)*[711] the abducting mother removed the children from the father who had abused and harassed the children and the mother. A rather controversial case

---

[701] [2002] 3 FCR 43, para 41.
[702] [2003] 2 FCR 151.
[703] *Re M (Abduction: Undertakings)* [1995] 1 FLR 1021.
[704] *N v N (Abduction: Article 13 Defence)* [1995] 1 FLR 107.
[705] *Re C (Abduction: Grave Risk of Psychological Harm)* [1999] 1 FLR 1145.
[706] *Re H (Children: Abduction)* [2003] 2 FCR 151, at para 30.
[707] [2000] 1 FLR 930.
[708] [2002] EWCA Civ 908, [2002] 3 FCR 43.
[709] See Freedman (2002) who is wary of ever using security concerns as a reason for not returning a child.
[710] [1999] 2 FLR 478.
[711] [1995] Fam 224.

is *Re G (Abduction: Psychological Harm)*,[712] where it was found that if the children were returned to the father this would have a severe effect on the mother's psychological health and this would harm the children. In *TB v JB (Abduction: Grave Risk of Harm)*[713] it was accepted that psychological harm to the mother if she were forced to return to New Zealand could lead to grave harm to the children, but that on the facts of the case the English court could assume that the New Zealand courts would protect the mother and children from being contacted or harassed by the father and that therefore the mother could be protected from psychological harm. Further the mother could receive medical assistance for any depression or other illness and thereby alleviate the harm to the children. Hale LJ vigorously dissented:

> primary carers who have fled from abuse and maltreatment should not be expected to go back to it, if this will have a seriously detrimental effect upon the children. We are now more conscious of the effects of such treatment, not only on the immediate victims but also on the children who witness it.

However, in *Re S (A Child) (Abduction: Grave Risk of Harm)*[714] Ward LJ emphasised that just because if the child was returned it would produce an intolerable position for the mother, did not mean that the position would be intolerable for the child, which was the question the court had to consider.[715] Freeman[716] argues on cases like these: 'So keen are we to uphold our international obligations to secure the return of abducted children that we forget that we also have an international obligation towards the children themselves ... to protect them from abuse.'

(c) The objection of children

A further defence is when 'the child objects to being returned and has attained an age and degree of maturity at which it is appropriate to take account of its views'. The court can consider not only whether the child objects to being returned to a particular country, but also whether the child objects to being returned to a particular person.[717] However, it should be stressed that the child's wishes will never determine the issue.[718] A court may decide that an objecting child is mature, but still decide to go against his or her wishes. Even though the court decides that a child is old enough to have his or her view taken into account, it does not mean that it must follow his or her view.[719] Normally, a trained officer will interview a child to ascertain his or her maturity. There is no particular age which a child must have reached before the child's wishes can be taken into account.[720] Obviously, the older the

---

[712] [1995] 1 FLR 64.
[713] [2001] 2 FCR 497, [2001] 2 FLR 515.
[714] [2002] 3 FCR 43 CA.
[715] For an argument that the courts have failed adequately to protect mothers who have abducted children to avoid violent situations, see Kaye (1999).
[716] Freeman (2000d: 7).
[717] *Re M (A Minor) (Child Abduction)* [1994] 1 FLR 390 CA.
[718] *Re S (Minors) (Abduction: Acquiescence)* [1994] 1 FLR 819.
[719] *Re L (Abduction: Child's Objections to Return)* [2002] 2 FLR 1042.
[720] *Re P (Abduction: Minor's Views)* [1998] 2 FLR 825.

child, the more likely it is that the court will decide the child is mature.[721] A recent example of the defence succeeding is *Re T (Abduction: Child's Objections to Return)*,[722] where the father removed the children from the mother in Spain to England because of the mother's drink problems. The older child, aged 11, objected to being returned. The court found her mature and her objections clear and reasoned. The Court of Appeal thought that to order the children's return would require too great a sacrifice of the children, and so permitted them to stay in Britain. Ward LJ explained that the court would take into account the child's perspectives, the reality and reasonableness of the reasons for his or her objection, the extent to which his or her reasons had been shaped by the abducting parent and the extent to which the objections might be overcome if the child is returned.

Cases relying on the child's objection must now consider the impact of the Human Rights Act 1998. In *Sylvester v Austria*[723] the Austrian Supreme Court overturned an enforcement order requiring the return of a child to her father on the basis that so much time had passed since the original order that the child had become alienated from her father. The European Court of Human Rights held that the delay had been caused by the Austrian state's failure to enforce the original order and hence it had infringed the father's and child's rights under article 8.

(d) Infringement of fundamental rights and freedoms

An English or Welsh court could refuse to return a child if that would be contrary to respect for human rights and fundamental freedoms. This ground is very rarely relied upon. In *Re S (Abduction: Intolerable Situation: Beth Din)*[724] a mother argued that if the child returned to Israel the case would be decided by a Jewish religious court, which would discriminate against her on the ground that she was a woman. However, Connell J rejected her argument, holding that as the mother was herself an Orthodox Jew and because it was her choice that the religious rather than civil courts in Israel would hear the case, her objection had little merit.[725]

(e) The residual discretion

Even if one of the defences above is not proved, the court still has a residual discretion to refuse to return a child. In *H v H (Abduction: Acquiescence)* Waite LJ suggested that in considering exercising the residual discretion the following factors should be considered:

---

[721] Although a child as young as 7 has had their views taken into account: *B v K (Child Abduction)* [1993] 1 FCR 382; *Re R (Child Abduction: Acquiescence)* [1995] 1 FLR 716; *Re S (A Minor) (Abduction: Custody Rights)* [1993] Fam 242. Contrast *Re C (Abduction: Grave Risk of Psychological Harm)* [1999] 1 FLR 1145 where boys aged 9 and 7 who had suffered severe physical abuse at their father's hands, were found to be insufficiently mature to object to their return to him. It is rare for teenagers to be returned against their wishes (see *Re L (Abduction: Child's Objections to Return)* [1999] 1 FCR 739).

[722] [2000] 2 FLR 193.

[723] [2003] 2 FCR 128.

[724] [2000] 1 FLR 454.

[725] For an interesting discussion of child abduction cases and the issue of cultural diversity, see Khaliq and Young (2001).

(a) the comparative suitability of the forum in the competing jurisdictions to determine the child's future in the substantive proceedings;
(b) the likely outcome (in whatever forum they be heard) of the substantive proceedings;
(c) the consequences of the acquiescence, with particular reference to the extent to which a child may have become settled in the requested state;
(d) the situation which would await the absconding parent and the child if compelled to return to the requesting jurisdiction;
(e) the anticipated emotional effect upon the child of an immediate return order (a factor which is to be treated as significant but not as paramount);
(f) the extent to which the purpose and underlying philosophy of the Hague Convention would be at risk of frustration if a return order were to be refused.[726]

In *B v El-B*[727] it was held that children should be returned to Lebanon, from where the mother had removed the children. Although the trial there would be under Sharia law, which would be very different from the approach in the English courts, the family were Muslim by birth and upbringing and it could not be concluded that Sharia law would not be concerned with the welfare of children.

F. The European Convention

The European Convention on the Recognition and Enforcement of Decisions Concerning Custody of Children and Restoration of Custody of Children (the Luxembourg Convention) applies to the 'improper removal' of any person under 16, unless the child has the right to decide their own place of residence.[728] Under article 1(d) an 'improper removal' is defined as:

> the removal of a child across an international frontier in breach of a decision relating to his custody which has been given in a Contracting State and which is enforceable in such a State; 'improper refusal' also includes:
> (i) the failure to return a child across an international frontier at the end of a period of the exercise of the right of access to this child or at the end of any other temporary stay in a territory other than that where the custody is exercised;
> (ii) a removal which is subsequently declared unlawful within the meaning of Article 12.

It is essential, therefore, under the Convention that an applicant has a court order in their favour. Without such an order the Luxembourg Convention cannot be utilised. However, in *Re S (A Minor) (Custody: Habitual Residence)*[729] the House of Lords held that under articles 12 and 23(2) the court had the power to make an order which could 'retrospectively' make the retention an 'improper removal'. Rather surprisingly, in *Re S (Abduction) (European Convention)*[730] Hollis J held that he was willing to make the declaration even though at the time of the abduction the father had no right to decide the child's residence. The father was then able to

---

[726] [1996] 2 FLR 570, at p. 576.
[727] [2003] 1 FLR 811.
[728] The law will be reformed if the draft EU Regulation on Parental Responsibility (Brussels II, as it is generally known) is approved. See the discussion in Karsten (2001).
[729] [1998] 1 FLR 122 HL.
[730] [1996] 1 FLR 660.

invoke the Luxembourg Convention on the basis of the interim residence order. It may not to be safe to rely on this case, given the criticism it has received.

(i) Refusing recognition or enforcement

If an application has been made after an improper removal, the child must be returned unless one of the exceptions applies. The position is a little complex because it depends on whether the state has signed article 8 of the Luxembourg Convention. If the state has, then if the application is made within six months of the child's removal the return is mandatory. However, most states have not implemented article 8, including the UK, and those states can refuse to return the child if article 9 or 10 applies.[731] Article 9 deals essentially with procedural defences; for example, if the defendant was not served with notice of the proceedings or the court lacked the competence to make the order. Article 10 is of greater interest:

> where it is found that by reason of a change of circumstances, including the passage of time but not including a mere change in the residence of the child after an improper removal, the effects of the original decision are manifestly no longer in accordance with the welfare of the child.

In considering the welfare of the child, the court is required by article 15 to ascertain the child's views, unless that would be impractical bearing in mind the child's age and understanding. It should be stressed that, in contrast to the Hague Convention, refusal is not permitted due to the child's objections per se; the child's objections are one factor to be considered when deciding what should be done for the welfare of the child.

G. Neither convention applies

(i) Children abducted to a non-Convention country

If the child has been removed from the UK to a country that has signed neither the Hague Convention nor the Luxembourg Convention, there are grave difficulties in recovering the child. There are two alternatives, although both are expensive and have only a limited chance of success. The first is to bring proceedings in the country to which the child has been taken; the second, to seek extradition of the abducting parent to England in connection with a criminal offence under the Child Abduction Act 1984. The latter is only an option if there is an extradition treaty between the UK and the country to which the child has been taken.

(ii) Children abducted to UK from a non-Convention country

Where a child is brought to England and Wales from a non-Convention country, the common law governs the position. Often wardship is used. The High Court, as

---

[731] Or in England and Wales if there is a pending application under the Hague Convention: Child Abduction and Custody Act 1985, s 16(4)(c).

always in wardship, will make its own assessment of what is in the child's best interests.[732] However, there is a presumption that it is in the best interests of the child for the child's future to be decided by the courts of the country from which the child has been abducted.[733] There are two crucial questions for the courts to look at:

1. Will the foreign court use principles similar to the ones used by the English or Welsh court? The court must be satisfied that the country will give sufficient protection to the children's interests.[734] This will be assumed where the state is a member of the European Union,[735] or where the state has historical roots with the UK.[736] It is not necessary to show that the other country has exactly the same attitude to children and their interests. In *Re JA (Child Abduction: Non-Convention Country)*[737] Ward LJ stressed that the courts have a responsibility to ensure that the child's welfare will be adequately protected by the courts in the other country.[738] However, more recently, in *Re E (Abduction: Non-Convention Country)*[739] the Court of Appeal took a rather different approach and argued that it was proper for a dispute within a Muslim family to be resolved according to the Muslim law in Sudan. They held that it would not be appropriate for the English courts to scrutinise the family justice regime of a particular country.
2. Is there any evidence that the child will suffer significant harm if he or she is returned to their country of origin?

The court will also consider whether there has been acquiescence or consent to the removal, but that is only one factor to be taken into account and there are no hard and fast rules on cases where there is acquiescence.[740]

9. CONCLUSION

This chapter has considered those cases where the courts have had to resolve private disputes concerning the upbringing of children. Much of this area of the law depends on the judiciary exercising their discretion and deciding each case on its own particular facts. Indeed, increasingly the courts are willing to accept that there is no one view which represents the child's best interests and it is rather a case of deciding which of the parents' wishes are to predominate. That said, there are some presumptions or assumptions (e.g. in favour of the 'natural' parent; in favour of contact with parents) which the courts have developed to provide a degree of predictability for some kinds of cases. Interestingly, some of the judiciary have begun to question whether the courtroom is the appropriate forum in which to resolve

---

[732] *Re L (Minors) (Wardship: Jurisdiction)* [1974] 1 All ER 913.
[733] *Re F (A Minor) (Abduction: Jurisdiction)* [1991] Fam 25; McClean and Beevers (1995).
[734] *Re S (Minors) (Abduction)* [1994] 1 FLR 297.
[735] *Re M (Abduction: Non-Convention Country)* [1995] 1 FLR 89.
[736] *Re M (Jurisdiction: Forum Conveniens)* [1995] 2 FLR 224 CA, concerning Malta.
[737] [1998] 1 FLR 231, concerning the Arab Emirates.
[738] *Re M (Minors) (Abduction: Peremptory Return Order)* [1996] 1 FLR 478, by contrast, suggested that the courts could presume that any state was in line with Britain's attitude.
[739] [1999] 2 FLR 642.
[740] *Re Z (Abduction: Non-Convention Country)* [1999] 1 FLR 1270.

family disputes. Whether this marks the beginning of the end for court resolution of family disagreements is unlikely, but it may well be that in the future the legal aid rules will be tightened so that courts will only be troubled by the arguments between members of richer families.

10

CHILD PROTECTION

Although the law generally assumes that parents will promote the interests of their children, some parents do not. In such cases the state has the power to remove children from their parents in order to protect them from harm. The power to remove children from parents is one of the greatest that the state has. For many parents, having their children compulsorily removed by the state would be one of the worst things that could happen to them. On the other hand, the appalling harm that children can suffer at the hands of their parents means that the state must intervene if children's rights are to be protected.

One of the great problems in the law concerning the protection of children is that if the wrong decision is made, enormous harm can be caused. Imagine that a social worker visits a home where a child has a broken arm and bruises. The social worker suspects this may have been caused by the parents, while the parents claim that the injuries were caused by a fall down the stairs. If the parents' explanation is untrue, but the social worker decides to believe it, she would be leaving the child with abusive parents and there would be a danger that the child could suffer serious injury or even death.[1] On the other hand, if the explanation is true and the social worker decides to remove the child, then the child and parents may suffer great harm through the separation. The history of the law on child protection reveals tragedies resulting from excessive intervention in family life as well as gross failure to intervene.[2] The difficulty is that it is only with hindsight that it would be apparent that in a particular case the approach was inappropriate.

The are four particular difficulties for the law in this area:

1. There are evidential problems. Lord Nicholls in the House of Lords recognised the difficulties facing a judge in care cases of having to 'penetrate the fog of denials, evasions, lies and half-truths which all too often descends'.[3] In other words, social workers and the courts often simply do not know the facts and have to deal with possibilities. Similarly, there are the difficulties of predicting the future. Predicting the likelihood that a parent will abuse a child on the basis of past conduct is far from easy. Yet such predictions are essential to child-care in practice.

2. Even if the facts are known, there is much controversy over how much suffering the child should face before it is suitable for the state to intervene to protect him or her. If a local authority finds a child living in a home which is dirty and untidy; where the family's diet is unhealthy; and the children spend nearly all

---

[1] For a recent horrific example see Laming (2003).
[2] Butler-Sloss (1989: 12); Department of Health (1995a); Masson (2000b).
[3] *Lancashire CC* v *B* [2000] 1 FLR 583 at p. 589.

506

their time watching television, what should be done? Many would argue that this kind of situation is not sufficiently serious to justify intervention. Others would argue that the state must offer support and help to the parents to improve the family's lifestyle, for the sake of the child. The issue here is whether protection of family privacy means the state should only intervene in the most serious cases, or whether the local authority is justified in acting in order to prevent abuse.

Fox Harding has outlined four basic approaches that the law could take in relation to suspected child abuse:[4]

(a) *Laissez-faire and patriarchy*.[5] Here, the core approach is that the role of the state should be kept to a minimum. The privacy of the original family should be respected. This is an 'all or nothing' approach. Family privacy should be protected unless it is absolutely necessary to remove a child. Critics argue that the approach promotes non-intervention except in the most extreme cases of violence, enabling men to exercise control over women and children within their families.

(b) *State paternalism and child protection*. This approach favours the intervention of the state in order to protect the child. It encourages state intervention, to whatever extent is necessary, to promote the welfare of children. Opponents of this policy claim that the approach places insufficient weight on the rights of birth families. The approach, they claim, can too easily slip into 'social engineering', and presumes that the state knows what is best for the child.

(c) *The defence of the birth family and parents' rights*. The emphasis in this approach is on the benefits of psychological and biological bonds between children and parents.[6] The birth family is seen as the 'optimal context' for bringing up children. Even where parents fail, the state should see its role as doing as much as possible to preserve the family ties. The approach is not opposed to state intervention, but argues that such intervention should be aimed at supporting the family as much as possible. Even where children do have to be removed, contact with the family should be retained and the aim should be to reunite the family if at all possible. Opponents of such an approach argue that it does not provide adequate protection for children. Given the levels of abuse within families, we cannot assume that children are always best cared for by their families.

(d) *Children's rights and child liberation*. Here the emphasis is on the child's viewpoints, feelings and wishes.[7] There is a range of approaches focusing on children's rights. At one extreme it could be argued that the state should only intervene if the child requests it.[8] In areas of suspected abuse placing weight on children's views must be treated with great caution,

---

[4] Fox Harding (1996).

[5] The leading proponents of this are Goldstein, Solnit, Goldstein and Freud (1996).

[6] For a radical challenge to the presumption that wherever possible children should be brought up by their parents see Bartholet (1999).

[7] Schofield (1998: 366) argues that many abused children want to remain with their parents, but the abuse to stop.

[8] For a more moderate approach based on children's rights, see Freeman (1983: 57).

given the complex psychological interplay that can exist between a child and his or her abuser.[9]

Fox Harding argues that aspects of all of these approaches can be found in the Children Act 1989. This, she suggests, is not necessarily a bad thing. In some areas the law may wish to place greater weight on the powers of parents, in other areas children's rights, and in others the protection of children.

3. Even where abuse is proved, there is much debate over the correct response to it.[10] Of particular concern is the level of abuse of children in care, and in particular of those in children's homes.[11] Removing a child from an abusive family only to place him or her into an abusive situation in a children's home is to heap harm upon harm.

4. A key issue in this area, and one that is often not made explicit, is the financial limitations local authorities face. As Hayes argues: 'Legislation on its own cannot ensure that children are protected from suffering significant harm. It is how it is resourced, how it is supplemented by policy documents, and how it is translated into the day-to-day practice of working with children and families which determines whether the child protection framework is operating in accordance with the apparent wishes of the legislature.'[12] As we shall see, the Children Act 1989 gives local authorities power to provide services to children in need in the hope of preventing child abuse, but unless they are adequately financed, such powers are useless. Another aspect of the funding problem is that there may be a level of assistance which is ideal for a particular child, but the local authority may not be able to resource it without depriving other children in their care of facilities they need.

1. THE CHILDREN ACT 1989 AND CHILD PROTECTION

The duties and responsibilities of local authorities towards families are located in Part III of the Children Act 1989. The powers granted to a local authority can be divided between those powers which give the local authority a discretion and those which impose a duty. Those which impose duties require local authorities to act in a particular way. Those which give a discretion leave the decision whether to use a power up to the local authority. It is also necessary to distinguish between those powers that permit the local authority to intervene in family life without the family's consent, and those which permit the local authority to offer voluntary services that a family may use as it wishes. However, this distinction is not watertight. This is because if there is the threat of compulsory intervention then the family may 'consent' to 'voluntary' intervention, aware that if they did not the local authority may intervene against the family's consent. So, to distinguish those services which are voluntary and those which are compulsory is not straightforward.[13]

---

[9] Jones and Parkinson (1995).
[10] Department of Health (1999c).
[11] E.g. Levy and Kahan (1991); The Stationery Office (2000b).
[12] M. Hayes (1998: 132).
[13] Masson (1992); Lord Chancellor's Department (1997).

It would be quite wrong to see the state's protection of children as limited to court intervention. Indeed, there has been much work by sociologists on the subtle ways in which the state polices families.[14] Health visitors, social workers, teachers and doctors can encourage the voluntary co-operation of parents and thereby encourage them to adhere to prevailing expectations about the appropriate care of children. This has been called the 'soft' policing of families.

The Children Act 1989 was produced after a major rethink over child protection policy and a number of themes emerged:

1. There should be a clear line drawn between the child being in care or not in care. A child in care is one looked after by the local authority, where the local authority effectively takes over the parental role. Under the previous legislation a child could be in an ambiguous position – formally not in care, but effectively in care. Under the Children Act a child can only enter care as a result of a court order and there are clear criteria which govern when a care order can be made.
2. The Act promotes 'partnership' between parents and local authorities. Parents and local authorities should work together for the good of the child. This has two aspects. The first is that the local authority should be regarded as a resource for parents to use, especially if the family is having difficulties.[15] The aim, therefore, is that parents experiencing difficulties in parenting will regard the local authority as there to provide support and assistance, rather than as a body to be feared. For example, if a mother is struggling in caring for her child, she should have the option of asking the local authority to accommodate her child temporarily, without there being a fear that the child will 'slip into care'. The second aspect is that even if the child is taken into care, parents should be involved with the care for the child to the greatest extent possible.

   Government guidance explains:

   > The objective of any partnership between families and professionals must be the protection and welfare of the child; partnership should not be an end in itself. From the outset workers should consider the possibility of a partnership with each family based on openness, mutual trust, joint decision making and a willingness to listen to families and to capitalise on their strengths. However, words such as equality, choice and power have a limited meaning at certain points in the child protection process. There are times when professional agencies have statutory responsibilities that they have to fulfil and powers that they have to use for the benefit of the child.[16]

There is a fear that there cannot be a partnership, or at least anything like an equal partnership, between a parent and a local authority.[17] The local authority has the 'sword of Damocles' of a care order hanging over the parents, and so there can be little equality in the 'partnership'.[18] The fear is that under the guise of 'partnership', social workers will be able to exercise even more power over parents than they would if they acknowledged the intervention was compulsory.

---

[14] Parton (1991).
[15] Masson (1995).
[16] Department of Health (1995b: 2.13).
[17] Kaganas (1995).
[18] For concerns, see Masson (1995).

3. Not only should parents and local authorities work in partnership, so also should local authorities and all the other bodies involved in child work (for example, the NSPCC, hospitals). The Children Act in various ways encourages co-operation between these different agencies. Reports into failings of the child protection system regularly cite a lack of communication between different bodies as being a cause of the absence of proper care.[19]

2. THE HUMAN RIGHTS ACT 1998 AND CHILD PROTECTION

English and Welsh law after the Human Rights Act 1998 must now start with a strong presumption that the state must respect the right to family and private life (article 8). However, it would be wrong to assume that the Human Rights Act supports a non-interventionist approach in child protection cases. There are three ways in which the Human Rights Act can permit or even require intervention:

1. Any removal by the state of a child from his or her parents will automatically constitute an infringement of article 8, but this may be justified by taking into account the welfare of the child. Paragraph 2 of article 8 permits an infringement of the right if it is necessary in the interests of others, and this would clearly include the interests of the child.[20] In deciding whether the infringement is necessary, the consideration of the welfare of the child is 'crucial'.[21] There is little difficulty justifying an intervention in family life in order to protect a child from abuse.

2. Although article 8 may readily be invoked to protect parents from state intervention, it could be argued that abused children have rights to respect for private life that can only be protected by intervention. Article 8 imposes positive obligations on the state and this will include obligations to protect a child from abuse.

3. Article 3 requires the state to protect children and adults from torture and inhuman and degrading treatment.[22] This is an absolute right in the sense that a breach of it cannot be justified by reference to the interests of others.[23] Therefore, if a local authority knows or should know that a child is suffering serious abuse then it is obliged to protect the child from that harm.[24] A local authority will have infringed a child's rights under article 3 if they failed to take measures that *could* have prevented the abuse. It is not necessary to show that had the local authority acted as it should the abuse *would* not have

---

[19] Laming (2003).

[20] See Chapter 8 for a general discussion.

[21] *K and T v Finland* [2000] 2 FLR 79; *L v Finland* [2000] 2 FLR 118.

[22] *A v UK (Human Rights: Punishment of Child)* [1998] 3 FCR 597 ECtHR; *X v UK* [2000] 2 FCR 245 EComHR.

[23] Therefore in *Re B (Care Proceedings: Diplomatic Immunity)* [2003] FL 8 a child had to be taken into care, even though the father might have been able to plead diplomatic immunity in relation to criminal and civil proceedings.

[24] *Z v UK* [2001] 2 FCR 246 and *E v UK* [2003] 1 FLR 348. See *DP v UK* [2002] 3 FCR 385 for an example of a case where it was held that because the local authority could not have known of the abuse they had not harmed the child's article 3 rights.

occurred.[25] A child who was not protected by a local authority from abuse could sue it under section 7 of the Human Rights Act 1998.

A significant concept which was introduced by the Human Rights Act 1998 is the notion of proportionality.[26] If the state is to intervene in a child's life, it must be shown that the level of state intervention is proportionate to the risk that the child is suffering. In *K and T v Finland*[27] a new-born baby was removed from the mother at birth. There were concerns that the mother suffered from various psychoses. As the mother had never behaved violently towards her other children and appeared calm at the birth, it was held to be a disproportionate response to remove the child.[28] In all of the recent cases in the public law area, the European Court has stressed that in deciding whether to remove a child the individual countries have a wide margin of appreciation. This concept of margin of appreciation has been used by the European Court to recognise that different states covered by the European Convention have different religious and cultural back-grounds and so states should be given some room for manoeuvre. Only where the state's response is clearly disproportionate, as in *K and T v Finland*,[29] will the Convention be infringed. A crucial question under the Human Rights Act will be how this margin of appreciation will be treated. It could be that the English courts will state that the local authority has a margin of appreciation and, unless the intervention in the right to respect for family life is clearly inappropriate, the courts will not hold a decision of the local authority to infringe the Act. However, it is possible that the doctrine has no place under the Human Rights Act because the Act applies just to the UK and so there is no need to take account of the different social and cultural backgrounds of different states. In such a case the court may be willing to take a stronger line than the European Court in requiring that a local authority acts proportionately when infringing a parent's rights. Bracewell J in *Re N (Leave to Withdraw Care Proceedings)*[30] has taken the latter view. She held that the margin of appreciation is not relevant and the question when considering a child being taken into care is whether it has been shown that 'there is a pressing social need for intervention by the State at this stage in family life and is the response proportionate to the need?'[31] This is a question for the courts, not the local authority.

The Human Rights Act 1998 also has important implications in the procedures used by a local authority before taking a child into care and in the decision-making process once a child has been taken into care. Both articles 6 (the right to a fair trial) and 8 have an impact when deciding the extent to which parents of children should be involved in local authority decision-making processes concerning their children.[32] This includes not only court hearings, but also meetings within the local authority about the child.[33] The key test is to be found in *W v UK*:[34]

---

[25] *E v UK* [2002] 3 FCR 700.
[26] *Re C and B (Children) (Care Order: Future Harm)* [2000] 2 FCR 614 CA.
[27] [2000] 2 FLR 79.
[28] See also *P, C, S v UK* [2002] 3 FCR 1, [2002] 2 FLR 631 ECtHR.
[29] [2000] 2 FLR 79.
[30] [2000] 1 FLR 134 at p. 141.
[31] [2000] 1 FLR 134 at p. 141.
[32] *Re L (Care: Assessment: Fair Trial)* [2002] 2 FLR 730.
[33] *TP and KM v UK* [2001] 2 FCR 289.
[34] (1988) 10 EHRR 29, at paras 63–4.

The decision-making process must ... be such as to secure that [the parents'] views and interests are made known to and duly taken into account by the local authority and that they are able to exercise in due time any remedies available to them ... what therefore has to be determined is whether, having regard to the particular circumstances of the case and notably the serious nature of the decisions to be taken, the parents have been involved in the decision-making process, seen as a whole, to a degree sufficient to provide them with the requisite protection of their interests.

Here are some examples of the potential impact of the Human Rights Act 1998 on the procedural protections for parents' rights:[35]

1. Reports which a local authority intends to rely upon in a court hearing should be disclosed to the parents,[36] unless there is a compelling justification rendering it necessary not to disclose the documents.[37] If there is any doubt over whether relevant information should be disclosed to parents the local authority should submit the issue to the court for approval.[38]
2. If the local authority has instructed the report of an expert (e.g. a psychologist's report) which is likely to have a preponderant effect on a court case then before the report is produced parents should have the opportunity to examine and comment on the documents being considered by the expert and to cross-examine witnesses interviewed by the expert.[39]
3. The parent must be provided with a lawyer during a hearing of an application for a care order or an application to free or place a child for adoption. This has been held to be an indispensable requirement of article 6.[40]
4. The parents should be kept informed of the local authority's plans in relation to the children.[41]

The courts have emphasised that in assessing whether or not there was unfairness in the local authority's procedure the court will consider the process as a whole. This means that although initially the local authority may have treated the parent unfairly, by subsequently fully involving the parents they can overcome the earlier unfairness.[42]

3. DEFINING AND EXPLAINING ABUSE

There are great difficulties in defining child abuse.[43] The problem is the great stigma attached to conduct which is labelled abuse. If the definition is too wide,

---

[35] And indeed for anyone who has family life with the child.
[36] *McMichael* v *UK* (1995) 20 EHRR 205.
[37] *Re B (Disclosure to Other Parties)* [2002] 2 FCR 32; *Venema* v *Netherlands* [2003] 1 FCR 153.
[38] *TP and KM* v *UK* [2001] 2 FCR 289.
[39] *Re C (Care Proceedings: Disclosure of Local Authority's Decision-Making Process)* [2002] 2 FCR 673.
[40] *P, C, S* v *UK* [2002] 3 FCR 1, [2002] 2 FLR 631 ECtHR, although see Lindley, Richards and Freeman (2001) for concerns over the legal advice and advocacy for parents in child protection cases.
[41] *C* v *Bury MBC* [2002] 3 FCR 608, [2002] 2 FLR 868.
[42] E.g. *Re C (Care Proceedings: Disclosure of Local Authority's Decision-Making Process)* [2002] 2 FCR 673. The courts may be willing to assume that the parent has only him- or herself to blame for the lack of involvement: *Re P (Care Proceedings: Father's Application)* [2001] 2 FCR 279.
[43] Fish (1997); Archard (1999).

there is a danger that the stigma will be lessened. If the definition is too narrow then this may weaken the protection offered to children. One definition is:

> Child abuse consists of anything which individuals, institutions, or processes do or fail to do which directly or indirectly harms children or damages their prospects of safe and healthy development into adulthood.[44]

Some would regard this as too wide a definition. Arguably, letting a child watch too much television or eat too much chocolate could fall into this definition, but most would not regard that as abuse.[45]

It is notable that the phrase 'child abuse' conjures up the notion of physical or sexual abuse of a child by an adult. However, this is far too narrow an understanding. In fact, a significant proportion of abuse is committed by children on other children. Further, other harms that children suffer, such as pollution, inadequate education or poverty are often not labelled abuse, but perhaps should be.[46]

What is widely accepted is that children who have been abused suffer in emotional, educational and social terms.[47] Because of the difficulty in defining abuse and detecting it[48] there is little consensus over the level of abuse which exists. The NSPCC, the highly respected children's charity, has claimed that one in eight people was abused as a child. Fretwell Wilson[49] claims that in Great Britain between 12 per cent and 24 per cent of girls[50] and 8–9 per cent of boys experience sexual abuse before their sixteenth birthday. What is noticeable is the common misperception that children are at greater risk of abuse from strangers than families. On average five or six children die a year at the hands of strangers, while between 70 and 100 will die at the hands of their families.[51]

It is perhaps easy to label child abuse as caused by social deviants. But we live in a country where one-third of children live in poverty; over 1 million schoolchildren work illegally; each year over 9,000 children are permanently excluded from schools; over 100,000 children live in temporary accommodation; 5,000 children under the age of 16 are used for prostitution; about 2,800 children between 15 and 17 are imprisoned in young offender's institutes; and a country that has the highest teenage pregnancy rate in Europe.[52] Abuse is the lot of far too many children in the UK and it is not just the 'sick' few who are to blame.

A. Explanations for abuse

Not surprisingly, there is no consensus on what causes abuse. The following are some of the explanations:

---

[44] Department of Health (1995a: para 1.4).
[45] For a description of the potential impact of emotional neglect and abuse on children, see Hobbs, Hanks and Wynne (1999).
[46] M. King (1997).
[47] Department of Health (1995a: 62).
[48] Particularly where the victim suffers from mental disability (see *Re D (A Child) (Wardship: Evidence of Abuse)* [2001] 1 FCR 707).
[49] Fretwell Wilson (2002).
[50] Whether it is 12 or 24 per cent depends on the definition of sexual abuse used.
[51] Lyon (2001).
[52] These statistics are taken from Butler-Sloss (2003).

1. *Psychological factors*. This explanation of the abuse lies in the psychology of the abuser. For example, there is some evidence that those who were themselves abused as children are more likely to abuse children when they become adults, although the fact that by no means all abused children then later abuse indicates that this cannot be the sole explanation.
2. *Sociological factors*. This explanation focuses on the position of children within society. For example, the sexualisation of children in advertising is pointed to as indicating the ambivalent attitude of society towards children and sexual relations.
3. *Feminist perspectives*. These focus on child sexual abuse as an example of patri-archy – the exercise of male power.[53] It is notable that the vast majority of sexual abuse is carried out by men.[54]
4. *Family systems*. Others point to family relationships as the key to explaining sexual abuse in the home. Furniss[55] argues that it is only if the other members of the family permit the abuse to occur (whether consciously or not) that it can. Some even claim that child abuse is caused by the wife's failure to meet the husband's sexual needs. Feminists have objected to this explanation on the basis that it can be read as blaming the mother for the abuse.[56]

4. PROTECTION OF CHILDREN BY THE CRIMINAL LAW

If a child is abused, as well as the question of whether the child should be taken into care there is the issue of whether criminal proceedings should be brought against the abuser. There is no one offence of child abuse; the general criminal law protects children, and so children could be the victims of the whole range of assaults in the Offences Against the Person Act 1861. There are also special offences designed to protect children.[57] For example, s 1 of the Children and Young Persons Act 1933 states that any wilful violent or non-violent neglect or ill-treatment which is 'likely to cause him unnecessary suffer-ing or injury to health (including injury to or loss of sight, or hearing, or limb, or organ of the body, and any mental derangement)' is an offence. The Sexual Offences Act 2003 has radically reformed the criminal law on sexual offences against children.[58]

Statute has intervened to make it easier for children to give evidence in criminal trials. For example, a video recording of a child explaining what happened may be admissible as evidence following the Criminal Justice Act 1991 and Youth Justice and Criminal Evidence Act 1999.[59] However, there is some concern that video recordings are less persuasive to a jury than live evidence.[60] There is no age limit on

---

[53] Edwards (1996: ch. 7).
[54] Smart (1989).
[55] Furniss (1991).
[56] Day Sclater (2000).
[57] See e.g. Punishment of Incest Act 1908; Sexual Offences Act 1956, ss 10–11, 14, 25 and 28. There has been an increasing number of criminal cases where the abuse is alleged to have taken place many years previously: Lewis and Mullis (1999).
[58] Home Office (2000b).
[59] Home Office (1989).
[60] Plotnikoff and Woolfson (1995). Further procedures to make it easier for children to give evidence are found in Part II of Youth Justice and Criminal Evidence Act 1999.

who can give evidence and so children are presumed to be competent to give evidence, whatever their age.

In preparing for a criminal trial, police and social workers must work closely together. However, this is not always an easy co-operation. Actions which might protect the child might not be those which best assist in the preparation of a trial.[61] For example, there are particular concerns that if a child is offered therapy after abuse this could be regarded as contaminating any subsequent evidence that the child may give at a trial.[62] The position is particularly difficult as the conviction rates for child abuse are so low. Spencer and Flin have suggested that only one in four trials of alleged abuse leads to conviction.[63] Of course, many other cases do not even reach trial. It must therefore be asked whether it is worth putting a child through the pain of a criminal trial, with the trauma of giving evidence, given the low rates of conviction. Further, even if there is a conviction, the child may suffer feelings of guilt if the abuser is imprisoned.

The arguments in favour of criminal prosecution centre on the fact that prosecution demonstrates society's condemnation of child abuse. To the child, the prosecution sends the message that the state acknowledges the abuse suffered and that harm has been done. If the perpetrator is imprisoned then, even if this does not guarantee that the abuser will not abuse again, at least it ensures that during the imprisonment he or she will commit no further abuse. On the other hand, if the prosecution fails, the abuser may feel vindicated and the child less protected. Fortin concludes: 'were it not for the risk of giving child abusers implicit permission to re-abuse with impunity there might be some basis for arguing that a child's rights to protection would be better served by child law alone, without involving the criminal justice system'.[64]

5. VOLUNTARY SERVICES PROVIDED BY LOCAL AUTHORITIES

The powers and duties of local authorities in respect of children whom it is feared may be suffering harm can be divided into three categories: provision of services; investigation; compulsory intervention. First, the provision of services will be considered.

A. Voluntary accommodation[65]

One of the most basic needs of a vulnerable child is accommodation. Not surprisingly, the Children Act 1989 sets out duties on a local authority to accommodate certain children in need. The Act draws a sharp distinction between children whose parents ask the local authority to accommodate their children ('voluntary accommodation') and children who have been compulsorily removed from parents under

---

[61] Fortin (1998a: 417).
[62] Keenan, Davis, Hoyano and Maitland (1999).
[63] Spencer and Flin (1993: 9).
[64] Fortin (1998: 433).
[65] The provision of housing for homeless families is referred to in Chapter 6.

a care order and accommodated by the local authority ('compulsory accommodation'). In this section voluntary accommodation will be discussed.

(i) Duty to accommodate

Section 20 of the Children Act 1989 sets out the circumstances in which a local authority *must* accommodate a child in need:

> Every local authority shall provide accommodation for any child in need within their area who appears to them to require accommodation as a result of:
> (a) there being no person who has parental responsibility for him;
> (b) his being lost or having been abandoned; or
> (c) the person who has been caring for him being prevented (whether or not permanently, and for whatever reason) from providing him with suitable accommodation or care.

There are basically two categories of people whom a local authority must accommodate. First, a local authority must accommodate orphaned or abandoned children (although a local authority will often prefer to apply for a care order in respect of an orphaned child so that it acquires parental responsibility for the child). Secondly, there is a duty to accommodate those children whose carers are prevented from looking after them.[66]

It should be stressed that there is no need for a court to approve the voluntary accommodation. But if a parent with parental responsibility for the child objects to the accommodation, the local authority may not accommodate the child. If the local authority wishes to accommodate a child despite the parent's objection, then the local authority must resort to compulsory measures, such as a care order. The accommodation is usually provided for by the local authority through foster parents or children's homes.

(ii) Discretion to accommodate

In addition to the duty just outlined, local authorities have a discretion to provide accommodation to a child even if the child is not in need, 'if they consider that to do so would safeguard or promote the child's welfare' under s 20(4).[67] This discretion exists even if there is a person who has parental responsibility who can provide accommodation. However, all those with parental responsibility must consent to the local authority accommodating the child.

(iii) The consent or objection of those with parental responsibility

As already mentioned, under s 20(7) no child under 16 can be accommodated without a court order where a person with parental responsibility objects; but there is no need for anyone positively to consent to the accommodation. If a person with

---

[66] Article 27(3) of the UN Convention on the Rights of the Child requires the signatory states to provide needy children with assistance with housing.
[67] Any person aged 16–21 can be accommodated if a local authority believes that this would safeguard or promote the child's welfare under the Children Act 1989 (hereafter CA 1989), s 20(5).

parental responsibility objects, then he or she must show that they are willing and able to provide accommodation for the child. There seems to be no requirement that the accommodation be suitable, although a court may decide that such a requirement be read into the statute. If the local authority believes that the child will be endangered if accommodated by that person, they must apply for a care order or other protective order. If a person is caring for a child under a residence order,[68] then only that person can object. If in such a case the non-resident parent objects, he or she could apply for a residence order or a prohibited steps order to prevent the child being accommodated by the local authority.[69]

The unmarried father without parental responsibility has no right to object to voluntary accommodation. If an unmarried father objects to the accommodation, he would need to apply for a residence order. If the parent with parental responsibility objects to the child being accommodated with a particular foster parent, the local authority must accede to that wish. They may return the child to the parents, or apply for a care order, but may not accommodate the child under s 20 against the objection of the parents.[70]

(iv) Children requesting accommodation

If the child requests accommodation him- or herself, the position depends on whether the child is above or below the age of 16.

(a) Children aged 16 and over

The local authority must accommodate any child aged 16 or 17 'in need', whose welfare it considers 'is likely to be seriously prejudiced if they do not provide him with accommodation'.[71] If the child is over 16 then there is no need for parental approval.[72] If the child is not in such dire need, the local authority is only required to provide advice on accommodation or housing and is not required to accommodate the child. The concern was that if the duty was not limited, local authorities might be inundated with requests for accommodation from 16- and 17-year-olds.[73] However, the high rates of homelessness among this age group have led some to call for this area of the law to be reconsidered. Another concern is that teenagers may seek local authority care as an act of rebellion, rather than really being in need. To prevent the teenager seeking accommodation, a parent could apply for a residence order, although that would only succeed in exceptional circumstances.[74]

(b) Children under 16

There is much doubt concerning the position of under 16-year-olds requesting local authority accommodation. It might be argued that, following *Gillick*,[75] a competent

---

[68] Or an order under the inherent jurisdiction allowing the child to stay with him or her.
[69] By analogy: *D v D (County Court Jurisdiction: Injunctions)* [1993] 2 FLR 802 CA.
[70] *R v Tameside MBC, ex p J* [2000] 1 FLR 942, [2000] 1 FCR 173.
[71] CA 1989, s 20(3).
[72] CA 1989, s 20(3).
[73] Fortin (1998a: ch 4).
[74] CA 1989, s 9(7).
[75] *Gillick v W Norfolk and Wisbech AHA* [1986] 1 FLR 229.

minor should have a decisive say as to whether they are accommodated by a local authority. Eekelaar and Dingwall have suggested that when a child is *Gillick*-competent then the parents lose the power to decide where the child is to live.[76] Those who oppose this view note that *Gillick* competent children do not have a power of consent where there are express statutory provisions to the contrary.[77] Here s 20(6) states that the court should:

> so far as is reasonably practicable and consistent with the child's welfare—
> (a) ascertain the child's wishes regarding the provision of accommodation; and
> (b) give due consideration (having regard to his age and understanding) to such wishes of the child as they have been able to ascertain.

This seems explicitly to fall short of giving the competent child the exclusive right to have themselves accommodated. Section 20(7) appears to be quite clear that a child cannot be accommodated under the Children Act against the wishes of a parent with parental responsibility. Bainham therefore argues that if a parent objects, then the competent child's wishes cannot prevail.[78] The matter could, however, be brought before the court by way of a s 8 application.[79]

(v) Removal from accommodation

Under s 20(8) of the Children Act 1989, anyone with parental responsibility 'may at any time remove the child from accommodation provided by or on behalf of the local authority'.[80] There is not even a requirement that parents give notice to the local authority of their intention to remove their child from voluntarily accommodation. It is not possible for the local authority to stop a removal by obtaining a s 8 order preventing the removal by the parent,[81] nor even to require a formal undertaking from parents not to remove their child.[82] But a parent with parental responsibility is not able to remove a child if the child was placed by another person with a residence order. Some argue that this is an inappropriate limitation on the rights of a parent with parental responsibility,[83] while others argue that the core element of a residence order is that the holder of the residence order can determine where the child should live.[84]

There are two main arguments in favour of the right of a parent to remove their children from accommodation. First, it is important to keep a clear distinction between voluntary and compulsory care, and the power of immediate removal maintains the clarity of this distinction. Secondly, it has been suggested that volun-

---

[76] Eekelaar and Dingwall (1990: 78).

[77] *Re W (A Minor) (Medical Treatment: Court's Jurisdiction)* [1993] 1 FLR 1, [1992] 2 FCR 785.

[78] Bainham (1998a: 341).

[79] Although a child cannot apply for a residence order in favour of him- or herself nor in favour of the local authority. CA 1989, s 9(2): *Re SC (A Minor) (Leave to Seek Section 8 Orders)* [1994] 1 FLR 96, [1994] 1 FCR 837.

[80] This might include an unmarried father with parental responsibility.

[81] *Nottinghamshire County Council v J* Unreported 26.11.93, cited in Lowe and Douglas (1998: 526).

[82] CA 1989, s 9(5), although *Re G (Minors) (Interim Care Order)* [1993] 2 FLR 839 at p. 843 suggested it was.

[83] Bainham (1998a: 339).

[84] Hayes and Williams (1999: 144).

tary accommodation should be made as attractive an option as possible, so that parents feeling under great pressure will be willing to use the 'service'.

There have been concerns that parents may misuse their power of automatic removal and remove their children in unsuitable circumstances. For example, a parent could turn up at the foster parents' house drunk, demanding the return of his or her child. The Children Act 1989 appears to suggest that the foster parents must hand the child over to the parent, but there are four options available for a local authority in such a case:

1. Some commentators[85] argue that a local authority is permitted to prevent the unsuitable removal of children by relying on s 3(5) of the Children Act 1989. However, a strong opposing argument is that s 3(5) cannot be used to prevent the exercise of the parental right to remove the child, especially where the parental right is explicitly granted in a statute.
2. A local authority could apply for an emergency protection order if the child is likely to suffer significant harm.
3. A foster parent from whom a child was removed could apply for a residence order or even rely on wardship[86] or the inherent jurisdiction.
4. Police protection may also be available in an extreme case.[87]

It may be that the threat of the local authority applying for a care order provides a suitable deterrent to children being inappropriately removed.

It seems that a child who is 16 or 17 can leave voluntary accommodation provided by the local authority at will. There is no statutory basis on which a local authority can detain a child against his or her wishes.[88]

(vi) Accommodation agreements[89]

If a child is accommodated, the local authority should enter an agreement with the person with parental responsibility. The agreement is likely to cover issues such as schooling, religious practices and contact arrangements. The agreement is not legally binding, but is intended to clarify the expectations of all involved and hence avoid any potential disputes.

(vii) Refusals to accommodate

If a local authority refuses to accommodate a child, parents have only a limited right to challenge that decision. It seems that, by analogy with *Re J (Specific Issue Order:*

---

[85] See the discussion in Cretney, Masson and Bailey-Harris (2002: 709).
[86] Although if foster parents started caring for the child as a ward of court they may lose the financial assistance of the local authority.
[87] CA 1989, s 46.
[88] There is a severe lack of resources for housing: see Fortin (1998a: ch. 4). Also see the problems in *R v Northavon DC, ex p Smith* [1994] 2 FCR 859, [1994] 2 FLR 671, with families being shunted around from department to department. The House of Lords case made it clear that there is an obligation for local authorities to change their housing policies in the light of CA 1989, s 27.
[89] Detailed in Department of Health (1991a: para 2.13 et seq.).

Leave to Apply),[90] a specific issue order could not be relied upon to compel a local authority to accommodate a child. Judicial review of a decision not to accommodate may be possible but it would be difficult to demonstrate that the local authority's decision was unlawful. For example, it would be difficult to show that the decision not to accommodate was so unreasonable that no reasonable local authority could have reached that decision.[91] The best route to challenge the decision would be to rely on the local authority's internal complaints procedure.

(viii) Effect of child being accommodated

A child accommodated by the local authority under s 20 is not put into care, and the local authority does not acquire parental responsibility. But the child will be 'looked after' by the local authority, and therefore the local authority will owe such a child the various duties discussed in Chapter 11.

B. Services for children in need

Clearly, prevention of abuse is better than dealing with its consequences. The Children Act 1989 therefore attempts to focus local authorities' attention on children in their area who are 'in need' and at danger of suffering significant harm.[92] The fact that a child is in need does not necessarily mean that his or her parents are mistreating them. A child may be 'in need' but be cared for so well by his or her parents that there is no fear of abuse or neglect[93] (e.g. such as a child brought up in an impoverished family). Part III of the Children Act requires the local authority to provide certain services to those children who are 'in need'. Once a local authority has decided that a child is in need, then it must provide services. Although a local authority cannot decide to provide no assistance to children in need, it is left to the local authority to decide what form the assistance will take. In considering what services to supply, a child's welfare is a relevant factor, but it is not paramount. Financial considerations will often play a significant role.[94]

The law governing children in need is a rather strange area because it appears there is no effective court enforcement of a local authority's duties, so the 'duties' are largely of a non-enforceable nature. However, a child whose needs are inadequately assessed could use judicial review, although that would be hard to prove.[95] The importance of the Children Act 1989 here is that it helps focus a local authority's attention towards vulnerable children. That said, after the Human Rights Act 1998 it is arguable that local authorities must ensure that children do not suffer

---

[90] [1995] 1 FLR 669, [1995] 3 FCR 799, where the child sought a declaration under CA 1989, s 8 that he was in need.
[91] *R v Kingston-upon-Thames RB, ex p T* [1994] 1 FLR 798, [1994] 1 FCR 232; *R v Birmingham City Council, ex p A* [1997] 2 FLR 841.
[92] Detailed guidance is found in Department of Health (1999c).
[93] For a useful discussion of the significance of child neglect see Tanner and Turney (2002).
[94] *Re M (Secure Accommodation Order)* [1995] 1 FLR 418. The issues are discussed in Masson (1992). Parry (2000) expresses concerns about the local authorities' care for ethnic minority children.
[95] *R (On the application of AB and SB)* v *Nottingham CC* [2001] 3 FCR 350 for a successful application for judicial review.

torture and inhuman or degrading treatment.[96] If the child is suffering so much that it could be said to be suffering inhuman and degrading treatment, then the local authority may be under an enforceable duty under the Human Rights Act to supply such protection necessary to prevent the child so suffering.[97] However, as we shall see, the House of Lords in *R (On the Application of G) v Barnet London Borough Council*[98] has held that s 17 of the Children Act 1989 does not give rights to individual children.

Crucial to understanding the extent of the local authority's responsibilities under the Children Act 1989 is the concept of being 'in need'.

(i) What does 'in need' mean?

A child is 'in need' if:

(a) he is unlikely to achieve or maintain, or to have the opportunity of achieving or maintaining, a reasonable standard of health or development without the provision for him of services by a local authority under this part;

(b) his health or development is likely to be significantly impaired, or further impaired, without the provision for him of such services; or

(c) he is disabled.[99]

'Development' includes 'physical, intellectual, emotional, social or behavioural development'; health includes 'physical or mental health'.[100] A disabled child is one who is 'blind, deaf, or dumb or suffers from mental disorder of any kind or is substantially and permanently handicapped by illness, injury or congenital deformity or such other disability as may be prescribed'.[101] The law here is not concerned with the causes of the need, but rather the fact of need. The need may arise from the lack of skills of the parent, or may be due to the disabilities of the child.

(ii) What services should be supplied?

Part III of the Children Act 1989 was intended to establish a single code to govern the voluntary services to children and all decisions of a local authority.[102] The general duty to provide services is set out in s 17(1):

It shall be the general duty of every local authority (in addition to the other duties imposed on them by this Part)—

(a) to safeguard and promote the welfare of children within their area who are in need; and

(b) so far as is consistent with that duty, to promote the upbringing of such children by their families

by providing a range and level of services appropriate to those children's needs.

[96] Applying *A v UK (Human Rights: Punishment of Child)* [1998] 2 FLR 959, [1998] 3 FCR 597.
[97] For a thorough discussion of the difficulties in enforcing a local authority's obligations under CA 1989, Part III see Murphy (2003).
[98] [2003] UKHL 57.
[99] CA 1989, s 17(10).
[100] CA 1989, s 17(11).
[101] CA 1989, s 17(11). Some have argued that this terminology is inappropriate: Freeman (1992a: 57).
[102] See Department of Health (1998b).

The duty is described as a general duty to indicate that an individual child cannot seek to compel a local authority to provide services by relying on this section.[103] The House of Lords in *R (On the Application of G)* v *Barnet LBC*[104] has held that the section does not create a right for a particular child to services, but rather describes a duty that the local authority owes to a section of the public (i.e. children in need). This is because it is for the local authority to decide how to spend their resources. The majority of their lordships held that s 17 did not impose a duty on a local authority even to assess the needs of a particular child.

Services are to be made available not only to children, but also to their parents and family members,[105] as long as the services are aimed at safeguarding the welfare of the child. 'Family' is defined to include 'any person who has parental responsibility for the child and any other person with whom he has been living'.[106] 'Services' can include the provision of assistance in kind and even cash in exceptional circumstances.[107] There is also a list of special duties in Sch 2 to the Children Act 1989. For example, there are duties to take reasonable steps to avoid the need to bring proceedings for care or supervision orders; duties to encourage children not to commit criminal offences; and duties to publicise the services that the local authority offers.[108]

C. The family assistance order

The family assistance order (FAO) is governed by s 16 of the Children Act 1989 and is a form of voluntary assistance provided to a family by the local authority.[109] The order requires either a probation officer or an officer of the local authority ('the officer') to be made available 'to advise, assist and (where appropriate) befriend any person named in the order'. The order can benefit anyone with whom the child is living and is not restricted to parents. The order is designed to provide short-term help to a family and may be as much directed at the parents as the child.[110]

The order can only be made in exceptional circumstances[111] and only by the court acting on its own motion. In other words, a parent cannot apply for a FAO. However, it is necessary that the person in whose favour the order is made has consented to the making of the order.[112] It seems the local authority must consent to the making of the order as well.[113]

---

[103] *R (On the Application of G)* v *Barnet London Borough Council* [2003] UKHL 57. *Re M (Secure Accommodation Order)* [1995] 1 FLR 418.

[104] [2003] UKHL 57.

[105] This includes any person with parental responsibility or any other person with whom the child is living (CA 1989, s 17(10)).

[106] CA 1989, s 17(10).

[107] CA 1989, s 17(6).

[108] A local authority is under a duty to provide day-care facilities to children in need as appropriate under CA 1989, s 18.

[109] Thorough reviews of the use of family assistance orders are to be found in James and Sturgeon-Adams (1999) and Seden (2001).

[110] Department of Health (1991b: 2.50).

[111] CA 1989, s 16(3)(a).

[112] CA 1989, s 16(3).

[113] CA 1989, s 16(7); *Re C (Family Assistance Order)* [1996] 1 FLR 424, [1996] 3 FCR 514.

The maximum length of the order is six months.[114] The only power of enforcement that the officer has is to refer the case to the court if he or she believes there is a need for variation. He or she could also report their concerns to the local authority that may wish to intervene by applying for a care order. The FAO should not be used for purposes unrelated to its primary purpose of assisting the family. So in *S v P (Contact Application: Family Assistance Order)*[115] it was said to be a misuse of the order to make it for the purpose of providing someone to accompany a child visiting his father in prison. An appropriate use of the order was found in *Re U (Application to Free for Adoption)*[116] when the court decided that a child should reside with her grandparents, but thought that a FAO could assist the child and grandparents in establishing a new life together.

In practice FAOs appear to be little used.[117] It has been suggested that this is because of concerns about the extent to which the order intervenes in family life. It also appears that there is much confusion among social workers as to their purpose.[118]

6. INVESTIGATIONS BY LOCAL AUTHORITIES

There are two provisions in the Children Act 1989 under which the local authority may be required to investigate a child's welfare. Section 47 sets out specific circumstances in which a local authority must investigate a child's well-being. Section 37 permits a court to require a local authority to investigate a child's welfare.

A. Section 47 investigations

Under s 47 of the Children Act 1989 the local authority is under a duty to investigate the welfare of a child in their area when:

1. a child is subject to an emergency protection order;
2. a child is in police protection;
3. a child has contravened a curfew notice;[119] or
4. the local authority has reasonable cause to suspect that a child is suffering, or is likely to suffer, significant harm.[120]

Local authorities may obtain information about potential abuse of children from a wide variety of sources. Neighbours, teachers, doctors, even children themselves may provide information to the local authority.[121] The local authority does not need proved facts before it carries out an investigation; suspicions are sufficient.[122] This means that even if a criminal prosecution against an alleged perpetrator of sexual

---

[114] CA 1989, s 16(5).
[115] [1997] 2 FLR 277, [1997] 2 FCR 185.
[116] [1993] 2 FLR 992.
[117] Seden (2001).
[118] James and Sturgeon-Adams (1999).
[119] Under Ch. 1, Part 1 of the Crime and Disorder Act 1998.
[120] CA 1989, s 47.
[121] Department of Health (2000c).
[122] *R (On the Application of S) v Swindon BC* [2001] EWHC 334, [2001] 3 FCR 702.

abuse had failed, the local authority might still be authorised to carry out a s 47 investigation.[123]

Under these circumstances the local authority must make 'such enquiries as they consider necessary to enable them to decide whether they should take any action to safeguard or promote the child's welfare'.[124] There is no power to enter a child's home against the parents' will. However, if parents fail to permit social workers to see a child then the local authority must apply for either an emergency protection order, a child assessment order, a supervision order, or a care order unless they are satisfied that the child can be satisfactorily safeguarded in other ways.[125] However, if the parents have permitted the local authority to see the child, the legislation leaves the choice of what to do next to the local authority. The main options are to do nothing, to offer the family services, or to apply to the court for a child assessment order, emergency protection order, or supervision or care order. As Eekelaar has pointed out, a local authority is not under a duty to apply for an order, even if it decides that the child would be best protected by applying for such an order. There is a duty to investigate and to decide what it *should* do, but there is no duty to do anything as a result of the investigation.[126] It may be that financial limitations would cause a local authority not to apply for an order which it thought desirable but not essential. In practice few s 47 enquires are undertaken due to staff shortages and lack of staff training.[127]

A court has no jurisdiction to prevent a local authority carrying out its investigative duties.[128] If a court was convinced that the investigations by a local authority were unjustified and causing harm to a child, it could make a prohibited steps order under s 8 of the Children Act 1989 to restrain a parent from co-operating with the investigation.[129] However, it would require a most unusual case for this to be an appropriate course of action.

B. Section 37 directions

The court cannot require a local authority to apply for a care order, nor can it force a care order upon a local authority which does not apply for one.[130] What the court may do is direct a local authority to investigate a child's circumstances under s 37 of the Children Act 1989. The court can make such a direction wherever 'a question arises with respect to the welfare of any child', and it appears to the court that 'it may be appropriate for a care or supervision order to be made with respect to him'.[131] The court must not make a s 37 direction if the case is not one where it may be appropriate to make a care or supervision order.[132] The local authority must

---

[123] *R (On the Application of S)* v *Swindon BC* [2001] EWHC 334, [2001] 3 FCR 702.
[124] CA 1989, s 47(1)(b).
[125] CA 1989, s 47(6).
[126] Eekelaar (1990).
[127] Department of Health (2002a: 6.8).
[128] *D* v *D (County Court Jurisdiction: Injunctions)* [1993] 2 FLR 802 CA.
[129] *D* v *D (County Court Jurisdiction: Injunctions)* [1993] 2 FLR 802 CA.
[130] *Nottingham CC* v *P* [1993] 2 FLR 134, [1994] 1 FCR 624 CA.
[131] CA 1989, s 37(1).
[132] *Re L (Section 37 Direction)* [1999] 1 FLR 984.

report back to the court within eight weeks. The court cannot seek to control the local authority's investigation.[133] If, following an investigation under s 37, the local authority does not apply for an order, it must explain this to the court and describe what services or assistance it intends to provide.[134] If the local authority after its investigations decides not to apply for a court order, the court cannot force it to do so.[135]

This area of the law may be open to challenge following the Human Rights Act 1998.[136] *A v UK (Human Rights: Punishment of Child)*[137] confirmed that if the state fails to ensure that children do not suffer torture or inhuman or degrading treatment, then the state may be in breach of article 3 of the Convention on Human Rights.[138] Although *A v UK* involved a child not being adequately protected by the criminal law concerning corporal punishment, an analogy could readily be made with the state failing to protect a child from abuse.[139] It is submitted that, following the Human Rights Act, where the local authority is aware that a child is suffering serious abuse following a s 37 or s 47 investigation, it is under a duty to protect the child.

A different concern in the light of the Human Rights Act 1998 is the number of investigations in which it was found that there was no evidence of abuse of children. It has been estimated that 25,000 investigations per year under s 47 find no evidence of abuse.[140] Arguably, an investigation launched without justification could constitute a lack of respect for family life and so breach article 8 of the Convention.

C. Multi-agency co-operation

A local authority should involve appropriate agencies when making investigations, and should consult them in deciding whether to make an application for a care order. There are two bodies in particular which are designed to facilitate multi-agency co-operation:

1. The area child protection committees have the mandate of advising and reviewing local practice for inter-agency training and co-operation. [141] Area child protection committees consist of representatives from various professions, including the social services, the NSPCC, the police, education, health and probation services, and certain voluntary organisations.

---

[133] *Re M (Official Solicitor's Role)* [1998] 3 FLR 815 suggested that it was inappropriate to use the Official Solicitor to ensure that a local authority carried out an investigation in the manner requested by the judge.
[134] CA 1989, s 37(3).
[135] *Nottingham CC v P* [1993] 2 FLR 134, [1994] 1 FCR 624 CA.
[136] See *KL v UK* (1999) 26 EHRR CD 113.
[137] [1998] 2 FLR 959, [1998] 3 FCR 597.
[138] *Z v UK* [2001] 2 FCR 246 EComHR.
[139] For an example of where the state's inadequate intervention led to a child suffering harm, see Greenwich London Borough Council (1987).
[140] The total number of investigations was 160,000: Gibbons, Gallagher, Bell and Gordon (1995).
[141] See Choudhry (2001) for a useful discussion of the impact of the Human Rights Act 1998 on the work of child protection conferences.

2. Child protection conferences must consider individual cases. A child protection conference is called after an investigation has been made under s 47. The first task is to decide whether the child should be placed on the child protection register.[142] This is a register 'of children for whom there are currently unresolved child protection issues and for whom there is an inter-agency plan'.[143] In 2001 there were 27,000 children on the register.[144] The second task is to consider the plan for the child's future, and to gather together all the available evidence from the various agencies.[145] A decision will then be made how best to secure a good outcome for the child. This may involve the child being taken into care, or may mean providing his or her family with support services.[146] Regular reviews should be carried out to ensure that the child is adequately protected and that the various agencies are working effectively together. Parents should be allowed to attend the child protection conference[147] unless there are exceptional circumstances.[148] However, parents do not have a right to contribute to the conference.[149] Children can also be involved in the child protection conferences if appropriate.[150]

D. Child assessment orders

A child assessment order is a preliminary order that allows assessments to take place to determine whether further orders may be necessary.

(i) When is a child assessment order appropriate?

A child assessment order (CAO) is appropriate where the local authority has concerns about a child but needs more information before it is able to decide what action to take.[151] The guidance makes it clear the CAO is 'emphatically not for emergencies'.[152] If the grounds for an emergency protection order (EPO) are made out, s 43(4) of the Children Act 1989 states that the court may not make a CAO but must make an EPO. In fact, it is difficult to envisage when a CAO may be appropriate.[153] If there is a serious concern that the child is being abused, and the parents refuse to have the child examined, then an EPO will normally be more appropriate; whereas if the parents are happy to agree to the examination, then

---

[142] The government has produced a Green Paper setting out its proposals for children at risk. See Department for Education and Skills (2003), discussed in Rogers (2003).
[143] Department of Health (1998b: 6.1).
[144] For further discussion on the statistics see Tanner and Turney (2002).
[145] There is a concern that too many children were placed on the protection register: Department of Health (1995a).
[146] Department of Health (1998b).
[147] With a friend or solicitor: *R v Cornwall CC, ex p LH* [2000] FLR 236.
[148] *R v Harrow LBC, ex p D* [1990] 1 FLR 79, [1989] FCR 729 CA. See also Savas (1996).
[149] *R v Harrow LBC, ex p D* [1990] 1 FLR 79, [1989] FCR 729 CA.
[150] Department of Health (1998b: 6.13).
[151] Discussed in Lavery (1996).
[152] Department of Health (1991b: 4.4).
[153] Parton (1991: 188–90).

there may be no need for a CAO at all.[154] It is therefore not surprising that few CAOs are granted. In the year ending September 1993 only 94 applications were made for CAOs, and only 55 were granted (26 were withdrawn).[155]

(ii) When can the CAO be made?

A CAO can only be requested by a local authority or an 'authorised person' (at present, only the NSPCC).[156] The court can make a CAO under s 43(1) where:

(a) the applicant has reasonable cause to suspect that the child is suffering, or is likely to suffer, significant harm;
(b) an assessment of the state of the child's health or development, or of the way in which he has been treated, is required to enable the applicant to determine whether or not the child is suffering, or is likely to suffer, significant harm; and
(c) it is unlikely that such an assessment will be made, or be satisfactory, in the absence of an order under this section.

The phrase 'significant harm' has the same meaning as in s 31, which will be discussed later in this chapter. The focus of the test is the applicant's belief of the risk of significant harm: it must be reasonable. The hurdle is lower than that for a care order, for example, because the CAO is less intrusive into family life.[157] Once the court is satisfied that s 43(1) is satisfied, it must still be persuaded that the making of the CAO is in the child's welfare under s 1(1) and satisfies s 1(5) of the Children Act 1989.[158]

(iii) The effects of a CAO

There are two automatic results of a CAO. First, the order requires any person who is able to do so to produce the child to a person named in the order (normally a social worker). The second effect is that the order authorises the named person to carry out an assessment of the child.[159] There are likely to be specific directions in the order relating to medical or psychiatric examinations: for example, who should conduct the examinations and where they should take place.[160] The local authority does not acquire parental responsibility, which remains with the parents. It seems that a child may refuse to submit to an examination if he or she is of sufficient understanding.[161]

---

[154] J. Dickens (1993: 94).
[155] Children Act Advisory Committee (1993). The numbers are so small that the government stopped collecting statistics on CAOs after 1993.
[156] Contrast with the emergency protection order, which can be applied for by anyone.
[157] One important difference between the CAO and the EPO is that an application for the CAO can be applied for *ex parte*.
[158] The checklist of factors in s 1(3) does not apply: *Re R (Recovery Orders)* [1998] 2 FLR 401.
[159] CA 1989, s 43(7).
[160] If the child is to be removed from home, this should be set out in the order: CA 1989, s 43(10).
[161] CA 1989, s 43(8); but note the interpretation of *South Glamorgan County Council v W and B* [1993] 1 FLR 574, [1993] 1 FCR 626 on the similarly worded s 44(7), that the court may override the refusal of a child.

The maximum duration of a CAO is seven days from the starting date specified in the order.[162] There is no power to extend this time period. Seven days is unlikely to be long enough for some psychological examinations.[163] The justification for the limitation is that seven days should be enough to tell the authority whether further orders are required.

7. COMPULSORY ORDERS: CARE ORDERS, SUPERVISION ORDERS AND EMERGENCY PROTECTION ORDERS

There are three main orders under which a local authority can intervene in a family's life even without the family's consent. For emergencies, the emergency protection order (EPO) is available. To provide long-term solutions the choice is between care or supervision orders.[164] Care and supervision orders should only be applied for as a last resort, if voluntary arrangements and the provision of services cannot adequately protect a child.[165] As Bainham has put it: 'Court orders for care and supervision are ... very much the ambulance at the bottom of the cliff while the support services are the (however inadequate) fence at the top.'[166] The Children Act 1989 makes it clear that a child can only be taken into care through one route, that is s 31.[167] The local authority cannot take a child into care except by applying for a care order.

A. Who can apply?

Section 31(1) states that only a local authority or the NSPCC can apply for a care or supervision order. There is provision for the Secretary of State to add to that list, but he has not. Before the NSPCC brings care proceedings, it should consult the local authority in whose area the child is ordinarily resident.[168]

B. Who can be taken into care?

Care and supervision orders can only be made in respect of a child who is under 18.[169] A married child cannot be taken into care. Can a care order be made in respect of a foetus?[170] There have been several cases where a local authority has become aware that a pregnant women is harming her unborn child, perhaps by taking drugs or excessive alcohol; or there may be a history of the woman abusing other children. The local authority may feel that the mother needs antenatal help and may even seek to restrict her behaviour. The court has consistently held that

---

[162] CA 1989, s 43(5).
[163] J. Dickens (1993: 96).
[164] The effects of the orders will be discussed in detail in Chapter 11.
[165] Department of Health (1991b: 3.2).
[166] Bainham (1998a: 325).
[167] *Re T (A Minor) (Care Order: Conditions)* [1994] 2 FLR 423, [1994] 2 FCR 721.
[168] CA 1989, s 31(6) and (7).
[169] CA 1989, s 105.
[170] Discussion in Wagstaff (1998).

the unborn child is not a person and so cannot be the subject of a care order, as was established in *Re F (In Utero)*.[171] However, harm done to the foetus might be relied upon as evidence to place a child in care shortly after birth.[172] This means that the local authority can only intervene to protect an unborn child if the mother consents to the intervention. The policy here seems to be that any intervention designed to assist the foetus will inevitably interfere with the mother's autonomy. The mother's freedom to take such alcohol she thinks fit, or refuse medication, for example, over-rides any interest that the foetus has.[173]

It is, of course, quite possible for a local authority to obtain an emergency court order once the child has been born.[174] However, the issue is not straightforward. If the child is born with foetal alcohol syndrome, for example, it is arguable that he or she might not be suffering harm (at least as compared with a similar child with foetal alcohol syndrome). Further, even if the child is suffering harm, it is arguable that the suffering is not caused by the parenting. The argument would be that if the foetus is not a child, then the care during the pregnancy cannot be parenting. Perhaps the best argument for the local authority would be that the lack of care shown towards the foetus during pregnancy is evidence that the parent is likely to cause the child significant harm in the future.[175] However, in *K and T v Finland*[176] the European Court of Human Rights took the view that removing a child at birth infringed the mother's rights under article 8 of the European Convention on Human Rights. The case concerned a mother who suffered on occasion from schizophrenia, although at the time of the child's birth she was in good health. The removal of the baby, without consultation, from the parents and without exploring the possibilities of reuniting the family, infringed the Convention. This was particularly so in the light of the fact the mother had no history of being violent towards children and the child had been taken from the hospital, which was a safe environment for the child and therefore there was no need for immediate intervention. The court were particularly concerned that the removal of the child prevented the mother from bonding with or breastfeeding the child.

C. The effect of a care order

The main effect of a care order is to give parental responsibility for the child to the local authority. The local authority may then remove the child from the parents (but does not have to). The local authority will be authorised to make decisions about the child and will be responsible for the child's welfare and deciding where the child will live. The effects of the care order will be discussed in more detail in Chapter 11.

---

[171] [1988] Fam 122 CA.
[172] *Re D (A Minor)* [1987] 1 FLR 422; *Re N (Leave to Withdraw Care Proceedings)* [2000] 1 FLR 134.
[173] *St George's Healthcare NHS Trust v S* [1998] 2 FLR 728.
[174] *Re R (A Child) (Care Proceedings: Teenage Pregnancy)* [2000] 2 FCR 556.
[175] *Re A (A Minor) (Care Proceedings)* [1993] 1 FLR 824.
[176] [2000] 2 FLR 79.

D. The nature and purpose of the supervision order

The supervision order aims to give the local authority some control over the child, without the degree of intervention involved in a care order.[177] Under a supervision order the child will remain at home, but will be under the watch of a designated officer of a local authority or a probation officer.[178] The making of the order does not alter the legal position of the parents; they retain full parental responsibility; the supervision order does not give parental responsibility to the local authority. The court cannot make a care order at the same time as a supervision order, although it can make a s 8 order and a supervision order.[179]

Although the supervision order is usually regarded as a less serious intervention in family life than a care order, the grounds for the orders are the same. This is because although the intervention into family life is less serious than with the care order, it is nevertheless a significant intrusion into the family's life.

E. Care or supervision order?

Where the threshold criteria have been made out, the local authority must decide whether a care order or a supervision order is more appropriate.[180] The following factors are relevant:

1. If the local authority wishes to remove a child from the home then it must apply for a care order.[181] It is not possible to remove a child under a supervision order.[182] If the local authority decides that the child should stay with the family, either a care order or a supervision order can be made. If a care order is made then the child can be removed by the local authority at any time.[183] If a supervision order is made then the child can only be removed if a further application is made to the court, for an emergency protection order for example. The supervision order, combined with the power to apply for an emergency protection order, should be regarded as a 'strong package', especially as the supervision order gives instant access into the child's home.[184] However, where there is very serious harm or sexual abuse, the courts have suggested that a care order should be made.[185]

2. Hale J in *Re O (Care or Supervision Order)*[186] stated that a supervision order normally requires co-operation from the parents and is therefore only appropriate where there is at least a reasonable relationship between the parent and the local authority. In *Oxfordshire CC v L (Care or Supervision Order)*[187] the parents had

---

[177] If the problems relate specifically to education then a special education supervision order is available.
[178] CA 1989, s 31(1)(b).
[179] E.g. *Re DH (A Minor) (Child Abuse)* [1994] 1 FLR 679, [1994] 2 FCR 3.
[180] For a useful summary of the relevant factors, see *Re D (Care or Supervision Order)* [2000] Fam Law 600.
[181] *Oxfordshire CC v L (Care or Supervision Order)* [1998] 1 FLR 70.
[182] Unless the child is voluntarily accommodated under CA 1989, s 20.
[183] *Re B (Care Order or Supervision Order)* [1996] 2 FLR 693, [1997] 1 FCR 309.
[184] *Re S(J) (A Minor) (Care or Supervision)* [1993] 2 FLR 919 at p. 947.
[185] *Re S (Care or Supervision Order)* [1996] 1 FLR 753 CA.
[186] [1996] 2 FLR 755, [1997] 2 FCR 17.
[187] [1998] 1 FLR 70.

co-operated with the local authority and responded well to assistance in the past. This indicated that a supervision order would be appropriate.

3. Where the local authority wishes to acquire parental responsibility, a care order is appropriate. *Re V (Care or Supervision Order)*[188] demonstrates this point well. There was a dispute between the parents and the local authority over what kind of education was appropriate for a disabled child. The local authority wanted to be able to make decisions relating to the child's education and so a care order was made, even though the child was to remain with the parents.

4. If a child was injured through an act of a parent that was thought to be out of character, then a supervision order may be more appropriate than a care order.[189]

5. If the parents would react very negatively to the making of a care order, but not to a supervision order, this could be a significant factor, especially if the children are going to remain with the parents.[190]

F. Grounds for supervision and care orders

The grounds for a supervision or care order are set out in s 31 of the Children Act 1989. Before a care order or a supervision order can be made, it is necessary to show four things:

1. The court must be satisfied that 'the child concerned is suffering, or is likely to suffer, significant harm'.[191]

2. '[T]hat the harm, or likelihood of harm, is attributable to: (i) the care given to the child, or likely to be given to him if the order were not made, not being what it would be reasonable to expect a parent to give him; or (ii) the child's being beyond parental control.'[192]

3. The making of the order would promote the welfare of the child.[193]

4. That making the order is better for the child than making no order at all.[194]

The first two requirements are commonly known as the 'threshold criteria'. It should be stressed that a care order or supervision order cannot be made simply on the basis that the child's parents agree that the child should be taken into care.[195] By contrast, simply because there is significant harm does not mean that an order must be made; it must also be shown that the making of the order will advance the child's welfare.[196] These four requirements will now be considered separately.

---

[188] [1996] 1 FLR 776 CA.
[189] *Manchester CC* v *B* [1996] 1 FLR 324.
[190] *Re B (Care Order or Supervision Order)* [1996] 2 FLR 693, [1997] 1 FCR 309.
[191] CA 1989, s 31(2)(a).
[192] CA 1989, s 31(2)(b).
[193] CA 1989, s 1(1).
[194] CA 1989, s 1(5).
[195] *Re G (A Minor) (Care Proceedings)* [1994] 2 FLR 69.
[196] *Humberside CC* v *B* [1993] 1 FLR 257, [1993] 1 FCR 613.

(i) 'Is suffering or is likely to suffer significant harm'

The following terms need to be examined.

(a) Harm

Harm is defined in s 31(9) of the Children Act 1989 as 'ill-treatment or the impairment of health or development'. 'Ill-treatment' includes 'sexual abuse and forms of ill-treatment which are not physical, including, for example, impairment suffered from seeing or hearing the ill-treatment of another'; 'development' is defined as 'physical, intellectual, emotional, social or behavioural development'; and 'health' means 'physical or mental health'.[197] Therefore, harm is not limited to physical abuse. For example, children can be harmed if their parents do not talk to them, or deprive them of opportunities of developing social skills. Similarly, not attending school[198] or not receiving adequate medical treatment[199] could amount to harm.

The harm can be due to positive or negative acts.[200] Of course, harm can be caused unintentionally. In *Re V (Care or Supervision Order)*[201] a mother, who was very protective of her son, sought to keep her son at home rather than sending him to a special school (he suffered from cystic fibrosis). This was held as amounting to harm, even though she was acting from the best of motives.

There can be difficulties in defining harm. Imagine a child who is brought up by devoutly religious parents who require the child to spend two hours a day in prayer and memorising holy texts. Some may say this is providing the child with an invaluable spiritual basis for his or her life. Others may regard this as abuse, hindering the child's social development. In *Re W (Minors) (Residence Order)*[202] the Court of Appeal considered a case involving a mother and stepfather who were naturists. The court accepted that nudity of adults before children per se did not fall within the definition of sexual abuse. The court required clear evidence that such conduct harmed the children. It did not follow that, because it might be disapproved of by many parents, it was therefore abuse.

(b) *Significant* harm

In the Department of Health's *Guidance and Regulations*[203] it is explained that 'minor shortcomings in health or minor deficits in physical, psychological or social development should not require compulsory intervention unless cumulatively they are having, or are likely to have, serious and lasting effects upon the child'. *Significant* harm can therefore be the result of several minor harms. Booth J in *Humberside CC v B*[204] suggested that 'significant' here meant 'considerable, note-

---

[197] CA 1989, s 31(9).
[198] *Re O (A Minor) (Care Order: Education: Procedure)* [1992] 2 FLR 7, [1992] 1 FCR 489.
[199] *F v Solfolk* [1981] 2 FLR 208.
[200] Bracewell J in *Re M (A Minor) (Care Order: Threshold Conditions)* [1994] Fam 95; approved [1994] 2 AC 424 HL.
[201] [1996] 1 FLR 776 CA.
[202] [1998] 1 FCR 75.
[203] Department of Health (1991b: 3.2).
[204] [1993] 1 FLR 257, [1993] 1 FCR 613.

worthy or important'. The court will readily assume that an abandoned child will be likely to suffer significant harm.[205]

It should be stressed that the word 'significant' focuses on the harm suffered by the child, rather than the blameworthiness of the parent's act. However, an act committed by a parent against their child which shows enormous indifference to the child's welfare, but in fact only causes a small amount of harm, might indicate that the child is likely to suffer significant harm in the future, which would be enough to establish the threshold criteria.

In deciding whether the child is suffering significant harm, 'the child's health or development shall be compared with that which could reasonably be expected of a similar child'.[206] Precisely what this means is open to debate. However, it seems clear that, for example, in determining whether a child with learning difficulties is suffering it is necessary to compare the child in question with a hypothetical child who also has learning difficulties. In other words, it cannot be said that the child with learning difficulties is suffering significant harm because he or she is less educationally developed than a child without such difficulties. The question is whether an average child with learning difficulties would have reached the same level of educational achievement. There are a number of debatable issues in considering the 'similar child' test:

1. There is particular controversy over the extent to which the cultural background of the child should be taken into account.[207] For example, if a particular religion or culture teaches that a teenage girl should not talk to anyone who is not related to her, and a local authority thought this was harming a girl's social development, should the girl be compared only with a girl brought up in the same culture?

   There are two main views on this. One is that 'Muslim children, Rastafarian children, the children of Hasidic Jews may be different and have different needs from children brought up in the indigenous white nominally Christian culture'.[208] This perspective would require the court to compare the child with a child from a similar culture or background. The other view is that there should be a minimum standard for all children;[209] that what is harmful to children should not depend on their cultural background. However, the fact that the harm was an aspect of cultural or religious practice may be very relevant in deciding whether making a care order would promote the welfare of the child.[210] In *Re D (Care: Threshold Criteria)*[211] the Court of Appeal adopted the second view, declaring that what amounts to significant harm should not depend on the child's cultural or ethnic background. On the other hand there are concerns also that a lack of appreciation of cultural differences may lead social workers to perceive harm where there is none.[212]

---

[205] *Re M (Care Order: Parental Responsibility)* [1996] 2 FLR 84, [1996] 2 FLR 521.
[206] CA 1989, s 31(10).
[207] Freeman (1992a: 107). See also Brophy, Jhotti-Johal, and Owen (2003).
[208] Freeman (1992a: 153). See also Freeman (1997a: ch. 7).
[209] Bainham (1998a: 383–4).
[210] CA 1989, s 1(3)(d).
[211] [1998] FL 656 CA.
[212] Brophy, Jhotti-Johal, and Owen (2003).

2. To what extent are the characteristics or capabilities of the parents to be taken into account? If a child is brought up by a parent with a disability, should the child be considered only in comparison with a similar child living with disabled parents?[213] The statutory test seems to focus on the child rather than the parents. The better view, therefore, is that the capabilities of the parents are not taken into account in the definition of harm.[214]

3. What if the child has brought about the harm him- or herself? In *Re O (A Minor) (Care Order: Education: Procedure)*[215] it was suggested that in relation to a 15-year-old truant, the 'similar child' was 'a child of equivalent intellectual and social development who has gone to school and not merely an average child who may or may not be at school'.[216] Crucially, the child was not to be compared with another truant child. The reason why truancy was not a relevant characteristic is not clear, but one interpretation of the decision is that factors that the child has brought upon himself or herself are not to be taken into account.

(c) Is suffering

Section 31 requires proof that the child either is or is likely to suffer significant harm. Notably, proof that the child has suffered harm in the past is insufficient, although harm in the past may be evidence that the child is likely to suffer harm in the future.

There has been much debate over what 'is' means in this context.[217] The leading case is now *Re M (A Minor) (Care Order: Threshold Conditions)*,[218] decided in the House of Lords. The father murdered the mother in front of the children. The father was convicted of murder and given a life sentence, and there was a recommendation that he be deported on his release. Three of the four children were placed with W (the children's aunt). The remaining child, M, was initially placed with foster parents, but later joined her siblings with W. By the time the case came before the House of Lords it was agreed by everyone that M should live with W, but the local authority still wanted a care order just in case it became necessary in due course to remove M from W's house.

The crucial issue in the case was whether the phrase 'is suffering' meant that it had to be shown that the child was suffering at the time of the hearing before the court. This was important because, by the time the matter came to court, the child was safely with the foster parents and it could not have been found by the court that 'she is suffering significant harm'. Lord Mackay LC rejected such a reading. He stated that the date at which the child must be suffering significant harm was 'the date at which the local authority initiated the procedure for protection under the Act'. If the child was suffering significant harm at the time the local authority first intervened, and the social work continued to the date of the court hearing, then the child 'is suffering significant harm' for the purpose of the Act. Subsequently the

---

[213] See Freeman (1992a: 107).

[214] More debatable may be whether the poverty of the family should be taken into account.

[215] [1992] 2 FLR 7, [1992] 1 FCR 489.

[216] Noted Fortin (1993).

[217] Only lawyers ...!

[218] [1994] 2 FLR 577, [1994] 2 FCR 871; discussed in Bainham (1994a); Masson (1994).

Court of Appeal in *Re G (Care Proceedings: Threshold Conditions)*[219] held that the local authority could rely on facts which subsequently came to light to demonstrate that at the time when the local authority first intervened the child was suffering significant harm, even if it did not know of those facts at the time.[220]

Applying this to the facts of the case in *Re M* it was clear that, at the time when the social work intervention started (i.e. just after the murder of the mother), it could have been said the child was suffering significant harm, and therefore a care order could be made. Lord Nolan explained:

> Parliament cannot have intended that temporary measures taken to protect the child from immediate harm should prevent the court from regarding the child as one who is suffering, or is likely to suffer, significant harm within the meaning of s 31(2)(a), and should thus disqualify the court from making a more permanent order under the section. The focal point of the inquiry must be the situation which resulted in the temporary measures taken, and which has led to the application for a care or supervision order.[221]

The decision is clearly correct because, if it is necessary to show that at the time of a court hearing a child is suffering significant harm, then the local authority may have to delay taking measures to protect the child until there has been a court hearing.[222] Although the House of Lords' interpretation of 'is' has been widely praised, another aspect of the decision has given cause for concern.

By the time the case was before the House of Lords, M was settled with W, but their Lordships approved the making of a care order. It may be questioned whether there really was a need for a care order at all. Lord Templeman justified their Lordships' decision by suggesting there was a need for 'a watching brief' on the child's behalf.[223] Although it is understandable that the local authority wanted to keep an eye on M, and also might want in emergency circumstances to be able to remove M, a supervision order and the potential to apply for an emergency protection order would seem to provide adequate protection.

Re M has been applied in several cases. In *Re SH (Care Order: Orphan)*[224] the child had spent spells in voluntary accommodation while the mother was in hospital. The mother died, and shortly afterwards the father died. The local authority then sought a care order. Hollis J, relying on *Re M*, held that the question was whether the child was suffering significant harm when the 'rescue operation' began. Here the 'rescue operation' began when the mother asked the child to be voluntarily accommodated.[225] At that time the child could be said to be suffering significant harm.

In *Re M (Care Order: Parental Responsibility)*[226] it was confirmed that the threshold condition may be satisfied in relation to an abandoned baby. The baby was

---

[219] [2001] FL 727.
[220] Although the Court of Appeal warned of 'Micawberish' actions being taken in the hope that the intervention will be justified by what will later be found out.
[221] [1994] 2 FCR 871, para 32.
[222] Lord Templeman and Lord Nolan specifically took this point.
[223] *Re M (A Minor) (Care Order: Threshold Conditions)* [1994] 2 AC 424 at p. 440.
[224] [1995] 1 FLR 746, [1996] 1 FCR 1.
[225] It was not relevant that the social work intervention was at the request of the mother.
[226] [1996] 2 FLR 84, [1996] 2 FLR 521.

found a few days old on the steps of a health centre. It was impossible to locate the child's family and the child was placed with foster parents, although a care order was not then sought. The local authorities became concerned because the baby was found to have medical difficulties, and so sought a care order which would give them parental responsibility. Cazalet J accepted that the baby was suffering significant harm because the child had been abandoned and no one had parental responsibility. The care order was granted, which gave the local authority parental responsibility.

(d) Is likely to suffer significant harm[227]

It is generally agreed that the state should be able to intervene and remove a child who is in real danger of suffering significant harm in the future, rather than wait until the harm occurs. However, removing a child on the basis of speculative harm, especially harm that may be a long way off, is controversial, because it is impossible to know whether or not the harm would materialise.

The simple words 'is likely to suffer significant harm' were discussed in detail by the House of Lords in *Re H (Minors) (Sexual Abuse: Standard of Proof)*.[228] The case divided the House of Lords three to two and revealed the real problems at issue. A 15-year-old girl alleged that she had been sexually abused by her mother's cohabitant. The cohabitant was tried for rape but he was acquitted by a jury. The local authority was still concerned about the situation, especially because the cohabitant still lived with the mother and her three younger children.[229] The local authority sought a care order in respect of the three younger girls. It argued that although it had not been proved beyond all reasonable doubt[230] that the older child had been abused, there was a substantial risk that the younger children could be abused. The judge at first instance accepted that there was 'a real possibility' that the older girl had been abused, but he felt that the 'high standard of proof' required for a care order had not been satisfied. He therefore dismissed the application for a care order. The House of Lords looked at five questions:

1. *What does 'likely' mean?* It was held unanimously that 'likely' meant that significant harm was a real possibility; that is, a possibility that could not sensibly be ignored. This is a comparatively 'low' risk of harm.[231] The phrase 'likely' did *not* require the court to find that the harm was more likely than not to occur. This is a remarkably 'pro-child protection' stance of the law to take. A child can be taken away from parents, even though the child has not been harmed and it is not even more likely than not that the child will be, if it can be shown that there is a real possibility the child will suffer significant harm.
2. *When must the harm be likely?* It needs to be shown that the child was likely to be harmed at the time the local authority first intervened. In other words, that the *Re M (A Minor) (Care Order: Threshold Conditions)*[232] approach to 'is' was also

---

[227] CA 1989, s 31(2)(a).
[228] [1996] AC 563; noted in Keating (1996); M. Hayes (1997); Keenan (1997).
[229] The 15-year-old child had moved to live elsewhere.
[230] The burden of proof in criminal proceedings.
[231] *Re O and N (Children) (Non-Accidental Injury)* [2003] 1 FCR 673, para 16.
[232] [1994] 2 FCR 871.

followed for 'is likely'. In *Re N (Leave to Withdraw Care Proceedings)*[233] Bracewell J stressed that the court was not restricted to looking at harm in the immediate future, but could also consider longer-term harms.

3. *What is the burden of proof?* It must be shown on the balance of probabilities that harm is likely. In other words, it must be more likely than not that there is a real possibility of harm. This was not controversial. However, the question has been made far more complex by *dicta* of Lord Nicholls in *Re H (Minors) (Sexual Abuse: Standard of Proof)*,[234] who argued: 'the more serious the allegation the less likely it is that the event occurred and, hence, the stronger should be the evidence before the court concludes that the allegation is established on the balance of probability'.[235] What he was arguing was that across the country there are very few cases of serious abuse of children, whereas there is numerically a higher number of low-level abuse cases. So in a randomly selected case it is less likely that serious abuse has occurred than that minor abuse has taken place. Therefore, more evidence is required to prove more serious abuse than to prove less serious abuse because serious abuse is statistically less likely. The flaw in this logic is that it has not been demonstrated that *where a child has alleged serious abuse* that serious abuse is less likely to have occurred than where a child has alleged more 'ordinary' abuse. In fact, one might think that the more horrific the allegations, the less likely it is that the child is making them up.[236] A further criticism of the *dicta* was made by Lord Lloyd (in the minority), who argued that under Lord Nicholls's approach, the more serious the feared injury, the harder the burden of proof is to satisfy, and the more difficult it is to ensure protection for the child. In the light of these criticisms, it is submitted that these *dicta* should not be followed.[237]

4. *Who has to prove that the child is likely to suffer significant harm?* The House of Lords agreed that the local authority had to prove that the significant harm was likely to occur. The burden did not lie on the parents to show that it was not likely to occur.

5. *From what evidence can the risk of harm be established?* The majority argued that in order to find that harm was likely, it was necessary first to find certain 'primary facts'. Each of these primary facts would have to be proved on the balance of probabilities. Then, looking at these primary facts, the court could consider whether they demonstrated that significant harm was likely (that is, that there was a real possibility of significant harm). In *Re H*, because it had not been found on the balance of probabilities that the older child had been abused (there was only a strong suspicion that she had), there were no primary facts proved. Therefore, it could not be shown that the younger girls were likely to suffer significant harm. Suspicion itself was an insufficient basis on which to decide that

---

[233] [2000] 1 FLR 134.
[234] [1996] AC 563; noted in Keating (1996); M. Hayes (1997); Keenan (1997).
[235] [1996] AC 563 at p. 586.
[236] It is also important to emphasise research which suggests that children who allege abuse but are disbelieved suffer harm: Sharland (1996: 184).
[237] They were not referred to in *Re M and R (Child Abuse: Evidence)* [1996] 2 FLR 195, [1996] 2 FCR 617.

there was a significant likelihood of abuse. One reason is that it would be unjustifiable for a parent to have his or her child removed (with the attendant shame and social exclusion which would probably follow) on the basis of a suspicion. Another reason is that, as Lord Nicholls explained subsequently in *Re O and N (Children) (Non-Accidental Injury)*,[238] otherwise a suspicion that a parent had harmed a child would not be sufficient to show the child had suffered significant harm, but could be relied upon to show that the child was likely to suffer significant harm. That would be 'extraordinary', he suggested.[239]

The majority's approach has been subject to several criticisms:

(a) The minority found the approach of the majority over-complicated. Lord Lloyd argued: 'Parliament has asked a simple question: is the court satisfied that there is a serious risk of significant harm in the future? The question should be capable of being answered without too much over-analysis.'[240] The minority argued that, looking at the case as a whole, there were sufficient worries (especially the fact that there was a strong suspicion that the cohabitant had abused the older girl) to justify the finding of likely harm. This, they thought, was sufficient to justify making the care order.[241] This argument was particularly strong on the facts of that case because, if the older girl had been abused as she had alleged, there was a very serious danger facing the younger children.

(b) Mathematically, the majority's approach looks dubious. Imagine two cases: in case A there are ten alleged facts pointing to abuse and there is a 45 per cent chance that each alleged fact was true; in case B there is one alleged fact pointing to abuse for which there is a 60 per cent chance that it is true.[242] The approach of the majority would allow for a finding of likely harm only in case B. In case A, as none of the facts were proved on the balance of probabilities, an order could not be made. Yet, in statistical terms, case A would be a stronger case than case B. The approach of the minority, looking at the totality of the circumstances, would permit the making of a care order in case A.

(c) The key underlying issue in the case has been explained by Hayes: 'The dilemma to be resolved is how the legal framework, and the legal process, can best reconcile safeguards for children suffering from significant harm with the obligation to respect parental autonomy and family privacy.'[243] There is an option of either threatening the parents' rights by removing the child from them without clear evidence, or threatening the child's rights by not providing protection even where there is a serious risk of danger. The House of Lords clearly preferred upholding parents' rights.

---

[238] [2003] 1 FCR 673.

[239] [2003] 1 FCR 673, para 16.

[240] *Re H (Minors) (Sexual Abuse: Standard of Proof)* [1996] AC 563 at p. 581.

[241] The majority did admit that the totality of the evidence established a worrying number of circumstances, but, as no facts were proved, this belief was mere suspicion.

[242] Assuming that the ten facts, if true, would provide as good evidence that future harm was likely as the single fact, if true.

[243] M. Hayes (1997: 1–2).

Whether this is consistent with the welfare principle in s 1 of the Children Act 1989 is open to debate.

(d) The question must now be viewed in the light of the European Convention on Human Rights. A child must be protected from 'torture' and 'inhuman and degrading treatment'.[244] Yet at the same time the state is required to respect the private and family life of all the family members.[245] It is certainly arguable that the approach taken in *Re H* places more weight on the parents' right to respect for family life than on the child's right to respect for private life and to be protected from inhuman and degrading treatment.

(ii) Harm attributable to the care given or likely to be given or the child's being beyond parental control

The court must be satisfied that the harm is attributable to the care of the child not being what it would be reasonable to expect a parent to give. This might involve acts by the parent harming the child, or a failure to protect the child from harm.[246] The requirement also means that if the harm is caused by someone who is not a carer of the child (e.g. if the child was abused by a stranger), that harm cannot form the basis of a care order, unless it could be argued that the harm is attributable to the parents because they failed to stop the third party from causing it. There is an exception to this where a parent shares the regular care of the child with a third party, which we shall discuss shortly. So, if the child is subject to bullying at school and suffers significant harm as a result, a care order could only be made if it could be shown that the parents had not taken reasonable steps to prevent the bullying. This requirement is in part explained on the basis that a parent who cannot be blamed for the harm should not have his or her child taken into care.

An argument which has been particularly difficult for the court is where it is clear that the child had been harmed, but it is not clear who caused the harm.

It is necessary to distinguish three situations:

1. *It is not clear which parent injured the child.* If it is shown that a child had suffered non-accidental injury at the hands of his or her parents but it could not be proved which of them caused the injury the threshold criteria will be met.[247]
2. *It is not clear whether a parent or another carer harmed the child.* The House of Lords in *Lancashire CC v B* examined this issue.[248] The case involved child A, who was being cared for by a childminder while her parents were out at work. It became clear that A had suffered serious non-accidental head injuries, but it was impossible to establish whether these injuries were caused by the mother, the father or the childminder. The parents argued that s 31(2)(b) required proof that it was the care of the parents (or primary carers) which was not of the standard

---

[244] Article 3.
[245] Article 8.
[246] *Re A (Children) (Interim Care Order)* [2001] 3 FCR 402.
[247] *Re O and N (Children) (Non-Accidental Injury)* [2003] 1 FCR 673.
[248] [2000] 1 FCR 583, discussed in Bainham (2000a).

expected of a reasonable parent and, as it was not clear that they had harmed the child, the care order should not be made. The local authority argued that all that needed to be shown was that the care given by *someone* who was caring for the child was below the standard expected of a reasonable parent. In other words, the reference to parents in s 31(2)(b) was a reference to the standard of care expected and not a requirement that it was a parent whose care was less than the required standard.

The House of Lords acknowledged that there were difficulties with either interpretation. If the parents' argument was accepted, then a child might undoubtedly be suffering significant harm but, because it was not clear who had caused the harm, no protection could be offered. As Lord Nicholls maintained: '[s]uch an interpretation would mean that the child's future health, or even her life, would have to be hazarded on the chance that, after all, the non-parental carer rather than one of the parents inflicted the injuries'.[249] On the other hand, if the view of the local authority was accepted, then a child could be taken into care even though the parents were blameless. The approach taken by the House of Lords was that if it is clear that either of the parents or one of the primary carers caused the harm, the attributable condition has been made out.

The difficulty with the House of Lords' decision is that it is far from clear who is 'a carer' in this context. If a child should not be denied protection because it is unclear whether the harm is caused by a parent or childminder, why should he or she be denied protection if it is unclear whether the harm is caused by a parent or a non-carer (e.g. a bully at school)? If, in the name of child protection, we are to permit children to be taken into care even if their parents may well be blameless, surely this should be so whoever else may have caused the harm?[250] The real problem at the heart of the House of Lords' decision is that it does not consider the purpose of the 'attributable' condition. Its purpose could have been seen as a form of protection of parental rights: 'your child will only be removed if you do not treat your child as a reasonable parent would'; or as a way of protecting children's interests: it will only be best for a local authority to remove a child from his or her parents if he or she is suffering significant harm. But the House of Lords' decision is not consistent with either approach and leaves the attributable condition without a clear role.

3. *It is not clear whether the parent or a third party (other than a carer) harmed the child.* In such a case, unless it is proved on the balance of probabilities that a parent or carer had harmed the child, a care order cannot be made.

It should be stressed that the test is essentially an objective one. The test refers to *a* parent, and not *this* parent. This makes clear that the test is satisfied even if the parent was doing his or her best, if the parent's best caused the child significant harm.

---

[249] *Lancashire CC* v *B* [2000] 1 All ER 97 at p. 103.
[250] Herring (2000b).

(a) 'The child's being beyond parental control'

The kind of situation here is where the child behaves in an uncontrolled manner. Commonly it is used where the child is dependent upon illegal drugs. It does not matter if it is unclear whether the harm is caused by the parent or the child being beyond parental control. Ewbank J in *Re O (A Minor) (Care Order: Education: Procedure)*[251] suggested: '... where a child is suffering harm in not going to school and is living at home it will follow that either the child is beyond her parents' control or that they are not giving the child the care that it would be reasonable to expect a parent to give'.

(iii) The order must promote the child's welfare

The court must not reason that, because the threshold criteria are satisfied, the care order must be made. It is crucial for the court to consider whether the making of the order is in the child's welfare.[252] When considering the welfare principle, the check-list of factors in s 1(3) must be taken into account.[253] Particularly relevant is whether there are any relatives[254] (or perhaps even a family friend) who can look after the child. A residence order in their favour, rather than a care order, may be more in the child's welfare. A crucial issue under the welfare criteria is whether the proposals of the local authority are proportionate to the harm. So even if there is significant harm, it may well be that taking the child into care would not be a proportionate response.[255] For example, in *Kutzner v Germany*[256] the European Court of Human Rights considered a case involving a married couple with learning difficulties. They had two children about whom the local authority became concerned. A psychologist's report suggested that there were concerns about the applicants' intellectual capacity to bring up children and the local authority placed the children with foster parents (and denied contact for the first six months). The European Court of Human Rights found that the parents' article 8 rights had been infringed. Although the local authority was justified in having concerns about the children, it had failed to consider whether additional measures of support to the couple would have sufficiently protected the children and thereby avoided the need for the 'most extreme measure' of removing the children.

The welfare stage is the point at which the court will consider whether it is more appropriate to make a care order or a supervision order. In theory, a court could grant a care order even though the local authority only applied for a supervision order,[257] although this would require 'urgent and strong reasons'.[258] In *Re K*

---

[251] [1992] 2 FLR 7.

[252] *Re O and N (Children) (Non-Accidental Injury)* [2003] 1 FCR 673, para 23, per Lord Nicholls.

[253] CA 1989, s 1(4)(b). Section 1(3)(g) is perhaps especially important in that it means that the court must consider whether making a s 8 order in favour of a relative is a better option than taking the child into care.

[254] *Re N-B and Others (Children) (Residence: Expert Evidence)* [2002] 3 FCR 259 CA. See Hunt (2001) for a discussion of the important role that relatives can play in child care cases.

[255] *Re O (A Child) (Supervision Order: Future Harm)* [2001] 1 FCR 289 CA.

[256] [2003] 1 FCR 249.

[257] In *Re M (A Minor) (Care Order: Threshold Conditions)* [1994] 2 AC 424 the House of Lords made a care order even though the local authority wished to withdraw its application; see also *Re K (Care Order or Residence Order)* [1995] 1 FLR 675, [1996] 1 FCR 365, where a care order was made contrary to the local authority's wishes.

[258] *Oxfordshire CC v L (Care or Supervision Order)* [1998] 1 FLR 70.

(Supervision Orders)[259] Wall J considered a case which was borderline between making a supervision order or no order. He stressed that the benefits of a supervision order were that the social workers would make the case a higher priority if a supervision order were granted and the mother would be more likely to co-operate if such an order were made.

In *Re K (Care Order or Residence Order)*[260] the question was whether it would be more appropriate to make a residence order or a care order. It was agreed that the children should be brought up by their grandparents. The local authority argued that the grandparents should be granted a residence order, whereas the grandparents argued that a care order was appropriate. This may sound odd, but the explanation lies in the financial consequences. If a care order were made and the children placed with the grandparents, the local authority would be responsible for providing financial support for the care of the children. However, if a residence order were made the local authority would not be obliged to make any financial contribution. Given that the children were disabled and needed specialist equipment, and that the grandparents were not well off, the Court of Appeal made a care order. It was fortunate for the grandparents that the local authority had originally applied for a care order and that its application was technically before the court, because the court could not have made a care order if the local authority had never applied for one.

What should the court do where the causes of the harm are unclear? In *Re O and N (Children) (Non-Accidental Injury)*[261] the House of Lords heard two appeals which they called cases of the 'uncertain perpetrator'. The cases concerned children whom it was clear had been harmed. The cases were therefore fundamentally different from *Re H*[262] where it had not been clear if any child had been harmed at all. In one case it was thought likely to be the father who had caused the harm, but the mother could not be ruled out. In the other case it was clear one of the parents caused harm, but it was unclear which. In both cases the mother and father had since separated. It was clear that in both cases the threshold criteria had been satisfied. The difficulty was at the stage when the court considered the welfare principle. Should the court not make a care order and return the child to the mother on the basis that it had not been established that she was a threat to the child, or were the suspicions over the mother sufficient to justify making a care order? Lord Nicholls thought it would be 'grotesque' if, because it could not be shown which parent had harmed the child, the child had to be treated as not at risk from either of them. Instead he suggested that:

> The preferable interpretation of the legislation is that in such cases the court is able to proceed at the welfare stage on the footing that each of the possible perpetrators is, indeed, just that: a possible perpetrator.[263]

---

[259] [1999] 2 FLR 303.
[260] [1995] 1 FLR 675, [1996] 1 FCR 365.
[261] [2003] 1 FCR 673.
[262] *Re H (Minors) (Sexual Abuse: Standard of Proof)* [1996] AC 563.
[263] [2003] 1 FCR 673 at para 28.

He went on to emphasise that social workers should be careful in such cases to treat the parents as potential perpetrators, not proved perpetrators. The decision does not make the decision of a judge in such a case any easier. But it does leave him or her with a wide discretion to decide whether or not it is safe to leave the child with a potentially abusive parent. The Court of Appeal in *North Yorkshire CC* v *SA*[264] has since explained that a person should be treated as a suspected abuser unless there is no real possibility that he or she has been involved in the abuse. They rejected a test that a person could be treated as a suspected abuser unless there was no possibility they had been involved.

An alternative way of dealing with such cases would be to say that in the unknown perpetrator cases each parent was either the perpetrator or was guilty of failing to protect their child from the other parent. Either way each parent posed a risk to the child. Lord Nicholls in *Re O and N* rejected this approach. He explained it could not be assumed that when one parent harmed the child, the other was blameworthy for not protecting the child. They may not have been present or the incident may have been a momentary loss of self-control, not giving the other parent a chance to intervene.

A similar issue arises where the case for a care order is made on the basis of two allegations. For example in *Re M and R (Child Abuse: Evidence)*[265] it was alleged that there had been sexual abuse, and also emotional neglect. The sexual abuse allegations were found to be unproved, but the neglect ones were found proved. The threshold criteria were therefore made out, but the question for the Court of Appeal was whether when deciding what order to make under the welfare principle the court should attach any significance to the sexual abuse allegation. The Court of Appeal held that the allegations should be ignored. Lord Nicholls in *Re O and N*[266] approved of the decision, but stated the court should at the welfare stage treat them as unproven allegations, which is not, perhaps, quite the same thing as ignoring them.

The effect of *Re O and N* is that suspicions (i.e. allegations which cannot be proved on the balance of probabilities) cannot be relied upon in establishing the threshold criteria, but they can be when the court decides what order, if any, to make under the welfare test. The mothers in *Re O and N* could with some justification feel that the decision enables the court to remove their children *from them* on the basis of suspicions. This was the very thing that Lord Nicholls in *Re H* said should not happen. A strong argument can be made that the law should be amended to permit suspicions to be relevant in deciding whether or not a supervision order should be made, but suspicions should not be relied upon to make a care order.[267]

---

[264] [2003] 3 FCR 118 CA.
[265] [1996] 2 FCR 617.
[266] [2003] 1 FCR 673.
[267] Bainham (2000b).

(iv) Section 1(5)

Section 1(5) requires the court to be persuaded that it is better for the child to make the care or supervision order than not to make an order at all. This provision was discussed in detail in Chapter 9.

(v) The role of the threshold criteria

One issue behind many of the cases interpreting s 31 is the role of the threshold criteria. Here are three popular views:

1. According to Lord Nicholls in *Re O and N*[268] the purpose of the threshold criteria is 'to protect families, both adults and children, from inappropriate interference in their lives by public authorities through the making of care and supervision orders'.
2. That the threshold criteria are there to reinforce the welfare principle and to remind courts that children are normally best brought up by their parents and only where there is a real danger will it be in the child's welfare for a care order to be made.
3. The threshold criteria exist to protect parents' rights. The state in effect guarantees to parents that unless they cause significant harm to their children, they will not be removed.

G. Care plans

It is well-established practice that a local authority applying for a care order should prepare a care plan.[269] This sets out what the local authority proposes should happen to the child while he or she is in care. It will suggest, for example, where he or she should live and what contact there should be with their family. The court, when considering whether to make the care order, should take into account the care plan.[270] The court can suggest alterations to the care plan but it cannot make a care order with certain conditions. So if the local authority refuses to change the care plan, then the court must either refuse to make the order or make the order on the basis of the local authority's plan. If a care order is made on the basis of the care plan, the local authority is not bound by the plan and can subsequently depart from it.[271]

The drafting of care plans can prove difficult, especially where the facts of the case are unclear.[272] This problem was considered by Bracewell J in *Re S (Care Proceedings: Split Hearing)*.[273] She suggested that there should be a split hearing: in the first hearing the court would establish the facts and the local authority could

---

[268] [2003] 1 FCR 673, para 14.
[269] *Manchester City Council v F* [1993] 1 FLR 419, [1993] 1 FCR 1000; Department of Health (1991a: 2.62).
[270] CA 1989, s 31(3A).
[271] See Chapter 11.
[272] Lord Chancellor's Department (1997).
[273] [1996] 2 FLR 773, [1996] 3 FCR 578.

then prepare a care plan; at the second hearing (if it is necessary) the court would consider precisely what order is appropriate in the circumstances.

(i) Does the basis of the care order matter?

There have been a few cases where the parents and the local authority agree that a care order should be made, but there is a dispute over the factual basis of the order. For example, in *Re B (Agreed Findings of Fact)*[274] the mother accepted that she was an inadequate mother and that a care order should be made. However, she denied an allegation that she had poisoned the child. The local authority wanted a full hearing so that the court could establish whether or not there had been a poisoning. The Court of Appeal, however, felt that the mother's acceptance that she was an inadequate parent was a sufficient basis upon which to make a court order, and that there was no need for a full hearing. This ruling, however, does not mean that a court can simply accept the parties' proposal that a care order should be made. In *Re G (A Minor) (Care Order: Threshold Conditions)*[275] it was stressed that the court (and not just the parties) had to be persuaded that the grounds for the care order existed, although there was no need for the court to decide disputed issues of fact if to do so was not necessary in deciding whether or not to make an order.

It is arguable that the lack of power of the courts to scrutinise a care plan, and the fact that they must accept or reject it as it is, is either in breach of article 6 (a right to a fair trial) or article 8 (a right to respect for family life) of the European Convention on Human Rights.[276] We shall return to the significance of care plans in Chapter 11.

H. Interim care orders

It may be that, having heard all the evidence, the court still feels it is not in a position to make a final decision of whether to make a care order or supervision order, or no order at all.[277] In such cases an interim order is appropriate.[278] An interim care order can only be made if the threshold and s 1 criteria are met and that making an interim care order is proportionate to the risk faced by the child.[279] If, when hearing an application for a care order or supervision order, the court is not convinced that the child is in need of immediate local authority care, it may consider just making an interim residence order[280] in favour of a relative. However, it may only do so if the court is persuaded that the child will be adequately protected without an interim care order or supervision order.[281]

These interim orders provide a legal framework until a final order can be made. It is important to stress that, as was made clear in *Re G (Minors) (Interim Care*

---

[274] [1998] 2 FLR 968.
[275] [1994] 2 FLR 69, [1995] Fam 16.
[276] Hall HHJ (2000).
[277] *Re S, Re W (Children: Care Plan)* [2002] 1 FCR 577 HL, para 90.
[278] *Re CH (Care or Interim Care Order)* [1998] 1 FLR 402, [1998] 2 FCR 347 CA.
[279] *Re H (A Child) (Interim Care Order)* [2003] 1 FCR 350.
[280] CA 1989, s 1(1) and (5) would have to be satisfied.
[281] CA 1989, s 38(3).

Order),[282] the fact that an interim order is made does not weigh on the court one way or the other in deciding the final order. To make an interim supervision order or interim care order the court must be satisfied that there are reasonable grounds for believing that the criteria under s 31(2) of the Children Act 1989 (the threshold criteria) have been satisfied, but they do not have to prove the conditions exist.[283]

On the making of an interim care order the local authority gains all the benefits and obligations of a care order: parental responsibility is placed on the local authority and the child is in the care of the local authority. There is a danger, therefore, that a court would be tempted to make an interim care order so that it could retain some control over the local authority and its care plan. However, Lord Nicholls in *Re S, Re W (Children: Care Plan)*[284] held that it would be wrong for a court to make an interim care order so that a court could exercise a supervisory role over the local authority. Lord Nicholls approved of the making of an interim care order in *C v Solihull MBC*[285] where the court was awaiting a report from an assessment of the parent's parenting skills and without that report it was not possible to decide whether or not to make a care order. However, when deciding whether there is sufficient certainty to make a care order the court should remember that to an extent uncertainty is inevitable and the local authority might have to be trusted to amend its care plan to deal appropriately with events as they unfold.[286]

What about cases where the care plan itself is rather unclear? Lord Nicholls explained that care plans had to be 'sufficiently firm and particularized for all concerned to have a reasonably clear picture of the likely way ahead for the foreseeable future'. He added that the plan had to be sufficiently clear to enable the parents and child to claim that the order would inappropriately interfere with their rights to respect for family life.[287] If the care plan is uncertain an interim care order may be appropriate.

More controversial are cases where the judge is persuaded that a care order is appropriate, but is not convinced that the care plan proposed by the local authority is appropriate. On the facts of *Re L (Sexual Abuse: Standard of Proof)*[288] the judge disagreed with the full care plan but decided that he should still make the care order because it was clear that the children needed protection and it would be wrong for him to make an interim care order to persuade the local authority to follow this view.

The leading case on attaching conditions to an interim care order is *Re C (Interim Care Order: Residential Assessment)*.[289] The House of Lords had to consider s 38(6), which states:

---

[282] [1993] 2 FLR 839, [1993] 2 FCR 557 CA.
[283] *Re B (A Minor) (Care Order: Criteria)* [1993] 1 FLR 815, [1993] 1 FCR 565.
[284] [2002] 1 FCR 577, para 90.
[285] [1992] 2 FCR 341.
[286] *Re S, Re W (Children: Care Plan)* [2002] 1 FCR 577 HL at para 98.
[287] *TP and KM v UK* [2001] 2 FCR 289, para 72.
[288] [1996] 1 FLR 116, [1996] 2 FCR 352.
[289] [1997] 1 FLR 1, [1997] 1 FCR 149: see C. Smith (1997a).

Where the court makes an interim care order, or interim supervision order, it may give such directions (if any) as it considers appropriate with regard to the medical or psychiatric examination or other assessment of the child . . .

The local authority had obtained an emergency protection order and an interim care order in relation to a child who had been taken to hospital with serious non-accidental injuries. The parents were young: 17 and 16 years old. The social workers involved favoured an assessment of the parents and child at a residential unit. The local authority disagreed on the basis of the cost of the programme (between £18,000 and £24,000) and because they feared that it would expose the child to risks. The House of Lords though it was permissible for the court to make an emergency protection order with conditions under s 38(6) that the parents and the child attend the centre. The House of Lords rejected two arguments of the local authority. The first was that under s 38(6) the assessment could only be ordered if it was of a medical or psychiatric nature, whereas here the assessment concerned the parents' abilities.[290] The House of Lords held that the assessment in question could fall within the definition of 'other assessment' in s 38(6), and so it was permitted.[291] The second argument of the local authority was that the condition was a wrongful attempt by the court to interfere with its care plan. The House of Lords rejected this argument, stating that although it was the preserve of the local authority to decide what should happen to a child in its care, it was the preserve of the court to decide whether a care order should be made. Here the assessment was necessary to enable the court to decide what order should be made. The decision in *Re C* does not sit easily with the general approach taken in the Children Act 1989 that the courts should not compel local authorities to spend their social services budget in a particular way.[292] In *Re C (Children) (Residential Assessment)*[293] the local authority argued that to be required to provide a residential assessment for the particular family would be to involve a disproportionate level of expenditure on one family, among all of those they had to care for. The Court of Appeal rejected this argument, but significantly on the basis that the local authority had not produced evidence to substantiate its claim. It was accepted that if such evidence had been forthcoming then the decision would have been different.

However, it is arguable that article 8(2) of the European Convention only permits the state to interfere with respect for family life if it is 'necessary', and the decision in *Re C (Children) (Residential Assessment)* is legitimate as part of the state's role in ensuring that a care order is necessary. Subsequently, in *Re B (Psychiatric Therapy for Parents)*,[294] the Court of Appeal made it clear that a condition could not be attached to an interim care order for the purpose of providing therapy for parents. This was applied by the Court of Appeal in *Re D (Jurisdiction: Programme of*

---

[290] See the useful discussion in R. Kennedy (2001) on the distinction between treatment and assessment.

[291] See also *Re B (A Child: Interim Care Order)* [2002] 2 FCR 367, [2002] FL 252 where the court was willing to state precisely where the assessment should be carried out.

[292] Hayes and Williams (1999: 181) suggest that it is an open question whether it would be possible to attach a condition to an interim care order requiring a child to be assessed in the home of the parents.

[293] [2001] 3 FCR 164.

[294] [1999] 1 FLR 701 CA.

Assessment or Therapy),[295] where the court confirmed that a programme of detoxification and psychotherapy for the mother could not be ordered under s 38(6). A programme must be one of assessment of the child, not treatment of a parent, although it could involve trying to improve the relationship between the parent and child while assessing them.[296]

Section 38(6) states that children can refuse to participate in the assessment if they have sufficient understanding. Very controversially, in *South Glamorgan County Council* v *W and B*,[297] the court held that a court order under the inherent jurisdiction could override the refusal of a child. This seems to go against the normal position that an order under the inherent jurisdiction cannot run counter to a statutory provision. Here s 38(6) explicitly gives the child the right to refuse.

(i) Exclusion orders

Under ss 38A and 44A of the Children Act 1989[298] exclusion orders are available to the local authority in addition to an emergency protection order and interim care orders. The exclusion requirement may include one or more of the following (s 38A (3)):

(a) a provision requiring the relevant person to leave a dwelling-house in which he is living with the child;

(b) a provision prohibiting the relevant person from entering a dwelling-house in which the child lives; and

(c) a provision excluding the relevant person from a defined area in which a dwelling-house in which the child lives is situated.

The circumstances in which an exclusion order can be made are (s 38A(2)):

(a) that there is reasonable cause to believe that, if a person ('the relevant person') is excluded from a dwelling-house in which the child lives, the child will cease to suffer, or cease to be likely to suffer, significant harm, and

(b) that another person living in the dwelling-house (whether a parent of the child or some other person)—

    (i) is able and willing to give to the child the care which it would be reasonable to expect a parent to give him, and

    (ii) consents to the inclusion of the exclusion requirement.

There are two important limitations on the exclusion order. First, the exclusion order can only be made if the grounds for an emergency protection order or interim care order are made out. Both of these orders are short-lived, and so the exclusion requirement offers only short-term protection. The second requirement is that there must be another person in the home who is able and willing to care for the child, and who consents to the inclusion of the exclusion requirement.[299] If, for example, the mother wishes to continue her relationship with the suspected abuser,

[295] [2000] 1 FCR 436.
[296] *Re D (Jurisdiction: Programme of Assessment or Therapy)* [2000] 1 FCR 436 CA.
[297] [1993] 1 FLR 574, [1993] 1 FCR 626.
[298] Inserted by Family Law Act 1996.
[299] *W* v *A Local Authority* [2000] 2 FCR 662.

she may well refuse to consent. She may then have to choose between consenting to the removal of her partner and having her child removed under a care order.

8. EMERGENCIES: POLICE PROTECTION AND EMERGENCY PROTECTION ORDERS

There are two main remedies available if children need immediate assistance.

A. Police protection

In cases requiring urgent action, the police have some powers to protect children. The powers enable the police to act immediately, without the delay of having to apply to a court. For example, in *Re M (A Minor) (Care Order: Threshold Conditions)*[300] the police were called to a house where a husband had murdered his wife in front of the children; the police were able to take the children immediately into their care.

These powers exist under s 46(1), where if a police constable has reasonable cause to believe that a child would be likely to suffer significant harm then the child can be removed by the constable to 'suitable accommodation'.[301] However, this section does not give the police the power to enter and search a building. This is an important limitation and means that, if the parents refuse to co-operate with the police, and the child is in the parents' house, the police have no powers under the Children Act 1989 to protect the child.[302]

The children can be kept in police protection for up to 72 hours. Once a child is taken into police protection, a designated officer will be appointed to be in charge of the case. He or she must inform the local authority of the decision to protect the child, and must let the parents or persons with parental responsibility know of the steps taken.[303] The police do not acquire parental responsibility when a child is in police protection, but the designated officer is required to do what is reasonable in all the circumstances to promote the child's welfare.[304] He or she must permit reasonable contact between the child and anyone with parental responsibility, or anyone else with whom the child was living.[305] The child must be released to the parent or person with parental responsibility unless there are reasonable grounds to believe that he or she is likely to suffer significant harm if released.[306]

---

[300] [1994] 2 AC 424.
[301] The constable may also take reasonable steps to remove the child to a hospital or other place.
[302] Unless the police are able to use their general powers to arrest people or search houses under the Police and Criminal Evidence Act 1984.
[303] CA 1989, s 46(3).
[304] CA 1989, s 46(9)(b).
[305] CA 1989, s 46(10).
[306] CA 1989, s 46(5).

B. The emergency protection order

(i) When is an emergency protection order appropriate?

Where it is clear that the child is suffering significant harm, but the local authority is not in a position to decide the long-term future of the child, then an emergency protection order (EPO) is appropriate. The guidance explains that the purpose of an EPO is 'to enable the child in a genuine emergency to be removed from where he is, or be kept where he is, if and only if this is what is necessary to provide immediate short-term protection'.[307] The EPO should only be used in emergencies, as it involves the immediate removal of a child, often without notice to the parents or time to prepare the child appropriately.

(ii) Who may apply?

Anyone can apply for an EPO. This is by contrast with a child assessment order, care order or supervision order. Restrictions on who can apply for the order seem inappropriate, given the kind of urgent situations in which the EPO is appropriate. The police, local authorities, teachers, doctors or close relatives are most likely to be the ones who will apply. If someone apart from the local authority is applying for the EPO, the local authority can take over the application if appropriate. As it is an emergency application, the EPO will normally be applied for *ex parte*.[308] It is arguable that an *ex parte* hearing would be in breach of article 6 of the European Convention on Human Rights. However, in *KA v Finland*[309] the European Court of Human Rights recognised that in urgent cases it was not possible always to involve the parents fully in the decision-making processes.

(iii) What are the grounds for the order?

There are three grounds for obtaining an EPO.

1. Where 'there is reasonable cause to believe that the child is likely to suffer significant harm if ... (i) he is not removed to accommodation provided by or on behalf of the applicant'.[310] This ground could be satisfied, for example, if there is reasonable cause to believe that the child is being abused.
2. Where 'there is reasonable cause to believe that the child is likely to suffer significant harm if ... (ii) he does not remain in the place in which he is then being accommodated'.[311] This might apply where the child is currently safe, but there is a fear that he or she will be removed to a place where they may be harmed. For example, if the child has run away to his or her grandparents, but the local authority fears that the father may be on the point of finding the child and taking him or her back to an abusive home life.

---

[307] Department of Health (1991b: 4.28).
[308] Family Proceedings Court (Children Act) Rules 1991, SI 1991/1395, r 4(5).
[309] [2003] 1 FCR 201, para 95.
[310] CA 1989, s 44(1)(a)(i).
[311] CA 1989, s 44(1)(a)(ii).

3. Under s 44(1)(b) a local authority or the NSPCC[312] can apply for an EPO where:

   (a) the applicant is making enquiries into the child's welfare; and
   (b) 'those enquiries are being frustrated by access to the child being unreasonably refused to a person authorised to seek access and that the applicant has reasonable cause to believe that access to the child is required as a matter of urgency'.[313]

   The NSPCC (but not local authorities) need to show also that there is reasonable cause to suspect that the child is suffering or is likely to suffer significant harm.

   These grounds are all prospective; they relate to the fear of harm in the future. So an EPO cannot be made on the basis of past harm unless the fact of past harm is evidence of a fear of future significant harm. The test attempts to strike a balance between ensuring that proceedings in these emergency situations do not get bogged down in complex questions of evidence, while at the same time ensuring that children are only removed when there is evidence to justify rapid intervention.

   Even if the grounds for an EPO are satisfied, the court must still decide whether or not to make an EPO using the welfare principle. Under article 8 of the European Convention the local authority will be required to consider whether there were any alternatives to removing the children under the emergency order.[314]

(iv) The effects of an EPO

Section 44(4) sets out the three legal effects of an EPO. The order:

   (a) operates as a direction to any person who is in a position to do so to comply with any request to produce the child to the applicant;
   (b) authorises—
      (i) the removal of the child at any time to accommodation provided by or on behalf of the applicant and his being kept there; or
      (ii) the prevention of the child's removal from any hospital, or other place, in which he was being accommodated immediately before the making of the order; and
   (c) gives the applicant parental responsibility for the child.

These will now be considered in more detail:

(a) Production of the child

The EPO requires any person who can comply with the request to produce the child to do so. The order also forbids the removal of the child from the place where the applicant has accommodated the child. If necessary, the applicant can enter any premises named in the EPO to search for the child,[315] although if force is required then the police should be involved and a warrant is required.[316]

---

[312] CA 1989, s 31(9).
[313] CA 1989, s 44(1)(b).
[314] *KA v Finland* [2003] 1 FCR 201.
[315] CA 1989, s 48(3) and (4).
[316] CA 1989, s 48(9).

(b) Acquisition of parental responsibility by applicant

The applicant will acquire parental responsibility on the making of the EPO. This is appropriate, as the applicant will remove the child and will be responsible for the child's welfare. However, the applicant obtains only limited parental responsibility – parental responsibility should only be exercised 'as is reasonably required to safeguard or promote the welfare of the child (having regard in particular to the duration of the order)'.[317] The applicant should therefore not make any decisions which are major or irreversible. For example, important medical treatment should not be performed under an EPO. Any major decisions should be brought before the court by way of an application for a specific issue order. The child should be returned home as soon as it appears to the applicant safe to do so.[318] If the child is returned to their parents, this will not automatically bring the EPO to an end. The applicant could again remove the child, if necessary, providing the EPO has not yet expired.

(c) Reasonable contact

During the length of the EPO there is a presumption of reasonable contact between the child and certain prescribed individuals, including parents; persons with parental responsibility; those with contact orders; those with whom the child was living before the EPO; and any person acting on their behalf.[319] If the court wishes, it can restrict any right of contact or impose conditions upon it when making the EPO.[320]

(d) Other directions

The court has the power when making an EPO to insert additional directions. The most likely additional directions are that medical or psychiatric examinations be carried out.[321] The competent child has a right to refuse such examinations under s 44(7).[322] An exclusion requirement can be added under s 44A of the Children Act 1989, as discussed above.

(v) How long does the EPO last?

Section 45(1) states that eight days is the maximum length of an EPO. The local authority or NSPCC can apply for an extension to a maximum total length of 15 days.[323] There is no appeal from the making of an EPO,[324] but it is possible to apply to discharge the order. The application to discharge can be brought by the child; the parents; persons with parental responsibility; and any person with whom the child was living immediately before the order. But the application for the discharge

---

[317] CA 1989, s 44(5)(b).
[318] CA 1989, s 44(10).
[319] CA 1989, s 44(13).
[320] CA 1989, s 44(6).
[321] CA 1989, s 44(6)(b) and (8).
[322] CA 1989, s 44(7); but see *South Glamorgan County Council v W and B* [1993] 1 FLR 574, [1993] 1 FCR 626, which suggests that a court can override refusal, although this is a controversial decision.
[323] On application by the NSPCC or local authority under CA 1989, s 45(4).
[324] CA 1989, s 45(10).

cannot be made until 72 hours have elapsed since the making of the EPO.[325] There is also no appeal against a refusal to grant an EPO.[326] It may be that if an application for an EPO fails, the local authority could seek to invoke the court's inherent jurisdiction.

A local authority has no right of appeal against the refusal to extend an EPO. This can give rise to problems, as revealed in *Re P (Emergency Protection Order)*.[327] In this case a young baby nearly died after what was thought to be an attempt to suffocate him. There was clear medical evidence by a paediatrician of the abuse. The magistrates, however, refused to extend the EPO. Johnson J subsequently heard an application for a care order and criticised the justices for failing to extend the EPO in the face of the life-threatening abuse. The only option available to a local authority whose application for an extension is denied is to apply for a care order or interim care order.

9. REPRESENTATION OF CHILDREN IN CHILD PROTECTION PROCEEDINGS

Under the Children Act 1989 children are normally represented by a solicitor and a guardian ad litem in public proceedings. Now the Children and Family Court Advisory and Support Services (CAFCASS) employs the guardian whose job it is to ensure the protection of children's interests in court proceedings. The solicitor is in the position of the advocate for the child. Normally the solicitor will take instructions from the guardian, but if the child is sufficiently mature the solicitor must follow the child's wishes.[328] Although there has been much praise for the representation of children in public law cases [329] there have been serious concerns expressed that children sometimes are not effectively involved or informed about the proceedings.[330]

10. LOCAL AUTHORITIES AND SECTION 8 ORDERS

A local authority may obtain a specific issue order or a prohibited steps order subject to the following restrictions:

1. A local authority may not apply for a specific issue order or prohibited steps order which has the same effect as a residence order or a contact order.[331] The policy behind this restriction is that if the child is not suffering sufficiently for a care order to be made then a local authority should not be seeking to arrange accommodation for the child against the parents' wishes.
2. If the child is in care then no s 8 order may be made apart from a residence order. As a local authority cannot apply for a residence order, the effect is that

---

[325] CA 1989, s 45(9).
[326] *Essex CC* v *F* [1993] 1 FLR 847, [1993] 2 FCR 289.
[327] [1996] 1 FLR 482, [1996] 1 FCR 637.
[328] Family Proceedings Rules 1991, SI 1991/1247, r 4.12.
[329] E.g. Fortin (2003b).
[330] Mason (2003).
[331] See Chapter 9.

a local authority cannot apply for a s 8 order in respect of a child it has in its care.

So there is limited scope for a local authority to use s 8 orders. They are appropriate, however, when a local authority might be concerned about a specific aspect of a parent's care of the child and, while not wanting to take the child into care, may wish to protect the child. For example, if parents are refusing to consent to necessary medical treatment the local authority might apply to the court for a specific issue order authorising the operation.[332] According to Charles J in *Re P (Care Orders: Injunctive Relief)*[333] a court can make injunctions under s 37 of the Supreme Court Act 1981 which are ancillary to a care order. In that case in addition to a care order injunctions were made stopping the parents from preventing the child from attending college.

11. THE PROBLEM OF OUSTING THE ABUSER

One situation which has troubled the courts and local authorities is where a child is living with the mother and a man who is suspected of abusing the child. The ideal solution may be to remove the suspected abuser, while leaving the child with the mother. This is certainly an acceptable solution where the mother agrees that the man should be removed.[334] However, where the mother wants the man to stay, there is a complex clash between the rights of the child and the rights of adults. For the state to force the mother to separate from her partner against her will would be a grave invasion of her rights, but that may be the only solution which protects the child. In such cases the options for the local authority are as follows:

1. The local authority will no doubt prefer to deal with the issue by informal co-operation and persuade the suspected abuser to leave the house voluntarily. The local authority may be able to offer assistance or alternative housing.[335]
2. The local authority could encourage the mother to apply for an occupation order, under the Family Law Act 1996, Part IV, to remove the man from the house.
3. The local authority could apply for a care order or a supervision order. It could then remove the child from the home under the care order. Alternatively, the child could remain with the mother under a care or supervision order and the local authority request that the abuser leave the home, with the threat that the child will be removed from the mother immediately if the abuser returns. However, the local authority cannot be forced to apply for a care or supervision order, and the court cannot make a care or supervision order unless the local authority applies for one. This is clear from *Nottingham CC v P*,[336] in which the Court of Appeal were deeply concerned that there was no power to compel the local authority to take steps to protect the children. A local authority may be

---

[332] E.g. *Re R (A Minor) (Wardship: Consent to Medical Treatment)* [1992] 1 FLR 190, [1992] 2 FCR 229.
[333] [2000] 3 FCR 426.
[334] Cobley and Lowe (1994).
[335] CA 1989, Sch 2, para 5.
[336] [1993] 2 FLR 134, [1994] 1 FCR 624 CA.

wary of applying for a care order and permitting a child to remain in the house because of the potential liability in tort if the child were abused. Further, if either a supervision or care order was relied upon a local authority may have grave difficulty in ensuring that the suspected abuser did not live in the house. A local authority, for these reasons, may prefer to remove a child from the house if a care order is made, and enable substantial contact between the child and his or her mother.

4. The availability of s 8 orders for the local authority in this kind of case is very limited. In *Nottingham CC* v *P* it was stressed that it was not possible for the local authority to obtain a s 8 order to remove the suspected abuser. Removing the man from the home is in the nature of a residence or contact order. Local authorities cannot apply for residence or contact orders. Nor may they apply for prohibited steps or specific issue orders which have the same effect as residence or contact orders. The Court of Appeal stressed that where the local authority was seeking to protect children who were suffering significant harm, it should look to Part IV of the Children Act 1989 for care and supervision orders, and not use private orders to protect children. The core reasoning behind this restriction is that a prohibited steps or specific issue order does not vest any power in the local authority. In *Nottingham CC* v *P* if a residence order with conditions had been made in the mother's favour then the local authority would not have been able to enforce it. The mother could have applied to discharge the order and the local authority would have had no standing to intervene. Therefore such an order provides inadequate protection for children in such cases.

The *Nottingham CC* v *P* decision does not prevent a prohibited steps order being granted on the application of a local authority where a suspected abuser is living apart from the mother and children. In *Re H (Minors) (Prohibited Steps Order)*[337] Butler-Sloss LJ argued that it was permissible to use a prohibited steps order to prevent a stepfather having contact with the children with whom he was no longer living.[338]

5. Exclusion orders are available under ss 38A and 44A of the Children Act 1989. These can only offer a short-term solution, as explained above.

6. The courts have also been willing to grant orders under the inherent jurisdiction removing a suspected abuser from the home, although the limits of this are unclear.[339] In *Devon CC* v *S* it was argued that where the court could not make an order which adequately protected the child then the court should rely on the inherent jurisdiction.[340] The court distinguished *Nottingham CC* v *P* on the basis that the court had found that it could have made an order that would have protected the child (a care order), but it had not been applied for by a local authority. If the court is persuaded that the child needs protection and no order could be made which would protect the child then an order under the inherent jurisdiction can protect the child. Although this decision is controversial in the

---

[337] [1995] 1 FLR 638, [1995] 2 FCR 547; discussed in M. Roberts (1995).
[338] See Chapter 9 for discussion of this case.
[339] *Re S (Minors) (Inherent Jurisdiction: Ouster)* [1994] 1 FLR 623; *Devon CC* v *S* [1994] 1 FLR 355, [1994] 2 FCR 409.
[340] [1994] 1 FLR 355, [1994] 2 FCR 409.

light of the Human Rights Act 1998 and article 3 of the European Convention on Human Rights, as interpreted in *Z* v *UK*,[341] the state is under an obligation to protect children suffering serious abuse and so the use of the inherent jurisdiction may be required.

7. The local authority could apply for a family assistance order, although this might provide only very limited protection to the child.

12. CONCLUSION

This chapter has considered the circumstances in which it is appropriate to take a child into care. This is a notoriously problematic and controversial issue. It is all too easy, with hindsight, to claim that the local authority was too interventionist or not interventionist enough, but making the decisions in some of these cases must be agonising. The Children Act 1989 has given the local authority the powers to provide services which are designed to prevent the authority having to use its more interventionist powers. Although the Children Act 1989 set up the threshold criteria before significant intervention in family life could be permitted, the interpretation of the criteria, particularly by the House of Lords, has had the effect of lessening the hurdle that they represent. The Human Rights Act 1998 will now play an important role, at least in formulating the language which will be used: it must be shown that the intervention in family life by the state is a necessary and proportionate response to the threat faced by the child. The change in language will not fundamentally change the key question, which is when the state is entitled to remove a child from his or her parents against their wishes. The issue involves the exercise by the state of one of its most coercive powers in order to fulfil its fundamental duties to protect the most vulnerable of its citizens.

---

[341] [2000] 2 FCR 245.

11

CHILDREN IN CARE

1. INTRODUCTION

This chapter will consider the law governing those children who are in the care of the local authority. On 31 March 2002, 59,700 children were being cared for by local authorities, a 1.4 per cent increase on the 2000 figure.[1] At that date there were 38,400 children under care orders. This was a 2 per cent increase on the previous year. Some 39,200 children were looked after in foster placements. In 1999, 62 per cent of those looked after by the local authorities were the subject of care orders and 34 per cent were in voluntary accommodation.[2] As article 20 of the UN Convention on the Rights of the Child explains, states owe duties of 'special protection and assistance' to children harmed by their families. Unfortunately, the history of state organised child-care in England and Wales is bleak, with widespread evidence of abuse and mistreatment of children in children's homes.[3] Indeed it is not difficult to find cases where the intervention of the state has made matters worse, not better, for children.[4] Fortin[5] has complained of the lot of children in care in the following terms:

> too many children still receive an inadequate service from social services departments. Planning for their future care is often poor or non-existent, too many experience numerous foster placements and the overall standard of physical and mental health and education of 'looked after' children continues to compare very unfavourably with children brought up at home.

The basic position under the Children Act 1989 is that local authorities (rather than courts) are responsible for deciding how children taken into care should be cared for. This is partly because the law recognises that decisions on how to look after a child in care involve careful interaction between the local authority, the parents, alternative carers and maybe other charitable bodies. These relationships might require ongoing and flexible negotiations of the kind unsuitable to court supervision. However, local authorities do not have unlimited discretion on how to bring up the child. There are four particular restrictions on local authorities' powers. First, there are financial restrictions which may limit the resources available

---

[1] Department of Health (2003a: 1).
[2] Performance and Innovation Unit (2000a: 3.7).
[3] For a survey, see Department of Health (1995a; 1999c). Tragically, the stories of abuse seem not to be abating: The Stationery Office (2000b). There is evidence of a small number of children being abused during foster care (Social Services Inspectorate (2002b: para 5.4)), especially private fostering (Philpot (2001)).
[4] E.g. *Re F* [2002] 1 FLR 217.
[5] Fortin (2003b: 486–7).

to a local authority.[6] Evidence suggests that this has meant that local authorities have failed to provide services needed by children in care.[7] The government has launched an initiative entitled *Quality Protects*, which is intended to improve the funding for support services for children in care.[8] Secondly, there are a few issues over which the courts retain some control. In particular, only a court can discharge a care order[9] and a court order is required to approve the termination of contact between the child in care and his or her parents.[10] Thirdly, parents retain parental responsibility (even when a child is taken into care) and will be encouraged to be involved in decisions relating to the way their child is brought up while in care. Fourthly, the children in care themselves play an important role in determining the way they are brought up under the care system.

The chapter will start with an outline of the approach to children in care taken by the European Convention on Human Rights because this will be highly influential on the development of the law in the future. We will then discuss the effect of supervision orders and care orders. In the light of these, we will consider the role of parents and courts following the making of a supervision or care order. The chapter will end by considering the role of adoption, which has traditionally been seen as an ideal way to treat many children removed by the state from their parents.

2. HUMAN RIGHTS ACT 1998 AND CHILDREN IN CARE

As noted in Chapter 10, because removing a child from his or her family automatically constitutes an infringement of the parents' and child's right to respect for family and private life, the removal must be justified under article 8(2) of the European Convention.[11] However, the significance of the right to respect for family life continues even after a child is taken into care.[12] The approach of the European Court of Human Rights is summarised in *L v Finland*:[13]

> The Court recalls that taking a child into care should normally be regarded as a temporary measure to be discontinued as soon as circumstances permit, and that any measure of implementation of temporary care should be consistent with the ultimate aim of reuniting the natural parent and the child ... In this regard a fair balance has to be struck between the interests of the child in remaining in public care and those of the parent in being reunited with the child ... In carrying out this balancing exercise the Court will attach particular importance to the best interests of the child, which, depending on their nature and seriousness, may override those of the parent. In particular the parent cannot be entitled under Art 8 of the Convention to have such measure taken as would harm the child's health and development.[14]

---

[6] E.g. *Re C (Children) (Residential Assessment)* [2001] 3 FCR 164.
[7] Lansdown (2001).
[8] This is discussed in M. Roberts (2001)
[9] Children Act 1989 (hereafter CA 1989), s 39.
[10] CA 1989, s 34.
[11] *W v UK* (1988) 10 EHRR 29.
[12] See further, Lindley, Herring and Wyld (2001).
[13] [2000] 2 FLR 118.
[14] At p. 140.

There are three points of particular note. First, care measures should be regarded as temporary and, if at all possible, should be designed to enable the child to be reunited with his or her parent. The local authority should keep under review the possibility of rehabilitation with the birth family.[15] This means that adoption should be used as a last resort because it normally terminates the link between the birth parent and child. However, the European Court in *KA* v *Finland*[16] accepted that there may come a time when the child's interests in not being moved from the stable arrangements that the state has made override the interests of the parents in being reunited with their child. Secondly, the rights of the parents to contact with children in care should be protected and any restriction on the rights of parents to see or have contact with their children must be justified as necessary and proportionate under article 8(2). In *Eriksson* v *Sweden*[17] the court emphasised that the length and severity of the restriction on contact would be taken into account when considering whether the infringement was permitted. The burden will be on the local authority to justify any restriction on contact between children and parents. The European Court in *Olsson* v *Sweden (No. 1)*[18] explained that the court 'cannot confine itself to considering the impugned decisions in isolation, but must look at them in the light of the case as a whole; it must determine whether the reasons adduced to justify the interference at issue are "relevant and sufficient" '. Thirdly, the response of the local authority to a child who is suffering harm must be proportionate to the harm which the child faced, as stressed by Bracewell J in *Re N (Leave to Withdraw Care Proceedings)*.[19] Hale LJ in *Re C and B (Children) (Care Order: Future Harm)*[20] explained:

> one comes back to the principle of proportionality. The principle has to be that the local authority works to support, and eventually to reunite, the family, unless the risks are so high that the child's welfare requires alternative family care.[21]

The local authority must demonstrate that there is no lesser level of intervention that would adequately protect the child.

In addition to article 8, article 6 of the Convention is important. It requires the state to provide a right of access to a court or tribunal to determine the parents' rights and obligations and this includes enabling parents to protect their rights under article 8.[22] In particular, this may mean that parents should have a right to challenge in court decisions of the local authority concerning children in care. In *Re G (Care: Challenge to Local Authority's Decision)*[23] the local authority had obtained a care order, but the child remained with the parents for two years. Then the local authority (without consulting the parents) decided to remove the children from their home. This was held to be in clear breach of the family's article 8 rights. If the

---

[15] *K and T* v *Finland* [2001] 2 FCR 673, at paras 154–5.
[16] [2003] 1 FCR 230, para 138.
[17] (1989) 12 EHRR 183.
[18] (1988) 11 EHRR 259 at para 68.
[19] [2000] 1 FLR 134.
[20] [2000] 2 FCR 614 CA.
[21] At p. 624.
[22] *McMichael* v *UK* (1995) 20 EHRR 205.
[23] [2003] FL 389.

local authority wished to carry out a significant change in the way a child in care was being looked after then the local authority would have to involve the parents effectively in the decision-making process (unless the case was an emergency).

When looking at the human rights of children in care there is sometimes seen to be a clash between the importance of partnership (the birth parents continuing to play as full a role as possible in the child's life) and the importance of permanency planning (that children should be placed in secure long-term arrangements, rather than floating in care uncertain as to the long-term plans for their future). This can be presented as a clash between the interests of parents and children. However, this could be misleading because children may have rights in retaining a link with their parents and existing family.[24]

3. THE EFFECT OF A SUPERVISION ORDER

On the making of a supervision order a supervisor will be appointed. Under s 35(1) of the Children Act 1989 the supervisor has three duties:[25]

    (a) to advise, assist and befriend the supervised child;
    (b) to take such steps as are reasonably necessary to give effect to the order; and
    (c) where—
        (i) the order is not wholly complied with; or
        (ii) the supervisor considers that the order may no longer be necessary,
  to consider whether or not to apply to the court for its variation or discharge.

So the key element of a supervision order is that a supervisor advises, assists and befriends the child. As well as befriending the child, the supervisor can advise the parents and make recommendations about the upbringing of children. For example, the supervisor might offer suggestions on methods of disciplining children. It is also possible to add specific conditions to a supervision order. Schedule 3 to the Children Act 1989[26] lists the conditions that a court can impose. These include requiring a child to live at a particular place, requiring the child to present him- or herself at a relevant place, or to participate in special activities. It is possible to impose conditions on a supervision order not listed in Sch 3, but only with the parents' consent.[27]

The whole ethos of the supervision order is based on the parents' consent and co-operation. The supervision order does not give the supervisor the right to enter any property and remove a child. Nor does the supervisor have the power to direct the child to undergo medical or psychiatric examination or treatment. It is not even possible to force the parents to comply with the conditions in the order or the requests of the supervisor. However, the failure to comply with requests from the supervisor may lead to the supervisor applying for a care order or emergency protection order. As the threshold criteria for the making of a care and supervision order are the same, the court may well be convinced that it would be appropriate

---

[24] Parkinson (2003).
[25] CA 1989, Sch 3 sets out their duties in further detail.
[26] *Re V (Care or Supervision Order)* [1996] 1 FLR 776 CA.
[27] CA 1989, Sch 3, para 3(1).

to make a care order if the parents are refusing to co-operate with the supervisor. This means that although the supervision order is apparently based on partnership and voluntary co-operation between the local authority and the parents, the threat of having the children removed under a care order gives the supervision order a coercive edge. However, supervision orders appear to be unpopular with some social workers who told researchers that the orders were 'a complete waste of time' and toothless.[28] A different kind of concern is indicated by research that children left with abusive parents are at risk of further abuse. In one study 40 per cent of children left with parents following local authority intervention suffered maltreatment in the 12 months following protective intervention. Fifteen per cent suffered serious maltreatment.[29] On the other hand, another study into cases where a care order or interim care order had been made found that in 46 per cent of cases the end result of the case could have been obtained without making an order[30] and that care orders were used to encourage parents to co-operate in the performance of assessment, rather than as a response to proved harms or risks.

4. THE EFFECTS OF A CARE ORDER

A. Distinguishing a child in care and a child voluntarily accommodated

In Chapter 10 it was noted that the Children Act 1989 draws a clear distinction between children in care and those voluntarily accommodated by the local authority under s 20 of the Act. The key difference is that local authorities have parental responsibility for a child in care,[31] whereas local authorities do not acquire parental responsibility over children who are voluntarily accommodated. The most significant practical consequence of this is that a person with parental responsibility can at any time remove a child who has been voluntarily accommodated, but cannot remove a child in care, without the consent of the local authority or approval of the court.[32]

B. The legal effects of the care order

Section 33 of the Children Act 1989 sets out the effects of a care order, which are as follows.

(i) Care orders and parental responsibility

Section 33(3) of the Children Act 1989 states that the local authority acquires parental responsibility by virtue of the care order and 'have the power (subject to the following provisions of this section) to determine the extent to which a parent

---

[28] Hunt and McLeod (1998: 237).
[29] Brandon (1999: 200–1).
[30] Brandon (1999: 151).
[31] CA 1989, s 33(3)(a).
[32] The court would have to discharge the care order.

or guardian of the child may meet his parental responsibility for him'.[33] So, on the making of a care order, the local authority acquires parental responsibility, but parents or guardians retain theirs. However, those who have parental responsibility by virtue of a residence order lose parental responsibility on the making of a care order. This is because a care order automatically brings to an end any residence order. Even though parents and guardians retain parental responsibility, they cannot exercise it in a way which is incompatible with the local authority's plans.[34] This means that although parental responsibility is shared between parents and local authorities, in fact it is the local authority that very much controls what happens to the children in its care. However, that is not to say that local authorities are completely unrestrained in their use of parental responsibility and parents are powerless. The Children Act 1989 sets out a number of limitations on the exercise of a local authority's powers over children in its care, which protect the interests of parents. The list is interesting because it reflects those issues which the law regards as so fundamental to the concept of being a parent that the local authority should not be able to override the parents' wishes:

1. Local authorities cannot permit the child to be brought up in a different religion from that which the parents intended for the child.[35]
2. Local authorities do not have the right to consent (or refuse to consent) to the making of an application for adoption or a freeing order.[36] The consent of the parents is required before an adoption order is made.[37]
3. Local authorities cannot appoint a guardian.[38]
4. Local authorities cannot cause the child to be known by a different surname, unless they have the consent of all those with parental responsibility, or the leave of the court.[39] An example of the kind of circumstances in which the court may be willing to give leave to change a surname is *Re M, T, P, K and B (Care: Change of Name)*,[40] where the children were in terror of their parents and had a pathological fear that their parents would remove them from their foster parents. Changing the children's name was seen as a means of preventing the parents from discovering the whereabouts of the children.
5. The child cannot be removed from the UK unless all those with parental responsibility consent or the court grants leave.[41]
6. The mother of a child in care is at liberty to enter a parental responsibility agreement, thereby giving the father parental responsibility, despite the local authority's opposition.[42]

---

[33] Although under CA 1989, s 33(4) the local authority can only restrict a parent's parental authority if satisfied that to do so is necessary to safeguard or promote the child's welfare.

[34] CA 1989, s 33(3).

[35] CA 1989, s 33(6)(a); Foster Placement (Children) Regulations 1991, SI 1991/910, reg 5(2); Children's Homes Regulations 1991, SI 1991/1506, reg 11.

[36] CA 1989, s 33(6)(b)(i).

[37] See page 601.

[38] CA 1989, s 33(6)(b)(iii). See Chapter 7.

[39] CA 1989, s 33(7).

[40] [2000] 1 FLR 645.

[41] 1989, Sch 2, para 19(3).

[42] *Re X (Parental Responsibility Agreement)* [2000] 1 FLR 517.

The sharing of the parental responsibility between the parents and the local authority is highly controversial.[43] Some argue that it is inappropriate that parents who have appallingly abused their children, so that their children have been taken into care, retain parental responsibility. Others argue that the retention of parental responsibility by parents weakens the powers of local authorities. A different objection is that the sharing of parental responsibility is artificial. It is claimed that parents have parental responsibility in name alone. The strength of this objection depends on the nature of parental responsibility.[44] If parental responsibility is essentially a status then maybe it is correct that a care order does not affect the status of parenthood. But if parental responsibility reflects the performance of day-to-day parenting of children then the retention of parental responsibility on the making of a care order may well be artificial.[45] The law can be seen as a compromise between those who wish to protect the rights of parents of children who have been taken into care and the concerns of social work professionals that giving parents too many rights will hamper their protection of children within their care. The present law on parental responsibility is consistent with the Human Rights Act 1998, as it can be seen as the minimum intervention in the rights of parents compatible with effective protection of children. Indeed, despite the academic criticism of the concept of shared parental responsibility, the reported cases do not indicate that local authorities are finding their powers unduly restricted by parents' retention of parental responsibility.[46] In fact, local authorities may be relieved that the parents must resolve controversial issues, such as religious upbringing and surnames.

The local authority should enter an agreement with the parents or those with parental responsibility concerning the arrangements for children in care. The agreement should deal with questions such as where the child should live and what services should be provided to the child.[47] The agreements are not binding contracts and they are not enforceable in the courts. The agreements should be in writing and copies of the agreement should be provided to those with parental responsibility. If appropriate, a copy should be given to the child in a comprehensible form.[48] The agreement may include a delegation to foster carers of the right to consent to medical treatment or give consent for the child to be involved in various activities arranged by the local authority.[49]

(ii) Duties imposed upon a local authority

The Children Act 1989 imposes upon local authorities a number of duties owed towards children who are looked after by them.[50] These duties are owed to children

---

[43] Eekelaar (1991c: 43).
[44] See Chapter 7.
[45] See Chapters 7 and 8 for discussion of the different understandings of parental responsibility.
[46] For an example of where the father did continue to pose a risk to the children in care and where the local authority were able to rely on CA 1989, s 33(3)(b) to limit the father's powers, see *Re P (Children Act 1989, ss 22 and 26: Local Authority Compliance)* [2000] 2 FLR 910.
[47] Arrangements for Placement of Children (General) Regulations 1991, SI 1991/890, reg 4 and Sch 4.
[48] Regulation 5(3).
[49] Department of Health (1991a: paras 2.30–2.39).
[50] CA 1989, s 22.

who are voluntarily accommodated by the local authority for more than 24 hours[51] and to those who are the subject of a care order.[52]

(a) The general duty
The general duty of the local authority is contained in s 22(3):

> It shall be the duty of a local authority looking after any child—
> (a) to safeguard and promote his welfare; and
> (b) to make such use of services available for children cared for by their own parents as appears to the authority reasonable in his case.

This duty is self-explanatory, but it should be noted that the local authority can owe duties to children even if the children are cared for by their parents.[53]

(b) The duty to decide where the child should live
The local authority must 'receive the child into their care and . . . keep him in their care while the order remains in force'.[54] So on the making of the care order the local authority becomes responsible for deciding where the child should live.

(c) The duty to consult
The Children Act 1989 in s 22(4) requires a local authority to consult with the child and his or her family:

> Before making any decision with respect to a child whom they are looking after, or proposing to look after, a local authority shall, so far as is reasonably practicable, ascertain the wishes and feelings of—
> (a) the child;
> (b) his parents;
> (c) any person who is not a parent of his but who has parental responsibility for him; and
> (d) any other person whose wishes and feelings the authority consider to be relevant regarding the matter to be decided.

The local authority must then give 'due consideration' to these views. The views of the child are taken into account as would be appropriate given the age and understanding of the child.[55] The local authority must also give due consideration to the child's 'religious persuasion, racial origin and cultural and linguistic background'.[56] These factors are likely to be most relevant when considering the placement of children with foster carers. Where possible, foster carers should be of the same religious and cultural background as the child, although that will be only one consideration when selecting suitable foster carers.

---

[51] CA 1989, s 22(2).
[52] CA 1989, s 22(1).
[53] For complaints that local authorities are more concerned with short-term solutions, rather than long-term ones for the child see Social Services Inspectorate (1999: 6.25).
[54] CA 1989, s 33(1).
[55] CA 1989, s 22(5)(a) and (b). If the local authority fails to consult with a parent or child, their decision is not necessarily void: *Re P (Children Act 1989, ss 22 and 26: Local Authority Compliance)* [2000] 2 FLR 910.
[56] CA 1989, s 22(5)(c).

(d) The duty to provide accommodation[57]

The local authority has a duty to accommodate a child in care. The Children Act 1989 sets out the alternative ways of providing accommodation:

1. to place the child with the parents, family or relatives;[58]
2. to place the child with foster carers;
3. to place the child in a community home;
4. to place the child in a voluntary home;
5. to place the child in a registered children's home;
6. to place the child in a home for special families;
7. such other arrangements as seem appropriate to the local authority.[59]

Before considering any other alternative accommodation, the local authority should first consider whether the child should be allowed to remain at home. There is a specific duty to make arrangements for the child to live with his or her family unless it is not reasonably practicable or consistent with his or her welfare.[60] There is also a duty to accommodate the child as close as possible to the parent's home[61] and to any siblings accommodated by the local authority.[62] In the light of the Human Rights Act 1998 the local authority would have to be convinced that it was necessary and proportionate in view of the child's interests to remove the child from his or her parents under article 8 and any interference with family life should be kept to the minimum necessary to promote the child's welfare.[63] This means that if it is possible for the child safely to spend short periods at home, the local authority should facilitate that. The Human Rights Act may well mean that the local authority will also have to take notice of the family life that exists between siblings and ensure that it is respected.[64]

It is a common misconception that children taken into care spend the rest of their childhood in children's homes. One study found that in less than half the cases where care proceedings were instigated were children removed from their parents.[65] In fact nine out of ten children taken into care are eventually returned to their families.[66] Indeed, it is becoming less common for children in care to be accommodated in children's homes, at least as a long-term solution. In part this is in response to a depressing procession of scandals about the physical and sexual abuse of children in children's homes. Foster carers are often seen as a preferable solution.

---

[57] CA 1989, s 23(1).
[58] CA 1989, s 23(5); Placement with Parents etc. Regulations 1991, SI 1991/893.
[59] CA 1989, s 23(2).
[60] CA 1989, s 23(5).
[61] CA 1989, s 23(7)(a).
[62] CA 1989, s 23(7)(b).
[63] *L v Finland* [2000] 2 FLR 118.
[64] Beckett and Hershman (2001).
[65] Hunt (1998: 287).
[66] Bullock, Malos and Millham (1993).

(e) The duty to maintain

There is a duty on the local authority to maintain a child, but in some circumstances it can recoup the cost by requiring a financial contribution to the child's maintenance from their parents or others, if reasonable to do so.[67]

(f) The duty to promote contact

A local authority is under a positive obligation[68] to promote contact between children and parents, family or friends unless such contact is not reasonably practicable or is inconsistent with the child's welfare. This is required under s 34 of the Children Act 1989 and would be required under article 8 of the European Convention.[69] Local authorities are also required to keep in touch with persons who have parental responsibility for the child and specifically to keep them informed of the child's whereabouts. However, there is no duty on the local authority to provide finance to promote the contact.[70] Parents and those with parental responsibility are required to keep the local authority informed of their addresses.

(g) Other miscellaneous powers and duties

There are other duties which are set out in Part II of Sch 2 to the Children Act 1989. These include, for example, assistance with travelling expenses for children in care; the appointment of an independent visitor; the arrangement for funeral expenses if a child dies while in care.

(h) Duty to review

The local authority is required to keep under review the long-term plans for each child in care. The local authority must review a child's case within four weeks of the child being first accommodated by the authority. A second review should be carried out within three months of the first and, thereafter, reviews every six months. The purpose of the review is to ensure that the child does not 'drift through care' and instead that the time in care is part of a co-ordinated programme designed to promote the child's welfare.[71] So it should be decided as early as possible whether the child is to be adopted and, if so, what steps should be put in place to enable that to take place. Parents and children should be included in the review, or at least consulted.[72] Following the Human Rights Act 1998, the review should constantly ensure that the children's and parents' rights to respect for family life should be maintained to the greatest extent possible and that, where appropriate, the care plan progresses towards reuniting the child and the parent.[73]

---

[67] CA 1989, Sch 2, para 21(2).
[68] CA 1989, Sch 2, para 15.
[69] *L v Finland* [2000] 2 FLR 118.
[70] CA 1989, Sch 2, para 16.
[71] For an appalling example of such drift see *Re F, F v Lambeth LBC* [2002] FL 8.
[72] Review of Children's Cases Regulations 1991, SI 1991/895.
[73] *L v Finland* [2000] 2 FLR 118.

(iii) Empowering children in care

There are a variety of provisions which seek to protect the rights of children in care:

1. Children's views must be given due consideration when making decisions about their time in care.[74]
2. Children can apply to the court for an order authorising contact with another person.[75]
3. Children can apply for a s 8 order.[76]
4. The child can institute the complaints procedures.[77]
5. The child can apply to discharge a care order.[78]

Despite these provisions, research suggests that children in care feel that their wishes are not being taken into account and are not listened to.[79] Some argue that the high levels of antisocial behaviour and running away among children in care is explained by the fact that they feel they are not being heard. There are particular concerns with the complaints procedure, which should be readily accessible to children in care. Some local authorities appoint a children's rights officer to promote good practice and to assist children to use the complaints procedure.[80] The hope was that the complaints procedures set out in s 26(3) of the Children Act 1989 would do much to resolve the problems of abuse. Lyon reports[81] that this has not happened because children are not confident about using the complaints procedure through fear of reprisals.[82] She also argues that even when complaints are made by children in care, they are not investigated effectively.[83] At least two separate reports[84] have found that both staff and children were not sufficiently informed about the existence of the complaints procedures.[85] Recently, the Waterhouse Report[86] found that children in care still feel that there is no one to whom they can complain and that they have little contact with people outside the care homes in which they live.

(iv) Contact arrangements for children in care

Even though a child has been taken into care, it may still be appropriate for the child to retain contact with his or her parents or other relatives.[87] There may be a number of reasons for encouraging contact between a child in care and their birth

---

[74] CA 1989, s 22(4)(a) and (5)(a).
[75] CA 1989, s 34(2) and (4).
[76] See Chapter 8.
[77] CA 1989, s 26(3)(a). Complaints procedures will be further discussed shortly.
[78] CA 1989, s 39(1).
[79] Department of Health (1996).
[80] CA 1989, Sch 2A; Ellis and Franklin (1995).
[81] Lyon (1997a).
[82] Dalrymple and Payne (1994).
[83] Lyon (1997a).
[84] Social Services Inspectorate (1996); Williams and Jordan (1996a).
[85] Williams and Jordan (1996b).
[86] The Stationery Office (2000b).
[87] Department of Health (1991a: ch. 6; 1991b: para 3.75).

family.[88] It may be that contact is part of a care plan designed ultimately to return the child to the parent. Even if that is not a possibility, contact may be regarded as important for providing the emotional support of a continuous relationship with his or her parents or providing the child with a sense of identity. Indeed even in a permanent placement, the success of that placement may depend on the benefit of contact with family members.[89] As already stressed, parents' rights to respect for family life under the Human Rights Act 1998 require the local authority to encourage contact unless it is necessary to prevent it in the child's interests. However, despite the legal position there can be practical and psychological problems which make contact between a child in care and his or her parents problematic.[90]

The issue of contact between the child in care and his or her family is one of the few issues concerning children in care where the court has a major say. There are two ways that the court may exercise control over contact between a child in care and his or her natural parents:

1. The making of the care order. When applying for a care order a local authority must present a 'care plan', which will include its proposals for contact.[91] If the court is dissatisfied with the arrangements for contact, it can refuse to make the care order, although it cannot make a care order on condition that a certain kind of contact take place.[92] This can leave the court with the choice between two evils: leave the child without the protection of a court order, or make a care order with a care plan of which the court disapproves.[93]

2. Section 34 creates a presumption in favour of contact between a child in care and his or her parents, guardians and anyone with whom the child had lived[94] under a residence order (or an order under the inherent jurisdiction).[95] Except in an emergency, the local authority can only refuse contact between the child and those people after applying to the court. In an emergency, s 34(6) of the Children Act 1989 permits a local authority to refuse contact for up to seven days if:

    (a) they are satisfied that it is necessary to do so in order to safeguard or promote the child's welfare; and
    (b) the refusal—
        (i) is decided upon as a matter of urgency; and
        (ii) does not last for more than seven days.[96]

If the local authority wishes to prohibit contact for a longer period than seven days, it must apply for an order under s 34 of the Children Act 1989 permitting

---

[88] Jolly (1994).
[89] Macaskill (2002), although contrast Browne and Moloney (2002).
[90] Miles and Lindley (2003).
[91] CA 1989, s 31(3A).
[92] *Re T (A Minor) (Care Order: Conditions)* [1994] 2 FLR 423, [1994] 2 FCR 721; see also Contact with Children Regulations 1991, SI 1991/891. However, the care order can contain a s 34 order authorising prohibition of contact.
[93] *Re S and D (Children: Powers of Court)* [1995] 2 FLR 456.
[94] Immediately before the making of the care order.
[95] Brasse (1993: 57).
[96] CA 1989, s 34(6).

it to do so. If such an application is made, the court must determine whether there is to be contact and, if there is, the frequency and place of contact.[97] However, the court has no jurisdiction to prohibit the local authority from permitting contact between the child and his or her parents.[98] All the court has the power to do is permit the local authority to prohibit contact.

When the courts consider cases where the local authority has sought to end contact between the child and his or her family the welfare principle and the s 1(3) checklist govern the discretion of the court.[99] A number of particular issues should be taken into account by the court in such cases.

(a) A presumption in favour of contact

Re E (A Minor) (Care Order: Contact)[100] confirms that there is a presumption in favour of contact. The burden of establishing that contact should be terminated rests on the local authority. Simon Brown LJ explained:

> Even when the s 31 criteria are satisfied, contact may well be of singular importance to the long-term welfare of the child: first in giving the child the security of knowing that his parents love him and are interested in his welfare; secondly, by avoiding any damaging sense of loss to the child in seeing himself abandoned by his parents; thirdly, by enabling the child to commit himself to the substitute family with the seal of approval of the natural parents; and fourthly, by giving the child the necessary sense of family and personal identity. Contact, if maintained, is capable of reinforcing and increasing the chances of a permanent placement, whether on a long-term fostering basis or by adoption.

Even in *Re DH (A Minor) (Child Abuse)*,[101] where there were fears that the mother suffered from Munchausen's syndrome, it was accepted that there was value in maintaining contact so that the mother did not become a fantasy figure to the child. The kind of cases where contact should be prohibited were where there is no likelihood of rehabilitation with the birth family and the child has been placed for adoption.[102]

(b) The Human Rights Act 1998

Under the Human Rights Act 1998 parents have a right of contact with their children and children a right of contact with their parents.[103] To justify a termination of contact under the Act, it would have to be shown that it was necessary in the child's interests and that it was proportionate to the harm faced by the child.[104] This approach will normally coincide with the application of the welfare principle.[105] However, the

---

[97] CA 1989, s 34(3).

[98] *Re W (Section 34(2) (Orders)* [2000] 1 FLR 512.

[99] *Re B (Minors) (Termination of Contact: Paramount Consideration)* [1993] 1 FLR 543, [1993] 1 FCR 363.

[100] [1994] 1 FLR 146, [1994] 1 FCR 584 CA.

[101] [1994] 1 FLR 679, [1994] 2 FCR 3.

[102] *Re L (Sexual Abuse: Standard of Proof)* [1996] 1 FLR 116 at p. 127, per Butler-Sloss LJ.

[103] *R v UK* [1988] 2 FLR 445 ECtHR. Although it will be easier to justify ending contact with a father who has had little contact with the child, than with a mother who has formed a close bond to the child: *Söderbäck v Sweden* [1999] 1 FLR 250.

[104] *S and G v Italy* [2000] 2 FLR 771.

[105] *Re F (Care: Termination of Care)* [2000] FCR 481.

requirement that the parents' rights can only be infringed if *necessary* in the child's interests might suggest that only if there is clear evidence that the child's interests require it can contact be terminated. Although the Human Rights Act 1998 may alter the language used to express the arguments, Wall J in *Re F (Care Proceedings: Contact)*[106] was of the view that it is unlikely that the Act will alter the ways decisions are reached in relation to s 34 applications. In *Re M (Care Proceedings: Judicial Review)*[107] Munby J, obiter, suggested that if a local authority plans to remove a child at birth, it must make arrangements for the mother to breastfeed the baby if she wishes, and to prevent her doing so would infringe the mother's and baby's article 8 rights.

(c) The plans of the local authority

When a local authority seeks to terminate contact this is often because contact is inconsistent with its plans for the child; for example, it wishes to place the child for adoption. So the issue is raised whether the court can refuse to permit termination of contact if the refusal will scupper the local authority's plans for the child. The approach taken by the courts to date is that, where an application is made under s 34, the court should give respect to the plans of the local authority, but at the end of the day the welfare principle governs the issue.[108] As was explained by Butler-Sloss LJ in *Re B (Minors) (Termination of Contact: Paramount Consideration)*:

> The proposals of the local authority, based on their appreciation of the best interests of the child, must command the greatest respect and consideration from the court, but Parliament has given to the court, and not to the local authority, the duty to decide on contact between the child and those named in section 34(1).[109]

So, if the court, even having given the plans of the local authority the greatest respect,[110] decides that the child's welfare requires the continuation of the contact, it will refuse the local authority's application to terminate contact.[111] In fact, it is unlikely that permitting occasional contact between a child and parent will render the local authority's plan impractical. Even if the plan is that the child should be adopted, it is nowadays common to have an 'open adoption', where the child retains contact with his or her birth family.[112] When considering whether to make an order under s 34, the court should not reconsider whether the care order should have been made in the first place.[113] It may be that after the Human Rights Act 1998 the court, in considering whether to terminate contact between a child and his or her family, will not be permitted to assume that the local authority's plans promote a child's welfare, but will be required to analyse them in greater detail.[114]

---

[106] [2000] 2 FCR 481.

[107] [2003] FL 479.

[108] *Berkshire CC v B* [1997] 1 FLR 171, [1997] 3 FCR 88.

[109] [1993] Fam 301 at p. 311. Supported in *Re E (A Minor) (Care Order: Contact)* [1994] 1 FLR 146, [1994] 1 FCR 584.

[110] In *Re D and H (Care: Termination of Contact)* [1997] 1 FLR 841 CA it was said to be inadvisable to disrupt the local authority plans by refusing to permit the termination of contact.

[111] *Berkshire CC v B* [1997] 1 FLR 171, [1997] 3 FCR 88.

[112] *Re S (A Minor) (Care: Contact Order)* [1994] 2 FLR 222, [1994] 2 FCR 414. A useful commentary is provided in C. Smith (1997a).

[113] *H v West Sussex CC* [1998] 1 FLR 862.

[114] See the discussion in *Re F (Care: Termination of Care)* [2000] FCR 481.

(d) Weight to be placed on the child's view

In *L v L (Child Abuse: Access)*[115] it was confirmed that the wishes of the children were to be taken into account when deciding whether to terminate contact. However, the weight placed on the child's wishes depends on the age of the child and circumstances of the case. Jones and Parkinson[116] have warned of the dangers of placing weight on abused children's wishes. This is because abuse can cause a complex psychological relationship between the child and an abuser. This factor was relevant in *Re G (A Child) (Domestic Violence: Direct Contact)*[117] in which an order was made under s 34 to deny contact between a child aged nearly 4 and her father. The child suffered from post-traumatic stress disorder and long-term trauma, having witnessed her father being violent to her mother, and the evidence was that contact would cause the child great harm.

(e) Contact with relatives other than parents

Section 34 provides a presumption of contact only between children and parents, guardians and those with whom the child has lived. The Court of Appeal has held that the duty of the local authority to promote contact extended to 'any relative, friend or other person connected with him'.[118] However, it needs to be stressed that, unlike parents, the local authority does not require the consent of the court to terminate contact with those not listed in s 34. This means that if a local authority does not permit contact, these other relatives and friends need to apply for a contact order under s 8 of the Children Act 1989.[119] In deciding whether to grant leave to a person seeking contact with a child, the court will be governed by the welfare principle, but will take into account the criteria set out in s 10(9):[120]

1. the nature of the contact being sought;
2. the connection of the applicant to the child;
3. any disruption to the child's stability or security; and the wishes of the parents and local authority which are important but not determinative.

In *Re M (Care: Contact: Grandmother's Application for Leave)*[121] the Court of Appeal considered that grandparents do not have a right of contact with children in care and must show that contact would be in the interests of the child. The court may well be prepared to assume that it is good for a child in care to maintain links with as many family members as possible if they are willing to go to the effort of visiting him or her.

(f) Application by children under s 34

The child can apply without leave of the court for contact with a named person and for an order permitting the authority to refuse to allow contact with a person.

---

[115] [1989] 2 FLR 16, [1989] FCR 697.
[116] Jones and Parkinson (1995).
[117] [2001] 2 FCR 134.
[118] CA 1989, Sch 2, para 15(1)(c).
[119] CA 1989, s 34(3)(b).
[120] *Re M (Care: Contact: Grandmother's Application for Leave)* [1995] 2 FLR 86, [1995] 3 FCR 550 CA.
[121] [1995] 2 FLR 86, [1995] 3 FCR 550 CA.

(g) Forcing an adult to have contact with children in care

The court has no power to force an adult to have contact with the child, according to Wilson J in *Re F (Contact: Child in Care)*.[122] The only person who can be forced to behave in a particular way by an order under s 34 is the local authority, who can be required to allow the parents to have contact with the child.

(h) Domestic violence

Where the child was taken into care following incidents of domestic violence, the factors listed in *Re L, V, M, H (Contact: Domestic Violence)*[123] will be taken into account. Particularly if the child was traumatised by the violence and the parent refuses to acknowledge the fact of or effects of the violence, then a court may authorise the denial of contact.[124]

Despite these efforts of the Children Act 1989 to encourage contact, in fact contact often breaks down.[125] The distances and difficulties of travel often discourage parents and other relatives from maintaining contact. Even if contact does take place, the strain of continuing a relationship on the basis of occasional contact can be great.[126] One study found that 51 per cent of children in care would like to see more of their family.[127]

(v) Abducting children from care

It is a criminal offence to abduct children from care. Section 49(1) of the Children Act 1989 provides that:

> A person shall be guilty of an offence if, knowingly and without lawful authority or reasonable excuse, he—
> (a) takes a child to whom this section applies away from the responsible person;
> (b) keeps such a child away from the responsible person; or
> (c) induces, assists or incites such a child to run away or stay away from the responsible person.

A 'responsible person' here means a person who has care of the child by virtue of a care order, an emergency protection order, or powers of police protection. The section is therefore designed to deal with people taking children away from public care, rather than people removing children from their parents or relatives.

5. QUESTIONING LOCAL AUTHORITY DECISIONS

A. Avoiding disputes

The Children Act 1989 is designed to prevent disputes between parents and local authorities arising in the first place. There are two main ways in which this is done.

---

[122] [1995] 1 FLR 510, [1994] 2 FCR 1354.
[123] [2000] 2 FLR 334.
[124] *Re G (Domestic Violence: Direct Contact)* [2000] Fam Law 789.
[125] Millham, Bullock, Hosie and Haak (1986).
[126] Millham, Bullock, Hosie and Haak (1986).
[127] Who Cares? Trust (2000).

The first is through the concept of partnership: this is the idea that local authorities should work in partnership with the child's family and others interested in the child's welfare. The second is through regular reviews: local authorities are required periodically to review each child looked after by them and have a duty to establish procedures to hear complaints or representations. The Review of Children's Cases Regulations 1991 require the local authority to take into account the views of parents; those with parental responsibility; and any other persons whose views are considered relevant when reviewing the care for children.

B. Procedures to challenge local authority decisions

Despite these attempts to avoid disputes, inevitably they arise and there are a number of routes of appeal for those seeking to challenge local authority decisions.[128]

(i) Internal complaints procedures[129]

The internal complaints procedure is primarily designed to work in cases where there is no dispute over what the facts are or the law is. The complaints procedure is most appropriate where the dispute is whether the local authority has misused its powers. *R v Kingston-upon-Thames RB, ex p T*[130] suggested that the complaints procedure should be preferred to judicial review in most cases.

Local authorities are required to establish procedures to deal with complaints.[131] The following can initiate the complaints procedure: children cared for by the local authority; parents of children in care; those with parental responsibility for children in care; and local authority foster carers.[132] The local authority may add to that list if it decides that an individual has sufficient interest in the child. The representations can relate to the way a particular child is cared for or refer to the carrying out of any of the local authority's functions under Part III of the Children Act 1989. The kinds of issues that might be involved include: complaints relating to day-care; after care; accommodation; or support services if the child lives at home. The procedures should involve a two-stage process. The local authority must appoint an officer who will be responsible for co-ordinating the complaint. The authority and an independent person must consider the complaint and formulate a response. If the complainant is not happy with the initial response then he or she has the right to have the complaint considered by a panel. The decision reached by the panel is not binding at law on the authority, but a local authority will normally abide by it.[133]

---

[128] See Bailey-Harris and Harris (2002) for an excellent discussion.
[129] General guidance is found in Representation Procedure (Children) Regulations 1991, SI 1991/894 and Department of Health (1991c). C. Williams (2002) provides a study of how the complaints procedures work in practice.
[130] [1994] 1 FLR 798, [1994] 1 FCR 232.
[131] Department of Health (1991a: ch. 10); Williams and Jordan (1996a; b).
[132] CA 1989, s 26(3).
[133] See *R v Brent LBC, ex p S* [1994] 1 FLR 203 CA.

If the local authority did not follow the recommendation of the panel then a judicial review application may well succeed.[134]

(ii) Human Rights Act 1998

Under s 7 of the Human Rights Act 1998 an individual can bring a claim against a local authority which has infringed or is about to infringe that individual's rights under that Act[135] Section 8 provides that if the application is successful then the court can provide such relief or remedy as is appropriate. This could include requiring the local authority to pay damages or reverse its decision and reconsider what should happen to the child.[136] In *C v Bury Metropolitan Borough Council*[137] a mother brought an action against a local authority under the Human Rights Act claiming that it had infringed her article 8 rights and those of her son who was in care. The case centred on the decision by the local authority to move the son to a residential school 350 miles away from the mother. Although it was accepted that their article 8 rights had been infringed it was held that the infringement was lawful, being in the son's interests and a proportionate interference. Perhaps of significance was the fact that the mother did not have a settled lifestyle and moved around the United Kingdom, and the finding that the local authority had acted reasonably given their financial responsibilities to all the children in their care. The decision has led one commentator to speculate that the Human Rights Act remedies may rarely differ in outcome from judicial review.[138] That would be surprising, but time will tell.

(iii) Judicial review

Judicial review is another court-based remedy when an individual is claiming that a local authority is acting illegally. Leave is required before an application for judicial review can be launched.[139] The court must be persuaded that the applicant has sufficient interest in the matter.[140] Clearly, a parent will have sufficient standing, as will other relatives if their relationship to the child was close enough. Before the court grants leave it will need to be satisfied that the applicant has a reasonable prospect of winning the case.[141] In *Re M; R (X and Y) v Gloucestershire CC*[142] Munby J held that judicial review was not appropriate to seek to prevent a local authority commencing emergency protection or care proceedings, unless there were

---

[134] As suggested *R v Kingston-upon-Thames RB, ex p T* [1994] 1 FLR 798 at p. 814, although not necessarily: *Re T (Accommodation by Local Authority)* [1995] 1 FLR 159, [1995] 1 FCR 517; *R v Avon County Council, ex p M* [1994] 2 FCR 259, [1994] 1 FCR 1006.

[135] Actions can only be brought in respect of acts after 2 October 2000 (Human Rights Act 1998, s 22(4)).

[136] *Re M (Challenging Decisions by Local Authority)* [2001] 2 FLR 1300.

[137] [2002] 2 FLR 868.

[138] Bailey-Harris (2002).

[139] Rules of the Supreme Court, Order 53, r 3.

[140] Clearly, parents and the child him- or herself will have sufficient interest but more remote relatives might have difficulty.

[141] *R v Lancashire CC, ex p M* [1992] 1 FLR 109, [1992] FCR 283 CA.

[142] [2003] FL 444.

exceptional circumstances. The purpose of judicial review is not to decide whether or not the decision was the right one but to decide whether the decision was reached in accordance with the law. So, even if the court thinks that the decision was the wrong one, it cannot overturn it unless the decision was outside the bounds of the law.

(a) Grounds for judicial review

There are three main grounds on which judicial review of a decision of a local authority could be sought:[143]

1. *Unreasonableness.* This phrase is given a special meaning in the law relating to judicial review. It must be shown that the local authority has acted in a way in which no reasonable local authority would act.[144]
2. *Illegality.* Several notions are included under this head. The core notion is that the local authority has acted outside the powers given to it by the law; for example, that the local authority has changed the surname of the child without the approval of the parents or the court. Another form of illegality is where the local authority has fettered its discretion. This means that it would be unlawful for a local authority to adopt a rigid policy or rule which determines every case that comes up for consideration (for example, that a child can never be adopted by a person of a different race). The reasoning is that where a local authority has been given a discretion by Parliament over a particular issue the local authority is obliged to consider each case separately and not apply a blanket rule. Of course, a local authority can adopt general policies which usually apply as long as each case is considered on its own merits. A local authority may also be acting illegally if it failed to take into account a factor it is required to take into account,[145] or takes a factor into account which it should not have taken into account.
3. *Procedural impropriety.* This would be relevant where the local authority has breached the rules of natural justice.[146] An example might be where a child is removed from foster carers without the child, foster carers or biological parents being consulted.[147]

The following list indicates the kind of complaints that have led to judicial review proceedings:

1. Removing a child from foster carers without consultation.[148]
2. Improperly removing a person from a list of approved adopters.[149]

---

[143] *Council of Civil Service Unions v Minister for the Civil Service* [1985] AC 374.
[144] E.g. *R v Kingston-upon-Thames RB, ex p T* [1994] 1 FLR 798, [1994] 1 FCR 232.
[145] E.g. *R v Avon CC, ex p K* [1986] 1 FLR 443, where a children's home was closed without considering the welfare of the children in the home.
[146] An example *R v Bedfordshire CC, ex p C* [1987] 1 FLR 239.
[147] *R v Wandsworth LBC, ex p P* [1989] 1 FLR 387. In *Re M (A Child)* [2002] 1 FCR 88 the child was found to have established the right to family life with the foster carer.
[148] *R v Hereford and Worcester County Council, ex p R* [1992] 1 FLR 448, [1992] FCR 497; *R v Lancashire CC, ex p M* [1992] 1 FLR 109, [1992] FCR 283 CA.
[149] *R v Wandsworth LBC, ex p P* [1989] 1 FLR 387.

3. Unjustifiably placing a child on a child protection register.[150]
4. Disclosing to third parties allegation of child abuse.[151]

Even if a local authority is found to have acted illegally, the remedies after a successful claim for judicial review are limited. The court will declare the decision unlawful and require the local authority to reconsider the issue. The court does not normally have the power to compel the local authority to act in a particular way. The limited remedies available under judicial review indicate that it is best used when an applicant is attempting to challenge a general policy of a local authority. Where the complaint is about the way a particular individual was treated, an application under the Human Rights Act 1998 may be more appropriate.

(iv) Secretary of State's default powers

The Secretary of State has the power to intervene in an extreme case. The Secretary of State will be reluctant to use this power in an individual complaint but may be persuaded to do so where a local authority has adopted what he or she regards as an undesirable policy. An example may be a local authority which has failed to set up a satisfactory complaints system.[152]

(v) The local government ombudsman

A complaint can be made to the relevant local government ombudsman if there is maladministration. Recourse to the local government ombudsman is only possible where there is no remedy by way of the internal complaints procedure or it would be unreasonable to use that procedure. The ombudsman will issue a report and can award an ex gratia payment.[153] However, the ombudsman has no power to order the local authority to act towards a child in a particular way.

(vi) Civil actions

There have in recent years been several attempts by parents and children to sue local authorities under the law of tort for compensation for harms caused by local authorities when performing their child-care obligations. The sorts of conduct complained of include a failure to act on reports of allegations of abuse;[154] removing a child from her mother after an incorrect identification of an abuser;[155] or failing to prevent abuse by a foster father after ineffective monitoring of the placement.[156] These claims are usually based on either the tort of negligence or the breach of statutory duty.[157] The

---

[150] E.g. *R v Hampshire CC, ex p H* [1999] 2 FLR 359.
[151] *R v Devon CC, ex p L* [1991] 2 FLR 541.
[152] *R v Dient LDO, ex p S* [1991] 1 FLR 203 CA.
[153] This is not enforceable.
[154] *X v Bedfordshire CC* [1995] 2 AC 633, [1995] 2 FLR 276 HL.
[155] *M v Newnham* [1995] 2 AC 633, [1995] 2 FLR 276 HL.
[156] *H v Norfolk* [1997] 1 FLR 384 CA.
[157] For an important recent decision on the doctrine of vicarious liability in the child-care context see *Lister v Hesley Hall Ltd* [2001] 2 FLR 307 HL.

cases involve some highly complex issues of tort law and so only a broad outline can be provided here. The position that the law has now reached is that each case depends on its facts. There is no blanket immunity that a local authority can rely upon when facing a claim of negligence. Instead a duty of care is owed where it is fair, just and reasonable. For example, in *W* v *Essex CC*[158] foster parents specifically told a local authority that they would not be willing to care for a child who was himself a known child abuser. Nevertheless, the local authority housed such a child with them and he abused the foster parents' own children. The House of Lords were willing to accept that, potentially, the local authority could be liable in tort for the harm caused to the foster parents and their children. In *Barrett* v *Enfield LBC*[159] a local authority was held liable for damages to a child whom it had taken into care, but then unsatisfactorily placed with foster carers. It was held that the courts should be more ready to find a duty of care where the claim was that a child taken into care had been mistreated, than in cases where the argument was that the taking into care was improper.

The law involves a delicate balance. On the one hand, in favour of liability for the local authority under the law of tort are arguments that tort liability will encourage the local authority to see that it has in place procedures to ensure that negligent acts do not take place. Also in favour of liability are arguments that children or adults who suffer as a result of local authority intervention or non-intervention deserve compensation for their loss. Indeed, they may be entitled to a remedy under article 6 of the European Convention. On the other hand, there are also arguments against tortious liability. It may be that local authorities may become too 'litigation conscious' in carrying out the delicate task of child protection, leading to social workers always adopting the safest course of action, which may not be the course which is the best policy for the child. A further complexity is that sometimes the decision over the form of intervention to protect a child is essentially a political one, involving allocation of resources. Such decisions, partly economic or political, are normally thought inappropriate for judicial review. Due to the difficulties in pursuing a tort action an applicant may prefer, where possible, to use the Human Rights Act 1998.

(vii) Private orders

An aggrieved parent or relative could use a s 8 order.[160] In *Re A (Minors) (Residence Orders: Leave to Apply)*[161] a foster mother sought to challenge a local authority's decision that she was no longer permitted to foster four children by applying for a residence order in respect of the children. The Court of Appeal took the view that, in considering whether to give leave, the authority's plans were very important.[162] The court was willing to assume that departure from the local authority's plan would not promote the child's welfare and therefore it declined to grant leave. This case indicates that it will be rare for a court to grant leave for a s 8 application which

---

[158] [2000] 1 FLR 657 HL.
[159] [1999] 3 WLR 79 HL.
[160] Non-parents may require the leave of the court: see Chapter 9.
[161] [1992] 2 FLR 154, [1992] 2 FCR 174 CA.
[162] As required under CA 1989, s 10(9)(d)(i).

the local authority opposes. Whether a court will have to be more willing to grant leave, relying on article 6 of the European Convention, is open to debate.

(viii) Inherent jurisdiction

If a child is in need and no other route is open to protect the child's welfare, the court may be willing to use the inherent jurisdiction in exceptional cases. In *Re M (Care: Leave to Interview Child)*[163] a father successfully applied under the inherent jurisdiction for an order that he could have his child interviewed to assist in his defence to a rape charge. The court will only make an order under the inherent jurisdiction if persuaded that the order sought will promote the welfare of the child.

(ix) The Care Standards Commission

The Care Standards Act 2000 has created a national Care Standards Commission, with the job of supervising, registering and inspecting children's homes and care homes. There are grave concerns over the outcomes of children in local authority care. One-quarter of adults in prison were once in care. Those adults who were in care are four times as likely to be unemployed and 60 times more likely to be homeless than those not brought up in care.[164] Whether the work of the Commission will improve the position of those who leave care remains to be seen.

6. THE POSITION OF LOCAL AUTHORITY FOSTER CARERS

Foster carers have proved highly successful in looking after children who have been taken into care. Children will live in the foster carers' homes and be brought up with their families. Foster carers are normally paid an allowance by local authorities to cover the costs of bringing up the child. Evidence suggests that children cared for by foster carers suffered less than children living in children's homes; and even children who have been adopted.[165] However, foster care is rarely intended to be a long-term solution for children in care. It is crucial that at the outset it is made clear to the foster carers and the child whether the arrangement is intended to be a long- or short-term one. Failure to do this could cause great hardship to all the parties.

The law is structured with the policy of making fostering an attractive option for both foster carers and local authorities. It seeks to strike a balance between enabling foster carers to make decisions in respect of children in their care, while ensuring that the local authority's long-term plans for the child are not hindered. Normally, the relationships between the local authority and foster carers are good and negotiations can deal with any problems that arise. However, the courts may become involved when the local authority and foster carers disagree over what should

---

[163] [1995] 1 FLR 825, [1995] 2 FCR 643.
[164] Performance and Innovation Unit (2000b: 2.3).
[165] Gibbons, Gallagher, Bell and Gordon (1995).

happen to the child and in particular if the local authority wishes to remove the child from the foster carers against their wishes.

The legal position of foster carers is precarious. Their status gives them the right to retain the child until there is a request from the local authority to return the child. The foster carers have limited recourse to the courts if required by the local authority to return the child:

1. The foster carers could apply for a residence or contact order. Foster carers can only seek leave to bring an application for a contact or residence order if:[166]

   (a) the child has lived with the foster carers for at least one year;[167] or
   (b) the local authority consents; or
   (c) they are relatives of the child.

   If none of these conditions exists then foster carers cannot bring an application. This puts foster carers in a weaker position than anyone else. Anyone else can apply for leave to bring an application for a s 8 order in respect of a child.
2. The foster carers could apply to adopt the child. If the foster carers issue a notice of their intention to apply to adopt the child, the court will refuse leave to remove the child until there has been a proper investigation of the adoption application.[168]
3. The foster carers could apply for judicial review of the local authority's decision to remove the child.
4. Foster carers are prevented by s 9(3) from applying for a residence order. However, in a controversial decision,[169] *Gloucestershire CC v P*,[170] the Court of Appeal stated that a court can make a residence order in favour of the foster carers on its own motion under s 10(1)(b), although only in exceptional cases.[171] Thorpe LJ dissented on the ground that this was to use s 10(1)(b) to get around the bar in s 9(3) preventing foster carers applying for residence orders.

It is possible that the relationship between a foster carer and a child could constitute family life and so be protected under article 8 of the European Convention on Human Rights. Whether the relationship does constitute family life seems to depend on the strength of the relationship between the child and foster carers.[172] In the light of this, local authorities will have to have strong justification before removing children from foster carers with whom they have lived for many years.

7. DURATION OF CARE AND SUPERVISION ORDERS

A supervision order lasts for up to one year initially, although it can be made for a shorter period.[173] It is possible for the supervisor to apply for an extension for up to

---

[166] These are the rules if the child is in care. If the child is not in care but accommodated by the local authority the position is slightly different: see Hayes and Williams (1999: 112–15).
[167] Not ending more than three months before the date of the application: CA 1989, s 10(5)(b).
[168] *Re C (A Minor) (Adoption)* [1994] 2 FLR 513, [1994] 2 FCR 839 CA.
[169] For criticism, see Lowe and Douglas (1998: 432).
[170] [1999] 2 FLR 61.
[171] See also Wall J in *Re MD and TD (Minors) (No. 2)* [1994] Fam Law 489.
[172] *Gaskin v UK* (1989)12 EHRR 36, para 49.
[173] See e.g. *M v Warwickshire* [1994] 2 FLR 593.

three years. The welfare principle will cover any application for an extension.[174] Any existing supervision order will be terminated if the court subsequently makes a care order.[175]

A care order lasts until any of the following events occur:

1. The child reaches the age of 18.
2. The court discharges the care order.[176] The child, the local authority and anyone with parental responsibility may apply for the discharge of a care order.[177] It should be noted that unmarried fathers without parental responsibility cannot therefore apply for a discharge, although the father could apply for a residence order which, if granted, would automatically discharge the care order.[178] According to *Re A (Care: Discharge Application by Child)*,[179] a child applying for discharge of a care order to which he or she is subject does not need leave. The welfare principle[180] governs applications to discharge care orders.[181] In some cases it may be appropriate to discharge a care order and replace it with a super-vision order.[182]
3. If the court grants a residence order in respect of a child, this will bring to an end any care order relating to that child.
4. An adoption order or freeing order will bring to an end a care order.

8. DUTIES TO CHILDREN LEAVING CARE

Children leaving care are often vulnerable. For example, one in seven girls leaving care is pregnant or has children of her own. It is therefore essential to ensure that there is proper provision for children who are moving out of care.[183] The basic duty of the local authority to a child leaving care is to 'advise, assist and befriend him with a view to promoting his welfare when he ceases to be looked after by them'.[184] The local authority can provide assistance, even exceptionally in cash.[185] Assistance in finding employment may be provided. The provision of services to children leaving care has been widely seen as inadequate.[186] Seven per cent of authorities did not monitor what happened to their children at all and 9 per cent did not monitor what had happened to children who had left their care. This area is now governed by the

---

[174] *Re A (A Minor) (Supervision Extension)* [1995] 1 FLR 335 CA.

[175] CA 1989, Sch 3, para 10.

[176] A supervision order can be varied or discharged on the application of the child; any person with parental responsibility; or the supervisor. Application to discharge supervision orders are also governed by the welfare principle, although if the court wished to substitute a supervision order with a care order this does necessitate proof of the significant harm test.

[177] CA 1989, s 39(1). Variation of a care order is not permitted because there is nothing to vary apart from discharging it.

[178] CA 1989, s 91(1).

[179] [1995] 1 FLR 599, [1995] 2 FCR 686, Thorpe J.

[180] CA 1989, s 1.

[181] *Re T (Termination of Contact: Discharge of Order)* [1997] 1 FLR 517.

[182] E.g. *Re O (Care: Discharge of Care Order)* [1999] 2 FLR 119.

[183] Recognised in Department of Health (1999b) and Social Exclusion Unit (1999b).

[184] CA 1989, s 24(1).

[185] CA 1989, s 24(8) and (9); restrictively construed in *R v Kent CC, ex p S* [2000] 1 FLR 155.

[186] Department of Health (2000c: para 2.4).

Children (Leaving Care) Act 2000. The aim of the Act is to ensure that children can move successfully from care to 'real life'. The local authority must have 'a pathway plan' which applies until the children are 21. The plan should cover their education, training and general plans for the future. There is a general duty to assess the needs of those leaving care. The Act is certainly an improvement on the present law.

9. THE BALANCE OF POWER BETWEEN COURTS AND LOCAL AUTHORITIES

A recurring theme through the past two chapters has been the delicate balance of power between the courts and local authorities.[187] Courts and local authorities have each complained that the other has exceeded its powers. In *Nottingham CC v P*[188] the court criticised the local authority for failing to apply for a care order, leaving the court powerless to help the child; while in *Re C (Interim Care Order: Residential Assessment)*[189] the local authority felt that the courts were exceeding their powers in ordering the local authority to assess the child at a specialist centre.

How does the Children Act 1989 balance the power between the courts and the local authority? At a simple level the answer is that the courts decide whether to make an order, but the local authority decides how to implement the order. The position has been summarised by the Court of Appeal in *Re R (Care Proceedings: Adjournment)*:[190]

> [T]he judge is not a rubber stamp. But if the threshold criteria have been met and there is no realistic alternative to a care order and to the specific plans proposed by the local authority, the court is likely to find itself in the position of being obliged to hand the responsibility for the future decisions about the child to the local authority ... To make other than a full care order on the facts of this case was to trespass into the assumption by the court of a control over the local authority which was specifically disallowed by the passing of the Children Act.

However, it is more complex than that. Dewar[191] has suggested two models that could describe the way that the court operates:

1. The first is the adjudicative or umpire model. Here the court simply decides whether a local authority has made out the threshold criteria for an order and will make the order without involving itself in planning issues. In other words, once the court is persuaded that the grounds for an order are made out, the local authority takes over control of what should happen during the order.
2. The second is the active or participatory model. The court should decide not only whether or not there should be an order but also what should happen once the order is made.

---

[187] M. Hayes (1996).
[188] [1993] 2 FLR 134, [1994] 1 FCR 624 CA.
[189] [1997] 1 FLR 1, [1997] 1 FCR 149.
[190] [1998] 2 FLR 390, [1998] 3 FCR 654.
[191] Dewar (1995). See also M. Hayes (1996).

There is support for both models in the Children Act 1989 and the case law. In favour of the adjudicative model being an accurate description of the role of the court in this area is the ethos of partnership, indicating that disputes over what should happen to the child in care should be resolved between the local authority, the parents and the child, without court intervention.[192] In particular, the local authority is required to set up a complaints procedure which is designed to resolve any disputes and avoid the need to refer issues to the court.[193] In favour of the participative model is the fact that the courts retain control over the contact arrangements, although it should be noted that the courts have the power only to require the local authority to ensure contact continues. The courts have no power to order a local authority to prevent contact.[194] The courts also have the power to revoke a care order, for example, by making a residence order.

There have been several cases revealing clashes between the courts and local authorities. Three revealing cases are the following:

1. In *Re S, Re W (Children: Care Plan)*[195] the House of Lords were required to consider the extent to which a court could require a local authority to carry out its care order. The Court of Appeal in that case clearly felt frustrated that a judge makes a care order on the basis of a particular care plan, but the local authority may then decide to do something completely different with a child, without having to return to the court.[196] An extreme example might be that the local authority in the care plan proposes keeping the child with the birth family, but providing them with services. The judge, approving of this, makes a care order but the local authority could then decide to place the child with fosterers, with a view ultimately to adoption: quite a different prospect from that foreseen by the judge who made the original care order.[197] It should be added that local authorities tend to depart from care plans not because of malice, but a shortage of funds. One study found that only 60 of the 100 children studied had their care plans fulfilled.[198] The same study suggests that where care plans are implemented this normally promotes the child's welfare better than where the plan is departed from.[199]

   The Court of Appeal in *Re S, Re W* therefore came up with a scheme under which on making the care order the court could star various items on the care plan (e.g. where the child was to live, crucial services which the local authority was to provide). If subsequently the local authority wished to depart from one of the starred items the local authority should take the matter back to court and

---

[192] Department of Health (1991b).
[193] CA 1989, s 26(3).
[194] *Re W (Section 34(2) Orders)* [2000] 1 FLR 512.
[195] [2002] 1 FCR 577 (HL), discussed in Herring (2002b); Miles (2002); Mole (2002); C. Smith (2002).
[196] In *Re O (Care: Discharge of Care Order)* [1999] 2 FLR 119 the care order was discharged because the care plan had been departed from so radically.
[197] A more realistic example may be that the child is placed with the birth parents under the care order but the promised services are not provided. For an example of a child 'lost in care' while a local authority failed to carry out a care plan see *F v Lambeth LBC* [2001] 3 FCR 738.
[198] Harwin and Owen (2003: 72).
[199] Harwin and Owen (2003: 78). See also Hunt and McLeod (1998: chs 7–9).

seek approval of the course of action. If they failed to do so the matter could be brought before the judge by the guardian.

It must be admitted that there were no sections in the Children Act 1989 which mentioned this starring system. However, the Court of Appeal justified its creation of it by reference to the Human Rights Act 1998. The argument was that on making a care order the state would, inevitably, be interfering in article 8 rights of the child and family. The court would have to make sure that the interference was justified and that the extent of the intervention was proportionate. The only way the court could do this would be to approve the extent of the intervention as set out in the care plan, and require court approval for any further intervention. The House of Lords, however, felt that the Court of Appeal's approach was illegitimate. The Court of Appeal had crossed the line from using the Human Rights Act to interpret legislation, which was permissible, to amending legislation, which was not.[200] The House of Lords pointed out that there were no words in the Children Act which the Court of Appeal were 'interpreting' to produce their starred system; rather, in effect, a new section was being added to the legislation.

The House of Lords went further and claimed that the Court of Appeal's interpretation infringed a cardinal principle in the Children Act 1989. Lord Nicholls explained:

> The court operates as the gateway into care, and makes the necessary care order when the threshold conditions are satisfied and the court considers a care order would be in the best interests of the child. That is the responsibility of the court. Thereafter the court has no continuing role in relation to the care order. Then it is the responsibility of the local authority to decide how the child should be cared for.[201]

In other words the court has the task of deciding whether or not to make a care order, but the local authority has the task of deciding what should happen to a child who has been taken into care.[202] As Lord Nicholls acknowledges, this principle is not without exception. A local authority cannot, for example, terminate contact between a child in care and his or her family, nor change the child's name or religion without the permission of the court. Indeed, supporters of the Court of Appeal's approach might even claim that the Children Act does leave the courts with control over crucial issues concerning the upbringing of a child in care and therefore the issue is not as straightforward as the House of Lords might have suggested. It is worth noting that Lord Nicholls was clearly not unsympathetic to what the Court of Appeal was doing. He described the Court of Appeal's approach as 'understandable'[203] and made it clear that his objection was that such an approach should be created by Parliament, not the courts.[204]

---

[200] *Re S, Re W (Children: Care Plan)* [2002] 1 FCR 577, para 39.
[201] Para 28.
[202] For criticism of this see Herring (2002b).
[203] Para 35.
[204] For calls for Parliament to reform the law and a useful summary of possible reform proposals see Geekie (2002).

Having decided that the Court of Appeal's use of the starring system was illegitimate Lord Nicholls then held that the present law (whereby the local authority could decide how to bring up a child in its care free from court supervision) was not incompatible with the rights of the child and his or her family under article 8. He explained that although the law gave the local authority the power to infringe the child's rights (e.g. by disproportionately interfering in his or her article 8 rights) that did not mean that the law itself thereby infringed the child's rights. The fact the Children Act provided only limited remedies where it was claimed that the local authority had interfered with the child or his or her family's right to family life did not thereby render the Act itself incompatible with the European Convention. This was because the absence of a provision in a statute could not render that statute incompatible with the European Convention.[205] In any event, as Lord Nicholls pointed out, whenever a local authority infringed a child or his or her family's article 8 rights they could bring proceedings against the local authority under s 7 of the Human Rights Act 1998. This also provided protection for an individual's article 6 rights.[206] He accepted that relying on parents bringing proceedings to protect the rights of a child in care was not fail-proof. A parent may not want or be unable to litigate. In such a case (unless the child was particularly mature) there would be no one who could enforce the child's rights.

In some ways the lesson to be learned from this litigation is that all too often local authorities lack the resources to implement care plans and this might lead to the infringement of the human rights of children in care. Although the temptation may be to enable the court to compel a local authority to abide by care plans, to do so might mean that local authorities will have to withdraw funding from other children in their care. The fact that all too often insufficient funds are available to ensure that the human rights of children in care are protected should shame our society.[207]

2. In *Nottingham CC v P*[208] the Court of Appeal held that it had no power to order a local authority to apply for a care order, even though it was convinced that a care order was necessary to protect the child. Sir Stephen Brown stated:

> The court is deeply concerned at the absence of any power to direct this authority to take steps to protect the children. In the former wardship jurisdiction it might well have been able to do so. The operation of the Children Act 1989 is entirely dependent upon the full co-operation of all those involved. This includes the courts, local authorities, social workers, and all who have to deal with children. Unfortunately, as appears from this case, if a local authority doggedly resists taking the steps which are appropriate to the case of children at risk of suffering significant harm it appears that the court is powerless.

---

[205] Para 59.

[206] Theoretically, if a parent's parental rights were infringed in a way which did not constitute an infringement of their article 8 rights, then it may be that the parent's article 6 rights could be infringed, but, as Lord Nicholls said, it is hard to think of an instance where this would happen.

[207] Herring (2002b).

[208] [1994] Fam 18, [1993] 2 FLR 134, [1994] 1 FCR 624 CA, discussed in Chapter 10.

No doubt concerns of this kind led Bracewell J in *Re N (Leave to Withdraw Care Proceedings)*[209] to hold that the court had the power to refuse to permit the local authority to withdraw an application for care proceedings when it felt that the children needed the protection of a care order. This does not sit easily with the argument that a care order cannot be made against the wishes of a local authority.

3. *Buckingham CC v M*[210] accepted that although a court cannot attach conditions to a care order in an effort to control the way a child is treated during a care order, a court can make an *interim* care order and then direct that the local authority arrange a planned rehabilitation between a child and his or her parents.[211] Hayes[212] has argued that this was improper and that the court had no jurisdiction to do this. She argued that the court order, with the direction that the child be rehabilitated with the mother,[213] involved giving the local authority parental responsibility for the child but then directing the local authority how it must exercise that parental responsibility. Hayes argued that it placed the local authority in an 'intolerable position – on the one hand it has the duty to look after the child and to keep him safe, on the other hand it cannot rely on its own assessment of whether the child will be protected if allowed to go home'.[214]

There is much to be said for the general approach of leaving day-to-day issues relating to the treatment of a child in care to the local authority. The first is a practical one and that is that the court cannot provide continuous guidance relating to children in care, responding to particular issues as they arise. Secondly, some issues relating to the care of abused children lie in the expertise of the local authority's social workers. Thirdly, the local authority will have to balance the needs of all children (and other vulnerable people) in their area with the resources they have available to spend. Although courts are adept in deciding specific issues relating to a particular child, court procedures are not suitable for formulating general policies in allocation of resources. Indeed this may have been the key policy behind the House of Lords' decision in *Re S, Re W (Children: Care Plan)*.[215]

10. SECURE ACCOMMODATION ORDERS

The secure accommodation order is only available to local authorities and is used to control the aggressive behaviour of children.[216] The aim is not necessarily to provide treatment, but to ensure that problematic children are in an environment where they pose no danger to themselves or others. If the child is to be placed in

---

[209] [2000] 1 FLR 134.

[210] [1994] 2 FLR 506, [1994] 1 FCR 859 CA.

[211] The House of Lords in *Re C (A Minor) (Interim Residence Order: Residential Assessment)* [1997] 1 FCR 149, [1997] 1 FLR 1 took a similar approach.

[212] M. Hayes (1996).

[213] Under the supervision of two doctors in the case.

[214] M. Hayes (1996: 203).

[215] [2002] 1 FCR 577.

[216] As well as the secure accommodation order, children can be detained under the Mental Health Act 1983; s 23 of the Children and Young Persons Act 1969; and s 38(6) of the Police and Criminal Evidence Act 1984.

secure accommodation[217] for more than 72 hours, court approval through a secure accommodation order is required. The order should only be used as a 'last resort'.[218] The grounds on which a child can be subject to a secure accommodation order are set out in s 25(1) of the Children Act 1989:[219]

(a) that—
  (i) he has a history of absconding and is likely to abscond from any other description of accommodation; and
  (ii) if he absconds, he is likely to suffer significant harm; or
(b) that if he is kept in any other description of accommodation he is likely to injure himself or other persons.

The court has no power to make a secure accommodation order in respect of a child over the age of 16.[220] The child's welfare is not the paramount consideration in deciding whether to make a secure accommodation order, as was made clear in *Re M (Secure Accommodation Order)*.[221] It will be recalled that one of the purposes of the order is for the protection of the public, in which case the order may be justifiable, even if it is not for the child's benefit.[222] The court's role is simply to test the evidence and fix the duration of the order, but not to determine what happens to the child during the accommodation.[223] A local authority must review the detention one month after the making of the order and thereafter every three months. The local authority must be satisfied that the criteria are still met and that detention is necessary.[224]

In *Re K (A Child)(Secure Accommodation Order: Right to Liberty)*[225] the Court of Appeal held that a secure accommodation order deprived a child of liberty and therefore fell within article 5 of the European Convention on Human Rights, which makes it clear that 'nobody shall be deprived of his liberty save in the following cases and in accordance with a procedure prescribed by law'.[226] The article lists the circumstances in which a detention may be permitted. A secure accommodation could be compliant with the article on the basis of article 5(1)(d), which permits: 'the detention of a minor by lawful order (i) for the purpose of educational supervision or (ii) his lawful detention for the purpose of bringing him before the competent legal authority'. Dame Elizabeth Butler-Sloss explained that education in article 5(1)(d) included education broadly defined. However, it would not be poss-

---

[217] For a discussion of what is secure accommodation, see *Re C (Detention: Medical Treatment)* [1997] 2 FLR 180, [1997] 3 FCR 49.
[218] Department of Health (1991a: para 5.1).
[219] Detailed regulation is found in the Child (Secure Accommodation) Regulations 1991, SI 1991/1505.
[220] A child under 16 in whose favour a secure accommodation order is made, but who subsequently becomes 16, could be accommodated under CA 1989, s 20(5): *Re G (Secure Accommodation)* [2000] 2 FLR 259, [2000] 2 FCR 385.
[221] [1995] 1 FLR 418 CA.
[222] Bates (1995).
[223] *Re W (A Minor) (Secure Accommodation Order)* [1993] 1 FLR 692.
[224] *LM v Essex CC* [1999] 1 FLR 988.
[225] [2001] 1 FCR 249 CA, discussed in Masson (2002b).
[226] In *Bouamar v Belgium* (1987) 11 EHRR 1, where a person with a history of aggressive behaviour was detained, the court suggested that the detention was only lawful if the matter was brought speedily before the court.

ible to use a secure accommodation order simply to punish or detain a child if there was no educational element in what was being done.[227]

11. ADOPTION

A. The use of adoption today

The history of adoption reveals changes within our society.[228] Legal adoption started with the passing of the Adoption of Children Act 1926.[229] Before then informal adoption had taken place under the guise of wet-nursing, apprenticeship and informal arrangements for the care of a child.[230] Traditionally adoption was regarded as a convenient way of handing children born to an unmarried mother to a married infertile couple.[231] It was seen as a blessing to all concerned: the unmarried mother could quietly and without embarrassment get rid of the child, who would otherwise be a public witness to her sin, and the married couple would be provided with the child they so longed for. Nowadays adoption is viewed rather differently, with the interests of the child, rather than the adults, being at the forefront of the law's concern.

Adoption is now seen as a service for children. It is one of the ways in which the state may arrange care for children whose parents are unable or unwilling to care for them. Infertile couples are now more likely to turn to assisted reproduction than an adoption agency. Unmarried mothers are unlikely to feel that such is the stigma of extramarital birth that they should put up their children for adoption. Indeed, only about 50 mothers a year place their babies for adoption and this is usually because of the child's disability or their mother's personal circumstances.[232] Further, in recent years half of all adoptions have involved the mother and stepfather adopting the mother's child,[233] so that the stepfather can become the child's father in the eyes of the law.

Traditionally, adoption was based on the 'transplant' model, namely that children would be transplanted from one family and inserted into a new family. The child would cease to be a member of his or her 'old family' and would become a full member of the new family. As Staughton LJ explained: 'The best thing for the children in the ordinary way is that he or she should become as nearly as possible the lawful child of the adopting parents.'[234] However, increasingly the transplant model is under challenge. One of the significant changes in the nature of adoption is that the average age of children being adopted has risen.[235] The older the child

---

[227] *Re M (A Child) (Secure Accommodation)* [2001] 1 FCR 692 CA emphasises that children have rights under article 6 to a fair trial in applications for secure accommodation orders.

[228] J. Goody (1983), Douglas and Philpot (2003), O'Halloran (2003) discuss the changing nature of adoption.

[229] Bridge and Swindells (2003: ch. 1). Cretney (2003a: ch. 17) provides an excellent history of adoption.

[230] J. Goody (1983).

[231] Department of Health (1999a).

[232] R. Parker (1999: 4).

[233] Lord Chancellor's Department (2000).

[234] *Re S (A Minor) (Blood Transfusion: Adoption Order Conditions)* [1994] 2 FLR 416 CA at p. 421.

[235] Lowe (1997a).

is, the more likely it is that he or she will be aware of who his or her biological parents are and that it will be appropriate for the adopted child to retain contact with his or her natural parents.[236] In such cases the transplant model is unsuitable.

There were 5,459 adoptions in 2002.[237] This was a 1.4 per cent increase on 2001, but 27 per cent fewer than 1992, when there were 7,466. The Department of Health has provided further details about adoptions of children in care:

> 3,400 looked after children were adopted in England in the year ending 31 March 2002, 11% (350) more than in the previous year and 25% (690) more than in 1999/00. 60% (2,000) of these children were aged between 1 to 4, whilst 29% (1,000) were aged between 5 to 9. 66% (2,250) of children had been looked after for less than 3 years prior to being adopted. The average time taken for looked after children to complete the adoption process was 2 years 10 months in 2001/02. 80% (2,700) of looked after children adopted during the year 2001/02 were placed for adoption within 12 months of the best interest decision. 16% (550) of children were adopted by their former foster carer in 2001/02, compared to 14% (430) in 2000/01.[238]

The Adoption and Children Act 2002 has completely reformed the law on adoption which had been set out in the Adoption Act 1976.[239] The road to reform has been a long one. In 1992 there was a major review of Adoption Law;[240] in 1993 there was a White Paper;[241] there followed various consultation documents leading to a draft Adoption Bill in 1996; followed by a further White Paper;[242] and ultimately the 2002 Act.

The government is convinced that adoption benefits children. This could be supported on the basis of psychological evidence that children in care permanently placed with a family suffer less than children living in institutional children's homes.[243] Research on adopted children even indicates that there is no difference between the well-being of adopted children and children living with their biological parents.[244] Indeed, the majority of adopted children fare better on various indicia than children with comparable starts in life who live with their birth parents.[245] Despite the widespread assumption that adoption benefits children in fact there has been remarkably little study into the benefits of adoption. Those studies that have been carried out tend to suggest that adoption is beneficial, but the picture is not straightforward and much more research needs to be done before we can confidently assert that adoption is superior to long-term fostering.[246] That said, when

---

[236] Ryburn (1998).

[237] Office for National Statistics (2003a).

[238] Department of Health (2003b).

[239] The Act is due to come into force at the end of 2004. Bridge and Swindells (2003) provide an excellent discussion of the Act.

[240] Department of Health and Welsh Office (1992).

[241] Department of Health and Welsh Office (1992).

[242] Department of Health (2000e); Performance and Innovation Unit (2000a), discussed in Barton (2000).

[243] Barton and Douglas (1995: 350); Department of Health (2000e). Judicially acknowledged in *Re F (A Minor) (Adoption: Parental Agreement)* [1982] 3 FLR 101.

[244] Bohman and Sigvardsson (1990).

[245] Reynor (1980); consider also Ryburn (1998: 55–6); Rushton (2002).

[246] Neil (2002); Eekelaar (2003a); Warman and Roberts (2003). Grotevant and McRoy (1998), for example, in a US study find no evidence that adoption benefits children.

considering the benefits of adoption it should not be forgotten that the statistics on children who remain in care are appalling: children in care are four times more likely to be unemployed than children not in care, 60 times more likely to be homeless, and that people who were in care as children constitute a quarter of the adult prison population.[247]

The 2002 Act is premised on the belief that adoption is presently underused by local authorities, is unco-ordinated[248] and riddled with delays.[249] As one report put it: 'society as a whole has a clear responsibility to provide these children with permanence – a safe, stable and loving family to support them through childhood and beyond – and a fresh start as quickly as possible'.[250]

The alleged problems with the law and practice of adoption before the 2002 Act comes into force include the following:

1. It has been claimed that the procedures by which adopters are selected are riddled with 'politically correct' values.[251] Craig has argued: 'It appears that only ideological arguments, racism and long-term investment in maintaining the status quo will stand in the way of our most vulnerable children growing up in permanent, loving families.'[252] The most common complaint is that adoption agencies have refused to permit people to adopt children of a different race, known as mixed-race adoption. Complaints have even been made that gay couples seeking to adopt have been favoured over married couples.[253] It is impossible to assess the validity of these claims. The assessment of the suitability of adopters involves consideration of such a large number of factors that it is hard to tell whether one factor dominated the decision.

2. There are also concerns over the length of time that the adoption process takes.[254] A research study by Ivaldi[255] shows that over half of adopted children were less than a year old when they entered into care but the average age at adoption was 5.5 years.[256] The government sees the problem to be this:

   > once a child has been admitted into local authority care the focus can too often tend to be exclusively on rehabilitation with the birth family. This is clearly the most desirable outcome but, if it turns out not to be achievable, a permanent home for the child may be delayed if contingency plans, including options for placement with extended family and for adoption or planned long-term fostering have not been considered.[257]

3. There are complaints that adoption is not used enough. It has been argued that too many children are left in care without attempts being made for them to be

[247] Performance and Innovation Unit (2000a: report box 2.3).
[248] Department of Health (2000e).
[249] See e.g. P. Morgan (1999a).
[250] Department of Health (2000e: 1.6).
[251] P. Morgan (1999a). Some of these concerns are reflected in Department of Health (2000e).
[252] Craig (1999: 67).
[253] P. Morgan (1999a).
[254] Department of Health (2000e); Performance and Innovation Unit (2000a).
[255] Ivaldi (1998).
[256] The average age of the child at placement was 3.5 years.
[257] Performance and Innovation Unit (2000a: 3.27).

adopted. In 1999 there were some 55,000 children being looked after by the local authority.[258] In 1999 there were 4,317 adoption orders,[259] whereas in 1975 there had been 21,299 orders. The Department of Health has accepted that couples who seek to adopt healthy white babies are likely to be disappointed.[260] Some commentators argue that lone parents should be encouraged to put their children up for adoption.[261] The government has also complained that there is a wide variety of percentages of children in care who are placed for adoption, ranging in one study from 19 per cent (in Sutton) to 1 per cent (in Darlington).[262] In 1997, 50 local authorities were placing ten or fewer children a year.[263] It should, however, be noted that Britain has a higher rate of children adopted out of care than many other countries.[264]

4. There are grave concerns over the 'failure' rate of adoptions, that is, the number of adoptions which have broken down after the adoption order has been made. A thorough review of the research has concluded that it is not possible to estimate the overall rate of disruption, so it is impossible to assess the size of the problem.[265] However, the very fact that we have no accurate figures on adoption breakdown rates suggests that the potential problem is not being adequately monitored.

By contrast with the difficulties with the law and practice under the 1976 Adoption Act, the government has stated that the following principles will govern the law and practice under the Adoption and Children Act 2002:

- Children are entitled to grow up as part of a loving family which can meet their needs during childhood and beyond.
- It is best for children where possible to be brought up by their own birth family.
- The child's wishes and feelings will be actively sought and fully taken into account at all stages.
- Children's ethnic origin, cultural background, religion and language will be fully recognised and positively valued and promoted when decisions are made.
- The role of adoptive parents in offering a permanent family to a child who cannot live with their birth family will be valued and respected.[266]

The government's dedication to adoption is demonstrated by its promise that it will spend £66.5 million over three years to improve adoption services.[267] How precisely will the Act improve adoption? It is to that question that we now turn.

---

[258] Department of Health (2000e); Performance and Innovation Unit (2000a).
[259] The Stationery Office (2000c).
[260] Department of Health, Home Office, Lord Chancellor's Department and Welsh Office (1993: 3.12). In *Re R (A Child) (Care Proceedings: Teenage Pregnancy)* [2000] 2 FCR 556 it was held that there should be no presumption that babies taken into care should be placed for adoption.
[261] P. Morgan (1999a).
[262] Ivaldi (1998).
[263] J. Richards (1999).
[264] Barton (2000).
[265] Department of Health (1999a).
[266] Department of Health (2003d; 2003e).
[267] Department of Health (2003c).

B. Encouraging adoption

For many years the numbers of adoptions have been in gradual decline and it had been forecast that adoption would become of little practical relevance for family lawyers. However, in *Adoption, a new Approach* and the *Prime Minister's Review: Adoption* the government[268] indicated its desire to greatly increase the number of adoption orders being made. Indeed the White Paper[269] has declared the government target to increase by 40 per cent by 2004/5 the number of children being looked after by a local authority who are adopted.[270] This aim has surprised some, given that the adoption rate from care of children in the UK is already one of the highest in the world.[271] Lowe and Murch express the concern that 'authorities, keen to meet their percentage target for adoption, may too hastily rule out rehabilitation with the birth parents or wider family, particularly for young children who are likely to be thought more adoptable'.[272] This target will only be reached if it is possible to increase the number of people willing to take on children whose abuse or disability will mean that there will be many challenges facing an adoptive parent. It will also mean that the local authority will have to increase the number of children it thinks suitable for adoption. It should be borne in mind that many children's experience of abuse means that they do not want ever again to live in a family environment.[273]

The Adoption and Children Act 2002 seeks to improve the adoption rates by the following means :

1. There will be a national register of people who wish to adopt a child and children who need to be adopted. Before the 2002 Act each local adoption agency made its own efforts in trying to match would-be adopters and children. In cases where children had particular needs (e.g. children from minority religious or cultural backgrounds) it could be difficult for small adoption agencies to find suitable adopters. The setting up of the national register should assist in such cases.

2. Local authorities are required to maintain an adoption service under s 3 of the Adoption and Children Act 2002. The adoption service must make arrangements for adoption and provide adoption support services.[274] Under s 5 of the 2002 Act local authorities must prepare a plan for adoption services in their area. Prior to the 2002 Act how adoption services were carried out was very much a matter for an individual local authority. A study by Lowe and Murch[275] found wide variations in the use made of adoption by different local authorities. These variations could not be explained simply on the basis of the kind of children in their care. The 2002 Act is intended to create a more co-ordinated approach which will be subject to greater central government control. The

---

[268] In Department of Health (2000e) and Performance and Innovation Unit (2000a) respectively.
[269] Department of Health (2001b: 5).
[270] Department of Health (2001b).
[271] Tolson (2002).
[272] Lowe and Murch (2002: 149).
[273] Fortin (2003b: 495).
[274] In this regard they must work in conjunction with other services.
[275] Lowe and Murch (2002).

Secretary of State will issue National Adoption Standards and other regulations which govern the way local authorities must perform their obligations concerning adoption. There will (inevitably) be targets in respect of adoption which the Department of Health will monitor.[276] The Adoption and Permanence Taskforce will 'assist' local authorities to develop adoption services. Voluntary organisations will continue to be permitted to operate as adoption agencies. However, they will have to register with the National Care Standards Commission and comply with the National Adoption Standards.

3. Under s 5 of the 2002 Act local authorities must consider whether or not to make an adoption plan in respect of every child in its care. If it is decided to pursue the adoption route then the local authority must take necessary actions. The National Adoption Standards expect local authorities to prepare a plan for permanence at the child's fourth-month review.[277] In this way it is intended to encourage local authorities to consider adoption for every child in care and where appropriate take steps to arrange the adoption as quickly as possible.

4. Section 1 of the Adoption and Children Act 2002 states: 'Whenever a court or adoption agency is coming to a decision relating to the adoption of a child the paramount consideration must be the child's welfare, throughout his life.' This is intended to discourage the court from refusing to make an adoption order because of the rights of the birth family. It is also thought that a child-centred adoption system is one that will have higher rates of adoption. Section 1 brings adoption in line with other areas of child law which are governed by the welfare principle in s 1 of the Children Act 1989.

C. Who can adopt?

As part of the attempt to encourage an increase in the rate of adoption the 2002 Act extends the category of those who can adopt. Now anyone can adopt, subject to the following restrictions:

1. An adoptive parent must be at least 21 years old. However, if a parent is adopting his or her own child then he or she need only be 18.[278]
2. If a couple wish to adopt together they must be married or 'living as partners in an enduring family relationship'.[279] This includes a same-sex relationship. If a couple are in a casual relationship this would mean they could not adopt together, but one of them could adopt a child alone.
3. A single person can adopt. But a married person can only adopt alone if he or she satisfies the court that his or her spouse cannot be found; or is incapable by reason of ill-health of applying for the adoption; or that the spouses have separated and it is likely to be a permanent separation.

[276] The National Care Standards Commission has the responsibility of inspecting local authority services: Care Standards Act 2000, Part 2. There is to be an Adoption and Permanence Taskforce (see Department of Health (2002d)).
[277] National Adoption Standards for England, Standards A2, A3.
[278] Adoption and Children Act 2002 (hereafter ACA 2002), s 50.
[279] ACA 2002, s 144(4). See Marshall (2003).

4. There are complex rules which set out domicile or habitual residence requirements for would-be adopters.[280]
5. An adoption agency cannot place any child for adoption where a person over the
age of 18 has been convicted or cautioned for a specified offence (e.g. child
abuse).

At the time one of the most controversial aspects of the 2002 Act was that it permitted adoption by a same-sex couple. In fact the change was not as dramatic as
might at first appear, for two reasons. First, even before the Act a gay or lesbian
person could adopt alone and then, together with his or her partner apply for a joint
residence order, granting them both parental responsibility for the child.[281]
Secondly, although the Act states that a same-sex couple may adopt a child, the Act
says nothing about whether or not the sexual orientation or marital status of an
applicant should count for or against a couple being considered for adoption. It is
submitted that it should be uncontroversial that if it is in the best interests of a child
to be adopted by a same-sex or unmarried couple the court should be able to permit
the adoption to go ahead. Otherwise one would have to take the view that it would
always be preferable for a child to remain in state care, rather than be adopted by
the most suitable unmarried or same-sex couple – a view it would be hard to accept.

The 2002 Act, however, is notable in its formal acknowledgement of same-sex
relationships. It also means that, for the first time in English and Welsh law, a child
could have two mothers or two fathers. It does not, however, allow a child to have
more than two parents in total.

D. Who can be adopted?

Only a person under the age of 19 can be adopted, although the application must
be made before that person's eighteenth birthday.[282] In other countries it is possible for one adult to adopt another. This is normally done to enable them legally to
become family members, which may have significance in relation to, for example,
inheritance rights. It has been used by some gay couples in the United States as a
way of enabling their relation to be recognised as a family one.[283]

E. Selecting adopters and matching adopters and children

Before setting out the procedures for matching adopters and children we need to
appreciate a tension in the law's goals here. A court will only be willing to make an
adoption order if it is decided that there is no realistic hope of the child living with
the birth family in the foreseeable future and that the adoption will promote the
child's welfare. There are therefore difficulties in cases where the birth family
objects to the adoption. When are their objections to be considered? If they are left

---

[280] ACA 2002, s 49(2), (3).
[281] *Re AB (Adoption: Joint Residence)* [1996] 1 FLR 27, [1996] 1 FCR 633.
[282] ACA 2002, ss 47(9) and 49(4). In *Re B (Adoption Order: Nationality)* [1999] 1 FLR 907 the House
of Lords approved of the making of an adoption order of a 16-year-old to enable her grandparents
to take care of her in this country.
[283] See also *Bedinger* v *Graybill's Trustee* (1957) (302) SW (2nd) 594 where a husband adopted his wife!

to the end of the process there could be a situation where the child has been placed with adopters for a trial period which has gone very well, with raised hope of the adopters and perhaps the child, which are dashed when at the final hearing the judge decides that the birth parents are justifiably objecting to the proposed adoption. However, if the consent of the birth parents is dealt with as the first issue the judge is in the difficult position of having to decide whether to dispense with the parents' consent, without knowing whether or not the proposed adopters will be suitable. The solution adopted by the 2002 Act is that the consent issue should be dealt with early on in the process, at the stage of the placement. However, if there is a change in circumstances then at the final hearing the parents have a further chance to object.

The road to adoption under the Adoption and Children Act 2002 involves the following stages:

1. *Planning for adoption.* The local authority should consider whether adoption is suitable for every child in its care. If it decides that a birth family are unable to meet a child's needs in the foreseeable future and that adoption is likely to provide the best means of doing so, then a plan for adoption should be drawn up.[284] As with all decisions that a local authority makes in relation to a child in care, his or her parents must be sufficiently involved in the planning process. This does not mean that they must be involved in every meeting, but they must be sufficiently involved to protect their interests.[285] In deciding whether to pursue adoption the local authority must also consider the likelihood of finding appropriate adopters. A severely disabled child may be harder to place; a child under the age of 4 with no direct links to family members will be much easier.[286]

   In making the decision to consider adoption a delicate balance has to be drawn. On the one hand, if the local authority believes that there is a hope of rehabilitation with the birth parents it will be reluctant to pursue an adoption. On the other hand, delaying adoption because of a faint hope of rehabilitation may mean the child has to spend years in limbo, making the chance of success of any later adoption more remote. Some local authorities use a process known as twin-tracking to deal with this difficulty: at the same time, work is done on the one hand with the family in an effort to pursue rehabilitation with the birth parent, while on the other hand preparations are made to find an alternative secure home for the child.[287] Such procedures can be difficult for all involved and require trust and commitment all round. There may also be concerns that such procedures may cause confusion for the child. Another scheme is known as concurrent planning where a child is placed with foster carers on the understanding that they will assist in attempts to rehabilitate the child with the birth parents, but, if that fails, the foster carers will be considered as adopters.[288]

---

[284] ACA 2002, s 1.
[285] *Scott v UK* [2000] 1 FLR 958.
[286] Lowe and Murch (2002: 141).
[287] The courts have approved such schemes: e.g. *Re R (Child of Teenage Mother)* [2000] 2 FLR 660.
[288] Monck, Reynolds and Wigfall (2003).

2. *Assessing would-be adopters.* When a couple or individual approaches an adoption agency, wishing to be considered as an adopter, they will be assessed by the agency. Many agencies take the view that the process should be as much about the agency deciding whether the couple are suitable to be adopters, as about assisting the couple to decide whether they wish to adopt. Applicants must be treated fairly, openly and with respect.[289] In the past there were concerns over the assessment of would-be adopters. Television programmes and newspaper articles claimed that some adoption agencies attached improper significance to irrelevant factors such as people's weight, smoking habits and religious beliefs. There were also complaints that the assessments used were improperly invasive. In response the government announced that the Department of Health would issue guidance on what factors should be taken into account.[290] This should at least ensure there is consistency in practice between the different agencies. The new scheme will also require local authorities to take some steps to recruit adopters.[291]

3. *The preparation of the report.* The adoption agency must interview and assess anyone who puts themselves forward for adoption and then prepare a detailed report for the agency's adoption panel.[292] The report might comment on the applicant's relationships, health and lifestyle, and will take up references.

4. *The adoption agency's decision on the applicant's suitability.* In the light of the report the adoption agency will decide whether or not to approve the adopters. Although the report prepared by the panel will be taken into account, the decision is ultimately one for the agency. At present it appears that 95 per cent of applicants put before the agency are approved. This figure may seem very high, but it should be appreciated that most candidates thought unsuitable for adoption will have withdrawn from the process before the final report is placed before the panel.

There is no right to adopt under the European Convention on Human Rights.[293] However, if an applicant could demonstrate that he or she was denied an adoption in a way which discriminated against him or her in a way prohibited by article 14 (e.g. on the grounds of race) then arguably that would infringe his or her rights. In *Fretté v France*[294] the European Court found that it was permissible for a state to prohibit a single homosexual man from adopting. It was held that the right to respect for family life presupposed the existence of a family and did not provide the right to found a family. Therefore it was not possible to claim a right to adopt a child under article 8. Because no Convention right had been infringed it was not possible for the applicant to rely on article 14 and claim that his Convention rights had been infringed in a way which had unlawfully discriminated against him.

---

[289] Department of Health, National Adoption Standards for England (2001) B 1–7.
[290] ACA 2002, s 45; Department of Health (2002f).
[291] Department of Health (2003e).
[292] This is required by the National Adoption Standards.
[293] *Fretté v France* [2003] 2 FCR 39 ECtHR.
[294] [2003] 2 FCR 49 ECtHR.

5. *Matching the child and adopter.* If the adopter(s) is or are approved, the agency must then consider whether there are any children needing to be adopted who are an appropriate match. If there are, the applicants will be given brief details of the children. If the applicants are keen to proceed then the adoption panel will prepare a report for the adoption agency on the proposed match.

6. *The agency approves the match.* The adoption agency will need to approve of the proposal that adoption between the child and would-be adopter should be pursued. It should be remembered that s 1 of the Act applies to the agency. Thus the agency should approve the match if to do so would promote the child's welfare. The agency will have to pay due regard to the child's religious persuasion, racial origin and cultural and linguistic background.[295] However, political policies (e.g. political objections to transracial adoption) should not be allowed to prevent the pursuing of an adoption which would promote the child's best interests.[296]

   The issue of transracial adoption is a controversial one.[297] At one extreme there are concerns that adoption can become a means of taking children away from deprived black families and giving them to infertile middle-class white couples. There is also conflicting evidence over whether children whose race differs from that of their primary carers suffer from confusions over their cultural identity. To others transracial adoption is to be encouraged as part of the creation of a racially and culturally diverse and mixed society.[298]

7. *The adopters are provided with a full report on the child.* The would-be adopters at this stage will be provided with a full report on the child's health, needs and history.[299]

8. *Placement of the child with the would-be adopters.* The next stage will be the placement of the child with the adopters for what is, in effect, a trial period. To place a child the agency must either have the consent of each parent with parental responsibility[300] or must have obtained a placement order from the court.[301] These two alternatives will now be considered:

   (a) Placement by consent. Parental consent can be specific (i.e. the parents consent to the child being placed with a particular person or people) or general (i.e. the parents consent to the child being placed with whomever the local authority believes to be appropriate). However, if at any time a parent withdraws his or her consent then the agency must apply for a placement order or return the child to the parents.[302] Once consent to placement is granted the agency acquires parental responsibility, but the

---

[295] See the discussion in *Re C (Adoption: Religious Observance)* [2002] 1 FLR 1119.

[296] Lowe and Murch (1999): 31 per cent of agencies said that they would not place a child transracially.

[297] See the discussions in P. Hayes (1995); P. Morgan (1999a); Gupta (2002).

[298] Murphy (2000).

[299] A local authority may be liable in tort if they fail to provide relevant information, which if disclosed would have persuaded the adopters not to go ahead with the adoption: *A and B v Essex CC* [2002] EWHC 2709.

[300] ACA 2002, s 19(1), unless care proceedings are pending (s 19(3)).

[301] ACA 2002, ss 21(3), 52.

[302] ACA 2002, ss 22, 31 and 32. If the birth parent(s) do not wish to be involved any further in the process they are entitled to ask that they are not informed of any application for adoption (s 20(4)).

birth parents do not lose it. However, the agency is entitled to restrict the way parents can exercise their parental responsibility.

(b) Placement by placement order.[303] The court can make a placement order only if all of the following are satisfied:

   (i) Either a care order has already been made in respect of the child or the court is satisfied that the significant harm test in s 31 of the Children Act 1989 (see Chapter 10) is satisfied.

   (ii) Parental consent has been given or been dispensed with.[304] Dispensing with parental consent will be dealt with in more detail in a later section, but in brief this can happen if to do so will promote the child's welfare.

   (iii) The court is persuaded that it is better to make the placement order than not to do so.[305]

The placement order grants the local authority parental responsibility.[306] It brings to an end any contact order in operation.[307] On the making of a placement order the prospective adopters will acquire parental responsibility while the child is with them. If the child is not with prospective adopters then the agency will have parental responsibility. The birth parents will retain parental responsibility if they have it, but the agency can decide the extent to which it can be exercised.[308] A placement order also prohibits the removal of the child from the adopters, by anyone (including most importantly the birth parents) except the local authority.[309] Once a placement order has been made only in exceptional circumstances will the birth family be able to raise objections to an adoption order. This means that once the placement order has been made the would-be adopters can go ahead with the placement secure in the knowledge that if the placement works well the birth family are very unlikely to undermine it.

Before making a placement order the court is required to consider the arrangements for contact between the child and birth family.[310] The placement order will terminate any existing contact order, but on making the placement order the court can make a contact order. It can also authorise the agency to refuse contact between the child and any named person.[311] The placement order can be subject to conditions. In particular the court can make the placement order subject to condition that the child keeps contact with the birth family. The placement order can be revoked if it is decided that there is no plan for adoption. The adoption

---

[303] Article 6 of the European Convention on Human Rights requires that legal aid be made available: *P, C, S* v *UK* [2002] 2 FLR 631.
[304] If consent has been given the local authority are likely to go down the route of placement by consent.
[305] ACA 2002, s 1(6).
[306] ACA 2002, s 26(1).
[307] ACA 2002, s 26(1).
[308] ACA 2002, s 24.
[309] ACA 2002, ss 34(1), 47(4).
[310] ACA 2002, s 27(4).
[311] ACA 2002, s 27.

agency can apply for a revocation. Birth parents cannot, unless they have the leave of the court. If the child was in care then the revocation of the placement order will lead to the care order taking full effect.[312]

9. *The agency applies for an adoption order.* If the placement has worked well the final stage will be for the adoption agency to apply for an adoption order. It is not possible to apply for an adoption order unless there has been a placement order or the parents are consenting to the adoption, with one exception: that is, foster carers who have looked after the child for at least 12 months, who can apply without satisfying any further requirements.[313]

F. Criminal prohibitions on illegal placements

It is illegal for anyone except an adoption agency to place a child for adoption with a person who is not a relative.[314] If parents wish to have their child adopted they should contact an adoption agency. Only local authorities and adoption societies can run adoption services.[315] There are even criminal offences if an unauthorised person seeks to run an adoption service.[316]

G. The making of an adoption order

It is not possible for an adoption to occur without a court order.[317] So, if a couple take into their home a child and raise him or her as their own child this will not be an adoption.[318] Without a court order they will have no formal status in respect of the child. Before considering an adoption order the court will have to be satisfied that the placement criteria have been met. The exact requirement depends on the nature of the applicants:

- If the adoption is arranged by an adoption agency then the child must have lived with the applicants for at least 10 weeks before the application is made.
- If the adoption is a non-agency case and the applicant is a step-parent or partner of the parent then the minimum period is 6 months.
- If the adoption is a non-agency case and the applicant is a local authority foster carer then a continuous period of 1 year is required.
- If the adoption is a non-agency case and the applicant is a relative then the child must have lived with the applicant for a cumulative period of 3 years during the preceding 5 years.[319]

---

[312] ACA 2002, s 29(1).
[313] ACA 2002, s 47.
[314] ACA 2002, ss 92, 93. See *Re MW (Adoption: Surrogacy)* [1995] 2 FLR 759, for a pre-2002 Act example.
[315] ACA 2002, s 92.
[316] ACA 2002, s 93.
[317] The government considered whether in simple cases court proceedings were necessary (Performance and Innovation Unit (2000a)), but the White Paper decided that the courts should be involved in all cases.
[318] Although such a child may become treated as a child of the family for the purposes of, for example, the Matrimonial Causes Act 1973.
[319] ACA 2002, s 42.

These requirements ensure that the child and would-be adopters have spent a sufficient amount of time together for the court to be able properly to assess whether the adoption is likely to benefit the child. If the placement criteria are satisfied the court will go on to consider the two key crucial requirements for an adoption order:

1. that the making of the adoption order is in the child's welfare, and
2. that the birth parent consents to the adoption or that consent has been dispensed with.

These requirements will be considered separately.

(i) That the making of the adoption order is in the child's welfare

In deciding whether or not an adoption order is in the welfare of the child the court must consider the checklist in s 1(4) of the Adoption and Children Act 2002. This is the following:

(a) the child's ascertainable wishes and feelings regarding the decisions (considered in the light of the child's age and understanding);
(b) the child's particular needs;
(c) the likely effect on the child (throughout his life) of having ceased to be a member of the original family and become an adopted person;
(d) the child's age, sex, background and any of the child's characteristics which the court or agency considers relevant;
(e) any harm (within the meaning of the Children Act 1989) which the child has suffered or is at risk of suffering;
(f) the relationship which the child has with relatives, and with any other person in relation to whom the court or agency considers the relationship to be relevant, including –

> (i) the likelihood of any such relationship continuing and the value to the child of its doing so;
> (ii) the ability and willingness of any of the child's relatives, or of any such person, to provide the child with a secure environment in which the child can develop, and otherwise to meet the child's needs;
> (iii) the wishes and feelings of the child's relatives, or of any such person, regarding the child.

Four points in particular will be emphasised about this list.[320] First, it should be noted that the court must consider the child's welfare not only during the child's minority, but for the rest of his or her life. Thus a court may be persuaded that making an adoption order in favour of a child just short of his or her eighteenth birthday will promote his or her welfare, if doing so will give him or her British citizenship. Secondly, as usual the child's own views about the proposed adoption are likely to be very important, if not crucial, to a determination of the child's welfare. At one time it was proposed that an adoption order could not be made in respect

---

[320] The list is similar, but not identical to, CA 1989, s 1(3).

of a child over the age of 12 without his or her consent. This did not appear in the final Act. However, it is hard to imagine a case where a court will decide that an adoption, against the wishes of a teenager, will promote his or her welfare. Thirdly, the Act requires the court specifically to consider the child's relationships with his or her birth family: not just his or her birth parents, but his or her wider family.[321] In particular the court must consider whether the child's blood relatives are in a position to care for the child.

A fourth point is that when considering an application for an adoption order the court must recall the alternative orders that it can make. These include: (i) a residence order in favour of the applicants;[322] (ii) a special guardianship; (iii) no order. The key issue in many contested adoptions is whether adoption is a preferable alternative to a residence order in favour of the would-be adopters, or a special guardianship in their favour. All of these options would lead to the child living with the applicants, but, unlike adoption, the birth parents would not lose their parental status. Also, significantly, the formal links between the child and his or her wider family (e.g. siblings, grandparents, etc.) would remain. The court will have to weigh up the benefits of retaining the broad links with the birth family with the benefits of security offered by an adoption. Holman J in *Re H (Adoption Non-patrial)*[323] summarised the benefits of an adoption order, over and above a residence order in favour of the would-be adopters:

> It is well recognised that adoption confers an extra and psychologically and emotionally important sense of 'belonging'. There is real benefit to the parent/child relationship in knowing that each is legally bound to the other and in knowing that the relationship thus created is as secure and free from interference by outsiders as the relationship between natural parents and their child.

In *Re B (A Child) (Sole Adoption by Unmarried Father)*[324] the Court of Appeal declined to make an adoption on the basis that the present fostering arrangements were working well and there was no particular benefit to be gained by an adoption. Mason has argued that it will be particularly difficult to justify making an adoption order, rather than a residence order, if a relative is seeking to adopt the child.[325]

In *Re M (Adoption or Residence Order)*[326] the views of a 12-year-old that she did not want to be regarded as no longer the sibling of her siblings were decisive in ordering a residence order in favour of the applicants, rather than an adoption. The Court of Appeal was brave in doing this because the applicants had stated that they would not be able to care for the child if only granted a residence order and threatened that if they were denied an adoption order they would return the child to the local authority. In the face of strong evidence that it was in the interests of the child to live with the applicants, the Court of Appeal trusted that the applicants would not carry through with their threats. In addition to a residence order, it also made

---

[321] Parkinson (2003).
[322] The ACA 2002 has amended s 12 of the Children Act 1989 so that a residence order can last until the child's eighteenth birthday.
[323] [1996] 1 FLR 717, at p. 726.
[324] [2002] 1 FCR 150.
[325] Mason (2003: 32).
[326] [1998] 1 FLR 570 CA.

an order under s 91(14) of the Children Act 1989, preventing the birth mother making an application for an order under that Act without the leave of the court. This would provide some limited protection to the applicants from concerns that the birth mother would be constantly seeking to interfere with the way they were raising the child.

When considering whether the adoption will promote the child's welfare the court will be aware of potential rights under the Human Rights Act 1998. The approach of the European Court of Human Rights towards adoption is rather ambiguous. In *Johansen* v *Norway*[327] the European Court considered the placement of the applicant's daughter in a foster home with a view to adoption. The court stated:

> These measures were particularly far-reaching in that they totally deprived the applicant of the family life with the child and were inconsistent with the aim of reuniting them. Such measures should only be applied in exceptional circumstances and could only be justified if they were motivated by an overriding requirement pertaining to the child's best interests.[328]

This statement, subsequently repeated in many cases, appears to suggest that adoption is only permissible in exceptional cases and only if there is a very strong case for it based on the child's interests. However, later cases suggested a more positive attitude towards adoption. In *Söderbäck* v *Sweden*[329] the European Court of Human Rights approved the making of an adoption order in favour of a mother and her new husband, despite the opposition of the child's father, who only ever had limited contact with the child. The court accepted that the stability that the adoption order would provide justified the making of the order. However, it is hard to see how the circumstances of that case were in any way exceptional. The case can be read as signifying a change in the European Court's attitudes towards adoption. Or it may be that as the only right to family life being infringed by the adoption order was that of the father and child who had only limited contact with each other, an adoption order was easier to justify than a case like *Johansen* where a child is being removed from a parent who has an established relationship with the child.[330]

(ii) The consent of the parents

Before an adoption order can be made the court must have the consent of the parents or dispense with that consent.

(a) Who must consent?

The consent of all parents with parental responsibility and any guardians is required. The consent of an unmarried father without parental responsibility is not required. The 1996 draft Adoption Bill required the consent of children over the age of 12 to being adopted but this is not required under the 2002 Act.[331] The

---

[327] (1996) 23 EHRR 33.
[328] Para 78.
[329] [1999] 1 FLR 250.
[330] *Söderbäck* v *Sweden* [1999] 1 FLR 250: paras 13–33 in the judgment appear to draw this distinction.
[331] See Piper and Miakishev (2003) for support for this proposal.

British Agencies for Adoption and Fostering (BAAF) objected to the consent requirement on the basis that children may feel they are being asked actively to reject their birth parents by consenting to adoption.[332]

If the birth parents consent to the adoption it might be thought that adoption is uncontroversial. Lord Nicholls expressed the view that if a mother consented to the adoption it could not be said to infringe her article 8 rights.[333] However, the right to respect for family life of the child should not be forgotten. Even where the parent is consenting to the adoption the child's rights are still being interfered with by the order.[334]

(b) The unmarried father without parental responsibility

As just noted, it is not necessary to have the consent of a father without parental responsibility before the court makes an adoption order. But that does not mean that he can be ignored by the adoption agency. The adoption agency should normally notify the father of the adoption proceedings. Where the father has family life for the purposes of article 8, the courts have held that he must be notified of the proceedings and involved sufficiently to protect his interests. Not to do so might infringe his rights under articles 8 and 6.[335] This human rights dimension means now that he should be informed of the proposed adoption unless there are very good reasons for not involving the father (e.g. where there is a concern that he will be violent towards the mother if he should learn of the child's birth and proposed adoption.)[336]

(c) What is consent?

Consent must be given 'unconditionally and with full understanding of what it involved'.[337] It is therefore not possible for a birth parent to consent to an adoption only under certain circumstances (e.g. that the adopter is a Chelsea supporter!).[338] The consent must be in writing on a form which sets out the effect of adoption and is witnessed by a CAFCASS officer. The intention of these requirements is that the consent be given freely and with full understanding.[339] This also explains why a birth mother's consent to adoption is only valid if the child is at least 6 weeks old.[340] Until this time she may not have full understanding of the significance of the decision she is making.

---

[332] Mason (2003: 26) complains that children are not able to be parties to the adoption proceedings.
[333] *Re B (Adoption by One Natural Parent to the Exclusion of Other)* [2001] 1 FLR 589 at para 29.
[334] Harris-Short (2002).
[335] *Re R (Adoption: Father's Involvement)* [2001] 1 FLR 302 CA.
[336] *Re M (Adoption: Rights of Natural Father)* [2001] 1 FLR 745; *Re J (Adoption: Contacting Father)* [2003] FL 368; *Re S (A Child) (Adoption Proceedings: Joinder of Father)* [2001] 1 FCR 158; *Re H (A Child) (Adoption: Disclosure); Re G (A Child) (Adoption: Disclosure)* [2001] 1 FCR 726.
[337] ACA 2002, s 52(5).
[338] If the birth parent is willing to consent to adoption only if the adopter has certain characteristics (e.g. is of a certain religion), he or she may be willing to give specific consent to adoption to named individuals, but not a general consent.
[339] Although see *Re A (Adoption: Agreement: Procedure)* [2001] 2 FLR 455 where the consent of a 15-year-old Kosovan rape victim to a freeing order was revoked on the basis that she had not understood what she was signing.
[340] ACA 2002, s 88(2).

(d) Consent to what?

The consent to the adoption can be consent to adoption to a specific person or general consent for the child being adopted by anyone. The consent can be given at the time of placement or subsequently. This reflects the variety of roles that the birth family may wish to play in an adoption case. It may be that the birth parents do not want any involvement in adoption and hand over the child to the adoption agency, happy for them to select an appropriate adopter. On the other hand, it may be that the birth family want a say in the selection of the adopter (particularly if the adoption is to be an open one) in which case they may prefer to consent to a particular adopter of whom they approve.

(e) Changes of mind

If the consent is given in advance of the adoption order it can subsequently be withdrawn, as long as an application for an adoption order has not been made. Further, if consent has been given and not withdrawn by the time of the application the parent cannot object to the making of the adoption order without the leave of the court. The court will give leave only if there has been a change in circumstances. Similarly, if a placement order has been made a parent cannot object to the making of the adoption order without the leave of the court.[341]

(iii) Dispensing with consent

The court can dispense with the consent of a parent whose consent is required in two circumstances:

1. 'The parent or guardian cannot be found or is incapable of giving consent.'[342] This provision will be used in cases where the parent or guardian has disappeared or is unknown (e.g. if the baby was found abandoned outside a hospital and the mother has never been identified). It is also used if the parent is suffering a mental disability which means she lacks capacity to consent.
2. 'The welfare of the child requires the consent to be dispensed with.'[343] Under the Adoption Act 1976 parents' objections to adoption could only be overridden if they were unreasonably withholding their consent to the adoption. Section 1 of the Adoption and Children Act 2002 makes clear that now the sole consideration for the court in dispensing with consent is the child's welfare. So the rights of the parents and questions about whether or not the parents were reasonable in their objections are irrelevant. This has led to heavy criticism by some who fear that to permit the adoption of children against the wishes of parents simply on the basis that it would be better for the child rides roughshod over the importance attached to parental rights. Can any parent be particularly confident that it is impossible to find someone else who would be better at raising his or her child?[344]

---

[341] ACA 2002, s 47.
[342] ACA 2002, s 52(1)(a).
[343] ACA 2002, s 52(1)(b).
[344] Barton (2001).

Such concerns, however, may be overblown. There are a number of ways in which, despite the wording of s 52(1)(b), the interests of parents could be taken into account:

(i) The subsection uses the word 'requires'. This might suggest that, if it is shown that adoption is only slightly in the interests of the child, this will be insufficient to *require* the consent to be dispensed with.

(ii) Under the Human Rights Act 1998 this subsection must be read in a way which is compatible with the European Convention if at all possible.[345] Clearly an adoption order is a grave interference with the right to respect for family life between the parent and child.[346] Indeed, it is harder to think of a graver one. It must therefore be a proportionate intervention. Only a substantial benefit to the child of adoption might be thought sufficient to make adoption a proportionate response and therefore permissible under article 8(2).[347]

It should be added that if the child has lived with the would-be adopters and has developed a close relationship with them it is arguable that the would-be adopters and child have developed family life which is also protected under article 8. Such an argument is likely to be strongest where the child has lived with the applicants for a considerable period of time.[348]

(iii) In interpreting the welfare test in the Children Act 1989 the courts have developed the 'natural parent presumption': that is, it is presumed that the child is best brought up by the natural (i.e. birth) family. It is true that this presumption has been questioned in recent years (see Chapter 9) but that has been in cases where there has been no effective relationship between the birth parent and child.

(iv) Professional practice. Most social workers working in this area regard adoption as a last resort, to be tried only where any hope of rehabilitation with the birth parents has been lost. This means that even if theoretically the law does not protect parents' rights, the practice of the professionals involved might mean that adoption will only be sought when there are very strong child welfare reasons for seeking it.

(v) Although at the adoption order stage the welfare test applies, at the placement stage the s 31 threshold criteria (see Chapter 10) will have to be satisfied. Therefore it will have to have been shown that the parenting of the child caused or risked the child significant harm before a child can be adopted against the parent's wishes.

Despite such arguments, Bridge and Swindells argue that there is a change in the law in that: 'Whereas parents (under the former law) could take a different view of

---

[345] Welbourne (2002) and Choudhry (2003) provide useful discussions on the potential impact of the Human Rights Act 1998 in this context.

[346] *P, C, S v UK* [2002] 2 FLR 631.

[347] *P, C, S v UK* [2002] 2 FLR 631, at para 118. See also *Re C and B (Children) (Care Order: Future Harm)* [2001] 1 FLR 611 CA.

[348] *Re B (A Child) (Adoption Order)* [2001] EWCA 347, [2001] 2 FCR 89.

their child's welfare and not be unreasonable, the court will now be able to impose its view on them.'[349] The point is that under the 1976 Act if it would be reasonable to take the view both that the child should be adopted and that the child should not (i.e. it was a borderline case) it would not be possible to dispense with the parent's consent. However, in such a case under the 2002 Act it would be open to the court to decide that an adoption was (just) in a child's welfare and therefore dispense with parental consent.

H. The effect of an adoption order

An adopted child is to be treated as the 'legitimate child of the adopter or adopters'.[350] This means that the adoption order will have the following effects:

1. Parental responsibility for the child is given to the adopters.[351]
2. Adoptive parents can make all decisions about the child which other parents can make, including appointing a guardian.[352]
3. An adoption order extinguishes the parental status and parental responsibility of any other person. There is one exception to this and that is where a step-parent adopts their partner's child, where their partner will retain parental responsibility and status.[353]
4. After the making of an adoption order an adopted child no longer has any right to inherit their birth parent's property.
5. On the making of an adoption order an adopted child who is not a British citizen will acquire British citizenship if the adopter is a British citizen.[354]

There are, however, some circumstances in which the adoption order does not treat the adopted child in exactly the same way as a natural child.

1. An adopted person is deemed within the prohibited degrees of relations for the purpose of marrying his or her birth relations.[355] Therefore, for example, if an adopted man marries his birth sister, entirely innocently, the marriage will be void. However, he can marry his adoptive relatives, including an adoptive sister, but not his adoptive mother.
2. A minor may retain the nationality he or she had acquired from his or her birth. However, a minor adopted in the UK court will be a British citizen if one of the adopters is a British citizen.[356]
3. Adoptions do not affect the right to succeed to peerages.
4. Section 69 of the Adoption and Children Act 2002 states that an adoption will not affect certain dispositions of property.[357]

---

[349] Bridge and Swindells (2003: 152).
[350] ACA 2002, s 67(1)–(3).
[351] ACA 2002, s 46(1).
[352] ACA 2002, s 67.
[353] ACA 2002, ss 51(2), 67(3)(d).
[354] British Nationality Act 1981, s 1(5).
[355] ACA 2002, s 74(1).
[356] British Nationality Act 1981, s 1(5).
[357] Bridge and Swindells (2003: 215–17) explain the detail of the law.

I. Open adoption

As originally conceived adoption was seen as a closed and secretive process. Birth parents were not told who had adopted the child, adoptive parents were not told who the birth parents were, and the child was not told that he or she had been adopted. Even if the child did find out this was a secret to be kept from the rest of the world.[358] This secrecy model changed with evidence that some adopted children needed detailed information of their birth background to establish a secure sense of who they were,[359] and birth parents needed to know that their child had been successfully and happily adopted.[360]

These concerns have led to an increase in willingness for local authorities to encourage open adoption. These are adoptions where the child maintains links with the birth parents or wider family. This may be indirectly through e-mails, or directly through face-to-face meetings.[361] Research suggests that open adoptions more often involve contact between the birth mother and her side of the family, rather than the birth father.[362] Research also suggests that in fact the possibility of contact is effectively determined at the time when the care order is made. If after the care order there is no contact, it is unlikely that contact will arise after adoption, while if contact has taken place after the care order this is likely to continue once the adoption order has been made.[363] At present at least 70 per cent of children who have been adopted retain some kind of contact with their birth families.[364]

The issue of open adoption is controversial.[365] In favour it is said that openly adopted children will feel less a sense of being rejected by their birth families;[366] it will provide them with a greater sense of security; and it might encourage birth families to be supportive of the adoption.[367] Indeed, one study interviewing adopted children found that many wanted greater contact with their birth families.[368] Against open adoption it must be recalled that some cases of adoption are those where the child has suffered or been at risk of significant harm because of the parenting they have received. Particularly where the birth family have abused the child the benefits of contact may be questioned. Further, there are concerns that contact with the birth family might undermine the position of the adopters.[369] It may also deter some would-be adopters from going through with the adoption.[370]

---

[358] Cretney (2003a: ch. 17).

[359] Triseliotis (1973).

[360] Howe and Feast (2000).

[361] National Adoption Standards (2001) A11.

[362] Neil (2000).

[363] M. Richards (1994).

[364] Department of Health (2002d: 15).

[365] Smith and Logan (2002) and Neil (2003) provide useful discussions. For an article sceptical about the benefits of open adoption see Quinton, Selwyn, Rushton and Dance (1998).

[366] Casey and Gibberd (2001). In *Re G (Adoption: Contact)* [2003] FL 9 the fear was expressed that without contact the children might view their birth families as 'ogres'.

[367] Lowe, Murch, Borkowski et al. (1999: 324); Smith and Logan (2002). *Re G (Child: Contact)* [2002] 3 FCR 377, [2002] EWCA Civ 761 acknowledges that research is generally in favour of open adoption.

[368] Thomas (2001).

[369] Lowe et al. (1999: 313). For an example see *Re C (Contempt: Committal)* [1995] 2 FLR 767.

[370] Lowe and Murch (2002: 62).

Interestingly the courts have been reluctant to make a court order requiring contact between the child and the birth family. The argument the courts have accepted is that if the adopters are happy for there to be contact then there is no need for the court to make an order requiring it.[371] And if the adopters do not want there to be contact it would be wrong to force them to do so.[372] Section 46(6) of the 2002 Act now requires the court to consider, when making an adoption order, whether to make a contact order in respect of the child. It remains to be seen whether this will be interpreted as encouraging the courts to make contact orders. Under the old law what tended to happen was that agencies produced written agreements which clearly set out the kind of contact between the child and the birth family that was expected.[373] These agreements are not, however, enforceable. If the adopted parents refuse to permit contact as expected it would be possible for the birth parents to apply for an article 8 contact order.[374] However, they will need the leave of the court before the court will hear their application. The court are only likely to grant leave where the maintenance of contact with the birth family is of such benefit to the child as to justify overriding the privacy of the adoptive family. Forcing contact against the wishes of the adopters is unlikely to benefit the child in the long run.[375] One of the few cases where the Court of Appeal held that leave should be granted was *Re T (Adopted Children: Contact)*[376] where the adopters had failed to provide an annual report to the adopted children's adult half-sister. Notably this case did not greatly interfere in the private and family life of the adoptive parents.[377]

J. Adoption by a parent

A parent may decide to adopt his or her own child. The reason for doing this is usually to eliminate the other parent from the picture. Nowadays this is very rare, but it sometimes arises. In *Re B (Adoption by the Natural Parent to Exclusion of Other)*[378] very shortly after the birth of her child a mother decided to place her children for adoption. The father, by chance, discovered this and offered to raise his child. The mother agreed to the arrangement. She did not want to play any role in the child's upbringing and was therefore happy for her maternal role to be ended. The Official Solicitor was appointed and objected on the basis that it was not in the child's welfare to terminate the link with her mother. At first instance the adoption order was made but the Court of Appeal allowed an appeal. Hale LJ held that only exceptional circumstances (e.g. disappearance of a parent or anonymous sperm donation) could justify single-parent adoptions. The House of Lords, however, allowed a further appeal and restored the adoption. It held, controversially, that an order which was in the child's best interests could not breach the child's rights. The

---

[371] *Re T (Adopted Children: Contact)* [1995] 2 FLR 251.
[372] *Re T (Adopted Children: Contact)* [1995] 2 FLR 251.
[373] Mason (2003: 57).
[374] Bridge and Swindells (2003: 233) discuss whether the welfare checklist in the CA 1989 or the ACA 2002 would be used.
[375] Eekelaar (2003a).
[376] [1995] 2 FLR 792.
[377] Contrast *Re S (Contact: Application by Sibling)* [1998] 2 FLR 897.
[378] [2002] 1 FLR 196 HL.

decision was reached under the Adoption Act 1976 under which the child's welfare was the first, but not paramount, consideration in any decision. It was held that as the mother did not want to have anything to do with the child an adoption could not be said to interfere improperly with the human rights of the mother or child.[379]

K. Adoption by parent and step-parent

Nearly a third of all adoptions involved step-parent adoptions in 2001.[380] Typical of such adoptions are where a mother remarries. Her new husband wishes to have a formal recognition of his status. He could enter into an agreement with his wife in relation to the child which would grant him parental responsibility.[381] However, he might still want the formal label of father and/or he may be concerned that the birth father may seek to interfere with the way that the stepfamily will care for the child. He may therefore consider adoption.[382] He might have two options:

1. The mother and her new husband adopt the mother's child. So rather strangely the mother adopts her own child. The purpose of doing this is that the birth father will lose entirely his parental status. The stepfather and birth mother will become the legal parents of the child. However, the attraction to some of adoption is that it means the stepfamily need no longer fear that the birth family will interfere with the way they raise the child.
2. The Adoption and Children Act 2002 enables the partner of a parent to adopt a child, without that affecting the parental status of the birth parents.[383] Thus a stepfather can adopt the child. He will become the father, but the mother will remain as the mother. Notably the procedure can be used not only by the spouse of a parent, but any partner (including a same-sex parent).

If there is an application for adoption involving a step-parent the application will be governed by the principles already outlined. It must be shown that the adoption will promote the welfare of the child and the necessary parental consents are obtained or dispensed with. It should be emphasised that the court must be persuaded that it is better to make an adoption order than to make no order at all.[384]

Many take the view that step-parent adoptions should not be permitted. In particular, while it is understandable why the stepfather might want some kind of recognition of his position in the child's life, that should not mean that the birth father and his side of the family lose their status in respect of the child.

---

[379] See Bainham (2002b) and Harris-Short (2002) for criticism of this decision.
[380] Eekelaar (2003a).
[381] CA 1989, s 4A.
[382] Note the comments of Thorpe LJ in *Re PJ (Adoption: Practice on Appeal)* [1998] 2 FLR 252, at p. 260, about the complex motives and emotions that surround a step-parent adoption.
[383] ACA 2002, s 52(2).
[384] ACA 2002, s 1(6). For an argument which is more positive towards kinship adoption see Talbot and Williams (2003).

L. Adoption by relatives

Relatives of the child may wish to adopt the child. This may be under an arrangement with the mother or through discussions with the local authority. A teenager
may ask her mother to raise her child for her. It may also be that the local authority
asks a relative to consider being an adopter, although this is rare.[385] There has been
a fair amount of criticism of adoption by relatives because it can distort the child's
family relationships (e.g. the child's birth grandmother becomes her mother and her
birth mother becomes her adopted sister). It is also thought to be unnecessary. A
residence order or special guardianship provides sufficient protection for the relative's position.[386] The Adoption and Children Act 2002 permits relatives to apply
to adopt, but only if they have cared for the child for at least three of the five previous years, or obtain the leave of the court to make the application.[387] The relative
must then satisfy the court that adoption is a better option than a residence order
or special guardianship. These hurdles may mean that very few adoptions by relatives occur.

M. Post-adoption support

Lowe has suggested that adoption has changed from the gift/donation model to a
contract/services model.[388] He points out that at one time a child being adopted was
regarded as a gift to be handed over by an adoption agency to an infertile couple.
Once the child was received by the couple, the local authority's role was at an end
and the adopter would be treated in the same way as a birth parent. Nowadays
adoption is seen as one of the ways of arranging the care of a child taken into care.
As the age of adopted children has increased and as a result children being adopted
may present a range of emotional and physical problems, it has become necessary
to rethink the assumption that the local authority carries no responsibility for
adopted children. This has led to increased awareness of the importance of providing support to children who have been adopted.[389] The task of adopting a child who
has been severely abused, or suffers from complex physical disability may be
beyond all but the most gifted of parents without the assistance, advice and support
of a local authority. The offering of services may help to decrease the rate of adoption breakdown and may encourage prospective adopters to adopt 'difficult' children.[390]

The Adoption and Children Act 2002 now requires adoption agencies to provide
for a wide range of adoption support services.[391] However, this does not create a
strong right to such services. Although adopted parents and children have the right

---

[385] Murch, Lowe, Borkowski et al. (1993: 11).
[386] This was the view taken by the Performance and Innovation Unit (2000a: para 5.8).
[387] ACA 2002, s 42(5), (6).
[388] Lowe (1997a).
[389] Lowe, Murch, Borkowski et al. (1999).
[390] Douglas and Philpot (2003: 109) emphasise that birth parents may also require services from the
local authority.
[391] ACA 2002, s 4(7); Adoption Support Services (Local Authorities) (England) Regulations 2003;
Department of Health (2003b).

to request that they be assessed for the provision of adoption support, the Act does not require the local authority to meet the need.[392] This would mean that the local authority may assess an adopted child to be in need of services, but then decide that it is unable to afford to provide them.[393] Special guardians (who will be discussed shortly) do not even have the right to be assessed, although a local authority may, if it wishes, provide services to them.[394]

N. Revocation of an adoption order

The adoption order continues to have effect unless another adoption order is made. In particular, the adoption order does not come to an end when the child reaches age 18. As mentioned above one of the main advantages of adoption is the security it creates. If adoption could be brought to an end it would undermine that benefit.[395] There are just three circumstances in which an adoption order can be overturned:[396]

1. If the child is adopted by his or her father, but his or her mother then marries the father. In such a case the father could apply under s 55 of the Adoption and Children Act 2002 for the adoption to be revoked and the child would then in law be the child of his or her parents. This provision is very rarely invoked.
2. It is possible to appeal against the making of the adoption order,[397] although it is necessary to show a flaw in the making of the order itself and exceptional circumstances need to be shown. The case law provides two examples of exceptional circumstances:

   (a) Where the consent of the parent to the adoption was given on the basis of a fundamental mistake. In *Re M (A Minor) (Adoption)*[398] a father agreed to the adoption of his children by his former wife and her new husband. Unknown to him, his ex-wife was terminally ill and she died shortly afterwards. The court allowed the appeal in what they regarded as a 'very exceptional case' on the basis that ignorance of the wife's condition negated his consent, which was based on a fundamental mistake.
   (b) Where the adoption procedures involved a fundamental defect in natural justice. In *Re K (Adoption and Wardship)*[399] an English foster carer had adopted a Muslim baby, who had been found under a pile of bodies in the former Yugoslavia. Unfortunately, the adoption process had been deeply flawed. No guardian ad litem had been appointed; the formal procedures at the Bosnian end had not been followed; ineffective notice had been given to the Home Office; and inadequate evidence provided of the death of the natural parents. The adoption order was set aside due to the lack

---

[392] ACA 2002, s 4.
[393] See, by analogy, *R (On the Application of A) v Lambeth* [2003] 3 FCR 419 HL.
[394] CA 1989, s 14F(1), (2).
[395] *Re B (Adoption: Setting Aside)* [1995] 1 FLR 1 at p. 7.
[396] *Re B (Adoption: Jurisdiction to Set Aside)* [1995] 2 FLR 1, [1994] 2 FLR 1297.
[397] If necessary, leave can be given to appeal out of time.
[398] [1991] 1 FLR 458, [1990] FCR 993.
[399] [1997] 2 FLR 221; [1997] 2 FLR 230 CA.

of protection for the birth family and the breach of natural justice caused by the faulty procedure. At the rehearing[400] for the adoption order it was decided that the child should be made a ward of court but that he remain with the foster carers who were required to bring him up with instruction in the Bosnian language and Muslim religion. Every three months they were required to report back to the Bosnian family.

3. If the child is adopted by a new set of parents this will end (but not revoke) the original adoption.

In the absence of one of these three grounds an adoption order cannot be set aside, however sympathetic the court may be to the application.[401] If the birth family are seeking to challenge an adoption order and are not able to overturn the adoption order, they could still apply for a residence order in respect of the child. It would be unlikely that such an application would succeed unless the adoption had completely broken down.[402]

O. The breakdown of adoption

Surprisingly there are no official statistics on the rate of breakdown of adoptions.[403] One study found that 9 per cent of the placements studied broke down before an adoption order was made and 8 per cent broke down after the order was made.[404] The impact of a failed adoption on the child and adoptive parents can only be imagined. Indeed, it is possible that failed adoptions will cause the child more harm than would have been suffered by the child if the adoption had not been attempted. It is therefore important that the government's attempts to increase the numbers of adoptions do not lead to an increase in the rate of adoption breakdown.

P. Access to birth and adoption register

One study estimated that a third of adopted people seek to obtain access to their birth records.[405] Of course, others may make less formal attempts to find the background to their births. One study found that 75 per cent in their sample sought their birth mother and 38 per cent their father.[406] An adopted person seeking to discover information about his or her birth family could seek access to the following:

1. *Birth certificates.* The Registrar-General is required under s 79 of the Adoption and Children Act 2002 to keep records to enable adopted people to trace their original birth registration. This would enable a person to discover the details of their birth, including the name of their mother. There is no absolute right to obtain a copy of the birth certificate. This is demonstrated by *R* v

---

[400] [1997] 2 FLR 230.
[401] *Re B (Adoption: Jurisdiction to Set Aside)* [1995] 2 FLR 1, [1994] 2 FLR 1297.
[402] *Re O (A Minor) (Wardship: Adopted Child)* [1978] Fam 196 CA.
[403] Department of Health (2002b).
[404] R. Parker (1999: 10).
[405] Rushbrooke (2001).
[406] Howe and Feast (2000).

Registrar-General, ex p Smith,[407] where the Court of Appeal held that the Registrar-General was entitled to restrict the access of Smith to his birth records. Smith was in prison in Broadmoor, having killed his cell-mate in the belief that he was killing his mother. It was held that he might use the knowledge of his birth mother to harm her and the court held that it was therefore proper for the registrar to deny him access.

2. *Information from adoption agencies.* When the Adoption and Children Bill was first introduced it sought to restrict access of adopted children to information about their birth. This was justified on the basis of data protection concerns and a need to protect the human rights of the birth parents.[408] However, these proposals were highly controversial and it was felt by many groups involved that they paid insufficient attention to the rights of adopted people to know their genetic identity. As a result the government amended the Bill and the Act requires adoption agencies to provide details which would enable an adopted person to obtain their birth certificate. They will also be able to obtain information from the court which made the adoption order.[409] If the agency does not wish to disclose the information it can obtain a court order permitting non-disclosure.[410] If it is 'protected information', in that it concerns private information about other people, then the agency can fail to disclose it although they should also take reasonable steps to ascertain the views of the people involved.

3. *The Adoption Contact Register.*[411] If birth families wish to contact adopted children then they can use the Adoption Contact Register. This is provided by the National Organisation for Counselling Adoptees and Parents (NORCAP). This facilitates contact between adopters and birth families. At 30 June 2001 just under 20,000 adoptees and 8,500 relatives had placed names on the register; 539 pairs of records were linked.[412]

Now a parent who has given up his or her child for adoption can seek an intermediary to find out further information about the adopted person. The individual must use an agency. This will normally be an adoption agency. The intermediary will contact the Registrar-General and seek to obtain the name of the agency who arranged the adoption. The intermediary will then seek to contact that agency, the court or local authority in an attempt to find out more information. The intermediary will only be able to disclose information to the birth family if they have the informed consent of the adopted adult.[413]

These measures go some way towards recognising a person's rights to know about their genetic origins,[414] which has been held to be an important aspect of a person's right to private life, protected by article 8 of the European Convention on Human

---

[407] [1991] FLR 255, [1991] FCR 403 CA.
[408] Adoption and Children Bill 2002, clauses 53–60.
[409] ACA 2002, s 60(4).
[410] ACA 2002, s 60(3).
[411] Department of Health (2003f).
[412] Eekelaar (2003a: 255).
[413] ACA 2002, ss 64(4), 65(1), 98(2) and (3).
[414] Howe and Feast (2000).

Rights.[415] It should be noted that in fact adopted children who do seek information about their birth parents are particularly interested in finding out about their mothers.[416] It is also important to appreciate that even where contact is made this does not usually lead to an ongoing relationship.[417]

Q. Intercountry adoption

The limits on the number of children available for adoption has caused some people to turn to adoption of babies from overseas. This practice is governed by the Adoption (Intercountry Aspects) Act 1999 and the Adoption and Children Act 2002, which give effect to the Hague Conference on Private International Law's Convention on Intercountry Adoption. This topic is not covered in detail in this book.[418]

R. Special guardianship

As already indicated one of the major concerns over the nature of adoption in England and Wales is the way that it terminates the parental status of the birth parents. Those troubled by this have sought to replace adoption with an institution which will provide security and an appropriate status for the new carer of the child, without ending completely the status of the birth parents. In the Adoption and Children Act 2002 the status of special guardian was introduced. This is not a replacement for adoption, but is an alternative to it. The White Paper mentions the kind of cases where special guardianship may be appropriate:

> Some older children do not wish to be legally separated from their birth families. Adoption may not be best for some children being cared for on a permanent basis by members of their wider birth family. Some minority ethnic communities have religious and cultural difficulties with adoption as it is set out in law. Unaccompanied asylum seeking children may also need secure, permanent homes, but have strong attachments to their families abroad.[419]

Special guardianship does not terminate the parental status of the birth parents and special guardians are not treated as the parents of the child.[420] However, they are given many of the rights of a parent. They are able to make almost every decision about a child's upbringing. They can even change the child's name, with the consent of those with parental responsibility.[421] The status of special guardianship

---

[415] *MG* v *UK* [2002] 3 FCR 289. See further O'Donnovan (1988); Van Bueren (1995).

[416] Sachdev (1992) found that only 20 per cent of adopted children said they ever thought about their birth father.

[417] Howe and Feast (2000) report a study that only 51 per cent of adopted children who had found their birth mother had continued the contact. However, 97 per cent of adopted people who had located their birth parents had no regrets about doing so.

[418] An excellent summary of the law on intercountry adoption can be found in Bridge and Swindells (2003: ch. 14).

[419] Department of Health (2000e: para 5.9).

[420] Even where a special guardian has been appointed the birth parents will retain their rights in respect of adoption.

[421] CA 1989, s 14C(3).

remains until revoked by an order of the court. A special guardianship can be varied or discharged on the application of the following:[422]

1. The special guardian.
2. The child's birth parents or guardian, with the leave of the court.
3. The child with the leave of the court.
4. Any individual who presently has the benefit of a residence order.
5. Any individual who had parental responsibility immediately before the making of the special guardianship order, with the leave of the court.
6. The local authority, but only where a care order is made in respect of the child.
7. The court on its own motion in any case where the welfare of the child arises.

Any application to revoke special guardianship must obtain the leave of the court.[423] Unless the application is by the local authority, the child or the special guardian him- or herself it needs to be shown that there has been a significant change in the circumstances from when the special guardianship order was made. This makes the special guardianship a little more secure than a residence order.[424]

Special guardianship is likely to be appropriate where there are good reasons why the child should retain formal links with the birth family. For example in *Re M (Adoption or Residence Order)*[425] the child was strongly of the opinion that she did not want her links with her mother and siblings to be destroyed, even though she wished to live with the applicants in a permanent relationship. This is the kind of case where special guardianship will now be considered. It may also be appropriate for some children from ethnic minorities. For example, the concept of adoption also sits unhappily with Islamic law which does not recognise the notion of the extinguishment of parental rights.[426] Special guardianship may therefore be more acceptable to some Muslim parents than adoption.

The success of special guardianship will depend on the extent to which both children and would-be adopters are satisfied that it will provide them with the sense of security and belonging together as a family which adoption has been said traditionally to provide. One difficulty, an odd, but important one, is terminology. Most people are very familiar with the concept of adoption and a child can introduce her adoptive parents (and vice versa) without explanation. A special guardianship order might require more explanation until it becomes a familiar term. An earlier attempt to introduce a similar concept was labelled 'custodianship'. This proved deeply unpopular, perhaps in part because, for example, of the difficulties a child might face in introducing her carer to her friends: 'Meet my custodian.'[427]

Anyone (including the child himself or herself![428]) can apply to be a special guardian of a child with the leave of the court.[429] Section 14A of the Children Act 1989 also provides a list of those who can apply without leave. This includes those

---

[422] CA 1989, s 14D.
[423] One exception is where the child is applying (CA 1989, s 14D(5)).
[424] Department of Health (2002e: 50).
[425] [1998] 1 FLR 570.
[426] Pearl and Menski (1998: 410).
[427] Custodianship was introduced by the Children Act 1975.
[428] The court must be satisfied that the child has sufficient understanding to make the application (CA 1989, s 10(8)).
[429] CA 1989, s 14A(3)(b).

who have a residence order in respect of a child, those with whom a child has lived for three of the last five years, and those who have the consent of all those with parental responsibility. It is possible for a cohabiting couple to apply to be special guardians. They do not need to be married or of opposite sex, but they must be over 18.[430] When considering an application for a special guardianship the court will, *inter alia*, take into account the applicant's connection with the child and (if the child is being looked after by a local authority) the local authority's plans for the child's future.[431]

12. CONCLUSION

The history of state care for children in England and Wales is littered with findings of abuse and mistreatment of these vulnerable children. It is therefore not surprising that there is now a move away from caring for children in children's homes and towards the use of adoption or fostering. The law on children in care involves a delicate balance between giving the local authority a discretion to care for a child as it thinks best and enabling parents to play an effective role in their children's lives, even though they have been taken into care. The Human Rights Act 1998 emphasises the rights of parents over children in care. Any intervention in family life must now be proportionate with the needs of the children. This might mean that the courts may be required to play a greater role in supervising the position of children in care than they have done to date. This chapter has also considered adoption, the most serious intervention by the state in family life. The Adoption and Children Act 2002 aims to increase adoption rates and produce a more co-ordinated approach to adoption. Time will tell whether adoption will be used at an increasing rate, or whether it will become an outdated institution.

---

[430] CA 1989, s 14A(1). Birth parents cannot apply to be special guardians (CA 1989, s 14A(2)).
[431] CA 1989, s 14A(12).

12

FAMILIES AND OLDER PEOPLE

1. INTRODUCTION

There is no legislative definition of 'older people'. It is most common to draw a definition in terms of the retirement age, or the age at which state pension becomes payable.[1] It is, in a way, odd to talk about older people as if they constituted a homogeneous group.[2] As the catchphrase states: 'you are only as old as you feel'.[3] Certainly there are stereotypes attached to old age – frailty and failing mental capacities – but many older people are highly active in their communities. As the government has acknowledged:

> we must not make the mistake of seeing older people as all the same. They are as varied, if not more varied, than any other age group in our society. Every day an older person does something – even going into space at age 77! – which shows that age is an increasingly unreliable sign of someone's needs and ambitions.[4]

Some may argue that it makes more sense to distinguish people with or without mental capacity or employment, rather than by using the category of age. Nevertheless, there are a number of particular issues that affect older people and this is recognised by the fact that the government has set up a Ministerial Group for Older People.[5]

In the family law context there are increasingly important questions about the extent to which families are and should be responsible for their older relatives. This chapter will consider whether adult children should be liable to support their impoverished parents in their old age and how to balance the interests of the old and young within society. It will also examine the complexities that surround the abuse of older people. The chapter will then outline what happens when older people are no longer able to look after themselves. Finally, the chapter will discuss what happens to the property of older people on their death. Before considering these issues it is necessary to quote some statistics which reveal something of the position of older people within our society.

---

[1] Age Concern (1984).
[2] Hence this chapter will use the phrase 'older people' rather than 'elderly people'.
[3] For a discussion of the biological process of ageing see Grimley Evans (2003).
[4] Department of Health (2000d).
[5] Department of Health (2000d).

2. STATISTICS ON OLDER PEOPLE

A. Number of older people

There has been much talk of a 'generational time bomb'. It has been claimed that there is an increasing number of older people and that a growing proportion of the population is older.[6] Certainly the statistics support this, although whether it is a 'bomb' and therefore something which should be a cause for concern is another issue. In 1901 there were 2.4 million men and women over 60; by 1981 there were 10 million; and it is predicted that by 2025 there will be 14.8 million.[7] The 2001 census found that there were 336,000 people aged 90 or over.[8] The percentage of people over 65 in Great Britain rose from 10.9 per cent in 1951 to 20 per cent in 1996[9] and by 2027 it is estimated that it will be 19.2 per cent.[10] The 2001 census stated that 21 per cent of the population was over 60.[11] Indeed, there are more people in the UK over 60 than there are under 16. The number of older people aged over 80 is predicted to increase by 50 per cent between 1995 and 2025.[12] In 2001, 1.9 per cent of the population was over 80.[13] By 2031 it has been estimated that 41 per cent of the population will be over 50, 23 per cent over retirement age and 6 per cent over 80.[14] These figures indicate that the ratio of employed people per number of elderly dependants is falling.[15] This is caused by both the decrease in the birth rate and the increase in life expectancy.

B. Older people and their families

It has been estimated that almost a third of all adults in the UK are grandparents.[16] Grandparents are now the single most important source of pre-school child-care after parents.[17] Even if they are not taking part in child-care, it appears that most older people are able to keep in contact with family or friends. The 1994 General Household Survey found that over three-quarters of older people aged 65 or over saw relatives or friends at least once a week.[18] Only 3 per cent of older people said they did not see relatives or friends at all. However, there is also evidence that older people, especially men, who divorce early on in life have weaker links with their families in old age.[19] Society has yet to see the full consequences of divorce.

---

[6] Ethnic minorities are under-represented with only 2 per cent of the over 60s being from black and ethnic communities. Ethnic minorities make up 7 per cent of the total population: Fredman (2003: 25).
[7] Tinker (1997: 11).
[8] Sixty-four per cent of those over 75 are women: Fredman (2003: 24).
[9] S. Gibson (2000: 41).
[10] Kiernan and Wicks (1990).
[11] Office for National Statistics (2001).
[12] Department of Health (2000b: 3).
[13] Office of National Statistics (2001).
[14] Department of Health (2000d).
[15] Hills (1997).
[16] Walsh (1998).
[17] Eden (2000).
[18] Office of Population and Census Surveys (1996).
[19] Solomou, Richards, Huppert et al. (1998).

The sharing of accommodation by adult children and their parents is not common, with only 2 per cent of men and 7 per cent of women over 65 living with their son or daughter.[20] Increasing percentages of older people are living alone.[21] This increase (again partly caused by increased divorce rates) has important social consequences because older people who live alone are much more likely to enter institutional care than those who live with a spouse.[22] In fact there is evidence that older people much prefer to live in their own homes than in institutional care.[23] Ninety-five per cent of those aged 65 or over live in private households and only 5 per cent live in communal establishments.[24] However, that 5 per cent constitutes 500,000 older people living in some form of institutional setting. Although it is rare for adult children to live with their infirm parents, it is common for them to provide day-to-day care for their parents. Most care is carried out by women aged 45–64.[25] It has been estimated that 2 million of the 5.7 million carers in the UK are over 60.[26]

C. Income

There is a wide disparity in the wealth of older people. The median income of pensioners is two-thirds that of non-pensioners.[27] About 60 per cent of pensioners are dependent on benefits.[28] Fifty per cent of all pensioners live either in or on the margins of poverty, and one-third of pensioners are at income support level.[29] Income support is thought to be the minimum necessary to live on in our society. In 10 per cent of households where one or both members are over 60 the home requires essential modernisation.[30] One particular difficulty (and cause of poverty) is that a high percentage of pensioners do not claim the benefits to which they are entitled. The failure to claim may result from a lack of knowledge, or a feeling that claiming benefits is similar to 'begging'. Poverty levels are particularly high among older women.[31] The poverty of pensioners leads us to ask whether wealthy adult children should be expected to support their impoverished older parents.

D. Age discrimination

Much of the recent legal discussion concerning older people has centred on the concept of age discrimination.[32] A sign of the growing recognition of age discrimi-

---

[20] Office of Population and Census Surveys (1996).
[21] Phillipson, Bernard, Phillips and Ogg (1999).
[22] Grundy (1992).
[23] D. Gibson (1998).
[24] Office of Population and Census Surveys (1993).
[25] Moynagh and Worsley (2000).
[26] Help the Aged (2002).
[27] M. Richards (1996a).
[28] Phillipson (1998).
[29] Fox Harding (1996: 43). In Britain, 1.63 million people aged 60 and over received income support in August 2000: Fredman (2003: 28).
[30] Fredman (2003: 28).
[31] Ginn and Price (2002).
[32] For an excellent discussion of age discrimination see Fredman (2003).

nation is that the European Union Framework Directive[33] requires legislation to outlaw discrimination on the grounds of age in employment matters. However, discrimination in employment is only part of the picture.[34] As Fredman has argued, unless discrimination against older people in health, housing and social security is combated, there will not be equality in the employment market.[35] It is easy to find evidence that older workers find it difficult to find or remain in employment. One-third of those aged between 50 and the state pension retirement age did not participate in paid employment.[36] Notably, although younger women are 50 per cent more likely to be employed than 20 years ago, the proportion of women in employment when approaching retirement has not increased. There is also evidence that older women of Indian, Pakistani or Bangladeshi origin are particular victims of discrimination.[37]

3. DO CHILDREN HAVE AN OBLIGATION TO SUPPORT THEIR PARENTS?

Some legal systems require adult children to support their aged parents.[38] In Britain such a legal obligation has not generally been accepted.[39] There is no equivalent of the Child Support Act which requires an adult child to support a parent in old age. Further, the social security system does not treat an adult child as a 'liable relative' of a parent, meaning that an adult child's resources are not taken into account when considering a parent's claim for income support. However, with the debate raging over how care for older people is to be financed, this question must be reconsidered. There is widespread feeling that there is at least a moral obligation on adult children to provide some support for their infirm parents; however, it is hard to find a convincing basis for this sense of obligation. There are a number of ways that one could establish an obligation on adult children to support parents:

1. *Reciprocated duty.* It could be argued that an obligation to support parents is a reflection of the obligation on parents to support young children. In other words, because parents provided for children in their vulnerability, children should support parents when parents become infirm. Despite the initial attraction of such an argument, there are difficulties with it. First, although parents can be said to have caused the child to be born in his or her vulnerable state, the adult child cannot be said to have caused the vulnerable state of his or her parents. A similar point is that although parents can be said to have chosen to have the child and so impliedly undertaken the obligation to care for the child, the same could not be said of children.[40] In the light of these objections it is clear

---

[33] Council Directive 2000/78/EC.
[34] See also Hepple (2003).
[35] Fredman (2003: 23).
[36] Performance and Innovation Unit (2000b).
[37] Fredman (2003: 25).
[38] E.g. J. Blair (1996).
[39] See Oldham (2001) for an excellent discussion of the English and French approaches to this issue.
[40] Daniels (1988).

that there is not necessarily a straightforward link between the duty of parents to care for children and an adult child's obligation to care for parents.

2. *Relational support*. It could be argued that an obligation to support parents flows from the relationship of love that exists between parents and children. The difficulty is that clearly not all parents and children are in loving relationships. However, even where children and parents do not love each other, adult children may feel a sense of obligation to support their parents. This suggests that the obligation to support comes not so much from a relationship of mutual love, but from some other source. A further difficulty with the relational argument is that people do not feel an obligation to support all those with whom they are in a loving relationship. Most people would not feel obliged to support a good friend in his or her old age, even though they may choose to do so. It has been suggested that what distinguishes family relationships from friendships is the notion of intimacy. The argument here is that family life involves bonds of sharing and intimacy, unlike that in any other relationship.[41] Parents and children reveal to each other aspects of their lives that they show to no other person. However, whether this intimacy is unique to families may be questioned. Some people may feel that they are more open to their friends than to their families. All these points suggest that although a loving relationship might form the basis of an obligation to support parents, there are other aspects that together complete a more complex picture of obligation.

3. *Implied contract*. It could be argued that there is an implied contract between parents and children that they will support each other. An obvious objection is that children are unable to consent to such a contract at birth. However, the law could assume that the child would have agreed to the contract at birth had he or she been competent to do so. This approach might carry some weight, especially if children were free to rescind the contract once they had reached sufficient maturity to decide whether to uphold it. Another objection to the contract approach is that to see the relationship between family members in terms of contract would not seem in accordance with the realities of family life. A family which regarded its relationships as governed by the terms of a formal contract would be a rather unusual family.

4. *Dependency*. Here the argument is that the obligation to support flows from the vulnerability of the parent. There is no doubt that some older people need care and financial help from someone. Our society would not accept that older people could be abandoned without any support. It is, then, a matter for society to decide who should provide that support. It could be argued that children are in the best position to give that care and therefore society is entitled to require adult children to supply it. This is a similar argument to the one used by Eekelaar to explain why parents are under a duty to care for their children.[42] Although children may be uniquely placed to provide emotional comfort for their older parents, whether the same is true for financial support is a different issue. This argument at its strongest could lead us to conclude that society

---

[41] English (1979).
[42] Eekelaar (1991b).

would be entitled, if it wished, to require some kind of support of older parents by adult children. However, although there is widespread acceptance that the law is right to require parents to fulfil their parental duties, the idea that children must support their parents is much more controversial.

A. Moral obligations or legal obligations?

English[43] has argued that although there may be moral obligations to support older relatives, these should not give rise to legal obligations. She argues that the law does not generally enforce obligations that arise out of love or friendship. Family members do not add up all they have given and all they have received from a relative in order to work out whether they should help them. Parents do not change nappies out of a sense of legal obligation, but as part of sacrificial love. These are strong arguments, but they could be used equally well in relation to adults and young children. We do place legal obligations on parents to care for young children, even though their relationship is one based on love. The law sets out the minimum required of parents, while accepting that it is just part of what is morally required of them. However, as we shall see, there is a fine line between legal obligations which compel people to provide care they may not wish to give, and the law encouraging and enabling people to give care and support voluntarily. So before deciding what the law's response should be, it is necessary to consider what obligations family members actually feel towards older people.

B. What obligations do people actually feel?

Despite the fact that it is difficult to pin down precisely *why* adult children owe a moral obligation to their parents, there is a widespread feeling that they do. However, such feelings of obligation are complex. Finch,[44] in her wide-ranging study of family obligations, distinguishes two kinds of moral obligation: a normative guideline; and a negotiated commitment. In basic terms, the normative guideline is an accepted standard that applies across the board to certain relationships: for example, that parents should care for their young children. The negotiated commitment is an agreement reached between two people which governs their behaviour: for example, the relationship between an elderly aunt and her nephew may develop over time to the stage where the nephew feels obliged to support his aunt even though, generally, nephews are not expected to support aunts. Finch found that in deciding whether a person felt under an obligation to provide assistance to another, there were guidelines rather than strict rules in operation. She[45] suggests that people tend to ask two key questions: Who is this person? (e.g. are they a relative?); and How well do I get on with this person? She found that parent–child links were the strongest family ties. In parent–child relationships the second question (How well do I get on with this person?) is less significant than the needs of the

---

[43] English (1979).
[44] Finch (1994).
[45] Finch (1989).

older person. So an adult child may feel little responsibility for a spry elderly parent, even if their relationship is close; whereas an adult child might feel a burden of responsibility for an infirm parent, even if their relationship is not close. That said, Finch notes that most people do not clearly reason out why they act in the way they do.

A further important aspect in the obligations that family members feel they owe to each other is gender. Ungerson[46] found that women have a clearer sense of obligation to family members than men. As noted earlier, it is women who perform the majority of practical care for older relatives.

C. Integrating family and state care

If, then, there is a sense of moral obligation towards older parents, how should the law respond? There has been some debate over whether the provision of state aid for older people has weakened the feeling of responsibility of adult children to support their parents. Finch thinks not, arguing: 'If anything it has been the state's assuming some responsibility for individuals – such as the granting of old age pensions – which has freed people to develop closer and more supportive relationships with their kin.'[47] Indeed, the existence of state services for older people has not meant that relatives do not care for each other. One survey found that 17 per cent of women and 13 per cent of men care for older relatives.[48] A high level of acceptance that children should care for their older parents has also been found. Although Finch argues that the sense of family obligation has not lessened, she accepts that the circumstances of modern life (e.g. the fact that more women are working) mean that the way people carry out their obligations has changed.[49] Such changes may lead to the result that social services will be required to perform more day-to-day services for older people.

There is increasing acceptance that it is necessary to integrate state support for older people with the support of relatives. Tinker suggests the aim should be:

> the interleaving of informal, usually family, care with statutory services that is so necessary but so difficult to achieve. What does seem evident is that without good basic statutory services, such as community nursing and help in the home, informal carers will not be able to support older people without cost to their mental and physical health. It is no use paying lip service to support for informal carers if help from professionals is not forthcoming.[50]

Not only can the role of the state be regarded as a necessary support for carers, there is also some evidence that older people perceive direct financial support from their children embarrassing and, in a sense, a lessening of their autonomy.[51] There is evidence that older people find it difficult to be in relationships with their children where they are receiving rather than giving. Therefore, receiving money

---

[46] Ungerson (1987).
[47] Finch (1994: 243).
[48] Office of Population and Census Surveys (1993).
[49] Finch (1989: 242); Qureshi and Walker (1989).
[50] Tinker (1997: 250).
[51] Wenger (1984).

directly from the government in the form of pensions, rather than from their children, may be regarded by many as a more acceptable form of financial assistance.

D. Conclusion

A case can be made for imposing obligations on adult children. Starting with the vulnerability and needs of older people, and accepting that they should be met somehow, society *could* choose to require adult children to provide that care, as they are often best placed to provide it. Such an obligation appears to be reflected in the attitudes and practices of most adult children. However, there are good reasons why our society may prefer to support older people through taxation rather than require financial support from relatives. First, there is the evidence mentioned above that older people dislike feeling that they are a drain on their younger relatives. Enforcing financial support and practical care may therefore damage the family relationships which can be so important in old age. Secondly, such a system could work against the interests of those older people who have no children. Thirdly, as we shall see shortly, there is clear evidence of the strain often incurred by those caring for vulnerable older relatives, and such strain may be exacerbated with an explicit legal obligation. So, it is submitted, a better option is for the state to seek to enable and encourage caring among family members, rather than compel it. As we shall now see, there is some attempt to do this in the present benefits system.

4. FINANCIAL SUPPORT FOR OLDER PEOPLE AND THEIR CARERS

The state provides a wide selection of benefits to the retired.[52] Most obviously there is the basic state pension, supplemented by the state earnings-related pension if paid into by the claimant during his or her employment. There is also a raft of other benefits including housing benefit, disability living allowance, incapacity benefit, and income benefit, as well as payments from the Social Fund, which are available to meet particular needs of the retired person. However, as mentioned earlier, these benefits are often not claimed by retired people. In addition to the state provision, the government in recent years has encouraged people to take out private pensions if their employers have not provided occupational pensions. Oldham, considering the public provision for older people, states: 'Public provision is in a mess. Levels of under-funding are such that the welfare system is no longer straining – it is actually failing – to achieve its goals.'[53]

Of particular interest is the state's support of those who care for older people and disabled adults. There is ample evidence that carers suffer great strain, both emotional[54] and financial.[55] The government has in recent years recognised the pressures that can be caused through caring for dependent relatives and has, following its

---

[52] For the details see Child Poverty Action Group (2000).
[53] Oldham (2001: 168).
[54] Healy and Yarrow (1997).
[55] Wright (1998).

report, *Caring About Carers*,[56] set up a national strategy for carers. For example, the local authority has the power to make special grants to enable carers to have breaks. Further, there are special benefits available for those who spend significant time caring for dependent relatives, for example invalid care allowance.[57] By offering these funds the state is recognising the benefits that carers provide not only to their dependants, but also to the state through saving the state the cost of providing the care. The details of these benefits are beyond the scope of this book, but three important points on a theoretical level can be made:

1. Parents who do not seek employment, and instead care for children, receive no special benefits in respect of their care.[58] Further, the government has developed the New Deal, through which the benefits system and other forms of assistance are designed to encourage lone parents with children to find employment.[59] So here the voluntary care by mothers (and especially lone mothers) of young children is not positively valued and encouraged by the state.[60] By contrast, the care of older people is supported and encouraged through the benefits system, although many argue that the support given to such carers is inadequate.[61] It may be that the government feels that carers of older people need financial incentives to provide care, which the parents of children do not need.

2. There are grave concerns that carers are inadequately valued within society. Gibson[62] suggests that social provision for frail and older people is predicated on the expectation that women provide the vast majority of the care at no fiscal cost to the state, and that the care the state does provide is subsidised by underpaid female care assistants. It is estimated that carers of dependent relatives (including disabled and elderly relatives) save the state some £34 billion a year.[63] However, there is a dark side to care of older people at home. The majority of carers described themselves as 'extremely tired' and some were depressed.[64] Both the older people and carers were terrified about the possibility of having to move the older person into a nursing home. It should not be assumed that, once the older person is in residential care, their carers are then free from strain.[65]

3. What is the state's obligation towards an older person who is wealthy enough to pay for support him- or herself? To what extent can the National Health Service and social services be expected to provide free care for an older person? There are large sums of money involved, with £10.5 billion being spent on long-term care in the year 2000.[66] The government undertook a review of the funding of long-term care for older people following a Royal Commission report.[67] The

---

[56] Department of Health (2002g). See also Carers (Recognition and Services Act) 1995.
[57] For the details see West (2000).
[58] Apart from child benefit, which is available to all parents.
[59] See Douglas (2000a).
[60] P. Morgan (2000) argues that lone parenthood is encouraged by the benefits system.
[61] See the campaigns of the Carers National Association. See also Oldham (2001).
[62] C. Gibson (2000).
[63] BMA figure quoted in Korgaonkar and Tribe (1995).
[64] Healy and Yarrow (1997).
[65] Wright (1998).
[66] Department of Health (2000b: 1.2).
[67] Royal Commission (1999).

Royal Commission had argued that the state should be responsible for ensuring that older people receive the basic care necessary for their health, and therefore the state should provide the health and essential personal care without charge. They proposed distinguishing between care which involves touching the patient and care which does not: if it does, it should be provided free of charge. Other expenses, including housing[68] and non-essential personal care, would not be provided without charge under the NHS. The government rejected this proposal, essentially on the ground that it would be too expensive. Instead, the government decided to distinguish between health care, which would be provided free of charge, and personal care (e.g. washing patients), which would only be provided free of charge if the patient had low income and few assets.[69] This distinction is problematic. As had been pointed out by the Royal Commission, a person would soon fall ill without washing. Further, if the inability to wash is caused by an illness, is it not a health issue? The government has supported its approach by arguing that there needs to be a 'fairer and lasting balance between taxpayers and individuals' over the financing of long-term care. It is clear that the approach proposed by the government will create artificial distinctions (between personal care and medical care), although this would happen wherever the line is drawn between what care is paid for and what is not. However, the idea that our society could accept that an older person who refuses to pay should be left unwashed seems unjustifiable in the light of the duty that society owes to all citizens to ensure that people do not suffer inhuman or degrading treatment under the Human Rights Act 1998.

5. INTER-GENERATIONAL JUSTICE

In the introduction to its plans for older people and the NHS, the government states: 'older people are not and must never be seen as a burden on society'.[70] It is revealing that the government felt it necessary to reject such a perception. There are few who would overtly claim that older people are a drain on society's resources. However, in the United States in particular, there has been much discussion of inter-generational justice.[71] This is an ethos that there should be fairness between the older members of society and the younger. There are some who argue that older people receive a disproportionate level of society's resources. Although those over 65 constitute 20 per cent of the population in the UK, half of all hospital and community health service expenditure is spent on them.[72] Some talk almost in terms of a battle between the older and younger generations, with the older generation calling for even greater health and pension provision for which the younger generation would have to pay through taxes.[73] There is no easy way of avoiding the fact that a

---

[68] Unless they had to be housed in a hospital.
[69] Department of Health (2000b).
[70] Department of Health (2000b: 1.2).
[71] E.g. G. Smith II (1997).
[72] Fox Harding (1996: 39).
[73] An American organisation, Americans for Generational Equity (AGE), argues that older people receive an undue proportion of available public resources and that it would be unreasonable to divert more funds to them.

society which distributes resources on the basis of need may well prefer one age group over another.

Daniels[74] wishes to move away from the image of competition between generations. He proposes the 'the lifespan approach', in which he suggests that society needs to consider whether the state should provide people with special resources in their young, middle or old age. The fact that the state might provide an especially high level of services in old age is not preferring the old to the young because the young will receive the same benefits when older. Across each person's lifetime the state expenditure will be the same, Daniels argues. In other words, 'transfers between age groups are really transfers within lives'.[75] Although his approach has much to recommend it to society, medicine and technology are changing too quickly for his approach to provide a satisfactory solution. For example, when a person is born, social attitudes and medical advances may mean that society wishes to focus provision on children, but by the time the person is older, social advances may mean that there is no need to spend so much on the young and those funds might be better spent on older people.

A. Health care and older people: health care rationing

It is generally accepted that it is not possible for the National Health Service to provide all of the treatments and medical services that are requested. It is therefore necessary to restrict medical provision, in other words, to ration it. The issue for this chapter is whether age should be a factor in deciding who should receive a particular treatment.[76] The official view is that age rationing is not permitted. The *National Service Framework for Older People* states:

> Denying access to services on the basis of age alone is not acceptable. Decisions about treatment and health care should be made on the basis of health needs and ability to benefit rather than a patient's age ... That is not to say that everyone needs the same health needs, the overall health status of the individual, their assessed social care need and their own wishes and aspirations and those of their carers, should shape the package of health and social care.[77]

However, the reality may be different. Jeffreys found in her survey that, in practice, surgeons and GPs accept that age is a factor in rationing health care.[78]

It is not controversial that if, because of someone's age, a certain form of treatment is not effective then the treatment should not be offered. What is controversial is whether effective treatment should be denied simply because of age. Two examples which highlight the issues are as follows: a heart becomes available for transplantation and a hospital must choose between a 25-year-old and a 50-year-old. Apart from their age, there are no other significant differences between the

[74] Daniels (1988: 5).
[75] Daniels (1988: 63).
[76] For a very useful discussion see Robinson (2003). The Health Care Standards for Elderly Persons Bill 2000 sought to prohibit age discrimination in the provision of medical or dental services.
[77] Quoted in Fredman (2003: 41). See also Health Advisory Service (2000).
[78] Jeffreys (1995). See also Age Concern (2000) and E. Roberts (2000) finding rationing on the basis of age throughout the NHS. For a useful general discussion see Robinson (2003: 101).

patients. Should the 25-year-old be given the heart on the basis of youth? Or take a health service trust which, because of budgetary constraints, can fund either treatment of a disease which is most common among the elderly or a disease which more commonly afflicts the young, but not both. Should it fund the latter because of the age factor?

One approach to such questions which has gained much support has become known as Quality-Adjusted Life Years (QALYs). Alan Williams explains:

> The essence of a QALY is that it takes a year of healthy life expectancy to be worth 1, but regards a year of unhealthy life expectancy as worth less than 1. Its precise value is lower the worse the quality of life of the unhealthy person (which is what the quality adjusted bit is all about) ... The general idea is that a beneficial health care activity is one that generates a positive amount of QALYs, and that an efficient health care activity is one where the cost-per-QALYs is as low as it can be. A high priority health care activity is one where the cost-per-QALY is low, and a low priority activity is one where the cost-per-QALY is high.[79]

So the approach attempts to calculate the improvement in life quality and life expectancy caused by the treatment. A key difficulty with the approach is that it can be hard to assess 'quality': how can one compare the increase in quality of life resulting from infertility treatment with that resulting from a hip replacement? In Oregon, in the United States, a vote was taken among the population to assess which operations were regarded as most improving the quality of life. Cosmetic breast surgery scored very highly on QALYs, in fact higher than hip replacements. This might suggest that relying on public opinion to decide what constitutes 'quality of life' would produce unacceptable results.

There are three particular difficulties in the way the QALY approach would operate in relation to elderly patients. First, the approach does not have built-in protection for the dignity of the patient. It is arguable that some treatments could be necessary even though they would not score highly on a QALYs assessment (e.g. pain relief in the last few days of a person's life). The second difficulty with the approach is that it assumes that time is equally precious to all people. A treatment denied to a person on their deathbed that would give them six months more to live is not directly comparable to treatment given to a 30-year-old, not in any mortal danger, which would increase their life expectancy by six months. Thirdly, some claim that the QALY calculation constitutes age discrimination as it would always work against older people. The elderly would always be at a disadvantage in their ability to demonstrate as many improved years as a younger person.

Some who reject QALY argue that like patients should be treated alike and if a patient would benefit from a hip replacement, the age of the patient should not be a relevant consideration. Treatment should instead focus on need,[80] although it is arguable that it is not age discrimination to distinguish between individuals on the basis of life expectancy.

In a highly controversial book, Callahan[81] argues that we need to work towards a society which appreciates the concept of 'a tolerable death'. He explains:

[79] A. Williams (1985: 3).
[80] Banner (1995).
[81] Callahan (1997).

My definition of a 'tolerable death' is this: the individual event of death at that stage in a life span when (a) one's life possibilities have on the whole been accomplished; (b) one's moral obligations to those for whom one has had responsibility have been discharged; and (c) one's death will not seem to others an offence to sense or sensibility, or tempt others to despair and rage at the finitude of human existence.[82]

He contrasts intolerable death (such as the death of a child) with tolerable death (that of a person in old age). He suggests that once someone has reached their natural life span (which he asserts may be late 70s or early 80s) then medical resources should not be used to resist death, although treatment can be provided to mitigate pain and suffering. At the heart of his argument is a belief that medicine must have limited aims and cannot be involved in a relentless effort to save life. Therefore, resources should not be spent on those who have reached their natural life span and should instead be focused on preventing intolerable (early) death. The problem with Callahan's argument is that while his concept of a timely and tolerable death may be acceptable to many, it will not be to all. Some may spend their youth and middle age working hard and looking forward to retirement, seeing their 70s and 80s as the prime of their life. Is it justifiable for our society to rule out this version of 'the good life'? Callahan's argument, however, makes a powerful case. If our society wishes not to adopt his approach, it must be willing to pay the extra taxes or health insurance payments to ensure that it does not occur.

6. INCAPABLE OLDER PEOPLE

A. Do older people have rights?

Clearly, old people who have mental capacity have rights. However, more difficult is the position of older people who through illness or old age lack capacity.[83] Of all people aged 80 or more over one in five will suffer some kind of dementia.[84] When children's rights were discussed in Chapter 8, it was noted that there are some difficulties in claiming that children have rights because they cannot choose whether to exercise their rights. The approach propounded by Eekelaar was that children's basic, developmental and autonomy interests should be promoted so that once children were sufficiently mature they would be in a position to make life choices for themselves.[85] Such an approach is not possible for incapable older people. Older people will already have developed their own style of life and values. Therefore the law cannot take a neutral position and make decisions for older people that would enable them to make their own once competent; this is because having lost competence, most older people will not regain their competence.

Goodin and Gibson suggest that, for these reasons, it is inappropriate to hold that an incompetent older person has rights and instead the law should move towards a different approach: 'A much more apt description of our duties and their due is couched in terms of a broader but in many ways more demanding notion of "right

---

[82] Callahan (1997: 66).
[83] Goodin and Gibson (1997).
[84] C. Gibson (2000: 42).
[85] Eekelaar (1986).

conduct" towards dependent others.'[86] So rather than talking about the protection of interests, 'it is rather, that there are certain sorts of things that we must, and certain sorts of things that we must not, do to and for particular sorts of people'.[87] This view therefore says that we cannot talk about rights for the older incapable person, because they cannot choose what they want, and the law cannot ascertain the interests that should be protected. However, this does not mean that older people should be unprotected because others are obliged to treat them with 'right conduct'. There is much to be said for such an approach, although talk of 'right conduct' lacks the punch of 'rights' in political rhetoric.

B. When does an older person lose capacity in the eyes of the law?

The answer to this question is the same as that for any adult.[88] Under the Mental Health Act 1983, s 7, a person can be the subject of a guardianship application if:

(a) he is subject to mental disorder, being mental illness, severe mental impairment, psychopathic disorder or mental impairment and his mental disorder is of a nature or degree which warrants his reception into guardianship under this section; and

(b) it is necessary in the interests of the welfare of the patient or for the protection of other persons that the patient be so received.

Guardianship enables a patient to receive community care even though he or she is unable to consent.[89] The guardian can, for example, require the patient to live in a particular place and attend a specified place for treatment, education, training or occupation. If the older person's condition is treatable, they can be taken into compulsory hospital care.[90]

In the absence of a guardian being appointed the individual is treated as competent even if he or she is in a vulnerable condition. The court reports have many examples of older people being persuaded to hand over large sums of money by people taking advantage of them.[91] Although older people are protected to some extent by the civil law[92] and the criminal law of theft, many feel such protection is inadequate.[93]

C. Incapacity and financial matters[94]

If an older person is incapable of looking after his or her financial affairs, what legal procedures are in place for taking care of them?[95] There is a range of options available in such a case.

---

[86] Goodin and Gibson (1997: 186).
[87] Goodin and Gibson (1997: 186).
[88] Whalley (2001) provides a detailed medical discussion of the effect of ageing on the brain.
[89] A useful comparative examination of guardianship can be found in Doron (2002).
[90] Mental Health Act 1983, s 3. For proposed reform of this law see Home Office (2000f), discussed in Cavadino (2002).
[91] See e.g. *Goldsworthy* v *Brickell* [1987] 1 Ch 378 and *Hammond* v *Osborn* [2002] EWCA Civ 885.
[92] Particularly the law on undue influence.
[93] See Burns (2002).
[94] For a useful discussion, see Langan (1997).
[95] For concerns that the law of undue influence fails to protect competent, but vulnerable, older people, see Burns (2002).

(i) Appointeeship

Appointeeship is a system for administering and spending social service benefits and pensions on behalf of people with mental incapacity. The appointees are responsible to the Secretary of State for claiming, receiving and spending the money. They are under a duty to report any changes in the individual's circumstances which may affect benefit entitlement. Usually relatives fulfil the role of appointee, but it can also be done by friends. The Benefits Agency will need to be persuaded that the person receiving benefits is 'unable for the time being to act'. The agency may seek medical evidence of this, but is not required to.

The real problem with the procedure is that it is open to abuse. There is no definition of mental incapacity and there is no requirement of medical evidence in order to establish it. There are no procedures in place for the person deemed with mental incapacity to challenge the appointeeship. This seems to infringe personal autonomy. Also, there is no real monitoring of the appointee to whom the money is sent. This is of particular concern, as some local authorities think it acceptable to let the owners of private nursing homes become appointees.

(ii) Short procedure order under the Court of Protection and receivership

The Court of Protection can appoint a receiver to take control of the mentally incapacitated person's property and financial affairs, including the receipt of social security benefits and other income. If the assets exceed £5,000, receivership will be used; if less then a short procedure order (SPO) will be issued. The Public Trust Office in an average year was responsible for 30,000 receiverships with assets totalling about £780 million.[96] The Court of Protection requires medical evidence of incapacity, demonstrating that the patient is incapable of managing their affairs,[97] although there have been complaints that insufficient effort is taken to ensure that the individual is truly incapable.[98] There are concerns that the criteria used are vague[99] and are unsuitable for those with fluctuating capacities.[100] Some claim that there are insufficient checks on whether receivers are acting with probity.[101] The National Audit Office found that many receivers submitted accounts late and some not at all.

(iii) Enduring Power of Attorney

Enduring Power of Attorney (EPA) is appropriate where the older person at present has capacity but fears that in the near future he or she may lose it.[102] The EPA takes effect from the moment it is signed and continues after the onset of mental

---

[96] National Audit Office (1994).
[97] As defined under the Mental Health Act 1983.
[98] Griffiths, Roberts and Williams (1993).
[99] Age Concern (1986).
[100] Law Commission Report 231 (1995).
[101] National Audit Office (1994).
[102] An ordinary power of attorney lasts for as long as the donor retains capacity.

incapacity. However, the donor (the person who signs the power) must have had capacity at the time the power was created. Recently the government[103] has accepted the validity of concerns that the law does not adequately ensure that the donor of the power truly lacks capacity.

If necessary, more than one person can be appointed. The EPA must be registered by the attorney with the Court of Protection at the time when the attorney believes the donor is, or is becoming, mentally incapable of dealing with his or her own affairs. A doctor need not be involved, but the donor and certain relatives[104] must be notified. There is provision to dispense with the notice requirement if, for example, the name and address of a relative cannot be ascertained or a relative is him- or herself mentally incapable. Once registered, the attorney steps into the shoes of the donor, and his or her actions are automatically subject to the Court of Protection or its administrative arm (the Public Trust Office). The EPA takes immediate effect unless there is some objection to the registration.[105] If there is no objection, the registration will proceed without any investigation as to the suitability of the attorney. If there is an objection, the court must make 'such inquiries (if any) as it thinks appropriate in the circumstances of the case'.[106] The grounds for objection include allegations that fraud or pressure was used to acquire the power, or 'that having regard to all the circumstances and in particular the attorney's relation to or connection with the donor, the attorney is unsuitable to be the donor's attorney'.[107] The burden of proving the lack of capacity or the unsuitability of the attorney rests on the objectors.[108]

Once the EPA is registered, the court can give directions to the attorney concerning the management or disposal of the donor's property[109] or require the attorney to produce documents to the court.[110] If the court becomes convinced that the attorney is unsuitable, the registration can be cancelled.[111] It is possible to challenge a decision of an attorney, but it must be demonstrated that the attorney is not dealing with the donor's finances properly. In one case a donor had been cared for by a companion for several years. The donor signed an EPA which made his nephew his attorney. The nephew sought possession of the flat in which the companion lived, relying on his powers under the EPA. The Court of Protection could not provide assistance to the companion because the attorney had dealt properly with the donor's money in the strictly financial sense, even if the attorney had been acting contrary to the donor's moral obligations.[112]

There are grave concerns that there is a lack of adequate supervision of EPAs. Some fear that unscrupulous people persuade vulnerable older persons to sign

---

[103] Lord Chancellor's Department (1999).
[104] Husband or wife; children; parents; siblings of the whole or half blood; grandchildren; nephews and nieces; uncles and aunts and their children. This list is in order of priority and at least three relatives must be informed.
[105] Enduring Powers of Attorney Act 1985 (hereafter EPA 1985), s 6(4).
[106] EPA 1985, s 6(4).
[107] EPA 1985, s 6(5).
[108] *Re W (Power of Attorney)* [2001] 1 FLR 832 CA.
[109] EPA 1985, s 8(2)(b)(i).
[110] EPA 1985, s 8(2)(b)(ii).
[111] EPA 1985, s 8(4)(g).
[112] *Re R (Enduring Power of Attorney)* [1990] 2 All ER 893.

EPAs and then use these to dispose of the older donors' assets without family members being aware of what is happening.[113] Although it is open to the Court of Protection to cancel registration if it is demonstrated that an attorney is unsuitable, that is dependent upon someone being willing to bring the matter to the court's attention and being able to find sufficient evidence of misuse.[114]

D. Reform

The government announced proposals to reform the law regarding incapacity.[115] These are now to be found in the Mental Incapacity Bill 2003.[116] The proposals centre on the creation of a new power: the lasting power of attorney (LPA). The government has suggested that it is necessary to have a clearer definition of when someone should be deemed incapable of looking after his or her own affairs. Clause 2 of the Bill proposes that the test be whether a person is unable to understand, retain or use relevant information for the purposes of making a decision. The LPA would give authority to an attorney to make decisions about the donor's finances or general welfare, subject to restrictions in relation to some health care matters.

7. SUCCESSION AND INTESTACY

This section will consider what happens to people's property on their death. What is particularly revealing is the law's acknowledgment that family members may have legally enforceable claims on the estate, even if there is no will. Before considering the law, the theoretical issues will be discussed.

A. Theory

It is important to distinguish between two situations: first, where the deceased has left a will; and second, where the deceased has not left a will or has left a will that does not deal with all of the deceased's property. These two scenarios give rise to quite different problems.

(i) Where there is a will

Where someone leaves a will it might be thought that the issue is straightforward. Our society accepts that people should be free to dispose of their property in whatever ways they wish, however foolish others may think them to be. If during their lives people wish to spend all of their hard-earned money on gambling or purchasing law textbooks, they may, and unless they are mentally incompetent there is no way of stopping them. If this is true in life, should it not also be true in death? Not necessarily, because on divorce the law feels entitled to redistribute a spouse's property to achieve a fair result. If the law is willing to do this when a relationship is

---

[113] Lord Chancellor's Department (1999: 2.3).
[114] E.g. *Re E (Enduring Power of Attorney)* [2000] 1 FLR 882.
[115] Lord Chancellor's Department (1999).
[116] Lord Chancellor's Department (1999).

ended by divorce, should it not also be able to do so if the relationship is ended by death?

As we shall see, the law's response to these arguments is to seek a middle course. A person is permitted to make a will directing what should happen to his or her property on death, but if anyone feels that the will has not provided for them adequately then they are allowed to apply to the court for an order that they receive a payment out of the estate under the Inheritance (Provision for Family and Dependants) Act 1975. What is interesting is that the class of potential claimants is not restricted to spouses. Other relatives may claim that the deceased has not adequately provided for them in the will. The intervention of the law could be based on two grounds. First, it could be argued that even though the deceased had made a will, he or she could not really have intended not to provide for the claimant and the law is intervening to ensure that the will truly reflects the wishes of the deceased. Alternatively, the law could be explained as being a recognition that legal claims can be made on the deceased's income. Neither of these arguments is satisfactory. With the first there is the difficulty that an award can be made under the Act even if the evidence is clear that the deceased did not want the claimant to receive any of his or her money. The problem with the second is that, while a person is alive, the law does not recognise a liability to provide for other relatives apart from spouses.[117] There does not seem to be a strong reason to explain why these obligations suddenly spring into existence on the death of a person. It may be argued that, while alive, a person has the right to govern what happens to their property and this trumps the claims of other family members; however, once deceased, a person has no rights and so the law can give effect to the claims of other family members.

(ii) Where there is no will: intestacy

There are different issues where the deceased has left no will. Here there are two main possible approaches. The law could attempt to ascertain what the wishes of the deceased were, considering all the evidence available. Or the law could decide objectively what would be a fair and just distribution of the property. The two approaches could be intermingled. We might presume that a deceased's intention would be a fair and just settlement, but there may be occasions when there is evidence that the deceased did not wish a fair distribution to be made.

In a way, the law on intestacy is easier to defend than the law where there is a will. The law makes it clear that if an individual does not make a will then the law will decide how the property will be distributed. If the deceased decides not to make a will, he or she can make no objection (were they able to!) about the distribution of the property. Given the difficulties and litigation that would inevitably surround a law based on attempting to ascertain the deceased's wishes, the law has developed a set formula which operates in cases of intestacy. It has been estimated that about 40 per cent of people over 60 have not made a will[118] and so it is important that the formula is predictable and discourages litigation. However, because a formula is not

---

[117] Unless a legally binding contract has been entered into.
[118] Law Commission Report 187 (1989).

appropriate in every case, English and Welsh law has established a procedure by which an application can be made to the court if the result of the statutory rules would produce injustice.

B. The law in cases where there is a will

The starting point is that the will is enacted and property is distributed according to it. There are, of course, ways to challenge a will. It can be argued that a will does not comply with the formalities in the Wills Act 1837, or that the will was made by the deceased while of unsound mind or as a result of undue influence[119] or that the will has been revoked.[120] The detail of the law cannot be covered here, but if the will is invalid for any of these reasons then the estate will be dealt with using the rules of intestacy. There may also be arguments that a particular piece of property does not belong (or does not wholly belong) to the deceased. For example, it may be argued that the house, although being in the name of the deceased, was in fact held on trust for the deceased and his wife under a constructive trust or proprietary estoppel.[121] In such a case, if the deceased purported in his will to give the house to his daughter, he would only be able to give her his share of the house.

If someone feels that they have not been adequately provided for under the will they may be able to make a claim under the Inheritance (Provision for Family and Dependants) Act 1975, which will be discussed shortly.

C. Intestacy

The rules that operate on intestacy apply where the deceased has not made a will or has made a will that does not dispose of his or her entire estate. The rules are rather complex and depend on whether the deceased has a surviving spouse or any surviving issue (that is, children of the deceased, including adopted children and children born outside marriage).

(i) If there is a surviving spouse and children or grandchildren

If there is a surviving spouse[122] and issue then the surviving spouse is entitled to all of the personal chattels,[123] and £125,000 (known as the statutory legacy), if there is that much in the deceased's estate. If there is still money or property left in the estate after these transfers are made then the spouse has a life interest in half the remainder. The balance of the estate (subject to the spouse's life interest) is held on statutory trust for the children. This will mean that the children will be

---

[119] See Kerridge (2000) for concerns that the law may fail adequately to protect vulnerable testators.
[120] E.g. divorce will revoke a will.
[121] See Chapter 4.
[122] It is necessary for the spouse to have survived the deceased by 28 days if he or she is to be seen as a surviving spouse: Administration of Estates Act 1925, s 46.
[123] In basic terms the furniture and personal objects of the parties. The term is defined in the Administration of Estates Act 1925, s 55(1)(x).

entitled to maintenance until they are 18 and then they will be entitled to the capital.[124]

(ii) If there is a surviving spouse, no issue, but close relatives

If there is a surviving spouse and no children, but there are surviving parents, brothers or sisters[125] then the spouse is entitled to the personal chattels absolutely, £200,000 statutory legacy and half of the balance absolutely (rather than just a life interest). The parents, or if no parents then brothers or sisters (or their issue[126]), are entitled to the other half of the remainder.

(iii) If there is a surviving spouse, but no issue or close relatives

If there is a surviving spouse but no parents or brothers or sisters or issue of brothers and sisters then the spouse will take the intestate's estate absolutely.

(iv) If there is no surviving spouse

If there is no spouse then there is a list of relatives who may be entitled to the estate in the following order. Whichever relatives are highest up the list will take the estate absolutely and those lower down the list will take nothing:

1. children of the deceased or grandchildren;
2. parents of the deceased;
3. brothers or sisters of the whole blood, or their issue;
4. brothers or sisters of the half blood, or their issue;
5. grandparents of the deceased;
6. aunts or uncles of the deceased, or their issue.

If there is more than one relative in a category they will share the estate equally. If there is no one related to the deceased in this list then the estate will go to the Crown, *bona vacantia*. It is open to the Crown to give as a matter of grace some of the property to friends or others who fall outside the terms of the intestacy rules. This power is most likely to be used in the case of cohabitants.

Any person who is unhappy about the operation of the intestacy rules can apply to the court under the Inheritance (Provision for Family and Dependants) Act 1975.

As has been noted, a spouse is entitled to the personal chattels of the deceased, for example, the television, the bed, any pets, etc. This seems only sensible and is largely uncontroversial. In addition, the spouse is given absolutely a lump sum which he or she may use to purchase somewhere to live,[127] and a life interest in the

---

[124] Cretney (1995). The Law Commission Report 187 (1989) found that the majority of people thought the surviving spouse should receive everything on the death of a spouse.

[125] They must be of the whole blood.

[126] 'Issue' here means the children of the brother and sister. They will take their parent's share if the parent has died.

[127] The spouse is entitled to take the matrimonial home in lieu of his or her lump sum.

rest of the estate which will provide him or her with an income. The rules do not mean that the spouse will automatically be able to live in the house. This may seem harsh but it is mitigated by two rules. The first is that if the family home is in the joint names of the deceased and the spouse then, on the deceased's death, under the rules of land law, the house will belong to the spouse absolutely and will not normally be regarded as part of the deceased's estate. So the spouse would have the house as well as the statutory legacy, and so should be well provided for. Secondly, even if the house is not in joint names then there are rules permitting the spouse to use his or her statutory legacy to purchase the house from the estate. Nevertheless, if the house is in the sole name of the deceased and is worth more than the statutory legacy, then the house may have to be sold. This has led some to argue that the spouse should be entitled to the entire estate of the deceased.[128] However, others argue that the present law is too generous to spouses. The circumstances in which it might appear too generous are where the deceased had remarried and the second spouse acquires the estate under the intestacy rules. The children of the deceased, especially if they do not get on well with their step-parent, may fear that the estate will ultimately be diverted to the step-parent's 'family' rather than the deceased's family. Another very important point about the intestacy rules is that they do not provide for unmarried cohabiting partners, nor good friends. The focus is very much on blood relations and spouses, not social relations. This is in contrast to other parts of the law[129] where social relationships are emphasised.

D. The Inheritance (Provision for Family and Dependants) Act 1975

Where relatives or dependants feel that an inadequate sum has been left to them as a result of the deceased's will or the rules on intestacy, an application can be made to the court for an order. The burden of persuading the court to make the order rests on the applicant. There are no rights to property under the Act; the legislation simply gives the court a discretion to decide the appropriate amount, if any, to be paid to a claimant. The court is entitled to provide for someone who is not mentioned in the will or would not be entitled to money on intestacy. An individual can claim under the Act even if the deceased had made it quite plain that he or she did not wish the individual to receive any money on their death. The policy of the Act has been to ensure that a person who has become dependent upon the deceased does not suffer an injustice on the deceased's death.[130]

(i) Who can apply?

The following can apply under the Act:

1. The spouse of the deceased.[131]

---

[128] Law Commission Report 187 (1989).
[129] See Chapter 7, for example.
[130] *Jelley* v *Iliffe* [1981] Fam 128 CA.
[131] Inheritance (Provision for Family and Dependants) Act 1975 (hereafter I(PFD)A 1975), s 1(1)(a). This includes people who in good faith entered a void marriage with the deceased: I(PFD)A 1975, s 25(4), but does not include former spouses.

2. The former spouse of the deceased, providing the applicant has not remarried.[132]
3. A person who '... during the whole of the period of two years ending immediately before the date when the deceased died ... was living—(a) in the same household as the deceased, and (b) as the husband or wife of the deceased.'[133]

   This category would include some cohabiting couples, but does not encompass gay or lesbian couples.[134] The test to be applied is whether a reasonable person with normal powers of perception would say the couple was living together as husband and wife.[135] In using this test the reasonable person should be aware of the multifarious nature of marriages.[136] Therefore, in *Re Watson*[137] a couple in their fifties who started living together companionably without engaging in sexual relations could be said to be living as husband and wife. Indeed, Neuberger J noted that many married couples in their mid-fifties do not have sexual relations. The requirement that the cohabitation last until 'immediately' before the death has to be interpreted sensibly. In *Re Watson*[138] the deceased spent the last few weeks of his life in hospital and that did not prevent the section applying.
4. Any child of the deceased, including posthumous, adopted and grown-up children.[139] An adopted child cannot claim under this ground against their biological parents, but can claim against their adopted parents.[140]
5. Any person 'treated by the deceased as a child of the family in relation to' a marriage.[141] This is similar to the concept 'child of the family' discussed in Chapter 7. It most commonly applies in relation to stepchildren.[142] It should be stressed that this category only exists in the context of a marriage. If the deceased cohabits with a woman and her child from a previous relationship, the child could not rely on this category.[143]
6. Any other person 'who immediately before the death of the deceased was being maintained, either wholly or partly, by the deceased'.[144] The phrase 'maintained' in this definition is clarified in s 1(3):

   > a person shall be treated as being maintained by the deceased, either wholly or partly, as the case may be, if the deceased, otherwise than for full valuable consideration, was making a substantial contribution in money or money's worth towards the reasonable needs of that person.

---

[132] I(PFD)A 1975, s 1(1)(b).
[133] I(PFD)A 1975, s 1A. This category of claimants is only available if the deceased died on or after 1 January 1996.
[134] See the reasoning in *Fitzpatrick v Sterling Housing Association Ltd* [2000] 1 FCR 21 HL.
[135] *Re Watson* [1999] 1 FLR 878.
[136] See Chapter 1 for a discussion of the factors a court is likely to take into account in deciding whether there was cohabitation.
[137] [1999] 1 FLR 878.
[138] [1999] 1 FLR 878.
[139] I(PFD)A 1975, s 1(1)(c).
[140] *Re Collins* [1990] Fam 56.
[141] I(PFD)A 1975, s 1(1)(d).
[142] See *Re Leach* [1986] Ch 226 CA for an example of the potential breadth of the section.
[143] Although they may be able to rely on I(PFD)A 1975, s 1(1)(e).
[144] I(PFD)A 1975, s 1(1)(e).

This could include unmarried cohabitees – homosexual or heterosexual – as well as two friends living together without a sexual relationship but with a degree of maintenance. A few points need to be stressed about fulfilling the definition of this category:

(a) The maintenance must be substantial. In *Rees v Newbery and the Institute of Cancer Research*[145] the deceased had provided the applicant (an actor) with a flat in London at a low rent. There was no cohabitation nor sexual or emotional relationship between them, but it was found that the applicant had been maintained by the deceased, by providing the flat.

(b) The contribution must be in 'money or money's worth'. There is some debate whether companionship and care could count as maintenance for 'money's worth'. As housework and nursing services and even 'companionship' can be bought, it is submitted that these can be regarded as being for money's worth.[146]

(c) It has to be shown that the maintenance was not paid for by valuable consideration.[147] This requirement has caused difficulties. Could it be said that although a deceased cohabitant provided the claimant with free accommodation this was in return for care and companionship and so the applicant was 'paid for' by valuable consideration? Although at one time it was suggested that it was necessary to weigh up the financial value of the maintenance provided by the deceased against the benefits to the deceased provided by the claimant, the courts no longer take such an approach. The courts will readily accept that one cohabitant was being maintained by the other. In *Bouette v Rose*[148] the Court of Appeal accepted that a mother was maintained by her disabled child. The child had been awarded a substantial sum of money as a result of her disability. The court took a practical approach and explained that the fund was used to support the lifestyle of both the mother and the child, and so the child was effectively maintaining the mother.

(d) The deceased must have been maintaining the claimant immediately before the death of the deceased. As *Re Watson*[149] makes clear, the fact that the deceased's last few weeks were spent in a hospital or a nursing home will not prevent the applicant's claim being accepted. However, if a couple clearly separate shortly before the death then a claim cannot be made. This is controversial: although the separation may indicate that the deceased would not have wanted to leave a former cohabitant any property, it does not necessarily mean that it would not be fair to make such an award.

---

[145] [1998] 1 FLR 1041.
[146] This seems to have been accepted in *Jelley v Illiffe* [1981] Fam 128.
[147] This, in simple terms, requires that the contribution had not been paid for.
[148] [2000] 1 FLR 363.
[149] [1999] 1 FLR 878.

(ii) What is reasonable financial provision?

The key question in deciding an order is whether reasonable financial provision was made for the claimant in the will. Rather strangely, the concept of reasonable provision depends on the exact relationship between the deceased and the claimant. If the claimant is the spouse, the question is simply whether the *provision* is 'reasonable'. For other cases, the question is whether the *maintenance* is reasonable. The emphasis on maintenance is important. A non-spouse applicant who is 'comfortably off' may have difficulty in persuading the court that they need to be maintained.[150] A spouse who is well off will more easily be able to argue that the provision was not reasonable. This is because a spouse may be entitled to a share in his or her spouse's property because of the length of the marriage, even though he or she may not need to be maintained.[151] Reasonable provision is not necessarily restricted to the minimum necessary to survive,[152] but will not stretch to luxuries.[153]

Under s 3, in considering a claim, the court should consider:

(a) the financial resources and financial needs which the applicant has or is likely to have in the foreseeable future;

(b) the financial resources and financial needs which any other applicant for an order ... has or is likely to have in the foreseeable future;

(c) the financial resources and financial needs which any beneficiary of the estate of the deceased has or is likely to have in the foreseeable future;

(d) any obligations and responsibilities which the deceased had towards any applicant for an order ... or towards any beneficiary of the estate of the deceased;

(e) the size and nature of the net estate of the deceased;

(f) any physical or mental disability of any applicant for an order ... or any beneficiary of the estate of the deceased;

(g) any other matter, including the conduct of the applicant or any other person, which in the circumstances of the case the court may consider relevant.

These factors are largely self-explanatory. It should be noted that factors (b), (c), (d), (f) and (g) require the court to consider the position of all those who may be seeking money from the estate. So although a claimant may show a close relationship to the deceased and be in great need, their claim may fail if there are others interested in the estate who are of greater need. Although it is not stated explicitly, the wishes of the deceased can be taken into account.[154] For example, in *Re Hancock (Deceased)*[155] there was a dramatic increase in the value of the estate (from £100,000 to £650,000) and the Court of Appeal accepted evidence that, had the deceased been aware that his estate would increase to this level, he would have provided for the applicant. There are some additional considerations that apply for specific kinds of applicants:

---

[150] *Re Jennings (Deceased)* [1994] Ch 256.
[151] I(PFD)A 1975, s 1(2).
[152] *Re Coventry* [1990] Fam 561.
[153] *Re Dennis* [1981] 2 All ER 140.
[154] According to I(PFD)A 1975, s 21, a statement of the deceased is admissible evidence.
[155] [1998] 2 FLR 346 CA.

(a) Spouses

For a surviving spouse reasonable financial provision means 'such financial provision as it would be reasonable in all the circumstances of the case for a husband or wife to receive, whether or not that provision is required for his or her maintenance'.[156] When considering the appropriate level for a spouse, the court will have regard to the age of the applicant; the duration of the marriage; the applicant's contribution to the welfare of the family of the deceased; and the provision the applicant may reasonably have expected to receive if the marriage had been terminated by divorce rather than by death.[157] Miller[158] has suggested that the court should separate two elements of provision for spouses: first, the spouse's share of the 'family property', and second the proportion of the estate which would be necessary to provide the spouse with sufficient support.

This emphasis on the amount that might have been awarded on divorce reflects the argument that a spouse whose marriage is ended by death should not be worse off than if the marriage had been ended by divorce. However, death and divorce are distinguishable. On divorce, the crucial question is how to divide up the property fairly between the two parties. On death, there is no division required except between the spouse and the other relatives. It could be argued, therefore, that on death a spouse might expect a greater share than on divorce. There has been some dispute in the case law whether the divorce analogy should be seen as just one factor, or the guiding criterion. The most recent authority, *Re Krubert*,[159] preferred the view that the divorce analogy was only one factor to be taken into account. This seems correct. First, as a matter of statutory interpretation – the divorce analogy relates to only one of several factors which should be taken into account. Secondly, as has already been mentioned, the two scenarios – death and divorce – are quite different.[160]

(b) Former spouses

A former spouse can only claim under the Act if he or she has not remarried.[161] It is rare for former spouses to claim under the Act because it is common on divorce for a court to order that an applicant cannot make a claim under the Act if the ex-spouse subsequently dies. If such an order is in place then an application cannot be made, whether or not the ex-spouse has remarried. Even if an ex-spouse is not prevented from bringing an application, the court may well take the view that it is reasonable provision for the deceased to leave a former spouse nothing in the will.[162]

(c) Child of the deceased

The court should have regard to the manner in which the child was being, or in which he or she might expect to be, educated or trained.[163] So if the intention was

---

[156] I(PFD)A 1975, s 1(2)(a).
[157] I(PFD)A 1975, s 3(2).
[158] Miller (1997).
[159] [1997] Ch 97 CA.
[160] Miller (1997).
[161] I(PFD)A 1975, s 1(1)(b).
[162] E.g. *Cameron v Treasury Solicitor* [1996] 2 FLR 716 CA; *Barrass v Harding* [2001] 1 FCR 297.
[163] I(PFD)A 1975, s 3(3).

that the child be privately educated, money from the estate could be claimed to provide such education.

(d) Adult children

The courts are generally reluctant to allow adult children who have sufficient earning capacity to succeed in making a claim against their parents' estate. The difficulty facing an employed adult child claimant is in showing that an award would be reasonable for his or her maintenance. The courts have usually required that an adult child establish a 'moral obligation' or some other special circumstances if the claim is to succeed. Examples of a moral obligation or special circumstances include a son who had worked on the family farm in the expectation that he would inherit it;[164] and an applicant whose father was left money by the applicant's mother on the understanding that he would leave the money in his will to the applicant but did not.[165] In *Re Hancock (Deceased)*[166] the Court of Appeal stressed that it would be wrong to say that an adult child can never succeed in an application unless there is a moral obligation or other special circumstances, but without those the application would be unlikely to succeed, especially if the applicant is in paid employment. In *Espinosa v Bourke*[167] the daughter had for a while cared for her father, but somewhat abandoned him when she ran off to Spain to live with a Spanish fisherman. Despite this being what some would regard as reprehensible conduct, she was entitled to an award based on her need, her doubtful earning capacity, and having no formal employment. This decision stresses that moral obligation is but one factor to be taken into account.[168]

(e) Child of the deceased's family

When the court is considering a child who was not biologically the deceased's, but whom he or she treated as a child of the family, the court should consider whether the deceased had assumed responsibility for the child and whether, in assuming responsibility, the deceased knew that the applicant was not his or her own child. The liability of any other person to maintain the applicant should also be taken into account.

(f) Dependants

In addition to the general factors, the court will consider 'the extent to which and the basis upon which the deceased assumed responsibility for the maintenance of the applicant, and ... the length of time for which the deceased discharged that responsibility'.[169] Megarry V-C stressed that the deceased must have assumed responsibility for the applicant: that maintenance on its own would not be enough, if the deceased had not undertaken responsibility.[170] The Court of

---

[164] *Re Pearce (Deceased)* [1998] 2 FLR 705.
[165] *Re Goodchild* [1996] 1 WLR 694.
[166] [1998] 2 FLR 346 CA.
[167] [1999] 1 FLR 747.
[168] Borkowski (1999).
[169] I(PFD)A 1975, s 3(4).
[170] *Re Beaumont* [1980] Ch 444.

Appeal, however, has suggested that it is willing to infer assumption of responsibility from maintenance.[171]

(g) Cohabitants

If the claimant relies on s 1A the following special factors apply:

- (a) the age of the applicant and the length of the period [of cohabitation] . . .;
- (b) the contribution made by the applicant to the welfare of the family of the deceased, including any contribution made by looking after the home or caring for the family.

However, a cohabitant cannot normally expect an award at a level which would enable him or her to retain the same standard of living as the couple had enjoyed together, even if it had been a lengthy relationship.[172] In *Re Watson*[173] the needs of the frail applicant were particularly significant.

8. ELDER ABUSE[174]

A. Defining elder abuse[175]

The National Council on Ageing has defined elder abuse as 'the mistreatment of an older person . . . it can be a single incident or part of a repeated pattern'.[176] The kinds of abuse include physical, sexual, psychological and financial abuse. The Social Services Inspectorate[177] found that physical abuse was the most frequent form of abuse among older people and the most common class of victim was women aged 81 or over.[178] The abuser is often the principal carer and a close relative.[179]

The Law Commission has defined abuse in this context as the:

> ill-treatment of that person (including sexual abuse and forms of ill-treatment that are not physical), the impairment of, or an avoidable deterioration in, the physical or mental health of that person or the impairment of his physical, intellectual, emotional, social or behavioural development.[180]

Notably, this definition includes abuse by omission (not providing the appropriate level of care) as well as abuse by act. It also makes it clear that abuse includes acts that were not intended to harm the dependent person.

Statistics on the level of abuse are hard to obtain, not least because much abuse goes unreported. The leading study in England and Wales found that 2 per cent of older people had suffered financial abuse and 5 per cent verbal abuse.[181] A smaller-

---

[171] *Jelley* v *Iliffe* [1981] Fam 128; *Bouette* v *Rose* [2000] 1 FLR 363, [2000] 1 FCR 385 CA.
[172] *Graham* v *Murphy* [1997] 1 FLR 860.
[173] [1999] 1 FLR 878.
[174] For a fuller discussion, see Pollard (1995); Brogden and Nijhar (2000); Pritchard (2002).
[175] Alternative definitions are discussed in Brammer and Biggs (1998).
[176] Quoted Pollard (1995: 257).
[177] Social Services Inspectorate (1992; 1993).
[178] Although see Pritchard (2002) for a discussion of the abuse of older men.
[179] Ogg and Bennett (1992).
[180] Law Commission Report 231 (1995: 9.8).
[181] Ogg and Bennett (1992).

scale study found that 27.5 per cent of pensioners had been the victim of abuse or neglect.[182]

B. The law

The criminal law applies as it does with any other group of people. The government rejected a proposal that there should be a new offence of ill-treatment or wilful neglect of a person without capacity.[183] The law provides a number of routes whereby an older person can obtain protection from abuse. Some of these remedies are the same as those available to cohabitants or spouses.

1. Non-molestation orders and occupation orders are available under the Family Law Act 1996.[184] To obtain a non-molestation order it is necessary to show that the older person is associated with the abuser. This can readily be established if the abuser is a relative. However, an older person who is living in a residential home will normally not be associated with a care assistant at the home.
2. The Protection from Harassment Act 1997 may afford protection. There is no need to prove that the parties are associated persons to use this legislation.
3. Older people are protected from abuse by the criminal law. However, this depends on the police being made aware of the abuse, which given the private nature of abuse and the reluctance or inability of the older person to report the abuse, may mean that it is rare for the criminal law to be invoked.
4. Under the Registered Homes Act 1984, local authorities have the right to cancel registration of an old persons' home; this Act could be invoked if there were allegations of serious abuse.[185] The local authority has the right to enter the home;[186] inspect records; and cancel or refuse registration.[187] There is an emergency procedure available to cancel registration if there is a serious risk to the life, health, or well-being of the residents.[188] There are, however, concerns that moving older people from their homes can lead to great distress and even premature death.[189]
5. There is a limited power in s 47 of the National Assistance Act 1948 to remove a person from care in a domestic setting. The application is on seven days' notice by a local authority to a magistrates' court. The main ground for such an application is that the person is living in unsanitary conditions and not receiving proper care and attention from other persons. The order initially lasts for three days. An emergency order can be applied for *ex parte* under the National Assistance (Amendment) Act 1951 for a maximum of three weeks. These

---

[182] Ogg and Munn-Giddings (1993).
[183] Lord Chancellor's Department (1999).
[184] Discussed in detail in Chapter 6.
[185] Many believe the power is not used effectively. See, for example, reports of abuse in elderly care homes: e.g. Kielder House, discussed Guardian (2000).
[186] Registered Homes Act 1984, s 17.
[187] The Care Standards Act 2000 creates the National Care Standards Commission, which monitors care services.
[188] Registered Homes Act 1984, s 11.
[189] *McKellar* v *Hounslow LBC* Unreported 28.10.2003 QBD.

powers are rarely used. This is in part because of the stigma that attaches to the phrase 'unsanitary conditions'.

The contrast with the protection available for children who are being abused is notable. In particular, there is no duty on a local authority to investigate a suspected case of abuse, as there is for children under s 47 of the Children Act 1989. Also, there is no equivalent to a child's being taken into care.

C. Issues concerning elder abuse

The question of the abuse of older people gives rise to some complex issues, which might explain why the law has struggled to find an effective response. The following are some of the difficulties:

1. *Autonomy.* Normally in a liberal democracy the state is not willing to remove adults from their homes, or to prevent them from seeing someone simply on the basis that it would not be good for them. We have seen when considering family violence that the law seeks to respect the autonomy of the victim, although there is a tension with other values that the law may seek to uphold. An example of the problem is that an older person may prefer to be cared for by a relative who is abusive, rather than being placed in a residential home. Should the state deprive the older person of that choice? One answer may be that it depends on whether the older person is competent to make that decision or not. However, there are real difficulties in deciding the level of competence of an older person, especially as the level of understanding may vary considerably from day to day. In any event, can we be sure that residential care is better for an older person than personal care by a loved one who is occasionally abusive? But does this last question reveal an attitude that would be regarded as unacceptable if we were talking about the care of a child?
2. *Definitions of self-neglect.* What might appear to be self-neglect to one person may be eccentricity to another. An older person who insists on sleeping all day and being awake at night might be exhibiting signs of self-neglect or neglect by carers, or might be eccentric. If older people are exhibiting eccentric behaviour, does this justify state intervention to protect them from themselves, or is this an unwarranted intrusion into the autonomy of older people?
3. *Problems in defining violence and neglect.* A carer who is rough in handling an older person or is irritable might be said to be abusive to the older person. But others might regard ill-temper as an inevitable part of the stresses involved in giving personal care.
4. *Proof.* As always with issues of abuse, there are great problems in proving the abuse. One solution would be regular visits of social workers to older people who are perceived to be vulnerable. However, there is a widespread feeling among older people that visits of social workers are an infringement of privacy.[190]
5. *Remedies.* If the abuse is taking place in the older person's home, there is the difficult question of remedy. Placing the older person in a residential home against

---

[190] Longres (1993).

his or her wishes could itself be seen as a form of abuse. Another issue is that even if the carer has physically abused the older person, this may be due in part to the lack of provision of adequate resources by the social services.

6. *Relationship of care-giver and care-receiver.* The relationship between the care-giver and care-receiver can be a complex one. The exhaustion and desperation that care-givers might feel could even be regarded as a form of abuse itself. Indeed, many cases of elder abuse are simply deeply sad stories that do not necessarily lead to blame of the kind that we place on the child abuser. Landau has pointed out that sometimes it is not clear who should be regarded as the social worker's client: the abused older person or the desperate carer. There is, in fact, an almost equal number of care-givers who report abuse as there are elderly charges who report being abused.[191]

9. CONCLUSION

The position of elderly people and their relatives is of increasing importance in family law. One key issue is the extent to which adult children should be required to provide financial support for elderly parents. Although there is widespread acceptance that there is a moral obligation owed by adult children to their parents, there are complex issues in the debate whether the obligation should become a legal one. The law on succession indicates that, at least once a person is dead, the law will give legal effect to moral obligations between a variety of relationships, including those between adult children and their parents. The chapter has also considered an issue which will become of increasing importance – inter-generational justice: how should society distribute its resources between the younger and older sections of society? The concluding discussion looked at the topic of abuse of older people and the complex issues that arise in protecting the rights, interests and dignity of the older person.

[191] G. Wilson (1994).

BIBLIOGRAPHY AND FURTHER READING

Adams, D. (2000) 'The Emerge Program', in J. Hanmer and C. Itzin (eds) *Home Truths About Domestic Violence*, London: Routledge.

Adhar, R. (1996) 'Religion as a factor in custody and access disputes', *International Journal of Law, Policy and the Family* 10: 177.

Age Concern (1984) *Community Care Handbook*, London: Age Concern.

Age Concern (1986) *The Law and Vulnerable Elderly People*, London: Age Concern.

Age Concern (2000) *New Survey of GPs Confirms Ageism in NHS*, London: Age Concern.

Akerstrom, M. (1998) 'Police persuasion: making battered women file a complaint', *International Journal of Law, Policy and the Family* 12: 62.

Alderson, P. (1993) *Children's Consent to Surgery*, Buckingham: Open University Press.

Alexander, G. (1998) 'The new marriage contract and the limits of private ordering', *Indiana Law Review* 1998: 503.

Altman, S. (1996) 'Divorcing threats and offers', *Law and Philosophy* 15: 209.

Altman, S. (2003) 'A theory of child support', *International Journal of Law, Policy and the Family* 17: 173.

Anderson, L. (1997) 'Registered personal relationships', *Family Law* 27:174.

Archard, D. (1993a) *Children: Rights and Childhood*, London: Routledge.

Archard, D. (1993b) 'Do parents own their children?', *International Journal of Children's Rights* 1: 293.

Archard, D. (1995) 'What's blood got to do with it? The significance of natural parenthood', *Res Publica* 1: 91.

Archard, D. (1999) 'Can Child Abuse Be Defined?', in M. King (ed.) *Moral Agendas for Children's Welfare*, London: Routledge.

Archard, D. (2001) 'Philosophical Perspectives on Childhood', in J. Fionda (ed.) *Legal Concepts of Childhood*, Oxford: Hart.

Archard, D. (2003) *Children, Family and The State*, Aldershot: Ashgate.

Ariès, P. (1986) *Centuries of Childhood*, London: Penguin.

Aris, R., Harrison, C., and Humphreys, C. (2002) *Safety and Child Contact*, London: LCD.

Armstrong, S. (2002) 'Is the jurisdiction of England and Wales correctly applying the 1980 Hague Convention on the Civil Aspects of International Child Abduction?' *International and Comparative Law Quarterly* 51: 427.

Arnold, W. (2000) 'Implementation of Part II: Lessons Learned', in Thorpe LJ and E. Clarke (eds), *No Fault or Flaw: The Future of the Family Law Act 1996*, Bristol: Jordans.

Ashton DJ (2000) 'Injunctions and mental disorder', *Family Law* 30: 39.

Ashworth, K. and Walker, K. (1994) 'Reeboks, a Game Boy and a cat', in S. Middleton, K. Ashworth and R. Walker (eds) *Family Fortunes*, London: Child Poverty Action Group.

Atiyah, P. (1982) 'Economic duress and the overborne will', *Law Quarterly Review* 98: 147.

Atkin, B. (2003) 'The rights of married and unmarried couples in New Zealand – Radical new laws on property and succession', *Child and Family Law Quarterly* 15: 173.

Axin, W. and Thornton, A. (1992) 'The relationship between cohabitation and divorce: Selectivity or causal influence?', *Demography* 29: 357.

BBC (2002a), 'Children want a voice in government', 7 October 2002, London: BBCNews online.

BBC (2002b), 'One third of British teenagers are overweight', 17 September 2002: BBCNews online.

BBC (2003) Internet Sperm Bank. www.bbc.co.uk/radio4

Backett, K. (1982) *Mothers and Fathers: A Study of the Development and Negotiation of Parental Behaviour*, Basingstoke: Macmillan.

Bagshaw, R. (2001) 'Children Through Tort', in J. Fionda (ed.) *Legal Concepts of Childhood*, Oxford: Hart.

Bailey-Harris, R. (1995) 'Financial rights in relationships outside marriage: A decade of reform in Australia', *International Journal of Law, Policy and the Family* 9: 223.

Bailey-Harris, R. (1996) 'Law and unmarried couples: Oppression or liberation?', *Child and Family Law Quarterly* 8: 137.

Bailey-Harris, R. (1998a) 'Dividing the Assets on Breakdown of Relationships Outside Marriage: Challenges for Reformers', in R. Bailey-Harris (ed.) *Dividing the Assets on Family Breakdown*, Bristol: Jordans.

Bailey-Harris, R. (1998b) 'Equality or Inequality Within the Family? Ideology, Reality and the Law's Response', in J. Eekelaar and T. Nahlapo (eds) *The Changing Family: International Perspectives on the Family and Family Law*, Oxford: Hart.

Bailey-Harris, R. (2000) 'New Families for a New Society', in S. Cretney (ed.) *Family Law – Essays for the New Millennium*, Bristol: Jordans.

Bailey-Harris, R. (2001a) 'Comment on White v White', *Family Law* 31: 14.

Bailey-Harris, R. (2001b) 'Dividing the assets on family breakdown: the content of fairness', *Current Legal Problems* 53: 533.

Bailey-Harris, R. (2001c) 'Same-Sex Partnerships in English Family Law', in R. Wintemute and M. Andenæs (eds) *Legal Recognition of Same-Sex Partnerships*, Oxford: Hart.

Bailey-Harris, R. (2001d) 'Contact – Challenging conventional wisdom', *Child and Family Law Quarterly* 13: 361.

Bailey-Harris, R. (2002) 'Comment on C v Bury MBC', *Family Law* 32: 810.

Bailey-Harris, R. (2003) 'Comment on GW v RW', *Family Law* 33: 386.

Bailey-Harris, R., Barron, J. and Pearce, J. (1999) 'Settlement culture and the use of the "No Order" Principle under the Children Act 1989', *Child and Family Law Quarterly* 11: 53.

Bailey-Harris, R., Davis, G., Barron, J. and Pearce, J. (1998) *Monitoring Private Law Applications Under the Children Act: A Research Report to the Nuffield Foundation*, Bristol: University of Bristol.

Bailey-Harris, R., and Harris, M. (2002) 'Local authorities and child protection – the mosaic of accountability', *Child and Family Law Quarterly* 14: 117.

Bainham, A. (1986) 'The balance of power in family decisions', *Cambridge Law Journal* 45: 262.

Bainham, A. (1989) 'When is a parent not a parent? Reflections on the unmarried father and his children in English law', *International Journal of Family Law* 3: 208.

Bainham, A. (1990) 'The privatisation of the public interest in children', *Modern Law Review* 53: 206.

Bainham, A. (1994a) 'The temporal dimension of care', *Cambridge Law Journal* 53: 458.

Bainham, A. (1994b) 'Non-Intervention and Judicial Paternalism', in P. Birks (ed.) *Frontiers of Liability*, Oxford: OUP.

Bainham, A. (1994c) 'Religion, human rights and the fitness of parents', *Cambridge Law Journal* 53: 39.

Bainham, A. (1995a) 'Contact as a fundamental right', *Cambridge Law Journal* 54: 255.

Bainham, A. (1995b) 'Family Law in a pluralistic society', *Journal of Law and Society* 23: 234.

Bainham, A. (1996) 'Sex Education: A Family Lawyer's Perspective', in N. Harris (ed.) *Children, Sex Education and the Law*, London: National Children's Bureau.

Bainham, A. (1997) 'Do babies have rights?', *Cambridge Law Journal* 56: 48.

Bainham, A. (1998a) *Children: The Modern Law*, Bristol: Jordans.

Bainham, A. (1998b) 'Changing families and changing concepts: Reforming the language of family law', *Child and Family Law Quarterly* 10: 1.

Bainham, A. (1998c) 'Honour Thy Father and Thy Mother: Children's Rights and Children's Duties', in G. Douglas and L. Sebba (eds) *Children's Rights and Traditional Values*, Aldershot: Dartmouth.

Bainham, A. (1999) 'Parentage, Parenthood and Parental Responsibility: Subtle, Elusive Yet Important Distinctions', in A. Bainham, S. Day Sclater and M. Richards (eds) *What is a Parent?*, Oxford: Hart.

Bainham, A. (2000a) 'Attributing harm: child abuse and the unknown perpetrator', *Cambridge Law Journal* 59: 458.

Bainham (2000b) 'Children Law at the Millennium', in S. Cretney (ed.) *Family Law – Essays for the New Millennium*, Bristol: Jordans.

Bainham, A. (2000c) 'Family rights in the next millennium', *Current Legal Problems* 53: 471.

Bainham, A. (2001a) 'Men and women behaving badly: Is fault dead in English family law?', *Oxford Journal of Legal Studies* 21: 219.

Bainham, A. (2001b) 'Resolving the unresolvable: The case of the conjoined twins', *Cambridge Law Journal* 60: 49.

Bainham, A. (2002a) 'Can we protect children and protect their rights?', *Family Law* 32: 279.

Bainham, A. (2002b) 'Unintentional parenthood: The case of the reluctant mother', *Cambridge Law Journal* 61:288.

Bainham, A. (2002c) 'Sexualities, Sexual Relations and the Law', in A. Bainham, S. Day Sclater and M. Richards (eds) *Body Lore and Laws*, Oxford: Hart.

Bainham, A. (2003) 'Contact as a Right and Obligation', in A. Bainham, B. Lindley, M. Richards. and L. Trinder (eds) *Children and Their Families*, Oxford: Hart.

Bainham, A., Lindley, B., Richards, M. and Trinder, L. (eds) (2003) *Children and Their Families*, Oxford: Hart.

Baker, A. and Townsend, P. (1996) 'Post-divorce parenting – rethinking shared residence', *Child and Family Law Quarterly* 8: 217.

Bala, N. and Jaremko Bromwich, R. (2002) 'Context and inclusivity in Canada's evolving definition of the family', *International Journal of Law, Policy and the Family* 16: 145.

Ball, C. and Connolly, J. (1999) 'Requiring school attendance: A little used sentencing power', *Criminal Law Review* 183.

Bamforth, N. (2001) 'Same-Sex Partnerships and Arguments of Justice', in R. Wintemute and M. Andenæs (eds) *Legal Recognition of Same-Sex Partnerships*, Oxford: Hart.

Banda, F. (2003) 'Global standards: Local values', *International Journal of Law, Policy and the Family* 17: 1.

Banner, R. (1995) 'Economic Devices and Ethical Pitfalls', in A. Grubb (ed.) *Choices and Decisions in Health Care*, Chichester: John Wiley & Sons.

Bar-Hava, G. and Pryor, J. (1998) 'Cinderella's challenge – adjustment to stepfamilies in the 1990s', *Child and Family Law Quarterly* 10: 257.

Barlow, A., Duncan, S., James, G. and Park, A. (2001) 'Just a Piece of Paper. Marriage and Cohabitation in Britain', in *British Social Attitudes: the 18th Report*, London: Sage.

Barlow, A., Duncan, S., James, G. and Park, A. (2003) *Family Affairs: Cohabitation, Marriage and the Law*, London: Nuffield Foundation.

Barnett, A. (2000) 'Contact and Domestic Violence: The Ideological Divide', in J. Bridgeman and D. Monk (eds) *Feminist Perspectives on Child Law*, London: Cavendish.

Barnett, S. (2000) 'Compatibility and religious rights', *Family Law* 30: 494.

Baron, J. (1990) *Not Worth the Paper*, London: Women's Aid Foundation.

Barrett, M. and MacIntosh, M. (1991) *The Anti-Social Family*, London: Verso.

Bartholet, E. (1999) *Nobody's Children*, Boston: Beacon Press.

Bartlett, K. (1984) 'Rethinking parenthood', *Virginia Law Review* 70: 879.

Bartlett, K. (1999) 'Improving the Law Relating to Postdivorce Arrangements for Children', in R. Thompson and P. Amato (eds) *The Postdivorce Family*, Thousand Oaks, Calif.: Sage.

Barton, C. (1996a) 'Adoption Bill – the consultation document', *Family Law* 26: 431.

Barton, C. (1996b) 'The homosexual in the family', *Family Law* 26: 626.

Barton, C. (1997) 'When did you next see your father?', *Child and Family Law Quarterly* 9: 73.

Barton, C. (1999) '*A v United Kingdom* – The Thirty-Thousand Pound Caning – An "English Vice" in Europe', *Child and Family Law Quarterly* 11: 63.

Barton, C. (2000) 'Adoption – the Prime Minister's Review', *Family Law* 30: 731.

Barton, C. (2001) 'Adoption and Children Bill 2001', *Family Law* 31: 431.

Barton, C. (2002a) 'Parental hitting – the "Responses" to "Protecting Children, Supporting Parents" ', *Family Law* 32: 124.

Barton, C. (2002b) 'White Paper weddings – The beginnings, muddles and the ends of wedlock', *Family Law* 32: 421.

Barton, C. (2003) 'The mediator as midwife – a marketing opportunity', *Family Law* 33: 195.

Barton, C. and Bissett-Johnson, A. (2000) 'The declining number of Ancillary Relief Orders', *Family Law* 30: 94.

Barton, C. and Douglas, G. (1995) *Law and Parenthood*, London: Butterworths.

Barton, C. and Hibbs, M. (2002) 'Ancillary financial relief and fat cat(tle) divorce', *Modern Law Review* 65: 79.

Bates, P. (1995) 'Secure Accommodation Order – in whose interests?', *Child and Family Law Quarterly* 7: 70.

Battersby, G. (1996) 'How not to judge the quantum (and priority) or a share in the family home', *Child and Family Law Quarterly* 8: 261.

Beatson, J. (2002) *Anson's Law of Contract*, 28th edn, Oxford: OUP.

Beck, C., Clavis, G., Barnes Jenkins, M. and Nadi, R. (1978) 'The rights of children: A trust model', *Fordham Law Review* 46: 669.

Beck, U. and Beck-Gernsheim, G. (1995) *The Normal Chaos of Love*, Cambridge: Polity Press.

Beckett, S. and Hershman, D. (2001) 'The human rights implications for looked-after siblings', *Family Law* 31: 288.

Beck-Gernsheim, E. (2002) *Reinventing the Family*, Cambridge: Polity Press.

Bennett, F. (1997) *Child Support: Issues for the Future*, London: Child Poverty Action Group.

Berger, P. and Kellner, H. (1980) 'Marriage and the Construction of Reality', in B. Cosin (ed.) *School and Society: A Sociological Reader*, London: Routledge.

Bergman, B. (1986) *The Economic Emergence of Women*, New York: Basic Books.

Bernardes, J. (1997) *Family Studies*, London: Routledge.

Bevan, G. and Davis, G. (1999) 'A preliminary exploration of the impact of family mediation on legal aid costs', *Child and Family Law Quarterly* 11: 411.

Bevan, H. (1989) *The Law Relating to Children*, London: Butterworths.

Bird, R. (1996) *Domestic Violence: The New Law*, Bristol: Jordans.

Bird, R. (2000) 'Pension sharing', *Family Law* 30: 455.

Bird, R. (2002) 'The reform of section 25', *Family Law* 32: 428.

Bird, R. and Cretney, S. (1996) *Divorce: The New Law – The Family Law Act 1996*, Bristol: Jordans.

Blackstone, W. (1770) *Commentaries on the Laws of England*.

Blair, A. (1997) *The Guardian*: 1 October 1997.

Blair, J. (1996) ' "Honour thy father and thy mother" – but for how long? Adult children's duty to care for and protect elderly parents', *Journal of Family Law* 35: 765.

Blustein, J. (1982) *Parents and Children: The Ethics of the Family*, Oxford: OUP.

Blyth, E. (1995) 'The United Kingdom's Human Fertilisation and Embryology Act 1990 and the welfare of the child: A critique', *International Journal of Children's Rights* 3: 417.

Bohman, M. and Sigvardsson, S. (1990) 'Outcomes in Adoption: Lessons from Longitudinal Studies', in D. Brodzinsky and M. Schechter (eds) *The Psychology of Adoption*, Oxford: OUP.

Bond, A. (1998) 'Reconstructing families – changing children's surnames', *Child and Family Law Quarterly* 10: 17.

Booth J (1985) *Report of the Matrimonial Causes Procedure Committee*, London: HMSO.

Booth J (1992) 'Life After Evans', *Family Law* 22: 178.

Booth J (2002) *A Scoping Study on Delay*, London: LCD.

Borkowski, A. (1994) 'Wilful refusal to consummate: "Just excuse" ', *Family Law* 24: 684.

Borkowski, A. (1999) 'Moral obligation and family provision', *Child and Family Law Quarterly* 11: 305.

Borkowski, A. (2002) 'The presumption of marriage', *Child and Family Law Quarterly* 14: 250.

Borkowski, A., Murch, M. and Walker, V. (1983) *Marital Violence. The Community Response*, London: Tavistock Publications.

Bornat, J., Dimmock, B., Jones, D. and Peace, S. (1999) 'The Impact of Family Change on Older People: The Case of Stepfamilies', in S. McRae (ed.) *Changing Britain*, Oxford: OUP.

Bowen, E., Brown, L. and Gilchrist, E. (2002) 'Evaluating probation based offender programmes for domestic violence offenders', *Howard Journal of Criminal Justice* 41: 221.

Bowker, L., Arbitell, M. and McFerron, J. (1989) 'On the Relationship Between Wife Beating and Child Abuse', in K. Yllo and M. Bograd (eds) *Feminist Perspectives on Wife Abuse*, London: Sage.

Bowlby, J. (1973) *Attachment and Loss,* London: Hogarth.

Bowley, M. (1995) 'A too fragile social fabric?', *New Law Journal* 145: 1883.

Bowley, M. (2000) 'Why some families are more equal than others', *The Times*: 9 May 2000.

Boyd, S. (1996) 'Is there an ideology of motherhood in (post) modern child custody law?', *Social and Legal Studies* 5: 495.

Bracher, M., Morgan, S. and Trussell, J. (1993) 'Marriage dissolution in Australia: Models and explanations', *Population Studies* 47: 403.

Bradley, D. (1987) 'Homosexuality and child custody in English law', *International Journal of Law and the Family* 1: 155.

Bradley, D. (1998) 'Politics, culture and family law in Finland: Comparative approaches to the institution of marriage', *International Journal of Law, Policy and the Family* 12: 288.

Bradley, D. (2001) 'Regulation of unmarried cohabitation in West-European Jurisdictions – determinants of legal policy', *International Journal of Law, Policy and the Family* 15: 22.

Bradney, A. (1983) 'Duress and arranged marriages', *Modern Law Review* 46: 499.

Bradney, A. (1993) *Religious Rights and Laws*, London: Sweet & Maxwell.

Bradney, A. (1994) 'Duress, family law and the coherent legal system', *Modern Law Review* 57: 963.

Bradshaw, J. and Millar, J. (1991) *Lone Parent Families in the UK*, DSS Research Report No. 6, London: HMSO.

Bradshaw, J., Stimson, C., Skinner, C. and Williams, J. (1999) *Absent Fathers?*, London: Routledge.

Brammer, A. and Biggs, S. (1998) 'Defining elder abuse', *Journal of Social Welfare and Family Law* 20: 285.

Brandon, M. (1999) *Safeguarding Children with the Children Act 1989*, London: The Stationery Office.

Brannen, J., Meszaros, G., Moss, P. and Poland, G. (1994) *Employment and Family Life*, London: University of London.

Brasse, G. (1993) 'Section 34: A Trojan horse?', *Family Law* 23: 55.

Brasse, G. (2002) 'Contact and money', *Family Law* 32: 691.

Brasse, G. (2003) 'Lambert v Lambert – Pandora's hostage to fortune', *Family Law* 33: 101.

Brazier, M. (1999) 'Can you buy children?', *Child and Family Law Quarterly* 11: 345.

Brazier, M., Campbell, A. and Golombok, S. (1998) *Surrogacy: Review for Health Ministers*, London: HMSO.

Brecher, B. (1994) 'What Is Wrong with the Family', in D. Morgan and G. Douglas (eds) *Constituting Families*, Stuttgart: Franz Steiner Verlag.

Bretherton, H. (2002) ' "Because it's me the decisions are about" – Children's experiences of private law proceedings', *Family Law* 32: 450.

Bridge, C. (1996) 'Shared residence in England and New Zealand – A comparative analysis', *Child and Family Law Quarterly* 8: 12.

Bridge, C. (1999) 'Religion, culture and conviction – the medical treatment of young children', *Child and Family Law Quarterly* 11: 1.

Bridge, C. (2000) 'Diversity, divorce and information meetings – ensuring access to justice', *Family Law* 30: 645.

Bridge, C. and Swindells, H. (2003) *Adoption. The Modern Law*, Bristol: Jordans.

Bridge, S. (1999) 'Assisted Reproduction and Parentage in Law', in A. Bainham, S. Day Sclater and M. Richards (eds) *What is a Parent?*, Oxford: Hart.

Bridge, S. (2001) 'Marriage and Divorce: The Regulation of Intimacy', in J. Herring (ed.) *Family Law – Issues, Debates, Policy*, Cullompton: Willan.

Bridge, S. (2002) 'The property rights of cohabitants – where do we go from here?', *Family Law* 31: 743.

Brinig, M. (2000) *From Contract to Covenant. Beyond the Law and Economics of the Family*, New York: Harvard University Press.

British Medical Association (1996) *Surrogacy*, London: BMA.

British Medical Association (2001) *Consent, Rights and Choices in Health Care for Children and Young People*, London: BMJ Books.

Broberg, P. (1996) 'The registered partnership for same-sex couples in Denmark', *Child and Family Law Quarterly* 8: 149.

Brogden, M. and Nijhar, P. (2000) *Crime, Abuse and the Elderly*, Cullompton: Willan.

Brophy, J. (1985) 'Child Care and the Growth of Power', in J. Brophy and C. Smart (eds) *Women in Law*, London: Routledge.

Brophy, J. (2000) ' "Race" and ethnicity in public law proceedings', *Family Law* 30: 740.

Brophy, J., Jhotti-Johal, J. and Owen, C. (2003) *Significant Harm*, London: Department for Constitutional Affairs.

Brown, J. and Day Sclater, S. (1999) 'Divorce: A Psychodynamic Perspective', in S. Day Sclater and C. Piper (eds) *Undercurrents of Divorce*, Aldershot: Ashgate.

Browne, D. and Moloney, A. (2002) ' "Contact irregular": A qualitative analysis of the impact of visiting patterns of natural parents on foster placements', *Child and Family Social Work* 7: 35.

Brunner, K. (2001) 'Nullity in unconsummated marriages', *Family Law* 31: 837.

Bryan, M. (1995) 'Parents as fiduciaries: A special place in equity', *International Journal of Children's Rights* 3: 227.

Bryan, P. (1992) 'Killing us softly: divorce mediation and the politics of power', *Buffalo Law Review* 40: 441.

Bryson, C., Budd, T., Lewis, J. and Elam, G. (2000) *Women's Attitudes to Combining Paid Work and Family Life*, London: Social and Community Planning Research.

Buchanan, A. and Hunt, J. (2003) 'Disputed Contact Cases in the Courts', in A. Bainham, B. Lindley, M. Richards. and L. Trinder (eds) *Children and Their Families*, Oxford: Hart.

Buchanan, A., Hunt, J., Bretherton, H. and Bream, V. (2001) *Families in Conflict*, Cambridge: Polity Press.

Buck, N. and Ermisch, J. (1995) 'Cohabiting in Britain', *Changing Britain* 3: 3.

Bullock, R., Malos, E. and Millham, S. (1993) *Going Home: The Return of Children Separated from Their Families*, Aldershot: Dartmouth.

Burch, C. (1983) 'Of work, family wealth and equality', *Family Law Quarterly* 17: 99.

Burch, C. (2002) 'Parental Alienation Syndrome and alienated children – getting it wrong in child custody cases', *Child and Family Law Quarterly* 14: 381.

Burggraf, S. (1997) *The Feminine Economy*, New York: Addison-Wesley.

Burns, F. (2002) 'The elderly and undue influence inter vivos', *Legal Studies* 23: 251.

Burrows, D. (2000) 'Mediation – The king's new clothes?', *Family Law* 30: 363.

Butler, A., Noaks, L., Douglas, G. et al. (1993) 'The Children Act and the issue of delay', *Family Law* 23: 412.

Butler, I. and Williamson, H. (1994) *Children Speak: Children Trauma and Social Work*, Harlow: Longman.

Butler, I., Scanlon, L., Robinson, M. (2002) 'Children's involvement in their parents' divorce: implications for practice', *Children and Society* 16: 89.

Butler, I., Scanlan, L., Robinson, M. et al. (2003) *Divorcing Children*, London: Jessica Kingsley

Butler-Sloss, E. (1989) *Report of the Inquiry into Child Abuse in Cleveland 1987*, London: HMSO.

Butler-Sloss, E. (2001) 'Contact and domestic violence', *Family Law* 31: 355.

Butler-Sloss, E. (2003) *Are we failing the family? Human rights, children and the meaning of family in the 21st Century*, London: LCD.

Buzawa, E. and Buzawa, C. (2003) *Domestic Violence: The Criminal Justice Response*, 3rd ed., London: Sage.

CICB (1990) *26th Report*, London: HMSO.

Caldwell, J. (2001) 'Child welfare defences in child abduction cases – some recent developments', *Child and Family Law Quarterly* 13: 121.

Callahan, D. (1997) *Setting Limits*, Georgetown, DC: Georgetown University Press.

Campbell, T. (1992) 'The Rights of the Minor', in P. Alston, S. Parker and J. Seymour (eds) *Children, Rights and the Law*, Oxford: Clarendon Press.

Cantwell, B. and Scott, S. (1995) 'Children's wishes, children's burdens', *Journal of Social Welfare and Family Law* 17: 337.

Carbone, J. (1996) 'Feminism, Gender and the Consequences of Divorce', in M. Freeman (ed.) *Divorce: Where Next?*, Aldershot: Dartmouth.

Carbone, J. (2000) *From Partners to Parents*, New York: Columbia University Press.

Carbone, J. and Brinig, M. (1988) 'The reliance interest of marriage', *Tulane Law Review* 62: 855.

Carbone, J. and Brinig, M. (1991) 'Rethinking marriage', *Tulane Law Review* 65: 953.

Carling, A. (2002) 'Family Policy, Social Theory and the State' in A. Carling, S. Duncan and R. Edwards (eds) *Analysing Families*, London: Routledge.

Carter, H. (2003) 'Marriage falls out of fashion ... or does it?', *The Guardian*: 21 March 2003.

Carter, R. (2001) 'Pilots, pre-pilots and protocols', *Family Law* 31: 867.

Casey, D. and Gibberd, A. (2001) 'Adoption and Contact', *Family Law* 31: 39.

Cavadino, M. (2002) 'New Mental Health Law for old – safety-plus equals human rights minus', *Child and Family Law Quarterly* 14: 175.

Chambers, D. (1984) 'Rethinking the substantive rules for custody in divorce', *Michigan Law Review* 83: 477.

Chau, P-L. and Herring, J. (2002) 'Defining, assigning and designing sex', *International Journal of Law, Policy and the Family* 16: 327.

Child Poverty Action Group (1994) *Putting the Treasury First*, London: CPAG.

Child Poverty Action Group (2000) *Paying for Care Handbook*, London: CPAG.

Child Poverty Action Group (2001) *Poverty: The Facts*, London: CPAG.

Child Poverty Action Group (2002) *Child Poverty Figures 'Very Disappointing'*, London: CPAG.

Child Support Agency (2000) *Annual Report*, London: CSA.

Children Act Advisory Committee (1993) *Annual Report*, London: HMSO.

Children Act Sub-Committee (2002a) *Making Contact Work*, London: LCD.

Children Act Sub-Committee (2002b) *Parental Contact with Children where there is Violence*, London: LCD.

Children's Law Centre (1999) *At What Age Can I...?*, London: Children's Law Centre.

Choudhry, S. (2001) 'The Child Protection Conference and the Human Rights Act 1998', *Family Law* 31: 531.

Choudhry, S. (2003) 'The Adoption and Children Act 2002, the welfare principle and the Human Rights Act 1998 – a missed opportunity', *Child and Family Law Quarterly* 15: 119.

Clarke, A. (1993) 'Insolvent Families', in H. Rajak (ed.) *Insolvency Law, Theory and Practice*, London: Sweet & Maxwell.

Clarke, K., Craig, G. and Glendinning, C. (1996a) *Small Change: The Impact of the Child Support Act on Lone Mothers and Children*, London: Family Policy Studies Centre.

Clarke, K., Craig, G. and Glendinning, C. (1996b) *Children's Views on Child Support*, London: The Children's Society.

Clive, E. (1994) 'Marriage: An Unnecessary Legal Concept?', in J. Eekelaar and M. Maclean (eds) *A Reader on Family Law*, Oxford: OUP.

Coady, C. (1992) 'Theory, Rights and Children', in P. Alston, S. Parker and J. Seymour (eds) *Children, Rights and the Law*, Oxford: Clarendon Press.

Cobley, C. (1998) 'Financial compensation for victims of child abuse', *Journal of Social Welfare and Family Law* 20: 721.

Cobley, C. and Lowe, N. (1994) 'Ousting Abusers – public or private solution?', *Law Quarterly Review* 110: 38.

Cohen, L. (2002) 'Marriage: the Long-Term Contract', in A. Dnes and R. Rowthorn (eds) *The Law and Economics of Marriage and Divorce*, Cambridge: CUP.

Collier, R. (1995) *Masculinity, Law and the Family*, London: Routledge.

Collier, R. (1999) 'The dashing of a "liberal dream"? – The information meeting, the "new family" and the limits of law', *Child and Family Law Quarterly* 11: 257.

Collier, R. (2000) 'Anxious Parenthood, the Vulnerable Child and the "Good Father"', in J. Bridgeman and D. Monk (eds) *Feminist Perspectives on Child Law*, London: Cavendish.

Collier, R. (2003) 'In Search of the "Good Father"', in J. Dewar and S. Parker (eds) *Family Law Processes, Practices, Pressures*, Oxford: Hart.

Commission on Children and Violence (1995) *Children and Violence*, London: Gulbenkian Foundation.

Conway, H. (2002) 'Homelessness and the family', *Family Law* 32: 911.

Cook, R. (2002) 'Villain, Hero or Masked Stranger: Ambivalence in Transaction with Human Gametes', in A. Bainham, D. Day Sclater and M. Richards (eds) *Body Lore and Laws*, Oxford: Hart.

Cook, R., Day Sclater, S. and Kaganas, F. (2003) *Surrogate Motherhood*, Oxford: Hart.

Cooke, E. (1994) 'Making the break squeaky clean', *Family Law* 24: 268.

Cooke, E. (1998) 'Children and real property – trusts, interests and considerations', *Family Law* 28: 349.

Cooper, D. (2001) ' "Like Counting Stars"? Restructuring Equality and the Socio-Legal Space of Same-Sex Marriage', in R. Wintemute and M. Andenæs (eds) *Legal Recognition of Same-Sex Partnerships*, Oxford: Hart.

Corbett, M. (1999) *Independent on Sunday*: 14 March 1999, 16.

Corker, M. and Davis, J. (2000) 'Disabled Children: Invisible under the Law', in J. Cooper and S. Vernon (eds) *Disability and the Law*, London: Jessica Kingsley.

Craig, P. (1999) 'What Next for the Children?', in P. Morgan (ed.) *Adoption: The Continuing Debate*, London: IEA.

Creighton, P. (1990) 'Spouse competence and compellability', *Criminal Law Review* 34.

Cretney, A. and Davis, G. (1996) 'Prosecuting "domestic" assault', *Criminal Law Review* 162.

Cretney, S. (1972) 'The Nullity of Marriage Act 1971', *Modern Law Review* 35: 57.

Cretney, S. (1995) 'Reform of intestacy: the best we can do?', *Law Quarterly Review* 111: 77.

Cretney, S. (1996a) 'Right and wrong in the Court of Appeal', *Law Quarterly Review* 112: 33.

Cretney, S. (1996b) 'Divorce Reform in England: Humbug and Hypocrisy or a Smooth Transition?', in M. Freeman (ed.) *Divorce: Where Next?*, Aldershot: Dartmouth.

Cretney, S. (1996c) 'From Status to Contract?', in F. Rose (ed.) *Consensus Ad Idem*, London: Sweet & Maxwell.

Cretney, S. (1998) *Law, Law Reform and the Family*, Oxford: OUP.

Cretney, S. (1999) 'Contract not apt in divorce deal', *Law Quarterly Review* 115: 356.

Cretney, S. (2000) 'Trusting the judges: Money after divorce', *Current Legal Problems* 53: 286.

Cretney, S. (2001) 'Black and white', *Family Law* 31: 3.

Cretney, S. (2002) 'Marriage, divorce and the courts', *Family Law* 32: 900.

Cretney, S. (2003a) *Family Law in the Twentieth Century – a History*, Oxford: OUP.

Cretney, S. (2003b) 'Private ordering and divorce – how far can we go?', *Family Law* 33: 399.

Cretney, S., Masson, J. and Bailey-Harris, R. (2002) *Principles of Family Law*, London: Sweet & Maxwell.

Cromack, V. and Parry, M. (1996) 'Welfare of the child – conflicting interest and conflicting principles: *Re T and E (Proceedings: Conflicting Interests)*', *Child and Family Law Quarterly* 8: 72.

Cronin, H. and Curry, O. (2000) 'The Evolved Family', in H. Wilkinson (ed.) *Family Business*, London: Demos.

Crook, H. (2001) 'Troxel et vir v Granville – grandparent visitation rights in the United States Supreme Court', *Child and Family Law Quarterly Review* 13: 101.

Crown Prosecution Service Inspectorate (1998) *The Inspectorate's Report on Cases Involving Domestic Violence*, London: Crown Prosecution Service Inspectorate.

Da Costa, E. (1998) 'Back door occupation orders', *Family Law* 28: 167.

Da Costa, E. (2002) 'Pensions – The Maskell approach', *Family Law* 33: 345.

Dalrymple, J. and Payne, M. (1994) *'They Listened to Him'*, Manchester: Manchester Metropolitan University.

Daniels, N. (1988) *Am I My Brother's Keeper?*, Oxford: OUP.

Davey, M. (1997) 'Creditors and the Family Home', in C. Bridge (ed.) *Family Law Towards the Millennium: Essays for P M Bromley*, London: Butterworths.

Davis, G. (1988) *Partisans and Mediators*, Oxford: Clarendon Press.

Davis, G. (2000) *Monitoring Publicly Funded Family Mediation*, London: Legal Services Commission.

Davis, G. (2001) 'Informing policy in the light of research findings', *Family Law* 31: 822.

Davis, G., Bevan, G, and Pearce, J. (2001) 'Family mediation – where do we go from here?', *Family Law* 31: 265.

Davis, G., Clisby, S., Cumming, Z. et al. (2003) *Monitoring Publicly Funded Family Mediation* London: Legal Services Commission.

Davis, G., Cretney, S., Barder, K. and Collins, J. (1991) 'The Relationship Between Public and Private Financial Support Following Divorce in England and Wales', in M. Maclean and L. Weitzman (eds) *The Economic Consequences of Divorce: The International Perspective*, Oxford: Clarendon Press.

Davis, G., Cretney, S. and Collins, J. (1994) *Simple Quarrels*, Oxford: Clarendon Press.

Davis, G., Finch, S., and Barnham, L. (2003) 'Family solicitors and the LSC', *Family Law* 33: 327.

Davis, G., Finch, S., and Fitzgerald, R. (2001) 'Mediation and Legal Services – The Client Speaks', *Family Law* 31: 110.

Davis, G. and Murch, M. (1988) *Grounds for Divorce*, Oxford: Clarendon Press.

Davis, G., Pearce, J., Bird, R. et al. (2000) 'Ancillary Relief Outcomes', *Child and Family Law Quarterly* 12: 1243.

Davis, G. and Roberts, S. (1989) 'Mediation and the battle of the sexes', *Family Law* 19: 305.

Davis, G. and Wikeley, N. (2002) 'National survey of Child Support Agency clients – the relationship dimension', *Family Law* 32: 523.

Davis, G., Wikeley, N. and Young, R. (1998) *Child Support in Action*, Oxford: Hart.

Daycare Trust, The (2003) *Towards Universal Child Care*, London: Daycare Trust.

Day Sclater, S. (1999) *Divorce: A Psychological Study*, Aldershot: Dartmouth.

Day Sclater, S. (2000) *Families*, London: Hodder & Stoughton.

Day Sclater, S. and Kaganas, F. (2003) 'Contact: Mothers, Welfare Rights', in A. Bainham, B. Lindley, M. Richards and L. Trinder (eds) *Children and Their Families*, Oxford: Hart.

Day Sclater, S. and Piper, C. (1999) *Undercurrents of Divorce*, Aldershot: Ashgate.

Day Sclater, S. and Yates, C. (1999) 'The Psycho-Politics of Post-Divorce Parenting', in A. Bainham, S. Day Sclater and M. Richards (eds) *What is a Parent?*, Oxford: Hart.

De Cruz, P. (1999) 'Adolescent autonomy, detention for medical treatment and *Re C*', *Modern Law Review* 62: 595.

Deas, S. (1998) 'Family lawyers sidestep the CSA', *Family Law* 28: 48.

Deech, R. (1980) 'The Case Against Legal Recognition of Cohabitation', in J. Eekelaar and S. Katz (eds) *Marriage and Cohabitation in Contemporary Societies*, Toronto: Butterworths.

Deech, R. (1990) 'Divorce law and empirical studies', *Law Quarterly Review* 106: 229.

Deech, R. (1993) 'The Rights of Fathers: Social and Biological Concepts of Parenthood', in J. Eekelaar and P. Sarcevic (eds) *Parenthood in Modern Society*, London: Martinus Nijhoff.

Deech, R. (1994) 'Comment: Not just marriage breakdown', *Family Law* 24: 121.

Deech, R. (1996) 'Property and Money Matters', in M. Freeman (ed.) *Divorce: Where Next?*, Aldershot: Dartmouth.

Deech, R. (1998) 'Family law and genetics', *Modern Law Review* 61: 697.

Deech, R. (2000) 'The Legal Regulation of Infertility Treatment in Britain', in S. Katz, J. Eekelaar and M. Maclean (eds) *Cross Currents*, Oxford: OUP.

Delphy, C. and Leonard, D. (1992) *Familiar Policy: A New Analysis of Marriage in Contemporary Western Societies*, Cambridge: Polity Press.

Dench, G. and Ogg, J. (2002) *Grandparenting in Britain*, London: Institute of Community Studies.

Department for Education and Employment (2000a) *Sex and Relationship Education Guidance 0116/2000*, London: DfEE.

Department for Education and Employment (2000b) *Bullying: Don't Suffer in Silence*, London: DfEE.

Department for Education and Employment (2002) *Pupil Absence in Schools in England*, London: DfEE.

Department for Education and Skills (2003) *Every Child Matters*, London: The Stationery Office.

Department of Health (1991a) *The Children Act 1989: Guidance and Regulations, Vol. 3, Family Placements*, London: HMSO.

Department of Health (1991b) *The Children Act 1989: Guidance and Regulations, Vol. 1, Court Orders*, London: HMSO.

Department of Health (1991c) *The Right to Complain – Practice Guidance on Complaints Procedures in Social Service Departments*, London: HMSO.

Department of Health (1991d) *The Children Act 1989: Guidance and Regulations, Vol. 2, Family Support, Day Care and Educational Provision for Young People*, London: HMSO.

Department of Health (1995a) *Child Protection: Messages from Research*, London: HMSO.

Department of Health (1995b) *The Challenge of Partnership in Child Protection: Practice Guide*, London: HMSO.

Department of Health (1996) *Focus on Teenagers: Research into Practice*, London: HMSO.

Department of Health (1998a) *Surrogacy Review*, London: The Stationery Office.

Department of Health (1998b) *Working Together to Safeguard Children*, London: The Stationery Office.

Department of Health (1999a) *Adoption Now*, Chichester: John Wiley & Sons.

Department of Health (1999b) *Me Survive Out There?*, London: DoH.

Department of Health (1999c) *The Government's Objectives of Children's Social Services*, London: DoH.

Department of Health (2000a) *Protecting Children, Supporting Parents*, London: The Stationery Office.

Department of Health (2000b) *The NHS Plan. The Government's Response to the Royal Commission on Long Term Care*, London: The Stationery Office.

Department of Health (2000c) *The Government's Objectives for Children's Social Services*, London: DoH.

Department of Health (2000d) *Building a Better Britain*, London: DoH.

Department of Health (2000e) *Adoption: a New Approach*, London: DoH.

Department of Health (2001a) *Analysis of Responses*, London: DoH.

Department of Health (2001b) *Local Authority Circular LAC (2001) 33*, London: DoH.

Department of Health (2002a) *Homelessness: Code of Guidance for Local Authorities*, London: DoH.

Department of Health (2002b) *Monitoring Adoption Disruption Rates Post Adoption Order*, London: DoH.

Department of Health (2002c) *Safeguarding Children*, London: DoH.

Department of Health (2002d) *Adoption and Permanence Taskforce Second Report*, London: DoH.

Department of Health (2002e) *Friends and Family Care (Kinship Care)* London: DoH.

Department of Health (2002f) *Adopter Preparation and Assessment and the Operation of Adoption Panels*, London: DoH.

Department of Health (2002g) *Caring About Carers*, London: DoH.

Department of Health (2003a) *Children Looked After in England 2001/2002*, London: DoH.

Department of Health (2003b) *Adoption Support Services Guidance*, London: DoH.

Department of Health (2003c) *Adoption and Permanence Project*, London: DoH.

Department of Health (2003d) *Draft Practice Guidance to Support the National Adoption Standards For England*, London: DoH.

Department of Health (2003e) *Adoption National Minimum Standards*, London: DoH.

Department of Health (2003f) *Adoption Register for England and Wales*, London: DoH.

Department of Health, Home Office, Lord Chancellor's Department and the Welsh Office (1993) *Adoption: the Future*, London: HMSO.

Department of Health and Welsh Office (1992) *Review of Adoption Law*, London: HMSO.

Department of Social Security (1990) *Children Come First*, London: HMSO.

Department of Social Security (1997) *Child Support Agency – Quarterly Summary of Statistics*, London: DSS.

Department of Social Security (1998) *Children First: A New Approach to Child Support*, London: DSS.

Department of Social Security (2000) *Children's Rights and Parents' Responsibilities*, London: DSS.

Department of Social Security (2001) *Child Support Agency Quarterly Summary of Statistics* London: DSS.

Department for Work and Pensions (2002) *Measuring Child Poverty*, London: DWP.

Devlin, P. (1965) *The Enforcement of Morals*, Oxford: OUP.

Dewar, J. (1992) *Law and the Family*, London: Butterworths.

Dewar, J. (1995) 'The courts and local authority autonomy', *Child and Family Law Quarterly* 7: 15.

Dewar, J. (1997) 'Reducing discretion in family law', *Australian Journal of Family Law* 11: 309.

Dewar, J. (1998) 'The normal chaos of family law', *Modern Law Review* 61: 467.

Dewar, J. (2000a) 'Family law and its discontents', *International Journal of Law, Policy and the Family* 14: 59.

Dewar, J. (2000b) 'Making Family Law New?', in M. McLean (ed.) *Making Law for Families*, Oxford: Hart.

Dewar, J and Parker, S. (2000) 'English Family Law since World War II: From Status to Chaos', in S. Katz, J. Eekelaar, and M. Maclean (eds) *Cross Currents*, Oxford: OUP.

Diamantides, M. (1999) 'Meditations on Parental Love', in M. King (ed.) *Moral Agendas for Children's Welfare*, London: Routledge.

Dickens, B. (1981) 'The modern function and limits of parental rights', *Law Quarterly Review* 97: 462.

Dickens, J. (1993) 'Assessment and the control of social work: Analysis of reasons for the non-use of the Child Assessment Order', *Journal of Social Welfare and Family Law* 15: 88.

Dickenson, D. and Jones, D. (1995) 'True wishes: The philosophy and developmental psychology of children's informed consent', *Philosophy, Psychiatry and Psychology* 2: 287.

Diduck, A. (1995) 'The unmodified family: the Child Support Act and the construction of legal subjects', *Journal of Law and Society* 22: 527.

Diduck, A. (2000) 'Solicitors and Legal Subjects', in J. Bridgeman and D. Monk (eds) *Feminist Perspectives on Child Law*, London: Cavendish.

Diduck, A. (2001) 'A family by any other name ... or Starbucks comes to England', *Journal of Law and Society* 28: 290.

Diduck, A. (2003) *Law's Families*, London: LexisNexis Butterworths.

Diduck, A. and Kaganas, F. (1999) *Family Law, Gender and the State*, Oxford: Hart.

Diduck, A. and Orton, H. (1994) 'Equality and support for spouses', *Modern Law Review* 57: 681.

Dingwall, R. (1988) 'Empowerment or Enforcement? Some Questions about Power and Control in Divorce Mediation', in J. Eekelaar and R. Dingwall (eds) *Divorce, Mediation and the Legal Process*, Oxford: Clarendon Press.

Dingwall, R. and Greatbatch, D. (1994) 'The Virtues of Formality', in J. Eekelaar and M. Maclean (eds) *A Reader on Family Law*, Oxford: OUP.

Dingwall, R. and Greatbatch, D. (2001) 'Family mediators – What are they doing?', *Family Law* 31: 379.

Dixon, M. (1998) 'Combating the mortgagee's right to possession: New hope for the mortgagor in chains?', *Legal Studies* 18: 279.

Dnes, A. (1998) 'The division of marital assets following divorce', *Journal of Law and Society* 25: 336.

Dnes, A. (2002) 'Cohabitation and Marriage', in A. Dnes and R. Rowthorn (eds) *The Law and Economics of Marriage and Divorce*, Cambridge: CUP.

Dobash, R. and Dobash, R. (1992) *Women, Violence and Social Change*, London: Routledge.

Dobash, R. and Dobash, R. (2000) 'Violence Against Women in the Family', in S. Katz, J. Eekelaar and M. Maclean (eds) *Cross Currents*, Oxford: OUP.

Doggett, M. (1992) *Marriage, Wife-Beating and the Law in Victorian England*, London: Weidenfeld & Nicholson.

Dolgin, J. (1998) *Defining the Family*, New York: New York University Press.

Donzelot, J. (1980) *The Policing of Families*, London: Hutchinson.

Doron, I. (2002) 'Elder guardianship kaleidoscope – a comparative perspective', *International Journal of Law, Policy and the Family* 16: 368.

Douglas, A. and Philpot, T. (2003) *Adoption – Changing Families, Changing Times*, London: Routledge.

Douglas, G. (1988) 'The family and the state under the European Convention on Human Rights', *International Journal of Law and the Family* 2: 76.

Douglas, G. (1991) *Law, Fertility and Reproduction*, London: Sweet & Maxwell.

Douglas, G. (1992) 'The retreat from *Gillick*,' *Modern Law Review* 55: 569.

Douglas, G. (1993) 'Assisted reproduction and the welfare of children', *Current Legal Problems* 46: 53.

Douglas, G. (1994a) 'In whose best interests?', *Law Quarterly Review* 110: 379.

Douglas, G. (1994b) 'The intention to be a parent and the making of mothers', *Modern Law Review* 57: 636.

Douglas, G. (2000a) 'Supporting Families', in A. Bainham (ed.) *The International Survey of Family Law*, 2000 Edition, Bristol: Jordans.

Douglas G. (2000b) 'Marriage, Cohabitation and Parenthood – from Contract to Status', in S. Katz, J. Eekelaar and M. Maclean, (eds) *Cross Currents*, Oxford: OUP.

Douglas, G. (2001) *An Introduction to Family Law*, Oxford: OUP.

Douglas, G. and Ferguson, N. (2003) 'The role of grandparents in divorced families', *International Journal of Law, Policy and the Family* 17: 41.

Douglas, G. and Lowe, N. (1992) 'Becoming a parent in English Law', *Law Quarterly Review* 108: 414.

Douglas, G. and Murch, M. (2002a) *The Role of Grandparents in Divorced Families*, Cardiff: Family Studies Research Centre, University of Wales.

Douglas, G. and Murch, M. (2002b) 'Taking account of children's needs at divorce', *Child and Family Law Quarterly*, 14: 57.

Douglas, G., Murch, M., Robinson, M. et al. (2001) 'Children's perspectives and experience of the divorce process', *Family Law* 31: 373.

Douglas, G., Murch, M., Scanlan, L. and Perry, A. (2000) 'Safeguarding children's welfare in non-contentious divorce: towards a new conception of the legal process', *Modern Law Review* 63: 177.

Douglas, G. and Philpot, T. (eds) (2003) *Adoption: Changing Families: Changing Times*, London: Routledge.

Downey, D. and Powell, B. (1993) 'Do children in single-parent households fare better living with same-sex parents?', *Journal of Marriage and the Family* 55: 55.

Drew, L. and Smith, P. (1999) 'The impact of parental separation on grandparent–grandchild relationships', *International Journal of Ageing and Human Development* 48: 191.

Duckworth, P. (2002a) 'We are family, Really?', *Family Law* 32: 91.

Duckworth, P (2002b) 'What is family? A personal view', *Family Law* 32: 367.

Duckworth, P. and Hodson, D. (2001) 'White v White – bringing section 25 back to the people', *Family Law* 31: 24.

Dunn, G. (1999) 'A Passion for Sameness? Sexuality and Gender Accountability', in E. Silva and C. Smart (eds) *The New Family*, London: Sage.

Dunn, J. (2003) 'Contact and Children's Perspectives on Parental Relationships', in A. Bainham, B. Lindley, M. Richards and L. Trinder (eds) *Children and Their Families*, Oxford: Hart.

Dunn, J. and Deater-Deckard, K. (2001) *Children's Views of Their Changing Family*, London: YPS.

Dupuis, L. (1995) 'The impact of culture, society and history on the legal process: an analysis of the legal status of same-sex relationships in the United States and Denmark', *International Journal of Law and the Family* 9: 86.

Dyer, C. (2000) 'Government drops plan for no-fault divorce', *The Guardian*: 2 September 2000.

Eaton, M. (1994) 'Abuse By Any Other Name: Feminism, Difference and Intralesbian Violence', in N. Fine and R. Myktiuk (eds) *The Public Nature of Private Violence. The Discovery of Domestic Abuse*, New York: Routledge.

Eden, R. (2000) *Traditional Family Life 'is in Decline'*, London: Family Policy Studies Centre.

Edwards, R., Gillies, V. and McCarthy, J. (1999) 'Biological parents and social families: legal discourses and everyday understandings of the position of step-parents', *International Journal of Law, Policy and the Family* 13: 78.

Edwards, S. (1996) *Sex and Gender in the Legal Process*, London: Blackstone.

Edwards, S. (2000) *Briefing Note: Reducing Domestic Violence*, London: Home Office.

Edwards, S., Gould, C. and Halpern, A. (1990) 'The continuing saga of maintaining the family after divorce', *Family Law* 20: 31.

Edwards, S. and Halpern, A. (1991) 'Protection for the victims of domestic violence: Time for radical revision', *Journal of Social Welfare and Family Law* 13: 94.

Edwards, S. and Halpern, A. (1992) 'Parental responsibility: An instrument of social policy', *Family Law* 22: 113.

Eekelaar, J. (1984) *Family Law and Social Policy*, London: Weidenfeld & Nicholson.

Eekelaar, J. (1986) 'The eclipse of parental rights', *Law Quarterly Review* 102: 4.

Eekelaar, J. (1987a) 'Second thoughts on illegitimacy reform', *Family Law* 17: 261.

Eekelaar, J. (1987b) 'Family Law and Social Control', in J. Eekelaar and J. Bell (eds) *Oxford Essays in Jurisprudence*, Oxford: OUP.

Eekelaar, J. (1988) 'Equality and the purpose of maintenance', *Journal of Law and Society* 15: 188.

Eekelaar, J. (1989) 'What is "critical" family law?', *Law Quarterly Review* 105: 244.

Eekelaar, J. (1990) 'Investigation under the Children Act 1989', *Family Law* 20: 486.

Eekelaar, J. (1991a) *Regulating Divorce*, Oxford: Clarendon Press.

Eekelaar, J. (1991b) 'Are parents morally obliged to care for their children?', *Oxford Journal of Legal Studies* 11: 51.

Eekelaar, J. (1991c) 'Parental responsibility: State of nature or nature of the state?', *Journal of Social Welfare and Family Law* 13: 37.

Eekelaar, J. (1991d) 'The wardship jurisdiction, children's welfare and parents' rights', *Law Quarterly Review* 107: 386.

Eekelaar, J. (1992) 'The importance of thinking that children have rights', *International Journal of Law, Policy and the Family* 6: 221.

Eekelaar, J. (1994a) 'The interests of the child and the child's wishes: the role of dynamic self-determinism', *International Journal of Law and the Family* 8: 42.

Eekelaar, J. (1994b) 'Non-Marital Property', in P. Birks (ed.) *Frontiers of Liability*, Oxford: OUP.

Eekelaar, J. (1994c) 'A jurisdiction in search of a mission: Family proceedings in England and Wales', *Modern Law Review* 57: 839.

Eekelaar, J. (1994d) 'Families and Children', in C. McCrudden and D. Chambers (eds) *Individual Rights and the Law in Britain*, Oxford: OUP.

Eekelaar, J. (1995) 'Family justice: Ideal or illusion? Family law and communitarian values', *Current Legal Problems* 48: 191.

Eekelaar, J. (1996) 'Parental responsibility – a new legal status?', *Law Quarterly Review* 112: 233.

Eekelaar, J. (1998) 'Do parents have a duty to consult?', *Law Quarterly Review* 114: 337.

Eekelaar, J. (1999) 'Family law: Keeping us "on message"', *Child and Family Law Quarterly* 11: 387.

Eekelaar J. (2000a) 'Family Law and the Responsible Citizen', in M. MacLean (ed.) *Making Law for Families*, Oxford: Hart.

Eekelaar, J. (2000b) 'Post-Divorce Financial Obligations', in S. Katz, J. Eekelaar and M. MacLean (eds) *Cross Currents*, Oxford: OUP.

Eekelaar, J. (2000c) 'The End of an Era?' in S. Katz, J. Eekelaar and M. MacLean (eds) *Cross Currents*, Oxford: OUP.

Eekelaar, J. (2001a) 'Asset distribution on divorce – the durational element', *Law Quarterly Review* 117: 24.

Eekelaar, J. (2001b) 'Back to basics and forward into the unknown', *Family Law* 31: 30.

Eekelaar, J. (2001c) 'Family law: The communitarian message', *Oxford Journal of Legal Studies* 21: 181.

Eekelaar, J. (2001d) 'Rethinking parental responsibility', *Family Law* 31: 426.

Eekelaar, J. (2002a) 'Beyond the welfare principle', *Child and Family Law Quarterly* 14: 237.

Eekelaar, J. (2002b) 'Contact – over the limit', *Family Law* 32: 271.

Eekelaar J. (2003a) 'Contact and the Adoption Reform', in A. Bainham, B. Lindley, M. Richards and L. Trinder (eds) *Children and Their Families*, Oxford: Hart.

Eekelaar, J. (2003b) 'Corporal punishment, parents' religion, and children's rights', *Law Quarterly Review* 119: 370.

Eekelaar, J. (2003c) 'Asset distribution on divorce – time and property', *Family Law* 33: 838.

Eekelaar, J. and Clive, E. (1977) *Custody After Divorce*, Oxford: OUP.

Eekelaar, J. and Dingwall, R. (1990) *The Reform of Child Care Law*, London: Routledge.

Eekelaar, J. and Maclean, M. (1986) *Maintenance After Divorce*, Oxford: Clarendon Press.

Eekelaar, J. and Maclean, M. (1990) 'Divorce law and empirical studies – a reply', *Law Quarterly Review* 106: 621.

Eekelaar, J. and Maclean, M. (1997) *The Parental Obligation*, Oxford: Hart.

Eekelaar, J., Maclean M., and Beinart, S. (2000) *Family Lawyers*, Oxford: Hart.

Eekelaar, J. and Nhlapo, T. (1998) 'Introduction', in J. Eekelaar and T. Nhlapo (eds) *The Changing Family: International Perspectives on the Family and Family Law*, Oxford: Hart.

Ellis, S. and Franklin, A. (1995) 'Children's Rights Officers: Righting Wrongs and Promoting Rights', in B. Franklin (ed.) *The Handbook of Children's Rights*, London: Routledge.

Ellison, L. (2002) 'Prosecuting domestic violence without victim participation', *Modern Law Review* 65: 834.

Ellison, R. (1998) 'Strengths and Weaknesses of the Law on Pension Splitting in the United Kingdom', in R. Bailey-Harris (ed.) *Dividing the Assets on Family Breakdown*, Bristol: Jordans.

Ellman, I. (2000a) 'Divorce in the United States', in S. Katz, J. Eekelaar and M. Maclean (eds) *Cross Currents*, Oxford: OUP.

Ellman, I. (2000b) 'The Misguided Movement to Revive Fault Divorce', in M. King White (ed.) *Marriage in America*, Lanham, Md.: Rowman & Littlefield.

Elster, J. (1987) 'Solomonic judgments: Against the best interests of the child', *University of Chicago Law Review* 54: 1.

Emery, R. (1994) *Renegotiating Family Relationships: Divorce, Child Custody and Mediation*, Guildford: Guildford Press.

Emery, R. (1998) *Marriage, Divorce and Children's Adjustment*, Thousand Oaks, Calif.: Sage.

Emery, R. (1999) 'Post Divorce Family Life for Children', in R. Thompson and P. Amato (eds) *The Postdivorce Family*, Thousand Oaks, Calif.: Sage.

English, J. (1979) 'What Do Grown Children Owe Their Parents?', in O. O'Neill and W. Ruddick (eds) *Having Children*, New York: OUP.

Ermisch, J. and Francesconi, M. (1998) *Cohabitation in Great Britain*, Colchester: University of Essex.

Ermisch, J. and Francesconi, M. (2001) *The Effects of Parents' Employment on Children's Lives*, London and York: Family Policy Studies Centre and Joseph Rowntree Foundation.

Ermisch, J. and Francesconi, M. (2003) *Working Parents: The Impact on Kids*, London: Institute for Social and Economic Research.

Evans State, J. (1992) 'Mandatory planning for divorce', *Vanderbilt Law Review* 45: 397.

Families Need Fathers (2003) *Safety and Justice: Reply to Consultation*, London: FNF.

Family Policy Studies Centre (1995) *Families in Britain*, London: Family Policy Studies Centre.

Family Policy Studies Centre (1997) *A Guide to Family Issues*, London: Family Policy Studies Centre.

Farmer, E. and Pollock, S. (1998) *Substitute Care for Sexually Abused and Abusing Children*, Chichester: John Wiley & Sons.

Fehlberg, B. (1997) *Sexually Transmitted Debt*, Oxford: OUP.

Feldman, D. (1997) 'The developing scope of article 8 of the European Convention on Human Rights', *European Human Rights Law Review* 1: 265.

Ferguson, P. (1993) 'Constructive trusts – a note of caution', *Law Quarterly Review* 109: 114.

Ferri, E. and Smith, K. (1998) *Step-Parenting in the 1990s*, London: Family Policy Studies Centre.

Field, M. (1989) 'Is Surrogacy Exploitative?', in S. Maclean (ed.) *Legal Issues in Human Reproduction*, Aldershot: Gower.

Finch, J. (1989) *Family Obligations and Social Change*, Cambridge: Polity Press.

Finch, J. (1994) 'The Proper Thing to Do', in J. Eekelaar and M. Maclean (eds) *A Reader on Family Law*, Oxford: OUP.

Fineman, M. (1988) 'Dominant discourse, professional language and legal change in child custody decision-making', *Harvard Law Review* 101: 727.

Fineman, M. (1995) *The Neutered Mother, the Sexual Family and Other Twentieth-Century Traditions*, London, New York: Routledge.

Fineman, M. (2002) 'Domestic violence, custody and visitation', *Family Law Quarterly* 36: 211.

Finlay, A. (2002) 'Delay and the Challenges of the Children Act', in Thorpe LJ and C. Cowton (eds) *Delight and Dole*, Bristol: Jordans.

Finlay, H. (1976) 'Farewell to affinity and the celebration of kinship', *University of Tasmania Law Review* 5: 10.

Finnis, J. (1994) 'Law, morality and "sexual orientation" ', *Notre Dame University Law Review* 69: 1.

Fionda, J. (2001) 'Legal Concepts of Childhood: An Introduction', in J. Fionda (ed.) *Legal Concepts of Childhood*, Hart: Oxford.

Fish, D. (1997) 'Child abuse – a legal practitioners' guide', *Family Law* 27: 665.

Fisher, L. (2002) 'The unexpected impact of *White* – taking "Equality" too far', *Family Law* 32: 108.

Flood-Page, C., Campbell, S., Harrington, V. and Miller, J. (2000) *Youth Crime*, London: Home Office.

Foley, E. (1996) 'Social justice and child poverty', *Ohio State Law Journal* 57: 485.

Ford, M. and Morgan, D. (2003) 'Addressing a misconception', *Child and Family Law Quarterly* 15: 199.

Forder, C. (1987) 'Might and right in matrimonial property law: A comparative study of England and the German Democratic Republic', *International Journal of Law and the Family* 1: 47.

Fortin, J. (1988) 'Can you ward a foetus?', *Modern Law Review* 51: 768.

Fortin, J. (1993) 'Significant harm revisited', *Journal of Child Law* 5: 151.

Fortin, J. (1996) '*Re F*: The gooseberry bush approach', *Modern Law Review* 57: 296.

Fortin, J. (1998a) *Children's Rights and the Developing Law*, London: Butterworths.

Fortin, J. (1998b) '*Re C (Medical Treatment)* – A baby's right to die', *Child and Family Law Quarterly* 10: 411.

Fortin, J. (1999a) 'The HRA's impact on litigation involving children and their families', *Children and Family Law Quarterly* 11: 237.

Fortin, J. (1999b) '*Re D (Care: Natural Parent Presumption)*: Is Blood Really Thicker than Water?', *Child and Family Law Quarterly* 11: 435.

Fortin, J. (2002) 'Children's Rights and the Impact of Two International Conventions: The UNCRC and the ECHR', in Thorpe LJ and C. Cowton (eds) *Delight and Dole*, Bristol: Jordans.

Fortin, J. (2003a) 'Children's Rights and the Use of Force "In Their Own Best Interests" ', in J. Dewar and S. Parker (eds) *Family Law Processes, Practices, Pressures*, Oxford: Hart.

Fortin, J. (2003b) *Children's Rights and the Developing Law*, London: LexisNexis Butterworths.

Foster, H. and Freund, D. (1972) 'A Bill of Rights for children', *Family Law Quarterly* 6: 343.

Fox, L. (2003) 'Reforming family property – comparisons, compromises and common dimensions', *Child and Family Law Quarterly* 15: 1.

Fox, M. and McHale, J. (1997) 'In whose best interests?', *Modern Law Review* 58: 700.

Fox Harding, L. (1996) *Family, State and Social Policy*, Basingstoke: Macmillan.

Francis, N. and Philipps, S. (2003) 'New light on prenuptial agreements', *Family Law* 33: 164.

Frantz, C. and Dagan, H. (2002) *On Marital Property: Research Paper 45*, New York University Law School.

Fredman, S. (2002) *Discrimination Law*, Oxford: OUP.

Fredman, S. (2003) 'The Age of Equality', in S. Fredman and S. Spencer (eds) *Age as an Equality Issue*, Oxford: Hart.

Freedman, E. (2002) 'International terrorism and the grave physical risk defence of the Hague Convention on International Child Abduction', *International Family Law* 6: 60.

Freeman, M. (1983) *The Rights and Wrongs of Children*, London: Frances Pinter.

Freeman, M. (1984) 'Legal Ideologies: Patriarchal Precedents and Domestic Violence', in M. Freeman (ed.) *The State, The Law and the Family*, London: Sweet and Maxwell.

Freeman, M. (1985) 'Towards a critical theory of family law', *Current Legal Problems* 40: 179.

Freeman, M. (1992a) *Children, Their Families and the Law*, Basingstoke: Macmillan.

Freeman, M. (1992b) 'Taking children's rights more seriously', *International Journal of Law, Policy and the Family* 6: 52.

Freeman, M. (1996) 'The new birth right?', *International Journal of Children's Rights* 4: 273.

Freeman, M. (1997a) *The Moral Status of Children*, London: Martinus Nijhoff.

Freeman, M. (1997b) 'The best interests of the child? Is the best interests of the child in the best interests of children?', *International Journal of Law, Policy and the Family* 11: 360.

Freeman, M. (2000a) 'Disputing Children', in S. Katz, J. Eekelaar and M. MacLean (eds) *Cross Currents*, Oxford: OUP.

Freeman, M. (2000b) 'Feminism and Child Law', in J. Bridgeman and D. Monk (eds) *Feminist Perspectives on Child Law*, London: Cavendish.

Freeman, M. (2000c) 'The end of the century of the child?', *Current Legal Problems* 55: 505.

Freeman, M. (2000d) 'Images of Child Welfare in Child Abduction Appeals', in J. Murphy (ed.) *Ethnic Minorities, Their Families and the Law*, Oxford: Hart.

Freeman, M. (2002a) *Human Rights*, Cambridge: Polity Press.

Freeman, M. (2002b) 'Human rights, children's rights and judgment', *International Journal of Children's Rights* 10: 345.

Freeman, M. (2003) 'The State, Race and the Family in England Today', in J. Dewar and S. Parker (eds) *Family Law Processes, Practices, Pressures*, Oxford: Hart.

Freeman, Marilyn (2003) *Outcomes for Children Returned after Hague Orders*, London: Reunite.

Fretwell Wilson, R. (2002) 'Fractured families, fragile children – the sexual vulnerability of girls in the aftermath of divorce', *Child and Family Law Quarterly* 14: 1.

Fried, C. (1978) *Right and Wrong*, Cambridge, Mass.: Harvard University Press.

Funder, K. (1988) 'Women, Work and Post-Divorce Economic Self-Sufficiency: An Australian Perspective', in M. Meulders-Klein and J. Eekelaar (eds) *Family, State and Individual Economic Security*, Brussels: Kluwer.

Funder, K. (1994) 'Australia: A Proposal for Reform', in J. Eekelaar and M. Maclean (eds) *A Reader on Family Law*, Oxford: OUP.

Furniss, T. (1991) *The Multi-Professional Handbook of Child Sexual Abuse, Integrated Management Therapy and Legal Intervention*, London: Routledge.

Future Foundation (1999) *Report for First Direct*, London: Future Foundation.

Galston, W. (1991) *Liberal Purposes*, Cambridge: CUP.

Gardner, J. (1998) 'On the ground of her sex(uality)', *Oxford Journal of Legal Studies* 18: 167.

Gardner, S. (1993) 'Rethinking family property', *Law Quarterly Review* 109: 263.

Gardner, S. (1998) 'Stalking', *Law Quarterly Review* 114: 33.

Gardner, S. (1999) 'Wives' guarantees of their husbands' debts', *Law Quarterly Review* 115: 1.

Garrison, M. (1998) 'Autonomy or community? An evaluation of two models of parental obligation', *California Law Review* 86: 41.

Gavison, R. (1994) 'Feminism and the Public–Private Distinction', in J. Eekelaar and M. Maclean (eds) *A Reader on Family Law*, Oxford: OUP.

Geekie, C. (2002) 'Protecting children's rights After *Re S* – the pressing need for reform', *Family Law* 32: 534.

Geldof, B. (2003) 'The Real Love that Dare Not Speak its Name', in A. Bainham, B. Lindley, M. Richards and L. Trinder (eds) *Children and Their Families*, Oxford: Hart.

Gelsthorpe, L. (1999) 'Youth Crime and Parental Responsibility', in A. Bainham, S. Day Sclater and M. Richards (eds) *What is a Parent?*, Oxford: Hart.

George, R. (1999) *In Defense of Natural Law*, New York: OUP.

Gerlis, S. (1996) 'Undertakings reconsidered', *Family Law* 26: 233.

Gershoff, E. (2002) 'Corporal punishment by parents and associated child behaviours and experiences: a meta-analytic and theoretical review', *Psychological Bulletin* 128: 539.

Ghandhi, P. and MacNamee, E. (1991) 'The family in UK law and the International Covenant on Civil and Political Rights', *International Journal of Law and the Family* 5: 104.

Ghate, D. and Hazel, N. (2002) *Parenting in Poor Environments*, London: Jessica Kingsley.

Gibbons, J., Gallagher, B., Bell, C. and Gordon, D. (1995) *Development after Physical Abuse in Early Childhood*, London: HMSO.

Gibson, C. (1994) *Dissolving Wedlock*, London: Routledge.

Gibson, C. (2000) 'Changing Family Patterns in England and Wales over the Last Fifty Years', in S. Katz, J. Eekelaar and M. MacLean (eds) *Cross Currents*, Oxford: OUP.

Gibson, D. (1998) *Aged Care*, Cambridge: CUP.

Giddens, A. (1989) *Sociology*, Cambridge: Polity Press.

Giddens, A. (1992) *The Transformation of Intimacy*, Cambridge: Polity Press.

Giddens, A. (1998) *The Third Way: The Renewal of Social Democracy*, Cambridge: Polity Press.

Giesen, D. (1997) 'Artificial Reproduction Revisited: Status Problems and Welfare of the Child – A Comparative View', in C. Bridge (ed.) *Family Law Towards the Millennium: Essays for P M Bromley*, London: Sweet & Maxwell.

Gill, D. and Jackson, B. (1983) *Adoption and Race*, London: Batsford.

Gillespie, G. (1996) 'Child support – the hand that rocks the cradle', *Family Law* 26: 162.

Gillespie, G. (2002) 'Child support – when the bough breaks', *Family Law* 32: 529.

Gilligan, C. (1982) *In a Different Voice*, London: Harvard University Press.

Gilmore, S. (2003) 'Parental responsibility and the unmarried father – a new dimension to the debate', *Child and Family Law Quarterly* 15: 21.

Gingerbread (2002) *A Quality Life for Lone Parents and Their Children*, London: Gingerbread.

Ginn, J. and Price, D. (2002) 'Do divorced women catch up in pension building?', *Child and Family Law Quarterly* 14: 157.

Gittens, D. (1993) *The Family in Question: Changing Households and Familiar Ideologies*, Basingstoke: Macmillan.

Glancy, M. (1997) 'Legal Aid Towards the Millennium – A Family Lawyer's View', in C. Bridge (ed.) *Family Law Towards the Millennium: Essays for P M Bromley*, London: Butterworths.

Glazebrook, P. (1984) 'Human beginnings', *Cambridge Law Journal* 43: 209.

Glendinning, G., Clarke, K. and Craig, G. (1996) 'Implementing the Child Support Act', *Journal of Social Welfare and Family Law* 18: 273.

Glendon, M. (1989) *The Transformation of Family Law*, Chicago: University of Chicago Press.

Glennon, L. (2000) '*Fitzpatrick v Sterling Housing Association Ltd* – An Endorsement of the Functional Family', *International Journal of Law, Policy and the Family* 14: 226.

Golding, J. (1999) 'Intimate partner violence as a risk factor for mental disorders', *Journal of Family Violence* 14: 99.

Goldstein, J., Solnit, A., Goldstein, S. and Freud, A. (1996) *The Best Interests of the Child*, New York: Free Press.

Golombok, S. (1999) 'Lesbian Mother Families', in A. Bainham, S. Day Sclater and M. Richards (eds) *What is a Parent?*, Oxford: Hart.

Golombok, S. and Cook, R. (1993) *A Survey of Semen Donations*, London: HFEA.

Golombok, S., Cook, R., Bish, A. and Murray, C. (1995) 'Families created by the new reproductive technologies: Quality of parenting and social and emotional development of the children', *Child Development* 64: 285.

Golombok, S., MacCallum, F., Goodman, E. and Rutter, M. (2002) 'Families with children conceived by donor insemination', *Child Development* 73: 952.

Goodin, R. and Gibson, D. (1997) 'Rights, young and old', *Oxford Journal of Legal Studies* 17: 185.

Goody, E. (1982) *Parenthood and Social Responsibility*, Cambridge: CUP.

Goody, J. (1983) *The Development of the Family and Marriage in Europe*, Cambridge: CUP.

Gordon, D., Adelman, L., Ashworth, K. et al. (2000) *Poverty and Social Exclusion in Britain*, York: Joseph Rowntree Foundation.

Gottlieb, C., Lalos, O. and Lindblad, E. (2000) 'Disclosure of donor insemination to the child: The impact of Swedish legislation', *Human Reproduction* 15: 2052.

Gosden, N. (2003) 'Children's surnames – how satisfactory is the current law?', *Family Law* 33: 186.

Government Actuary's Department (1994) *Ninth Survey of Occupational Pension Schemes*, London: HMSO.

Gower, L. (1948) '*Baxter v Baxter* in perspective', *Modern Law Review* 11: 176.

Grace, S. (1995) *Home Office Research Study 139: Policing Domestic Violence in the 1990s*, London: HMSO.

Graham, P., Turk, J. and Verhulst, F. (1999) *Child Psychiatry*, Oxford: OUP.

Gray, K. (1977) *Reallocation of Property on Divorce*, Abingdon: Professional Books.

Greenwich London Borough Council (1987) *A Child in Mind: The Report of the Commission of Inquiry into the Circumstances Surrounding the Death of Kimberly Carlile*, London: Greenwich LBC.

Gregory, J. and Foster, K. (1990) *The Consequences of Divorce*, London: Lord Chancellor's Department.

Gregson, N. and Lowe, M. (1994) *Servicing the Middle Classes*, London: Routledge.

Grenfell, L. (2003) 'Making sex: Law's narratives of sex, gender and identity', *Legal Studies* 23: 66.

Griffiths, A., Roberts, G. and Williams, S. (1993) 'Elder Abuse and the Law', in P. Decalmer and F. Glendenning (eds) *The Mistreatment of Elderly People*, London: Sage.

Grillo, T. (1991) 'The mediation alternative: Process dangers for women', *Yale Law Journal* 100: 1545.

Grimley Evans, J. (2003) 'Age Discrimination: Implications of the Ageing Process', in S. Fredman and S. Spencer (eds) *Age as an Equality Issue*, Oxford: Hart.

Grotevant, H. and McRoy, R. (1998) *Openness in Adoption: Exploring Family Connections*, New York: Sage.

Grundy, E. (1992) 'The Household Dimension in Migration Research', in T. Champion and T. Fielding (eds) *Migration Processes and Patterns, Volume 1: Research Progress and Prospects*, London: Belhaven.

Guardian, The (2000) 'Finding the breathing space for quality time', 18 March 2000.

Gunn, M. and Smith, J. (1985) 'Arthur's case and the right of life of a Down's Syndrome child', *Criminal Law Review* 705.

Gupta, A. (2002) 'Adoption, Race and Identity', in A. Douglas and T. Philpot (eds) *Adoption – Changing Families, Changing Times*, London: Routledge.

Hakim, C. (2003) *Models of the Family of Modern Societies*, Aldershot: Ashgate.

Haldane, J. (1994) 'Children, Families, Autonomy and the State', in D. Morgan and G. Douglas (eds) *Constituting Families*, Stuttgart: Franz Steiner Verlag.

Hale LJ (1999) 'The view from Court 45', *Child and Family Law Quarterly* 11: 377.

Hale LJ (2000) 'The Family Law Act 1996 – Dead Duck or Golden Goose?', in S. Cretney (ed.) *Family Law – Essays for the New Millennium*, Bristol: Jordans.

Hall HHJ (2000) 'Care Planning', *Family Law* 30: 343.

Hamilton, C. (1995) *Family, Law and Religion*, London: Sweet & Maxwell.

Hamilton, C. and Watt, D. (1996) 'A discriminatory education – collective worship in schools', *Child and Family Law Quarterly* 8: 28.

Hanlon, J. (2001) 'Till divorce do our pension plan part', *Child and Family Law Quarterly* 31: 51.

Hanmer, J. (2000) 'Domestic Violence and Gender Relations', in J. Hanmer and C. Itzin (eds) *Home Truths About Domestic Violence*, London: Routledge.

Hanna, C. (1996) 'No right to choose: Mandated victim participation in domestic violence prosecutions', *Harvard Law Review* 109: 1850.

Hantrais, L. and Letablier, M.-T. (1996) *Families and Family Policy in Europe*, London: Longman.

Harding, L. (1987) 'The debate on surrogacy legislation – time for change', *Journal of Social Welfare Law* 9: 37.

Harris, J. (1998) 'Rights and Reproductive Choice', in J. Harris and S. Holm (eds) *The Future of Human Reproduction*, Oxford: Clarendon Press.

Harris, J. (1999) 'Clones, Genes and Human Rights', in J. Burley (ed.) *The Genetic Revolution and Human Rights*, Oxford: OUP.

Harris, N. (1996) 'Unmarried cohabiting couples and social security in Great Britain', *Journal of Social Welfare and Family Law* 18: 123.

Harris-Short, S. (2002) 'Putting the child at the heart of adoption?', *Child and Family Law Quarterly* 14: 325.

Harrison, M. (2002) 'Australia's Family Law Act', *International Journal of Law, Policy and the Family* 16: 1.

Hart, S., Cohen, C., Erickson, M. and Flekkoy, M. (2001) *Children's Rights in Education*, London: Jessica Kingsley.

Harvard Law Review (1991) 'Looking for a family resemblance: The limits of the functional approach to the legal definition of family', *Harvard Law Review* 104:1640.

Harwin, J. and Owen, M. (2003) 'The Implementation of Care Plans and its Relationship to Children's Welfare', *Child and Family Law Quarterly* 15: 71.

Haskey, J. (1983) 'Marital status before marriage and age at marriage: Their influence on the chance of divorce', *Population Trends* 32: 4.

Haskey, J. (1984) 'Social class and socio-economic differentials in divorce in England and Wales', *Population Trends* 38: 419.

Haskey, J. (1992) 'Pre-marital cohabitation and problems of subsequent divorce', *Population Trends* 69: 70.

Haskey, J. (1994) 'Stepfamilies and stepchildren in Great Britain', *Population Trends* 76: 17.

Haskey, J. (1996a) 'Divorce statistics', *Family Law* 26: 301.

Haskey, J. (1996b) 'Population review: (6) Families and households in Great Britain', *Population Trends* 85: 7.

Haskey, J. (1997) 'Children who experience divorce in their family', *Population Trends* 87: 5.

Haskey, J. (2001) 'Demographic aspects of cohabitation in Great Britain', *International Journal of Law, Policy and Family* 15: 51.

Hasson, E. (2003) 'Divorce law and the Family Law Act 1996', *International Journal of Law, Policy and the Family* 17: 338.

Hawthorne, J., Jessop, J., Pryor, J. and Richards, M. (2003) *Supporting Children Through Family Change,* York: Joseph Rowntree Foundation.

Hayes, M. (1994) ' "Cohabitation clauses" in financial provision and property adjustment orders – law, policy and justice', *Law Quarterly Review* 110: 124.

Hayes, M. (1996) 'The proper role of courts in child care cases', *Child and Family Law Quarterly* 8: 201.

Hayes, M. (1997) 'Reconciling protection of children with justice for parents in cases of alleged child abuse', *Legal Studies* 17: 1.

Hayes, M. (1998) 'Child protection – from principles and policies to practice', *Child and Family Law Quarterly* 10: 119.

Hayes, M. and Williams, C. (1999) *Family Law Principles, Policy and Practice,* London: Butterworths.

Hayes, P. (1995) 'The ideological attack on transracial adoption in the USA and Britain', *International Journal of Law and the Family* 9: 1.

Hayton, D. (1993) 'Constructive trusts of homes – a bold approach', *Law Quarterly Review* 109: 485.

Health Advisory Service (2000) *Not Because They Are Old,* London: HAS.

Healy, J. and Yarrow, S. (1997) *Family Matters,* Bristol: Policy Press.

Help the Aged (2002) *Caring in Later Life: Reviewing the Role of Older Carers,* London: Help the Aged.

Hencke, D. (2002) 'Child Support Agency writes off £2bn', Guardian Unlimited, http://www.guardian.co.uk, 7 August 2002.

Hendricson, C. (2003) *Government and Parenting,* York: Joseph Rowntree Foundation.

Henley, T. and Hershman, D. (2001) 'The representation of children in private law', *Family Law* 31: 540.

Hepple, B. (2003) 'Age Discrimination in Employment: Implementing the Framework Directive 2000/78/EC' in S. Fredman and S. Spencer (eds) *Age as an Equality Issue,* Oxford: Hart.

Herman, J. (1981) *Father–Daughter Incest,* Cambridge, Mass.: Harvard University Press.

Herring, J. (1997) 'Children's abortion rights', *Medical Law Review* 5: 257.

Herring, J. (1998a) ' "Name this child" ', *Cambridge Law Journal* 57: 266.

Herring, J. (1998b) 'Book review', *Cambridge Law Journal* 57: 213.

Herring, J. (1998c) 'The criminalisation of harassment', *Cambridge Law Journal* 57: 10.

Herring, J. (1999a) 'The Welfare Principle and the Rights of Parents', in A. Bainham, S. Day Sclater and M. Richards (eds) *What is a Parent?*, Oxford: Hart.

Herring, J. (1999b) 'The Human Rights Act and the welfare principle in family law – conflicting or complementary?', *Child and Family Law Quarterly* 11: 223.

Herring, J. (2000a) 'The Caesarean Section Cases and the Supremacy of Autonomy', in M. Freeman and A. Lewis (eds) *Law and Medicine*, Oxford: OUP.

Herring, J. (2000b) 'The suffering children of blameless parents', *Law Quarterly Review* 116: 550.

Herring, J. (2001) 'Parents and Children', in J. Herring (ed.) *Family Law: Issues, Debates, Policy*, Cullompton: Willan.

Herring, J. (2002a) 'Gay rights come quietly', *Law Quarterly Review* 118: 31.

Herring, J. (2002b) 'The human rights of children in care', *Law Quarterly Review* 118: 534.

Herring, J. (2002c) *Criminal Law*, Basingstoke: Palgrave.

Herring, J. (2003a) 'Connecting Contact', in A. Bainham, B. Lindley, M. Richards and L. Trinder (eds) *Children and Their Families*, Oxford: Hart.

Herring, J. (2003b) 'Children's Rights for Grown-Ups', in S. Fredman and S. Spencer (eds) *Age as an Equality Issue*, Oxford: Hart.

Herring, J. and Chau, P-L. (2001) 'Assigning sex and intersexuals', *Family Law* 31: 762.

Hester, M. (2002) 'One step forward and three steps back? Children, Abuse and Parental Contact in Denmark', *Child and Family Law Quarterly* 14: 267.

Hester, M. and Pearson, C. (1997) 'Domestic violence and children – the practice of Family Court Welfare Officers', *Child and Family Law Quarterly* 9: 281.

Hester, M., Pearson, C. and Harwin, N. (2000) *Making an Impact: Children and Domestic Violence*, London: Jessica Kingsley.

Hester, M., Pearson, C. and Radford, L. (1997) *Domestic Violence*, Bristol: Policy Press.

Hester, M. and Radford, L. (1996) *Domestic Violence and Child Contact Arrangements in England and Wales*, Bristol: Policy Press.

Hetherington, M. and Kelly, J. (2002) *For Better or For Worse*, New York: WW Norton & Co.

Hibbs, M. (1997) 'Surrogacy legislation – time for change', *Family Law* 27: 564.

Hibbs, M., Barton, C. and Beswick, J. (2001) 'Why marry? Perceptions of the affianced', *Family Law* 31: 197.

Hill, J. (1991) 'What does it mean to be a "parent"? The claims of biology as the basis for parental rights', *New York University Law Review* 66: 353.

Hill, M. (1995) 'Family Policies in Western Europe', in M. Hill, R. Hawthorne-Kirk and D. Part (eds) *Supporting Families*, Edinburgh: HMSO.

Hill, M. and Tisdall, K. (1997) *Children and Society*, London: Longman.

Hills, M. (1997) *The Future of Welfare*, York: Joseph Rowntree.

Hobbs, C., Hanks, H. and Wynne, J. (1999) *Child Abuse and Neglect* London: Churchill Livingston.

Hobbs, T. (2002a) 'Parental Alienation Syndrome and the UK Family Courts, Part 1', *Family Law* 32: 182.

Hobbs, T. (2002b) 'Parental Alienation Syndrome and the UK Family Courts – The dilemma', *Family Law* 32: 568.

Hochschild, A. (1996) 'The Emotional Geography of Work and Family Life', in L. Morris and S. Lyons (eds) *Gender Relations in Public and Private: Changing Research Perspectives*, London: Macmillan.

Hodson, D., Green, M. and De Souza, N. (2003) '*Lambert* – shutting Pandora's box', *Family Law* 33: 37.

Hoggett, B. (1994) 'Joint parenting systems: The English experiment', *Journal of Child Law* 6: 8.

Hoggett, B., Pearl, D., Cooke, E. and Bates, P. (2003) *Family Law and Society*, London: Butterworths.

Hollingsworth, K. and Douglas, K. (2002) 'Creating a children's champion for Wales? The Care Standards Act 2000 (Part V) and the Children's Commissioner for Wales Act 2001', *Modern Law Review* 65: 58.

Holt, J. (1975) *Escape from Childhood*, London: Dutton.

Home Office (1989) *Report of the Advisory Group on Video Evidence*, London: HMSO.

Home Office (1990a) *Crime, Justice and Protecting the Public*, London: HMSO.

Home Office (1990b) *Children Come First*, London: HMSO.

Home Office (1993) *Local Authority Circular (93) (13)*, London: HMSO.

Home Office (1997) *Bringing Rights Home: The Human Rights Bill*, London: HMSO.

Home Office (1998) *Supporting Families. A Consultation Document*, London: The Stationery Office.

Home Office (1999) *Living Without Fear*, London: Home Office.

Home Office (2000a) *Report of the Interdepartmental Working Group on Transsexual People*, London: Home Office.

Home Office (2000b) *Setting the Boundaries*, London: Home Office.

Home Office (2000c) *A Choice By Right*, London: Home Office.

Home Office (2000d) *Domestic Violence: Break the Chain*, London: Home Office.

Home Office (2000e) *Government Policy Around Domestic Violence*, London: Home Office.

Home Office (2000f) *Reforming the Mental Health Act*, London: Home Office.

Home Office (2002) *Civil Registration: Vital Change; Birth, Marriage and Death Registration in the 21st Century*, London: The Stationery Office.

Home Office (2003a) *Safety and Justice*, London: Home Office.

Home Office (2003b) *Government Policy Around Domestic Violence*, London: Home Office.

Homer, S. (1994) 'Against marriage', *Harvard Civil-Rights Civil-Liberties Law Review* 29: 505.

Horowitz, M. and Harper, M. (1995) 'A code for cohabitees – fairness at last?', *Family Law* 25: 693.

House of Commons Joint Committee on Human Rights (2003) *Eighth Report*, London: The Stationery Office.

Howard, M. and Wilmott, M. (2000) 'The Networked Family', in H. Wilkinson (ed.) *Family Business*, London: Demos.

Howe, D., Brandon, M., Hinings, J. and Schofield, G. (1999) *Attachment Theory, Child Maltreatment and Family Support*, Basingstoke: Palgrave.

Howe, D. and Feast, J. (2000) *Adoption, Search and Reunion*, London: The Children's Society.

Hoyle, C. (1998) *Negotiating Domestic Violence: Police, Criminal Justice and Victims*, Oxford: Clarendon Press.

Hoyle, C. and Sanders, A. (2000) 'Police responses to domestic violence: from victim choice to victim empowerment', *British Journal of Criminology* 40: 14.

Humphreys, C. (2001) 'The Impact of Domestic Violence on Children', in P. Foley, J. Roche and S. Tucker (eds) *Children in Society*, Buckingham: Open University Press.

Humphreys, C. and Harrison, C. (2003) 'Squaring the circle – contact and domestic violence', *Family Law* 33: 419.

Humphreys, C., Hester, M., Hague, G. et al. (2002) *From Good Intentions to Good Practice: Mapping Services Working with Families where there is Domestic Violence*, York: Policy Press.

Hunt, J. (1998) 'A moving target – care proceedings as a dynamic process', *Child and Family Law Quarterly* 10: 281.

Hunt, J. (2001) 'Kinship Care, Child Protection and the Courts', in B. Broad (ed.) *Kinship Care*, Lyme Regis: Russell House.

Hunt, J. and Lawson, J. (1999) *Cross the Boundaries*, London: National Council for Family Proceedings.

Hunt, J. and Macleod, A. (1998) *The Best-Laid Plans*, London: The Stationery Office.

Illman, J. (1996) *The Guardian*: 9 July 1996.

Ince, S. (1993) 'Inside the Surrogacy Industry', in M. Minow (ed.) *Family Matters*, New York: New York Press.

Independent on Sunday (2000) 'Gay couple's twins to get right to stay', *Independent on Sunday*: 9 January.

Ingleby, R. (1992) *Solicitors and Divorce*, Oxford: OUP.

Ingleby, R. (1997) 'The De-Bromleyfication of Australian Family Law', in C. Bridge (ed.) *Family Law Towards the Millennium: Essays for PM Bromley*, London: Butterworths.

Inglis, A. (2001a) 'We are family (after all) – inclusive family law', *Family Law* 31: 895.

Inglis, A. (2001b) 'We are family? The uneasy engagement between gay men, lesbians and family law', *Family Law* 31: 830.

Inglis, A. (2003) ' "The ordinary run of fighting"? Domestic violence and financial provision', *Family Law* 33: 181.

Irvine, S. (1999) 'Resourcing the Family', in C. Smart and E. Silva (eds) *The New Family*, London: Sage.

Ivaldi, G. (1998) *Children Adopted from Care*, London: BAAF.

Jackson, E. (2002) 'Conception and the irrelevance of the welfare principle', *Modern Law Review* 65: 176.

Jackson, E., Wasoff, F., Maclean, M. and Dobash, R. (1993) 'Financial support on divorce: The right mixture of rules and discretion?', *International Journal of Law, Policy and the Family* 7: 230.

Jagger, G. and Wright, C. (1999) *Changing Family Values*, London: Routledge.

James, A. (1992) 'An open or shut case? Law as an autopoietic system', *Journal of Law and Society* 19: 271.

James, A. (2002) 'The Family Law Act 1996', in A. Carling, S. Duncan and R. Edwards, *Analysing Families*, London: Routledge.

James, A. (2003) 'The Social, Legal and Welfare Organisation of Contact', in A. Bainham, B. Lindley, M. Richards and L. Trinder (eds) *Children and Their Families*, Oxford: Hart.

James, A., Jenks, C. and Prout, A. (1998) *Theorizing Childhood*, Cambridge: Polity Press.

James, A. and Sturgeon-Adams, L. (1999) *Helping Families after Divorce: Assistance by Order*, London: Policy Press.

Jeffreys, M. (1995) 'Geriatric Medicine: Some Ethical Issues Associated with its Development', in A. Grubb (ed.) *Choices and Decisions in Health Care*, Chichester: John Wiley & Sons.

Jeffs, T. (2002) 'Children's Educational Rights in a New Era?', in B. Franklin (ed.) *The New Handbook of Children's Rights*, London: Routledge.

Jeffs, T. and Smith, M. (1996) *Informal Education*, London: Eduction Now.

Jenks, C. (1996) *Childhood*, London: Routledge.

Jenks, C. (2002) 'Schooling, Education and Children's Rights', in B. Franklin (ed.) *The New Handbook of Children's Rights*, London: Routledge.

Jepson, R. (2000) *The Effectiveness of Interventions to Change Health-related Behaviours*, London Medical Research Council.

John, M. (2003) *Children's Rights and Power*, London: Jessica Kingsley.

Johnson, A., Mercer, C., Erens, B. et al. (2001) 'Sexual Behaviour in Britain', *The Lancet* 358: 1835.

Johnson, M. (1999) 'A Biomedical Perspective on Parenthood', in A. Bainham, S. Day Sclater and M. Richards (eds) *What is a Parent?*, Oxford: Hart.

Jolly, S. (1994) 'Cutting the ties – the termination of contact in care', *Journal of Social Welfare and Family Law* 16: 299.

Jolly, S. (1995) 'Implacable hostility, contact and the limits of law', *Child and Family Law Quarterly*, 7: 228.

Jones, G., Lockton, D., Wood, R. and Kashefi, E. (1995) 'Divorce applications: An empirical study of one court', *Journal of Social Welfare and Family Law* 17: 67.

Jones, E. and Parkinson, P. (1995) 'Child sexual abuse, access and the wishes of children', *International Journal of Law, Policy and the Family* 9: 54.

Jones-Purdy, C. (1998) 'The Law and Morality of Support in the Wider Family', in J. Eekelaar and T. Nhlapo (eds) *The Changing Family: International Perspectives on the Family and Family Law*, Oxford: Hart.

Joshi, H. and Davies, H. (1992) 'Pensions, divorce and wives' double burden', *International Journal of Law and the Family* 6: 289.

Kaganas, F. (1995) 'Partnership Under the Children Act 1989 – An Overview', in F. Kaganas, M. King and C. Piper (eds) *Legislating for Harmony*, London: Jessica Kingsley.

Kaganas, F. (1996) 'Responsible or feckless fathers?', *Child and Family Law Quarterly* 8: 165.

Kaganas, F. (2002) 'Domestic Homicide, Gender and the Expert', in A. Bainham, S. Day Sclater and M. Richards (eds) *Body Lore and Laws* Oxford: Hart.

Kaganas, F. and Day Sclater, S. (2000) 'Contact and domestic violence – the winds of change?', *Family Law* 30: 630.

Kaganas, F. and Piper, C. (1994) 'Domestic violence and divorce mediation', *Journal of Social Welfare and Family Law* 16: 265.

Kaganas, F. and Piper, C. (1999) 'Divorce and Domestic Violence', in S. Day Sclater and C. Piper (eds) *Undercurrents of Divorce*, Aldershot: Ashgate.

Kaganas, F. and Piper, C. (2001) 'Grandparents and contact: "rights v welfare" revisited', *International Journal of Law, Policy and the Family* 15: 250.

Kaganas, F. and Piper, C. (2002) 'Shared parenting – a 70% solution?', *Child and Family Law Quarterly* 14: 365.

Kaltenborn, K. and Lemrap, R. (1998) 'The welfare of the child in custody disputes after parental separation or divorce', *International Journal of Law, Policy and the Family* 12: 74.

Kandel, R. (1994) 'Which came first: The mother or the egg? A kinship solution to gestational survey', *Rutgers Law Review* 47: 165.

Kapp, M. (1982) 'The father's lack of rights and responsibilities in the abortion decision', *Ohio University Law Review* 9: 370.

Karsten I. (2001) 'The Draft EC Regulation on Parental Responsibility', *Family Law* 31: 885.

Katz, I. (1999) 'Is Male Circumcision Morally Defensible?', in M. King (ed.) *Moral Agenda for Children's Welfare*, London: Routledge.

Katz, S. (1999) 'Emerging models for alternatives to marriage', *Family Law Quarterly* 33: 663.

Kaufmann, F-X., Kuijsten, A., Schulze, H-J. and Strohmeier, K. (eds) (2002) *Family Life and Family Policies in Europe*, Oxford: OUP.

Kavanagh, L. (2000) 'Independent yet committed', *The Times*: 29 February 2000.

Kaye, M. (1996) 'Domestic violence, residence and contact', *Child and Family Law Quarterly* 8: 285.

Kaye, M. (1999) 'The Hague Convention and the flight from domestic violence: how women and children are being returned by coach and four', *International Journal of Law, Policy and the Family* 13: 191.

Keating, H. (1996) 'Shifting standards in the House of Lords – *Re H and Others (Minors) (Sexual Abuse: Standard of Proof)*', *Child and Family Law Quarterly* 8: 157.

Keenan, C. (1997) 'Finding that a child is at risk from sexual abuse', *Modern Law Review* 60: 857.

Keenan, C., Davis, G., Hoyano, L. and Maitland, L. (1999) 'Interviewing allegedly abused children with a view to criminal prosecution', *Criminal Law Review* 863.

Kelly, J. (2003) 'Legal and Education Interventions for Families in Residence and Contact Disputes', in J. Dewar and S. Parker (eds) *Family Law Processes, Practices, Pressures*, Oxford: Hart.

Kennedy, J. (2000) *Family Law in 2000 and Beyond*, London: LCD.

Kennedy, R. (2001) 'Assessment and treatment in family law – a valid distinction?', *Family Law* 31: 676.

Kerridge, R. (2000) 'Wills made in suspicious circumstances: the problem of the vulnerable testator', *Cambridge Law Journal* 59: 310.

Khaliq, U. (1996) 'Transsexuality and English law: latest developments', *Journal of Social Welfare and Family Law* 18: 365.

Khaliq, U. and Young, J. (2001) 'Cultural diversity, human rights and inconsistency in the English courts', *Legal Studies* 21: 192.

Kidner, R. (1988) 'The duty of occupiers towards children', *Northern Ireland Law Quarterly* 139: 150.

Kiernan, K. (1999) 'Cohabitation in Western Europe', *Population Trends* 96: 25.

Kiernan, K. (2001) 'The rise of cohabitation and childbearing outside marriage in Western Europe', *International Journal of Law, Policy and the Family* 15: 1.

Kiernan, K. and Estaugh, V. (1993) *Cohabitation, Extramarital Childbearing and Social Policy*, London: Family Policy Studies Centre.

Kiernan, K. and Mueller, G. (1999) 'Who Divorces?', in S. McRae (ed.) *Changing Britain*, Oxford: OUP.

Kiernan, K. and Wicks, M. (1990) *Family Change and Future Policy*, York: Rowntree and Family Policy Studies Centre.

Kilkelly, U. (2000) *The Child and the European Convention on Human Rights*, Aldershot: Ashgate.

King, A. (1988) 'No legal aid without mediation – section 29', *Family Law* 18: 331.

King, M. (1974) 'Maternal love, fact or myth', *Family Law* 4: 61.

King, M. (1987) 'Playing the symbols – custody and the Law Commission', *Family Law* 17: 186.

King, M. (1997) *A Better World for Children*, London: Routledge.

King, M. (1999) 'Introduction', in M. King (ed.) *Moral Agendas for Children's Welfare*, London: Routledge.

King, M. (2000) 'Future uncertainty as a challenge to law's programmes: the dilemma of parental disputes', *Modern Law Review* 63: 523.

King, M. and Piper, C. (1995) *How the Law Thinks About Children*, Aldershot: Arena.

Korgaonkar, G. and Tribe, D. (1995) *Law for Nurses*, London: Cavendish Press.

Krause, H. (1994) 'Child Support Reassessed: Limits of Private Responsibility and the Public Interest', in J. Eekelaar and M. Maclean (eds) *A Reader on Family Law*, Oxford: OUP.

Krause, H. and Meyers, M. (2002) 'What family for the 21st century?' *American Journal of Comparative Law* 50: 101.

Kruk, E. (1998) 'Power imbalance and spouse abuse in domestic disputes', *International Journal of Law, Policy and the Family* 12: 1.

Lacey, L. (1992) 'Mandatory marriage "for the sake of the children": A feminist reply to Elizabeth Scott', *Tulane Law Review* 66: 1434.

Lacey, N. (1993) 'Theory into Practice? Pornography and the Public/Private Dichotomy', in A. Bottomley and J. Conaghan (eds) *Feminist Theory and Legal Strategy*, Oxford: Blackwell.

Lafollete, H. (1980) 'Licensing parents', *Philosophy and Public Affairs* 9: 182.

Laming, Lord (2003) *The Victoria Climbié Report*, London: The Stationery Office.

Lane, M. (2003) 'Ethical Issues in Surrogacy Arrangements', in R. Cook, S. Day Sclater and F. Kaganas (eds) *Surrogate Motherhood*, Oxford: Hart.

Langan, J. (1997) 'In the best interests of elderly people? The role of local authorities in handling and safeguarding the personal finances of elderly people with dementia', *Journal of Social Welfare and Family Law* 19: 463.

Lansdown, G. (2001) 'Children's Welfare and Children's Rights', in P. Foley, J. Roche and S. Tucker (eds) *Children in Society*, Buckingham: Open University Press.

Lasch, C. (1977) *Haven in a Heartless World*, New York: Basic Books.

Laslett, P. (1979) *The World We Have Lost*, Methuen: London.

Laurance, J. (2000) 'The booming baby market', *Independent on Sunday*, 7 April 2000.

Lavery, R. (1996) 'The Child Assessment Order – a re-assessment', *Child and Family Law Quarterly* 8: 41.

Law Commission Consultation Paper 173 (2003) *Partial Defences to Murder*, London: The Stationery Office.

Law Commission Report 6 (1966) *Reform of the Grounds of Divorce – The Field of Choice*, London: HMSO.

Law Commission Report 26 (1969) *Breach of Promise of Marriage*, London: HMSO.

Law Commission Report 33 (1970) *Report on Nullity of Marriage*, London: HMSO.

Law Commission Report 170 (1988) *Facing the Future*, London: HMSO.

Law Commission Report 172 (1988) *Family Law: Review of Child Law*, London: HMSO.

Law Commission Report 175 (1988) *Family Law: Matrimonial Property*, London: HMSO.

Law Commission Report 187 (1989) *Distribution on Intestacy*, London: HMSO.

Law Commission Report 192 (1990) *Family Law: The Ground of Divorce*, London: HMSO.

Law Commission Report 207 (1992) *Report on Domestic Violence and Occupation of the Family Home*, London: HMSO.

Law Commission Report 231 (1995) *Mental Incapacity*, London: HMSO.

Law Commission Report 234 (1995) *Sixth Programme of Reform*, London: HMSO.

Law Commission Report 278 (2002) *Sharing Homes*, London: The Stationery Office.

Law Society (2002) *Cohabitation: The Case for Clear Law*, London: Law Society.

Laws, J. (1998) 'The limitation of human rights', *Public Law* 1998: 254.

Lenard, D. (1980) *Sex and Generation: A Study of Courtship and Weddings*, London: Tavistock.

Levy, A. and Kahan, B. (1991) *The Pindown Experience and the Protection of Children*, London: HMSO.

Lewis, J. (1999) 'Marriage and cohabitation and the nature of commitment', *Child and Family Law Quarterly* 11: 355.

Lewis, J. (2001a) 'Debates and issues regarding marriage and cohabitation in the English and American Literature', *International Journal of Law, Policy and the Family* 15: 159.

Lewis, J. (2001b) *The End of Marriage?*, Cheltenham: Edward Elgar.

Lewis, J. (2002) 'The Problem with Fathers', in B. Hobson (ed.) *Making Men into Fathers*, Cambridge: CUP.

Lewis, J., Arthur, A., Fitzgerald, R. and Maclean, M. (2000) *Settling Up*, London: NCSR.

Lewis, P. and Mullis, A. (1999) 'Delayed criminal prosecutions for childhood sexual abuse: Ensuring a fair trial', *Law Quarterly Review* 115: 265.

Liddy, J. (1998) 'The concept of family law under the ECHR', *European Human Rights Law Review* 1: 15.

Lim, H. and Roche, J. (2000) 'Feminism and Children's Rights', in J. Bridgeman and D. Monk (eds) *Feminist Perspectives on Child Law*, London: Cavendish.

Lind, C. (1995) 'The time for lesbian and gay marriages', *New Law Journal* 145: 1553.

Lind, C. (1997) 'Perceptions of sex in the legal determination of fatherhood – *X, Y, Z v UK*', *Child and Family Law Quarterly* 9: 401.

Lindley, B. (1997) 'Open adoption – is the door ajar?', *Child and Family Law Quarterly* 9: 115.

Lindley, B., Herring, J. and Wyld, N. (2001) 'Public Law Children's Cases', in J. Herring (ed.) *Family Law – Issues, Debates, Policy*, Cullompton: Willan.

Lindley, B., Richards, M. and Freeman, P. (2001) 'Advice and advocacy for parents in child protection cases – what is happening in current practice', *Child and Family Law Quarterly* 13: 167.

Lindley, R. (1989) 'Teenagers and Other Children', in G. Scarce (ed.) *Children, Parents and Politics*, Cambridge: CUP.

Loken, G. (1999) 'Gratitude and the map of moral duties towards children', *Arizona Law Journal* 31: 1121.

Longres, J. (1993) 'Self-neglect and social control', *Journal of Gerentological Social Work* 22: 3.

Lord Chancellor's Advisory Committee on Legal Education and Conduct (1999) *Mediating Family Disputes: Education and Conduct for Mediators*, London: LCD.

Lord Chancellor's Department (1995) *Looking to the Future: Mediation and the Ground for Divorce*, London: HMSO.

Lord Chancellor's Department (1996) *Striking the Balance. The Future of Legal Aid in England and Wales*, London: HMSO.

Lord Chancellor's Department (1997) *The Children Act Advisory Committee Final Report*, London: LCD.

Lord Chancellor's Department (1998) *Court Procedures for the Determination of Paternity*, London: HMSO.

Lord Chancellor's Department (1999) *Making Decisions*, London: LCD.

Lord Chancellor's Department (2000) *Judicial Statistics*, London: LCD.

Lord Chancellor's Department (2001) *Guidelines for Good Practice on Parental Contact in Cases where there is Domestic Violence*, London: LCD.

Lord Chancellor's Department (2002a) *Making Contact Work*, London: LCD.

Lord Chancellor's Department (2002b) *Moving Forward Together*, London: LCD.

Lord Chancellor's Department (2002c) *Scoping Study on Delay in Children Act Cases*, London: LCD.

Lord Chancellor's Department (2002d) *The Government's Response to the Children Act Sub-Committee's Report, 'Making Contact Work'*, London: LCD.

Lord Chancellor's Department (2003a) *Reducing Delays in Family Proceedings Courts*, London: LCD.

Lord Chancellor's Department (2003b) *Domestic Violence. A Guide to Civil Remedies and Criminal Sanctions*, London: LCD.

Lord Chancellor's Department (2003c) *Results of the 2003–04 Grant Programme to Marriage and Relationship Support Services*, London: LCD.

Lord Chancellor's Department (2003d) *Judicial Statistics*, London: LCD.

Lowe, N. (1988) 'The limits of the wardship jurisdiction: who can be made a ward?', *Journal of Child Law* 1: 6.

Lowe, N. (1994) 'Problems relating to access disputes under the Hague Convention on International Child Abduction', *International Journal of Family Law* 8: 374.

Lowe, N. (1997a) 'The changing face of adoption – the gift/donation model versus the contract services model', *Child and Family Law Quarterly* 9: 371.

Lowe, N. (1997b) 'The House of Lords and the Welfare Principle', in C. Bridge (ed.) *Family Law Towards the Millennium: Essays for P M Bromley* London: Butterworths.

Lowe, N. (1997c) 'The meaning and allocation of parental responsibility – a common lawyer's perspective', *International Journal of Law, Policy and the Family* 11: 192.

Lowe, N. (2000) 'English Adoption Law', in S. Katz, J. Eekelaar and M. McLean (eds) *Cross Currents*, Oxford: OUP.

Lowe, N. (2002) 'The Family Law Act 1986 – a critique', *Family Law* 32: 39.

Lowe, N. and Douglas, G. (1998) *Bromley's Family Law*, London: Butterworths.

Lowe, N. and Murch, M. (1999) *Supporting Adoption*, London: BAAF.

Lowe, N. and Murch, M. (2001) 'Children's participation in the family justice system – translating principles into practice', *Child and Family Law Quarterly* 13: 137.

Lowe, N. and Murch, M. (2002) *The Plan for the Child*, London: BAAF.

Lowe, N. and Murch, M. (2003) 'Translating Principles into Practice', in J. Dewar and S. Parker (eds) *Family Law: Processes, Practices, Pressures*, Oxford: OUP.

Lowe, N., Murch, M., Borkowski, M. et al. (1999) *Supporting Adoption*, London: BAAF.

Lowe, N. and Perry, M. (1998) 'The operation of the Hague and European Conventions on International Child Abduction between England and Germany', *International Family Law* 1: 8.

Lui, S. and Weaver, S. (1994) 'A survey of demand donors' attitudes', *Human Reproduction* 1994: 9.

Lye, D. and Waldron, I. (1997) 'Attitudes towards cohabitation, family and gender roles', *Sociological Perspectives* 410: 199.

Lyon, C. (1997a) 'Children Abused within the Care System', in N. Parton (ed.) *Child Protection and Family Support*, London: Routledge.

Lyon, C. (1997b) 'Children and the Law – Towards 2000 and Beyond', in C. Bridge (ed.) *Family Law Towards the Millennium: Essays for P. M. Bromley*, London: Butterworths.

Lyon, C. (2000) 'Children's Participation in Private Law Proceedings', in Thorpe LJ and E. Clarke (eds) *No Fault or Flaw: The Future of the Family Law Act 1996*, Bristol: Family Law.

Lyon, C. (2001) 'Children's rights and human rights', *Family Law* 31: 329.

Lyon, C., Surrey, E. and Timms, N. (1999) *Effective Support Services for Children and Young People when Parental Relationships Break Down*, Liverpool: Liverpool University.

McAllister, F. (1995) *Marital Breakdown and the Health of the Nation*, London: One plus One.

McAllister, F. (2000) 'Choosing Childlessness?', in H. Wilkinson (ed.) *Family Business*, London: Demos.

Macaskill, C. (2002) *Safe Contact? Children in Permanent Placement and Contact with their Birth Relatives*, Lyme Regis: Russell House.

McCall Smith, A. (1990) 'Is Anything Left of Parental Rights', in E. Sutherland and A. McCall Smith (eds) *Family Rights: Family Law and Medical Ethics*, Edinburgh: Edinburgh University Press.

McCarthy, P. (2001) *The Provision of Information and the Prevention of Marriage Breakdown*, London: The Stationery Office.

McCarthy, P., Walker, J. and Hooper, D. (2000) 'Saving marriage – a role for divorce law?', *Family Law* 30: 412.

McClean, D. (1997) 'International child abduction – some recent trends', *Child and Family Law Quarterly* 9: 387.

McClean, D. and Beevers, K. (1995) 'International child abduction – back to common law principles', *Child and Family Law Quarterly* 7: 128.

McColgan, A. (1993) 'In defence of battered women who kill', *Oxford Journal of Legal Studies* 13: 219.

MacCormick, N. (1976) 'Children's rights: a test-case for theories of rights', *Archiv für Rechts und Sozialphilosophie* 62: 305.

McGee, C. (2000) 'Children's and Mother's Experiences of Support and Protection Following Domestic Violence', in J. Hanmer and C. Itzin (eds) *Home Truths About Domestic Violence*, London: Routledge.

McGillivray, A. (1994) 'Why children do have equal rights: In reply to Laura Purdy', *International Journal of Children's Rights* 2: 243.

McGillivray, A. (1997) ' "He'll learn it on his body": Disciplining childhood in Canadian law', *International Journal of Children's Rights* 5: 193.

Mackay, Lord (2000) 'Family Law Reform', in S. Cretney (ed.) *Family Law – Essays for the New Millennium*, Bristol: Jordans.

McLanahan, S. and Bumpass, L. (1988) 'Intergenerational consequences of marital disruption', *American Journal of Sociology* 94: 130.

Maclean, M. (1991) *Surviving Divorce*, New York: New York University Press.

Maclean, M. (2000) 'Access to Justice in Family Matters', in S. Katz, J. Eekelaar and M. MacLean (eds) *Cross Currents*, Oxford: OUP.

Maclean, M. (2002) 'The Green Paper: Supporting Families 1998', in A. Carling, S. Duncan and R. Edwards (eds) *Analysing Families*, London: Routledge.

Maclean, M., Lewis, J., Arthur, S. et al. (2002) 'When cohabiting parents separate – law and expectations', *Family Law* 32: 373.

Maclean, M. and Mueller-Johnson, K. (2003) 'Supporting Cross-Household Parenting', in A. Bainham, B. Lindley, M. Richards and L. Trinder (eds) *Children and Their Families*, Oxford: Hart.

Maclean, S. (1990) 'Mothers and Others: The Case for Surrogacy', in E. Sutherland and A. McCall Smith (eds) *Family Rights: Family Law and Medical Ethics*, Edinburgh: Edinburgh University Press.

Maclean, S. and Maclean, M. (1996) 'Keeping secrets in assisted reproduction – the tension between donor anonymity and the need of the child for information', *Child and Family Law Quarterly* 8: 243.

McLellan, D. (1996) 'Contract marriage – the way forward or dead end?', *Journal of Law and Society* 23: 234.

Macooby, E. (1999) 'The Custody of Children of Divorcing Families', in R. Thompson and P. Amato (eds) *The Postdivorce Family*, Thousand Oaks, Calif.: Sage.

Macooby, E. and Mnookin, R. (1992) *Dividing the Child*, Cambridge, Mass.: Harvard University Press.

McRae, S. (1997) 'Cohabitation: A trial run for marriage?', *Sexual and Marital Therapy* 12: 259.

Mahoney, M. (1991) 'Legal images of battered women: Redefining the issue of separation', *Michigan Law Review* 90: 1.

Maidment, S. (1998) 'Parental Alienation Syndrome – A judicial response?', *Family Law* 28: 264.

Maidment, S. (2001a) 'Children and psychiatric damage – parents' duty of care to their children', *Family Law* 31: 440.

Maidment, S. (2001b) 'Parental responsibility – is there a duty to consult?', *Family Law* 31: 518.

Mama, A. (2000) 'Violence Against Black Women in the Home', in J. Hanmer and C. Itzin (eds) *Home Truths About Domestic Violence*, London: Routledge.

Mansfield, P., Reynolds, J. and Arai, L. (1999) *What Policy Developments would be most likely to Secure an Improvement in Marital Stability*, London: LCD.

Mantle, G. (2001) *Helping Families in Dispute*, Aldershot: Ashgate.

Marsh, A., Ford, R. and Finlayson, L. (1997) *Lone Parents, Work and Benefits. DSS Research Report No. 61*, London: The Stationery Office.

Marshall, A. (2003) 'Comedy of adoption – when is a parent not a parent?' *Family Law* 33: 840.

Marshall, P, (2003) 'Divorce and the family business', *Family Law* 33: 407.

Martin, C. and Thery, I. (2001) 'The PACS and marriage and cohabitation in France', *International Journal of Law, Policy and the Family* 15: 135.

Mason, J. (2003) 'Paternalism, Participation and Placation', in J. Dewar and S. Parker (eds) *Family Law: Processes, Practices, Pressures*, Oxford: Hart.

Masson, J. (1984) 'Old Families into New: A Status for Step-Parents', in M. Freeman (ed.) *State, Law and the Family*, London: Tavistock.

Masson, J. (1992) 'Managing risk under the Children Act 1989: Diversion in child care?', *Child Abuse Review* 1: 103.

Masson, J. (1994) 'Social engineering in the House of Lords: Re M', *Journal of Child Law* 6: 17.

Masson, J. (1995) 'Partnership with Parents: Doing Something Together under the Children Act 1989', in F. Kagan, M. King and C. Piper (eds) *Legislating for Harmony*, London: Jessica Kingsley.

Masson, J. (1996) 'Right to Divorce and Pension Rights', in M. Freeman (ed.) *Divorce: Where Next?*, Aldershot: Dartmouth.

Masson, J. (2000a) 'From Curtis to Waterhouse', in S. Katz, J. Eekelaar and M. MacLean (eds) *Cross Currents*, Oxford: OUP.

Masson, J. (2000b) 'Thinking about contact – a social or a legal problem?', *Child and Family Law Quarterly* 12: 15.

Masson, J. (2002a) 'Letter', *Family Law* 32: 568.

Masson, J. (2002b) 'Securing human rights for children and young people in secure accommodation', *Child and Family Law Quarterly* 14: 77.

Masson, J. and Winn Oakley, M. (1999) *Out of Hearing: Representing Children in Care Proceedings*, Chichester: John Wiley & Sons.

Matheson, J. and Babb, T. (2003) *Social Trends 2002*, London: The Stationery Office.

Maushart, S. (2001), *Wifework*, London: Bloomsbury.

Mayall, B. (2002) *Towards a Sociology for Childhood*, Buckingham: OUP.

Mayes, G., Gillies, J., MacDonald, R. and Wilson, G.(2000) 'Evaluation of an information programme for divorced or separated parents', *Child and Family Law Quarterly* 15: 85.

Mears, M. (1991) 'Getting it wrong again', *Family Law* 21: 231.

Mee, J. (1999) *The Property Rights of Cohabitees*, Oxford: Hart.

Meli, M. (1993) 'Towards a Restructuring of Custody Decision-Making at Divorce: An Alternative Approach to the Best Interests of the Child', in J. Eekelaar and P. Sarcevic (eds) *Parenthood in Modern Society*, London: Martinus Nijhoff.

Meltzer, H. and Gatward, R. (2000) *The Mental Health of Children and Adolescents in Great Britain*, London: The Stationery Office.

Mendoza, L. (1995) 'Bankruptcy and family breakdown', *Family Law* 25: 558.

Merrick, R. (2000) *Grandparents Suffering as Divorces Rise*, London: Family Policy Studies Centre.

Merron J., Baxter, P. and Bates, M. (2001) 'Is *Duxbury* misleading? Yes it is', *Family Law* 31: 747.

Michalowski, S. (1997) 'Is it in the best interests of a child to have a life-saving liver transplantation?', *Child and Family Law Quarterly* 9: 179.

Middleton, S. and Adelman, L. (2003) 'The Poverty and Social Exclusion Survey of Britain', in J. Bradshaw (ed.) *Children and Social Security*, Aldershot: Ashgate.

Middleton, S., Ashworth, K. and Braithwaite, I. (1997) *Small Fortunes*, York: Joseph Rowntree Foundation.

Miles, J. (2001) 'Domestic Violence', in J. Herring (ed.) *Family Law: Issues, Debates, Policy*, Cullompton: Willan.

Miles, J. (2002) 'Mind the gap . . .: Child protection, statutory interpretation and the Human Rights Act', *Cambridge Law Journal* 61: 533.

Miles, J. and Lindley, B. (2003) 'Contact for Children Subject to State Intervention', in A. Bainham, B. Lindley, M. Richards and L. Trinder (eds) *Children and Their Families*, Oxford: Hart.

Millar, J. (1996) 'Mothers, Workers, Wives: Comparing Policy Approaches to Supporting Lone Mothers', in E. Silva (ed.) *Good Enough Mothering?*, London: Routledge.

Miller, G. (1997) 'Provision for a surviving spouse', *Conveyancer* 61: 442.

Miller, G. (2002) 'Bankruptcy as a means of enforcement in family proceedings', *Family Law* 32: 21.

Millham, S., Bullock, R., Hosie, K. and Haak, M. (1986) *Lost in Care*, Aldershot: Gower.

Minow, M. (1986) 'Rights for the next generation: A feminist approach to children's rights', *Harvard Women's Law Journal* 9: 1.

Mirless-Black, C. (1999) *Home Office Research Study 191: Domestic Violence*, London: Home Office.

Mirless-Black, C. and Bayron, C. (2000) *Domestic Violence: Findings from the BCS Self-Completion Questionnaire*, London: Home Office.

Mnookin, R. (1975) 'Child custody adjudication', *Law and Contemporary Problems* 39: 226.

Mnookin, R. (1981) 'Thinking about children's rights – beyond kiddie libbers and child savers', *Stanford Lawyer* 1981: 24.

Moen, P. (2003) *It's About Time,* Ithaca, NY: Cornell University Press.

Mole, N. (2002) 'A note on the judgment from the perspective of the European Convention for the Protection of Human Rights and Fundamental Freedoms 1950', *Child and Family Law Quarterly* 14: 447.

Moloney, L. (2001) 'Do fathers "win" or do mothers "lose"? A preliminary analysis of closely contested parenting judgments in the Family Court of Australia', *International Journal of Law Policy and the Family* 15: 363.

Monck, E., Reynolds, J. and Wigfall, V. (2003) *The Role of Concurrent Planning*, London: BAAF.

Monk, D. (2002) 'Children's rights in education – making sense of contradictions', *Child and Family Law Quarterly* 14: 45.

Montgomery, J. (1988) 'Children as property', *Modern Law Review* 51: 323.

Mooney, J. (2000) 'Women's Experiences of Violence', in J. Hanmer and C. Itzin (eds) *Home Truths About Domestic Violence*, London: Routledge.

Morgan, D. (1994) 'A surrogacy issue: Who is the other mother', *International Journal of Law and the Family* 8: 386.

Morgan, D. (1995) 'Undoing What Comes Naturally – Regulating Medically Assisted Families', in A. Bainham, D. Pearl and R. Pickford (eds) *Frontiers of Family Law*, London: John Wiley & Co.

Morgan, D. (2003) 'Enigma Variations: Surrogacy, Rights and Procreative Tourism', in R. Cook, S. Day Sclater and F. Kaganas (eds) *Surrogate Motherhood*, Oxford: Hart.

Morgan, P. (1999a) 'Adoption and the Care of Children', in P. Morgan (ed.) *Adoption: The Continuing Debate*, London: IEA.

Morgan, P. (1999b) *Farewell to the Family?*, London: IEA.

Morgan, P. (2000) *Marriage-Lite*, London: Institute for the Study of Civil Society.

Morgan, P. (2002) *Children as Trophies*, Newcastle: Christian Institute.

Morley, P. (2000) 'Domestic Violence and Housing', in J. Hanmer and C. Itzin (eds) *Home Truths About Domestic Violence*, London: Routledge.

Morley, R. and Mullender, A. (1992) 'Hype or hope? The importance of pro-arrest policies and batterers' programmes from North America to Britain as key measures for preventing violence to women in the home', *International Journal of Law and the Family* 6: 265.

Morley, R. and Pascall, C. (1996) 'Women and homelessness: Proposals from the Department of the Environment, Part II, Domestic Violence', *Journal of Social Welfare and Family Law* 18: 327.

Morris, A. and Nott, S. (1995) *All My Worldly Goods*, Aldershot: Dartmouth.

Morrow, V. (1998) *Understanding Families*, London: National Children's Bureau.

Mostyn, N. (1999) 'The Green Paper on child support – Children First: A new approach to child support', *Family Law* 29: 95.

Mouffe, O. (1995) 'Democracy and pluralism: A critique of the rationalist approach', *Cardozo Law Review* 16: 1533.

Mount, F. (1982) *The Subversive Family*, London: Jonathan Cape.

Moynagh, M. and Worsley, R. (2000) *Tomorrow*, King's Lynn: Tomorrow Project.

Muir, H. (2003) 'Women's baby hope cut back', *The Guardian*: 27 June 2003.

Mumford, S. (1998) 'The judicial resolution of disputes involving children and religion', *International and Comparative Law Quarterly* 47: 117.

Murch, M. (2003) *The Voice of the Child in Private Family Law Proceedings*, Bristol: Family Law.

Murch, M., Douglas, G., Scanlan, L. et al. (1999) *Safeguarding Children's Welfare in Uncontentious Divorce*, Cardiff: Cardiff University.

Murch, M., Lowe, N., Borkowski, M. et al. (1993) *Pathways to Adoption*, London: HMSO.

Murch, M., Lowe, N., Borkowski, M. et al. (1999) *Adoption: Reframing the Approach*, London: Department of Health.

Murphy, J. (2000) 'Child Welfare in Transracial Adoption', in J. Murphy (ed.) *Ethnic Minorities, Their Families and the Law*, Oxford: Hart.

Murphy, J. (2002) 'The recognition of same-sex families in Britain: The role of private international law', *International Journal of Law, Policy and the Family* 16: 181.

Murphy, J. (2003) 'Children in need: The limits of local authority accountability', *Legal Studies* 23: 103.

Murphy, M. (1985) 'Demographic and socio-economic influences on recent British marital breakdown patterns', *Population Studies* 39: 441.

Murphy, M. and Wang, D. (1999) 'Forecasting British Families into the Twenty-First Century', in S. McRae (ed.) *Changing Britain*, Oxford: OUP.

National Audit Office (1994) *Report by the Comptroller and Auditor General: Looking After the Financial Affairs of People with Mental Incapacity*, London: HMSO.

National Audit Office (2000) *Report on Accounts 1999–2000*, London: National Audit Office.

National Family and Parenting Institute (2001a) *Marriage in the European Union Today*, London: NFPI.

National Family and Parenting Institute (2001b) *Work and The Family Today*, London: NFPI.

National Family and Parenting Institute (2001c) *The Family Today*, London: NFPI.

National Inter-Agency Working Party (1992) *Report on Domestic Violence*, London: Victim Support.

National Statistics (2001) *Britain 2001*, London: The Stationery Office.

National Statistics (2003a) *Marriage, Divorce and Adoption Statistics*, London: ONS.

National Statistics (2003b) *Census 2001*, London: ONS.

Neale, B. and Smart, C. (1997) 'Good and bad lawyers? Struggling in the *shadow of the new law?*', *Journal of Social Welfare and Family Law* 19: 377.

Neale, B. and Smart, C. (1999) *Agents or Dependants?*, Leeds: Centre for research on Family, Kinship and Childhood, Leeds University.

Neil, E. (2000) 'The reasons why young children are placed for adoption', *Child and Family Social Work* 11: 303.

Neil, E. (2003) 'Adoption and Contact: A Research Review', in A. Bainham, B. Lindley, M. Richards and L. Trinder (eds) *Children and Their Families*, Oxford: Hart.

Nelson, H. and Nelson, J. (1989) 'Cutting motherhood in two: Some suspicions concerning surrogacy', *Hypatia* 4: 85.

Newcastle Conciliation Project (1989) *Report to the Lord Chancellor on the Costs and Effectiveness of Conciliation in England and Wales*, London: Lord Chancellor's Department.

Newell, P. (1989) *Children Are People Too*, London: Bedford Square Press.

Newell, P. (1995) 'Respecting Children's Right to Physical Integrity', in B. Franklin (ed.) *The Handbook of Children's Rights*, London: Routledge.

Newell, P. (2002) 'Global Progress on Giving Up the Habit of Hitting Children', in B. Franklin (ed.) *The New Handbook of Children's Rights*, London: Routledge.

New Policy Institute (2002) *Monitoring Poverty and Social Exclusion*, York: Joseph Rowntree Trust.

Nield, S. (2003) 'Constructive trusts and estoppel', *Legal Studies* 23: 311.

Nielsen, L. (1990) 'Family rights and the "Registered Partnership" in Denmark', *International Journal of Law and the Family* 4: 297.

Noble, M., Smith, G. and Chong, S. (1998) *Lone Mothers Moving In and Out of Benefits*, York: Joseph Rowntree Foundation.

Noddings, N. (2003) *Caring*, Berkeley: University of California Press.

Northern Ireland Office of Law Reform (2001) *Physical Punishment in the Home*, Belfast: Office of Law Reform.

Nourin Shah-Kazemi, S. (2000) 'Cross-cultural mediation', *International Journal of Law, Policy and the Family* 14; 302.

NSPCC (2000) *Child Maltreatment Survey*, London: NSPCC.

O'Connor, P. (1993) 'Ireland: Nullity and the judiciary', *Journal of Family Law* 32: 345.

O'Donnovan, K. (1982) 'Should all maintenance of spouses be abolished?', *Modern Law Review* 45: 424.

O'Donnovan, K. (1984) 'Legal marriage – who needs it?', *Modern Law Review* 47: 111.

O'Donnovan, K. (1988) 'A right to know one's parentage', *International Journal of Law, Policy and the Family* 2: 27.

O'Donnovan, K. (1993) *Family Law Matters*, London: Pluto.

O'Donnovan, K. (1998) 'Who is the Father? Access to Information on Genetic Identity', in G. Douglas and L. Sebba (eds) *Children's Rights and Traditional Values*, Aldershot: Ashgate.

O'Donnovan, K. (2000) 'Constructions of Maternity and Motherhood in Stories of Lost Children', in J. Bridgeman and D. Monk (eds) *Feminist Perspectives on Child Law*, London: Cavendish.

Office of the Deputy Prime Minister (2003) *Statutory Homelessness Statistics*, London: The Stationery Office.

Office for National Statistics (1994) *Social Trends 1994*, London: HMSO.

Office for National Statistics (1996) *Social Trends 1996*, London: HMSO.

Office for National Statistics (1999) *Population Trends*, London: ONS.

Office for National Statistics (2000) *Living in Britain*, London: ONS.

Office for National Statistics (2001) *The 2001 Census*, London: ONS.

Office for National Statistics (2002) *Omnibus Survey*, London: ONS.

Office for National Statistics (2003a) *Marriage and Divorce 2001, Adoptions in 2002 in England and Wales*, London: ONS.

Office for National Statistics (2003b) *Divorce in 2002*, London: ONS.

Office of Population and Census Surveys (1993) *Great Britain 1991 Census*, London: HMSO.

Office of Population and Census Surveys (1996) *Living in Britain: Results from the 1994 General Household Survey*, London: OPCS.

Ofstead (2002) *Sex and Relationships*, London: HMI.

Ogg, J. and Bennett, G. (1992) 'Elder abuse in Britain', *British Medical Journal* 305: 990.

Ogg, J. and Munn-Giddings, M. (1993) 'Researching elder abuse', *Ageing and Society* 13: 389

Ogus, A., Jones-Lee, M., Cloes, M. and McCarthy, P. (1990) 'Evaluating alternative dispute resolution: Measuring the impact of family conciliation on costs', *Modern Law Review* 53: 57.

O'Halloran, K. (2003) 'Adoption – A Public or Private Legal Process?' in J. Dewar and S. Parker (eds) *Family Law: Processes, Practices, Pressures*, Oxford: Hart.

Okin, S. (1992) *Justice, Gender and The Family*, New York: Basic Books.

Oldham, M. (1995) ' "Neither a borrower nor a lender be" – The life of *O'Brien*', *Child and Family Law Quarterly* 7: 104.

Oldham, M. (2001) 'Financial obligations within the family – aspects of intergenerational maintenance and succession in England and France', *Cambridge Law Journal* 60: 128.

Oliver, D. (1982) 'Why do people live together?', *Journal of Social Welfare and Family Law* 4: 209.

Oliver, D. (1999) *Common Values and the Public–Private Divide*, London: Butterworths.

Olsen, F. (1992) 'Children's Rights: Some Feminist Approaches to the United Nations Convention on the Rights of the Child', in P. Alston, S. Parker and J. Seymour (eds) *Children, Rights and the Law*, Oxford: Clarendon Press.

Olsen, F. (1998) 'Asset Distribution after Unmarried Cohabitation: A United States Perspective', in R. Bailey-Harris (ed.) *Dividing the Assets on Family Breakdown*, Bristol: Jordans.

O'Neill, O. (1992) 'Children's rights and children's lives', *International Journal of Law and the Family* 6: 24.

O'Neill, O. (2002) *Autonomy and Trust in Bioethics*, Cambridge: CUP.

O'Neill, O. and Ruddick, W. (1979) *Having Children*, Oxford: OUP.

Oppenheim, C. and Lister, R. (1996) 'The Politics of Child Poverty 1979–1995', in J. Pilcher and S. Wagg (eds) *Thatcher's Children*, London: Falmer Press.

O'Quigley, A. (1999) *Listening to Children's Views and Representing Their Best Interests*, York: Joseph Rowntree Foundation.

Orentlicher, D. (1998) 'Spanking and other corporal punishment of children by parents: Overvaluing pain, undervaluing children', *Houston Law Review* 35: 1478.

Owusu-Bempah, K. (2001) 'Racisim: An Important Factor in Practice with Ethnic Minority Children and Families', in P. Foley, J. Roche and S. Tucker (eds) *Children in Society*, Buckingham: Open University Press.

Pahl, J. (1989) *Money and Marriage*, Basingstoke: Macmillan.

Palmer, G., Rahman, M. and Kenway, R. (2002) *Monitoring Poverty and Social Exclusion*, York: Joseph Rowntree.

Parker, A. (2002) 'Mutual Consent Divorce', in A. Dnes and R. Rowthorn (eds) *The Law and Economics of Marriage and Divorce*, Cambridge: CUP.

Parker, R. (1999) *Adoption Now*, London: DoH.

Parker, S. (1991) 'Child support in Australia: Children's rights or public interest?', *International Journal of Law and the Family* 5: 24.

Parker, S. (1992) 'Rights and utility in Anglo-Australian family law', *Modern Law Review* 55: 311.

Parker, S. (1998) *New Balances in Family Law*, Melbourne: Griffith University.

Parkinson, P. (1996) 'Multiculturalism and the Recognition of Marital Status in Australia', in G. Douglas and N. Lowe (eds) *Families Across Frontiers*, London: Kluwer.

Parkinson, P. (2003) 'Child protection, permanency planning and children's right to family life', *International Journal of Law, Policy and the Family* 17: 147.

Parkinson, P. and Humphreys, C. (1998) 'Children who witness domestic violence – the implications for child protection', *Child and Family Law Quarterly* 10: 147.

Parry, M. (2000) 'Local Authority Support for Ethnic Minority', in J. Murphy (ed) *Ethnic Minorities, Their Families and the Law*, Oxford: Hart.

Parsons, T. and Bales, B. (1955) *Family, Socialization and Interaction Process*, Glencoe: Free Press.

Parton, N. (1991) *Governing the Family*, London: Macmillan.

Pascoe, S. (1998) 'Can English law uphold the sanctity of marriage?', *Family Law* 28: 620.

Passport Agency (1994) 'Passport agency guidance', *Family Law* 24: 651.

Patterson, C., Fulcher, M. and Wainright, J. (2002) 'Children of Lesbian and Gay Parents', in B. Bottoms, M. Kovera and B. McAuliff (eds) *Children, Social Science and the Law*, Cambridge: CUP.

Pawlowski, M. (2002) 'Beneficial entitlement – do indirect contributions suffice?', *Family Law* 32: 190.

Pawlowski, M. and Brown, J. (2002) *Undue Influence and the Family Home*, London: Cavendish.

Pearce, J., Davis, G. and Barron, J. (1999) 'Love in a cold climate – section 8 applications under the Children Act 1989', *Family Law* 29: 22.

Pearl, D. and Menski, W. (1998) *Muslim Family Law*, Bristol: Jordans.

Performance and Innovation Unit (2000a) *The Prime Minister's Review of Adoption*, London: Performance and Innovation Unit.

Performance and Innovation Unit (2000b) *Winning the Generation Game*, London: Performance and Innovation Unit.

Perry, P., Douglas, G., Murch, M. et al. (2000) *How Parents Cope Financially on Marriage Breakdown*, London: Joseph Rowntree.

Phillips, C. (2003) 'Who's who in the pecking order?', *British Journal of Criminology* 43: 710.

Phillipson, C. (1998) *Reconstructing Old Age*, London: Sage.

Phillipson, C., Bernard, M., Phillips, J. and Ogg, J. (1999) 'Older People in Three Urban Areas: Household Composition, Kinship and Social Networks', in S. McRae (ed.) *Changing Britain*, Oxford: OUP.

Philpot, T. (2001) *A Very Private Practice*, London: BAAF.

Pickford, R. (1999) 'Unmarried Fathers and the Law', in A. Bainham, S. Day Sclater and M. Richards (eds) *What is a Parent?*, Oxford: Hart.

Piper, C. (1993) *The Responsible Parent: A Study in Divorce Mediation*, Hemel Hempstead: Harvester Wheatsheaf.

Piper, C. (1996) 'Norms and Negotiation in Mediation and Divorce', in M. Freeman (ed.) *Divorce: Where Next?*, Aldershot: Dartmouth.

Piper, C. (1999) 'How do you define a family lawyer?', *Legal Studies* 19: 93.

Piper, C. and Miakishev, A. (2003) 'A child's right to veto in England and Russia – another welfare ploy', *Child and Family Law Quarterly* 15: 57.

Pirrie, J. (2002) 'Time for the courts to stand up to the Child Support Act', *Family Law* 32: 114.

Pirrie, J. (2003) 'Report of the Child Support Agency', *Family Law* 33: 105.

Pizzey, E. (1978) *Scream Quietly or the Neighbours will Hear*, Harmondsworth: Pelican.

Pleasence, P., Balmer, N., Buck, A. et al. (2003) 'Family problems – what happens to whom', *Family Law* 33: 497.

Plomer, A. and Martin-Clement, N. (1996) 'The limits of beneficence: Egg donation under the Human Embryology and Fertilisation Act 1990', *Legal Studies* 16: 434.

Plotnikoff, J. and Woolfson, R. (1995) *Prosecuting Child Abuse*, London: Blackstone.

Pollard, J. (1995) 'Elder Abuse – The public law failure to protect', *Family Law* 25: 257.

Pontifical Council for the Family (2000) *Family, Marriage, and 'De Facto' Unions*, Rome: Pontifical Council for the Family.

Poulter, S. (1987) 'Ethnic minority cultural customs, English law and human rights', *International and Comparative Law Quarterly* 36: 589.

Poulter, S. (1998) *Ethnicity, Law and Human Rights*, Oxford: OUP.

Poussin, E. and Martin-LeBrun, G. (2002) 'A French study of children's self-esteem after parental separation', *International Journal of Law, Policy and the Family* 16: 313.

Poyser, A. (2001) 'The Way Forward: CAFCASS and the Future for the Representation of Children in Family Proceedings', in M. Ruegger (ed.) *Hearing the Voice of the Child*, London: Russell House.

Price, F. and Cook, R. (1995) 'The donor, the recipient and the child – human egg donation in UK licensed clinics', *Child and Family Law Quarterly* 7: 145.

Priest, J. and Whybrow, J. (1986) *Custody Law in Practice in the Divorce and Domestic Courts*, London: HMSO.

Pritchard, J. (2002) *Male Victims of Elder Abuse*, London: Jessica Kingsley.

Probert, R. (2002a) 'Sharing homes – a long-awaited paper', *Family Law* 32: 834.

Probert, R. (2002b) 'When are we married? Void, non-existent and presumed marriages', *Legal Studies* 22: 398.

Pryor, J. (2003) 'Children's Contact with Relatives', in A. Bainham, B. Lindley, M. Richards and L. Trinder (eds) *Children and Their Families*, Oxford: Hart.

Pryor, J. and Daly Peoples, R. (2001) 'Adolescent attitudes toward living arrangements after divorce', *Child and Family Law Quarterly* 13: 197.

Pryor, J. and Seymour, F. (1996) 'Making decisions about children after parental separation', *Child and Family Law Quarterly* 8: 229.

Purdy, L. (1994) 'Why children shouldn't have equal rights', *International Journal of Children's Rights* 2: 223.

Quinton, D., Selwyn, J., Rushton, A. and Dance, C. (1998) 'Contact with birth parents in adoption – a response to Ryburn', *Child and Family Law Quarterly* 10: 349.

Qureshi, H. and Walker, A. (1989) *The Caring Relationship*, London: Macmillan.

Rabinovitch, D. (2002) 'Mothers matter more', *The Guardian*: 20 April 2002.

Radford, L. (1999) *Unreasonable Fears? Child Contact in the Context of Domestic Violence*, London: Women's Aid.

Ragoné, H. (2003). 'The Gift of Life', in R. Cook, S. Day Sclater and F. Kaganas (eds) *Surrogate Motherhood*, Oxford: Hart.

Rao, R. (2003) 'Surrogacy Law in the United States', in R. Cook, S. Day Sclater and F. Kaganas (eds) *Surrogate Motherhood*, Oxford: Hart.

Rasmusen, E. (2002) 'An Economic Approach to Adultery Law', in A. Dnes and R. Rowthorn (eds) *The Law and Economics of Marriage and Divorce*, Cambridge: CUP.

Rasmusen, E. and Evans State, J. (1998) 'Lifting the veil of ignorance: Personalising the marriage contract', *Indiana Law Journal* 73: 453.

Raz, J. (1984) 'Legal rights', *Oxford Journal of Legal Studies* 4: 1.

Raz, J. (1986) *The Morality of Freedom*, Oxford: OUP.

Raz, J. (1994) 'Multiculturalism: A liberal perspective', *Dissent* 1994: 67.

Reece, H. (1996) 'The paramountcy principle: consensus or construct?', *Current Legal Problems* 49: 267.

Reece, H. (2000) 'Divorcing the Children', in J. Bridgeman and D. Monk (eds) *Feminist Perspectives on Child Law*, London: Cavendish.

Reece, H. (2003) *Divorcing Responsibly*, Oxford: Hart.

Rees, O. (2002) 'Beyond the hype – A year in the life of the Children's Commissioner for Wales', *Family Law* 32: 748.

Regan, M. (1993a) *Family Law and the Pursuit of Intimacy*, New York: New York University Press.

Regan, M. (1993b) 'Reason, tradition and family law: A comment on social constructionism', *Virginia Law Review* 79: 1515.

Regan, M. (1999) *Alone Together: Law and the Meaning of Marriage*, New York: OUP.

Regan, M. (2000) 'Morality, Fault and Divorce Law', in M. King White, *Marriage in America*, Lanham, Md.: Rowman & Littlefield.

Reynolds, J. and Mansfield, P. (1999) *The Effect of Changing Attitudes to Marriage on its Stability*, London: The Stationery Office.

Reynor, L. (1980) *The Adopted Child Comes of Age*, London: Allen and Unwin.

Rhoades, H. (2002) 'The "No contact mother": Reconstructions of motherhood in the era of the "new father" ', *International Journal of Law, Policy and the Family* 16: 71.

Rhoades, H. (2003) 'Enforcing contact or supporting parents?' Unpublished paper presented to the Oxford Centre for Family Law and Policy.

Ribbens McCarthy, J., Edwards, R. and Gillies, V. (2003) *Making Families*, Durham: Sociologypress.

Richards, C. (2001) 'Allowing blame and revenge into mediation', *Family Law* 31: 775.

Richards, J. (1999) 'A Denial of the Right to Family Life', in P. Morgan (ed.) *Adoption: The Continuing Debate*, London: IEA.

Richards, M. (1989) 'Joint custody revisited', *Family Law* 19: 83.

Richards, M. (1994) 'Divorcing Children: Roles for Parents and the State', in M. Maclean and J. Kurczewski (eds) *Families, Politics and the Law: Perspectives for East and West Europe*, Oxford: Clarendon Press.

Richards, M. (1995a) 'Private Worlds and Public Intentions: The Role of the State at Divorce', in A. Bainham, D. Pearl and R. Pickford (eds) *Frontiers of Family Law*, London: John Wiley & Co.

Richards, M. (1995b) 'But What About the Children? Some Reflections on the Divorce White Paper', *Child and Family Law Quarterly* 4: 223.

Richards, M. (1996a) *Community Care for Older People*, Bristol: Jordans.

Richards, M. (1996b) 'Divorce and divorce legislation', *Family Law* 26: 151.

Richards, M. (1997) 'The Interests of Children at Divorce', in M. Meulders-Klein (ed.) *Familles et Justice*, Brussels: Bruylant.

Richards, M. (2003) 'Assisted Reproduction and Parental Relationships', in A. Bainham, B. Lindley, M. Richards and L. Trinder (eds) *Children and Their Families*, Oxford: Hart.

Richards, M. and Connell, J. (2000) 'Children and the Family Law Act', in Thorpe LJ and E. Clarke (eds) *No Fault or Flaw: The Future of the Family Law Act 1996*, Bristol: Jordans.

Richards, M. and Dyson, M. (1982) *Separation, Divorce and the Development of Children*, London: DHSS.

Richards, M. and Stark, C. (2000) 'Children, parenting and information meetings', *Family Law* 30: 484.

Rippon, P. (1998) 'Mistresses I have known — unmarried cohabitants and land ownership', *Family Law* 28: 682.

Robb, M. (2001) 'The Changing Experience of Childhood', in P. Foley, J. Roche and S. Tucker (eds) *Children in Society*, Buckingham: Open University Press.

Roberts, E. (2000) *Age Discrimination in Health and Social Care*, London: King's Fund.

Roberts, M. (1995) 'Ousting abusers – Children Act 1989 or inherent jurisdiction *Re H (Prohibited Steps Order)*', *Child and Family Law Quarterly* 7: 243.

Roberts, M. (2000) 'Children by Donation: Do they have a Claim to their Genetic Parentage?', in J. Bridgeman and D. Monk (eds) *Feminist Perspectives on Child Law*, London: Cavendish.

Roberts M. (2001) 'Childcare Policy', in P. Foley, J. Roche and S. Tucker (eds) *Children in Society*, Buckingham: Open University Press.

Roberts, S. (1988) 'Three Models of Family Mediation', in J. Eekelaar and R. Dingwall (eds) *Divorce, Mediation and the Legal Process*, Oxford: Clarendon.

Roberts, S. (1995) 'Decision-making for life apart', *Modern Law Review* 58: 714.

Roberts, S. (1996) 'Family mediation and the interests of women – facts and fears', *Family Law* 26: 239.

Roberts, S. (2000) 'Family Mediation in the New Millennium', in S. Cretney (ed.) *Family Law – Essays for the New Millennium*, Bristol: Jordans.

Robertson, J.(1994) *Children of Choice*, Princeton: Princeton University Press.

Robinson, J. (2003) 'Age Equality in Health and Social Care', in S. Fredman and S. Spencer (eds) *Age as an Equality Issue*, Oxford: Hart.

Roche, J. (1999) 'Children and Divorce: A Private Affair?', in S. Day Sclater and C. Piper (eds) *Undercurrents of Divorce*, Aldershot: Ashgate.

Rodger, J. (1996) *Family Life and Social Control*, Basingstoke: Macmillan.

Rogers, B. and Pryor, J. (1998) *Divorce and Separation*, York: Joseph Rowntree.

Rogers, C. (2003) *Children at Risk 2003–4*, London: NFPI.

Roman Catholic Church (1987) *Instruction on Respect for Human Life in its Origin and on the Dignity of Procreation*, London: Catholic Truth Society.

Rose, N. (1987) 'Beyond the Public/Private Division: Law, Power and the Family', in P. Fitzpatrick and A. Hunt (eds) *Critical Legal Studies*, Oxford: Basil Blackwell.

Rowthorn, R. (1999) 'Marriage and trust', *Cambridge Journal of Economics* 23: 661.

Rowthorn, R. (2002) 'Marriage as a Signal', in A. Dnes and R. Rowthorn (eds) *The Law and Economics of Marriage and Divorce*, Cambridge: CUP.

Royal Commission (1999) *Royal Commission Report on Long Term Care*, London: HMSO.

Ruegger, M. (2001) *Hearing the Voice of the Child*, Lyme Regis: Russell House.

Rushbrooke, R. (2001) *The Proportion of Adoptees who have Received their Birth Records*, London: ONS.

Rushton, P. (2002) *Adoption as a Placement Choice*, London: King's College London.

Rusk, P. (1998) 'Same sex spousal benefits', *Toronto Faculty of Law Review* 52: 170.

Ryburn, M. (1998) 'In whose best interests? Post adoption contact with the birth family', *Child and Family Law Quarterly* 10: 53.

Sachdev, P. (1992) *Adoption, Reunion and After*, Washington: Child Welfare.

Salter, D. (2000) 'A practitioner's guide to pension sharing', *Family Law* 30: 489.

Salter, D. (2003) 'Maskell unmasked', *Family Law* 33: 344.

Sarat, A. and Felstiner, W. (1995) *Divorce Lawyers and their Clients*, New York: OUP.

Savas, D. (1996) 'Parental participation in case conferences', *Child and Family Law Quarterly* 8: 57.

Save the Children and National Children's Bureau (1998) *It Hurts You Inside – Children Talking About Smacking,* London: Save the Children and National Children's Bureau.

Sawyer, C. (1995) 'The competence of children to participate in family proceedings', *Child and Family Law Quarterly* 7: 180.

Sawyer, C. (2000) 'Hitting people is wrong', *Family Law* 30: 654.

Sawyer, C. (2001) 'Applications by children: Still seen but not heard?', *Law Quarterly Review* 117: 203.

Schaffer, R. (1990) *Making Decisions About Children: Psychological Questions and Answers,* Oxford: Blackwell.

Schneider, C. (1991) 'Discretion, rules and law: Child custody and the UMDA's Best Interest Standard', *Michigan Law Review* 89: 2215.

Schneider, C. (1995) 'On the duties and rights of parents', *Virginia Law Review* 81: 2477.

Schneider, E. (1994) 'The Violence of Privacy', in M. Fineman and R. Myktiuk (eds) *The Public Nature of Private Violence,* London: Routledge.

Schneider, E. (2000a) *Battered Women and Feminist Law Making,* New Haven: Yale University Press.

Schneider, E. (2000b) 'Law and Violence Against Women in the Family at Century's End', in S. Katz, J. Eekelaar and M. Maclean (eds) *Cross Currents,* Oxford: OUP.

Schofield, G. (1998) 'Making sense of the ascertainable wishes and feelings of insecurely attached children', *Child and Family Law Quarterly* 10: 363.

Schofield, G. and Thoburn, J. (1996) *Child Protection: The Voice of the Child in Decision Making,* London: Institute for Public Policy Research.

Schuz, R. (1996) 'Divorce and Ethnic Minorities', in M. Freeman (ed.) *Divorce: Where Next?,* Aldershot: Dartmouth.

Schwartz, P. (2000) 'Peer Schwartz', in M. Whyte (ed.) *Marriage in America,* Lanham, Md.: Rowman & Littlefield.

Scott, E. (1990) 'Rational decision making about marriage and divorce', *Virginia Law Review* 76: 9.

Scott, E. (2003) 'Marriage Commitment and the Legal Regulation of Divorce', in A. Dnes and R. Rowthorn (eds) *The Law and Economics of Marriage and Divorce,* Cambridge: CUP.

Scott, E. and Scott, R. (1995) 'Parents as fiduciaries', *Virginia Law Review* 81: 2401.

Scott, K. and Warren, M. (2001) *Perspectives on Marriage,* New York: OUP.

Scottish Law Commission Report 135 (1992) *Report on Family Law,* Edinburgh: HMSO.

Scully, A. (2003) 'Big money cases, judicial discretion and equality of division', *Child and Family Law Quarterly* 15: 205.

Seden, J. (2001) 'Family Assistance Orders and the Children Act 1989: Ambivalence about intervention or a means of safeguarding and promoting children's welfare?', *International Journal of Law, Policy and the Family* 15: 226.

Select Committee (1975) *Report on Violence in Marriage,* HC 553, London: HMSO.

Select Committee (1977) *Violence in the Family,* HC 329, London: HMSO.

Sevenhuijsen, S. (1997) *Citizenship and the Ethics of Care,* London: Routledge.

Sevenhuijsen, S. (2000) 'Caring in the third way', *Critical Social Policy* 20: 5.

Sevenhuijsen, S. (2002) 'An approach through the ethic of care', in A. Carling, S. Duncan and R. Edwards (eds) *Analysing Families,* London: Routledge.

Seymour, J. (2000) *Childbirth and the Law,* Oxford: OUP.

Sharland, E. (1996) *Professional Intervention in Child Sexual Abuse,* London: HMSO.

Sharp, C. (2003) 'Bigamy and financial relief', *Family Law* 33: 414.

Sharpe, A. (2002) *Transgender Jurisprudence,* London: Cavendish.

Shaw, M. (2002) 'When Young People Refuse Treatment: Balancing Autonomy and Protection', in Thorpe LJ and C. Cowton (eds) *Delight and Dole,* Bristol: Jordans.

Shaw Spaht, K. (2002) 'Louisiana's Covenant Marriage Law', in A. Dnes and R. Rowthorn (eds) *The Law and Economics of Marriage and Divorce,* Cambridge: CUP.

Sheldon, S. (2001) ' "Sperm bandits", birth control fraud and the battle of the sexes', *Legal Studies* 21: 460.

Sheldon, S. (2003) 'Unwilling fathers and abortion: Terminating men's child support obligations', *Modern Law Review* 66: 175.

Shelter (2003) *Relationship Breakdown and Housing,* London: Shelter.

Shultz, M. (1982) 'Contractual ordering of marriage', *California Law Review* 70: 204.

Shultz, M. (1990) 'Reproductive technology and intent-based parenthood: An opportunity for gender neutrality', *Wisconsin Law Review* 1990: 297.

Silva, E. and Smart, C. (1999) *The New Family,* London: Sage.

Simons, J. (1999) *Can Marriage Preparation Courses Influence the Quality and Stability of Marriage?,* London: One Plus One.

Simpson, B., Jessop, J. and McCarthy, P. (2003) 'Fathers after Divorce', in A. Bainham, B. Lindley, M. Richards and L. Trinder (eds) *Children and Their Families,* Oxford: Hart.

Singer HHJ (2001) 'Sexual discrimination in ancillary relief', *Family Law* 31: 115.

Singer, J. (1997) 'Husbands, wives and human capital: Why the shoe won't fit', *Family Law Quarterly* 31: 119.

Slaughter, M. (2002) 'Marital Bargaining', in M. Maclean (ed.) *Making Law for Families,* Oxford: Hart.

Smart, C. (1984) *The Ties that Bind,* London: Routledge.

Smart, C. (1989) *Feminism and the Power of Law,* London: Routledge.

Smart, C. (1991) 'The legal and moral ordering of child custody', *Journal of Law and Society* 19: 485.

Smart, C. (2000a) 'Divorce in England 1950–2000: A Moral Tale', in S. Katz, J. Eekelaar and M. Maclean (eds) *Cross Currents,* Oxford: OUP.

Smart, C. (2000b) 'Stories of a family life', *Canadian Journal of Family Law* 17: 20.

Smart, C. (2003) 'Children and the Transformation of Family Law', in J. Dewar and S. Parker (eds) *Family Law: Processes, Practices, Pressures,* Oxford: Hart.

Smart, C. and Neale, B. (1997) 'Argument against virtue – must contact be enforced?', *Family Law* 27: 332.

Smart, C. and Neale, B. (1999) *Family Fragments?*, Cambridge: Polity Press.

Smart, C. and Neale, B. (2000) ' "It's my life too": Children's perspectives on post-divorce parenting', *Family Law* 30: 163.

Smart, C., Neale, B. and Wade, A. (2001) *The Changing Experience of Childhood*, Cambridge: Polity Press.

Smart, C. and Stevens, P. (2000) *Cohabitation Breakdown*, London: Joseph Rowntree.

Smith, C. (1997a) 'Judicial power and local authority discretion – the contested frontier', *Child and Family Law Quarterly* 9: 243.

Smith, C. (1997b) 'Children's rights: Judicial ambivalence and social resistance', *International Journal of Law, Policy and the Family* 11: 103.

Smith, C. (2002) 'Human rights and the Children Act 1989', *Child and Family Law Quarterly* 14: 427.

Smith, C. and Logan, J. (2002) 'Adoptive parenthood as a "legal fiction" – its consequences for direct post-adoption contact', *Child and Family Law Quarterly* 14: 281.

Smith, D. (2003) 'Making Contact Work in International Cases: Promoting Contact Whilst Preventing International Parental Child Abduction', in A. Bainham, B. Lindley, M. Richards and L. Trinder (eds) *Children and Their Families*, Oxford: Hart.

Smith II, G. (1997) *Legal and Healthcare Ethics for the Elderly*, Washington: Taylor and Francis.

Smith, L. (1989) *Home Office Research Study 107: Domestic Violence: An Overview of the Literature*, London: Home Office.

Smith, L. (1993) 'Children, Parents and the European Human Rights Convention', in J. Eekelaar and P. Sarcevic (eds) *Parenthood in Modern Society*, London: Martinus Nijhoff.

Smith, M. (2003) 'New stepfamilies – a descriptive study of a largely unseen group', *Child and Family Law Quarterly* 15: 185.

Smith, M., Robertson, J., Dixon, J. and Quigley, M. (2001) *A Study of Step Children and Step Parenting*, London: Thomas Coram Research Unit.

Smith, R. (2000) *Property Law*, Harlow: Longman.

Smith, S. and Cook, R. (1991) 'Ovarian hyperstimulation: Actual and theoretical risks', *British Medical Journal* 1991: 127.

Snodgrass, G. (1998) 'Creating family without marriage: The advantages and disadvantages of adult adoption among gay and lesbian partners', *Journal of Family Law* 36: 75.

Social and Community Planning Research (2000) *Women's Attitudes to Combining Paid Work and Family Life*, London: SCPR.

Social Exclusion Unit (1998) *Truancy and School*, London: SEU.

Social Exclusion Unit (1999a) *Teenage Pregnancy*, London: SEU.

Social Exclusion Unit (1999b) *Bridging the Gap*, London: SEU.

Social Services Inspectorate (1992) *Confronting Elder Abuse*, London: HMSO.

Social Services Inspectorate (1993) *No Longer Afraid: The Safeguard of Older People in Domestic Settings*, London: HMSO.

Social Services Inspectorate (1996) *Complaints Procedures in Local Authorities Social Services Departments: A Third Overview*, London: HMSO.

Social Services Inspectorate (1999) *Someone Else's Children*, London: DoH.

Social Services Inspectorate (2002) *Fostering for the Future*, London: DoH.

Solberg, A. (1997) 'Negotiating Childhood', in A. James and A. Prout (eds) *Constructing and Reconstructing Childhood*, 2nd edn, London: Falmer.

Solomou, W., Richards, M., Huppert, F. et al. (1998) 'Divorce, current marital status and well-being in an elderly population', *International Journal of Law, Policy and the Family* 12: 323.

Spencer, J. and Flin, R. (1993) *The Evidence of Children*, London: Blackstone.

Spon-Smith, R. (2002) 'The man is father of the child – or is he?', *Family Law* 32: 26.

Stainton Rogers (2001) 'Constructing Childhood, Constructing Child Concerns', in P. Foley, J. Roche and S. Tucker (eds) *Children in Society*, Buckingham: Open University Press.

Stalford, H. (2002) 'Concepts of family under EU law – lessons from the ECHR', *International Journal of Law, Policy and the Family* 16: 410.

Stanko, E. (2000) *Press Release*, London: Reuters.

Stanko, E., Crisp, D., Hale, C. and Lucraft H. (1998) *Counting the Costs: Estimating the Impact of Domestic Violence in the London Borough of Hackney*, Swindon: Crime Concern.

Stationery Office, The (2000a) *Social Inequalities*, London: The Stationery Office.

Stationery Office, The (2000b) *The Waterhouse Report: Lost in Care*, London: The Stationery Office.

Stationery Office, The (2000c) *Marriage, Divorce and Adoption Statistics 1998*, London: The Stationery Office.

Stone, P. (1992) 'The habitual residence of a child', *Journal of Child Law* 4: 130.

Strauss, M. and Donnolly, P. (1993) 'Corporal punishment of adolescents by American parents', *Society* 24: 419.

Strong, S. (2000) 'Between the baby and the breast', *Cambridge Law Journal* 59: 259.

Stumpf, A. (1986) 'Redefining mother: A legal matrix for the new reproductive technologies', *Yale Law Journal* 96: 187.

Sturge, C. and Glaser, D. (2000) 'Contact and domestic violence – the experts' court report', *Family Law* 30: 615.

Sutherland, E. (1997) 'The unequal struggle – fathers and children in Scots law', *Child and Family Law Quarterly* 9: 191.

Sutherland, E. (2001) 'Parentage and Parenting', in J. Scoular (ed.) *Family Dynamics: Contemporary Issues in Family Law*, London: Butterworths.

Sutherland, E. (2003) ' "Man not included" – single women, female couples and procreative freedom in the UK', *Child and Family Law Quarterly* 15: 155.

Swindells, H., Neaves, A., Kushner, M. and Skilbeck, R. (1999) *Family Law and the Human Rights Act 1998*, Bristol: Family Law.

Swisher, P. (1997) 'Reassessing fault factors in no-fault divorce', *Family Law Quarterly* 31: 269.

Symes, P. (1985) 'Indissolubility and the clean break', *Modern Law Review* 48: 44.

Taitz, J. (1988) 'A transsexual's nightmare: The determination of sexual identity in English Law', *International Journal of Family Law* 2: 139.

Talbot, C. and Williams, M. (2003) 'Kinship care', *Family Law* 33: 502.

Tan, Y. (2002) 'New Forms of Cohabitation in Europe: Challenges for English Private International Law', in K. Boelle-Woelki (ed.) *Perspectives for the Unification and Harmonisation of Family Law in Europe,* Antwerp: Intersentia.

Tanner, K. and Turney, D. (2002) 'What do we know about child neglect?' *Child and Family Social Work* 8: 25.

Tasker, F. and Golombok, S. (1991) 'Children raised by lesbian mothers', *Family Law* 21: 184.

Tax Law Review Committee (2003), *Response to Civil Partnerships,* London: Tax Law Review Committee.

Tee, L. (2001) 'Division of Property upon Relationship Breakdown', in J. Herring (ed.) *Family Law: Issues, Debates, Policy,* Cullompton: Willan.

Teitelbaum, L. (1999) 'Children's rights and the problems of equal respect', *Hofstra Law Review* 27: 799.

Teitelbaum, L. and Dupaix, L. (1994) 'Alternative Dispute Resolution and Divorce: Natural Experimentation in Family Law', in J. Eekelaar and M. Maclean (eds) *A Reader on Family Law,* Oxford: OUP.

Ten Downing Street (2003) *Child Support Agency Praised,* London: Ten Downing Street.

Thatcher, M. (1990) *The Independent,* 19 July 1990.

Thatcher, M. (1995) *The Downing Street Years,* London: HarperCollins.

Thatcher, M. (1999) *Marriage After Modernity,* Sheffield: Sheffield Academic Press.

Thoburn, J. (1988) *Child Placement: Principles and Practice,* London: Wildwood.

Thomas, N. (2001) 'Listening to Children', in P. Foley, J. Roche and S. Tucker (eds) *Children in Society,* Buckingham: Open University Press.

Thomson, M. (1998) 'When mortgaged property should be sold', *The Conveyancer* 62: 125.

Thomson, R. (2000) 'Legal, Protected and Timely: Young People's Perspectives on the Heterosexual Age of Consent', in J. Bridgeman and D. Monk (eds) *Feminist Perspectives on Child Law,* London: Cavendish.

Thornton, M. (1997) 'The Judicial gendering of citizenship: A look at property interests during marriage', *Journal of Law and Society* 24: 486.

Thornton, R. (1989) 'Homelessness through relationship breakdown', *Journal of Social Welfare Law,* 11: 67.

Thorpe LJ (1994) 'Independent representation for minors', *Family Law* 24: 20.

Thorpe LJ (1998a) 'Should Section 25 be reformed?', *Family Law* 28: 469.

Thorpe LJ (1998b) 'The English System of Ancillary Relief', in R. Bailey-Harris (ed.) *Dividing the Assets on Family Breakdown,* Bristol: Jordans.

Thorpe LJ (1998c) *Report to the Lord Chancellor of the Ancillary Relief Advisory Group,* London: Ancillary Relief Advisory Group.

Thorpe LJ (2000) 'Introduction', in Thorpe LJ and E. Clarke (eds) *No Fault or Flaw: The Future of the Family Law Act 1996,* Bristol: Jordans.

Thorpe LJ (2002) 'Property rights on family breakdown', *Family Law* 32: 891.

Tilley, J. (2000) 'Cultural relativism', *Human Rights Quarterly* 19: 461.

Tinker, A. (1997) *Older People in Modern Society,* Harlow: Longman.

Tolson, R. (2002) 'Goals and the teams performance', *Family Law* 32: 491.

Tong, R. (1985) 'Feminist Perspectives and Gestational Motherhood', in J. Callaghan (ed.) *Reproduction, Ethics and the Law*, Bloomington, Ind.: Indiana University Press.

Treitel, G.H. (2003) *The Law of Contract*, London: Sweet & Maxwell.

Trinder, L. (2003) 'Working and not Working Contact after Divorce', in A. Bainham, B. Lindley, M. Richards and L. Trinder (eds) *Children and Their Families*, Oxford: Hart.

Trinder, L., Beek, M. and Connolly, J. (2002) *Making Contact: How Parents and Children Negotiate and Experience Contact After Divorce*, York: Joseph Rowntree.

Triseliotis, J. (1973) *In Search of Origins*, London: Routledge.

Ungerson, C. (1987) *Policy is Personal: Sex Gender and Informal Care*, London: Tavistock.

UNICEF (2000) *The State of the World's Children*, Geneva: UNICEF.

United Kingdom College of Mediators (1998) *Standards and Code of Practice*, London: UK College of Mediators.

United Nations Committee on the Rights of the Child (2002), *Consideration of Reports Submitted by State Parties Under Article 44 of the Convention*, New York: United Nations.

United Nations Human Rights Committee (1995) *United Kingdom of Great Britain and Northern Ireland CRC/C/15/SR/205*, Geneva: Centre for Human Rights.

Van Bueren, G. (1995) 'Children's access to adoption records – State discretion or an enforceable right?', *Modern Law Review* 58: 37.

Van Praagh, S. (1997) 'Children, custody and a child's identity', *Osgoode Law Journal* 35: 309.

Veitch, E. (1976) 'The essence of marriage – A comment on the homosexuality challenge', *Anglo-American Law Review* 5: 41.

Waddington, W. (2000) 'Marriage: An Institution in Transition and Redefinition', in S. Katz, J. Eekelaar and M. Maclean (eds) *Cross Currents* Oxford: OUP.

Wagstaff, C. (1998) 'Harming the unborn child – the foetus and the threshold criteria', *Family Law* 28: 160.

Waite, L. (2000) 'Cohabitation: A Communitarian Perspective', in M. Whyte (ed.) *Marriage in America*, Lanham, Md.: Rowman & Littlefield.

Walker, J. (ed.) (1998) *Information Meetings and Associated Provision within FLA 1996. Second Interim Evaluation Report*, Newcastle: Newcastle Centre for Family Studies.

Walker, J. (ed.) (1999) *Information Meetings and Associated Provision within FLA 1996. Third Interim Evaluation*, Newcastle: Newcastle Centre for Family Studies.

Walker, J. (2000a) 'Whither the FLA, Part II?', in Thorpe LJ and E. Clarke (eds) *No Fault or Flaw: The Future of the Family Law Act 1996*, Bristol: Jordans.

Walker, J. (2000b) 'Information meetings revisited', *Family Law* 30: 330.

Walker, J. (2001a) *Information Meetings and Associated Provisions within the Family Law Act 1996*, London: Lord Chancellor's Department.

Walker, J. (2001b) 'The information pilots – using and abusing evidence', *Family Law* 31: 817.

Walker, J., McCarthy, P. and Timms, N. (1994) *Mediation: The Making and Remaking of Co-operative Relationships*, Newcastle: Relate Centre for Family Studies.

Wall HHJ (1997) 'Domestic violence and contact', *Family Law* 27: 813.

Wallbank, J. (1998) 'Castigating mothers: The judicial response to wilful women in cases concerning contact', *Journal of Social Welfare and Family Law* 20: 257.

Wallbank, J. (2002a) 'Clause 106 of the Adoption and Children Bill: Legislation for the "good" father?' *Legal Studies* 22: 276.

Wallbank, J. (2002b) *Challenging Motherhoods,* London: Prentice Hall.

Wallerstein, J. and Kelly, J. (1980) *Surviving the Breakup,* New York: Basic Books.

Wallerstein, J. and Kelly, J. (1998) 'The long-term impact of divorce on children', *Family and Conciliation Courts Review* 36: 368.

Wallerstein, J. and Lewis, J. (1998) 'The long-term impact of divorce on children', *Family and Conciliation Courts Review* 12: 368.

Walsh, J. (1998) *Across the Generations,* London: Age Concern.

Wardell, L. (1998) 'Same-Sex Marriage and the Limits of Legal Pluralism', in J. Eekelaar and T. Nhlapo (eds) *The Changing Family: International Perspectives on the Family and Family Law,* Oxford: Hart.

Wardell, L. (2002) 'Parental infidelity and the "no harm" rule in custody litigation', *Catholic University Law Review* 52: 81.

Wardle, T. (1996) 'The use and abuse of rights rhetoric', *Loyola University Chicago Law Journal* 27: 321.

Warman, C. and Roberts, C. (2003) *Adoption and Looked After Children – an International Comparison,* Oxford: Oxford Centre for Family Law and Policy.

Warner, K. (2000) 'Sentencing in cases of marital rape: Towards changing the male imagination', *Legal Studies* 20: 592.

Warnock Report (1984) *Report of the Committee of Inquiry into Human Fertilisation and Embryology,* London: HMSO.

Warren, E. (2002) 'Bankrupt Children', *Minnesota Law Review* 86: 1003.

Weeks, J., Donovan, C. and Heaphy, B. (2001) *Same-Sex Intimacies: Families of Choice and Other Life Experiments,* London: Routledge.

Weitzman, L. (1985) *The Divorce Revolution,* New York: The Free Press.

Welbourne, P. (2002) 'Adoption and the rights of children in the UK', *International Journal of Children's Rights* 10: 269.

Wellings, A. (1995) 'Provision of sex education and early sexual experience: The relationship examined', *British Medical Journal* 311: 417.

Wells, C. (1997) 'Stalking: The criminal law's response', *Criminal Law Review* 463.

Wenger, G. (1984) *The Supportive Network,* London: Allen & Unwin.

West, S. (2000) *Your Rights,* London: Age Concern.

Weyland, I. (1995) 'Judicial attitudes to contact and shared residence since the Children Act 1989', *Journal of Social Welfare and Family Law* 17: 445.

Weyland, I. (1997) 'The blood tie: Raised to the status of a presumption', *Journal of Social Welfare and Family Law* 19: 173.

Weyrauch, W. (1980) 'Metamorphosis of marriage', *Family Law Quarterly* 13: 415.

Whalley, L. (2001) *The Ageing Brain,* London: Weidenfeld & Nicholson.

White House Working Group on the Family (1985) *The Family: Possessing America's Future,* Washington: White House.

Whittle, S. (2002) *Respect and Equality,* London: Cavendish.

Who Cares? Trust (2000) *Remember my Messages,* London: Who Cares? Trust.

Wikeley, N. (2000) 'Child support – the new formula', *Family Law* 30: 820.

Wikeley, N. (2001) 'Private cases and the Child Support Agency', *Family Law* 31: 37

Wild, L. and Richards, M. (2003) 'Exploring parent and child perceptions of inter-parental conflict', *International Journal of Law, Policy and Family* 17: 366.

Willbourne, C. and Stanley, G. (2002) 'Contact under the microscope', *Family Law* 32: 687.

Williams, A. (1985) 'The value of QALYs', *Health and Social Service Journal* July 1985: 3.

Williams, C. (2002) 'The practical operation of the Children Act complaints procedure', *Child and Family Law Quarterly* 14: 25.

Williams, C. and Jordan, H. (1996a) *The Children Act 1989 Complaints Procedure*, Sheffield: University of Sheffield.

Williams, C. and Jordan, H. (1996b) 'Factors relating to publicity surrounding the complaints procedure under the Children Act 1989', *Child and Family Law Quarterly* 6: 337.

Williams J. (2002) 'Prisoners and artificial insemination – Have the courts got it right?', *Child and Family Law Quarterly* 14: 216.

Wilson, G. (1994) 'Abuse of elderly men and women among clients of a community psychogeriatric service', *British Journal of Social Work* 24: 81.

Wilson J (1999) 'Ancillary relief reform', *Family Law* 29: 159.

Wilson J (2003) 'The misnomer of family law', *Family Law* 33: 29

Wilson, S. (1997) 'Identity, genealogy and the social family: The case of donor insemination', *International Journal of Law, Policy and the Family*, 11: 270.

Wilson, W. (1998) *Criminal Law*, London: Longman.

Wintemute, R. and Andenæs, M. (eds) (2001) *Legal Recognition of Same-Sex Partnerships*, Oxford: Hart.

Woelke, A. (2002) 'Family credo', *Family Law* 32: 475.

Women & Equality Unit (2003) *Civil Partnership*, London: DTI.

Women's Aid (1998) *Women's Aid Annual Report 1997/8*, Bristol: Women's Aid Federation.

Women's Aid (2003) *Failure to Protect*, London: Women's Aid.

Woodhouse, B. (2000) 'The Status of Children', in S. Katz, J. Eekelaar and M. Maclean (eds) *Cross Currents*, Oxford: OUP.

Woolf, M. (2000) 'Children to get details of sperm donor men', *The Independent*: 18 September 2000.

Wright, C. (1998) *Continuing to Care*, York: Joseph Rowntree.

Yell, G. (1992) 'Point of order', *Law Society's Guardian Gazette* 89: 20.

Yllo, K. and Bograd, M. (1988) *Feminist Perspectives on Wife Abuse*, London: Sage.

Young, I. (1999) 'Mothers, Citizenship and Independence', in U. Narayan and J. Bartkowiak (eds) *Having and Raising Children*, Pennsylvania, Pa.: Pennsylvania State University Press.

INDEX

Abduction
  criminal law, 491–2
  European convention, 502–3
  Hague convention, 494–502
  nature of, 490–1
  non–convention cases, 503–4
  prevention of, 492–3
Adoption
  adopters, 592–3
  agencies, 591–2
  birth parents, 611–13
  consent, 601–5
  contact, 606–11
  crisis in, 589
  effect of, 605
  encouraging, 591–2
  gay, 592
  open, 606–1
  relatives, 609
  revocation, 610–11
  selecting adopters, 593–8
  setting aside, 610–11
  special guardianship, 613–14
  step–parent, 608
  support, 609–10
  transracial, 596
  use of, 587–90
  welfare and, 599–601
Ancillary relief
  see Financial support on
    divorce
Assisted reproduction
  DIY, 293
  fathers and, 290–3
  rights to, 337–40
Autopoietic theory
  definition of, 17–18

Bankruptcy
  families and, 151–4
  financial relief, 226–7

Care order
  applicants for, 528
  care plans, 544–5
  contact order, 567–72
  duration of, 579–80
  effects of, 529, 561–72
  exclusion order, 548–9
  grounds for, 531–44
  interim, 545
  police protection, 549
  subjects of, 528–9
  supervision order, 530–1
  threshold criteria, 532–41
Child of the family
  definition of, 302–4
  financial support, 183–4
Child protection
  abuse, 512–13
  accommodation, 515–20
  care order, 528–49
  child assessment orders, 526–8
  criminal law, 514–15
  emergency protection, 549–53
  family assistance order, 522–3
  human rights, and, 510–12
  investigations, 523–8
  nature of, 506–8
  ousting abuser, 554–6
  services, 520–2
  supervision order, 528–49
Child support
  acts, 169–80
  children act under, 180–3
  matrimonial causes act, 183–4
  theory, 160–8
Children
  abduction, 491–2
  contract law, 417–18
  corporal punishment, 414–17
  court, in, 402–8
  criminal law, 412–14

definition, 348–50
divorce, 102–3, 111, 436–8
duties, 419–20
education law, 408–12
emigration, 466–8
inheritance, 634–6, 640–1
medical law, 393–402
names, 460–6
older parents, 619–23
publicity, 459–60
religion, 452–4
rights, 383–93
tort law, 418
Children in care
care order, 561–2
foster carers, 578–9
general, 557–8
human rights, 558–60
secure accommodation, 585–7
supervision order, 560–1
Cohabitation
definition, 59–60
domestic violence, 262–3
inheritance, 633–42
law on, 59–68, 133–47
Contact order
adoption and, 606–11
child in care, 567–72
domestic violence, 475–7
enforcement, 479–82
meaning, 423–6
when ordered, 468–85
Contract Law
children, 417–9
married couples, 64
pre–marriage, 222–3

Discretion
financial support, 192–3
rules, and, 25–6
Divorce
aims of, law, 82–85
causes of, 80–81
children and, 102–3, 111–12, 426–8
defence to, 92–3
economic consequences, 185

fault, 105–9
ground of, 88–93
history of, 85–6
individualisation of, 104–5
information meeting, 96–104
procedure, 86–7
rate of, 79
reform, 96–104
religion, 110–11
separation orders, 112
statistics, 79
Domestic violence
causes, 241–2
children, 262
contact, 475–7
criminal law, 272–9
definition, 238–9
enforcement of orders, 249, 267
ex parte orders, 265
harassment, 267–9
history, 242–3
housing, 269–72
human rights, 263–4
incidence, 239–41
non–molestation, 244–9
occupation orders, 250–65
older people, 642–5
power of arrest, 266–7
state liability, 279
undertakings, 266

Education Law
children's rights, 408–12
Elder abuse, 642–5
Emergency protection order, 549–53
Engaged couples
domestic violence, 69, 245
property, 68–9
Evidence
married couples, 65

Families
crisis in, 23–4
definition of, 1–7
finances, 124–6
human rights, 309–11

'new', 6, 9–10
promotion of, 8
state and, 18–20
statistics, 6–7
Family Law
chaos, 16–17
definition of, 10
functionalism, 11–12
messages, 22
moral judgements, 20–21
non-legal, 24–5
privatisation of, 19–20
Father
definition of, 288–93
parental responsibility, 314–20
Financial support on divorce
bankruptcy, 226–7
children and, 202–3
clean break, 197–200
conduct, 207–8
consent orders, 223–4
disabilities, 207
discovery, 195
enforcement, 225–6
equality, 209–13
factors to be considered, 201–13
housing, 218–22
human rights, 194
orders, 195–7
pensions, 214–8
poor, 213–4
reform, 234–6
rich, 214
tenancies, 232–3
theoretical issues, 186–95
variation, 228–30
Foster parents
definition of, 300–2
legal position of, 578–9

Gay and lesbian relationships
adoption, 592
domestic violence, 69–71
family as, 1, 5–6, 69–71
inheritance, 637
marriage, 47–9

residence orders, 455–6
Guardians
law on, 296–300

Human rights
act, 28–9
child protection, 510–2, 558–60
child support, 174
children's welfare, 375–9
consequentialism and, 25
contact, 470–3
divorce, 110
domestic violence, 263–4
family life, respect for, 309–12
gay relationships, 47–9, 455–6
know parent, to, 336, 611–13
maintenance, 194
marriage, 44–9
older people, 628–9
parent, to be, 337–45
parental responsibility, 321
religion, 452–4

Illegitimacy
'abolition' of, 345–6
Inherent jurisdiction, 488–90
Inheritance
children, 637, 641
intestacy, 633–4, 634–6
theoretical issues, 632–4

Legal aid
reform and, 23
Local authority
care order, 516–72
courts and, 581–5
investigations, 523–8
judicial review, 573–6
parental responsibility, 313–14
questioning decisions of, 573–8
section 8 orders, 553–4
voluntary services, 515–23

Maintenance
marriage during, 131–3
Marriage

alternatives to, 76–7
consequences of, 60–8
consortium, 67–8
contract, 35–6
death and, 112–13
financial consequences, 61–2, 131–3
meaning, 32–5
non–marriage, 38
presumption of, 36–7
sham, 56
statistics, 31–2
status, 35–6
unity, 67
void, 37–59
voidable, 37–59
Mediation
    advantages of, 116–19
    definition of, 113–16
    disadvantages of, 119–12
    encouragement of, 101–2
Medical Law
    children and, 393–402
Mother
    definition of, 286–7
    parental responsibility, 314
    presumption in favour of, 448–9
Multiculturalism
    family law, 26–8

Nullity
    age, 41
    approbation, 56–7
    bars, 56–8
    bigamy, 43
    consent, 52–6
    consummation, 50–2
    drunkenness, 55
    duress, 52–4
    effects of decree, 58–9
    formalities, 42–3
    fraud, 55
    intersexuals, 46–7
    mental disorder, 55–6
    mistake, 54
    pregnancy, 56
    prohibited degrees, 40–1

reform, 59
same–sex marriage, 43–9
transsexuals, 43–9
unsoundness of mind, 54–5
venereal disease, 56

Older people
    abuse of, 642–5
    attorney, power of, 630–2
    families and, 617–18
    family support for, 619–23
    incapable, 628–32
    inter–generational justice, 625–8
    rights, 628–9
    state support for, 623–5
    statistics, 617–19

Parental responsibility
    care order and, 561–3
    losing, 325–6
    meaning of, 356–61
    sharing, 361–6
    who has, 312–20
Parents
    basis of parenthood, 326–36
    definitions of, 284–96
    discretion, 350–6
    foster parents, 300–2
    genetic, 327–8
    guardians, 296–300
    intent–based, 327–8
    licensed, 346
    losing, 296
    parental orders, 294–6
    rights, 350–6
    social, 296–306, 330
    step–parents, 304–5
    surrogacy, 294–6, 341–5
Partnership
    child protection, 509–10
    local authorities, 26, 509–10
Prohibited steps orders
    domestic violence, 269
    local authorities, 553–4
    meaning, 426
    restrictions on, 426–9

Property
  bankruptcy, 151–9
  constructive trusts, 135–9
  family home, 133–59
  matrimonial home rights, 148–9
  occupation rights, 147–9
  personal, 128–30
  proprietary estoppel, 139–41
  reform, 144–7
  resulting trusts, 134–5
  sale of home, 149–50
  theory, 126–7
Public–private divide
  definition of, 14–16
  domestic violence, 280–1

Relatives
  adoption, 609
  contact, 483
  definition, 245
  legal rights of, 306–9
Residence order
  disabled parents, 456–7
  gay parents, 455–6
  joint, 423, 458–9
  meaning, 422–3

Section 8 orders
  conditions, 429–32
  leave for, 433–4
  local authorities, 553–4
  restricting applications, 435–6
  restrictions, 435–6
Secure accommodation orders,
  585–7
Solicitors
  domestic violence, 282
  negotiation, 122, 193–4
  role of, 24
Special guardianship, 613–14

Specific issue orders
  domestic violence, 269
  local authorities, 553–4
  meaning, 426
  restrictions, 426–9
Step–parents
  adoption, 606
  contact, and, 483
  definition of, 304–5
Supervision order
  care order, 530–1
  duration of, 579–80
  effects of, 560–1
  grounds for, 531–44
  nature of, 530–1
Surrogacy
  regulation of, 294–6, 341–5

Taxation
  married couples, 66
Tort Law
  children, 418–19
  local authorities, 576–7
  married couples, 64

Unmarried couples
  see Cohabitation

Wardship
  effect of, 487
  law on, 486–8
Welfare principle
  adoption and, 592
  alternatives to, 380–3
  application, 438–48
  criticisms of, 379–80
  delay and, 445–6
  meaning, 366–8
  natural parent, 449–51
  no order principle, 446–8